The Oxford History of Christian Worship

The Oxford History of Christian Worship

GEOFFREY WAINWRIGHT
KAREN B. WESTERFIELD TUCKER
Editors

OXFORD
UNIVERSITY PRESS

2006

OXFORD
UNIVERSITY PRESS

Oxford University Press, Inc., publishes works that
further Oxford University's objective of excellence
in research, scholarship, and education.

Oxford   New York
Auckland   Cape Town   Dar es Salaam   Hong Kong   Karachi
Kuala Lumpur   Madrid   Melbourne   Mexico City   Nairobi
New Delhi   Shanghai   Taipei   Toronto

With offices in
Argentina   Austria   Brazil   Chile   Czech Republic   France   Greece
Guatemala   Hungary   Italy   Japan   Poland   Portugal   Singapore
South Korea   Switzerland   Thailand   Turkey   Ukraine   Vietnam

Library of Congress Cataloging-in-Publication Data

The Oxford history of Christian worship / Geoffrey Wainwright,
Karen B. Westerfield Tucker, editors. p. cm.
Includes bibliographical references and index.
ISBN-13: 978-0-19-513886-3 (alk. paper)
ISBN-10: 0-19-513886-4 (alk. paper)
   1. Public worship.   I. Wainwright, Geoffrey, 1939–   .
II. Westerfield Tucker, Karen B. (Karen Beth), 1954–   .
BV15.O95 2005
264'.009—dc22
2005021054

9 8 7 6 5 4 3 2 1

Printed in the United States of America
on acid-free paper

Contents

Preface

Christian worship has a history of two thousand years and, by now, a global reach. This book traces its winding course and describes its varied manifestations in ways suited to the general reader as well as to historians, theologians, and scholars of religion in a broader sense. At the same time it provides a compendium for the use of teachers and students in the special field of liturgy and for those who have direct responsibility for the conduct of worship in their communities. After the manner of other Oxford histories, it combines fluent text, pictures, and boxed inserts.

The focus rests on the corporate worship of the Church, predominantly celebrated in cathedrals, parishes, and other congregational settings, though attention is given also to monastic communities. The presentations are largely descriptive, including liturgical texts but also going "beyond the text." They treat concrete performances and set the liturgical actions within a particular cultural context. The emphasis falls on the principal Sunday service (whether word and eucharist or word alone), on events and occasions observing the main festivals, on the ceremonies of Christian initiation, on sacramental rites and pastoral offices such as weddings and funerals, and on the constant round of prayer. For pedagogical purposes, orders of service are outlined, and contemporary accounts set off from the main text are cited in extract or in full. In their own writing, authors pay close attention to the social incidences of worship, providing thick descriptions of the liturgical life in their periods and areas.

The book combines several grids in its arrangement. The principal sequence is chronological, but this is diversified according to geography and, where necessary, confessional identity. While the majority of chapters treat the material details of worship in their particular time and place, there are also thematic chapters that give a longitudinal reading of such features as music, spatial setting, and the visual arts. These topics are treated at least in an indicative way in the other chapters. Throughout the book care is taken to acknowledge the contributions of women to liturgical practice.

The editors have engaged an international and ecumenical team of writers with expertise in many areas. The contributors range across the confessions (Orthodox, Catholic, the Reformation churches, Mennonite, Baptist, Methodist, and Pentecostal), the continents (Africa, the Americas, Asia, Australia, and Europe), and the languages (the editors have translated chapters from the French, the German, and the Portuguese, and others write from the Netherlands, Sweden, and Korea).

The editors are grateful to the following collaborators at Oxford University Press: Cynthia Read, who first proposed this project; Theo Calderara, who helped manage some of the details early in the project; Timothy J. DeWerff for overall project management; Stephen Wagley and Eric Stannard, who developed the book and oversaw the editing; and Martin A. Levick and Susan Gamer, who tracked down numerous illustrations. The index was compiled by Julia Marshall of Marshall Indexing Services. Among university colleagues, the editors wish to thank Lucas Van Rompay for help in standardizing transliterations from various Middle Eastern languages; Marchita Mauck for advising on artistic matters; Kerry McCarthy for searching out several musical references; and Reed Criswell for invaluable electronic assistance. Particular mention must be made of the library staff at the Boston University School of Theology and at Duke University Divinity School as well as those in the Rare Book and Special Collections at Duke. Cooperation in the search for illustrations was gladly afforded by Joyce Borger, Christian Reformed Church; Joan Cambitsis, Publications Office, World Council of Churches, Geneva; Michael DuBose, United Methodist News Service; Amy Heckert, Brethren Historical Library and Archives; Laurie Oswald, Mennonite Church USA; Ken Shaffer, Brethren Historical Library and Archives; and Mark Shenise, General Commission on Archives and History, United Methodist Church.

The editors express their deep appreciation to the Louisville Institute for providing a General Grant toward the illustration program of the book.

Geoffrey Wainwright
Karen B. Westerfield Tucker

The Feast of the Transfiguration, AD 2005

Editors and Contributors

The Editors

Karen B. Westerfield Tucker, a United Methodist minister, is Professor of Worship at Boston University. The editor of *The Sunday Service of the Methodists* (1995) and the author of *American Methodist Worship* (2001), she is the Chair of the Worship and Liturgy Committee of the World Methodist Council. She is Editor-in-Chief of the international and ecumenical journal *Studia Liturgica*.

Geoffrey Wainwright, a British Methodist minister who previously taught in Cameroon and England, occupies the Cushman Chair of Theology at Duke University in North Carolina. He is a past president of the international Societas Liturgica and of the American Theological Society. His *Doxology* (1980), "a systematic theology written in liturgical perspective," was followed by *Worship with One Accord* (1997) and *For Our Salvation* (1997).

The Contributors

John F. Baldovin, S.J., is Professor of Historical and Liturgical Theology at Weston Jesuit School of Theology, Massachusetts. A former President of the North American Academy of Liturgy and of Societas Liturgica, he has served as an adviser to the (U.S.) Bishops' Committee on the Liturgy, and with the International Commission on English in the Liturgy. Among his numerous publications are *The Urban Character of Christian Worship* (1987, 2002); *Worship: City, Church and Renewal* (1991); and *Bread of Life, Cup of Salvation: Understanding the Mass* (2003).

M. Bradford Bedingfield, a practicing attorney in Boston, Massachusetts, earned the D.Phil. in English Literature from Oxford University and has taught in the United States, England, and Japan. An editor for Old English entries in the third edition of the *Oxford English Dictionary*, he has published on Anglo-Saxon topics, including: *The Dramatic Liturgy of Anglo-Saxon England* (2002); and "Ritual and Drama" in *Ritual and Belief: The Rites of the Anglo-Saxon Church* (2005).

Teresa Berger teaches theology at the Divinity School of Duke University, North Carolina. She is a Roman Catholic, originally from Germany, with doctorates both in dogmatic theology and in liturgical studies. Berger is the author and editor of several books, including *Liturgie und Frauenseele. Die liturgische Bewegung aus der Sicht der Frauenforschung* (1993), *Women's Ways of Worship: Gender Analysis and Liturgical History* (1999), *Dissident Daughters: Feminist Liturgies in Global Context* (2001), and *Fragments of Real Presence* (2005).

Bruno Bürki, a pastor of the Swiss Reformed Church currently serving in Neuchâtel, taught for ten years on the interconfessional faculty in Yaoundé (Cameroon) and has held positions in the Catholic Faculty of Theology at Fribourg. Among his books are studies on Christian death (*Im Herrn enschlafen*, 1969), the liturgies of Protestant churches in Africa (*L'assemblée dominicale*, 1976), and Reformed eucharistic liturgies in France and Switzerland (*Cène du Seigneur, Eucharistie de l'Église*, 1985). A former President of Societas Liturgica, he is a Council member of the Federation of Swiss Protestant Churches.

Christine Chaillot, an Orthodox laywoman (Greek Orthodox Patriarchate of Constantinople) from Switzerland, has studied Oriental Orthodox communities throughout the Middle East and elsewhere. She has written numerous articles and books, among them *Rôle des images et vénération des icônes dans les Églises Orthodoxes Orientales* (1993), *The Syrian Orthodox Church of Antioch and All the East* (1998), and *The Ethiopian Orthodox Tewahedo Church Tradition* (2002).

Anscar J. Chupungco, O.S.B., is Rector-President of San Beda College in the Philippines, having previously been Director of the Paul VI Institute of Liturgy in the Philippines and a professor at the Pontifical Liturgical Institute in Rome. He has written widely on the topic of liturgical inculturation, and has contributed to liturgical renewal especially in the Philippines. He is the editor of the multivolume *Handbook for Liturgical Studies*.

Conrad L. Donakowski is Professor Emeritus of the Humanities and Music at Michigan State University; Director of Music at St. Thomas Aquinas Church in East Lansing, Michigan; and visiting professor of liturgy and culture in the Liturgical Institute at Mundelein Seminary, Chicago. His publications include the book *A Muse for the Masses: Ritual and Music in an Age of Democratic Revolution* and articles on religious ritual as mass medium in the *Aufklärung*, the civic cult of French revolutionary *fêtes*, and opera as propaganda for the *Risorgimento*.

Michael S. Driscoll, a Roman Catholic presbyter, teaches on the faculty of the University of Notre Dame, Indiana. He wrote *Alcuin et la pénitence à l'époque carolingienne* (1999) and has published numerous articles in journals such as *Worship, Ecclesia Orans*, and *Traditio*. A former President of the North American Academy of Liturgy, he was an advisor to the (U.S.) Bishops' Committee on the Liturgy. He serves as a member of the executive Council of Societas Liturgica.

Nwaka Chris Egbulem studied African philosophy and theology in Nigeria and the Congo before completing graduate studies at the University of Notre Dame and the Catholic University of America. The author of *The Power of Africentric Celebrations*

(1996), he is a visiting professor in Nigeria and at the Institute for Black Catholic Studies at Xavier University, New Orleans. He is the founder and CEO of two international nonprofit organizations: the Amen Foundation, Inc., and Action Africa, Inc.

Christopher Ellis is the Principal of Bristol Baptist College in Bristol, England, and the author of *Gathering: A Theology and Spirituality of Worship in Free Church Tradition* (2004). He moderates the Faith and Unity Executive of the British Baptist Union, is a member of the Worship and Spirituality Commission of the Baptist World Alliance, and is a former member of the Joint Liturgical Group of Great Britain.

William T. Flynn is Lecturer at the University of Leeds, Institute for Medieval Studies. He is the author of *Medieval Music as Medieval Exegesis* (1999), has published articles and chapters on music and theology, and has received awards and commissions for musical compositions. He participates in the study group *Sapientia-Eloquentia* based at the University of Stockholm, which is investigating developments in liturgical poetry from the eleventh to the twelfth centuries.

Duncan B. Forrester served early in his career as a Church of Scotland missionary in educational ministry in India, and later as a Lecturer at the University of Sussex in England. In 2001 he retired from his position as Professor of Christian Ethics and Practical Theology at Edinburgh University, where he had also served as Dean of the Faculty of Divinity and the Director of the Centre for Theology and Public Issues. He has published widely, principally in Indian politics and religion and in ethics and political theology.

Robert Gribben is Professor of Worship and Mission in the United Faculty of Theology in Melbourne, Australia, and a minister of the Uniting Church in Australia. He has served on the national liturgical bodies of his church and wrote the authorized commentary on its worship book. He has been Chair of the English Language Liturgical Consultation, has twice been elected President of the Australian Academy of Liturgy, and currently chairs the Ecumenics Committee of the World Methodist Council.

André Haquin, a Belgian priest, is a professor at the Catholic University of Louvain-la-Neuve. He devoted a study to a pioneer of the Liturgical Movement, *Dom Lambert Beauduin et le renouveau liturgique* (1970), and has written on the eucharist in *L'eucharistie au coeur de l'Église et pour la vie du monde* (2004).

David R. Holeton is Professor of Liturgy at the Charles University, Prague, Czech Republic. Ordained in the Anglican Church of Canada, he taught liturgy in Vancouver and Toronto before assuming his present position in 1997. His main academic interests lie within the areas of Christian initiation, communion of all the baptized and the Bohemian sacramental and liturgical movement.

Maxwell E. Johnson is Professor of Liturgy at the University of Notre Dame, Indiana, and a minister in the Evangelical Lutheran Church in America. He is a coauthor of *The Apostolic Tradition: A Commentary* (2002) and revised and expanded E. C. Whitaker's *Documents of the Baptismal Liturgy* (2003). He is the author of *The Rites of Christian Initiation: Their Evolution and Interpretation* (1999), *The Virgin of Guadalupe:*

Theological Reflections of an Anglo-Lutheran Liturgist (2002), and *Worship: Rites, Feasts, and Reflections* (2005).

Seung-Joong Joo, educated in Korea and the United States, is Assistant Professor of Preaching and Worship and Dean of the Graduate School of Ministry at the Presbyterian College and Theological Seminary in Seoul, Korea. His research and pastoral interests include the inculturation and adaptation of historic Christian practices for the Korean context.

Kyeong-Jin Kim is Professor of Worship at the Busan Presbyterian University in Gimhae City, South Korea, and serves as senior pastor of the Gurutugy Presbyterian Church in Seoul. The history and practices of Presbyterian worship in Korea are the principal areas of his scholarly investigation.

Harry Klaassens has served several parishes as a minister of the Protestant Church in the Netherlands and is currently pastor of the Ichthus Church in Emmen. His doctoral work addressed the history and theology of Pentecost and their interpretation for congregational practices. He has published principally in the areas of practical theology and pastoral liturgy.

Jaime Lara is chair of the Program in Religion and the Arts and Associate Professor of Christian Art and Architecture at Yale Divinity School and Yale Institute of Sacred Music. He has been vice president of the National Hispanic Institute for Liturgy (USA) and was editor of the Spanish-language lectionary for the United States and of the Spanish translation of *Environment and Art in Catholic Worship*. He is the author of *City, Temple, Stage: Eschatological Architecture and Liturgical Theatrics in New Spain* (2004).

Marchita Mauck is Professor of Art History at Louisiana State University and Associate Dean of the College of Art and Design. She is a medievalist by specialization with additional interest in contemporary art and architecture. Her books include *Shaping a House for the Church* (1990) and *Places for Worship* (1995). She has served as a liturgical design consultant for renovation and new church projects throughout the United States.

Elsie Anne McKee, Archibald Alexander Professor of Reformation Studies and the History of Worship at Princeton Theological Seminary, has published primarily in the area of sixteenth-century Reformed history and theology. She has written *John Calvin on the Diaconate and Liturgical Almsgiving* (1984), *John Calvin: Writings on Pastoral Piety* (2001), and several critical studies of the life and work of Katharina Schütz Zell.

Nathan D. Mitchell is on the faculty of the Department of Theology at the University of Notre Dame, Indiana, and concurrently the associate director of the Notre Dame Center for Liturgy. His most recent books include *Eucharist as a Sacrament of Initiation* (1994), *Liturgy and the Social Sciences* (1999), and *Real Presence: The Work of Eucharist* (2001). Since 1991, his column "The Amen Corner" has appeared in each issue of *Worship*.

Nils-Henrik Nilsson, a pastor in the Church of Sweden, taught at the University of Lund from 1982-1987, and since 1989 has been the Secretary for Liturgy in the Church of Sweden. He is the author of several books including: *Gudstjänst i Svenska kyrkan*, 1994 (Worship in the Church of Sweden); *Evangelieboken i gudstjänst och förkunnelse*, with LarsOlov Eriksson, 2003 (The Lectionary in Worship and Preaching); and *Gudstjänsten och vi själva*, 2005 (Worship and We Ourselves).

Joanne M. Pierce is an associate professor in the Department of Religious Studies at the College of the Holy Cross, Massachusetts. Her published articles address medieval topics, among them "The Evolution of the *ordo missae* in the Early Middle Ages" (1997) and "'Green Women' and Blood Pollution: Some Medieval Rituals for the Churching of Women after Childbirth" (1999). She is a coeditor of *Source and Summit: Commemorating Josef A. Jungmann, S.J.* (1999).

Samson Prabhakar is an ordained minister of the Church of South India and received the Doctor of Theology in Religious Education from the University of Bern, Switzerland. He is presently the Director of Research at the South Asia Theological Research Institute (SATHRI) of The Board of Theological Education of the Senate of Serampore College, Bangalore. He taught in the Department of Christian Ministry at the United Theological College from 1982 to 2001.

John Rempel is a minister in the Mennonite Church USA and Assistant Professor of Historical Theology at the Associated Mennonite Biblical Seminary in Indiana. He was a member of the Worship Committee of the Church of the Brethren—Mennonite Church Canada & USA that produced *Hymnal: A Worship Book* (1992), the author of *The Lord's Supper in Anabaptism* (1993), and the editor of the 1998 *Mennonite Minister's Manual*. In 1991, he became the first representative of the Mennonite Central Committee at the United Nations, a position he held until 2003.

Alexander Rentel is Assistant Professor of Canon Law and Byzantine Studies at St. Vladimir's Orthodox Theological Seminary in New York. He received his S.E.O.D. from the Pontifical Oriental Institute (Rome), and did his dissertation on the Patriarchal Liturgical *Diataxis* of Dimitrios Gemistos. He is an ordained Eastern Orthodox priest and serves as Canon Law adviser to the Holy Synod of Bishops of his Church.

Hans-Christoph Schmidt-Lauber, after a pastoral ministry at Kiel in northern Germany, became Professor of Practical Theology at the University of Vienna, Austria. His published works run from *Die Eucharistie als Entfaltung der verba testamenti* (1957) to the manual *Handbuch der Liturgik* (3rd ed., 2003). A former President of Societas Liturgica, he played a prominent part in the development toward a new service book for the Lutheran and United Churches in Germany, *Evangelisches Gottesdienstbuch* (1999).

Bryan D. Spinks is Professor of Liturgical Studies at Yale Institute of Sacred Music and Yale Divinity School, and Chair of the Liturgy Program. A priest of the Church of England, he served on the Church of England Liturgical Commission from 1986 until 2000. Among his most recent publications are *Mar Nestorius and Mar Theodore the Interpreter: The Forgotten Eucharistic Prayers of East Syria* (1999) and *Sacraments, Ceremonies, and the Stuart Divines. Sacramental Theology and Liturgy in England and Scotland 1603–1662* (2003).

S. Anita Stauffer, a pastor of the Evangelical Lutheran Church in America, is the former study secretary for worship of the Lutheran World Federation, Geneva, Switzerland. She has published her archaeological work on early Christian fonts and baptisteries as well as studies on worship and culture, most notably the series produced by the Lutheran World Federation.

Timothy M. Thibodeau is Professor of History at Nazareth College in Rochester, New York, and has also served as adjunct Professor of Church History at the Colgate-Rochester Divinity School. He has published extensively on the history of Christianity and the development of medieval legal studies. He coedited, with Anselme Davril, O.S.B., the modern critical edition of William Durandus of Mende's *Rationale divinorum officiorum*, published by *Corpus Christianorum, Continuatio Mediaevalis*.

Lucas Van Rompay, formerly on the faculty of the University of Leiden in the Netherlands, is currently Professor of Eastern Christianity at Duke University, North Carolina. His publications include text editions with annotated translations of Syriac Old Testament commentaries, such as *Théodore de Mopsueste: Fragments syriaques du Commentaire des Psaumes* (1982), as well as numerous articles on Syriac literature and the cultural history of Eastern Christianity.

Wilhelm Wachholz teaches church history at the Evangelical Lutheran seminary in São Leopoldo, Brazil. His dissertation, which studied the "Evangelical Society for Protestant Germans in America," was published as *"Atravessem e Ajudem-nos"; a atuação da "Sociedade Evangélica de Barmen" e de seus obreiros e obreiros enviados ao Rio Grande do Sul (1864–1899)*. His research interests include Reformation history and Protestantism in Latin America.

James F. White taught for twenty years each at Southern Methodist University and the University of Notre Dame, and most recently served as Bard Thompson Professor of Liturgical Studies at Drew University in New Jersey. His widely used *Introduction to Christian Worship* is in its third edition and has been translated into multiple languages. A prolific author, he wrote on *Roman Catholic Worship* (1995, 2003), while his books on Protestant liturgies particularly in North America made a specially significant contribution to scholarship. As an ordained United Methodist minister, he helped to guide his denomination's production of liturgical resources from the 1960s until his death in 2004.

Telford Work is Assistant Professor of Theology at Westmont College, California, and the author of *Living and Active: Scripture in the Economy of Salvation* (2002). His articles have appeared in Oxford University Press and Eerdmans books, *Theology Today*, *Scottish Journal of Theology*, *International Journal of Systematic Theology*, *Pro Ecclesia*, *St. Vladimir's Seminary Quarterly*, *Studies in Interreligious Dialogue*, and *Re:generation Quarterly*.

Common Abbreviations
Used in this Book

BELK *Bekenntnisschriften der evangelisch-lutherischen Kirche*. Göttingen: Vandenhoeck & Ruprecht, 1930.

CCCM *Corpus Christianorum, Continuatio Mediaevalis*. Turnhout: Brepols, 1966– .

CPG *Clavis Patrum Graecorum*. 4 volumes. Edited by Maurice Geerard and F. Glorie. Turnhout: Brepols, 1974-1987.

CCSL *Corpus Christianorum*. Series Latina. Turnhout: Brepols, 1953– .

DMA *Dictionary of the Middle Ages*. Edited by Joseph R. Strayer. 13 volumes. New York: Scribner, 1982–1989.

LXX The Septuagint.

PG *Patrologia Graeca*. Edited by J.-P. Migne. Paris: 1857–1866.

PL *Patrologia Latina*. Edited by J.-P. Migne. Paris: 1844–1855.

ST *Studi e Testi*. Rome: Biblioteca Apostolica Vaticana, 1900– .

WA *Luthers Werke*, Weimar edition.

The Oxford History of Christian Worship

1

Christian Worship: Scriptural Basis and Theological Frame

GEOFFREY WAINWRIGHT

And God spoke all these words saying, "I am the Lord your God, who brought you out of the land of Egypt, out of the house of bondage. You shall have no other gods before me. You shall not make for yourself a graven image, or any likeness of anything that is in heaven above, or that is in the earth beneath, or that is in the water under the earth; you shall not bow down to them or serve them; for I the Lord your God am a jealous God." (Exod. 20:1–5)

The One God and the Many Gods (So-Called)

In expounding the first commandment thus given to the People of God, Martin Luther in the Large Catechism proposed a pragmatic definition of divinity: "What your heart clings to and trusts in, that is really your god." For his part, John Calvin observed in the *Institutes* that "just as waters boil up from a vast, full spring, so does an immense crowd of gods flow forth from the human mind," and these "specters" take concrete form as "idols" (1.5.12). While Moses himself was still on Mount Sinai "conversing with God," the people in the wilderness said to Aaron, "Up, make us gods, who shall go before us"; and the Lord said to Moses, "They have turned aside quickly out of the way which I commanded them; they have made for themselves a molten calf, and have worshiped it and sacrificed to it, and said, 'These are your gods, O Israel, who brought you up out of the land of Egypt'" (Exod. 32). Whether the graven image represented the Lord or "other gods" (from whose worship indeed the people's own remote, pre-Abrahamitic ancestors had not been exempt; Josh. 24:2), the condemnation from heaven was unequivocal.

From the singing and dancing around the golden calf onward, Moses and the Old Testament prophets inveighed recurrently against idolatry and summoned the people and their rulers to repentance (e.g., 2 Kings 17:7–18, 21:1–15; Isa. 10:10–11; Ezek. 6, 14, 20, etc.; Hosea 4, 8, 13–14). The God who delivered Israel from Egypt is the true God, being the universal Creator; the handmade gods of the nations are mere idols. The nations themselves are invited to join Israel in worshiping the Lord:

> O sing to the Lord a new song;
> sing to the Lord all the earth!
> Sing to the Lord, bless his name;
> tell of his salvation from day to day.
> Declare his glory among the nations,
> his marvelous works among all the peoples!
> For great is the Lord, and greatly to be praised;
> he is to be feared above all gods.
> For all the gods of the peoples are idols;
> but the Lord made the heavens.
> Honor and majesty are before him;
> strength and beauty are in his sanctuary.
> Ascribe to the Lord, O families of the peoples,
> ascribe to the Lord glory and strength!
> Ascribe to the Lord the glory due his name;
> bring an offering and come into his courts!
> Worship the Lord in holy array;
> tremble before him, all the earth! (Ps. 96:1–9)

At the time of Israel's exile in Babylon, the prophet Isaiah first mocks the folly of idolatry with stinging sarcasm: ironsmiths and carpenters deludedly worship what they themselves have made; then he summons the ends of the earth to find their salvation instead in Israel's redeemer, the Lord of hosts, who made the heavens and the earth: "I am the first and the last; and besides me there is no God" (Isa. 44–46). A final vision has all nations and tongues coming to Jerusalem to see the glory of the Lord in his temple (66:18–21; cf. Zech. 14).[1]

The New Testament sees that prophecy as having started to be fulfilled through a decisive intervention on God's part—the redemptive incarnation, death, and resurrection of the Son, and the outpouring of the pentecostal Spirit for the spread of the Gospel. Paul, apostle and evangelist, delights that the Thessalonian converts, through the preaching of the Word and the power of the Holy Spirit, have "turned from idols to serve the living and true God, and to wait for his Son from heaven, whom he raised from the dead, Jesus who delivers us from the wrath to come" (1 Thess. 1:2–10). Those are the events—the message, the response, the expectation—that mark the faith that comes to expression in worship addressed to the God who is their origin and their goal. Phenomenologically speaking, there are, in the sense of Luther and Calvin, "many (so-called) gods" and "many (so-called) lords," but the Christian confession is that "there is one God, the Father, from whom are all things and for whom we exist, and one Lord, Jesus Christ, through whom are all things and through whom we exist" (1 Cor. 8:4–6; cf. John 17:3; 1 John 5:20–21).

In his phenomenological classic on "the idea of the holy" (*Das Heilige*, 1917; English trans. 1923), Rudolf Otto designated by the term "numinous" the "mysterium tremendum et fascinans" that provokes worship from human beings at its manifestation. In biblical religion, the object and experience of awe have taken on a personal and ethical character. The Wholly Other has become the transcendent Creator. If the Creator inspires fear ("terrifies"), it is on account of his power and his purity; if he attracts ("fascinates"), it is by his creating love and his redeeming grace. If the creature feels fear, it is on account of the creature's own weakness and sin; if the creature is drawn toward God, it is because the love that made the creature will not let it go. Even further: God's power shows itself *as* love for the creature; God's purity shows itself *as* grace to transform the sinner. Whether in power and purity or in love and

The Tall Cross at Monasterboice. West face of the Tall Cross at Monasterboice, County Louth, Ireland, probably dating to the ninth century. Testifying to scriptural study in the monastic tradition, Irish high crosses may have served local instructional purposes (a kind of *biblia pauperum*) as well as being gathering points for processions and pilgrimages. They are regularly dominated by the crucified Christ on one main face, and often by Christ in majesty on the other. On the east face of the Tall Cross at Monasterboice appear typologically interpreted scenes pointing forward from the Old Testament to Christ and the Church (the sacrifice of Isaac, Moses smiting the rock, Samson's display of strength against the Philistines, the anointing of David, the ascension of Elijah, the three children in the fiery furnace), while the west face probably depicts (reading upward on the shaft from the lowest firmly decipherable panel) the baptism of Christ, the myrrh-bearing women coming to the tomb, Christ with Peter and Paul, the initial incredulity of Thomas (?), and the casting of lots for Jesus' robe. Surrounding the crucified Christ at the head of the cross are various incidents from the story of his Passion. (See Peter Harbison, *The High Crosses of Ireland: An Iconographical and Photographic Survey*, 3 vols., Bonn: R. Habelt, 1992, vol. 1, pp. 146–52 [text], vol. 2, figures 488–499 [photographs].) ART DIRECTORS AND TRIP/PHOTOGRAPH BY HÉLÈNE ROGERS

grace, there is an irreducible majesty about God. According to the Letter to the Hebrews (12:28–29), "worship with reverence and awe" is due to "our God [who] is a consuming fire"; according to an ancient prayer for Pentecost in the Gelasian Sacramentary, it was as "the burning fire of divine love" that the Holy Spirit descended upon the disciples of the risen Lord ("in ignis fervore tui amoris").

The Christian understanding of worship can be found in a concentrated way in Paul's Letter to the Romans. A close reading of that—accompanied by other references as appropriate—will provide a scriptural basis for the history that is presented in this book and the beginnings of a theological frame in which to view what is here described.[2] Christian worship recognizes its own scriptural basis by the fact that the continual reading of the scriptures is a constitutive part of the liturgy: these scriptures narrate the fundamental story, up to and including its awaited consummation; they contain the promises, commands, and patterns that worshipers take up as they play their own part in the story. The theological frame is vital because scripturally derived doctrine concerning God, man, and their proper relationship provides the standards by which Christian worshipers seek to abide as they embody and enact the ongoing life of the Church before God that is Tradition. In very broad lines, there is a consistency in the content and structures of Christian worship across the centuries; and this becomes apparent in the history that is told in the present book. It is, however, also the case that the liturgy has been an arena of doctrinal disputes over the Trinity, christology, and the modalities of salvation. These, too, are reflected in the arrangement of the book, where (for example) distinctions are made between Chalcedonian churches and non-Chalcedonian ("Oriental Orthodox"), between the Byzantine East and the Latin West, between the Roman Catholic Church and the Protestant churches (and among these latter).

The Letter to the Romans

In the first chapter of the epistle, the apostle sets his opening announcement of the Gospel in counterpoise to the fallen condition from which humankind is to be saved. The primordial sin consists in idolatry. From the beginning God's eternal power and

Saint James's Episcopal Church, Goose Creek, South Carolina. The church was built between 1708 and 1719. Typically for the Anglican tradition at that time, this building contains apsidal plaques displaying the Ten Commandments (the first of which continues to ground Christian worship), the Lord's Prayer, and the Apostles' Creed (the baptismal and perennial profession of faith). The pulpit and altar-table embody the centrality of word and sacrament in the liturgy of the Church.
G. E. KIDDER-SMITH/CORBIS

deity has been appropriately revealed to call forth honor and thanks, yet human beings have mistakenly attributed the divine glory to the creation that simply declares it (cf. Ps. 19:1–4): they have inexcusably "exchanged the truth about God for a lie and worshiped and served the creature rather than the Creator"; they have foolishly "exchanged the glory of the immortal God for images resembling mortal man or birds or animals or reptiles." Whether as the manifestation or as the consequence of this idolatry, human beings engage in lethally reprehensible behavior of body, mind, heart, and tongue.

After showing the universality of human wickedness (whether among Jew or Gentile, "none is righteous, no, not one"), Paul moves in chapter 3 to God's gracious redemptive action, which is described in cultic terms: "Since all have sinned and fall short of the glory of God, they are justified by his grace as a gift, through the redemption which is in Christ Jesus, whom God put forward as an expiation [*hilastêrion*] by his blood, to be received by faith" (vv. 23–24). The Letter to the Hebrews develops the fullest sacrificial account of Christ's atoning work. In accordance with the instituted sacrifices of the Old Testament, where God provided the blood or the life (Lev. 17:11), the author insists that it was the incarnate Son who once and for all made atonement by his self-offering to God through the eternal Spirit and thus entered the holy place, where he lives for ever to make intercession as high priest (Heb. 1:1–3; 2:17; 5:5–9; 6:19–20; 7:26–28; 9:1–14, 23–26; 10:11–14). In the heavenly dispensation Christ himself now takes the place of the "mercy seat" (*hilastêrion*) under the first covenant (Heb. 9:5). In the language and gestures of sacrifice that continue to mark the Christian liturgy, the worshipers can only faithfully appropriate the oblation of Christ and thus find through him access to the "throne of grace" (Heb. 4:14–16; 10:19–22; 12:22–24; 13:15).

In the fourth and fifth chapters of Romans Paul says more about being "set right" ("justified") by God and about the faith by which the free gift of salvation is received. He then needs, however, to warn his readers that divine grace is the very opposite of an excuse for continuance in sin. This he does, in chapter 6, in baptismal terms:

> Do you not know that all of us who have been baptized into Christ Jesus were baptized into his death? We were buried therefore with him by baptism into death, so that as Christ was raised from the dead by the glory of the Father, we too might walk in newness of life. . . . So you also must consider yourselves dead to sin and alive to God in Christ Jesus. (vv. 3–4, 11)

The life in Christ is lived according to the indwelling Spirit of God, as chapter 8 shows.

The eighth chapter is in fact rich in implications for Christian worship.[3] It speaks of the access to the Father that the Spirit gives to those who are thus joined to Christ, and of the intercessory power of the Spirit, who groans with them and helps them in their weakness as they await final redemption. To be led by the Spirit is to be sons and daughters of God; it is to "have received the Spirit of adoption, in whom we cry, Abba, Father" (vv. 14–15). Jesus himself prayed to his Father "in the Spirit" (Luke 10:21–22); and in teaching his disciples to pray "Our Father" (Matt. 6:9–13; Luke 11:2–4), Jesus gave them the privilege of using the Son's own form of address ("Abba" conveys both respect and familiarity, both gratitude and confident petition). When his disciples assemble in his name, he promises his presence among them and thus the Father's hearing of their prayers (Matt. 18:19–20). In Ephesians 2:18–22, the "access" to the Father through Christ in the Spirit is represented in corporate and cultic terms, believers becoming "a holy temple in the Lord" (cf. 1 Pet. 2:1–10).

Whereas in Romans 8:15 Christians pray in the Spirit, in the thematically similar passage of Galatians 4:1–6 it is the Spirit of God's Son, sent by God into the hearts of his adopted children, who cries "Abba, Father." The difference may not be great, as the continuation of Romans 8 shows. We have, says the apostle, "the first fruits of the Spirit," but still—or, more precisely, therefore—we "groan inwardly" as we "await" the fullness of our inheritance as God's adopted children, namely "the redemption of our bodies" (8:23); and in this we share the "groaning of the entire creation," for creation cannot be released from futility and decay until fallen humanity has fully regained its liberty in Christ. The "new creation" of 2 Corinthians 5:17–21 has individual, communal, and cosmic dimensions. The current inward groaning may indicate that "we do not know how or what to pray"; but then "the Spirit helps us in our weakness"; the Spirit "intercedes" by his own "ineffable groanings" (Rom. 8:26). Ernst Käsemann links the groanings by and in the Spirit with the "unutterable words" that Paul heard in his heavenly rapture (2 Cor. 12:4). Whereas "enthusiasts" at Corinth and elsewhere may interpret glossolalia in the congregation's worship as already "the language of heaven" in the manner of a radically realized eschatology (1 Cor. 13–14), Paul in Romans 8 (so Käsemann) understands such Spirit-inspired utterances as participation, still under the Cross, in the sighs of all that yearns, hopes, and waits for the final accomplishment of God's saving rule for which Christ the high priest is interceding in heaven (cf. Rom. 8:31–38). In any case, the Spirit's prayers, or prayers inspired by the Spirit, are sure to be heard, because "He who searches hearts knows what is the mind of the Spirit" and "the Spirit intercedes for the saints according to [the will of] God" (Rom. 8:27; cf. 1 Cor. 2:9–16). According to Revelation 22:17, it is together that the Spirit and the Church as Christ's Bride say "Come": "Come, Lord Jesus" (22:20).

The long argument in Romans 9–11 about Israel and the Gentiles includes the claim that the word of God is brought near by the preaching of the gospel of Christ (10:14–17), which makes possible the faith in the heart that "God raised [Jesus] from the dead" and the confession with the lips that "Jesus is Lord," whereby salvation comes—for "every one who calls upon the name of the Lord will be saved" (10:8–13). Those chapters conclude with a doxology to the merciful God whose final purpose it is that all—both Jew and Gentile—may be saved (11:25–36). When faith gains a voice, it becomes a vehicle for the extension of God's grace to others, and the chorus of thanksgiving swells to the glory of God (2 Cor. 4:13–15).

On the basis of all that he has said in Romans so far, the apostle summons his believing brothers and sisters to "present your bodies as a living sacrifice, holy and acceptable to God, which is your reasonable worship [*logikê latreia*]" (Rom. 12:1). According to Hebrews 13:15–16, what can now be offered through Christ is "a sacrifice of praise to God, the tribute of lips that acknowledge his name," without neglecting "to do good and to share what you have, for such sacrifices are pleasing to God." In Romans 12, Paul then goes on to describe Christians, with their varied gifts and ministries, as constituting one Body in Christ, into which they are incorporated by baptism (so 1 Cor. 12:13). In that light, Christian worship appears as vocal, corporeal, and corporate, embracing both liturgical assembly and mutual service among the congregation.

In Romans 13:1–7 Paul recognizes the God-given functions of the civil authorities, which grounds the practice in Christian worship of praying on their behalf, not least with a view to the peace that facilitates the course of the gospel (so 1 Tim. 2:1–7). By Romans 13:11–14 the present age is set in the eschatological perspective that marks all Christian worship: "Salvation is nearer to us now than when we first believed; the night is far gone, the day is at hand." That is the fact that grounds Paul's exhortation in 12:2 and renders the *logikê latreia* possible: "Do not be conformed to this age/world but be transformed by the renewal of your mind, that you may prove what is the good and acceptable and perfect will of God." Such worship is experienced by the Church as a foretaste of the heavenly liturgy adumbrated in the book of Revelation.

The need for mutual love, announced in Romans 13:8–10 according to the commandment, is applied in chapter 14 to a controversy in the Roman congregation which the apostle does not consider sufficient to divide the parties in fundamental faith. In chapter 15 Paul prays for them that they be of one mind (*to auto phronein*), one heart or will (*homothumadon*), and one mouth or voice (*en heni stomati*), for only so can they properly "glorify the God and Father of our Lord Jesus Christ" (vv. 5–6). The indispensability of mutual love in the celebration of the Lord's supper is made clear in 1 Corinthians 10–11.

In Romans 15:15–16 Paul speaks in liturgical or priestly terms of his evangelizing mission among the nations: by God's grace, he is a minister (*leitourgos*) of Christ Jesus to the Gentiles, serving as a priest (*hierourgountos*) the gospel of God, so that the offering (*prosphora*) of the Gentiles may be acceptable (*euprosdektos*), sanctified (*hagiasmenê*) by the Holy Spirit. Thus the Gentiles may come to praise and glorify God along with his people of the old covenant (vv. 8–12). The "offering of the Gentiles, sanctified by the Holy Spirit" (v. 16) rejoins the first part of Romans 8 and the Spirit of God dwelling in believers, resembling closely the figure of the temple, which the apostle uses in 1 Corinthians 6:19–20: "Do you not know that your body is a temple of the Holy Spirit within you, which you have from God? You are not your own; you were bought with a price. So glorify God in your body." The inclusion of "the nations" hints at the geographical and cultural spread that will positively characterize Christian worship, though the significance of geography and culture will always be qualified by the transcendent fact that the Father seeks those who will worship him in Spirit and in Truth (cf. John 4:20–26). Early Christian writers saw the eucharist as a fulfillment of the prophecy of Malachi 1:11 concerning the pure sacrifice that would be offered to the Lord of hosts from the rising of the sun to its setting.

The interweaving between mission and praise, between evangelical witness and the worship of God, is striking. It recurs in the doxology that concludes the Letter to the

Saint Paul's evangelizing mission. The Apostle Paul viewed his work of evangelism in terms of worship, employing a Greek vocabulary that had cultic resonances. *Saint Paul Preaching in Athens*, tapestry after a design by Raphael, c. 1515–1516. Pinacoteca Vaticana, Vatican Museums and Galleries, Vatican City/Scala/Art Resource, NY

Romans (16:25–27), the importance of which it is hard to overestimate for the understanding and practice of Christian liturgy:

> Now to him who is able to strengthen you according to my gospel and the preaching of Jesus Christ, according to the revelation of the mystery which was kept secret for long ages but is now disclosed and through the prophetic writings is made known to all nations, according to the command of the eternal God, to bring about the obedience of faith—to the only wise God be glory for evermore through Jesus Christ! Amen.

"Mystery" does not here refer immediately to God's incomprehensible transcendence, though that—"the King of kings and Lord of lords, who alone has immortality and dwells in unapproachable light"—is the infinite horizon of Christian worship (1 Tim. 6:15–16). Mystery here denotes the divine purpose and plan to bring human beings to salvation, which has now been brought to light as never before through its embodiment in Jesus Christ, the incarnate Son. Christ himself is "the mystery of our religion: manifested in the flesh, vindicated in the Spirit, seen by angels, preached among the nations, believed on in the world, taken up in glory" (1 Tim. 3:16). In the Christian liturgical assembly, that mystery is conveyed not only in "the prophetic writings" but also, and more directly, in the apostolic gospel and preaching, as Old and New Testaments are read, expounded, apprehended, and implemented, and in what came to be called "sacraments" (the Latin *sacramenta* corresponding to the Greek *mysteria*). Martin Luther, in *The Babylonian Captivity of the Church*, could say that, biblically speaking, there is but one sacrament, the Church's "sacraments" being "sacramental signs" of Christ himself (WA 6:501). The Flemish Dominican Edward Schillebeeckx's twentieth-century classic of sacramental theology was entitled *Christ the Sacrament of the Encounter with God*; the various sacraments are diverse enactments of the one encounter. Christ figures at the heart of worship as the mediator not only of God to man but of human praise and prayer to the only wise God: *soli Deo gloria*. That glory, as the doxology of Romans instantiates, is to be ascribed "for evermore." The "history of Christian worship" is the story of its occurrence under the reserve of an age in which, as believers are authoritatively warned, idolatry under many guises still tempts and threatens (1 Cor. 10:10–22; Gal. 5:20; Col. 3:5; Phil. 3:19): "Little children, keep yourselves from idols" (1 John 5:21).

If Romans 16 provides in "mystery" a basic category for the understanding and practice of Christian worship, it supplies also another in "glory," though we shall return rather to Romans 3, where the occurrence of that word, taken in conjunction with the associated notion of image, may lead into a more systematic account of our subject: "All have sinned and fall short of the glory of God" (Rom. 3:23). That negative declaration provides a clue for the positive interpretation of Christian worship. A first, and rather dense, statement of such an interpretation will then be unfolded in three ways in the rest of this chapter.

God's glory, in the first instance, is the sheer "godness"—the deity—of God, which is love (1 John 4:16). Christian theological speculation, prompted by the self-revelation of God in history, will figure this as the love among the Three Persons of the Blessed Trinity in all eternity. It can be said—after the event—that it was God's love that freely undertook the creation of a world other than himself, and that it was God's good purpose especially to create humankind in the expectation of a loving response that would also please God. In the words of the late-second-century bishop Irenaeus of Lyons (*Against the Heresies* 4.20.7), "the glory of God is man alive," whose "life is the vision of God" (*gloria Dei vivens homo, vita autem hominis visio Dei*). Humankind, however, in its God-given freedom has preferred to go its own way: idolatry is, at root, creaturely self-worship. Thus humankind has failed to reflect the radiant, self-diffusive goodness of God (cf. Exod. 33:17–23). In so doing, humanity has missed its vocation, as made in the image of God, to "render" glory to God. True worship occurs when human beings are restored to their original vocation and final end. This has happened redemptively in Jesus Christ, who is the image of God both from the divine side (2 Cor. 4:6; Col. 1:15–20; Heb. 1:1–3) and from the Adamic side (Rom. 5:15–21; 1 Cor. 15:42–50), being himself (in Chalcedonian terms) one Person, the Son, known in two natures.[4] "And the Word became flesh and dwelt among us, full of grace and truth; we have beheld his glory, glory as of the only Son from the Father. . . . No one has ever seen God; the only Son, who is in the bosom of the Father, he has made him known" (John 1:14, 18).

Those who adhere to Christ by faith and are incorporated into him by baptism are being renewed after the image of their Creator (Col. 3:1–10), conformed to the image of the firstborn Son (Rom. 8:29), and may thus, in the power of the Holy Spirit, render God the glory that is theirs by reflection (Rom. 8:30; 2 Cor. 3:17–18). Their daily lives and their cultic acts will not be at variance. Eschatologically, Hans Urs von Balthasar suggests, the bringing home of humankind to God may be considered an "additional gift" (*zusätzliches Geschenk*) in the eternal and ever-new mutual self-giving of the Father, Son, and Spirit, an "enrichment" (*Bereicherung*) or "enhancement" (*Steigerung*) of the divine life through its inclusion of the redeemed creature to which God grants participation in himself.[5] God's generosity in creation and salvation is his own "greater glory."

What has there been densely stated can be explicated through a consideration of three traditional accounts of humankind's creation "in the image of God" (as *imago Dei*), bringing out their implications for the theology of worship and for liturgical performance. The three strands, distinguishable though they are, will naturally interweave. They may be designated the personal, the social, and the cultural. Their interaction matches the overlap among their areas of reference.[6]

Imago Dei: Made for Communion with God

Whether the correspondence be located in freedom or reason or speech, humankind is seen throughout Scripture as made by God sufficiently like himself for communication to take place between the Creator and the human creature, a personal exchange in which each partner is meant to find satisfaction. The relationship, though mutual, is not symmetrical. It is well expressed in the opening exchange of the Westminster Assembly's Shorter Catechism of 1647–1648:

> What is the chief end of man?
>
> Man's chief end is to glorify God, and to enjoy him for ever.

The principle and the sentiment are hymnically enacted in the paraphrase of Psalm 147 by Isaac Watts (1674–1748), where our "duty" of praise is also our "delight":

> Praise ye the Lord! 'Tis good to raise
> Your hearts and voices in His praise:
> His nature and His works invite
> To make this duty our delight.

The delight, however, is also God's, as the final stanza makes clear:

> But saints are lovely in His sight,
> He views His children with delight;
> He sees their hope, He knows their fear,
> And looks, and loves His image there.

Humankind, in another lapidary formulation of Irenaeus, was made in the "image" of God, in order to grow into God's "likeness."[7] According to Augustine of Hippo, in *The City of God* (8.17.2), the height of religion is to imitate the object of worship: *imitari quem colis*. The moral perfections of God are to be reflected in the character of the worshiper as virtues. Therefore Augustine can also say, in the *Enchiridion* (1.3), that "God is to be worshiped by faith, hope, and love" (*fide, spe, caritate colendus est Deus*). The liturgy is the point at which this worship comes to concentrated symbolic expression in rites that are received as divinely given and in words that resonate with God's own.

The "nature" and "works" of God that invite worship are typically spelled out in the anaphora or great thanksgiving of the eucharist, where the presiding minister summons the assembly, "Lift up your hearts," and all consent that "it is right to give God thanks and praise."[8] This prayer may begin with awe at the transcendent being of God, characteristically expressed in such apophatic or negative attributions as "in-finite," "in-visible," "im-mortal," and "un-changing." Then may come recognition of the properties displayed in God's positive relation to the world, such as "wisdom," "power," and "mercy." The climax of this part of the prayer is the Sanctus, in which the Church on earth associates itself with the whole company of heaven in singing "Holy, Holy, Holy is the Lord God of hosts: Heaven and earth is full of your glory." To call God holy is a tautology, but this assertion and ascription is also an acclamation and an acknowledgment on the part of the worshipers. If it has not done so already, the praise of God then moves into thanks for God's action in history, culminating in the redemption of the world by the gift of the incarnate Son, Jesus Christ. The pivot of the prayer comes in the recital from the Last Supper, when Jesus gave to his disciples the rite by which to recall his death and resurrection until he should return. The sacramental reception of Christ and his benefits is envisaged under the bread and wine laid out on the altar-table, and his followers affirm in some way their association with his sacrifice. The Holy Spirit is invoked to make all these things possible. Then the present and local congregation petitions God for the sake of the universal Church and looks forward to sharing in the enjoyment of God's bliss with all God's saints from every time and place in the kingdom to come. The prayer concludes with a doxology that anticipates the everlasting glorification of God.

The communication between God and humankind is such that liturgy may be understood as a dialogue.[9] The primary pattern is that of call and response, the gracious initiative residing with God. The exchange occurs throughout the service, although at some points the voice may be God's and at others his people's. The reading of the scriptures, their explication, and their application are heard as a word from God. The human response may come as a word to God in the confession of faith and in prayers of thanksgiving, petition, and intercession. The dialogue is not pursued by oral and aural means only, though these predominate. According to the Scriptures, there is a certain material density about "the word of the Lord" (*dᵉbar-YHWH*). The prophet can "see the word of the Lord" in an object or a gesture (Amos 1:1; 7:1, 4, 7; 8:1; 9:1; Jer. 1:11–14). Moreover, "the hand of the Lord" can be upon Elijah, Elisha, or Ezekiel at crucial moments (1 Kings 18:46; 2 Kings 3:15; Ezek. 1:3; 3:14; 8:1; 37:1). According to the Psalmist it is possible to "taste and see the goodness of the Lord" (34:8). Lest all this be thought to remain at the level of metaphor, the Word took solid flesh in Jesus Christ (John 1:14). The voice from heaven, at Jesus' transfiguration, said "Listen to him." He not only told parables but enacted them, as in the feeding of the crowds, the turning of the water into wine, the entry into Jerusalem on a donkey, the cleansing of the Temple. Joining actions to words, by his touch he healed people from leprosy, cured blindness, and even raised Jairus's daughter from the dead. On the eve of his Passion, the Lord and Master washed his own disciples' feet, and on that same night he gave them the bread as his body and the cup of wine as his blood. Correspondingly, after Jesus' death and resurrection, the First Letter of John harks back to the prologue of John's Gospel in describing the continuing conveyance of the Word of life:

> That which was from the beginning, which we have heard, which we have seen with our eyes, which we have looked upon and touched with our hands, concerning the word of life . . . we proclaim also to you, so that you may have fellowship with us; and our fellow-ship is with the Father and with his Son Jesus Christ. (1:1–3)

It is entirely in line with this, then, that God's address comes to the worshiping assembly by other means as well as by the spoken word. Martin Luther, in the Large Catechism, called baptism a *Gotteswasser*, in which "God's Word is contained." God there does what he says, cleansing from sin and generating a new life destined for eternity (Titus 3:4–7). Instituted by Christ, sacraments are believed to effect what they signify. The imposition of hands may convey specified blessings. Anointings may be performed for healing (James 5:14–15). Perfumed oils signify spiritual gifts in chrismation and ordination. Body language functions in a Godward direction also. The human voice comes into play in speech and song. Gestures and postures have their place: "holy hands" may be lifted in prayer, as in the traditional *orans* position or in a charismatic assembly (cf. 1 Tim. 2:8), and standing or kneeling will mark different attitudes before God. Praise may be offered through processions and dance. Incense may be swung in adoration. Icons may be kissed, being themselves understood as signs of the presence of the incarnate Son and his saints.[10]

The Supper at Emmaus. On the first Easter Sunday the risen but unrecognized Lord expounded to two of his disciples on the road to Emmaus the things in the Law, the Prophets, and the Psalms concerning himself as the Christ, and then he "made himself known to them in the breaking of the bread" (Luke 24:13-35). The story sets a paradigm for the liturgy of the Church as "word and table." Painting (1648) by Rembrandt van Rijn (1606–1669). MUSÉE DU LOUVRE, PARIS/ SCALA/ART RESOURCE, NY

Liturgical worship has certain ethical presuppositions and consequences, since it is properly the symbolic focus that both gathers up and irradiates the whole of life, at the very heart of which is the relationship between human beings and God. The Old Testament prophets inveighed against solemn assemblies, feasts and sacrifices, the noise of songs, and the melody of harps, when these were belied by the people's conduct; they were unacceptable to the Lord unless and until the would-be worshipers repented of doing evil and learned to do good (Isa. 1:10–17; Amos 5:21–24; Hosea 6:6). The prophetic theme is carried over into the reported and reflected teaching of Jesus: to make an offering of what ought to have gone to father or mother is to break God's commandment (Mark 7:9–13); an offering should not be made to God before peace has been made with the brother or sister (Matt. 5:23–24); the house of prayer is desecrated when it is made a den of robbers (Mark 11:17). The implication of the "double commandment" and of the parable of the Good Samaritan is that love of God includes love of neighbor (Luke 10:25–37). Love of the invisible God is a lie without love of the visible brother or sister (1 John 4:19–21). By apostolic teaching, the imitation of Christ's self-offering occurs through "walking in love" for one another, which is the proper context for "speaking to one another in psalms and hymns and spiritual songs, singing and making melody to the Lord with all your heart, always and for everything giving thanks in the name of our Lord Jesus Christ to God the Father" (Eph. 5:1–20).

What has been said so far has been implicitly trinitarian; it is time now to bring the watermark to the surface. Baptism is administered "in the name of the Father and of the Son and of the Holy Spirit" (Matt. 28:18–20). The New Testament shows Christians addressing praise and prayer to "the Father" whom Jesus so addressed (Matt. 11:25 = Luke 10:21; Mark 14:36; Luke 23:34, 46; John 11:41; 12:27–28; 17 passim; 2 Cor. 1:3–4; Gal. 1:3–5; Eph. 1:3–10; 3:14–21; Col. 1:3; 1 Thess. 1:2–3; 1 Peter 1:3–5). Worship was also very early addressed to Christ himself: apart from the acts of obeisance (*proskunêsis*) in the synoptic gospels and the "My Lord and my God" of Thomas (John 20:28), there are hymns in praise of Christ's sovereignty (Phil. 2:5–11; Rev. 1:5–6; 5:13; cf. 2 Tim. 4:18; 2 Peter 3:18), and individuals prayed to him in time of need (Acts 7:59; 2 Cor. 12:8). As formal doctrine matured amid theological controversy, the Council of Nicaea in 325 located the Son's eternal generation in the very being of the Father, and the Nicenes argued against the Arians that the reduction of Christ to a creature would (unthinkably!) turn Christians into idolaters.[11] When the debate turned to the deity of the Holy Spirit also, Athanasius of Alexandria and the Cappadocians

Saint Basil the Great. Basil (c. 330–379), bishop of Caesarea in Cappadocia from 370, celebrating the holy liturgy. His treatise *On the Holy Spirit* provides the classic theological rationale for trinitarian worship. Scholars recognize, down to the details of phraseology, the strong impress of Basil's thought on the eucharistic anaphora that, in historically and geographically varied versions, goes under his name. Mural in the Church of Saint Sofia, Ohrid, Macedonia, Macedonian School, eleventh century (detail). BRIDGEMAN ART LIBRARY

appealed to the confession of the threefold name in baptism: since only God can save, any other baptism would have been salvifically useless.[12] In his treatise of c. 373 *On the Holy Spirit*, Basil of Caesarea was able to point to an existing tradition of addressing doxologies to the Holy Spirit alongside the Father and the Son, and this position was canonized by the Council of Constantinople in 381 in the creed: "And [we believe] in the Holy Spirit, the Lord and Giver of life, who proceeds from the Father, who with the Father and the Son together is worshiped and glorified." Basil's treatise justified two grammars of address in worship. Since all good gifts from the Father of lights are mediated by the Son and reach humankind in the Holy Spirit, it is appropriate to return thanks *in* the Spirit *through* Christ to the Father. In contemplating God in Himself, however, a coordinated form of address is appropriate, given the coinherence of the Three Persons.[13] In the classic liturgies of Christianity, the former structure is indeed the predominant mark of thanksgivings and petitions, while sheer doxology often punctuates the liturgy as

> Glory be to the Father and to the Son and to the Holy Spirit,
> As it was in the beginning, is now, and ever shall be, world without end.
> Amen.

Imago Dei: Made for Life in Society

The opening chapters of Genesis picture humankind as created "male and female," for the sake of companionship and with a view to continuing the race (Gen. 1:27–28; 2:21–25). These are the constituents of society. By the grace of God they remain such in the order of preservation, even after human disobedience to the divine command brings dislocation between the sexes and across the generations as well as among siblings (3:8–4:26). The social constitution of humankind finds redeemed embodiment in the Christian community at worship, even if its realization remains imperfect.

The rite of baptism is the sacrament of entry into a new set of family relationships. Rebirth as sons and daughters of God implies the acquisition of new brothers and sisters in the persons of all the Father's children. That is the basis of the *philadelphia* in which the apostle Paul encourages Christians to persist (Rom. 12:10; 1 Thess. 4:9–10; cf. 1 Peter 3:8). Refusal of love to the sister or brother is a denial of one's own filial relationship to the Father (1 John 3–4).

From apostolic times, however, the internal practice of the Christian assembly has not been without problems in the matter. The Letter of James castigates those who pay special attention to "the man with gold rings and in fine clothing," while they dishonor "the poor man in shabby clothing" (2:1–17). Whatever the details concerning the disorders in the Corinthian assembly, they clearly included feasting by some while others went hungry; and for the apostle Paul, that was to "despise the church of God" (1 Cor. 11:22). The Letter of Jude speaks of people who "are blemishes on your love feasts, as they boldly carouse together, looking after themselves" (v. 12). On the more positive side, we find care deliberately taken to feed the widows, although even that was not without its troubles (Acts 6). At the end of the second century in North Africa, Tertullian describes a meal by which the poor were helped (*Apologeticum*, 39). An early church order, *The Apostolic Tradition*, gives the following instruction for a love feast or agape: "If you are invited all to eat together, eat sufficiently, but so that there remain something over that your host may send to whomever he wills, as the superfluity of the saints, and the person to whom it is sent may rejoice with what is left over." Eventually, the agape disappeared from the main stream of Christian practice, although it has occasionally been revived among "purist" or "enthusiastic" groups such as the Paulicians, the Mennonites, the Moravians, and the early Methodists. At some point (scholars differ as to when), a separation took place between the agape and the sacramental eucharist, probably on account of the kind of abuses recorded in 1 Corinthians 11. Celebrated "unworthily" (one might say "unethically"), the Lord's supper could, according to the apostle, be morbidly counterproductive. On the other hand, mutual care is demonstrated sacramentally when Justin Martyr reports, in second-century Rome, that deacons carried the elements from the communal celebration to those who were prevented from attending by sickness or imprisonment (*First Apology* 67).

The sacramental eucharist, its character as a meal having been reduced to minimal proportions, has for most of history been left to bear the weight of symbolically expressing the brotherly and sisterly love to which those who address God as "Abba" are called. Drawing on a possible underlying Hebraic idiom, a creative interpretation of Romans 14:17 may provide a scriptural basis and theological frame for the Lord's supper as the social embodiment of the Christian community: "The kingdom of God *is* food and drink *insofar as* eating and drinking express and foster justice, peace, and joy in the Holy Spirit."[14] A responsibly celebrated eucharist exemplifies justice because thankful people are welcomed by the merciful Lord into his table fellowship and all together share in the fruits of redemption and in the foretaste of the new heavens and the new earth in which right will prevail (cf. 2 Peter 3:13). The eucharist, responsibly celebrated, also exemplifies peace, because reconciled people are there at peace with God and with one another (cf. Matt. 5:23–24). Responsibly celebrated, the eucharist finally exemplifies joy in the Holy Spirit, because the participants "do not get drunk with wine" but rather the cup of blessing conveys to all who partake of it a taste of that "sober inebriation" that the Spirit gives (cf. Eph. 5:18). Having learned and experienced all this in the paradigm of the eucharistic meal, the Christian community is committed—in terms of mission—to an everyday witness in word and deed that will give the opportunity for all the material resources of creation and all occasions of human contact to become the medium of that communion with God and among human beings which is marked by justice, peace, and joy in the Holy Spirit, and in which the kingdom of God consists. In that line of worldly extension, some twentieth-century Orthodox theologians took to speaking of "the liturgy after the Liturgy."[15]

Orthodox liturgy. Festal patriarchal divine liturgy for the Feast of the Entrance of the Mother of God into the Temple. The Patriarch of Moscow, Alexsy II, distributes communion to the faithful in the Kremlin's Dormition Cathedral (built in the fifteenth century) in Moscow on 21 November (Gregorian calendar)/4 December 2004 (Julian calendar). The Christian liturgy celebrates and embodies in the present moment the communion of the saints that transcends the generations. PHOTOGRAPH COURTESY OF REV. ALEXANDER RENTEL

Each local congregation must first be gathered and shaped. In his theological exposition of the course of the Byzantine liturgy, Alexander Schmemann speaks fundamentally of "the sacrament of the assembly," for it is at the eucharist that "you assemble as a church" (1 Cor. 11:18) and the presider and people "concelebrate." In ancient churches, the very icons "seem to take part in the assembly of the Church, they express its meaning, they provide its eternal movement and rhythm. The entire Church, the entire assembly, with all its 'ranks'—prophets, apostles, martyrs and saints—seems to ascend to heaven, elevated and lifted up by Christ to his table in his kingdom." Critical of what he terms the "Western captivity" of much modern Orthodoxy, Schmemann seeks a model in a more classic piety according to which

> each member knew from the very beginning, from the deacon's exclamation "*kairos!*" ("It is time to begin the service to the Lord") to the concluding "Let us depart in peace," he was taking part in a single *common task*, in one sacred reality, wholly identified with what the Church is revealing, manifesting, and granting in the given moment, in her ascent to the heavenly table of the kingdom.

Finally, the eucharist is "the sacrament of the kingdom."[16]

In its Constitution on the Sacred Liturgy, the Second Vatican Council spoke of the liturgical assembly of the particular church as the "preeminent manifestation of the Church," comprising "the full, active participation of all God's holy people . . . especially in the same eucharist, in a single prayer, at one altar at which the bishop presides, surrounded by his college of presbyters and his ministers" (41). Thus is displayed and enacted, in its differentiated ordering, the social constitution of the Catholic Church as a *plebs sancta*, a royal priesthood unto God (cf. 1 Peter 2:9; Rev. 1:6; 5:10). Other ecclesial bodies may structure assemblies and distribute roles differently. Thus the congregations of classic Protestantism—given the Reformers' purpose of a critical correction of the Church according to Scripture—have typically centered on a pastor in his pulpit amid a community of listeners and learners. A Pentecostal service may find more fluid leadership among the momentarily inspired. As early as the first- or second-century *Didache*, there could apparently be a risk of tensions over liturgical presidency and preaching between a local leader (say, a bishop with a character and functions modeled on the "head of a household"; 1 Tim. 3:4–5) and a wandering prophet.[17] In the Constantinian era, the bishop's status and function as an imperial official brought with it some features of civil ceremonial. Rises in the general social status of women, especially in modern times, have been followed, to varying degrees in different churches, by the appointment of women to positions of liturgical leadership, although such shifts have sometimes occurred first in the churches and then influenced society at large. The social structures and behavior of the worship assembly may not only borrow from the ambient world but may also challenge it, as with the "black churches" of America in the face of a (formerly) slave-holding society.[18]

At the very beginning of the modern Liturgical Movement, Dom Lambert Beauduin perceived that the worship assembly was the chief locus for the formation of Christian faith and life and the shaping of the Christian community (see Chapter 27 "The Liturgical Movement and Ritual Revision in the Catholic Church"). In patristic times, the process began with the catechumenate, in which converts received verbal instruction from appointed teachers, had their conduct examined, and underwent ritual exorcism from the forces of evil. As the moment for their baptism approached, they had the words of the creed and of the Lord's prayer "delivered" to them, which they then "returned." It was usually only after their baptism that the full meaning of the sacramental rites was explained to them in a "mystagogical catechesis." While some such pattern has continued to be practiced in missionary situations (though often in truncated forms), the growth of a Christendom in which the subjects of baptism have predominantly been infants entailed the temporal transposition of even basic teaching into a feature of the already constituted liturgical community. It is there that participants principally learn the language—both words and gestures—of the faith.

Liturgy and/as Language

Christian ritual constitutes a complex symbolic system—employing verbal, gestural, and material signs—by which the Church and the churches explore, describe, interpret, and fashion reality; express and form their thoughts, emotions, and values; and communicate across time and space in ways that both build and convey traditions as well as both allowing and reflecting social relations in the present. In the twentieth century, liturgical theologians and practitioners worked in an intellectual and cultural context that was marked by the linguistic turn in philosophy, the hermeneutical approach in literary studies, the iconological attention to meaning in the visual arts, and the preoccupation of sociology and psychology with questions of identity. The case of Christian worship is perennially rendered special by the fundamental fact that God, who is both transcendent and self-communicating, is believed to speak and act through rites that he has instituted and to receive the praise and the prayers that are addressed to him.

From linguistic philosophy, liturgists have found help in the notions of "performative language" and "speech acts," or "how to do things with words" (Austin, 1962): words and gestures "take effect," for example, in the pouring of water and the invocation of the Triune Name of God. Hermeneutical theory emphasizes the importance of a tradition in the "reading" of "texts," broadly understood, thus enacting the communion of the saints across the worshiping generations. Visual signs have a scriptural ancestry in the prophetic "seeing" of the word of the Lord (as in Amos and Jeremiah), a christological basis in the incarnate Son as revelation of the Father and "image of the invisible God," and an eschatological future in salvation as the face-to-face "vision of God" (expected in 1 Cor. 13:12, Heb. 12:14, and Rev. 22:4). From the human sciences, liturgists have drawn on sociology and psychology for understanding how communal and personal identity is both expressed and shaped by rituals: the churches have rites for the admission, nourishment, suspension, expulsion, and restoration of their members as well as the appointment of officers in their community; the stages of an individual's life, from birth through maturity, vocation, marriage, perhaps sickness, and certainly death may have a Christian stamp put on them by "rites of passage."

The linguistic philosopher Richard Schaeffler has helpfully analyzed how the doxological dialogue builds up the community of believers. Semantically, grammatically, and pragmatically, the faith is transmitted from the past by the reading of canonical texts and the performance of consecrated actions that allow present experience of reality to be shaped, tested, expressed, and enriched in interpretive interaction with the normative events of salvation. Moreover, this takes place within a fellowship of mutual help among contemporary members (a "horizontal" dialogue), and in the perspective of ongoing renewal through orientation to the definitive sight of God's glory, which in each generation is anticipated by God's gracious address and its response in praise.[19] Enunciating a principle that goes beyond the circumstances of the particular controversy in which he was engaged, the French Catholic bishop J.-B. Bossuet (1627–1704) could say that "le principal instrument de la tradition de l'Église est renfermé dans ses prières."[20] From the viewpoint of the particular worshipers, participation in the liturgy is an act by which they associate themselves with a continuing community; they thereby themselves become carriers of the living Tradition.

In Wittgenstinian terms, the worship assembly may be regarded as the concentrated instantiation of an entire "form of life." It plays its own "language game": Christians at worship are not engaging in scientific description or everyday conversation, nor even theological discourse; rather, they are conversing with God, who is their creator and redeemer. This game has its ontological rules (at the level of the objective difference and relation between humanity and God), it includes technical moves whose efficacy has been proved in past play, and the present enjoyment and permanent point of the game lie in a growing communion of the worshipers with God. By virtue of its role in the encounter with God, human language—drawing on the biblical records of the original and normative self-communication of God in revelation and redemption and on the continuing divine-human dialogue in the history of the Church—operates in a characteristic "register" in the liturgy. Within the linguistic register of worship, there are several subregisters that correspond to different aspects or moods of the communion with God: adoration toward the God of majesty and mercy; confession of sin and lament for misery; proclamation of the divine message of redemption; profession of faith and the giving of thanks for salvation; self-oblation in obedience to God, whose service is perfect freedom; petition and intercession in the face of all that stands in the way of God's kingdom; and expectation and anticipation of the delights of heaven and the final renewal of creation.

In the second half of the twentieth century, several processes took place affecting the language of worship in the churches in various ways and to different degrees. At least six may be mentioned: the shift of the Latin rite into the vernaculars; the widespread recasting of service books among the Protestant churches; the proliferation of new translations of the Bible; the secularization of much of older Christendom and the spread and growth of Christianity in other parts of the world; the flourishing of pentecostal or charismatic versions of the faith; and the developing concern for inclusivity in society at large. These were arenas in which historically recurrent tensions in the practice of worship took contemporary linguistic form: between mystery and intelligibility, between sacral and mundane, between inheritance and novelty, between universality and particularity, between unity and diversity, and between fixity and freedom.

Tradition through time signals the transgenerational character of the church in a deeper sense than the merely historical. Christian liturgy brings to expression in various ways the belief that its social relations are not finally severed by death but rather are enfolded in the eternal keeping of God and to be consummated in God's final Kingdom. The present form of relationships across death has been differently envisaged and cultivated according to history and geography, sometimes to the point of theological controversy. The offering of the eucharist for the benefit of the departed seems to be implied in Tertullian's ironic remarks in early-third-century North Africa about a widower who has remarried and perhaps now "offers for" both a living and a deceased wife (*On Chastity*, 11); and the notion is certainly present in Augustine's distinction at the altar between martyrs, whose prayers Christians should request, and the other departed, for whom prayer is commended (*Sermons* 159, 1; PL 38:868). The medieval West developed an intricate system of prayers and masses for the faithful departed on their way through Purgatory, which was conceptually criticized by the Orthodox East and pragmatically attacked by the Protestant Reformers on account of the accompanying papal

The most spectacular linguistic change was the rapid switch from Latin to modern languages in the Roman Catholic Church. At the Council of Trent (1545–1563), echoes persisted of the medieval argument that the three languages in which Pilate wrote what he wrote—Hebrew, Greek, and Latin—were the only ones fit for use in divine worship; but in face of the move by the Protestant Reformers into what the Anglican Articles called language "understanded of the people," the Tridentines justified the maintenance of Latin on the grounds of its universality (it was still the language of educated Western culture) and of the dangers of doctrinal error arising from the translation of liturgical texts (Schmidt, 1950). As late as 1947, Pope Pius XII in his encyclical on the sacred liturgy, *Mediator Dei*, argued for the continuing use of Latin as "an imposing sign of unity and an effective safeguard against the corruption of true doctrine." Under pressure from the Liturgical Movement, however, the Second Vatican Council in 1963, while preserving the normative status of Latin in the liturgy, gave prudent encouragement to some translation of the liturgy for use in modern vernaculars (*Constitution on the Sacred Liturgy*, 36); local episcopal conferences quickly exploited their authority in this matter, no doubt as part of the implementation of the equally conciliar principle of "full, conscious, and active participation" by the faithful in liturgical celebrations (*Constitution on the Sacred Liturgy*, 14). After several decades along these lines, the Roman Congregation for Divine Worship and the Discipline of the Sacraments in 2001 judged it necessary to issue, in *Liturgiam Authenticam*, a very detailed and cautionary "instruction on vernacular translation of the Roman liturgy."

Over that same period of time, many Protestant churches were recasting their service books and revising their liturgical language. Ecumenical convergences were achieved through a return to patristic structures in the rites (*ressourcement*), whereas linguistic revision moved rather in the direction of updating (*aggiornamento*). While a transitional phase allowed for the parallel continuance of "traditional" language (as in modest revisions of, say, the *Book of Common Prayer*), the "contemporary" forms have achieved increasing favor. The most noticeable sign in English at the early stage was the move from "Thou" (once both intimate and dignified but then

grant, and even sale, of indulgences. In the canon of the Roman mass, God is simply asked to "remember his servants who preceded us with the sign of faith" and to grant to "all who rest in Christ . . . a place of refreshment, light and peace."

Martyrs were early believed to gain direct access to heaven, where they joined the apostles (themselves martyred), the Blessed Virgin Mary, and (finally) other persons of conspicuous sanctity. Both the Orthodox East and the Catholic West "honor" the saints at the offering of the eucharist, expect help from their intercessions, and ask at the last to be given a share in their heavenly joys. Again, however, the Protestant Reformers attacked the "cult" of the saints, alleging an infringement of the sole mediatorship of Christ, an illicit notion of the transferability of merits earned by works of supererogation (that is, works performed beyond the call of duty), and the superstitious attribution of miraculous properties to the bodily relics of the saints. The confessional documents of the Reformation churches nevertheless claim to honor the saints by giving thanks to God for his exemplary grace at work in their lives and by imitating their faith and other virtues, or by "loving them as brothers," and desiring to "share eternal salvation with them, to dwell eternally with them in the presence of God, and to rejoice with them in

archaic) to "You" in the address to God. The shift to the contemporary occurred, more broadly, at a time when many intellectuals, and some theologians, considered that "mankind" had now "come of age" and outgrown the dependence on a sovereign and transcendent God signified by worship as hitherto understood and practiced; correspondingly, the newer liturgical language itself took on a somewhat immanentist and humanistic cast, provoking many worshipers in turn to complain about the loss of a sense of the divine mystery. Another linguistic tension caught liturgical revision between the bureaucratic prose of mid-century committee work and the risk of poetic idiosyncrasy, which can be accommodated in an occasional hymn but not in ordinaries and propers for regular use. (Something of both the ideological and the aesthetic struggle can be caught in Prayer II C—nicknamed "the Star Trek eucharist"—of the 1979 Prayer Book of the Episcopal Church in the United States.) Ecumenical agreements within a language area—say, English or German—on "common texts" for standard canticles and creeds were a positive accomplishment, although the wording of the Lord's Prayer remains contested in English.

Again, progress has been made in ecumenically agreed translation of the Bible. In French, there is the *Traduction oecuménique de la Bible* (*TOB*; 1975), in German the *Einheitsübersetzung* (1979), and since 1995 a new translation of the whole Bible into contemporary Tamil, sponsored by both the United Bible Societies and the Roman Catholic Church. In English, the *Revised Standard Version* (1951) functioned well for a couple of generations until it was overtaken by the *New RSV* (1989). However, the twentieth century also witnessed, especially in English, a proliferation of other translations of varying quality and for various purposes; and their often eclectic use in worship has contributed to the loss of a relatively common "scriptural language." Some communities, especially among African Americans and classic Evangelicals, have preferred to retain the King James Version. Conservatism in biblical translation in no way disqualifies but rather invites an imaginative and provocative application of the scriptural message in the sermon, the homily now being recognized, even in the Roman Catholic Church, as "part of the liturgy itself (*pars ipsius liturgiae*)" (*Constitution of the Sacred Liturgy*, 52).

Christ."[21] These sentiments might have left room for (say) the calendrical commemoration of saints, but while a modest such *sanctorale* was retained in the Anglican Books of Common Prayer, the Lutheran churches left very little, and the Reformed churches in the Swiss, Dutch, and Scottish areas none at all. The twentieth-century Liturgical and Ecumenical Movements brought a new interest among some mainstream Protestants in a liturgical observance of saints' days and a recognition that the Church on earth joins its worship of God to that offered by the saints in heaven; but most would still hesitate to extend to the invocation of the help of a named saint in heaven the principle that "the prayer of a righteous person availeth much" (James 5:16).[22]

Imago Dei: Made to Administer the Earth

In the ancient Near East, it was a custom of rulers to set up statues of themselves in distant provinces in order to assert their claim to sovereignty over the territory. A third traditional strand in the interpretation of humankind as made in the image of God

The secularization (and perhaps the paganization) of much of older Christendom and the spread and growth of Christianity in various other parts of the world raises again the question—manifested also and perhaps especially at the level of liturgical language—of the interaction between the gospel and culture. What was true for Europe during the conversion of the Western nations is now recurring elsewhere: the studies of Lamin Sanneh (1989) have demonstrated the transformative effect of Bible translation and use on language and society in parts of Africa and Peter Phan (1998) has shown the same in a more limited way in connection with catechetical work in parts of Asia. In initial phases, crucial decisions are required in the evaluation of the other religious beliefs and practices that already permeate the receptor languages. In the reevangelization of the West, the issue may be the retrieval of the stories, images, and concepts that shaped the languages for a thousand years and more. The transmission by radio of the linguistically traditional Service of Lessons and Carols on Christmas Eve from King's College Chapel, Cambridge, retains a remarkable global popularity, and many local churches have borrowed from it.

The Pentecostal Movement dates from the turn into the twentieth century. Whether in "tongues" or in natural language, Pentecostal worshipers have been said to construct "cathedrals in sound." (For a sympathetic study of glossolalia by a professional linguist, see Samarin, 1972). The milder Charismatic Movement has fostered free prayer also in mainstream denominations, as had long been the practice in the "free churches." Even staid parishes have been known to improvise the biddings at the time of intercessions. The tension between fixity and freedom reaches back to the beginnings of Christian worship. According to Justin Martyr in Rome (c. 150), it appears that the presider extemporized the eucharistic prayer "to the best of his power" (*First Apology* 67), although it may have been according to a template or paradigm such as the so-called *Apostolic Tradition* of Hippolytus provided for the newly ordained bishop a couple of generations later. However, various North African synods around AD 400 document that the later moves toward complete fixity were due at least in part to the need to ensure the doctrinal orthodoxy of new prayers even when written down (Bouley, 1981). Other factors making for fixity are the social need for formality in large assemblies and the psychological need for the regularity that confirms relationships. Even Pentecostal and "black church" worship falls into patterns in both its larger and its smaller units, although its pneumatic dynamism allows for spontaneity and surprises.

In the area of social inclusivity, especially between male and female, many Protestant churches using European languages have diminished the use of "generic masculines" in their service(book)s, adopting instead the line of "men and

has taken it to signify appointment as God's viceroy upon the earth. In the mid-twentieth century, some theologians invoked the command of Genesis 1:28 to "subdue and have dominion" in order to explain historically the rise of technology in a Western culture where a biblically de-divinized nature had been set free for human use; further, the text was claimed morally to justify the exploitation of the earth's resources. More recently, growing awareness of the modern ecological crisis has led theologians to turn rather to the other creation story in Genesis: the human task is to "till the earth and *keep*

women." In reference to God, some have expanded their language by drawing on various scriptural metaphors and similes with female resonances (see Ramshaw, 1995), but no substantial Christian body has abandoned the normative nominal use of "Father, Son, and Holy Spirit." The Roman Catholic Church, as evidenced in *Liturgiam Authenticam*, has been very hesitant to authorize linguistic change even in reference to human beings, for fear of losing nuances in the biblical and traditional texts.

Theologically, all Christian use of language is governed by the Incarnation of the Word, as Athanasius makes clear in his treatise bearing that title, and also Augustine in *De doctrina christiana*. Christian liturgy stands under that rubric, and in turn helps to keep believers aware of it.

References

Austin, J. L. *How to Do Things with Words.* Cambridge, Mass.: Harvard University Press, 1962.

Bouley, Allan. *From Freedom to Formula: The Evolution of Eucharistic Prayer from Oral Improvisation to Written Texts.* Washington, D.C.: Catholic University of America Press, 1981.

Jasper, David, and R. C. D. Jasper, eds. *Language and the Worship of the Church.* New York: St. Martin's Press, 1990.

Justin Martyr. *First Apology* 67.

McCabe, Herbert. "The Eucharist as Language." *Modern Theology* 15 (1991) 131-141.

Phan, Peter. *Mission and Catechesis: Alexandre de Rhodes and Inculturation in Seventeenth-Century Vietnam.* Maryknoll, N.Y.: Orbis, 1998.

Ramshaw, Gail. *God beyond Gender: Feminist Christian God-Language.* Minneapolis, Minn.: Fortress Press, 1995.

Samarin, William J. *Tongues of Men and Angels: The Religious Language of Pentecostalism.* New York: Macmillan, 1972.

Sannah, Lamin. *Translating the Message: The Missionary Impact on Culture.* Maryknoll, N.Y.: Orbis, 1989.

Schmidt, Herman. *Liturgie et langue vulgaire: Le problème de la langue liturgique chez les premiers réformateurs et au Concile de Trente.* Translated from the Dutch by Dom Suitbert Caron. Rome: Gregorian University, 1950.

Wainwright, Geoffrey. "Babel, Barbary, and the Word Made Flesh: Liturgy and the Redemption of the World." *Antiphon* 3.3 (1998) 5–14.

it" (2:15), and the power to "name" the nonhuman creation (2:19–20) is less the right to exploit it than the duty to give it meaning. A theology of Christian worship has to look at the liturgy's paradigmatic function between nature and culture as the human being stands before God and administers the divine gift of creation.

Frederick Dillistone derived two primordial patterns of worship from a distinction that emerged in the earliest history of the human race between the gatherers and the hunters, between "centripetal" and "centrifugal" communities:

> Within the community able to survive through dependence on the resources of a par-
> ticular territory, there tends to be a sense of regularity, of repetition, promoted by the
> regular movements of the heavenly bodies, by dependence on predictable rainfall and by
> the rhythm of the annual seasons. Humans and the natural order are thus closely allied.
> The dance is a natural expression of solidarity; so too is the procession to the accompa-
> niment of drums. There is continuity from generation to generation as rhythmic chants
> are intoned. . . .
>
> In contrast to the sedentary, repetitive pattern characteristic of a settled society, there
> exists another pattern expressed by an outward-moving, goal-seeking social group. . . . A
> sudden appearance, an unexpected confrontation, a period of suspense—all found a place in
> a successful hunt. And when the prey had been captured, the opportunity came to celebrate
> symbolically by dramatic reconstruction of the contest, by song or by story-telling. . . .
>
> Thus, in ritual theory and practice, there has been a signal divide. On the one hand,
> ritual action and vocal prayer constantly repeated; on the other, a story (recording some
> surprising event) and dramatic celebration. In the one case, religious exercises have been
> directed towards superhuman powers whose nature has been revealed in and through
> the wonderful constancies of the created order: birth and death, seedtime and harvest,
> the regular supplies of water and the control of fire. In the other case, they have been
> directed towards the power who has guarded a particular people through the vicissitudes
> of their historic experiences, sustaining them by surprising deliverances in the past and
> promises for the future, such deliverances and promises being dramatised by means of
> ritual activities.

Recognizing that such a distinction could never be absolute, and certainly not in the
case of Christian worship, Dillistone is nevertheless ready to speak of "liturgy in the
round" and "liturgy on the road."[23]

Set broadly in some such perspective, Christian liturgy can be seen as human creatures—in their archetypal experiences with time, space, and matter—having the redeeming stamp of the Bible's God put upon them as God works out his purposes for
humankind and the world and gives humans an active share in their achievement in
ways that have implications for culture, prior as well as consequent, universal as well
as particular.

Time

Clearly, the liturgy is an occasion and locus for worshipers to deal symbolically—
coram Deo—with the natural data of time and space. The passage of time is the most
ineluctable experience of human beings. Its chief markers are the alternance of day
and night as the earth turns on its own axis, and the annual cycle as the earth circles
the sun. "Morning and evening"—a refrain in the story of creation in Genesis 1—are
the daily moments for sacrifice and prayer in the Old Testament (Exod. 29:38–46;
Pss. 5:1–3; 59:16–17; 141:1–2), and lauds and vespers figure as the principal services
in the Christian office of the hours. Morning, in particular, carries associations with
the constantly renewed gift of life, as in the hymn of John Keble (1792–1866):

> New every morning is the love
> Our wakening and uprising prove. . . .

With "each returning day" come "new mercies" that allow "our daily course," "the
common task," to become "a road / To bring us daily nearer God." Morning has
acquired special historical resonances through the divine provision of manna in the
wilderness (Exod. 16) and the resurrection of Christ (Matt. 28; Mark 16; Luke 24;

John 20). According to "the last words of David," the early morning graciousness of God can be reflected in the just rule of the Lord's Anointed (2 Sam. 23:1–7); and the morning hymns of the Church can hail the risen and ascended Christ as the Sun of Righteousness (as in Charles Wesley's "Christ, whose glory fills the skies"). Characteristic themes of evening, beyond thanks for the day spent, are prayers for protection through the darkness and for repose in expectation of a final awakening, as in the hymn of Thomas Ken (1637–1711):

> Glory to Thee, my God, this night
> For all the blessings of the light;
> Keep me, O keep me, King of kings,
> Beneath Thy own almighty wings. . . .
>
> Teach me to live, that I may dread
> The grave as little as my bed;
> Teach me to die, that so I may
> Rise glorious at the awful day.

The annual seasonal cycle of pastoral and agricultural feasts received in biblical Israel a commemorative function in the history of salvation. The springtime lambs were taken into Passover as the yearly celebration of the Exodus from Egypt; the harvest feast of Weeks, fifty days later (*pentêkostê* in the Septuagint at Tob. 2:1), came to be associated in rabbinic Judaism with the lawgiving and covenant of Sinai. Under the New Testament, the apostle Paul could declare that "Christ our Passover has been sacrificed for us" (1 Cor. 5:7), and the death and resurrection of Christ—as the "Exodus" that he accomplished at Jerusalem (Luke 9:31)—early came to be celebrated as the "paschal mystery" at Easter.[24]

In Christian usage, the developed feast of Pentecost was the occasion for late patristic preachers to relate the new covenant of the Spirit to the old covenant of the Law, and to present the gift of the Holy Spirit for apostolic witness (Acts 2) as a reversal of Babel (Gen. 11), bringing unity and catholicity to the Church and its mission.[25] According to a familiar though not uncontested hypothesis, the festival of Christ's nativity took its date from the winter solstice and the late Roman imperial feast of *Sol invictus*, or at least acquired its popularity as a substitute for the solar celebration.[26] The "historicization" of the annual cal-

Harvest festival. Harvest festival in a Methodist church in Britain. Photograph by Hélène Rogers/Art Directors and Trip

endar ("liturgy on the road") still leaves room for the rhythms of nature and culture to be celebrated, as for instance when the feast of the Transfiguration becomes on Greek soil the occasion for welcoming the grape harvest, or when churches in the Protestant North hold their "harvest festivals" in thanksgiving that "All is safely gathered in / 'Ere the winter storms begin" (so the nineteenth-century hymn by Henry Alford, "Come, ye thankful people, come").

The phases of the moon carry some cultic significance in the Old Testament in connection with the deliverance from Egypt, as in Psalm 81:

> Blow the trumpet at the new moon,
> at the full moon, on our feast day.
> For it is a statute for Israel,
> an ordinance of the God of Jacob,
> when he went out against the land of Egypt.[27]

It is, however, the seven-day week from the creation story in Genesis 1 that remains imprinted on Christian worship. Justin Martyr, in second-century Rome, gives the theological reasons in favor of Sunday as the day of liturgical assembly: it is "the first day of the week," when God "made the world," and when "Jesus our Savior rose from the dead" (*First Apology* 67).[28] Eastern Orthodox Christians consider every Sunday a "little Easter," and Athanasius of Alexandria called the span of fifty days from Easter to Pentecost "the great Sunday" (*magna dominica*, according to the Latin version of his festal letters). The appellation of Sunday in many languages as "the Lord's day" makes the connection with the resurrection and may also point forward to Christ's return on "the Day of the Lord," since there is a traditional expectation that the Second Advent will take place on a Sunday.[29] The eschatological associations of Sunday are seen also in its patristic designation as the "eighth day," going beyond the present "week" into the future age.

Some features of the Old Testament seventh-day sabbath have been carried over to the Christian Sunday, including the notion of "rest" in an eschatological sense (Heb. 4). For God, however, work and rest are not ultimately opposed, as may be inferred from the acts and words of Jesus when he heals the lame man on the sabbath by the pool of Bethsaida (John 5). Work and rest find a resolution in play, and Romano Guardini was bold enough to speak of "the playfulness [*Spielhaftigkeit*] of the liturgy," and Jean-Jacques von Allmen of worship as "an eschatological game." The German Romantic theologian Friedrich Schleiermacher saw the cultus as "festival" in the "pauses" of the everyday.[30]

Space

As embodied creatures, human beings occupy space. For its place of worship, Israel had in its journeyings the tent of meeting (Exod. 40); in its settlement, the Jerusalem temple (1 Kings 8); in its exile, room for weeping (Ps. 137)—though the people knew that the Lord's presence was inescapable (Ps. 139). While Christian worship occurs "in Spirit and in Truth" (John 4:24), it also requires a physical place. This may range from a room in a "house church" or *domus ecclesiae* (where the social dimension of the gathering is particularly evident) to a naturally impressive site (where the wonders of creation are readily evoked). At least from the fourth century on, local congregations have purposely constructed entire buildings for the celebration of the liturgy, sometimes following civic models (existing basilicas were indeed occasionally comandeered for new use), sometimes adopting ground plans that made a doctrinal statement (say, in the shape of a cross), sometimes elevating mystical aspirations in towers and steeples ("prayers in stone") or prefiguring the courts of heaven in vast domes adorned inside by, say, a painting or mosaic of Christos Pantokrator (that is, Christ the Universal King).

As James White demonstrates in "The Spatial Setting," chapter 31 of this book, the internal disposition of the worship space and the relative size and prominence of its fixed items may bear theological significance: the altar table, a reading ambo (pulpit or desk), a preaching pulpit, a baptismal font, a presidential chair. Again, the facilities for kneeling, sitting, standing, processing, and so forth, may favor certain concepts, modes, and moods of worship.

The wandering patriarchs of Israel erected shrines to mark their encounters with the Lord (Gen. 12:7–8; 28:10–22; 35:1–5). The scenes of marvelous events in the history of God with the world and with his people attract worshipers, as do the places associated with outstanding saints. Pilgrimages enact in a sustained way "liturgy on the road." Pilgrims may take back home with them ideas and items that then find a place in the liturgy of their churches. The ceremonies of Holy Week from Jerusalem—the classic early account is found in the *Travel Diary* of the Spanish nun Egeria in the late fourth century—or Rome are reproduced in many localities. By these routes and channels the catholicity of the Church in the topographical sense is enhanced.

The custom of orientation in church architecture and in burial practices bespeaks the expectation that, at his final advent, Christ will come, like the rising sun and the lightning (Matt. 24:27), from the east.

Matter

God's creatures are "good" (Old Testament scholars reckon that the nuance of *tôb* in the context of Genesis 1 is "meeting its purpose"), when they are "received with thanksgiving" (1 Tim. 4:3–5). As gifts they convey the divine blessing; they allow people to respond with gratitude. Their use thereby becomes a medium of communion between humanity and God. That is their meaning and destiny.

For human beings, as themselves corporeal creatures, the body is the point of contact with the rest of the material creation. We apply matter to ourselves, we take it into ourselves, we work outwardly upon it. In baptism, the water is applied in more or less its raw state (though with accompanying prayer and invocation). In the sacramental oils, cultivation and manufacture come to the fore. The prayers of the Roman Missal strikingly combine the parts played by nature and culture in the provision of materials for the eucharist, the whole being set within the context of God's creation and salvific purposes:

> Blessed are you, Lord, God of all creation. Through your goodness we have this bread to offer, which earth has given and human hands have made. It will become for us the bread of life.

> Blessed are you, Lord, God of all creation. Through your goodness we have this wine to offer, fruit of the vine and work of human hands. It will become our spiritual drink.

When human beings administer the earth as the means of divine blessing, they are fulfilling a royal function on behalf of God; when they give God thanks and praise, they are fulfilling a priestly function on behalf of creation. In the traditional rites of Easter Eve, the natural elements of earth, fire, wind, and water are assumed into the story of redemption as the flint is struck, the paschal candle lit, and the Spirit or Breath of God invoked upon the baptismal font [see color plate 2].

Artistic production

The negotiation of time, space, and matter can be extended from the elementary level to the aesthetic, where again the liturgy has a paradigmatic role to play, now in the realm of artistic production. Roughly speaking, time is handled through sound; space through sight (veering toward touch); and matter chiefly through touch (though often sight may suffice).

As to sound, music allows and requires time, which means it can accommodate story, complex layerings of actions and events, developments and surprises, tensions and resolutions.[31] In interaction with texts, musical performance—both vocal and instrumental—may not only embellish but also interpret a rite or a feast, as William Flynn makes clear in this volume (see "Liturgical Music"). Physiologically, singing brings out more deliberately than does simple speech the corporeality of worship. Sheerly instrumental music—say, Olivier Messiaen's compositions for organ—may surpass words without evacuating them, hinting at the ineffability of God.

Sight is engaged by paintings, mosaics, and such like (as Marchita Mauck develops in "The Visual Arts"). In the funereal art of the catacombs, faith in the ultimate victory of life over death is confessed through a congeries of Old Testament types, gospel scenes, and sacramental acts that evoke the saving work of God in Christ. Eastern icons were vindicated by the iconodule councils after the iconoclastic disputes in the eighth and ninth centuries. By an extension of the incarnational principle, icons are believed to mediate both the presence of their subjects and the honor returned to these; they invite veneration by the touch of hands or lips. Said John of Damascus (c. 675–c. 749), in his defense of the practice:

> I do not worship matter, I worship the Creator of matter, who for my sake became matter, and accepted to dwell in matter, and through matter wrought my salvation. I will not cease honoring matter, for it was through matter that my salvation was effected. (*On the Holy Images*, 1.16; PG 94:1245)

Orthodox iconographers follow a regime of prayer and ascetic discipline that makes their work of art an act of cooperation with God.

The Church in the West remained more at the level of pedagogy in visual matters. Pope Gregory I of Rome (c. 540–604) declared that "in a picture, the illiterate are able to read."[32] Throughout the Middle Ages the notion of, say, carved stone portals or stained glass windows as the "bible of the poor" obtained in the West.[33] Sculpted fonts could depict the salvific significance of baptism, or even of all the sacraments.[34] As the Middle Ages went on, painted altarpieces came to occupy a more directly liturgical function, both affectively and effectively; a prime example is the complex polytych painted by Matthias Grünewald for the Antonine convent of Isenheim that was devoted to the care of sufferers from Saint Anthony's fire, or the *ignis plaga*.[35] The genre continued into the Renaissance and Baroque periods and even beyond.[36]

Technical skills contribute to the material enactment of liturgy. Scripturally, the beautification of the sanctuary and the vesting of its principal ministers go back to Exodus 25–39, where the designers and workers in wood, metals, stones, and textiles are considered to be "filled with the Spirit of God, with ability and intelligence, with knowledge and all craftsmanship" (31:1–11; 35:30–39:43), and the various materials came as "freewill offerings" from "all the men and women, the people of Israel" (35:20–29). These features returned to Christianity particularly when, in the fourth century, the religion "went public" with the conversion of Constantine and the imperial establishment of the Church under Theodosius. Ministerial vestments and cultic utensils have acquired varying weights of theological significance over the course of liturgical history, as the essay by Joanne Pierce in this book describes (see "Vestments and Objects").

Inculturation

The liturgy is probably the area of the churches' life in which the question of "inculturation" was most discussed in twentieth-century theology, as the essays by

Anscar Chupungco and Chris Egbulem in this volume illustrate (see "Mission and Inculturation: East Asia and the Pacific" and "Mission and Inculturation: Africa"). It is in fact a perennial issue in Christian thought and practice: Josef Jungmann, for instance, showed how attitudes and habits shifted in the patristic period before and beyond the Constantinian turn, with Christians usually waiting until pagan words and performances had become "empty husks" before filling them with new content and associations.[37] Theologically, the positive diversities among humankind can be viewed as the work of a richly resourceful Creator and providential Lord of history, into whose final kingdom all the treasures of the nations will be brought (cf. Hag. 2:7; Matt. 2:11; Rev. 21:26). Some differences in human culture, however, can be attributed, theologically, to a greater or less present conformity among a fallen and not-yet-fully-redeemed humankind to the will of God and the destiny to which God is calling it.

Rather than taking H. Richard Niebuhr's five "typical" attitudes as fixed and divergent stances of the Christian faith toward all human culture, it may be more appropriate to see them as indicating the possibility of, and need for, a discriminating attention on the part of Christians toward every human culture at all times and in all places.[38] Whereas a particular cultural configuration may appear as predominantly positive or negative in relation to the saving purposes of God, it is likely that most cultures will contain some elements to be affirmed; some to be negated, resisted, and even fought; some to be purified and elevated; some to be held provisionally in tension; and some to be transformed. The liturgy can function not only to sift but also to inspire a surrounding public culture. Christian worship can bring artists and craftspeople to undertake their regular work to the glory of God, and the churches may discerningly take their best and most appropriate products into the direct service of the liturgy.[39]

Conclusion: Cooperation, Community, and Communion

When culture is viewed as cooperation with the Creator, the congruity among the three understandings of humankind as *imago Dei* that find concentrated embodiment in Christian worship becomes especially apparent, for such cooperation is a form of the communion with God for which the human being is made, and the social constitution of humanity as community is exercised in cultural production. In philosophical categories, the quest for truth, goodness, and beauty finds its unity through reference to the one and only God as source, standard, and goal of the three transcendentals: ultimate *truth* lies in the knowledge of God, which is given and received in the communion whose concentrated form is praise and prayer; *goodness* is encountered and spread through the reception and sharing of God's grace, focally in and among the liturgical assembly; *beauty* is perceived and magnified when the glory of God is glimpsed and reflected in the splendor of the liturgy. In characteristically modern terms, it might be said that the liturgy affords the opportunity for human beings to "discover meaning" and "make sense" of their lives and the world—provided always that the anthropological and cosmological categories be embraced within a divine transcendence that, according to the Christian faith, is the gracious being and action of the Triune God.[40]

All this is both made possible by an eschatological prospect and qualified by an eschatological reserve. Those "upon whom the ends of the ages have come" (1 Cor. 10:11) live in the overlap of this world and its passing forms (1 Cor. 7:31; 1 John 2:17)

The Vision of the Lamb. From a tenth-century Spanish manuscript of the *Commentary on the Apocalypse* by Beatus of Liébana (died 798). In the early chapters of the book of Revelation (4, 5, and 7), Christ receives worship from the angelic creatures, the elders, and the martyrs as "the Lamb that was slain"; in the later chapters (19 and 21–22), the Lamb becomes the Bridegroom who takes the Church as his Bride. According to the seer, worship in the city of God consists in hymns of praise and the wedding feast that have been anticipated in the Sanctus and the communion of the eucharist. That is "to glorify God, and to enjoy him for ever" (Westminster Catechism). THE PIERPONT MORGAN LIBRARY MS. M 644, FOL. 87/ART RESOURCE, NY

with the new creation that has already begun in Christ (2 Cor. 5:17). What can now be seen "in a mirror dimly," perhaps often only as "puzzling reflections" (1 Cor. 13:12: *di' espotrou en ainigmati*), will one day be encountered "face to face." The celestial city will need no temple, "for its temple is the Lord God Almighty and the Lamb" (Rev. 21:22). Meanwhile the liturgical assembly is granted in ritual mode an anticipatory share in the worship that, in accordance with the inspired prophecy of Isaiah (Isa. 6; John 12:37–50), the entire cosmos will one day render to the Thrice-Holy God. A hymn by Richard Mant (1776–1848) expresses this faith:

> Bright the vision that delighted
> Once the sight of Judah's seer;
> Sweet the countless tongues united
> To entrance the prophet's ear.
>
> Round the Lord in glory seated
> Cherubim and seraphim
> Filled His temple, and repeated
> Each to each the alternate hymn:
>
> "Lord, Thy glory fills the heaven;
> Earth is with its fullness stored;
> Unto Thee be glory given,
> Holy, Holy, Holy Lord."
>
> Heaven is still with glory ringing,
> Earth takes up the angels' cry,
> "Holy, Holy, Holy," singing,
> "Lord of hosts, the Lord most high."
>
> With His seraph train before Him,
> With His holy Church below,
> Thus conspire we to adore Him,
> Bid we thus our anthem flow:
>
> "Lord, Thy glory fills the heaven;
> Earth is with its fullness stored;
> Unto Thee be glory given,
> Holy, Holy, Holy Lord."

Bibliography

Allmen, Jean-Jacques von. *Worship: Its Theology and Practice*. New York: Oxford University Press, 1965.

Brunner, Peter. *Worship in the Name of Jesus*. Translated by M. H. Bertram. St. Louis, Mo.: Concordia, 1968.

Lathrop, Gordon. *Holy Things: A Liturgical Theology*. Minneapolis, Minn.: Fortress, 1993.

Smart, Ninian. *The Concept of Worship*. New York: St. Martin's Press, 1972.

Vagaggini, Cipriano. *Theological Dimensions of the Liturgy*. Translated by Leonard J. Doyle and W. A. Jurgens. Collegeville, Minn.: Liturgical Press, 1976.

Wainwright, Geoffrey. *Doxology: The Praise of God in Worship, Doctrine, and Life*. New York: Oxford University Press, 1980.

Notes

[1] For worship practices in the Old Testament, see Roland de Vaux, *Ancient Israel: Its Life and Institutions*, trans. John McHugh (London: DLT, 1961) 269–517; Hans-Joachim Kraus, *Worship in Israel: A Cultic History of the Old Testament*, trans. Geoffrey Buswell (Oxford: Blackwell; Richmond, Va.: John Knox, 1965); H. H. Rowley, *Worship in Ancient Israel: Its Forms and Meaning* (London: SPCK, 1967); John Eaton, *Vision in Worship: The Relation of Prophecy and Liturgy in the Old Testament* (London: SPCK, 1981); Samuel E. Balentine, *The Torah's Vision of Worship* (Minneapolis, Minn.: Fortress, 1999).

[2] For present purposes a particularly valuable commentary is Franz-J. Leenhardt, *L'épître de saint Paul aux Romains* (Neuchâtel and Paris: Delachaux & Niestlé, 1957). See also Ernst Käsemann, *An die Römer*, 2nd ed. (Tübingen: Mohr-Siebeck, 1974); and Heinrich Schlier, *Der Römerbrief* (Freiburg: Herder, 1977). At some points my reading takes exegetical decisions that there is no room to substantiate here, though they can find support in respectable New Testament scholarship.

[3] On Romans 8 and 15, see Geoffrey Wainwright, "*Veni, Sancte Spiritus*: The Invocation of the Holy Spirit in the Liturgies of the Churches," in *The Holy Spirit, the Church, and Christian Unity*, ed. Doris Donnelly, Adelbert Denaux, and Joseph Famerée (Leuven: Leuven University Press & Peeters, 2005) 303-326.

[4] For a Pauline understanding of image, which also (the author argues) helps to account for the deliberate lack of icons in the first Christian generations as well as allow for later developments in art, see C. Kavin Rowe, "New Testament Iconography? Situating Paul in the Absence of Material Evidence," in *Picturing the New Testament: Studies in Ancient Visual Images*, ed. Annette Weissenrieder, Friederike Wendt, and Petra von Gemünden (Tübingen: Mohr-Siebeck, 2005) 289–312.

[5] Hans Urs von Balthasar, *Theodramatik*, vol. 4 (Einsiedeln: Johannes-Verlag, 1983) 453–476 (Eng. trans., *Theodrama*, vol. 5, trans. Graham Harrison [San Francisco: Ignatius Press, 1998] 506–521).

[6] For a similar threefold interpretation of the *imago Dei* by a biblically conversant scholar writing in this case as a dogmatician, see H. J. Kraus, *Reich Gottes, Reich der Freiheit: Grundriss systematischer Theologie* (Neukirchen: Erziehungsverein, 1975) 141–149. Kraus stresses the character of the *imago* as a promise and a destiny (*Bestimmung*).

[7] Irenaeus exploits the binome of Genesis 1:26: "in our image, after our likeness." This has rendered him exegetically suspect to some scholars, but Hebraic doublets are not necessarily synonymous, and the second member may rather develop the first.

[8] On the basic genus and the historically variable species of this central prayer, see W. J. Grisbrooke, "Anaphora," in *A New Dictionary of Liturgy and Worship*, ed. J. Gordon Davies (London: SCM, 1986). For theologically sensitive analyses of two important anaphoras from different areas of language studies, see Daniel J. Sheerin, "The Anaphora of the Liturgy of St. John Chrysostom: Stylistic Notes," and (on the Roman canon within the total rite) David Crystal, "Liturgical Language in a Sociolinguistic Perspective," in *Language and the Worship of the Church*, ed. David Jasper and R. C. D. Jasper (New York: St. Martin's Press, 1990) 44–81 and 120–146 respectively.

[9] E. J. Lengeling, *Liturgie: Dialog zwischen Gott und Mensch* (Freiburg im Breisgau: Herder, 1981). For detailed examinations of biblical, patristic, and later vocabulary and usage in connection with worship, see Lengeling's articles "Kult" and "Liturgie" in *Handbuch Theologischer Grundbegriffe*, ed. Heinrich Fries (Munich: Kösel), vol. 1 (1962) 865–880, and vol. 2 (1963) 75–97 respectively.

[10] For a more elaborate discussion of the role of all five physical senses as channels of revelation and response, see Geoffrey Wainwright, "Senses of the Word," in his *For Our Salvation: Two Approaches to the Work of Christ* (Grand Rapids, Mich.: Eerdmans, 1997) 1–96.

[11] Athanasius, *Letter to Adelphius*, 3–4 (PG 26:1073–1077); also Gregory Nazianzen, *Oration 40, On Holy Baptism*; and Gregory of Nyssa, *On the Holy Spirit, against Macedonius*.

[12] Athanasius, *First Letter to Serapion*, 29–30 (PG 26:596–600); also Gregory of Nyssa, *Sermon on the*

Baptism of Christ; cf. Theodore of Mopsuestia, *Fourteenth Catechetical Homily* 14–21; Ambrose of Milan, *On the Mysteries* 5.28.

[13]Basil of Caesarea, *On the Holy Spirit*, particularly 1 (3); 7 (16); 10 (24–26); 25 (58–60); 26 (63–64); 27 (68).

[14]Romans 14:17 reads literally "The kingdom of God is not food and drink but justice and peace and joy in the Holy Spirit." Behind the "creative interpretation" in the text I am postulating an idiom where negation together with an adversative functions not as a cancellation but as a qualification. Thus in Hosea 6:6, for example, "I desire mercy, not sacrifice" is not an abrogation of the cult but a declaration that sacrifices are unacceptable in the absence of mercy. Certainly the apostle Paul in 1 Corinthians 11 makes a connection between the content and manner of a meal, on the one hand, and present and future salvation, on the other.

[15]Ion Bria, *The Liturgy after the Liturgy: Mission and Witness from an Orthodox Perspective* (Geneva: WCC, 1996); and Emmanuel Clapsis, "The Eucharist as Missionary Event in a Suffering World," in his *Orthodoxy in Conversation: Orthodox Ecumenical Engagements* (Geneva: WCC; Brookline, Mass.: Holy Cross Orthodox Press, 2000) 191–197.

[16]Alexander Schmemann, *The Eucharist: Sacrament of the Kingdom*, trans. Paul Kachur (Crestwood, N.Y.: St. Vladimir's Seminary Press, 1988), in particular 21, 217.

[17]*Didache*, 9–15; see Karl-Heinrich Bieritz, "Anthropologische Grundlegung," in *Handbuch der Liturgik: Liturgiewissenschaft in Theologie und Praxis der Kirche*, ed. Hans-Christoph Schmidt-Lauber, Michael Meyer-Blanck, and Karl-Heinrich Bieritz, 3rd ed. (Göttingen: Vandenhoeck & Ruprecht, 2003) 95–128, here 109–110.

[18]See James H. Cone, "Sanctification, Liberation, and Black Worship" in *Theology Today* 35 (1978–1979) 139–152.

[19]Richard Schaeffler, "*Doxologia kai oikodomê*: Der Lobpreis Gottes und der Aufbau der Glaubensgemeinschaft," in *Ecumenical Theology in Worship, Doctrine, and Life: Essays Presented to Geoffrey Wainwright on His Sixtieth Birthday*, ed. David S. Cunningham, Ralph Del Colle, and Lucas Lamadrid (New York: Oxford University Press, 1999) 55–68.

[20]J.-B. Bossuet, "Instruction sur les états d'oraison" (1697), section 6, in *Œuvres*, ed. J. P. Migne, vol. 4 (Paris: 1856) 115.

[21]For example, the Confession of Augsburg, and the Apology thereof (article 21), and the Second Helvetic Confession, 5:4–5. See Jaroslav Pelikan and Valerie Hotchkiss, eds., *Creeds and Confessions of Faith in the Christian Tradition*, vol. 2 (New Haven, Conn., and London: Yale University Press, 2003) 75, 466.

[22]See Geoffrey Wainwright, "The Saints and the Departed: Confessional Controversy and Ecumenical Convergence," *Studia Liturgica* 34 (2004) 65–91.

[23]F. W. Dillistone, "Liturgical Forms in Word and Act," in *Language and the Worship of the Church*, ed. Jasper and Jasper, 3–25.

[24]Thomas J. Talley, *The Origins of the Liturgical Year*, 2nd ed. (Collegeville, Minn.: Liturgical Press, 1991); cf. Irmgard Pahl, "The Paschal Mystery in Its Central Meaning for the Shape of Christian Liturgy," *Studia Liturgica* 26 (1996) 16–38.

[25]René Cabié, *La Pentecôte: L'évolution de la cinquantaine pascale au cours des cinq premiers siècles* (Tournai: Desclée, 1965); and John Gunstone, *The Feast of Pentecost: The Great Fifty Days in the Liturgy* (London: Faith Press, 1967).

[26]Susan K. Roll, *Towards the Origins of Christmas* (Kampen: Kok Pharos, 1995); and Hans Förster, *Die Feier der Geburt Christi in der Alten Kirche: Beiträge zur Erforschung der Anfänge des Epiphanie- und Weihnachtsfests* (Tübingen: Mohr Siebeck, 2000).

[27]In both the first and the second Temples, new moons are appointed times for sacrifices (1 Chron. 23:31; 2 Chron. 2:4 and 31:3; Ezra 3:5; Ezek. 45:17 and 46:1–8).

[28]For further details on the connections between Sunday as the day of resurrection ("the Lord's day") and as the day for the eucharist ("the Lord's meal"), see Geoffrey Wainwright, *Eucharist and Eschatology*, 2nd ed. (New York: Oxford University Press, 1981) 74–77.

[29]In line with Jewish messianic expectations at Passover, there is evidence that early Christians—as late as Jerome (died 420) and Isidore of Seville (died 636)—expected the return of Christ precisely during the Easter vigil; see Wainwright, *Eucharist and Eschatology*, 22–24 and 77.

[30]Romano Guardini, *The Spirit of the Liturgy*, trans. Ada Lane (London: Sheed and Ward, 1930); Jean-Jacques von Allmen, *Prophétisme sacramentel* (Neuchâtel: Delachaux & Niestlé, 1964) 287–311; and his "Worship and the Holy Spirit," *Studia Liturgica* 2 (1963) 124–135. For Schleiermacher, see Christoph Albrecht, *Schleiermachers Liturgik* (Göttingen: Vandenhoeck & Ruprecht, 1963), in particular 15–19.

[31]See Jeremy S. Begbie, *Theology, Music, and Time* (Cambridge: Cambridge University Press, 2000).

[32]Gregory the Great, *Epistles* 11.13 (*PL* 77:1128–1129). The idea was not abandoned by John of Dam-

ascus: "What the book is to the literate, the image is to the illiterate" (*On the Holy Images*, 1.17; *PG* 94:1248).

33See the classic work of Émile Mâle, *Religious Art in France of the Thirteenth Century*, trans. Dora Nussy (New York: Dutton, 1913), reprinted as *The Gothic Image* (New York: Harper & Row, 1958). For glass, see Jean Rollet, *Les maîtres de la lumière* (Paris: Bordas, 1980). For both stone and glass, Jean Favier, *L'univers de Chartres* (Paris: Bordas, 1988), translated as *The World of Chartres* (New York: Abrams, 1990).

34Ann Eljenholm Nichols, *Seeable Signs: The Iconography of the Seven Sacraments, 1350–1544* (Woodbridge, Suffolk: Boydell, 1994).

35See Andrée Hayum, *The Isenheim Altarpiece: God's Medicine and the Painter's Vision* (Princeton, N.J.: Princeton University Press, 1989).

36Barbara G. Lane, *The Altar and the Altarpiece: Sacramental Themes in Early Netherlandish Painting* (New York: Harper & Row, 1984); and Peter Humfrey, *The Altarpiece in Renaissance Venice* (New Haven, Conn.: Yale University Press, 1993).

37Josef Andreas Jungmann, *The Early Liturgy to the Time of Gregory the Great*, trans. Francis A. Brunner (Notre Dame, Ind.: University of Notre Dame Press, 1959), esp. chapters 11–13.

38H. Richard Niebuhr, *Christ and Culture* (New York: Harper & Row, 1951). See my discussions: "Culture," in *Doxology*, 357–398; and "Canons, Cultures, and the Ecumenically Correct," in *Worship with One Accord* (New York: Oxford University Press, 1997) 251–276.

39From the mid-twentieth century see the illustrated writings of the French Dominican Marie-Alain Couturier selected from his journal *L'art sacré* and translated as *Sacred Art* (Austin: University of Texas Press, 1989). Couturier marshaled the collaboration of such as Léger, Matisse, Rouault, Chagall, and Le Corbusier for the chapels at Assy (1950), Vence (1951), Audincourt (1951), and Ronchamp (1955).

40See Graham Hughes, *Worship as Meaning: A Liturgical Theology for Late Modernity* (Cambridge: Cambridge University Press, 2003). Hughes is writing from within an Australian context—in particular, Sydney—that he finds deeply marked by "disenchantment" (in Max Weber's sense of *Entzauberung*). Hughes might also have been writing from Europe, except that secularization may there be yielding in part to neopaganism; cf. Geoffrey Wainwright, "Religiöse Sprache und sakrale Symbole in einer säkularisierten Welt," in *Kirchen im Kontext unterschiedlicher Kulturen: Auf dem Weg in das dritte Jahrtausend*, ed. Karl Christian Felmy et al. (Göttingen: Vandenhoeck & Ruprecht, 1991) 119–133. Forward-looking books that seek anchorage in the classical faith are Kenan Osborne, *Christian Sacraments in a Postmodern World: A Theology for the Third Millennium* (New York and Mahwah, N.J.: Paulist, 1999); and Keith F. Pecklers, *Worship: New Century Theology* (London and New York: Continuum, 2003). Certainly, the facts of the persistence, revitalization, and expansion of the Christian Tradition demand full attention in the formulation of a theology of worship that illuminates the liturgical history and is illuminated by it.

2

The Apostolic Tradition

MAXWELL E. JOHNSON

The title of this chapter is a provocation. It raises the question of what coherence exists among the bits and pieces that have come down to us from the worship practices of the early Church. An older scholarship supposed a unified origin of Christian liturgy which time and space then varied. More recent work favors a multiple beginning which then converged at certain points. On one hand, as Georg Kretschmar noted several years ago with specific regard to the variety of practices encountered in the pre-Nicene development of the rites of Christian initiation, "a plurality of possibilities is itself apostolic."[1] What Kretschmar stated about Christian initiation would also apply easily, for example, to the eucharistic liturgy, daily prayer (the liturgy of the hours), the liturgical year, and other liturgical-sacramental rites. Hence, to say that this essay is about the historical development of "*the* apostolic tradition" of Christian worship would be simply incorrect. For what is encountered in that history is not a single tradition but various traditions, some of which may be apostolic in their origins and others not. On the other hand, the term "apostolic tradition" is itself also the title of a famous church order, the *Apostolic Tradition*, frequently ascribed to bishop Hippolytus of Rome (c. 215). This influential document has been long thought to be, if not exactly what its title claims, an authentic, authoritative, and dependable witness to early third century Roman liturgical practice, composed by the famous traditionalist and antipope himself, and reflecting what the "tradition" of liturgy in Rome had been up to and including his own time. Today, however, the emerging scholarly view is that this *Apostolic Tradition* probably was not authored by Hippolytus, not even necessarily Roman in its content, and probably not early third century in date, at least not as it exists in the various extant manuscripts in which it has come down to us—the (incomplete) Verona Latin (fifth century) and the Oriental versions (Sahidic, Ethiopic, Arabic, and Bohairic, all medieval or later in date).[2] Hence, the "tradition" of this so-called *Apostolic Tradition* may well reflect a synthesis or composite text of various and diverse liturgical patterns and practices, some quite early and others not added until the time of its final redaction.[3]

To attempt, then, to describe the various traditions of Christian worship, "apostolic" or otherwise, in the first three centuries of the church is an enormously complex endeavor. For, contrary to the assumptions often held by earlier scholars, contemporary liturgical scholarship increasingly realizes and emphasizes that Christian worship was diverse even in its biblical-apostolic origins, multilinear rather than monolinear in its development, and closely related to the several cultural, linguistic, geographical, and theological expressions and orientations of distinct churches through-

The *Apostolic Tradition*

The so-called *Apostolic Tradition* belongs to the genre of ancient "church orders," early Christian documents claiming to contain various authoritative "apostolic" rules and commands regarding liturgical practice, church structure, and the moral life of Christians. For much of the past century this particular document has been attributed to Hippolytus of Rome, a martyr-presbyter or antipope, or both, who supposedly compiled it at the beginning of the third century for the use of his community. Originally composed in Greek, the *Apostolic Tradition* now survives only in a Latin translation in a fifth-century manuscript (the Verona Palimpsest) and in later translations into Sahidic Coptic (eleventh-century ms.), Arabic (fourteenth-century ms.), Ethiopic (fifteenth-century ms.), and Bohairic Coptic (nineteenth-century ms.). Portions of the *Apostolic Tradition* appear in other fourth- or fifth-century church orders which today are seen as being derivative documents in some way, such as Book VIII of the *Apostolic Constitutions* along with its *Epitome*, the *Canons of Hippolytus* (today recognized as the earliest derivative document, perhaps as early as the 330s), and the *Testamentum Domini*, as well as in some Greek fragments that may provide some witness to the original.

In the late nineteenth century, only the Coptic and Ethiopic versions were known, and so this anonymous and untitled work was given the name "The Egyptian Church Order" by Hans Achelis (1891). At the beginning of the twentieth century, a Latin version was published in 1900 by Edmund Hauler, and an Arabic version in 1904 by George Horner. Two years later, Eduard von der Goltz suggested that this document might in fact be the lost *Apostolic Tradition*, ascribed to Hippolytus of Rome on the base of a statue supposedly of him that had been found somewhere between the Via Nomentana and the Via Tiburtina and now stands at the entrance to the Vatican Library. (Recent studies have demonstrated that this statue was originally that of a female figure and was transformed into that of a male bishop in the sixteenth century.) Von der Goltz was followed by Eduard Schwartz in 1910 and then by R. H. Connolly in 1916. Significant studies by B. S. Easton (1934), Gregory Dix (1937), and Bernard Botte (1963) accepted this conclusion and, with some exceptions (e.g., that of J. M. Hanssens in 1959, who argued for an Alexandrian origin), the theory that this document represents authoritatively the authentic liturgical tradition of the Roman church in the early third century has been commonly accepted by scholars and liturgical reformers alike.

Contemporary scholarship on this document is challenging previous assumptions. Marcel Metzger (1988, 1992), building on the work of Jean Magne (1975) and Alexandre Faivre (1980), has underscored that the *Apostolic Tradition* – a "phantom document"—belongs to the genre of "living literature" and was a composite work reflecting various traditions. Based on the important study of Allen Brent (1995), Alistair Stewart-Sykes (2001) has interpreted the document as

out the early centuries of Christianity.[4] Apart, then, from some rather broad (but significant) commonalities discerned throughout various churches in antiquity, the traditions of worship during the first three centuries were rather diverse in content and interpretation, depending on where individual practices are to be located. Indeed, already in this era, together with the diversity of christologies, ecclesiologies, and, undoubtedly, liturgical practices encountered in the New Testament itself,[5] the early history of the "tradition" of Christian worship is simultaneously the early history of

Statue identified as Hippolytus of Rome.
Discovered in Rome in 1551, the statue
displayed on the base a list of writings, among
them titles known to have come from
Hippolytus (c. 170–c. 236). The seated figure
was thus identified as Hippolytus, although
many of his writings catalogued by Eusebius
and Jerome did not figure on the statue's list.
Among the titles inscribed was *The Apostolic
Tradition*, leading to the connection between
that church order and the controversial
theologian. T. APIRYON

the product of a church-school at
Rome—the "School of Hippolytus"—reflecting the transition from
a loose federation of house
churches to the establishment and
acceptance of the monarchical
episcopate. While Stewart-Sykes
sees the text as a composite work,
he also interprets all strata of the
text as reflecting authentic and authoritative early Roman liturgy and
regards the final form of the document itself, essentially the reconstructed form of Gregory Dix and
Bernard Botte, as having been
completed by the mid-third century. A very different approach
from Stewart-Sykes has been taken
by Paul Bradshaw, Maxwell Johnson, and Edward Phillips (2002).
Building further upon the work of
Metzger, these authors judge the
work to be "an aggregation of material from different sources, quite
possibly arising from different geographical regions and probably
from different historical periods,
from perhaps as early as the mid-
second century to as late as the
mid-fourth." They thus think it
"unlikely that it represents the
practice of any single Christian
community"; rather, "it is best understood by attempting to discern
the various individual elements and
layers that constitute it" (Bradshaw, 2000).

The so-called *Apostolic Tradition*,
therefore, must be used with great

the developing liturgical traditions of several different Christian communities: the early
Aramaic or Syriac-speaking Christians centered in Edessa and, later, in Nisibis, Syria
(extending into modern Iraq, Iran, and portions of Turkey); the Greek-speaking Syrian
Christians centered in Antioch of Syria and in Jerusalem of Syro-Palestine, and from
the beginning of the fourth century also in Armenia; the Greek-speaking Christians of
Lower Egypt and the Coptic-speaking Christians of Upper Egypt, where already by the
third century both liturgy and scripture had been translated into Coptic; the Latin-
speaking members of the North African churches; and the no doubt multilinguistic
groups that made up the Christian communities living in Rome. We should not, then,

caution in attempting to discern the patterns, theology, and ritual practices of early Christianity. In other words, while the *Apostolic Tradition* may certainly be seen as a "tradition," this document which has exercised considerable influence on twentieth-century ritual revision in the Roman Catholic Church and beyond can no longer so confidently be claimed as either Roman, Hippolytan, or early third century.

References

Bradshaw, Paul. "Hippolytus Revisited: The Identity of the So-Called Apostolic Tradition," *Liturgy* 16 (2000) 9–10.

Bradshaw, Paul, Maxwell E. Johnson, and L. Edward Phillips. *Apostolic Tradition: A Commentary*. Hermeneia Commentary Series. Minneapolis: Fortress Press, 2002.

Brent, Allen. *Hippolytus and the Roman Church in the Third Century*. Leiden: Brill, 1995.

Hanssens, J. M. *La liturgie d'Hippolyte*, Orientalia Christiana Analecta 155. Rome: Pontificale Institutum Orientalium Studiorum, 1959.

Stewart-Sykes, Alistair. *Hippolytus, On the Apostolic Tradition*. Crestwood, N.Y.: St. Vladimir's Seminary Press, 2001.

expect to find only one "apostolic" liturgical practice or theology surviving in this period of the church's history before the Council of Nicaea (325) but, rather, great diversity both within the rites themselves and in their theological interpretations.

Similarly, the early liturgical traditions we encounter in this period would ultimately contribute, especially during the great formative period of the fourth and fifth centuries, to the composition of the distinct liturgical "rites" of East and West that still characterize Christianity today. But these distinct "rites," it should be noted, resulted not from what liturgical scholars used to describe as a process of "diversification of rites" from an allegedly original or pristine apostolic unitive or ritual "core," but rather from a process of "unification of rites," and from what John Fenwick has called a process of liturgical "cross-fertilization,"[6] as the liturgical practices of local churches were brought into conformity with those of the great patriarchal sees and influential pilgrimage centers, and as liturgical structures and practices that had developed in one church were borrowed and copied by others.

This chapter will be limited in scope to the principal occasions for Christian worship in the first three centuries for which the textual-liturgical evidence is most abundant: Christian initiation, the eucharistic liturgy, daily prayer (the liturgy of the hours), and the liturgical year. There is certainly evidence from this period for the existence of other early liturgical rites, especially for those associated with the development of *exomologesis* (the one-time postbaptismal "canonical penance"), understood, in the words of Tertullian, to be the plank thrown to drowning sinners after the shipwreck of serious postbaptismal sin.[7] Similarly, as John Baldovin notes, "major conflicts—with the Jews, with gnostic brands of Christian faith, and with secular authorities—forced the [Christian] movement to define itself, especially in the latter half of the second century, and thus to canonize its own Scripture . . . and line of authoritative tradition, called apostolic succession."[8] Hence, together with the *regula fidei*, centered in developing trinitarian creedal expressions and the monarchical episcopacy, there is some (but very limited) evidence for ordination rites associated with the development of the threefold office of bishops, presbyters, and deacons, and for other ministries (e.g., confessors, widows, lectors, and subdeacons).[9] Later liturgical evidence permits us to

Banquet scene. The intentions of early Christian art—like early liturgical texts—are not always clear. A third-century wall painting from the catacomb of Callistus in Rome may depict the eucharist or it may represent a refrigerium ("refreshment"), the funeral feast practiced also by non-Christians that was believed to connect the living with the dead. The Church tolerated the refrigerium until around the fifth century. SCALA/ART RESOURCE, NY

make some assumptions about the existence during this period of rites for ministry to the sick, for Christian burial,[10] and for marriage. It is, however, primarily the rites of Christian initiation and the eucharistic liturgy, together with its great prayer and, to a somewhat lesser extent, daily prayer, and the liturgical year for which the evidence is most abundant, so this chapter will focus only on these. Finally, in the conclusion I will draw out some implications from this brief study of pre-Nicene Christian liturgy, theological and otherwise, for how this "apostolic tradition" of Christian worship might still function in helping to provide at least broad authoritative norms for ongoing liturgical celebration and renewal in the churches today. I am convinced that diversity of liturgical practice and theology, whether in the early pre-Nicene period or the so-called contemporary postmodern period, does not necessarily lead to either liturgical or doctrinal relativism.

The Rites of Christian Initiation

Christian baptism, as witnessed to in the New Testament accounts of Jesus' own baptism in the Jordan by John the Baptizer (Matt. 3:13–17, Mark 1:9–11, Luke 3:21–22, John 1:31–34), finds its immediate origins in the baptismal practice of John himself. We are not certain, however, how John derived his baptismal practices or how he himself became a "baptizer." Earlier scholarship tended to locate the origins of his practice either in what were considered to be parallel Jewish "baptismal" rituals performed among the Essene community at Qumran near the Dead Sea, or in the tradition of Jewish "proselyte" baptism as an initiatory rite for gentile converts to Judaism. But differences between John's once-for-all baptism and the repeatable Qumran washings, and the fact that the documentary evidence for Jewish proselyte baptism is later than the known existence of Christian baptism, make it difficult to maintain either as definitive sources. Alternatively, in view of a number of Old Testament prophetic texts that speak of God's new creation and restoration as beginning with a divine washing away of sin (e.g., Isa. 1:16–17, Ezek. 36:25–28), Adela Collins has suggested that John's "baptism of repentance" was a ritually enacted prophetic sign which anticipated the very coming of God in human history and the ultimate cleansing with water that would inaugurate the new creation of God itself.[11] This was no repeatable immersion of ritual or cultic purity, nor was John's baptism a way to make Jewish converts out of gentiles. What John proclaimed, anticipated, and ritually enacted, in typical prophetic fashion, was the dawning of God's decisive intervention in history, the beginning of God's cleansing, restoration, and transformation of God's people.

Nevertheless, based possibly also on Jesus' own baptismal practice (John 3:22, 26; 4:1) in continuity with John's practice, and in general continuity with an overall context of ritual washings and bathing customs within first-century Judaism,[12] new converts to Christianity, apparently at least from the first Christian Pentecost on (Acts 2:38–42), were initiated into Christ and the church by a ritual process which included some form of "baptism" with water. This process, of course, would eventually be based in the command of the risen Jesus himself (Matt. 28:19). Unfortunately, the New Testament records little detail about this baptismal practice or what additional ceremonies may have been included. Although we might assume that some kind of profession of faith in Jesus as Lord was present, we do not know, for example, if any particular formula—for example, "I baptize you in the name of the Father and of the Son and of the Holy Spirit" from the dominical command for baptism (Matt. 28:19), or "in the name of Jesus" (Acts 3:6)—was employed, or even if these were actually "liturgical" formulas to be recited at baptism or merely catechetical-descriptive formulas *about* baptism.[13] Nor do we know precisely *how* baptisms were regularly administered (by immersion, complete submersion, or pouring),[14] whether infants were ever candidates for baptism in the New Testament period,[15] what kind of preparation may have preceded adult baptism, whether anointings were already part of the process, or if occasional references to the apostolic conferral of the postbaptismal gift of the Holy Spirit (cf. Acts 8 and 19) were regular features of baptismal practice in some early communities or exceptional cases in particular situations. The account in Acts 8, for example, appears to be concerned with the conversion and Christian initiation of Samaritans, which came about not by or under the direction of the Jerusalem apostles but through the mission of Philip. So, by having the apostles Peter and John go to Samaria to lay hands on these converts, Luke may well be underscoring one of his key emphases in Acts: that all Christian missionary work must somehow be subordinated to or ratified by the apostles in Jerusalem themselves. Along similar lines, the context and situation in Acts 19:1–7 concerns those who had received only *John's* baptism, not *Christian* baptism. Such situations as these can hardly be seen as reflecting any sort of normative pattern; rather, they are specific and unique occasions.[16] Indeed, had postbaptismal handlaying related to the gift of the Holy Spirit been an "apostolic" and regular baptismal practice, it is difficult to understand why that practice did not continue everywhere in the rites of the first few centuries. For that matter, Martin Connell's recent study of foot washing in the Gospel of John suggests that among some early Johannine communities it was not baptism at all but a foot washing ceremony that constituted the "rite" of Christian initiation,[17] and hence the possibility emerges that many of the ceremonies that came to be attached to baptism as additional or supplementary rites (e.g., handlaying, anointing, foot washing) once constituted complete rites of initiation, perhaps even without the water bath, in some early communities.

If liturgical clarity and precision with regard to initiation rites are not present in it, the New Testament does provide a rich collection of baptismal images and metaphors. Among these are forgiveness of sins and the gift of the Holy Spirit (Acts 2:38); new birth through water and the Holy Spirit (John 3:5, Titus 3:5–7); putting off the "old nature" and "putting on the new," that is, "being clothed in the righteousness of Christ" (Gal. 3:27, Col. 3:9–10); initiation into the "one body" of the Christian community (1 Cor. 12:13; see also Acts 2:42); washing, sanctification, and justification in Christ and the Holy Spirit (1 Cor. 6:11); enlightenment (Heb. 6:4 and 10:32, 1 Peter 2:9); being "anointed" and/or "sealed" by the Holy Spirit (2 Cor. 1:21–22, 1 John

2:20, 27); being "sealed" or "marked" as belonging to God and God's people (2 Cor. 1:21–22; Eph. 1:13–14; 4:30; Rev. 7:3); and, of course, being joined to Christ through participation in his death, burial, and resurrection (Rom. 6:3–11, Col. 2:12–15). Two of these would be particularly emphasized within the developing liturgical traditions: Christian initiation as new birth through water and the Holy Spirit (John 3:5ff.); and Christian initiation as being united with Christ in his death, burial, and resurrection (Rom. 6:3–11). Around these, several other New Testament images would eventually cluster as specific rites to accompany baptism.

Our earliest extra-biblical sources for the rites of Christian initiation provide only a few more details, but important ones. Chapter 7 of the (probably Syrian) late-first or early-second-century proto-church order called the *Didache* directs that, after instruction (presumably the kind of ethical formation supplied by chapters 1–6 of the document) and one or two days of fasting by the candidates, baptizers, and community alike, baptism is to be conferred as follows:

> 1. As for baptism, baptize in this way: Having said all this beforehand, baptize in the name of the Father and of the Son and of the Holy Spirit, in running water. Regarding baptism. 2. If you . . . do not have running water, however, baptize in another kind of water; if you cannot [do so] in cold [water], then [do so] in warm [water]. 3. But if you have neither, pour water on the head thrice in the name of the Father and Son and Holy Spirit. 4. Before the baptism, let the person baptizing and the person being baptized—and others who are able— fast; tell the one being baptized to fast one or two [days] before.[18]

Only the baptized, we are instructed further in chapter 9, are to receive the eucharist.

There is, however, a great deal that the *Didache* does not tell us about the initiation rite—for example, the duration of prebaptismal catechesis, whether the trinitarian language is a reference to a baptismal "formula," or whether the baptismal rite culminated immediately in the eucharist. Nor does the *Didache* indicate any preferred day or season for baptism; it is silent about what sort of profession of faith may have been expected from the baptismal candidates, offers no information about the "ministers" of baptism, and makes no reference to any additional rites that may have accompanied baptism itself. Equally absent from this document is any definitive theological interpretation of, or reflection on, the meaning of baptism. Unfortunately, then, the information provided by the *Didache* about the rites of Christian initiation is only of the most general kind.

In the middle of the second century at Rome, chapters 61 and 65 of the *First Apology* of Justin Martyr addressed to the Roman emperor Antoninus Pius not only corroborate the information provided by the *Didache* but also add some other elements:

> (*Chapter 61*): . . . those who believe in the truth of our teachings and discourses promise that they can live in accordance with it. Then they are taught to pray and, while fasting, to ask God for the forgiveness of their past sins. We, for our part, pray and fast with them. . . . Next, we bring them to a place where there is water, and they are reborn in the same way as we ourselves were reborn before them. That is to say, they are cleansed with water in the name of God the Father and Master of the universe, and of our Savior Jesus Christ, and of the Holy Spirit. For Christ said: "Unless you are born again, you shall not enter the kingdom of heaven." . . . Upon the person who wishes to be reborn and who repents of his sins, we invoke the name of God the Father and Master of the universe. . . . We call this washing an "enlightenment," because those who are taught as we have described have their minds enlightened. . . . (We also invoke) upon the person who is enlightened and cleansed the name of Jesus Christ, who was crucified under Pontius Pilate, and the name of the Holy Spirit, who through the prophets foretold the entire story of Jesus.

(*Chapter 65*): After we have thus cleansed the person who believes and has joined our ranks, we lead him in to where those we call "brothers" are assembled. We offer prayers in common for ourselves, for him who has just been enlightened, and for all . . . everywhere. . . . When we finish praying, we greet one another with a kiss. Then bread and a cup of wine mixed with water [literally, "water and wine mixed with water"] are brought to him who presides over the brethren.[19]

Because Justin refers in this description to what may be called "creedal" language, it is not clear if a baptismal formula pronounced by the administrator is intended, or if he is alluding to an early example of the Western threefold profession of faith by the candidate as constituting the "formula" of baptism. At the same time, although it is often assumed that Justin describes Roman liturgical practice, his theology of baptism as "new birth" and his reference to baptism as *phôtismos* ("enlightenment"), characteristic emphases in the Christian East, may instead reflect an Eastern Christian tradition (Justin was from Flavia Neapolis in Syria) or, possibly, a Syrian community at Rome. Nevertheless, the overall ritual pattern he describes underscores that some kind of prebaptismal catechesis preceded baptism, and that this entire process of becoming a Christian culminated in sharing in the prayers, kiss, and eucharist of the community.

It is only in the early third century that we begin to see a more complete picture of the various processes of early Christian initiation emerging, together with detailed evidence of several additional ritual elements. The extent to which any of these elements are present, however, varies according to liturgical tradition. In early Syrian documents (e.g., the *Didascalia Apostolorum* and the *Apocryphal Acts of the Apostles*), a pattern of initiation exists wherein the baptism of Jesus is seen as the primary paradigm for Christian baptism and the theology of baptism flows from the "new birth" focus of John 3:5. These documents place minimal stress on catechesis but strong emphasis on a prebaptismal anointing of the head (and eventually the whole body), interpreted as a "royal" anointing by which the Holy Spirit assimilates the candidate to the messianic kingship and priesthood of Christ, baptism accompanied by the Matthean trinitarian formula, and the concluding reception of the eucharist, with no other postbaptismal ceremonies such as handlaying or anointing(s) involved.[20] Without question it is this prebaptismal anointing, derived from the anointing of kings and priests in ancient Israel, that was the high point of the "baptismal" ritual. During the course of the fourth century, at least in Syro-Palestine and the Greco-Roman coastland, that ritual was transformed to accommodate a *postbaptismal* pneumatic anointing and a reinterpretation of the prebaptismal anointing as exorcistic, purificatory, and preparatory. It is also possible, but by no means proved, that one of the principal occasions for initiation in the early Syrian tradition was January 6, the Feast of the Epiphany or Theophany, interpreted primarily as the feast of Jesus' baptism.[21] Alternatively, based on later Armenian liturgical sources, it is also possible that prebaptismal catechesis was limited to a three-week period prior to baptism, whenever it was celebrated.[22]

Several scholars have also suggested that early Egyptian initiation practice provides a close parallel to that of Syria,[23] including a similar liturgical structure of anointing(s), baptism, and eucharist. Indeed, the later Coptic tradition, primarily through legends about earlier practice, preserves a memory of the fourth century as a time of baptismal innovation with the adoption of a postbaptismal anointing in Egypt. At the same time, the writings of both Clement of Alexandria and his famous student Origen indicate that a central baptismal metaphor in Egyptian Christianity was the crossing of the Red Sea, understood not as baptism but as entrance into the catechumenate, followed by baptism itself, interpreted as the Israelites' crossing of the Jordan under Joshua (Jesus), thus underscoring again Jesus' baptism in the Jordan as the dominant baptismal paradigm.[24] In terms of the duration of the Egyptian catechumenate, it appears that candidates for baptism were enrolled *on* Epiphany, when the opening section of Mark's gospel, the principal gospel in Egyptian Christianity, would have been read, and they were then baptized forty days later in mid-February, with catechetical instruction given during a fast already associated with Jesus' forty-day fast in the wilderness. It is also possible that at the time of baptism a passage inserted between the canonical Mark 10:32–34 and Mark 10:35–45—a secret or mystic gospel in which Jesus "initiates" a Lazarus-like figure he had raised from death six days earlier—was read to those being initiated.[25] This passage, the "Mar Saba Clementine Fragment," increasingly recognized today as being among the authentic writings of Clement of Alexandria, together with this early forty-day, post-Epiphany fast in Egypt, may help to explain not only the origins of "Lazarus Saturday" (the day before Palm Sunday) in the later Byzantine tradition—including, significantly, baptisms still being administered on this day in tenth-century Constantinople—but also the origins of the specific forty days of the pre-Easter "Lent," which would emerge almost everywhere after the Council of Nicaea.

Western sources of the third century provide alternative patterns to the early Syrian, and possibly Egyptian, practice. In North Africa, Tertullian's *De baptismo* (c. 200) describes a ritual process which included "frequent" prebaptismal vigils and fasts, a renunciation of Satan, a threefold creedal question-and-answer profession of faith in the context of the conferral of baptism, a postbaptismal "christic" anointing related to priesthood, a handlaying "blessing" associated with the gift of the Holy Spirit, and participation in the eucharist, which also included the reception of milk and honey as symbols of entering into the "promised land."[26] Tertullian's description is corroborated generally a bit later in North Africa by Cyprian of Carthage,[27] and for Rome, presumably, in the *Apostolic Tradition*.[28]

According to this so-called *Apostolic Tradition*, prebaptismal catechesis was to last for as long as "three years" and included frequent prayer, fasting, and exorcism, with

entrance into the "catechumenate" itself accompanied by a detailed interrogation of the motives and lifestyles of those seeking admission. For those eventually "elected" to baptism, the rites themselves took place at the conclusion of a night-long vigil (perhaps held Saturday to Sunday, but possibly Friday to Saturday[29]) and consisted of a renunciation of Satan, a full-body anointing with the "oil of exorcism," a threefold, creedal interrogation accompanied by the three immersions of baptism itself, a postbaptismal anointing by a presbyter with

Baptismal scene. Relief on a sarcophagus from Lungotevere, Rome, that dates from the third century. The naked candidate stands knee-deep in water supplied from what appears to be a natural source. The baptizer's hand is placed on the candidate's head as part of the rite. Museo Nazionale Romane, Terme di Diocleziano, Rome/Erich Lessing/Art Resource, NY

the "oil of thanksgiving," an entrance into the assembly (where the bishop performed a handlaying with prayer and a second anointing), and, after the kiss of peace, the sharing of the eucharist, including the cup of water and the cup of milk and honey, the latter of which is also referred to by Tertullian. Since, as noted above, authorship, date, provenance, and influence of this church order are all subject to intense scholarly debate and revision today, the details provided by it must be received with due caution. It is possible that several of these elements reflect later (fourth-century) additions or interpolations: examples are the "three-year catechumenate," for which there is no undisputed corroborative evidence in the first three centuries; the use of "exorcised" oil for a prebaptismal anointing (neither of these first two elements is documented for the West until later); the precise wording of the creedal formula, which corresponds most closely only to fourth-century and later versions of the Roman and, ultimately, Apostles' Creed[30]; and the second (episcopal) postbaptismal anointing.[31]

With regard to the episcopal handlaying prayer and anointing, the Latin version of the *Apostolic Tradition* does not interpret these ritual actions in relationship to a "giving" of the Holy Spirit to the newly baptized but provides, instead, the following rubrics and texts:

> And the bishop shall lay his hands on them and invoke saying: Lord God, you have made them worthy to receive remission of sins through the laver of regeneration of the holy Spirit: *send upon them your grace*, that they may serve you according to your will; for to you is glory, to Father and Son with the holy Spirit in the holy Church, both now and to the ages of ages. Amen.
>
> Then, pouring the oil of thanksgiving from his hand and placing it on his head, he shall say: I anoint you with holy oil in God the Father almighty and Christ Jesus and the holy Spirit.[32]

The subsequent "Oriental" versions of this document transform the handlaying prayer precisely into an explicit invocation of the Holy Spirit on the newly baptized. Hence, it is not surprising that one of the principal scholarly debates over Christian initiation in the *Apostolic Tradition* has concerned the interpretation of these postbaptismal "episcopal acts" in relationship to what would become later, in the Roman rite, the separate sacrament called "confirmation."

In treating these episcopal rites, Aidan Kavanagh has argued that they reflect only the traditional structure of what may be termed an episcopal *missa*.[33] That is, this episcopal unit has the overall structure of a "dismissal" rite used to dismiss various categories of people (e.g., catechumens and penitents) from the liturgical assembly, a practice known to have occurred frequently in Christian antiquity at the close of various liturgies. Different groups of people, before leaving the liturgical assembly, would go before the bishop and receive his blessing, often by a handlaying rite. Consequently, just as these neophytes had often been "dismissed" from both catechetical instruction and from other liturgical gatherings by a rite that included the laying on of hands, so now, after baptism and anointing by the presbyter, they were again dismissed by means of a similar ritual structure; however, this time the "dismissal" was *from* the baptismal bath *to* the eucharistic table. Although this dismissal rite would later develop theologically into a postbaptismal conferral of the Holy Spirit and ultimately would be separated from baptism itself, the origins of what later became the independent rite called "confirmation" are thus *structural* rather than theological.

In a response, Paul Turner questions Kavanagh's interpretation of these episcopal acts as constituting an actual "dismissal," and suggests, alternatively, that they should be viewed as "the first public gesture of ratification for the bishop and the faithful who did not witness the pouring of water," as it is quite clear that both baptism and the presbyteral anointing happened at a place outside the liturgical assembly itself.[34] In other words, this unit of the bishop's handlaying prayer and anointing constitutes a rite of "welcome" rather than dismissal, a rite by which those newly born of water *and* the Holy Spirit are now welcomed officially into the eucharistic communion of the church. And they are welcomed there by the chief pastor of the community, the bishop, who prays for God's grace to guide the neophytes that they might be faithful to what their baptism has already made them. In its origins, therefore, what through various historical accidents and developments became "confirmation" may simply have been the way in which the baptismal rite itself was concluded and the eucharist begun in some communities.

Along with these specific ritual details, third-century sources also show that infant baptism, including infant communion, was being practiced widely. When the question of infants is considered in this period of history, it is not simply their baptism but their complete initiation, including the reception of communion, that is implied. Tertullian (*De baptismo* 18) strongly cautions against infant initiation, arguing that people should be "made Christians" only "when they have become competent to know Christ." Origen, however, calls it an "apostolic custom" (*In Romanos commentaria* 5, 9). *Apostolic Tradition* 21 makes provision for those "who cannot answer for themselves." Cyprian (*Epistle* 64) gives a theological defense based on the inheritance from Adam of the "disease of death," if not yet "original sin."

Tertullian is the first author known to express a preference for initiation taking place at Easter, writing:

> The Passover [i.e., Easter] provides the day of most solemnity for baptism, for then was accomplished our Lord's passion, and *into it we are baptized* . . . . After that, Pentecost is a most auspicious period for arranging baptisms, for during it our Lord's resurrection was several times made known among the disciples, and the grace of the Holy Spirit first given. . . . For all that, every day is a Lord's day: any hour, any season, is suitable for baptism. If there is any difference of solemnity, it makes no difference to the grace.[35]

It may be that something similar is intended in *Apostolic Tradition* 21, but since this document refers only to initiation at a nighttime vigil, which could have been even a Friday to Saturday vigil, there is no compelling reason to assume automatically that it is the Easter vigil that is meant, especially when *Apostolic Tradition* 33 can refer to Pascha itself without making any reference to Christian initiation. Indeed, the modern assumption that "the" early Church regularly baptized at Easter finds support *only* in Tertullian's marked preference for the practice and in Hippolytus of Rome's *Commentary on Daniel* 13:15, both of which are Western sources.[36] Even so, Tertullian's reference to the season of Pentecost ("a most auspicious *period*"), and to "every day" as "a Lord's day" with the result that "any hour, any season, is suitable for baptism," suggests that he also knew a variety of occasions for Christian initiation within the North African church of his day. In fact, the biblical precedent for Pentecost baptism in Acts 2:37–42, together with the documented practice of an annual "covenant renewal" ceremony at Qumran on the Jewish feast of Pentecost, may well suggest that baptism on (or during) Pentecost actually antedates the development of a preference for Easter baptism in the church's history.[37]

Although not directly related to the early development of the rites of Christian initiation, it is important to note that in the middle of the third century the churches of Rome and North Africa found themselves involved in an intense controversy about baptism with special regard to the reconciliation of heretics and schismatics who sought to return to the unity of the Church. This controversy began with the "Novatianist Schism," a split in the church at Rome resulting in a rather puritanical and exclusivist Christian sect of Novatianists, who refused to readmit to communion any who had lapsed (i.e., denied the Christian faith) during the recent Decian persecution of 250. Established in opposition to the church of Rome and its duly elected bishop Cornelius, who permitted the reconciliation of those who had lapsed after a period of penance, this sect, under the leadership of its own bishop, Novatian, saw itself as the only legitimate church. The Novatianist church was excommunicated as "heretical," but its continued existence raised the question of the validity of the sacraments administered by those outside the unity of the church, and it is within this context that the real baptismal controversy arose.

Cyprian of Carthage followed what had been the traditional teaching of the North African church[38] and stressed the invalidity of baptism given by heretics and schismatics alike. Simply put, baptism administered outside of unity with the Catholic Church, according to Cyprian, was invalid and so had to be repeated for those seeking to come back into unity.[39] So strong, in fact, was Cyprian's insistence on the proper and necessary *ecclesiological* context of baptism that he wrote in *De unitate ecclesiae* 5 that "he can no longer have God for his Father, who has not the Church for his mother."

Cyprian was careful not to call what he considers the baptism of heretics and schismatics a "re-baptism." Rather, since baptism itself did not exist outside the church, "those who come thence are not *re-baptized* among us, but are baptized" (*Letter 71, to Quintus*, 1). It is on this point that Cyprian and Stephen, by then the Bishop of Rome, entered into a profound disagreement that threatened to break off communion between the churches of North Africa and Rome.[40] At Rome itself, those baptized in schism or heresy were merely received back into communion, as in the reconciliation of apostates and penitents, by the imposition or laying on of hands by the bishop. They were not (re-)baptized. Stephen, in fact, was so adamant about this as the practice to be followed—a practice based, in his opinion, on the authority of Saint Peter the Apostle himself—that he threatened to break off communion with the North African church if they continued in this "innovative" manner.

Cyprian's arguments, however, were not really "innovations" but were based on the decisions of the Council of Carthage (220), presided over by his immediate predecessor, Agrippinus. This council had decided in favor of "re-baptism" in such contexts, and this is the traditional view that Cyprian vigorously defended. Under Cyprian's leadership, in fact, three other councils were held at Carthage in order to discuss this matter further (one in 255 and two in 256). In spite of Stephen's threats, the North African tradition of "re-baptism" was upheld. As there was only one Church, there could only be one baptism. Even if properly celebrated and administered elsewhere, baptism could not and did not exist outside of unity with the one Church.

History demonstrates that it was the view of Stephen and the church of Rome that largely prevailed in this controversy. But the problem remained unresolved in the lifetimes of Cyprian and Stephen, both of whom were to suffer martyrdom during the Valerian persecution of 257. Nevertheless, although this controversy would return in the context of the Donatist schism in the time of Augustine, communion between North Africa and Rome was not broken off as a result. In other words, unity and communion were maintained in spite of a serious threat to that communion over something so fundamental and basic as differing approaches to ecclesiology and baptismal theology. In fact, in Augustine's own response to the Donatists, who appealed to Cyprian's theology in support of their own re-baptism practices against the Catholic Church of North Africa, he used Cyprian's maintenance of communion precisely as an argument against schism and disunity.[41]

The Eucharistic Liturgy and Its Anaphoral Prayer

The origins of the central practice of Christian worship, variously known as the "breaking of bread," "Lord's Supper," "Eucharist, "Mass," or "Divine Liturgy," and celebrated in obedience to Jesus' command to "do this" table ritual as his "memorial," are similarly complex and unclear. Apart from some notable exceptions,[42] traditional scholarship and catechesis tended to look almost exclusively at these origins as deriving from the "Last Supper" accounts in the Synoptic Gospels (Matt. 26:26–29, Mark 14:22–25, Luke 22:14–20), where the context is clearly the annual celebration of the Jewish Passover, and where the "institution" of the eucharist by Christ takes place during the Passover ritual. Among twentieth-century liturgical scholars, the most widely influential hypothesis about eucharistic origins in relation to this Passover context is proposed by the Anglican Benedictine scholar Gregory Dix in his 1945 classic, *The Shape of the Liturgy*.[43] According to Dix, there is discernible a definite liturgical structure or shape implied in the New Testament narratives of Christ's "institution," especially in the earliest account supplied by Paul in 1 Corinthians 11:23–26: a "seven-action shape" of the eucharistic meal. That is, before the Passover meal proper, (1) Jesus *took* bread, (2) said the *blessing* (a Jewish form of *berakah*) over the bread, (3) *broke* the bread, and (4) *gave* the bread to his disciples accompanied by the new interpretative words that this bread was his body. After the meal proper, (5) Jesus *took* the cup of wine, (6) said a prayer of *thanksgiving* (*eucharistia*), and (7) *gave* the cup to his disciples with the interpretive words that this wine was his blood of the new covenant. When, in the course of the late first or early second centuries, the eucharistic meal itself was discontinued, surviving as the occasional agape of the Christian community, a "four-action shape" of the eucharist proper resulted. That is, the eucharistic "meal" came to be structured around the actions of (1) *taking* bread and cup, (2) *blessing* and *thanking* God over the bread and cup, (3) *breaking* the bread, and (4) *giving* both the bread and cup to the members of the gathered assembly. By a fusion of this eucharistic "shape" with the Jewish synagogue's "liturgy of the word," the overall two-part structure of the eucharistic liturgy itself, discernible ever thereafter in the traditions of both East and West, developed fully with the *taking* becoming offertory or preparation rites, the *blessing* and *thanking* turning into the anaphora or eucharistic prayer, the *breaking* into fraction rites, and the *giving* of the bread and cup into the distribution and reception of communion.

    Dix also suggests that the precise Jewish origins of the eucharistic anaphora can be discerned from this Last Supper Passover (or Pauline) context, in that when instituting the eucharist Jesus naturally would have used, after the meal, the tripartite Jewish grace said over a cup of wine, the *birkat ha-mazon*, consisting of a *blessing* of God for food, a *thanksgiving* for the gift of the land, and a *supplication* for Jerusalem. Extant, at the earliest, in the tenth-century manuscript of the *Siddur Rav Saadya Gaon*, the text of this *birkat ha-mazon* is:

BLESSING OF HIM WHO NOURISHES

Blessed are you, Lord our God, King of the universe, for you nourish us and the whole world with goodness, grace, kindness, and mercy.

Blessed are you, Lord, for you nourish the universe.

BLESSING FOR THE LAND

We will give thanks to you, Lord our God, because you have given us for our inheritance a desirable land, good and wide, the covenant and the law, life and food. . . .

. . . And for all these things we give you thanks and bless your name for ever and beyond.

Blessed are you, Lord, for the land and for food.

BLESSING FOR JERUSALEM

Have mercy, Lord our God, on us your people Israel, and your city Jerusalem, on your sanctuary and your dwelling place, on Zion, the habitation of your glory, and the great and holy house over which your name is invoked. Restore the kingdom of the house of David to its place in our days, and speedily build Jerusalem. . . .

. . . Blessed are you, Lord, for you build Jerusalem.[44]

Stemming from Dix's initial suggestion, one of the clear goals of liturgical scholarship on eucharistic origins, until just recently, has been to trace what was considered to be a single line of literary evolution from the *birkat ha-mazon*, presumed to have been used by Jesus at the Last Supper, through the table prayers of *Didache* 9 and 10, the Syrian anaphora called *Addai and Mari*, the anaphora included in conjunction with the ordination of bishops in the *Apostolic Tradition*, and other possible, primarily Egyptian, anaphoral fragments (e.g., the *Strasbourg Papyrus*), all the way to the fourth-century and later development of the classic anaphoras of both East and West.[45]

More recent scholarship on eucharistic origins, however, has called into serious question not only the derivation of "the" eucharistic anaphora from the *birkat ha-mazon*, but also the historical reliability and authority of the Last Supper accounts themselves as a liturgical "source" for the eucharist, including the presumed Passover context found in only the Synoptic Gospels. At the same time, recent scholarship has also drawn attention to the various problems associated with trying to determine what kinds of "Jewish" prayers the historical Jesus himself may or may not have used within the context of a first-century Judaism increasingly recognized to have been widely diverse in its own liturgical prayers and practices. Hence, together with the New Testament Last Supper narratives of eucharistic "institution"—which may well be theologically motivated etiologies rather than either historical reminiscences of what Jesus actually did and said at the Last Supper or liturgical patterns reflecting or even "rubrics" prescribing liturgical practice[46]—contemporary scholarship would demand that, when seeking eucharistic origins, we take into account the following: Jesus' table companionship with "tax collectors and sinners" as the celebration of the in-breaking of the eschatological "reign" or "kingdom of God"; his several feeding miracles (John 6, in particular); the meal contexts of his post-resurrection appearances (cf. Luke 24 and John 21); and the continued meal customs of the apostolic church (Acts 2:42, 46). Similarly, in addition to the annual Passover meal as one source, contemporary liturgical scholarship points to the meal practices of the Greco-Roman *symposion* or

---

Didache

Chapters 1–6: "The two ways"

Chapter 7: Baptism

Chapter 8: Fasting

Chapter 9:

About the thanksgiving: give thanks thus:

First, about the cup:

We give thanks to you, our Father, for the holy vine of your child David, which you made known to us through your child Jesus;
glory to you for evermore.

And about the broken bread:

We give thanks to you, our Father, for the life and knowledge which you made known to us through your child Jesus;
glory to you for evermore.

As this broken bread was scattered over the mountains, and when brought together became one, so let your Church be brought together from the ends of the earth into your kingdom;
for yours are the glory and the power through Jesus Christ for evermore.

But let no one eat or drink of your thanksgiving but those who have been baptized in the name of the Lord. For about this also the Lord has said, "Do not give what is holy to the dogs."

Chapter 10

And after you have had your fill, give thanks thus:

We give thanks to you, holy Father, for your holy Name which you have enshrined in our hearts, and for the knowledge and faith and immortality which you made known to us through your child Jesus;
glory to you for evermore.

You, almighty Master, created all things for the sake of your Name, and gave food and drink to mankind for their enjoyment, that they might give you thanks; but to us you have granted spiritual food and drink and eternal

---

convivium (the post-meal "drinking party") and to possible Jewish parallels with or adaptations of this practice in the first century AD (e.g., the *chavurot*) as providing another influential context for early Christian eucharistic meal practice.[47] Moreover, together with the *birkat ha-mazon*, oral forms of which undoubtedly existed early on,[48] the variety of then existing Jewish prayer forms from diverse Jewish contexts (e.g.,

life through your child Jesus. Above all we give you thanks because you are mighty;
glory to you for evermore. Amen.

Remember, Lord, your Church, to deliver it from all evil and to perfect it in your love; bring it together from the four winds, now sanctified, into your kingdom which you have prepared for it;
for yours are the power and the glory for evermore.

May grace come, and may this world pass away.

Hosanna to the God of David.

If any is holy, let him come; if any is not, let him repent.

Marana tha. Amen.

[*But about the words over the sweet savor, give thanks thus, as we say:*

We give thanks to you, Father, for the sweet savor which you made known to us through your Son Jesus; glory to you for evermore. Amen.]

Chapters 11–13: Prophets

Chapter 14

On the Lord's day of the Lord, come together, break bread, and give thanks, having first confessed your transgressions, that your sacrifice may be pure.

But let none who has a quarrel with his companion join with you until they have been reconciled, that your sacrifice may not be defiled.

For this is that which was spoken by the Lord, "In every place, and at every time, offer me a pure sacrifice; for I am a great king, says the Lord, and my Name is wonderful among the nations."

Chapter 15: Church discipline

Chapter 16: The last day

Reference

Jasper, R. C. D., and G. J. Cuming. *Prayers of the Eucharist: Early and Reformed,* 3d ed. New York: Pueblo, 1980, pp. 23–24.

from Dura-Europos and from Qumran and later rabbinic legislation, where it is indicated that "blessings" over both bread and wine might occur together at the *beginning* of a communal meal rather than separated by an intervening meal[49]) makes it extremely difficult to assume that early Christian eucharistic practice followed only one structure or pattern. For that matter, as Bryan Spinks has pointed out, there is no compelling reason to assume that either Jesus himself or the early Christian communities, especially in the absence of written official texts, would have used even such standardized prayers as the *birkat ha-mazon* when other meal-grace choices were available or when original creations were an option. For, in spite of the obvious continuity between Christianity and Judaism, Christianity also represents a *discontinuity* in practice and thought that must be taken seriously.[50]

Furthermore, if we do not know with certainty what the liturgical structure of the eucharistic meal or its prayers may have been early on, we also cannot be certain about what may have constituted the food and drink of such "eucharistic" gatherings. Both these issues have been addressed in compelling studies by Andrew McGowan. With regard to the former, McGowan has demonstrated that there is considerable evidence for early eucharistic meals (e.g., 1 Cor. 10:16, *Didache* 9, a fragment of Papias preserved in Irenaeus, and the agape meal in *Apostolic Tradition* 41) where the cup ritual actually comes before the bread ritual, much as in the so-called shorter version of the Last Supper narrative in Luke 22:15–19.[51] With regard to the latter, McGowan has underscored that, in addition to bread and wine (or water), and sometimes even bread alone, other elements, such as cheese, milk, honey, fruits, or fish, were surely a part of some gatherings. If such additional elements have often been associated with agape meals rather than with eucharistic meals proper, it is important to question whether early Christians themselves would have made such precise distinctions with regard to their communal meal practices.[52] Of particular note in this context of both eucharistic meal structure and contents is the documented use of water rather than wine, or the references to "cup" without specifying its contents, in some early Christian communities of a more ascetic orientation. Indeed, polemics against the eucharistic use of water were widespread, including writings by Clement of Alexandria, Irenaeus, and Cyprian of Carthage, who underscored the necessity of mixing water and wine at the eucharist, and there is a rather odd reference to "water and wine mixed with water" in Justin Martyr's description of the eucharistic liturgy in his *First Apology* 65; these may well suggest that the origins of the liturgical practice of the mixed cup reflect not only the ancient practice of mixing wine with water before drinking but also a deliberate synthesis of diverse eucharistic practices themselves.[53]

A fish, a basket of bread, and a glass of red wine. Located in the crypt of Lucina of the catacomb of Callistus at Rome, the third-century wall painting combines images of the miracle of the loaves and the fishes with the bread and wine of the eucharist. The fish might have been part of the eucharistic meal or it might represent Christ or Christian baptism. Christ was the great fish, claimed Tertullian in his treatise on baptism (c. 200), and Christians were little fishes who began and continued life in the (baptismal) water. SCALA/ART RESOURCE, NY

All of this evidence militates against the attempts of Dix and others to find an original, pristine, and "apostolic" core of the eucharistic liturgy as having derived from a "seven-action" shape into a "four-action" shape. Since other early meal ritual patterns indicate a blessing of bread and cup together *before* a meal, it becomes difficult to maintain the hypothesis that these two actions merged into a unified rite only after the meal itself disappeared from early Christian eucharistic assemblies. Furthermore, to maintain that one can infer the development of later "offertory," preparation, or "fraction" rites from such necessary and utilitarian actions such as "taking" and "breaking," or that these actions should even be accorded the same ritual weight as blessing or thanking and eating, seems rather far-fetched, especially when one considers that not all eucharistic liturgies developed either specific "offertory" or "fraction" rites in their histories. Hence, instead of either a seven or four-action "shape of the liturgy," the most that can probably be inferred from the diversity of early Christian eucharistic meals (if one wants to use such "shape of the liturgy" language at all) is that the early eucharist had but a "two-action shape": the sharing of bread and cup in the context of blessing, thanksgiving, and praise.[54] To say any more than this is sheer speculation.

Furthermore, even the long-standing hypothesis that the twofold "liturgy of the word" and "liturgy of the eucharist" was derived from a fusion between the Jewish synagogue service and the Christian eucharistic meal, while neither implausible nor impossible, needs to be juxtaposed to two facts: (1) we know clearly neither the nature and contents of the synagogue service in the first century, nor whether the synagogue "service" was already more than a kind of "Bible study" before the destruction of the Temple in 70 AD[55]; and (2) communal meals themselves, whether Jewish, Greco-Roman, or early Christian, would have already included what may be called religious or philosophical conversation and the singing of hymns, which may themselves also have functioned as the source for this section of the liturgy.[56] In other words, while services or liturgies of the word, including catechetical assemblies, are known from early Christianity, eucharistic celebrations without some kind of word component are not. The only real question is whether such "liturgies of the word" always came *before* the eucharistic meal or if, consistent with the *symposion* or *convivium*, they were part of an extended discourse on the word occuring *after* the meal.[57]

Nevertheless, whatever conclusions may be drawn about eucharistic origins, our earliest documents (1 Cor. 11 and *Didache* 9 and 10) do confirm that the eucharist was initially a literal meal, held most likely in the evening within a domestic, "house church" setting, with the contents of the meal provided by members of the assembly. By the

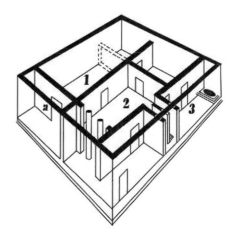

Floor plan of the house church at Dura-Europos (Syria). A private home was renovated to accommodate Christian worship c. AD 232–256 by the removal of a partition wall from two rooms to create a larger common space (1). A raised platform at the east end likely held an altar (a, on this wall in area 1). A third room of the house was converted for use as a baptistery (3), with apparently a courtyard between the two rooms (2). DRAWING BY BENJAMIN W. TUCKER AFTER ARMANDO GARZON-BLANCO IN BRADSHAW AND HOFFMAN, 1991

Third-century baptistery at Dura-Europos. Frescoes on the walls depicting biblical scenes surrounded the canopied font, which was approximately three feet deep. Baptism was probably performed with the candidate standing in the font with water poured over the head, although submersion may have been possible. Excavation photo in situ, 1932. YALE UNIVERSITY ART GALLERY

middle of the second century, the "meal" itself had in some places disappeared from the eucharist proper, with only the specific ritual sharing of bread and cup in the context of praise and thanksgiving, increasingly transferred to Sunday morning and remaining as the central focus of worship [see color plate 3]. Again, it is Justin Martyr, in chapter 67 of his *First Apology*, who provides our earliest overall description of what constituted this Sunday worship:

> And on the day called Sunday an assembly is held in one place of all who live in town or country, and the records of the apostles or the writings of the prophets are read as time allows.
>
> Then, when the reader has finished, the president in a discourse admonishes and exhorts (us) to imitate these good things.
>
> Then we all stand up together and send up prayers; and as we said before, when we have finished praying, bread and wine and water [literally], are brought up, and the president likewise sends up prayers and thanksgivings to the best of his ability, and the people assent, saying the Amen; and the elements over which thanks have been given are distributed, and everyone partakes; and they are sent through the deacons to those who are not present.
>
> And the wealthy who so desire give what they wish, as each chooses; and what is collected is deposited with the president.
>
> He helps orphans and widows, and those who through sickness or any other cause are in need, and those in prison, and strangers sojourning among us; in a word, he takes care of all those who are in need.
>
> And we assemble together on Sunday, because it is the first day, on which God transformed darkness and matter, and made the world; and Jesus Christ our Savior rose from the dead on that day; for they crucified him the day before Saturday; and the day after Saturday, which is Sunday, he appeared to his apostles and disciples, and taught them these things which we have presented to you also for your consideration.[58]

The liturgical outline provided by Justin for Sundays—assembly, readings, prayers (of the faithful), exhortation or homily, kiss of peace (inferred from Justin's description

of Christian initiation in *First Apology* 61), preparation of the bread and cup, eucharistic prayer, the "Amen" of the community, and distribution—is corroborated for North Africa in the writings of Tertullian.[59] Tertullian is also our first witness to the use of the "orans" posture for Christian prayer, to psalmody being sung during the liturgy of the word (*De anima* 9:4), and to the use of the "Our Father" preceding the kiss of peace (the "seal" of the prayer) at the conclusion of the prayers of the faithful before the eucharist proper began (*De oratione* 18:1–2).[60]

A Christian at prayer. The common posture for prayer in the early Church was standing with upraised hands. The late-third-century wall painting is located in the catacomb of Priscilla, an old quarry used by Roman Christians for burials from the late second century to the fourth century. SCALA/ART RESOURCE, NY

The Eucharistic Liturgy in the Second and Third Centuries

Sunday Assembly
Biblical Readings with Psalmody
Homily
Prayers of Intercession
(Our Father)
Kiss of Peace
Presentation of the Bread and Mixed Cup of Wine and Water
Eucharistic Prayer
Amen of the Assembly
Reception of Communion
(Dismissal)
(Collection for the support of widows and orphans)
Taking of Communion to those unable to be present
Reservation of the Eucharist at Home

References

Justin Martyr. *First Apology* 61, 65.
Tertullian. *Apologeticum* 39.

On the basis of Justin's description, and taking into account the meal contexts of Jesus' post-resurrection appearances in the gospels (especially the Emmaus account in Luke 24), Gordon Lathrop has deduced what might be called an ecumenical, transcultural, and possibly even "apostolic" authoritative *ordo* for Christian worship. He writes that

> these are the essentials of Christian worship. A community *gathers in prayer* around the scriptures *read* and *proclaimed*. This community of the word then tastes the meaning of that word by keeping the meal of Christ, *giving thanks* over bread and cup and *eating* and *drinking*. It is this word-table community, the body of Christ, which gathers other people to its number, continually *teaching* both itself and these newcomers the mercy and mystery of God and *washing* them in the name of that God. All of these essential things urge the community toward the world—toward prayer for the world, sharing with the hungry of the world, caring for the world, giving witness to the world. . . . Around these central things, which will be most evident in Sunday and festival worship, other gathering of Christians may also take place.[61]

Other elements of the liturgical celebration, according to Lathrop, flow from this central core as well. He continues:

> The very centrality of bath, word, and table, and the very reasons for their centrality . . . do begin to give us some characteristics of the mode of our celebration. These characteristics . . . are corollaries which ought not be easily ignored. A list of such characteristics should include *ritual focus*, a *music which serves*, the importance of *Sunday* and other festivals, a *participating community*, *many ministries*, and a *recognized presider* who is in communion with the churches.[62]

Although it is certainly true that the liturgical skeleton provided by Justin is discernible in every Christian eucharistic tradition thereafter, there are several things we simply do not know clearly from his description. We do not know, for example, whether Sunday worship took place on Sunday morning, or if the rite Justin knew actually took place in the evening; whether the "kiss of peace" at the end of the intercessory prayers in *First Apology* 61 was a standard feature of eucharistic worship in this period or something reserved for the baptismal eucharist alone; whether the "mixed cup" of wine and water to which he refers was a universal practice or, as suggested above, may represent the beginnings of a synthesis of distinct eucharistic practices or may even be an interpolation into Justin's text; whether the prayer of thanksgiving prayed extemporaneously by the "president" (*proestôs*) was a single, integral *eucharistia* over the bread and cup or, like other surviving examples from the pre-Nicene period (e.g., the *Didache* and *Didascalia Apostolorum*), was but a series of separate prayers accompanying an actual meal; and whether the collection for the poor actually took place at the end of the eucharistic rite or at some other point before, during, or after the rite itself. To abstract some recognizable or authoritative *ordo* for Christian liturgy from such brief descriptions, in which the precise details the historian would actually need or want are lacking, may be rather risky if the aim is to find a normative pattern for what the church *should* do in its liturgical assemblies as a result. In fact, one might argue that the construction of such an *ordo* is but an attempt to replace Gregory Dix's "shape of the liturgy" with a new, alternative "shape." Similarly, John Baldovin has written that a pure liturgical "core" never really exists independently from its "code" (i.e., what is done and how it is actually done) or its culture.[63] And, unfortunately, it is precisely both "code" and "culture" that are missing from Justin's all too brief description.

Although Justin is clear that the "eucharistic prayer" or "anaphora" (prayer of offering) was extemporized by the presider or "president," some models for eucharistic praying are provided in other documents of the first three centuries. Undoubtedly in some relationship to the evolving Jewish meal prayers (e.g., the *birkat ha-mazon*), anamnesis (remembrance of God's saving acts in Christ) and epiclesis (invocation or supplication for the promised fulfillment of those acts) would come to characterize early Christian eucharistic praying. But the particular structures of those anaphoral prayers would vary. In some extant texts, such as the meal prayers in *Didache* 9 and 10 (Syria), undoubtedly inspired by some form of the *birkat ha-mazon*, we note a tripartite structure of thanksgiving, praise, and supplication.[64] In others, such as that of *Addai and Mari* (Syria), a classic anaphoral prayer still in use with some additions within East Syrian Christianity today, a bipartite structure of thanksgiving and supplication appears evident.[65] Still others—for example, the anaphoral fragment called the *Strasbourg Papyrus* (Egypt)—appear to have a bipartite structure of thanksgiving and supplication linked together by offering:

> To bless [you] . . . [night] and day . . .

> [you who made] heaven [and] all that is in [it, the earth and what is on earth,] seas and rivers and [all that is] in [them]; [you] who made man [according to your] own image and likeness. You made everything through your wisdom, the light [of?] your true Son, our Lord and Savior Jesus Christ; giving thanks through him to you with him and the Holy Spirit, we offer the reasonable sacrifice and this bloodless service, which all the nations offer you, "from sunrise to sunset," from south to north, [for] your "name is great among all the nations, and in every place incense is offered to your holy name and a pure sacrifice."

Over this sacrifice and offering we pray and beseech you, remember your holy and only Catholic Church, all your peoples and all your flocks. Provide the peace which is from heaven in all our hearts, and grant us also the peace of this life. The . . . of the land peaceful things towards us, and towards your [holy] name, the prefect of the province, the army, the princes, councils . . .

[for seedtime and] harvest . . . preserve, for the poor of [your] people, for all of us who call upon [your] name, for all who hope in you. Give rest to the souls of those who have fallen asleep; remember those of whom we make mention today, both those whose names we say [and] whose we do not say . . . [Remember] our orthodox fathers and bishops everywhere; and grant us to have a part and lot with the fair . . . of your holy prophets, apostles, and martyrs. Receive(?) [through] their entreaties [these prayers]; grant them through our Lord; through whom be glory to you to the ages of ages.[66]

Addai and Mari

Prayers of preparation
Psalms
Prayers
Trisagion ["Holy God, holy and strong, holy and immortal . . ."]
Readings (Old Testament, Acts)
Psalm
Epistle
Alleluia
Gospel
Dismissal of catechumens
Prayers of the faithful
Prayer of inclination
Transfer of gifts
Creed
Preparation for anaphora
Peace

Priest:	Peace be with you.
Answer:	And with you and your spirit.
Priest:	The grace of our Lord (Jesus Christ and the love of God the Father, and the fellowship of the Holy Spirit be with us all now and ever world without end).
Answer:	Amen.
Priest:	Up with your minds.
Answer:	They are with you, O God.
Priest:	The offering is offered to God, the Lord of all.
Answer:	It is fitting and right.

The priest says privately: Worthy of glory from every mouth and thanksgiving from every tongue is the adorable and glorious name of the Father and of the Son and of the Holy Spirit. He created the world through his grace and its inhabitants in his compassion; he saved men through his mercy, and gave great grace to mortals.

Your majesty, O Lord, a thousand thousand heavenly beings adore; myriad myriads of angels, and ranks of spiritual beings, minister of fire and spirit, together with the holy cherubim and seraphim, glorify your name, crying out and glorifying (unceasingly calling to one another and saying):

People: Holy, holy (holy, Lord God almighty; heaven and earth are full of his praises).

The priest says privately: And with these heavenly armies we, also even we, your lowly, weak, and miserable servants, Lord, give you thanks because you have brought about us a great grace which cannot be repaid. For you put on our human nature to give us life through your divine nature; you raised us from our lowly state; you restored our Fall; you restored our immortality; you forgave our debts; you set right our sinfulness; you enlightened our intelligence. You, our Lord and our God, conquered our enemies, and made the lowliness of our weak nature to triumph through the abundant mercy of your grace.

(aloud) And for all (your helps and graces towards us, let us raise to you praise and honor and thanksgiving and worship, now and ever and world without end).

People: Amen.

The priest says privately: You, Lord, through your many mercies which cannot be told, be graciously mindful of all the pious and righteous Fathers who were pleasing in your sight, in the commemoration of the body and blood of your Christ, which we offer to you on the pure and holy altar, as you taught us.

And grant us your tranquillity and your peace for all the days of this age *(repeat)* [*People:* Amen.]. That all the inhabitants of the earth may know you, that you alone are the true God and Father, and you sent our Lord Jesus Christ, your beloved Son, and he, our Lord and our God, taught us through his life-giving gospel all the purity and holiness of the prophets, apostles, martyrs, confessors, bishops, priests, deacons, and all sons of the holy Catholic Church who have been sealed with the living seal of holy baptism.

And we also, Lord, *(thrice)* your lowly, weak, and miserable servants, who have gathered and stand before you, [and] have received through tradition the form which is from you, rejoicing, glorifying, exalting, commemorating, and celebrating this great mystery of the passion, death and resurrection of our Lord Jesus Christ.

May your Holy Spirit, Lord, come and rest on this offering of your servants, and bless and sanctify it, that it may be to us, Lord, for remission of debts, forgiveness of sins, and the great hope of resurrection from the dead, and new life in the kingdom of heaven, with all who have been pleasing in your sight.

And because of all your wonderful dispensation towards us, with open mouths and uncovered faces we give you thanks and glorify you without ceasing in your Church, which has been redeemed by the precious blood of your Christ, offering up (praise, honor, thanksgiving and adoration to your living and life-giving name, now and at all times forever and ever). *People:* Amen.

Apologia

Fraction and signing

Lord's Prayer

Elevation

> *The priest proceeds:*   The holy thing to the holies is fitting in perfection.
>
> *People:*   One holy Father, one holy Son, one holy Spirit. Glory be to the Father and to the Son and to the Holy Spirit to the ages of ages. Amen.

Communion
The body of our Lord for the pardon of offences.
The precious blood for the pardon of offences.

Thanksgiving for communion
Dismissal

Reference

Jasper, R. C. D., and G. J. Cuming. *Prayers of the Eucharist: Early and Reformed*, 3d ed. New York: Pueblo, 1980, pp. 41–44.

Scholarly debate continues on whether or not this *Strasbourg Papyrus* ever constituted a complete anaphora or is but a fragment of a longer, non-extant prayer.[67] Nevertheless, some liturgical scholars have seen the *Strasbourg Papyrus* in the background of several of the classic fourth-century anaphoras. Geoffrey Cuming, for example, suggested that the *Strasbourg Papyrus*—or something like it—lies not only behind the description of the anaphora provided by Cyril of Jerusalem's *Mystagogical Catechesis* 5 but also behind the later anaphoras called "St. James" and "St. Mark"[68]; and John Fenwick drew similar conclusions with regard to "St. Basil."[69] Whether or not the *Strasbourg Papyrus* text was ever used by itself as a complete anaphora, it was apparently recognized and used as such in the construction of later anaphoral prayers. According to both Fenwick and Cuming, it is also possible that a short anaphoral core, discernible in the "preface" section of later texts, also lies behind the late-fourth-century anaphoras of the *Apostolic Constitutions* 8, the anaphora of the "Twelve Apostles" and that of "St. John Chrysostom."[70] What the first three centuries may have produced with regard to eucharistic prayers, therefore, were but relatively brief meal prayers, or even non-meal prayers, that would later be woven together and/or incorporated with other prayers and prayer fragments to produce the great anaphoral constructions known to us later.

With one notable exception to be considered below, a common characteristic of all these early texts is the absence of several elements that would later become standard components of eucharistic praying in general: the "preface," the Sanctus from Isaiah 6, the "institution narrative" from the New Testament Last Supper and/or Pauline accounts, explicit anamneses (memorial sections), and epicleses of the Holy Spirit. Indeed, it is largely because of the absence of an "institution narrative," and undoubtedly owing in part to predetermined ideas of what a "eucharistic" prayer *should* contain, that previous scholars were often led to conclude that the meal prayers of *Didache* 9 and 10 were not "eucharistic" but were intended for the community's agape meal instead.

One prayer that has certainly captured the imagination of contemporary liturgists in the West, and that now appears in some form in the modern liturgical books of several different churches, Roman Catholic and Protestant alike, is the following model bipartite anaphora provided among the materials for the ordination of a bishop in the *Apostolic Tradition*:

> The Lord be with you.
>   And with your spirit.
> Up with your hearts.
>   We have them with the Lord.
> Let us give thanks to the Lord.
>   It is fitting and right.

> We render thanks to you, O God, through your beloved child Jesus Christ,
> whom in the last times you sent to us as saviour and redeemer and angel of your will; who is your inseparable Word, through whom you made all things, and in whom you were well pleased. You sent him from heaven into the Virgin's womb; and conceived in the womb, he was made flesh and was manifested as your Son, being born of the holy Spirit and the Virgin. Fulfilling your will and gaining for you a holy people, he stretched out his hands when he should suffer, that he might release from suffering those who have believed in you.

And when he was betrayed to voluntary suffering that he might destroy death, and break the bonds of the devil, and tread down hell, and shine upon the righteous, and fix a term, and manifest the resurrection, he took bread and gave thanks to you, saying, "Take, eat: this is my body, which shall be broken for you." Likewise also the cup, saying, "This is my blood, which is shed for you; when you do this, you make my remembrance."

Remembering therefore his death and resurrection, we offer to you the bread and the cup, giving you thanks because you have held us worthy to stand before you and minister to you. And we ask that you would send your holy Spirit upon the offering of your holy Church; that, gathering (it) into one, you would grant to all who partake of the holy things (to partake) for the fullness of the holy Spirit for the strengthening of faith in truth, that we may praise and glorify you through your child Jesus Christ, through whom be glory and honour to you, with the holy Spirit, in your holy Church, both now and to the ages of ages. Amen.[71]

This anaphora obviously includes already both a brief "institution narrative" and an explicit epiclesis of the Holy Spirit in relationship to the reception of the "fruits" of communion. But since it is becoming accepted today that such elements were not incorporated into anaphoral structures until the fourth century, it is quite possible that their presence in this text (if not the entire prayer itself) are but fourth-century additions to an earlier "core." That is, within the first three centuries, the institution narrative may have functioned either as a "distribution formula" at the reception of communion, as providing a dominical "warrant" at some point *for* the church's celebration, or, alternatively, as part of ongoing catechesis on the *meaning* of the eucharist.[72] Indeed, the removal of such elements as the "institution narrative" and the epiclesis from this prayer reveals what may well have been originally a simple bipartite prayer of christological thanksgiving and supplication concluded by a doxology.

John Fenwick's work, referred to above, has underscored the plausibility of seeing the fourth century as a time of standardization and cross-fertilization in which various anaphoral elements began to be incorporated into and added to earlier anaphoral "cores" across different ecclesial traditions. Although it is possible that the Sanctus itself, known from both Jewish and early Christian non-eucharistic worship, may have already begun to enter into eucharistic worship in some third-century contexts,[73] the proposal of Gabriele Winkler that the origins of the anaphoral use of epicleses of the Holy Spirit derive from the consecration of the prebaptismal oil within the initiation rites of the early Syrian tradition suggests even further reasons why the epiclesis in the *Apostolic Tradition* anaphora may be viewed as a later addition. That is, the language of "*send* your holy Spirit upon the offering of your holy Church" in the text, in light of what both Sebastian Brock[74] and Winkler[75] have argued with regard to earlier epicletic language in the Syrian tradition (e.g., "Come, Lord Jesus," "Come, Holy Spirit," or "let your Spirit come"), appears to correspond to Greek usage known elsewhere only from the fourth century. As such, it is quite possible that the version of this prayer that has come down to us, and from which it has been recently adapted and incorporated into modern liturgical usage, more closely reflects a stage within the fourth-century developmental process than anything in the first three centuries.

Whatever the early eucharistic usages of the "institution narrative" and epicleses may have been, however, they certainly did not function early on as "consecration formulas" for setting apart the bread and cup in the context of an anaphoral prayer. Rather, what "consecrated" the bread and wine appears to have been the prayer of thanksgiving (*eucharistia*), the anaphora itself. Nevertheless, it is also clear that Christians of the first three centuries understood the eucharistic bread and wine to be identified in a realistic manner with the "body" and "blood" of Christ. So Ignatius of Antioch (c. 98–117) could refer to the eucharist as the "medicine of immortality" (*To the Ephesians* 20.2) and could draw a christological parallel between the incarnation of Christ and the eucharist, claiming that certain "Docetists," who denied the reality of the incarnation, also abstained from the eucharist because "they do not acknowledge the eucharist to be the flesh of our Saviour Jesus Christ" (*To the Smyrnaeans* 7.1). Justin Martyr noted that the eucharist was not "common bread or common drink" but the "flesh and blood of [the] incarnate Jesus" (*First Apology* 66). Irenaeus of Lyons (ca. 180) asserted that "the bread . . . when it receives the invocation of God is no longer common bread, but the eucharist, consisting of two realities, the earthly and the heavenly" (*Adversus Haereses* 4, 18, 4). And Origen of Alexandria, in *Contra Celsum* (8.3), said: "We give thanks to the Creator of the universe and eat the loaves that are presented with thanksgiving and prayer over the gifts, so that *by prayer* they become a certain holy body which sanctifies those who partake of it with a pure intention." If Tertullian could refer to the bread or wine as the *figura* ("figure") of the body or blood of Christ (*Adversus Marcionem* 4, 40), this should not be interpreted as a repudiation of realistic in favor of symbolic language, but within an overall philosophical context where "symbol" participates in the reality being signified and is the key to unlocking that reality. Indeed, such language of the eucharist as *figura, typos, antitypos, similitudo*, and *homoiôma* of the body and blood of Christ would become characteristic eucharistic language in the later patristic period.[76]

Related to the so-called consecration of the eucharist is the early Christian notion of the eucharistic action as the church's "sacrifice" or "offering," an association made as early as *Didache* 14:1. Viewing it as the fulfillment of the "pure sacrifice" of Malachi 1:11, the earliest interpretation of this eucharistic sacrifice appears to have been the offering of prayer and thanksgiving itself as the church's "bloodless" offering *of praise* in contradistinction to the "blood" sacrifices of Judaism and the religions of the Greco-Roman world. The *Strasbourg Papyrus*, for example, makes this relationship clear in saying "We offer the reasonable sacrifice and this bloodless service, which all the nations offer you, 'from sunrise to sunset,' from south to north, [for] your 'name is great among all the nations, and in every place incense is offered to your holy name and a pure sacrifice.'"[77] The sacrificial interpretation of the eucharist thus had to do primarily with the great eucharistia, the *prayer* "offered" over the bread and cup; as such, even the language of the later (fourth-century) Roman *canon missae*, the Roman eucharistic prayer categorically repudiated and rejected by the churches of the sixteenth-century Protestant Reformation, refers to the eucharistic sacrifice as but the Church's *sacrificium laudis* ("sacrifice of praise"), in a manner quite consonant with these earlier texts.

At the same time, as suggested by the fact that early Christians themselves still brought gifts of bread, wine, and other food to the eucharist for both eucharistic use and distribution to the poor, and by the response to Gnostic dualism and denial of the overall importance of the material world, the "eucharistic sacrifice" came to be seen as somehow embodied also in these material "gifts." Hence, the anaphora of the *Apostolic Tradition*, whatever its date, can refer to the bread and cup as the "oblations" which the church now "offers." Cyprian of Carthage draws a parallel between Christ's own sacrifice and that which is offered in the eucharist by the "priest" (i.e., bishop), "who discharges the office of Christ"; Cyprian states that the latter is done "in commemoration" of the former (*Epistle* 63:14).

With regard to this, however, one must proceed cautiously. Recent scholarship has attempted to argue that early eucharistic use of sacrificial terminology may have been a deliberate attempt to subvert the religious meaning of sacrifice altogether and to assert that the *Christian* sacrifice was no cultic sacrifice at all but the "offering" of praise and thanksgiving leading to and expressing the priestly life of the community in its ethical service to the poor and in grateful response for God's own gifts.[78] While undoubtedly true, this probably should not be pushed too far as a specifically Christian interpretation. Similar "spiritualization" of the sacrificial cult was already common among both Jews and pagans in antiquity.[79] Ultimately, then, one can say little more for this period than that what is "offered" *in* the eucharist "is what the New Testament has Jesus order us to offer: the memorial of his own self offering,"[80] that is,

the liturgical *doing* of the eucharist in obedience to his command. Or, as Kenneth Stevenson has shown in his work *Eucharist and Offering*, the metaphor of eucharistic sacrifice has several possible referents and can point simultaneously to the self-offering of the community, to the gifts (bread and cup) that are offered, and to the entire eucharistic rite itself as that which is offered in thanksgiving for God's gift of salvation.[81] At the same time, it is important to underscore that the eucharist in the first three centuries was certainly widely understood theologically as the church's "sacrifice"; thus, the burden of proof to the contrary has always been (and remains) on those who wish somehow to deny this interpretation and who seek to avoid using sacrifical terminology altogether in their eucharistic practice and theology.

Apart from its common celebration on Sundays, it is not clear how frequently the eucharist would have been celebrated on other days throughout the first three centuries.[82] Practice probably varied from place to place. In some places the Christian fasting days of Wednesdays and Fridays (*Didache* 8) may have concluded with a public service of the word and the reception of communion from the reserved eucharist (Alexandria), or they may have become occasions for the celebration of the eucharistic liturgy itself (North Africa). Occasional celebrations in cemeteries, at the tombs of the martyrs, in homes, in prisons, and elsewhere are known to have become so common in North Africa that by the middle of the third century Cyprian could refer to a "daily" celebration at Carthage.

The "Capella Greca" or Greek Chapel.
Located in the second-century catacomb of Priscilla in Rome, the underground rectangular chamber with a long masonry bench is named for two Greek inscriptions located in a niche. The ceilings and upper walls were painted with biblical scenes. The eucharist was celebrated in this room, which also housed the remains of the deceased faithful. Scala/Art Resource, NY

Local expansions of liturgical calendars from the end of the second century on to include the "anniversary" days of martyrs' deaths also contributed to a growing frequency of the eucharistic liturgy in the early churches, especially at the tombs and shrines of the martyrs (those churches called *martyria*). There is also evidence that Christians regularly took enough of the eucharistic elements home with them each Sunday to be able to receive communion at other times during the week, even daily (Tertullian, *Ad uxorem* 2.5), a practice that would persist for several centuries both among the laity and within monastic circles. Hence, in the first three centuries it already becomes necessary to distinguish the full celebration of the eucharistic liturgy, including the reception of communion, from other occasions when communion would be distributed and received apart from the full eucharistic liturgy.

Daily Prayer (the Liturgy of the Hours)

In the early fourth century, the church historian Eusebius of Caesarea described what he considered to be the universal practice in churches of his era of what has been called, thanks to the seminal work of Anton Baumstark,[83] the "cathedral" or parochial office:

> For it is surely no small sign of God's power that throughout the whole world in the churches of God at the morning rising of the sun and at the evening hours, hymns, praises, and truly divine delights are offered to God. God's delights are indeed the hymns sent up everywhere on earth in his Church at the times of morning and evening. For this reason it is said somewhere, "Let my praise be sung sweetly to him" (cf. Ps. 146:1). And "Let my prayer be like incense before you" (Ps. 140 [141]:2).[84]

But if this is clear for the early fourth century, and no doubt in broad continuity with what went before, it is difficult to determine the precise nature and structure of daily prayer prior to Eusebius's account. That is, Christians of the first three centuries, whether in private, with family members, or in small communal gatherings, certainly knew regular patterns of prayer at intervals throughout the day, but there is no single pattern that can be taken as universally fixed or normative in this period. Rather, the mandates in the New Testament to "pray always" (1 Thess. 5:17), to "sing psalms, hymns, and spiritual songs to God" (Col. 3:17), the Pentecostal descent of the Holy Spirit at the third hour (Acts 2:15), and the apostolic precedents of Peter's vision during prayer at noon (Acts 10:9) and Peter's and John's praying at the Temple at the ninth hour (Acts 3:1) resulted in various patterns within the early Christian communities. *Didache* 8, for example, directs that Christians are to pray the "Our Father" three times each day, without specifying exactly when during the day. Early Eastern sources (e.g., Clement of Alexandria, *Stromata* 7:7; Origen, *Treatise on Prayer* 12.2) appear to know a threefold daily pattern (morning, noon, and evening) with an additional period during the night. Some Western sources (Tertullian, *De oratione* 25) emphasize a twofold pattern of morning and evening as comprising "official" or "statutory" prayers (*legitimae orationes*), while indicating that a fivefold daily pattern was also known (morning, third hour, sixth hour or noon, ninth hour, and evening, together with prayer during the night). In fact, a short time later Cyprian of Carthage (*De oratione dominica* 34) could use the same terminology, *legitimae orationes*, to refer not to morning and evening prayer but, in light of the precedent in Daniel 6:10, to prayer at the third, sixth, and ninth hours. Still other possible Western sources (e.g., *Apostolic Tradition* 41) know an *horarium* consisting similarly of a fivefold pattern: morning, third hour, sixth hour (noon), ninth hour, and evening, with prayer during the night. But it should be noted here that this *horarium* in *Apostolic Tradition* 41 refers to "morning prayer" as both a time for private prayer and a communal assembly for "instruction" (or catechesis), with the added rubric that those unable to attend the public assembly should read the scriptures (a "holy book") privately, and it refers to evening prayer as an assembly for the communal agape, rather than to communal "morning" and "evening" *prayer* properly speaking. Hence, even in the *Apostolic Tra-*

dition the actual pattern for prayer during the day appears to have been primarily threefold: the third, sixth, and ninth hours, interpreted christologically in relation to Christ's passion and death and not to Acts.

Earlier scholarship sought to demonstrate that daily morning and evening prayer were public liturgical gatherings in direct continuity with Jewish synagogue practice, with prayer at the third, sixth, and ninth hours added as merely "private" occasions.[85] More recent scholarship, however, has shown that Jewish patterns of prayer were also quite diverse, and that the most that can probably be said of the relationship between prayer in Judaism and early Christianity is that both Jews and Christians prayed at fixed times.[86] Even at Qumran at least two patterns for daily prayer are discernible, one apparently correlated with the Temple sacrifices (late in the morning and at the ninth hour in the afternoon) and one corresponding to the rising and setting of the sun, both of which appear to have been conflated into the threefold daily pattern known from rabbinic Judaism.[87]

If any pattern is the "original" Christian practice, then, it is probably a similar threefold one, but this appears to have been organized variously within the early communities. In some places the pattern may have been correlated with the natural divisions of the day (morning, noon, and evening) and in others with the divisions of the workday throughout the Roman Empire (at the third, sixth/noon, and ninth hours). What sources like Tertullian, Cyprian, and the *Apostolic Tradition* demonstrate, therefore, is probably an early conflation or synthesis of various daily prayer patterns which would ultimately form the "classic" *horarium* adapted and expanded into the "cathedral" and various "monastic" offices in the fourth century.[88] If the later cathedral office and Egyptian type of monastic office came to focus on morning and evening as times for daily communal prayer, the equally ancient early Christian precedent and alternative of prayer at the third, sixth, and ninth hours remained a characteristic of communal daily prayer preserved within the liturgical synthesis of "urban monasticism." To say, then, that "Lauds as morning prayer and Vespers as evening prayer are the two hinges on which the daily office turns," and so "are to be considered as the chief hours and are to be celebrated as such,"[89] while true enough in relationship to *contemporary* versions of the office, is an assertion for which there appears to be little authoritative support in the first three centuries of the church's history.

Unfortunately, we also know very little about the contents of daily prayer in these first three centuries, though we can assume that psalms, readings from scripture, and hymns were frequently used. It is possible that the early Christian vesperal hymn *Phôs hilaron* ("O joyous light"), a characteristic of the *lucernarium* or "lamplighting" in later "cathedral vespers," the antiquity of which is underscored by Basil of Caesarea, was already being used within a domestic context as a christological thanksgiving to greet the lighting of the lamps in the evening.[90] It is also possible that the later traditional evening psalm of cathedral vespers in the East, Psalm 141, with its reference to the "evening sacrifice" (Ps. 141:2), was already a regular feature of evening prayer at least in Egypt, but this is not certain.[91] And it seems likely that Psalms 147–150 (the "*laudate* psalms") early on became a standard component of morning prayer, ultimately suggesting even the term "lauds" for morning prayer in the West. But explicit evidence for this too is only later. Hence, rather than emphasizing specific contents, from early on theologians saw the principal focus of prayer at these fixed intervals as an expression of eschatological watchfulness and readiness (cf. Col. 4:2 and Eph. 6:18), an expectant and continual "vigil" (cf. Matt. 25:1–13, Mark 14:32–37, and Luke 12:32ff.) for the imminent return of the Lord.[92] Together with this, and ultimately replacing it in overall emphasis, daily prayer, like the eucharist itself, would come to be seen as part of the spiritual "sacrifice of praise" expressing the self-offering of Christians in their lives of service to God.

The Liturgical Year

At the conclusion of his description of the eucharistic liturgy in *First Apology* 67, Justin Martyr wrote, as noted above:

> And we assemble together on Sunday, because it is the first day, on which God trans-formed darkness and matter, and made the world; and Jesus Christ our Savior rose from the dead on that day; for they crucified him the day before Saturday; and the day after Saturday, which is Sunday, he appeared to his apostles and disciples, and taught them these things which we have presented to you also for your consideration.

Sunday, therefore, might well be called the original Christian *feast*; and, together with the Wednesday and Friday fasting days already known from *Didache* 8, the *dies dominica* appears to have constituted the original Christian *week*. Both fasting and kneeling for prayer on Sundays early became forbidden as incompatible with what Sunday celebrated.

Although the precise relationship between the Christian Sunday and the Jewish Sabbath remains a subject of scholarly debate for the New Testament and earliest periods of church history,[93] Justin's description reveals that, by the middle of the second century, Sunday had become (at least in Rome) *the* Christian day for the liturgical assembly. Apart from the appearances of the risen Lord on Easter Sunday night oc-curring most often in the context of evening community meals (cf. Luke 24), New Testament texts referring to Sunday are few and difficult to interpret (i.e., Acts 20:7–12; 1 Cor. 16:2, and Rev. 1:10); however, it is important to note that the New Testa-ment nowhere contradicts Sunday as the preferred day for Christian assembly. Thus, several terms and other designations would become closely attached to it early in the church's history: the "Lord's day," which, according to Willy Rordorf, may have arisen because of the weekly meal, the "Lord's supper," celebrated on this day by the post-resurrection Christian community[94]; the day of "resurrection," the day of "encoun-ter" with the risen Lord through word and meal; the "day of light," as the first day of creation, now associated with the "light" of Christ; the "eighth day," the day of *new* creation beyond the seven-day cycle; and the day of the "epiphany" or manifestation of the church.

The early Christian celebration of Sunday, then, was neither a "little Easter" (to the contrary, Easter would become a "big Sunday"), nor the Christian fulfillment of the Jewish Sabbath, the Christian version of the Sabbath, or the Christian replace-ment for the Sabbath. Rather, if the language of type and fulfillment is to be used at all in this context, then Christ himself (see Matt. 11:26), not Sunday, is the "fulfill-ment" of the Sabbath. Pope John Paul II in his 1998 apostolic exhortation on Sunday, *Dies Domini*, clearly reflects this early Christian understanding:

> Because the third commandment depends upon the remembrance of God's saving works and because Christians saw the definitive time inaugurated by Christ as a new beginning, they made the first day after the Sabbath a festive day, for that was the day on which the Lord rose from the dead. The Paschal Mystery of Christ is the full revelation of the mystery of the world's origin, the climax of the history of salvation and the anticipation of the eschatological fulfillment of the world. What God accomplished in creation and

wrought for his people in the Exodus has found its fullest expression in Christ's death and resurrection, through which its definitive fulfillment will not come until the *Parousia*, when Christ returns in glory. In him, the "spiritual" meaning of the Sabbath is fully realized, as Saint Gregory the Great declares: "For us, the true Sabbath is the person of our Redeemer, our Lord Jesus Christ." . . . In the light of this mystery, the meaning of the Old Testament precept concerning the Lord's Day is recovered, perfected, and fully revealed in the glory which shines on the face of the Risen Christ (cf. 2 Cor. 4:6). We move from the "Sabbath" to the "first day after the Sabbath," from the seventh day to the first day: the *dies Domini* becomes the *dies Christi*![95]

Sunday, then, is not so much the commemoration of a single past event—for instance, the resurrection of Christ—but the icon or symbol of ongoing and present communion with the risen Lord. As Mark Searle wrote:

> Sunday, with its assembly, its preaching, its breaking of bread, is essentially a post-resurrection appearance of the Risen Christ in which he breathes his Spirit upon his disciples for the forgiveness of sins and for the life of the world. As such, it is the point at which all the central images of the Christian life converge and, because the liturgical year is but the spinning out of these images from week to week, the Christian Sunday may properly be claimed as the heart, not only of the liturgical year, but of the Christian life itself.[96]

Christians of the first three centuries also came to celebrate the annual feast of Pascha as the time of Jesus' death and resurrection, but scholarship has long sought to determine if the earliest celebrations of the feast took place on a Sunday or on a fixed calendrical date. Earlier scholarship tended to favor an early and near-universal Sunday observance of Pascha, with other documented observances relegated to the status of idiosyncratic aberrations, but recent studies have argued the opposite. Modern liturgical scholarship is moving increasingly to the position that the most primitive celebration of Pascha (possibly reflected in the New Testament itself) was not in connection with a Sunday but was an all-night vigil held by Christians in Asia Minor (and elsewhere) on the night of 14 Nisan, the day of Passover in the Jewish calendar and the calendrical date of Jesus' death according to the chronology of John's gospel (the equivalent of either March 25 or April 6, according to various versions of the Julian calendar), which culminated in the celebration of the eucharist at cock-crow, the conclusion of the Jewish Passover.[97] Strongly eschatological in orientation as a vigil awaiting the return of the Lord, the overall emphasis of this christianized passover, called the "Quartodeciman (fourteenth, from 14 Nisan) Pascha," was the *death* of Christ, the true paschal lamb, and there is no record of baptisms ever having been part of the celebration. Similarly, together with Exodus 12 as one of the key readings for the vigil, it is also possible, based on the "Poem of the Four Nights" for Passover in the Palestinian Targum on Exodus, that both the creation account (Gen. 1) and the narrative of Abraham's binding of Isaac (Gen. 22:1–18), all three of which appear in the Easter vigil readings within the Jerusalem-based, fifth-century *Armenian Lectionary*, were already employed in continuity with Judaism during the Quartodeciman paschal celebration.[98] On a theological level, our sources for the Quartodeciman Pascha (especially the treatise *On the Pascha* by Melito of Sardis) indicate the common interpretation that the word "Pascha" itself had been derived from the Greek verb *paschein* ("to suffer"). Thus, while Jesus' resurrection was of course a component of the celebration, a parallel might surely be drawn between Paul's statement about the eucharist in 1 Cor. 11:26 ("For as often as you eat this bread and drink the cup, you proclaim the Lord's *death* until he comes"), his reference in 1 Cor. 5:7 ("For Christ our paschal lamb has been sacrificed"), and the commemorative and eschatological nature of this paschal celebration.

The fourth-century historian Eusebius of Caesarea[99] described a late-second-century "paschal controversy" between these Quartodecimans (in the person of bishop Polycrates) and Rome (in the person of bishop Victor, who attempted excommunication) over whether the Pascha was to be celebrated on a calendrical date or at a Saturday-to-Sunday vigil *after* the Jewish Passover, a practice presumably followed by churches elsewhere (Egypt and Jerusalem). But if it is true that in the late second century the controversy was over both the date of Pascha and when one was to begin and end the pre-paschal fast, Thomas Talley has argued that evidence prior to this controversy suggests that before the year 165 (during the pontificate of Soter) Rome itself did not yet celebrate an annual feast of Pascha at all.[100]

Although the precise calculation of the annual Pascha was not completely determined until the Council of Nicaea (325), the Sunday celebration of Pascha, preceded by one, two, or even six days of fasting, would become normative practice by the end of the second century. Along with this, an annual Sunday celebration—with its natural associations of Jesus' resurrection, and the Egyptian theology of Clement and Origen, which, inspired by the exegetical methodology of Philo of Alexandria, interpreted Pascha as *transitus* or "passage"—would suggest eventually that the celebration of Pascha was not only about the passage of *Christ* from death to life but also about Christian participation in this passage through baptism and eucharist. Raniero Cantalamessa interprets this as a shift from seeing Christ as the "protagonist" of the feast to viewing the assembled community as the protagonist.[101] Hence, in some places, as we have seen for North Africa and Rome, the paschal vigil would soon become the preferred occasion for Christian initiation in the West.[102] Also discernible in this period are a nascent but aliturgical "paschal triduum" (primarily fasting from Friday through the end of the vigil), Holy Week (the association of specific days with events in Jesus' last week), Lenten season (at least at Rome and possibly only three weeks in duration[103]), and a fifty-day paschal season called "Pentecost" (from *pentekostê* "fifty"), during which, similar to Sundays themselves, both

Tablet for calculating the date of Easter. The Council of Nicaea (325) decreed that Easter would be observed on the first Sunday following the first full moon of spring (northern hemisphere). To assist with worship planning, tables were produced that determined the proper date. Though from a later period, an example is the marble tablet from Ravenna that provided the dates for Easter for the years 532 to 626. Museo Arcivescovile, Ravenna, Italy/ Scala/Art Resource, NY

fasting and kneeling were forbidden; however, these practices were not yet fully liturgicized according to any particular scheme.[104]

Although scholars tend to agree that the feast of the Epiphany is older than that of Christmas, the origins of both feasts have customarily been interpreted on the basis of the "religionsgeschichtliche ('history of religions') hypothesis" that both were intentional and polemical fourth-century Christian replacements for popular Greco-Roman feasts in the ancient world—Epiphany in the East and Christmas in the West.[105] Recent scholarship on their origins, however, has brought new life to the "computation hypothesis," first advanced by Louis Duchesne as early as 1899[106] and defended further by Hieronymus Engberding in the early 1950s.[107] This hypothesis, simply put, is that the origins of the dates of these feasts, in a manner similar to a Jewish reckoning of the supposed relationship between the death dates and birth dates of the Hebrew patriarchs, depend on an early Christian calculation made by correlating the widely accepted historical date of Christ's death with that of his conception (either March 25 or April 6, the equivalent of 14 Nisan), leading to his "birth" nine months later on either December 25 or January 6, depending on the specific calendars of local churches in the ancient world. As such, the possibility is raised that Christmas itself is actually earlier than either Aurelian's establishment of the pagan feast of *Sol Invictus* (274) or what has been assumed to be a deliberate fourth-century institution by Constantine. This hypothesis has been reinvigorated and defended by Thomas Talley, who sees the origins of Christmas in third-century North Africa rather than in Rome.[108]

The January 6 feast of the Epiphany, long associated in the West with the coming of the Magi (Matt. 2:1–12), celebrates in the East the event of Jesus' baptism in the Jordan by John, a celebration already attested among some communities in Egypt in the late second century by Clement of Alexandria (*Stromata* I, 21, 146, 1–2), who also claimed that January 6 was known in Egypt as the date of Jesus' "birth." Gabriele Winkler[109] not only underscores the overall Eastern origins of this feast and argues for a date within the earliest stratum of Christian history, but also, by means of a detailed analysis of early Syrian and Armenian texts, proposes that the earliest layer of celebration had to do with Jesus' "pneumatic birth" in the Jordan, where, according to these texts, the Holy Spirit comes to "rest" on

Adoration of the Magi before the seated Mother and Child. The third-century stone epitaph of Severa from the catacomb of Priscilla in Rome illustrates the account in Matthew 2:11 as testimony of the deceased woman's faith. The figure at the far right may be Joseph pointing to Mary or it may be the prophet Balaam motioning toward the star (Num. 24:17). Severa herself, nobly dressed, almost certainly is represented in the left corner next to the inscription that reads *in Deo vivas*: "May you live in God." BIBLIOTHECA APOSTOLICA VATICANA, VATICAN MUSEUMS/SCALA/ART RESOURCE, NY

him and the divine voice and fire or shining light reveal the moment of his "birth." As a result of later christological development in the church, together with the eventual acceptance of the December 25 Christmas in the East, the apparent adoptionist overtones of this earlier theology of Jesus' pneumatic "birth" in the Jordan were suppressed, resulting in reinterpretation of Epiphany not as the "birth" of Christ in the Jordan but as a commemoration of his baptism alone.

Although it is probably true that the principal content of both feasts was a unitive celebration of Jesus' beginnings—his birth, his baptism, and even his first miracles—

it has been suggested that these dates were also selected for the beginning of an annual course of reading particular gospels, and that it is these readings that determined the specific contents of these feasts. Consequently, reading Mark 1 on January 6 in Egypt, for example, would naturally bring to expression Jesus' baptism in the Jordan, whereas in Jerusalem, also on January 6, the first chapters of Matthew would suggest a focus on Jesus' nativity and the visit of the Magi, precisely the contents of Epiphany we find in later Jerusalem sources.

The final type of feast to be noted in this period is that of the martyrs, celebrated on the anniversary of their deaths, their *natale* or "heavenly birthday."[110] Intensely local in character, these feasts were tied inseparably to a community's possession of a martyr's tomb, remains, or relics around which the community would assemble. Our best surviving example of this is the famous early account of the martyrdom of Polycarp, which states in part:

> So we later took up his [Polycarp's] bones, more precious than costly stones and more valuable than gold, and laid them away in a suitable place. There the Lord will permit us, so far as possible, to gather together in joy and gladness to celebrate the day of his martyrdom as a birthday, in memory of those athletes who have gone before, and to train and make ready those who are to come hereafter.[111]

Only later, as relics were transferred to other churches, would the martyr cult spread. As those who had given the ultimate witness in the face of persecution, the martyrs became concrete embodiments of Christ's own passion and were regularly believed to have been accorded immediate entrance into heaven. Hence, the veneration of the martyrs as faithful disciples of Christ and prayers asking for their intercession also became characteristic emphases.

Together with this developing cult of the martyrs, there is also some evidence for a growing devotion to the Virgin Mary in this period. The title "Theotokos," possibly first used theologically either by Hippolytus of Rome or by Origen of Alexandria, appears with a direct invocation of Mary in an early (third-century or perhaps earlier) Greek liturgical hymn known as the *Sub tuum praesidium*: "To your protection we flee, holy Mother of God (*Theotokos*); do not despise our prayers in [our] needs, but deliver us from all dangers, glorious and blessed Virgin."[112] Walter Ray has proposed that the August 15 date of the feast of Mary Theotokos in the fifth-century *Armenian Lectionary*, a document which reflects clearly the liturgical tradition of Jerusalem, actually belongs to the earliest, even first-century, stratum of the developing Jerusalem calendar. According to Ray, the date of August 15 may have already had some Marian connotations related to the date of the conception of Isaac within a sectarian Jewish calendar known from the Book of Jubilees and Qumran documents.[113] Certainly the widespread liturgical and other devotion to the saints and Mary in the later patristic period would be an evolution consistent with such early pre-Nicene features.

Assessment

The liturgical theologian Geoffrey Wainwright has written that "rather than present *experience* being allowed to hold sway over the inherited tradition," we should let "the inherited *tradition* shape and govern present experience,"[114] and further that "[a] deeper replunging into its own tradition will . . . be necessary if the church is to survive in recognizable form, particularly in our western culture."[115] No doubt Wainwright meant the word in the broad and complex sense that "Tradition"—with a capital "T"—has acquired in the modern ecumenical movement. As this chapter has demonstrated, it has become extraordinarily difficult in the light of contemporary liturgical scholarship to say clearly from within this formative period of the first three centuries what this "inherited tradition" actually is. That is, the history of Christian worship in these centuries is not the history of a *single* tradition of worship that undergirds the diversity of liturgical practices stemming from some pristine, unitive, or "apostolic" core; rather, it is itself the history of a plurality of liturgical practices from the very beginning. There is no one clearly deduced "apostolic tradition" of Christian worship, but, as we have seen, a variety of traditions. As a consequence, it becomes next to impossible to begin sorting out from this variety what should be considered as constituting—authoritatively or normatively—the "inherited tradition" of worship into which the church today is to "replunge" itself. Indeed, there are no clear historical grounds for asserting that the pattern of Christian initiation in *Apostolic Tradition* 21, for example, is somehow *the* authentic pattern according to which rites of Christian initiation today should be constructed and celebrated as the norm for initiatory practice, especially when it looks as though the text itself is a composite document reflecting a conflation of different patterns from different periods and churches, and when other extant practices and patterns elsewhere are also discernible. There are equally no historical grounds for asserting that the eucharistic prayer in *Apostolic Tradition* 4, or even its so-called model anaphoral pattern, should be *the* model for constructing eucharistic prayers today, especially when other early examples of anaphoral prayers with other structures and contents, even without the time-honored Western inclusion of "institution narratives," are available. Similarly, authoritative assertions about the historical priority of morning and evening prayer in the cycle of daily prayer, the theological priority of Romans 6 for baptismal theology, and the concomitant correlation between Easter and Christian initiation are all difficult to maintain today in light of the available historical evidence. What we see instead in these centuries is not a single tradition of Christian worship ready-made or fully formed in a tightly constructed package to be handed on unchanged to subsequent generations of the church. Rather, what is encountered here are what we might call the various building blocks of that "tradition" in development. And it is from these building blocks that the Church in subsequent generations throughout history, both through evolution in continuity with these centuries and by means of occasional revolution or reform in discontinuity, will pick and choose as it seeks to understand and express its ecclesial identity liturgically within changed historical, social, and cultural contexts in order to continue being faithful to the gospel.

Such a view of the "apostolic tradition" of Christian worship in the first three centuries, however, does not mean that all is relative, nor that there is nothing authoritative or normative that emerged for the church's subsequent tradition(s) of worship from these centuries of development. *Au contraire!* Although there are some difficulties in the recent attempt of Gordon Lathrop to abstract an authoritative, transcultural, timeless, and ecumenical liturgical *ordo* from Justin Martyr's brief description of liturgical practice in his *First Apology* 61 and 67, the mere fact that Justin's (and, for that matter, Tertullian's) overall *pattern* or skeleton for Christian worship obviously survives as easily discernible throughout the distinct rites of the first Christian millennium and beyond does grant a certain legitimacy to Lathrop's attempt. That is, even if we do not know from the earliest period what exactly constituted Christian liturgy in precise detail, the fact remains that all of our liturgical evidence from at least Justin

Martyr on through the sixteenth-century Reformation clearly indicates the continued existence of some kind of "baptismal" rite of initiation in water and the Holy Spirit, the continued assembling of the churches on Sundays and other feasts on a liturgical calendar to hear the word and share in some form of eucharistic meal with its great eucharistia as the "memorial" of Christ and central act of its worship of God, the existence of patterns for daily prayer (whether private or communal), some form of "order," and some form of ministry outside of the community. All of this points indeed to some kind of universal pattern or *ordo* of worship that the diverse churches of Christian antiquity *did* see as providing a universal norm which determined its understanding of what constituted Christian worship and which did appear to transcend local diversity and variety. The diversity we encounter in the churches of the first few centuries, then, is precisely a diversity in *how* things were done: how baptism and its various supplemental rites were celebrated; how Sunday and festival observance were structured (e.g., whether Pascha occurred on a calendrical date or a Sunday); how the meal, together with its proclamation of the word, was celebrated and its gifts gathered and distributed; how the meal prayers were to be prayed and what their various structural components were to be; how catechumens were prepared for initiation; and how the various ministries of oversight and service might be ordered. But no one, to my knowledge, actually questioned the very existence, structure, and contents of Christian worship as having to do precisely with these liturgical acts. These, it seems, are givens and are constitutive parts of the "inherited tradition," which may indeed serve to "shape and govern present experience." To that end, Lathrop's model of a liturgical *ordo* remains not only, in the words of James F. White, one of "the finest available description[s] of classical Christian worship,"[116] but commends itself even today as a fruitful model in the contemporary search for some kind of ecumenical-liturgical "norm."

Even more than this, though, can be said about what may be considered authoritative or normative for Christian worship from this "apostolic tradition" of the first three centuries. Significant elements that may serve to make authoritative challenges to contemporary Christianity include at least the following: the emerging trinitarian faith, the *regula fidei*, that is reflected already in the developing creedal questions and answers associated with Christian initiation in Justin, Tertullian, Cyprian, and the *Apostolic Tradition*; the development of a clear (and nowhere contradicted) theology of the real presence of Christ (his body ["flesh"] and blood) in the eucharistic bread and cup, expressed as early as Ignatius of Antioch; the developing theology of the eucharist itself (also nowhere contradicted) as the church's "sacrifice," expressed as early as *Didache* 14:1; and the fact that, by the third century at the latest, the baptism of infants and small children (and by implication their communion) was apparently widespread in both East and West. Might something similar be said for the emerging theology of the communion of saints expressed in the developing devotion to the martyrs and the Virgin Mary in this same period? Indeed, the "deeper plunging" of the church today into its "inherited tradition," as this tradition developed in the first three centuries, would seem to imply not only the liturgical tradition but precisely the theological and doctrinal positions that the liturgical tradition both constitutes and expresses. That is, continuity with the so-called "apostolic tradition" is not only about a broad continuity in liturgical practice but, perhaps even more, about a continuity in *faith*.

Finally, these centuries might also provide a worthy model of ecumenism that the churches today would do well to emulate. That is, what Kretschmar called an apostolic "plurality of possibilities," specifically in regard to early rites of Christian initiation, may suggest some kind of "apostolic" norm for a plurality of possibilities for liturgical and other issues within the context of unity and communion for the contemporary Church. If such reconciled diversity may be inferred from the maintenance of communion and unity between North Africa and Rome during the third-century "re-baptism" controversy of Cyprian and Stephen, another earlier and potentially church-dividing controversy provides an even stronger model. Within the context of narrating the accounts of the late second century "Quartodeciman Controversy," during which bishop Victor of Rome threatened to break off communion with the churches of the East, Eusebius related the following earlier event from the time of Polycarp of Smyrna and Anicetus of Rome, written by Irenaeus of Lyons:

> [W]hen the blessed Polycarp arrived in Rome in the time of Anicetus, while they had minor differences about certain other matters, they made peace immediately, not wishing to quarrel over this matter [of the date]. For neither was Anicetus able to persuade Polycarp not to observe, since he had always done so with John the disciple of our Lord and with the rest of the apostles, with whom he had lived; nor did Polycarp persuade Anicetus to observe, for he said it was incumbent upon him to maintain the practice of the presbyters before him. And still they remained in communion with each other, *and in the church Anicetus ceded the Eucharist to Polycarp*, obviously out of respect, and they parted from one another in peace, while the whole Church, both observants and non-observants, were at peace. (*Ecclesiastical History* 5.14)[117]

Anicetus ceding "the Eucharist to Polycarp," that is, permitting Polycarp to preside at the Roman eucharistic liturgy in his place, speaks volumes about Christian unity and communion within a diversity of practice and theology. Indeed, if the "apostolic tradition" of these first three centuries has anything normative to say to the churches today, its greatest contribution may well be that Christian unity does not mean uniformity and that the bonds of communion can be maintained—or repaired—in spite of great diversity. If, according to Eusebius, Irenaeus's own words in this context earned him the title of "peacemaker," which his name signified already, perhaps the model of Anicetus ceding the Eucharist to Polycarp still suggests itself as a worthy ecumenical model, and perhaps it can still function to bring peace and unity to a Christianity divided over other questions even in our own day.[118]

Bibliography

Adam, Adolf. *The Liturgical Year: Its History and Its Meaning after the Reform of the Liturgy.* Collegeville, Minn.: Liturgical Press, 1981.

Aune, David. "Worship, Early Christian." In *The Anchor Bible Dictionary*, vol. 6, 973–989. New York: Doubleday, 1992.

Bradshaw, Paul. *Early Christian Worship: A Basic Introduction to Ideas and Practice.* London: SPCK, 1996.

Bradshaw, Paul. *The Search for the Origins of Christian Worship.* 2nd ed. New York and Oxford: Oxford University Press, 2002.

Bradshaw, Paul, and Lawrence Hoffman, eds. *The Making of Jewish and Christian Worship.* Two Liturgical Traditions, 1. Notre Dame, Ind.: University of Notre Dame Press, 1991.

Bradshaw, Paul, and Lawrence Hoffman, eds. *Passover and Easter.* Two Liturgical Traditions, 5 and 6. Notre Dame, Ind.: University of Notre Dame Press, 1999.

Bradshaw, Paul, Maxwell E. Johnson, and L. Edward Phillips. *Apostolic Tradition: A Commentary*. Hermeneia Commentary Series. Minneapolis: Fortress Press, 2002.

Brown, Peter. *The Cult of the Saints: Its Rise and Function in Latin Christianity*. Chicago: University of Chicago Press, 1981.

Gerlach, Karl. *The Antenicene Pascha: A Rhetorical History*. Liturgia Condenda 7. Louvain: Peeters, 1998.

Giraudo, Cesare. *La struttura letteraria della preghiera eucharistica*. Rome: Biblical Institute Press, 1981.

Jasper, R. C. D., and G. J. Cuming. *Prayers of the Eucharist: Early and Reformed*. 3rd ed. Collegeville, Minn.: Liturgical Press, 1987.

Johnson, Maxwell E. *The Rites of Christian Initiation: Their Evolution and Interpretation*. Collegeville, Minn.: Liturgical Press, 1999.

Johnson, Maxwell E., ed. *Between Memory and Hope: Readings on the Liturgical Year*. Collegeville, Minn.: Liturgical Press, 2000.

Johnson, Maxwell E., ed. *Living Water, Sealing Spirit: Readings on Christian Initiation*. Collegeville, Minn.: Liturgical Press, 1995.

Mazza, Enrico. *The Origins of the Eucharistic Prayer*. Translated by Ronald E. Lane. Collegeville, Minn.: Liturgical Press, 1995.

Roll, Susan K. *Toward the Origins of Christmas*. Liturgia Condenda 5. Kampen: Kok Pharos, 1995.

Taft, Robert. *Beyond East and West: Problems in Liturgical Understanding*. Rome: Edizioni Orientalia Christiana, 1997.

Taft, Robert. *The Liturgy of the Hours in East and West: The Origins of the Divine Office and Its Meaning for Today*. 2nd ed. Collegeville, Minn.: Liturgical Press, 1993.

Talley, Thomas. *The Origins of the Liturgical Year*. 2nd rev. ed. Collegeville, Minn.: Liturgical Press, 1986.

Whitaker, E. C. *Documents of the Baptismal Liturgy*. 2nd rev. ed. London: SPCK, 1970.

Winkler, Gabriele. *Das armenische Initiationsrituale: Entwicklungsgeschichtliche und liturgievergleichende Untersuchung der Quellen des 3. bis 10. Jahrhunderts*. Orientalia Christiana Analecta 217. Rome: Pontificale Institutum Studiorum Orientalium, 1982.

Notes

[1] Georg Kretschmar, "Recent Research on Christian Initiation," in Johnson, *Living Water, Sealing Spirit*, 33.

[2] See Paul F. Bradshaw, "Redating the Apostolic Tradition: Some Preliminary Steps," in *Rule of Prayer, Rule of Faith: Essays in Honor of Aidan Kavanagh, OSB*, ed. John Baldovin and Nathan Mitchell (Collegeville, Minn.: Liturgical Press, 1996) 3–17; and his "Hippolytus Revisited: The Identity of the So-called 'Apostolic Tradition,'" *Liturgy* 16 (2000) 8–12. See also Bradshaw, Johnson, and Phillips, *Apostolic Tradition*.

[3] The attempt of Allen Brent, in *Hippolytus and the Roman Church in the Third Century* (Leiden: Brill, 1995), to identify this document as the liturgical *ordo*

or product of a distinct ethnic and/or dissident Christian community in early Rome is unconvincing. Although he shows some awareness of the more recent scholarly debates on the *Apostolic Tradition*, Brent still assumes that the document was already in its final form in the early third century. The developing scholarly consensus does not exclude, however, that certain portions of the document may go back to the early third century or even earlier.

[4] The best guide to the development of the varieties of Christian worship in the first three centuries is Bradshaw, *The Search for the Origins of Christian Worship*. See also Bradshaw, *Early Christian Wor-*

ship; John Baldovin, "Christian Worship to the Eve of the Reformation," in Bradshaw and Hoffman, *The Making of Jewish and Christian Worship*, 156–183; Kenneth Stevenson, *The First Rites: Worship in the Early Church* (Collegeville, Minn.: Liturgical Press, 1989); and the classic, if now surpassed, studies by Gregory Dix, *The Shape of the Liturgy* (London: Dacre, 1945), and Josef Jungmann, *The Early Liturgy to the Time of Gregory the Great*, trans. Francis A. Brunner (Notre Dame, Ind.: University of Notre Dame Press, 1959).

[5]Cf. Ferdinand Hahn, *Worship in the Early Church* (Philadelphia: Fortress, 1973); Aune, "Worship, Early Christian"; and Larry W. Hurtado, *At the Origins of Christian Worship: The Context and Character of Earliest Christian Devotion* (Grand Rapids, Mich.: Eerdmans, 1999).

[6]See John Fenwick, *The Anaphoras of St. Basil and St. James. An Investigation into Their Common Origins*, Orientalia Christiana Analecta 240 (Rome: Pontificium Institutum Orientale, 1992); and his *Fourth Century Anaphoral Construction Techniques*, Grove Liturgical Study 45 (Bramcote, Notts.: Grove, 1986).

[7]See Tertullian, *De penitentia*; and James Dallen, *The Reconciling Community* (Collegeville, Minn. and New York: Pueblo, 1986).

[8]Baldovin, "Christian Worship to the Eve of the Reformation," 157.

[9]See Paul F. Bradshaw, *Liturgical Presidency in the Early Church*, Grove Liturgical Study 36 (Bramcote, Notts.: Grove, 1983); and his *Ordination Rites of the Ancient Churches of East and West* (Collegeville, Minn.: Liturgical Press, 1990). See also John Baldovin, "The Development of the Monarchical Bishop to 250 A.D.," in his *Worship: City, Church, and Renewal* (Washington, D.C.: Pastoral Press, 1991) 151–170.

[10]See Richard Rutherford, *The Death of a Christian: The Order of Christian Funerals*, rev. ed. (Collegeville, Minn.: Liturgical Press, 1990).

[11]See Adela Collins, "The Origin of Christian Baptism," in Johnson, *Living Water*, 46–47.

[12]Collins, "Origin," 35–47; see also Gordon Lathrop, "Baptism in the New Testament and Its Cultural Settings," in *Worship and Culture in Dialogue*, ed. S. Anita Stauffer (Geneva: Lutheran World Federation, 1994) 23–31.

[13]See L. Hartman, *"Into the Name of the Lord Jesus": Baptism in the Early Church*, Studies of the New Testament and Its World (Edinburgh: T & T Clark, 1997).

[14]See S. Anita Stauffer, "Cultural Settings of Architecture for Baptism in the Early Church," in *Worship and Culture in Dialogue*, 57–66.

[15]See the classic debate on infant baptism between Kurt Aland, *Did the Early Church Baptize Infants?* (London: SCM, 1963) and Joachim Jeremias, *The Origins of Infant Baptism* (London: SCM, 1963).

[16]See the summary of scholarly approaches in Kilian McDonnell and G. T. Montague, *Christian Initiation and Baptism in the Holy Spirit: Evidence from the First Eight Centuries* (Collegeville, Minn.: Liturgical Press, 1991) 31–39.

[17]Martin F. Connell, "*Nisi Pedes*, Except for the Feet: Footwashing in the Community of John's Gospel," *Worship* 70 (1996) 20–30.

[18]The best critical edition of the Greek text of the *Didache* is W. Rordorf and A. Truillier, eds., *La doctrine des douze apôtres*, Sources Chrétiennes 248 (Paris: Éditions du Cerf, 1978). This English translation is from the edition and commentary by Kurt Niederwimmer, *The Didache*, Hermeneia—A Critical and Historical Commentary on the Bible (Minneapolis: Fortress, 1998) 125.

[19]Text adapted from Lucien Deiss, *Springtime of the Liturgy: Liturgical Texts of the First Four Centuries* (Collegeville, Minn.: Liturgical Press, 1979), p. 92.

[20]Winkler, *Das armenische Initiationsrituale*; and her "The Original Meaning of the Prebaptismal Anointing and Its Implications," in Johnson, *Living Water*, 58–81.

[21]See Merja Merras, *The Origins of the Celebration of the Christian Feast of Epiphany: An Ideological, Cultural and Historical Study* (Joensuu, Finland: Joensuu University Press, 1995) 164ff.

[22]Cf. Maxwell E. Johnson, "From Three Weeks to Forty Days: Baptismal Preparation and the Origins of Lent," in his *Living Water*, 118–136.

[23]See Georg Kretschmar, "Beiträge zur Geschichte der Liturgie, insbesondere der Taufliturgie in Ägypten," *Jahrbuch für Liturgik und Hymnologie* 8 (1963) 1–54; Paul Bradshaw, "Baptismal Practice in the Alexandrian Tradition, Eastern or Western?" in *Essays in Early Eastern Initiation*, ed. Paul Bradshaw, Alcuin/GROW Liturgical Study 8 (Bramcote, Notts.: Grove, 1988) 5–17; and Maxwell E. Johnson, *Liturgy in Early Christian Egypt*, Alcuin/GROW Liturgical Study 33 (Bramcote, Notts.: Grove, 1995) chap. 1.

[24]See especially Kilian McDonnell, *The Baptism of Jesus in the Jordan: The Trinitarian and Cosmic Order of Salvation* (Collegeville, Minn.: Liturgical Press, 1996) 43–44; and Johnson, *Liturgy in Early Christian Egypt*, chap. 1.

[25]See Talley, *The Origins of the Liturgical Year*, 194–213. For a critique of Talley's hypothesis on the relationship between the Lenten traditions of Alexandria and Constantinople, see Gabriel Bertonière, *The*

Sundays of Lent in the Triodion: The Sundays without a Commemoration, Orientalia Christiana Analecta 253 (Rome: Pontificio Istituto Orientale, 1997) 29–42.

[26]For texts see Whitaker, *Documents of the Baptismal Liturgy*, 7–10.

[27]For texts see Whitaker, *Documents*, 10–12.

[28]A convenient text of the initiation rites, based primarily on the fifth-century Verona Latin manuscript, is provided in Geoffrey Cuming, *Hippolytus: A Text for Students*, Grove Liturgical Study 8 (Bramcote, Notts.: Grove, 1976) 15–22. The following discussion of Christian initiation in *Apostolic Tradition* is based on Bradshaw, Johnson and Phillips, *Apostolic Tradition*, 82–135.

[29]See J. M. Hanssens, *La Liturgie d'Hippolyte*, Orientalia Christiana Analecta 155 (Rome: Pontificale Institutum Orientalium Studiorum, 1959) 448–451.

[30]See especially W. Kinzig, "'. . . natum et passum etc.' Zur Geschichte der Tauffragen in der lateinischen Kirche bis zu Luther," in W. Kinzig, C. Markschies, and M. Vinzent, *Tauffragen und Bekenntnis: Studien zur sogenannten "Traditio Apostolica," zu den "Interrogationes de fide" und zum "Römischen Glaubensbekenntnis"* (Berlin and New York: de Gruyter, 1999) 128–132. It is important to note here as well that the baptismal use of the full text of the Apostles' Creed in question-and-answer form is not a characteristic of the Roman liturgical tradition and, in fact, did not become incorporated in this manner until the liturgical rites published in 1969 and 1972.

[31]See Bradshaw, "Redating the Apostolic Tradition: Some Preliminary Steps," 3–17; and Maxwell E. Johnson, "The Postchrismational Structure of *Apostolic Tradition* 21, the Witness of Ambrose of Milan, and a Tentative Hypothesis Regarding the Current Reform of Confirmation in the Roman Rite," *Worship* 70 (1996)16–34.

[32]Text from Cuming, *Hippolytus*, 20 (emphasis added).

[33]Aidan Kavanagh, "Confirmation: A Suggestion from Structure," in Johnson, *Living Water*, 148–158. See also Aidan Kavanagh, *Confirmation: Origins and Reform* (Collegeville, Minn.: Liturgical Press, 1988).

[34]Paul Turner, "The Origins of Confirmation: An Analysis of Aidan Kavanagh's Hypothesis," in Johnson, *Living Water*, 255.

[35]Tertullian, *De baptismo* 19; English translation adapted from Whitaker, *Documents*, 9 (emphasis added).

[36]On the development of the "ideal" of Easter baptism in the history of the church, see Paul Bradshaw, "'Diem baptismo solemniorem:' Initiation and Easter in Christian Antiquity," in Johnson, *Living Water*, 137–147.

[37]I owe this reference to Qumran practice to Professor James Vanderkam.

[38]See Tertullian, *De baptismo* 15. For a recent study of the rebaptism controversy in the time of Cyprian, see J. P. Burns, "On Rebaptism: Social Organization in the Third Century Church," *Journal of Early Christian Studies* 1 (1993) 367–403.

[39]See Cyprian, *Letter 69, to Magnus*, 3, 7, and 11; *Letter 73, to Jubaianus*, 2 and 21.

[40]Geoffrey Willis, *Saint Augustine and the Donatist Controversy* (London: SPCK, 1950) 147–148.

[41]See Augustine, *De baptismo contra Donatistas*, 1.18.27.

[42]Cf. Hans Lietzmann, "Vom urchristlichen Abendmahl," *Theologische Rundschau* 9 (1937) 168–227, 273–312; 10 (1938) 81–99; and his "Das Abendmahl in der Urgemeinde," *Journal of Biblical Literature* 56 (1937) 217–252. Lietzmann distinguishes between the joyful, eschatological fellowship meal of early Jewish-Christian communties (Acts 2:42) and the "Pauline" (1 Cor. 11:23–26) type of eucharist connected to the memorial of the death of Christ.

[43]Dix, *The Shape of the Liturgy*.

[44]Text from Jasper and Cuming, *Prayers of the Eucharist*, 10–11.

[45]Cf. Louis Ligier, "The Origins of the Eucharistic Prayer: From the Last Supper to the Eucharist," *Studia Liturgica* 9 (1973) 161–185; Louis Bouyer, *Eucharist* (Notre Dame: University of Notre Dame Press, 1968); and Herman Wegman, "Généalogie hypothétique de la prière eucharistique, "*Questions Liturgiques* 61 (1980) 263–278. See also Thomas Talley, "From Berakah to Eucharistia: A Reopening Question," *Worship* 50 (1976) 115–137; and Talley, "The Literary Structure of the Eucharistic Prayer," *Worship* 58 (1984) 404–419, who, while certainly following in the overall lines of this evolutionary schema, is much more carefully nuanced in his treatment of the sources. A notable exception to this approach is the study of Allan Bouley, *From Freedom to Formula: The Evolution of the Eucharistic Prayer from Oral Improvisation to Written Texts* (Washington, D.C.: Catholic University of America Press, 1981). In this significant work, Bouley underscores the oral and spontaneous nature of early Christian eucharistic praying.

[46]See Andrew McGowan, "Is There a Liturgical Text in This Gospel? The Institution Narratives and Their Early Interpretative Communities," *Journal of Biblical Literature* 118 (1999) 73–87.

⁴⁷For these various meal practices, see Jan Michael Joncas, "Tasting the Kingdom of God: The Meal Ministry of Jesus and Its Implications for Contemporary Worship and Life," *Worship* 74 (2000) 329–365. See also Aune, 983–986; Lawrence Hoffman, "The Passover Meal in Jewish Tradition," in Bradshaw and Hoffman, *Passover and Easter*, 9–11; and in the same volume, Blake Leyerle, "Meal Customs in the Greco-Roman World," 29–61.

⁴⁸See Joseph Tabory, "Towards a History of the Paschal Meal," in Bradshaw and Hoffman, *Passover and Easter*, 62–80.

⁴⁹For references to the diversity of structure in Jewish meal practices see Bradshaw, *Search*, chap. 3.

⁵⁰See Bryan D. Spinks, "Beware the Liturgical Horses! An English Interjection on Anaphoral Evolution," *Worship* 59 (1985) 211–219.

⁵¹See Andrew B. McGowan, "First Regarding the Cup . . . : Papias and the Diversity of Early Eucharistic Practice," *Journal of Theological Studies* 46 (1995) 551–555.

⁵²See Andrew McGowan, "Naming the Feast: *Agape* and the Diversity of Early Christian Meals," *Studia Patristica* 30 (1997) 314–318.

⁵³Such was the original suggestion of Adolf von Harnack, "Brot und Wasser: Die eucharistischen Elemente bei Justin," in *Über das gnostische Buch Pistis-Sophia: Brot und Wasser; die eucharistischen Elemente bei Justin. Zwei Untersuchungen*, Texte und Untersuchungen 7 (Leipzig: J. C. Hinrichs, 1891) 115–144.

⁵⁴Such is the compelling hypothesis of Bryan Spinks. See his "Mis-shapen: Gregory Dix and the Four-Action Shape of the Liturgy," *Lutheran Quarterly* 4 (1990) 161–177.

⁵⁵Cf. Lawrence Hoffman, *The Canonization of the Synagogue Service* (Notre Dame, Ind.: University of Notre Dame Press, 1979); and Thomas Talley, "Word and Sacrament in the Primitive Eucharist," in *Eulogema: Studies in Honor of Robert Taft, S. J.*, ed. Ephrem Carr, Stefano Parenti, Abraham-Andreas Thiermeyer, and Elena Velkovska, Studia Anselmiana 110 / Analecta Liturgica 17 (Rome: Centro Studi San Anselmo, 1993) 497–510.

⁵⁶See Bradshaw, *Search*, 139.

⁵⁷See Joncas, 363.

⁵⁸Text from Jasper and Cuming, *Prayers*, 29–30.

⁵⁹*Apologeticum* 39, 2–6. On Tertullian and the eucharist in general, see Victor Saxer, "Tertullian," in Willy Rordorf et al., *The Eucharist of the Early Christians* (New York and Collegeville, Minn.: Pueblo, 1978) 132–155.

⁶⁰On the kiss of peace in early Christianity see L. Edward Phillips, *The Ritual Kiss in Early Christian Worship*, Alcuin/GROW Liturgical Study 36 (Cambridge: Grove, 1996).

⁶¹Gordon Lathrop, *What Are the Essentials of Christian Worship?* (Minneapolis: Augsburg Fortress, 1994) 22. See also his *Holy Things: A Liturgical Theology* (Minneapolis: Fortress, 1993).

⁶²Lathrop, *What Are the Essentials*, 23.

⁶³John Baldovin, "The Church in Christ, Christ in the Church," in *The Many Presences of Christ*, ed. T. Fitzgerald and D. Lysik (Chicago: Liturgy Training Publications, 1999) 13–31.

⁶⁴Among proponents of the tripartite structure of the eucharistic prayer Enrico Mazza is dominant; see his *The Origins of the Eucharistic Prayer*.

⁶⁵See Bryan D. Spinks, *Addai and Mari—The Anaphora of the Apostles: A Text for Students*, Grove Liturgical Study 24 (Bramcote, Notts.: Grove, 1980). The leading scholar today arguing for an overall bipartite pattern for early eucharistic praying in continuity with Judaism is Cesare Giraudo, *La struttura letteraria della preghiera eucharistica*.

⁶⁶Text from Jasper and Cuming, *Prayers*, 53–54.

⁶⁷With the notable exception of Bryan Spinks ("A Complete Anaphora? A Note on Strasbourg Gr. 254," *Heythrop Journal* 25 [1984] 51–55), who has urged caution in accepting uncritically the *Strasbourg Papyrus* as a complete anaphora on account of, especially, its fragmentary state, most contemporary liturgical scholars view it as both early and complete. See Geoffrey Cuming, "The Anaphora of St. Mark: A Study in Development," *Muséon* 95 (1982) 115–29, reprinted in Bradshaw, *Essays on Early Eastern Eucharistic Prayers*, 57–72; Cuming, *The Liturgy of St. Mark*, Orientalia Christiana Analecta 234 (Rome: Pontificale Institutum Studiorum Orientalium, 1990); Enrico Mazza, "Una anafora incompleta? Il Papiro Strasbourg Gr. 254," *Ephemerides Liturgicae* 99 (1985) 425–436; Walter Ray, "The Strasbourg Papyrus," in *Essays on Early Eastern Eucharistic Prayers*, 39–56; and Herman Wegman, "Une anaphore incomplète?" in R. van den Broek and M. J. Vermaseren, eds., *Studies in Gnosticism and Hellenistic Religions* (Leiden: Brill, 1981) 435–450. To this list of those who accept the *Strasbourg Papyrus* as a complete anaphora should now be added Jürgen Hammerstaedt, *Griechische Anaphorenfragmente aus Ägypten und Nubien*, Papyrologica Coloniensia 28 (Opladen and Wiesbaden: Westdeutscher Verlag, 1999) 22–41.

⁶⁸Geoffrey Cuming, "The Shape of the Anaphora," *Studia Patristica* 20 (1989) 341.

[69]Fenwick, *The Anaphoras of St Basil and St James*. But see the critical review of Fenwick's work by Gabriele Winkler in *Oriens Christianus* 78 (1994) 269–277.

[70]See especially Geoffrey Cuming, "Four Very Early Anaphoras," *Worship* 58 (1984) 168–172.

[71]Text adapted from Jasper and Cuming, *Prayers*, 34–35. For a more complete discussion of this eucharistic prayer, see Bradshaw, Johnson, and Phillips, *Apostolic Tradition*, 37–48.

[72]See Aune, 984; Edward Kilmartin, "*Sacrificium Laudis*: Content and Function of Early Eucharistic Prayers," *Theological Studies* 35 (1974) 268–287; and Emmanuel J. Cutrone, "The Liturgical Setting of the Institution Narrative in the Early Syrian Tradition," in *Time and Community*, ed. J. Neil Alexander (Washington, D.C.: Pastoral Press, 1990) 105–114.

[73]See Robert Taft, "The Interpolation of the Sanctus into the Anaphora: When and Where? A Review of the Dossier," Part I, *Orientalia Christiana Periodica* 57 (1991) 281–308, and Part II, 58 (1992) 531–552; Gabriele Winkler, "Nochmals zu den Anfängen der Epiklese und des Sanctus im Eucharistischen Hochgebet," *Theologisches Quartalschrift* 74 (1994) 214–231; and Winkler, "Weitere Beobachtungen zur frühen Epiklese (den Doxologien und dem Sanctus): Über die Bedeutung der Apokryphen für die Erforschung der Entwicklung der Riten," *Oriens Christianus* 80 (1996) 177–200.

[74]Sebastian Brock, "The Epiklesis in the Antiochene Baptismal *Ordines*," in *Symposium Syriacum 1972*, Orientalia Christiana Analecta 197 (Rome: Pontificale Institutum Orientalium Studiorum, 1974) 183–218.

[75]See Winkler, "Nochmals zu den Anfängen der Epiklese" and "Weitere Beobachtungen." See also Maxwell E. Johnson, "The Origins of the Anaphoral Use of the Sanctus and Epiclesis Revisited: The Contribution of Gabriele Winkler and Its Implications," in *Crossroad of Cultures: Studies in Liturgy and Patristics in Honor of Gabriele Winkler*, ed. Hans-Jürgen Feulner et al., Orientalia Christiana Analecta 260 (Rome: Pontificio Istituto Orientale, 2000) 405–442.

[76]On this see the study of Enrico Mazza, *Mystagogy: A Theology of Liturgy in the Patristic Age* (Collegeville, Minn.: Liturgical Press, 1989).

[77]Jasper and Cuming, *Prayers*, 53–54.

[78]Robert Daly, *The Origins of the Christian Doctrine of Sacrifice* (Philadelphia: Fortress, 1978); and Lathrop, *Holy Things*, 139–158.

[79]I owe this insight to the essay, "Metaphor and Sacrifice: A Survey and Critique," by the Notre Dame New Testament doctoral student Leslie Baynes.

[80]Robert Taft, "Understanding the Byzantine Anaphoral Oblation," in Mitchell and Baldovin, *Rule of Prayer*, 45.

[81]Kenneth Stevenson, *Eucharist and Offering* (Collegeville, Minn.: Liturgical Press, 1986) 3–4.

[82]Robert Taft, "The Frequency of the Eucharist throughout History," in his *Beyond East and West*, 87–110.

[83]See Anton Baumstark, *Comparative Liturgy* (London: A. R. Mowbray, 1958) 112.

[84]Eusebius, *Commentary on Ps. 64*, PG 23, 630; English translation from Taft, *Liturgy of the Hours*, 33.

[85]C. W. Dugmore, *The Influence of the Synagogue upon the Divine Office* (London: Oxford University Press, 1944).

[86]Taft, *Liturgy of the Hours*, 3–11.

[87]See L. Edward Phillips, "The Early Christian Prayer Offices: Origin and Development," *Liturgy* 16 (2000) 44–47.

[88]Bradshaw, *Early Christian Worship*, 70.

[89]*Constitution on the Sacred Liturgy*, 89.

[90]See Taft, *Liturgy of the Hours*, 36–38.

[91]See Johnson, *Liturgy in Early Christian Egypt*, 40–42.

[92]Taft, *Liturgy of the Hours*, 15ff.

[93]See Samuel Bacchiocchi, *From Sabbath to Sunday: A Historical Investigation of the Rise of Sunday Observance in Early Christianity* (Rome: Pontifical Gregorian University Press, 1977).

[94]Willy Rordorf, *Sunday* (Philadelphia: Westminster, 1968).

[95]John Paul II, *Dies Domini: On Keeping the Lord's Day Holy*, para. 18 (Boston: Pauline Books & Media, 1998) 25–26.

[96]Mark Searle, "Sunday: The Heart of the Liturgical Year," in Johnson, *Between Memory and Hope*, 76.

[97]Talley, *Origins*, 1–32. See also Paul Bradshaw, "The Origins of Easter," in Johnson, *Between Memory and Hope*, 111–124; and the detailed study of Gerlach, *The Antenicene Pascha*.

[98]See Talley, *Origins*, 3, 47–50.

[99]For Eusebian texts related to this controversy see the convenient collection in Raniero Cantalamessa, *Easter in the Early Church*, trans. and ed. James M. Quigley and Joseph T. Lienhard (Collegeville, Minn.: Liturgical Press, 1993) 33–37.

[100]See Talley, *Origins*, 13–27.

[101]See Cantalamessa, *Easter*, 8ff.

[102]See Bradshaw, "'*Diem baptismo sollemniorem*,'" 137–147.

[103]But see the description of the forty-day catechumenal period in Egypt under the section on Christian initiation earlier in this chapter. Recent scholarship, in fact, has argued that the forty days of a pre-paschal "Lent," known only after the Council of Nicaea, may well have their origins in this pre-Nicene, post-Epiphany fasting period. See also Johnson, "From Three Weeks to Forty Days," 118–136.

[104]Talley, *Origins*, 33–37.

[105]Cf. Adam, *Liturgical Year*, 121ff.

[106]See Louis Duchesne, *Origines du culte chrétien*, 5th ed. (Paris: Fontemoing, 1920).

[107]Hieronymus Engberding, "Der 25. Dezember als Tag der Feier der Geburt des Herrn," *Archiv für Liturgiewissenschaft* 2 (1952) 25–43.

[108]Talley, *Origins*, 79–162. But see also Roll, *Toward the Origins of Christmas*; and Hans Förster, *Die Feier der Geburt Christi in der Alten Kirche—Beiträge zur Erforschung der Anfänge des Epiphanie- und Weihnachtsfests* (Tübingen: Mohr-Siebeck, 2000).

[109]Gabriele Winkler, "Die Licht-Erscheinung bei der Taufe Jesu und der Ursprung des Epiphanie-festes," *Oriens Christianus* 78 (1994) 177–229. This essay appears in the English translation of David Maxwell in Johnson, *Between Memory and Hope*, 291–348.

[110]Brown, *The Cult of the Saints*.

[111] "The Martydom of Polycarp, Bishop of Smyrna, as Told in the Letter of the Church of Smyrna to the Church of Philomelium," in *Early Christian Fathers*, ed. Cyril C. Richardson (New York: Macmillan, 1970) 156.

[112]See the summary of the issues provided by Kilian McDonnell, "The Marian Liturgical Tradition," in Johnson, *Between Memory and Hope*, 387–388.

[113]Walter Ray, *August 15 and the Development of the Jerusalem Calendar* (Ph.D. diss., University of Notre Dame, 2000).

[114]Geoffrey Wainwright, "Divided by a Common Language," in his *Worship with One Accord: Where Liturgy and Ecumenism Embrace* (New York and Oxford: Oxford University Press, 1997) 156 (emphasis added).

[115]Geoffrey Wainwright, "Renewing Worship: The Recovery of Classical Patterns," in *Worship with One Accord*, 138.

[116]James F. White, "How Do We Know It Is Us?," in *Liturgy and the Moral Self: Humanity at Full Stretch Before God*, ed. E. Byron Anderson and Bruce Morrill (Collegeville, Minn.: Liturgical Press, 1998) 55–65.

[117]English translation from Cantalamessa, *Easter*, 36 (emphasis added).

[118]I have dealt with many of these issues in a more summary fashion in several publications elsewhere. See Maxwell E. Johnson, "Worship, Practice and Belief," in *The Early Christian World* (London and New York: Routledge, 2000) 475–499. Especially for the section on Christian initiation see Johnson, *The Rites of Christian Initiation*, chapters 1 and 2. Portions of the conclusion to this chapter are based on Johnson, "Can We Avoid Relativism in Worship? Liturgical Norms in the Light of Contemporary Liturgical Scholarship," *Worship* 74 (2000) 135–154.

3

The Empire Baptized

JOHN F. BALDOVIN, S.J.

But how can anyone describe those vast assemblies, and the multitudes that crowded together in every city, and the famous gatherings in the houses of prayer; on whose account, not being satisfied with the ancient buildings, they erected from the foundation large churches in all the cities. (Eusebius, *Ecclesiastical History* 8.1.5)

After this, the sight was seen which had been desired and prayed for by us all; feasts of dedication in the cities and consecrations of the newly built houses of prayer took place, bishops assembled, foreigners came together from abroad, mutual love was exhibited between people and people, the members of Christ's body were united in complete harmony. (Eusebius, *Ecclesiastical History* 10.3.1)

The church historian Eusebius wrote the first of these passages during a period of relative calm after the persecution of Christians under the Roman emperor Decius in the mid-third century. The second passage was written in the flush of Christianity's imperial acceptance after the vicious persecutions of Diocletian at the beginning of the fourth century. Both passages serve to illustrate the continuity and discontinuity of Christian worship in the course of the transformation brought about by Emperor Constantine's acceptance of Christianity. It is still necessary to dispel the popular myth that before Constantine Christians were a tiny persecuted group huddled in the catacombs where they conducted their worship in secret.[1] The rest of the myth goes something like this: Christians worshiped with great evangelical simplicity and had no elaborate calendar of liturgical observances because they lived in intense expectation of the final coming of Christ—at least until acceptance by the empire made them feel at home in the world.[2]

Another frequently encountered myth, already dispelled in the previous chapter, supposes Christian worship, uniform at the beginning, only later diversified. The story of Christian worship from Constantine to the rise of Islam shows, however, that an original diversity began to come together in remarkably similar ritual patterns in the fourth century only to diversify subsequently into the major rites still known in the early twenty-first century.[3]

The period covered by this chapter—roughly from the legalization of Christianity by Constantine (312) up to the birth of Islam (622) saw major developments in every aspect of Christian worship. These individual developments can only be surveyed in broad lines. Beginning with the physical setting of church buildings, we shall move from there to the origin and development of the major rites. At that point we shall

The Emperor Baptized. Roundel from the left wing of the Stavelot Triptych, c. 1156–1158. Although Constantine attributed his military victory at the Milvian Bridge in 312 to the God of the Christians and took a strong interest in the affairs of the Church (including the Council of Nicaea), it seems he was not himself baptized until the end of his life in 337, a not uncommon choice in his time. By the fifth century, the legend arose that the emperor was baptized by Pope Sylvester at the Lateran Baptistery in Rome. ART RESOURCE, NY

turn our attention to Christian initiation and the eucharist. We will move from there to considering the development of patterns of daily prayer and the calendar, finally touching on other rituals important to Christian life: the ritualization of public penance, marriage, rituals for the sick and funerals, and rites for ordination to Christian ministry.

The Setting for Worship

In the first three centuries Christians worshiped mainly in private houses. Some of these houses, like the well-known house-church of Dura-Europos (on the Syrian frontier of the Roman Empire), were modified to accommodate Christian worship. One of the larger rooms served as a baptistery, another for the celebration of the eucharist, and a third possibly for the instruction of catechumens. But even prior to the fourth century we know from Eusebius that Christians were constructing their own buildings for worship. With Constantine's legalization of Christianity, not to mention the enormous imperial financial support, the building of churches virtually exploded in the course of the fourth century. Much of the story attached to the development of the eucharistic liturgy and the calendar is associated with what was required by the sheer scale of the new buildings and by the fact that Christians could now make the public plazas and thoroughfares of the major cities their own.[4] Understandably this process took much longer in Rome, entrenched as it was in its traditional past, than it did in a "new" city like Constantinople or in Jerusalem, which had been turned into a Roman army camp in the middle of the second century.

Vast amounts of money were poured into the construction of church buildings and the shrines of the saints. One can get some sense of the extravagance of the imperial donations from the list of gifts to the Lateran basilica in the *Liber Pontificalis*.[5] For example, Constantine gave seven altars of finest silver, each weighing two hundred pounds, seven gold patens, each weighing thirty pounds, two censers of finest gold, each weighing thirty pounds. And this is not even a fraction of the gifts that are enumerated for this building alone.

Eusebius devotes a part of the last book (Book 10) of his church history to the panegyric he delivered on the occasion of the dedication of a new basilica built at Tyre. He initiates a literary tradition that reaches a kind of crescendo in Paul the Silentiary's magnificent descriptions of Justinian's rebuilt Hagia Sophia in Constantinople in the sixth century.[6]

PAUL THE SILENTIARY—DESCRIPTION OF HAGIA SOPHIA

Thus, as you direct your gaze towards the eastern arches, you behold a never-ceasing wonder. And upon all of them, above this covering of many curves, there rises, as it were, another arch borne on air, spreading out its swelling fold, and it rises to the top, to that high rim upon whose back is planted the base of the divine head-piece of the center of the church. Thus the deep-bosomed conch springs up into the air: at the summit it rises single, while underneath it rests on triple folds; and through fivefold openings pierced in its back it provides sources of light, sheathed in thin glass, through which, brilliantly gleaming, enters rosy-ankled Dawn. . . .

Cross-section of Hagia Sophia. The structure originally known as the Great Church of Constantinople was later given the name Hagia Sophia ("Holy Wisdom"). Constantine the Great is believed to have founded the church, which in 381 was the setting for the Second Ecumenical Council. The current building dates from the sixth century. FOTO MARBURG/ART RESOURCE, NY

And towards the west one may see the same forms as towards the dawn, though there is a small difference. For there in the central space it is not drawn in a curved arc as it is at the eastern end, where the priests, learned in the art of sacrifice, preside on seats resplendent with an untold wealth of silver; at the west is a great, richly-wrought portal, not a single one, but divided into three at the boundary of the temple.

By the doors there stretches out a lengthy porch receiving those that enter beneath wide gates. It is as long as the wondrous church is broad; this space is called narthex by the Greeks. Here through the night there rises a melodious sound pleasing to the ears of Christ, giver of life, when the psalms of God-fearing David are sung with alternate voice by the sacred ministers. . . . Into the porch there open wide seven holy gates inviting the people to enter; one of these is on the narrow face of the narthex facing south, and another on the northern wing; the rest on their groaning pivots are opened by the warden in the west wall which marks the end of the church. Whither am I driven? What wind, as upon the sea, has carried away my roaming Speech? The center of the church, the most renowned place, has been neglected. Return, my song, to behold a wonder scarcely to be believed when seen or heard. . . .

Rising above this into the immeasurable air is a helmet rounded on all sides like a sphere and, radiant as the heavens, it bestrides the roof of the church. At its very summit art has depicted a cross, protector of the city. It is a wonder to see how [the dome], wide below, gradually grows less at the top as it rises. It does not, however, form a sharp pinnacle, but is like the firmament which rests on air. . . .

At the very navel the sign of the cross is depicted within a circle by means of minute mosaic so that the Saviour of the whole world may for ever protect the church; while at the base of the half-sphere are fashioned forty arched windows through which the rays of fair-haired Dawn are channelled. . . .

Now, towards the east and the west, you will see nothing beneath the arches: all is air. But towards the murmuring south wind and the rainless north there rises a mighty wall up to the chin of the rounded arch, and it is illuminated by twice four windows.

Paul the Silentiary—Description of the Ambo of Hagia Sophia

In the center of the wide church, yet tending rather towards the east, is a kind of tower, fair to look upon, set apart as the abode of the sacred books. Upright it stands on steps, reached by two flights, one of which extends towards the night, the other towards the dawn. These are opposite to one another; but both lead to the same space that is curved like a circle; for here a single stone circumscribes a space that resembles a circle, but is not altogether equal to a complete curve, for it contracts a little and so draws out the outline of the stone. And towards the west and east the stone forms a neck projecting from the circle and resting upon the steps. Up to the height of a man's girdle our divine Emperor has erected beauteous walls, crescent-shaped, sheathed in silver. For he has not bent the silver right around the stone, but the silver slabs unfold into glorious curves in the middle and form a wall. The skillful craftsman has opened the curve sufficiently on either side so as to provide access to the flights of steps. Nor does fear seize those who descend the sacred steps because their sides are unfenced; for walls of shining marble have been artfully reared here, and they rise above the steps to such height as is needed to guide a man's hand. By grasping them, a man eases his toil as he mounts upwards. So, in a slanting line, these [parapets] rise on either side together with the steps that are between them and come to a stop.[7]

In terms of the effect on the conduct of worship, the adoption of the form of a basilica was a significant move. Unlike traditional temples, whose main feature was the enshrining of a cult object, the basilica (the word comes from the Greek for king: *basileus*) was a large building originally meant to house the conduct of public business, whether a law court, an imperial audience chamber, or even a market. The ruins of these civic buildings can still be seen in the Roman Forum. The Christians transformed the basilican style by arranging the building on a longitudinal axis, as can be seen in the floor plan of the fifth-century Santa Sabina. Thus provision was made for a very important feature of the eucharistic liturgy—the procession. Basilicas were open, pewless halls with a central nave and two or four side aisles terminating in an apse on which the bishop was enthroned, surrounded by his presbyters. Such buildings could be provided with galleries, like Hagia Sophia, whose gallery was reserved for women. An entry hall, or narthex, would serve as an intermediate space between an open-air atrium and the nave. The narthex would serve as a kind of in-between space for those who were not admitted to eucharistic com-

Lunette from Hagia Sophia. The mosaic from the late tenth century portrays Justinian I (*left*), who offers the enthroned Virgin and Child a model of Hagia Sophia, and Constantine I (*right*), who gives them a walled city representing Byzantium. Hagia Sophia, Istanbul/Erich Lessing/Art Resource

munion: the catechumens, the mentally ill (energumens). Those doing public penance would stand at the back of the church. Basilicas usually had a large number of doors, which enabled the faithful to enter en masse from public processions. It is rather difficult for people in modern postindustrial urban societies to get a sense of the interplay between indoor and outdoor worship in the late antique world. Perhaps the best analogy in the early twenty-first century would be a religious rally or worship service in a sports stadium.

The basilica's interior was arranged to facilitate the conduct of worship—especially the eucharist. Often a processional pathway was arranged through the midst of the nave to allow the clergy and other ministers easy access. Low barriers like those in Santa Sabina would enable ease of movement in

Nave of the basilica of Santa Sabina, Rome. The church was completed around 440, presumably on the site of the original *titulus Sabinae*, a church in the home of Sabina, who had been martyred. The longitudinal building is simple: a central nave culminates in an apse and there are two side aisles. Much of the interior decoration from the fifth century has disappeared, but the original wooden front door carved with biblical stories survives. Scala/ Art Resource, NY

Extracts from Ambrose of Milan's teaching on baptism:
De Sacramentis **(On the Sacraments)**
(see the discussion on page 92)

Book 2

16. We must now examine what it is we mean by baptism. You came to the font, you went down into it, you turned towards the high priest [the bishop], you saw, there at the font, the levites and the presbyter . . . .

20. You were asked: "Do you believe in God the Father almighty?" You replied: "I believe," and you were immersed: that is, buried. You were asked for a second time: "Do you believe in our Lord Jesus Christ and in his cross?" You replied: "I believe," and you were immersed: which means that you were buried with Christ. For one who is buried with Christ rises again with Christ. You were asked a third time: "Do you believe also in the Holy Spirit?" You replied: "I believe," and you were immersed a third time, so that the threefold confession might absolve the manifold lapses of the past.

Book 3

1. Yesterday the subject of our instruction was the font, which has the shape and appearance of a sort of tomb. When we believe in the Father, the Son and the Holy Spirit, we are received and immersed in it; then we rise up: that is, we are restored to life. You also receive the *myron*, that is, the chrism, over your heads. Why over your heads? Because "the faculties of the wise man are situated in his head," says Solomon. Wisdom without grace is inert; but when wisdom receives grace, then its work begins to move toward fulfillment. This is called regeneration.

4. You came up out of the font. What then? You listened to the reading. The high priest put on an apron: for though the presbyters did the same, it belongs to the high priest to begin the liturgy. What does this mystery mean? You must have heard it read that when the Lord had washed the feet of the other disciples he came to Peter, and Peter said to him: "Do you wash my feet?" That is to say: Do you, the master, wash the feet of the servant? Do you, the spotless one, wash my feet? Do you, the creator of the heavens, wash my feet? You have the same thing elsewhere. He came to John, and John said to him: "I need to be baptized by you, and do you come to me? I am a sinner, and you have come to the sinner in order to make a pretence of putting away your sins: you who never committed sin." See all the righteousness, to see the humility, see the grace, see the holiness. "If I do not wash your feet," he said, "you have no part in me."

the area reserved for the choir and the ministers around the altar. In Western churches an ambo for the proclamation of the scriptures rose from one or both sides of the choir. In the East the ambo would often be a separate structure in the middle of the nave. In fact in Syria a structure called the "bema" housed the clergy for the entire liturgy of the word and contained an altar called "golgotha" for the enshrinement of the Book of the Gospels.

Basilicas were not the only important form of Christian church building. A number of places for worship were shrines built over the remains of the martyrs and later

5. We are aware that the Roman Church does not follow this custom, although we take her as our prototype, and follow her rite in everything. But she does not have this rite of the washing of the feet. Perhaps it is because of the large numbers that she has ceased to practice it. But there are those who try to excuse themselves by saying that it should not be performed as a mystery, not as part of the baptismal rite, not for regeneration, but that this washing of the feet should be done as a host would do it for his guests. However, humility is one thing, sanctification another. You must know that this washing is a mystery and sanctification. "If I do not wash your feet, you shall have no part with me." I am not saying this as censuring others; I am simply recommending our own rite. I wish to follow the Roman Church in everything: but we too are not devoid of common sense. When a better custom is kept elsewhere, we are right to keep it here also.

6. We follow the apostle Peter himself; it is to his devotion that we cling. What does the Roman Church say to this? He indeed it is who is the source of our argument, and he was the priest of the Roman Church: Peter himself, who says, "Lord, not my feet only, but also my hands and my head." Consider his faith. When he refused at first, this was because of his humility. The submission he made afterwards came from devotion and faith.

8. The spiritual sealing follows. You have heard about this in the reading today. For after the ceremonies of the font, it still remains to bring the whole to perfect fulfillment. This happens when the Holy Spirit is infused at the priest's invocation: "the Spirit of wisdom and understanding, the Spirit of counsel and strength, the Spirit of knowledge and piety, the Spirit of holy fear." These might be called the seven "virtues" of the Spirit.

11. What happens after this? You can approach the altar. When you have arrived, you can see what you could not see before.

References

Whitaker, E. C. *Documents of the Baptismal Liturgy*, 3rd ed., rev. and expanded by Maxwell E. Johnson. Alcuin Club Collections 79. London: SPCK, 2003, pp. 179–181. (Source for text.)

Yarnold, Edward. *The Awe-Inspiring Rites of Initiation: The Origins of the R.C.I.A.*, 2nd ed. Collegeville, Minn.: Liturgical Press, 1994, pp. 116–125. (Source for translation. See also pp. 30–31, citing evidence for the connection of foot washing with baptism from Turin [Maximus], Aquilea [Chromatius], North Africa [Augustine], Spain [Council of Elvira], and possibly Syria [Aphrahat].)

other saints. The greatest shrines had to do, of course, with Christ. A complex of buildings was constructed at the traditional site of Golgotha and the Holy Sepulchre in Jerusalem. A five-aisled basilica, called the Martyrium, was placed across an open atrium from a domed building called the Anastasis for the resurrection of Christ. Also in the complex were a small shrine chapel enclosing the place of crucifixion as well as a baptistery and lodging for the bishop and clergy.

As with the Anastasis, many of the shrine churches in the East had domed roofs or circular plans. The shrine, or *memoria*, of a martyr could be located within a basilica, as in the case of Saint Peter's on the Vatican Hill in Rome, or next to it, as in the case of Saint Lawrence Outside-the-Walls, also in Rome.[8] Most of these shrines, since they were located in cemeteries, were to be found outside a city's walls.

The last important building that provided a space for Christian worship is the baptistery. The practice of baptizing naked adult candidates made it necessary to initiate them in a distinct building. Such buildings were often octagonal in shape, to symbolize the Christian conquest of time—beyond the perfection of seven. They also typically had antechambers where the candidates undressed and made their renunciation of evil. The baptismal pool itself could be located in a large domed room with glittering mosaics from floor to ceiling, as in the Baptistery of the Orthodox in Ravenna.[9] As we shall see below, the separation of baptism from the basilica influenced the unfolding of the initiation rites themselves.

Most Christian church buildings must have been relatively modest affairs compared to the famous monuments that have just been surveyed, but their shapes, functions, and decorations were all determined by models in the larger cities.

The Emergence of the Major Rites

This period also witnessed the emergence of the major ritual families of Christianity. The previous chapter demonstrated that there was no original single apostolic liturgy from which different churches diverged. Rather, the fourth century is a time of ritual consolidation. For example, the new ease of communication made it possible for different traditions of eucharistic praying to borrow from one another. John Fenwick has suggested that the Egyptian tradition of prayer found in the *Strasbourg Papyrus* may have been combined with other elements to form the Anaphora, or eucharistic prayer, of Saint Basil.[10] In addition, the basic structure of the eucharistic liturgy developed in a remarkably similar fashion throughout the Christian world, as Robert Taft has demonstrated using the method of comparative liturgy.[11] The fourth century and early fifth century were a period of cross-fertilization for Christian worship.

But gradually, and especially after the dissolution of the western Roman Empire in the late fifth century, what have come to be known as the classic rites of Christianity came into their own. These rites consolidated around the major urban centers and were in many ways influenced by the liturgy that was characteristic of each particular city. Some rites had great influence well outside their own territories. For example, one of the earliest Christian calendars comes from Armenia and was constructed in the first half of the fifth century.[12] The calendar and its lectionary provide notices of the Jerusalem church in which each feast is celebrated. Moreover, as we shall see when we come to considering the development of the calendar, many of the readings were very specific not only to the calendar date but also to the places of their celebration. We can suppose that these factors had little relevance in Armenia. They show, however, how one rite could influence another. By the seventh century we can distinguish a number of distinct rites or families of rites. It is important to note that rites can transcend church boundaries. For example, Russian Orthodox, Greek Catholics, and Syrian Melkites all use the Byzantine rite.

First the East. The Alexandrian rite, centered on the patriarchate of Alexandria in Egypt, is characterized by the use of the Anaphora of Saint Mark. The West Syrian rite developed out of the traditions of two major urban centers: Jerusalem and Antioch. Its characteristic eucharistic prayer is the Anaphora of Saint James. The East Syrian rite, on the other hand, was centered on Edessa and became the rite of those Persian and Indian Christians who became known as "the Church of the East". Their best-known anaphora is that of Addai and Mari. The Byzantine rite has close affinities with the West Syrians. As a relatively "young" church, beginning in the fourth century, Constantinople drew from Antioch, Cappadocia, and (later) Jerusalem for its liturgical practices. Its major eucharistic prayers are named for two outstanding saints from Antioch and Cappadocia respectively: John Chrysostom and Basil the Great.

The Roman rite has been the most influential in the West. The churches in Rome seem originally to have been polyglot with perhaps a preponderance of Greek. In the third century, however, we begin to find a Latin Christian literature, although mainly coming from North Africa. It is not until late in the fourth century that something like a Roman rite—in Latin—appears, and even then the source is a text of the Roman canon quoted by Ambrose of Milan (in *On the Sacraments* 4.21ff.). A letter from Pope Innocent I to an Umbrian bishop, Decentius of Gubbio, in 416 reveals that even in the city of Rome itself there were three distinct practices: that of the bishop, another of the neighborhood churches (called *tituli*), and finally that of the martyrs' shrines that lay outside the city walls.[13] Somewhat of a hybrid of the Roman rite and the usage of the churches beyond the Alps was the Ambrosian rite, centered on the city of Milan and related to other northern Italian cities, such as Aquileia, Turin, and Brescia. Very little is known of the liturgical texts of North Africa, but Frederik van der Meer has pieced together a picture of Augustine's liturgical practice in the early fifth century.[14] Finally, the churches north of the Alps and to the west had the Gallic (modern France and Germany) and Mozarabic (or more accurately Visigothic—in the Iberian Peninsula) rites. These rites were influenced by their contact with the Christian East and can be characterized by their flowery language and tendency toward elaborate ceremonial, as Edmund Bishop demonstrated in a classic essay, "The Genius of the Roman Rite."[15]

Although the various rites of Christian worship reveal a good deal of diversity developing in the late patristic period, they are similar enough to be dealt with together, as we can see in turning to individual aspects of the liturgy.

Christian Initiation

A distinctive feature of early Christian initiatory practice that was recovered in the twentieth century is the catechumenate, a period of instruction, training, and rituals leading up to the sacramental rites of baptism, anointing, and participation in the eucharist. References to the length of the catechumenate vary throughout the period, and one must be cautious about assuming that the same rigor was applied everywhere. Ramsay MacMullen begins his treatment of the conversion of the Roman Empire with a story from the mid-fifth-century church historian Theodoret, who describes the descent of tribes of Bedouins upon Simeon the Stylite in the desert forty miles east of Antioch:

> They arrived in companies, 200 in one, 300 in another, occasionally a thousand. They renounced with their shouts their traditional errors; they broke up their venerated idols in the presence of that great light; and they foreswore the ecstatic rites of Aphrodite, the demon whose service they had long accepted. They enjoyed divine religious initiation and received their law instead spoken by that holy tongue (of Symeon).[16]

We are not told specifically that these tribespeople were baptized. But Theodoret clearly considers them initiated in some sense. The point is that in this scene there is

no arduous struggle with demons or long periods of fasting and instruction. Therefore one must be rather cautious about overstating the seriousness of the catechumenate,
at least in this period. By the end of this period—in the seventh-century Gelasian
Sacramentary (Rome)—it is presumed that the catechumens are infants carried in the
arms of acolytes as the creed is presented to them.

Notwithstanding these cautions, we do have a number of texts that can give a picture of the catechumenate. In the mid-fourth century, Cyril, bishop of the newly
(re)founded church in Jerusalem, speaks to those who have just been enrolled for
Easter baptism (*Procatechesis* 1):

> Already there is an odour of blessedness upon you, O ye who are soon
> to be enlightened; already ye are gathering the spiritual flowers, to
> weave the heavenly crowns: already the fragrance of the Holy Spirit
> has breathed upon you: already ye have gathered round the vestibule
> of the King's palace; may ye be led in also by the King. . . . Thus far
> there has been an inscription of your names, and a call to service, and
> torches of the bridal train, and a longing for heavenly citizenship, and
> a good purpose, and hope attendant thereon.

Cyril goes on to speak of "forty days of repentance" and the
terrors instilled by the exorcists as the candidates are scrutinized. There are eighteen lectures after this preparatory one in
Cyril's series, whose "syllabus" is basically the points of the
Christian creed. There is no clear evidence for a uniform period of preparation for initiation. The *Apostolic Tradition* (whose
evidence may only hold good for the fourth, not the third, century as the previous chapter argued) presumes a catechumenate
of three years' duration after an initial severe examination of
motives, occupations, and manner of living. It could well be
that the catechumenate took on greater rigor in the course of
the fourth century, when becoming a Christian was an easier
task that promised more pleasant prospects than it had during
the centuries before Constantine. In the preaching of the fourth
century onward—especially that of John Chrysostom—there is
a renewed appreciation of the Pauline death and resurrection
motifs, as in Romans 6 and other passages, which had not been
as much in evidence during the previous centuries. Exorcisms
and secrecy (the so-called *disciplina arcani*) may have been in-
ventions of a Christian faith that was in need of more serious
attention from the crowds that flooded into the church than
they may have been willing to imagine.

Fortunately we have a firsthand account of the preparation
for baptism from a pilgrim in fourth-century Jerusalem. A religious of some sort from northwest Spain (Galicia), Egeria spent
three years visiting the major cities and holy sites of the eastern
Mediterranean. The travel diary she wrote for her sisters back
home is one of the most precious witnesses of liturgy for this
period, precisely because it is not a liturgical book but an eyewitness report. Her description of the preparation, the initiation itself, and postbaptismal instruction is worth citing in full
(*Travel Diary* 45–47):

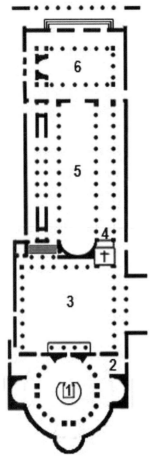

**Constantine's Jerusalem
Church in the late fourth
century.** (1) Tomb; (2)
Anastasis; (3) Court
"Before the Cross"; (4)
Chapel "Behind the Cross";
(5) Martyrium; (6) Court.
Drawing by Benjamin W.
Tucker after Wilkinson,
2d ed., 1981

I feel I should add something about the way they instruct those who are about to be baptized at Easter. Names must be given in before the first day of Lent, which means that a presbyter takes down all the names before the start of the eight weeks for which Lent lasts here, as I have told you. Once the priest has all the names, on the second day of Lent at the start of the eight weeks, the bishop's chair is placed in the middle of the Great Church, the Martyrium, the presbyters sit in chairs on either side of him, and all the clergy stand. Then one by one those seeking baptism are brought up, men coming with their fathers and women with their mothers. As they come in one by one, the bishop asks their neighbours questions about them: "Is this person leading a good life? Does he respect his parents? Is he a drunkard or a boaster?" He asks about all the serious human vices. And if his inquiries show him that someone has not committed any of these misdeeds, he himself puts down his name; but if someone is guilty he is told to go away, and the bishop tells him that he is to amend his ways before he may come to the font. He asks the men and the women the same questions. But it is not easy for a visitor to come to baptism if he has no witnesses who are acquainted with him.

. . . They have here the custom that those who are preparing for baptism during the season of Lenten fast go to be exorcized by the clergy first thing in the morning. . . . As soon as that has taken place, the bishop's chair is placed in the Great Church, the Martyrium, and all those to be baptized, the men and the women, sit round him in a circle. There is a place where the fathers and the mothers stand, and any of the people who want to listen (the faithful, of course) can come and sit down, though not catechumens, who do not come in while the bishop is teaching.

His subject is God's Law; during the forty days he goes through the whole Bible, beginning with Genesis, and first relating the literal meaning of each passage, and then interpreting its spiritual meaning. He also teaches them at this time all about the resurrection and the faith. And this is called *catechesis*. After five weeks' teaching they receive the Creed, whose content he explains article by article in the same way as he explained the Scriptures, first literally and then spiritually. Thus all the people in these parts are able to follow the Scriptures when they are read in church, since there has been teaching on all the Scriptures from six to nine in the morning all through Lent, three hours' catechesis a day.

. . . When seven weeks have gone by, and only the week of Easter remains, the one which the people here call the Great Week, the bishop comes early into the Great Church, the Martyrium. His chair is placed at the back of the apse, behind the altar, and one by one the candidates go up to the bishop, men with their fathers and women with their mothers, and repeat the Creed to him. When they have done so, the bishop speaks to them all as follows: During these seven weeks you have received instruction in the whole biblical Law. You have heard about the faith, and the resurrection of the body. You have also learned all you can as catechumens of the content of the Creed. But the teaching about baptism itself is a deeper mystery, and you have not the right to hear it while you remain catechumens. Do not think it will never be explained; you will hear it all during the eight days of Easter after you have been baptized. But as long as you are catechumens you cannot be told God's deep mysteries.

Then Easter comes, and during the eight days from Easter Day to the eighth, after the dismissal has taken place in the church and they have come with singing to the Anastasis, it does not take long to say the prayer and bless the faithful: then the bishop stands against the inner screen of the cave of the Anastasis, and interprets all that takes place in baptism. . . . as he does so, the applause is so loud that it can be heard outside the church. Indeed the way he expounds the mysteries and interprets them cannot fail to move his hearers.[17]

Such detailed descriptions are a luxury for those who desire some sense of the experience of Christian worship in late antiquity. We can be sure that there were variations on these practices throughout the Christian world, but at the same time there are several common features in the catechetical process.

1. There is an enrollment of names of the candidates at the beginning of Lent.[18] Various names were given to these candidates: *competentes* (seekers), *electi* (chosen), and *phôtizomenoi* (about to be enlightened).
2. The candidates have sponsors who speak up for them—called "mothers" and "fathers" by Egeria.
3. The candidates undergo daily exorcisms. Cyril (*Procatechesis* 9) makes it clear that these exorcisms were designed to be terrifying experiences.
4. The Lenten catechesis is a lengthy exposition of Christian scripture and faith. It is closed to those who are catechumens but have not yet reached the stage of enrollment for baptism.
5. Candidates are formally given the creed, which is ritually handed back to the bishop shortly before Easter. In some places the same procedure was followed for the Lord's prayer.[19]
6. A series of lectures, elsewhere called "Mystagogy," were given after baptism in Easter Week.

In the fourth century a number of individuals, among them Ambrose of Milan, Augustine of Hippo, and Emperor Constantine, postponed their Christian initiations, remaining catechumens for years. For some it was a case of a later conversion, but for others—since baptism was considered a one-time "free" remission for the sins of one's past—postponing baptism was an attempt to avoid the rigors of public penance.

The actual sacramental ceremonies of Christian initiation took different forms in the various churches, as can be seen from the chart depicting practice in the East.[20]

In the East a richly elaborated ritual of initiation at the paschal vigil between Holy Saturday and Easter Sunday is described in the homilies of Cyril of Jerusalem (died 387), John Chrysostom (died 407), and Theodore of Mopsuestia (died 428). In the West a similar description is given in the postbaptismal homilies of Ambrose of Milan (died 397).[21] Each begins with a ritual that connotes a separation from the individual's

INITIATION RITES IN THE EAST

Cyril	Chrysostom	Theodore	East Syria	Egypt
			Anointing	
Renunciation	Renunciation	Renunciation	Renunciation	Renunciation
Syntaxis (?)	*Syntaxis*	*Syntaxis*	*Syntaxis*	*Syntaxis*
Anointing (head)	Anointing (head)	Anointing (head)		Anointing
Stripping	Stripping	Stripping		
Anointing (body)	Anointing (body)	Anointing (body)		
Interrogations				
Baptism	Baptism (formula)	Baptism (formula)	Baptism (formula)	Baptism (formula)
Anointing with chrism		Kiss		Anointing with chrism
White garment?	Radiant garment			
		Signing		
	Kiss			
Eucharist	Eucharist	Eucharist	Eucharist	Eucharist

former life. For Cyril the ceremony begins in the outer room of the baptistery with a renunciation of sin. The candidates face westward—the position of darkness and the setting sun. He writes in *Mystagogical Catechesis* 1.9:

> So when you renounce Satan, you trample underfoot your entire covenant with him and abrogate your former treaty with Hell. The gates of God's Paradise are open to you, that garden which God planted in the east. . . . When you turned from west to east, the region of light, you symbolised this change of allegiance.

The ritual is clearly meant to instill a dramatic sense of transformation in the candidates. The gates of paradise may well have been the doors to the brightly lit baptistery itself, whose mosaics would glimmer in the light of candles and oil lamps. John Chrysostom mentions that the candidates are kneeling with their hands outstretched to heaven as they make their renunciation and then immediately an act of allegiance to Christ (*syntaxis*): "And I pledge myself, Christ, to you" (*Baptismal Homily* 2.21). For Theodore the candidate stands barefoot on sackcloth with his or her outer garment removed and then kneels to renounce Satan and evil. The candidate then pledges faith in the triune God. Ambrose begins his description of the ritual on Holy Saturday morning with a ceremony called the *ephphetha*, in which the bishop "opens" the ears and mouths of the candidates by touching their ears and nostrils (cf. Mark 7:31–35). In the evening at the baptistery the candidates are first anointed all over (like athletes, says Ambrose) by presbyters and deacons, and then they make their renunciation.

Cyril, John, and Theodore all describe the stripping of the candidates and an anointing that takes place after the renunciation of evil and adherence to Christ. As the previous chapter has shown, it is probable that originally there was only one anointing associated with baptism and that it preceded the baptismal bath. In the course of the fourth century that anointing with chrism seems to have been replaced with an anointing of the forehead or the entire body with olive oil. This prebaptismal anointing is variously described with athletic or military metaphors that indicate a more prophylactic or protective significance as opposed to the royal and priestly identification with Christ in the postbaptismal chrismation. John Chrysostom in Antioch is the exception, for he includes only one anointing—with chrism—before the baptismal bath. But even John seems to have adopted a somewhat prophylactic interpretation of the act:

> You are now a soldier and have signed on for a spiritual contest. Accordingly the bishop anoints you on the forehead with spiritual *myron* (chrism), placing a seal on your head and saying: N. is anointed in the name of the Father, the Son and the Holy Spirit. Now the bishop knows that the Enemy is enraged and is sharpening his teeth going around like a roaring lion, seeing that the former victims of his tyranny have defected. Renouncing him, they have changed their allegiance and publicly enlisted with Christ. It is for this reason that the bishop anoints you on your forehead and marks you with the seal, to make the devil turn away his eyes. He does not dare look at you directly because he sees the light blazing from your head and blinding his eyes. From this day onwards you will confront him in battle, and this is why the bishop anoints you as athletes of Christ before leading you into the spiritual arena. (*Baptismal Homily* 2.22)

As Robert Taft has written, "in the history of liturgical *development*, structure outlives meaning."[22] The rite that Chrysostom is describing retains the old Syrian structure but has endowed it with a new meaning, more suitable to the late-fourth-century context of baptism understood in terms of Paul's death and resurrection theology in Romans 6. On the other hand, Theodore retains something of the old meaning of prebaptismal anointing despite the fact that his rite has added a postbaptismal chrismation. In Theodore's rite sponsors put linen stoles over the heads of the candidates and raise them to their feet as a sign of their newly won freedom.

Now the stage is set for the baptismal bath. In strikingly similar ways both Ambrose and Theodore speak of the bishop's blessing of the baptismal water as the transforming work of the Holy Spirit. A developing theology of the Holy Spirit seems operative in emphasizing the consecration of an object for use. We shall find a similar development in the epiclesis of the eucharistic prayers. The presumption in the fourth and following centuries is that baptism is performed by either a total immersion of the body or by pouring water over the head of a person standing in water, as in the baptism of Christ in the Ravenna baptisteries [see color plate 5]. All four of the bishops speak quite clearly of a threefold immersion. Two of them (Ambrose and Cyril) describe the baptism of the individual in an interrogatory form; that is, there is no declaratory baptismal formula spoken by the minister but rather the candidate's affirmative answer to three questions based on the three persons of the Trinity. Chrysostom and Theodore, on the other hand, witness a baptismal formula in the indicative: "N. is baptized in the name of the Father and of the Son and of the Holy Spirit."

The Neonian or Orthodox baptistery, Ravenna. Baptisteries in the early centuries were separated from the main church building and sometimes, like the fifth-century Orthodox baptistery at Ravenna, were eight sided to symbolize new life in Christ. The font during the time of Bishop Neon (451–475) was circular. The twelfth-century font now visible is octagonal. SCALA/ART RESOURCE, NY

Of these four homilists, Cyril gives perhaps the clearest explanation of a theology of ritual mimesis when he tells the newly baptized of the significance of their baptismal dying in Christ:

What a strange and astonishing situation! We did not really die, we were not really buried, we did not really hang from a cross and rise again. Our imitation was symbolic, but our salvation a reality. Christ truly hung from a cross, was truly buried, and truly rose again. All this he did gratuitously for us, so that we might share his sufferings by imitating them, and gain salvation in actuality. . . . In his case all these events really occurred; but in your case there was a likeness of death and suffering, but the reality, not the likeness, of salvation. (*Mystagogical Catechesis* 2.5, 7)

The other fourth-century homilists employ similar approaches to typology and symbolism—all in an effort to help the newly baptized appreciate how their experience participates in that of Christ. Christians in late antiquity lived in a cultural universe richly populated with invisible realities—a world in which symbol and ritual were not the counterfeit of reality but rather the privileged means to access reality. It is often stated that this worldview rested upon a Platonic theory of knowledge and being. This is true, but it is also somewhat like saying that contemporary individuals are Freudians when they employ concepts like "superego" or "unconscious motivation." Such an attitude toward to the world is not so much orthodox Freudianism as part of the cultural air one breathes.

We have already suggested that the original prebaptismal anointing was shifted (except for Chrysostom) to a point immediately following the baptismal bath. For Cyril this anointing communicates the Holy Spirit in a manner similar to the consecrated bread of the eucharist communicating Christ:

> But be sure not to regard the myron merely as ointment. Just as the bread of the Eucharist after the invocation of the Holy Spirit is no longer just bread, but the body of Christ, so the holy myron after the invocation is no longer ordinary ointment but Christ's grace, which through the presence of the Holy Spirit instills his divinity to us. (*Mystagogical Catechesis* 3.3)

Ambrose speaks of a postbaptismal *spiritale signaculum* (spiritual seal) as the gift of the spirit. Maxwell Johnson urges caution in interpreting this seal as an anointing,[23] especially since later North Italian practice has only one postbaptismal anointing, which Ambrose had already referred to, citing the formula recited by the priest:

> God the Father Almighty, who has brought you to a new birth by water and the Holy Spirit and has forgiven your sins, himself anoints you into eternal life. (*De sacramentis* 2.24)

We have already noted that there is no postbaptismal anointing in Chrysostom. Theodore's evidence is somewhat more complex. Since he is writing around the same time and place as Chrysostom, it is difficult to know what he is referring to when he speaks in *Baptismal Homily* 2.27 of the "seal" that the bishop puts on the person's forehead after baptism, especially since he takes pains to argue that the Spirit has been given in the baptismal bath.[24] It could well be, as Kilian McDonnell has argued, that it is only in the fourth century that the baptismal ritual was accommodated to the scriptural witness of the Spirit coming down upon Jesus after he emerged from the Jordan.[25]

These details are significant since they later evolve into the practice of confirmation in the West and chrismation considered as a distinct sacrament in the East. At the end of the fourth century, however, it is better to conceive of these rites as forming a whole, just as contemporary bathing practice involves not only water but might also involve soap, shampoo, powders, and lotions. Remember as well that these bishops were giving homilies to enrich the experience of the newly baptized, not writing treatises in doctrine or systematic theology. Finally, in attempting to understand liturgical history, one is always in danger of importing later practices into earlier events in order to make sense of them in one's own mental framework.

Several other rites are mentioned by our homilists. Theodore speaks quite explicitly of the white garment given to the neophytes, the others somewhat more obliquely. Chrysostom mentions the kiss of peace that is given to the newly baptized. The *Apostolic Tradition* mentions that the kiss is reserved to the baptized since the kiss of the catechumens is not yet holy. Our appreciation of the post-Nicene initiatory practice would not be complete without mention of participation in the eucharist. Later Western practice divorces baptism, confirmation, and the reception of the eucharist. In this period it seems to be taken for granted that receiving the eucharistic elements is the logical culmination of the initiation—a literal "in-corp-oration" into the community of the faithful. Similarly, a bishop's sealing of the newly baptized who are being admitted to the eucharist—whether by anointing or imposition of the hand—would be the public ritual affirmation of the individual's baptism, which had to take place in the (private) baptistery for the sake of modesty.

Two other practices should be accounted for at the end of the fourth century. The first is rather curious. Ambrose speaks of a washing of the feet that follows the baptismal bath. He supports the practice with a reference to the serpent biting Adam's heel that now needs special protection from sin (*De sacramentis* 3.7). He admits that the Roman church does not practice this ritual but claims that common sense requires his church to adopt whatever better practices it finds. As was suggested in the previous chapter, Milan may have adopted an initiatory practice from a Johannine community that had foot washing as its main rite of initiation. Finally, Egeria makes mention of a practice in Jerusalem that can illustrate how significant locale, culture, and situation can be in the development of worship. After the baptismal bath and while the people are still in the Great Church keeping vigil, the bishop leads the neophytes into the Anastasis, the shrine of Christ's resurrection, where they sing a hymn and have a prayer (*Travel Diary* 38.1–2). What better way to impress upon the newly baptized that they have been raised with Christ who was raised in this very spot?

To fill in the picture of Christian initiation in the centuries following Constantine, we shall turn to the West and especially to Rome. We have a fairly good picture of initiation around the mid-seventh century in two related documents: *Ordo Romanus XI* and the Gelasian Sacramentary.[26] By the seventh century the major exorcisms or scrutinies that had taken place on the third, fourth, and fifth Sundays of Lent were now transferred to the weekdays, presumably because the candidates were now fewer and most were literally infants. The post-Constantinian era sees a shift from predominantly adult conversion and initiation to a Christian world where most are baptized as infants. This should come as no surprise given the fact that the social and civil world has been Christianized. It is also related to the triumph of Augustine of Hippo's theology of original sin, which itself drew in part on the Church's practice of initiating infants.

The Roman rite (but not the rest of the Western churches at this time) witnesses a twofold chrismation of the newly baptized, first by the presbyter and then by the bishop. The prayers are instructive and hint at a theological development with regard to the giving of the Holy Spirit. One suspects that two traditions are being conflated here since the first part of the second prayer reduplicates the presbyter's formula of anointing.

After the baptism, the presbyter signs the head of the neophyte with a formula reminiscent of the *Apostolic Tradition*:

> God Almighty, the Father of our Lord Jesus Christ, who granted you regeneration by water and the Holy Spirit and who has given you forgiveness of all your sins, himself anoints you with the chrism of salvation in Christ Jesus to eternal life.

The bishop then bestows the sevenfold gift of the Spirit with the imposition of the hand and this prayer:

> God Almighty, Father of our Lord Jesus Christ, who granted regeneration to your servants by water and the Holy Spirit, and who have given them forgiveness of all their sins, send on them, Lord, your Holy Spirit, the Paraclete, and give them the Spirit of wisdom and understanding, the Spirit of counsel and might, the Spirit of knowledge and godliness, fill them with the Spirit of fear of God, in the name of our Lord Jesus Christ, with whom you live and reign God forever with the Holy Spirit, forever and ever. Amen.

Finally, the bishop signs the forehead of each with chrism and says, "The sign of Christ to life eternal," and then gives the kiss of peace.[27]

The Gelasian Sacramentary also provides a blessing of the water of the baptismal font whose interest lies in the fact that it first exorcizes the water and only then blesses it. *Ordo Romanus XI* adds the fact that the bishop pours chrism into the font in the form of a cross toward the end of the baptismal prayer, after which the water is sprinkled on the faithful. At this point the West still retains the interrogatory form of baptism (that is, without a formula recited by the priest) and a dipping three times in response to three questions on the articles of the creed.

This period also witnesses the beginnings of a distinct sacrament of confirmation in the West. As noted above, the bishop's consignation of the candidate seems to have originated in the public affirmation of what had been of necessity a private ritual. What happened when there was no bishop present to baptize and anoint? Pope Innocent I in a letter to the bishop Decentius of Gubbio (Umbria) writes the following:

> About the signing of the newly baptized: it is quite clear that no one may perform it except the bishop. For although presbyters are priests, they do not have the highest degree of the priesthood. It is not only the custom of the Church which demonstrated that the signing and the gift of the Holy Spirit is restricted to bishops, but the passage in the Acts of the Apostles which declares that Peter and John were sent to give the Holy Spirit to those already baptized. For when presbyters baptize, whether in the absence of the bishop or in his presence, they may anoint the baptized with chrism (provided that it is consecrated by the bishop) but they do not sign the forehead with the same oil. That is reserved to the bishops when they give the Spirit, the Paraclete.[28]

In similar fashion fourth- and fifth-century church councils in Gaul make it clear that the bishop is to confirm or perfect the ministry of presbyters when the postbaptismal chrismation has for some reason been omitted.[29] In both cases, I would argue, such "confirmation" has more to do with the role of the bishop in initiation than with the effects of a sacramental act.

A fitting conclusion to this section on Christian initiation can be found in the poetic inscription in the Lateran Baptistery in Rome, often attributed to the mid-fifth-century pope, Sixtus III:

> Here is born in Spirit-soaked fertility
> a brood destined for another City,
> begotten by God's blowing
> and borne upon this torrent
> by the Church their virgin mother.
> Reborn in these depths they reach for
>   heaven's realm,
> the born-but-once unknown by felicity.
> This spring is life that floods the world,
> the wounds of Christ its awesome source,
> Sinner sink beneath this sacred surf
> that swallows age and spits out youth.
> Sinner here scour sin away down to innocence,
> for they know no enmity who are by

The baptistery at the basilica of Saint John Lateran. The baptistery connected with the cathedral of Rome was in the early fourth century a circular building containing a central circular pool approximately twenty-seven feet in diameter and three feet deep. In the late fourth century, the baptistery was reconstructed in octagonal form. SCALA/ART RESOURCE, NY

one font, one Spirit, one faith made one.
Sinner, shudder not at sin's kind and number,
for those born here are holy.[30]

The Eucharistic Banquet

> But why in bread? I provide nothing of my own at this point, rather let us listen together to the Apostle, who said, when he was speaking about this sacrament, "We, though many, are one bread, one body." Understand and rejoice. Unity! Verity! Piety! Charity! "One bread." What is this one bread? "Many . . . one body." Remember that bread is not made from one grain, but from many. When you were exorcized, you were, after a fashion, milled. When you were baptized you were moistened. When you received the fire of the Holy Spirit you were baked. Be what you see, and receive what you are.[31]

Augustine of Hippo, speaking to the newly baptized in his congregation early in the fifth century, describes the eucharistic banquet in memorable terms. For him the eucharist is an evocative symbol of the unity between the members of the church as the body of Christ and the sacramental body of Christ. Augustine is speaking at a time when it is not difficult to make the connections between the eucharistic action and the eucharistic elements and the relevance of both to the living church. At the same time, the period between Constantine and the rise of Islam is one of profound development in all areas affecting this central Christian ritual: the shape and structure of the eucharist, the eucharistic prayer, and movements in theology.

A number of factors inspired the expansion of the structure of the eucharistic liturgy. Prominent among them are the numbers that now flooded the churches as well as the ability to use the public spaces and thoroughfares of the cities for religious processions and outdoor celebrations.[32] As time went on, the rites of the major cities were adapted in smaller cities and churches in the countryside. As noted above, in the letter of Pope Innocent to Decentius, even the city of Rome itself had some variations in practice. The major basilicas were required to shelter thousands of worshipers and so required an expansion of the scale of the service and more elaborate ceremonial.[33]

Robert Taft has outlined a very helpful hypothesis for understanding the general development of the eucharistic liturgy across the various families of rites. The description of the service by Justin Martyr in the mid-second century presents these main features: scripture readings; preaching; common prayers; kiss of peace; bringing of bread and wine to the presider; anaphora; communion. Such an order implies three "soft points" or "points of action without words": (1) the entrance into church, which preceded the readings; (2) the kiss of peace and the transfer of gifts, which took place between the word service and the eucharistic prayer; and (3) the breaking of bread, communion, and subsequent dismissal. These were the points at which additional items would then be inserted in the course of liturgical developments.[34]

In both East and West the fourth-century eucharistic rite began with the greeting of the bishop followed straightaway by the readings. One can find the same abrupt beginning in the pre-1955 Roman rite celebration of Good Friday—an illustration of Anton Baumstark's theory that the most solemn days tend to retain the most ancient practices.[35] There was no prayer to open the liturgy, nor were there (prescribed) chants. By the beginning of the fifth century this situation has changed. The *Liber Pontificalis* informs us that Pope Celestine I (422–432) ordered the 150 psalms of David "should be performed antiphonally by everyone."[36] Most scholars hold that this is a reference

The apse of Santa Maria Assunta, Torcello, Italy. The cathedral was founded in 639, but the current building dates from around the thirteenth century. The location of the bishop's chair (*cathedra*) in the apse surrounded by seats for the presbyters conforms to the disposition of space used in the earliest building. BRIDGEMAN ART LIBRARY

to the entrance psalm ("introit"). Just shortly after, around the middle of the fifth century, we begin to see short prayers, called collects or *orationes*, that come after the major processions in the celebration: entrance, presentation of the gifts, and holy communion. In his classic work, *The Mass of the Roman Rite*, Josef Jungmann showed that each of the action points in the eucharistic liturgy had a similar structure:

- procession
- covered by a chant
- concluded with a prayer[37]

Thus antiphonal psalmody was sung at the entrance, at the presentation of the gifts, and at the procession to receive communion. Psalms in responsorial form were sung between the readings. In the course of time a litany that accompanied processions from church to church was added to the beginning of the liturgy and eventually became the Kyrie eleison, or "Lord, have mercy."[38] The hymn "Glory to God in the Highest," derived from morning prayer in the East, was added to the entrance rite on solemn occasions presided over by a bishop and then gradually extended to eucharists presided over by presbyters as well. Finally, in the Roman rite a variable prayer or "collect" brought the entrance rite to an end. These prayers began their lives as booklets (*libelli*) that were eventually collected into what is now known as the classic sacramentaries of the Western churches.

The entrance rite of the Byzantine liturgy also expanded to meet the requirements of larger space and greater numbers. Processional psalmody and litanies accompanied both outdoor processions and the entrance into the churches. The Office of Three Antiphons, with which the Byzantine eucharist still begins, originated most probably in the outdoor processions into the churches. The Trisagion, often referred to as a hymn, was originally the antiphon (troparion) for a processional psalm.

In like fashion the rites at the presentation of gifts (offertory) and communion were filled in with elements of prayer and song and so expanded greatly. The Byzantine

Procession of martyrs. A sixth-century mosaic line of martyrs proceeds along the upper nave wall of San Apollinare Nuovo, Ravenna, toward an enthroned Redeemer. Leading the group and shown here are Martin, Clement, Sixtus, and Lawrence, wearing white (cf. Rev. 7:13–14) and carrying crowns of glory. On the opposite wall, richly-dressed virgins in line approach the Madonna and Child. Scala/Art Resource, NY

procession of the gifts from the outdoor sacristy through the nave to the sanctuary of Hagia Sophia was a grandiose spectacle, prompting some to confuse the still unconsecrated elements of bread and wine with the body and blood of Christ.[39]

As the rites at the "action points" of the liturgy expanded, the old core of the liturgy tended to shrink. In the fourth century at Antioch the *Apostolic Constitutions*, a handbook of church order, required four readings at the eucharistic liturgy. In the Roman rite a second chant that preceded the proclamation of the gospel probably followed what had been a second reading. With rare exceptions, by the end of the sixth century the liturgy of the word in both East and West contained only two readings: a Gospel and one other (usually New Testament) reading that went before it. The eucharistic prayer, not a visually stimulating part of the liturgy, lapsed into silent recitation. The chart shows how the liturgy expanded in the West up to the High Middle Ages. The second-century elements are printed in capital letters. The second column, *Ordo Romanus Primus*, represents the development of the eucharistic liturgy at Rome.

The chart shows that a number of significant elements were added to the celebration of the eucharist in the course of the post-Constantinian period. Cyril of Jerusalem is the first to mention the washing of the hands by the priest before he begins the eucharistic prayer:

> You saw the deacon offering water for the washing to the priest and to the presbyters encircling God's altar. Of course he did not do this because their bodies were dirty. Not at all; we did not enter the church with grimy bodies in the first place. No, the washing is a symbol of the need for you to be clean of all sins and transgressions. . . . So there is no doubt that the washing of the hands represents symbolically freedom from sins. (*Mystagogical Catechesis* 5.2)

Later evidence from Jerusalem suggests that the priest's hands were washed before leaving the bema and entering the sanctuary space around the altar.[40] The same Cyril witnesses to the presence of the Lord's prayer after the eucharistic prayer—as a preparation for holy communion. Some have suggested that in North Africa the Lord's prayer concluded the intercessory prayers before the presentation of the gifts. In the Gallican rites and some Eastern rites the "Our Father" follows the fraction, whereas

DEVELOPMENT OF WESTERN EUCHARIST

Justin Martyr ca. 150	Ordo Romanus Primus ca. 700	Gallican Rite ca. 650	Medieval Roman Rite ca. 1300
Liturgy of the Word	**Liturgy of the Word**	**Liturgy of the Word**	**Liturgy of the Word**
			Private prayers
	Introit	Introit	Introit
	Kyrie	GREETING	Kyrie
	Gloria in excelsis	Trisagion	Gloria in excelsis
GREETING	GREETING	Benedictus	GREETING
READINGS &	Collect	Collect	Collect
PSALMODY		OLD TESTAMENT READING	
	EPISTLE	PSALMODY	PSALMODY
	PSALMODY	NEW TESTAMENT READING	EPISTLE
		ACCLAMATION	ACCLAMATION
	GOSPEL	GOSPEL	GOSPEL
INTERCESSIONS	Dominus vobiscum/ Oremus	Litany?	Dominus vobiscum/ Oremus
PEACE			
Liturgy of Eucharist	**Liturgy of Eucharist**	**Liturgy of Eucharist**	**Liturgy of Eucharist**
PRESENTATION OF GIFTS	PRESENTATION OF GIFTS	PRESENTATION OF GIFTS	Preparation of Table
	Chant	Procession/Chant	Chant
	Prayer over Gifts	Diptychs	Offertory Prayers
		Collect	Prayer over Gifts
		PEACE/collect	
EUCHARISTIC PRAYER	EUCHARISTIC PRAYER	EUCHARISTIC PRAYER	EUCHARISTIC PRAYER
(FRACTION)	Lord's Prayer	FRACTION	Lord's Prayer
	PEACE	Lord's Prayer	PEACE
COMMUNION	COMMUNION	Blessing	COMMUNION
	Postcommunion Collect	2 collects	Postcommunion Collect
			DISMISSAL
DISMISSAL	DISMISSAL	DISMISSAL	Blessing
COLLECTION			

in the Roman rite Pope Gregory the Great (590–604 CE) placed it immediately after the doxology and amen that conclude the eucharistic prayer.[41] Cyril of Jerusalem also describes the invitation to holy communion:

> Next the celebrant says: *What is holy for the holy*. The offerings are holy since they have received the descent of the Holy Spirit, and you are holy because you have been accounted worthy of the Holy Spirit. The holy things therefore correspond with the holy people. Then you say: *There is one holy, one Lord, Jesus Christ*. For in truth there is only one holy, in the sense of holy by nature. We are not holy by nature, but by participation, practice and prayer. (*Mystagogical Catechesis* 5.19)

The other significant Eastern innovation was the introduction of the Nicene Creed prior to the eucharistic prayer in the Byzantine tradition in the early sixth century.

Finally, we should mention one other peculiarity with regard to the structure of the eucharist. The Roman rite (along with North Africa) placed the exchange of peace following the Lord's prayer rather than between the intercessory prayers and the eucharistic prayer, as in most of the other rites. Thus at Rome the peace served as an immediate introduction to holy communion rather than the whole of the eucharistic action.

The eucharistic prayers also achieved their classic form during the three centuries following Constantine. Developments in these prayers were to affect the piety and belief of Christians for centuries, even up to the present. As with the general trends in the structural development of initiation and the eucharistic liturgy, so also the eucharistic prayers showed first some important convergences and then gradually the unfolding of different sequences in their structure. As was suggested in the previous chapter, with the exception of the anaphora in the *Apostolic Tradition* (which as far as manuscripts are concerned only goes back to a Latin translation of the late fourth century), there are no certain indications of the eucharistic institution narrative forming a part of the eucharistic prayer in the first four centuries. This can be puzzling, even troubling to Westerners, who are accustomed to thinking that the institution narrative ("On the night he was betrayed . . .") is the center from which the rest of the prayer springs, a formula of consecration enshrined in a prayer. On the other hand, research has suggested that an original core consisting of praise, thanksgiving, and petition was elaborated by three additions in the course of the fourth and fifth centuries—depending on the tradition. The three elements are the angelic hymn (Sanctus or "Holy, Holy, Holy"), the institution narrative or recital of Jesus' words and actions at the Last Supper, and finally an explicit request (epiclesis) for the Holy Spirit to sanctify the elements and the communicants.[42] These elements were added to the already existing prayers at different places, thus creating diverse theologies. The introduction of the Sanctus may well have preceded the fourth century but does not seem to have been adopted in the Roman rite until the fifth.

How did the various structures affect the development of piety and theology? An illustration: in the West Syrian or Antiochene tradition one finds a request for consecration of the gifts and various blessings upon the communicants following the memorial (including the institution narrative) part of the prayer. As can be seen in the chart, this makes for a rather logical trinitarian progression of ideas: thanks and praise centering on the Father leads to memorial of the Son and request for the sanctification wrought by the Holy Spirit. This focus comes as no surprise given the fourth century as the time of great controversy (the Councils of Nicaea and Constantinople) over the nature of the Trinity. The history of the liturgy constantly bears witness to the dialectic between belief and worship. At times theology is the engine that drives liturgical development; at times the process is reversed: piety and worship shape the development of doctrine and theology.

Other traditions, notably the Roman rite eucharistic prayer (or canon of the mass), place the request for the consecration of the gifts before the institution narrative. Cesare Giraudo has considerably advanced the study of the ancient anaphoras by dividing them into anamnetic and epicletic traditions. In the former the institution narrative comes at the end of a series of thanksgivings for what has been accomplished in Christ. In the latter, however, a request for consecration precedes the institution narrative.[43] Later theology was influenced by the very structure of the prayers. In the West the institution narrative became the focus of a consecratory moment, when the bread and wine are transformed into the body and blood of Christ. In the East that moment came at the epiclesis. To put it simply, the notion of consecration is affected by the point at which God is asked to "do something" in the prayer: before or after the institution narrative. Though there are suggestions of such a "moment of consecration" theology in some authors (Cyril of Jerusalem, Ambrose, and John Chrysostom), this notion is anachronistic in this period. What affected piety and theology most was probably not so much the structure and content of the various prayers but rather the gradual decline in the reception of the elements that led to a divorce between the eucharistic action as a whole and something "happening" during the prayer.

This decline begins already in the fourth century, betokened by the vocabulary of awe and fright that can be found in Cyril, John Chrysostom, and Theodore of Mopsuestia. Alexander Schmemann saw this as the development of a "mysteriological" piety that transformed Christian worship significantly.[44] As with the development of the *disciplina arcani* and the severity of the catechumenate in the fourth century, it should come as no surprise that preachers would warn their hearers about the seriousness of what they were about in receiving holy communion. After all they no longer had persecutions to ensure the sincerity of believers.

Let us, then, survey the various traditions of eucharistic praying as they developed by the middle of the seventh century with the help of the following chart:

Eucharistic bread. An impression from a sixth-century terra-cotta bread stamp from Tunisia bears the words "ego sum panis vivus qui de caelo descendi" ("I am the living bread that came down from heaven") from John 6:51. The words frame the image of a deer or stag that gives symbolic reference to Psalm 42:1: "As a deer longs for flowing streams, so my soul longs for you, O God." Museo della Civiltà Romana, Rome/Dagli Orti/Art Archive

EUCHARISTIC PRAYER TRADITIONS			
West Syrian	**East Syrian**	**Alexandrian**	**Roman**
Dialogue	Dialogue	Dialogue	Dialogue
Praise and Thanks	Praise and Thanks	Praise for creation	Praise and Thanks (variable)
Sanctus	Sanctus	Offering	Sanctus
Post-Sanctus (Praise and Thanks)	Thanksgiving (addressed to Christ)	Intercessions	Prayer for acceptance of offering
Institution narrative	Intercessions for the living and the dead	Sanctus	Intercession for the living
Anamnesis/Oblation	Anamnesis	1st epiclesis	Commemoration of saints
Epiclesis	Epiclesis	Institution narrative	2d prayer for acceptance
Intercessions	Doxology	Anamnesis	Prayer for consecration
Doxology	Amen	2d offering	Institution narrative
Amen		2d epiclesis	Anamnesis/Oblation
		Doxology	3d prayer for acceptance
		Amen	2d prayer for consecration
			(Intercession for the dead)
			2d commemoration of saints
			Blessing of other gifts
			Doxology
			Amen

A quick glance reveals the reasonableness of the hypothesis that what eventually came to be unified prayers were originally individual prayers that were assembled differently in the various rites. This is particularly evident in the Alexandrian tradition, where both the expression of offering and the epiclesis are repeated. As was noted in the previous chapter, *Papyrus Strasbourg Gk. 254* can be construed as a complete anaphora with expression of thanks and praise, offering, and intercession. The addition of the Sanctus to the prayer enabled it to comprise as well invocations of the Holy Spirit, the institution narrative, and a more explicit anamnesis and a second offering. A characteristic that differentiates this tradition from the West Syrian is the choice of word to connect the Sanctus with the rest of the anaphora. In the case of the Anaphora of Saint Mark, the primary representative of the Alexandrian tradition, the word is "fill," playing off "heaven and earth are full of your glory." In the West Syrian anaphoras of Saint James, Saint John Chrysostom, or Saint Basil, the word "holy" was chosen as verbal link with the hymn to the thrice-holy.

The other prayer that betrays its origins in a diversity of prayers is the Roman canon. In the chart it contains more structural elements than any of the other traditions. The intercession for the dead appears in the manuscripts only in the ninth century. A significant development in the prayer, indeed in the theology of eucharistic consecration, can be seen in the difference between the received text of the Roman canon and the fourth-century description of the prayer by Ambrose:

FIRST PRAYER FOR CONSECRATION IN THE ROMAN TRADITION	
Ambrose: *On the Sacraments* 4.21	Roman Canon
Make this offering for us approved, spiritual, pleasing; it is the figure of the body and blood of our Lord Jesus Christ.	Vouchsafe, we beseech you, O God, to make this offering wholly blessed, approved, ratified, reasonable, and acceptable; that it may become to us the body and blood of your dearly beloved Son, Jesus Christ our Lord.[45]

In the earlier prayer a kind of typology is at work, a typology in which symbol and ritual participate in the reality that they image. In the Roman canon, on the other hand, it seems that a further blessing by God is needed for the bread and wine to be consecrated; that is, a blessing beyond their symbolic participation by likeness to Christ. In the process of development a more explicit expression of consecration was considered necessary than had previously been the case.

The Roman canon was to stand virtually untouched as *the* Roman eucharistic prayer for some fourteen centuries. One factor that can account for the longevity of this prayer is the variability of its first part, the so-called "preface." The Latin *praefatio* unfortunately has received the interpretation of something that comes before, like the introduction to a book. The word, however, means "to set before in a spatial sense," in other words, "to declaim publicly." It would have stood for the entire prayer. This is all the more important since in the Roman canon the preface is the only place where thanks and praise are mentioned explicitly. The prefaces provided a specific motive for the giving of thanks and praise, the making of eucharist. For example, the fifth- through sixth-century collection of mass formulas, sometimes called the *Verona Sacramentary*, contains some 290 sets of prayers from the months of April through

December, almost all containing a preface. Such variety hearkens back to a period, before Nicaea, when a eucharistic prayer could be improvised, although surely according to an established formula and structure in each local church.

One of the more intriguing features of the Roman canon is the second prayer for consecration that follows the anamnesis/oblation and reads:

> We humbly beseech you, almighty God, bid these things be borne by the hand of your angel to your altar on high, in the sight of your divine majesty, that all of us who have received the most holy body and blood of your Son by partaking at this altar may be filled with all heavenly blessing and grace, through Christ our Lord.[46]

Edward Kilmartin has found in this prayer an example of the twofold consecration of the body and blood of Christ in the Roman eucharist.[47] Here the elements are hallowed by being lifted on high so there is a marvelous exchange (*admirabile commercium*) between heaven and earth. As we shall see below, this prayer has as its equivalent that part of the West Syrian epiclesis that invokes blessings upon the communicants.

One of the most fascinating of the ancient anaphoras is the East Syrian prayer attributed to the Apostles Addai and Mari. Some scholars think that parts of the prayer may well go back to the third century.[48] The most distinctive (and controverted) characteristic of this prayer is the fact that to the early twenty-first century it lacks an institution narrative. Opinions vary as to whether it ever had one. Certainly a related prayer, the Maronite Third Anaphora of Saint Peter, does contain the institution narrative. A further oddity of this prayer is that the part after the Sanctus is addressed not to the Father, as in most prayers, but to Christ.

We return to the West Syrian tradition for our final example of a eucharistic prayer. The Byzantine anaphora of Saint Basil has good claim to go back to Saint Basil the Great, a late-fourth-century bishop in Cappadocia. Basil was one of the prime defenders of the divinity of the Holy Spirit, was significant in the development of theological terminology with regard to the Trinity, and wrote a rule for monks, still honored in the Byzantine churches in the early twenty-first century. This text is a later recension of the Egyptian prayer attributed to the same author. Here is the text:[49]

THE ANAPHORA OF SAINT BASIL

Priest: The grace of our Lord Jesus Christ and the love of the God and Father, and the fellowship of the Holy Spirit be with you all.

People: And with your spirit.

Priest: Let us lift up our hearts.

People: We have them with the Lord.

Priest: Let us give thanks to the Lord.

People: It is fitting and right (to worship the Father, the Son, and the Holy Spirit, the consubstantial and undivided Trinity).

And the priest begins the holy anaphora: I AM, Master, Lord God, Father almighty, reverend, it is truly fitting and right and befitting the magnificence of your holiness to praise you, to hymn you, to bless you, to worship you, to give you thanks, to glorify you, the only truly existing God, and to offer to you with a contrite heart and a humble spirit this our reasonable service. For it is you who granted us the knowledge of your truth; and who is sufficient to declare your powers, to make all your praises to be heard, or to declare all your wonders at all times? Master, Master of all, Lord of heaven and earth and all Creation, visible and invisible, you sit on the throne of glory and behold the depths, without beginning, invisible, incomprehensible, infinite, unchangeable, the Father of our Lord Jesus Christ the great God and savior of our hope, who is the image of your goodness, the identical seal, manifesting you the Father in himself, living Word, true God, before all ages wisdom, life, sanctification, power, the true Light by whom the Holy Spirit was revealed, the spirit of truth, the grace of sonship, the pledge of the inheritance to come, the first fruits of eternal good things, lifegiving power, the fountain of sanctification, by whose enabling the whole rational and spiritual Creation does you service and renders you the unending doxology; for all things are your servants. For angels, archangels, thrones, dominions, principalities, powers, virtues, and the cherubim with many eyes praise you, the seraphim stand around you, each having six wings, and with two covering their own faces, and with two their feet, and with two flying, and crying one to the other with unwearying mouths and never-silent doxologies, (*aloud*) singing the triumphal hymn crying aloud and saying:

People: Holy, (holy, holy, Lord of Sabaoth; heaven and earth are full of your glory. Hosanna in the highest. Blessed is he who comes in the name of the Lord. Hosanna in the highest.)

The priest says privately: With these blessed powers, Master, lover of men, we sinners also cry and say: you are truly holy and all-holy, and there is no measure of the magnificence of your holiness, and you are holy in all your works, for in righteousness and true judgment you brought all things upon us. For you took dust from the earth and formed man; you honored him with your image, O God, and set him in the paradise of pleasure, and promised him immortality of life and enjoyment of eternal good things in keeping your commandments. But when he had disobeyed you, the true God who created him, and had been led astray by the deceit of the serpent, and had been subjected to death by his own transgressions, you, O God, expelled him in your righteous judgment from paradise into this world, and turned him back to the earth from which he was taken, dispensing to him the salvation by rebirth which is in your Christ. For you did not turn away finally from your creature, O good one, nor forget the works of your hands, but you visited him in many ways through the bowels of your mercy. You sent forth prophets; you performed works of power through your saints who were pleasing to you in every generation; you spoke to us through the mouth of your servants the prophets, foretelling to us the salvation that should come; you gave the Law for our help; you set angels as guards over us. But when the fullness of the times had come, you spoke to us in your Son himself, through whom also you made the ages, who, being the reflection of your glory and the impress of your substance, and bearing all things by the word of his power, thought it not robbery to be equal with you, the God and Father, but he who was God before the ages was seen on earth and lived among men; he was made flesh from a holy virgin and humbled himself, taking the form of a slave; he was conformed to the body of our humiliation that he might conform us to the image of his glory. For since through man sin had entered into the world, and through sin death, your only-begotten Son, who is in your bosom, O God and Father, being born of a woman, the Holy Mother of God and ever-Virgin Mary, born under the law, was pleased to condemn sin in his flesh, that those who died in Adam should be made alive in him, your Christ. And having become a citizen of this world, he gave us commandments of salvation, turned us away from the error of the idols, and brought us to the knowledge of you, the true God and Father; he gained us for himself, a peculiar people, a royal priesthood, a holy nation; and when he had cleansed us with water and sanctified us by the Holy Spirit, he gave himself as a ransom to death, by which we were held, having been sold under sin. By means of the cross he descended into hell, that he might fill all things with himself, and loosed the pains of death; he rose again on the third day, making a way to resurrection from the dead for all flesh, because it was not possible for the prince of life to be conquered by corruption, and became the firstfruits of those who had fallen asleep, the first-born from the dead, so that he might be first in all ways among all things. And ascending into the heavens, he sat down at the right hand of the majesty in the highest, and will also come to reward each man according to his works. And he left us memorials of his saving passion, these things which we have set forth according to his commandments. For when he was about to go out to his voluntary and laudable and life-giving death, in the night in which he gave himself up for the life of the world, he took bread in his holy and undefiled hands and showed it to you, the God and Father, gave thanks, blessed, sanctified, and broke it, and gave it to his holy disciples and apostles, saying, "Take, eat; this is my body, which is broken for you for the forgiveness of sins."

People: Amen.

Likewise also he took the cup of the fruit of the vine and mixed it, gave thanks, blessed, sanctified, and gave it to his holy disciples and apostles, saying, "Drink from this, all of you; this is my blood, which is shed for you and for many for the forgiveness of sins. (*People*: Amen.) Do this for my remembrance. For as often as you eat this bread and drink this cup, you proclaim my death, you confess my resurrection."

Therefore, Master, we also, remembering his saving Passion, his lifegiving cross, his three-day burial, his resurrection from the dead, his ascension into heaven, his session at your right hand, God and Father, and his glorious and fearful second coming; (*aloud*) offering you your own from your own, in all and through all,

People: We hymn you, (we bless you, we give you thanks, O Lord, and pray to you, our God.)

Therefore, Master, all-holy, we also, your sinful and unworthy servants, who have been held worthy to minister at your holy altar, not for our righteousness, for we have done nothing good upon earth, but for your mercies and compassions which you have poured out richly upon us, with confidence approach your holy altar. And having set forth the likenesses of the holy body and blood of your Christ, we pray and beseech you, O holy of holies, in the good pleasure of your bounty, that your all-Holy Spirit may come upon us and upon these gifts set forth, and bless them and sanctify and make (*he signs the holy gifts with the cross three times, saying:*) this bread the precious body of our Lord and God and Savior Jesus Christ. Amen. And this cup the precious blood of our Lord and God and Savior Jesus Christ, Amen. which is shed for the life of the world (and salvation). Amen (*thrice*).

Prayer:
Unite with one another all of us who partake of the one bread and the cup into fellowship with the one Holy Spirit; and make none of us to partake of the holy body and blood of your Christ for judgement or for condemnation, but that we may find mercy and grace with all the saints who have been well-pleasing to you from of old, forefathers, Fathers, patriarchs, prophets, apostles, preachers, evangelists, martyrs, confessors, teachers, and every righteous spirit perfected in faith; (*aloud*) especially our all-holy, immaculate, highly blessed (glorious) Lady, Mother of God and ever-Virgin Mary; (*while the diptychs are read by the deacon, the priest says the prayer:*) Saint John the (prophet,) forerunner and Baptist, (the holy and honored apostles,) this saint N. whose memorial we are keeping, and all your saints: at their entreaties, visit us, O God.

And remember all those who have fallen asleep in hope of resurrection to eternal life, and grant them rest where the light of your countenance looks upon them.

Again we pray you, Lord, remember your holy, catholic, and apostolic Church from one end of the world to the other, and grant it the peace which you purchased by the precious blood of your Christ, and establish this holy house until the consummation of the age, and grant it peace.

Remember, Lord, those who presented these gifts, and those for whom, and through whom, and on account of whom they presented them.

Remember, Lord, those who bring forth fruit and do good work in your holy churches and remember the poor. Reward them with rich and heavenly gifts. Grant them heavenly things for earthly, eternal things for temporal, incorruptible things for corruptible.

Remember, Lord, those in deserts and mountains and in dens and in caves of the earth.

Remember, Lord, those who live in virginity and piety (and self-discipline) and an honest way of life.

Remember, Lord, our most religious and faithful Emperor, whom you thought fit to rule the land: crown him with the weapon of truth, with the weapon of your good pleasure; overshadow his head in the day of war; strengthen his arm, exalt his right hand; make his empire mighty; subject to him all the barbarous people that delight in war; grant him help and peace that cannot be taken away; speak good things to his heart for your Church and all your people, that in his peace we may lead a quiet and peaceful life in all godliness and honesty.

Remember, Lord, all rule and authority, our brothers at court and all the army; preserve the good in their goodness, make the wicked good in your bounty.

Remember, Lord, the people who stand around and those who for good reason are absent, and have mercy on them and on us according to the abundance of your mercy. Fill their storehouses with all good things, preserve their marriages in peace and concord; nourish the infants, instruct the youth, strengthen the old; comfort the fainthearted, gather the scattered, bring back the wanderers and join them to your holy, catholic, and apostolic Church; set free those who are troubled by unclean spirits; sail with those that sail, journey with those that journey; defend the widows, protect the orphans, rescue the captives, heal the sick. Be mindful, O God, of those who face trial, those in the mines, in exile, in bitter slavery, in all tribulation, necessity, and affliction; of all who need your great compassion, those who love us, those who hate us, and those who commanded us, though unworthy, to pray for them.

Remember all your people, O Lord our God, and pour out upon all your rich mercy, granting to all their petitions for salvation. Be mindful yourself of those whom we have not mentioned through ignorance or forgetfulness or the number of the names; O God, you know the age and the title of each, you know every man from his mother's womb. For you, Lord, are the help of the helpless, the hope of the hopeless, the savior of the tempest-tossed, the haven of sailors, the physician of the sick: yourself be all things to all men, for you know every man and his petition, his house, and his need.

Rescue, Lord, this flock, and every city and country, from famine, plague, earthquake, flood, fire, the sword, invasion by foreigners, and civil war.

(*aloud*) Above all, remember, Lord, our Father and bishop N.: grant him to your holy churches in peace, safety, honor, health, and length of days, rightly dividing the word of your truth.

The diptychs of the living are read.

(*Deacon*: N. the all-holiest metropolitan or bishop, and him who presents these holy gifts ... and all men and women. *People*: And all men and women.)

Remember, Lord, all the orthodox episcopate who rightly divide the word of your truth.

Remember, Lord, also my unworthiness, according to the multitude of your mercies: forgive me every offence, willing and unwilling; and do not keep back, on account of my sins, the grace of your Holy Spirit from the gifts set forth.

Remember, Lord, the priesthood, the diaconate in Christ, and every order of the clergy, and do not put to shame any of us who stand round your holy altar.

Look upon us, Lord, in your goodness; appear to us in your rich mercies; grant us temperate and favorable weather; give kindly showers to the land for bearing fruit; bless the crown of the year of your goodness, Lord. End the divisions of the churches; quench the ragings of the nations, quickly destroy the uprising of heresies by the power of your Holy Spirit. Receive us all into your kingdom, making us sons of light and sons of the day; grant us your peace and your love, Lord our God, for you have given us all things; (*aloud*) and grant us with one mouth and one heart to glorify and hymn your all-honourable and magnificent name, the Father and the Son and the Holy Spirit, now , and always and to the ages of ages.

People: Amen.

This prayer has a similar structure to the anaphoras of the *Apostolic Constitutions* Book 8, Saint John Chrysostom, and Saint James. It is also very much like the prayer found in the *Apostolic Tradition*, quoted in the previous chapter, with the exception of the Sanctus and the intercessions. Prayers in this West Syrian tradition move from praise and thanksgiving to the hymn of the thrice-holy and on to a passage connecting the Sanctus to the institution narrative. The recital of the Last Supper narrative is followed by a memorial of God's acts in Christ together with a formula of offering. Then comes the invocation of the Holy Spirit upon the gifts and the communicants and finally the intercessions. The section of the prayer beginning with the epiclesis is the first time that God is actually asked to do something and therefore, following Giraudo's terminology, we can call it an anamnetic prayer.

The first part of the prayer is an exuberant paean of praise to God, especially for the revelation given in Christ. Christ himself is described with attributes drawn mainly from the Bible, for example, firstfruits of the eternal good things (Paul) and living word (John). The transition to the Sanctus enables the assembled to join the whole creation in praising God. As was noted above, the word "holy" connects the Sanctus with the rest of the prayer. In Byzantine Basil the post-Sanctus consists of a lengthy recital of the history of salvation: creation, fall, the prophets, the incarnation, the teaching of Christ, and redemption. The institution narrative caps this retelling of salvation, leading to a further recapitulation (technically the anamnesis of the prayer) and a formula of offering back to God what is after all God's own in the first place.

The invocation of God's Holy Spirit upon the offerers and upon the gifts initiates the part of the prayer where God is asked to do something. We have already seen this dynamic in the prayers of the ante-Nicene era; it is a dynamic of remembrance and petition, reminiscent of the psalms of Israel. First, God is praised and thanked for what has been done, and then because of confidence in God's goodness in the past, a request that God act in a similar way is made in the present. Though the formula need not be read as pointing to a "moment of consecration," the prayer at this point makes it very clear that the gifts are to be transformed into the body and blood of Christ by the Holy Spirit.

The prayer proceeds to ask for communion both with the Holy Spirit and with one another, leading into a quite lengthy series of intercessions for practically every conceivable category of people, beginning with the saints and the dead. Little wonder that the much shorter Anaphora of Saint John Chrysostom eventually supplanted Basil as the usual eucharistic prayer in the Byzantine rite. This anaphora ends, as all do, with a doxology and the affirming "amen" of the people.

The eucharistic prayer in the West Syrian tradition proceeds with a logic that has made it attractive to modern liturgical reform. It runs smoothly from praise and thanks to memory, offering, petition, and intercession. Basil and prayers like it represent a classic stage in the development of Christian prayer.

Some of the important theological themes that were developed in the period after Constantine have been alluded to above. The sense that the eucharist unified believers not only with Christ but with one another was a most important element of piety [see color plate 4]. At the risk of painting too rosy a picture, one can argue that the period between Constantine and the rise of Islam witnessed an admirable balance among the significant elements of eucharistic piety and theology: the unity of believers, the presence of Christ in the elements of communion, entering into Christ's sacrifice by means of the celebration, and even issues of justice and charity for the poor. All of these are evident in the preaching of people like Ambrose, Augustine, and John Chrysostom. But toward the end of the period in the early seventh century, one of the last patristic writers, Isidore of Seville (martyred 636), could mistakenly interpret the etymology of *eucharistia* (thanksgiving) as *bona gratia* (good grace). Isidore reveals how objectified the notion eucharist had become. When communion was no longer a logical conclusion to the eucharistic action, it was easier to distinguish the sacred food from the action. This was a process that began, somewhat ironically, with the widespread acceptance of Christianity in the fourth century. One can say that success ruined the integral understanding of eucharist as the repeatable conclusion of the rites of initiation. The popularity of Christianity made it necessary to emphasize the importance of Christian rituals, the fact that they could not be taken lightly. This "mysteriological piety" in turn discouraged the frequent reception of holy communion, which in turn helped to separate the liturgical action from the elements of bread and wine. Medieval theology would reap the consequences of this development. At the same time it became difficult to hold together the understanding of symbolic reality that undergirded so much of this period's preaching about the eucharist. Once again, this was a process that was to bear bitter fruit much later, in the eleventh-century disputes between Berengar of Tours and Lanfranc of Bec, among others.

Our consideration of the eucharist concludes with a feature of the Roman rite that serves to illustrate how the celebration could manifest the unity of the church in time and space. The letter of Innocent I, which was referred to above, describes a rite that takes place after the fraction of the consecrated bread:

> Concerning the fermentum, which we send to the titular churches on Sundays, it is needless for you to ask, for all our churches are set up within the city. As to the presbyters who are not able to join with us [in the main eucharist] on Sundays because of the people they serve, these receive the fermentum made by us from the acolytes, so they may not consider themselves separated from our communion, especially on Sundays. This practice ought not be observed in the outlying churches nor in the cemeterial churches, for we have assigned presbyters there who have the right to confect the sacrament (which in the first place should not be carried too far).[50]

Innocent's letter is a response to an Umbrian bishop's questions about liturgical practices. The rite of *fermentum* consists in sending particles of the broken consecrated bread to presbyters at churches within the city walls. They would in turn place the particle into the chalice of consecrated wine before holy communion. The symbolism is clear—there is (ideally) only one eucharist that takes place in the city on a given Sunday. All of the churches participate in this one celebration of the sacrament of unity. A later source (the *Ordo Romanus Primus*, c. 750) describes the bishop of Rome dropping a piece of bread consecrated at his most recent liturgy into the chalice during his own celebration. This was referred to as the *sancta*. Thus we can observe a very tangible sense of how the eucharist communicated continuity and unity in the post-Constantinian Christian world.

Patterns of Daily Prayer

The post-Constantinian period witnessed the first full-blown descriptions of public services of daily prayer among the early Christians. We know certainly that Christians prayed together (and alone) at set times during the day in the first three centuries, but we know very little of what that prayer consisted in or how it was conducted. With the public acceptance of Christianity throughout the Roman Empire, however, we begin to find examples of prayer services held in the churches. Anton Baumstark conveniently distinguished between two kinds of daily prayer, which he called the cathedral office and the monastic office.[51] This distinction describes not so much any single office as it does styles of prayer that come from diverse contexts. Gregory Dix thought the offices of daily prayer grew out of the monastic movement in the early fourth century.[52] Thereby he perpetuated the notion that such prayer is originally monastic in its genius and only gradually was adapted in the rest of the churches. Baumstark's distinction helps one understand that there are two rather different origins to the practice of daily prayer at set hours. What he called the cathedral office was characterized by:

- use of selective psalms
- attention to the time of day
- ceremonial: lights and incense
- observance of ecclesiastical ranks
- emphasis on intercessory prayer

The aim of this kind of office was clearly to praise God publicly and in a way that enabled the participation of large numbers of diverse people. Thus (in an era when books were scarce indeed) a popular form of psalmody was responsorial. It consisted in soloists (or a chorus) singing the verses of a psalm while the congregation sang an easily memorized refrain. This is also the genius of litanies that have a repeated prayer like "Lord, have mercy" as a response to any number of petitions. Thus one modern author calls this style "the people's office."[53] It was also a form of prayer that had an appeal to the senses through the use of incense, lights, and processions.

The other style of prayer Baumstark termed the monastic office. It was characterized by:

- psalms read in numerical order
- little ceremony
- little emphasis on ecclesiastical rank
- readings from scripture for meditation

Monasticism, it must be remarked, was originally a movement of laypersons who left the cities to live as hermits or in communities with little or no emphasis on the ecclesiastical structures of the churches. The aim of their prayer was constancy in contemplation, complete absorption in God. Thus we have two very different approaches to daily public prayer: one that is truly public and the other that happens to be done in common.[54] But these two styles did not stay distinct for long. They mixed to become hybrid offices, both in the monasteries and in the cities.

Once again one of the most accessible sources for the origins of public daily prayer is the fourth-century pilgrim Egeria. Egeria describes the daily services of prayer in Jerusalem and other places of pilgrimage in the eastern Mediterranean. She gives a particularly full picture of the round of services at Golgotha and the Holy Sepulchre. There are five daily services, which take place in the Anastasis rotunda:

Cockcrow	-	Hymns, psalms, antiphons, prayers
Dawn	-	Morning hymns with the bishop
Sixth hour	-	Psalms and antiphons with the bishop
Ninth hour	-	Psalms and antiphons with the bishop
Tenth hour	-	*Luchnikon* (Lamplighting)—Psalms and antiphons
		Arrival of bishop, prayers, litanies, processions to Golgotha and the Martyrium church.

Of the services Egeria narrates, the most important for the subsequent history of the liturgy is a special vigil of the resurrection that takes place on Sunday mornings. Here is her description (24.8–11):

Ruins of the Church of Saint Simeon near Aleppo, Syria. The centerpiece of the courtyard that was surrounded by four basilicas in cruciform arrangement was the pillar upon which the hermit Simeon lived, prayed, and preached for thirty-six or thirty-seven years. The fifth-century church became known as Qal'at Sim'ân ("the mansion of Simeon") and was for a time a destination for pilgrims. Only the base of the column remains at the site. PHOTOGRAPH BY CHRIS RENNIE/ART DIRECTORS AND TRIP

But on the seventh day, the Lord's Day, there gather in the courtyard before cock-crow all the people, as many as can get in, as if it was Easter. The courtyard is the "basilica" beside the Anastasis, that is to say, out of doors, and lamps have been hung there for them. Those who are afraid they may not arrive in time for cock-crow come early, and sit waiting there singing hymns and antiphons, and they have prayers between, since there are always presbyters and deacons there ready for the vigil, because so many people collect there, and it is not usual to open the holy places before cock-crow.

Soon the first cock-crows, and at that the bishop enters, and goes into the cave in the Anastasis. The doors are all opened, and all the people come into the Anastasis, which is already ablaze with lamps. When they are inside, a psalm is said by one of the presbyters, with everyone responding, and it is followed by a prayer; then a psalm is said by one of the deacons, and another prayer; then a third psalm is said by one of the clergy, a third prayer, and the commemoration of all. After these three psalms and prayers they take censers into the cave of the Anastasis, so that the whole Anastasis basilica is filled with the smell. Then the bishop, standing inside the screen, takes the Gospel book and goes to the door, where he himself reads the account of the Lord's resurrection. At the beginning of the reading the whole assembly groans and laments at all the Lord underwent for us, and the way they weep would move even the hardest hearts to tears. When the Gospel is finished, the bishop comes out, and is taken with singing to the Cross, and they all go with him. They have one psalm there and a prayer, then he blesses the people, and that is the dismissal. As the bishop goes out, everyone comes to kiss his hand.

This service has been called a "cathedral vigil." In Baumstark's categories the cathedral elements are fairly obvious: ecclesiastical order, responsorial psalmody, processions, and the use of lights and incense. But the service also seems to take the place of the daily monastic vigil at cockcrow and is the only service of daily prayer at Jerusalem that contains a reading. The service lives on in the Byzantine "all-night vigil," which combines vespers and a resurrection vigil and is celebrated every Saturday evening.

There are several specific elements that can be identified as part of the content of the cathedral style of prayer. The characteristic psalms of morning and evening prayer respectively are Psalm 63 and Psalm 141. Each of these psalms contains a verse that makes it appropriate to the time of day:

Psalm 63:5–6   My soul is satisfied as with a rich feast,
        and my mouth praises you with joyful lips
when I think of you on my bed,
        and meditate on you in the
watches of the night.

Psalm 141:2   Let my prayer be counted as
        incense before you,
and the lifting up of my hands
        as an evening sacrifice.

In addition we can be fairly sure that the canticle "Glory to God in the Highest" (adapted from Luke 2) was employed in morning prayer and that an ancient hymn "O Radiant Light" (*Phôs hilaron*) was used in the evening. There is some controversy with regard to whether the last three psalms of the psalter (148–150), the so-called "lauds psalms," originally concluded a recital of the entire psalter by the monks every night or served as the normal conclusion of cathedral morning prayer. After a careful review of the evidence, Taft concludes that the native soil of these psalms in the office is cathedral morning prayer.[55]

Daily liturgical prayer was not originally the preserve of monks and nuns as though popular or "cathedral" forms were an afterthought or adaptation that came later. This certainly was an image that lasted for centuries among Christians—the office was for specialists. But this was simply not the case in the churches of the fourth and fifth centuries, as Egeria quite clearly witnesses.

Robert Taft has concluded that both the cathedral and monastic traditions of praying had a daily *horarium* in common. Both types prayed in the morning and in the evening, with the monks rising to pray at cockcrow and the cathedral tradition beginning at dawn.[56] The early monks and nuns, however, did develop distinctive forms of prayer that were to be influential in the history of the daily office. There were actually two liturgical traditions in early Egyptian monasticism: the eremitic tradition of Scete in northern Egypt and the cenobitic tradition of the Pachomians in the South. Following John Cassian, who as a young monk lived in Egypt in the last two decades of the fourth century, Taft outlines the daily office among the hermits, which was done in common on Saturday and Sunday, as follows. Twelve psalms would be recited by a soloist or soloists according to the course of the psalter (1, 2, 3 . . .). After each psalm, the seated monks stand and pray silently with arms extended, they prostrate themselves and then stand again and pray silently. The leader concludes each of these units with a collect. The twelfth psalm is an alleluia psalm, and the doxology, "Glory to the Father . . . ," concludes the psalmody. There follow two readings from the Bible. On weekdays one of these is taken from the Old Testament.[57] The cenobitic form of prayer took place daily at cockcrow and in the evening and most probably consisted of six passages of scripture that were read aloud as the monks continued weaving baskets and mats.[58] The genius of daily liturgical prayer in the monastic tradition had to do more with contemplation than with praise.

As we have already seen with regard to Jerusalem, the two styles of liturgy quickly began to cross-fertilize. Toward the end of this period, in the *Rule of Saint Benedict*, c. 540, the most influential monastic rule in the West, one finds a hybrid office that combined features of the office of the city of Rome and monastic traditions that can be found in *The Rule of the Master*, Benedict's early-fifth-century predecessor, and earlier sources. Robert Taft argues that Benedict followed the Roman usage when it came to psalmody but the Master when it came to other elements in the hours. Not unlike what one sees in the construction of eucharistic prayers, the office consisted of elements from different sources that were patched together more or less elegantly. This is also true of the offices themselves. The first office of the day in the cathedral style was morning prayer (later commonly called lauds). The first office of the day in the monastic style was vigils (later called matins). The hybrid offices contained both vigils and morning prayer, with the eventual addition of a short office called "prime" for good measure. Archbishop Cranmer was to recombine matins and lauds in the sixteenth-century English offices, just as he was to combine evening prayer (vespers) with compline, bedtime prayer.

There are eight daily offices in the *Rule of Benedict*. They are:

vigils (matins)
lauds
prime
terce
sext
none
vespers
compline

The four middle hours are often referred to as the "Little Hours" and are performed throughout the daily regimen. These hours tend to add the psalms that are not distributed among the major hours in an effort to sing all 150 psalms in the course of a week—the monastic ideal.

What can be gleaned from this evidence? In the first place, each of these offices bears out the fact that cathedral and monastic elements have been mixed. There are a number of elements that suggest an origin in the cathedral type of office:

- the use of fixed psalms (matins—3, 95; lauds—67, 51, 148–150)
- the use of fixed canticles (matins—Te Deum, Te decet laus; lauds—Benedictus; vespers—Magnificat)
- metric hymns (ecclesiastical compositions)
- litanies

**STRUCTURE OF THE OFFICES OF MATINS, LAUDS, AND VESPERS
IN THE *RULE OF SAINT BENEDICT*[39]**

Matins (Sundays/Feasts)
O Lord, open . . . (3 times)
Psalm 3
Psalm 95 with antiphon
Hymn
1st nocturn
6 psalms with antiphons
Versicle
Blessing
4 readings with responsory
Gloria
2nd nocturn
6 psalms and antiphons
Versicle
4 readings with responsory
Gloria
3rd nocturn
3 Old Testament canticles and alleluia
Versicle
Blessing
4 readings with responsory
Te Deum
Gospel of the day
Te decet laus
Blessing

Lauds
Psalm 67 (solo)
Psalm 51
2 (variable) psalms
Canticle
Psalms 148–150
Apostle reading
Responsory
Hymn
Versicle
Benedictus
Litany
Lord's prayer (*aloud by superior*)

Vespers
4 consecutive psalms (110, 111, . . .)
Apostle reading
Responsory
Hymn
Versicle
Magnificat
Litany
Lord's prayer (*aloud by superior*)

On the other hand, monastic origins are suggested by the use of continuous psalmody, especially at vespers, and the preponderance of readings. On this basis, of the three offices, lauds is clearly the most "cathedral" in inspiration; that is, it has the most elements that can be memorized easily. Of course it should be remembered that in these centuries we are far from the invention of the printing press. Therefore books were very scarce, and most of the office had to be done by memorization in any case. We presume, however, that the monks, being professionals, were able to memorize more than lay folk.

We mentioned earlier that a popular misconception holds to a purely monastic origin for the daily office. Toward the end of this period, the mid-seventh century, as Latin was less and less known and as the monasteries became more clerical, the cathedral office did become the preserve of monks and clergy, but the daily office itself had origins as well in popular parochial practice, as we have seen.

The Calendar

One of the most fascinating and complex developments in the centuries after Constantine was the creation of the Christian calendar, roughly as it is still known in the early twenty-first century. To be sure the origins of the celebration of Christmas and Epiphany, Easter and the days devoted to the saints can be found in the first three centuries, as the previous chapter has demonstrated. Gregory Dix hypothesized that the original eschatological expectation that characterized the Christian attitude toward time was transformed after Constantine into a more domesticated acceptance of history and therefore of historical anniversaries in the calendar. After the work of Thomas Talley and Robert Taft, this hypothesis no longer holds. The development is far more complex. Eschatology and history go hand in hand even in the first three centuries. The shift from the third to the fourth centuries was not as radical as Dix had supposed.[60] On the other hand, there is an unmistakable connection between the development of the calendar and the possession of property that became more possible in the fourth century.

The first known Christian calendar is in an almanac of civic and religious feasts together with lists of bishops and consuls. The so-called Chronograph of 354 was a manuscript dedicated by Furius Dionysius Philocalus, a Roman calligrapher, to Valentinus, a wealthy Christian aristocrat.[61] One of the lists is called a *depositio martyrum*, or list of martyrs' burials. The early Christians celebrated the dead on their dates of death rather than birth. As it was customary for family members to

Saint Lawrence and the gospel cupboard. The mosaic lunette in the fifth-century mausoleum of Galla Placidia in Ravenna, Italy, portrays the martyr Lawrence carrying an open book and a cross of triumph while proceeding quickly toward the instrument of his own death. The open cupboard on the opposite side reveals four books inscribed with the names of the four evangelists. SCALA/ART RESOURCE, NY

gather at the tombs of their loved ones on their birthdays once a year, so also the Christians gathered not only at the tombs of their traditional families but at those of the great representatives of their larger family, the martyrs of the church, on their true birthdays—the days they entered eternal life. As the families of non-Christians had feasts (*refrigeria*), so did the Christians combine a meal with their signal feast, the eucharist.

There are twenty-four days marked in the martyr list of the calendar of 354. Most are for local Roman saints, accompanied by the cemetery in which they were buried. One of the most significant features of the early calendars is their localized nature. In general, a eucharistic celebration was (originally) held on a feast of a martyr only where the body was buried, that is, near his or her relics. It is difficult to overstate the significance of relics for late antiquity and indeed for the Middle Ages. As Peter Brown has written, they were like an X-ray of social relations in Europe.[62] There were some feasts, however, that were popular enough to be celebrated without relics. The early Roman calendar lists two such feasts, both of North African martyrs: Perpetua and Felicity (7 March) and Cyprian (14 September).[63] The list of martyrs is headed by a curious item:

> [25 December] VIII Kalends of January—Christ born in Bethlehem of Judea.

This is the first certain mention we have of the celebration of the nativity of Jesus Christ on 25 December. In the list of civic feasts the same day is called the *Natalis Solis Invicti* (Birthday of the Unconquered Sun), a winter-solstice feast that had been introduced under Emperor Aurelian in the year 274. Finally, the martyr list has another feast that is not strictly speaking the anniversary of a death; 22 February is called the *Natale Petri de Catedra* or the "Birthday of Peter at the Chair." In the early twenty-first century this is a feast on the Roman Catholic calendar that commemorates Peter's episcopacy in Rome, but originally 22 February was a Roman festival of the dead, called the *Cara Cognatio*, at which an empty chair was left at the head of the table for the deceased paterfamilias. Since the Apostle Peter was considered the deceased paterfamilias of the Roman church, this feast of the dead honored him.

Another illustrative and significant calendar from this period is the so-called Old Armenian Lectionary. This calendar, which consists of feasts, dates, indications of readings, places of celebration (stations), and some rubrics, reflects the life of the church at Jerusalem in the late fourth century and early fifth century.[64] Epiphany (6 January) marks the beginning of the annual liturgical cycle. It begins with a night vigil eucharist at the Constantinian basilica in Bethlehem and continues the next day at the Martyrium in Jerusalem. The feast is an octave, with the eucharist celebrated by the bishop in a different church for eight days:

> 2d Day   Martyrium of Saint Stephen
> 3d Day   Martyrium (Jerusalem)
> 4th Day Sion
> 5th Day Eleona (Mount of Olives)
> 6th Day Lazarium (in Bethany)
> 7th Day Golgotha
> 8th Day Anastasis

The Jerusalem church was slow to accept the Western celebration of the nativity on 25 December. Its Epiphany feast was originally a nativity feast, as the readings from the Armenian Lectionary bear out. Thomas Talley has pointed out that the feast celebrating the Incarnation was in the fourth century the starting point of the liturgical cycle of readings. The church's primary gospel (in this case Matthew) was begun on the feast.

Three feasts in the course of a Jerusalem year have octaves: Epiphany, Easter, and the Dedication of the Holy Places (13 September). Epiphany also has a series of twelve readings for its vigil. Four of them are also read at Easter.

The monthly calendar is interrupted at the end of March by the insertion of readings for the catechumenate and for noneucharistic liturgical services on the weekdays of Lent. Analysis of the Lenten series of readings has suggested that the earliest Lent at Jerusalem may have lasted for three weeks like the original Lent at Rome.[65] As in the pilgrimage diary of Egeria, a complex series of services for Holy (Great) Week is described in the Armenian Lectionary. On the Saturday before Palm Sunday there is a procession out to Bethany, where Lazarus was raised. Palm Sunday includes a morning eucharist at the Martyrium and a long afternoon service, including a procession with palms down the Mount of Olives. Monday, Tuesday, and Wednesday all have special afternoon services. Thursday is called "Thursday in the Old Passover" and includes a triple celebration of the eucharist, at the Martyrium, Golgotha, and Sion, as well as an all-night vigil culminating in a procession down the Mount of Olives to the Holy Sepulchre. On Good Friday morning the wood of the cross is venerated in the small chapel behind Golgotha. Egeria has given a charming description (37.1–2):

> The bishop's chair is placed on Golgotha Behind the Cross (the cross there now), and he takes his seat. A table is placed before him with a cloth on it, the deacons stand round, and there is brought to him a gold and silver box containing the holy Wood of the Cross. It is opened, and the Wood of the Cross and the Title are taken out and placed on the table.
>
> As long as the holy Wood is on the table, the bishop sits with his hands resting on either end of it and holds it down, and the deacons round him keep watch over it. They guard it like this because what happens now is that all the people, catechumens as well as faithful, come up one by one to the table. They stoop down over it, kiss the Wood, and move on.

Starting at midday there is a series of psalms, readings from scripture, and prayers for three hours in the courtyard between the Martyrium basilica and the Holy Sepulchre. Among the readings are Old Testament prophecies and New Testament passages related to Christ's passion as well as all four Gospel passion narratives. The reading service ends at the ninth hour (midafternoon) and is followed immediately by a short prayer service in the Anastasis commemorating Jesus' burial.

The next day, Saturday, marks the great vigil of Easter. Here is what the Armenian Lectionary says:

> On Saturday evening in the holy Easter the bishop sings this psalm (Ps. 114, antiphon v. 2) in the holy Anastasis. At the same hour they ascend to the Martyrium and the bishop lights a candle; at once the clergy begin the Vigil of holy Easter, and twelve lessons are read. At each lesson there is prayer with kneeling.

The lessons are:

1. Genesis 1:1–3:24	Creation
2. Genesis 22:1–18	Abraham and Isaac
3. Exodus 12:1–24	Passover Meal
4. Jonah 1:1–4:11	Jonah
5. Exodus 14:24–15:21	Crossing of the Red Sea
6. Isaiah 60:1–13	Arise, shine for your light has come
7. Job 38:1–28	God out of the Whirlwind

8. 2 Kings 2:1–22   Ascension of Elijah
9. Jeremiah 31:31–34   New Covenant
10. Joshua 1:1–9   Crossing Jordan
11. Ezekiel 37:1–14   Dry Bones
12. Daniel 3:1–90   Song of the Three Children

And while the hymn is said, at midnight, the throng of the newly baptized enters with the bishop. Readings: Psalm 66 (antiphon v.1); 1 Cor. 15:1–11; Matthew 28:1–20. At the same hour the Offering (= Eucharist) is made.

After the dismissal at the same hour of the night the Offering is made at the Anastasis before Golgotha.[66]

Although it is dangerous to generalize from one liturgy to all others, one can get some idea of how one very influential Easter vigil was celebrated in the early fifth century. First of all the vigil begins just as a normal vespers would with the lighting of lamps (and, one can guess, the hymn *Phôs hilaron* and accompanying psalmody). Then the vigil readings are done with prayers and psalms. These clearly are meant to be performed while the bishop and others are baptizing in the baptistery. Egeria comments that the Jerusalem vigil differs from her own in northwest Spain because the baptismal party detours through the Anastasis on the way back to the basilica. Evidence from medieval Constantinople suggests that the readings went on in the basilica as long as the baptisms did.

Thomas Talley has noted the similarity between the Jerusalem vigil readings and a Palestinian Targum on Exodus, "The Poem of the Four Nights," already mentioned in the previous chapter with regard to Quartodeciman practice. The four nights in this Targum are: creation, the binding of Isaac, the Passover, and the final redemption. Talley points out that the first three readings in the Jerusalem scheme are precisely the first three nights, while the last nine readings can easily be interpreted as the night of final redemption.[67]

The readings for the eucharist are 1 Corinthians 15 (the resurrection of the body) and Matthew 28 (the finding of the empty tomb). Talley has also pointed out that Matthew is the base gospel at Jerusalem. He has shown that each church in antiquity developed its lectionary from one of the four gospels and that one can discern later strata in the use of other gospels. Matthew is clearly the gospel of choice in the Armenian Lectionary. It even ousts the Lukan infancy gospel when it comes to the celebration of Epiphany.

The stational churches and reading for the octave of Easter reveal just how intimately connected

The tomb of the crucified Jesus. Located in the Church of the Holy Sepulchre in Jerusalem, the long-recognized place of Jesus' burial has been a site for pilgrimage and devotion. In the fourth century, the pilgrim Egeria referred to the building surrounding the tomb as the "Anastasis" or place of resurrection. The tomb is now enclosed in an edicule constructed in the early nineteenth century after the fire of 1808 had damaged the eleventh-century edifice that had itself replaced the original monument destroyed by Hakin in 1009. Lithograph by Louis Haghe from a drawing by David Roberts (1796–1864). NEW YORK PUBLIC LIBRARY

locations and the liturgical lessons are in the imagination of late antiquity. Here they are:

EASTER OCTAVE IN THE OLD ARMENIAN LECTIONARY				
Day	**Church**	**1st Reading**	**2nd Reading**	**Gospel**
Sunday	Martyrium	Acts 1:1–14		Mark 15:42–16:1
Monday	Martyrium	Acts 2:22–41		Luke 23:50–24:12
Tuesday	Saint Stephen's	Acts 2:42–3:21		Luke 24:13–35
Wednesday	Sion	Acts 3:22–4:12	James 1:1–12	Luke 24:36–40
Thursday	Eleona	Acts 4:13–31	James 1:13–27	Matthew 5:1–12
Friday	Before Golgotha	Acts 4:32–5:11	James 2:1–13	John 21:1–14
Saturday	Anastasis	Acts 5:12–33	James 2:14–26	John 21:15–25
Sunday	Martyrium	Acts 5:34–6:7	James 3:1–13	John 1:1–17

The first noteworthy element is that Egeria had reported (some fifty years before the Armenian Lectionary) that the stational church used for Tuesday was the Martyrium. The shrine of Saint Stephen was built only after his relics had been discovered in 415. It is clear that Easter marks the beginning of the reading of the Acts of the Apostles—a feature common in the early lectionaries—as if to say, "This is what happens when people respond to the Risen Lord Jesus." In addition, there are two features of this octave that show the connection between place and celebration. The first is the reading of the letter of James that begins on Wednesday at Sion, traditionally the earliest church center in the city. The name James is particularly associated with the Jerusalem church, for James was considered its first bishop. Therefore the holiest days of the year are associated with this community's own unique history. Similarly, the gospel reading for Thursday at the Eleona (or Mount of Olives basilica) is the Matthean version of the Beatitudes, presumably chosen because Jesus gave this sermon on the "mount."

The fifth-century lectionary for Jerusalem also reveals a number of different kinds of celebration, all of which have heirs in the medieval church. The earliest and most traditional of the commemorations were those of the martyrs, like Stephen (27 December) or the Forty Soldier-Martyrs of Sebaste (9 March). For the first time one sees a church's bishops commemorated on its calendar (Cyril, 18 March; John, 29 March) as well as a figure renowned for his holiness (Antony the Hermit, 17 January). Emperors too are remembered in the calendar (Theodosius, 19 January; Constantine, 22 May). Surely this is a sign that the empire has been "baptized." Old Testament prophets and other figures, whom it would be natural to remember in Jerusalem, are on the list as well: Jeremiah, 1 May; Isaiah, 6 July; Elisha, 14 June; David, 25 December. There are a number of commemorations of the apostles: Thomas, 23 August; Philip, 15 November; Andrew, 30 November; Peter and Paul, 28 December; James and John, 29 December. We have already mentioned the feast of the dedication of the holy places, 13 September, which had an octave. Such days, like that of the dedication of a church to Mary, mother of Jesus, as a feast of the Theotokos (Mother of God) on 15 August, were subsequently to become important feasts. The second day of the 13 September octave was the occasion of the showing of the relic of the cross of Jesus. It eventually became the feast of the Triumph of the Cross. The 15 August feast took place at a church dedicated to Mary at the "Second Mile from Bethlehem." The church marked the spot where Mary rested (according to the apocryphal Protoevangelion of James) on her way to giving birth to Jesus. The readings in the Armenian Lectionary are clearly geared to Mary as mother (Isa. 7:10–15; Gal. 3:29–4:7; Luke 2:1–7). But the Greek for rest (*koimêsis*) means the "rest" of death as well, and so the date eventually commemorated Mary's death (and in some traditions her bodily assumption into heaven).

Other important dedication feasts also originated in Jerusalem. A church in honor of Saint Anne, mother of Mary, was dedicated in the fifth century. Tradition held that it was the place of Mary's birth, and so this dedication became the feast of the Nativity of Mary (8 September). In 543 Emperor Justinian had a church dedicated to Mary. It was located near the ruins of the Jewish Temple. Called New Saint Mary's, its dedication date on 21 November became a very important Byzantine feast, the Presentation of Mary in the Temple, once again based on an apocryphal legend from the Protoevangelion of James, which reports that Mary was sent to live in the Temple from the age of three.

What we have seen in the calendar of the Armenian Lectionary is a good example of how feasts and commemorations evolved throughout this period. A Christian reshaping of time and space enabled people throughout the empire to orient themselves to a new religious imagination, one that was very much geared to each particular culture, its martyrs and local history, as well as the broader drama of Christian salvation.

Let us shift our attention back to the Roman church, this time to the end of the sixth century. A listing of epistles and stational churches is found in MS Würzburg Codex 62. The same codex contains a very similar, but slightly later, gospel list noting the stational churches. We shall focus here on two parts of the liturgical calendar: the celebration of Christmas and the character of Lent. The Roman Christmas liturgy in the late sixth century can be analyzed on the basis of the following chart:

CHRISTMAS, ROME, SIXTH CENTURY				
Celebration	**Station**	**1st Reading**	**2nd Reading**	**Gospel**
Vigil	Saint Mary Major	———	Romans 1:1–6	Matthew 1:18–21
1st mass	Saint Mary Major	Isaiah 9:2–6	Titus 2:11–15	Luke 2:1–14
2nd mass	Saint Anastasia	Isaiah 61:1–3; 62:11–12	Titus 3:4–7	Luke 2:15–20
3rd mass	Saint Peter's	Isaiah 52:6–10	Hebrews 1:1–12	John 1:1–14

In the fourth and fifth centuries the stational church for the major liturgy of the day was Saint Peter's on the Vatican Hill. We know that Pope Leo the Great (440–461) preached there on Christmas morning.

> From such a system of teaching proceeds also the ungodly practice of certain foolish folk who worship the sun as it rises at the beginning of daylight from elevated positions: even some Christians think it is so proper to do this that, before entering the blessed Apostle Peter's basilica, which is dedicated to the One living and true God, when they have mounted the steps which lead to the raised platform, they turn round and bow themselves towards the rising sun and with bent neck do homage to its brilliant orb. We are full of grief and vexation that this should happen, which is partly due to the fault of ignorance and partly to the spirit of heathenism: because although some of them do perhaps worship the Creator of that fair light rather than the Light itself, which is His creature, yet we must abstain even from the appearance of this observance: for if one who has abandoned the worship of gods finds it in our own worship, will he not hark back again to this fragment of his old superstition, as if it were allowable, when he sees it to be common both to Christians and to infidels?[68]

Whether or not Christmas originated in response to the Roman civic feast of the Unconquered Sun, some Christians were clearly hedging their bets by reverencing the sun rising over the city on the date of the old winter solstice. Saint Peter's was the perfect location for this practice since it looked out over the city from the West. The gospel reading at this original celebration, the prologue to John's Gospel, suggests that originally this feast was a unitive celebration, focusing on the Incarnation as a whole rather than exclusively on the nativity of Christ. The presence of two readings before the gospel also suggests earlier practice; that is, before the insertions at the "soft points" of the liturgy began to shift the weight of celebration from the original core.

The second liturgy was added to the Roman celebration sometime after the Council of Ephesus (431) with its affirmation of Mary as Theotokos, Mother of God, and the subsequent dedication of a basilica in her honor in the city of Rome: Saint Mary Major. There the relic of the crib of Bethlehem was kept in a chapel, and the church served as the site of celebration during the night. What has become the traditional Christmas gospel reading, the Lucan account of Jesus' birth, was read at this celebration.

A final liturgy, at dawn in the church of Saint Anastasia, appeared in the sixth century. Anastasia was a martyr in the persecution of Diocletian (304) whose cult was observed in Constantinople on 25 December. In the sixth century, with the Byzantine conquest of the city of Rome, the basilica of Anastasia at the foot of the Palatine Hill became a kind of chapel for the imperial court. This liturgy was most probably added out of respect for the Byzantine rulers. The gospel is a continuation of the Lucan infancy narrative, and therefore the liturgy became referred to as the "Mass of the Shepherds."[69]

The feast of the Epiphany, which originated in the East and was adopted in Rome toward the end of the fourth century, focused on the visit of the Magi in Matthew's Gospel. It is probable that the baptism of Christ, the original focus of this Incarnation feast in some Eastern churches, was not accepted at Rome because of the trinitarian and christological questions concerning the person of Christ that arose precisely at this time. Too much attention on the baptism of Jesus might lend credibility to a more adoptionist version of christology.

The basic lines of the Roman Lent are also evident in the Würzburg epistle list and gospel list and suggest the formation of this enormously complex system sometime in the late fifth century.[70] The Roman Lent begins on Ash Wednesday and continues for six weeks (with forty fast days) until Easter. The forty-day Lent most probably began at Rome as a continuous preparation for Easter sometime in the late fourth century. Prior to that we can discern a three-week preparatory period for Easter baptism, characterized by the old title given to the fifth Sunday (Sunday *in Mediana*) and by the reading of John's Gospel during those weeks.[71] At some point before the late fifth century, four more days were added to Lent to ensure forty days of *fasting* during the period. Thus what originally began on the first Sunday of Lent now began on a Wednesday (Ash Wednesday). By the time of the Würzburg epistle list three Sundays had been added as a kind of preparation for the preparatory season. They were numbered with a roughly decimal approach to the days before Easter: Septuagesima (seventy), Sexagesima (sixty), and Quinquagesima (fifty). Each of these Sundays contained prayers and chants that evoked protection in time of trouble, and with good reason: these Sunday formulas were developed in the sixth century, when the fortunes of the city were at a very low ebb given invasions, plagues, and droughts.

Each day in the Lenten scheme was celebrated at a different church in the city of Rome. The larger churches were employed for Sundays and other significant celebrations, such as the Ember Days (special fast days in the first week) or days that related to baptismal preparation (Wednesday in the fourth week at Saint Paul's Basilica, a date for the enrollment of candidates). The link between the churches chosen as stations and the readings for each day in the Lenten cycle reveals a rich symbolic imagination at work in the development of liturgy in this period. Let us take just a few of many possible examples.

SOME ROMAN LENTEN CELEBRATIONS			
Day	Station	1st Reading	Gospel
Monday, Week 1	Saint Peter-in-Chains	Ezekiel 34:1–16	Matthew 25:1–46
Friday, Week 2	Saint Vitalis	Genesis 37:6–22	Matthew 21:33–46
Tuesday, Week 3	Saint Pudenziana	2 Kings 5:1–15	Matthew 18:15–22

Saint Peter-in-Chains was one of the "penitential" churches in the city; that is, a place where one could enroll for public penance and reconciliation. The gospel reading (the separation of the sheep and goats) mentions judgment and Peter (as *pastor* or "shepherd" of the Roman church). The prayer over the gifts found in the Gelasian Sacramentary refers to the "chains of sin" (*vincula peccatorum*). Saint Vitalis was a church built on the site of an ancient well. The first reading is the story of Joseph tossed into the well by his brothers, while the gospel makes the connection via the phrase: "Here is the heir. Let us kill him." (Matthew 21:38). Finally, Saint Pudenziana is a fourth-century church with an excellent mosaic in its apse that may depict the

Apse mosaic, Santa Pudenziana. One of the *tituli* or parish churches, Santa Pudenziana is the only Roman church to have originally served as a civil basilica, and was renovated for Christian purposes in the late fourth century. In the apsidal mosaic depicting the enthroned Christ surrounded by the apostles there are edifices in the background that may correspond to Emperor Constantine's building projects. SCALA/ART RESOURCE, NY

holy places in Jerusalem and Bethlehem. The church had legendary associations with the Roman senator Pudens, where the apostle Peter stayed. Peter is a major figure in the Gospel reading. He asks if one should forgive as many as seven times. The connection is made with the story of Naaman, the leprous Syrian commander, who is instructed to bathe seven times in the Jordan.

Thus the liturgical calendar developed at Rome and elsewhere with a rich imagination that combined the basic narrative of salvation history with attention to the history and topography of the local church. Because of the innate conservatism of liturgy, many of these scripture readings were to last for centuries beyond their original and very particular inspirations. They were also imported to cities and lands that had no association with their particular genius beyond that of wanting to adopt the liturgy of a very important church.

Other Rites

In the course of the three hundred years after Constantine accepted Christianity, a number of other rites developed among Christians. Not that they did not marry, bury, or require reconciliation before this, but our sources are more plentiful for this period. We shall begin with the ritual most closely associated with baptism; that is, penance and reconciliation.

Penance and Reconciliation

By the mid-second century Christians had come to the realization that not all would live the life expected of them. Writings such as *The Shepherd of Hermas* (Rome, second century) and the works of Tertullian (Carthage, turn of the third century) had to struggle with those who had fallen into serious sin. Just what constituted serious sin was a matter of some dispute. In his Montanist treatise *On Chastity*, Tertullian had listed idolatry, blasphemy, murder, adultery, fornication, false witness, and participation in spectacles.[72]

In the fourth through the seventh centuries the process of public reconciliation of sins is called "canonical penance" because the rules for it are established by church councils in their "canons." It is impossible in this brief space to give anything but the most general overview of the varieties of penitential practice. Sources for various times within this period, not to mention the many different local churches, make generalization a perilous enterprise.[73]

Augustine may serve as illustrative of the attitude toward formal penance. In one of his sermons preached sometime during Lent in 398, after speaking of repentance that comes with preparation for baptism and then daily penitence for ordinary sinning, the bishop of Hippo turns to our subject:

> There remains the third kind of repentance, about which let me say something briefly, so that with the Lord's help I may keep my promise and complete what I have proposed. It involves a heavier and more sorrowful kind of penance, for those who are properly called penitents in the Church, who are barred from sharing in the sacrament of the altar, in case by receiving it unworthily they should eat and drink judgment upon themselves. There is a serious wound involved; perhaps adultery has been committed, perhaps murder, perhaps some sacrilege, a grave matter, a grave wound, lethal, deadly; but the doctor is almighty. Already, after the suggestion of the deed, and the liking of the idea and consent to it, and finally the perpetration of it, let the sinner be like one four

days dead, and stinking. But not even this one has the Lord forsaken, but he has cried out, Lazarus, *come forth outside* (John 11:39–43). The weight of the grave has yielded to mercy, death has yielded to life, the underworld has yielded to the world on high.

Lazarus was raised up, he came forth from the burial mound; and he was bound, as people are who do penance when they confess their sins. They have already come forth from death; because they wouldn't confess unless they were coming forth. The very act of confessing is a coming forth from a hidden and dark place. But what does the Lord say to his Church? *Whatever you loose*, he says, *on earth, shall be loosed in heaven* (Matt. 18:18). Accordingly, after Lazarus has come forth, because the Lord has exercised his prerogative of mercy by bringing to confession one who was dead, hidden away and stinking; now the ministers of the Church carry out the rest: *Loose him, and let him go free* (John 11:44).

But, my dearest friends, none of you should propose this kind of penance to yourselves, none of you prepare yourself for this kind; still, if it does happen to come to it, none of you should despair.[74]

Clearly public penance of this kind was considered a very serious matter. In a famous line, Jerome referred to it as "the second plank in shipwreck."[75] There was to be only one opportunity for public penance. Little wonder that, just as many postponed baptism until later in life, so many postponed penance until their deathbeds. Perhaps it was for this reason, in light of the Church's compassion, that the Council of Nicaea insisted that every Christian should be allowed to receive the eucharist as viaticum on his or her deathbed.[76]

It should be noted that throughout this period public penance was understood to be more therapeutic than punitive. There were various categories of public penitent: those who had to be at the back of the church during the liturgy, those who had to kneel, those who could remain only for the word service and not the eucharist proper, those who could remain for the whole of the liturgy but not receive holy communion.

Toward the end of this period, as witnessed in the Gelasian Sacramentary, Ash Wednesday marked the initiation of public penance, and Holy Thursday marked its end.[77] That way the church received its full complement in time for Easter baptism.

One cannot overestimate the influence the penitential system would eventually have on the piety and liturgical life of Western Christians. But that is a story best left to a later chapter.

Anointing the Sick

My son the deacon Celestine has added in his letter that your Grace has raised the question about what was written in the letter of the blessed Apostle James, "If anyone among you is sick, let him call the presbyters and let them pray over him, anointing him with oil in the name of the Lord, and the prayer of faith will heal the sick and the Lord will raise him up, and if he has committed sin, he will be forgiven." No doubt this must be understood to refer to baptized Christians who are ill, who can be anointed with the holy oil of the chrism which has been consecrated by the bishop and may be used not only by sacred ministers but by all Christians for anointing in the case of their own or other people's sickness.[78]

This passage from the already-quoted letter of Pope Innocent I to Bishop Decentius of Gubbio toward the beginning of the fifth century demonstrates that ordinary Christians were anointing themselves and others with consecrated oil in the case of sickness. Laypersons could anoint right up until the end of the seventh century. But Innocent's letter also sows the seeds of the later practice of anointing those at the point of death. Of the oil of anointing he says:

> It cannot be poured onto penitents, because it is a sacrament. How can it be thought that something of this kind can be allowed to those to whom the other sacraments are denied?[79]

As more and more Christians put off reconciliation with the Church, they became unable to receive the anointing of the sick (or any other sacrament for that matter) until their deathbeds. For Innocent the term "sacrament" must surely be thought of in a broad sense since here we are a long way from a limitation to the idea of seven sacraments.

From the fourth century on we possess a number of blessing prayers for the oil used both in the anointing of the sick and of catechumens, because in both cases, according to Stefano Parenti, exorcistic motifs are involved.[80] Some prayers are quite specific with regard to illness. In the prayer collection of Bishop Serapion of Thmuis (fourth-century Egypt) we read, for example:

> Father of our Lord and Savior Jesus Christ, having all authority and power, the savior of all people, we call upon you and we implore you that healing power of your only-begotten may be sent out from heaven upon this oil. May it become to those who are anointed . . . for a rejection of every disease and every sickness, for an amulet warding off every demon, for a departing of every unclean spirit, for a driving away of all fever and shiverings and every weakness, for good grace and forgiveness of sins, for a medicine of life and salvation, for health and wholeness of soul, body, spirit, for perfect strength. Master, let every satanic energy, every demon, every plot of the opposing one, every blow, every lash, every pain, or every slap in the face, or shaking, or evil shadow be afraid of your holy name, which we have now called upon, and the name of the only-begotten; and let them depart from the inner and outer parts of these your servants so that the name of Jesus Christ, the one who was crucified and risen for us, who took to himself our diseases and weaknesses, and is coming to judge the living and the dead, may be glorified. For through him (be) to you the glory and the power in holy Spirit both now and to all the ages of ages. Amen.[81]

We have no texts of actual rituals for the anointing of the sick for the fourth to the seventh centuries, but this prayer for the blessing of the oil gives us the sense that such anointings may have been performed quite frequently and for a variety of reasons.

Burial of the Dead

One of the most distinctive features of Christianity in the world of late antiquity was the nature of its belief in life after death. We have already seen, when dealing with the anniversaries of the martyrs, how Christians transformed the death rituals of their surrounding cultures by celebrating the anniversaries of the deaths rather than the births of loved ones. Here is a classic expression of the liturgy of death and burial. It is Augustine's description of the funeral of his mother, Monica:

> When she breathed her last, the boy Adeodatus [her grandson] burst out in lamentation, but he was hushed by all of us and fell silent. . . . We did not think it fitting to solemnize that funeral with tearful cries and groans, for it is often the custom to bewail by such means the wretched lot of those who die, or even their complete extinction. But she did not die in misery, nor did she meet with total death. . . .
>
> After the boy had been stopped from weeping, Evodius took up the psalter and began to sing a psalm. The whole household answered him in the psalm, "I will sing of mercy and judgment unto you, O Lord." When they heard what had happened, many of the brethren and devout women gathered there. According to custom, those whose duty it was made ready the burial. . . .

> Lo, when her body was carried away, we went out, and we returned without tears. Not even in those prayers we poured forth to you when the sacrifice of our redemption was offered up in her behalf, with the corpse already placed beside the grave before being lowered into it, as is the custom of that place, not even during those prayers did I shed tears.[82]

Several aspects of Augustine's description are noteworthy: the tendency to disallow outward mourning, the care for the corpse, the singing of psalms, and the celebration of the eucharist at graveside. Christian funerals were clearly understood as occasions of both grieving and rejoicing in the fourth and fifth centuries. In writing of the funeral of Fabiola, Jerome describes: "Psalms were chanted and the gilded ceilings of the temples were shaken with uplifted shouts of Alleluia."[83]

By the sixth and seventh centuries, however, a shift in the attitude toward death may be detected among Christians. From a more hopeful view of dying as union with Christ, Christians moved to the more ominous sense of death as a summons to "judgment and inevitably to punishment for sin."[84] The two attitudes had always existed side by side, but the shift was one of emphasis, and it would be very significant for the liturgical practice of later centuries. One feature that remained constant was the funeral procession inherited from the surrounding culture.

Weddings

Christian weddings were another liturgical practice inspired greatly by the cultures in which Christians found themselves. We know that Christians adopted the Mediterranean (and Jewish) customs of celebrating a marriage first by an agreement (betrothal) and then by the wedding ceremony (nuptials) itself. Western Christian sources are familiar with ordinary social practices, such as the giving of a ring for betrothal, the joining of right hands, the procession to the house of the husband, and the kiss of the spouses.[85] In the East, Christians adopted the Greek practice of crowning the couple. In the West, a veil was used, a practice that itself may have been borrowed from the Jews, who employed a wedding canopy over the couple.[86] Although we have no extant wedding rituals as such until the Byzantine Barberini Euchologion (eighth century), we know that from the fourth century at least some weddings were celebrated in church. The beautiful (if somewhat sober) wedding poem, or *epithalamium*, that Paulinus, bishop of Nola, wrote for Julian and Titia (both children of bishops) makes it clear that their wedding took place in a church:

> May your father the bishop bless you,
> and lead in the singing of the holy chants
> along with the choir of singers.
> Kindly Memor, lead your children to the Lord
> and before the altar commend them
> with a prayer and a blessing of the hand.[87]

The same poem refers to the nuptial veil but not to the exchange of rings or vows, which it may be surmised took place at home. The nuptial veil is well attested in Rome and Milan. Gaul and Spain witness to a blessing being given by a priest in the bridal chamber.

The earliest full text of a nuptial blessing can be found in the so-called *Verona Sacramentary*, the collection of prayer booklets, many of which may go back to the sixth century.[88] The blessing is found together with a set of mass prayers (including an embolism for the Roman canon at the Hanc igitur) in a section titled "Incipit velatio nuptialis" ("The beginning of the wedding veiling"). The veiling was considered by metonymy for the whole of the wedding liturgy. The nuptial blessing focuses mainly on the bride. It has the typical structure of formal Christian prayer: narrative statement of what God has done, followed by a petition. The scriptural images employed are those the Old Testament figures of Rachel, Sarah, and Rebecca.

It should be noted that it is a long time before Christians are required to marry in church. All the same the Church's blessing seems to have been desirable from the third century on.

Rites of Ordination

Understandably we have much more information about ordination rites than about weddings. Church orders from the *Apostolic Tradition* on provide ordination prayers and rubrics.[89] Several church orders, the Egyptian *Canons of Hippolytus* (fourth century), and the Syrian *Apostolic Constitutions* (fourth century) and *Testamentum Domini* (fifty century) are dependent on the *Apostolic Tradition*. By the fourth century the threefold ministerial organization of bishop-presbyter-deacon was universal among Christians. Eastern churches also ordained deaconesses, especially for service at baptism and in charitable enterprises. There are scattered references to deaconesses in the West (and Egypt) but no solid information on their being ordained.[90]

There are a number of common factors that we find in the ordination rites in the sources from the fourth to the seventh centuries. Some form of popular election or approval is found—at least in the ordination of a bishop. With the exception of *Apostolic Constitutions*, the imposition of hands is the visible sign of ordination. In that document the Book of the Gospels is held over the head of the candidate. Bradshaw suggests that this practice may come from a period when a conflict between having the local presbytery or visiting bishops lay on hands was resolved by adopting this practice. Ordinations in this period involved both the silent prayers of the people for the descent of the Spirit and the vocalized prayer of the bishop. In the ordination of a bishop a kiss was exchanged with the entire assembly—at least in the case of the bishop.

In our attempt to avoid overgeneralizing, we shall limit ourselves to the illustrative example of ordinations in the *Apostolic Constitutions*. In this fourth-century Syrian text the ordination rite for a bishop begins with the approval of all the people gathered together on a Sunday. They have apparently chosen the man for bishop and are asked three times if the candidate is worthy (*axios*). One of the (visiting) bishops prays the prayer of blessing while two others stand near, and other bishops and presbyters pray in silence. Deacons hold the Book of the Gospels over the candidate's head. The prayer takes the traditional form of narrative/request. After describing God's governance of the world through ministers, the bishop turns to petition:

> Now through the mediation of your Christ pour forth through us the power of your princely Spirit, which was at the service of your beloved child Jesus Christ, which was given by your will to the holy apostles of you, the eternal God. Grant in your name, God who know the heart, to this your servant, whom you have chosen as bishop, to feed your holy flock and to exercise the high-priesthood for you, blamelessly serving night and day and propitiating your countenance; to gather the number of those being saved, and to offer to you the gifts of your holy church.[91]

The prayer goes on to ask that the bishop may have the power to forgive sins and to offer "a pure and bloodless sacrifice." At the conclusion of the prayer, the new bishop presides at the eucharist. The text says that "in the morning" (the next morning?) the new bishop is "enthroned in the place reserved for him by the rest of the bishops, all giving him the kiss in the Lord."

The rubrics for the ordination of presbyters are far less detailed. *Apostolic Consitutions* merely says that the bishop lays his hand on the head of the candidate and prays with the presbytery and deacons standing round. The prayer is an expansion on the one found in *Apostolic Tradition*. There is very little in the prayer that sounds cultic. Presbyters are appointed to share in the governance of the church, "admitted into the presbytery by the vote and judgment of the whole clergy."[92] It could be that this prayer signals a period of transition from election of ministers by the people to election by clergy. The prayer implies that presbyters help the bishops without stating so explicitly, thus witnessing to the ambiguity of differentiating bishops' orders from presbyters that lasts until the early twenty-first century. Note, however, that the existing presbyters are not associated in the imposition of hands on the new presbyter as they are in *Apostolic Tradition*. We can only surmise that there is a negotiation of power going on beneath the text of this document. Certainly the power of bishops was to grow enormously in both the church and civic society in the course of the fourth century.[93]

The ordination of deacons follows. The same rubric about the laying on of hands applies as was the case with presbyters. Since only the bishop lays hands on the presbyter, there is no need to differentiate between orders in the way that *Apostolic Tradition* does when it insists that only the bishop lays hands on deacons. The prayer of blessing for deacons has nothing specific to say about the nature of diaconal ministry, referring instead to Stephen the protomartyr as a type and as imitator of the sufferings of Christ. The prayer has a curious phrase that asks that the deacon "may be worthy of a higher rank." It would be anachronistic to interpret this phrase to mean that fourth-century Syrians had a "stepping-stone" approach to ordinations. It is probably an allusion to 1 Timothy 3:13 ("for those who serve well as deacons gain a good standing for themselves and great boldness in the faith that is in Christ Jesus").[94]

A somewhat more cultic allusion can be discerned in the "keeping of the gates" in the ordination prayer for deaconesses:

> Eternal God, Father of our Lord Jesus Christ, creator of man and woman, who filled with the Spirit Miriam and Deborah and Anna and Huldah; who did not disdain that your only-begotten Son should be born of a woman; who also in the tent of the testimony and in the temple appointed women to be guardians of your holy gates; now look upon this your servant who is being appointed for ministry, and give her the Holy Spirit and cleanse her from every defilement of body and spirit so that she may worthily complete the work committed to her, to your glory and the praise of your Christ, through whom [be] glory and worship to you in the Holy Spirit for ever. Amen.[95]

Apostolic Constitutions also provides prayers (and the rubric of imposition of hands) for ordaining subdeacons and readers. The spirit and tone of these prayers differ greatly from the far more elaborate and cultic prayers found in the so-called *Verona Sacramentary*, prayers that served as models in the Roman rite for a millennium and a half. Just as the eucharistic rite itself became far more mysteriological in the course of the fifth and sixth centuries, so the process of clericalization and mystification of the ordained proceeded apace and had a significant impact of the practice and theology of Christian worship.

Legacy

We have surveyed the development of various aspects of Christian worship in the three centuries following Constantine's edict of toleration, attempting to avoid the generalization that what happened in one church necessarily happened in all the others at roughly the same time. Despite the great similarities and convergence that one can detect in the consolidation of rites in the fourth century, we have also seen the beginnings of the differentiation of the major rites. Each major local church (Alexandria, Rome, Jerusalem, Constantinople, Edessa) began to develop a system of worship that responded to the needs of its own history and culture. Historical events like the schisms that followed the Councils of Ephesus (431) and Chalcedon (451) further encouraged the creation of various rites.

With the rise of Islam in the mid-seventh century, Mediterranean civilization was being transformed, and Christian worship was taking different directions in places as diverse as Persia and the British Isles. But for all the differentiation, the comparative study of liturgy can still find important similarities in the ways Christians attempted to respond to God by worship in the name of Jesus. Thus the story has been one of continuity and discontinuity, similarity and difference that continue on into the Middle Ages.

Bibliography

Baldovin, John F. *The Urban Character of Christian Worship: The Origins, Development, and Meaning of Stational Liturgy.* Rome: Pontificale Institutum Studiorum Orientalium, 1987.

Baldovin, John F. "The Fermentum at Rome in the Fifth Century: A Reconsideration," *Worship* 79 (2005) 38-53.

Bradshaw, Paul F. *Ordination Rites of the Ancient Churches of East and West.* New York: Pueblo, 1990.

Bradshaw, Paul F. *The Search for the Origins of Christian Worship.* 2nd ed. New York and Oxford: Oxford University Press, 2002.

Cantalamessa, Raniero, comp. *Easter in the Early Church.* Translated and edited by James M. Quigley and Joseph T. Lienhard. Collegeville, Minn.: Liturgical Press, 1993.

Dix, Gregory. *The Shape of the Liturgy.* London: Dacre Press, 1945.

Finn, Thomas M. *Early Christian Baptism and the Catechumenate: Italy, North Africa, and Egypt.* Collegeville, Minn.: Liturgical Press, 1992.

Finn, Thomas M. *Early Christian Baptism and the Catechumenate: West and East Syria.* Collegeville, Minn.: Liturgical Press, 1992.

Giraudo, Cesare. *La struttura letteraria della preghiera eucaristica.* Rome: Biblical Institute Press, 1981.

Jasper, R. C. D., and G. J. Cuming, eds. and trans. *Prayers of the Eucharist: Early and Reformed.* 3rd ed. New York: Pueblo, 1987.

Jeanes, Gordon P., ed. and trans. *The Origins of the Roman Rite.* Bramcote, Notts.: Grove Books, 1991.

Johnson, Maxwell. *The Rites of Christian Initiation: Their Evolution and Interpretation.* Collegeville, Minn.: Liturgical Press, 1999.

Jungmann, Josef A. *The Early Liturgy to the Time of Gregory the Great.* Translated by Francis A. Brunner. Notre Dame, Ind.: University of Notre Dame Press, 1959.

Krautheimer, Richard. *Early Christian and Byzantine Architecture.* 4th ed. Revised by Richard Krautheimer and Slobodan Curcic. New York: Penguin, 1986.

Mazza, Enrico. *The Origins of the Eucharistic Prayer.* Translated by Ronald E. Lane. Collegeville, Minn.: Liturgical Press, 1995.

Renoux, Athanase. *Le codex arménien Jérusalem 121.* Patrologia Orientalis, vols. 35–36. Turnhout, Belgium: Brepols, 1969–1971.

Riley, Hugh M. *Christian Initiation*. Washington, D.C.: Catholic University of America Press, 1974.

Rutherford, Richard. *The Death of a Christian: The Rite of Funerals*. Rev. ed. Collegeville, Minn.: Liturgical Press, 1990.

Schuster, Ildefonso. *The Sacramentary*. 5 vols. Translated by Arthur Levelis-Marke. London: Burns, Oates, and Washbourne, 1924.

Searle, Mark, and Kenneth W. Stevenson. *Documents of the Marriage Liturgy*. Collegeville, Minn.: Liturgical Press, 1992.

Sheerin, Daniel J. *The Eucharist*. Message of the Fathers of the Church. Wilmington, Del.: M. Glazier, 1986.

Stevenson, Kenneth. *Nuptial Blessing*. New York: Oxford University Press, 1983.

Taft, Robert F. *Beyond East and West: Problems in Liturgical Understanding*. Rome: Edizioni Orientalia Christiana, Pontifical Oriental Institute, 1997.

Taft, Robert F. *The Liturgy of the Hours in East and West: The Origins of the Divine Office and Its Meaning for Today*. 2nd ed. Collegeville, Minn.: Liturgical Press, 1993.

Talley, Thomas J. *The Origins of the Liturgical Year*. 2d rev. ed. Collegeville, Minn.: Liturgical Press, 1991.

Vogel, Cyrille, ed. and trans. *Le pécheur et la pénitence dans l'église ancienne*. Paris: Éditions du Cerf, 1966.

Whitaker, E. C. *Documents of the Baptismal Liturgy*. 2d rev. ed. London: SPCK, 1970.

Wilkinson, John, ed. and trans. *Egeria's Travels*. 3d ed. Warminster, Wilts.: Aris and Phillips, 1999.

Yarnold, Edward. *The Awe-Inspiring Rites of Initiation*. 2nd ed. Collegeville, Minn.: Liturgical Press, 1994.

Notes

[1] A fine treatment of the continuity between pre- and post-Constantinian Christian worship can be found in Bradshaw, *The Search for the Origins of Christian Worship* 211–213.

[2] Gregory Dix's *The Shape of the Liturgy* dispelled the first myth by describing the lavish appointments of the North African church at Cirta in 303 (pp. 24–27). Unfortunately he reinforced the second myth in treating the fourth century as "the sanctification of time" (pp. 303–396). Among others, Robert Taft has shown that Christians had a very complex understanding of time from the very beginning; cf. his "Historicism Revisited" in *Beyond East and West*, 31–50.

[3] Taft, "How Liturgies Grow: The Evolution of the Byzantine Divine Liturgy," in *Beyond East and West*, 203–205; and "The Structural Analysis of Liturgical Units: An Essay in Methodology," *Beyond East and West*, 200–202.

[4] See Baldovin, *The Urban Character of Christian Worship*.

[5] Raymond Davis, ed., *The Book of Pontiffs (Liber Pontificalis)* (Liverpool: Liverpool University Press, 1989) 16–17, under Pope Silvester; on the disposition of churches in Rome, see Richard Krautheimer, *Three Christian Capitals* (Berkeley: University of California Press, 1983) 7–40.

[6] Cyril Mango, *The Art of the Byzantine Empire 312–1453* (Toronto: University of Toronto Press, 1986) 80–96.

[7] Paul the Silentiary, "Description of Hagia Sophia" and "Description of the Ambo of Hagia Sophia" (24 December 562), in Mango, *Art of the Byzantine Empire*, 80–82, 91–92.

[8] See Krautheimer, *Early Christian and Byzantine Architecture*; and Robert Milburn, *Early Christian Art and Architecture* (Berkeley: University of California Press, 1988) 83–144.

[9] See Spiro Kostof, *The Orthodox Baptistry of Ravenna* (New Haven, Conn.: Yale University Press, 1965); also S. Anita Stauffer, *On Baptismal Fonts: Ancient and Modern* (Bramcote, Notts.: Grove Books, 1994).

[10]John Fenwick, *The Anaphoras of St. Basil and St. James: An Investigation into Their Common Origins*, Orientalia Christiana Analecta 240 (Rome: Pontificium Institutum Orientale, 1992).

[11]Taft, "How Liturgies Grow," *Beyond East and West*, 203–205.

[12]Athanase Renoux, *Le codex arménien Jérusalem 121*.

[13]See Robert Cabié, *La lettre du Pape Innocent Ier à Decentius de Gubbio* (Louvain: Publications Universitaires de Louvain, 1973).

[14]Frederik van der Meer, *Augustine the Bishop* (London: Sheed and Ward, 1962) 317–402.

[15]In Edmund Bishop, *Liturgica Historica* (Oxford: Oxford University Press, 1918) 1–19.

[16]Theodoret of Cyrrus, *Religious History* 26, in Ramsey MacMullen, *Christianizing the Roman Empire (AD 100–400)*, (New Haven, Conn.: Yale University Press, 1984) 2.

[17]Cited in Wilkinson, *Egeria's Travels*, 161–163. Other citations of Egeria are from this edition.

[18]The enrollment of candidates takes place at Epiphany in Milan and Turin in northern Italy. See Johnson, *The Rites of Christian Initiation*, 135.

[19]See Edward Yarnold, "Initiation: The Fourth and Fifth Centuries," in *The Study of Liturgy*, rev. ed., ed. C. Jones, G. Wainwright, E. Yarnold, and P. Bradshaw (New York: Oxford University Press, 1992) 134.

[20]The chart is adapted from Johnson, 122.

[21]Edward Yarnold, in *The Awe-Inspiring Rites of Initiation*, gives the texts for the baptismal catecheses of Cyril, John Chrysostom, Theodore Mopsuestia, Ambrose; citations come from this edition of Yarnold. For a thorough analysis and commentary on the mystagogical homilies, see Riley, *Christian Initiation*.

[22]Taft, "Structural Analysis," in *Beyond East and West*, 189. Emphasis in the original.

[23]See Johnson, 137.

[24]See Yarnold's helpful note, 199.

[25]Kilian McDonnell, *The Baptism of Jesus in the Jordan: The Trinitarian and Cosmic Order of Salvation* (Collegeville, Minn.: Liturgical Press, 1996) 231; cited in Johnson, *Rites*, 109.

[26]For these and other baptismal texts, see Whitaker, *Documents of the Baptismal Liturgy*, 166–203.

[27]Jeanes, *Origins of the Roman Rite*, 17.

[28]Cabié, *La lettre*; this translation in Jeanes, 44–45.

[29]See the summary of opinions on this question in Johnson, 144.

[30]Translated by Aidan Kavanagh in his *The Shape of Baptism: The Rite of Christian Initiation* (Collegeville, Minn.: Liturgical Press, 1978) 49. Original in Ernst Diehl, ed., *Inscriptiones Latinae Christianae Veteres* (Berlin: Weidmann, 1925) 285, #1513.

[31]Augustine of Hippo, Sermon 272, in Sheerin, *The Eucharist*, 95.

[32]See Baldovin, *Urban Character*.

[33]We need to be careful not to easily accept the thesis that Christians simply copied imperial ceremonial. See Thomas Mathews, *The Clash of Gods: A Reinterpretation of Early Christian Art* (Princeton, N.J.: Princeton University Press, 1993).

[34]Taft, "Structural Analysis," *Beyond East and West*, 200–201.

[35]Anton Baumstark, *Comparative Liturgy* (Westminster, Md.: Newman, 1958) 26ff.

[36]Davis, *Liber Pontificalis*, 34.

[37]Josef Jungmann, *The Mass of the Roman Rite (Missarum Sollemnia)*, 2 vols., trans. Francis A. Brunner (New York: Benziger Brothers, 1951–1955) 1:266.

[38]Gregory the Great to Bishop John of Syracuse (598) in Jeanes, 47–48.

[39]See Robert Taft, *The Great Entrance*, 2nd ed. (Rome: Pontificale Institutum Studiorum Orientalium, 1978).

[40]See John Baldovin, *Liturgy in Ancient Jerusalem* (Bramcote, Notts.: Grove, 1989) 24–25.

[41]See the thorough treatment in Jungmann, *Mass of the Roman Rite*, 2:277–293.

[42]See Mazza, *The Origins of the Eucharistic Prayer*.

[43]Giraudo, *La struttura letteraria della preghiera eucaristica*.

[44]Alexander Schmemann, *Introduction to Liturgical Theology*, 2nd ed. (Crestwood, N.Y.: St. Vladimir's Seminary Press, 1975) 72–90.

[45]Jasper and Cuming, *Prayers of the Eucharist*, 164–165. Jasper and Cuming translate the Ambrose passage: "*because* it is the body and blood."

[46]Jasper and Cuming, *Prayers of the Eucharist*, 165.

[47]Edward Kilmartin, *The Eucharist in the West: History and Theology*, ed. Robert Daly (Collegeville, Minn.: Liturgical Press, 1998) 167–176.

[48]See Anthony Gelston, *The Eucharistic Prayer of Addai and Mari* (Oxford: Oxford University Press, 1992), for a survey of modern scholarship. This prayer is employed in the Assyrian Church or the "Church of the East."

[49]Jasper and Cuming, *Prayers*, 116–123. The text is taken from a ninth-century manuscript, Vatican MS gr. 336, also called the Barberini manuscript, and its omissions are supplied by Grottaferrata MS G b vii, somewhat later. That the priest here says some of the prayers aloud and others in a low voice is a result of yet later influences. For a full study of this text in relation to another well-known West Syrian anaphora, see Fenwick, *Anaphoras of St. Basil and St. James.*

[50]Cabié, *La lettre* 26 (my translation).

[51]See Taft, *Liturgy of the Hours*, 62.

[52]Dix, 304–332.

[53]George Guiver, *Company of Voices: Daily Prayer and the People of God* (Collegeville, Minn.: Liturgical Press, 1988) 53.

[54]See Paul Bradshaw, *Two Ways of Praying* (Nashville, Tenn.: Abingdon, 1995).

[55]Taft, *Liturgy of the Hours*, 200–205

[56]Taft, *Liturgy of the Hours*, 65–66.

[57]Taft, *Liturgy of the Hours*, 60–61; see John Cassian, *Institutes* 2–3.

[58]Taft, *Liturgy of the Hours*, 64, following Armand Veilleux, *La liturgie dans le cénobitisme pachômien au quatrième siècle* (Rome: Herder, 1968).

[59]Adapted from Guiver, 251–252. Guiver provides a valuable guide to the sources for the daily office in part 5 of his book.

[60]See Bradshaw, *Search*, 211–213; Talley, *Origins of the Liturgical Year*; and Taft, "Historicism Revisited," 31–49.

[61]Michele Renee Salzman, *On Roman Time: The Codex-Calendar of 354 and the Rhythms of Urban Life in Late Antiquity* (Berkeley: University of California Press, 1990).

[62]Peter Brown, *The Cult of the Saints: Its Rise and Function in Latin Christianity* (Chicago: University of Chicago Press, 1981) 89.

[63]For the full list, see Noële M. Denis-Boulet, *The Christian Calendar*, trans. P. J. Hepburne-Scott (New York: Hawthorn, 1960) 53–55.

[64]Renoux, *Codex*; for an English translation, see Wilkinson, 175–194.

[65]See Maxwell Johnson, "Preparation for Pascha? Lent in Christian Antiquity," in *Between Memory and Hope: Readings on the Liturgical Year*, ed. M. Johnson (Collegeville, Minn.: Liturgical Press, 2000) 207–222; on the possibility of a Sunday lectionary in the Jerusalem Lent, see John Baldovin, "A Lenten Sunday Lectionary in Fourth Century Jerusalem?" in

Time and Community, ed. J. Neil Alexander (Portland, Ore.: Pastoral Press, 1990) 115–122.

[66]Renoux, 294–311; Wilkinson, 187–188, 193. For extended commentary, see Gabriel Bertonière, *The Historical Development of the Easter Vigil and Related Services in the Greek Church* (Rome: Pontificale Institutum Studiorum Orientalium, 1972).

[67]Talley, 48–49.

[68]Leo the Great, *Sermon 27 (On the Nativity 7)*, in *A Select Library of the Nicene and Post-Nicene Fathers of the Christian Church*, 2nd ser., vol. 12, ed. Philip Schaff (repr. ed. Grand Rapids, Mich.: Eerdmans, 1979) 140.

[69]For this and many other historical details, see Schuster, *The Sacramentary*, 1:368–369.

[70]See Baldovin, *Urban Character*, 147–153.

[71]See Pierre Jounel, "The Preparation for Easter," in *The Church at Prayer IV: The Liturgy and Time*, 2nd ed., ed. A. G. Martimort, trans. Matthew J. O'Connell (Collegeville, Minn.: Liturgical Press, 1986) 67.

[72]See Vogel, *Le pécheur et la pénitence*, 23; for similar lists in Augustine (fifth century) and Caesarius of Arles (sixth century), see p. 29.

[73]For an overview, see Antonio Santantoni, "Reconciliation in the First Four Centuries" and "Reconciliation in the West," in *Handbook for Liturgical Studies*, ed. Anscar J. Chupungco, vol. 4: *Sacraments and Sacramentals* (Collegeville, Minn.: Liturgical Press, 2000) 93–104, 121–130.

[74]Augustine, Sermon 352, in *The Works of St. Augustine*, pt. 3, vol. 10: *Sermons (341–400) on Various Subjects*, trans. E. Hill (Hyde Park, N.Y.: New City Press, 1995) 147.

[75]Jerome, Letter 80.9, in Bernhard Poschmann, *Penance and the Anointing of the Sick* (New York: Herder and Herder, 1964) 104.

[76]Canon 13, in Vogel, 189.

[77]See Santantoni, 98–99; and Vogel, 200–204.

[78]Innocent I to Decentius of Gubbio, in Jeanes, 47.

[79]Innocent I to Decentius of Gubbio, in Jeanes, 47.

[80]Stefano Parenti, "Anointing of the Sick during the First Four Centuries," in *Handbook for Liturgical Studies*, ed. Anscar J. Chupungco, vol. 4: *Sacraments and Sacramentals*, 159.

[81]Maxwell Johnson, *The Prayers of Sarapion of Thmuis* (Rome: Pontificio Istituto Orientale, 1995) 67.

[82]Augustine, *Confessions* 9.12, trans. John K. Ryan (New York: Doubleday, 1960) 224–225.

[83]Jerome, Letter 77.11, in *A Select Library of the Nicene and Post-Nicene Fathers of the Christian Church*, 2nd ser., vol. 6, ed. Philip Schaff (repr. ed. Grand Rapids, Mich.: Eerdmans, 1979) 162.

[84]Rutherford, *Death of a Christian*, 28.

[85]Adrien Nocent, "The Christian Rite of Marriage in the West," in *Handbook for Liturgical Studies*, ed. Anscar J. Chupungco, vol. 4: *Sacraments and Sacramentals*, 277–285.

[86]See the summaries in Stevenson, *Nuptial Blessing*, 25–29.

[87]Paulinus of Nola, Carmen 25, in Searle and Stevenson, *Documents of the Marriage Liturgy*, 38.

[88]Searle and Stevenson, 40–44.

[89]For the question of the dating of the *Apostolic Tradition*, see Maxwell Johnson in the previous chapter, "Apostolic Tradition," n.2.

[90]For this and what follows I am greatly indebted to Bradshaw, *Ordination Rites of the Ancient Churches*.

[91]*Apostolic Constitutions* 8.5, in Bradshaw, *Ordination Rites*, 114.

[92]Bradshaw, *Ordination Rites*, 115.

[93]See Harold A. Drake, *Constantine and the Bishops: The Politics of Intolerance* (Baltimore: Johns Hopkins University Press, 2000).

[94]Bradshaw, *Ordination Rites*, 115.

[95]Bradshaw, *Ordination Rites*, 116.

4

The Ancient Oriental Churches

CHRISTINE CHAILLOT

Introduction

Origins and Spread

At the origins of Christianity stand the first communities that grew up in Palestine, where Jesus lived, and in the neighboring countries of Syria and Egypt, where Patriarchates were organized at Antioch and Alexandria. Around those two ancient capitals one can distinguish two principal families of Churches, which themselves became divided on account of various theological divergences although political and cultural factors also intervened. At the Council of Ephesus in 431, the most debated question was the title of Mary as God-bearer or Mother of God (Theotokos). The proponents of the title saw it as a confession of Christ's origin in the very being of the Godhead. Nestorius, Bishop of Constantinople, who had expressed reservations about the title, was condemned for making too sharp a contrast between the divinity and the humanity of Christ. The Church of Persia did not condemn Nestorius and was then labeled by others "Nestorian." This Church rejects that name and prefers to be called the Church of the East or the Assyrian Church; it recognizes the Virgin as Mother of Christ.[1]

At the Council of Chalcedon in 451, a new terminology was used to express the divinity and the humanity of Christ. He was said to be one person "in two natures" (*en duo physesin*). Certain Christians, particularly the Copts and the Syrian Orthodox, considered that this terminology implied a separation between the divinity and the humanity of Christ. They rejected it and remained faithful to the christological formula of Saint Cyril of Alexandria, "one nature (*mia physis*) of God the Word, Incarnate," a formula that mentions both the divinity and the humanity in Christ but insists on their union. That provoked a schism within the Patriarchates of Alexandria and of Antioch—between the Melkites or the Imperials, who followed the doctrine of Chalcedon and constituted Patriarchates called "Greek Orthodox" (recently called "Eastern Orthodox"), and, on the other hand, those who were given the name of "Monophysites." From the 1960s, theologians and scholars have recognized that this term is misleading and should be avoided, and these churches should now be called "Oriental Orthodox."[2]

The Oriental Orthodox family includes Copts, Ethiopians, Armenians, and Syrian Orthodox. Heirs of the Pharaohs, the Copts live along the Nile in Egypt, and indeed the word "Copt" means "Egyptian." The Coptic Orthodox Church of Alexandria has its patriarchal See in Cairo. Comprising about 7 million people, the Coptic community in Egypt is the largest in the Middle East. The Ethiopian Christians constitute

Christ feeding the multitude. Four Gospels, Ethiopic, 1664–1665. Private
Collection/Topham Picturepoint/Bridgeman Art Library

the oldest black Church in Africa. The Ethiopian Church was linked to the Coptic
Patriarchate of Alexandria until it gained autocephaly in 1959; in 1998 a Patriarchate
was instituted in Eritrea following the political independence of 1991. In Ethiopia the
Oriental Orthodox Church numbers about 30 million, and in Eritrea about 1.5 million. The Armenian and Syrian Orthodox Churches have found themselves historically in geopolitically strategic areas between Europe and Asia, disputed since time
immemorial between the great powers that surrounded them. The Armenian Church
is organized in two Catholicosates (Etchmiadzin, in Armenia, which is the main one,
and the ancient one of Sis, now centered in Lebanon), and two Patriarchates
(Constantinople and Jerusalem). The Armenians around the world number about 8
million, including about 3 million in Armenia itself. The Syrian Orthodox Patriarchate of Antioch has had its See in various places and is, as of 1959, established in Damascus; it has at most 400,000 faithful in the Middle East and around the world. After
various twists and turns in an earlier history that is believed to go back to the Apostle
Thomas, a community of Christians in Kerala, southwestern India, lived from the
seventeenth century under the Syrian Orthodox Patriarchate of Antioch. Part of that
community continues to recognize the supreme authority of Antioch, while since 1912,
another part, having declared its independence, goes under the name of the Malankara
Orthodox Syrian Church of India. Both of these groups, numbering about 1 million
each, are viewed as part of the Oriental Orthodox family of Churches.

The Assyrian Church—whose language is East Syriac and whose rite is called by
liturgical scholars East Syrian—numbered, in the early twenty-first century, only a few
hundred thousand members in the Middle East (Iraq, Iran, North Syria, Lebanon) and
elsewhere, principally in India and the United States. Because of disagreements over the

calendar, the community has been split since 1968 into two Patriarchates, one in Chicago and the other in Baghdad. It was with the Church of the East that Indian Christianity appears to have been chiefly associated before the sixteenth century.

The present and future situation of the Christians in several of these regions remains delicate. In Egypt and in other places of the Middle East, the rise of Islamic fundamentalism sometimes causes tension. The number of Christians is steadily decreasing; for political and economic reasons, many emigrate and organize new communities in the diaspora. A French author, Jean-Pierre Valognes, has even entitled a book *Vie et Mort des Chrétiens d'Orient* (1994); a similar tale is told in William Dalrymple's *From the Holy Mountain* (1998). Despite these historical difficulties, one can nevertheless observe a renewal among the Oriental Churches at both the administrative and the spiritual levels, and their liturgical heritage remains very much alive.

All these Churches, both Oriental Orthodox and Assyrian, have parishes in the diaspora, in North and South America, in Europe, and in Australia. From these ancient Churches have also emerged, through contact with Western Christianity from the Crusades onward, communities that are attached to Catholic or, especially since the nineteenth century, Protestant traditions.

A Few Historical Markers

Christians have undergone intermittent persecutions of various kinds from the beginning. The stories of numerous martyrs are written in the Synaxaries of the various Churches, and they are read with the stories of the saints on their feast days. Persecution was severe under the Roman emperors Decius (reigned 249–251) and Diocletian (284–305). In the Sassanid Empire, where Zoroastrianism had been the state religion since 227, persecution of the Christians occurred throughout the fourth century, especially in the Syro-Mesopotamian area; and in the middle of the fifth, after the confrontation between the Persian authorities and the Armenians, Christians suffered under the Persian king Yazdgard II. After the schisms resulting from Chalcedon in 451, non-Chalcedonian Christians were pursued by the Byzantines. The political and cultural situation in the Middle East changed with the Muslim conquests and the constitution of the Umayyad Empire in Damascus (650–750) and the Abbasid Empire in Baghdad (750–1258). At the beginning of the eighth century, the Umayyad Empire extended from central Asia to Spain. Islam rapidly became implanted as the dominant and state religion in the Middle East. In the early period, Muslims were conciliatory toward Christians, but they soon imposed a status that has become known as "dhimmitude," a sort of submission that, although it allowed the Christians to play some role in society, nevertheless implied an obligation to pay heavy taxes as well as subjection to all kinds of annoyances in everyday life. All the Oriental Churches have experienced over the centuries periods of intolerance, indeed persecution, including the most distant Ethiopia, whose neighbors are Muslims. But this must not make us forget rich intellectual encounters; thus numerous philosophical, scientific, and other works were translated from Greek into Arabic via Syriac by Christian scholars, for example, during the ninth century in Baghdad. The Oriental Christians witnessed various invasions, principally the Saljuk Turks (1077–1308) and the Mamelukes (1250–1517). The destructive violence of the Mongols (1257–1336) struck a blow to the Oriental Christian communities, from which they have never properly recovered. From the end of the fifteenth century, the Ottomans began to take over the Middle East (1453–1922). By the end of the nineteenth century, massacres were committed against the Syrian Orthodox and especially against the Armenians and also the Assyrians. This violence reached its culmination in the genocide of 1915. Almost a third of these three peoples were exterminated: more than a million Armenians, about a hundred thousand Syrian Orthodox, and perhaps a hundred thousand Assyrians. The victims of the genocide are commemorated by the Armenians in an office for the repose of the dead on 24 April, the anniversary of the beginning of the massacres in Turkey in 1915.

Following the spread of the Arabs and of Islam, Arabic became the principal language of the Middle East. Most prayers in Coptic and Syrian Orthodox communities are now spoken and sung in the everyday language of Arabic, except for the most important parts of the Liturgy such as the epiclesis. The Armenians, the Assyrians, and the Ethiopians preserve their ancient liturgical language.

Common Liturgical Features

There are few specialist scholars in the study of the liturgical traditions of the Oriental Churches, and the documentation remains fragmentary. Despite work in the last decades of the twentieth century, truth remains in what Irénée Dalmais wrote in 1960:

> The surviving commentaries are very few, and mostly still unpublished, and the information to be gleaned from religious or secular writers, among them historians and hagiographers, has not yet all been brought together. . . . Without that, we have to stop short at a simply external description, which does not allow us to penetrate to the inner significance of this or that rite or to set out the different interpretations given it in the course of time, often for accidental reasons. This makes it very difficult to attain the main object of liturgical science, which is to meet the living soul of a community as it expresses itself in its official religious celebrations.[3]

In the light of those remarks, what I shall present here is a description of the rites as they are celebrated at the time of this writing.

An observer of liturgical life in the Orthodox Churches, both Byzantine and Oriental as well as Assyrian, will find numerous similarities in the symbolically important matters of space, vestments, gestures, and liturgical objects, the conduct of the Liturgy and the Daily Offices, and the life of both laypeople and monastic communities. For example, the general structure of the Liturgy of the Eucharist remains the same (preparatory prayers; Scripture readings; prayers of intercession; eucharistic prayer or anaphora, with anamnesis and epiclesis; communion under two kinds; and the dismissal of the faithful);[4] confession is regularly practiced before communion, which is received fasting. The Liturgy of the Hours has seven daily offices.[5] Concerning sacramental life, the baptism of children is followed by their chrismation and communion; in weddings the couple receives crowns; there are prayers for the departed, especially after eight days, forty days, and a year; relics and icons are blessed and venerated, although the Armenians and the Assyrians venerate more the Cross. The same annual cycle of the great feasts is followed: the feasts of Christ, of the Virgin, and of the saints, sometimes accompanied by processions. The feast of feasts is Easter, or the Resurrection. Easter is preceded by Great Lent, when penitential exercises are undertaken, such as numerous prostrations, and fasting is even stricter than in the other annual periods of fasting before the great festivals and on the weekly fasts of Wednesday and Friday. The ceremonies in the various Churches are similar for the blessing of water at Epiphany, the blessing of olive or palm branches on Palm Sunday, the washing of the feet and the consecration of the holy oil, or *myron*, on Holy Thursday. Peculiar to the Oriental Orthodox Churches is the fact that the clergy goes shoeless to celebrate the Liturgy among the Copts and the Ethiopians, with liturgical slippers being worn among the Armenians and Syrians.

The kiss of peace has been preserved in all the Oriental Orthodox Churches. Before the Anaphora the priest greets the deacon at the altar, and then the deacon comes down among the faithful to transmit this sign of peace, from row to row or all around the church. The gesture itself is performed in different ways. Among the Syrians, the faithful touch hands and sometimes also the face. Among the Copts it is similar, except that one touches one's mouth with one's hand before passing the peace on to the next person. Among the Armenians the kiss is on both cheeks. Among the Ethiopians one bows to both left and right in order to greet one's neighbors.

The practice of pilgrimage is common to all the Oriental Churches. There are various centers of pilgrimage; the central or royal pilgrimage obviously remains Jerusalem, where all the Oriental Orthodox Churches have their own church buildings and monasteries.

Among all the Oriental Orthodox it is important for spiritual guidance to have a spiritual father. The Ethiopians call him "soul father."

There is no ordination of women to the priesthood. It is known that a female diaconate existed in some Oriental Orthodox traditions. There exist ancient texts and prayers for consecrating deaconesses, except in the Coptic and Ethiopian traditions; to bless those whom the Copts call deaconesses or "consecrated girls/virgins," different texts of the Byzantine tradition have been compiled. Some decades before the twenty-first century, a woman was ordained to the diaconate in the Armenian Patriarchate of Constantinople. In the parishes of the Syrian Orthodox tradition, including the diaspora, girls called "deaconesses" sing in the choir.

For the Oriental Christians it is, above all, essential to remain faithful to a specific tradition, and especially to the apostolic faith proclaimed in the course of the liturgies and the other offices. Certain prayers narrate the history of their Churches and the martyrdoms they have undergone. The sole refuge of these Christians always remained their Church and their faith, so one can understand why it is of primary importance for them to keep intact their heritage, whether religious, cultural, liturgical, or other, as their most precious possession. The recitation of all these prayers prompts the faithful to reflect on the principal aims of the religious life—salvation and eternal life. The Eucharistic Liturgy, which is the central rite, as well as the other prayers are like a long catechism sung or recited. The liturgical texts also contain teaching from the Bible or from the Fathers of the Church. The most popular prayers are learned by heart. That allows them also to pass through the heart and to penetrate into the deepest part of the person in a transformative way. Thus all these prayers are maxims for the spiritual and ascetical life, not only for the faithful of the Oriental Churches but also for all who will read them or listen to them. To that must be added the poetic beauty of the texts.

The Copts

Copts are proud that the infant Jesus found refuge in their country (Matt. 2:15), and they sing of the Lord's Flight into Egypt, which is kept as a feast of the second level in their calendar: "God who is glorified in the council of the saints [Ps. 89:8], who sits upon the cherubim [Ps. 99:1], appeared in the land of Egypt, we sing unto Him. . . . Let us sing unto Christ who visited us, His people." Another doxology explains that Saint Mark is the Apostle and Evangelist of Alexandria and Egypt: "You have enlightened us by Your Gospel. You have informed us of the Father, the Son, and the Holy

Spirit. You have brought us forth from the darkness, while yet we were sitting under the shadow of death. You have given us the Bread of Life which came forth from Heaven."

The first kernel of the Church in Egypt was formed in Alexandria. The ancient papyri show that worship was first celebrated in Greek and later translated into Coptic. Coptic derives from the ancient language of the Pharaohs but is written in Greek characters with the addition of seven or eight letters derived from the hieroglyphic script. In the twelfth century, Patriarch Gabriel II imposed the Bohairic form of Coptic as the liturgical language, and it continues to be a liturgical language of the Copts to this day, especially in the monasteries.[6] Coptic has not been spoken in everyday life since around the eleventh to the fourteenth century. In the parishes, Arabic is predominant, having been introduced into the liturgy already before the fourteenth century. There still exist numerous texts common to the Greek Orthodox and Coptic traditions: for example, the Monogenes hymn to Christ, some Theotokia or hymns to the Virgin, some *troparia*, and some offices. At the beginning of the fifteenth century, Patriarch Gabriel V caused liturgical usages to be fixed.

Like other Eastern liturgies, the Coptic rite derives from a fusion between the ritual of the cathedral (or parish) and monastic practices. It was in Egypt that monastic life began, in the desert with Saint Anthony (died 356), "the father of monks"; with Pachomius (died 346), the initiator of cenobitic, or community, life; with Shenoute (died c. 465); and with Saint Macarius and the other monks of the Wadi Natrun and elsewhere.

Liturgical Space

The archeological remains of ancient Coptic churches and monasteries can be visited all around Egypt. A number of ancient monasteries, with their churches, still exist and flourish; the most famous are the Monastery of Saint Anthony, and the Wadi Natrun Monasteries. The typical Coptic church takes the form of a basilica, but one can still find ancient churches built according to irregular plans; in a few churches there is a gallery over the narthex, reserved in the past for women.

Typical of the churches is the wooden screen (*hijâb*) before the altar sanctuary (*haikal*) [see color plate 6]. The screen is beautifully carved, sometimes with scenes from the Gospels, and sometimes also inlaid with ivory and mother of pearl in the shape of small crosses or geometric patterns. Icons are placed on top of the screen or elsewhere on the iconostasis. In the sanctuary of ancient churches there are two little windows (*taqah*) on either side of the central doorway to the altar, and sometimes, on the east side of the altar, a kind of hole (*bahr*) where, some say, deacons used to hide the Holy Gifts in case of threat or danger. Before the sanctuary door there is a curtain that remains closed when no ceremony is taking place. The door of the iconostasis remains open throughout the Liturgy. In some ancient churches one can see behind the altar some circular steps—the *synthronos*—where in the past sat the bishop and concelebrants.

Ostrich eggs, also found in Ethiopian Churches, may be suspended from the roof or door of the sanctuary. As explained in the *Precious Pearl* by John ibn Sabbâ‎ Zakariah (fourteenth century), the ostrich hatches her eggs by fixing her eyes on the spot in the sand where she has buried them; so the Christian during prayer should fix his or her whole attention on God for fear of losing spiritual fruits. The faithful prostrate themselves and recite the Our Father in front of the altar curtain whenever they enter the church, and they kiss its hem. The curtain of the iconostasis, which is usually red, is black for Holy Week and then white until Pentecost.

On the church walls one can see multiple icons. Relics may be lodged in a type of sarcophagus, and when the faithful come to ask intercession of the saint, they rest their head on the container or lie flat on the ground in front of it. Relics are also kept in cylindrical bolsters placed under the icon of the saint. The relics are taken in procession on the saint's day. When they are taken out, the piece of linen covering them is removed and they are anointed with a mixture of perfumed oil (*ḥanut*) and aromatics; it is closed again and put back in place after the procession in the church.

Liturgical Vestments

Liturgical vestments are mostly long white robes with long sleeves embroidered with crosses. Married priests wear a kind of cloth miter (*ṭailasân*). For the Liturgy, monastic priests replace their black hood (*qalanswa*) with a white one. Priests may wear a sort of white linen cloth covering the head for the celebration of the Liturgy. Bishops replace their black turbans by white ones. On Good Friday, from the Sixth Hour until the end of the offices, all the clergy wear a black burnus, and the pillars of the church are covered with black cloths.

Daily Office

The Offices of the Hours are fixed. In the monasteries one monk will go from monk to monk telling each which Psalm to recite; the Psalms are recited in a low voice. To the Psalms is added an invariable reading from Holy Scripture and other prayers such as the Creed, the Gloria, and the Theotokia. Every celebration of the Eucharist must be preceded by the two Offices of the Incense, evening and morning.

Eucharist

To start the Liturgy the priest says prayers of preparation and washes his hands.[7] Then comes the procession of the "Lamb" (*ḥamal*)—the eucharistic bread—to the altar. The Lamb is a round loaf, stamped with a cross composed of thirteen squares: the largest one in the middle represents Christ (it will be for the celebrant's communion), and the others represent the Apostles. The loaf bears the inscription of the beginning of the Trisagion in Greek letters and is pierced by five holes symbolizing the wounds of Christ on the Cross. An uneven number of such loaves are presented in a basket to the priest, who eyes them carefully and chooses the best looking, "a spotless lamb" (Exod. 12:5), for consecration. He "cleans" it with a white cloth and blesses it by making the sign of the cross in different places with wine on his thumb; he then wraps it in the cloth and puts it on his head for the procession to and around the altar. The loaves that were not chosen will be distributed as blessed bread at the conclusion of the Liturgy. The priest also sniffs the wine.

Eucharistic loaf.

After a prayer of thanksgiving, the absolution of the officiants and the people takes place. Then come three readings from an Epistle of Saint Paul, a Catholic Epistle, and the Acts of the Apostles. These are followed by the Trisagion and the reading of the Gospel (which is preceded by a Psalm verse).

Next come the sermon, prayers of intercessions, the Creed, and the kiss of peace. Then begins the Anaphora, the central part of the Liturgy, which includes the consecration of the Holy Gifts and various commemorations and intercessions. Communion is preceded by Our Father and a prayer of preparation for reception. Finally comes the dismissal. In general, the liturgical sequence is quite similar among all the Oriental Churches.

Everyone receives communion without shoes. The faithful go into rooms alongside the altar, men on the left of the sanctuary, women on the right, or all are in front of the sanctuary door. Communion is given under both kinds. The Body of Christ is placed in the mouth of the faithful, and the Blood is given separately from a liturgical spoon. The faithful place a handkerchief before their mouth to prevent the Gifts from falling, and a sip of water taken after communion ensures that the elements are consumed. Women's heads are covered. At the end of the Liturgy the priest distributes the blessed bread to the faithful. After the priest has finished washing the sacred vessels, he takes the pitcher and sprinkles water with his right hand on the faces and heads of the faithful, going all around the church.

Two rites of absolution are especially characteristic of the Coptic celebration: the absolution "of the Son" after the presentation of the gifts, and the absolution "of the Father" before communion. When the celebrant elevates the Holy Gifts before communion, he also recites a magnificent christological confession of faith that speaks of the unity of divinity and humanity in Christ without the humanity being absorbed:

Coptic priest giving the Holy Body.
Photograph courtesy of Christine Chaillot

> Amen, amen, amen. I believe, I believe, I believe and confess to the last breath that this is the Life-giving Flesh, that of the Only-begotten Son, our Lord and our God, our Savior Jesus Christ. He took it from our Lady and Queen, the Mother of God, the pure and the holy Saint Mary, and made it one with His Divinity without mingling and without confusion and without alteration. He confessed the good confession before Pontius Pilate, and by His own will He gave Himself up on the Cross to redeem us. In truth, I believe that His Divinity was never separated from his Humanity for one moment nor for the twinkling of an eye. (Anaphora of Saint Basil)

These same words are also recited in the Ethiopian rite, in the Anaphora of the Apostles.

Long intercessory prayers, or litanies, include all people and situations: the living and the dead, the sick, travelers, the offerings and the offerers, celestial beings (angels, cherubim and seraphim; prayers are made for clergy and laity, for reconciliation, for natural events, including the rising of the Nile. The Egyptian year is, in fact, divided into three parts, based on the vital rhythm of the Nile River before the construction of the Aswan Dam. The ecological intercessory prayer acquires a universal scope:

> Raise [the waters of the Nile] to their measure according to Your grace. Give joy to the face of the earth. May its furrows be abundantly watered and its fruit be plentiful. Prepare it for sowing and harvesting. Manage our life as You deem fit. Bless the crown of the year with Your goodness for the sake of the poor of Your people, the widow, the orphan, the traveler, the stranger, and for the sake of us all who entreat You and seek Your Holy Name. For the eyes of all wait upon You, for You give them their food in due season. Deal with us according to Your goodness, O You who give food to all flesh. Fill our hearts with joy and gladness, that we too, having sufficiently in everything, always may abound in every good deed.

The Liturgy is sung in its entirety, with direct participation by the people.

Until the twelfth century the Copts had many anaphoras, but the twenty-sixth canon of Patriarch Gabriel II then ordered the use of only three, which are the ones that have been retained. The Anaphora of Saint Basil in the Alexandrine version is the most frequently used. On feast days the so-called Anaphora of Saint Gregory Nazianzen is used, it, too, being of Cappadocian origin. On the other hand, the Anaphora of Saint Cyril—which evolved from the ancient liturgy of Saint Mark, an authentic Egyptian composition—has almost disappeared from use.

Liturgical Books

The famous commentator on the liturgy in the thirteenth and fourteenth centuries, Abu'l Barakat, in his *Book of the Lamp*, lists liturgical books that have continued in use in the Coptic Church. These comprise the Euchologion, the Rituals, the Pontifical, the Synaxary or Book of Propers, the Lectionary, and the Book of Hours or Horologion (*agbia*).

The Coptic tradition makes a distinction between the canonical Hours and the Office of Psalmody (*tasbeha*), which is sung daily. The Psalmody includes four biblical odes (*hos*), some beautiful hymns to the Mother of God (Theotokia), one for each of day of the week, doxologies (praises to the saint of the day), and intercessions, as well as some other hymns (*psali, lobsh, tarh* . . .) and other prayers (such as Creed, Trisagion). In the month of Kiyahk there are special nighttime psalmodies for the Virgin and for Advent.

Liturgical Year

The era of Diocletian, who became Roman emperor in 284 and under whose reign many Christians were killed, became the Era of the Martyrs and the beginning of the Coptic calendar. The annual calendar follows the old Egyptian calendar, divided into twelve months of thirty days each and a final short month of five days (or six days in a leap year). The names of the Coptic months go back to names of pharaonic gods and feasts. For instance, the first month, Tut, was dedicated in pharaonic Egypt to Thot, god of wisdom and sciences. This religious calendar governed also agricultural life and its seasons (flooding, planting, harvesting). The liturgical year begins on 1 Tut, which is presently 10 September of the Gregorian calendar (and 11 September in leap year).

During the Liturgy of the first day of the Coptic New Year (Nayruz), the Gospel reading of Luke 4:14-30 recalls the commission to preach the Good News and to proclaim a year full of grace. It is a summons to become new creatures in Christ: "Let us abandon all evil inclinations. Let us purify our hearts in the name of the Lord";

"Let us sing to the Lord a new song of praise because He has made a covenant of salvation with us."

There are fourteen feasts of Christ. The seven major feasts are as follows: Christmas, or Nativity (7 January, 29 Kiyahk); Epiphany (19 January, 11 Tuba), Annunciation (considered as the feast of Incarnation, 7 April, 29 Baramhat); Palm Sunday; Easter; Ascension; and Pentecost. On Easter Monday an early morning Liturgy is celebrated with the reading of the appearance of Christ to the disciples on the road to Emmaus (Luke 24:13–35); this day is kept as a spring feast, Sham al-Nasim, and Copts organize picnics. The seven minor feasts of Christ are Circumcision (14 January, 6 Tuba), the First Miracle at the Wedding at Cana (21 January, 13 Tuba), Presentation in the Temple (15 February, 8 Amshir), Maundy Thursday, the Sunday of Saint Thomas (the first Sunday after Easter), the Flight of the Holy Family to Egypt (1 June, 24 Bashans), and Transfiguration (19 August, 13 Misra). Two other feasts may be added in this list, feasts of the Cross (27 September, 17 Tut; and 19 March, 10 Baramhat). There are three "monthly commemorations": on the twelfth of every month, when memory is made of archangel Michael; on the twenty-first, for remembering Our Lady Mary; and on the twenty-ninth, for remembering the Annunciation and the Birth and Resurrection of Christ. Two other archangels (Gabriel and Raphael) also have commemorations on specific days.

There are more than thirty feasts dedicated to the Virgin. The main ones are the Annunciation of her Birth, her Birth, her Presentation in the Temple, her Dormition, her Assumption, and the Dedication of the first church in her name.

As in other Oriental calendars, the main saints of the Synaxarion are: Patriarchs; martyrs, several of whom are knightly saints (like George), and other local saints (for example, Mercurius/Abu Sefein, Victor, Theodore, Menas the miracle worker, Mary the Egyptian); and numerous monks. From the Apocalypse (4:4–11) are celebrated the "four living creatures" and the twenty-four elders around the throne of the Lamb. The main saints are well represented in the iconography, as for example on the walls of the newly restored ancient church of the Monastery of Saint Anthony by the Red Sea.

Some Sacraments

In the baptismal rite[8] the newly baptized is dressed in white with a red ribbon that is attached around the chest (the ribbon symbolizing the blood of Christ, which has cleansed us). Then the newly baptized is crowned because he or she becomes a new son or daughter of the divine King. In the wedding rite the priest presents the rings and puts oil on the couple's foreheads. The priest puts the crowns (*al-iklil*) on their heads. The bride stands on the right of the bridegroom, who is dressed in a gold-embroidered cloak symbolic of his spiritual priesthood in his new family.

Music

In Coptic music there are eight tones, as in the Byzantine rite. Coptic church music is accompanied at certain times by cymbal and the triangle. In the second half of the twentieth century, Ragheb Moftah devoted his life to the recording and analysis of the music with the help of the best chanters. Ernest Newlandsmith compiled thirteen volumes of notation of tunes. Coptic melodies are rather slow and repetitive. In some songs the same part of a word may be sung for several minutes in different notes and modulations.

Monasticism

When he was elected Patriarch of the Coptic Church, Cyril VI (1959–1971), a holy and wonder-working monk, decided above all to reorganize monastic life. Since then there have been many new vocations, in particular among the university educated. The hospitality of the monks is legendary, owing to their reception of every visitor as if he or she were Christ himself. Formerly a hymn of welcome was sung to clergy and laypeople who visited an Egyptian monastery. It is given here from a manuscript of the Monastery of Saint Macarius: "This is the place where hearts are weighed. Whoever comes here with faith finds forgiveness of sins and offenses. This is the habitation of saints, of athletes, of ascetics, and worshipers. This is the place of the pure of heart which makes their glory shine over the whole world, which spreads the perfume of their good reputation and of their joy." The prayer ends by asking God to protect the pilgrims by way of the prayers of the martyrs and saints. As in all the Oriental Christian traditions, it is usual for Coptic laypeople, and even certain Muslims who have been touched by this fraternal hospitality, to visit the monasteries regularly in order to pray at the tombs and relics of the holy monks and to converse with the monks and ask for their spiritual counsel. Pilgrimages bring together thousands of the faithful, especially those to the Monastery of Saint Demiana in the Delta and those of Al-Muharraq and al-Rizaiqat in Upper Egypt. Apparitions of the Virgin in Cairo, in ʿAyn al-Zaytun in 1968, and in Shubra in 1986, have attracted crowds of Christians and non-Christians.

The Ethiopians

The largest Oriental Orthodox Church community resides in Ethiopia. The traditional liturgical language is Ge'ez, which belongs to the south semitic family. Some prayers, however, may be said in the vernaculars, mostly in Amharic. The same liturgical rite is used in Eritrea.

A Christian Kingdom

Ethiopia lasted longest of the Christian kingdoms of the East; in 1974 the Emperor Haile Selassie was assassinated, and the Kingdom fell to a Marxist regime. The first Ethiopian Christian king of Axum, Ezana by name, was converted by Frumentius, a Syrian by origin, who was consecrated by Saint Athanasius of Alexandria as the first bishop of Ethiopia before the year 350. Local tradition tells that at the end of the fifth century the so-called Nine Saints, perhaps monks coming from the Eastern Byzantine Empire, evangelized more places around Axum, meriting the title of "Second Apostles." They would also have founded the first monasteries. Translations of the Bible and other books (probably including some liturgical ones) were made from Greek to Ge'ez during that period. The fall of Axum around the ninth century as well as the invasion of the Muslim leader Muhammad Gran in the sixteenth century explain why the material and manuscripts remaining from before those times are rare. In the fourteenth century, under the Coptic Metropolitan in Ethiopia, Abba Selama, some liturgical books were translated from Arabic into Ge'ez. In fact the Ethiopian Church continued to depend on the Coptic Church in Alexandria, which sent bishops to govern it until it gained its autocephaly in 1959.

Because of the links with the Coptic Church of Alexandria, a certain similarity exists at the level of the liturgy. In addition, there is creativity of indigenous Ethiopian material: for example, the *Book of Hours* by George of Gasetsha in the fifteenth century, and several anaphoras, two of which were composed (as Getatchew Haile has suggested) by famous Ethiopian monks, Samuel of Waldebba and (again) George of Gasetsha. A period of great development in hymnography in Ethiopia occurred in the fifteenth century, at the time of King Zara Yacob, who himself is said to have authored some prayers—"The Lord Reigneth" (*Egziabher nagsa*); "Praise of the Beloved" (*Sebhata fequr*); a prayer of anointing or the Book of the Pearl (*Mashafa bahrey*); and, above all, his compositions for the Virgin.[9]

Because of Ethiopia's peculiar position in Christian history and geography, its relationships with the liturgies of other ancient Churches (East and West) is eclectic and complex. For instance, there are connections with the Syriac rite. Some prayers are of Greek origin (the Anaphoras of Saint Mark and Saint James). One text, that of the Good Thief ("Remember me, O Lord, in your kingdom"), is still sung in distorted Greek on Good Friday. These foreign influences, including the Coptic, were indirect, often through Arabic translations, and the complicated paths of transmission largely remain to be clarified. According to Ugo Zanetti, the Ethiopian liturgy is apt to give us valuable information especially concerning the ancient Coptic liturgy.

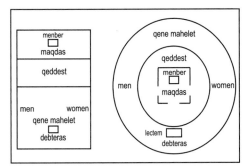

Plans of Ethiopian churches. (*Left*) rectangular; (*right*) circular. DRAWING BY BENJAMIN W. TUCKER BASED ON AN ILLUSTRATION BY CHRISTINE CHAILLOT

Liturgical Space

The most ancient churches of Ethiopia are in the style of a basilica, as can be seen in the ruins at the ancient capital of Axum and in other churches in Tigray province (for example, the church of the Debre Damo Monastery, which is the oldest church still standing in Ethiopia), as well as in Eritrea. The famous rock-hewn churches at Lalibela were built in the late twelfth and the early thirteenth century under the Zagwe king of that name. Lalibela and its surroundings are considered the "Holy Land" of Ethiopia.

In the rectangular churches, divided into three zones, the singers (*debteras*), who are a choir composed only of men, usually stand at the back of the church. In round-shaped churches, they stand in the outer ambulatory, facing the altar door. The circular churches are very typical of Ethiopia and are very similar in configuration to domestic dwellings in the villages, with conical thatched roofing. Inside these churches the space is divided into three rings. In the center is the sanctuary (*maqdas*). In the middle ring (*qeddest*), communion is given and the readings are made during the eucharistic liturgies. During festivals, readings before the Liturgy are made in the outside ring (*qene mahelet*), where the choir stands. The altar is called *menber*.

Church of Saint George at Lalileba. The Church of Saint George at Lalileba, Ethiopia, was hewn from the living rock; thirteenth century. WERNER FORMAN/ART RESOURCE, NY

What corresponds to the altar slab used in other churches is the *tabot*, generally a piece of wood with inscriptions, in particular that of the Holy Trinity, of the Virgin, and of the name of the patron saint after whom the church is dedicated. The *tabot* is consecrated with holy chrism. It is seen by Ethiopians as a replica of the Ark of the Covenant, or the Tables of the Law. The *tabot* is very important in Ethiopian spirituality, and thus great respect is expressed toward it, as is demonstrated when it is carried in procession at festivals.

Liturgical Vestments

Liturgical vestments are very colorful. So also are the umbrellas that are, as a sign of respect, held over the Gospel book during reading and over the Eucharist during distribution. During processions, umbrellas are held over the beautiful gold or silver gilt crosses, the icons, the heads of the prelates, and the *tabots*. Deacons and priests during the Liturgy cover their heads with a kind of crown made of metal or fabric. The bishops wear white clothes and turbans for the Liturgy, and black ones in daily life.

The Liturgy of the Eucharist

In the Eucharistic Liturgy, called *Qeddase*, the liturgy of the Word and the pre-anaphora are more or less invariable. After the Gospel has been read, the book is wrapped in a cloth and carried by the deacon among the faithful for them to kiss it and place it against their foreheads. Officially, fourteen anaphoras are used for various special occasions, but others also are known. Two Early Church anaphoras are preserved, that named after Our Lord Jesus Christ and that named after the Apostles, which is in fact the older one; both are frequently used.[10]

The eucharistic bread is stamped with a cross of thirteen squares. It is prepared by deacons in a special house east of the church called "the house of bread" (*bethlehem*). The deacon rings a bell when bread is brought from the *bethlehem* to the *maqdas* and at other liturgical times. To celebrate the Liturgy it is in principle necessary to have the participation of at least two priests and three deacons. At communion it is the celebrating priest who distributes the Body of Christ, and the main deacon the Blood.

When the priest dips his finger into the Blood and signs the Body, he says: "Grant to all those who partake of it, that it may be unto them a sanctification and a filling with the Holy Spirit, and for strengthening of the true faith, that they may hallow and praise You and Your beloved Son Jesus Christ with the Holy Spirit." The people answer, "Amen." And then the priest continues, "Grant us to be united through Your Holy Spirit, and heal us by this oblation that we may live in You for ever." After the Our Father, the people sing: "The hosts of the angels of the Savior of the world stand before the Savior of the world and encircle the Savior of the world, even the Body and Blood of the Savior of the world. Let us approach the face of the Savior of the world. In the faith which is of Him let us submit ourselves to Christ. . . . In the faith which is of Him, the Apostles followed His steps" (Anaphora of the Apostles). Many churches in Ethiopia are named after the Savior of the world (Medhane Alem).

The texts used for the sacraments of baptism and marriage reflect the Coptic texts, but Ethiopian practice is not always exactly the same.[11] Funerals are demonstrative affairs; everybody weeps, shouts, and beats their chest, raising their arms skyward, although the ecclesiastical authorities discourage these things because of the Christian hope in resurrection.

Offices and Other Prayers

The seven daily offices of the monks and nuns are found in the Book of the Hours (Mashafa Sa'atat), composed in the fourteenth century by the Ethiopian George of Gasetsha: it replaced the Book of Hours from the Coptic Horologion. For a detailed explanation of the offices, there is only one study to be referred to, that of Habtemichael Kidane.[12] The Ethiopian Lectionary follows the Coptic system, but revised. The main Antiphonary for the year (Degwa) is attributed to Saint Yared (sixth century). For Lent the Soma Degwa is used. The structure and the ordinary—the fixed parts—of the Divine Office are contained in the Me'eraf.[13] At the end of the Hours and before the Eucharist, the Prayer of the Covenant (Kidan) is used.

The Book of David (Dawit) includes Psalms, biblical Canticles, and the Praises of the Virgin (Weddase Maryam), one for each day of the week. The Praises of Mary are related to the Coptic Theotokia. The Ethiopians attribute them to Saint Ephrem the Syrian.

The following is a short extract from the Weddase Maryam that is rich in christology:

> Rejoice, O Mother of the Lord, joy of the angels; rejoice, O Pure Virgin announced by the prophets, rejoice, for you have found favor. . . . Rejoice, O Mother of the Only-begotten who was never separated from the bosom of his Father. . . . He came and was made man from you. Rejoice, O burning bush which the fire of the Godhead did not consume: rejoice, O Handmaid and Mother, Virgin and Heaven, who bore in your flesh the Heavenly Being who sits astride the cherubim.

Monks and nuns also pray with beads in a special way, making frequent prostrations as they proceed. The prayers involve manifold repetitions of "Lord Christ, have mercy upon us," " For the sake of our Lady Mary, Christ have mercy upon us," "Remember me in your Kingdom," "Lord have mercy upon us according to Your mercy," and the Our Father. The prayers are counted either on chaplets or on the joints of the fingers. Devout laypeople use these prayers as well.

Pious Ethiopians may privately recite the "Daily Prayers" (Selote Zewetir) and also other typical Ethiopian prayers, such as the Weddase Maryam, the Melke Iyesus, and the Melke Maryam. The *melke* is a spiritual portrait in which the parts of the body are greeted. Here is an example addressed to Krestos Samra, a famous woman saint of the fifteenth century, whose name literally means "Christ has been pleased with her": "Hail to your ears which were summoned to listen! The sword of the Gospel word thus penetrated inside your heart. . . . Hail to your mouth which took scrupulous care by keeping silent so as not to tell lies."

Devotion to the Virgin

Devotion to the Virgin is very prominent in Ethiopia and in the other Oriental Churches, but always with references back to Christ. At the beginning of the cathedral Office of the Vigil (*wazema*) comes a famous hymn to Mary called "Gate of Light" (Anqasa Berhan): "O Holy and Happy One, glorious and blessed, honored and exalted, the gate of Light, the ladder of Life, the dwelling place of the Divinity. . . . You are, my Lady, the golden basket in which is found the fresh manna which is offered continually and without fail, giving to the whole world grace and justice."

A canticle from the fifteenth century, called "The Hymn of the Flower" (Mahlete Sige), is the most famous Marian hymn in Ethiopia. It is sung during the month of flowers that follows on the rainy season, which is also the time when the Flight of the Holy Family into Egypt is commemorated:

Mary, Flower, whose season is spring, perfume the stench [of my sins] by your scent. . . . Now is the time of blossom and pleasant aromas; here is your Miracle, your Ointment which delights the Church. While by Him, Mary, you set me running on the road of the Redemption, make me flee like a gazelle or a young stag far from the face of error, the serpent's sister, whose poison kills.

Here, an allusion is made to a much read work in the Ethiopian Church, "The Miracles of Mary." Some of its stories are local stories of miracles from Egypt and Ethiopia; others, originated in France, were brought to Palestine by the Crusaders, translated into Arabic, and then finally translated into Ge'ez. In Ethiopian iconography the Virgin is very often shown surrounded by angels.

The faithful have also a special devotion to angels and saints. The Synaxary is similar to the Coptic, with additions of Ethiopian saints, and was completed at the latest by the end of the sixteenth century. It includes also short poems (*salam*). The Act, or literally "the fight" (*gedl*), shows the heroic aspects of the life of a saint and is read at church as part of the service on the saint's feast day, or privately at any time, in order to be imitated.

The Calendar[14]

The calendar of the days is similar to the Coptic. Specific to the Ethiopian calendar is that each year is placed under the patronage of an Evangelist. The calendar follows the Roman Empire system of two parts to the day, with twelve hours each for day and night: one o'clock in the day in Ethiopian time is seven o'clock in the morning in Western reckoning.

The Ethiopian tradition has a monthly repetition of feasts. There are four each month in honor of the Virgin. The archangel Michael is honored on the 12th, and Gabriel on the 19th. Among the saints, Gebre Manfas Qeddus ("The Servant of the Holy Spirit") is honored on the 5th, Abba Aragawi on the 14th, and Tekle Haymanot ("The Plant of Faith") and Krestos Samra on the 24th. On the 7th of every month is commemorated the feast of the Trinity; on the 10th, that of the Cross; on the 27th, that of the Savior of the world; on the 29th, that of the Nativity ("Hail to Your Nativity, O God Most High, which took place from the Virgin without fleshly union or seed. To manifest the face of Your Nativity in those days, the earth produced its greenery as you had ordered it to sprout, without a drop of rain or dew").

There are nine major feasts of Christ in the year: Incarnation/Annunciation (Tesbe'et), Nativity (Lidet), Baptism/Epiphany (Timkat), Transfiguration (Debre Tabor), Palm Sunday (Hosanna), Good Friday/Crucifixion (Siklet), Easter (Tensaye), Ascension (Erget), and Pentecost (Paraklitos). There are nine minor feasts: the Finding of the True Cross (Maskal), the three Sundays of Advent (Sibkat, or the Preaching of Prophets foretelling the Messiah; Berhan, or the Light of the world; and Nolawi, or the Good Shepherd), Christmas Eve (Genna), Circumcision of the Lord (Gezrat), Presentation of the Lord in the Temple (Ledeta Se'meon), the Miracle of Cana (Kana za Galila), and the Mount of Olives (Debre Zeit), which looks for the Second Coming of Christ (see Matthew 24). Other ways of listing the feasts may be found. There are thirty-three feasts of the Virgin, related to her life, her name, her miracles, and her sanctuaries.

The liturgical year comprises a movable paschal cycle and twenty fixed periods. The year begins on Maskaram (11 September, or 12 September in a leap year). The feast of the Holy Cross (Maskal), on 27 September, is celebrated in a special way with a big fire in Addis Ababa on the square of the same name. One of the greatest festivals is Epiphany or Timkat: the waters are blessed in commemoration of the Baptism of Christ, and the people wash or sprinkle themselves abundantly.

The names of the seven Lenten Sundays are usually taken from the Gospel readings. The first is Zewerede, or the descent of Jesus into the world (John 3:10–24); the second is Qeddest, or "Sanctity" (Matt. 6:16–24); then come the "Temple" (Mek'wrab) of John 2:12–25, the "Paralytic" (Mesagu) of John 5:1–24, the "Mount of Olives" (Debre Zeit, or the apocalyptic discourse of Jesus) from Matthew 24:1–35, the "Good Servant" (Gebr'her) of Matthew 25:14–30, and finally "Nicodemus" (Niqodimos) of John 3:1–11.

On Holy Saturday morning a ceremony takes place, during which the faithful receive green reeds (*qetema*), which they plait and bind on their heads. Like Noah's olive branch, these are a sign of peace, for "Christ made peace by His Cross."

During festivals the people, and especially the women, move in circles, clapping hands and singing songs of the day. After the Liturgy a meal is shared by the members of prayer associations (*tsewa mahebar*), which may be dedicated to the Holy Trinity, Christ, the Virgin, or a saint.

Music and Poetry

Church music is said to go back to the time of Yared (sixth century), but Western scholars think that it was not composed before the fifteenth century, with later revisions.[15] The melodies of the chants are in three modes: *ezel*, *ge'ez*, and *araray*, which is used in combination with the two other modes. Also ascribed to Yared for accompanying worship are the use of long drums (*kebero*), sistra (*senasile*), the clapping of hands, and rhythmic movements of the body (*shibsheba*), in a performance (*aqwaqwam*, or "way of standing") that recalls the dance of David before the Ark, in 2 Samuel 6, even though the Ethiopians do not like to call it a dance because of the secular associations of the term.

During the great feasts, after the Liturgy, the *tabots* are carried in procession three times around the church. Then, in two parallel ranks facing each other, the *debteras*, holding staves (*maqwamia*) and sistra and accompanied by drums, advance and retreat while chanting, first in a slow way and then faster until the end [see color plate 7]. The congregation claps hands and the women ululate, as is the practice in all Oriental Churches for celebrative occasions. The drum is mostly used for Mahelet, the chanting service of the choir. It is beaten before and after the Eucharist and also after the distribution of communion. No drums or other instruments are used during Lent. Some even say that musical instruments like the sistra, and "dances" by the *debteras*, go back to the time of the Levites dancing in front of the Ark in Solomon's Temple in Jerusalem. The use of drums to give rhythm to the songs of the *debteras* is certainly more of African origin. A great center of church music and chanting was the capital at Gondar, established in the seventeenth century.

In keeping with the traditional, oral pattern of religious instruction, the liturgical chant (*zema*) is learned by heart. Some students learn to compose liturgical poems (*qene*), which they submit to the teacher for correction. When they have been well trained, the young *debteras* will join the church choir, in which they may be asked to produce a *qene*. Qenes are sung at least every Sunday and for festivals, when *debteras* are present. The *qene* can also be prepared for other occasions, such as weddings or funerals. The newly composed poem is used only once. Each poem must contain words chosen for their double meaning so as to have both a literal and a hidden sense, called "wax and gold." The student must not only know very well the Ge'ez language but must also be acquainted with the Bible and Ethiopian history and legends, as the following example shows: "The tree has grown, as the tree flourishes when watered by the peasant" could be rendered, too, as, "Tekle Haymanot [meaning The Plant of Faith] became sanctified by his tears," meaning also that Tekle Haymanot, the great Ethiopian saint and ascetic (died 1313), aided in the "restoration" of the Solomonic dynasty after the period of the Zagwe kings. At present a few women also teach the art of the *qene*.

Gestures of Piety

The gestures of Ethiopian Christians are particularly pious. From the gate of the church compound and several times until reaching the church and inside, they bow, prostrate themselves, and lift up their hands to heaven. On feast days, which as has been seen are numerous, they spend entire nights and days praying in the church in a standing position. It is an impressive sight to see thousands of the faithful dressed in their white veil (*shama*) rushing in and out of church. This piety is also manifest during pilgrimages to the great historic centers, such as Axum, Lalibela, and Gondar, and in the monasteries. Two of the most popular pilgrimages are those to Kulubi and to the Monastery of Zeqwala, which is dedicated to Saint Gebre Manfas Qeddus. Many pilgrims come on foot, even barefoot. On arrival, some of them go around the church several times on their knees. In the holy places there are, most of the time, springs of water (*tsebel*, or "holy water") from which the pilgrims drink or wash for therapeutic reasons. It is the custom to make gifts on the occasion of pilgrimages or feasts—for example, the offering of a cow whose meat will be distributed to the poor. Families also distribute alms and food to beggars on the occasion of baptisms, weddings, or funerals, and some also have churches built. When an Ethiopian man or woman is widowed, it is traditional for them to take up the monastic life, either in a monastery or at home. It is also customary for other people to supply them with food, just as is done for students in the traditional religious schools. Beggars make their requests and express their thanks for the gifts they receive in the name of the Holy Trinity, of the saint whose day it is, and very often in the name of the Virgin.

The Armenians

Armenian Church tradition has built its apostolicity on the disciples Thaddeus and Bartholomew. There was surely an early evangelization by Greek- and Syriac-speaking missionaries through contacts with the important centers of Caesarea in Cappadocia and Edessa. What is certain is that Saint Gregory the Illuminator, after being ordained (c. 301) by the bishop of Caesarea, Leontius, became the first head of the Armenian Church. The propers of the Liturgy for the Feast of the Church at Etchmiadzin summarize the conversion of Armenia. In a vision, Gregory was shown to build the first church in the country, in Etchmiadzin, and he converted the king, Tiridat. This made Armenia the first nation in which Christianity was established, and the event is sung in a hymn (*sharagan*): "The Only-Begotten Son has descended [which is the meaning of "Etchmiadzin"], and the light of glory was with Him; voices resounded in the depths of Hades. Gregory saw the great light, and joyfully told of it to the king, who believed. Come, let us build the sanctuary of the light, for therein shone forth light unto us in the land of Armenia."

After the invention of the Armenian alphabet around 405 by Mesrob (also known as Mashtots), the Bible, the Liturgy, and other books were translated from Greek and Syriac into Armenian by a group called the "Holy Translator Doctors." Their feast is considered a national feast of culture.

A great portion of Armenia was made a Persian province at the end of the fourth century. The Persians of Zoroastrian religion did not view positively the new Christian faith, and some persecution ensued until 484. Because he died with his men, in 451, for safeguarding the Christian faith against the Zoroastrians, the Armenian Vartan is considered a martyr. The event is celebrated every year as a martyrs' commemoration and a national feast by the Armenian Church: "A victor filled with supernal power, valiant among soldiers, O blessed Vartan . . . Together with their glorious and holy children, the watchful shepherds quenched the flame of the fire-worshiping Persians with the fire of the Spirit."

After the fall of the Bagratid dynasty (885–1045), many Armenians fled to Cappadocia and Cilicia, where a kingdom was founded. A new ecclesiastical See was established in Cilicia in the twelfth century, and contacts were then made with the Crusaders from the West. Latinisms in the Armenian rite date from that time (11th–14th centuries). This was, in fact, one of several waves of influences on the Armenian liturgy: first from Mesopotamian Syrian and Cappadocian Greek; then in the fifth century from Jerusalem, especially in the Lectionary and Calendar, and with the translation of the Anaphora of Saint James into Armenian; and again around the turn of the second millennium, from Byzantium. The rite reached its full dimensions around the fourteenth century, with some small additions occurring after that date.

Owing to the schools that they build in the Middle East and in the diaspora, the Armenians continue to speak their language, and they fiercely preserve the use of  classic Armenian for their prayer life, with some exceptions in the United States, where some translations have been made into English. Classical Armenian remained the literary language until the nineteenth century.

Liturgical Space

An Armenian church is easily recognizable by its architecture. The central dome is surmounted by a conical roof. The oldest archeological remains of churches, some in basilican shape, are found at Zwarthnots, near Etchmiadzin (seventh century), and at Ani (tenth–eleventh century), as well as at Dvin (fifth century) and Aghthamar (tenth century). The church building is divided into a vestibule, the nave, the chancel, and the sanctuary. The chancel, raised by a step from the nave, is closed by a low screen or balustrade. From the chancel, one mounts to the elevated platform known as the *bem* or *bema*, upon which the altar table is located. To reach the

The Cathedral at Etchmiadzin, Armenia.
PHOTOGRAPH COURTESY OF CHRISTINE CHAILLOT

sanctuary or altar area (*srbaran*), there are three steps (or an odd-numbered set) on each side. The rectangular altar itself is elevated by three to twelve slight raises, on which are placed candelabra, the Gospel book, and, at the highest level, a picture of the Mother of God presenting the Savior (in a pose called "Mother and Child Enthroned"). This picture is sometimes replaced by a representation of the Resurrection from Easter until Ascension, and by the appropriate picture at Christmas. Although there may not be many pictures, they are always present, especially in the cathedral in Etchmiadzin, in Jerusalem, and in the churches of the New Julfa in Isfahan (Iran).

In the north wall of the apse, to the left of the altar, is a tabernacle closed by a door or a little curtain, where the Holy Gifts are kept for the sick; it is there, on the table, that the preparation of the oblations takes place, unless that is done at the altar table itself. A cupboard located on the right side of the altar stores the liturgical vessels and the *myron*. A single curtain (*varakoyr*) stretched on wires in front of the sanctuary is open during most of the Liturgy, but is closed on three occasions: during the preparation of the gifts; when the celebrant himself receives holy communion; and immediately following the communion of the faithful, when the chalice is cleaned and the vessels are put in their places. During Lent a large picture of the Crucifixion, or else a cross, is placed in front of the altar curtain (a black fabric is used for that season).

Typically Armenian are the large stones known as *khatchkars*, on which crosses are sculpted. The decorative carving can be highly intricate. These monuments may be found both in and around the churches and graveyards as well as across the countryside.

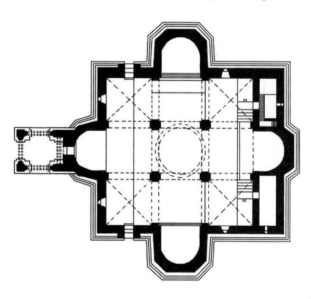

Plan of the Cathedral at Etchmiadzin. Drawing by Benjamin W. Tucker after Adriano Alpago Novello et al., 1995

Liturgical Vestments

The priest and bishop wear a cope over which is placed a large and hard collar or amice (*vakas*); underneath the cope are the alb (*shapik*) and the pectoral stole (*porourar*). A girdle (*goti*) and maniples on the forearms (*bazpan*) are also worn. The bishop's attire has two components taken from the Latin tradition, the miter and a pastoral cross or crozier (*gavazan*). Bishops also have the *omophorion* taken from the Byzantine tradition, and the Panagia medal (*panaké*) with a representation of Christ and his Mother. Learned celibate clergy, given the title of "doctor" or "teacher" (*vartapet*), may carry a T-shaped staff decorated with heads of snakes and reminiscent of Aaron's rod as a sign of their authority to preach. In daily life the *vartapets* and bishops wear a black cassock accompanied with a black and pointed headgear that is worn for the daily offices, but not for the eucharistic liturgy. The Catholicos, or Patriarch, is distinguished by his wearing, on the right side of the *goti*, an *epigonation* (*konk'er*), presently a lozenge-shaped piece of embroidery. During his consecration the Catholicos's head is covered by a large veil (*kogh*).

Eucharist

A primitive recension of the Anaphora of Saint Basil is preserved in Armenian and ascribed to Saint Gregory the Illuminator. Catholicos Yovhannes Mandakuni (478–490) translated other Cappadocian Greek anaphoras, and one of them, attributed to Saint Athanasius, eventually supplanted all others in Armenian usage. It seems to be the only anaphora in use during the mid-tenth century at the time of Khosrov (died c. 963), who devotes some of his commentary to it, even if he mentions the existence of other anaphoras. In the ninth and tenth centuries, the Liturgy of Saint Basil was again translated into Armenian in a more developed Byzantinized redaction. The Byzantine Liturgy of Saint John Chrysostom was also translated, by the thirteenth century. Later commentators on the liturgy include Nerses Lambronts'i (died 1198) and Yovhannes Archishets'i (died c. 1330).

The first part of the Divine Liturgy, or preparation, is conducted in the chancel, down from the sanctuary. The Liturgy of the Word, or Synaxis, is known to the Armenians as the Midday Office (Djashou). Before the Lesser Entrance the Monogenes hymn is sung, as in the Byzantine Liturgy of Saint John Chrysostom. Prior to the reading of the Gospel, the deacon says, "Let us hear," and the people respond, "God speaks."

The Great Entrance with the bread and wine is similar to that in the Byzantine tradition. It is accompanied by a hymn: "The Body of the Lord and the Blood of the Savior are laid before us. The heavenly hosts invisibly sing and say with unceasing voice 'Holy, Holy, Holy, Lord of Hosts.'" The Anaphora includes the Offertory of the Gifts, the Thanksgiving or Eucharistic Prayer, the Fraction, and Communion.

Latinization of the beginning and the end of the Armenian Divine Liturgy began in the fourteenth century under the influence of the Dominican friars. It includes the reading of the Last Gospel, John 1:1–14, at the end of the service. These Latin usages were slow to take hold in the Armenian liturgy. As late as the middle of the seventeenth century, some manuscript euchologies still did not contain them. What is also specific is the use of unleavened bread (*azyme*) stamped with Christ on the Cross or with the Resurrection monogram, and pure red wine, unmixed with water.

Offices and the Life of Prayer

The main liturgical books are the Book of the Liturgy or Mystery (Khorhurt'atetr) for the priest, the Book of Rituals (Mashtots) for use at the other sacraments, the Book of Hymns (Sharakan), the Book of Hours for the daily services (Jhamakirk'), and the Lectionary (Casoc).

The cathedral Sunday offices of fifth-century Jerusalem probably shaped the Liturgy of the Hours. The Armenian offices were enriched by hymns composed by Nerses Shnorhali (died 1173). It seems that the sunrise office is an indigenous Armenian composition. "Peace" and "Rest" are Compline services that are offered late at night and just before retiring for bed. They were compiled in Armenia, and they contain many hymns and prayers that are uniquely Armenian, yet they also include elements that are found in the Byzantine and other traditions. There are very short daytime offices (*voghormias*) that are based on Psalm 50 (51).

The Office of the Myrrh-Bearing Women takes place within Sunday matins. It is not a preparation for the Divine Liturgy, but a weekly celebration of the Lord's Resurrection on the Lord's Day.

Liturgical Year

The liturgical year is divided into eight periods: Epiphany, Lent, Easter, "Holy Spirit" (from Pentecost to Transfiguration), Transfiguration (the seventh Sunday after Pentecost), Assumption of the Mother of God (on the Sunday nearest to 15 August), Exaltation of the Holy Cross (on the Sunday nearest to 14 September), and Hifnag (the fifty days before Epiphany). This last begins with the Sunday nearest to 25 November. Armenians celebrate Christmas and Epiphany on the same day (6 January), thus maintaining the ancient custom of all Christians until perhaps the fourth century. All major feasts must be celebrated on a Sunday.

At the Second Council of Dvin in 551, a correction of the date of Easter was made by Moses II, whereby the year 552 became the first year of the new cycle. In 1922, according to an encyclical of Catholicos Georg V, the Armenians adopted the Gregorian calendar. As of this writing, only the Armenians in Jerusalem use the Julian calendar.

On the evening of Palm Sunday, Armenians have an office called the "Opening of Doors" (Turnpatsek). It symbolizes the entrance into the heavenly Jerusalem.

On Holy Thursday (Avak), an Office of the Sufferings or Darkness (Khavaroum) takes place in the evening, in memory of the last night of Christ on earth. The lights of the church are extinguished after each of the readings, which are canonically twelve in number (covering the betrayal, arrest, trials, and passion of Christ). On Holy Saturday evening, all lights are extinguished but are put on again (Jrakalouits, "lighting candles") at the reading of Isaiah 60. Three readers, representing the three young men who were not consumed in the fiery furnace, "psalmodize" from Daniel 3:1–30. For Easter (Zadig) and the following forty days, the people repeat, "Kristos hariav ee merelots" ("Christ is risen from the dead"), as is done in other Oriental Churches.

On the seventh Sunday after Pentecost is celebrated the feast of the Transfiguration of Christ, which supplanted the ancient and "pagan" feast of "Rose Garlands" in memory of the temple of the goddess Astghig, decorated with flowers. People splash each other with water during the feast.

Because grapes ripen and are harvested in the middle of August in Armenia, it is a custom in all Armenian Churches to bless and distribute them after the liturgy of the Assumption of the Virgin. The "first fruits" are used to make wine for the Eucharist. Various hymn writers call Christ "the Good Fruit."

The various feasts of the Holy Cross include: the remembrance of the Apparition of the Holy Cross in 351 over Mount Zion in Jerusalem (the Fifth Sunday after Easter); the Exaltation of the Holy Cross (14 September, but celebrated on the nearest Sunday); the Holy Cross of Varak (near Van), where it is said that a piece of the Cross was hidden by Saint Hripsime (second Sunday after the Exaltation of the Holy Cross); and the Discovery of the Cross by Empress Helena in the fourth century (sixth Sunday after the Exaltation of the Holy Cross). There are seven feasts of the Virgin. Besides the feasts of the Annunciation (7 April) and of Mary's Assumption (the Sunday nearest 15 August), the major feasts of the Virgin are the Birth of the Mother of God (8 September), the Presentation of the Mother of God in the Temple (21 November), and the Conception of the Mother of God (9 December). Two minor feasts of the Virgin are associated with the discovery of the box containing the Virgin's veil (fifth Sunday after Pentecost) and the discovery of her belt (second Sunday after the Assumption).

The Lectionary (Tshashots) used today by the Armenians is a developed form of the ancient Lectionary of Jerusalem. Saints' days are on Mondays, Tuesdays, and Thursdays, and, for the main saints, Saturdays. Saints are never commemorated on Sundays nor on the days after the five great festivals, and never on Wednesdays and Fridays. The latter are days of abstinence with a penitential spirit, except during the fifty days following Easter.

In the Armenian calendar of saints are found not only Armenian names but also biblical ones as well as non-Armenian saints (Greek, Syrian, early Latin, Persian, Arab, and others). Highly venerated are the martyrs of Avarayr (451), namely Saint Vartan and his Companions, mentioned above, including the Catholicos Saint Hovsep (Joseph) and the priest Saint Ghevond (Leontius). On the feast day of Saint Thaddeus, Saint Sandoukht, the daughter of King Sanadrouk and the first woman martyr and saint of Armenia, is also celebrated.

Other Sacraments

The Armenian liturgy of initiation is substantially close to the oldest Syrian understanding of baptism, although the pre-baptismal anointing is no longer practiced.[16] For the blessing of the baptismal braid (*narod*), the priest twists red and white ribbons and ties them around the neck of the child. Crowns may replace the *narod*.

For betrothal and matrimony the priest puts braids on the couple to keep them holy and united in spirit. With crowns on their heads, the bride and groom face each other while holding right hands. The best man holds a cross over the heads of the couple while the priest asks God to bless the crowning of the couple. The deacon then brings a tray with a cup of sweet wine that is consumed by the newly wedded couple.

For the memorial of the deceased, and on other special occasions, Armenians offer *madagh*, a custom that has its roots in pre-Christian animal sacrifice. An animal is blessed, sacrificed, and the meat is then divided. The family that offered the *madagh* keeps a portion, which is consumed at a festive gathering. Other portions are distributed to neighbors, the poor, the sick, and the clergy. The ceremony is still observed in Armenia and elsewhere but is discouraged by the ecclesiastical authorities.

The hymn "In Jerusalem Above," attributed to Saint Nerses Shnorhali, is a beautiful funeral hymn: "In Jerusalem above, in the dwellings of the angels where Enoch and Elijah live in old age in dove-like form, radiant in the Garden of Eden: have mercy, Merciful Lord, on the souls of those that are asleep." Other funeral hymns offer words such as these: "All the nations of men rejoiced when they heard of Your Resurrection. With new feathers were they adorned at Your Resurrection, O You Holy Only-Begotten. Merciful Lord, have mercy on the souls of those that are asleep"; "O You Life from Life and Light from Light, who have made us out of the earth and have renewed us again by the second birth of the font and have saved us by grace from that first death: In Your Father's mansions of light give rest to those of us that are asleep"; and "In gladness did the heavenly hosts come down from heaven into the earth, when You arose from the dead and shone forth as a Light to all creatures. By Your holy and

Blessing the myron. The Armenian Catholicos in Etchmiadzin blessing the holy myron, 2001. PHOTOGRAPH COURTESY OF CHRISTINE CHAILLOT

life-giving Resurrection, raise those who are asleep unto the deathless life. Make them enter with full lamps into the nuptial chamber with the wise, holy virgins."

Music and Poetry

The creation of church hymns is attributed to Saint Mesrob and Saint Sahak. Armenian melodies are sung according to eight modes. These are said to have been adapted from the Byzantine, possibly in the fifth century. Makar Yegmalian and Vatarpet Komitas produced new compositions in the nineteenth century. The Armenian repertoire includes hundred of hymns (*sharagans*) that are recognized as ecclesiastical poetry.

Many manuscripts exist of music that is no longer used but are the subject of scholarly study. Liturgical fans (*kshotz*) surrounded with small bells are shaken during the liturgy.

Prayers from *The Book of Lamentations* by Gregory of Narek (tenth century) are considered to be curative, and they may be "psalmodized" over the sick. Thus from the third prayer is the following:

> Make of the composition of this Book of Lamentations, which was begun in Your Name, O Most High, a life-giving remedy to heal Your creatures from their sicknesses of soul and body. What I have begun, I pray You to complete. Let Your Spirit be intimately united with it. Let the breath of Your great power be joined to these poems which are Yours and which Your grace inspired me to write.[17]

Nerses Shnorahli was consecrated as Catholicos in 1166. One of the most popular prayers he wrote is of twenty-four verses and begins with, "I confess with faith, and adore You, O Father, Son, and Holy Spirit." He enriched the Book of Hours with compositions such as "Aravot Louso" and "Aysor Anjar." Prime by Nerses sounds like a cosmic prayer:

> From the east to the west, from north and from south, all races and peoples praise You in a new hymn, the Maker of all things, who this day have shot forth the sunlight into the world. Churches of the righteous, glorifiers of the Holy Trinity, at the dawning of light, praise Christ the Dawn of Peace, with the Father and the Holy Spirit, who has shot forth the light of his knowledge into us.

The Syrians

In the region of Antioch, at the beginning of Christianity, Greek was spoken mostly in towns on the seacoast, and Syriac was used in the countryside, around Edessa, Nisibis (that is, in Mesopotamia), and also in Palestine. So, the Syriac language was spoken by many Christians, and was also used liturgically, in the Eastern Roman Empire and in the Persian Empire (modern-day Iraq and western Iran). Syriac is a semitic language close to the Aramaic spoken by Christ. Syriac is divided into two dialects: West Syriac, which is used by the Syrian Orthodox, the Syrian Catholics, and the Maronites (with many words ending in *o*); and East Syriac, which is used by the Church of the East and by the Churches that sprang from it, the Chaldean Catholic and the Syro-Malabar Catholic in India (words ending in *a*). In this section I deal with only the Syrian Orthodox, which is one of the Oriental Orthodox Churches. Liturgical scholars call their rite "West Syrian."

Following the christological misunderstanding of Chalcedon (451), the Syrian Orthodox community had a separate Patriarchate located in different places, though then with the main seat in the Monastery of Deir Zafaran (1293–1933). In the beginning of the twenty-first century the Syrian Orthodox are still found living in Turkey, Syria, Iraq, and Lebanon. Syriac continues in use for the liturgy but it is being displaced more and more by local languages, such as Arabic, or by translations in the diaspora. The Syrian Orthodox community in South India uses Syriac less and less and substitutes Malayalam, the language of daily life. English is much used by Indian communities in the diaspora.

Three principal liturgical centers had a major influence in the origins of the Syrian Orthodox rite: part of the liturgy was translated from Greek into Syriac, borrowing from the traditions of both Antioch and Jerusalem; the third center, in Syriac, was Edessa. So Syrian Orthodox prayers come partly from the Greek and partly from original Syriac compositions, especially the hymns. The hymns are an important element in the Syriac liturgical tradition. They were composed in Syriac by great poet-theologians. The most famous is Ephrem the Syrian (died 373), who is called Harp of the Holy Spirit and regarded as the father of all the Syriac liturgical traditions. The repertoire was increased by new compositions in continuity with the basic common legacy of Saint Ephrem. The principal contributor was James of Serugh (died 521), called Cithara of the Holy Spirit on account of the beauty of his metrical homilies (*mimre*) and his hymns (*sughyotho*).

In the course of the seventh century, Syriac imposed itself on the Syrian Orthodox as the sole liturgical language and what still existed in Greek was abandoned. The structure of the anaphora was fixed in the seventh century. James of Edessa (died 708) is believed to be the author or compiler of most of the West Syrian liturgical texts. The present form of the eucharistic celebration belongs to the sixteenth century.

Liturgical Space

In northern Syria, especially between Antioch and Aleppo, one may see the ruins of hundreds of ancient churches. The churches of Qirk Bize and Qalb Loze are typical architectural examples. Other ancient churches are found at Tur Abdin in southeast Turkey, and in the north of Iraq. The church is generally rectangular with a single longitudinal nave or a nave and two side aisles. It is divided into three parts: the sanctuary (*beth qudsho*, with one or three altars); the choir (*qestromo*); and the nave (*haiklo*), or nave and aisles. In the choir area are two lecterns (singular *gudo*), around which the choirs alternate their prayers and readings. The altar is consecrated by a piece of wood (*tablito*). Above the altar there traditionally stands a canopy, which is said to be a symbol of the tabernacle of Moses or of Heaven. The altar is separated off by a long curtain that is often decorated. Older icons are extremely rare and have been replaced by modern paintings. Among the most beautiful murals may be mentioned those of the Monastery of Mar Moussa at Nebek, in Syria, which date from the eleventh and twelfth centuries.

As soon as they enter the church, the faithful go to kiss the Gospel book, which is always displayed before the altar on a special lectern (*golgotha*). The baptismal font is generally located at the front of the nave, on the south side. One may find relics kept in the "house of saints" (*beth qadishe*), which is called *beth sohde* if they are the relics of martyrs. Peculiar to the ancient churches of the Syriac rite is a platform (*bema*) situated in the middle of the nave, sometimes elevated, where certain read-

Ground plan of a traditional Syrian Orthodox church. Key: 1, sanctuary (*beth qudsho*); 2, nave (*haiklo*); 3, area for the choir and deacons, one step above the nave (*qestromo*); 4, two lecterns (sing. *gudo*) for prayers and readings sung by two choirs in alternation; 5, three (or more) altars (sing. *madbho*) in large buildings; 6, a special lectern called the "golgotha" (*gogultho*) located in front of the large altar curtain; 7, baptismal font; and 8, platform used for readings and chanting (*bema*). DRAWING BY BENJAMIN W. TUCKER BASED ON AN ILLUSTRATION BY CHRISTINE CHAILLOT

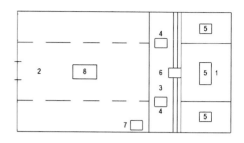

ings and chants are performed. This practice was influenced by the reading of the Torah from the *bema* in the synagogue.

Liturgical Vestments

Patriarchs, bishops and monks always wear a small hood (*eskimo*) falling to the back. For celebrating the Liturgy the married priests wear a little flat cap similar to the Jewish men's cap (*kippa*). On top of other liturgical vestments, all wear the cope, which can be very colorful. Slippers are prescribed for celebrants and deacons.

Eucharist

Anaphoras continued to be composed until the end of the Middle Ages. More than seventy anaphoras are counted in the Syrian Orthodox tradition, and about a dozen are still in use.[18] Many are attributed to famous Syrian Orthodox doctors, Patriarchs or prelates, such as Mar James of Serugh (died 521), Mar Severus of Antioch (died 538), Mar Philoxenus of Mabbug (died 523), Mar Dionysius James bar Salibi (died 1171), and Bar Hebraeus (died 1286) as well as Maphrian Marutha (died 649), John the bishop of Dara, and his contemporaries Dionysius of Tell Mahre (ninth century) and Moses bar Kepha (died 903), and Michael the Great (died 1199). Other anaphoras carry the names of Apostles or early Church Fathers: Saint Mark, Saint Peter, Saint John the Evangelist, Saint Xystus and Saint Julius of Rome, Saint John Chrysostom, and Saint Cyril of Alexandria. The two most frequently used eucharistic anaphoras are those of the Twelve Apostles (Antioch) and Saint James (Jerusalem).[19]

The post-Sanctus prayer in the Anaphora of Saint James presents the economy of salvation: "In the fullness of time You sent into the world even Your Only-Begotten Son, who being incarnate of the Holy Spirit and of the Virgin Mary renewed Your image that was impaired in mankind." And before the dismissal in the Anaphora of the Twelve Apostles, the celebrant says, "O Lord God of our salvation, Who for our sake became Man and redeemed us by the sacrifice of Your own Person, save us from all destructive corruption and make us temples for Your Holy Name because we are Your people and Your inheritance."

The basic structure of the Syriac anaphoras is very similar to that of the Greek anaphoras of Saint John Chrysostom and of Saint Basil. Small differences include the placement of the Creed, which comes before the Offertory and Peace in the Syrian (Antiochene) rite but after in the Byzantine rite; and the Fraction, which precedes the Our Father in the Syrian rite but follows in the Byzantine.

Certain Syrian Orthodox authors wrote commentaries on the liturgy, such as James of Edessa, John of Dara, Moses bar Kepha, Dionysius bar Saliba, Bar Hebraeus, and not forgetting a famous anonymous commentary written under the name of George, Bishop of the Arab tribes.[20]

Several times the priest flutters his hands over the Gifts at the consecration as a symbol of the descent of the Holy Spirit. Liturgical fans (*marwahotho*) are agitated at several times in the liturgy to emphasize the importance of the liturgical action, such as at the reading of the Gospel, at the Offertory, during the Epiclesis, and before the Communion. The fans are made of metal disks with symbols of the cherubim and seraphim on top of the poles; tiny bells are also attached.

The Offices and the Life of Prayer

The main books used for the Daily Offices are the Shehimo (for ordinary week days, with Psalms and hymns), Fenqitho or festal hymnary (with different hymns for Sundays and feasts of the year and of selected saints' days), and Hussoyo (with prayers known as *sedre* for feasts, Sundays, saints' days, Lent, and Holy Week). During the Liturgy the deacons and subdeacons use the book *Tekso d-Qurobho*. A reference guide to the biblical lections throughout the year is to be found in the *Mehawyono d-Qeryone*. The *Slawotho d-Kohne* is the book used by the priest for all prayers in the Church and when visiting people, for blessings, confession, for the sick, and so on. It includes the Anaphora of Saint James.

Hearing the Gospel. Worshipers listening to the reading of the Gospel during prayers at the Syrian monastery of Deir Zafaran, Turkey. PHOTOGRAPH COURTESY OF CHRISTINE CHAILLOT

Sunday Compline includes a trinitarian doxology focused on the Resurrection: "Glory to the Father who has woven garments of glory for the Resurrection; worship to the Son who was clothed in them at His Rising; thanksgiving to the Spirit who keeps them for all the saints."

The introductory prayer at weekday night offices looks to the divine vigilance for rescue from torpor: "Awaken us, Lord, from our sleep in the sloth of sin that we may praise Your watchfulness, You who watch and do not sleep. Give life to our mortality in the sleep of death and corruption, so that we may adore Your compassion, You who live and do not die."

Liturgical Year

The book *Kronikon* is like a church calendar (Surgodo), giving the dates of the movable observances for each year (for instance, the Fast of Nineveh and Easter Day) as well as the days of the saints' feasts.[21] The liturgical year is divided into seven seasons of about seven weeks: Annunciation; Nativity and Epiphany; Great Fast and Passion Week; Resurrection and Pentecost; the Apostles; the Transfiguration; the Cross.

According to Mar Ephrem Barsaum (died 1957), in his book *The Golden Key to Divine Worship*, the liturgical year begins with the "Sunday of the Consecration of the Church," which is followed by the "Sunday of the Rededication of the Church." Then come the Sundays of Advent, devoted to the Annunciations to Zechariah and the Mother of God, the Visitation of the Virgin to Elizabeth, the Birth of John the Baptist, the Revelation to Joseph, and the "Sunday before Christmas." At Christmas matins this is heard: "O Christ Jesus, Light from Light, You gave light by Your Epiphany to those who sit in darkness and the shadow of death. Give light, Lord, to our minds so that with the shepherds we may gaze on the Light of Your luminous Nativity from the Virgin, and offer You pure songs of praise on this day when You appeared in the flesh."

Most Sundays in the Great Fast are dedicated to some miracles of Christ: the wedding at Cana and the healings of the leper, the paralytic, the daughter of the Canaanite woman, and the man born blind. The parable of the Good Samaritan is read on the fifth Sunday in Lent.

Specific on Good Friday is the procession during which the celebrant carries a cross on the right shoulder around the inside of the church building.[22] Then the cross is fixed on a stand in front of the sanctuary, with two lighted candles symbolizing the two thieves. In the Ninth Hour the lights are put out. After a second procession of the cross, its "burial" takes place: it is washed with rose water, perfumed with frankincense, covered with pure cotton, wrapped in a cloth, and placed in a box symbolizing the coffin. At the end of the prayer the faithful pass under it and drink a bitter mixture reminding them of the Passion. Then the "coffin" is placed inside the altar in a place sealed with wax until Saturday. When the Resurrection is announced, the cross, decorated with a red scarf, is put on a stand in front of the altar with two lighted candles; the cross remains there until Ascension.

During the Pentecost Liturgy the deacon sprinkles the faithful with leaves to signify the descending gifts of the Holy Spirit.

There are seven feasts of the Virgin: Annunciation (25 March), Dormition (15 August), Birth (8 September), Glorification as Mother of God (26 December), Our Lady of the Sowing (15 January), Our Lady of the Blessing of the Harvest (15 May), and the Dedication of the first church named after the Virgin in Yathrib (15 June). A feast of the Virgin's belt (*zunoro*) is celebrated in Homs (where a piece is said to be kept) on the day of her Dormition.

Saints include Saint Peter, considered the first Patriarch of Antioch; Patriarchs such as Severus, Maphrians of the East such as Ahudemmeh, Marutha, and Bar Hebraeus; and others such as Philoxenus and Moses bar Kepha. Then there are monks such as A̱ho or Awgin, who is said to be of Egyptian origin and to have founded monasticism around Nisibis in the fourth century. Simeon the Stylite (386-459), a great ascetic who lived on top of a column, is mentioned in the poems of James of Serugh. Saint James Baradaeus reorganized the Syrian Orthodox Church in the sixth century and helped other non-Chalcedonian communities. Saint Gabriel founded the great Monastery named after him in Tur Abdin in the seventh century. The feast days of King Abgar of Edessa (who exchanged letters with Jesus, as reported in Eusebius of Caesarea's *Ecclesiastical History*, and who received a cloth—the *mandylion*—with the imprint of Christ's Face) and Saint Ephrem change according to Lent. Many martyrs are commemorated on their special days, such as Saint Ignatius of Antioch, the Forty Martyrs of Sebaste, Saint Behnam and his sister Sara (10 December), and the nun Saint Febronia (24 June).

Pilgrims visit ancient monasteries where relics are kept, such as in Zafaran Monastery (southeast Turkey), which was the seat of the Patriarchate from 1293 to about 1933; Mor Gabriel Monastery, presently the seat of the bishop of Tur Abdin; and Mar Mattai Monastery near Mosul, in Iraq. The relics of Saint James of Nisibis are still in the original church, in southeast Turkey. The faithful ask the intercession of certain saints for specific problems—for instance, Mar Malke, the disciple of Awgin, for cures from epilepsy and insanity.

Other Sacraments

After baptism and chrismation a piece of cloth (*klilo*) is put around the child's head, symbolizing a crown. Crowns are used also for weddings. For a funeral a bishop is carried seated on a throne to the church and to the grave.

Music and Poetry

The book that contains the main melodies and hymns is the *Beth Gazo* or *Octoechos*. The eight modes or tones are put into categories called cold and hot, wet and dry, joyful and mourning, active and passive. Nuri Iskandar recently transcribed the notation. Two tones are used during the same week. The chants are organized in an eight-week modal cycle in the following order: 1-5; 2-6; 3-7; 4-8; 5-1; 6-2; 7-3; 8-4. Each tone also has a specific use, such as the first tone for the joy of Easter. The manner of singing and the liturgical tradition may differ from one place to another. There are two

Wedding in a Syrian church. Photograph courtesy of Christine Chaillot

main liturgical centers: Tur Abdin (southeast Turkey) and Mosul (northern Iraq, the former seat of the Maphrian).

Many typical Syrian Orthodox hymns are found in all liturgical books. Among the oldest and best-known types of hymns are the *madroshe*, didactic strophes sung by a soloist while the choir repeats a refrain between each strophe. Many *madroshe* are attributed to Saint Ephrem. The *sughitho* is a type of *madrosho* with short stanzas, sometimes with alphabetic acrostic and in the form of dialogues. James of Serugh is considered a master of this form.

The most characteristic West Syrian prayer is the *sedro* ("a row, order or series"), a theologically rich prayer normally said at the offering of incense. It is a long prayer in the form of a series of expositions or meditations. Famous for their *sedre* are Marutha of Tikrit, Athanasius of Balad, Bar Salibi, Michael the Great, and, above all, Patriarch John III (died 648).

Metrical homilies (*mimre*), or poems in couplets, are the most original contribution of the Syrian tradition. There were originally designed to be sung during liturgical or sacramental celebrations. *Mimre* ascribed to Mar Balai, bishop of Balis in the fifth century (in present Maskane, Syria), are used in daily matins and vespers. Saint Ephrem's famous *mimro* on the prophet Jonah and the repentance of Nineveh is used in the three-day Fast of the Ninevites, which precedes Great Lent. The *quqoyo* is a *qolo*, or stanzaic hymn, in a special meter, and is associated with Simon the Potter (sixth century).

In the Anaphora of Saint James of Jerusalem, the deacons sing the following metrical homily attributed to Saint James of Serugh during the closing acts of the Liturgy when, after communion and before departing, the faithful receive a last blessing by kissing the Gospel book and eating a piece of blessed bread:

> The Lord Whom the seraphs fear to look at, the same you behold in Bread and Wine on the altar. The lightning-clothed hosts are burned if they see Him in His brilliance, yet the contemptible dust partakes of Him with confidence. The Son's mysteries are fire among the heavenly beings; Isaiah bears witness with us to having seen them. The mysteries which were in the Divinity's bosom are distributed to Adam's children on the altar. The altar is fashioned like the cherubim's chariot and is surrounded by the heavenly hosts; on the altar is laid the Body of God's Son, and Adam's children carry it solemnly in their hands.

The third of Saint Ephrem's Hymns on the Nativity begins thus: "Blessed be the Child Who today delights Bethlehem. Blessed be the Newborn Who today made humanity young again. Blessed be the Fruit Who bowed Himself down for our hunger. Blessed be the Gracious One Who suddenly enriched all of our poverty and filled our need. Blessed be He Whose mercy inclined Him to heal our sicknesses." An extract from one of Saint Ephrem's Hymns on the Resurrection reads as follows:

> From on high did power descend to us, from a womb did hope shine out for us, from the grave salvation appeared for us, and on the right hand the King sits for us: blessed in His Glory! . . . From on high He came down as Lord, from the womb He came forth as a servant, death knelt before Him in Sheol, and life worshiped Him in His Resurrection. Blessed is His victory! . . . His birth gives us purification, His baptism gives us forgiveness, His death is life to us, His ascension is our exaltation. How should we thank Him! . . . Whom have we, Lord, like You—the Great One Who became small, the Wakeful who slept, the Pure One who was baptized, the Living One who died, the King who abased Himself to ensure honor for all! Blessed is Your honor! *Refrain*: Blessed is Your rising![23]

The Indians

Traditionally, the Apostle Thomas is considered to be the one who brought the Gospel to India, and some relics of Saint Thomas are said to be kept in Mosul (northern Iraq) and in India. The reputed place of Saint Thomas's martyrdom at Mylapore, near Madras, remains the great place of pilgrimage for Indian Christians.

When the Portuguese arrived in India (1498), accompanied by Catholic missionaries, they found Christians celebrating according to the East Syrian rite. In fact the first so-called Saint Thomas Christians had long been in contact with the Church of the East in Persia. But following the Synod of Diamper (1599), the liturgy was completely Latinized and most of the books written in Syriac were burned. A group of local Christians rebelled—the Coonen Cross revolt—in 1653 and asked for help from the Oriental Churches. Thus a Syrian Orthodox bishop, Mar Gregorios, was sent to India in 1665. At that point, the West Syrian Orthodox rite was adopted in India. The Syrian Orthodox in this tradition are divided into two communities: the ones that still acknowledge the Patriarch of Antioch; and (since declaring their autocephaly in 1912) those that go by the name of Malankara Orthodox Syrian Church of India, or sometimes simply the Malankara Orthodox Church. They both continue to follow the West Syrian rite.

Local Customs

Daily prayer is held during the morning and evening in many homes. A brass lamp, similar in shape to those used by Hindus, is lighted. Such lamps are also found in churches, where they are lighted at all times. The brass lamp is put in front of the house during church festivals and on days when processions are held. As is true for Coptic villages in Egypt, Christian homes in India may be marked with a cross. The old churches, like Hindu temples, stand in the center of a large yard with oil lamps in the walls. The architecture of such churches, especially the roof and porches, is inspired by local design. Some churches have also been influenced by the Portuguese baroque style.

On the day celebrating the parish's patron, processions are made around the church and sometimes through the village with drums and wind instruments (*nagawatam*), ornamental umbrellas, elephants (more so in northern Kerala), and occasionally firecrackers. The path is decorated with cut palm leaves. For festivals of the Lord, especially at Easter and Christmas, liturgical processions are made only around the church. During church festivals and other social occasions, a theatrical play (*margamkali*) may take place outside the church building. A type of dance may be performed by men who sing songs narrating biblical stories and the account of Saint Thomas coming to India, although this practice is disappearing. Old women still wear white saris for taking communion. The liturgical vestments are of very bright colors. Since the 1960s, prayers are said most often in the local language, Malayalam, but Syriac is still used.

Living in India, these Christians have adapted some Hindu rites in Christian ceremonies. For instance, as soon as a baby is born, a golden object is traditionally rubbed in honey and is put into the child's mouth, for a "sweet, golden life." There is another ceremony at the beginning of formal education (*vidyarambham*). When the child is five, a teacher or learned person will place the child onto a mat. The home's brass lamp will be lit. A plate of uncooked rice will be brought. The teacher will take the right hand of the child and make the index finger write the first letter of the alphabet in the grains of rice. The Hindu teacher will then invoke the god Ganapathi, but the Christian teacher will say, in Sanskrit, "Adoration to You, Jesus Christ." The teacher will also take his golden ring and write the first letter on the child's tongue, in order that the child may have a "golden mouth." At a wedding a golden ornament, or *thali*, taken from Hindu tradition, is made in the shape of a cross to christianize it. Immediately after tying the *thali* around the bride's neck, the bridegroom puts a new cloth (*sari*) over her head. The giving of a dowry is illegal, but it is privately given as a girl's share of her parents' property. As is still the custom in several Oriental Churches, marriage ceremonies last for several days.

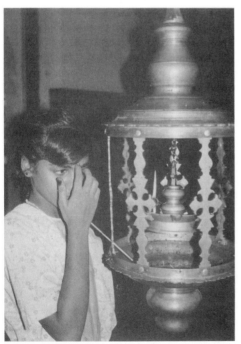

Indian girl crossing herself with oil from a brass lamp. Photograph courtesy of Christine Chaillot

Other Indian Churches

In addition to the two Syrian Orthodox communities, there are two groups from among them that passed to the Roman obedience. Since 1932, one of these has been known as the Syro-Malankarese Church and uses basically the West Syrian rite; it numbers about 360,000 adherents. The largest community of all, however, is the Syro-Malabar Church, of some 3 million members, which has remained attached to Rome since the sixteenth century and uses a liturgy that is historically East Syrian. Malabar and Malankar are ancient names for the modern state of Kerala in southwest India where these Christian communities live.

The Assyrians

One cannot speak of worship in the Ancient Oriental Churches without mentioning the Assyrian Church, which is also called the Church of the East. Christianity seems to have spread to Mesopotamia before the end of the first century. The Church of the East is said to descend from Addai and Mari, two of the Seventy-Two (Luke 10:1) who, according to tradition, evangelized Edessa. The Church of the East developed independently, laboring in outside eyes under the epithet "Nestorian." The first seat of the Church of the East was in Seleucia-Ctesiphon, south of modern Baghdad, and then from 766 in Baghdad. These communities first developed in the Persian Empire, which was supplanted by the Caliphate of Baghdad. The Church of the East undertook great missionary efforts in Asia until the Mongol conquest in the fourteenth century. Numerous monks founded monasteries as far as Mongolia and China, and many Asiatic people converted to Christianity. It was with the Church of the East that the Saint Thomas Christians of India had their closest connections until the sixteenth century.

The East Syrian rite seems to derive from Edessa, not Antioch, even though there is a common heritage. The rite was little influenced by Hellenism and thus preserves traces of a Semitic background. Some scholars have emphasized structural and stylistic parallels between a prayer of the Anaphora of Addai and Mari and the Jewish form of table blessing, the *birkat ha-mazon*.[24]

Few manuscripts exist that are older than the fourteenth century. But commentaries from between the seventh and ninth centuries show that the liturgical reorganization made by Catholicos Ishoʿyab III (in the mid-seventh century) was maintained, despite later additions.[25]

Liturgical Space

In mountainous areas, churches were built like little fortresses and refuges because of possible incursions. The door at the entrance was low and narrow, and on top of it there was an engraved cross, venerated by the faithful before entering the church.

In the plains, one can often find to the east of ancient churches an open yard with an altar, the "house of prayer" (*beth-slutha*), for offices to be held outside during the warm season, from May to October—that is, from Ascension to the Sunday of the Dedication of the Church (Quddash ʿEdta).

The *bema*, an elevated platform situated in the middle of the church, allows the Gospel to be read and preached among the people. The *bema* symbolizes the earthly Jerusalem; it can be shaped in a square, an elongated rectangle, or a horseshoe. There the daily offices and the preparation and first part of the Liturgy, before the anaphora, take place. In the center of the *bema* is a table (symbol of Golgotha) and on it are placed the Gospel book and a cross, along with two candles to symbolize the two Testaments. However, during the reading of the Gospel, the two candles are understood to represent the disciples who are to be lights to the world.

On the south side of the *bema* is a lectern for the reading of the Old Testament and the Acts of the Apostles; a lectern on the north side is for the reading of Saint Paul and the Gospels. A thurible hangs nearby for the purification of the priest's hands.

The sanctuary is on an elevated platform. On the altar are placed one cross, two candlesticks, and the Gospel book. Another cross is located in front of the altar in order that the faithful may venerate it as they enter the church. There are two niches in the sanctuary: north for the paten, and south for the chalice and for the oil used during baptism and confession. An extension of the sanctuary juts out beyond the sanctuary veil into the nave: it, the *qestroma*, symbolizes the earthly paradise.

Before the readings, the clergy go in procession from the sanctuary to the *bema* through the passage called *sheqaqona*, which symbolizes the narrow way leading from earth to heaven; later they go back to the altar to celebrate the eucharistic anaphora.

The *martyrion* with relics (*beth sahde*) is located on the north side of the nave. That is where the martyrs' anthems (*ᶜonyatha d-sahde*) are recited. Near the sanctuary may also be found a niche (*shkhinta*) with relics or soil (*ḥnana*) from the burial place of the saint to whom the church is dedicated.

Liturgical Vestments

Priests and bishops wear an alb (*kotina*) girded by a belt (*zunara*), over which are placed a semicircular piece of cloth ornamented with crosses on the shoulders (*maᶜpra*), a stole (*ourara*) similar in style to the Byzantines, and sleeves (*kape*). The Patriarch is distinguished by colored headgear (*kaphila*).

When holding the paten during the distribution of communion by the priest, the deacon covers his shoulders with a veil (*mqablana*).

Eucharist

When the bread for the Eucharist is being mixed from fine flour, olive oil, and warm water, a portion of the dough from the previous celebration is added in. This establishes a continuity of the sacrament through the ages.

In the opening part of the Liturgy, two prayers of special interest are said. One, an expansion of the Our Father, insisting on the holiness of God, is recited both at the beginning of the Liturgy and at the end: "Our Father in Heaven, hallowed be Your name. Your kingdom come. Holy, Holy, You are Holy, our Father in Heaven, for heaven and earth are full of the greatness of Your glory. Watchers and men cry out to You, Holy, Holy, you are Holy. Our Father in Heaven, hallowed be Your name. Your kingdom come." Then, when the veil of the sanctuary is opened for the first time (before the Trisagion and the readings), the ancient Resurrection hymn (Lakhu Mara), attributed to Catholicos Mar Shemᶜon bar Sabbaᶜe (fourth century), is: "You, Lord of all, we confess, and You Jesus Christ we glorify, for You give life to our bodies and salvation to our souls."

The pre-anaphora also includes three Psalms (15, 150, 117), alternating with prayers. Before the reading of the Epistle and before the reading of the Gospel, a lengthy hymn or *turgama* is each time sung. After the homily a litany (*karozutha*) invites prayer for prosperity. Before the anaphora another *karozutha* is said by the deacon. The kiss of peace is made just before the beginning of the anaphora.

There are three anaphoras used in the Church of the East. The Anaphora of Theodore of Mopsuestia, most probably first composed in Greek, is used from Annunciation to Palm Sunday. The Anaphora of Nestorius is used only five times each year. The most frequently used anaphora is that of the Apostles, also called Addai and Mari, and is an original Syriac composition.[26]

In the course of the Anaphora, typical Assyrian prayers are recited; known as *ganatha* (from the verb *ghan*, "to bow"), they are said in a low voice by the celebrant before the altar. This example of a *ghanta* comes at the beginning of the eucharistic prayer of Addai and Mari:

> Worthy of praise from every mouth, and confession from every tongue, and adoration and exaltation from every creature is the worshipful and glorious Name of Your glorious Trinity, O Father, Son, and Holy Spirit, for You created the world in Your grace and its inhabitants in Your Mercifulness; You saved humankind in Your compassion, and showed great grace unto mortals. Thousands upon thousands of those on high bow down and worship Your majesty, O my Lord, and ten thousand times ten thousand holy angels and spiritual hosts, the ministers of fire and spirit, glorify Your name, and with holy cherubim and spiritual seraphim offer worship to Your Lordship.

For communion the priest and one deacon present the Body and Blood to the faithful. The Body and Blood are given separately. The priest places the Body into the hands of the communicants, as in ancient practice, but the believer is also given the choice to receive the Eucharist directly into the mouth.

During the communion of the people, hymns by Saint Ephrem, Saint Yazdin, and others are sung. An example is a hymn of praise, called a *teshbohta*, such as the following, which is attributed to Saint Ephrem:

> O our Lord Jesus, worshipful
>   King, Who conquered the
>   tyrant, death, by Your
>   suffering;
> O Son of God, Who promised
>   us new life in the kingdom
>   on high:
> Remove from us all harm, and
>   make tranquility and mercies
>   to dwell in our land,
> That on the day of Your
>   appearing we may live before
>   You, and go out to meet You
>   according to Your will.
> With hosannas we will give
>   thanks to Your Name for Your grace toward our race.
> For Your mercies have multiplied toward our humanity, and Your love has shone forth
>   upon our mortality.
> You have blotted out our debts with Your pardon. Glory to Your Name for Your gift.
> Blessed is Your honor from within Your place, You who forgive debts because of Your
>   mercies,

Communion in the Assyrian Church. The distribution of communion in the Assyrian Church, London. Photograph courtesy of Christine Chaillot

And Who by Your grace make us worthy to confess and worship Your Godhead.
And to Your Lordship at all seasons we will lift up glory. Amen and amen.

Another hymn of praise sung during communion on feasts of the Lord is believed to have been composed by Saint Yazdin:

Strengthen, O our Lord, the hands which reach out and take the sacrament for the pardon of debts.
Make them worthy every day to yield fruit to Your Godhead.
Make worthy to sing glory the mouths which have given praise within the sanctuary.
May the ears, which have heard the sound of Your praises, never hear, O my Lord, the sound of disquiet.
May the eyes, which have seen Your great compassion, O my Lord, see again Your blessed hope.
So form the tongues, which have cried out "holy," that they may always speak the truth.
Lead the feet, which have walked within the churches, into the land of light.
Renew the bodies, which have eaten Your living Body with new life.
Strengthen Your assistance to our assembly, which worships Your Godhead.
May Your great love remain with us, and by it may we excel in rendering glory.
Open the door to the petition of us all, and may our service also enter in before You.[27]

The final blessing (*ḫuttama*) on Sundays and feast days is said at the door of the sanctuary while the inner veil is shut:

He who blesses us with all spiritual blessings in Heaven through Jesus Christ our Lord, and summons us to His kingdom, and calls us and brings us near to His desirable blessings which do not pass away, nor cease, nor depart—as He advised and promised in His life-giving Gospel, saying to the blessed company of His disciples, "Amen, amen, I say to you, whoever eats my body and drinks my blood remains in me and I in him, and I will raise him up at the last day, and he does not come to judgment but passes from death to eternal life": may He bless our company and guard our standing. May He beautify our people who came and took delight in the power of His glorious, holy, life-giving, and divine Mysteries. By the living sign of the Cross of the Lord may you be sealed and preserved from all harm, hidden and open, now, always, and for ever and ever.

Liturgical Books

The book of prayers for Sundays is called Ḥudra. For the Daily Office, different books are used as well as the Psalter: the "Before and After" (Qdam wa-dbatar), the Kaskoll, and the Gazza (for feasts).

The cathedral offices are Vespers (*ramsha*), Vigil on Sundays (*shahra*), and Morning Prayers (*ṣapra*).[28]

The Rogation of the Ninevites (Baʿotha d-Ninwaye) is a collection of hymns. It was composed, according to the Assyrian tradition, after a plague in the eighth century was stopped—following Jonah's example—by the fasting and prayers of the bishop of Kirkuk, Mar Sorisho, and his people.

Famous commentaries on the East Syrian liturgy were written by Narsai (died 503) and Gabriel Qatraya (seventh century), and the Anonymous Author's Exposition dates from perhaps the eighth century.

Music

Chanting is said to go back to Saint Ephrem's time (died 373). It was reformed by Babai of Gabilta in the eighth century. Chanting is no longer accented by the playing of triangles and cymbals. Some melodies are fixed, with different rhythms and modes, And some use a 3/4 tone that is rarely found in Western music. The Liturgy says, "As the melodies of our chants are beautiful, so let our conduct be the same in His presence, so that with our words and our deeds we may please the Lord."

The Liturgical Year

It is said that Patriarch Isho῾yab III, in the mid-seventh century, made a liturgical reorganization and arranged the year in groups of more or less "seven weeks" each (*shabbo῾e*): Christmas, with four Sundays before Christmas, called "of Annunciation," and two Sundays after Christmas; Epiphany (Den<u>h</u>a), with seven or eight Sundays; Lent (<u>S</u>awma) and Holy Week; Resurrection (Qyamta) or Eastertide until Pentecost; then the "time of the Apostles" (Shli<u>h</u>e), followed by "Summer" (Qay<u>t</u>a). The Feast of the Cross (14 September) is surrounded by Sundays dedicated to Elijah and Moses, a complex period called "Elijah/Cross/Moses" (Elia-<u>S</u>liwa-Mushe). The last four Sundays of the liturgical year are called "of the Dedication of the Church." On the first Friday of this last group is remembered Mar Awgin (died 370), who is said to have founded monastic life in the region of Mesopotamia.

The memorials of saints and martyrs are, in fact, usually celebrated on Fridays. The Friday after Easter commemorates Mar Shem῾on bar Sabba῾e's martyrdom, which occurred on Good Friday in 341, and the other confessors martyred under Sapor II. The Friday after Pentecost is named "golden" in memory of the healing of the lame man by Saint Peter—the first miracle of the Apostles. On the seventh Friday after Pentecost, remembrance is given to the Seventy-Two Disciples. The feasts of the saints on Fridays of the Epiphany period include Syriac- and Greek-speaking Fathers of the Church.

Funerals and Some Sacraments

Modern practice for funerals stipulates that only the bodies of the clergy may enter the altar area from the nave. The bodies of the laity are prepared, brought to the church, and then carried to the grave for burial. Only men, however, are allowed to go to the cemetery for the burial rite. Women are allowed to visit the gravesite on the third day. This custom may be modeled upon Jewish practice; nevertheless, it is similar to the account in the Gospels of the women visiting Jesus' tomb on the third day.

Clay or dust (<u>h</u>nana) taken from the tombs of revered saints, and often mixed with water, is sometimes given as a cure for the sick. The clay or dust may also be added to the mixture of wine and water in the chalice, and is consumed by a couple during the marriage rite. Before blessing the couple the priest immerses the cross into it. The chalice with water and wine symbolizes the union (*shawtaputa*) of the new couple, and <u>h</u>nana (meaning "pity" or "compassion") symbolizes the mercy of God for the husband and wife. The marriage rite preserves semitic customs, such as the blessing of the bridal chamber.

A popular prayer by Narsai expounds the mysteries thus:

> On the Mysteries of the Church my thoughts dwelt mystically,
> And I desired to show the musing of the heart by word of mouth.
> By word of mouth I desired to tell of their greatness,
> And with words to describe the image of their splendor;
> On their splendor to fix my mind with precision.
> And a trembling seized me, released me, and left me motionless.
> Motionless I remained; I stood in terror,

And I began to call out sorrowfully with the son of Amoz.
With the son of Amoz I cried, Woe to my unclean person,
Who in his uncleanness fixes his mind on the mysteries of his Lord.
I meditated upon these things and in dread I turned back,
And the Spirit of his beckoning encouraged me to enter the Holy of Holies.
Into the Holy of Holies of the glorious Mysteries He bid me to enter,
And make plain the beauty of their splendor to the sons of the mysteries.
Come, then, O son of the divine mysteries,
Hear the narration, marvelous in the telling, of the mysteries of the Church.
Mystery to me, Mystery to me, Mystery to me and to mine, the prophet cried.
With the reason therefore hear the Mysteries made known to you.
Truly high and exalted is this Mystery,
Which the priest accomplishes in the sanctuary mystically.
Mystically the Church depicts the glorious Mysteries,
And as in an image makes manifest to all men the things that have happened.
The things which took place in the death of the Son she recalls in the Mysteries.
And also His Resurrection from the dead she reveals in the sight of all.
A Mystery signifies mystically what has been and what will be,
And the Church signifies mystically that which has taken place only by way of her
    Mysteries.
The Church signifies her Mysteries in secret, away from outsiders,
And the priest completes [them] mystically in the sanctuary.
To her children and sons alone, baptized [and] sealed, she brings the joy
Of participation in these adored Mysteries, which she fulfills.

The Chaldean Church

Since the sixteenth century a community of Assyrian Christians has been in communion with Rome. Known as the Chaldeans, they employ the ancient Anaphora of Addai
and Mari, brought into conformity with Roman doctrine.*

Bibliography

Badger, G. P. *The Nestorians and their Rituals.* 2 vols. London: J. Masters, 1852; re-
    print, London: Darf, 1987.
Brock, Sebastian P., ed. "The Hidden Pearl: The Syrian Orthodox Church and Its An-
    cient Aramaic Heritage." 4 vols. Rome: Trans World Film Italia, 2001. [VHS tape]
Brown, Leslie W. *The Indian Christians of St. Thomas: An Account of the Ancient Syrian
    Church of Malabar.* 2nd ed. Cambridge: Cambridge University Press, 1982.
Burmester, O. H. E. *The Egyptian or Coptic Church: A Detailed Description of her Litur-
    gical Services and the Rites and Ceremonies Observed in the Administration of her Sacra-
    ments.* Publications de la Société d'Archéologie Copte. Cairo: French Institute of
    Oriental Archaeology, 1967.
Chaillot, Christine. *The Coptic Orthodox Church.* Paris: Inter-Orthodox Dialogue, 2005.
Chaillot, Christine. *The Ethiopian Orthodox Tewahedo Church Tradition: A Brief Intro-
    duction to Its Life and Spirituality.* Paris: Inter-Orthodox Dialogue, 2002.
Chaillot, Christine. *The Malankara Orthodox Church: Visit to the Oriental Malankara
    Orthodox Syrian Church of India.* Geneva: Inter-Orthodox Dialogue, 1996.
Chaillot, Christine. *Rôle des images et vénération des icônes dans les Églises orthodoxes
    orientales: syrienne, arménienne, copte, éthiopienne.* Geneva, Switzerland: Dialogue entre
    Orthodoxes, 1993.

Chaillot, Christine. *The Syrian Orthodox Church of Antioch and All the East: A Brief Introduction to Its Life and Spirituality.* Geneva: Inter-Orthodox Dialogue, 1998.

Conybeare, F. C., ed. *Rituale Armenorum; Being the Administration of the Sacraments and the Breviary Rites of the Armenian Church.* Translated by A. J. MacLean. Oxford: Clarendon, 1905.

Dalmais, Irenée-Henri. *Eastern Liturgies.* Translated by Donald Attwater. New York: Hawthorn, 1960.

Findikyan, Daniel, and Lilit Amirchanian. *A Walk through the Divine Liturgy of the Armenian Church.* New York: Diocese of the Armenian Church in America, 2001.

Innemée, Karel C. *Ecclesiastical Dress in the Medieval Near East.* Leiden and New York: Brill, 1992.

The Liturgy of the Ethiopian Church. Translated by Marcos Daoud. Revised by H. E. Blatta Marsie Hazen. Cairo: Egyptian Book Press, 1959.

Madey, John, ed. *The Eucharistic Liturgy in the Christian East.* Kottayam, India: Prakasam Publications; Paderborn: Ostkirchendienst, 1982.

Mattam, Mar Abraham. *Forgotten East: Mission, Liturgy, and Spirituality of the Eastern Churches: A Study with Special Reference to the Church of St. Thomas Christians.* Satna, India: Ephrem's Publications, 2001.

Spinks, Bryan D. *Worship. Prayers from the East.* Washington, D.C.: Pastoral Press, 1993.

Notes

[1]See Sebastian Brock, "The 'Nestorian' Church: A Lamentable Misnomer," *Bulletin of the John Rylands Library* 78 (1996) 23–35. In the historic christological controversy, much depends on the understanding of the Syriac word *qnoma* (plural *qnome*)—whether "person" or "substance" or "nature"—of which a duality was maintained in Christ by the Church of the East.

[2]In the centuries after the Council of Chalcedon, various attempts at union were made, without success; but in 1964, with the help of the World Council of Churches, a series of unofficial theological dialogues began between the Eastern Orthodox Churches and the Oriental Orthodox Churches, and in 1985 this dialogue became official. It was able to recognize that the christological faith of the two families was similar although formulated in different words, and that the problem resided in a terminological misunderstanding about the word *physis*. In the Cyrilline formula it can be understood as "person," the very term used at Chalcedon. For both Eastern and Oriental Orthodox, Christ is fully God and fully Man without confusion, change, separation, or division. Unofficial consultations organized by the Pro-Oriente Institute in Vienna since 1971 have reached similar conclusions between the Ori-

ental Orthodox and the Roman Catholic Church. In 1994, after fifteen centuries of christological misunderstanding, Pope John Paul II and Mar Dinkha IV, Patriarch of the Assyrian Church of the East, signed a common declaration that Catholics and Assyrians are "united today in the confession of the same faith in the Son of God," and a dialogue between Rome and the Church of the East has followed on sacramental theology and on ecclesiological questions.

[3]Irenée-Henri Dalmais, *Eastern Liturgies*, 42. For work in the earlier decades of the twentieth century, see Joseph-Marie Sauget, *Bibliographie des liturgies orientales 1900–1960* (Rome: Pontificium Institutum Studiorum Orientalium, 1962).

[4]See John Madey, ed., *The Eucharistic Liturgy in the Christian East*; Ioannes Malak, "The Eucharistic Divine Liturgy According to the Rite of the Coptic Church of Alexandria" (pp. 3–34); Paulos Tzadua, "The Divine Liturgy according to the Rite of the Ethiopian Church" (pp. 37–68); Eustathios Joseph Mounayer, "The Eucharistic Liturgy of the Syrian Church of Antioch" (pp. 71–98); Emmanuel Khoury, "Genesis and Development of the Maronite Divine Liturgy" (pp. 101–131); P. T. Givergis

Paniker, "The Holy Qurbano in the Syro-Malankara Church" (pp. 135–171 plus unpaginated appendix); Petros Yousif, "The Divine Liturgy according to the Rite of the Assyro-Chaldean Church" (pp. 175–237); Varghese Pathikulangara and Jacob Vellian, "The Eucharistic Liturgy of the Chaldeo-Indian Church" (pp. 241–272); and Garabed Amadouni, "The Divine Liturgy or Canon of Ministration of the Church according to the Armenian Rite" (pp. 327–380).

[5]For the various ways in which, historically and geographically, the Churches have synthesized or juxtaposed features from "cathedral" (or "parish") and "monastic" practices in the Offices, see Robert Taft, *The Liturgy of the Hours in East and West* (Collegeville, Minn.: Liturgical Press, 1986).

[6]See Ugo Zanetti, "Bohairic Liturgical Manuscripts," *Orientalia Christiana Periodica* 61 (1995) 65–94.

[7]The Office of the Morning Incense and the Eucharistic Liturgy are translated in John, Marquis of Bute, *The Coptic Morning Service for the Lord's Day* (London: Cope and Fenwick, 1908).

[8]For a translation, see R. M. Woolley, *Coptic Offices* (London: SPCK, 1930) 1–58; cf. O. H. E. Burmester, "The Baptismal Rite of the Coptic Church (A Critical Study)," *Bulletin de la Société d'Archéologie copte* 11 (1945) 27–86; and M. de Fénoyl, "Les sacrements de l'initiation chrétienne dans l'Église copte," *Proche-Orient Chrétien* 7 (1957) 7–25. Woolley's *Coptic Offices* contains also the services for holy matrimony, the anointing of the sick, and the burial of the dead.

[9]See Getatchew Haile, "Ethiopic Literature," in *African Zion: The Sacred Art of Ethiopia*, ed. Marilyn Heldman, S. C. Munro-Hay, and Roderick Grierson (New Haven and London: Yale University Press, 1993) 47–55.

[10]The whole service—translated by Marcos Daoud and revised by Blatta Marsie Hazen—is found in *The Liturgy of the Ethiopian Church*. Translations of the anaphoras only are given in J. M. Hardin, *The Anaphoras of the Ethiopic Liturgy* (London: SPCK, 1928). For detailed technical work, see Ernst Hammerschmidt, *Studies in the Ethiopic Anaphoras*, 2nd ed. (Stuttgart: Steiner, 1987).

[11]See S. Grébaut, "Ordre du baptême et de la confirmation dans l'Église éthiopienne," *Revue de l'Orient chrétien* 26 (1927–1928) 105–180.

[12]Habtemichael Kidane, *L'ufficio divino della Chiesa etiopica*, Orientalia Christiana Analecta 257 (Rome: Pontificium Institutum Studiorum Orientalium, 1998).

[13]See Bernard Velat, "Études sur le Me'eraf. Commun de l'office divin éthiopien. Introduction, traduction française, commentaire liturgique et musical," *Patrologia Orientalis* 33, nos. 1–4 (1966), and his "Me'eraf. Commun de l'office divin éthiopien pour toute l'année. Texte éthiopien avec variantes," *Patrologia Orientalis* 34, nos. 1–2 (1966); cf. Peter Jeffery, "The Liturgical Year in the Ethiopian Deggwa (Chantbook)," in *Eulogema: Studies in Honor of Robert Taft, S. J.*, ed. Ephrem Carr et al., Studia Anselmiana 110 and Analecta Liturgica 17 (Rome: Centro Studi S. Anselmo, 1993) 199–234.

[14]See E. Fritsch, *The Liturgical Year of the Ethiopian Church*, special issue of *Ethiopian Review of Cultures* vol. 9-10 (Addis Ababa: 2001).

[15]See, for example, Kay Kaufman Shelemay and Peter Jeffery, eds., *Ethiopian Christian Liturgical Chant: An Anthology*, Recent Researches in the Oral Traditions of Music, 3 vols. (Madison, Wisc.: A-R Editions, 1993–1997) [printed music]; also digital sound disc, 1994.

[16]See Gabriele Winkler, "The Original Meaning of the Prebaptismal Anointing and its Implications," *Worship* 52 (1978) 24–45, and (especially) her *Das armenische Initiationsrituale: entwicklungsgeschichtliche und liturgievergleichende Untersuchung der Quellen des 3. bis 10. Jahrhunderts*, Orientalia Christiana Analecta 217 (Rome: Pontificium Institutum Studiorum Orientalium, 1982); cf. Joseph Chalassery, *The Holy Spirit and Christian Initiation in the East Syrian Tradition* (Rome: Mar Thoma Yogam, 1995); and Sebastian P. Brock, *The Holy Spirit in the Syrian Baptismal Tradition*, 2nd ed. (Pune, India: Anita Printers, 1998).

[17]French translations from the Armenian are found in *Grégoire de Narek: Le livre de prières*, ed. Isaac Kéchichian, Sources chrétiennes 78 (Paris: Éditions du Cerf, 1961) 72.

[18]In *Ephemerides Liturgicae* 102 (1988) 436–445, Sebastian Brock called attention to "Two Recent Editions of Syrian Orthodox Anaphoras," in which, taken together, access may be found to some fifteen anaphoras: one edition printed from calligraphic script at the Syrian Orthodox Monastery of Saint Ephrem, near Hengelo, in the Netherlands; the other, bilingual in Syriac and Malayalam, printed at the Mar Julius Press at Pampakuda in Kerala, India. In the same article Brock lists the seventy-odd known West Syrian anaphoras and indicates where printed editions from the past four centuries, sometimes in Latin translation, are available. More generally, see Brock's *Syriac Studies: A Classified Bibliography (1960–1990)* (Kaslik, Lebanon: Parole de l'Orient, 1996) 184–208, with updates in the periodical *Parole de l'Orient* 23 (1998) for the years 1991–1995, and 29 (2004).

[19]See Baby Varghese, *The Syriac Version of the Liturgy of St. James: A Brief History for Students*, Alcuin/GROW Liturgical Studies 49 (Cambridge: Grove, 2001).

[20]See the English translations in Baby Varghese, *Dionysius bar Salibi: Commentary on the Eucharist*, and *John of Dara: De Oblatione—Commentary on the Eucharist*, Kottayam, India: St. Ephrem Ecumenical Research Institute, 1998 and 1999, respectively. German translations of three commentaries are found in Andreas Heinz, *Die Eucharistiefeier in der Deutung syrischer Liturgieerklärer: Die Liturgiekommentare von Georg dem Araberbischof (+724), Mose bar Kepha (+903), Dionysius bar Salibi (+1171)* (Trier: Paulinus, 2000).

[21]On the year, see Athanasius Y. Samuel, ed., *Ma'de'dono: The Book of the Church Festivals according to the Ancient Rite of the Syrian Orthodox Church of Antioch*, trans. Murad Saliba Barsom (Lodi, N.J.: Metropolitan Mar A. Y. Samuel, 1984).

[22]See Baby Varghese, "Holy Week Celebrations in the West Syrian Church," in *Hebdomadae Sanctae Celebratio*, ed. Antony G. Kollamparampil (Rome: C.L.V.-Edizioni liturgiche, 1997) 165–186.

[23]Selections from the poetry of Saint Ephrem may be found in Sebastian P. Brock, *The Harp of the Spirit: Eighteen Poems of St. Ephrem*, 2nd ed. (London: Fellowship of St. Alban and St. Sergius, 1982), and in *St. Ephrem: Hymns on Paradise*, intro. and trans. Sebastian Brock (Crestwood, N.Y.: St. Vladimir's Seminary Press, 1990). The Hymns on the Nativity are included in K. E. McVey, *Ephrem the Syrian: Hymns* (New York: Paulist Press, 1989).

[24]For a discussion, see Anthony Gelston, *The Eucharistic Prayer of Addai and Mari* (Oxford: Clarendon, 1992) 7–11, where the author is skeptical on this point. The book contains text, translation, and detailed commentary on the Anaphora in question.

[25]For scholarly literature on the East Syrian rite, see Pierre Yousif, *A Classified Bibliography on the East Syrian Liturgy* (Rome: Mar Thoma Yogam, 1990).

[26]See Bryan D. Spinks, *Addai and Mari—The Anaphora of the Apostles: A Text for Students*, Grove Liturgical Study 24 (Bramcote, Notts.: Grove, 1980), and his *Mar Nestorius and Mar Theodore the Interpreter: The Forgotten Eucharistic Prayers of East Syria*, Alcuin/GROW Liturgical Studies 45 (Cambridge: Grove, 1999). For the liturgy of Addai and Mari as currently used, see *The Order of the Holy Qurbana (Liturgy of the Blessed Apostles Mar Addai and Mar Mari)* (San Jose, Calif.: Adiabene Publications, 2001).

[27]A close paraphrase of this hymn, by C. W. Humphreys and Percy Dearmer, is found in *The English Hymnal*.

[28]A. J. MacLean, *East Syrian Daily Offices* (London: Rivington, 1894; repr. Farnborough, Hants.: Gregg, 1969). For numerous studies concerning the liturgy of the hours in the Assyrian/Chaldean rite, see the writings of Juan Mateos. For example: *Lelya-Sapra: essai d'interprétation des matines chaldéennes*, Orientalia Christiana Analecta 156 (Rome: Pontificium Institutum Orientalium Studiorum, 1959); "L'office paroissial du matin et du soir dans le rite chaldéen," *La Maison-Dieu* 64 (1960) 65-89; and "L'office divin chez les Chaldéens," in *La prière des heures*, ed. Mgr. Cassien and B. Botte, Lex Orandi 35 (Paris: Cerf, 1963) 253–281.

Editors' note: In a mutual agreement with the Church of the East, the Roman authorities in 2002 permitted Chaldean Catholics in pastoral need to receive communion at an Assyrian eucharist, even when the Anaphora of Addai and Mari was used in its ancient form without direct citation of the words of institution. In an important article for the history and theology of eucharistic consecration, Robert Taft justified this move liturgically, dogmatically, and ecumenically: "Mass Without the Consecration? The Historic Agreement between the Catholic Church and the Assyrian Church of the East Promulgated 26 October 2001," *Worship* 77 (2003) 482–509.

Excursus: The Maronites

LUCAS VAN ROMPAY

The Maronites represent one specific branch within the broader tradition of Syriac Christianity. Demographically, their traditional center is in Lebanon; ecclesially, they are in communion with the See of Rome. Historically, the Maronites are close to the Greek Orthodox of the Patriarchate of Antioch (the so-called Melkites), with whom they share adherence to the Council of Chalcedon (451). Whereas the Greek Orthodox, however, in the course of their history became fully part of Byzantine Christianity and thus belong to Eastern Orthodoxy, the Maronites developed their own type of Syriac Chalcedonianism, which increasingly became disconnected from Byzantine, "Melkite" Christianity.

In the sixth century the monks of the Monastery of Saint Maron—named after an ascetic who lived in the fourth and the early fifth century—took the lead in defending the Council of Chalcedon against its opponents, who were in the process of developing a "Miaphysite" christology and their own church structure, and later became the Syrian Orthodox (now one of the Oriental Orthodox churches). The Monastery of Saint Maron, which was perhaps at the head of a confederation of like-minded monasteries, was situated near Apamea in the Roman province of Syria Secunda, a region that maintained close contacts with Edessene Christianity and, in the sixth century, was divided between supporters and opponents of the council. Chalcedonian Christians of this region subsequently became divided as a result of the discussions concerning "monenergism" and "monotheletism," formulas of compromise between the one-nature and the two-nature doctrines proposed by the Byzantine Imperial Church in 638 and later condemned at the Sixth Ecumenical Council (680–681). The exact involvement of the Maronite monks and their followers in these discussions is unclear and remains a matter of dispute. In all likelihood, however, the estrangement between the Maronites and the Imperial Church goes back to this period and to the Maronites' unwillingness to accept the decisions of the Sixth Council. Increasingly isolated by the expansion of Islam, the Maronites developed their own identity, based on their Syriac cultural background, and elected their own patriarch of Antioch. After the destruction of the Monastery of Saint Maron, probably in the tenth century, the ecclesiastical center of the Maronites was transferred to Mount Lebanon, where henceforth the Maronite patriarch resided in various monasteries, including Mayfuq and Qannubin (in the north Lebanese Qadisha valley), and later in Bkerke and Diman.[1]

Of vital importance to the Maronites has been their alliance with the See of Rome. Contacts between the Maronite monks and the pope of Rome are attested as early as the sixth century. But it was in the period of Crusader presence in the Middle East that a more solid relationship was created, leading to the full incorporation of the Maronites in the Catholic Church, a long process that was concluded at the Council of Ferrara-Florence (1438–1445). As an early example of what later would be known as "Uniatism," the Maronite Church had to walk the fine line between full acceptance of Roman Catholicism and Latinization on the one hand, and preservation of local traditions on the other.

The extent to which Maronite liturgy was brought into conformity with Western Catholic tradition may be judged from different angles. In their zeal to eradicate all remains of alleged monothelete and other heresies, some Roman emissaries, particularly in the sixteenth century, went so far as to ban certain liturgical practices and expressions, and even to burn manuscripts, thus destroying much of the earlier literary heritage. Others were more moderate and exhibited greater respect for the Maronites' tradition. Among the Maronite church leaders and intellectuals, no one was more influential than Patriarch Stephan al-Duwayhî (1670–1704); he was able to steer a middle course between conservatives and reformers and, with many significant publications, contributed to the revitalization and consolidation of Maronite liturgical tradition. The Maronite college in Rome, founded in 1584, was instrumental in keeping Maronite church life and education well under Roman control; but several Maronite intellectuals—among them the three famous scions of the Assemani family, Joseph Simon (1687–1768), Joseph Aloysius (1710–1782), and Stephan Evodius (1707–1782)—took advantage of their Western experience in Rome to study their own Syriac and Christian Arabic tradition, and this subsequently became an important frame of reference in further liturgical reform. J. S. Assemani served as the papal delegate at the Lebanese Synod of 1736. As a distant echo of the Council of Trent (1545–1563), this synod marked a further step in the Latinization of the Maronite Church but also exposed underlying tensions between the Latinizers and those who wanted to strengthen the indigenous, Eastern character of the Maronite Church.

Although Arabic had long since become the spoken and written language of the Maronites, Syriac was maintained as an important language of literature and liturgy. Duwayhî, who as a youth lived in Rome for fourteen years, published both in Syriac and in Arabic upon his return. Several books on liturgical and pastoral topics were in Syriac, but Duwayhî's comprehensive theological–liturgical work on the eucharist, *al-Manâra* (The Candelabrum) was in Arabic.[2]

The major liturgical texts have all been preserved in Syriac, with some portions in Arabic or Karshuni (Arabic written in Syriac characters). The printing press greatly facilitated the codification of the texts and their expurgation according to Roman Catholic lines. In Rome between 1592 and 1594, the Maronite missal (*Qurbono*) was first printed. It contained a limited number of anaphoras, among which the venerable anaphora attributed to Saint Peter, known as "Sharrar" (after its opening word, meaning "confirm"). Later editions were increasingly Latinized: the anaphora of the Latin mass was inserted and the Sharrar was removed. Earlier Maronite manuscripts contained a great number of anaphoras, several of which were attributed to Syrian Orthodox leaders and bishops such as Maruta of Takrit, Jacob of Edessa, Dionysius bar Salibi, and Michael the Syrian. The presence of these anaphoras attests to the high degree of interaction between the Syrian Orthodox and the Maronites in Syria and northern Lebanon. They were seen, however, as "Jacobite" infiltrations, and, in the process of liturgical reform, they were eliminated from further transmission.

It is clear, therefore, that Maronite liturgical texts, printed first in Rome and later in Lebanon, are of a hybrid nature, containing an old layer of authentic Syriac materials—cleared, however, of all kinds of "heterodox" elements—along with numerous insertions and innovations of Western Catholic origin. Unfortunately, earlier manuscripts, giving us access to the pre-Latin phase of Maronite tradition, are very rare. Genuine early Syriac elements can sometimes be identified with the help of the East Syrian liturgical tradition, preserved mainly in Iraq and Iran. The above-mentioned "Sharrar" anaphora, for example, has much in common with the East Syrian Anaphora of the Apostles Addai and Mari.[3] The survival of these very similar texts at the two extremes of the Syriac geographical area points to their great antiquity. Similarly, the Maronite weekday office (Shehimto) contains a number of hymns that are also found in the Church of the East or in the Chaldean Catholic Church. Although the possibility of later borrowing cannot always be ruled out, in most cases we must be dealing with independent witnesses of the earliest Syriac Christian tradition. The "Hymn of Light" ("Nuhro dnah l-zaddiqê"), very popular among twenty-first-century Maronites and sung by all choirs, may serve as an example. It is attributed to either Ephrem of Edessa or Theodore of Mopsuestia, and has the name of Jesus Christ (Yeshu͗ Mshihâ) as an acrostic. Its opening lines are as follows:

> Light has shone out for the righteous, and for the upright of heart, joy.
> Jesus our Lord Christ has shone out for us from the womb of His Father,
> He has come and brought us out of darkness and illumined us with His glorious light.
> Daytime has shone out over human beings and the dominion of darkness has fled;
> Light has shone out for us from His light and given light to our darkened eyes.
> His glory has shone out in the midst of the universe and given light to the depths
>   below:
> Death is extinguished and darkness has fled and the gates of Sheol have been shattered.[4]

The Latinization and Western orientation that have marked the Maronite Church for centuries are now being challenged by Maronite Christians in Lebanon, the other Middle Eastern countries, and the worldwide diaspora. In the process of renewed self-reflection, the Maronites tend to stress their being rooted in Syriac and Antiochene Christian tradition. This explains why, despite the increased role of the vernacular language (Arabic or any Western language), Syriac remains an integral, albeit modest, part of Maronite liturgy. An entirely new edition of the "Qurbono" ("According to the Rite of the Syriac Antiochene Maronite Church") was published by the Maronite Patriarchate in 1992. Exactly 400 years after the first Qurbono publication in Rome, the new edition aims at "bringing back the Service of the Qurbono to its authentic Maronite tradition" (Archbishop Boutros Gemayel).

Not only have Syriac liturgical and theological texts been studied with renewed enthusiasm and effort by the Maronites in the years leading up to the twenty-first century, the musical and artistic traditions have received much attention as well.[5] Along with the academic study of these subjects in the Maronite institutions of higher education, choirs have brought Syriac sacred music and Ephrem's hymns to new and powerful life in the churches. In church decoration, particularly in wall paintings and icons, Maronite artists have found their main source of inspiration in medieval wall paintings in Lebanon and Syria as well as in the illuminations of the famous "Rabbula Gospels." This sixth-century manuscript of exceptional beauty, probably created in a Syrian Orthodox monastery of the Apamea region, came into the possession of the Maronites at an early date. For centuries it belonged to the Maronite patriarchal library, at Mayfuq and Qannubin, before being transferred in the early sixteenth century to Florence, where it is presently housed in the Medicea-Laurenziana Library.

Plate 1. Praying couple. Linen and woolen screen curtain in the loop-weave technique representing a couple praying beneath an apse and a Coptic inscription written in Greek script. The curtain comes from a monastery at Antinoë and dates from the fifth to the sixth century. [See chapter 4.] BENAKI MUSEUM, ATHENS

(2)

(3)

(4)

(1)

Plate 2. The Paschal Vigil. Scenes from medieval southern Italian Exsultet rolls depicting rites and ceremonies from the Paschal Vigil: (1) the blessing of the baptismal font; (2) the celebrant breathing on baptismal water; (3) the celebrant plunging the paschal candle into the font; and (4) the baptism of an infant. The designation "Exsultet" derives from the first word of the deacon's opening proclamation summoning heaven and earth and the Church to "rejoice" at the new exodus accomplished through Christ's death and Resurrection. [See chapter 1.] BIBLIOTECA CASANATENSE, ROME, CAS 724

Plate 3. The breaking of bread. One of the earliest representations of what is believed to be the eucharist is found in the Capella Greca in the catacomb of Priscilla, Rome. The second-century wall painting located above the apse niche shows seven persons, one a veiled woman, reclining at table. A bearded presider extends his arms to break a loaf, hence the name "fractio panis" (*he klasis tou artou*) given to this scene. Visible in front of him is a two-handled cup. On the table are two plates, one with two fish and the other with five loaves, and to the right and left are seven baskets of bread, all of which connect this image with the feeding of the multitude (cf. Mk. 6:30–44 and other gospel accounts). [See chapter 2.] Scala/Art Resource, NY

Plate 4. The Last Supper. Sixth-century mosaic on a wall in the nave of the church of S. Apollinare Nuovo, Ravenna. The sacramental presence of Christ is represented by the fish, which in the early Church was a symbol of Christ. The Greek word *ichthus* allows the formation of an acronym with the meaning "Jesus Christ, Son of God, Savior" (*Iêsous Christos Theou 'Uios Sôtêr*). [See chapter 3.] Scala/Art Resource, NY

Plate 5. The baptism of Christ. The Neonian or Orthodox baptistery in Ravenna, Italy, was erected in the fifth century. In the central dome mosaic a naked Jesus wades in the Jordan while the Holy Spirit descends like a dove. John the Baptizer stands on the riverbank; on the other side, the personification of the river rises from the water. John's hand may have originally rested on Christ's head and not held a bowl, the change coming as the result of tampering at restoration. [See chapter 3.] SCALA/ART RESOURCE, NY

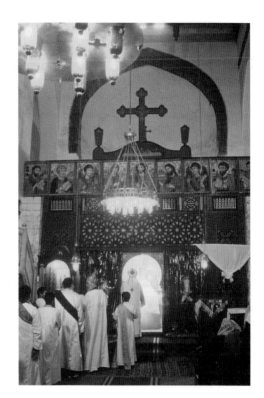

Plate 6. Coptic procession. Entering the ḥijâb through the haikal, Church of St. Barbara, Old Cairo. [See chapter 4.] PHOTOGRAPH COURTESY OF CHRISTINE CHAILLOT

Plate 7. Ethiopian music and procession. *Debteres* with staves, sistra, and drums, Lalibela, Ethiopia. [See chapter 4.] PHOTOGRAPH COURTESY OF CHRISTINE CHAILLOT

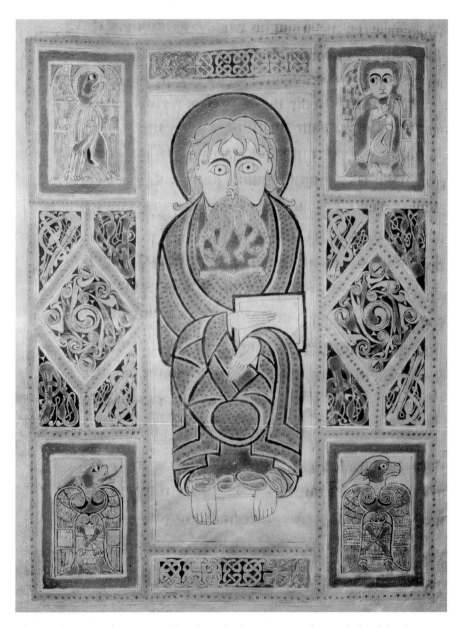

Plate 8. Saint Mark. Saint Mark and, in the four corners, the symbols of the Four Evangelists (for the origins of which see Revelation 4:7). From the St. Gall Gospels (vellum) by the Irish School (eighth century). [See chapter 5.] STIFTSBIBLIOTHEK, ST. GALLEN, SWITZERLAND/BRIDGEMAN ART LIBRARY

Ascension of Christ. The presence of Mary the Mother of the Lord in an attitude of prayer derives from a conflation of Acts 1:14 with Luke 24:50-52 and Acts 1:6-11. From the Rabbula Gospels, folio 13b, Zagba on the Euphrates, Syria, c. 586. SCALA/ ART RESOURCE

Providing a direct link with sixth-century Syriac Christianity and embodying the peregrinations of the Maronites themselves, from the region of Apamea to Mount Lebanon, the images of this unique codex—reproduced in Maronite liturgical and pastoral publications and imitated in wall paintings—serve as markers of Maronite identity.

Whether this new orientation will succeed in reinvigorating the Maronite communities remains to be seen. Following the devastating Lebanese civil war (1975–1991),

Maronite Christians, once the guardians of Lebanese national identity, represented only one-quarter (between 0.5 and 1 million) of the Lebanese population, with far greater numbers of Maronites living in the worldwide diaspora, particularly North and South America, Europe, and Australia. To address the new challenges, the Maronite Church convened a patriarchal synod, the first of its kind since the Lebanese Synod of 1736. It was inaugurated in 2003, with several follow-up meetings scheduled. The "discovery of the Maronite heritage and traditions" and the "consolidation of the Maronite identity" are among its official goals. Whatever its outcome, it is obvious that the rich liturgical tradition, now in the process of being reaffirmed and reshaped, will have to play a vital role in the spiritual survival of the Maronites, well into the new millennium.

Bibliography

Gemayel, Archbishop Boutros. "The Maronite Divine Liturgy." *Eastern Churches Journal* 9 (2002) 33–62.

Hayek, Michel. *Liturgie maronite. Histoire et textes eucharistiques*. Tours, France: Mame, 1964.

Maronite Patriarchal Synod. Official web site: http://www.maronitesynod.org/

Notes

[1] Harald Suermann, *Die Gründungsgeschichte der Maronitischen Kirche*, Orientalia Biblica et Christiana 10 (Wiesbaden: Harrassowitz, 1998), as well as Mariam de Ghantuz Cubbe, "Quelques réflexions à propos de l'histoire ancienne de l'Église Maronite," *Parole de l'Orient* 26 (2001) 3–69.

[2] Tanios Noujaim, "Duwayhî et les langues syriaque et arabe," *Parole de l'Orient* 20 (1995) 371–397.

[3] See Bryan D. Spinks, *Addai and Mari—The Anaphora of the Apostles: A Text for Students*, Grove Liturgical Study 24 (Bramcote, Notts.: Grove, 1980), which surveys the scholarship up to the date of publication and sets out "Addai and Mari" and "Sharrar" in parallel on facing pages; and Sarhad Jammo, "The Anaphora of the Apostles Addai and Mari: A Study of Structure and Historical Back-

ground," *Orientalia Christiana Periodica* 68 (2003) 5–35.

[4] Syriac text in Paul Rouhana, *L'Église Chante* (Kaslik, Lebanon: Université Saint-Esprit, 1992) 22—24; English trans. in Sebastian Brock, "Some Early Witnesses to the East Syriac Liturgical Tradition," *Journal of Assyrian Academic Studies* 18 (2004) 34–35.

[5] For the study of Maronite music, see particularly Louis Hage, *La musique maronite*, 1–7, Bibliothèque de l'Université Saint-Esprit 4: 22–25, 42–44 (Kaslik, Lebanon: Université Saint-Esprit, 1972–2001); for some comments on the "Rabbula Gospels" within Maronite tradition, see Antoine Khoury Harb, *The Maronites. History and Constants* (Beirut: The Maronite Heritage, 2001).

Plate 9. Altar of the Seven Sacraments. Rogier van der Weyden (c. 1399–1464) painted the altarpiece for Jean Chevrot, the Bishop of Tournai, around 1453. The sacraments were defined as seven by the Second Council of Lyons in 1274: baptism, confirmation, penance, eucharist, orders, marriage, and extreme unction. [See chapter 6.] KONINKLIJK MUSEUM VOOR SCHONE KUNSTEN, ANTWERP, BELGIUM/ERICH LESSING/ART RESOURCE, NY

Plate 10. Celebration of mass. Scenes from
Ulrich von Richtenthal's Chronicle of the
Council of Constance, c. 1450. [See chapter 6.]
NEW YORK PUBLIC LIBRARY, ASTOR, LENOX, AND
TILDEN FOUNDATIONS/SPENCER COLLECTION MS.
32, PAGES 415 AND 274/ART RESOURCE, NY

5

The Conversion of the Nations

MICHAEL S. DRISCOLL

The medieval history of Europe can be told, from a liturgical point of view, as the sometimes complex, and certainly nuanced story of the conversion of the nations from paganism to the Christian faith. The term "medieval" is occasionally confusing because it refers both to a historical era in Europe and also to certain stylistic characteristics associated with that era.[1] So while Saint Augustine (died 430) assuredly lived within the period known as late antiquity, he is often treated as a medieval thinker. Such treatment is based on his style of theological and philosophical inquiry and on the fact that he established the trajectory that came to fruition centuries later during the medieval era. Peter Cramer, in his 1993 history of baptism in the early Middle Ages, establishes the beginning date for that period at approximately the year 200.[2] For present purposes we may begin with the conversion of the Frankish king Clovis, for the story of his baptism in 496 or thereabouts, as told by Gregory of Tours three quarters of a century later, opens the door to the ritual and social realities of Christianity's adoption across a swathe of Western Europe. Then medieval European liturgy can be typified by an analysis of the years between 590 and 1085. Beginning and ending with the reigns of the popes Gregory the Great and Gregory VII respectively, this particular period represents the most seminal period in the formation of liturgical life in the West as the conversion of the nations to the Christian faith proceeded. Within this broad sweep of five hundred years three key moments pertaining to the liturgical and sacramental life of the Latin Church require particular attention: the two reforms of Gregory the Great and Gregory VII and, roughly halfway between them, the Carolingian *renovatio*.[3]

Painting the Picture

How can the picture of medieval liturgy and spirituality be painted? One approach is by way of liturgical books, the production of which, in various kinds, is a hallmark of the Middle Ages, and the developing genres of books attest to increasing liturgical complexity.[4] In treating the essential moments of medieval liturgical history, attention must be drawn to the growing literary contribution. However, it can be justly argued that the study of liturgical texts examines the liturgy only from the perspective of those using these books, namely monks and priests, and the elite few who understood the Latin language in which these books were written. What about those great numbers of laity for whom Latin was unintelligible, yet who nonetheless were nourished by the liturgy? It would be false to think that one had to understand Latin in

order to know what was being transacted in the liturgy. The language of the liturgy is not only verbal; it includes posture, gesture, music, visual aspects, and a number of other elements to which the conscious person would be susceptible. Thus semiotics and ritual studies help to assess how the rites actually worked, while the histories of the visual and auditory arts assist in broadening our understanding.[5] Moreover, even when liturgy moved away from earlier forms of improvisatory prayer to textually determined prayer,[6] the question of orality—that is, of the basis on which the actual speaking rested—remains prevalent. For in the Middle Ages a large part of prayer, including liturgical prayer, was not committed to writing. Rather, memorization played a determinant role in ensuring that certain aspects of prayer continued within the realm of orality.[7] Nevertheless, medieval liturgy became increasingly dependent on written sources. In general, throughout the early Middle Ages liturgical texts can be characterized by an increasing complexity, keeping pace with the development of the liturgy and helping to govern a proper and aesthetic performance of the rites.

A second methodological approach centers on the various liturgical reforms and on papal history. The advantage of this approach is that it focuses the study of the liturgy around certain key figures, permitting the identification of certain texts and characteristics with influential people. However, one of the disadvantages is that reforming popes cannot be assessed apart from relationship with their predecessors and successors. In naming a few individual popes, the assumption is sometimes made that these historical reforms were put into effect immediately and that liturgical practices were centralized and uniform throughout the Latin West. In reality, however, reform movements in the Middle Ages took decades to be implemented on account of the slow process of manuscript copying and dissemination before the advent of the printing press and movable type. A monastery or church first had to determine whether they needed and/or could afford a new liturgical book. And then, even after the order was placed, there could be considerable delay before the book's delivery. Since delays were so lengthy, it is difficult to gauge the immediate response to a reform, especially in estimating its value at the popular level.

This leads to a third methodological approach, which involves extending one's peripheral vision to include mystical and hagiographical sources. The value of this approach is that it helps to determine the degree and character of reception of the liturgical reforms, taking into consideration whether there was indeed reception, or indifference and hostility to the reform measures. The drawback is that the ever-widening focus leaves more and more room for subjective interpretation on the part of the scholar.

Each of these approaches merits use, and all are here applied to three moments that bear great importance for medieval liturgy: the papacy of Gregory the Great, the renewal associated with Charlemagne, and the reform of Gregory VII. Because the number and genres of liturgical texts grew so rapidly and extensively in the early Middle Ages, only four liturgical genres will be considered, namely the sacramentaries, the *ordines romani*, the pontificals, and the customaries. To help gauge the impact of the reforms of each of these three periods, anecdotal examples will be drawn from popular piety and practice. These sources, whether they are hagiographic, mystical, or euchological, shed light on how the reforms were received and implemented.

It will be helpful to bear in mind, in a general way, the relationship between the liturgy as it was celebrated in Rome and the liturgy as it was celebrated in other parts of the West. Cyrille Vogel warns against the false assumption that "the Latin liturgy sprang up full-blown or that it originated in a single region or city (Rome) and then spread to other countries as they underwent the process of Christianization."[8] Rather, great regional divergences existed and geographical autonomy marked the particular Western rites in Gaul, Milan, Spain, and the British Isles. In distinction from the Roman rite, which seems to have been at first the local use of the city of Rome, some writers use the term "Gallican" to cover not only the rite characteristic of Gaul itself but also the Ambrosian, Mozarabic, and Celtic rites, inasmuch as these seem to be more closely connected with each other than any one of them is with the Roman. Curiously, they all also appear to bear some Eastern characteristics not present in the Roman.[9]

In the period from the sixth to the ninth century, the Roman rite gradually widened its influence, not indeed without incorporating into itself some Gallican features. The process began first in England with the transplantation of Roman ecclesiastical organization in the south of England.[10] However, on the Continent each region maintained primary jurisdiction over the liturgical rites. Only with the rise of Pepin the Short and Charlemagne in the eighth century did the Roman liturgy begin to dominate the others.[11] The dissemination of Roman rites and practices, initially due to private initiatives, was implemented by the Frankish rulers in the region of Neustria (north-central Gaul), most notably by Charlemagne in the decade preceding his imperial coronation on Christmas, AD 800. The Roman rite ended by superseding virtually all the Gallican rites; these remained in use only in a few places, having on their part incorporated some Roman features. Yet it should be noted that the "Roman" rites were by no means the same everywhere. Many dioceses had their own characteristic variations. Thus in England there were Sarum, York, Lincoln, Hereford, and Bangor liturgical practices, and there were similar variations on the Continent. Moreover the monastic orders had their own forms so that there were Benedictine practices, and later unique liturgical usages of Franciscans, Carthusians, and other orders. By 1000 the Roman rite itself was pretty well fixed apart from minor details, and these in ceremony rather than in ritual. Between 1000 and 1570 small changes continued to take place.

Entrance into the Faith

Treatment of conversion of the Western nations must start with the practice of initiation by which persons—individually and in some sense communally—were admitted to the Church. Since baptism shaped the identity of rulers and subjects alike, our story may begin paradigmatically with the historical, if not legendary, baptism of Clovis the Frank. Gregory of Tours (died 594) is responsible for keeping alive the memory of Clovis, and in his narrative we can at least discover aspects of baptism important at the time of Gregory.[12]

How did Clovis, a barbarian tribal king who converted to Christianity, become for the Carolingians and later for Christian France a symbol of identity and destiny?[13] Toward the time of Clovis's coming to power (481), a Roman army under Syagrius occupied part of Gaul. Barbarian principalities divided up the rest of the territory: Visigoths and Burgundians in the central and southern parts of Gaul had already joined forces for several decades and the Frankish tribes fought among themselves in the northern part of the country. With the collapse of the imperial authority in the West, each military authority, either Roman or barbarian, sought to assure the continuity of the state and to become the territorial authority. The support of the Gallo-Roman elites and of the Church, the only power within the cities, was therefore essential. Furthermore, the people of the Gallo-Roman cities were Catholic, while the Visigoths and the Burgundians were Arians and the Franks remained pagan.

Clovis at fifteen years of age inherited the federated Frankish kingdom of Tournai. Quickly, toward 486, the young king seized the last Roman enclave and reestablished the unity of the country by eliminating the rival chiefs one by one. Seeking an alliance against the perennial enemy the Visigoths, Clovis wed (c. 492–494) Clotilde, a Catholic Burgundian, niece of Gondebaud. Clotilde, for her part, actively encouraged her husband to convert to Christianity, helped by Remigius, the bishop of Reims. Clovis did not oppose the baptism of his first son, who died within a year. In spite of this bad omen, his second son had also been baptized, only to fall ill, but was later healed by the prayers of his mother. Thus, in 496, Clovis invoked the God of the Christians at Tolbiac during battle: "If you give me victory over my enemies, I will believe in you and will be baptized

The Baptism of Clovis. Clovis I, Merovingian king of the Salian Franks, was baptized by St. Remigius at Reims around 496. From a fourteenth-century manuscript of the *Grandes Chroniques de France*. Musée Goya, Castres, France/Giraudon/Art Resource, NY

in your name." The decision of Clovis initially was surrounded in great secrecy, but later the king undertook measured steps to assure the help and the fidelity of his warriors. The baptismal ceremony took place with great pageantry in the cathedral of Reims. Gregory of Tours narrates the event thus:

> Then the queen asked saint Remigius, bishop of Reims, to summon Clovis secretly, urging him to introduce the king to the word of salvation. And the bishop sent for him secretly and began to urge him to believe in the true God, maker of heaven and earth, and to cease worshipping idols, which could help neither themselves nor any one else. . . . [Remigius] bade them get ready the baptismal font. The squares were shaded with tapestried canopies, the churches adorned with white curtains, the baptistery set in order, the aroma of incense spread, candles of fragrant odor burned brightly, and the whole shrine of the baptistery was filled with a divine fragrance: and the Lord gave such a grace to those who stood by that they thought they were placed amid the odors of paradise. And the king was the first to ask to be baptized by the bishop. Another Constantine advanced to the baptismal font, to terminate the disease of ancient leprosy and wash away with fresh water the foul spots that had long been borne. And when he entered to be baptized, the saint of God began with ready speech: "Gently bend your neck, Sicamber;[14] worship what you burned; burn what you worshipped." . . . And so the king confessed the all-powerful God in the Trinity, and was baptized in the name of the Father, Son and Holy Spirit, and was anointed with the holy ointment with the sign of the cross of Christ. And of his army more than 3000 were baptized.[15]

The conversion to Catholicism of the barbarian king was a great event. Gregory evokes the image of a new Constantine given to the Church as a young conqueror. Clovis was now ready to convert the West and conversely he won the Church as an ally. According to Gregory, numerous were those among the Gauls who burned with desire to have the Franks as masters.

After having defeated the Allamans (496–506), Clovis launched an assault in 507 on the Visigothic kingdom in a crusade declared against Arianism. At his death in 511, his kingdom stretched from the Low Countries to the Pyrenees and from the Atlantic to present-day Germany. His sons annexed the kingdom of the Burgundians and Provence, which was under Ostrogothic control. The dynasty of Clovis endured until the eighth century. The official entrance into the Church of the first barbarian kingdom permitted the amalgamation of the Franks with the Gallo-Romans, which could not have happened with the other barbarian kingdoms. Thus emerged a new nation, which would be called "France, the eldest daughter of the church."

There were probably three stages in the process of conversion of a monarch: first of all, intellectual acceptance of Christ's message—the "conversion" proper; second, the decision to announce this publicly to followers who might be hostile to the change; third, the ceremony of baptism and membership in the community of Christians.[16] Generally the Gallican rite as described by later sacramentaries and *ordines* consisted of six elements: the catechumenate; baptism; anointing of the candidate; *pedilavium*; vesting in white robes; and communion at the mass of the Easter vigil. Only the first stage of intellectual acceptance would be considered as private between the king and the bishop. Thereafter what the monarch does affects the kingdom.

From early days, the baptistery has had a special form and placement, housing the font into whose purifying water the future Christian would be plunged. In the West, the traditional plan of the baptistery was octagonal rather than circular, the number eight symbolizing resurrection and rebirth in line with Christ's Resurrection on the first day of a new week. Until the Carolingian period, the baptistery was one of the

buildings in the overall architectural plan of a cathedral, being an autonomous structure, situated most often directly facing the main entrance of the church, or sometimes near the façade but preferentially on the south side.

At the time of Clovis, it would seem that baptism was by partial if not full immersion. The catechumen descended into the water, and manuscript and artistic depictions show the person waist-deep in water receiving the anointing. It was therefore
necessary that the baptistery have an immersion pool, even though it may have been
shallow. Flowing water fed the pool, a symbol of living water, like the Jordan River,
where John baptized Christ; unfortunately, no vestiges have survived of the plumbing
by which water was channeled to the font. As the cathedral at Reims was built over the
former Roman baths from the Constantinian era, we can suppose that this water was
at least tepid.

Our most complete source for early initiation is the Gelasian Sacramentary. The
reign of Clovis overlaps with the reign of Pope Gelasius (492–496), after whom the
Gelasian Sacramentary is named. The principal manuscript of this book, *Vaticanus
regenensis 316*, was compiled in Gaul in the first half of the eighth century, more than
two hundred years after the appearance of the archetype. Michel Andrieu posits that
it represents a collection of Frankish usages over three centuries.[17] Antoine Chavasse
has argued that the "old Gelasian" that stands at its core was itself compiled at Rome
from two earlier sources, the younger of which certainly was in existence in the sixth
century.[18] Three other documents testify to the baptismal rite in Gaul in the eighth
century: the *Missale gothicum*, the *Missale gallicanum vetus*, and the *Missale bobbiense*.

It remains difficult to distinguish with certitude elements that might have been
practiced in Gaul at the end of the fifth century from Roman and Frankish elements
that have been blended later. Gregory of Tours, who was born when Clovis was coming to power, is writing his account of the baptism several decades later. His is by no
means an eyewitness account, nor is he interested in giving much detail about the rite
itself. Other than the mention of the bending of the neck, which in the past has been
interpreted to mean baptism by infusion, the baptism in the name of the Trinity and
the anointing with chrism (consecrated oil), Gregory is sadly silent. Even if he had
supplied more details, one would be forced to ask whether he was faithful to the practice of Clovis's time or whether he was reflecting on this event through the lens of the
liturgical practice at the end of the sixth century. We do not know, for example, if
there were any scrutinies that preceded the baptism, nor what the preparatory period
would have looked like. Nor can we ascertain the number and shape of the secondary
rites surrounding the initiatory event itself.

What more can be learned from Gregory about the initiatory tradition surrounding Clovis? The day for the baptism of Clovis was fixed as Christmas. Now Easter was
the principal season for baptism, but perhaps that date seemed too far away. Clovis
and those around him may have been in a hurry to seize this unique opportunity,
especially from a political perspective. There is evidence suggesting that in Gaul as
well as Milan, dates other than Easter were also appropriate for baptism. The feast of
Epiphany, combining the adoration of the Magi with the baptism of Jesus in the Jordan, was especially appropriate as a secondary baptismal feast.[19] If Clovis was impa-
tient to be baptized, why did he not wait a little longer until early January? Here
again, the sources are silent. Michel Rouche indeed argues that the actual baptism
could not have occurred in the same year as the battle of Tolbiac (496), since some
sort of catechumenate would have been obligatory; moreover, the attendance of so
many bishops at the baptism would have required more advanced warning.[20] He ar-

gues that the real date was more likely Christmas Day 497 or even 499. In that case, the choice of Christmas for the baptism would have been particularly deliberate: to insist on the new birth of Clovis in Christ and the new birth of the Franks as a Christian nation. A contemporary source, a letter to Clovis from the bishop Avitus of Vienne, sends his regrets for not attending the event and beautifully explores the meaning of the Christmas date. He writes:

> It is well that the birth of our Redeemer has inaugurated this glory in such a way that the day when the regenerating water will prepare you for salvation was also the day when the world received him who was born for its redemption, the master of heaven. This is why the day when we celebrate the birth of the Lord, may also be your day; that is to say, the day when you are born in Christ is also the day when Christ was born in the world; it is the day when you have consecrated your soul to God, your life to your contemporaries, your fame to posterity.[21]

Some translations of Gregory's account insist that Clovis bends his neck in order that water might be poured over his head. Rather than "bend your neck," however, another translation offered by Rouche attempts to contextualize the action and renders the expression as "humbly take off your neck piece."[22] The verb *deponere* can mean "take off," while *colla* (neck) is possibly a literary conceit meaning *collaria* (a neckpiece worn by the Franks similar to those worn by the Celts as a sign of power). Thus it would mean: throw down this sign of worldly power associated with the pagan gods. In this context, the expression "adore what you burn and burn what you adore" would make more sense. This phrase might be derived from the ritual itself, when one renounces Satan and all his pomp. We know from other sources that the Visigothic pagan priests wore neckpieces as well as armpieces. These talismans furnished a sacred power and were a part of the priestly garb. Saint Ambrose complained also to have seen an Arian bishop of Roman origins adorn himself with these emblems.[23] In throwing down these pagan symbols of power, the king of the Franks crosses over into a new sphere, the Christian sphere, where power is delegated by God and not insured by the wearing of talismans.

The minister of baptism either poured water over the candidate three times or immersed the candidate thrice, while pronouncing the formula in the name of the Trinity. After being baptized in the name of the Father and the Son and the Holy Spirit, Clovis would emerge from the font and put on a white garment, symbol of his entrance into eternal life. Next his sister Albofleda would be baptized. Following the water rite was the anointing of the head with sacred chrism, a rite that signified accession of the Christian neophyte to the royal, priestly, and prophetic dignity of the people of God.[24] Besides Clovis and Albofleda, another sister, Lantechilde, was anointed. She had already been baptized into Arianism. The fact that she is only anointed indicates the Church recognizes the validity of the first baptism. However, she as a reformed heretic must make her declaration of adhesion to the Holy Trinity, stating that the Son is equal to the Father and the Holy Spirit. After Lantechilde is anointed with sacred chrism, hands are laid as a sign of penance and reconciliation.

The distinction between baptism as a water rite and christening as an anointing rite eventually led—as the performance of the two became separated in time—to the sacrament of confirmation. The name "confirmation" was first used by the Gallican Councils of Riez (439) and Orange (441). Since baptism was necessary for salvation, and since the Church was spreading quickly throughout the empire, particularly into rural areas, bishops delegated priests to perform the water rite in their parishes but retained for themselves the oil rite as a way of confirming the baptism; and the interval between the two acts could vary, extending to years.[25] Around 460 Faustus, the bishop of Riez, delivered a Pentecost sermon in which he attempts to make sense of the practice of separating the two rites.[26] He stresses the importance of the episcopal confirmation, noting that those previously baptized were now more fully Christian. But a confusion entered regarding the meaning of the anointing rite. Surrounding baptism there were in fact several anointings and the kind of oil and the prayers used with the anointing help determine the specificity of each anointing. Anointing with chrism—pure olive oil perfumed with balsam—bore the sense of a consecration, usually associated with priests, prophets, and kings. The use of the oil of catechumens, on the other hand, held the idea of anointing for strengthening. Faustus, in his attempt to justify the separation of the anointing with chrism from baptism, preached that in baptism the Holy Spirit gives new life but in confirmation the Spirit gives an additional strength needed for battle with sin. Consequently, as a result of this confusion, the theology of confirmation stressed the effect of strengthening for the fight (*robur ad pugnam*). To this was joined in Carolingian times the notion of confirmation as equipment for "preaching to others the same gift as one has received in baptism."[27]

It appears that the use of chrism in Christian initiation inspired the anointing of the later French kings. The ceremonial installation of a king is called a consecration (*le sacre du roi*) rather than a coronation, underscoring the importance of the anointing ritual. Paul Jacobson convincingly argues that the later Carolingian regal anointings have their foundations in the baptismal anointings as practiced in early medieval Gaul.[28]

In the Carolingian period, Clovis's fame spread. Beginning with Pepin the Short, the father of Charlemagne, the kings of France exalted Clovis as the founder of the Frankish monarchy. Pepin was the first of them to receive the royal anointing. Pepin's solemn consecration confirmed the divine origins of his power and was explicitly associated with the baptism of Clovis, which furnished a dynastic legitimacy to this usurper of the Merovingians. Charlemagne would give to his son the name of the founder (Louis = Clovis), and it would be the most widely used name among the French kings. The confusion between baptism and the alleged consecration of Clovis, cultivated by the archbishops of Reims, would assure them a monopoly of the royal anointing after the twelfth century and make Reims the city of its occurrence.

The Carolingian period saw the importance of baptism not only as a sacrament to be received but also as a way of thinking about identity in the Holy Roman Empire. In a "society of the baptized," infants became the primary candidates. Consequently the ritual of baptism underwent revision,[29] providing rich material for commentators.[30] In 811 or 812 Charlemagne sent to the ecclesiastical officials of the empire a circular letter in which he explores the meaning of the rites of initiation and provides an exposition on the church that celebrated them.[31] Evidence from the region of Gaul indicates that the baptismal liturgy had been in serious decline. The rites of the catechumenate had all but disappeared, although traces of the former initiatory regime remained preserved in some liturgical books without any longer being practiced.[32] Now, under Charlemagne, emphasis was placed on the creed as the heart of the baptismal rite. The creed as the symbol of faith was the glue to hold the Holy Roman Empire together. As Susan Keefe notes:

> The rite of baptism, comprising the entire initiation process for a Christian from catechetical preparation to reception of the Eucharist as a full member of the Church, put its stamp on every individual not only as part of the Church, but as a member of society. It was often the only thing that distinguished the people of the newly conquered borders of the Carolingian empire from the pagan tribes.[33]

In principle, of course, this was the very ritual pattern by which the bounds of Christendom were extended as new nations continued to be brought into the faith.

As ancient liturgical books began to wear out and were discarded, new ritual books were needed. One of the oldest liturgical sources, dating from the eighth century, is the *Ordo Romanus XI.*[34] Compiled in Gaul, this baptismal ordo attests to Roman usage as it was transported north of the Alps for Gallican clergy who had never seen Roman liturgical ceremonies. Thus the ordo is quite detailed in the description of how the rite of baptism should take place. Liturgical ritual books by nature tend to be very conservative because compilers hesitate to eliminate elements that are no longer in use. In the case of Ordo XI, for example, the candidates—although they were now primarily infants—are commanded to sit, stand, kneel, pray, and speak, thus pointing to the need for baptismal sponsors or godparents who can respond on behalf of the infant candidates. One salient feature of this ordo is that the seven scrutinies take place between the third week of Lent and Holy Saturday morning. It is easy to gauge how the catechumenate has been reduced temporally and altered to accommodate infants. The third scrutiny is particularly interesting because it includes the presentation and explanation of the Creed and the Our Father as well as a general presentation about the four gospels. After the abridged catechumenate, the infants are presented for baptism. Thus, Joseph Lynch observes: "From this it can be seen that the compiler of the fully developed scrutinies in *Ordo XI* had worked out a way to initiate helpless infants while at the same time respecting venerable usages."[35]

Ordo XI barely mentions the blessing of the paschal candle and the liturgy of the word. The text only alludes to the blessing of the font, which is followed immediately by the baptism. We know only that the bishop (*pontifex*) baptizes one or two infants and that he deputes a deacon to baptize the remainder. Following the baptismal bath, the godparents present the child to a priest who signs the child on the forehead with chrism and says a prayer, but this anointing is not considered confirmation, because confirmation is described in greater detail as a second anointing with chrism by the bishop. After a prayer evoking the sevenfold gifts of the Holy Spirit, the bishop traces the sign of the cross with chrism on the foreheads of the neophytes and pronounces the formula: "In the name of the Father and of the Son and of the Holy Spirit. Peace be with you." The language is clear in calling this ritual confirmation, using the terms *confirmans* and *confirmatur*. The infants are then given holy communion at the mass that follows. A final note indicates that this ceremony of baptism for the Easter Vigil can also be celebrated at the Vigil of Pentecost.

A final witness to baptismal liturgical revision is found in *Ordo Romanus L*, which represents the full flowering of the Carolingian liturgical *renovatio*.[36] The sacramental liturgical forms underwent definitive redaction at Mainz at the monastic scriptorium of Saint Alban between 950 and 962. The *Romano-Germanic Pontifical*, and Ordo Romanus L as its fundamental section, are the two great monuments of this effort.[37] Ordo L seems very similar to Ordo XI but the compilers of Ordo L have modified the ritual of baptism to incorporate the liturgical modifications that occurred over the two intervening centuries. A notable change is the omission of the parents in the rite of infant baptism, which corresponded with a canon law in Mainz forbidding parents to be the sponsors of their children in baptism.[38] Ordo L faithfully reproduces the first six scrutinies found in Ordo XI, but greatly expands and modifies the seventh scrutiny. One explanation for the liturgical conservatism in the case of the first six scrutinies is that it is unlikely that they were still in use. Archaic in form, they were nonetheless maintained in the liturgical book. It is more than likely that infants were baptized in one session without the benefit of the preceding six scrutinies. On Holy Saturday the priests were instructed to catechize the infants (*primum qualiter cathecizantur infantes*),[39] which simply means to prepare the babies for baptism through hand-laying, signing with the cross, and placing salt on the tongue. From this directive it is clear that the catechumenate has been telescoped and abridged to include only the seventh scrutiny. Ordo L then calls for the recitation of the Lord's prayer and the Creed with one notable adaptation. In Ordo XI the priest recited these texts first over the boys and then over the girls, but in Ordo L the Creed and Our Father are used to test the sponsors for their aptness. Furthermore, rather than the parents being asked if it was their will that their child be baptized (as found in Ordo XI), now the child is addressed directly and the godparents respond in the child's stead. The role of the parents in the rite of baptism diminished in favor of the expanding responsibilities of the godparents. In the Carolingian period, the godparent was reminded often of his or her responsibilities and thus became an ever more significant partner for insuring that Christian instruction was carried out in the larger context of religious and intellectual renewal.

In summary, a few observations can be made concerning baptism as entrance into the Church and as a first step in the ongoing conversion of persons and their society. In comparing the eighth-century Ordo XI with the earlier Gelasian Sacramentary that reflects sixth-century liturgical practice, a conflicting tendency is apparent. On the one hand, the eighth-century liturgical revisers show their reluctance to discard venerable rituals and prayers, which terminates in ritual conflation and elaboration. On the other hand, the revised ceremonies, instead of taking place over an extended

Saint Boniface. Saint Boniface (or, by his English name, Wynfrith) baptizing, and himself suffering martyrdom (754). From a Fulda mass book of the early eleventh century. The "Apostle of Germany" offers only his gospel book as protection against his attackers. Seminary Library Udine/Dagli Orti/Art Archive

period of time, are abridged so as to be performed in rapid succession. It is conceivable that the rites described in Ordo XI could be carried out in two sessions, alleviating the burden on parents and godparents dealing with restless infants. Secondly, the ritual of baptism described in Ordo XI presumes the presence of many priests and deacons. A question arises about its feasibility in rural settings of Francia and Germania. Ritual simplification is not only conceivable, but necessary, particularly in light of reports from Saint Boniface during his four decades of missionary work.[40] Third, in the post-Carolingian period, baptism according to Ordo L still captured the religious and political imagination of rulers and religious thinkers because it was the way that citizens became Christians in an empire that declared itself Holy and Roman. In spite of ritual revision and possible deformation, the sacrament of baptism remained a *locus theologicus* for commentators and a means to solidify the empire.

After baptism, the question turns, as it always did: how is the Christian then nourished in the faith? What role do the other sacraments play in sustaining Christians? How does the regular liturgy, most particularly the eucharist and the office of prayer, contribute to the continuing conversion of the Western nations?

The First Gregorian Reform: Gregory the Great

Gregory the Great (reigned 590–604) referred to himself as "the servant of the servants of God." Such a description seems fitting, given what another Gregory, the historian bishop of Tours, writes about him as a deacon, before his election as bishop of Rome:

> He belonged to one of the first senatorial families and from his youth was devoted to God and with his own means had established six monasteries in Sicily and a seventh within the Roman walls; and giving to these such an amount of land as would suffice to furnish their daily food, he sold the rest and all the furniture of his house and distributed money among the poor; and he who had been used to appear in the city arrayed in silken robes and glittering jewels was now clad in cheap garments, and he devoted himself to the service of the Lord's altar and was assigned as seventh levite to aid the pope.[41]

Gregory, having in 590 been elected pope, continued the vast reforming project of his predecessors Leo the Great (died 461) and Gelasius I (died 496). In addition to affirming the primacy of Rome over Byzantium and the Lombards, Gregory the Great worked for clerical and liturgical reform within the Latin Church. But while Gregory is credited with reforming prayer life, little is known directly about liturgical life in Rome during his time. Nonetheless, the so-called histories and hagiographic writings from late antiquity or early medieval times do provide an invaluable, if incomplete, source for discerning the importance of the liturgy in the church's life as expressed by the saints. The *vitae sanctorum* (lives of the saints) were intended as spiritual writings to edify their hearers and provide *exempla* (models) for their moral lives. They also were used as propaganda to promote the cults of the various saints. They are not history in the purview of modern historiographers; they do, however, furnish oblique references to the liturgy, especially how the liturgy and sacraments nourished the spiritual lives of the saints or fended off evil from believers. These hagiographic sources can be helpful witnesses in determining the success of Gregory's reform.

Gregory lent his name to several medieval liturgical books: a sacramentary, containing sacerdotal mass prayers and materials for administration of some sacraments;

the *ordines*, or brief documents containing directions for the ritual implementation of the mass and other sacramental rites; and the *capitulare evangeliorum*, a book used by a deacon indicating which gospel text was to be used for any given liturgical celebration. In the course of the early Middle Ages, the sacramentary emerged as the primary book used in the celebration of the mass. It contained a collection of prayers or orations that the priest presider used. The canon of the mass, from the Sanctus onward, was basically a fixed prayer, while a series of prayers for each day varied according to the liturgical feast and season. This series normally included four prayers: the opening collect, the prayer over the gifts, the preface leading into the Sanctus, and the prayer after communion. In addition to prayers for the mass, the sacramentary included the liturgical calendar, an *ordo missae* (a list delineating the order of the various parts of the mass) and the rituals for some of the other sacraments, including baptism, funerals and penance, and some blessings. Two principal types of sacramentary emerged from the early Middle Ages: one bearing the name of Pope Gregory; and the other bearing the name of his predecessor, Gelasius.

The Gregorian Sacramentary is a collection of prayers, prefaces, and rubrical material of the Roman Church originally collected at the time of Gregory I. In its original form it presented the liturgy celebrated at the Lateran Church, the cathedral of the diocese of Rome. Although the Gregorian Sacramentary was well suited for a papal liturgy, it remained little adapted for the needs of small churches outside of Rome. It contained ceremonies that the bishop of Rome would have needed, such as the dedication of churches, and other ceremonies reserved to a bishop. The Gelasian Sacramentary, on the other hand, also emanating from Rome, provided a less formal liturgy for the use of priests. There were various attempts during the sixth and seventh centuries to produce a sacramentary that would combine both the papal liturgy and the less formal presbyteral liturgy. Ultimately these failed to bring about the desired unity.

It was not until the Carolingian renewal that there was any serious attempt to disseminate these sacramentaries in all of Western Christendom. Charlemagne, in his attempt to unify the empire, saw a single liturgy as a possible aid to the endeavor and asked Pope Hadrian I for a copy of the Gregorian Sacramentary, which could be copied and disseminated throughout the Holy Roman Empire.[42] This book, however, because of its limited papal usage, was unpopular outside of Rome. Eventually a sacramentary composed of elements from both the ancient Gregorian Sacramentary and an edition of the Gelasian Sacramentary was adopted in northern Italy and France. This hybrid sacramentary was in use by the tenth century and is the forerunner of the present sacramentary.

The sacramentary, however, contained only the texts of prayers, and was therefore lacking any indications of the ritual actions to be used in conjunction with these prayers. So, it was necessary to consult another liturgical document—the ordo. Various rites became increasingly sophisticated and directions needed to be provided in separate documents called ordines, of which only fifty have survived.[43] Ordines are invaluable because they provide indications as to how the liturgy and the sacraments were celebrated in various locations at different times.

Another passage from the *History of the Franks* by Gregory of Tours provides insight into the power of prayer, especially psalmodic prayer. In response to the great epidemic plague of 590, Pope Gregory

> made an address to the people of Rome to meet it by prayer. When he spoke these words bands of clergy gathered and he bade them sing psalms for three days and pray for God's

mercy. Every three hours choirs of singers came to the church crying through the streets of the city "Kyrie eleison." Our deacon who was there said that in the space of one hour while the people uttered cries of supplication to the Lord eighty fell to the ground and died. But the bishop did not cease to urge the people not to cease from prayer. (10.1)

Especially associated with Gregory the Great is the so-called major litany, sung on 25 April (the feast of Saint Mark). A description of the use of the great litany at the time of Gregory the Great is found in Ordo L.[44] The *litania septena*—its sevenfold structure has outlasted the circumstances of its origin—was recited by seven distinct social groups as they departed simultaneously from seven different churches in the city of Rome: clerics from Saint John the Baptist, men from Saint Marcellus, monks from Saints John and Paul, handmaids of the Lord (virgins) from Saints Cosmas and Damian, married women from Saints Peter and Stephen, widows from Saint Vitale, and the poor and children from Saint Cecilia. Provisions were made for time of war, how the people should dress, and what their demeanor should be for the sake of penitence. As a liturgical document, Ordo L gives a small indication of liturgical life in the city of Rome. It can be better understood against the backdrop of the papal stational liturgies, where the pope during Lent would visit the different churches of Rome, each day of the week except Thursday.[45] The idea of stational churches was adapted in the context of rural monasteries. In the absence of separate churches to and from which one processed, one moved from altar to altar within a single church building.[46]

In his *Eight Books of Miracles*, Gregory of Tours gives an account of a miracle that bears on the understanding of Sunday as the Lord's day, a day of rest:

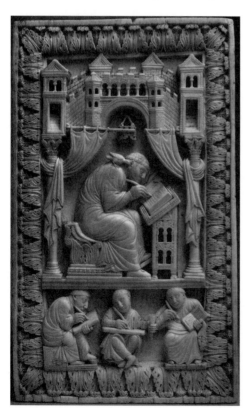

In the territory of the city [Tours] at Lingeais, a woman who lived there moistened flour on the Lord's day and shaped a loaf, and drawing the coals aside she covered it over with hot ashes to bake. When she did this her right hand was miraculously set on fire and began to burn. She screamed and wept and hastened to the village church in which relics of the blessed John are kept. And she prayed and made a vow that on this day sacred to the divine name she would do no work, but only pray. The next night she made a candle as tall as herself. Then she spent the whole night in prayer, holding the candle in her hand all the time, and the flame went out and she returned home safe and sound.[47]

Saint Gregory the Great Writing.
Gregory, Bishop of Rome (590–604), is often depicted with a dove perched on his shoulder and whispering into his ear, a symbol of the inspiration of his musical compositions by the Holy Spirit. Ivory from Metz, c. 968–980.
KUNSTHISTORISCHES MUSEUM, VIENNA/
ERICH LESSING/ART RESOURCE, NY

The miraculous power of the relics to heal the woman and to bring her back to a more frequent practice of the eucharist on Sunday is striking. This kind of story gives some indication how the liturgical life, especially Sunday observance, modeled the popular piety. Many of the miracle stories obliquely reflect the liturgical reforms of Gregory and their effect on the people.

Finally, the name of Gregory the Great is associated with the reform of liturgical music. The so-called Gregorian Antiphonary contains the musical parts composed for the liturgy of the eucharist and the office sung by a cantor or a *schola cantorum*. "Gregorian Chant" is plainchant of the Roman rite named after Gregory the Great, although Gregory probably had little to do directly with the composition of the texts or the music. In the past scholars held that the form of plainchant that survived is based on older Roman chant with subsequent pruning of long florid passages and the incorporation of other elements from the eighth- and ninth-century Gallican liturgy of Carolingian France. The chant was diffused throughout the Frankish empire as part of a Romanizing policy of the imperial court. Eventually it supplanted most other forms of local or regional plainchant, but ultimately was itself influenced by the traditions it supplanted, keeping pace with the evolution of the Roman-rite mass and divine office. Recent scholarship, however, argues in favor of Roman provenance dating to the latter part of the seventh century.[48] The ancient repertory of texts and melodies has been progressively enriched up to modern times.

Interior of the Octagon in the Palatine Chapel at Aachen. Under Charlemagne, sole ruler of the Franks from 771 and crowned emperor in 800, the court and church at Aix-la-Chapelle (Aachen) became an important center of liturgical scholarship and renewal. FOTO MARBURG/ART RESOURCE, NY

The Carolingian *Renovatio*[49]

In the late-eighth and early-ninth centuries, Charlemagne undertook a major reform of cultural and religious aspects of the Holy Roman Empire. In the case of his liturgical reform, it is important to note that the initiative belonged to the emperor, Charles the Great, rather than to Pope Hadrian I. However, Hadrian provides a point of historical reference, because one of the sacramentaries used as an instrument of the reform, the Hadrianum, bears his name. Charlemagne invited a number of scholars to come to the court to assist him, most notably Alcuin, the celebrated deacon from York. In addition to the founding of schools and the improvement of existing ones, Charlemagne's *renovatio* comprised several notable elements: the development of the Caroline minuscule script; the appearance of a new edition of the Vulgate, containing corrections derived from the fathers and ancient scribes; the promulgation of important legislation, notably the *Annales regni francorum*, and especially the *Admonitiones generales*, which were to be applied in a uniform way in the kingdom of the Franks in order to level out regional differences; the reformation of monasticism based on a single manuscript of the Rule of Saint Benedict, brought from Monte Cassino in 787; and the general reform of the liturgy based on a standardization of liturgical books, such as sacramentaries, lectionaries, homilaries containing sermons of the Fathers, and antiphonals. The liturgical aspect of the Carolingian renewal must be situated in the broader context of political maneuvering and the centralization of authority. Stronger schools staffed by monks all observing the same liturgical practices guaranteed Charlemagne's campaign a certain success.

Of great importance for understanding Charlemagne's strategy for liturgical uniformity is the so-called Hadrianum, a type of Gregorian Sacramentary.[50] The emperor had requested a book from the pope, and he sought to make it the authentic liturgical source. Unfortunately the pontiff sent a book that was useful for papal practice but not particularly helpful outside of the papal court. Furthermore, the book was liturgically incomplete and frankly insufficient for Charlemagne's purposes. Work was undertaken to adapt it through the addition of a supplement.[51] Consequently, what was considered to be pure Roman liturgical style was, in reality, a hybrid of Roman practices mixed with Gallican elements. With the help of the imperial court, this mixed liturgy spread with amazing speed to all parts of northern Europe as a primary aspect of the *renovatio imperii*, being accorded the same authority as the Hadrianum. Despite its drastically different style of composition, it was assumed to be of Roman origin. Charlemagne was generally successful in imposing liturgical uniformity throughout the Frankish kingdom extending from Frisia and Saxony in the north to southern Italy, from the Pyrenees to Bohemia. In the end, this mixed liturgy returned in the tenth century to Rome itself and became the established liturgical practice there under the Ottonian emperors.

In addition to the sacramentary and the ordines, another book emerged onto the liturgical scene in the ninth and tenth centuries that combined certain features from the two other types: the pontifical. This book, designed for episcopal use, contained noneucharistic rites that the bishop alone could perform. One of the best examples of this episcopal book is the Romano-Germanic Pontifical.[52] The development of the pontifical was an important step in the centralization of power and helped to galvanize further liturgical uniformity. This liturgical genre continued to develop into the twelfth century thanks to the efforts of William Durand, the bishop of Mende, who brought the pontifical to its apogee. Although the pontifical has been revised since Vatican II, one can still discern the hand of Durandus.

Between the time of Gregory the Great and the time of Charlemagne there had in fact been a gradual shift from geographical and liturgical autonomy to uniformity in liturgical practice. Probably the most important factors in this centralization were monastic organization and practices. Monastic civilization is truly based on the book [see color plate 8 for an image from the Sankt Gallen Gospels]. Thus, the monks, working in their *scriptoria* copying liturgical books, Bibles, and other writings, could play a key role in the realization of Charlemagne's dream of a liturgically and thereby politically united Holy Roman Empire.[53] Entailed in the Carolingian *renovatio* was the intense cross-fertilization of liturgies.

The native liturgy that had existed in much of the Frankish empire—the old Gallican rite—was thus exposed to Roman influence. In point of fact, however, what resulted from this meeting of two different ritual families was neither Gallican nor Roman, but a ritual hybrid. This Gallican-Roman hybrid, the result of a cross-fertilization of liturgical traditions, eventually made its way back to Rome itself. At the same time, the Gallican rite vanished except in a few local churches that maintained a strong attachment to native customs.[54]

A linguistic factor also entered into the equation, contributing to the demise of the regional liturgies and an important shift in spirituality. The lingua franca was no longer Latin, and the use of Latin was reserved almost exclusively for the liturgy. The movement toward the general use of the vernacular in the ninth and tenth centuries brought profound cultural and intellectual change. Because Latin was reserved to the liturgy and private prayer could be said in the vernacular, a split was created between liturgical and private prayer.

The prayers of the Carolingian period bore a personal and devotional character. Several good examples of prayer books (*libelli precum*—small booklets of prayer) have survived. It has long been held that Alcuin was the compiler of *libelli* such as these.[55] While questions of authority and textual originality are far from settled, the choice of texts and their compilation prove especially revelatory of the spirituality of the early Middle Ages and serve to delineate the boundaries of the penitential and confessional discipline of this period.[56] Far from being original, the *libelli* are rather evidence of prayer collections that had been fairly well circulated.[57] The books are punctuated by prayers of Irish and Anglo-Saxon origin, called confessions, along with many other penitential prayers. Furthermore, these booklets, which were compiled principally in the Celtic and Anglo-Saxon lands, are patterned after the monastic psalter. Most of the prayers that are of a devotional nature seem to have been intended for private use, a characteristic typical of Irish spirituality at this time.[58] The prayer forms reveal the provenance of the prayers and the influence of Celtic and Anglo-Saxon patterns as well as classical Roman prayer forms upon the composition of prayers. The Roman style is characterized by its simplicity and sobriety.[59] Perhaps resulting from the precision of the Latin language, the tone of these prayers seems juridical—normally the prayers of Roman origin are short and extremely well refined, eliminating excess verbiage. They are addressed to the Father through the Son and in the Holy Spirit. In the case of these *libelli*, one notes the ample use of Roman collect prayers that followed the psalms in the praying of the divine office. The brevity and precision of these psalter collects is notable. Contained within the prayer booklets are the seven Psalms of Penitence (Psalms 6, 31, 37, 50, 101, 129, and 142 in the Vulgate numbering), which played an important role in penitential spirituality and the satisfaction of penance.[60] Each of these seven psalms was followed by a collect, the majority of which are of Roman origin. The collect following Psalm 129 (*De profundis*) provides an example of the Roman collect:

> We pray, Lord,
> that the ears of your mercy be attentive to prayers of supplication,
> because with you is forgiveness of sins,
> so that you may not notice our iniquities,
> but grant to us your mercies,
> through our Lord . . .[61]

The prayer summarizes and echoes the psalm that has just been said and focuses the mind of the person praying on redemption through God's loving mercy without wasting a single word. The prayer transmits, illustrates, and applies the mystery of Christ as fully as possible. In these few brief lines, a complete theology of redemption and reconciliation is sketched and articulated. The form of the prayer is telegraphic in order to celebrate in a few words the mysteries of faith.

By contrast, the Irish forms are much more prolix. They witness eloquently to a penance understood from a psychological perspective. One feature of the Celtic prayers is the confession of sins (*confessio peccatorum*). The sinner enumerates all the parts of the body as though each part has been guilty of perpetrating sin. By way of this anatomical catalog, every imaginable sin is mentioned that could possibly be committed by the eyes, ears, nostrils, mouth, hands, feet, tongue, throat, neck, breast, and heart. Then the interior parts of the body are enumerated, such as bones, marrow, and kidneys. Even teeth, hair, fingernails, tears, and spittle are accused of having sinned. The penitent prays as though all of these sins are applicable to his or her life . In reality, the form is less a confession of real sins than an examination of conscience. As a prayer, it was intended to be recited slowly so as to allow consideration of the implications of sin in act, word, and thought.

Such a spirituality was promoted by the monasteries, especially those founded by the Irish both in the British Isles and on the Continent that served as great penitential centers for monks and laity alike. Penitents sought out a confessor or a director of conscience in these monasteries, corresponding to the *amnchara*, or soul friend—a name indicating the importance of this person in the spiritual development of the one being directed. Considering, therefore, both the penitential manuals and the very detailed and exhaustive nature of the Celtic prayers, penance should be considered more a way of life than merely a confession of sins.[62]

Another typical form of Irish prayer, strikingly parallel to the confessions, is the *lorica* or the "breastplate" prayer, in which the petitioner prays to God to protect all the parts of the body. Again the anatomical catalog is recited as the penitent exhausts all the possibilities of danger.

> Watch over my mouth lest it speak in vain and tell profane stories.
> Watch over my eyes lest they look at a woman with carnal desire.
> Watch over my ears lest they hear with disparagement or idle words of liars.
> Watch over my feet lest they frequent brothels.
> Watch over my hands lest they often tend to give gifts.[63]

Contrasted with the Roman style of prayer, these texts are marked by affective exuberance, a trait characteristic of Irish devotion.

The confession attributed to the pen of Alcuin is of an equivalent length to the Irish examples and contains the typical anatomical list.[64] However, this list is in reverse order, beginning with the feet and terminating with the head. Composed for Charlemagne, this prayer demonstrates the Celtic influence on the deacon from York. The way in which sins are spoken of is very dynamic: the feet are slow to obey the commandments of the Lord, the knees bend more in fornication than in prayer, and the stomach swells with gluttony and drunkenness.

During the Carolingian period the link between liturgy and civilization was both extensive and problematic. According to Étienne Delaruelle,

> We know that the Carolingian civilization was on many counts a liturgical civilization. This was a *populus christianus*, truly a Holy People, which recognized itself in the collective practice of the same rites, whose biblical and symbolic meaning was expounded by the writers of the time. But at this time the liturgy was the law as much as it was exegesis, history, or theology. Councils, synods, and princes established rules. The life of the Christian, as never before, was inserted into a network of strict obligations: Sunday mass, Easter communion, observance of certain feasts, interdiction of servile work, fasting.[65]

After Alcuin, under the direction of Benedict of Aniane, the liturgy grew in importance in the life of the monks. This growth came, however, at the expense of apostolic activity, an aspect of monastic life so important since the time of Saint Columba and Saint Boniface. The liturgy, which played an important role in the reform of the monastic orders, ceased to be the communal expression of an entire people at prayer. Rather it became a collection of rites performed by monks and clerics, from which the people hoped to derive benefits.

By the Carolingian period, the Latin liturgy, formerly intelligible, had become a sacred spectacle performed by clergy in a sacral language no longer grasped by the community. Correct liturgical observances, that is, those that conformed (or were thought to conform) to what was practiced in Rome, the model of orthodoxy, became a subject of great concern in the Carolingian empire at the same time that the clerical elite took control of the entire liturgical action in a way that cemented their leadership position. As a result, the mass was no longer seen as an actual participation in the saving mystery of Christ—past, present, and to come—but as a sacred drama that, like scripture, was to be given an allegorical reading to uncover its dogmatic and moral meaning. Modern liturgists have much lamented this shift, but it may well have been inevitable, given linguistic changes, the decay of ancient urban Christianity, and other factors. This important shift did not mean that liturgy could no longer function as a favored setting for the cultivation of mystical consciousness, as it had so often in the ancient church. It did mean, though, that it was likely to do so mostly for monks and clergy, and to a lesser extent than it had in previous ages.[66]

Ritualism increased with the encouragement of the emperor himself. Legal stipulations, promulgated in the capitularies, dictated how the rites were to be performed. At Aachen in 802 specific questions were listed concerning the knowledge and skills required of clerics in general, and in particular of priests before they could be ordained: whether they knew, understood, and were able to expound the Apostles' and Athanasian Creeds, the Lord's prayer, the gospels, the homilies of the orthodox Fathers, mass "according to the Roman order," the divine office "according to the Roman rite," the calendar, baptism, penance, exorcisms, and the commendation of souls.[67] Furthermore, because of rampant illiteracy among the secular clergy, steps had to be taken to protect the sacraments from ritual abuse. This ultimately led to scrupulous respect for the rites themselves by the clergy.

Individualism was one of the ingredients of the religious atmosphere of the era. The Carolingian period saw private masses multiply, in which was manifest a need for the immediate and frequent presence of God to the detriment sometimes of solemnity and liturgical rhythm. At the same time the use spread for the priest to celebrate the mass not facing the people, but turning his back to them. This revealed a lack of comprehension at what the mass had been in the time of the early church: an engagement and dialogue between God and his people. Henceforth the people, no longer having direct access to the supernatural world, depended on the priest to ask for needed graces on their behalf.[68] Priests began to celebrate private masses as well as votive masses for special intentions.[69] The laity were further removed from a role in worship. Their part had been given over to specialists. An example of the professionalism of the liturgy can be seen in liturgical music. The amount of music expanded radically, especially for the monastic office. The style became increasingly difficult, moving from syllabic chant to longer and more complicated melodic motifs, often having many notes per syllable and rendering the text unintelligible. Clearly the music had to be executed by practiced singers from cathedral and monastic schools. Under the influence of Charlemagne, Gregorian (or Roman) chant was uniformly adopted. Metz became a leading center for Roman chant under the aegis of Chrodegang. By the tenth century, polyphony was introduced (first in two voices, then in three and four). The musical development toward greater and greater complexity parallels the general development within the sacramental rites and the liturgy.

Church architecture provides another example of how the lay faithful were separated from the liturgy. People stood in the nave, separated from the sanctuary by the chancel, and from the altar by the choir of clerics who sang the psalms in the *schola cantorum*. The separation between clerics and people is also reflected in a subtle change in the language of the Roman canon emphasizing that the priest was offering the sacrifice on behalf of the people.[70] A huge gap was developing between clergy and laity both physically and figuratively. People attended mass as though it were a brilliant spectacle. The popular ignorance of Latin, already noted, added to the problem: the language of worship was known exclusively by educated clerics and so their liturgy became an exercise in archaism.[71] The mass was becoming a private affair of clerics.

In addition, Josef Jungmann demonstrates the rise of a new concept of eucharist.[72] The Carolingian mass was less a thanksgiving raised to God than a gift given by God, who descended for the purpose. Jungmann writes:

> In the earlier periods of liturgical life we saw the emphasis placed on the Mass as a *eucharistia*, as a prayer of thanks from the congregation who were invited to participate by a *Gratias agamus*, and whose gifts, in the course of the Mass, were elevated by the word of the priest into a heavenly sacrificial offering. But now an opposite view was taking precedence in men's minds. . . . The Eucharist is the *bona gratia*, which God grants us, and which at the climactic moment of the Mass, the consecration, descends to us.[73]

The ritual with many of the prayers spoken sotto voce heightened the importance of the words of consecration, underlining the mysterious change of the bread and wine into Christ's body and blood. The evolution of the rites separated the idea of sacrifice from daily life. The practice of the people presenting offerings of bread and wine that were brought from home (along with other foodstuffs to be distributed to the poor) was now replaced with taking up a collection to represent their offerings. The "breaking of the bread" (*fractio panis*), a ritual action replete with meaning in the Acts of the Apostles, no longer used real bread that the people could recognize as such. Rather, the Carolingian *renovatio* introduced unleavened bread pressed with irons into the form of wafers. At best, there was a ritualized fraction rite, but it was reduced to a token gesture. The consecrated wine was no longer distributed to laity except on rare occasions. Communicants kneeling at rails that separated the clergy from the lay faithful received communion on the tongue. Realism was replaced by allegory, often fanciful and sometimes exaggerated. Commentators such as Amalarius gave symbolic interpretations to the mass: the successive parts of the mass, the vestments, and the vessels recalled Old Testament types; the mass represented a commemorative allegory of the life of Christ. Prone to excesses, these interpretations were eventually condemned by the Synod of Quiercy (838). Yet still they endured.

Reception of the eucharist was infrequent. Saint Boniface, for example, recommended in the eighth century that people go to communion on great occasions, the great feasts of the liturgical year, namely Christmas, Easter, and Pentecost. Yet the faithful were warned about committing sacrilege with communion. Additionally, emphasis was placed on their religious obligation to fast, to give alms, and to practice acts of mortification, which heightened people's sense of sinfulness and unworthiness to receive the eucharist. The liturgy became more magical than spiritual, and stories of people desecrating hosts and of bizarre eucharistic miracles abounded. One particular

genre of eucharistic story deals with stealing hosts to fertilize the ground for improved and more abundant crops.[74] In general the penitential character of the time led
to a general hesitancy of the clergy to give communion to the people.

A further monument to the spirituality of the age is found in a type of document
called a *speculum*, or mirror. Dhuoda, a Christian noblewoman from Septimania, in
843 wrote a manual for her son on how to live his faith according to his state in life.[75]
The treatise is thorough and helpful, but this kind of writing was reserved to an educated elite, the former pupils of monastic schools. Jonas of Orléans (c. 830) also tried
to establish the basis for an *ordo laicorum*, that is, a form of Christian life adapted for
the laity.[76]

The penitential spirit that defined this age was highlighted by a new form of sacramental penance deriving from Irish and Anglo-Saxon monastic usage. Sometimes called
tariffed penance, this regimen assessed a person's life and attempted to prescribe the
proper penance as a medicine for each and every sin. Next to the three classic sins—
murder, adultery, and apostasy (renunciation of the faith)—the seven or eight deadly
sins were added, variously named and listed as pride, conceit, covetousness, envy, lust,
gluttony, anger, and dejection, or sloth. Penance was a medicine applied so as to heal
the soul from the illness of sin.[77]

The popular religious usage of psalms and other prayers found in the *libelli precum*
was very much inspired by their use in liturgical prayer. Again, however, social factors
intervened. The illiterate tended to imitate what the educated did as best as they were
able. Instead of praying all 150 psalms, they would substitute 150 *Aves* or *Paters*. Thus
the full rosary was born. Their spiritual practices, however, revolved more around
moral actions than prayer—they might abstain from conjugal relations and have prolonged fasting during Lent. In the mix of religion with popular culture, many examples of superstition can be noted.[78] This gave rise to the *Indiculus superstitionum* (for
Saxons). In confession, penitents were questioned whether they prayed outside of
church near wells, rocks, trees, or road crossings, and they were chided for superstitious acts such as the use of talismans and incantations. The cult of the dead became
particularly pronounced among the people, and it was during this time that All Saints'
Day became established as a part of popular piety. To Alcuin is attributed the introduction of the *memento* of the departed into the canon of the mass.

The image of God as the stern and distant though ever present judge aided in
terrifying people, occasioning a rise in the felt need for intermediaries such as saints,
angels, and archangels. It is at this time that the angelic bodies became highly indi-
vidualized: Michael, Gabriel, and Raphael each had certain special powers and deserved special honors.

André Vauchez argues that "in the Carolingian age the practice of religion was less
the expression of an interior adherence than an obligation of the social order."[79] On
two occasions, the Roman liturgy, that is, the mass and the liturgy of the hours, benefited from the reform of the clergy: first during the time of Chrodegang (died 766),
bishop of Metz, a great admirer of the Roman liturgy, and second at the Council of
Aix-la-Chapelle in 816–817, where many initiatives begun by Pepin the Short and
Charlemagne were incorporated. With the exception of the Iberian Peninsula, the
Roman rite from the Carolingian period onward was well implanted in the West. But
it was not until the end of the eleventh century and the pontificate of Gregory VII
(1073–1085) that the Roman rite was imposed on the curia, the diocesan and religious
clergy, the monks, and the laity.

Anglo-Saxon Holy Week

M. Bradford Bedingfield

Evidence for Holy Week commemoration in England before the tenth century is somewhat scarce. In the time of Bede (died 735), there is no indication of a Palm Sunday procession, and the liturgy for the day was apparently dominated by the reading of the Passion according to Matthew. Good Friday may or may not have featured an "adoration of the cross" in addition to the traditional reading from John and the "solemn prayers" that go back to the earliest Western witnesses, whereby all of Christendom, and all of humanity in need of Christendom, is brought under the shadow of the cross. The Easter Vigil itself was apparently an all-night affair, ending with Easter baptisms for catechumens in the early morning hours.

By the time of the tenth-century Benedictine reform, the liturgy for Holy Week had changed dramatically, at least in the major ecclesiastical centers of Canterbury, Winchester, Exeter, and Worcester, from where most of the surviving liturgical manuscripts derive. The monastic *Regularis Concordia* (c. 972) describes much of the liturgy for the week, as do some vernacular sermons from the period, especially those of Ælfric of Eynsham (died c. 1020).[1] These sources, in addition to the liturgical books that have survived, attest to a diverse and experimental liturgical landscape, in which models from the Continent (primarily supplemented Gregorian) were rather freely combined, adapted, and revised. The most complete extant sources describe the monastic liturgy, but the general reform-era desire to extend monastic observance to the laity created a much more fluid, and more inclusive, relationship between monastic observance and lay piety.

Late Anglo-Saxon Palm Sunday featured a procession from one church, where the palms were blessed, to another church, where they were offered at mass. Sources indicate that both *hadode* (monks) and *lærwede* (laity) participated in the procession, which culminated in a dramatic entry into the mother church (signifying Jerusalem). Maundy Thursday featured, in addition to the washing of the altars and the *mandatum* (the washing of the feet and the feeding of the poor), two episcopal ceremonies: the consecration of the chrism and the reconciliation of public penitents. *Tenebrae* and the lighting of the new fire also began on Maundy Thursday, and were repeated on Friday and Saturday. The liturgy for Good Friday featured many traditional elements, including the reading of the Passion from John (during which, according to the *Concordia*, two "thieves" would strip away the altar cloth at the point where Christ's garments are divided), the *orationes sollemnes*, and the *adoratio crucis*, which included the dramatic "reproaches," in which deacons playing the part of Christ would chastise those gathered before the cross: "My people, what have I done to you? How have I offended you?" The Easter Vigil itself was anticipated on Saturday afternoon, beginning at the hour of none and ending with *æfensang* (evensong). The paschal candle was lit from the new fire, the Gloria and the Hallelujah were reintroduced into the liturgy, and the Resurrection was celebrated. On Easter morning, the office of matins commemorated the revelation of Christ to the holy women. By the late Anglo-Saxon period, baptism was no longer a central feature of Holy Week commemoration.

In many respects, this overall structure of Holy Week in England is similar to that found elsewhere in Christendom at the time. However, the Anglo-Saxon services also included some of the earliest dramatic elaborations to the medieval liturgy. Crafted to follow *Tenebrae*, which took place during the night office, a ritual described in the *Concordia* takes advantage of the darkened church to allow participants to feel *tenebrarum terror, qui tripertitum mundum . . . timore perculit insolito* ("the terror of the darkness that struck the threefold world with unusual fear") at the time of Christ's death. Once the lights were extinguished, pairs of children sang of Christ's death, one pair at a time, from three sides of the church. This was repeated three times, and was performed again on Friday and on Saturday. On Friday, after the *adoratio crucis*, followers of the *Concordia* performed a *depositio*, whereby the cross, having been praised and adored at the time of Christ's death, was taken down and placed in a "tomb" (a part of the altar marked off by a curtain). The tomb was guarded by brethren until the Easter Vigil. Directions in the *Concordia* indicate an awareness of both the ceremony's mimetic qualities ("as if for the burial of the body of our Lord") and its educational and edificatory value ("worthy to be followed for the strengthening of the faith of unlearned common persons and neophytes"). The *Concordia's visitatio sepulchri* is perhaps its most famous dramatic ceremony. In the early hours of Easter morning, three brethren, dressed in copes, approached the tomb, where another brother sat, holding a palm. As the three approached, the "angel" would sing, *"Quem quaeritis"* ("Whom do you seek?"), and upon receiving their answer, would reply, *"Non est hic; surrexit"* ("He is not here; he has risen"). The angel would show them the empty tomb, and the three "women" would then take up the grave-cloth and show it to the congregation. This version of the *visitatio* is one of the earliest, and one of the most complete, to be found in Europe during this time.

Many of these rituals were imported from the Continent, where some of the monks who drafted the *Concordia* were trained. Other ceremonies, such as *Tenebrae* and the *adoratio crucis*, already had some purchase in Anglo-Saxon England. Rarely, in any case, was the reception of continental liturgy a passive one. Anglo-Saxon reformers creatively arranged, expanded, and elaborated the Holy Week liturgy. A driving concern for making the laity active and intelligent participants in the liturgy encouraged the reformers to instruct layfolk by means of dramatic identification and by treatment of the liturgy in vernacular preaching texts. Ælfric, at least, was concerned that his congregation appreciate that they had an active, and imitative, role to play in liturgical commemoration. In a sermon for Palm Sunday, he explains that "[w]e geefenlæcað þam geleaffullum of ðam folce mid þysre dæde, for ðan þe hi bæron palmtwigu mid lofsange togeanes þam hælende" ("We imitate the faithful of that people with this deed because they bore palm-twigs with praise-singing to the Savior"). Reflection of the liturgy in Anglo-Saxon art, architecture, and poetry attests to the creative vigor of Anglo-Saxon commemoration during Holy Week: *The Dream of the Rood*, for instance, depicts a dramatic interaction between an adorer and the cross, waiting thane-like to bear the approaching Christ, and then heroically standing firm while Christ dies and is buried.

Note

[1] Editions of *Regularis Concordia* include Lucia Kornexl, ed., *Die Regularis concordia* (Munich: Fink, 1993) and Thomas Symons, ed. and trans., *Regularis concordia* (London: Nelson, 1953). On Ælfric's homilies, see Peter Clemoes, ed., *Ælfric's Catholic Homilies: The First Series: Text*, EETS s.s. 17 (Oxford: Oxford University Press, 1997).

References

Bedingfield, M. Bradford. *The Dramatic Liturgy of Anglo-Saxon England*. Woodbridge, Suffolk: Boydell and Brewer, 2002.

Blair, John, and Richard Sharpe, eds. *Pastoral Care before the Parish*. Leicester: Leicester University Press, 1992.

Clemoes, Peter, ed., *Ælfric's Catholic Homilies: The First Series: Text*, EETS s.s. 17.

Cubitt, Catherine. *Anglo-Saxon Church Councils c. 650–c. 850*. London: Leicester University Press, 1995.

Kornexl, Lucia, ed. *Die Regularis concordia*. Munich: Fink, 1993.

Pfaff, Richard, ed. *The Liturgical Books of Anglo-Saxon England*. Kalamazoo, Mich.: Medieval Institute Publications, 1995.

Symons, Thomas, ed. and trans. *Regularis concordia*. London: Nelson, 1953.

Second Gregorian Reform: Gregory VII

The second Gregorian reform, although designated by the name of its most ardent champion, has its roots in the tenth century, and was invigorated by the monastic reforms of houses such as Cluny and Gorze.[80] Leo IX (1049–1054), who sought to eradicate widespread abuses in the church, gave great impetus to the reform. Beginning with the Council of Reims (1049), he pushed through changes in papal election procedures, defined the roles of cardinals, assured the appointment of reformers to key positions in the church, and summoned provincial councils for the implementation of his reforms. Nicholas II (1058–1061) continued his work, determining the course of ecclesiastical history for the next half century, and preparing the way for Hildebrand, who became Gregory VII.

Hildebrand had served Gregory VI as chaplain, and upon that pope's death in 1047 had entered a Cluniac monastery (probably Cluny itself), but was soon called back to Rome, where he enjoyed great influence under several popes. An ardent reformer and stubborn idealist, he himself was elevated to the papal throne in 1073. His general ban on lay investiture led him directly into conflict with the German emperor Henry IV. Though having submitted in penitence before the pope at Canossa in 1077, Henry in 1084 seized Rome and set up his own candidate on the papal throne. Even though Gregory was able to escape through Norman intervention, he died in exile in 1085.

As pope, Gregory took into his hands the task of leadership of the Roman liturgy, which for almost three hundred years had been governed by rulers and bishops north of the Alps. He undertook the restoration of the Roman Ordo, calling into question the Romano-Frankish liturgy, which had taken root in Rome. In this matter of the

---

Mozarabic Marriage

The earliest extant form of this Spanish rite dates from the tenth or eleventh century but it preserves some features attested already by Isidore of Seville in the seventh. The sprinkling of salt is probably exorcistic. The custom of "arrhas" is explained below.

ORDER FOR BLESSING THE WEDDING CHAMBER
First, at the third hour on the Sabbath [Saturday], according to custom, salt is to be sprinkled in the dwelling or bridal chamber. Then, when the priest arrives to bless the marriage chamber, he recites this verse, saying:
Look upon your servants and upon your works, O Lord, and direct their children with blessings (Ps. 89/90:16-17).

Then this prayer:
O Lord, those things which are blessed by invocation of your name are sustained by the fullness of your blessing. Bless this room, set aside for honest marriage, that no onslaught of evil may touch it. May the chastity of marriage alone reign here and may your compassion attend its worthy celebration.
Our Father.

Blessing:
May the all-powerful Lord pour forth his plenteous blessings upon this marriage chamber and bless with everlasting holiness those who meet here together. Amen.

May all evil spirits be turned back from this place and may the angels take up their awaited station here. Amen.

Here by God's grace may marriage so be celebrated that the virtue of the married couple is never debased. Amen.

May the words and actions of those who enter here to celebrate their marriage be so proper that they are never swept away by desire to the shipwreck of passion. Amen.

Thus may modest decency protect the newlyweds and everlasting peace sustain those who are joined in the joys of matrimony. Amen.

ORDER FOR THOSE MARRYING
[Here one or more folios are missing from the manuscript. They will have contained the Vespers for Saturday evening and perhaps also the Lauds of Sunday morning. The manuscript resumes with the ending of this prayer:]

---

local rite, however, Gregory's reform was confined to details of lesser importance, such as the number of psalms and lections to be read in the monastic office. The nature of his wider reforms was primarily clerical rather than liturgical as such; they concerned more the discipline and administration of the rites than their structure. This clerical orientation served the centralization of the liturgy. Recognizing that it was impossible to return to the "Roman liturgy of ancient Roman usage,"[81] the sec-

. . . May they offer you the dedication of their marriage vow. May they love one another and love you not the less. Living in peace and serving you faithfully, may they never cease to beseech you with us, saying:
Our Father.

Blessing:
May Christ the Lord receive the faithful vows of his servants, N. and N., and forgive you all your sins. Amen.

May an unbreakable bond of love be his gift to those who now enter upon the grace of marriage, that they might pass through this world in peace. May they who are about to enter into chaste wedlock be kept unharmed in heart and body before God at all times.

ORDER OF THE ARRHAS
If anyone wishes to give arrhas, he should approach the priest. A dish is presented; on it he lays a clean cloth and two rings.
Prayer:
Lord, all-powerful God, you commanded Abraham to give Isaac to Rebecca through the exchange of arrhas, as an image of holy matrimony, so that by the offering of rings the number of children might be increased. We pray you to sanctify with your power this offering of arrhas which your servant, N., makes to his beloved bride, N. Graciously bless both them and their gifts so that, protected by your blessing and joined in the bond of love, they may rejoice to be counted among your faithful for ever.

Blessing:
May the Lord fill you with sweet reverence for his name and fructify you with the seed of holiness. Amen.

May your life together be like the fragrance of the lilies, that your minds may rise easily to heaven at all times. May you remain true, with God's help, to the exchange of arrhas you have made that they may be signs of united hearts and that you may be the parents of virtuous children.

ORDER FOR THE BLESSING OF NEWLY-WEDS
When people come to be married, Mass is celebrated according to custom and then, before the deacon dismisses the congregation, those to be married approach the priest at the gates of the sanctuary.
The parents of the girl, or other relatives if she has no parents, come forward and hand the girl over to the priest. The priest veils the couple with a pall or sheet, placing on top of it a cord of white and purple.
Then he recites this preface with the two prayers which follow it.

ond Gregorian reform demanded that episcopal sees of the Latin Church should rigorously follow the customs of the Roman see by obeying all the liturgical prescriptions it issued. As a result, ancient rites such as the Ambrosian and Mozarabic in Milan and Spain were imperiled by centralization. The liturgy became "Romanized."

The reform was fundamentally concerned with worldly practices that had been allowed to intrude into the church. The three goals of the reform were to curtail three

Preface:
Dearly beloved, let us call upon almighty God . . . . May they, by his favor, have the children they desire and may these children, being his gift, also be endowed with his blessing, so that these his servants, N. and N., may serve in humility of heart him whom they acknowledge to be their creator. Amen.

Prayer:
O God, when the world itself was new-born, you shaped woman out of the bone of man, for the purpose of continuing the human race, thereby revealing the unity of genuine love; for, in making the two out of one, you have shown that the two are one. Thus you established the basis of the first marriage, namely, that the man should take to wife what was part of his own body, knowing it to be made out of part of himself.

Look graciously down from your heavenly throne and be pleased to hear the prayers we offer for your servants whom we have joined in marriage by blessing their union. Bless them with your merciful kindness and by the kindness of your mercy sustain them. Amen.

Grant them, Lord, to be of one mind in the fear of your Name and to show their love in the goodness of their mutual behavior. Amen.

May they love one another and never be estranged from you. Amen.

May they render to one another the debt of marriage in such a way as never to cause offense to you. Amen.

May they never turn aside after another, but please you by remaining faithful to one another. Amen.

Grant them, Lord, an abundance of this world's goods and a large family of children. Amen.

Let the sweetness of your blessing so surround them that whatever children may be born of their union may find favor with their fellows and be blessed by you. Amen.

Grant them, Lord, to enjoy length of days in this life and to desire the unending life that is to come. Amen.

Let them so negotiate all temporal business that they will continue faithfully to long for eternal things. Amen.

Grant them so to love all passing goods that they may not lose those goods that last forever. Amen.

Loving each other truly and serving you faithfully, let them see their children's children and, after a long life in this present world, let them come to the heavenly kingdom. Amen.

abuses: simony (the buying and selling of sacramental functions, notably ordination); nicolaitism (the marriage or concubinage of priests); and lay investiture (the investment of priests with symbols of spiritual powers by lay people, for example, a bishop's ring and staff). All three of these practices had been sanctioned by enduring usage, yet the reform attempted to remove them.

BLESSING OF THE GIRL ALONE

O God, by the teaching of the Holy Spirit, you commanded that Rebecca should be veiled when she first saw Isaac, and by angels you ordered that women should veil their heads. Vouchsafe to bless this your servant, N., who intends to marry. May her chastity be her covering. As she receives the veil of modesty may the grace of modesty be hers. Let her cleave to one man. Let her marry one man in Christ. Let her be aware that she marries not in fornication but in truth. Let her look to her father Abraham; let her look to Sarah, her mother and model, the mother of all holy children who marry. And let her work out her salvation in the bearing of faithful children.

Our Father.

Blessing:

May the Lord bless you by the word of our mouth and may he join your hearts in the everlasting bond of sincere love. May you flourish with an abundance of this world's goods; may you be fittingly blessed with children; may you always rejoice in your friends. May the Lord grant you the goods that last, to your parents a happy old age, and to all everlasting happiness. Amen.

Having finished these prayers, the priest hands the girl over to the man, admonishing them that, out of respect for the Holy Communion, they should keep themselves from pollution that night. And so they receive Communion.

Afterwards the deacon gives the dismissal, saying:

In the name of our Lord Jesus Christ, the Mass is over. Let us go in peace.

And as they begin to process and to leave the church, the following antiphon is sung:

You who to the grace of marriage.

Then he says:

Blessing:

May the three-fold majesty and single Godhead bless you. Amen. The Father, the Son, and the Holy Spirit. May you be found on the day of judgement just as you were when you left the font.

The Latin text is found in Marius Férotin, ed., *Le Liber Ordinum en usage dans l'église wisigothique et mozarabe d'Espagne du cinquième au onzième siècle*, Monumenta Ecclesiae Liturgica 5 (Paris: Firmin-Didot, 1904) 433-443. The translation is taken from Mark Searle and Kenneth W. Stevenson, *Documents of the Marriage Liturgy* (Collegeville, Minn.: Liturgical Press, 1992) 122-129. Searle and Stevenson (ibid., 120-121) explain thus the Blessing of the Arrhas or marriage gift: "Originally this would have been a form of bride price paid to the woman's family when the marriage was contracted (i.e., at betrothal). The ceremony of

The overall reform plan also affected the liturgy and sacraments more directly. Not only were sacraments both outward (physical) signs and inward (spiritual) signs of participation in the Body of Christ, they were also very useful as instruments toward the centralization of church order; and consequently, sacramental uniformity in practice was desired. Thus, the Gregorians sought to supplant local rites with the

the giving of the arrhas constituted a binding betrothal rite, celebrated some time – often years – before the actual marriage. By the eleventh century, however, the old Germanic bride price had long since been confused with the Roman custom of making provision for the bride's future in the form of a settlement against the eventuality of her being widowed, a settlement which could often be quite extensive. In this rite, however, the arrhas is simply a gift from the groom to the bride and appears to be identified, in any case, with the two rings. This suggests that the exchange of rings – which first appears here – has come to replace the bridal gift by the eleventh century. More significantly, it seems as though the solemn betrothal with arrhas has now been absorbed into the celebration of the marriage itself, since it is placed between Vespers and the Nuptial Mass."

Roman rite and worked consistently to uproot local deviations from the Roman norm. Although sacramental theology was relatively undeveloped, the Gregorians asserted the universality of Roman sacramental norms.

It is clear that while the Gregorian reform bears Gregory's name, the reform really began under Leo IX. It extended, moreover, beyond Gregory's life to Pope Callistus II and the First Lateran Council of 1123. Its importance lies in the fact that it was not limited to a particular diocese, kingdom, or religious order, or to the lifetime of any one inspired leader. The second Gregorian reform affected the political and spiritual life of all Western Europe and greatly influenced the direction of future reforms. In order to understand the goals, achievements, and failures of the Gregorian reform, one must place it in the wider context of the many attempts in the eleventh and twelfth centuries to bring about renewal in Christian life.[82] Principally, it encouraged a form of church unity that centered on absolute papal headship. Sacerdotalism and the papal monarchy, therefore, were the guiding principles of the Gregorian movement, and, in time, became the reform's self-justifying ends.

Monastic life: Psalters and Customaries

Abbo, the abbot of Fleury in the late tenth century, recognized the key role of the monks in the reform of the church: "The life of the clergy is a faithful mirror of the whole Church, as the habit and profession of the monk is the example of all that is highest in penance."[83] In the Benedictine West, from the time of the Carolingian *renovatio* onward, a uniform conception of monastic life prevailed, which allowed for few differences between monasteries. Much of the monastic reform was due to the efforts of the Carolingian abbot Benedict of Aniane, but the abbots of Cluny from the tenth through the twelfth centuries gave it renewed impetus. The uniformity of monasteries was one of the reform's goals and this could be achieved through the imposition of rules, thus giving rise to another genre of document: the customary. Prayer occupied the largest part of the customaries, since monks were devoted to praying the divine office as provided by the Rule of Benedict. Throughout the course of time the office had been adapted and inflated with extra psalms, offices, processions, litanies, prayers, and ceremonies, which in turn gave rise to new forms of religious art and music. The customaries addressed the practical concerns within monastic life, including the liturgical practices. They also affected the practices of the individual monks, even making provision for "private prayer." For example, in the *Ordo Qualiter*, com-

Saint Benedict of Nursia. Saint Benedict (c. 480–c.550) handing his Rule (c. 540) to a monk. The alternance or interweaving of prayer and work ("ora et labora") has been characteristic of the Benedictine order from its beginnings, although the modes and proportions have been variable. Benedictines have played an important part in the modern Liturgical Movement. BIBLIOTHÈQUE NATIONALE, PARIS, LATIN MS. 10062, FOLIO 98/SNARK/ART RESOURCE, NY

posed in the early ninth century, a rule was laid down that after compline "all shall keep the strictest silence of tongue and heart and shall pray in secret, remembering their sins not without tears, sighs and groans, but in such a way as not to disturb each other."[84] This rule is better understood by considering some of the eucharistic practices of the day. While the host was being elevated, the monks were encouraged to make audible salutations, groaning and begging the Lord, present in the eucharist, for divine assistance. This exercise often was a noisy and prolonged affair on account of the monks' fervent exuberance.

Because monasticism was considered the highest order of life at this time, monastic forms of liturgy and religious life dominated in the Church at large. Liturgy, even in the rural parishes, was necessarily patterned after monastic usage. Attempts were made to transform the laity into quasi-monastics. Monasticism greatly encouraged devotional practices and ways of life among the laity that were thought to serve affective union with God. The two chief forms of monastic life (cenobitic, or community life, and eremitic, or solitary life) were augmented by the collegial form. Groups of secular priests living a semicenobitic life became more and more prevalent. Such collegial chapters of canons were established in many cathedrals in an attempt to reform the clergy. One notable monastic reformer was Norbert of Xanten (1080–1134). A member of the chapel of Emperor Henry V, he withdrew to solitary life after the degradation of Pope Paschal II (1112), and founded the order of Prémontré (Premonstratensians, or Norbertines). At the apogee of collegial life, there were about a thousand houses of canons regular.

If the eucharist was the normal liturgical form for Christianity in general, the liturgy of the hours was more characteristically a monastic preserve, although forms of the office were adapted to all Christian lifestyles.[85] The enjoinder to pray without ceasing became the raison d'être of the monastic communities.[86] Although the origins of the office predate the tenth and eleventh centuries by at least six hundred years, the liturgy of the hours as it existed at this moment in history included two types: the Roman and the Benedictine. Before Saint Benedict, an office existed at Rome, possibly from the fourth century. It was this form that Saint Benedict used and adapted for the prayer of the monastic communities he founded, as he mentions in his Rule. The earliest extant sources of the Benedictine *cursus* date from the eighth and ninth centuries, primarily after the monastic reform spearheaded by Benedict of Aniane. Once this office had been established, it remained virtually the same to the present, undergoing only minor modifications that dealt primarily with the distribution of the psalms. In the eighth century, especially through the efforts of Pepin the Short, the Roman *cursus* was resurrected alongside Benedictine usage as a means toward overall clerical reform. Except for the Iberian Peninsula, the Roman rite from the Carolingian period onward was implanted throughout the West. In the eleventh century, however, through the efforts of Gregory VII, the monastic office was imposed on all from the level of the curia downward.[87] Suffice it to say that the hours became gradually inflated and the musical interventions grew in importance. Perverting Saint Benedict's motto *ora et labora in laetitia pacis*, the era tended to emphasize the praying over the working, and often the prayer itself was considered to be the work of the monks.

One historical oddity concerning the office deals with the recitation of the hours in private. Originally to be prayed in common, the office was gradually transformed into a form of private prayer. For while the Rule of Benedict (ch. 50) and the Rule of Chrodegang (ch. 4) include a prescription that those who for some reason are outside the monastery or away from a church body should recite the office in private, from the tenth century onward this practice became more and more usual, especially since the clergy did not always live in community. For monks and canons living in collegial communities, however, communal prayer remained the norm. It is the development of the private recitation, however, that led to changes in the form of the office in the later Middle Ages, especially among the mendicant orders of Franciscans and Dominicans. Private recitation also gave rise to the famous books of hours, usually ornate and richly decorated books used by royalty and aristocrats. These books included the Little Office of the Blessed Virgin Mary as well as the Office for the Dead. Often in late medieval and Renaissance paintings of the Annunciation, we find the Blessed Virgin kneeling at her prie-dieu reading from her book of hours, much like the elegant woman of the Renaissance would have done.

Monastic piety revolved around daily and yearly cycles of liturgies, special devotions (for example, to the Blessed Virgin Mary), and prayer and meditation on scripture. Monastic disciplines aimed at the mortification of the will and body by means of exercises of self-flagellation performed while reciting the penitential psalms. Devotions for poverty and the suffering of Christ and other pious practices were joined to liturgical prayer in order to intensify the spiritual life. Customaries became an essential document to help the monks and to govern these general practices in each monastery. Although not purely liturgical texts, the customaries did deal with the liturgy, and could perhaps be considered to be the monastic equivalent of the *ordines romani*— they were used in conjunction with other liturgical texts to indicate how the liturgy should be executed in each given monastery.

The customaries have recently enjoyed great scholarly attention, particularly among specialists in monasticism. These documents have proven quite illuminating, especially in the study of Cluny and Gorze in the tenth and eleventh centuries.[88] But while each monastery was autonomous or semiautonomous, the customaries reflect the dominating influence of the great monasteries of the time, such as Fleury, Fulda, Cluny, Ratisbon, Saint Gall, Monte Casino, and Canterbury. The documents are of two types: one focuses on customs concerning liturgical usage and the other focuses on customs concerning community life. In some customaries, there exists a combination of the two. The liturgical ceremonies are described in meticulous detail, usually following the provision of the liturgical year. The several rites (the mass, sacraments, and various sacramentals) are described with mention made of the liturgical vessels and objects that were to be employed. Often processions are described in wonderful detail, to such an extent that historians of architecture have been able to reconstruct the appearance of abbatial churches at certain given moments in history.[89] The description of each ceremony is often preceded by the preparations necessary for the liturgical event, prescribing what articles are needed and who will use them. They give witness to the general complexity of the monastic liturgy. The customaries, however, go beyond the bounds of simple stage directions, since they also carried juridical weight and were regulatory for a given monastery or an affiliation of monasteries. They also represent a type of reform document. The customary, for example, at the Abbey of Cluny is very revealing of the process of reform, since the editions that we possess were all compiled by monks in other monasteries. One customary, the *Liber tramitis*, was compiled in Italy and seems to represent the usages of the monastery of Farfa.[90] It is important for its description of the Cluniac liturgy in the tenth and eleventh centuries and demonstrates the far-reaching influence of Cluny, which at its apogee had over twelve hundred houses across Europe.

There were exchanges between monastic prayer and popular forms of piety. Many movements espousing apostolic poverty, inspired by Acts 4, arose in the Middle Ages. These lay movements, to some degree, represented a kind of denunciation of papal power, and, at times, a harsh critique of monasticism itself, which was not always faithful to the vow of poverty.

Two other expressions of popular piety were the crusades and pilgrimages. The crusades gave rise to some of the new orders, such as the Knights Templar and the Knights of Saint John, that provided ways in which lay people engaged in public life could exercise their faith in semimonastic ways. On the other hand, pilgrimages as a popular form of penitential piety were partially responsible for the construction of many of the cathedral churches. Built along the famous pilgrimage routes, they housed the pilgrims on their way to the great shrines. Certainly this is the backdrop to Chaucer's *Canterbury Tales*.

Mysticism: Hildegard of Bingen

To assess the success of the second Gregorian reforms in monastic matters, attention must be given to the following

Saint Hildegard of Bingen. Inspired by heavenly fire, Saint Hildegard of Bingen at age 43 begins to write down her visions. From a twelfth-century codex of her *Scivias* (Codex Rupertsberg, now lost). ERICH LESSING/ART RESOURCE, NY

century. Hildegard of Bingen (1098–1179), at the monastery of Rupertsberg in Germany, provides an example of both monastic and mystical renewal. At the time of her birth the Cistercian order was in its infancy. While she first felt stirrings toward the apostolic poverty movement, she was entrusted rather to Benedictine monasticism, which had remained a real option only for the elite. In her childhood Hildegard was offered by her parents as an oblate to a hermitage associated with Jutta. She made formal profession of virginity when she was in her teens and professed the Benedictine Rule. In her thirties she was elected abbess. In her forties and fifties she composed her mystical visions, *Scivias*,[91] which upon completion received the immediate approval of Pope Eugenius III, undoubtedly contributing to the work's great success. It consists of three books of unequal length, dealing with creation, redemption, and sanctification. Each chapter begins with a vision followed by a simple description. The genre of a "text" interpreted line by line makes one think of a monastic commentator doing a gloss on a text from scripture. Book one explores the created order, while book two is dominated by the figure of *Ecclesia*, or the Church. This is where Hildegard presents her teaching on the sacraments of redemption: baptism, confirmation, priesthood, penance, and eucharist. Monastic vows are considered at great length as a sacrament, while marriage is discussed in book one as a sacrament of the original order. Book three, where the virtues receive allegorical treatment, has a double structure, historical and moral.

In book two, in the sixth vision, Hildegard beholds the eucharist, which for her is above all the sacrament of Christ's passion. Her record maintains a strong visionary aspect:

> And you *see* that the calm light shines around the altar until the sacred rite is ended and the priest has withdrawn from it. For that light is an eternal *sight*, and shows itself by miracle with great brightness until the mysteries of this hallowed office are finished and the dispenser of the sacred rites, having completed them, withdraws from the holy spot. Why is this? Because it is fitting that the Divine Majesty manifests Its power most fully in these blessed rites, and because as long as a person remains within these things that belong to God, God's will never leaves him. (2.6.10)

At this point, seeing the eucharist is more important than eating it. Hildegard explores the nature of vision by asking "why humans cannot take this spiritual gift in *visible form*":

> But you, O human, cannot take this spiritual gift *visibly*, as if eating *visible* flesh and drinking *visible* blood; for you are filth of filth. But, as the living spirit in you is *invisible*, so also the living sacrament in that oblation is *invisible* and must be received *invisibly* by you. For as the body of My Son came about in the womb of the Virgin, so now the body of My Only-Begotten arises from the sanctification of the altar. What does this mean? The human soul, which is *invisible*, *invisibly* receives the sacrament, which exists *invisibly* in that oblation, while the human body, which is *visible*, *visibly* receives the oblation that *visibly* embodies that sacrament. (2.6.14; author's emphasis)

For Hildegard, steeped in platonic thought, the sacrament is a source of contemplation—a kind of icon:

> In the sacrament of the altar Christ's mysteries appear as in a mirror—and therefore, while you are looking at these things, suddenly there appear before your eyes as if in a mirror the symbols of the Nativity, Passion and burial, Resurrection and Ascension of our Savior, God's Only-Begotten, as they happened to the Son of God while He was on earth. For, as you see in a true vision, the mysteries of Him who came to earth to save humanity . . . shine brightly in the sacrament of the altar, since when God's Only-

Begotten lived for a time among people of the world these things happened to Him in His body by the will of the Father for the redemption of the human race. (2.6.17)

Finally, as the Agnus Dei is sung, the faithful communicate. At this point movement is made from the sense of sight to taste, though the other senses are also evoked:

> And as Heaven closes, you hear the voice from thence saying that believing and faithful people should eat and drink with true devotion the body and blood of their Savior, Who for them suffered temporal death, to wash away the contamination our first parents brought into the world. . . . For the Son of God, fulfilling the precepts of His Father, offered Himself for people's salvation and gave His body and blood to be eaten and drunk for their sanctification. (2.6.20)

What does eating mean for Hildegard? Citing the Song of Songs 5:1 ("Eat, my friends; drink, and be inebriated, my dearly beloved!"), she responds that it is to eat in faith. Food is provided for those who, through holy baptism, have come to divine friendship. Drinking the wine provides a taste of the spilled blood of Christ that purges all from Adam's fall. But here it must be asked if this is food or something else, because she speaks of chewing the true *medicine* in the body of Christ, which mercifully wipes away the repeated deeds of crime and injustice. To drink is to take in hope from this vine, bringing one out of eternal punishment. The act of eating and drinking is less associated with a meal than with taking in the cup of salvation and the bread of faith, "that you may firmly and strongly believe in that grace by which you have been redeemed" (2.6.21).

Provision is made for the reception of communion under both kinds, except for those who are "weak in mind," for whom receiving the chalice would pose a problem of spilling.[92] Hildegard writes: "But if the person has enough discernment to keep the mystery safe, when the sacred flesh is given him to eat let him also be given the blood of that flesh to drink" (2.6.46). Provision is also made that the priest celebrating the mass must himself communicate. This would seem to indicate that the laity often attended without receiving.[93]

In her vision of the eucharist, Hildegard provides an indication of the importance of sacramental practice in her spiritual life. Generally there were five specific moments within the eucharistic liturgy that had particular significance in provoking her mystical visions: the procession and entry into the church, the moments involving conversation with God, the elevation of the host, the approach to communion, and the actual reception of the eucharist.[94] It was as important to reverence the eucharist at the moment of the elevation of the host as to receive it in communion. Gazing

A priest celebrates communion. From the *Scivias* of Hildegard of Bingen (Codex Rupertsberg). ERICH LESSING/ART RESOURCE

upon the consecrated species as it was exposed on the altar or carried in procession constituted a kind of ocular communion. The elevation therefore was a high point in the liturgy because it was then that Christ, in his humanity and divinity, came into direct contact with the assembly. In the later Middle Ages, actual reception would be completely replaced by spiritual ocular communion. People would hurry from church to church in order to catch a glimpse of the real presence at the moment of the elevation. Perhaps this was because of a growing sense of unworthiness. Nonetheless, the "elevation" became an essential part of the medieval mass, and consequently, of popular piety. However, it produced many abuses, such as priests showing the host by placing it on their heads and prancing about, while people shouted at the priest to heave the host higher so that they might see it, producing exaggerated elevations lasting for several minutes.

In her eucharistic vision, Hildegard delineates five states for intending communicants, in order "that they may healthfully receive the sacrament" (2.6.51). Only those in the first group who are "bright of body and fiery of soul" are eligible to receive the eucharist. This means that they are clear in faith about the sacrament and, "stirred to a blaze by the wind, they are inspired by this sacrament to burn with celestial love." The other four states are first in need of penance before communicating. Yet, "the fountain of salvation will still flow for them if they take care to wash themselves from this wickedness of theirs by worthy penitence" (2.6.56). Sinners should first make recourse to confession:

> Let him bare these wounds to Me by making a humble confession to a priest. And why this? Because true confession is a second resurrection. How? The human race was slain by the fall of the old Adam; the new Adam by His death raised it up. And so the resurrection of souls arose in the death of the new Adam. And so a person should confess his sins, as the old Adam did not; for he concealed his transgression instead of confessing it. (2.6.82)

Those who communicate without having undergone penance bring about their own demise: "Therefore, O human, if you receive the body and blood of My Son unwashed, not self-purified by confession or penance, in the terrible day of inquiry you will be tried for your presumption about your filthy sins, as new wine when it ferments throws off and is purged of the impurities in it" (2.6.58). Hildegard includes long tirades about those who should not approach the altar—women, cross-dressers, fornicators, sodomites, those involved in bestiality and those who commit the sin of masturbation. Hildegard also uses her vision of the eucharist to address and condemn the pressing and current questions of simony (2.6.61) and clerical concubinage (2.6.62–75). What percentage, finally, of the population according to Hildegard figured into the group of eligible communicants? Or is her vision somewhat akin to Dante's thirteenth-century perception, where he saw far more people he knew in *Inferno* than in *Purgatorio* or *Paradiso* combined?

Evaluating the Second Gregorian Reform

How, in the end, are we to evaluate the second Gregorian reform? The Gregorians gave great importance to participating in the Body of Christ by affective union; they fostered doctrines and institutions to serve that union. Still, they wished affective devotion to stay within limits set by their principles of sacerdotalism and papal monarchy. The torrent of popular devotions that strengthened their program flowed out and around those restraints and, for many, undermined it.[95]

It must be added that the second Gregorian reform had only partial success in its disciplinary measures. Toward the end of his life, Gregory VII lamented how few feared God, and how few there were to perform priestly offices for good Christians. Simony and nicolaitism continued, as well as the gross immorality of clergy, and the exploitation of the poor to support clerical luxury. In the tenth and eleventh centuries, two contrary movements coexisted: a drift toward decadence, and a movement for reform. This was an age known for its great abuses within the church, leading to schisms and scandals in the papacy. Churches and monasteries were seized by seculars, and, among the clergy, simony and incontinence were ubiquitous. Gregory VII took a courageous lead in religious revival and the reform named after him endured for two centuries. Nevertheless, decadence and reform continued to exist side by side. Monasticism was the unifying force in the Gregorian reform, beginning with the abbots and filtering down through the ranks. This monastic vision had consequences for the laity and popular piety. The reforms had two principal ends with regard to the laity: to integrate them more into the ecclesiastical community by closer participation in the prayer and work of the church; and to loosen their hold on the clerical appointments and ecclesiastical institutions. As for the clergy, the provided remedy for vice insisted on life in common in chapters of canons that distinguished between the *vita regularis* and the *vita canonica*. While monks lived a life of contemplation, the canons regular united the contemplative and active life, combining liturgical duties with the *cura animarum*. In one of the first rules drawn up for regular canons, much was borrowed from the Rule of Saint Benedict and adapted by Gregory around the theme of conversion. Ascetic detachment, purity of heart, fear and love, a sense of sin and hope, and daily observances of prayer were the goals of the whole church. Each person was encouraged to live a kind of asceticism adapted to his or her situation.

Conclusion

Looking back over the entire early and central medieval period in the West, four tendencies may be noted regarding the eucharist: the movement away from eating and toward looking; the use of communion prayers to accompany and explain liturgical action; the devotion to the host centered on Christ's passion and death; and the notions about an enduring real presence to combat heretical intellectual tendencies. The fourth often led particularly to an exaggeration of eucharistic piety and abuses, such as visions of hosts that bled or turned into bloody fingers, stories about desecration of the host, targeting especially Jews, and finally general superstition.

Regarding the overall movement of liturgical reform aimed at the continuing conversion of the Western nations, four points must be made. While much liturgical diversity existed at the time of Gregory I, by the time of Gregory VII there was much uniformity. Monasticism was the leading impulse behind the great reforms, which produced a monastic vision of the Church with monastic forms of liturgy and prayer offered as the model for all to follow but in fact leading to a growing breach between clergy and laity. Those educated in monastic schools constituted a religious elite who were able to adapt the monastic spiritual forms to their own use. Those who were illiterate also had spiritual needs, but often their methods of adaptation led to widespread superstition and gross abuse, since the official liturgy lay beyond them.

Bibliography

Andrieu, Michel. *Les "ordines romani" du haut moyen âge.* 5 vols. Spicilegium Sacrum Lovaniense, nos. 11, 23, 24, 28, 29. Louvain: Spicilegium Sacrum Lovaniense, 1931–1961.

Blumenthal, Uta-Renate, ed. *Carolingian Essays: Andrew W. Mellon Lectures in Early Christian Studies.* Washington, D.C.: Catholic University of America, 1983.

Byer, Glenn C. J. *Charlemagne and Baptism: A Study of Responses to the Circular Letter of 811/812.* San Francisco: International Scholars Publications, 1999.

Cowdrey, Herbert E. J. *The Cluniacs and the Gregorian Reform.* Oxford: Clarendon, 1970.

Cramer, Peter. *Baptism and Change in the Early Middle Ages: c. 200–c. 1150.* Cambridge: Cambridge University Press, 1993.

Fisher, J. D. C. *Christian Initiation: Baptism in the Medieval West.* London: SPCK, 1965; reprint Chicago and Mundelein, Ill.: Hillenbrand Books, 2004.

Fliche, Augustin. *La réforme grégorienne.* 3 vols. Louvain: Spicilegium Sacrum Lovaniense, 1924, 1925, 1937.

Klauser, Theodor. *A Short History of the Western Liturgy.* Oxford: Oxford University Press, 1965.

Larson-Miller, Lizette, ed. *Medieval Liturgy: A Book of Essays.* New York and London: Garland, 1997.

Macy, Gary. *Treasures from the Storeroom: Medieval Religion and the Eucharist.* Collegeville, Minn.: Liturgical Press, 1999.

Palazzo, Éric. *A History of Liturgical Books: From the Beginning to the Thirteenth Century.* Collegeville, Minn.: Pueblo, 1998. Translation of *Le Moyen Age: Des origines au XIIIᵉ siècle.* Paris: Beauchesne, 1993.

Vogel, Cyrille. *Medieval Liturgy: An Introduction to the Sources.* Translated and revised by William Storey and Niels Rasmussen. Washington, D.C.: Pastoral Press, 1986.

Notes

[1]"The term medieval can often be used in a pejorative sense in the area of current liturgical practice. To be too medieval in structure, gesture, or phrasing seems to suggest ritual action which is not responsive to the needs of the late-twentieth-century Christian community, something archaic or antiquarian in outlook or preference." See Joanne Pierce, "Early Medieval Liturgy: Some Implications for Contemporary Liturgical Practice," *Worship* 65 (1991) 509–522.

[2]Peter Cramer, *Baptism and Change in the Early Middle Ages.*

[3]Donald A. Bullough, *Carolingian Renewal: Source and Heritage* (Manchester and New York: Manchester University Press, 1991).

[4]Cyrille Vogel, *Medieval Liturgy: An Introduction to the Sources*; Éric Palazzo, *Le moyen âge: Des origines au XIIIᵉ siècle*; and Richard Pfaff, *Medieval Latin Lit-*

urgy: A Select Bibliography (Toronto: University of Toronto, 1982).

[5]Edward Foley, *From Age to Age: How Christians Celebrated the Eucharist* (Chicago: Liturgy Training Publications, 1991).

[6]Allan Bouley, *From Freedom to Formula: The Evolution of the Eucharistic Prayer from Oral Improvisation to Written Texts* (Washington, D.C.: Catholic University of America Press, 1981).

[7]Thomas Elich, *Le contexte oral de la liturgie médiévale et le rôle du texte écrit* (Ph.D. diss., Paris IV-Sorbonne and Institut Catholique de Paris, 1988).

[8]Vogel, 1.

[9]See Louis Duchesne, *Origines du culte chrétien: Étude sur la liturgie avant Charlemagne,* 3rd ed. (Paris: Fontemoing, 1903) 86–105, and in English as *Christian Worship: Its Origin and Evolution: A Study of the*

Latin Liturgy up to the Time of Charlemagne, trans. M. L. McClure (London: SPCK, 1903) 86–105; and Josef A. Jungmann, *The Early Liturgy to the Time of Gregory the Great*, trans. Francis A. Brunner (Notre Dame, Ind.: University of Notre Dame Press, 1959) 227–237. For a detailed bibliography on "the non-Roman Western rites," see Vogel, 273–289.

10Wilhelm Levison, *England and the Continent in the Eighth Century* (Oxford: Clarendon, 1946).

11J. M. Wallace-Hadrill, *The Frankish Church* (Oxford: Clarendon, 1983).

12It must be said that the story of Clovis owes greatly to the work of Gregory of Tours. His account, however, is often discredited as a piece of propagandist legend. In 1925, L. Halphen developed his extremist thesis: "Not only did Gregory not know the Frankish king, having been born more than twenty-five years after his death, but he was separated at the time he wrote it by three quarters of a century or more from the decisive events which marked the kingdom of the founder of the Merovingian dynasty. Here we see how a half dozen paragraphs of brief notes, together with some lives of the saints and two or three letters from St. Rémy and St. Avit, have been used to stuff the annals of history with legends and anecdotes" ("Grégoire de Tours, historien de Clovis," in *Mélanges d'histoire du moyen âge offerts à M. Ferdinand Lot*, ed. Achille Luchaire [Paris: 1925] 235–244).

13The English historian J. M. Wallace-Hadrill more than most depicted Clovis as the barbarian long-haired king; see his *The Long-Haired Kings* (London: Methuen, 1962) and his *Early Germanic Kingship in England and on the Continent* (Oxford: Clarendon, 1971). More recently Roger Collins has challenged the barbarian stereotype that owes partly to Gregory of Tours's hagiographical account of Clovis. Collins goes so far as to suggest that Clovis may have been Arian before his conversion to Catholicism; see *Early Medieval Europe, 300–1000*, History of Europe (New York: St. Martin's, 1991) 104–108.

14Gregory uses the word "Sicamber" in place of the barbarous "Frank," having been inspired by the *Life of St. Remigius*, where the term is used; see Edward James, *The Franks* (Oxford: Basil Blackwell, 1988) 121–137.

15Gregory of Tours, *History of the Franks by Gregory Bishop of Tours*, trans. Ernest Brehaut (New York: Columbia University Press, 1916) 2.31. Later citations are from this edition.

16The emperor Constantine reached the first stage in 312, never seemed to have grasped the nettle of the second stage, and reached the third only on his deathbed in 337. According to Gregory of Tours, the Burgundian king Gundobad reached the first stage of conversion from Arianism to Catholicism,

but did not dare to progress to the second stage for fear of the followers. Clovis, on the other hand, progressed through all three stages.

17Michel Andrieu, *Les "ordines romani" du haut moyen âge*, vol. 2: *Les textes—ordines I–XIII*, Spicilegium Sacrum Lovaniense 23 (Louvain: Spicilegium Sacrum Lovaniense, 1948) 380–381.

18Antoine Chavasse, *Le sacramentaire gélasien (Vaticanus Regenensis 316)*, Bibliothèque de Théologie 4/1 (Tournai: Desclée, 1959) 155–176.

19See Martin Connell, *The Liturgical Year in Northern Italy (365–450)* (Ph.D. diss., University of Notre Dame, 1994).

20Michel Rouche, *Clovis* (Paris: Fayard, 1996) 255.

21*Alcimi ecdicii aviti opera quae supersunt*, in *Monumenta Germaniae Historica: Auctores Antiquissimi*, vol. 6/2, ed. Rudolf Peiper (Berlin: 1883) 75.

22Rouche, 280–281.

23Epistle 39, to Emperors Gratian, Valentinian, and Theodosius, May 381, in *Saint Ambrose: Letters*, ed. Mary Melchoir Beyenka, The Fathers of the Church, 26 (New York: Fathers of the Church, 1954) 211.

24See M. Dudley and G. Rowell, *The Oil of Gladness: Anointing in the Christian Tradition* (London: SPCK; Collegeville, Minn.: Liturgical Press, 1993). The ancient blessing prayer of chrism at the Chrism Mass found in the Gelasian Sacramentary adds the mention of martyrs: "it is from Christ's holy name that chrism takes its name and with chrism you have anointed for yourself priests, kings, prophets and martyrs (*a cuius sancto nomine chrisma nomen accepit, unde unxisti sacerdotes reges prophetas et martyres tuos*)." L. Mohlberg, *Liber sacramentorum romanae aeclesiae ordinis anni circuli* (Rome: Herder, 1968) #388.

25See J. D. C. Fisher, *Christian Initiation: Baptism in the Medieval West*. Fisher calls his book "a study in the disintegration of the primitive rite of initiation."

26L. A. van Buchem, *L'homélie pseudo-eusébienne de pentecôte: L'origine de la "confirmatio" en Gaule méridionale et l'interprétation de ce rite par Fauste de Riez* (Nijmegen: Janssen, 1967).

27Rabanus Maurus, *De clericorum institutione*, 1.30; PL 107:314.

28Paul Jacobson, "*Sicut Samuhel unxit David*: Early Carolingian Royal Anointings Reconsidered," *Proceedings of Annual Meeting of the North American Academy of Liturgy* (1997) 109–131.

29See Joseph H. Lynch, *Godparents and Kinship in Early Medieval Europe* (Princeton, N.J.: Princeton University Press, 1986).

30See Susan A. Keefe, *Water and the Word: Baptism and the Education of the Clergy in the Carolingian*

Empire (Notre Dame, Ind.: University of Notre Dame Press, 2002), and her "Carolingian Baptismal Expositions: A Handlist of Tracts and Manuscripts," in *Carolingian Essays: Andrew W. Mellon Lectures in Early Christian Studies*, 169–273.

[31] Byer, *Charlemagne and Baptism*.

[32] See Louis Duchesne, *Origines du culte chrétien*, 318; Eng. trans., 318. The *Missale bobbiense* retained the rites *Ad Christianum faciendum*, marking the traditional beginning of the catechumenate, but these survived in vestigial form only as a part of the Easter Vigil or for baptism *in extremis*.

[33] Keefe, "Handlist," 171.

[34] Andrieu, 2:363–447, hereafter Ordo XI.

[35] Lynch, 293.

[36] Michel Andrieu, *Les "ordines romani" du haut moyen âge*, vol. 5: *Les textes* [suite]—*Ordo L*, Spicilegium Sacrum Lovaniense 29 (Louvain: Spicilegium Sacrum Lovaniense, 1961).

[37] Cyrille Vogel and Reinhard Elze, *Le pontifical romano-germanique du dixième siècle*, 3 vols., ST 226, 227, 269 (Vatican City: Biblioteca Apostolica Vaticana, 1963, 1972) 1:1–173: these pages contain the Ordo Romanus L.

[38] Joseph Lynch comments that the ban of parents as sponsors at baptism was expanded to include confirmation and was symptomatic of the parents' growing exclusion from the entire baptismal liturgy (p. 198).

[39] Andrieu, 5:261.

[40] The English bishop Boniface, evangelizer of the Saxons, was particularly troubled by the lack of a proper ritual of baptism. It is safe to say that the elaborate scrutinies as mentioned in Ordo XI were not a part of missionary baptisms. Regarding the water rite itself, Boniface, writing to Pope Gregory II in 726, asks whether a baptism is valid if the priest omits the traditional questions about the creed. The pope assures him that it was, as long as the baptismal formula was trinitarian in form. In 739, Boniface writes to Pope Gregory III because one of his priests pronounced the baptismal formula in the vernacular. The pope assured Boniface that a vernacular baptismal formula did not invalidate the sacrament. Then in 746 Boniface writes to Pope Zachary to inquire about the case of a priest who baptized "in the name of the fatherland, the daughter and the Holy Spirit" (*in nomine patria et filia et spiritus sancti*). The pope responded that as long as the priest intended to baptize as the church desires and did not mean any heresy or error, then the baptism is valid, notwithstanding the ignorance of Latin on the part of the priest. See *Die Briefe des heiligen Bonifatius und*

Lullus, in *Monumenta Germaniae Historica: Epistolae Selectae*, vol. 1, ed. Michael Tangl (Berlin: 1916) 46, 73, 141.

[41] Gregory of Tours, *History of the Franks*, 10.1. Later citations are from this edition.

[42] "In nomine Domini hic sacramentorum de circulo anni expositio a sancto Gregori papa Romano editum ex authentico libro bibliothecae cubiculi scriptum" is the eighth-century title; see Jean Deshusses, *Le Sacramentaire Grégorien: Ses principales formes d'après les plus anciens manuscrits*, vol. 1, Spicilegium Friburgensis 16 (Fribourg, Switzerland: Éditions Universitaires, 1971) 85.

[43] See the five volume work of Michel Andrieu, *Les "ordines romani" du haut moyen âge*.

[44] Andrieu, 5:314–315: Ordo L, chapter 35: De letania maiore.

[45] The "stations" indicate special churches in the city of Rome recognized for their historical and spiritual importance in the eternal city.

[46] An example here is of Sankt Gallen in Switzerland, the floor plan of which comes from a ninth-century manuscript from the Stiftsbibliothek in Sankt Gallen. See Lorna Price, *The Plan of St. Gall in Brief* (Berkeley: University of California Press, 1982).

[47] Gregory of Tours, *Les livres des miracles et autres opuscules de Georges Florent Grégoire*, ed. and trans. H. L. Bordier (Paris: Renouard, 1857–1864) chapter 15.

[48] See James McKinnon, *The Advent Project: The Later-Seventh-Century Creation of the Roman Mass Proper* (Berkeley: University of California Press, 2000).

[49] On the term, see Donald Bullough, "Roman books and Carolingian Renovatio," *Renaissance and Renewal in Christian History*, ed. Derek Baker, Studies in Church History 14 (Oxford: Blackwell, 1977). In more detail, his *Carolingian Renewal: Sources and Heritage* (Manchester: Manchester University Press, 1991).

[50] Henri Barré and Jean Deshusses, "À la recherche du Missel d'Alcuin," *Ephemerides Liturgicae* 82 (1969) 3–44; Jean Deshusses, *Le sacramentaire grégorien: Ses principales formes d'après les plus anciens manuscrits*, vols. 2–3, Spicilegium Friburgensis 16 and 28 (Fribourg, Switzerland: Éditions Universitaires, 1971, 1982); and his "Le 'Supplément' au sacramentaire grégorien: Alcuin ou Benoît d'Aniane?" *Archiv für Liturgiewissenschaft* 9/1 (1965) 48–71.

[51] The supplement in the past was thought to be of Alcuin's hand. The extensive scholarship of Jean Deshusses now attributes the supplement to Benedict of Aniane.

[52]See Vogel and Elze, *Le pontifical romano-germanique.*

[53]Amalarius of Metz, *Opera liturgica omnia*, ed. J. M. Hanssens, ST, 138–140 (Vatican City: Biblioteca Apostolica Vaticana, 1948–1950).

[54]Nathan Mitchell, *Cult and Controversy: The Worship of the Eucharist outside Mass* (New York: Pueblo, 1982) 67–68.

[55]André Wilmart, *Precum libelli quattuor aevi karolini (prior pars)* (Rome: Ephemerides Liturgicae, 1940) 5–6. Wilmart takes great pains to study the manuscripts from a codicological and paleographical perspective in order to show Alcuin's familiarity with these four *libelli*. See also Michael S. Driscoll, *Alcuin et la pénitence à l'époque carolingienne* (Münster, Germany: Aschendorff, 1999).

[56]Michael S. Driscoll, "The *Precum Libelli* and Carolingian Spirituality," *Proceedings of the North American Academy of Liturgy* (1990) 68–76; see also Pierre-Marie Gy, "The Different Forms of Liturgical *Libelli*," in *Fountain of Life*, ed. Gerard Austin (Washington, D.C.: Pastoral Press, 1991) 23–34.

[57]A strong resemblance exists between the *libelli* of Alcuin and those of Nunnaminster; see *The Book of Nunnaminster (London, British Library, Harley Ms 2965)*, ed. W. de Gray Birch, Hampshire Record Society, no. 5 (Winchester: 1889), reprinted in Bibliotheca "Ephemerides liturgicae," Subsidia Instrumenta liturgica quarreriensia Supplementa (Rome: C. L. V., 2001). See also *The Prayer Book of Aedeluald the Bishop, Commonly Called the Book of Cerne*, ed. Arthur B. Kuypers (Cambridge: Cambridge University Press, 1902); and *The Book of Cerne*, ed. Michelle P. Brown, British Library Studies in Medieval Culture (London: British Library; Toronto: University of Toronto Press, 1996).

[58]See Jean Leclercq, *La spiritualité du moyen âge* (Paris: Aubier, 1961) 86.

[59]See Kathleen Hughes, "Types of Prayer in the Liturgy," in *The New Dictionary of Sacramental Worship*, ed. Peter E. Fink (Collegeville, Minn.: Liturgical Press, 1990) 959–967. The classic essay is Edmund Bishop's "The Genius of the Roman Rite," in his *Liturgica Historica* (Oxford: Clarendon, 1918) 1–19.

[60]See Michael S. Driscoll, "The Seven Penitential Psalms: Their Designation and Usages from the Middle Ages Onwards," *Ecclesia Orans* 17 (2000) 153–201. The notion that certain of the psalms had a penitential significance for the Christian reader is already to be found in Origen and Augustine, but the first commentator to single out seven psalms as being specifically penitential was Cassiodorus. See

Cassidore, *Expositio Psalmorum I–LXX*, Corpus Christianorum 97 (Brepols: 1958), commentary on Psalm 50, 469. Also see Ursula Jaitner-Hahner, *Cassiodors Psalmenkommentar: Sprachliche Untersuchungen* (Munich: Arbeo-Gesellschaft, 1973).

[61]"Intendant quaesumus domine pietatis tuae aures supplicum preces, quia apud te est propitiatio peccatorum, ut non observes iniquitates nostras, sed inpercias nobis misericordias tuas, per dominum" (Wilmart, 30, 53, 78).

[62]See Ludwig Bieler, "The Irish Penitentials: Their Religious and Social Background," *Studia Patristica* 8,2 (1966) 335–339.

[63]*The Prayer Book of Aedeluald the Bishop*, #10.

[64]For Alcuin's confession prayer entitled "Deus inaestimabilis misericordiae," see Wilmart, 21–23.

[65]Étienne Delaruelle, *La piété populaire au moyen âge* (Torino: Bottega d'Erasmo, 1980) 12. See also his "La Gaule chrétienne à l'époque franque: L'époque carolingienne," *Revue d'Histoire de l'Église de France* 38 (1952) 64–72.

[66]Bernard McGinn, *The Growth of Mysticism: Gregory the Great through the Twelfth Century*, vol. 2 (New York: Crossroads, 1994) 23.

[67]*Monumenta Germaniae Historica: Leges*, vol. 1, ed. Georg Pertz, (Hannover: Impensis Bibliopolii Avolici Hahniani, 1837) 107–108.

[68]Delaruelle, *La piété populaire*, 13–14.

[69]This and many other of the developments about to be mentioned are treated in the first chapter of André Vauchez, *La spiritualité du moyen âge occidental, VIIIᵉ–XIIIᵉ siècle* (Paris: Seuil, 1994). The first edition of that book (Paris: Presses Universitaires de France, 1975) appeared in translation by Colette Friedlander as *The Spirituality of the Medieval West: From the Eighth to the Twelfth Century* (Kalamazoo, Mich.: Cistercian Publications, 1993).

[70]Until the eighth century the priest offered the eucharistic sacrifice, referring to all the assembled people, *"qui tibi offerunt hoc sacrificium laudis"* ("who offer you this sacrifice of praise"). Now he felt compelled to add the formula *"vel pro quibus tibi offerimus"* ("or for whom we offer it to you").

[71]Latin enjoyed a prestige without rival—vernacular was not always written, whereas Latin was the literary language. Also, Rome and its culture fascinated the Carolingian clergy. They made great efforts to maintain the high literary level of antiquity by using classical linguistic forms.

[72]Josef Jungmann, *Missarum sollemnia*, vol. 1, trans. Francis A. Brunner (New York: Benzinger, 1951) 74–103.

[73]Ibid., 82.

[74]Miri Rubin recounts some "uses and abuses" of the consecrated host in *Corpus Christi: The Eucharist in Late Medieval Culture* (Cambridge: Cambridge University Press, 1991) 334–342. She also deals with stories about Jews stealing hosts and desecrating the sacrament, which heightened the degree of anti-Semitism.

[75]Dhuoda, *Manuel pour mon fils*, ed. Pierre Riché, Sources Chrétiennes 225 bis (Paris: Cerf, 1991).

[76]Jonas d'Orléans, *Les idées politico-religieuses d'un évêque du IXe siècle: Jonas d'Orléans et son "De institutione regia,"* ed. Jean Reviron (Paris: Vrin, 1930).

[77]It was believed that opposites heal illness and sin. The Latin expression is *contraria contrariis sanantur*.

[78]In the penitential books we find superstitious elements: see *Corrector sive medicus*, Burchard of Worms (ninth c.); he speaks about consulting the lunar cycles for building or contracting marriage, howling at the moon, or crying to the stars for healing. See Cyrille Vogel, *Le pécheur et la pénitence au moyen âge* (Paris: Cerf, 1966) 15–27.

[79]Vauchez, *La spiritualité du moyen âge occidental*, 12; cf. Eng. trans., 14.

[80]"On the continent the reforming movement was dominated by three names, Cluny, Gorze and in Italy, Monte Cassino. Cluny, which was founded in Burgundy in 910, spread [the style of its monastic life] throughout France, into Spain and Italy, to England and even in the north and east of Europe and as far as Poland. Gorze was founded in Lorraine in 933, and its influence was chiefly felt in northeast Europe and throughout the Empire. . . . Gorze and Cluny, however, typify the two main streams of reform" (Jean Leclercq, "From St. Gregory to St. Bernard: From the Sixth to the Twelfth Century," in *A History of Christian Spirituality*, vol. 2: The Spirituality of the Middle Ages [London: Burns and Oates, 1968; repr. New York: Seabury, 1982] 102).

[81]"*Ordinem romanum et antiquum morem*"; see Theodor Klauser, *A Short History of the Western Liturgy* (Oxford: Oxford University Press, 1965) 94.

[82]Karl Morrison, "The Gregorian Reform," in *Christian Spirituality: Origins to the Twelfth Century*, ed. B. McGinn, J. Meyendorff, and J. Leclercq (New York: Crossroads, 1986) 177–193.

[83]Abbo of Fleury (died 1004), *Apologeticus*, PL 139: 465 A.

[84]"*Secrete orare*": see Leclercq, "From St. Gregory to St. Bernard," 103.

[85]From the early centuries Christians prayed in common. Two distinguishable, though partially confluent, forms appeared in the Latin West: the Christian communities in cities gathered for the cathedral or parish office, while monks and nuns gathered for the monastic office. See Paul Bradshaw, *Two Ways of Praying* (Nashville, Tenn.: Abingdon, 1995).

[86]See Robert Taft, *Liturgy of the Hours in East and West* (Collegeville, Minn.: Liturgical Press, 1986) 138–140. The simplified structure of the hours in the Roman monastic office consisted of vigils, lauds, intermediate hours (prime, terce, sext, and none), vespers, and compline. In the monastic custom the monks and nuns in the course of each week would complete the entire psalter of one hundred and fifty psalms, assigning them throughout the week at the various hours of prayer. In addition, other psalms for special occasions or intentions, such as psalms of penance, were prayed. As a consequence, those who prayed the office more than likely knew the psalter by heart. In many of the *precum libelli*, for example, only the first line of the psalm is indicated, which would have been sufficient as an aide-mémoire to stimulate the person to the recitation of the psalm by heart.

[87]The study of the office has been of special interest to medieval musicologists on account of its richness and the gradual complexity of the forms of prayer and chant. In addition to the psalms and biblical canticles, other elements studied include antiphons, responses, verses, hymns, and lessons. One genre that developed in the Middle Ages was the trope: usually original in composition, these were inserted into existing liturgical texts and served almost as a gloss or a commentary on the text or the liturgy. Tropes serve as a rich expression of medieval piety and theology. Notker of Sankt Gallen (died 1022) was one of the chief composers of tropes. See the numerous critical editions of tropes produced by the *Corpus Troporum* project of the University of Stockholm, Sweden.

[88]Kassius Hallinger, *Consuetudinum saeculi X, XI, XII monumenta: Introductiones*, Corpus Consuetudinum Monasticarum 7/1 (Siegburg, Germany: F. Schmitt, 1984).

[89]Carol Heitz, *L'architecture religieuse carolingienne: les formes et leurs fonctions* (Paris: Picard, 1980), *Recherches sur les rapports entre architecture et liturgie à l'époque carolingienne* (Paris: Picard, 1961).

[90]Peter Dinter, ed. *Liber tramitis aevi Odilonis abbatis*, Corpus Consuetudinum Monasticarum 10 (Siegburg, Germany: F. Schmitt, 1984).

[91]Hildegard of Bingen, *Scivias* (New York: Paulist Press, 1990). The title is short for "Scito vias Domini" or "Know the Ways of the Lord."

[92]By the time of John Hus in the late fourteenth century, communion under both kinds became a rallying cry and the refusal to give the people the cup was interpreted by the Hussites as a claim to clerical privilege.

[93]*Scivias*, 2.6.49.

[94]Joy Schroeder, "Encountering Christ in the Eucharistic Rite: The Experience of Medieval Women," paper submitted in a course on liturgical theology at the University of Notre Dame, December 1995.

[95]Morrison, "The Gregorian Reform," 191.

6

Western Christendom

TIMOTHY THIBODEAU

Papal and Monastic Reform

Any extended analysis of the liturgy of the Latin Church in the Gothic age (c. 1100–1500) must begin with a basic understanding of the political, cultural, and religious forces that played a pivotal role in the development of the Church's rites in that epoch. The liturgy of the Gothic age was profoundly influenced by two sweeping movements of earlier origin that were of lasting consequence in the history of medieval Christianity: the reform of the papacy and the triumph of Cluniac monasticism. These reforms helped to precipitate a great crisis of Church and state which modern historians call the Investiture Controversy (c. 1075–1122). This intense conflict pitted the Holy Roman Emperor and the reform popes in a battle for control of the Church within the boundaries of a German Empire that stretched from Saxony to Lombardy.[1]

The ostensible center of this controversy—the investiture of higher clergy by a theocratic ruler—was, properly speaking, a liturgical ceremony in which an ordinand was consecrated bishop by an archbishop or several bishops, thereby becoming a sacramental minister of the church. The new bishop was immediately "invested" with the symbols of his pastoral office, the ring and staff, by the temporal magnate by whom he was appointed, thereby becoming the magnate's feudal vassal. This confusion of the spiritual and temporal roles of the bishop became the locus of a protracted and acrimonious dispute between the papal reformers, who battled mightily against "lay investiture," and the imperialists, who could conceive of no practical alternative for the administration of the German church.

The fierce debate over lay investiture was accompanied by a variety of hard-fought victories for the reform party in Rome: the canonical election of a pope by a conclave of cardinals; a spirited condemnation of simony (the purchase or sale of ecclesiastical offices); and the universal ban on clerical marriage (defined as "concubinage") in the Latin Church. At the height of the papal reform, some of the most extreme theories of papal sovereignty ever espoused by any medieval pope were forcefully articulated. Gregory VII (reigned 1073–1085) declared, in his *Dictates of the Pope*, that not only could he excommunicate the German emperor, he could also strip him of his imperial title. Gregory did in fact excommunicate and depose Henry IV (reigned 1056–1106) on two separate occasions (in 1076 and 1080), plunging the Holy Roman Empire into a state of anarchy and warfare. This same pope also affirmed in his *Dictates*: "He should not be considered as Catholic [i.e., Christian] who is not in conformity with the Roman Church."[2] To paraphrase a well-known gospel maxim, no faithful Christian could serve two masters: the only master of Christendom was Saint Peter's vicar and successor, the pope.

The Investiture Controversy technically came to a close in 1122 with the Concordat of Worms, a compromise negotiated by Emperor Henry V (reigned 1106–1125) and Pope Callistus II (reigned 1119–1124). This treaty was eventually ratified by the First Lateran Council (1123), the same council that codified the far-reaching decrees of the reform popes and synods.[3] The German emperor, now considered a "layman," would no longer appoint or invest bishops or abbots with the symbols of their spiritual office, the ring and staff. He could, however, be present for their election and resolve disputed elections. The emperor could also require homage from the higher clergy in return for the *regalia* attached to their episcopal or abbatial sees (principally the lands and material possessions attached to the ecclesiastical office).

In his assessment of the outcome of the Investiture Controversy, Gerd Tellenbach argues convincingly that this conflict can be understood as a battle between rival ecclesiologies or definitions of church governance.[4] When the German emperor gave up his right to clerical investiture, a "sacramental" model of the Church had triumphed over a "royal" or "theocratic" ecclesiology. Put another way, the "priestly" authority of *sacerdotium* (from the Latin term for priest or bishop, *sacerdos*) had superseded the royal power or *regnum*. The world could now be sharply divided into a sacred and a profane sphere, each with its own authority structure: an *ordo clericus* and an *ordo laicus*. In the sacred sphere of the liturgical and sacramental rites of the Church, only the clergy could preside or exercise any kind of authority. Even the emperor was, in a strict sense, a member of the *ordo laicus*, or a layman who must, by definition, be a passive observer of the sacred liturgy. In such a scheme, there was, ecclesiologically, no substantial difference between an emperor and a peasant, since they were both laymen. Gregory VII said as much in a famous letter to Bishop Herman of Metz (1081): "[G]reater power is granted to an exorcist when he is made a spiritual emperor for the casting out of devils than can be conferred upon any layman for the purpose of earthly dominion."[5]

The triumph of the reform papacy was accompanied by one of the most important religious reform movements of the central Middle Ages: Cluniac monasticism.[6] In 909 the dying Duke of Aquitaine, William III, handed over his best hunting lands in Burgundy to the Benedictine monk Berno of Baume (William had no direct male heir).[7] It was not unusual for a dying magnate to make amends with God for his sins by establishing a religious house to pray for his deceased soul. What was atypical was that the duke gave away his rights in perpetuity to appoint the abbot of the monastery of Cluny, or to interfere in any way with the internal workings of the monastic community; the abbey was placed under the patronage of saints Peter and Paul. William was convinced that the spiritual benefits of the daily prayers of reformed monks far outweighed the financial or administrative losses that might accompany the canonical election of the abbot of Cluny. It did, however, trouble the duke that Berno had chosen the best hunting grounds among all of his scattered holdings for the foundation of his new monastery, at the villa of Cluniacum. His hesitation ceased when Berno assured him that his deceased soul would be better served by the prayers of holy monks than by the barking of hounds. From such humble origins developed one of the mightiest religious foundations of the Middle Ages.

By the close of the eleventh century, Cluniac monasteries dotted the French, German, and Italian countryside; by 1100 there were about 600 Cluniac monasteries and roughly 10,000 Cluniac monks in Latin Christendom. Unlike the early Benedictine

foundations, these monastic houses constituted an international *ordo* or religious order. Although the governance of the monasteries remained autonomous, they were
bound by the same *consuetudines Cluniacensis*, the liturgical customs of Cluny.[8] Frequent meetings of Cluniac abbots ensured a remarkable degree of liturgical uniformity in these widely scattered foundations. The Cluniac monks' close connection
with the reformed papacy, their reputation for devout observance of the *Rule for Monks*
of Saint Benedict (c. 480–550), their exemption from monarchic, ducal, and episcopal
control, their ornate churches and elaborate liturgies, and the reputed efficacy of their
prayers for the dead became known throughout Christendom. Cluny's reputation for
commemorating and interceding in prayer for its deceased benefactors evolved into
the celebration of All Souls' Day, which immediately followed the Feast of All Saints
in the liturgical calendar. Abbot Odilo (reigned 994–1049) imposed the observance of
this holy day on all Cluniac houses in the eleventh century; it eventually became a
universal observance for the Latin Church.

Cluniac monks eventually moved into the highest reaches of ecclesiastical authority, serving first as cardinals and then as popes in the age of the Investiture Controversy. The First Crusade was preached by a former Cluniac monk who as pope took
the name Urban II (reigned 1088–1099). In 1095 he dedicated the main altar of the
Abbey Church of Cluny, which became the largest church building in Western

Consecration of Cluny. Consecration of the Abbey of Cluny by Pope Urban II, c. 1095.
Manuscript illustration. Bibliothèque Nationale de France, Paris, MS. 17716, folio 91/
Snark/Art Resource, NY

Christendom until the sixteenth century; the same year, he called for a crusade in the East. The attack on simony, the insistence on clerical celibacy, and the defense of the "liberty" of the Church (the canonical election of the pope and the abolition of lay investiture) were all, in the minds of many of the papal reformers, associated with the ideals of the Cluniac monasticism.[9]

The Cluniac reforms of the liturgy led to a fundamental transformation of the liturgical performance and piety of both monastic and cathedral churches. The Benedictine Rule defined monasticism as a life of "prayer and work," *ora et labora*. For Saint Benedict, prayer was a *divinum officium*, a "divine work" or duty, hence the liturgical term "divine office" for the liturgy of the hours prescribed by the rule. As a work of prayer, what Benedict called the *Opus Dei*, the divine office was distinguishable from other forms of "work," namely the manual labor required of all monks by the rule. At Cluny, however, "prayer and work" became indistinguishable. While claiming to adhere closely to Benedict's rule, Cluny inaugurated a radical reconfiguration of Benedictine monastic life. Even though Benedict was never ordained a cleric, nor were the majority of Benedictine monks in the early Middle Ages, priestly ordination became the *sine qua non* of Cluniac monasticism. Even though the rule prescribed manual labor, the Cluniac monk was too busy with the "work of prayer" to do physical labor, which could actually be done by the numerous serfs attached to Cluniac foundations. The Cluniac monk's life was consecrated to a daily round of prayers, which took up practically every waking moment of his day. According to his medieval biographer, Saint Anselm (c. 1033–1109) had considered becoming a Cluniac monk but quickly abandoned the idea when he realized that the liturgical schedule left no room for private study.[10]

The lion's share of the Benedictine Rule is devoted to the precise legislation of the biblical lessons and prayers that constitute the divine office. Divided into seven daily "canonical hours" of prayer, the twin pillars of the liturgical schedule of the rule were the weekly recitation of the entire psalter and the yearly reading of the entire Bible.[11] In the ninth century, the Carolingian monastic reformer Benedict of Aniane (c. 750–821) imposed additional observances—principally the Office of the Dead and the Fifteen Gradual Psalms (Ps. 119–133)—on all of the Benedictine foundations in the Carolingian empire of Charlemagne's son and successor, Louis the Pious (reigned 814–840). In the mid-eleventh century, the original Benedictine monastic office was burdened with numerous other "little offices" such as votive offices for saints, the Virgin Mary, commemorations, and "suffrages" or intercessory prayers at lauds and vespers.

By the time of the monastic-papal reform, the Benedictine Office had clearly departed from the simple principle of moderation displayed by the original rule and had evolved into an elaborate regime which, in some monasteries, consumed a choir monk's entire day. The Cluniac monk had the added obligation of celebrating daily mass and commemorating the deceased benefactors of the monastic foundation, whose names were carefully recorded in necrologies or obituaries, the official lists of dead patrons. It was at Cluny that the custom originated of reciting the so-called *Psalmi familiares*, the excerpts from the Seven Penitential Psalms (Ps. 6, 31, 37, 50, 101, 129, 142) for patrons, benefactors, and friends at each of the canonical hours.

The sacerdotal ecclesiology of the reform popes worked in tandem with the sacerdotalism of Cluniac monasticism. Thanks in large part to Cluny, the solemn celebration of the mass eclipsed the divine office as the summit and quintessence of monastic worship, not only for Cluniac monks but also eventually for all Latin monks of the later Middle Ages. This new Cluniac emphasis on the priestly function of the monk is inextricably connected to contemporary theological controversies associated with the real presence of Christ in the eucharistic host. A heightened sense of the mass as the miraculous re-creation of the body and blood of Christ in the tangible objects of bread and wine lent a new sense of drama to the eucharistic liturgy. The awesome sacramental power entrusted to the priest required, in the Cluniac scheme of monastic and clerical reform, that the priest who approached the altar of the Lord be worthy of "confecting" the body and blood of Christ. This explains to a considerable degree the reform papacy's adamant enforcement of clerical celibacy, even when the vast majority of diocesan priests (and some bishops) were in some sort of matrimonial state. The cardinal-deacon Peter Damian (c. 1007–1072) articulated this passion of the reformers for the ritual purity of clerics when he declared in *Against the Intemperate Clerics*: "The hands that have been dedicated to the service of the heavenly table, preparing the food of angels, should not be subjected to touching the obscene parts and filthy contagion of women."[12]

Although the practice predated the foundation of Cluny, Cluniac piety rapidly accelerated the trend toward the private celebration of the daily mass in the monasteries and cathedrals of Europe. It became common for several private masses—a eucharistic liturgy without a congregation—to be celebrated simultaneously in the various chapels of a monastic or cathedral church. The Cluniac conception of private mass as intercessory prayer for the deceased saw its logical development well outside the confines of the monastery in the person of the "chantry priest," a secular priest whose occupation was to "chant" private masses for the dead. Such clerics really had a sinecure (from the Latin *sine cura*, a clerical appointment without pastoral care, or *cura animarum*). By the late thirteenth century, such endowed private masses for the dead proliferated in the cathedral and parish churches of Latin Christendom.

The chantry priest is also emblematic of the objectification of the eucharist and a concomitant arithmetical form of piety which viewed the daily sacrifice of the mass as a talisman that offered spiritual benefits beyond the here and now. In this exchange of temporal for spiritual currency, wealthy and not-so-wealthy patrons endowed and prescribed the daily celebration of mass and other devotions for the passage of their souls or the souls of deceased loved ones from the sorrows of purgatory to the beatific vision of heaven.[13] This sacred mercantilism was accompanied by a crude theological architecture which placed purgatory (a scholastic innovation) in between heaven and hell.[14]

In 1274, the Second Council of Lyons ratified this popular piety by decreeing that the souls "undergoing purification after death could benefit from the suffrages of the living faithful, namely by the sacrifice of the mass, almsgiving, and other pious practices done by the faithful for other faithful, according to the custom of the Church."[15] By the mid-fourteenth century, the foundation of chantries became a major preoccupation of the numerous religious confraternities, whose primary mission was to engage in charitable works for their living and deceased members. As we will see, the chantry priest was also the product of a culture that no longer viewed the eucharist as a communal celebration (in the patristic sense), but rather as a sacred object to be adored and venerated from a distance, or manipulated (as in the endowment of chantries) for one's own spiritual interests.

Abbot Suger and the Gothic Age of Liturgy

Perhaps the most celebrated proponent of Cluniac liturgy was Suger (c. 1081–1151), abbot of the royal monastery of Saint-Denis.[16] With Suger's abbacy (1122–1151) in one of the oldest and most renowned monastic foundations in the French royal domain, we witness the full flowering of Cluniac liturgy (even though Saint-Denis was not, strictly speaking, part of the Cluniac order). Suger's magnificently reconstructed abbey church became the cradle of a bold architectural style which we now call "Gothic" to distinguish it from its "Romanesque" predecessor. Although scholarly debate continues about whether Suger should be credited with single-handedly introducing Gothic architecture to medieval France, there is no doubt that his achievements at Saint-Denis left an indelible mark on the art, architecture, and liturgy of the Gothic age.[17] Friend and confidant of the French King Louis VI, "the Fat" (reigned 1108–1137), Suger was the tireless monk-architect for whom no stone was too precious, no expense too great, no object too ornate to be put in the service of worshiping the Lord Jesus Christ, whose body and blood were worthy of the most sacred and sublime edifice:

> To me, I confess, one thing has always seemed preeminently fitting: that every costlier or costliest thing should serve, first and foremost, for the administration of the Holy Eucharist. *If* golden pouring vessels, golden vials, golden little mortars used to serve, by the word of God or the command of the Prophet, to collect the *blood of goats or calves or the red heifer: how much more* must the golden vessels, precious stones, and whatever is most valued among all created things, be laid out, with continual reverence and full devotion, for the reception of *the blood of Christ!*[18]

The Royal Abbey of Saint-Denis had long been associated with the Frankish monarchy. Richly patronized by the early Merovingian King Dagobert I (reigned 621–637), the monastery was named after an early Christian martyr who was, according to pious legend, apostle to the Franks. The Frankish hagiographer bishop Gregory of Tours (c. 540–594) claimed that Saint Denis was the first bishop of Paris and was martyred during the Decian persecution (c. 250–251). The ninth-century abbot Hilduin (reigned 814–840) erroneously conflated this early Christian martyr with the Greek mystical theologian known as Dionysius the Areopagite in the hagiography that he composed, thus beginning the medieval legend of Dionysius/Denis. In Hilduin's version of the story, Saint Denis was converted to Christianity in Athens by Saint Paul; he was then ordained a bishop in Rome before embarking on his mission to the pagan Franks. His ministry ended when he was decapitated in Paris during the reign of Domitian (c. 96). A ninth-century Latin translation of the original Greek Pseudo-Dionysian corpus (which we now know was written in Syria in the early sixth century) was housed in the library of Suger's abbey and lent further credibility to this legend.[19]

The Christian Neoplatonic theories of celestial, angelic, and ecclesiastical hierarchies in these texts served as the whetstone for Abbot Suger's theological and architectural designs. The epigraphic inscription that adorns the exterior of the church, just above the tympanum, clearly alludes to the Pseudo-Dionysian association of God with Light:

> Whoever you may be, if you wish to extol these doors, do not marvel at their gold or their cost, but instead at their craftsmanship. This work shines nobly, but being nobly bright, the work should enlighten men's minds to move through the [visible] lights to the True Light, where Christ is the true gateway. The golden door determines how [this light] is present; the dull mind rises to the Truth through the material world, and in seeing this light it is resurrected from its former submersion.[20]

The fact, too, that Saint-Denis was the favored burial place of a succession of Frankish monarchs justified, in the mind of Suger, the exorbitant sums by which he financed his ambitious construction projects.

The church Suger inherited as abbot was a magnificent Carolingian structure that had been consecrated in 775. It continued to be patronized by Carolingian rulers, and a new chapel was attached to the apse in 832. Between 1137 and 1144, Suger undertook a massive reconstruction of that church—principally the façade, the narthex, and the choir—in honor of God and the deceased patrons and benefactors of the monastery. Amazingly, the magnificent choir, where the new architectural style is most strikingly displayed, was constructed in little more than three years. On 14 June 1144, Suger crowned his grandiose projects with the solemn consecration of the rebuilt church's twenty altars (eleven in the choir and nine in the crypt). His splendid liturgy was attended by King Louis VII (1137–1180), Eleanor of Aquitaine, a great many nobles, and no fewer than seventeen archbishops and bishops.[21] (This also more or less marks the end of major work on the abbey church; after Suger died in 1151, almost a century passed before new construction commenced.) The clerics who attended Suger's ceremony in the summer of 1144 were undoubtedly dazzled by its opulence, and when they returned home, they were eager to undertake comparable construction projects.

In Solomonic tones, Suger provides us with a first-hand account of his accomplishments in two treatises: *On His Administration* and *On the Consecration* (of the new church). These remarkable documents give full voice not only to the ideals of an ambitious abbot, but also to the whole Cluniac conception of sacred liturgy as it had evolved in the twelfth century; Suger was laying the foundations of Christian worship in the Gothic age. In *Administration*, he delights in the liturgical "ornaments" that adorn his renovated church, even as he attempts to defend himself against the charges of vanity and *superbia* (the mortal sin of pride). Suger once again invokes Pseudo-Dionysian theology when justifying his costly artworks:

> Often we contemplate, out of sheer affection for the church our mother, these different ornaments both new and old. . . . Thus, when—out of my delight in the beauty of the house of God—the loveliness of the many colored gems has called me away from external cares, and worthy meditation has induced me to reflect, transferring that which is material to that which is immaterial, on the diversity of the sacred virtues: then it seems to me that I find myself dwelling, as it were, in some strange region of the universe which neither exists entirely in the slime of the earth, nor entirely in the purity of Heaven; and that, by the grace of God, I can be transported from this inferior to a higher world in an anagogical manner.[22]

By the time that Suger's rebuilt abbey church was consecrated, Cluniac liturgy and architecture had been challenged polemically by a new group of religious idealists: the monks of Cîteaux, or Cistercians. Nicknamed the "white monks" because they refused to dye their monastic habit (the *cuculla*) black as was the custom of Cluny, the Cistercians were ardent reformers of religious life who claimed that they had restored the original ideals of the founder of Western monasticism, Saint Benedict of Nursia. They were ably led by one of the most prolific authors and most towering religious figures of the twelfth century, Saint Bernard of Clairvaux (c. 1090–1153).[23]

Adviser to kings and popes, nemesis of the dialectician Pierre Abelard (1079–1142), and scathing critic of the extravagances of Gothic art, Bernard held to the spiritual ideals of Benedictine simplicity, humility, and poverty, which clashed with what he identified as Cluniac luxury. Cistercian oratories imitated the new architectural style of the Gothic age in only the simplest terms; the ribbed vault allowed for better fenestration, bathing the monastic church with light. But in stark contrast to the Cluniac churches and monasteries, the Cistercian houses were isolated and remote, with unadorned and simple interiors. The inherent simplicity of Cistercian art (no porches, no towers, no stained glass windows) served as a palpable reminder of the movement's ideal of material poverty and the rejection of worldly glory.

For Bernard and the Cistercians, the very name of Cluny immediately conjured up images of the regal splendor and aristocratic privileges that they were sworn to renounce (the majority of the monks at Cluny, were in fact aristocrats). Situated in a tiny village in the Mâconnais, Cluny had become home to roughly three hundred choir monks, who celebrated their elaborate liturgies in what became the largest church in western Europe before the construction of Saint Peter's Basilica in Rome in the sixteenth century. In fact, this magnificent abbey church—which art historians designate as Cluny III—had received its finishing touches only a few years before Suger undertook his own ambitious projects at Saint-Denis. (Built between c. 1088 and 1130, virtually none of Cluny III survived the desecrations of the French Revolution.)

While Bernard wrote letters praising Suger's efforts as abbot to reform the community of monks at Saint-Denis, he also offered stinging criticisms of the costly and flamboyant architectural designs of Cluny that Suger was so eager to surpass. In a letter to the Cistercian abbot William of St. Thierry, Bernard excoriated Cluniac extravagance as imitating the superfluous rites of Judaism while being inimical to the gospel itself: "O vanity of vanities, but not as vain as insane! Each part of the church glitters and the poor go hungry; her walls are clothed in gold and her sons are abandoned to nakedness. . . . The curious come and are filled with delight; the destitute come and find nothing to sustain them."[24]

Bernard's denigration of Cluniac artwork as a vainglorious enterprise obviously took a psychological toll on Suger, who, unlike the aristocratic critic Bernard, was a man of exceedingly humble origins (his father was probably a serf). In his *Administration*, Suger took great pains to justify the splendor of his abbey church; it was, after all, a fitting vessel for the miraculous re-creation of the body and blood of Christ in the daily sacrifice of the mass:

> The detractors also object that a saintly mind, a pure heart, a faithful intention ought to suffice for this sacred function; and we, too, explicitly and especially affirm that it is these that principally matter. [But] we profess that we must do homage also through the outward ornaments and sacred vessels, and to nothing in the world in an equal degree as to the service of the Holy Sacrifice, with all inner purity and with all outward splendor.[25]

Despite its intensity, the conflict between the Cluniacs and the Cistercians remained, in the history of art and architecture, an intramural quarrel among monks that was relatively short-lived. Within a half-century of Bernard of Clairvaux's death, the Gothic style and its accompanying liturgical glitter could be found throughout the length and breadth of France; by the end of the thirteenth century, it had been replicated all over Christian Europe. The Romanesque abbey churches and cathedrals, which the new architecture had replaced, seemed increasingly alien in the vibrant, optimistic, and expanding culture of the twelfth- and thirteenth-century Renaissance. Their ponderous, fortresslike exteriors and dimly lit interiors were reminders of a more primitive, even barbarous age when brute force rather than brains ruled the world. In that not-too-distant past the relics of saints, enshrined in the dark bowels of monastic churches, offered the frightened masses more protection from adversity than did any written law code or centralized organ of government.

The age of Scholasticism saw the towering spires of Gothic cathedrals overtake the townscapes of the Loire River valley. The Gothic age witnessed a new surge of civic pride, as the expanding cities and towns of Capetian France competed in an "arts race," so to speak, to build ever larger and more splendid cathedrals. Undoubtedly one of the most impressive of these structures, the cathedral of Chartres,[26] was emblematic of the optimism and technical virtue of the architecture of the Gothic age—a marvel of speed, size and splendor.

The story of the construction of this particular cathedral underscores the dramatic interplay of the religious, social, political, and artistic ideals of the twelfth century. The present structure arose from the ashes of a catastrophic fire (June 1194) which consumed the eleventh-century cathedral, the episcopal palace, and a good portion of the surrounding town. Ironically, the eleventh-century cathedral had been built by bishop Fulbert of Chartres when the Carolingian edifice he inherited was itself destroyed by a disastrous fire in 1020.[27] A well-known center of Marian devotion, the eleventh-century cathedral had long been a locus of pilgrimage because it housed a most marvelous relic: the *Sancta Camisia* or "Sacred Tunic," which the Virgin Mary was purported to have worn when she gave birth to Christ. The relic, which first appeared in Europe in Carolingian times, was presented to the cathedral by Charlemagne's grandson, Charles the Bald, in 867.

When the conflagration of 1194 destroyed the cathedral—taking with it, so it was thought, the Sacred Tunic—the citizens of Chartres despaired, believing that the Virgin Mary had abandoned them. When the precious relic was recovered unscathed in the crypt of the church where it had been hidden, it was taken as a miraculous sign that a more magnificent church should be built in honor of the Mother of God. The cathe-

Window at Chartres. Angel with a censer. Detail of the Noah window, Chartres Cathedral, thirteenth century. ERICH LESSING/ART RESOURCE, NY

dral chapter dedicated vast sums of money for the project, as did the townspeople and the regional aristocracy; even the kings of France, Castile, and England participated in this pious benefaction.[28] In an astoundingly brief twenty-six years, an anonymous architect designed the cathedral, supervised its construction, and brought to near completion an edifice whose total length reached 422 feet and whose vaults stood a dizzying 116 feet above the church floor.[29] (Although most of the work was finished by 1233, the cathedral was not officially consecrated until October 1260.) The completed structure immediately became paradigmatic for the construction of High Gothic cathedrals; with some variations, the plan of Chartres was imitated in the cathedrals of Soissons, Reims, and Amiens.[30]

Not surprisingly, the citizens of Chartres came to view their cathedral in much the same way the citizens of Periclean Athens did their Parthenon. Every craft guild in Chartres wanted its own stained glass window in the refurbished church. Like the Parthenon, the cathedral of Chartres is the artistic creation of a particular culture in a particular place and time; like its Greek predecessor, it also transcends that time and place and belongs to the ages.

The towering monuments of the Gothic age were paralleled by no less lofty intellectual edifices, the theological *Summae* of the great schoolmen of the thirteenth century.[31] Despite the protestations of Bernard of Clairvaux, the Cluniac conceptions of sacred liturgy emerged victorious in the great cathedral and abbey churches of Europe, while in the renowned University of Paris, situated squarely in the heartland of Gothic art and architecture, the scholastic method of the logicians triumphed over the Cistercian monastic ideals of simplicity and renunciation of the world.

The Liturgy of the Latin Church

The Investiture Controversy centered on a liturgical practice that was emblematic of broader theological and ecclesiological disputes within the body of European Christendom in the eleventh century. Not only had the reform popes battled to divest the German emperor of his legal authority over the higher clergy, they also labored to centralize the liturgy of the Latin Church by making the Roman rite (that is, the liturgy of the diocese of Rome) normative for all of Christian Europe. This attempt at "restoring" the integrity of the Roman liturgy and purifying it of "Germanic" influences accompanied the bold new primatial claims of the reformed papacy. Moreover, the era of papal reform witnessed not only the estrangement of *regnum* (imperial power) and *sacerdotium* (priestly authority of the pope) in Christian Europe but also a schism between the Latin and Greek churches which was animated, in part, by the burgeoning theological claims of the popes regarding their authority over all Christian bishops. In the summer of 1054, the pope's legates and the patriarch of Constantinople excommunicated each other in a sad turn of events, presaging the intense conflicts that lay ahead for the reform party in Rome.

Gregory VII's extreme Petrine claims, as they relate to the ecclesio-political disputes in which he was embroiled, are well documented.[32] His political theories were clearly based on his literal reading of Matthew 16:18–24, in which Christ gives Peter the power to "bind and loose," a passage interpreted as giving Peter's successors in the papal office direct spiritual authority over all Christians. What is often overlooked is how Gregory VII's deep personal devotion to Saint Peter also fueled his desire to "reform" the liturgy of the Latin Church along purely Roman lines. The imposition of the liturgy of Saint Peter's see in every corner of the Western church was a logical extension of Gregory's theological claims for the primacy of the bishop of Rome over all dioceses of Christendom.[33]

Gregory VII lived, however, under the illusion that there was in fact some pristine Roman rite dating to the Latin patristic era that could be "restored" in the eleventh-century church. Modern liturgical scholarship has put to rest such claims and presents us with a far more diverse and complex story of the development of the liturgy of the Western church in the early Middle Ages. Gregory VII could not have known, for example, that the diocese of Rome itself had tolerated a variety of liturgical practices that existed side by side, even in the supposed halcyon days of this reform pope's hero, Gregory the Great (reigned 590–604). Nor could he have known an axiomatic principle of modern liturgical studies, that most of the liturgical texts of the early Middle Ages are anonymous compositions that were often misattributed to some great figure. For example, medieval liturgists believed that Gregory the Great, under the inspiration of the Holy Spirit—often depicted in medieval manuscripts as a dove perched on the pope's shoulder as he works—single-handedly composed a vast corpus of plainsong liturgical music which we still call "Gregorian chant."

This is not to say, however, that the early liturgy of Rome lacked any substantive norms. By the time of Gregory the Great's pontificate, the eucharistic liturgy celebrated by the pope himself in the "stational churches" of Rome had crystallized in the form of a *Sacramentarium* (also called a *Liber missalis*) or sacramentary. This book of prayers—which included the invariable canon of the mass—had no rubrics per se, and contained only the prayer texts for the various rites celebrated by the pope over the course of the entire year. The sacramentary would accompany the pope as he presided at each of the "stations" in his diocese, alternately celebrating the Sunday eucharistic liturgy from basilica to basilica, as a symbol of the unity of his flock. Other separate service books complemented the papal sacramentary: an antiphonary used by the *schola cantorum*, the choir that would chant liturgical antiphons during the mass; a *capitulare evangeliorum*, the book that contained the gospel lessons recited by the deacon (also called a lectionary); and *ordines romani*, booklets which described the exact procedures of liturgical celebrations, something like an instruction manual for a master of ceremonies.[34]

Even in the time of Gregory I, who is credited with putting the final touches to his own sacramentary, the so-called Gregorian Sacramentary—a task that was more likely completed by Honorius I (reigned 625–648)—we witness remarkable liturgical diversity in the Latin Church as a whole and in the diocese of Rome itself. Several early sacramentaries, some of which were erroneously attributed to Leo I (reigned 440–461) and Gelasius I (492–496)—the so-called Leonine and Gelasian sacramentaries—existed contemporaneously and were in fact used in the Latin Church at precisely the same time.[35] North of the Alps in the seventh and eighth centuries, we are confronted with an even more complex situation: native "Gallican" sacramentaries were mixed with "Roman" books to produce hybrid service books, such as the "Frankish Gelasian" sacramentaries of the eighth century.

As both Theodor Klauser and Cyrille Vogel have argued, it is impossible to speak of the "absolute unity" of the Roman liturgy in the seventh and eighth centuries in any canonical or juridical sense.[36] Gregory the Great used his own sacramentary, while the presbyters of the *tituli* or titular churches of his diocese (what would eventually become the autonomous "parish" churches of medieval Rome) continued to use their own *libelli missarum*, booklets with which they celebrated the eucharistic liturgy. Neither the pope nor his presbyters believed that a papal mass should be normative for the whole diocese of Rome, let alone for the entire Latin Church.

In fact, the first full-fledged attempts at imposing liturgical uniformity in Latin Christendom came not from popes but from the Frankish monarchs of the eighth and ninth centuries, principally Pepin III and his son Charlemagne.[37] Cyrille Vogel has conclusively shown that a sweeping liturgical renaissance and reform began with Pepin after he was crowned king of the Franks by Pope Stephen II (754).[38] The so-called Frankish-papal alliance manifested itself in Pepin's military defense of the "patrimony of Saint Peter" (later called the Papal States), and in Pepin's personal devotion to the see of Saint Peter and his successor, the pope.

Pepin had a passion, liturgically speaking, for all things "Roman." In reviving and reforming the church in his kingdom, he insisted on importing Roman exemplars of service books and imposing them unilaterally on all of his churches and monasteries. This proved logistically impossible, even under the best of circumstances, since not enough exemplars could be found, nor could enough copies be made for each of the churches of Carolingian Christendom. In fact, Pepin's reforms had the unintended effect of producing even *more* diversity as "Gregorian," "Gallican," and "Gelasian" sacramentaries interacted and produced new hybrids.

Charlemagne continued his father's attempts at fully "romanizing" the Frankish liturgy, with more measurable success. Aside from importing Roman clerics and having them teach the *cantus romanus* or Roman chant to his monks, the Frankish king took great pains to procure from the pope himself, Hadrian I (reigned 772–795), the most complete, "authentic" Gregorian sacramentary to serve as an exemplar for his copyists in his imperial capital of Aachen. In this respect, Charlemagne, like Gregory VII, also lived with the erroneous assumption that such a thing as a "pure" Gregorian sacramentary (without later accretions) actually existed in the papal curia. The coveted codex, called the *Hadrianum*, or the Gregorian sacramentary of Hadrian I, finally arrived around 785. It was a deluxe manuscript, but it was neither complete nor, as we now know, purely Gregorian. The gaps in the text were eventually filled in or supplemented during the reign of Charlemagne's son and successor, Louis the Pious (reigned 814–840). Between 810 and 814, the monastic reformer Benedict of Aniane, amended the Roman exemplar with the Gallican elements of the so-called Frankish Gelasians. The resulting additions are known collectively as the *Supplementum* (which until recently was wrongly attributed to Alcuin of York).[39] This sacramentary was widely used in Carolingian lands and represents a landmark in the evolution of medieval Latin liturgy. In his *General Admonition* (789), Charlemagne mandated that his bishops conform as closely as possible to the newly compiled codex; this decree facilitated the uniformity of liturgical prayer so ardently pursued by the Frankish kings.

With the promulgation of the *Hadrianum* and the *Supplementum* in Frankish lands, a tremendously fruitful period in liturgical history in the diocese of Rome came to an abrupt end. The popes of the tenth century were notorious for their lack of interest in liturgics, not to mention the questionable character of their morals. However, the dearth of liturgical activity in Rome ended by the turn of the millennium, thanks largely to two "foreign" influences: the spread of the Cluniac monastic customs, and the Ottonian renaissance of monastic life and the liturgy. With good cause, historians of the Latin liturgy refer to this as the period of Franco-German leadership, for it was in this era (c. 962–1050) that the rites and ceremonies of the church in Rome were overtaken by the Frankish and Germanic elements imported to Italy by Cluniac monks and the German emperors.[40] The intrinsic austerity of the Roman liturgy was suddenly overwhelmed by the dramatic, emotive elements of the Franco-German liturgies of the Ottonian court, first brought to the city of Rome when Otto I (reigned 936–972) arrived there for his imperial coronation in the winter of 962. To the liturgies of the sacred Triduum of Holy Week, for example, were added new, captivating ceremonies such as the Veneration of the Cross on Good Friday, and the dramatic elements associated with the Easter vigil (the singing of the Exsultet, and the lighting of fire). Thus the "Roman liturgy" had been restored in a distinctly Franco-Germanic form. One of the most palpable examples of this "restoration" was the *Franco-German Pontifical*. A pontifical is a "bishop's book" which provides instructions for the performance of liturgical rites reserved for a bishop; the *Franco-German Pontifical* (c. 950–962) was employed by the papal court down to the time of the Investiture Controversy.[41]

It was this Ottonian liturgy that Gregory VII sought to reform when he became pope. His reforms, strictly speaking, amounted to little more than the regulation of psalms and lessons in the liturgy of the hours; any sweeping changes would have created insurmountable problems, including the disintegration of the Roman liturgy. Gregory's efforts did lead, eventually, to the creation of a "reformed" pontifical for use in the Roman Curia, the so-called *Roman Pontifical of the Twelfth Century*.[42] Of greater significance was Gregory VII's demand that all episcopal sees of the Latin church strictly obey and adhere to the liturgical decrees of the pope, which set the stage for the final development of the medieval Latin liturgy. Within a century of Gregory VII's pontificate, the right of canonization of feasts would, for example, be reserved to the pope.

At a time when the Investiture Controversy had reached a dramatic crescendo, the pro-papal liturgist and canonist Bernold of Constance (1054–1100) produced an important treatise on the liturgy, the *Micrologus of Ecclesiastical Observances* (c. 1086–1100), which helped to promote this new papal liturgical hegemony.[43] Although the purpose of Bernold's liturgical commentary was not new, his method was. Beginning in the Carolingian era, principally with the lengthy commentaries of Amalarius of Metz (died 852/3), the genre of liturgical exposition had been dominated by an allegorical or figurative reading of the rites of the church. Bernold's concise treatise largely abandoned the florid allegories of Amalarius in favor of a "historical" interpretation of the development of the mass, the divine office, the church's fasts, and the calendar. That is, his rhetorical purpose was to champion the integrity and superiority of the Roman rite over Germanic or Gallican liturgies by embracing the newly developing science of canon law. Where previous monastic expositors had indulged in imaginative and sometimes obtuse allegorical interpretations, Bernold systematically marshaled papal decretals, patristic citations, and conciliar decrees from the early church to his own era to champion the cause of *romanitas* ("Romanness").

This "historical" approach produced, to his mind, sufficient evidence to support Gregory VII's objective of making the Latin liturgy more "Roman" and suppressing such indigenous rites as the Milanese, Armenian, and Visigothic. In fact, Bernold, more than Gregory VII, can be credited with centralizing the Roman mass in the late eleventh century. For example, his widely disseminated treatise caught the attention of a synod of Hungarian bishops around 1100, which decreed that Bernold's presentation of the mass (both the rubrics and prayer texts) would be the norm for celebration of the eucharist in the Hungarian Church.[44]

Within a half-century of Bernold's liturgical work, one of the finest collections of medieval canon law—and one of the most important books of the later Middle Ages—was produced by an enigmatic Italian monk named Gratian. Although it was never promulgated as an "official" code of law, his gargantuan *Decretum* (c. 1140) became the textbook par excellence for students of canon law all over Europe.[45] Gratian's work also did much to validate the juridical model of liturgical exposition first attempted by Bernold. The last portion of his collection in particular, the *De consecratione* (On consecrations)—which may or may not have been compiled by him—offered an exemplary and systematic organization of patristic, papal, and conciliar liturgical texts which could be consulted by future popes and liturgists in the continued quest to define and centralize the Roman liturgy. From the time of Gratian to the end of the thirteenth century, we witness the development of a complex and sophisticated system of sacramental and liturgical jurisprudence.[46]

Yet the final phase of the unification of the Roman liturgy in the Middle Ages had much less to do with the study of canon law than it did with the pressing business of the papal curia and the missionary activity of the mendicant friars, particularly the Franciscans, who adopted the liturgy of the papal court and transported it to every corner of Latin Christendom. By the early 1200s, the old monastic paradigm of spirituality had been eclipsed by the Scholasticism of the universities. The new mendicant orders existed in a symbiotic relationship with university culture, and they were prepared to meet the intellectual, social, and cultural challenges faced by the Latin Church at the beginning of a new century. Both the Franciscans and the Dominicans had close personal ties with the papal curia and eagerly became foot soldiers in the papacy's battle against the various heretical movements that threatened to undermine the hegemony of a papally governed church in Europe. The mendicants also remedied many of the spiritual frustrations of the laity with their dramatic preaching, the exemplary personal conduct of their clergy (principally their chastity and material poverty), and their work to spread a variety of popular devotional practices among laypeople (the rosary and the Stations of the Cross, for example).[47]

Because of their devotion to university education and preaching, the mendicants exhibited a tremendous degree of flexibility in their liturgical practices. Where the liturgical observances of the Cluniac monk consumed nearly every moment of his day—the liturgy was, in fact, the *sine qua non* of his existence—the friar was preoccupied with the *vita activa*, the "active life" of pastoral care and preaching. The mendicant friars and clergy of the papal court, including the pope himself, had a practical problem not faced by the cloistered monks: they had to "put in a day's work," and the liturgy could be seen, perhaps to overstate the case, as something that interrupted the work day. Such liturgical flexibility and brevity undoubtedly troubled some observers of the liturgical "reforms" (c. 1213–1216) of Pope Innocent III (reigned 1198–1216). One such critic, writing in the mid-thirteenth century, was Ralph van der Beke, the dean of Tongres cathedral in Belgium. His protestations, which really represent a minority view, are nonetheless illuminating because he provides a succinct and mostly accurate description of the thirteenth-century curial liturgy:

> [T]he clerics of the papal chapel always shortened and often altered (*semper breviabant et saepe alterabant*) the Office either by command of the pope or on their own initiative, according to the whim of pope and cardinals. In Rome I saw an ordinal of that Office. It was compiled in the days of Innocent III; and the Friars Minor [i.e., the Franciscans] follow this shortened Office. Hence they entitle their books as "according to the use of the Roman Curia."[48]

The books to which Ralph refers were the *Ordinal of the Papal Court* (c. 1213–1216),[49] which regulated the celebration of the mass and the divine office, and the *Pontifical of the Roman Curia*, begun by Innocent III and revised by Gregory IX (1227–1241) and Innocent IV (1243–1254).[50]

Yet despite the liturgical reforms of Innocent III and other thirteenth-century popes, and the development of a uniform breviary and "full" missal employed by the mendicants, a tremendous amount of liturgical diversity persisted in the monasteries, cathedrals, and parishes of Europe to the end of the Middle Ages. Uniformity, in the modern sense, became a reality in the Roman Catholic Church only when the printing press could codify and effectively impose what Klauser terms the rigid rubricism of the Counter-Reformation papacy and its Congregation of Rites.[51]

William Durandus of Mende (c. 1230–1296), undoubtedly the best known and most widely read liturgical expositor of the late Middle Ages, composed his *Rationale for the Divine Offices* (c. 1292–1296) at the close of the very century that saw the widespread dissemination of the liturgy of the papal court. Durandus himself was a curial official—he had been a papal chaplain, no less—but in his magisterial commentary on the rites of the Church he underscored the liturgical pluralism and diversity that still prevailed throughout Latin Christendom at the end of the Middle Ages:

> The reader should not be disturbed if he reads about things in this work which he has not found to be observed in his own particular church, or if he does not find something that is observed there. For we shall not proceed to discuss the peculiar observances of any particular place but the rites that are common and more usual, since we have labored to set forth a universal teaching and not one of particular bearing, nor would it be possible for us to examine thoroughly the peculiar observances of all places.[52]

Eucharistic Controversies and Devotions

The theological battles of the Investiture Controversy ensured that the mass would no longer be viewed as a congregational celebration of presbyter and people. It was now largely conceived as a theatrical performance of the ordained, within the confines of a sacred space, the sanctuary, accessible only to the clerical *ordo*. In the early Roman mass, however, the liturgy was a dialogue between the presider and the people; the canon was recited out loud by the bishop or presbyter, who faced his congregation so that everyone could hear it and thus participate in the eucharistic liturgy. Eventually the canon, with its awesome "words of consecration," was recited inaudibly by the bishop or priest out of reverence for the sacred words, as if they were formulae from an arcane discipline. Throughout the Middle Ages, the liturgy came more and more to be defined as a clerical prerogative, with the priest standing *in persona Christi* at the altar as he offered the daily sacrifice of the mass. Passive onlookers, who no longer participated in the celebration, except perhaps for moments of private devotion, viewed the priest from a distance.[53]

Despite centuries of development and marked change, the nucleus of the medieval mass remained the ritual reenactment of the Last Supper, or the eucharistic prayer. In a formula harmonized from Saint Jerome's Vulgate translation of the Synoptic Gospels (Matt. 26:26–29, Mark 14:22–25, Luke 22:19–20), the "words of consecration" uttered by Christ at the Last Supper would be recited by a bishop or priest when he prayed over the bread and wine: *Hoc est enim corpus meum*, "This is my body"; *Hic est calix sanguinis mei*, "This is the cup of my blood."[54]

That Christ was miraculously present in the eucharistic elements—the doctrine of the "real presence"— was a truism for the patristic church. Precisely *how* that presence occurred or how it could be described was a *mysterion*, a sacred mystery that defied, at least for early Christian theology, the precise categories of natural philosophy. In the Latin tradition, Saint Augustine of Hippo (354–430) shied away from technical or empirical definitions of the real presence. In his *Commentary on Saint John's Gospel*, for example, he declares: "Believe, so that you may eat the Body of Christ."[55] The implication was that Christ's presence in the eucharistic bread could be grasped only by a faithful recipient. Still, for a variety of reasons, from the mid-eighth century to the early fourteenth, Latin theologians struggled mightily to define, both qualitatively and quantitatively, one of the core mysteries of the Christian belief system. In the process of debating the real presence, the medieval Latin Church soon discovered the limitations, even poverty, of its theological vocabulary. Even when invoking Latin patristic authorities, both monastic and scholastic theologians discovered that key theological terms often lacked the stability and uniform definition demanded by later theological controversies. It was increasingly clear that the Church Fathers, most notably Saint Ambrose (c. 339–397) and Saint Augustine, could be interpreted as having substantially different conceptions of the presence of Christ in the eucharistic bread and wine.

The earliest medieval debates on the sacrament of the altar come from the Carolingian era.[56] Despite the eloquence of its Latin, the beauty of its illuminated manuscripts, the vitality of its monasteries, and the theocratic rule of its monarchs, the Frankish Church of the eighth and ninth centuries was, to a considerable extent, a missionary or frontier church. Masses of ignorant peasants who continued to indulge in blatantly pagan practices and recent converts to Christianity (most notably the Saxons) presented the Carolingian church with herculean tasks in the realm of pastoral care. Seemingly simple questions of ritual purity (e.g., could a menstruating woman receive communion?) could and did evolve into complex questions about the nature of the sacrament itself. Moreover, to an unlettered mind, the priest's act of turning ordinary objects into Christ's body and blood could easily be perceived as a magical feat of shamanism, particularly since the "words of consecration" were recited *sotto voce* in a foreign tongue. It was within this milieu—a missionary church training monastic clergy to evangelize and indoctrinate illiterate barbarians—that Carolingian writers produced the first treatises on eucharistic theology.

One such writer, who was not a theologian in the strictest sense, was the Carolingian bishop Amalarius of Metz (c. 775/780–852/853). The first medieval Latin expositor of the entire liturgy, he wrote extended commentaries on the mass, the divine office, the church year, and the ordination of clergy.[57] Amalarius dealt with the problem of eucharistic theology through allegorical interpretation of the various parts of the mass, including the eucharistic prayer. Rather than attempting to use a grammatical approach to explicating the words of consecration, Amalarius contented himself, in his expositions of the mass, with elaborate allegories which linked its prayer texts and ceremonial to events in salvation history in a dramatic, almost theatrical manner.

When addressing the eucharist itself, Amalarius was on shaky ground theologically. His adversaries Agobard and Florus of Lyons secured his condemnation at the Synod of Quiercy (838) for some of his allegorical interpretations of the mass. His discussion of the "fraction rite," or the tripartite breaking of the host, contained in his short exposition written in 821, attempted to relate the pieces of the host to the "triform body of Christ." That these pieces of the host correspond to Christ's historical body, the Church militant, and the deceased faithful was expressly condemned as heretical by the synod, since it divided the one body of the Lord into three bodies. This did nothing, however, to diminish either the popularity of Amalarius's works or of the allegorical approach to liturgical theology, which continued unabated to the end of the Middle Ages.

A contemporary of the controversial Carolingian liturgist took a distinctly different approach to understanding the eucharist. Paschasius Radbertus (c. 785–860), abbot of the monastery of Corbie (842–847), is credited with provoking the first medieval "eucharistic controversy," properly speaking, when he composed his *Treatise on the Body and Blood of the Lord* (c. 831–833; revised 843–844).[58] Unlike Amalarius, who resorted to speculative allegories, Paschasius attempted a more formal or systematic theology of the eucharist, taking a grammatical approach to the problem of real presence. Here he had as his guide Saint Ambrose, whose writings display a concretizing impulse in stressing the historical reality of Christ's body and blood in the consecrated bread and wine. Christ's words "This is my body" required no abstract speculation; he was, in fact, really offering his body to his disciples, in sacramental form; however, later writers, including Paschasius, took extreme positions which are not entirely in conformity with Ambrose's views. Paschasius also emphasized the sacrificial character of the mass: it was not simply a remembrance or recollection of a past event, but a *reenactment* of the sacrifice of Christ at Calvary every time a priest celebrated the eucharist. This emphatic sacrificial language has a clear antecedent in the writings of the last Latin Church Father, Pope Gregory the Great, who spoke of the daily "sacrifice of the saving victim" (*hostiam salutarem immolare*).[59]

Scarcely a decade had passed before Paschasius's eucharistic theology came under sharp criticism from various well-known Carolingian authors, including Ratramnus (died 868), a monk in Paschasius's own abbey of Corbie. In his own treatise on the eucharist, *On the Body and Blood of the Lord*,[60] which he composed at the request of the Carolingian emperor Charles the Bald, Ratramnus attacked (perhaps unfairly) what he perceived to be the crass realism of Paschasius's conception of the eucharist. Implicit in his attack was a demonstration of how his abbot Paschasius contradicted Saint Augustine's theology of the sacraments.

In the *City of God*, Augustine offered what became for the medieval church a textbook definition of the term "sacrament": "A sacrament is an invisible grace in a visible form."[61] When applying such language to eucharistic theology, Augustine had been careful to distinguish between the eucharistic bread as the "thing itself" (*res ipsa*) and the body of Christ as the "thing symbolized" (*sacramentum* or *signum*). This nuanced conception is comparable to the Platonic notion of the "participation" of visible things in the invisible realm of Ideas or Forms. Augustine's position undoubtedly posed major challenges for later theologians because his eucharistic theology was neither strictly materialistic (claiming that a particular piece of bread is the historical body of Christ) nor strictly symbolic or figurative (claiming the bread remains bread after the eucharistic prayer). Moreover, the fact that Augustine left no extended treatment of the eucharist in his voluminous corpus of works compounded the problem of reconciling his disparate references to the sacraments and the eucharist, scattered as they are across a wide range of treatises, sermons, and letters.

Still, Paschasius's concrete equation of the historical body of Christ with the eucharistic host threatened to overturn the Augustinian paradigm of sacramental theology. Ratramnus himself returned to a mystagogical interpretation by comparing Christ's real presence in the communion bread and wine to the presence of the Holy Spirit in the waters of baptism. It was repugnant and erroneous to speak of bones and flesh on the altar in any physical sense; to speak of Christ's presence in bread and wine, then, is to emphasize the reality of the *spiritual* presence of the resurrected Christ, in a figural or a symbolic sense. Ironically, Ratramnus's treatise, with its radically Augustinian approach to sacramental theology, was condemned at the Synod of Vercelli in 1050, where it was wrongly attributed to the heterodox Neoplatonist philosopher John Scotus Eriugena (c. 810–877).

The Carolingian eucharistic controversy, which ended within a generation of its inception, was limited to a relatively small number of antagonists and was over almost as soon as it had begun. In fact, "controversy" may be too strong a term, since it largely amounted to an in-house debate among a handful of monks at Corbie. The dispute was important, however, in demonstrating the diversity of thinking not only in the Carolingian Church but also among the Church Fathers themselves on so central a Christian doctrine. It revealed, too, some of the inherent weaknesses of the Latin language when it attempted to settle matters which seemed beyond its grasp (a problem that would supposedly be solved by scholastic theologians with numerous neologisms). Finally, the controversy displayed the limitations of Carolingian theology, even in the heyday of a "renaissance." Though it figured prominently as one of the seven liberal arts, dialectic (or formal logic) scarcely had been brought to bear in any developed or systematic manner to the formulation of Christian dogma.

The next medieval eucharistic controversy erupted in the politically charged environment of the monastic-papal reform of the eleventh century. In 1049, Berengar of Tours (999–1088) quite deliberately revived the controversial views of Ratramnus, whose treatise on the eucharist was now assumed to have been written by the Carolingian philosopher Eriugena. This was the opening salvo in a bitter theological battle that would span virtually the entire period of the Investiture Controversy. In resurrecting the views of Ratramnus, Berengar attempted to remain faithful, as he understood it, to the Augustinian tradition of eucharistic theology by maintaining a distinction between the sacramental power (*virtus*) of the consecrated bread and the sensible presence of the historical body of Christ. He lambasted as ridiculous the proposition that the physical body of Christ was replicated in bits and pieces in scattered churches throughout the world. His critique of Paschasian eucharistic theology once more brought into sharp relief the two seemingly contradictory traditions of eucharistic theology in the West, one Ambrosian and the other Augustinian. The eucharistic controversy of the eleventh century was as much a battle over the correct exegesis of proof texts from the Latin Fathers as it was a fight over the theology of the real presence.

Berengar's opponents seized upon his figural language as amounting to an outright denial of the real presence of Christ in the sacrament of the altar—this at a time when Cluniac conceptions of the monastic priesthood and the efficacy of masses for the dead had taken root. Among his many critics were the monks of the Norman monastery of Bec, one of whom in particular led a spirited and successful assault on his works: Lanfranc (c. 1010–1089), the future archbishop of Canterbury. His own treatise, *On the Body and Blood of the Lord, against Berengar of Tours* (c. 1063),[62] was the most nuanced and sophisticated rebuttal of Berengar produced by his enemies; it also offers us the only surviving fragments of Berengar's original work on the eucharist. In a scathing critique, Lanfranc systematically refuted Berengar's exegesis of Augustine. Moreover, Lanfranc proposed a return to Paschasius's interpretation of Ambrose's theology of the eucharist, equating it with the "natural" body of the resurrected Christ. This was a "glorified body," no doubt, but a historical body nonetheless: "The sacrament of the body of Christ . . . is his flesh, which exists in the form of bread."[63]

Aside from being a passionate polemicist, Lanfranc made a positive step in the direction of developing a "scholastic" theology of the eucharist, employing the tools of dialectic when he attempted to distinguish the "substance" of the consecrated bread (the body of Christ) and the physical qualities of the bread, or its outward appearance: it is "changed incomprehensibly and ineffably into the substance of [Christ's] flesh and blood."[64] Here we see, perhaps in embryonic form, a theory of transubstantiation.

Even before Lanfranc's attack on his theology, Berengar had been condemned *in absentia* on two separate occasions by church synods. He was eventually forced at the Synod of Rome (1059) to make a profession of faith—crafted by the papal reformer cardinal Humbert of Silva Candida—which not only repudiated his extreme Augustinianism but also required him to embrace the most grotesque understanding of Christ's "somatic" or bodily presence in the consecrated host:

> I agree with the Holy Roman Church and the Apostolic See, and in my heart and in my words profess that I have the same belief concerning the sacrament of the Lord's table that my lord the venerable Nicholas and this holy synod have, that by evangelical and apostolic authority they have commanded me to hold: that the bread and wine placed on the altar are, after consecration, not only a sacrament but also the true body and blood of our Lord Jesus Christ; that they are truly and physically handled and broken by the priest, not just sacramentally, and are ground by the teeth of the faithful.[65]

Not surprisingly, Berengar soon disavowed this oath, which, given the circumstances, was of questionable validity. Yet this very oath found its way into one of the most important collections of medieval canon law, the *Decretum* of Gratian. Despite his best efforts to clarify his position, including a point-by-point rebuttal of Lanfranc, some twenty years later Berengar was once again compelled at a Roman synod (1079), this time by Gregory VII, to take another oath affirming his belief in the real presence. This oath, however, abandoned the extremism of the previous one, substituting a far more nuanced description of Christ's presence in the sacrament of the altar. What had previously amounted to the "bodily" presence of Christ now came to be defined as his "substantial" presence in the bread and wine.[66] Although the acrimony and polemical attacks on Berengar abated with the end of the Investiture Controversy, the debate on eucharistic theology would engage some of the best minds in Latin Christendom during the next two centuries.

The Renaissance of the twelfth century, with its revival of Roman jurisprudence, its systematic study of canon law, and the initial recovery of portions of Aristotle's treatises on logic, allowed the theologians of the Latin Church to take a quantum leap in the history of sacramental theology. A new scholastic method of "question, disputation, solution" and a new scholastic theological vocabulary could be brought to bear on some of the central mysteries of the Christian faith, including the theology of the eucharist. The greatest contribution of twelfth-century theology to this discussion was a scholastic neologism that originated in the Parisian schools: "transubstantiation."[67] This term was an attempt by early scholastic theologians to employ Aristotelian language when explaining the miraculous change of bread into the body of Christ, even as the material object of bread retained its outward physical appearance and qualities. According to their conception, the "accidents" (perceptible qualities) of bread were unchanged before and after its consecration, but its "substance" or essence was "transformed" into the body of Christ through a miracle that could not be observed in any physical sense. The term "transubstantiation" gained immediate popularity and was regularly employed not only by theologians but also by liturgical expositors, even though there were diverse and often contradictory opinions over its precise meaning.

Yet at the turn of the thirteenth century, when the Latin Church offered a dogmatic proclamation of what Roman Catholics must believe about the presence of Christ in the eucharist, it employed this scholastic neologism. The Fourth Lateran Council (1215) employed the term to "settle" thorny theological debates about the mystery of the real presence and to counter the heterodox beliefs of the Cathars or Albigensians, who denied the validity of priestly ministry and any sort of real presence in the sacraments. The council declared:

> There is truly one universal Church of the faithful, outside of which no one can be saved; in this Church Jesus Christ is the priest and sacrifice, whose Body and Blood are truly contained in the sacrament of the altar under the appearance of bread and wine, with the bread transubstantiated into his Body and wine into his Blood by divine power.[68]

Even in the face of a conciliar decree promulgated by a pope of Innocent III's stature, theologians continued to disagree about the precise meaning of the term "transubstantiation," since the terms "substance" and "accidents" were still open to a variety of philosophical interpretations. But the Latin theologians' penchant for precision was animated and tremendously enriched by the reception, in the university milieu, of the full Aristotelian corpus in Latin translation. Natural philosophy could now become the handmaiden of systematic Christian theology, moving the discussion to a level that Carolingian theologians scarcely could have imagined.

Thomas Aquinas, Dominican priest and Parisian master, made a significant contribution to the discussion of the meaning of transubstantiation in the third part of his *Summa Theologiae* (c. 1272–1273). There Aquinas offered a much more systematic and philosophically refined definition of transubstantiation than anything put forth by Innocent III or Lateran IV. He argued that immediately after the words of consecration, the substance of bread and wine cease to exist, miraculously replaced by the substance of the body and blood of Christ, which is imperceptible to the physical senses, since men would be revolted by the prospect of consuming real flesh and blood.[69]

Still, the scholastic method of defining and discussing eucharistic theology was accompanied by some absurdities, which eventually became the locus of scorn and derision on the part of the Christian humanists of the Renaissance and Reformation eras. Pope Innocent III himself, writing before he was elected pope, pondered at some length the precise meaning of the term "transubstantiation" in his well-known treatise *On the Mysteries of the Mass* (c. 1195).[70] In the context of that discussion he wondered openly what became of a consecrated host when, if by chance, a mouse consumed it. He concluded that the body of Christ miraculously ceased to exist in the transubstantiated bread as soon as the mouse nibbled it. Such trifles were unfairly invoked by humanist scholars to invalidate all of medieval Scholasticism.

Leaving aside its relative strengths and weaknesses, scholastic theology helped to facilitate the divorce of the eucharist from its patristic roots. Generally speaking, both the Greek and Latin fathers had defined the eucharist as an act of both thanksgiving and communion. Augustine, for example, linked the sacramental mystery of the eucharist to the incorporation of individual believers, through their faith in the sacrament, into the mystical body of Christ, symbolized also by the ecclesial community. Thus, when Augustine presided at the eucharistic liturgy, men and women of his congregation brought their own bread and wine to the celebration which they placed on the altar. They would receive their bread and wine after it had been consecrated by their bishop, stressing the unity of the Christian community and the active participation of its members in the celebration of the Christian mysteries.

By the end of the Middle Ages, however, the eucharist had been reduced to an *object*, the eucharistic host consecrated by the hands of a properly ordained priest. The late twelfth century practice of elevating the host at the moment of consecration—which first appeared in northern France at the close of that century—was the logical outcome of this reification of the eucharist into a sacred object or relic par excellence of Christ's body, to be seen, reverenced, and adored but not regularly received at communion. Even as it produced a dogmatic declaration of eucharistic theology, the Fourth Lateran Council required reception of communion only once per year. The Feast of Corpus Christi (made universal throughout the church in 1264), with its paraliturgical processions of a consecrated host in a sealed monstrance, paraded through streets and villages, is an even more extreme case of treating the eucharist as both a relic and a talisman. For a great majority of the laity, "seeing" the host had become an acceptable substitute for "receiving" it.

On a more popular level, the high eucharistic theology of the later Middle Ages was propelled by the intense personal devotion of some of the mendicants, principally Francis of Assisi (1182–1226), and a number of female mystics, among whom Catherine of Siena (c. 1347–1380) figures prominently. In his final words to the Order of Friars Minor, the so-called *Testament*, Saint Francis underscores the centrality of his devotion to the eucharist to his christocentric piety:

> [I] desire to fear, love and honor them [priests] and all others as my masters. And I do not wish to consider sin in them because I discern the Son of God in them and they are my masters. And I act in this way since I see nothing corporally of the Most High Son of God in this world except His Most Holy Body and Blood which they receive and which they alone administer to others. And these most holy mysteries I wish to have honored above all things and to be reverenced and to have them reserved in precious places.[71]

The intense devotionalism of individual saints and mystics was rooted not in any elaborate scholastic system but rather in the idiosyncrasies of a handful of figures who played tremendously important roles in the formation of late medieval Christian spirituality. Devotion to the eucharistic presence of Christ worked in tandem with a spirituality in which the sufferings of the crucified Christ seemed to overwhelm all other themes in Christian piety. Christ's wounds, and particularly the effusion of his blood, became common themes in the art, poetry, and music of late medieval Christianity. For example, the famed eucharistic hymn *Adoro te devote*, at-

Miracle of the host. At the elevation of the host, the body of Christ (*corpus Christi* or *corpus Domini*) appears in place of the consecrated bread. Mural (c. 1357–1364) by Ugolino di Prete Ilario in the Chapel of the Corporal in the cathedral of Orvieto, Italy.
CATHEDRAL OF ORVIETO, ITALY/DAGLI ORTI/THE ART ARCHIVE

Durandus's definition of allegory is not only faithful to patristic biblical hermeneutics but also encapsulates the whole Amalarian approach to liturgical exposition,
which is the *sine qua non* of Durandus's mammoth treatise (as well as the overwhelming majority of medieval liturgical expositions):

> Allegory is present when what is said literally has another meaning spiritually; for ex-
> ample, when one word or deed brings to mind another. If what is said is visible, then it is
> simply an allegory; if it is invisible and celestial, then it is called anagogy. Allegory also
> exists when an unrelated state of affairs is shown to exist through the use of strange or
> alien expressions; for example when the presence of Christ or the sacraments of the
> Church are signified in mystical words or signs: [when Isaiah says] *A branch shall come
> forth from the root of Jesse* [Isa. 11:1], by which he clearly means: "The Virgin Mary shall
> be born of the stock of David, who was the son of Jesse." Mystical deeds can signify in
> the same fashion the freedom of the people of Israel from Egyptian slavery by the blood
> of the [paschal] lamb, which signifies the Church snatched away from the clutches of the
> devil through the passion of Christ.[85]

For Amalarius and his heir, Durandus of Mende, the proper celebration of the
liturgy was not simply the correct recitation of set texts. It involved a keen understanding of how the daily liturgies, both the mass and the divine office, work in concert to present a dramatic, "iconographic" representation of the key events of "salvation
history" in much the same way that liturgical time and its distinct seasons are emblematic of this sacred time-scheme. The mass, in particular, functioned as an iconographic set of "portraits" or reenactments of key events in the economy of salvation.
In his *Exposition of the Mass* (c. 813–814), Amalarius outlined the mass liturgy in bold
typological strokes. For example, the Introit or opening prayer symbolizes the Old
Testament prophets who predicted Christ's coming; the Kyrie or "Lord have mercy"
represents John the Baptist's proclaiming Christ's advent; the Gloria in Excelsis or
"Glory to God in the highest" refers to the company of angels who brought tidings of
great joy to the shepherds watching their sheep.[86] The deacons who stand behind the
priest at the altar during the celebration of the mass represent the apostles who were
hiding in fear during Christ's passion; the subdeacons on the opposite side of the altar
figuratively represent the holy women who stood at the foot of the cross, and so on.[87]

Amalarius's commentaries on the divine office (the seven canonical hours of prayer
celebrated by medieval monks and secular clergy) also provide eloquent testimony to
his ability to explicate otherwise obscure liturgical texts by demonstrating how they fit
within the broader theological framework of salvation history. His crowning achievement in this regard is his *Book on the Order of the Antiphons*, which consists of eighty
chapters dealing with the night and day offices and the antiphons sung during Lent and
special feasts. In the following passage, Amalarius offers an allegorical interpretation of
the arrangement of the twelve psalms of the first nocturn of the night office on Sunday:

> After this antiphon [Ps. 95:1], twelve Psalms are sung before the lessons and responses;
> this twelvefold number contains within itself the totality of all time and creation. In the
> twelve Psalms the clergy are inspired by the memory of the holy fathers who cultivated
> the vineyard of the Lord before the Law. Those who hasten to the night Office are
> instructed by this number to remember that from the beginning of the world, the Lord
> has had preachers in his Church who tended to the people of God through their labors,
> so that they might gain their reward in their heavenly homeland through the resurrec-
> tion of Christ. The first Psalm, *Happy is the man* [Ps. 1:1], in a sense celebrates the just
> man Abel whose blood was shed as a type of Christ's. The Psalm, *In you, O Lord, have I
> trusted* [Ps. 7:1], celebrates Noah and his sons and their wives who were saved during the

flood; and the Psalm, *Save me, O Lord, for there are none who are holy* [Ps. 11:2], refers to Abraham, who alone resisted the adoration of idols while others fell down before them.[88]

As we have already seen, Amalarius's foray into the realm of eucharistic theology showed the limits of his methods, though it gained him notoriety. His adversaries Agobard and Florus of Lyons produced polemical treatises savaging his allegorical approach to the liturgy. At the Synod of Quiercy (838), in the midst of a protracted dispute over Amalarius's episcopal appointment, they secured a formal condemnation of heresy for Amalarius's allegorical interpretation of the fraction rite. Remarkably, this sentence—which was more politically than theologically motivated—did nothing to diminish the popularity of his works, which continued to be copied in manuscript form well into the twelfth century. More importantly, the exegetical method Amalarius introduced dominated the landscape of formal liturgical exposition down to the end of the Middle Ages. In fact, the succeeding centuries of medieval liturgical exposition can be seen, with a few interruptions, as an elaboration and refinement of the Amalarian tradition.

With the collapse of the Carolingian empire came a sudden disappearance of new commentaries on the liturgy. Although the Ottonian age witnessed significant religious and liturgical reforms, it was not until the era of the Investiture Controversy, some two hundred years after the death of Amalarius, that full-scale liturgical commentaries were generated once more, this time with some notable differences. For example, Bernold of Constance's *Micrologus of Ecclesiastical Observances* (c. 1086–1100)[89] offered an approach to liturgical exposition startlingly different from the allegorical tradition. Written when the polemical debates over lay investiture had reached a dramatic crescendo, this treatise took a historical-canonical approach to explaining the form and content of the mass and the church calendar. Bernold's purpose was itself polemical; he attempted, by marshalling an impressive display of canonical sources, to argue for the supremacy of the liturgy of the diocese of Rome over other indigenous rites (e.g., Visigothic, Milanese, Armenian). Whereas Amalarius had exercised his creative capacities by creating marvelous allegories, Bernold invoked the historical authority of papal decrees and the canons of church councils and regional synods in his analysis of the divine rites.

As the ferocious polemics of the Investiture Controversy began to diminish, Bernold's historical and canonical method was largely abandoned when monastic commentators such as Rupert of Deutz (c. 1075–1129) and Honorius of Autun (c. 1075/1080–1156) reworked the Amalarian corpus and proposed even more typological readings of the liturgy for the moral exhortation of a predominantly monastic audience. Despite the increasing importance of the liturgy in the era of monastic-papal reform, Rupert's *Book on the Divine Offices* (c. 1111/1112)[90] was really the first full-scale allegorical exposition of the entire liturgy since the works of Amalarius began to circulate. Among its copious and elaborate allegories, it is difficult to find any trace of the polemics of the era of papal and monastic reform. Written a short time later by a prolific and equally enigmatic cleric named Honorius Augustudonensis (who was not, despite his nickname, from Autun), the *Spiritual Gems* (c. 1130)[91] repackaged and refined the Amalarian tradition in encyclopedic form, adding even more allegorical interpretations of the liturgy as iconographic portraits linked symbolically to key events in the life of Christ. Soon another succinct allegorical exposition began to circulate in France, which was erroneously attributed the well-known spiritual master Hugh of Saint Victor. This treatise, *The Mirror of Church Mysteries* (c. 1160–1165),[92] survives in scores of medieval manuscripts and had a huge impact on succeeding commentators

Baptismal font. Saint Mary's Church, Rostock, Germany. © Courtauld Institute of Art, London/Conway Collections

because of its lucid yet concise presentation of Amalarian interpretations of the mass, the divine office, and clerical ordination rites.

It is not until the anonymous publication of the *Liber Quare*[93] (the Book of Why [we celebrate]) in the early twelfth century that we detect the first hints of Scholasticism in liturgical exposition. This has much more to do with the rhetorical structure of the text—with its scholastic question-and-answer format—than it does with the actual content of the work, which is clearly derived from Amalarius's expositions. John Beleth's *Summa of the Ecclesiastical Offices* (c. 1160–1164),[94] which soon followed the *Liber Quare*, was the first major liturgical exposition, per se, to bear the scholastic title of "Summa." Yet the title of this grand treatise is misleading if we expect a historical or dialectical approach to explicating the liturgy. True, Beleth demonstrated a considerable knowledge of canon law, used a scholastic rhetorical structure, and introduced scholastic terminology (namely transubstantiation) to his discussion of the eucharist. But his long treatise stands squarely within the Amalarian tradition of allegorical liturgical commentary.

It is quite remarkable, then, that the "monastic" allegorical methods of liturgical exposition not only survived but flourished in the age of Scholasticism (c. 1100–1300). While it is true that some liturgical commentaries came structurally to resemble the plan and format of the theological *Summae* of the scholastic era, by and large the basic description and explication of the liturgical texts and ceremonies of the church remained predominantly figurative or allegorical.

From the late twelfth century to the mid-thirteenth the number of scholastic commentators increased dramatically; the overall length of their treatises also increased proportionately. Among the most important of these authors were the canon lawyer Sicard of Cremona (c. 1150–1215),[95] Pope Innocent III (c. 1160–1216),[96] and the Parisian master of theology William of Auxerre (c. 1150–1231).[97] Much of what they say about the liturgy can be traced back to Amalarius or other allegorists who relied on him (Rupert, Honorius, and Pseudo-Hugh of Saint Victor). Although Sicard, Innocent III, and William of Auxerre all employed scholastic terminology in their discussion of the real presence, including the term transubstantiation, they broke little new ground in their overall approach to liturgical exposition.

The best-known allegorical exposition of the entire Middle Ages was produced in the heyday of Scholasticism: the *Rationale for the Divine Offices* of William Durandus, bishop of Mende. Because of the success of his liturgical exposition, not to mention the production of his famous *Pontifical*,[98] which superseded the previous pontificals of the Roman Curia, Durandus is arguably the best-known Latin liturgist from the entire medieval period. After receiving a doctorate in canon law from the University of Bologna, he soon produced a number of works in both law and liturgy, including his *Pontifical*, or "bishop's book," which regulated liturgical rites reserved to a bishop. Durandus's best-known work, however, was his mammoth exposition of the liturgy, which he composed in two recensions after he became bishop of the diocese of Mende in Provence.

The *Rationale*, which survives in hundreds of medieval manuscripts, was undoubtedly popular because of its scope and its synthetic or encyclopedic quality (the modern critical edition of the complete text numbers close to 1700 pages). Durandus himself noted that he was a "compiler" of previous works, likening himself to a honeybee that gathered what he deemed useful from other commentaries. The full commentary is divided into eight separate books which treat a wide range of subjects: (1) the symbolism of the church building, (2) the clerical orders, (3) the symbolism of clerical vestments, (4) the mass, (5) the divine office, (6) the temporal cycle, (7) the sanctoral cycle, and (8) the *computus* and calendrical sciences.

Because of the depth and breadth of his treatise, Durandus's allegorical commentary immediately became *the* definitive work in the field of liturgics. The famed nineteenth-century liturgist and restorer of the monastery of Solesmes, Dom Prosper Guéranger, thus declared with good cause that Durandus's treatise can be "considered the final word from the Middle Ages on the mystery of divine worship."[99]

This "final word" is allegorical. The *Rationale* opens with a lengthy excursus on how the enigmatic arrangement of the divine rites figuratively reflects a higher order of things that can be unveiled only by the most "diligent examiner":

> All things associated with the services, furnishings and vestments of the Church are full of signs and symbols of the divine, and they all overflow with a celestial sweetness when they are scrutinized by a diligent observer who can extract *honey from rock and oil from the stoniest ground* [Deut. 32:13]. Who knows *the order of the heavens and can apply its rules to the earth* [Job 38:33]? Certainly, he who would attempt to investigate the majesty of heaven would be overcome by its glory. It is, in fact, a deep well from which I cannot drink [cf. John 4:11], unless he who *gives all things abundantly and does not reproach us* [Jas. 1:5] provides me with a vessel *so that I can drink with joy from the fountains of the Savior* [Isa. 12:3] *which flow between the mountains* [Ps. 103:10]. A reason cannot always be given for everything which has been handed down to us by our predecessors . . . therefore, I, William, Bishop of the holy church of Mende by the indulgence of God alone, knocking at the door, will continue to knock, until the key of David deigns to open it for me [cf. Rev. 3:20], so that the *king might bring me into his cellar where he stores his wine* [Cant. 2:4]. Here the celestial model which was shown to Moses on the mountaintop will be revealed to me [cf. Ex. 20], so that I can unveil and explain clearly and openly each furnishing or ornament which pertains to the ecclesiastical services, what each of these signifies or represents figuratively and to set forth their rationale, according to that which has been revealed to me by Him *who makes the tongues of infants speak eloquently* [Wis. 10:21], *whose Spirit blows where it wishes* [John 3:8], and *gives to each one as it deserves* [1 Cor. 12:11], to the praise and glory of the Trinity.[100]

Liturgical Performance

In his classic study of medieval monastic culture, *The Love of Learning and the Desire for God*, Jean Leclercq describes the sacred liturgy as both the "stimulus" and "outcome" of medieval monastic life:

The liturgy is at once the mirror of a culture and its culmination. Just as the Office of Corpus Christi, in the composition of which St. Thomas surely participated, crowns his doctrinal work, so the hymns, sequences, and innumerable poems written by the monks are the culmination of their theology. . . . In the liturgy, grammar was elevated to the rank of an eschatological fact. It participated in the eternal praise that the monks, in unison with the angels, began offering God in the abbey choir, and will be perpetuated in Heaven. In the liturgy, the love of learning and the desire for God find perfect reconciliation.[101]

Leclercq's dictum can be expanded well beyond the monks of the early Middle Ages to include the musicians, artists, and dramatists of the scholastic centuries, for whom the liturgy remained a continual source of inspiration and artistic challenge [see color plates 9–14].

One of the most noteworthy and aesthetically enduring legacies of the monastic centuries was the gargantuan corpus of Latin chants composed by monks for the celebration of the mass and the divine office.[102] For medieval monks and clerics, to pray was, in effect, to chant or sing the various parts of the liturgy. No less an authority than Saint Augustine was invoked by medieval authors to elevate chant to the highest form of divine praise when they attributed to him a pseudonymous saying, *Qui bene cantat, bis orat*—"He who sings well prays twice."

The Carolingian renaissance, with its ambitious program of monastic liturgical renewal, was accompanied by a reform and systematization of handwriting. This script, the so-called Carolingian minuscule, helped to facilitate the evolution of musical notation and allowed for a far greater degree of stability in the transmission of manuscripts from one monastery to another and from one generation of monks to the next. Monks no longer relied solely on memorization and the oral transmission of liturgical music. However, the modern musicologist faces the daunting task of comprehending exactly how medieval chant was sung, since the precise meaning of the notations that accompany early medieval manuscript texts is subject to a variety of interpretations (involving principally pitch and rhythm). The earliest musical manuscripts with clearly transcribable notations date no earlier than the eleventh century. Scattered references in theoretical treatises and isolated fragments of musical manuscripts—some of which date from many centuries later—offer us inconclusive evidence for the precise reconstruction of early medieval chant. Until quite recently, most modern performances of medieval chant have relied on the reconstructions of the French abbey of Saint-Pierre, the so-called Solesmes system of rhythm and accentuation of Dom

Monks in choir. Illuminated initial from a late fourteenth- or early fifteenth-century manuscript. SANTA CROCE, FLORENCE, ITALY, CODEX A, FOLIO 131 VERSO/SCALA/ ART RESOURCE, NY

Mocquereau (1849–1930), which may or may not bear any resemblance to how medieval chant was actually performed.[103]

Medieval liturgists themselves often labored to explain the origins of many of their liturgical customs and texts. They were sometimes troubled, too, by the inexplicable diversity of practice from diocese to diocese, monastery to monastery, since they lived with the illusion that the core elements of the Latin liturgy had been handed down mostly intact from the patristic era. By the ninth century, it was the commonly held view of the monastic musicians and liturgists that Pope Gregory the Great had arranged the order of the psalms and antiphons in the current liturgy. Gregory the Great's biographer, John the Deacon (825–880), codified this legend and explicitly credited the pope with compiling a *Liber antiphonarius*, or *Book of Antiphons*.[104] Ironically, one of the popularizers of this view, Amalarius of Metz, went to Rome to procure an "official" copy of this Gregorian antiphonary, only to come back empty-handed. In his famed *Book on the Order of the Antiphons*, Amalarius related how his numerous questions to the Roman clergy about the order and arrangement of antiphons were met with mostly inconclusive or vague answers.[105] He was left to his own devices, principally some sort of allegorical exegesis, when he attempted systematically to analyze the form and content of the antiphons. Amalarius also discovered that what the Franks and the Romans called an "antiphonary" could mean quite different things; the Frankish antiphonary seemed to be far more capacious and included many chants that the Romans had in separate books (e.g., the gradual and responsorial psalms).[106] This was particularly troubling to a Carolingian liturgist, since the Carolingian royal court issued numerous decrees mandating the adoption of the *cantus romanus*, or Roman form of chant, throughout its empire, according to Roman exemplars of liturgical books.

In the absence of any reliable documentary evidence, medieval liturgists often indulged in fabulous legends to account for some of their most beloved hymns. For example, they attributed the composition of the "Te Deum," which was sung by the monks at the end of the night office, to a patristic miracle. According to Durandus of Mende,[107] this venerable hymn was composed antiphonally by Saint Ambrose of Milan and Saint Augustine during the Easter vigil, when Augustine was baptized by the archbishop of Milan. As he baptized Augustine, Ambrose sang, "Te Deum laudamus," to which Augustine responded, "Te Dominum confitemur"; this antiphonal chanting continued until the entire hymn was completed.

Although medieval liturgical commentators often turned to miraculous or allegorical explications to account for the otherwise obscure origins of medieval hymnody, the earliest Christian music theorists viewed music first and foremost as a philosophical exercise. The most influential musical theorist of the early Middle Ages, Boethius (c. 480–524), composed a lengthy technical treatise, *On the Fundamentals of Music*,[108] which remained authoritative even in the thirteenth-century university classroom. The "true musician," according to Boethius, was the learned critic who engaged in rigorous philosophical inquiry, not the composer or performer.[109] This mathematical or quantitative approach to music originated with Pythagoras. The Pythagorean, Platonic, and Aristotelian philosophical traditions developed an elaborate musical taxonomy which classified music into philosophical and mathematical systems that evolved into rhythmic and melodic "modes." The patristic encyclopedists—Boethius, Cassiodorus, (c. 485–585), and Isidore of Seville (c. 560–636)—refined, synthesized, and codified this philosophical paradigm of musical cosmology. They bequeathed an epitome of Greco-Roman music theory to the medieval monks, while laying the foundations of the medieval curriculum of seven liberal arts, in which the *ars musica* figured prominently in the quadrivium (a grouping of four subjects among the seven).

Still, the overwhelming majority of musical texts from the Middle Ages are eminently practical rather than theoretical works. For monks, music could not remain a philosophical exercise but had to be devoted to the regulation of monastic worship. In short, liturgical compositions were not incidental music or accompaniment to the liturgy; they *were* the liturgy. Medieval sources invariably refer to priests and bishops "singing the mass" (*cantare* or *decantare missam*).

In a more technical sense, early medieval chant was an exclusively vocal performance that could assume a variety of forms depending upon its location in the liturgy. As a general rule, the Latin text of the liturgy dictated the form of music that the chant would take. For example, the gospel in the mass would be chanted in a "recitational" tone; that is, the text would be chanted more or less in a single pitch.[110] In the divine office, the chants could be "direct," in which case psalms would be set to music and sung in full; or they could be "responsorial," with portions of a psalm or scriptural lesson set to music and sung in response to another text. Over time the chants became increasingly complex and variegated, moving from simple recitation to ornate melodies, depending upon their position in the mass or office, the liturgical season, and the solemnity of the feast day.

By the Carolingian era, we witness a dynamic tension between the simplicity of spirit and purity of worship demanded by the asceticism of monastic Christianity on one hand, and on the other the creative impulses of composers who strove for grammatical and rhetorical refinement, modeling Christian prayer texts on the idioms of classical pagan authorities. Simultaneously, the musicians of the monastic milieu endeavored to produce more elaborate and complex hymnody by employing neumatic (breathing) and melismatic (melodic) devices, transforming such simple texts as a Kyrie or an Alleluia into melodies of astonishing variety and beauty. Medieval liturgical expositors produced florid theological interpretations to match the melodies by fitting them into a well-developed allegorical scheme of music theory. For instance, in his mammoth *Rationale for the Divine Offices*, Durandus of Mende explicated the neumatic ornamentation of the vowels "e" and "a" in the Kyrie and Alleluia as representing the spiritual joy of humanity when the Virgin Mary was born; the "second Eve," Mary, transformed the transgressor's name, "Eva," into the angelic salutation "Ave."[111]

To summarize, the music from the monastic centuries of Christendom that we still call "Gregorian chant" was largely produced in Franco-German monasteries and cathedrals, mostly by anonymous composers. As Jungmann notes, thanks to the Franco-Germanic leadership in liturgical reform and renewal in both the Carolingian and Ottonian courts, a "Gallicanized version" of the liturgy—including liturgical chants—supplanted the "old Roman" forms even in the very diocese of Rome itself.[112]

The Gothic age produced, within the span of a century, an unprecedented transformation of the repertoire of liturgical music. As we have seen, twelfth- and thirteenth-century Paris and its immediate environs experienced the convergence of the scholastic theology of the new university, the active spirituality of the mendicant friars, and the flowering of Gothic art and architecture. Before the close of the twelfth century, the newly constructed Gothic choir of the cathedral of Notre Dame—whose cornerstone was laid in 1163 and which was completed in 1182—reverberated with the sounds of striking new forms of liturgical music, the various styles of polyphony that marked a conceptual breakthrough in the history of medieval music. Parisian polyphony was of such exceptional quality that modern musicologists refer to a "School of Notre Dame" in the production of sacred music in the Gothic age.[113] Just as Gothic architecture overtook its Romanesque predecessor, the polyphony of the late Middle Ages and early Renaissance superseded the monophonic chant of the monastic centuries. At the same time, dramatic new modes of liturgical and paraliturgical performance added a new sense of the spectacular to medieval worship; among these were the new liturgical dramas and a drama of another sort, the Feast of Corpus Christi.

The newly constructed cathedral of Notre Dame became the vehicle for the new style of music when a poet, master of arts, and musician called Master Leo or Leoninus (c. 1135–1200) first began experimenting with a complex new rhythmic system which combined two "autonomous voices" in one musical composition. Modern scholars have struggled to identify precisely who this Master Leo was; some have even questioned his very existence. For the few clues we have about his identity we must rely on a treatise produced by an English student at the University of Paris in the latter part of the thirteenth century (the so-called Anonymous IV).[114] Musicologists designate the work attributed to Leoninus, the *Magnus liber organi* (Great Book of Polyphony, c. 1160–1180), as the first full-scale presentation of two-part polyphonic settings for the mass and the divine office (namely, responsorial chants for the great feast days). Although liturgical polyphony predates Leoninus's work—the monks of Santiago de Compostela and Saint-Martial of Limoges had already experimented with it—his *Magnus liber* set a new benchmark for melismatic (or florid) and discant (note-against-note) polyphony.[115]

Leoninus's work was, according to some modern musicologists, the equivalent of a theological *Summa* for the musicians of the scholastic era, and its contents were immediately copied and imitated by other composers who attempted to expand the new musical style from two-part to three- or even four-part vocal arrangements. Chief among these composers was the enigmatic Parisian master Perotinus. Perotinus (or Petrus), about whom we know a little more than we know about his predecessor Leoninus, worked closely with the bishop of Paris in a substantive reform of the liturgy of Notre Dame cathedral; he reworked the *Magnus liber* and produced a series of magnificent discant polyphonic compositions (some in three or four parts) for major church feasts.[116]

As the infant steps of the new musical styles of performance were being taken, liturgical drama—theatrical presentations in Latin, staged in church—had also made its mark in the cathedrals of the Gothic age.[117] From the eleventh century to the early Renaissance, the Latin Church witnessed the full-fledged development of three forms

of liturgical drama: the miracle play, the mystery play, and the morality play. The first type of performance was associated with a fundamental component of medieval popular piety, the cult of the saints. Medieval hagiographies followed standard literary tropes which largely ignored

Mystery play. Medieval mystery plays have been revived in modern times, as at Worsborough, Yorkshire, England, in July 1986. PHOTOGRAPH BY GEOFFREY WAINWRIGHT

mundane biographical details of a saint's life and instead focused on miracles per-formed by the saint either while alive or after his or her death.[118] The dramatic reen-actment of these miracles was by far the most popular sort of paraliturgical performance. These plays were not viewed by the onlookers simply as allegories, but as vivid repre-sentations of the *reality* of the saint's continued presence in a sacred locus, and of the continued efficacy of intercessory prayers to the saints who still worked miracles for the faithful.

The mystery play took its cue from biblical lessons, focusing on key events in salva-tion history—the creation of the world, the resurrection of Christ, and the Last Judg-ment. As we have previously noted, the early medieval expositors of the liturgy viewed the mass and the divine office as an iconographic presentation of key events in the economy of salvation. A "stage performance" of some of these events was the logical outcome of Amalarius of Metz's initial approach to medieval liturgiology with his elaborate scheme of allegorical interpretation. Although scholarly debate continues over the precise origins of liturgical drama, properly speaking, it is generally accepted that by the ninth century sung tropes to the Introit of the mass for Easter Sunday took a dialogue form that eventually became the nucleus of more elaborate performances. The so-called *visitatio sepulchri* or "visit to the sepulchre" of Christ begins with the angel asking the "three Marys" at the Lord's tomb, "Quem quaeritis" ("Whom do you seek?"). Thus, this early drama is called the *Quem quaeritis* play.[119] By the twelfth century, the biblical stories of the birth of Christ and of his resurrection became the centerpiece of elaborately staged Christmas and Nativity plays, with appropriate scenery and costumes. One noteworthy feature of these performances is the fact that they were *sung*, not spoken dramas; and although they were performed in an age when polyphony was proliferating, the music remained simple monophonic chant.[120]

The morality play, which flourished only at the very end of the Middle Ages, was often an allegorical presentation of the vices or virtues, designed for the moral exhor-tation of a predominantly illiterate audience. Such plays must be viewed within the larger context of late medieval piety and the cultivation of the *ars moriendi*, the art of preparing for one's death and the spiritual battle that ensued between the devil and angels for the soul of a dying "Everyman" figure.[121] Perhaps one of the finest examples of this sort of drama is a vernacular play which itself bears the title *Everyman* (before 1485). This short play features a cast of characters whose very names are the vices and virtues which they are intended to communicate allegorically to the audience (e.g., Knowledge, Confession, Beauty, Discretion).[122]

With the promulgation of the Feast of Corpus Christi, we observe the establish-ment of drama of a different sort: the paraliturgical cult of the eucharist.[123] By the end of the thirteenth century, when it had evolved into a universal feast of the Latin Church and its more dramatic components had crystallized in the form of public processions of the consecrated host, this feast threatened to undermine the celebration of the eucharist within the context of the mass. The piety associated with Corpus Christi must be viewed against the backdrop of powerful trends in medieval Christianity that reach back to the era of papal and monastic reform: the "sacerdotalism" of the twelfth- and thirteenth-century Church, and the "high" eucharistic theology generated by cen-turies of eucharistic controversies and devotions.

Around the year 1209, the Augustinian nun Juliana of Liège (c. 1193–1258) claimed that she had visions that she and the clergy with whom she consulted interpreted as a divine mandate to establish a new feast in honor of the eucharist. In 1247, the arch-deacon of Liège, Jacques Pantaléon, convinced the bishop of the diocese, Robert of

Turotte, to institute a diocesan celebration of the Feast of Corpus Christi. This diocesan feast immediately drew the attention of the Order of Friars Preachers, or Dominicans. The Parisian master and Dominican cardinal, Hugh of Saint Cher, was instrumental in bringing the new feast to Germany and eastern Europe in his official capacity as cardinal-legate to Germany (1251). The Dominican order itself added the new feast to its liturgical calendar in 1304.[124]

When Jacques Pantaléon was elected pope and took the name Urban IV (reigned 1261–1264), he extended the feast to the universal Church in the bull *Transiturus de hoc mundo* (1264).[125] This was, in fact, the first papally sanctioned universal feast in the history of the Latin Church. However, the untimely death of the pope and the ineffectual manner in which the feast was proclaimed led to its uneven reception in various regions of Europe. Durandus of Mende—himself a former papal chaplain and curial official under Urban IV—gives us a brief account of the institution of Corpus Christi in his *Rationale for the Divine Offices*: "And it should be known that Pope Urban IV decreed that a feast of Corpus Christi be celebrated the fifth day after this Sunday [i.e. the first Sunday after Pentecost], granting great indulgences for both clerics presiding at its offices and the people gathered for these divine services."[126] During the pontificate of the Avignon pope John XXII (1316–1334), when the collection of papal decretals of his predecessor Clement V was promulgated (the so-called Clementines of 1317), the Feast of Corpus Christi finally attained the enduring status of a universal feast in the Latin Church.

By the time this feast was widely celebrated, the mass had long since eclipsed all other forms of liturgical worship in both the clerical and the popular mind. Furthermore, as the number of sacred relics proliferated in Europe, especially in the wake of several crusades in the Holy Land, and the medieval cult of the saints continued to intensify, the eucharist itself began to compete with these sacred objects as *the* relic of Christ par excellence in any locale in Christendom. Moreover, the eucharistic host had a tremendous advantage over other holy relics: through the miracle of transubstantiation, the body of Christ could be "created" and "reserved" anywhere by a properly ordained priest or bishop.

The Office of Corpus Christi. Saint Thomas Aquinas submits the office of Corpus Christi to Pope Urban IV. Painting by Taddeo di Bartolo (1363–1422). THE PHILADELPHIA MUSEUM OF ART, JOHN G. JOHNSON COLLECTION, 1917/ART RESOURCE, NY

Although clerical authorities insisted that the consecrated host was not to be treated as a relic per se, it was in fact subjected to the same sort of devotionalism as other objects associated with the cult of the saints. In the popular mind, a monstrance could be seen as a reliquary for the body of Christ. The earliest documentation we have of a paraliturgical procession of the host as relic comes from Cologne (1279). Within a century, the practice of publicly processing with the eucharist existed all over Europe, and these processions shared a high level of pageantry, popular enthusiasm, and considerable expenditure of money by secular and clerical authorities. Another noteworthy feature of the feast was that the procession of the consecrated host "sacralized" the temporal boundaries of any given town, village, or city; the most important public places—bridges, mills, fields—were "blessed" or "sanctified" through their contact with the objective presence of the body of Christ.

Mystics, spiritual writers, and the laity alike approached the consecrated host with a certitude that when it was elevated by the priest at the sacring, or when it was paraded publicly in a monstrance, they could say quite literally that they had "seen God." In the waning years of the Gothic age, "seeing God" had become a substitute for receiving the body of Christ. The groundwork for this mentality had already been put in place by the Fourth Lateran Council; even as it offered a formal dogmatic declaration for the real presence of Christ in the eucharistic bread and wine, the Council required sacramental confession and communion only once per year.

The objectification of the eucharist as a sacred relic created a rigid sacramental paradigm that endured to the very end of the Middle Ages. This model was only radically challenged and eventually undermined by Protestant theologians, who attempted to restore what they took to be the pristine eucharistic celebration of the Lord's Supper.

Bibliography

Harper, John. *The Forms and Orders of Western Liturgy from the Tenth to the Eighteenth Centuries: A Historical Introduction and Guide for Students and Musicians.* Oxford and New York: Oxford University Press, 1991.

Jungmann, Josef A. *The Mass. An Historical, Theological, and Pastoral Survey.* Translated by Julian Fernandes. Collegeville, Minn.: Liturgical Press, 1976.

Jungmann, Josef A. *The Mass of the Roman Rite: Its Origin and Development.* 2 vols. Translated by Francis A. Brunner. Westminster, Md.: Christian Classics, 1986.

Klauser, Theodor. *A Short History of the Western Liturgy: An Account and Some Reflections.* 2nd ed. Translated by John Halliburton. Oxford and New York: Oxford University Press, 1979.

Mitchell, Nathan. "The Liturgical Code in the Rule of Benedict." In *The Rule of St. Benedict in Latin with English Notes,* edited by Timothy Fry, 379–414. Collegeville, Minn.: Liturgical Press, 1981.

Panofsky, Erwin. *Abbot Suger on the Abbey Church of Saint-Denis and Its Art Treasures.* 2nd ed. Princeton, N.J.: Princeton University Press, 1979.

Rubin, Miri. *Corpus Christi: The Eucharist in Late Medieval Culture.* Cambridge: Cambridge University Press, 1991.

Stoddard, Whitney S. *Monastery and Cathedral in France.* Middletown, Conn.: Wesleyan University Press, 1966.

Vogel, Cyrille. *Medieval Liturgy: An Introduction to the Sources.* Translated by William Storey and Niels Rasmussen. Washington, D.C.: Pastoral Press, 1986.

Yudkin, Jeremy. *Music in Medieval Europe.* Englewood Cliffs, N.J.: Prentice-Hall, 1989.

Notes

[1]For an introduction to the controversy, see Uta-Renate Blumenthal, *The Investiture Controversy: Church and Monarchy from the Ninth to the Twelfth Century* (Philadelphia: University of Pennsylvania Press, 1988). For English translations of key documents from the controversy, see Brian Tierney, *The*

Crisis of Church and State 1050–1300 (Englewood Cliffs, N.J.: Prentice-Hall, 1964). For a comprehensive analysis of the papacy in the age of reform, see I. S. Robinson, *The Papacy 1073–1198: Continuity and Innovation* (Cambridge: Cambridge University Press, 1990).

[2]Tierney, 50.

[3]Robinson, 134–135.

[4]Gerd Tellenbach, *Church, State and Christian Society at the Time of the Investiture Controversy*, trans. R. F. Bennett (repr. ed., Atlantic Highlands, N.J.: Humanities Press, 1979); see also Tellenbach, *The Church in Western Europe from the Tenth to the Early Twelfth Century*, trans. Timothy Reuter (New York: Cambridge University Press, 1993).

[5]Tierney, 70.

[6]For a study of Cluny in the era of papal reform, with a detailed analysis of sources, see Noreen Hunt, *Cluny Under Saint Hugh 1049–1109* (Notre Dame, Ind.: University of Notre Dame Press, 1967); see also H. E. J. Cowdrey, *The Cluniacs and the Gregorian Reform* (Oxford: Oxford University Press, 1970). For more recent research see Giles Constable, *Cluny from the Tenth to the Twelfth Centuries: Further Studies*, Variorum Collected Studies Series 671 (Aldershot, Hants.: Ashgate, 2000).

[7]For an English translation of the foundation charter, see Tierney, 28–29.

[8]For the specifics of Cluniac liturgy, see Hunt, 99–117; Appendix I, 208–210. For a bibliography of primary and secondary sources for Cluniac liturgy, see Vogel, *Medieval Liturgy*, 286–287.

[9]For an analysis of the complex relationship of Cluny to the papal reform, see Cowdrey, xiii–xvii.

[10]R. W. Southern, ed. *The Life of St. Anselm, Archbishop of Canterbury* (London and New York: T. Nelson, 1962) 9.

[11]A study of the Benedictine Office in English is Nathan Mitchell, "The Liturgical Code in the Rule of Benedict," 379–414. An analysis of the evolution of the medieval Benedictine Office can be found in J. B. L. Tolhurst, *The Monastic Breviary of Hyde Abbey, Winchester*, Henry Bradshaw Society 80 (London: Harrison, 1942).

[12]*Contra intemperantes clericos*, c. 4, PL 145:393. For an analysis of the regulation of sex in canon law in the age of papal reform, see James A. Brundage, *Law, Sex, and Christian Society in Medieval Europe* (Chicago: University of Chicago Press, 1987) 176–255.

[13]English chantries are among the best documented; see K. L. Wood-Legh, *Perpetual Chantries in Britain* (Cambridge: Cambridge University Press, 1965);

and Joel K. Rosenthal, *The Purchase of Paradise: Gift Giving and the Aristocracy, 1307–1485* (London: Routledge and K. Paul, 1972).

[14]See Jacques Le Goff, *The Birth of Purgatory*, trans. Arthur Goldhammer (Chicago: University of Chicago Press, 1984).

[15]H. Denizger and H. Schönmetzer, eds., *Enchiridion Symbolorum*, 32nd ed. (Barcelona: Herder, 1963) 276, n.856.

[16]For the liturgy of Saint-Denis through the entire medieval period, see Anne Walters Robertson, *The Service-Books of the Royal Abbey of Saint-Denis: Images of Ritual and Music in the Middle Ages* (Oxford: Oxford University Press, 1991).

[17]For an overview of French Romanesque and Gothic art, see Stoddard, *Monastery and Cathedral in France*. Though dated, this lavishly illustrated book is still a standard work on the topic. The best complete study of the social, cultural, and artistic interchanges of the Gothic age remains Georges Duby, *The Age of the Cathedrals: Art and Society, 980–1420*, trans. Eleanor Levieux and Barbara Thompson (Chicago: University of Chicago Press, 1981).

[18]Panofsky, *Abbot Suger*, 65. For more recent work on Suger and the Church of Saint-Denis, see Paula Lieber Gerson, ed., *Abbot Suger and Saint-Denis, A Symposium* (New York: Metropolitan Museum of Art, 1986); and Sumner McKnight Crosby, *The Royal Abbey of Saint-Denis, from its Beginnings to the Death of Suger, 475–1151* (New Haven, Conn.: Yale University Press, 1987).

[19]For the precise details of Hilduin's conflation of three "Dionysiuses," see Robertson, 33–42.

[20]The Latin text is in Panofsky, 46–48; in this case, the translation of Suger's tortuous Latin is my own.

[21]Crosby, 117.

[22]Panofsky, 63–65.

[23]For an overview of the various monastic reform movements of the later Middle Ages, see Jean Leclercq, "From St. Gregory to St. Bernard," in *A History of Christian Spirituality II: The Spirituality of the Middle Ages*, ed. Louis Boyer et al. (New York: Seabury, 1968) 127–220.

[24]*Apologia ad Guillelmum Sancti-Theoderici Abbatem* c.12, PL 182: 915.

[25]Panofsky, 67.

[26]Stoddard, 173–196. For an illustrated study, see Malcolm Miller, *Chartres Cathedral* (New York: Riverside, 1985).

[27]Miller, 6.

[28]Miller, 10.

[29]Stoddard, 173.

[30]Stoddard, 179.

[31]For a study of the interchanges between scholastic thought and Gothic architecture, see Charles M. Radding and William W. Clark, *Medieval Architecture, Medieval Learning: Builders and Masters in the Age of Romanesque and Gothic* (New Haven, Conn.: Yale University Press, 1992).

[32]An analysis of his papal reign can be found in Tellenbach, *The Church in Western Europe*, 185–252. Gregory's views are well documented in his numerous letters, some of which are available in the English translation of Ephraim Emerton, *The Correspondence of Pope Gregory VII* (New York: Norton, 1969).

[33]For a discussion of the context of Gregory VII's attempts at liturgical reform, see Chrysogonus Waddell, "The Reform of the Liturgy from a Renaissance Perspective," in *Renaissance and Renewal in the Twelfth Century*, ed. Robert L. Benson and Giles Constable (Cambridge, Mass.: Harvard University Press, 1982) 88–109.

[34]A summary of these developments can be found in Klauser, *Short History*, 5–59. For more recent critical scholarship on the earliest Christian liturgies, see Paul F. Bradshaw, *The Search for the Origins of Christian Worship*, 2nd ed. (New York and Oxford: Oxford University Press, 2002). The definitive treatment of sources for the study of medieval liturgy is Vogel, 357–360.

[35]S. J. P. Van Dijk, "Urban and Papal Rites in Seventh- and Eighth-Century Rome," *Sacris Erudiri* 12 (1961) 411–487.

[36]See Klauser, 5–59 and Vogel, 357–360.

[37]See Rosamund McKitterick, *The Frankish Church and the Carolingian Reforms 789–895* (London: Royal Historical Society, 1977).

[38]Cyrille Vogel, "Les échanges liturgiques entre Rome et les pays francs jusqu'à l'époque de Charlemagne," in *Chiese nei regni dell'Europa occidentale e i loro rapporti con Roma sino all'800*, Settimane di Studio Centro Italiano di Studi sull'Alto Medioevo 7 (Spoleto: Sede del Centro, 1960) 185–295.

[39]For the specifics on the final production of this sacramentary, see Vogel, *Medieval Liturgy*, 79–82.

[40]Klauser, 54–95.

[41]C. Vogel and R. Elze, eds., *Le Pontifical romano-germanique du X siècle*, 3 vols., ST 226, 227, 269.

[42]Michel Andrieu, ed., *Le Pontifical romain au moyen-âge, I. Le Pontifical du XIIᵉ siècle*, ST 86.

[43]*Micrologus de ecclesiasticis observationibus*, PL 151:973–1022. The definitive study of this work is by Daniel S. Taylor, "Bernold of Constance, Canonist and Liturgist of the Gregorian Reform: An Analysis of the Sources of the *Micrologus de ecclesiasticis observationibus*" (Ph.D. diss., University of Toronto, 1995).

[44]Roger E. Reynolds, "Liturgical Scholarship at the Time of the Investiture Controversy: Past Research and Future Opportunities," *Harvard Theological Review* 71 (1978) 114–115.

[45]The best-known modern edition of the work is that of Emil Friedberg, *Corpus Iuris Canonici*, 2 vols. (Leipzig: Bernard Tauchnitz, 1879). For an introduction to Gratian and his methods, see *Gratian, The Treatise on the Laws (Decretum DD.1-20)*, trans. Augustine Thompson and James Gordley, Studies in Medieval and Early Modern Canon Law 2 (Washington, D.C.: Catholic University of America Press, 1993).

[46]I have treated this subject in "The Influence of Canon Law on Liturgical Exposition c.1100–1300," *Sacris Erudiri* 37 (1997) 185–202.

[47]For an overview see C. H. Lawrence, *The Friars: The Impact of the Early Mendicant Movement on Western Society* (New York: Longman, 1994). For the mendicants and liturgical developments in the thirteenth century, see Klauser, 94–108.

[48]S. J. P. Van Dijk and J. Hazelden Walker, *The Origins of the Modern Roman Liturgy: The Liturgy of the Papal Court and the Franciscan Order in the Thirteenth Century* (Westminster, Md.: Newman, 1960) 3.

[49]S. J. P. Van Dijk and J. Hazelden Walker, *The Ordinal of the Papal Court from Innocent III to Boniface VIII, and Related Documents*, Spicilegium Friburgense 22 (Fribourg: University Press, 1975).

[50]Vogel, *Medieval Liturgy*, 252.

[51]Klauser, 117–35.

[52]*Rationale divinorum officiorum*, Pro. 14, CCCM 140:9.

[53]A general introduction to the Latin patristic liturgy can be found in Klauser, 5–72.

[54]The complete Latin text can be found in Jean Deshusses, ed., *Le Sacramentaire grégorien: Ses principales formes d'après les plus anciens manuscrits*, Spicilegium Friburgense 16 (Fribourg: University Press, 1971) 89.

[55]*In Iohannis Evangelium Tractatus*, 25.12; 26.1; CCSL 36:260.

[56]For a discussion of this subject, see Gary Macy, *The Theology of the Eucharist in the Early Scholastic*

Period: A Study of the Salvific Function of the Sacrament According to Theologians c. 1080–c. 1220 (Oxford: Oxford University Press, 1984).

57*Amalarii episcopi opera liturgica omnia*, ST 138–140.

58*De corpore et sanguine Domini*, CCCM 16.

59Jungmann, *The Mass*, 58–59; see also Carole Straw, *Gregory the Great: Perfection in Imperfection* (Berkeley: University of California Press, 1988) 180–181.

60*De corpore et sanguine Domini liber*, PL 121:125–170.

61*De civitate Dei*, 10.5, CCSL 47:277.

62*De corpore et sanguine Domini adversus Berengarium Turonensem liber*, PL 150:407–441. Treatment of the Berengarian controversy can be found in Margaret Gibson, *Lanfranc of Bec* (Oxford: Oxford University Press, 1978) 63–97. A philosophical analysis of the crisis can be found in Henry Chadwick, "Ego Berengarius: Reply to Lanfranc by Berengar of Tours," *Journal of Theological Studies* 40 (1989) 415–445.

63*De corpore et sanguine Domini* c. 14, PL 150:423.

64*De corpore et sanguine Domini* c. 8, PL 150:419.

65Denziger and Schönmetzer, 227, n.690.

66Denziger and Schönmetzer, 230, n.700.

67For the history of the term, see Joseph Goering, "The Invention of Transubstantiation," *Traditio* 46 (1991) 147–170; cf. Macy, *Theologies of the Eucharist*; and James F. McCue, "The Doctrine of Transubstantiation from Berengar through the Council of Trent," *Harvard Theological Review* 61 (1968) 385–430. Thibodeau reviews some of the literature on this subject in "The Doctrine of Transubstantiation in Durand's *Rationale*," *Traditio* 51 (1996) 308–317.

68For the complete text of the decree see Antonio García y García, ed., *Constitutiones Concilii quarti Lateranensis una cum Commentariis Glossatorum*, Monumenta Iuris Canonici, ser. A, vol. 2 (Vatican City: Biblioteca Apostolica Vaticana, 1981) 42.

69William Barden, ed., *St. Thomas Aquinas Summa Theologiae*, vol. 58: *The Eucharistic Presence*, III.75.1–77.7 (New York and London: Blackfriars, 1965) 52–161.

70*De missarum mysteriis* 4.9, PL 217:861-862.

71Regis J. Armstrong and Ignatius C. Brady, *Francis and Clare: The Complete Works* (New York: Paulist Press, 1982) 154.

72Theodore Graesse, ed., *Jacobi a Voragine Legenda Aurea* (Dresden and Leipzig: Imprensis Librariae Arnoldianae, 1846) 198–199.

73Caroline Walker Bynum, *Holy Feast and Holy Fast: The Religious Significance of Food to Medieval Women* (Berkeley: University of California Press, 1987).

74Bynum, 3.

75A general introduction to this topic can be found in Joseph R. Strayer, ed., *Dictionary of the Middle Ages*, vol. 7 (New York: Scribner, 1986), "Liturgy, Treatises on" by Roger E. Reynolds.

76See Vogel, *Medieval Liturgy*, 10–11, for a detailed list of patristic texts on the liturgy.

77See Vogel, 62–134, for a discussion of the history and development of the Romano-Frankish and Romano-Germanic sacramentaries. A definitive treatment of the Carolingian church is in McKitterick, *The Frankish Church and the Carolingian Reforms*.

78For a short biography see A. Cabaniss, *Amalarius of Metz* (Amsterdam: North-Holland, 1954).

79Thibodeau treats the complex nature of medieval liturgical allegory and its relationship to patristic modes of scriptural exegesis in "*Enigmata figurarum*: Biblical Exegesis and Liturgical Exposition in Durand's *Rationale*," *Harvard Theological Review* 86 (1993) 65–79.

80Jungmann, *The Mass of the Roman Rite*, 1:87–92. For a more recent discussion of liturgical theology and "salvation history," see I. H. Dalmais, "The Liturgy as Celebration of the Mystery of Salvation," in *The Church at Prayer: An Introduction to the Liturgy*, ed. A. G. Martimort, et al., vol. 1, trans. Matthew J. O'Connell (Collegeville, Minn.: Liturgical Press, 1987) 253–72.

81Jean Leclercq, "From Gregory the Great to Saint Bernard," in *The Cambridge History of the Bible: The West From the Fathers to the Reformation*, ed. G. W. H. Lampe (Cambridge: Cambridge University Press, 1969) 2:189.

82*Rationale divinorum officiorum I–IV; V–VI; VII–VIII*, CCCM 140, 140A, 140B.

83*Rationale*, Pro. CCCM 140:9–12.

84*Rationale*, Pro. 12, CCCM 140:8.

85*Rationale*, Pro. 10, CCCM 140:7.

86*Amalarii episcopi opera liturgica omnia* vol. 1, ST 138:255–281; summarized by Jungmann, *Mass of the Roman Rite*, 1:89–90.

87Jungmann, *Mass of the Roman Rite*, 1:90.

88*Liber de ordine antiphonarii*, 1.2–5, ST 140:19–20.

89*Micrologus de ecclesiasticis observationibus*, PL 151:973–1022.

90*Liber de divinis officiis*, CCCM 7.

91*Gemma animae*, PL 72:541–738.

92*Speculum de mysteriis Ecclesiae*, PL 177:335–380.

[93]*Liber Quare*, CCCM 60.

[94]*Iohannis Beleth Summa de ecclesiasticis officiis*, CCCM 41–41A.

[95]*Mitrale seu de ecclesiasticis officiis summa*, PL 213:13–434.

[96]*De sacro altaris mysterio*, PL 217:775–961; for a modern partial critical edition see David. F. Wright, "A Medieval Commentary on the Mass: *Particulae 2–3* and *5–6* of the *De missarum mysteriis* (c. 1195) of Lothario of Segni (Pope Innocent III)" (Ph.D. diss., University of Notre Dame, 1977).

[97]There is no printed edition of his *Summa de officiis ecclesiasticis*; in my own research, I have employed an early-fourteenth-century manuscript of this work.

[98]Michel Andrieu, ed., *Le Pontifical Romain au Moyen Age III: Le Pontifical de Guillaume Durand*, ST 88 (1940).

[99]*Institutions liturgiques*, vol. 1 (Paris: Débécourt, 1840) 355.

[100]*Rationale*, Pro. 1, CCCM 140:2–3.

[101]Jean Leclercq, *The Love of Learning and the Desire for God: A Study of Monastic Culture*, trans. Catharine Misrahi (New York: Fordham University Press, 1982) 250–251.

[102]Among the many works on the subject of medieval music: Willi Apel, *Gregorian Chant* (Bloomington: Indiana University Press, 1958); Richard H. Hoppin, *Medieval Music* (New York: Norton, 1978); Giulio Cattin, *Music of the Middle Ages I*, trans. Steven Botterill (Cambridge: Cambridge University Press, 1984); and Yudkin, *Music in Medieval Europe*.

[103]For a discussion of the development of modern systems of reconstruction and performance in the Catholic Church, see Cattin, 94–100.

[104]*Vita Gregorii*, 2.6, PL 75:90.

[105]*Liber de ordine antiphonarii*, Prologus, 1–7, ST 140:13–14.

[106]For the Roman antiphonaries, see Vogel, *Medieval Liturgy*, 357–360.

[107]*Rationale divinorum officiorum*, V.3.31, CCCM 140A:68.

[108]*De insitutione musica libri quinque*, ed. Gottfried Friedlein (Leipzig: Teubner, 1867); for an introduction and translation, see Calvin A. Bower, *The Fundamentals of Music, Anicius Manlius Severinus Boethius* (New Haven, Conn.: Yale University Press, 1989).

[109]Bower, 1.1, 8.

[110]Yudkin, 43–45.

[111]*Rationale*, V.2.33, CCCM 140A:28.

[112]Jungmann, *Mass of the Roman Rite*, 95. See also Van Dijk, "Urban and Papal Rites," 411–487. For a review of the scholarly literature on the differences between "Gregorian" and "Paleo-Roman" or Old Roman chant, see Cattin, 26–31.

[113]For a comprehensive analysis of the liturgy of Notre Dame, see Craig Wright, *Music and Ceremony at Notre Dame of Paris 500–1550* (Cambridge: Cambridge University Press, 1989), esp. 235–359.

[114]For the debate over Leoninus' identity, see Stanley Sadie, ed., *The New Grove Dictionary of Music and Musicians*, vol. 10 (London: Macmillan; Washington, D.C.: Grove's Dictionaries of Music, 1980), "Léonin," by Ian D. Bent. For an analysis of the *Magnus liber*'s content, see Yudkin, 363–371 and Wright, 243–258. The earliest manuscripts of the work date from the mid-thirteenth century.

[115]For a comprehensive study and transcription of one manuscript of the *Magnus liber*, see G. Waite, *The Rhythm of Twelfth-Century Polyphony* (New Haven, Conn.: Yale University Press, 1954).

[116]See Wright, 288–294, who makes the case for Petrus *Succentor*, "subcantor" of the cathedral (c. 1207–1238).

[117]Representative works on the subject include F. Collins, Jr., *Medieval Church Music Dramas: A Repertory of Complete Plays* (Charlottesville: University Press of Virginia, 1976); and Hoppin, 175–186.

[118]Two representative works on this subject are Peter Brown, *The Cult of the Saints: Its Rise and Function in Latin Christianity* (Chicago: University of Chicago Press, 1981); and Patrick J. Geary, *Furta Sacra: Thefts of Relics in the Central Middle Ages*, rev. ed. (Princeton, N.J.: Princeton University Press, 1990).

[119]Hoppin, 175–176.

[120]Hoppin, 179.

[121]Johan Huizinga, *The Autumn of the Middle Ages*, trans. Rodney J. Payton and Ulrich Mammitzsch (Chicago: University of Chicago Press, 1996) 179.

[122]For the text of the play, see M. H. Abrams, ed., *The Norton Anthology of English Literature*, vol. 1, 6th ed. (New York and London: Norton, 1993) 363–384.

[123]See Rubin, *Corpus Christi*.

[124]Rubin, *Corpus Christi*, 164–196.

[125]Denziger and Schönmetzer, 273, n.846.

[126]*Rationale divinorum officiorum*, VI.115.6, CCCM 140A:544.

7

Byzantine and Slavic Orthodoxy

ALEXANDER RENTEL

Therefore, what [Christ's Church] received from the beginning, it enacts continually and teaches what is beyond understanding through sacred symbols. Those things which are visibly enacted have partaken of such great glory, and so they are marvelous to all.

Symeon of Thessalonika (martyred early 15th century)[1]

Historical Overview

In the early twenty-first century well over 130 million Christian faithful worship according to traditions that can be traced back to the liturgical practices of the Orthodox Church in the Byzantine Empire.[2] Today the largest concentration of believers that follow this liturgical tradition naturally live as they have for centuries in areas that were once part of the Byzantine Empire: Greece, Serbia, Bulgaria, and concentrated pockets of Turkey, southern Italy, Egypt, Syria, Lebanon, and Palestine. Vast numbers of believers are also found in countries that gradually became part of the larger Byzantine commonwealth, that is, countries that fell under the sway of Byzantine culture: Romania, Georgia, Ukraine, and Russia. Modern practitioners of this tradition, however, no longer live exclusively in the eastern Mediterranean basin or in the Balkan Peninsula or even in eastern Europe. Because of missionary work, the mass emigrations and immigrations of the eighteenth and nineteenth centuries, and the revolutions of the early twentieth century, they can now be found in countries far afield from the patriarchal sees of the ancient Eastern Orthodox Churches. New centers of ecclesiastical life have multiplied throughout the world in such places as western Europe, North America, Australia, Southeast Asia, and Africa. So today, modern Orthodox clergy in Paris, Sydney, San Francisco, Buenos Aires, and Hong Kong, together with their concelebrants in the traditional Orthodox countries, regularly utter in prayer an anaphora, attributed to John Chrysostom (c. 340–407), whose origin can be traced back to two great Roman-Hellenistic poleis of late antiquity: Antioch and Constantinople. Similarly Orthodox communities in both the old and new worlds of Byzantine Christianity continue to celebrate the aggregate daily cycle of the divine office, which was forged by the end of the first millennium in the monasteries and cathedrals of Jerusalem and Constantinople and in the rugged gullies of the Palestinian desert.

Three broadly delineated epochs emerge from an examination of the 1,700-year history of the Byzantine-Slavic rite: the Byzantine era, the post-Byzantine era, and the post-Enlightenment or modern period. The rite becomes a distinct liturgical tradition in the 300-year period that commences in the fourth century in the early days of the East Roman or Byzantine Empire and ends in the seventh century. Although the rite was never quite coterminous with the geographical boundaries of the Byzantine Empire, and certainly the Orthodox Church existed before the Roman Empire became Christian, nevertheless the Orthodox Church over the centuries became more and more centered around the capital city of the empire, Constantinople. For long the Church's fortunes mirrored those of the empire. Thus the Church's Byzantine era begins with the founding of the new capital of a Christian empire, and its first phase closes with the end of late antiquity, shrinking borders, and growing insularity marked by the Council in Trullo (691–692). Initially, as the new capital city springs to life, it draws to it people and ideas from the most important cities throughout the Christian world who arrive in Constantinople and spur the development of the nascent Byzantine liturgical tradition. Conversely, with the establishment of a Christian empire, the avenues of communication throughout the length and breadth of the empire allow for a lively exchange of liturgical practice. This is especially the case between Constantinople, the monasteries of Palestine, and the holy city of Jerusalem. As the great imperial period draws to a close and as the borders of the empire shrink, so too does the outlook of the church. With the doctrinal controversies of the fifth, sixth, and seventh centuries and the growing political estrangement between East and West, the vision of the one Church that encompasses all Christendom is lost. What remains in the Byzantine world is a lingering suspicion toward what falls outside the borders of the empire.

Under these new circumstances, a new phase in the Byzantine era opens in the eighth and ninth centuries with the iconoclast controversy, which caused tumult in the Church for almost 150 years. Aside from the obvious changes in church decoration, the iconoclasm controversy inadvertently brought about one of the greatest periods of liturgical development, namely, the achievement of the new Studite liturgical synthesis and the spread of the Byzantine liturgical traditions to countries outside the borders of the empire (eighth–thirteenth centuries). The Studite tradition represents the monastic rite, one of two traditions within the broader Byzantine liturgical life, the other being the cathedral liturgical tradition. This period saw these two traditions living equally side by side. An abrupt end came with the sack of Constantinople by the Western crusaders in 1204. The final phase began almost as abruptly when the Byzantines recaptured Constantinople in 1264. The greatly reduced scope of the empire set the stage for the complete decline of the ancient urban cathedral traditions and the prevalence of the monastic rite over all aspects of the liturgical rites (fourteenth–fifteenth centuries). The entire Byzantine era is the period when the liturgical rites were shaped, and each of its stages laid down a peculiar stratum of liturgical practices that is still evident upon close examination. By the end of this era nearly all the structures of the office and the sacraments were present. Later times saw further adaptation and addition, but by the end of the empire in 1453, almost all aspects of the rite as it is known up until the modern era were completely in place.

The Great Imperial Age

Although the Orthodox Church is not identical to the Byzantine Empire, the Church and its liturgical practices could not help but reflect the changes that empire underwent. In the process a distinct liturgical tradition was formed that would eventually be passed on to other cultures and that would long outlive the empire. Obviously the

The "Harrowing of Hell." According to the Apostles' Creed, Christ "descended to the dead" (cf. 1 Peter 3:19–20; 4:6) between his crucifixion and resurrection. An eleventh-century image in the Greek monastery of Hosios Loukas shows Christ raising up Adam, Eve, King David, and King Solomon. ERICH LESSING/ART RESOURCE, NY

ultimate origins of the Orthodox Church in the Byzantine Church are in the apostolic mission following the divine plan of salvation that "repentance and forgiveness of sins should be preached in his name to all nations beginning from Jerusalem" (Luke 24:47). From that apostolic era to a point just prior to the emergence of Constantinople, the Christian Church had already existed for almost three hundred years. A unity of faith manifested in a rich diversity of traditions marked this early period of the Church's existence. This diversity meant that, just within the geographical confines of the eastern Mediterranean, local churches formulated theological expressions differently. Communities in one region organized their churches along lines that differed from a neighboring region with alternate hierarchical structures. Above all, churches celebrated the liturgical rites in many and diverse ways. Over time, however, much of this vast diversity of Christian life in the East eventually coalesced around the imperial capital Constantinople, and from these diverse traditions an aggregate liturgical tradition was formed. This dynamic process, which involved countless actors and took centuries, gave shape and cohesion to the Orthodox Church. At some point Christianity was brought to Byzantium by an unknown missionary, traditionally considered to be the Apostle Andrew, but little is actually known about this period of the proto-Byzantine Church. At the time of its dedication as the capital in AD 324, Byzantium was still a city within the ecclesiastical jurisdiction of the bishop of Heraclea in Thrace, Asia Minor, within the larger civil prefecture of Oriens. All of this would quickly change with the arrival of the emperor, the imperial court, and the senate, and at once the sleepy backwater town of Byzantium was suddenly transformed into the center of the civilized world. At the same time the church of ancient Byzantium was transformed into the imperial Church of Constantinople and given a position within Christendom second only to the Church of Rome. The third canon of the Second Ecumenical Council, First Constantinople (AD 381), codified this process of transformation that had begun over half a century earlier: "The bishop of Constantinople is to have the privileges of honor after the bishop of Rome because it is the New Rome."

The course of development had already been put in place in the first quarter of the fourth century. In AD 324 the Roman emperor Constantine the Great made a fateful decision to move the capital of his empire from Rome to a more strategically advantageous location, the ancient Greek city of Byzantium. He chose Byzantium, modern-day Istanbul, because it was closer to the sites of his most pressing military campaigns and because it was easily defended, as it is located on a peninsula overlooking the Bosphorus. Byzantium would eventually become known as Constantinople, named after its founder, and for its entire life as the capital city, Constantinople was the heart of the political, cultural, and religious life of what would later be known as the Byzantine Empire. At this earliest stage of development, the liturgical traditions of the Church of Constantinople began to be formed by innumerable factors. Certainly the imperial ritual of ancient Rome influenced the development of the Church's liturgical tradition. All the trappings of the imperium, of power and authority, such as lights, incense, processions, found a ready home in the rapidly developing liturgical ritual idiom that now had to speak to the large crowds of new converts to Christianity. Constantinople naturally drew people from all over the empire with the lure of opportunities that could be found in the new capital of the empire and the preeminent church in the East. The liturgical traditions these persons brought with them from the other great cities of Christian late antiquity provided the Byzantine Church with a vibrant and constant source of liturgical influences. Antioch, for example, helped shape the early Church of Constantinople simply by its close proximity and by virtue of its great prestige. Antioch also supplied Constantinople with many of its leading early ecclesiastical figures, John Chrysostom and Nestorius, for example, who brought with them elements of an Antiochene liturgical tradition that was itself based on a unique combination of Hellenism and Semitic Christianity.

Among the cities whose liturgical practices influenced those of Constantinople, perhaps no other city influenced the Byzantine liturgy to a greater degree than the Church of Jerusalem. For almost a millennium the holy city would continue to serve the Byzantine Church as a perpetual and inexhaustible source for new liturgical practices. Around 384 a traveler from the West, the great pilgrim (and first liturgical scholar) Egeria, visited Jerusalem and found a well-established liturgical tradition. Unlike most of the Christian world, this liturgical tradition had a keen sense of place. For example, there was already a developed liturgical calendar focused on biblical events and persons. And corresponding liturgical services were held at the appropriate places—the Anastasis or Holy Sepulchre for Pascha, the Church of the Nativity at Bethlehem, the Mount of Olives for Pentecost—driving home that here was the place where Christ lived. One can only imagine the impression made on the Spanish nun and countless other Christians who traveled to Jerusalem from the distant corners of the Christian world. In their monasteries or dusty little villages far away from Palestine, it would be one thing to contemplate the events recounted in the gospel and maybe celebrate them on a modest scale. It would be quite another to come to Jerusalem and stand in the very place where Christ was crucified and buried. There at the church constructed over the place, at a vigil for the day of the Lord's Resurrection, the faithful would wait outside in the courtyard, huddled in the dark, singing preliminary hymns. At cockcrow the bishop of Jerusalem would enter the cave of the Anastasis, and the doors of the church would be flung open. The faithful would then get their first glimpse of the church, with candles blazing, pouring their light out in the still-dark morning. Inside the church the faithful would be confronted with clouds of incense billowing out of the cave of the Anastasis, clergy resplendent in their fineries, and innumerable other people from all over the Christian world praying and singing psalms, which were chosen exactly for their appropriateness of time or day. At the climax of this ceremony, the bishop of Jerusalem himself would have come out of the cave of the Anastasis and would stand in its door and read the account of the Passion and Resurrection of Christ. The impact this must have had on the Christian faithful cannot be overestimated.

Not only Jerusalem but also the cities (Bethlehem, for example) and especially the desert that surrounded Jerusalem played an important role in the liturgical development of the Eastern Christian Churches. The monasteries were built in the gullies of the Palestinian desert by men who first came to the area because of Jerusalem. With the foundation of these monasteries, the lives of the monks were inexorably linked to Jerusalem, the holy places, and ecclesiastical politics. Perhaps a combination of the fame of these monks and their association with Jerusalem gave them a prestige in the Eastern Churches far outstripping any other monastic community of the day, with the exception of Egyptian monasticism. Like Jerusalem, the prestige of the Palestinian monastic foundations can be witnessed in the liturgical influence they exerted over the various Eastern Churches. This liturgical influence continued long after the doctrinal splits of the fifth and sixth centuries. That the Byzantine liturgical tradition was influenced by Palestinian monasteries is an understatement. The prevalent book of liturgical direction for the Byzantine Church, the *Typikon*, is precisely the *Typikon of the Ecclesiastical Order of the Holy Lavra in Jerusalem of Our Venerable and God-Bearing Father Sabas*. An examination of the history of the Byzantine liturgical tradition shows that influence of the ecclesiastical order of Palestine and Jerusalem was so strong that it even supplanted the native imperial Constantinopolitan tradition. For example, in numerous Byzantine *Typika* there is a direction for the liturgical rites of Holy Friday that says, "We have received the tradition from the fathers in Palestine, not to celebrate the liturgy of the Presanctified Gifts on this day." This rubric contradicts the authentic Constantinopolitan tradition that in fact celebrated the Presanctified Liturgy on this day (in the liturgy of the Presanctified Gifts, there is no anaphora, but provision is made for communion under elements reserved from a previous celebration). What is known therefore as the Orthodox Church in the Byzantine Empire is at its origins really the sum of numerous parts from throughout the Christian world.

Perhaps equally characteristic of this early phase is the involvement of emperors and the imperial family in the liturgical life of the church. The level of imperial involvement ranged from participation in the liturgical services, where they were accorded all deference as befitted their imperial office, to the introduction of specific hymns, such as in the year 576, when Emperor Justin II commanded that the Cherubikon and Cenae tuae be sung at the transfer of gifts during the Divine Liturgy. No other emperor, however, was as important in the development of the liturgical traditions as Emperor Justinian I the Great. His influence can be seen at many levels in the Byzantine liturgical tradition. For example, in 535/6 he introduced into the entrance rites of the Divine Liturgy the hymn "Ho monogenês," which either he wrote or at least sanctioned. In any event the hymn reflects a concise summary of Nicene and Chalcedonian Orthodox dogma, in fact being little more than a pastiche of various creedal statements:

> Only begotten Son and Word of God who, being immortal, accepted for our salvation to take flesh from the holy Theotokos and ever virgin Mary, and without change became man and were crucified, O Christ our God, trampling down death by death, being one of the holy Trinity, glorified together with the Father and the Holy Spirit: Save us.

The doctrinal content of this hymn fits squarely within its historical context. Justinian, himself an accomplished theologian, was interested in reconciling and uniting the Orthodox Churches with those groups that had broken communion in the wake of the Council of Chalcedon. This hymn presents not only a doctrinal statement but also somewhat of a compromise by including a version of the controversial *Theopaschite* formula ("the crucified God"). Justinian was involved in many other aspects of church life and additionally left his mark on the church's liturgical year. In a letter from the year 561, he established, among other things, common dates throughout the empire for the liturgical cycle of Annunciation and Christmas and fixed the date of Hypapante, the Presentation of the Lord in the Temple, to forty days after the feast of the Nativity of Christ.

Justinian's most enduring legacy, however, must be his extensive building projects. During his reign and under his patronage, numerous churches and cathedrals were built, including the masterpiece of Byzantine ecclesiastical architecture, the Hagia Sophia, which was dedicated on 24 December 537. In his definitive study of the early churches of Constantinople and the liturgical rites that were held in them, Thomas Mathews has pointed out that the early churches, no matter what their size, share a common idea: enclosed porticos that allowed for the faithful to gather and await the arrival of the clergy; numerous entrances that allowed everyone, both clergy and laity, to enter into the church buildings at the same time; and finally, vast open interior spaces that permitted large numbers of people to attend the services.[3] As Mathews points out, these characteristics allow the inference that the early churches of Constantinople were built for a decidedly urban cathedral liturgy. While ecclesiastical architecture continued to develop, the great Church of the Hagia Sophia and the liturgy celebrated in it remained the liturgical model for the Byzantine Church. Of course this naturally meant that when other communities in the Byzantine Church emulated the liturgy celebrated there, a process of transmission and adaptation was involved, simply because no other community could hope to duplicate the liturgy of the Hagia Sophia with its immense interior, its elaborate adornment, and the large number of trained clergy and singers who served there.

By the end of the great imperial period in the seventh century, the church as well as Byzantine society was marked by a growing sense of insularity. By this point in the history of the empire, all of its former territory in Syria, Palestine, North Africa, and northern Italy had been lost. Successive invasions by Arabs from the East and Slavs from the North put the Byzantines on the defensive. A telltale sign of the anxiety of this era is the fifty-fifth canon of the Council in Trullo, which compares the fasting discipline of the Roman Church to that of Constantinople and says the Roman practice runs contrary to the "ecclesiastical order." This council equated the "ecclesiastical order" with Constantinopolitan practices and considered it normative, even though the Roman practice might well have been ancient and up to this point no one had had any problems with it. Canons from the Council in Trullo neatly summarize the state of the Byzantine liturgy at the end of the seventh century just prior to the iconoclast controversy. The Church of Constantinople is the primary see in the East (Trullo 36). The Church's hierarchy has a celibate episcopacy (Trullo 12) but a married presbytery and diaconate (Trullo 14). These ministers are commanded to give homilies every day but especially on Sundays (Trullo 19). Trullo 29 speaks of a Divine Liturgy being celebrated on Holy Thursday in the context of a question of fasting. Trullo 53, however, commands that the Presanctified Liturgy be celebrated on all other days during Great Lent except on weekends and Annunciation (compare with 58, which forbids self-communion). Trullo 32 mentions the Byzantine practice of a mixed chalice. Trullo 78 alludes to prebaptismal preparations that are to include catechesis and learning the creed. Canon 81 forbids the singing of the Trisagion hymn ("Holy God, Holy and Mighty, Holy and Immortal, have mercy on us") with the *theopaschite* interpolation "who wast crucified for us, have mercy on us." (The Byzantine Church in Constantinople had long interpreted the Trisagion as being addressed to God, but non-Chalcedonian Christians sang it with the interpolation, which changed the addressee from the triune God to Christ.)[4] Trullo 89 describes when the fast on Holy Saturday is to be broken. Trullo 90 provides precious information on the daily office, indicating when the clergy enter the sanctuary and the reckoning of liturgical time. Finally, Trullo 95 describes the various methods the Byzantine Church used to receive converts to the Orthodox Church.

The Iconoclasm Controversy and the Studite Synthesis

Within half a century of the Council in Trullo, Emperor Leo III in AD 726 had the image of Christ that was over the *Chalke* gate of the imperial palace destroyed. This event is considered the beginning of iconoclasm, a controversy that raged in various degrees of intensity for almost 150 years within the Byzantine Church. As an imperially sanctioned movement, iconoclasm sought the removal and destruction of figurative images from the church. The precise reasons for the initial outbreak of iconoclasm are murky, but with the accession of Leo III's son, Constantine V, the controversy presented serious theological challenges to the church that were met first by John of Damascus, then by Patriarch Nikephorus and Theodore of Stoudion. Iconoclasts opposed figurative images of Christ because, they said, it was impossible to depict the nature of God and so any image limited God's nature or split the person of Christ by just portraying his human-

Iconoclasm. The iconoclastic emperor Leo V (813-820) receives the icon-advocating patriarch Nicephorus I while an icon is whitewashed at right. BRITISH LIBRARY, LONDON, ADD. 19352, FOL. 27V/BRIDGEMAN ART LIBRARY

ity. The iconodules, those who favored the use of icons, countered this and argued that it was not God's nature being depicted but the person of Jesus Christ, both God and man, who was incarnate and lived on earth at a particular point in history. The iconoclast controversy went on for over a century, and its intensity waned at various points. It is difficult to judge the impact this controversy had in the daily lives of the church and society. Nonetheless along the way church councils were called to resolve the issue, supporters of icons were sent into exile, and documents in support of icons and against them were written and distributed, but in the end the issue was settled not with a large church council but when Patriarch Methodios I, an ardent iconodule, ascended the patriarchal throne on 11 March 843.

The effects of the iconoclasm controversy on the church are numerous. Most obviously, as a result of the final victory of iconodules, which is annually celebrated in the Orthodox Church on the first Sunday of Great Lent, icons and specific iconographic programs regularly adorn Orthodox church buildings as objects of devotion. These icons cannot be considered simply as decoration; rather, and especially since iconoclasm, they have played an integral role in liturgical services. From this time forward icons were regularly carried around city walls in procession by clergy during prayers of intercession for deliverance from wars or natural disasters. Icons were venerated and kissed by the faithful as part of the liturgy. During the services, clergy censed icons, which were illumined by candles and lights, as part of their circuit of the church building. Later iconographic programs that decorated church buildings illustrated the entire festal liturgical year with images that would include the feasts of Christ and his mother. Soon after the end of iconoclasm, iconographic programs took on a slightly different role and were used to reveal a key aspect of Byzantine liturgical theology, the

unity of heavenly and earthly worship. To do this Byzantine churches typically were built with a large dome, which was then decorated with a mosaic of Christ, here called Pantocrator or "the Almighty." An image of the Virgin often was placed

The triumph of Orthodoxy. The icon commemorates the restoration of icons to Orthodox worship on the First Sunday of Lent, 11 March 843, following a period of iconoclasm. Since that date, the First Sunday of Lent has been commemorated as the "Triumph of Orthodoxy." The image of the Virgin Mary Hodegetria attributed to the artistry of Luke the Evangelist appears as an icon within an icon. To the left are regent Empress Theodora and her son Emperor Michael III; to the right is Patriarch Methodios. Among the figures in the lower section is St. Theodosia of Constantinople. Byzantine, c. 1400. BRITISH MUSEUM, LONDON/HIP/SCALA/ ART RESOURCE, NY

in the apse of the church, where she would seem to be hovering, overseeing and join-ing in the liturgical worship of her son. In a homily from 867, the patriarch of Constantinople Photius, commenting on a new image of the Mother of God that was added to the apse of the Hagia Sophia [see color plate 16], says:

> before our eyes stands motionless the Virgin carrying the Creator in her arms as an infant, depicted in painting as she is in writings and visions, an interceder for our salva-tion and a teacher of reverence to God, a grace of the eyes and a grace of the mind, carried by which the divine love in us is uplifted to the intelligible beauty of truth.[5]

Additionally images of angels and prophets from the Old Testament would be added, forming a choir. When Orthodox believers entered into such a church, they were presented with a structure that revealed neither a remote God nor a mere image. Rather, Patriarch Photius insisted, such a structure was anchored in "truth and real-ity" and revealed "grace and Spirit."[6]

Inadvertently iconoclasm helped spur one of the most profound transformations in the history of the Byzantine liturgical tradition. This was accomplished by the rise of a chief proponent of the anti-iconoclastic movement, the great monastic leader and reformer Theodore of Stoudion (759–826). The name Stoudion comes from the neigh-borhood of Constantinople where the monastery of Saint John the Forerunner was located. It was in this monastery that Theodore became abbot and ascended to the height of his influence and fame. Prior to Theodore's arrival at the monastery of Saint John, it had been inhabited at one time by a group of monks called the *akoimetoi* or the "sleepless ones." They were given this name because the monks maintained a twenty-four hour liturgical cursus (in shifts, to be sure), and consequently the monastery never slept. In the course of the sixty-five years of his life, Theodore was involved in every major theological controversy of his day. Because of his activities, he was for-mally exiled on three different occasions while at other times serving as chief counse-lor to the emperor and giving different emperors advice not only on ecclesiastical matters but on military matters, such as encouraging Emperor Michael I Rhangabe to invade the Bulgars at one point. More central to the development of the liturgy, Theodore witnessed to Byzantine monasticism and served as its leading inspiration, activist, and promoter. Through his work, he formed what he himself called *ta tagma*, a monastic confederation or "order" that took root and provided the subse-quent basis for the types of monasticism found in Constantinople, southern Italy, and Mount Athos and then throughout the empire and the Orthodox world.

Theodore began his monastic career at a monastery on a family estate in Asia Mi-nor but then moved to a monastery in Sakkoudion under the direction of his uncle Plato. In 799 he and the other monastics at Sakkoudion were invited to take over the monastery of Saint John the Forerunner in the Stoudion area of Constantinople. This fateful move begins the establishment of the Studite monastic confederation as Theodore becomes abbot of the Stoudion monastery as well as remaining coabbot of the Sakkoudion monastery, a position he had been appointed to in 794. Once at Stoudion, Theodore continues a program of monastic life, undoubtedly started while still at Sakkoudion, that has at its core the idea of returning to the monastic traditions laid down by the great monastic figures of the East, most especially Basil the Great and Dorotheus of Gaza. Time and again Theodore refers to the "tradition of the fathers" as the guiding principles of what can be recognized now as a process of mo-nastic reform. The reforms consisted in a strong emphasis on learning, which was manifested in time given over to reading and catechism, a highly structured cenobitic monastic life with almost complete subservience to the abbot, a recognition of the importance of physical activity, and finally, a rigorous liturgical life with liturgical traditions that were a synthesis of native Constantinopolitan practices and the traditions of the great monasteries of Palestine.

For the most part Theodore created this synthesis by combining the Palestinian monastic tradition with the Constantinopolitan cathedral tradition. Liturgical scholarship has tended to think that the synthesis was formed when Theodore invited Palestinian monks to his monastery in Constantinople to bolster the orthodoxy of his order of monks in their struggle in the iconoclasm controversy. It was simply assumed that, in his letters inviting the monks from Palestine, Theodore was referring to his resistance to the official imperial iconoclasm. But Thomas Pott has shown from the chronology of the letters that Theodore wrote them much later in life and in exile (AD 808–811 and 818), and so they could speak to the origin of his liturgical synthesis. Additionally Theodore was defending Orthodoxy not against iconoclasm but in a fight he waged against the imperial house over a marriage he deemed illicit. Furthermore Theodore held the ecclesiastical traditions of his monastic elders as unwritten law; it would have been inconceivable for him to create something new contrary to what he had learned. The origins of his liturgical synthesis, therefore, point not toward Constantinople but toward his origins in monastic life at Sakkoudion in Asia Minor under his uncle Plato. Indeed after the Arab invasions in Palestine beginning in the seventh century, it is well known that Palestinian monks found refuge deep in the heart of the Byzantine Empire on Mount Olympus in Asia Minor, near the Sakkoudion monastery where Theodore entered monasticism. There is contemporary liturgical evidence from other parts of the empire that exactly shows the far-flung dispersion of Palestinian monastic traditions melding together with Constantinopolitan liturgical practices, such as the eighth-century *Euchologion* contained in codex Barberini Greek 336.[7] Theodore's liturgical work— he was above all an inspired hymnographer—betrays the hand not of someone creating new forms but of someone who worked in a familiar medium. In other words, he is credited with writing hymns, but the hymns ascribed to him are written to be used in already established ways. Theodore's legacy looms large in the Byzantine liturgical tradition. He spent a life developing his synthesis, which was codified in writing within a generation after his death. This facilitated its easy transmission throughout the Byzantine world through his monastic confederation. And as his liturgical practices were spread through his confederation, the distinctive character of the Studite liturgical synthesis—the aggregation of Constantinopolitan cathedral and Palestinian monastic traditions as well as his emphasis on catechism—in turn marked the confederation and held it together.

Christos Pantocrator. The enthroned Christ, the ruler of the world, gazes from the dome into the interior of the Church of the Katholikon at the monastery of Hosias Loukas located on the slopes of Mount Helikon in Greece. The building and many of its decorations date from the tenth and eleventh centuries. ERICH LESSING/ART RESOURCE, NY

The Cathedral and the Monastic Traditions

The modern rites of the Orthodox Church stand at the end of a long process of historical development. The Studite synthesis represents an important turning point in the liturgical process. The history of the liturgy, however, is not linear or confined to a small group of people or even simply the history of the monastic tradition. Rather, the history of the liturgy is made up of countless actors and innumerable factors that have extended over a huge geographical area. In fact two distinct traditions of celebrating the daily office coexisted for a long period of the history of the church, namely, cathedral and monastic traditions. The liturgical manuscripts themselves witness to these two traditions. For example, a note placed at the beginning of the music for *orthros* or morning prayer in a fifteenth-century musical manuscript from the Monastery of Saint Catherine's on Mount Sinai (Sinai Greek 1293) speaks of a florid arrangement of a particular psalm verse, Psalm 142:10 (LXX), "Lead me on a level ground," that is characteristic of cathedral orthros. The manuscript notes that this psalm verse

> is sung in the Catholic [i.e., non-monastic] Churches on designated feasts when Great Vespers is not sung. But in monasteries it is not like this. After the end of Great Vespers, a reading takes place, and after this, the *Hexapsalmos*, then the Great Litany, and, after the exphonesis, "God is the Lord ... ," in the tone of the troparion.

Described here is a key difference between the late cathedral rite, otherwise designated as the "sung office," and the monastic rite. The difference noted consists in alternative ways of celebrating the office on feast days. The cathedral rite has one way, characterized by elaborate singing of psalm verses, and the monastic has another, that of the all-night vigil, where vespers is combined with orthros, separated only by a reading from the New Testament or a patristic commentary. When analyzing these two liturgical traditions, great care needs to be taken in drawing lines of demarcation if for no other reason than that monastics were found in almost every cathedral community throughout the empire. Furthermore at least one major monastic liturgical tradition, the Studite, originated from a monastery that existed in the middle of Constantinople. The Studite tradition itself, in fact, was a synthesis of monastic and cathedral. Moreover as the cathedral rite waned toward the end of the fourteenth century, its practitioners borrowed more and more from the monastic rites and inserted these elements into the venerable cathedral traditions. Nevertheless broad descriptions for the two traditions can be sketched, even though their coexistence involved the interaction of persons and the exchange of liturgical rites and texts.

Within these broadly defined traditions, innumerable local practices existed side by side. As difficult as it is to define the cathedral rite, it is even harder to define the monastic rite because it is a conglomeration of various monastic liturgical traditions. Each monastery, even if it followed a similar liturgical tradition to another, would still have its own distinct practices. Nevertheless certain characteristics of the monastic rite can be adduced, especially in comparison with the cathedral rite. Obviously, as the name implies, the monastic rite was developed in monasteries by and for monks who had withdrawn from the worldly life and entered a life of contemplation and prayer. Any work they did was secondary to their life of prayer. Thus the monastic daily cursus had not only evening and morning worship but also worship throughout the day and the night. Another hallmark of monastic liturgy is vigils and keeping vigil, both throughout the day and throughout the night. The services were developed precisely to occupy the monks through their labors and their long vigils. Psalmody was read not for its appropriateness to time and day but in large blocks, just one psalm after another. Other parts of scripture were read in a similar fashion. Indeed some of our earliest descriptions of monastic vigils describe simply the entire Psalter being read along with other texts from scripture. For example, the description of a monastic vigil found in the *Narration of the Abbots John and Sophronius* from the early seventh century records little more than the Psalter read in three parts, along with the epistles of James, Peter, and John, and concluding with some early Christian hymns.[8] As with the cathedral rite, the monastic rite can in no way be considered monolithic. The rite that the Orthodox Churches throughout the world celebrate in the early twenty-first century is more or less a dialect, as it were, of a particular form of the monastic rite that finds its origins in an aggregate of monastic traditions from Egypt, Asia Minor, and Syria, above all the monasteries of Palestine, and finally, the urban monasticism of Jerusalem and Constantinople.[9]

Many monastic writers recognized the aggregate character and variegated forms of the monastic liturgy and commented on it. For example, in a simple glance through manuscript copies of *Typika*, one regularly encounters compilers ruminating on diversity of liturgical practice. They say such things as "We have discovered in the order of the Holy Mountain and monasteries in the city of Byzantium," and then they describe the particular difference great or small.[10] Or:

> It is necessary to know that in the Lavra of our Blessed father Saba, Compline is not sung in the Church, but each [does it] in [their] cells, and we have received this; but in the cenobitic houses of Palestine, it is sung like this.[11]

The compiler then continues with the difference in the order of psalmody enumerated. Other monastic leaders, when confronted with diverse usages, try to make sense of it. Prominent among these is a figure from the environs of Antioch named Nikon of the Black Mountain (1025–c. 1088). While Nikon was compiling the *Typikon* for his monastery, he says that he

> came upon and collected different *Typika*, of Studios [i.e., a form of urban monasticism centered in Constantinople] and of Jerusalem, and one did not agree with the other, neither Studite with another Studite one, nor Jerusalem ones with Jerusalem ones. And, greatly perplexed by this, [he] interrogated the wise ones and the ancients, and those having knowledge of these matters and seasoned in things pertaining to the office of ecclesiarch and the rest, of the holy monastery of our holy father Saba in Jerusalem, including the office of hegumen.[12]

Nikon then went about compiling the *Typikon* for his monastery by synthesizing what he considered best from the different monastic traditions. His methodology is interesting: in the end he did not create something out of whole cloth but fashioned together a *Typikon* out of extant sources, grounding himself in "the tradition of the holy fathers firmly in all respects."[13] Thus at once he created a brand new *Typikon*, but one based on the venerable traditions of the monastic life. This method of creating what modern scholarship would designate as a new liturgical document out of existing sources reveals much about Nikon and other Byzantine churchmen. It would have been inconceivable for Nikon to do whatever he felt in terms of the liturgy. Whatever he did, or whatever countless other Orthodox churchmen throughout the ages did, it had to be done within the context of what had been given over to him. This does not mean that everything received was considered of equal value or that the Nikon and the Church regularly fell prey to fundamentalism. Nikon himself sifted and sorted through a great amount of material searching for authentic answers to his liturgical questions. For Nikon and other churchmen, an inestimable value was placed on what was received from those who were considered authentic witnesses of the Church's tradition. For Nikon, the great monastic leaders—Basil the Great, Pachomios, Theodore of Stoudios, all his predecessors—were shown to be authentic teachers of the authentic tradition and therefore it was necessary to emulate them and their lives.

Shortly after the initial Studite synthesis, the Byzantine churchmen began transmitting the rite throughout the geographical sphere of influence of the Byzantine Empire. The Studite monks passed along their synthesis by way of the network of Studite monasteries. But at the same time the Byzantine rite was moving beyond the strict borders of the empire. In the ninth century the great Slavic missionary brothers, Cyril and Methodios, and their immediate disciples translated the Byzantine liturgy from Greek into Slavonic and bequeathed to the Slavs the great liturgical treasure of the Byzantine Church. Not too much later, in AD 988, the glories of the Byzantine liturgy helped convert another group of people of Slavic origins, the Rus' of Kiev. The *Russian Primary Chronicle* recounts how the great prince of Kiev, Vladimir, sent out emissaries to the neighboring kingdoms to find a suitable religion for his people. Vladimir's emissaries were unimpressed with all the other faiths save that of the Byzantine Empire. For when the emissaries arrived in Constantinople, they were immediately taken to the greatest Christian cathedral in the world, the Hagia Sophia. The emissaries assured Vladimir that the religion of the Byzantines was the one to adopt because when they witnessed the liturgy being celebrated in the Hagia Sophia they were overcome by its beauty. They reported to Vladimir:

> We knew not whether we were in heaven or on earth. For on earth there is no such splendor or such beauty, and we are at a loss how to describe it. We know only that God dwells there among men, and their service is fairer than the ceremonies of other nations. For we cannot forget that beauty.[14]

Even though in the middle- and late-Byzantine periods the rite was undergoing a rapid expansion all the way to Kiev and eventually to the Arctic Circle, the heart of the rite remained in the Byzantine Empire. This transmission to the Slavs, nevertheless, points to the rite's future, to continued adaptation and assimilation of the rite in lands far away from the Byzantine Empire by people who were neither subject to the Byzantine Empire nor even Greek speakers.

The conversion stories of Vladimir's emissaries testify to visual splendor and the overwhelming power of the Byzantine rite. The services these emissaries witnessed were not celebrated according to the monastic tradition but according to the cathedral rite, the other great liturgical tradition within the Byzantine Church. The cathedral rite originated in the great cities of antiquity—Rome, Alexandria, Constantinople, Antioch, and Jerusalem—and was developed precisely for urban life. Often centered around the great episcopal cathedrals and parish churches of these cities, morning and evening services framed the day with regular processions taking place, which were meant to emphasize the unity of all the Christians in the one city.[15] The services themselves were highly organized and required large numbers of higher and lower clergy, along with trained singers who could sing complex melodies and also lead the entire congregation in psalmody in the long services. It is indicative of the large number of clergy needed for the celebration of the cathedral rite that Emperor Justinian in the sixth century had to limit the number of clergy for the patriarchal churches in Constantinople. In *Novella III* the emperor allows for no more than 60 priests, 100

Russia becomes a Christian nation. The Radziwill Chronicle (fifteenth century), which records the history of Russia from the fifth through the thirteenth centuries, includes the story of the conversion of Vladimir, Prince of Kiev. One page of the Chronicle shows Vladimir's emissaries attending the Orthodox liturgy. Another page pictures Vladimir's baptism at Cherson in 987/988 and the subsequent baptism of his entire court. ACADEMY OF SCIENCE, SAINT PETERSBURG, RUSSIA/ERICH LESSING/ART RESOURCE, NY

male deacons and 40 deaconesses, 90 subdeacons, 110 readers, 25 chanters, and 100 hundred doorkeepers.[16] Certainly all of these clergy rarely, if ever, served together all at once. Rather, they were needed to maintain a number of patriarchal churches in Constantinople. Nevertheless a large contingent of clergy likely served the daily services, during which the various liturgical duties were distributed to the appropriate ministers. In other words, at any given service singers would chant responses or psalms, priests would recite prayers, deacons would lead the faithful in litanies, and a bishop might only make an entrance after the service began when he was needed.

An important document that witnesses to such a distribution of duties among the clergy of a cathedral is the now lost manuscript *Codex Pyromalus*, published by Jacques Goar in his monumental collection of euchological materials, *Euchologion sive Rituale Graecorum*.[17] This manuscript, a *Diataxis*, or Rubric Book, describes the celebration of the Divine Liturgy of Saint Basil "according to the order of the Great Church [i.e., the Hagia Sophia in Constantinople]." Through comparison with other liturgical texts, scholars have been able to date the liturgy described in this document to the tenth century.[18] The first directions given in the text read:

> Prayer which the patriarch makes over the offering of the holy bread, "O God, our God. . . ." Before the arrival of the patriarch, the priests and the concelebrating deacons enter into the Church. When all are standing before the holy doors, the first of the priests bows his head and quietly says this prayer, "O Lord, our God, whose power is . . . " Then the chanters sing two or three verses of the psalm, "It is good to give thanks to the Lord." And the deacon who is slightly above and behind them on the second step of the ambon, proclaims the *eirinika*, "In peace let us pray to the Lord."[19]

This brief passage displays many elements characteristic of cathedral services: numerous clergy are mentioned (bishops, priests, deacons, chanters), all of whom await the arrival of the patriarch. The patriarch himself is designated as the chief celebrant, though he is not present for the beginning of the service. Mention of a patriarch or bishop is an obvious sign that a document describes a cathedral service. Likewise the document refers to specific architectural features of cathedrals, notably the *ambon*, which was a raised platform in the center of the nave upon which ministers ascended to read scripture or, as here, deacons ascended to recite litanies.

The *Codex Pyromalus* fits well in the taxonomy of documents that describe the services celebrated in the great cathedrals throughout the Byzantine Empire. Reading them, the power of the services is easy to imagine. Not only would they have been elaborately celebrated, with highly trained singers, long processions in fine vestments, and candles and incenses, but also the most important officials of the church participated in these services. For many, this would have been the only chance to see the high officials of the church. Conversely, these grand liturgical ceremonies were occasions when the high officials of the church wanted to be seen and could therefore make deliberate gestures. In fact much of the cathedral rite was about making a particular point. Early cathedral or urban liturgy, for example, was concerned about maintaining the unity of the church in a geographically diffuse city. So in Rome the Church developed the practice of sending to the various "parishes" of the city a portion of the sacramental bread, the *fermentum*, to emphasize the unity of the Church around the eucharist. Similarly in Constantinople as elsewhere official processions wound their way through the city, stopping at different stations to say a litany, read a gospel lesson, and recite a prayer. The point of such procession was to give a visual sign of the unity of the Church.

These grand ritual gestures were by no means confined to late antiquity. At the end of the fourteenth century, as the Byzantine Empire was rapidly crumbling, one of the last documents describing the cathedral rite appears. Written by a powerful deacon of the patriarchal chancery, Dimitrios Gemistos, who was more a bureaucratic functionary than a liturgical theologian, this document, an Ordinance of the Patriarchal Liturgy, describes how the patriarch served the Divine Liturgy at his cathedral in Constantinople, the Hagia Sophia. The contents of this ordinance betray not the slightest hint that what was happening outside was but a mere shadow of the once-glorious Byzantine Empire. However, reading between the lines and deciphering its ritual code, the immense power of the Byzantine patriarch at the end of the fourteenth century becomes evident. Perhaps nowhere is this power more apparent than when the document describes the preliminary rites of episcopal ordination. During these rites, the ordinand stood before the patriarch and read a confession of faith. This rite took place in the back of the Hagia Sophia, and the patriarch, surrounded by other bishops, priests, and the most important deacons and officials of his chancery, sat on a high throne directly under an image of Christ. This image, called the *Chalke* image of Christ, depicted Christ standing with his right arm extended, bestowing a blessing. When the ordinand finished his confession of faith, the patriarch himself stood and extended his own in blessing in imitation of Christ, mimicking the exact posture and action of Christ. A clear connection was being asserted between Christ and the patriarch, one that equated the patriarch to Christ himself. Contemporary literature regularly speaks more explicitly of this identification. A mere ten to fifteen years after the composition of the *Diataxis*, Patriarch Anthony of Constantinople expressed clearly his view on where the patriarch ultimately derived his authority. In the midst of chastising the Muscovite prince for neglecting the commemoration of the Byzantine emperor in the liturgy, he says:

> Do you not know that the patriarch holds the position of Christ and sits on the very throne of the Master? You despise not a man, but Christ Himself, since he who honors the patriarch honors Christ himself.[20]

Equally characteristic of the cathedral rite was the particular way psalms were sung, antiphonally, and selected especially for their relevance to the time of day or the liturgical commemoration. Already in the fourth century the pilgrim Egeria remarked on the practice of the Jerusalem Church in selecting psalms that were "always appropriate, whether at night, in the early morning, at the day prayers at midday or three o'clock, or at Lucernare. Everything is suitable, appropriate, and relevant to what is being done."[21] This careful selection of psalms for the daily office entailed the antiphonal singing of only a few select psalm verses. The cathedral churches in Constantinople followed a similar method of selecting particular psalm verses and singing them antiphonally at set times of the day. The cathedral Psalter in use in Constantinople, which is attributed to Patriarch Anthimos (535–536) of Constantinople, divided the Psalter into seventy-four or seventy-six groups of psalms that were sung both in a set pattern in the office and on a rotating cycle. The psalms were further divided into over two thousand psalm verses, each with its own refrain.[22] Even though Constantinople and Jerusalem shared a method of psalmodizing, it can by no means be inferred that the cathedral rite was in any way monolithic. In and around Jerusalem, for example, the liturgical life was anchored on the holy sites throughout the city and in the surrounding countryside. For the Byzantine Empire, the ritual topography was entirely different. In the cathedral services in Constantinople, the services were also marked by the participation of the emperor, who took part in entrances, occasionally joined in the singing, and censed the altar table and blessed it with the candles.

Even within Constantinople the liturgical rites of the city differed greatly depending on where one went. An interesting note is found in an eleventh-century *Euchologion* compiled by Strategios, a presbyter of the Great Church and the patriarchal chapels in Constantinople who, after providing the necessary service texts for the celebration of Vespers with the Kneeling Prayers on the evening of Pentecost, comments:

> And, as was written, this is how the Great Church of God does the Office of Kneeling Prayers for Pentecost. But for the other Catholic Churches, the house Churches, and the monasteries, one does it one way and another does it another way.[23]

He then goes on to describe at least five different ways of celebrating the same service. This Constantinopolitan tradition of the cathedral form of worship remained in force in Constantinople and other great cities of the empire until the beginning of the thirteenth century. After this its practitioners could only be found in Thessalonika, the second city of the empire, and occasionally in Constantinople.

For over a thousand years of its existence, the cathedral rite had psalm verses with a short refrain as almost the sole content of its hymnal. This exclusive use of psalms in the cathedral rite meant that these services had a strong Old Testament flavor and gave them, in the words of Alexander Lingas, a "coolly majestic 'imperial'" character.[24] But in the face of the monastic traditions with compelling and vivid hymnography, it was a natural development for the cathedral rite to incorporate into itself a large measure of these hymns. This development happens only at the very end of the existence of the cathedral rite, in the fourteenth century, when hymns of monastic origin, canons, *troparia*, and so forth, are introduced into the order of the cathedral rite. Archbishop Symeon of Thessalonika, who not only commented on the liturgy in the fourteenth and fifteenth centuries but was instrumental in changing the cathedral services, admits to adding monastic hymnography. He says this was done to preserve but also revive interest in the cathedral services. He remarks:

> But wishing that order to be preserved and kept from harm, we ourselves have introduced the canons as a sort of spice or sweetening so that no lazy or indifferent person grumbling about beauty and knowing nothing of order may find a pretext to destroy it, alleging that he does not hear the familiar canons that are sung by all.[25]

It is not surprising that as the empire was passing away, so too would this last great witness to late antiquity.

By the end of the fourteenth century the Byzantine cathedral rite gave way almost completely to the monastic rite. Archbishop Symeon is an important witness to this, but the shift can also be seen in other documents. The *Diataxis* of Dimitrios Gemistos likewise witnesses to the complete prevalence of the monastic tradition in the fourteenth century. When Gemistos sat down to compose his *Diataxis*, which was to describe how the patriarch of Constantinople served the Divine Liturgy in the Hagia Sophia, he utilized as one of his chief sources the Athonite monastic *Diataxis* of Philotheos Kokkinos. Thus he mixed the practices of a small monastic church with those of the vast patriarchal, urban cathedral. By so doing Gemistos helped assure the victory of the monastic rite over the cathedral rite and unwittingly cemented a process that had been going on for centuries. Gemistos, however, was only one actor in a drama, which had been going on for almost a thousand years and involved countless people. In fact the victory of the monastic rite—of Byzantine liturgical history—is not a story of a few people but of many. If Gemistos did reflect on what he was doing, he probably thought that he was merely codifying existing traditions and liturgical practices. His view on this would be perfectly akin to another contemporary Byzantine liturgist, Archbishop Symeon of Thessalonika, who also is said to have reformed the liturgy. But Alexander Lingas, who has evaluated the content of Symeon's reforms, concludes that far from being "revolutionary," the reforms "represented the harmonization and systematization of existing precedents for the inclusion of texts and music from outside the Byzantine cathedral tradition."[26] When the Byzantine Empire fell to the Ottoman Turks in May 1453, what was left was simply the monastic liturgical tradition in its various forms. The shape of the Byzantine liturgy at the end of the fourteenth century is essentially the shape the liturgy has retained into the modern era.

The Post-Byzantine Period and the Rise of Russia

Within a hundred years after the fall of the Byzantine Empire, after a couple of generations had already lived in the new reality of the Ottoman Empire, around the middle of the sixteenth century, a new period of the Byzantine-Slavic liturgical rite opened, that of the post-Byzantine or premodern period. In this period there is no longer a geographical center of the rite. The Byzantine Empire had fallen, and though the Church continued, its members struggled with the fact that Church and state were no longer inexorably intertwined. At the same time a new Orthodox power, the Russian Empire, was beginning to emerge as the dominant force in the Orthodox Churches. But while there was no center to the rite, there was a common desire to consolidate and codify the rite. For the Greek-speaking Christians in the Ottoman Empire, this was done in the face of social instability and insecurity about their place in a Muslim-dominated society. It was a time not to change but to maintain. For the Russians, the consolidation and codification of the rites was born out of different motivations, namely under the pretense of becoming more like the Greeks, more like the Byzantine Empire of old, and hence more like a real Orthodox empire.

Concretely the consolidation and codification of the rites take place in the seventeenth century under the directions of the Muscovite patriarch Nikon. Even by medieval Russian standards, Nikon was a forceful personality. Convinced that the Russian service books were not fully "orthodox" but rather corrupted because they were not identical to Orthodox service books in Greek, Nikon set out on an official policy of reforming the Russian service books. To accomplish this reform, he sent church officials to the important ecclesiastical centers in the Greek-speaking churches to find Greek service books that could be used to correct the Russian liturgical books. The officials returned and began the process of translation and correction immediately. What Nikon's correctors brought back with them and subsequently used as the basis for their work differed from the official account. Officially the correctors worked from the best and oldest liturgical manuscripts; in reality it is estimated that of the approximately five hundred manuscripts brought to Russia, fewer than ten were liturgical. What was really used, and recognized at the time, were the early printed Greek books published in Venice, especially the *Euchologion* published in Venice in 1602. Naturally Nikon's corrections aroused a firestorm of protest on the part of those who were committed to the old books and the older liturgical traditions contained in the books. This group, called Old Believers, was led by a fiery priest, Avvakum, among others and eventually split away from the Russian Church in protest over Nikon's liturgical reforms. Nikon predicated his reforms on the superiority of all things Greek. If Russian practice differed in any way from Greek practice, he felt Russian practice had to be brought in line with the Greeks. He was reported to have said, "Although I am a Russian and the son of a Russian, my faith and my convictions are Greek." To this end he changed not only the liturgical books but insisted on other changes as well, such as adopting Greek-style ecclesiastical dress. Rather famously he also insisted that Russians begin making the sign of the cross as in the Greek manner, with their right index and middle finger held together with the thumb, as opposed to making the cross with two fingers (the index and middle finger). The Great Russian Council of 1666–1667 officially endorsed Nikon's reforms but condemned and deposed him due to the heavy-handed ways that he went about enforcing his reforms.

Both Nikon and his opponents struggled to present what they considered to be the "authentic" Orthodox liturgy. While they differed in the details, they both suffered under the same misapprehension that there was such a thing in the Orthodox Church as one, authentic liturgical rite. Authenticity for them both meant monolithic. For Nikon's opponents, the one way was the Russian tradition that they had inherited; and in fact this Russian tradition they defended was simply an older liturgical tradition. For Nikon, the authentic tradition was the Greek way, but the Greek way he advocated stood at the end of a long line of liturgical development. Neither Nikon nor the Old Believers appreciated the facts of liturgical development of the Byzantine liturgy and of diversity of liturgical practices that had always existed in the Byzantine rite. An awareness of these issues would only come later with the dawn of the post-Enlightenment, modern era. During this period the history of the liturgy is marked by a change in interpretation brought about by a new historical consciousness and

Transfiguration of our Lord Russian Orthodox Church. Located in the village of Ninilchik on the west coast of the Alaskan Kenai peninsula, the present church building dates from 1901 and was designed by a local architect, Aleksei Oskolkoff. The congregation in Ninilchik was founded in 1846; the Orthodox faith arrived in Alaska (Kodiak Island) in 1797 through the efforts of St. Herman and others. PHOTOGRAPH BY VINCE STREANO AND CAROL HAVENS/ART DIRECTORS AND TRIP

new developments in scholarship. Naturally the historical development and even the modern diversity of the Byzantine liturgical rite are equally predicated in the diversity of human culture, which conditions the liturgy through adaptation. This is a more fundamental reason for liturgical change and diversity. Adaptation can easily be seen in the historical record, and some of it at least can be categorized under the rubric of organic development. Even further, as in all Christian worship, the faithful apprehend the Byzantine liturgy through their capacity for rational thought, which is itself the sum of multiple factors. Christian faithful in the post-Enlightenment modern era have a much different worldview than their ancestors in the Byzantine Empire. So in order for the liturgy to remain intelligible for the countless number of Christian believers who have worshiped according to the Byzantine rite and therefore fulfill its salvific purpose, the liturgy has had to renew itself in every generation.

The Modern Era and Cultural Diversity

Throughout the history of the venerable Byzantine liturgical rite, the transmission of its traditions beyond the lands of its formation to the far corners of the world has brought with it necessary adaptation. Today the faithful no longer celebrate their liturgy only in the Greek language of late antiquity or in a descendent language of Old Slavic but also in Arabic, English, French, German, Spanish, Japanese, and various native Alaskan dialects, among others. In western Europe and North America a new emphasis and concern has been placed on the involvement of the laity in the liturgy, reflecting the democratic ideals of the Western world. Even in regions of Africa where the Byzantine rite has been taken, some accommodations to the liturgy have been made in response to the traditions of African tribal life. Thus the Byzantine liturgical tradition is no longer a liturgical rite solely of the eastern Mediterranean, the Balkan Peninsula, or even eastern Europe, but it is also western, northern, and southern as its adherents can now be found in all parts of the world. This has not come about without challenges, however. In each new region of the world where the tradition has come, the communities of believers struggle to remain faithful to their liturgical inheritance while living in a new situation and facing all the problems of the modern world. Indeed given the rapid technological developments and the prevalence of secularism in the second half of the twentieth century, the countries in whose soil the rich Byzantine liturgical tradition took root and grew strong must now face these same challenges while at the same time authentically preserving their legacy.

While united today as inheritors of the liturgical legacy of the Byzantine Empire, the followers of this rite are by no means united in ecclesiastical allegiance. By far the vast majority of believers belong to the Orthodox Church and are members of one of the fifteen autocephalous (self-governing) Orthodox Churches. These churches continue to be ranked in order of precedence, first according to the ancient reckoning of the Ecumenical Councils (cf. the thirty-sixth canon of the Council in Trullo) and then according to a variety of ecclesiastical and nonecclesiastical factors. The first four patriarchal churches, which are also the most ancient, are supranational churches:

1. the patriarch of Constantinople, whose primary authority covers Turkey, the Greek Islands, and the monastic communities on Mount Athos as well as ethnic communities, including those of Greek, Russian, Ukrainian, and Carpatho-Russian ancestry, throughout the world;
2. the patriarch of Alexandria, whose authority extends throughout Egypt and all Africa;
3. the patriarch of Antioch, whose authority extends throughout all Syria and also Arab Orthodox communities throughout the world;
4. the patriarch of Jerusalem, whose territory is confined mostly to Palestine and Jordan.

After these first four, a national or ethnic identity characterizes the rest of the autocephalous Orthodox Churches:

5. the Church of Russia;
6. the Church of Georgia;
7. the Church of Serbia;
8. the Church of Romania;
9. the Church of Bulgaria;
10. the Church of Cyprus;
11. the Church of Greece;
12. the Church of Albania;
13. the Church of Poland;
14. the Church of the Czech Republic and Slovakia;
15. the Orthodox Church in America.

Like the patriarchs of Constantinople and Antioch, a number of these other autocephalous churches have ethnic communities that exist well beyond the boundaries of their given countries.

Alongside the autocephalous Orthodox Churches, there are a handful of autonomous local Orthodox Churches, which means that they are nominally dependent on an autocephalous church. The number of churches considered officially autonomous differs slightly from church to church, but they usually include the following:

1. the Church of Mount Sinai;
2. the Church of Finland;
3. the Church of Japan;
4. the Church of Ukraine;
5. the Church of Estonia.[27]

Each of the local Orthodox Churches is served by a hierarchy of ordained ministers, deacons, priests, and bishops and is ultimately guided by one bishop, who holds the rank of a patriarch, archbishop, or metropolitan. The specific method of governance varies from local church to local church. In some local Orthodox Churches the chief bishop holds a great deal of authority, whereas in others a synod of bishops serves as the ultimate authority in the church, and in still others the lower clergy and the laity are involved to a greater degree in the management of the church's affairs. But while governing themselves independently of one another, the Orthodox Churches remain united in their faith in Jesus Christ and the Holy Trinity. Among the Orthodox Churches, the bishop or patriarch of Constantinople fulfills the unique ministry of serving as "the first among equals." By acknowledging the Constantinopolitan patriarch's primacy, the Orthodox Churches consequently see communion with him as a visible sign of their unity. Far from being an Eastern equivalent of a pope, however, his authority outside the Church of Constantinople is limited and chiefly involves the maintenance of the unity among the Orthodox Churches.

Outside the strict canonical boundaries of the Orthodox Church, there are believers who follow the Byzantine liturgical rite and the traditions of the various local Orthodox Churches but who are not in full communion with the other Orthodox Churches. These groups have broken communion with some or all of the Orthodox Churches for different reasons, ranging from the political fallout in the aftermath of the Russian Revolution to the adoption of the revised Gregorian calendar in the 1920s by the patriarch of Constantinople and the Orthodox Church of Greece.[28] Each of these groups, even though outside canonical Orthodoxy, nevertheless considers itself fully Orthodox in practice and theology. In the early twenty-first century some steps toward reconciliation of these schisms have taken place, especially within the Russian Orthodox Church. Alternatively another sizable group follows the liturgical practices and canonical discipline of the Byzantine rite but is instead in communion with the Church of Rome and consequently not with any of the Orthodox Churches. These Catholic groups are known in modern times as Greek Catholics in central Europe or Melkites in the Middle East or are lumped together and pejoratively referred to as Uniates.[29] These Catholic groups left communion with the Orthodox Churches for diverse political and theological reasons and entered into communion with the Church of Rome at various times. Perhaps the most famous events in this regard were the unions with Rome established in the sixteenth century in what is now western Ukraine and in the eighteenth century with the Melkites in Lebanon and Syria.[30]

The Orthodox Understanding of Worship

The expectation that the essential purpose of liturgical worship is the remission of sins and the "sanctification of the faithful" stands at the core of the Byzantine-Slavic liturgical tradition. As Archbishop Symeon of Thessalonika says, the purpose of liturgy is the same as the Incarnation, namely, that believers "become partakers of God and gods according to grace."[31] The worship of God the Father in the person of his Son, Jesus Christ, through the grace of the Holy Spirit fulfills this expectation in the liturgy. This worship is an encounter that is at once personal and corporate, brought about by both a direct experience and a remembrance of God's salvific work [see color plate 15]. Entering into a liturgical service, Orthodox believers receive these gifts by encountering God through a complex ritual structure that expresses in word, place, and action both God's presence and his salvific work. Already in the eighth century Patriarch Germanus I (715–730) articulated this basic premise of the Byzantine rite: "The Church is heaven on earth, in which the heavenly God has made his home and dwells; it resonates with the cross, the tomb, and the resurrection of Christ."[32] Throughout the history of this liturgical tradition, encounter and remembrance have been accomplished and contemplated through various means: the proclamation of scripture, the recitation of psalmody, the chanting of hymns, the petitions of prayer, and the performance of ritual action. Archbishop Symeon of Thessalonika stated forcefully that

> what [Christ's Church] received from the beginning, it enacts continually, and teaches what is beyond understanding through sacred symbols. Those things which are visibly enacted have partaken of such great glory, and so they are marvelous to all.[33]

What the Church has received from the beginning is, of course, the apostolic deposit: the proclamation of Jesus Christ dead, buried, and raised from the dead. This, Symeon says, the Church has received and enacts through liturgical customs and practices, which in turn is what the believers are presented in the liturgy, though how the Church has taught or portrayed this has changed through the centuries. Nicholas Cabasilas, another fourteenth-century Byzantine theologian, concurs with Symeon and explains: "In them [i.e., the rites] Christ and the deeds he accomplished and the sufferings he endured for our sakes are represented."[34] According to Cabasilas, this representation is meant to initiate faith in unbelievers, but it also "preserves, renews, and increases" the faith already present in believers. He goes on to say that in this encounter with God in the liturgy,

> beholding the unutterable freshness of the work of salvation, amazed by the abundance of God's mercy, we are brought to venerate him who had such compassion for us, who saved us at so great a price: to entrust our souls to him, to dedicate our lives to him, to enkindle in our hearts the flame of his love.

For Cabasilas, mere contemplation of liturgy as a didactic enterprise or even the nurturing of faith are not enough; these are only the journey to union with Christ. Commenting on the rites of baptism he says, "It is not merely to the extent of reasoning, thinking, and believing that the baptized may know God; something far greater and closer to reality may be found in these waters."[35] The greater reality in baptism, as it is for all the other rites, is the reception of union with Christ by the Holy Spirit. As Cabasilas says in another place: "In the sacred mysteries, we depict his burial and proclaim his death. By them we are begotten and formed and wondrously united to the Savior."[36]

According to this liturgical theology, contemplation and prayer induces faith, which stimulates desire for the Lord in the believers, who are then prepared to receive the divine mysteries. It is in the reception of these mysteries, in the reception of the body and blood of the resurrected and glorified Lord, that sanctification is added "to sanctification, that of sacred rite to contemplation, 'we are transformed from glory to glory,' that is to say, from the lesser to that which is greatest of all."[37] Centuries earlier than Cabasilas, Maximus the Confessor (580–662), Byzantium's first great mystagogue, had asserted the same thing:

> In having God through prayer as its mystical and only Father by grace, the soul will center on the oneness of his hidden being by a distraction from all things, and it will experience or rather know divine things all the more as it does not want to be its own nor able to be recognized from or by itself or anyone else's but only all of God's who takes it

up … penetrating it completely without passion and deifying all of it and transforming it unchangeably to himself.[38]

Archbishop Symeon again puts it quite simply: "These mysteries have been given to us in order that we become one with him."[39]

The Byzantine liturgy can be likened to a vibrant tapestry that portrays Christ's saving Passion. The composition of this rich tableau ranges from the darkened contemplative hues of the solitary midnight office to the stunningly bright joy of paschal midnight liturgy in a church overflowing with people. On closer inspection the tapestry is seen to be woven from diverse threads: Holy Scripture supplies the canvas on which the threads of hymnography and prayer are interwoven, ritual adorns it and gives further texture. Plainly speaking, the liturgy functions as a unitary whole, but the Church has constructed the entire liturgical symbolic structure and even each liturgical service out of diverse components, which fulfill their common purpose differently. While the Byzantine liturgy represents the divine economy in all that it does, the liturgy itself has never devolved into a mere play where Christ's Passion has been literally acted out, nor has it fostered a fanciful idea that it is possible to return to the past through magical incantations. Rather, the Orthodox Church has developed a liturgy that proclaims the Gospel by means of an intricate, complex liturgical system that speaks in many different voices. Unquestionably though, the power of these events is direct and is transmitted to the faithful in the liturgy: Christ's death and Resurrection offer believers a passage from life to life and union with him. This complex structure also forms the faithful; it gives them a way of understanding above all the Orthodox faith but also how they should live their lives being united with Christ. Even beyond deeds and works, the liturgical rites provide the faithful with suitable words, metaphors, and symbols, which they can use to understand and communicate their faith to the world around them.

Scripture

The Holy Scriptures form the backbone of the liturgy; every service makes use of them in one way or another. Moreover, the use of scripture by the Orthodox Church anchors believers in the God of the scriptures, who reveals himself to them in word. The Orthodox Church employs scriptures in various ways in order to bring out different levels of meaning of the texts. The long recitation of psalms or the reading of passages from the Old Testament prophetically points to Christ, while the reading of a gospel pericope or a passage of the Pauline corpus directly portrays Jesus Christ's saving economy. The particular context within the services where the scriptures are read provides the all-important hermeneutic tool for understanding how and why the scriptures are used in the liturgy. For example, on feast days celebrating the Lord or during Holy Week, the gospel accounts read during matins construct a historical narrative, which hymns then expand further. Miracle accounts, Jesus' ethical teachings, and the parables dominate the Sunday gospel lectionary, those readings that are read during the Divine Liturgy. But far from being a simple recitation of the life and teachings of a first-century itinerant Jewish rabbi in Palestine, the eucharistic context of these readings affects their meaning. All his teachings, parables, and miracles, which reveal his messianic identity in the Gospels, are considered within the Church, which has been gathered together for communion. So the one who speaks or is spoken of in the Gospel is identified as the one who offers his body and blood in the bread and wine. With his identity revealed and his presence assured, the liturgy reveals itself as a

Twelve Feasts of the Church. The left panel of the fourteenth-century icon shows (from left to right, top to bottom) the Annunciation, the Nativity, the Presentation, Baptism, the Transfiguration, and the raising of Lazarus. The right panel illustrates the Triumphal Entry, the Crucifixion, the Harrowing of Hell, the Ascension, Pentecost, and the Assumption of the Virgin. Museo dell'Opera del Duomo, Florence, Italy/Nicolo Orsi Battaglini/Art Resource, NY

place where God manifests his power in an encounter with his faithful people. That the gospel readings themselves reveal the presence of Jesus Christ, the Son of God the Father, in the liturgical assembly can be seen in an ancient ritual described in a liturgical document from around the turn of the first millennium, the so-called *Typikon of the Great Church*. The *Typikon of the Great Church*, a book of rubrics that described the liturgical celebration in the patriarchal cathedral in Constantinople, speaks of an enthronement of the Gospel book on the *synthronon*, which was the patriarchal throne set up in the apse of the cathedral. On the eve of the feast of the Nativity of Christ, this *Typikon* prescribes that "a Gospel book [be] placed on the *synthronon* and another on the altar table."[40] This enthronement took place during the singing of the Trisagion, at that point of the Divine Liturgy when the patriarch and concelebrating clergy ascended the synthronon and took their seats there to listen to the daily scripture readings. The *Typikon* further directs that the patriarch must sit to the left of the Gospel, in a place normally reserved for a clergyman of lower rank than the patriarch. In this ritual act the solemn enthronement of the Gospel book not only proclaims the presence of Christ but also his presidency through his word within the liturgical assembly. Although this ritual is no longer in use today, the Gospel book rests on the altar table, is elaborately decorated, and is regularly venerated and kissed by the faithful both as an object of pious devotion and a testimony to God's continued presence in the community of believers.

The gospel readings during Sunday orthros or morning prayer have a different focus and identify Christ's Resurrection as the fulfillment of the messianic expectation of the Old Testament. To do this the Church has selected eleven accounts of Christ's Resurrection culled from each of the four Gospels, which are read in a recurring cycle throughout the liturgical year.[41] These resurrection accounts are juxtaposed between set responsorial psalmody (called *prokeimena*, which rotate along a different eight-week cycle) and hymnography. The texts of responsorial psalmody are select texts taken from the Psalter, which express expectation for deliverance from God. The particular texts heighten the tension of the service as the initial psalm verse expresses the hope for deliverance and the alternating verse affirms the faithfulness of God. For example, one of the initial psalm verses for this unit of psalmody speaks of God's intention to deliver his faithful: "'Now I shall arise,' says the Lord, 'I shall place him in salvation, and speak boldly in him'" (Ps. 11:6, LXX). To this promise of a Lord who will rise up and offer salvation, the alternating verse answers in assurance: "The Lord's words are pure words, silver tried by fire, tested in earth, seven times refined" (Ps. 11:7, LXX). Thus a brief liturgical dialogue has ensued, one that proclaims God's salvation and faithfulness. This responsorial psalmody then sets the stage for the reading of one of the eleven resurrection Gospels, which specifies exactly what is the fulfillment of God's promise to deliver his people Israel: the Resurrection of his Son, Jesus Christ. This entire liturgical unit closes with a hymn that ruminates on the implications of contemplating Christ's Passion and Resurrection:

> Having beheld the resurrection of Christ, let us worship the holy Lord Jesus, the only sinless one. We venerate your cross, Christ, and we hymn and glorify your holy resurrection. You are our God; apart from you, we know no other and we call upon your name. Come, all faithful, let us worship the holy resurrection of Christ, because through the cross joy has come into all the world. Let us hymn his holy resurrection through always blessing the Lord. For by enduring the cross for us, he has destroyed death by death.

This hymn ties up the various threads of this liturgical unit and brings the Resurrection into the present life of the believer by the recurring pattern it articulates. Note that the Church does not imagine that through the recitation of psalmody and the singing of hymns the faithful are somehow magically stepping back into history to a time before the Resurrection of Christ. Rather, the hymn places Christ's Resurrection—pointed toward in the prokeimenon, proclaimed in the gospel—immediately into the life of the believer. Indeed the hymn exhorts believers to respond now to Christ's Resurrection by worshiping, hymning, and glorifying him. The doubt hinted at in the psalmody gives way to faith in the risen Lord, hope is confirmed by fulfillment, and the believer's sole response is to be one of thankful worship.

Notably the Church does not employ the entire Bible as a liturgical book but uses instead a number of different books, each containing only that part of Holy Scripture appropriate for a particular use in the services. In other words, one liturgical book contains the Gospels, another the Epistles, another the Psalms, and so forth. The Gospel book comes in two traditional forms: first, the *Evangelion*, which has the full text of the four Gospels in order with rubrics for when a passage is to be read in the margin or in a separate index; the other form, the *Lectionary*, has the text of the Gospels broken up into pericopes for daily use. The liturgical book that contains the readings from the Acts of the Apostles and the different epistles, the *Praxapostolos*, likewise comes in two forms: either the complete text with rubrics in the margin or broken up into the daily readings.[42] Two cycles govern the order in which the New

Testament is read annually. The first begins on the date of Pasch and thus follows a lunar cycle. This cycle sets forth readings for every day of the year except for the weekdays of Great Lent, when the eucharistic liturgy is not celebrated, so that most of the text of the New Testament is read annually in order. The lectionary system during Lent covers only Saturdays and Sundays. Scholars date the formation of the complete annual cycle of gospel readings to at least the ninth century, when it first begins to appear in the manuscript tradition.[43] To be sure the formation of the cycle of readings for Saturdays and Sundays dates from much earlier, though the exact time is difficult to pin down. The second cycle, following the solar cycle of months, begins on the ecclesiastical New Year, 1 September. This cycle assigns readings for festal days and for the various sanctoral commemorations. Originally these two cycles were actually part of one annual cycle; they only became separated, probably in the sixth century, as the number of sanctoral commemorations grew and the cycle simply became unwieldy. The long development of the Church's festal cycle obviously therefore influenced the development of this second cycle of gospel readings, and while it is difficult to know when this cycle fully came in existence, some elements can in fact be specifically dated.[44] Like the first cycle, the pattern for this festal-sanctoral cycle was almost completely in place by the ninth century. In liturgical practice the readings of these two cycles regularly overlap, and the readings from the festal cycle will either replace the daily readings or be simply joined to them.[45]

Passages from the Old Testament are used extensively in the liturgy with the underlying presupposition of the fundamental connection between the Old and New Testaments in that they both speak in their respective ways of Christ. For example, on the feast of the Transfiguration (6 August), selections from the Old Testament that are read at vespers connect the appearances of the Lord to Moses on Mount Sinai (Exod. 24:18; 3:4–6, 8) and to Elijah on Mount Horeb (1 Kings 19:3–16) to the transfiguration of Christ to his disciples on the high mountain (Matt. 17:1–9). The juxtaposition of these Old Testament readings with the specific festal hymnography makes a confession of faith as the God of the Old Testament is identified with the person of Jesus Christ in the New Testament, who once again speaks to Moses and Elijah about the salvation of his people, namely, "his departure, which he was to accomplish in Jerusalem" (Luke 9:31). At one time in the history of the rite, the passages from the Old Testament that are read in church were collected in a book called the *Prophetologion*, but for many centuries they have been incorporated into other books for the sake of convenience.[46]

Perhaps no other part of scripture is read during the liturgy as widely as the Psalms. In so doing the Orthodox Church utilizes a wide range of methods for chanting psalmody. To begin with an invariable group of psalms form the skeleton structure of the daily office. The service book, the *Horologion*, or the Book of Hours, contains the invariable psalms along with the other regular material that form these services.[47] During some of these services, the long continuous recitation of a variable group of psalms, called a *kathisma*, is interspersed. The Orthodox Psalter, or Book of Psalms, contains the psalms divided into twenty such kathismata, which are further broken into three *stasis* each.[48] The recitation of the kathisma results in the entire Psalter being read at least once a week throughout most of the year and twice a week during fasting periods.[49] This meditation on scripture indeed reveals the mystery of Christ, but the Church also sees a further purpose in this lengthy recitation. Namely, the ethical implications implied in the mystery of Christ can be taught and transmitted to the faithful. In his homily *On the Sacred Assembly*, Anastasius of Sinai (c. seventh century) draws this point out clearly:

> The grace of the Holy Spirit always encourages us through the entirety of the Divine
> Scripture to the carrying out of his divine commands. But even better is the exhortation
> by the prophet David that is chanted daily in psalmody. The Psalter instructs piety, it
> gives the law concerning faith, teaches chastity, directs in the fear of God, it illustrates
> punishment, compunction, continence, repentance, sympathy, love of God, submission
> to God, purity, long-suffering, fasting, and goodness. The diligence and attentiveness of
> prayer and the Divine Scriptures is the mother of all virtues.[50]

Anastasius concludes his sermon with a summation on a fundamental aspect of all the
liturgical services:

> Not frequently I hear many say, "Alas, poor me! How can I achieve salvation? I am too
> weak to fast, do not know how to keep vigil, am incapable of observing virginity, unable
> to retire from the world—how shall I obtain salvation?" How? I will show you: Forgive
> and you will be forgiven (Luke 6:37). Pardon and you will be pardoned—behold the
> short and quick way to salvation. But come, I will show you another way too. Which?
> Judge not and you will not be judged (Luke 6:37). That is the other way, without fasting,
> vigils, and efforts.[51]

At times the Orthodox Church still employs yet other ancient method of psalmody,
such as the chanting of select psalm verses antiphonally and responsorially. Strict
responsorial psalmody is the more common of the two and regularly appears throughout
the Divine Liturgy and in the office. The most common form of responsorial psalmody
still in use in the Byzantine tradition is the prokeimenon. The prokeimenon is structured quite simply: a psalm verse is first chanted by a reader, then the same verse is
sung by the singers in a particular melody. After the reader chants another verse, the
choir responds with the first verse. Some prokeimena continue this back-and-forth
recitation, but most conclude after the second verse, when the reader reads just the
first half of the verse and the choir sings the second half. Prokeimena can stand alone,
as they do at vespers, or they can introduce the epistle lection at the Divine Liturgy.
By and large strictly antiphonal singing has fallen into disuse in the Byzantine tradition, though remnants of antiphons can be found throughout different services. For
example, Robert Taft has demonstrated that there was an antiphon sung during the
distribution of communion at the Divine Liturgy in Constantinople by the sixth century. The structure of the communion antiphon at the height of its use was classic,
with psalm verses interspersed with a brief hymn, called a *koinonikon*, and concluding
with a doxology and a concluding hymn, a *perisse*. However, this antiphon was already
in decay by the twelfth century. From the time of its initial decay until the modern
era, only fragments of this original antiphon remain, the koinonikon, the doxology,
and the perisse:[52]

> Let our mouths be filled with your praise, O Lord, so that we may hymn your glory;
> because you have made us worthy of communion with your holy, immortal, and pure
> mysteries. Keep us in your holiness, meditating on your righteousness all our days.

Other select psalm verses appear intercalated with hymns. For example, at the chanting of the classic vespertine psalm, Psalm 141 (LXX 140), numerous hymns are inserted between its verses and chanted.[53] The relationship between the hymns and the
invariable psalmody is virtually nonexistent, however. A famous hymnographer of the
Church, John of Damascus, even admits as much: "When we recite a text—from a
psalm, perhaps, or a canticle—we often add to it a troparion or refrain having no
bearing on its meaning."[54]

Hymnody

Over the centuries the Church has developed a rich tradition of hymnody to proclaim, explain, and defend the faith but also to inform the faithful of the specific liturgical commemoration of a given day. The quality of these hymns varies, from a brief
couple of stanzas to a terse theological formulation. In fact for a long period Byzantine hymnographers drew inspiration from the highly theological, but also highly rhetorical, homilies of Gregory the Theologian, sometimes borrowing entire sections
outright.[55] The hymnographic tradition is diverse in its literary genres as it has been
formed over centuries and has diverse geographical origins. While early scholars have
often postulated a Syriac origin for the Byzantine hymnographic tradition, more recent scholars have pointed out that it is more likely that both traditions have a similar
origin in the earliest pieces of Syriac and Greek Christian literature.[56] Such metrical
homilies as the second-century homily by Melito of Sardis, *Peri Pascha*, originally
written in Greek, witness to a very early inspiration if not outright antecedent to the
later Greek hymnographic tradition. While the exact steps are unknown, the trajectory from homily to hymnody is not difficult to follow. For example, *Peri Pascha* reads
in one section:

> 71. He is the lamb being slain, this is the speechless lamb, this is the one born of Mary
> the fair Ewe, this is the one taken from the flock, and led to slaughter; who was sacrificed
> in the evening, and buried at night; who was not broken on the tree, who was not undone
> in the earth, who rose from the dead and resurrected humankind from the grave below.[57]

Later Greek hymns will take this exact same imagery from Isaiah 53:7b–8 of the messianic figure as a blameless lamb who will be slain by lawless men, and identify it clearly
with Christ and his Passion just as Melito did. For instance, a hymn sung during the
office on Good Friday (also found in a Syriac translation) echoes Melito's words:

> As a lamb that is led to the slaughter, O Christ King, and like a sheep without guile you
> were nailed to the cross by wicked men for our sins, O Lover of man. (Second troparion,
> First Hour, Good Friday)

To be sure Christ has been identified with the Lamb of God since at least John the
Baptist (John 1:29), but along with content, the metrical homilies and metered hymns
share a method of scriptural exegesis that interprets a passage by an interpolated word,
or a parallel verse structure, or even succinct summaries of scriptural verses.[58]

All of this is not to say that the Syriac Christian literary tradition did not have an
influence on the development of Byzantine hymnody. Historians of Byzantine
hymnography have long cited the influence of fourth-century Ephrem the Syrian's
poetry on the first known Byzantine hymnographer, Romanos the Melodist (sixth
century).[59] Romanos, himself of Syrian origin, wrote in a genre of hymnography called
a *kontakion*.[60] The structure of the entire kontakion involves a short poetic introductory piece, a *prooimion*, which establishes both the literary theme and the musical pattern that govern the rest of the kontakion. This introductory stanza is followed by an
ikos, a short hymn that takes up and develops the theme while following the musical
pattern established in the prooimion. Usually some type of refrain or alternating refrains follow each ikos, either a series of strophes with the same concluding phrase or
a simple "alleluia." A kontakion could contain as many as twenty-four ikoi with refrains. This whole structure was repeated up to twelve or thirteen times, though each
unit ended with the same refrain. The most famous kontakion, though likely not written by Romanos, must be the *Akathistos* hymn in honor of the Mother of God, which

is still prescribed to be sung on the fifth Saturday of Great Lent, though out of devotion it is often sung throughout the year by the faithful ("Akathistos" literally means "not sitting"; in other words, the hymn to be said standing). The *Akathistos* to the Mother of God follows the usual pattern of kontakia, with a short introduction, the prooimion:

> To thee, our leader in battle and defender, O Theotokos, we thy servants, delivered from calamity, offer hymns of victory and thanksgiving. Since thou art invincible in power, set us free from every peril, that we may cry to thee: Hail, Bride without Bridegroom.

The ikos comes next:

> A prince of the angels was sent to the Theotokos from heaven, to say to the Theotokos, Hail! And seeing thee, O Lord, take bodily form at the sound of his bodiless voice, filled with amazement he stood still and cried aloud to her.

Then the numerous strophes begin:

> Hail, for through thee joy shall shine forth: hail, for through thee the curse shall cease. Hail, recalling of fallen Adam: hail, deliverance from the tears of Eve. Hail, height hard to climb for the thoughts of men: hail, depth hard to scan even for the eyes of angels. Hail, for thou art the throne of the King: hail, for thou holdest him who upholds all. Hail, star causing the Sun to shine: hail, womb of the divine incarnation. Hail, for through thee the creation is made new: hail for through the Creator becomes a newborn child.

The strophes conclude with a refrain that will carry on throughout the entire *Akathistos*:

> Hail, Bride without Bridegroom!

The second ikos continues the theme of the ineffability of her conception of Jesus the Son of the Most High:

> The Holy Maiden, seeing herself in all her purity, said boldly unto Gabriel: "Strange seem thy words and hard for my soul to accept. From a conception without seed how dost thou speak of childbirth," crying: Alleluia.[61]

According to the structure of the kontakion, this whole pattern is then repeated up to twelve times. At one time the kontakion was the centerpiece of Byzantine hymnography. Over the centuries, however, it gave way to a new hymnographic structure that had monasteries and not urban cathedrals as its point of origin. Nevertheless the kontakion, and especially the *Akathistos* hymn, as has been stated, never entirely disappeared from the Byzantine liturgical tradition. New kontakia continued to be written and performed as part of a regular liturgical cycle well into the twelfth century and even into the modern era.[62]

In the seventh and eighth centuries hymnographers from the environs of Jerusalem and the great monastery of Saint Saba in Palestine introduced a new genre of hymnography to the Byzantine Church: the canon.[63] Such men as Andrew of Crete and John of Damascus[64] and his adopted brother Kosmas the Melodist, wrote great numbers of canons, which were then transmitted to the Byzantine Church in Constantinople most likely on account of their popularity and their sound Orthodox doctrine and through a dynamic process of liturgical interaction and borrowing between Jerusalem and Constantinople. In the ninth century Theodore of the Stoudion monastery in Constantinople was instrumental both in composing canons and in introducing their use into Byzantine worship.[65] The structure of the canon is rather simple: it is a series of anywhere from two to three to four or even eight or nine groups of hymns, each loosely based on one of nine biblical odes.[66] Each ode begins with a *heirmos*, which is followed by a series of other hymns, called *troparia*, and is concluded by a final hymn called a *katavasia*. The heirmos establishes the music and the poetic meter for the rest of the hymns that belong to that ode. When a hymnographer sat down to compose a canon, he or she could compose a new heirmos for that particular canon, or he or she could choose an extant one from a repertoire of heirmoi contained in the liturgical book called the *heirmologion* or the Book of Heirmoi. Strictly speaking, therefore, the heirmoi do not necessarily make up part of the composed canon, while the troparia always do. This point is made clear in a commentary on music, where the author says:

> Whoever wishes to create a canon must first sing the heirmos, then create troparia with the same number of syllables and the same metre as the heirmos and preserving the theme.[67]

The content of the heirmos typically makes concrete allusion to the biblical ode it is associated with and also sets forth another theological theme that will be carried through the ode. The canon for Holy Thursday, attributed to Kosmas the Melodist, demonstrates the structure of the canon well. The heirmos of the first ode, which in this canon was written by Kosmas himself, has as its biblical theme the song of Moses from Exodus 15:1–19, in which the Israelites praise God for delivering them from Pharaoh and his army. The heirmos of this canon begins:

> The Red Sea was parted by a blow from Moses' staff, and the deep with its waves grew dry. It served as a path to the unarmed people of Israel, but to the Egyptians in full armour it proved a grave. A hymn of praise was sung, well-pleasing to God: Christ our God is greatly glorified.

The mention of Christ being glorified in the last phrase serves a double purpose: at once it acknowledges that Christ was the deliverer of ancient Israel. At the same time Christ's glory obviously alludes to his death and Resurrection, the new Passover. The troparia of this ode of the canon then build from the biblical theme of the Passover described in Exodus 15 to the theological theme of Christ the Wisdom of God, who is the true Passover. According to the canon, as the Passover of old was celebrated with food and drink, the celebration of this new Passover is the consumption by the faithful of the Wisdom and Word of God who is glorified by his Passion. The first troparion of this ode makes the first connection by praising the Incarnation of Christ:

> Cause of all and bestower of life, the infinite Wisdom of God has built his house, from a pure Mother who has not known man. For, clothing himself in a bodily temple, Christ our God is greatly glorified.

The stage is thus set as the canon calls to mind the Incarnation of Jesus Christ. The canon passes over the subsequent occurrences between his Incarnation and incidents commemorated on Holy Thursday because a summoning of historical events is unnecessary. Christ, the Wisdom of God—"the cause of all and bestower of life"—has become incarnate and offers himself as food to the faithful. The next two troparia make the connection clear:

> Instructing his friends in the mysteries, the true Wisdom of God prepares a table that gives food to the soul, and he mingles for the faithful the cup of the wine of life eternal. Let us approach with reverence and cry aloud: Christ our God is greatly glorified.

Throughout these troparia, Kosmas has added a further level of theological depth by referencing Proverbs 9. And in both instances the tangible nature of food and drink is exploited as a medium to commune with the Wisdom of God. In the concluding troparion Kosmas cites Psalm 33:9 (LXX) and mixes the imagery and makes explicit that the feasting and drinking of this Passover celebration is the consumption, or the hearing, of the "exalted preaching" of the Word and Wisdom of God:

> Ye faithful, let us all give ear to the exalted preaching of the uncreated and consubstantial Wisdom of God, for he cries aloud: "O taste and see that I am good! Sing: Christ our God is greatly glorified."

The structure of this canon is typical, and as with any other canon, the basic structure and theological themes are then carried through in the remainder of the canon. This canon from Holy Thursday concludes both structurally and theologically, as do all canons, with the ninth ode. The heirmos and first troparion of this ode return unambiguously to what was put forward at the beginning of the canon:

> Come, ye faithful, let us raise our minds on high and enjoy the Master's hospitality and the banquet of immortal life in the upper room; and let us *hear the exalted teaching of the Word* whom we magnify.

> "Go", said the Word to the disciples, "and prepare the Passover of those whom I call to share in the Mystery: *with the unleavened bread of the word of truth* prepare the Passover in the upper room where the mind is established, and magnify the strength of grace."[68]

Aside from kontakia and canons, hymns of varying length, generically referred to as troparia, or sometimes as *stichera*, make up the bulk of the Byzantine hymn repertoire. Troparia and stichera show up throughout the Byzantine liturgy fulfilling numerous functions. At times they stand alone and form a liturgical unit by themselves, such as the *apolytikia*, or dismissal hymns. At other times they are interspersed between psalm verses, such as during the singing of the vespertine Psalm 141. Unlike canons and kontakia, hymns such as these do not share any sort of formal structure beyond perhaps common music patterns. Throughout all the liturgical services, numerous types of these hymns may be heard, and whereas the names and function of these hymns differ, the methods used to convey the message of the hymns are even more varied. For example, during the Lenten season one finds hymns that are homiletic in nature and do nothing less than exhort the faithful to a higher way of life:

> All the names of the Old Testament have I set before you, my soul, as an example. Imitate the holy acts of the righteous and flee from the sins of the wicked.[69]

Or hymns present a simple exposition of the fundamental ethical teaching implicit in the gospel in song:

> Come, ye faithful, and in the light let us perform the works of God; let us walk honestly as in the day. Let us cast away every unjust accusation against our neighbour, not placing any cause of stumbling in his path. Let us lay aside the pleasures of the flesh, and increase the spiritual gifts of our soul. Let us give bread to those in need, and let us draw near unto Christ, crying in penitence: O our God, have mercy on us![70]

Many hymns simply serve as basic prayers and end with nothing other than a plea for God's great mercy:

> Do not demand from me worthy fruits of repentance, for my strength has failed with me. Give me an ever contrite heart and poverty of spirit that I may offer these to thee as an acceptable sacrifice, O only Savior.[71]

Festal hymnography draws out the meaning of a given feast. One commonly encounters hymns that are deeply theological in content on feast days. Often they ruminate on or develop a theological point, as at the feast of Transfiguration:

> Thou hast appeared to Moses both on the Mountain of the Law and on Tabor: of old in darkness, but now in the unapproachable light of the Godhead.[72]

Or a hymn can bring out a tightly woven doctrinal statement that emanates from the given feast. The feast of the Dormition of the Theotokos offers the perfect opportunity for the Church to make a concise statement on the place of Mary through the hymns:

> O pure Virgin, sprung from mortal loins, thine end was conformable to nature: but because thou hast borne the true Life, thou hast departed to dwell with the divine Life Himself.[73]

Perhaps even more dramatically, a hymn can recast an event and explain its universal significance:

> When Augustus ruled alone upon the earth, the many kingdoms of men came to end: and when thou wast made man of the pure virgin, the many gods of idolatry were destroyed. The cities of the world passed under one single rule; and the nations came to believe in one sovereign Godhead. The peoples were enrolled in the decree of Caesar; and we, the faithful, were enrolled in the Name of the Godhead, when thou, our God, wast made man. Great is thy mercy: glory to thee.[74]

The hymns from the Holy Week cycle often paint a vivid and dramatic picture of the Divine Passion:

> The whole creation was changed by fear, when it saw thee, O Christ, hanging on the cross. The sun was darkened and the foundations of the earth were shaken; all things suffered with the Creator of all. Of thine own will, thou hast endured this for our sakes: O Lord, glory to thee.[75]

Within this body of hymnody, some present a familiar event from an entirely different vantage point:

> When the most pure virgin saw thee hanging upon the Cross this day, O Word, she wept bitterly with the love of a mother, her heart was wounded. From the very depths of her soul she groaned in torment. She struck her face in her grief and tore her hair. Beating her breast she lamented, "Woe is me, my divine child! Woe is me, O Light of the World! Why do you vanish from my sight, Lamb of God?"[76]

In the end many hymns, though, seek nothing else but to praise God for his wondrous economy of salvation:

> Let everything in heaven rejoice, let everything on earth be glad, for the Lord has shown strength with his arm; by death he has trampled on death; he has become the first-born from the dead; from the belly of Hell he has delivered us, and granted the world his great mercy.[77]

For the most part the hymns are sung according to specific guidelines that direct the melody, rhythm, style, and performance, which add further nuance to the hymns. Alongside the hymns has grown up a rich musical tradition with both ancient chants and modern compositions.[78]

The texts of these hymns are found in various service books used in the Church according to different cycles. Throughout the year, for instance, the hymnody is drawn from the *Oktoechos* or the *Menaion*.[79] The *Oktoechos* follows more or less an eight-week cycle with each week's hymns sung according to a different set of musical patterns. The themes of the hymnody found in *Oktoechos* vary from short hymns in praise of Christ's Resurrection, which is the theme given over on Saturday night and Sundays; hymns in honor of the apostles, monks, and saints; or the moving hymns attributed to John of Damascus, which meditate on the meaning of life and death:

> I weep and I wail when I contemplate death, when I behold our beauty fashioned after the image of God lying in the tomb, disfigured, dishonored and empty of form.[80]

> What earthly pleasure remains unmixed with grief? What earthly glory remains unchanged? All things are feeble shadows and deceitful dreams; death shall come in a moment and wipe them all away. But you, Christ, in the light of your countenance, in the sweet beauty of your holiness, give rest to those whom you have chosen.[81]

The *Menaion*, or Book of Months, comes in twelve volumes, one for every month of the year, and contains an entry for every day of the year. The *Menaion* contains the variable service texts in honor of saints or the hymns for a particular feast. The *Triodion* is the choir book for the period of Great Lent. Its name is derived from the canons sung at weekday matins. The canon, as stated above, is a group of hymns that usually comes in eight parts or odes, but the canons in the *Triodion* are made up of only three or four odes, hence the name *Triodion*, or Three Odes. The *Triodion* contains all the material necessary for chanters and singers beginning with the four preliminary Sundays of Lent and continuing with the six weeks of Lent, the weekend of Palm Sunday, and all of Holy Week.[82] The *Triodion* concludes with the very last service on Holy Saturday before the annual celebration of Pasch. During the period of Pentecost, another book, the *Pentecostarion*, provides all the variable hymns sung in church.[83]

Procession in the Kursk province. The procession, perhaps for Easter, was painted by Ilya Repin (1844–1930) between the years 1878–1883. TRETYAKOV GALLERY, MOSCOW/SCALA/ ART RESOURCE, NY

The *Typikon* or the *Ordo*, or Rule, regulates how all these books are combined and fitted together with the invariable parts of the office. The development of the *Typikon* is long and complicated, but ultimately derives from two different sources.[84] The first source is the *Synaxaria*, which were often found appended to the *Praxapostolos*. A *Synaxarion* contains the list of daily commemorations, rubrics for the appointed scriptural readings, and rudimentary directions for what hymns were to be sung on a given day. Eventually the contents of this type of book grew more and more detailed as the number of hymns that could be sung on any given day likewise grew. A *Synaxarion* could be written for either a monastic house, such as the famous *Synaxarion of the Monastery of Theotokos Evergetis*,[85] or for the magnificent cathedral churches of the empire, such as the so-called *Typikon of the Great Church*.[86] The specific contents of a *Synaxarion* could differ greatly from document to document. The other source was monastic foundation documents, or *ktetor typika*, which, in the course of detailing every aspect of monastic life, provided rules for the celebration of the liturgical cycle within a monastery.[87] The authors of *ktetor typika* took great pains to enumerate carefully even the minutest detail of the liturgical service because of the underlying presumption of the importance of the liturgical cycle in the monastic life. Christodoulos (eleventh century), the founder of the monastery of Saint John the Theologian on the island of Patmos, says:

> Before all else it is assuredly fitting to speak of our true employment, that which has priority over all others, I mean the doxology of praise to God. For it is in view of this one thing that, from very "not being" (of this I am convinced) "we have been brought into being" and adorned with reason, in order to honor the Creator with uninterrupted hymn-singing.[88]

As in the case of the Byzantine monastery of Theotokos Evergetis, these two types of documents were transmitted together. By the thirteenth century these two streams would become fused, and a particular monastic *Typikon*, the *Typikon* of Saint Sabas monastery in Palestine, primarily liturgical in nature, would gain prevalence over most of the Orthodox world.[89] This dominance was not complete, as many of the Greek-speaking parochial churches throughout the world never completely adopted this *Typikon* but maintained a more parochial-oriented liturgical rule.

While most Byzantine hymnographers were men, the tradition also knows of woman composers such as Thekla the Nun,[90] and, of course, the most famous Byzantine woman hymnographer, Kassia, who penned a number of hymns.[91] One of Kassia's hymns is, in fact, among the most celebrated of all Byzantine hymns:

> The woman who had fallen into many sins, perceiving thy divinity, O Lord, fulfilled the part of a myrrh-bearer; and with lamentations she brought sweet-smelling oil of myrrh to thee before thy burial. "Woe is me," she said, "for night surrounds me, dark and moonless, and stings my lustful passion with the love of sin. Accept the fountain of my tears, O thou who drawest down from the clouds the waters of the sea. Incline to the groaning of my heart, O thou who in thine ineffable self-emptying hast bowed down the heavens. I shall kiss thy most pure feet and wipe them with the hairs of my head, those feet whose sound Eve heard at dusk in Paradise, and hid herself for fear. Who can search out the multitude of my sins and the abyss of the judgments, O Savior of my soul? Despise me not, thine handmaiden, for thou hast mercy without measure"[92]

The power of Kassia's hymn surely derives from figurative language and its affective tone but also from its deceptive simplicity. In it the woman who anointed Jesus' feet connects her own actions to the coming Passion and to its universal significance. She connects her actions that take place directly before the opening of the kingdom to all by

Christ's death and Resurrection to Adam and Eve's expulsion from paradise and slavery to death. By putting these words in this woman's mouth, Kassia gives the hymn a direct-ness that is built up by rhetorical flourishes rather than obscured by them.

Obviously the Orthodox Churches of necessity continue to compose new hymns for the various needs, whether they be for newly canonized saints or for new annual commemorations. The hymns for these new services follow the classic models of Or-thodox Christian hymnody. Nevertheless new services, while following older styles, reflect upon the concerns of the modern era. Patriarch Dimitrios I of Constantinople (1972–1991) commissioned a monk on Mount Athos, Gerasimos, to compose an en-tire service for the preservation of creation. This service is meant to be sung annually on 1 September, traditionally the date of the ecclesiastical New Year. The hymns of the service continue along the lines of older ecclesiastical poetic meter and use famil-iar phrases and metaphors, but the content is entirely new:

> Lord and Saviour, who as God brought all things into being by a Word, establishing laws and governing them unerringly to your glory, at the prayers of the Mother of God, keep secure and unharmed all the elements which hold the earth together, and save the universe.[93]

Euchology and Rubrics

The Byzantine liturgical rite has an extensive euchological tradition with origins that go back to the earliest centuries of Christianity. This tradition is contained within the liturgical book, the *Euchologion*, or Prayer Book, and has evolved over the centuries from individual scrolls that contained one service or a handful of prayers that were later gathered together in larger compilations. The earliest known *Euchologion*, the manuscript Barberini Greek 336, a manuscript with a southern Italian provenance, dates from the late eighth century.[94] Nascent *Euchologia* surely existed in some form before this time, but from this point onward *Euchologia* begin to emerge in the manu-script tradition as a distinct type of liturgical book. Until the development of the printing press, it seems that no two *Euchologion* manuscripts had exactly the same contents unless one was an exact copy of another. Nevertheless a typical *Euchologion* would contain all the texts necessary for the celebrant to complete the various liturgi-cal rites. Hence the earliest *Euchologia* are missing the texts for chanters or readers; these texts are found in other books, the *Horologion*, the *Menaion*, the *Triodion*, and so forth. *Euchologia* also omit the texts necessary for a deacon; the diaconal texts were kept in another book altogether, the *Diakonikon*.[95]

Naturally the *Euchologion* has the prayer texts necessary for the celebration of the eucharist, whether it be the Divine Liturgy of John Chrysostom or Basil the Great or the Presanctified Liturgy.[96] Most *Euchologia* included the prayers that were said dur-ing the celebration of the daily office. Typically the *Euchologion* would also have many of the prayers that mark the entire life cycle of a person, with the prayers and services for baptism and chrismation, weddings, services for healings, exorcisms, and funerals. But not even every *Euchologion* contained these basic services. The contents of a given *Euchologion* could vary widely according to the needs of the owner. If the owner of the *Euchologion* was a bishop, beyond the typical euchology contents it might also contain prayers for ordination. If the *Euchologion* was to be used in a monastery, it might contain the specific prayers for monastic tonsure and the distinct funeral service for a monastic. The printed versions of the *Euchologia* all include a great number of services for all sorts of needs beyond the major sacramental services. In fact the Slavonic ver-

Rite of baptism. Converts prepare for baptism at St. Ivan's Church, Moscow, 2003. PHOTOGRAPH BY CHRIS NIEDENTHAL/TIME LIFE PICTURES/ GETTY IMAGES

sion of the *Euchologion* is called simply the *Trebnik* or Book of Needs. Over time condensed versions of the *Euchologion* were compiled. For example, a *Leitourgikon* is basically an abbreviated *Euchologion* that chiefly contains the texts of the Divine Liturgy. Similarly the *Archieratikon* has those texts appropriate to an *archiereus*, a hierarch, such as the Divine Liturgy, but also includes ordination, the prayers for the consecration of a church building, and so forth.[97]

Like all traditional Christian prayers, those of the Byzantine euchology tradition give thanks to God, bless God's marvelous works, ask for aid and assistance for various needs through his Son, by his Holy Spirit. For example, the prayer for the blessing of the water at a baptism opens with praise to God, as the celebrant raises his arms and exclaims in a loud voice:

> Great art thou: O Lord, and wonderful are they works, and no words are sufficient to sing thy wonders!

The prayer then recites the history of God's plan of salvation and states that everything in the cosmos has been ordered by God. As such the cosmos joins together in a liturgy with the heavenly angels giving glory to God:

> All powers and intelligences dread thee: the sun hymns thee, the moon praises thee, the stars hold converse with thee, the light obeys thee, the depths shudder before thee, the springs of water serve thee … the angels worship thee: the choirs of archangels praise thee: the many-eyed cherubim and six-winged seraphim encircle thee, they wing around thee with fear and veil thy unapproachable glory.

After this identification of God, and the delineating of God's central position in the universe, the prayer goes on and remembers how God "would not bear to look upon the race of men in servitude to the devil, but came and saved us." And so the prayer asks that the "our loving king be present now in the visitation of thy Holy Spirit and sanctify this water. Give it the grace of redemption, the blessing of Jordan … a gift of sanctification, a way of remission of sins."[98] The full form of the text of this prayer is already found in the earliest known texts of the *Euchologion*.[99] It is safely assumed therefore that the origins of this prayer, as with so many of the prayers found in the *Euchologion*, go back to late antiquity, but it is difficult to ascertain with any certainty their precise origins. The two major exceptions to this, though, are the anaphoral prayers authentically ascribed to Basil the Great and John Chrysostom.[100] In both cases these two Church Fathers took extant anaphoral prayers and edited them in particular ways, adding to them their own theological concerns and vocabularies. Scholars assume that Basil the Great heavily redacted an extant anaphora at least

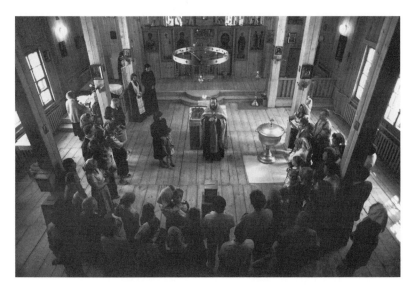

Liturgy in a Russian Orthodox church. The community at the Church of All Saints in Akademgorok/ Novosibirsk, Russia, gathers around the font. The iconostatis or wall decorated with icons is visible that separates the nave from the altar. © 2004 PETER WILLIAMS

two different times over the course of his life, which gave rise to numerous versions of his anaphora found in Greek but also in Coptic, Syriac, and Armenian translations. Only one of these versions is still in use by the Byzantine Church.[101]

John Chrysostom seems to have brought an anaphoral prayer with him from Antioch when he arrived in Constantinople at the end of the fourth century to become bishop of that city. In fact there are parts of Chrysostom's anaphoral text that are common with a Syriac anaphora, *The Anaphora of the Apostles*, which has led scholars to hypothesize a common underlying text to both anaphoras. When these two anaphoras are placed in comparison, the sections that are unique to Chrysostom can further be isolated. On further study much of the text unique to his anaphora can be shown by electronic verbal and stylistic analysis to be fully unique to Chrysostom alone. Such phrases found in the middle of the anaphora text, "For you are God, *ineffable, inconceivable, incomprehensible, always existing, ever the same,* you and your only-begotten Son and your Holy Spirit," appear only in the Liturgy of Chrysostom and in his authentic writings. The ascription of the anaphora to his name, therefore, at least in terms of his heavy redaction of an Antiochene anaphora, seems sure. His motivation was a reaction against Eunomian polemics of the mid-fourth century: Chrysostom added specific theological phrases to an extant anaphora, which countered the claims of the Eunomian party (a later form of Arianism).[102]

Books of rubrics as a type of liturgical book develop relatively late in the history of the Byzantine rite, and this development seems to have been in response to the almost complete absence of rubrics in earliest euchology texts. The few rubrics in the earliest *Euchologia* and the distribution of liturgical roles were limited to the titles of prayers indicating their places in the service, to directions as to which celebrant said a particular item, or even perhaps to the barest outline of a service. Examples of each of these rubrics may be seen in the eighth-century *Euchologion* Barberini Greek 336. For instance, the title of many prayers runs quite simply: "Prayer of the entrance" or "First prayer of the faithful, after the unfolding of the *eiliton*." Beyond these brief rubrical indications in these titles, the ceremonial directions necessary for a liturgical service were left to oral tradition or to the memory of the celebrants. Rubric books or *Diataxeis* filled this textual vacuum, providing instructions for the celebrants of the liturgy that were obviously meant to be used in conjunction with the *Euchologion*. At the beginning of the second millennium, especially on the Italo-Greek periphery of the Byzantine rite, rubrics begin to develop in the euchology texts themselves. André Jacob suspects that the growth of the euchology rubrics was motivated by the instability of the region brought about by successive invasions of Arabs and Normans, isolating it from contact with the other areas of the Byzantine rite.[103] It would only be natural in such a situation to rely more on the authority of written texts when the transmission of the oral traditions from the center of the rite, Constantinople, had been interrupted. Instability and social upheaval would also stimulate the codification of traditions in the face of competing ritual traditions and practices.

Byzantine churchmen wrote books of rubrics for many different liturgical services. Ordinances for the vespers or matins exist side by side with those for the Great Blessing of Water on Theophany. Most often *Diataxeis* were written in order to describe the celebration of the Divine Liturgy. Easily the most famous *Diataxis* in the Byzantine liturgical tradition is the *Diataxis* of Philotheos Kokkinos (1300–1377/8), twice patriarch of Constantinople.[104] Philotheos composed this *Diataxis* while he was the abbot (1342–1345) of the Great Lavra on Mount Athos and naturally relied on Athonite monastic traditions. The large number of extant manuscripts of Philotheos's *Diataxis* and the widespread diffusion of his *Diataxis* throughout the Byzantine world testify to its popularity. Further witness to the popularity of the Philothean *Diataxis* can be seen in its Slavonic translations. Toward the end of Philotheos's life and immediately after his death, his *Diataxis* was translated into Slavonic by two of his disciples, Patriarch Euthymius of Trnovo in Bulgaria and Metropolitan Cyprian of Rus', who then introduced the *Diataxis* into their countries for use in their churches.[105] The final stage in the Philothean *Diataxis* acquiring prevalence in the Byzantine rite happened when a heavily redacted version was used for the first Greek edition of the Divine Liturgy published in Rome by Dimitrios Doukas in October 1526.[106] Doukas's edition was then used by Iakovos Leonginos (Giacomo Leoncini) in his Greek edition of the *Leitourgikon* published in Venice in 1578, which was used in turn by the Venetian printers for the subsequent Greek editions of both the *Leitourgikon* and *Euchologion*. The *Diataxis* was once again translated into Slavonic and introduced for use into Slavic countries as these printed Greek editions of the *Euchologion*, based on Doukas, provided the basis for the so-called reformed books of Patriarch Nikon in Russia.[107] The personal prestige of Patriarch Philotheos provided the likely impetus for the wide diffusion of the *Diataxis* he composed rather than its being an official promulgation. Indeed it remains an open question in the field of Byzantine liturgical studies how far documents such as *Diataxeis* or even *Typika* were considered prescriptive or descriptive by churchmen.

Liturgical Orders and Their Interpretation

The Byzantine-Slavic liturgical tradition has always placed great value on ritual actions in the liturgy. The tradition has not been content simply to proclaim Christ in words alone but has developed a ritual that is full of visual splendor, with grand gestures meant to be seen and understood by all but also with minute actions that are seen only by those performing them. The sources of this ritual idiom are manifold. Some ritual elements must have come from the imperial court, such as the processions with candles and incense or sumptuous vestments. Other elements seem to have descended from domestic rituals. Another source has been the theological commentaries on the rites. Using principles drawn from patristic biblical exegesis, Byzantine liturgical commentators such as Maximus the Confessor, Patriarch Germanus I of Constantinople, Nicholas and Theodore of Andida (late eleventh century), Nicholas Cabasilas, and Symeon of Thessalonika wrote lengthy treatises that sought to explain the underlying meaning of the rites.[108] Their comments, however, have served not only to explicate ritual but also influence its development.[109] The early development of the preliminary rites to the Divine Liturgy, the *prothesis*, when the bread and wine and liturgical vessels are prepared, provides an apt example for this interplay. At one time this rite was a simple matter. The deacons put in order the vessels needed for the liturgy, then prepared the bread and wine; a priest or bishop then said a prayer to complete the rite. This simple service is still evident in earliest euchology sources. For example, the *Euchologion* Barberini Greek 336 describes this brief rite in the title of the prayer, "Prayer which the priest says in the *skeuophylakion* after the bread has been placed on the *diskos*."[110] But at the same time of this manuscript, Patriarch Germanus, in his liturgical commentary, identifies the bread that is prepared with the Lamb of God, spoken of in Isaiah 53:7–8.[111] As the prothesis developed over the next centuries, these verses from Isaiah began to be said in conjunction with the actions done by the priest in the preparation of the bread.[112]

At the level of interpretation, however, formal liturgical commentators cannot be considered as the only driving force. Popular liturgical piety must have played as important a role in the shaping of the actual liturgical rites. This is not to say that Byzantine churchmen were necessarily concerned about popular opinion with regard to likes or dislikes of the liturgical rites. Rather, because it is the nature of liturgy, as Anton Baumstark famously said, "to relate itself to concrete situations of time and place,"[113] the liturgy, whether the rites themselves, their settings, or their interpretations, cannot but reflect the cultural milieu from which it grows. As Byzantine culture changed, various aspects of the liturgy changed with it. Any number of examples could be adduced from the tradition, but perhaps the most striking is the development of the transfer of the gifts within the Divine Liturgy. Originally and functionally this was the moment in the liturgy when the gifts, which were prepared earlier, were moved from a small outer building, the *skeuophylakion*, to the altar table. As time went by, at precisely the same time that the entire liturgy began to be seen by some commentators as a vivid portrayal of Christ's earthly life, this one rite within the liturgy began to take on greater importance as the transfer became associated with the burial procession and the deposition on the altar table with the deposition into the tomb. Consequently, in order to highlight these themes developed in the liturgical commentators, various elements were layered around this rite: the liturgical cloth that covered the chalice and discos were embroidered with images of Christ lying naked in his tomb. Likewise priests were appointed to recite different formulae as they placed the chalice and discos on the altar table:

> The noble Joseph, when he had taken down thy pure body from the tree, wrapped it in fine linen and placed it in a new tomb.

> Bearing life and more fruitful than paradise, brighter than any royal chamber, thy tomb, O Christ, is the fountain of our resurrection.

The long development of this rite, called the Great Entrance, which went from a simple transfer of gifts to an elaborate procession, was influenced by the Byzantine liturgical commentators, but it was just as certainly moved along by popular piety, to which this rite must have had a great deal of resonance. Likewise the original setting of this rite in late antiquity, the vast open cathedral space of the Hagia Sophia in Constantinople, was greatly different from the later, post-iconoclasm setting of much smaller Byzantine churches. These later churches were often decorated in rich iconographic programs that represented the life of Christ. Hence they were natural places for a shift in understanding from a sober but ultimately functional rite to a rite that imitates one aspect of Christ's earthly life. However, the ultimate cause of such a shift is found neither in church decoration, nor the liturgical commentators, nor even the development of the rites themselves but in the larger context of Byzantine society. Again the solemn ceremonies of the Great Entrance of the Divine Liturgy had great resonance in the piety of Byzantine faithful and continue to have so among Orthodox believers. Often the Great Entrance is seen as one of the central elements of the entire Divine Liturgy, so much so that, by the fourteenth century, frescos created to decorate the walls of churches and monasteries began to have a new image, one that was called "the Divine Liturgy," a depiction of the Great Entrance being served by angels, who are dressed in all the appropriate vestments and carry all the necessary vessels, at the heavenly altar.[114]

Mystagogical commentaries did not originate with the Byzantine Church, and they are not unique to the Byzantine tradition. In fact all of the Byzantine mystagogues were influenced by early ecclesiastical writers who first commented on the liturgical rites: John Chrysostom, Theodore Mopsuestia, Pseudo-Dionysius, and even Origen.[115] Nicholas Cabasilas, while commenting on the rites of baptism, goes so far as to place the same import on ritual as on the text of prayers: "The Trinity is named in prayer, but the passion and the bodily death we represent by means of the water, and conform ourselves to that blessed image and form."[116] According to the Byzantine liturgical mind, the ritual did not merely provide the framework for the words uttered in prayer or the scripture readings but complemented them both by equally, though differently, portraying the salvific work of Christ.

Even beyond this idea, the concern that the Byzantine Church had for liturgical rubrics such as *Diataxeis* or *Typika* witnesses to the great interest that this church has always had in maintaining good order in ecclesiastical life. Indeed this concept of order was central to the Byzantine worldview. As Alexander Kazhdan has pointed out, the order that was manifested in these ecclesiastical rites was to the Byzantines nothing less than "an image of the divine world."[117] Documents exclusively rubrical in content attempted to prescribe this order in the earthly ritual, which was but a mirror of the heavenly ritual and the heavenly order. Archbishop Symeon of Thessalonika could well speak for all Byzantine churchmen when he thundered against his congregation for their seeming lack of concern for proper liturgical order:

> Do you not know that this order encompasses all things, as it is written? And that God is not a God of disorder, as the one speaking from God has said, but of peace and order? And that the good order in heaven is also in the Church?[118]

And so while these liturgical documents were made with the practical idea that someone would use them, at the same time they had a grander purpose in mind at their creation. They were not simply reference materials; rather, they attempted to convey an ideal image of the ritual which was itself an image of the heavenly liturgy.

In any given service the different components of the liturgical rites come together to form one service with one basic proclamation, though carried out through many means. For example, the basic structure of the morning office, matins or orthros, in broad outline is as follows:[119]

    I.   Invocation
    II. Fixed psalmody (Pss. 3, 38, 63, 88, 103, 143)—the *hexapsalmos*
    III. Litany or *Synapte*
    IV. Responsorial psalmody (Ps. 118:27, 29, 10, 22) and variable hymnody
    V. Continuous psalmody with variable hymnody—the kathisma
    VI. Psalm 51 (50)
    VII. Canon
    VIII. Psalms 148, 149, 150
    IX. Great Doxology, "Glory to God in the highest"
    X. Litanies
    XI. Dismissal

Liturgy, however, cannot be described merely by a list of successive actions. To do so would be akin to reducing a ballet to its choreography and not to actual dancers dancing. From a list like this, a structure alien to the liturgy can mistakenly be inferred and be superimposed, dramatically changing the way the services are understood. The temptation to view the services as a type of journey with a beginning, middle, and end or cast the services in terms of theater with plot development and a climax implies a unidirectional movement that is entirely absent from most of the services. The interior logic of the services is, in fact, quite different. The ritual of the Divine Liturgy, for example, already in the preparatory rites, points to the bread as the "Lamb of God who takes away the sins of the world" and who is "sacrificed for the life of the world and its salvation" and whose side is pierced where "straightway there came forth blood and water and he who saw bore witness and his witness is true." The theme of the lamb being sacrificed is only resumed again later, right before communion at the fraction, when the priest says, "Broken and divided is the Lamb of God, who is broken, but not disunited, who is ever-eaten, but never consumed, but sanctifies all the faithful." Here there is no movement, no intervening climax; the liturgy began where it ends. Obviously, according to the Orthodox Church, something does happen in the liturgy that changes the bread and wine into the body and blood of Christ, but this something cannot be reduced to an efficacious word or phrase or a single moment or even the arc of a series of moments. It is simply a mystery effected by the power of God. If there is an overarching unidirectional movement, it is intended to be on the part of believers, who in one unitary contemplation of the salvation offered by God, with many voices proclaiming it and many layers enriching it and giving it depth, move toward union with him.

Divine liturgy. Father Alexander Schmemann, noted Orthodox liturgical scholar, celebrating liturgy. PHOTOGRAPH COURTESY OF ALEXANDER RENTEL

An understanding of the liturgy that is different from what the liturgy says about itself can have any number of disastrous results. For example, a mistaken understanding of the liturgy can serve as a catalyst for the estrangement between the Orthodox and Catholic Churches. For almost a millennium, Eastern Orthodox and Western Roman Catholics argued contentiously over the exact moment of the consecration of the bread and wine. The argument was regularly pointed to as a vast and insurmountable gulf that separated the two churches. Roman Catholics understood the moment to be the words of institution; the Orthodox understanding differs by a few minutes in the liturgy and argues that it is at the epiclesis or the moment when the Holy Spirit is called down over the gifts that are offered. Recent scholarship, however, has shown that such a simplistic view is entirely foreign to the liturgical texts and rites themselves and to the earliest understanding of the eucharist itself. Regardless of Roman Catholic liturgical theology, for the Orthodox Church the epiclesis cannot be seen as the one moment when bread and wine are transformed into the body and blood of Christ because, as in the liturgy attributed to Basil the Great, the holy gifts are spoken of as the bread and wine/chalice both before and after the epiclesis. Byzantine liturgical commentators will even see what transpires at the epiclesis, with the descent of the Holy Spirit, as completed only at the addition of hot water, the *zeon*, to the chalice directly after the fraction and commixture. This ritual vividly portrays Christ's resurrected body and blood being enlivened by the warmth and "fullness of the Holy Spirit."[120] Commenting on the nature of traditional Christian liturgies, Robert Taft points out that

> there is one single offering of the Church within which several things happen. These things are expressed in various ways and moments. . . . These classical anaphoras express that the Eucharist is a sacrifice, the sacramental memorial of Christ's own sacrifice of the Cross, in which the Church, repeating what Jesus did at the Last Supper, invokes God's blessing on bread and wine so that it might become Jesus' body and blood, our spiritual food and drink.

He goes on to say:

> All attempts to squeeze more out of the words of the prayer ... is an inference that can be made only by imposing on the text the results of later theological reflection and/or polemics.[121]

To be sure no liturgical unit exists in isolation. These units and the words and ritual that make them up interact with one another, resuming and developing earlier themes, then ending them abruptly as new ones are introduced. The movement of a service rarely goes forward, more often sideways, and sometimes backwards. At times the liturgy soars to a crescendo of intensity and then pulls back to a decrescendo of quiet contemplation. At times the different liturgical elements go on at the same time: the priest can be standing at the altar quietly reading the set prayers of the office to himself, while a deacon can be incensing the whole church, while at the same time the choir can be singing hymns. The hymns themselves might use any number of images to convey one point. Likewise a group of hymns sung together in a liturgical unit might build on one theme after another, piling verbal images on top of one another.

So when the believers gather together for orthros, they are immediately reminded that though they lay down and slept, they woke again, for the Lord has sustained them (Ps. 3). They can hear all that the psalmody can teach them here (II) and throughout the service. At the same time the priest, on behalf of the community of believers, offers quiet prayers giving thanks that, through a holy bidding, they have all been able to come and stand before the presence of the glory of God. There the priest offers further thanksgiving and asks for the pardon and remission of their sins so they may become children of the light and of the day.[122] Then the community prays, through the priest, a litany "for the peace of the whole world ... for [their] bishop ... for civil authorities ... for this city, for every city ... for seasonable weather" (III). The faithful can then give themselves over to the meditation of God's saving economy, contemplating him "who has been revealed to us" in psalmody and through hymns (IV–V). As the office goes on, they can yet again ask for remission of sins (VI) and hear again in hymns, now during the canon (VII), the subject or subjects of the daily commemoration. After this their worship is revealed to be joined together with the choir of the cosmos—the angels, the sun and the moon, the stars, the firmament of heaven, the mountains, the hills, the trees, the animals, all the people of the earth—and they sing God's praises "because he has raised up a horn of salvation for us" (Ps. 148:14), namely his Son, Jesus Christ, the Lamb of God, who takes away the sin of the world and who sits at the right hand of the God the Father (VIII–IX). According to the liturgical books, the morning service is even to culminate at the same time the sun rises. The *Typikon* states, "It is necessary for the ecclesiarch [the monastic who is charged with the order of services] to be strict at both the psalmody and the readings, so that the dismissal takes place as the sun is rising."[123] So in the newness of the dawn's first light, having made a passage from darkness to light, the faithful conclude their services and prepare to enter the world, praying one more litany, asking for an "angel of peace, a faithful guide, a guardian of our souls ... all things that are good and profitable for [their] souls" (X). The precise order of this service differs depending on what day of the week it is and what commemoration is called for, but the movement of orthros generally follows this trajectory.

The Message of the Gospel and the Identity of the Church

Taking a step back and looking at the services from a broader perspective also reveals that the services through all of their diverse units still proclaim the basic message of the Christian gospel, Christ's victory over death. The theme of Byzantine vespers uses the natural metaphor of the encroaching evening darkness being conquered by the presence of light in the church. In the evening office the faithful again gather and bless God, this time meditating especially on the marvels of creation, affirming in a presbyteral prayer that "the good things of this earth are given to us a pledge of the kingdom to come" (Sixth Prayer of Light).[124] During this service a ritual offering of incense is made as a sign of prayers rising to heaven coming before the face of God. Here again psalmody is chanted, and hymns in praise of God and his saints are sung. The prayers seek deliverance from all temptations that seek after the souls of the believers, because, as the priest prays on behalf of the faithful:

> To you, O Lord, do we lift up our eyes, and on you have we hoped that you will not put us to shame, O our God. (Prayer of the Entrance)

The expectation of this hope is fulfilled in the celebration in song of Jesus Christ, the light of the world, the light that shines in the darkness, the light that makes the night bright as day, with the singing of the ancient Christian hymn "Phôs hilaron":

> O joyful light of the holy glory of the immortal, heavenly, holy, blessed Father: O Jesus Christ. Coming to the setting of the sun and seeing the evening light, we hymn Father, Son and Holy Spirit, God. Right it is for you to be hymned at all times with voices of praise, Son of God, giver of life. Therefore the world glorifies you.

In the Divine Liturgy prayers and hymns of praise and thanksgiving are offered to God, and in return, by the descent of the Holy Spirit, bread and wine are transformed into the body and blood of Christ. The believers partake of the body and blood of the risen Christ believing that they share in his death, Resurrection, and glory. As communicants they receive the "purification of [their] souls, remission of sins, the communion of the Holy Spirit, the fullness of the Kingdom of Heaven" (from the Anaphora of Chrysostom). This communion places the believers in a relationship with God so close that the believer can now be so bold as to call on God as Father and therefore possesses a filial relationship, sharing by God's grace as a son does in all that God is. Maximus the Confessor, in his *Mystagogy*, makes this clear when he says that through the reception of communion "we are given fellowship and identity with him by participation in likeness by which man is deemed worthy to become God."[125] All of this begins now in this life but will reach full perfection in the future age, when, according to Maximus, "we shall pass from the grace which is in faith to the grace of vision, when our God and Savior Jesus Christ will indeed transform us into himself ... and will bestow on us the original mysteries which have been represented for us through sensible symbols here below."[126] The Divine Liturgy, following the Lord's own command, is also an act of making remembrance of the Lord and his saving acts, "the cross, the tomb, the resurrection on the third day, the ascension into heaven, the seating at the right hand of Father, and the second coming" (Anaphora of Chrysostom). Recalling these saving acts and ever mindful of the revelation of God the Father, by his Son Jesus Christ, and the gift of the Holy Spirit, the Christian believer is drawn up from temporal earthly worship into the timeless realms of heavenly worship with the angels who themselves are "concelebrants" and who "co-glorify" God together with the believers (Prayer of the Entrance). Being both "here on earth" and "there in heaven," the believer sings the hymn of the angels, "Holy, holy, holy," to God because his Son, Jesus Christ, has entered into the true sanctuary in order to appear in the presence of God and offers himself once and for all for the putting away of sin by the sacrifice of himself.

As with all the sacred rites, the Divine Liturgy gives the faithful a way of understanding themselves. One way it does this is to inform them of who they are as a Church. In other words, through participation in the celebration of the Divine Liturgy, what it means to be "Church" is revealed. At one time at the beginning of the liturgy the community of faithful literally waited outside the church building and entered together. Everyone, from the patriarch to the emperor, would wait outside until all was ready to proceed. Everyone would wait, because everyone was gathered together for a common purpose, the glorification of God, who would visit them in his own body and blood. When the time came for the entrance, the patriarch, standing before the open doors of the cathedral, beholding the physical beauty of the temple and the shining brightness of sun streaming through the windows, would pray the appointed prayer:

> Master, Lord our God, who have appointed in heaven orders and hosts of angels and archangels of the ministry of your glory, grant that with our entrance there may be an entrance of your holy ones with us, co-glorifying and concelebrating with us your goodness. For to you is due all glory, honor, and worship, to the Father, and to the Son, and to the Holy Spirit, now and ever and unto ages of ages.[127] (Prayer of the Entrance)

As this prayer sets out, the task for all the members of the faithful, from those who have been ordained for particular service to those who attend contemplating their own salvation, is to enter into the presence of God, glorifying him and offering to him thanksgiving "for all things of which we know and which we know" (Anaphora of Chrysostom). It is to enter into reality where life in this world and in the next is acknowledged to be a gift from God. It is to join together with all the cosmos, with what is visible and invisible, and give thanks to God for this great gift. Even though today the initial part of the Divine Liturgy is celebrated differently, as the priest begins the service in the altar, which is demarcated off from the rest of the church building by a wall of icons called the *iconostasis*, the assembly still gathers, hymns are sung, prayers are prayed, and litanies are chanted. The community has been brought together by the will of God to fulfill his purpose.

A central idea, whether it be the pattern of light emerging from darkness or the light overtaking the evening darkness, both of which imitate Christ's Resurrection from the dead, can interpret part or whole of the rite but only because the entire Christian faith is predicated on the salvation offered to believers by Christ. Everything in the liturgy finds its source in this. Therefore the liturgy not only represents Christ's salvific act but forms believers in the newness of life brought about by this salvation. Ultimately the liturgy is the place where this newness of life begins, where it is sustained, and where it will be fully realized as a believer transfers from this life to eternal life.

Iconostasis. The monastery church of St. John Bigorski in Macedonia, rebuilt in the nineteenth century, contains a wooden iconostatis that was intricately carved by the Miyak craftsmen Petre Filipovski and Makarie Frchkovski from 1830 to 1840. Six horizontal squares are decorated with flora, fauna, and human figures in local costume. DAGLI ORTI/THE ART ARCHIVE

The contemporary use of the Byzantine liturgical rite by so many Christians who have no connection to the Byzantine Empire, whether by cultural similarity or even geographical proximity to its former boundaries, or who are not even in ecclesiastical unity with the Orthodox Church testifies to one of the greatest strengths of the rite: its ability to conform itself to times and places while remaining a coherent liturgical tradition. In other words, a dynamic interplay between transmission, acceptance, adaptation, maintenance, rejection, and conservatism marks the present experience and the historical development of Byzantine liturgical rite. To be sure, far from being something static or unchanging, the history of the Byzantine rite is indeed one of change as each generation of Orthodox churchmen has sifted through what has been handed over to them. Entire forms of the rite, such as the cathedral practice, simply disappeared as the practices of urban monasticism rapidly and completely overtook it. But vast and dramatic changes like this need to be understood within the context of why they were carried out. Orthodox churchmen were less exercising a personal freedom that allowed them to change the liturgy than they were operating from a conservative mentality that sought to preserve the liturgical traditions of those who had gone before them and bore witness to the authenticity of the rite. It would have been inconceivable to a figure such as Theodore the Studite that he was innovating the liturgy when he invited Palestinian monks to join his monastic community in Constantinople and bring with them their liturgical practices. In fact this importation of Palestinian monks finally had an enormous impact on the development of the liturgy. In retrospect this may appear as innovation, but Theodore, in his own eyes, was merely importing an authentic and staunchly Orthodox liturgical tradition to help bolster his monastery in the face of persecution. Theodore, as well as the countless other actors who affected the evolution of the Byzantine rite, had the assurance that underlying all liturgical change was the vitality of an unchanging core that could be articulated in a diversity of traditional and authentic ways.

Bibliography

Cabasilas, Nicholas. *A Commentary on the Divine Liturgy*. Translated by J. M. Hussey and P. A. McNulty. London: SPCK, 1960.

Cabasilas, Nicholas. *The Life in Christ*. Translated by Carmino J. deCatanzaro. Crestwood, N.Y.: St. Vladimir's Seminary Press, 1974.

The Festal Menaion. Translated by Mother Mary and Kallistos Ware. London: Faber, 1969.

Germanus of Constantinople. *On the Divine Liturgy*. Edited and translated by Paul Meyendorff. Crestwood, N.Y.: St. Vladimir's Seminary Press, 1984 (*Ecclesiastical History and Mystical Contemplation*, CPG 8023).

The Lenten Triodion. Translated by Mother Mary and Kallistos Ware. London: Faber, 1978.

Ouspensky, Leonid, and Vladimir Lossky. *The Meaning of Icons*. 2nd ed. Translated by G. E. H. Palmer and E. Kadloubovsky. Crestwood, N.Y.: St. Vladimir's Seminary Press, 1982.

Pott, Thomas. *La réforme liturgique byzantine: Étude de phénomène de l'évolution non-spontanée de la liturgie byzantine*. Bibliotheca Ephemerides Liturgicae, Subsidia, [BELS] 104. Rome: C. L. V., Edizioni Liturgiche, 2000.

Roberson, Ronald G. *The Eastern Christian Churches: A Brief Survey*. 6th rev. ed. Rome: Orientalia Christiana, 1999.

Schmemann, Alexander. *The Eucharist: Sacrament of the Kingdom*. Translated by Paul Kachur. Crestwood, N.Y.: St. Vladimir's Seminary Press, 1988.

Schmemann, Alexander. *Of Water and the Spirit: A Liturgical Study of Baptism*. Crestwood, N.Y.: St. Vladimir's Seminary Press, 1974.

Taft, Robert F. *A History of the Liturgy of St. John Chrysostom*. Vol. 2: *The Great Entrance: A History of the Transfer of Gifts and Other Preanaphoral Rites of the Liturgy of St. John Chrysostom*, 2nd ed., Orientalia Christiana Analecta 200. Rome: Pontificium Institutum Studiorum Orientalium, 1978. Vol. 5, *The Precommunion Rites*. Orientalia Christiana Analecta 261. Rome: Pontificium Institutum Studiorum Orientalium, 2000.

Taft, Robert F. *The Liturgy of the Hours in East and West: The Origins of the Divine Office and Its Meaning for Today*. Collegeville, Minn.: Liturgical Press, 1986.

Taft, Robert F. "Mount Athos: A Late Chapter in the History of the Byzantine Rite." *Dumbarton Oaks Papers* 42 (1988) 179–194.

Notes

[1] Symeon of Thessalonika, *Expositio de sacro templo*, PG 155:700.

[2] Official numbers are notoriously difficult to ascertain, but this rough estimate of 130 million is arrived at by adding together the numbers provided in Ronald Roberson's *The Eastern Christian Churches*, for the Orthodox Churches, 43–148, and those churches in communion with Rome that follow the Byzantine rite, 161–188.

[3] Thomas F. Mathews, *The Early Churches of Constantinople: Architecture and Liturgy* (University Park: Pennsylvania State University Press, 1971) 105–115.

[4] Sebastià Janeras, "Les byzantins et le *trisagion* christologique," in *Miscellanea liturgica in onore di Sua Eminenza il Cardinale Giacomo Lercaro*, vol. 2 (Rome: Desclée, 1967) 469–499.

[5] Cyril Mango, ed. and trans., "The Homilies of Photius, Patriarch of Constantinople," *Dumbarton Oaks Studies* 3 (1958) 295.

[6] Cyril Mango, "The Homilies of Photius, Patriarch of Constantinople," 188.

[7] Pott, *La réforme liturgique byzantine*, 110–113.

[8] The text of this narration is available in A. Longo, "Il testo integrale della *Narrazione degli abati Giovanni e Sofronio* attraverso le *Hermeneiai* di Nicone," *Rivista di studi bizantini e neoellenici* 12–13 (1965–1966) 223–267. The text is discussed in Taft, *Liturgy of the Hours*, 198–200.

[9] For the history of the monastic office, see Taft, *Liturgy of the Hours*, 57–91.

[10] A. Dmitrievsky, *Opisanie liturgicheskikh rykopisei*, 3 vols. (Kiev: Tip. Universiteta sv. Vladimira, 1895–1901; Petrograd: Tip. V. F. Kirshbauma, 1917), 3: 131.

[11] Dmitrievsky, *Opisanie liturgicheskikh rykopisei*, 3: 173.

[12] Translation taken from Taft, "Mount Athos," 179.

[13] *Byzantine Monastic Foundation Documents: A Complete Translation of the Surviving Founders' Typika and Testaments*, ed. John Thomas and Angela Constantinides Hero, 5 vols. (Washington, D.C.: Dumbarton Oaks Research Library and Collection, 2000) 1:391.

[14] Samuel H. Cross and Olgerd P. Sherbowitz-Wetzor, eds. and trans., *The Russian Primary Chronicle: Laurentian Text* (Cambridge, Mass.: Mediaeval Academy of America, 1953) 110–111.

[15] The classic treatment of the cathedral services in late antiquity is John F. Baldovin, *The Urban Character of Christian Worship: The Origins, Development, and Meaning of Stational Liturgy*, Orientalia Christiana Analecta 228 (Rome: Pontificale Institutum Studiorum Orientalium, 1987). See also Taft, *Liturgy of the Hours*, 31–56, 141–213.

[16] *Corpus Iuris Civilis*, III (Berlin: Weidmann, 1893) 21.

[17] Jacques Goar, *Euchologion sive Rituale Graecorum*, 2nd ed. (Venice: 1730; repr. Graz: Akademische Druck- und Verlagsanstalt, 1960) 153–156.

[18] The evidence for dating the liturgy described in

this codex to the tenth century is summarized in Robert F. Taft, "*Quaestiones disputatae*: The Skeuophylakion of Hagia Sophia and the Entrances of the Liturgy Revisited; Part II," *Oriens Christianus* 82 (1998) 67–71.

[19]Goar, *Euchologion*, 153.

[20]Translation from John Barker, *Manuel II Palaeologus (1391–1425): A Study in Late Byzantine Statesmanship* (New Brunswick, N.J.: Rutgers University Press, 1969) 106. For Gemistos and his *Diataxis*, see Alexander Rentel, *The 14th Century Patriarchal Liturgical Diataxis of Dimitrios Gemistos: Edition and Commentary*, Orientalia Christiana Analecta, forthcoming.

[21]John Wilkinson, ed. and trans., *Egeria's Travels* (London: SPCK, 1971) 126.

[22]For the distribution of this Psalter and the various refrains, see Oliver Strunk, "The Byzantine Office at the Hagia Sophia," *Dumbarton Oaks Papers* 9–10 (1955–1956) 200–201. For the exact order of cathedral services, the bibliography is growing rapidly, but above all the work of the liturgical musicologist Alexander Lingas is an excellent place to start; see his article "Festal Cathedral Vespers in Late Byzantium," *Orientalia Christiana Periodica* 63 (1977) 421–459; see also his "Sunday Matins in the Byzantine Cathedral Rite: Music and Liturgy" (Ph.D. diss., University of British Columbia, 1996).

[23]Miguel Arranz, *L'Eucologio costantinopolitano agli inizi del secolo XI: Hagiasmatarion e Archieratikon (Rituale e Pontificale) con l'aggiunta del Leiturgikon (Messale)* (Rome: Pontificia Università Gregoriana, 1996) 21.

[24]Lingas, "Sunday Matins," 276.

[25]Symeon of Thessalonika, *De sacra precatione*, PG 155:556; translation from Strunk, "Byzantine Office," 195.

[26]Lingas, "Sunday Matins," 218.

[27]For more information on the different autocephalous and autonomous Orthodox Churches, see Roberson, *The Eastern Christian Churches*, 43–148.

[28]Roberson, *The Eastern Christian Churches*, 120–137.

[29]Roberson, *The Eastern Christian Churches*, 161–188. On Uniatism from an Orthodox perspective, see Jean-Claude Roberti, *Les Uniates*, Bref 44 (Paris: Cerf; Montreal: Fides, 1992). From a Catholic perspective, see above all the classic work by Cyril Korolevsky, *L'uniatisme*, Collection Irénikon 5–6 (Amay-sur-Meuse, Belgium: Prieuré d'Amay-sur-Meuse, 1927), an English translation of which is available in Cyril Korolevsky, *Metropolitan Andrew (1865–1944)*, trans. Serge Keleher (L'viv, Ukraine:

Stauropegion, 1993) 543–598; and Robert F. Taft, "The Problem of 'Uniatism' and the 'Healing of Memories': Anamnesis, not Amnesia," *Logos: A Journal of Eastern Christian Studies* 41–42 (2000–2001) 155–196.

[30]For the union in western Ukraine, see Borys Gudziak, *Crisis and Reform: The Kyivan Metropolitanate, the Patriarchate of Constantinople, and the Genesis of the Union of Brest* (Cambridge, Mass.: Ukrainian Research Institute, Harvard University, 1998). For the so-called Melkites, see Cyril Charon (Korolevsky), *History of the Melkite Patriarchates*, 3 vols., ed. Nicholas Samra, trans. John Collorafi (Fairfax, Va.: Eastern Christian Publications, 1998–2001) (*Histoire des patriarcats Melkite* [n.p., 1909]).

[31]Symeon of Thessalonika, *Expositio de sacro templo*, PG 155:700.

[32]Germanus, *On the Divine Liturgy*, 56–57.

[33]Symeon of Thessalonika, *Expositio de sacro templo*, PG 155:700.

[34]Cabasilas, *A Commentary on the Divine Liturgy*, 26.

[35]Cabasilas, *The Life in Christ*, 99.

[36]Cabasilas, *The Life in Christ*, 49.

[37]Cabasilas, *A Commentary on the Divine Liturgy*, 29.

[38]Maximus, *Mystagogy*, in *Maximus Confessor: Selected Writings*, trans. George C. Berthold (New York: Paulist, 1985) 206 (CPG 7704).

[39]Symeon, *De sacro ordine sepulturae*, PG 155:672.

[40]Juan Mateos, *Le Typikon de la Grande Église: Ms. Saint-Croix n° 40 Xᵉ siècle*, vol. 1: *Le cycle de douze mois*, Orientalia Christiana Analecta 165 (Rome: Pontificium Institutum Orientalium Studiorum, 1962), vol. 2: *Le cycle des fêtes mobiles*, Orientalia Christiana Analecta 166 (Rome: Pontificium Institutum Orientalium Studiorum, 1963) 1:152.4–6. A similar rite is found on the eve of the Feast of Epiphany, but three Gospel books are used for this feast: one is placed on the altar table, the second one is read from, and the third is placed on the synthronon. See 1:180.19–23.

[41]These eleven gospel readings, called *eothina*, or morning gospels, are Matt. 28:16–end; Mark 16:1–9; Mark 16:9–end; Luke 24:1–13; Luke 24:12–36; Luke 24:36–end; John 20:1–11; John 20:11–19; John 20:19–31; John 21:1–15; John 21:14–end.

[42]The history of the liturgical books that contain the New Testament texts is complex and not entirely understood. The work done has been mainly on the text itself and not the liturgical use of the text. Nevertheless the studies by Yvonne Burns remain indispensable. See her "A Comparative Study of the

Weekday Lection Systems Found in Some Greek and Early Slavonic Gospel Lectionaries" (Ph.D. diss., University of London, 1975), and her article "The Greek Manuscripts Connected by Their Lection System with the Palestinian Syriac Gospel Lectionaries," *Journal for the Study of the New Testament*, supp. ser. 2 (1980) 13–28. A summary review of lectionary scholarship is in Bruce Metzger, "Greek Lectionaries and a Critical Edition of the New Testament," in *Die alten Übersetzungen des Neuen Testaments, Die Kirchenväterzitate und Lektionare*, ed. Kurt Aland, Arbeiten zur Neutestamentlichen Textforschung 5 (Berlin: De Gruyter,1972) 479–497. Almost no work has been done on the formation of the *Praxapostolos*. There is a brief description of its content in Caspar R. Gregory, *Textkritik des Neuen Testamentes*, vol. 1 (Leipzig: J. C. Hinrichs, 1900), 335–342, 465–478. There is also an important unpublished dissertation on the *Praxapostolos*: E. Velkovska, "Il Praxapostolos A.b. V della Biblioteca di Grottaferrata" (SEOD diss., Pontificio Istituto Orientale, 1994).

⁴³W. C. Braithwaite, "The Lection System of the Codex Macedonianus," *Journal of Theological Studies* 5 (1904) 265–274.

⁴⁴Yvonne Burns, "The Historical Events That Occasioned the Inception of the Byzantine Lectionaries," *Jahrbuch der Österreichischen Byzantinistik* 32.11.4 (1982) 119–127.

⁴⁵The structure of the Byzantine gospel and epistle lectionary cycle is neatly summarized in Irmgard M. De Vries, *The Epistles, Gospels, and Tones of the Byzantine Liturgical Year*, Eastern Churches Quarterly Reprint 3 (Antwerp: Vita et Pax, 1954). It can also be found in older works, such as Frederick Scrivener, *Plain Introduction to the Criticism of the New Testament*, vol. 1 (London and New York: George Bell, 1894) 80–89.

⁴⁶The text of the *Prophetologion* was edited by Carsten Hoeg and Günter Zuntz, *Prophetologium*, Monumenta Musicae Byzantinae, Lectionaria I.1:1–6 (Copenhagen: Munksgaard, 1939–1970), and II.1–2, ed. Gudrun Engberg (Copenhagen: Munksgaard, 1980–1981). On the history of the *Prophetologion*, see S. G. Engberg, "The Greek Old Testament Lectionary as a Liturgical Book," *Cahiers de l'Insitut du Moyen-âge grec et latin* 54 (1986) 39–48.

⁴⁷A convenient summary of the history of the *Horologion* can be found in the introduction written by Nicolas Egender, *La prière des Église de rite byzantin*, vol. 1: *La prière des heures: Horologion* (Chevetogne, Belgium: Éditions de Chevetogne, 1975) 11–90. For the oldest known text of the *Horologion*, see Juan Mateos, "Un horologion inédit de S. Sabas: Le codex sinaïtique grecque 863 (IXe siècle)," ST 233 (1964) 49–54.

⁴⁸Robert Taft discusses this distribution of the Psalter as well as others in "Mount Athos," 181–182.

⁴⁹For the division of the Psalms into kathismata and kathismata into stasis and the distribution of the Psalter throughout the liturgical year, see *The Festal Menaion*, 530–534.

⁵⁰Anastasius of Sinai, *Oratio de sacra synaxi*, PG 89:825 (CPG 7750).

⁵¹Anastasius of Sinai, *Oratio de sacra synaxi*, PG 89:845 (CPG 7750); translation from Taft, *Precommunion Rites*, 151.

⁵²Details of the history of the communion antiphon are in Taft, *Precommunion Rites*, 261–318.

⁵³For examples of this, see *The Festal Menaion*, 82–83, 100–101.

⁵⁴John of Damascus, *De hymno Trisagio epistola*, PG 95:36 (CPG 8049); translation from Oliver Strunk, *Essays on Music in the Byzantine World* (New York: Norton, 1977) 168.

⁵⁵P. Karavites, "Gregory Nazianzinos and Byzantine Hymnography," *Journal of Hellenic Studies* 113 (1993) 81–98.

⁵⁶Egon Wellesz, *A History of Byzantine Music and Hymnography* (Oxford: Clarendon, 1961) 10–11. This book is still a good, accessible history of Byzantine hymnography.

⁵⁷Melito of Sardis, *On Pascha: With the Fragments of Melito and Other Material Related to the Quartodecimans*, trans. Alistair Stewart-Sykes (Crestwood, N.Y.: St. Vladimir's Seminary Press, 2001) 56.

⁵⁸The connection between Melito's *Peri Pascha* and later Byzantine hymnography was first noted by Egon Wellesz in his important article "Melito's Homily on the Passion: An Investigation into the Sources of Byzantine Hymnography," *Journal of Theological Studies* 44 (1943) 41–52. A more precise connection between Melito and the hymn from Good Friday mentioned above is drawn out by Sebastià Janeras in his study on the Byzantine Church's celebration of Holy Friday: *Le Vendredi-Saint dans la tradition liturgique byzantine*, Studia Anselmiana 99/Analecta Liturgica 12 (Rome: Pontificio Anteno S. Anselmo, 1988) 261–270.

⁵⁹W. L. Peterson, "The Dependence of Romanos the Melodist upon the Syriac Ephrem," *Vigilae Christianae* 39 (1985) 171–187.

⁶⁰Romanos's life and work along with the relevant bibliography is in the critical edition of his kontakia: Romanos le Mélode, *Hymnes*, Sources chrétiennes (SC) 99 (Paris: Cerf, 1964); SC 110 (Paris: Cerf, 1965); SC 114 (Paris: Cerf, 1965); SC 128 (Paris: Cerf, 1967); and SC 283 (Paris: Cerf, 1980). An

English translation of a selection of Romanos's kontakia can be found in *Kontakia of Romanus, Byzantine Melodist*, 2 vols., trans. Marjorie Carpenter (Columbia: University of Missouri Press, 1973); and also *On the Life of Christ: Kontakia*, trans. Ephrem Lash (San Francisco: HarperCollins, 1995).

[61] *The Lenten Triodion*, 422–423.

[62] On the continued use of this form, see Alexander Lingas, "The Liturgical Use of the Kontakion in Constantinople," in *Liturgy, Architecture, and Art of the Byzantine World: Papers of the XVIII International Byzantine Congress (Moscow, 8–15 August 1991) and Other Essays Dedicated to the Memory of Fr. John Meyendorff*, ed. C. Akentiev, Byzantinorussica 1 (Saint Petersburg: Vizantinorossika, 1995) 50–57.

[63] The work of the Sabaitic hymnographers are reviewed in Christian Hannick, "Hymnographie et hymnographes Sabaïtes," in *The Sabaite Heritage in the Orthodox Church from the Fifth Century to the Present*, ed. Joseph Patrich, Orientalia Lovaniensia Analecta 98 (Louvain: Uitgeveij Peeters en Departement Oosterse Studies, 2001) 217–228.

[64] For an analysis of John of Damascus's hymnography, see Andrew Louth, *St. John Damascene: Tradition and Originality in Byzantine Theology* (Oxford: Oxford University Press, 2002) 252–282.

[65] Theodore's liturgical reforms are most recently summarized in Pott, *La réforme liturgique byzantine*, 99–129. For his hymnographic work, see esp. 117–120. For the style of other ninth-century composers, see A. Kazhdan, "An Oxymoron: Individual Features of a Byzantine Hymnographer," *Rivista di studi bizantini e neoellenici* 29 (1992) 19–58.

[66] The nine biblical odes are Exod. 15:1–19; Deut. 32:1–43; 1 Sam. 2:1–10; Hab. 3:1–19; Isa. 26:9–20; Jon. 2:3–10; Dan. (LXX) 3:26–56; Dan. (LXX) 3:57–88; Luke 1:46–55, 68–79. On these, see Taft, "Mount Athos," 181, 188–190.

[67] J. B. Pitra, *Analecta Sacra Spicilegio Solesmensi*, vol. 1 (Paris: A. Jouby et Roger, 1876; repr. Farnborough, Hants.: Gregg Press, 1966) xlvii.

[68] *The Lenten Triodion*, 548–549, 553.

[69] Sixth troparion of the eighth ode, Great Canon of Saint Andrew at Great Compline. *The Lenten Triodion*, 227.

[70] First sticheron at vespers, first Friday of Great Lent. *The Lenten Triodion*, 273.

[71] Fourth troparion of the ninth ode, Great Canon of Saint Andrew at Great Compline. *The Lenten Triodion*, 265.

[72] Third troparion of the first ode, second canon of matins, the Feast of the Transfiguration. *The Festal Menaion*, 483

[73] First troparion of the third ode, second canon of matins, the Feast of the Dormition. *The Festal Menaion*, 516.

[74] Sticheron after the Glory at "Lord, I call," vespers, the Feast of the Nativity. *The Festal Menaion*, 254. Note this hymn is also ascribed to Kassia.

[75] First sticheron from the Aposticha of the Office of the Holy Passion. *The Lention Triodion*, 598.

[76] Third sticheron from the Aposticha of the Office of the Holy Passion. *The Lenten Triodion*, 599.

[77] Resurrectional Apolytikion, tone 3. Translation from *The Divine Liturgy of Our Father among the Saints John Chrysostom* (Oxford: Oxford University Press, 1995) 61.

[78] A concise history of music that covers the entire span of the history of the Orthodox Church does not exist. For the Byzantine era and the Greek-speaking churches, see Dimitri Conomos, *Byzantine Hymnography and Byzantine Chant* (Brookline, Mass.: Hellenic College Press, 1984); also *New Grove Dictionary of Music and Musicians*, 2nd ed., ed. Stanley Sadie and John Tyrell (London: McMillan, 2001), "Byzantine Rite, Music of the," by K. Levy. For the Russian tradition of music, see Johann von Gardner, *Russian Church Singing*, trans. Vladimir Moroson, vol. 1: *Orthodox Worship and Hymnography* (Crestwood, N.Y.: St. Vladimir's Seminary Press, 1980), vol. 2: *History from the Origins to the Mid-Seventeenth Century* (Crestwood, N.Y.: St. Vladimir's Seminary Press, 2000).

[79] For the history of *Oktoechos*, see Christian Hannick's introduction to *Dimanche, offices selon les huit tons: Oktoéchos* (Chevetogne, Belgium: Éditions de Chevetogne, 1972) 11–60; for the early history of this book, see A. Cody, "The Early History of the Oktoechos in Syria," in *East of Byzantium: Syria and Armenia in the Formative Period*, ed. Nina G. Garsoïan, Thomas F. Mathews, and Robert W. Thomson (Washington, D.C.: Dumbarton Oaks, Center for Byzantine Studies, Trustees for Harvard University, 1982) 89–113.

[80] Sticheron from the Aposticha, Friday night Octoechos, tone 8.

[81] Sticheron from the Aposticha, Friday night Octoechos, tone 1.

[82] The introduction to the English translation of the Lenten *Triodion* provides a good summary in English of its history, contents, and nature; see *The Lenten Triodion*, 13–98. For an academic study of the formation of part of the *Triodion*, see Gabriel Bertonière, *The Sundays of Lent in the Triodion: The Sundays without a Commemoration*, Orientalia Christiana Analecta 253 (Rome: Pontificio Istituto Orientale, 1997).

[83]Very little work has been done on the history of the *Pentecostarion*. An older work summarizes what is known: P. de Meester, *Riti e particolarità liturgiche del Triodio e del Pentecostario* (Padua, Italy: 1943).

[84]On the history of the liturgical *Typikon*, see Miguel Arranz, "Les grandes étapes de la Liturgie Byzantine: Palestine-Byzance-Russie; Essai d'aperçu historique," *Liturgie de l'église particulière et liturgie de l'église universelle*, BELS 7 (Rome: C.L.V., Edizioni Liturgiche, 1976) 43–72; and Taft, "Mount Athos."

[85]*The Synaxarion of the Monastery of the Theotokos Evergetis*, vol. 1, *September to February*, ed. and trans. Robert Jordan, Belfast Byzantine Texts and Translations 6.5 (Belfast, Ireland: Belfast Byzantine Enterprises, Institute of Byzantine Studies, Queen's University of Belfast, 2000). For a study of this document, see John E. Klentos, "Byzantine Liturgy in Twelfth-Century Constantinople: An Analysis of the Synaxarion of the Monastery of the Theotokos" (Ph.D. diss., University of Notre Dame, 1995).

[86]This *Typikon* has been edited by Mateos in *Le Typicon de la Grande Église*.

[87]The history of these documents is neatly summarized in C. Galatariotou, "Byzantine Ktetorika Typika: A Comparative Study," *Revue des Études Byzantines* 45 (1987) 77–138; and A.-A. Thiermeyer, "Das Typikon-Ktetorikon und sein literarhistorischer Kontext," *Orientalia Christiana Periodica* 58 (1992) 475–513.

[88]Christodoulos, "Christodoulos: *Rule, Testament*, and *Codicil* of Christodoulos for the Monastery of St. John the Theologian on Patmos," trans. P. Karlin-Hayter, in *Byzantine Monastic Foundation Documents*, 2:586.

[89]This well-known influence of the *Typikon* of Saint Sabas is conveniently summarized by Nicholas Egender in his article "La formation et l'influence du *Typikon* liturgique de Saint-Sabas," in *Sabaite Heritage*, 209–216. The lesser known history of the adoption of the Sabaitic *Typikon* by the Serbs in the early fourteenth century is discussed by Svetlana Popovic, "Sabaite Influences on the Church of Medieval Serbia," in *Sabaite Heritage*, 401–403.

[90]E. Catafygiotou-Topping, "Thekla the Nun: In Praise of Woman," *Greek Orthodox Theological Review* 25 (1980) 353–370. Catafygiotou-Topping also lists two other Byzantine woman hymnographers: Theodosia (ninth century) and Palaiologina (fifteenth century).

[91]Antonia Tripolitis, in *Kassia: The Legend, the Woman, and Her Work*, Garland Library of Medieval Literature 84, Series A (New York: Garland, 1994), includes a translation of Kassia's recognized

works (pp. 2–105) and briefly details what is known of her life (pp. xi–xxi).

[92]Sticheron after the Glory of the Aposticha, matins, Holy Wednesday. *The Lenten Triodion*, 540–541. For a study of this hymn in depth, see A. Dyck, "On Cassia, *Kyrie, he en pollais*," *Byzantion* 56 (1986) 63–76.

[93]*Orthodoxy and Ecology: a Resource Book*, Alexander Belopopsky and Dimitri Oiknomou (Bialystok, Poland: Orthdruk: Orthodox Printing House, 1996). The service was first published in Thessalonika in 1997.

[94]Edition and study by Stephano Parenti and Elena Velkovska, *L'Eucologio Barberini gr. 336*, BELS 80 (Rome: C.L.V., Edizioni Liturgiche, 1995). For the history of the *Euchologion*, see above all M. Arranz, "Les Sacrements de l'ancien Euchologe constantinopolitan (1). Étude préliminaire des sources," *Orientalia Christiana Periodica* 48 (1982) 284–335.

[95]Taft, *The Great Entrance*.

[96]On the general history of the presanctified liturgy, see Stefanos Alexopoulos, "The Presanctified Liturgy in the Byzantine Rite: A Comparative Analysis of its Origins, Evolution, and Structural Components" (Ph.D. diss., University of Notre Dame, 2004).

[97]For a history of the *Archieratikon*, see Robert F. Taft, "The Pontifical Liturgy of the Great Church according to a Twelfth-Century Diataxis in Codex *British Museum Add. 34060*," *Orientalia Christiana Periodica* 45–46 (1979–1980) 297–307; 89–124. Also see the older work by C. Korolevskij, "Le Pontifical dans le rite byzantin," *Orientalia Christiana Periodica* 10 (1944) 202–215.

[98]Translation from E. C. Whitaker, ed., *Documents of the Baptismal Liturgy*, 2nd ed. (London: 1970) 79–80.

[99]Parenti and others.

[100]Translations of these anaphoras are in R. C. D. Jasper and G. J. Cuming, *Prayers of the Eucharist: Early and Reformed*, 3rd ed. (New York: Pueblo, 1987) 114–123 for Basil; 129–134 for Chrysostom.

[101]The extremely complicated details of the origins of Basil's anaphora are neatly summarized in D. R. Stuckwisch, "The Basilian Anaphoras," in *Essays on Early Eucharistic Prayers*, ed. Paul Bradshaw (Collegeville, Minn.: Liturgical Press, 1997) 109–130. See also John R. K. Fenwick, *The Anaphoras of St. Basil and St. James: An Investigation into their Common Origin*, Orientalia Christiana Analecta 240 (Rome: Pontificium Institutum Orientale, 1992). For older important works that compare the theology of the received text of the anaphora with Basil's other theological works, see Boris Bobrinskoy, "Liturgie et ecclésiologie trinitaire de Saint Basile,"

Verbum Caro 23 (1969) 1–32; and Bernard Capelle, "Les liturgies basiliennes et S. Basile," in *Un témoin archaïque de la liturgie copte de S. Basile*, ed. Jean Doresse and Emmanuel Lanne, Bibliothèque du Muséon 47 (Louvain: Publications Universitaires, 1960) 42–74.

[102]For a detailed account on the origin and attribution of this anaphoral prayer, see Robert Taft, "The Authenticity of the Chrysostom Anaphora Revisited: Determining the Authorship of Liturgical Texts by Computer," *Orientalia Christiana Periodica* 56 (1990) 5–51; the translation of Chrysostom's anaphora is from p. 28.

[103]André Jacob, "Histoire du formulaire grec de la Liturgie de Saint Jean Chrysostome" (Ph.D. diss., Université Catholique de Louvain, 1968) 29.

[104]The text of Philotheos' *Diataxis* can be found in any number of editions. Perhaps most convenient is the noncritical edition of the earliest dated manuscript of the *Philothean Diataxis*, *Athos Panteleimon 770*, in P. N. Trempelas, *Hai treis leitourgiai kata tous en Athinais Kodikas* [The three liturgies according to the codices in Athens], Texte und Forschungen zur Byzantinisch-neugriechischen Philologie 15 (Athens: M. Patriarchikes Epistemonikes Epitropes pros Anatheoresin kai Ekdosin ton Leitourgikon Vivlion, 1935) 1–16. A later recension of the *Diataxis* can also be found that is fully integrated into the euchology text of the Divine Liturgy in F. E. Brightman, ed., *Liturgies Eastern and Western* (Oxford: Clarendon, 1896; repr. 1967) 353–399. Philotheos Kokkinos was a towering figure in the Byzantine Empire during the fourteenth century. Yet even though his influence was enormous, no single work that studies him or his theology exists. On his role in the hesychast controversy and in the Byzantine political sphere, see John Meyendorff, *Byzantium and the Rise of Russia* (Cambridge and New York: Cambridge University Press, 1981) 173–199. For his liturgical influence, see Pott, *La réforme liturgique byzantine*, 187–196; and Taft, "Mount Athos," 191–194.

[105]Taft, "Mount Athos," 193–194.

[106]Dimitrios Doukas, *Hai theiai leitourgiai tou hagiou Ioannou tou Chrysostomou, Basileiou tou Megalou, kai he ton Proegiasmenon: Gemanou Archiepiskopou Konstantinopoleos Historia Ekklesiastike kai mystike theoria* [The Divine Liturgies of St. John Chrysostom, Basil the Great, and Presanctified: The ecclesiastical history and mystical contemplation of Germanus, Archbishop of Constantinople] (Rome: 1526). Doukas's edition is reprinted in C. A. Swainson, ed., *The Greek Liturgies Chiefly from Original Authorities* (Cambridge: Cambridge University Press, 1884) 101–144. Doukas and his publishing activities are summarized in Evro Layton, *The Sixteenth-Century Greek Book in Italy: Printers and Publishers for the Greek World*, Library of the Hellenic Institute and Post-Byzantine Studies 16 (Venice: Istituto ellenico di studi bizantini e postbizantini di Venezia, 1994), 276–280; and D. J. Geanakoplos, *Greek Scholars in Venice: Studies in the Dissemination of Greek Learning from Byzantium to Western Europe* (Cambridge, Mass.: Harvard University Press, 1962) 223–255.

[107]Paul Meyendorff, *Russia, Ritual, and Reform: The Liturgical Reforms of Nikon in the 17th Century* (Crestwood, N.Y.: St. Vladimir's Press, 1991) 185–186.

[108]The definitive work on the Byzantine mystagogical tradition is René Bornert, *Les commentaires byzantins de la Divine Liturgie du VIIe au XVe siècle*, Archives de l'Orient Chrétien 9 (Paris: Institut français d'études byzantines, 1966).

[109]A good description of this process is in Hans-Joachim Schultz, *Die byzantinische Liturgie: Vom Werden ihrer Symbolgestalt* (Freiburg im Breisgau: Lambertus, 1964); in English, *The Byzantine Liturgy*, trans. Matthew J. O'Connell (New York: Pueblo, 1986).

[110]Parenti and Velkovska, *Barberini 336*, 1.2.

[111]Germanus, *On the Divine Liturgy*, 71.

[112]The development of the prothesis rite is the subject of a section of Pott's *La réforme liturgique byzantine*, 169–196.

[113]Anton Baumstark, *Comparative Liturgy*, rev. Bernard Botte, trans. F. L. Cross (Westminster, Md.: Newman, 1958) 18.

[114]The complex development is described in Taft's *The Great Entrance*.

[115]A convenient summary of the Church's mystagogical tradition and how it influenced the Byzantine tradition can be found in Robert F. Taft, "The Liturgy of the Great Church: an Initial Synthesis of Structure and Interpretation on the Eve of Iconoclasm," *Dumbarton Oaks Papers* 34–35 (1980–1981) 45–75.

[116]Cabasilas, *The Life in Christ*, 75.

[117]Alexander Kazhdan and Giles Constable, *People and Power in Byzantium: An Introduction to Modern Byzantine Studies* (Washington, D.C.: Dumbarton Oaks Center for Byzantine Studies, Trustees for Harvard University, 1982) 158.

[118]Symeon of Thessalonika, *De ordine sepulturae*, PG 155:680.

[119]More detailed outlines of orthros are in *The Festal Menaion*, 75–76; D. Touliatos-Banker, "The Byzantine Orthros," *Byzantina* 9 (1977) 325–383; and also Taft, *The Liturgy of the Hours*.

[120]For the history and understanding of this rite, see Taft, *The Precommunion Rites*, 441–502.

[121]Robert F. Taft, "Understanding the Byzantine Anaphoral Oblation," in *Rule of Prayer, Rule of Faith: Essays in Honor of Aidan Kavanagh, O.S.B.*, ed. Nathan Mitchell and John Baldovin (Collegeville, Minn.: Liturgical Press, 1996) 53–54. See also Taft's article "Ecumenical Scholarship and the Catholic-Orthodox Epiclesis Dispute," *Ostkirchliche Studien* 45 (1996) 201–226.

[122]On the history of these morning prayers, see Miguel Arranz, "Les prières presbytérales des matines byzantines," *Orientalia Christiana Periodica* 37 (1971) 406–436; 38 (1972) 64–115.

[123]Dmitrievsky, *Opisanie liturgicheskikh rykopisei*, 3: 25.

[124]The prayers of light are presidential prayers said quietly during the vesper service. On their history, see Miguel Arranz, "Les prières sacerdotales des vêpres byzantines," *Orientalia Christiana Periodica* 37 (1971) 85–124.

[125]Maximus, *Mystagogy*, 207.

[126]Maximus, *Mystagogy*, 207–208.

[127]See Taft, "Liturgy of the Great Church," 50–51.

8

Reforms, Protestant and Catholic

NATHAN D. MITCHELL

Introduction

Had consumers living in Siena, Italy, during July of the year 1423 been prosperous
enough to afford fresh fabric for new gowns or doublets, they might have noticed a
sudden increase in prices. That summer the prestigious Sienese guild of wool merchants (the Arte della Lana) began imposing a tax on cloth to finance the painting of
a new altarpiece, a triptych to be used each year during the feast of Corpus Christi, as
celebrated in the church of the Carmelite friars (the "Carmine" or *ecclesia sanctae Mariae
de Monte Carmello*). What, one may ask, does an altarpiece commissioned by wool
merchants in an early-fifteenth-century Italian city have to do with "sixteenth-century liturgical reforms, Protestant and Catholic?" Quite a lot, as it turns out. The
artist selected to paint the triptych was Stefano di Giovanni (c. 1450), known today as
Sassetta. Enough of Sassetta's completed predella survives to convince modern art
historians that his work was not only extraordinarily innovative, but that it also "opens
a new chapter in the history of Sienese painting."[1]

Just as important, Sassetta's triptych provides tantalizing clues about how fifteenth-
century Sienese Catholics viewed the eucharist in the religious life of their church and
city. Because the Carmine was eventually razed and its altarpiece dispersed, the precise arrangement of Sassetta's work had to be reconstructed from literary records.
Eighteenth-century descriptions tell us that the overarching theme of the triptych
was *The Glory of the Blessed Sacrament*. The central panel depicted the consecrated host
housed in a gothic monstrance, carried by flying angels, and accompanied by a band
of angel-musicians. On the predella beneath this main panel were seven paintings, six
of which survive: the first two showed scenes from the life of Saint Anthony; the final
two depicted Saint Thomas Aquinas in prayer; and the middle three portrayed eucharistic themes.[2]

Not surprisingly, one of these middle paintings is a Last Supper; the other two,
however, may trouble twenty-first-century viewers. The first of these two panels, sometimes called *The Miracle of the Holy Sacrament*, shows the interior of a chapel where a
group of well-dressed male and female onlookers stand or kneel behind a group of
Carmelite friars, who shrink back from the scene unfolding before their eyes. A fully
vested priest turns from the altar to offer the host, which rests on a paten, to a fainting
young friar whose soul is being snatched by a fleeing devil. Looking closely, one sees
that the host is bleeding; indeed, blood covers almost the entire surface of the paten
and spills over onto the (sinful? unbelieving?) friar's black mantle. In the Middle Ages,

of course, reports of bleeding hosts were not rare; Thomas Aquinas even found it necessary to comment on such eucharistic "miracles" in his *Summa Theologiae.*[3] Sassetta's painting is not, therefore, unique—other narrators and artists of the period chose the same theme—but the naturalistic intensity of the Arte della Lana panel makes it quite memorable.

While the *Miracle of the Holy Sacrament* is shocking, a greater jolt awaits viewers in *The Burning of a Heretic*, the remaining scene among the three eucharistic panels of Sassetta's altarpiece. In the open air outside a walled city, at either dusk or dawn, an altar has been erected where a priest, assisted by an acolyte, is elevating the host while rapt worshipers (including a cardinal and a Carmelite friar) gaze upward. Mounted soldiers—one of them carrying a banner emblazoned with the arms of the Arte della Lana—stand guard over the scene. Meanwhile, just slightly to the left of the painting's center, a bound figure (whose bearded face is turned away from the elevated host) is being burned alive. A servant adds fodder to the flames, while additional bundles of faggots lie near the condemned man's feet, which are completely engulfed by the mounting fire. The sumptuous red, gold, and ochre of the celebrating priest's chasuble eerily reflect the colors of the flames that consume the bound man's body. Most art historians agree that this panel is meant to depict the violent torture and execution of someone who has denied the Roman church's teaching about the eucharist (namely, the theology of transubstantiation and the doctrine of Christ's real presence in the consecrated elements).

Miracle of the Holy Sacrament. Predella painting (1423) by Sassetta (1394–1450). Bowes Museum, Barnard Castle, County Durham, U.K./Bridgeman Art Library

Precisely who this "someone" might be is debatable. Some scholars suggest it was the Bohemian theologian John Hus, burned outside the walls of Constance (in modern-day Germany) on 6 July 1415; others say the scene depicts the execution of accused heretic Francesco di Pietro Porcari, consigned to the flames outside the gates of Siena on 3 July 1421, a scant two years before Sassetta began working on the Arte della Lana altarpiece. But it is also possible that the scene is generic and does not portray any specific historical episode. As Keith Christiansen notes, a church council meeting at Siena in 1423–1424 had

The Burning of a Heretic. Predella painting by Sassetta, 1423. © National Gallery of Victoria, Melbourne, Australia/Bridgeman Art Library

reiterated the condemnations of Hus, Wyclif, and any other person who, in the words of Sienese painter Bindino da Travale, dared to say that "the body of Christ . . . did not become blood and flesh . . . [that] the host was a [mere] semblance of Christ . . . [and that] the host does not become blood and flesh and bones."[4]

Da Travale's comments reveal, of course, a eucharistic realism redolent of the recantation that the theologian Berengarius of Tours was forced to make in the mid-eleventh century.[5] Moreover, the denunciation of heretical views and a fierce reassertion of eucharistic "realism" would have been quite compatible with the Arte della Lana's purpose, which was to provide an altarpiece for the celebration of Corpus Christi, a feast that boldly reaffirmed medieval Catholic doctrine about the eucharist. And what was that doctrine? As Miri Rubin deftly summarizes it, medieval eucharistic doctrine centered on the use and transmission of social power:

> Power defined the center of the discussion: the sacrament was a central symbol or test of orthodoxy and dissent throughout the later Middle Ages. Christ's presence in the sacrament, the need for sacerdotal mediation, the practice of gazing at the sacrament, the notion of certain inherent magical properties of the host, the body of Christ: all these could be crucial tests. And we find them conducted by people across the social spectrum, just as we now know that Lollard criticism and dissent were alive not only among the poor.[6]

Surely such power is reflected in Sassetta's horrific panel, *The Burning of a Heretic*. In it, the authority of "spiritual church" and "secular state" unite to destroy dissent by fire—and to consign the dissenter to hell (in Sassetta's painting, a winged devil is swooping down from the dark sky to claim the heretic's soul). Medieval theologies of real presence and transubstantiation (perhaps imperfectly understood) thus provided a symbolic framework within which it was possible to claim that "through sacerdotal ritual action matter could be transformed into something quite different, a repository of supernatural power, and that only such sacerdotal action could effect this change."[7] Nor were these views found only on the European continent; they are also represented in the homiletic traditions of late medieval England, where preachers reminded communicants of the truths that "holy churche techeth thee" about the eucharist:

> the . . . Hoste is Goddes bodie in the forme of brede. . . . For it semeth to thine eye but as a litill brede, but yitt it is no brede but Goddes owen flesh and [h]is blode. And to thine eye it semeth litill, and yitt it is ful mekell; why-for it fulfilleth bothe heven and erthe. Also in the savour in thi mouthe it semeth brede, and it is not so; for-why certeynly it is the same flessh that was borne of Oure Ladye Seynt Mary on Cristemasse day.[8]

Small wonder, then, that eucharistic doctrine became a crucial litmus test of orthodoxy in the sixteenth century. While the Reformers protested "the disgraceful masses of the papists"[9] and claimed that "where there are no real and genuine Christians. . . . one should abandon the monstrances and the Corpus Christi processions,"[10] the Catholic Counter-Reformation championed the doctrine of real presence, the theology of transubstantiation,[11] and the formation of new religious societies and "confraternities" devoted to fostering adoration of the Blessed Sacrament.[12]

This chapter will explore the liturgical reforms proposed by leading Reformers (for example, Luther, Zwingli, Calvin, Cranmer), as well as Catholic reforms launched after the Council of Trent (1545–1563). Because it became such a "lightning rod," I will pay close attention to the eucharist as it was treated by both Protestant Reformers and Catholic Counter-Reformers in the sixteenth century. As I hope to show, leaders of both camps agreed that the Church's public worship was in need of an overhaul, although they disagreed on the best way to achieve reform. It is possible, moreover, that leaders in both groups overdramatized the "rift between clerical and lay experience of the late medieval mass," and that their conclusion (medieval lay participation was radically "impoverished") may have been mistaken. Virginia Reinburg contends it is wrong to assume that "the medieval laity had some physical, but no intellectual involvement with the words of the Gospel or the doctrine of the eucharist."[13] Medieval liturgy was not, she argues, a mere clerical monopoly; rather, lay participants assigned meanings to the rites quite different from those of their clerical counterparts. The "laity's mass," writes Reinburg, "was less sacrifice and sacrament than a communal rite of greeting, sharing, giving, receiving, and making peace. . . . [T]he mass was less a ceremonial representation of eucharistic doctrine on Christ's original sacrifice than a sacred rite uniting them with God, the Church, and each other." The medieval lay congregation, she concludes, experienced the liturgy as "a ritual drama in which both priest and congregation had distinct, but equally necessary parts to play."

It might be said, therefore, that medieval laypersons participated in the eucharist not so much by "understanding" the words and rites but by "observing proper demeanor toward its Lord and his acts." For example:

> Late medieval French expositions of the mass suggest that the clergy expected lay people to participate in the liturgy in a distinctive way—a way distinguishable from the clergy's more doctrinally instructed participation, but possessing its own integrity. . . . The mass meant what it did to lay participants at least in part because it was conducted in a ritual language of gestures and symbols they knew from secular life.

Some of these gestures and symbols were learned from family and village life, some from the marketplace, some from the royal court. In effect, medieval lay participants "understood" the liturgy with their bodies, and so their connection to the ritual flowed from "a rich layering of associations, of social relationships and rituals expressing those relationships." This point is confirmed by the many medieval illustrations (especially from late-fifteenth-century sources), which show strong gestural connections between the liturgy and the rituals of secular life. "In this sense," Reinburg asserts, "the late medieval liturgy can be viewed as the establishment of social and spiritual solidarity among God, the Church, and the lay community."[14]

As will be seen, however, the approach to reform adopted by the Council of Trent had more in common with a Protestant emphasis on "doctrinally informed lay participation" than with medieval notions of lay involvement in the mass. Both Trent and the Reformers pursued a goal that can be described as "modern"—informed, educated, well-catechized people who understand, intellectually, the significance of the Church's public, ritual actions. At the end of the day, both Protestant and Catholic leaders of the sixteenth century found themselves agreeing that the proper solution to the liturgical "problem" was "intellectually informed participation by layfolk." The Reformers sought to achieve this goal through the use of vernacular languages, the restoration of the word to its rightful place in public worship, and frequent evangelical preaching. Similarly, although the bishops present at Trent's twenty-second session (17 September 1562) rejected the idea "that [mass] should be celebrated everywhere in the vernacular tongue," they admitted that the mass "contains much instruction for the people," and so "the holy council commands pastors and all who have the *cura animarum* that they, either themselves or through others, *explain frequently during the celebration of the mass some of the things read during the mass, and that among other things they explain some mystery of this most holy sacrifice, especially on Sundays and festival days.*"[15]

Preaching. Known as "The Preaching of the Church or the Calling of St. Anthony," a painting from c. 1535 by an unknown "Master of the Preaching of the Church" features a congregation gathered to listen to a sermon. In the distant left, a table at the entrance to the choir is readied for the sacrament. At the distant right, bread is distributed, suggesting that the subject of the sermon was the Lord's prayer ("our daily bread") or that the painting was connected with St. Anthony, patron of the poor, or the brotherhood founded in his name. RIJKSMUSEUM, AMSTERDAM/ PHOTOGRAPH BY KAREN WESTERFIELD TUCKER

In its emphasis on the need for "explanation" and its tendency to equate "lay participation in the liturgy" with "well-informed cognitive access," Trent was conceding points to the Reformers while essentially rejecting the typical medieval layperson's approach to participation in Catholic worship. If pastors or their surrogates had acted on Trent's admonition to "explain frequently during the celebration of the mass some of the things read during the mass," the eucharist would have become a service of instruction quite puzzling to most lay participants.[16] In actual fact, the catechetical mandate from Trent's twenty-second session was rarely acted upon. Still, it can truthfully be said that the drive toward Roman Catholic liturgical "modernism" (with its emphasis on clarity, cognitive access, intelligibility, and "full, conscious, active participation" in ritual forms) actually began, not at the Second Vatican Council in the mid-twentieth century, but at the Council of Trent in the mid-sixteenth.

Reformed Liturgies of the Sixteenth Century

The "Reformation" before the Reformation

The history of Christian liturgical reforms in the sixteenth century begins, however, not with Roman Catholic initiatives, but with Protestant ones. In several important respects, the Reformation had already begun well before Luther posted his ninety-five theses on the door of the castle church at Wittenberg (in modern-day Germany), on

31 October 1517. Indeed, it can be argued that in some regions of Europe (for example, Lombardy, in present-day Italy, and Languedoc, in present-day France) the medieval church's ability to impose compliance with its doctrines had already begun to break down by the end of the twelfth century.[17] Sometimes a heterodox movement—for instance, Catharism—expanded well beyond its place of origin and became a truly "supranational heresy," successful not so much because of its charismatic leaders but because of "its developed ritual and organization and the dogmatic envelope it gave to dissent."[18] The Cathars were literally "purists" (from Greek *katharos* [pure]) who claimed to be reviving the freshness, fervor, and simplicity of the early church. Like the adherents of Manichaeism in an earlier epoch, they embraced philosophical dualism, rejecting matter as evil and repudiating doctrines or practices that affirmed the goodness and redemptive potential of the body (for example, marriage, sacraments, the true humanity of Christ, the resurrection of the body).

Although the Cathars were eventually "eradicated by force" or simply "outgrown," other movements—the Waldensians, for instance—survived until the Reformation of the sixteenth century, adhering to the Protestant side perhaps already in 1532 or certainly by the 1550s or 1560s.[19] Throughout the thirteenth, fourteenth, and fifteenth centuries, therefore, dissenters continued to debate or deny church doctrine on a

---

The Bohemian Brethren

David R. Holeton

Beginning in the second half of the fourteenth century, Bohemia was the center of an important though little-known sacramental and liturgical movement. When Charles IV became Holy Roman Emperor in 1346, he kept Prague as his capital. The city witnessed a period of rapid growth and change which, compounded by an outbreak of plague and later by a divided papacy, caused a widespread sense of eschatological expectation. In the midst of this, the reform-minded priest Milíč of Kroměříž founded a community that attracted clergy, laity (both single and married), and a number of former prostitutes. There he celebrated the eucharist daily, preaching in the vernacular and distributing communion to all who desired it. The social and sacramental life of this "Jerusalem" community awakened a renewed appreciation for frequent communion among the laity, as well as a new understanding of the role of the eucharist as a means of social transformation by gathering together social classes not usually in contact with one another.

By the end of the fourteenth century, the frequent-communion movement had won strong theological support from a number of the reform-minded masters of Prague University, notably in Mathias of Janov's monumental *Regulae Veteris et Novi Testamenti* as well as in the writings of Adalbertus Ranconis, Matthew of Cracow, and Henry of Biterfeld. Eventually the movement received the approbation of both the synod and the archbishop of Prague (Jan of Jenštejn) and was popularized throughout the kingdom of Bohemia through the vernacular writings of the layman Tomáš Štítný of Štítné. By the early years of the fifteenth century, frequent communion (at least weekly and often daily) was widespread throughout Bohemia.

Inspired by the pastoral success of the frequent-communion movement and supported by the extensive collections of texts—biblical, patristic, scholastic, and canonical—that had been compiled to justify it, some theologians (notably

wide range of matters, from clerical celibacy and sexual ethics to priestly mediation and the sacramental system (especially eucharist). Some dissenters, like the fourteenth-century English divine John Wyclif, took issue with medieval eucharistic doctrine on both philosophical and pastoral grounds. Although Wyclif was deeply devoted to the sacrament, he "disliked what he interpreted as idolatry in the reaction to the elevation of the Host at mass or to the Corpus Christi processions," and he found he could not "both accept transubstantiation and maintain his metaphysics."[20] Although some of Wyclif's doctrines were eventually condemned at the Council of Constance (1415), his death in 1384 allowed him to escape John Hus's fiery fate.[21]

But the steady drumbeat of religious dissent was not the only force at work. The Protestant historian James F. White identifies five other factors that had already begun to reshape Christianity by the beginning of the sixteenth century: (1) the spirit of exploration and discovery that led to state sponsorship of voyages to the New World in the late-fifteenth century; (2) the consequent expansion of Christian missionary activity into new territories that virtually encircled the globe; (3) the emergence of a "new national consciousness on the level of new nation states"; (4) the technological revolution resulting from the invention of printing about 1450; and (5) the expansion of commerce and education in cities (fueled in part by the printed word).[22]

Jakoubek of Stříbro and Nicholas of Dresden) began promoting the restoration of the chalice to the laity. The practice was instituted in Prague in 1414, while the religious reformer Jan Hus was in prison in Constance awaiting trial before the council. Hus' death at the stake on 6 July 1415 served as the catalyst to make the lay chalice—which had been condemned by the council—the symbol of Bohemian resistance to the Roman authorities. (It is from their practice of communion under both bread and wine—*sub utraque specie*—that the reform movement came to be known as Utraquism and its members Utraquists; "Hussite" was a term used only by the movement's enemies.) Two years later, in 1417, using the same collection of texts employed to support frequent communion, now supplemented by others supporting the lay chalice, Jakoubek and others extended communicant status to all the baptized, including infants. For more than two hundred years, the regular reception of communion by all the baptized, regardless of age, remained a fundamental premise of Utraquism and was regarded as "the Law of God" and nonnegotiable in any discussion with the authorities in Rome.

When the "Hussite" Revolution broke out in 1419, largely over the king's attempt to restrict the lay chalice and infant communion, some extreme groups within Utraquism began making demands for a more radical liturgical reform. Centered in southern Bohemia, groups that came to be known as Taborites gave up the traditional rites and returned to what they believed to be "biblical" simplicity, abandoning all liturgical practices for which they could find no scriptural justification. After their defeat at the battle of Lipany in 1434, these radical initiatives were forced underground, but they surfaced later in the century in the small reforming group that called itself the Jednota Bratrská (Unity of Brethren, or *Unitas Fratrum*, the spiritual ancestors of what later became known as the Moravian Church). This latter group developed a rite of confirmation for adolescents which was popularized through the writings of Erasmus and eventually became the model for the new confirmation practices of the sixteenth-century reformers.

As a part of the wider Bohemian reform movement, Czech had become a "sacred" language alongside Latin during the second half of the fourteenth century. A variety of Czech translations of the Bible were produced, and experiments were made using those translations for the liturgical readings. Books of hours and other devotional literature in Czech were also quite common by the end of that century, and Štítný's writings had provided a Czech vocabulary for lay theological discourse. In this context, it is not surprising that initiatives began to be undertaken to translate into the vernacular the entire Roman liturgy—eucharist, office, and all pastoral services. The *Jistebnice Kancionál*, dating from the 1420s, is the first extensive example in Europe of an attempt to translate the whole medieval liturgy into the local language. From the early days of the fifteenth century, vernacular hymnody also played an important role in worship, and the growing corpus of Czech hymns (many of which were later borrowed in the German Reformation) were used alongside traditional plainchant in Utraquist worship. The pace at which Czech overtook Latin in Utraquist worship is still unclear because there was no central authority to regulate liturgical use, and the balance between languages appears to have been determined by the preferences of the local parish.

Utraquism, as the majority church, saw itself in continuity with the historic church of Bohemia, insisting on the "historic" or "apostolic" succession and most of the traditional rites and ceremonies of the Prague use of the Roman rite. The appearance of Utraquist worship was decidedly "Catholic," so that foreign observers, even at the end of the sixteenth century, often remarked that it was like Roman Catholic worship except for the use of the vernacular, communion *sub utraque* for all, and the celebration of the feast of Saint Jan Hus on July 6.

The defeat of the Bohemian Estates by the Hapsburgs in 1620 saw the triumph of the Counter-Reformation in the Bohemian lands. Although there was some initial accommodation to Utraquist liturgical practice (frequent communion *sub utraque specie* and vernacular lections), absolute conformity to the norms of the post-Tridentine liturgical books was soon demanded, and any religious practice other than Roman Catholicism and Judaism became a capital offense.

References

David, Zdeněk. *Finding the Middle Way: The Utraquists' Liberal Challenge to Rome and Luther*. Baltimore: Johns Hopkins University Press, 2003.

DeVooght, Paul. *Jacobellus de Stříbro (+1429), premier théologien du hussitisme*. Bibliothèque de la Revue d'Histoire Ecclésiastique 54. Louvain: Publications Universitaires de Louvain, 1972.

Holeton, David R. "The Bohemian Eucharistic Movement in Its European Context." *Bohemian Reformation and Religious Practice* 1 (1996) 23–47.

Holeton, David R. "The Evolution of Utraquist Eucharistic Liturgy: A Textual Study." *Bohemian Reformation and Religious Practice* 2 (1998): 97–126.

Jistebnice Kancionál. Edited by Jaroslav Kolár, Anežka Vidmanová, and Hana Vlhová-Wörner. Monumenta Liturgia Bohemica 2. Prague: 2004.

The impact of these factors on the church's life and worship was extraordinary. As White notes, "In 1450, a *Book of Common Prayer* would have been an oxymoron; a century later it was a reality." For better or worse, Christianity was exploding into a "worldwide faith encompassing the globe." Such success was bought at a price, however; explorers and missionaries of this period are still justly criticized for their violent exploitation of native peoples and for their brutal imposition of Eurocentric political and religious systems on the indigenous cultures of the Americas.

The Ritual Negotiation of Social Life

There was yet another potential peril in the phenomenal expansion of Christianity during the immediate pre-Reformation period. The new political consciousness that led to "nationalized churches" in England and Scandinavia and to "royal Catholicism" in France[23] also led to important changes in the "ownership" of rituals that people regularly used to negotiate their roles in society. As the Middle Ages waned and early modern Europe emerged, social tasks and functions that in late medieval life had been assigned to the Christian liturgy (especially the eucharist) became state sponsored. To citizens of the twenty-first century, this may seem quite logical. Contemporaries of this time live in societies where social cohesion—that is, the creation and maintenance of a just, peaceful, inclusive, productive society—is considered the proper work of government, a primary goal of the political process. Uniting people is seen as a secular goal, especially in complex, industrialized societies (like the United States) whose populations are diverse culturally, ethnically, racially, and linguistically. Citizens in this period see "public order" as a secular enterprise, not a religious one; it is the province of presidents and legislatures, parliaments and prime ministers, courts and tribunals.

But transferring the power to control social life from Church to state was in fact a long, complex process. In the medieval West, social unity was understood as a distinctively religious project—indeed, as a *eucharistic* project. This is the argument of a famous essay published in the 1980s by John Bossy that examined the sociological assumptions supporting the medieval Latin mass.[24] He concluded that from the High Middle Ages (c. 1200) until the Reformation (and perhaps thereafter), Christians saw the mass not as a ritual enactment of power relations between priest and people but as a complex social algebra that helped participants understand relations between the living and the dead, and the distinctions between "insiders" and "outsiders" in society. This algebra, Bossy argued, decisively shaped the medieval layperson's experience of the eucharist as both a sacrifice and a sacrament. For lay participants, the latter two terms were not so much theological as social in nature. Sacrifice was a metaphor for the social body seen in its diverse parts, while sacrament served as a metaphor for the social body seen in its wholeness. Thus, in the minds and experience of medieval lay folk, sacrifice is to sacrament as parts are to whole. As Bossy declared,

Celebration of a Mass with Musical Instruments. Engraving by Adriaen Collaert (1560–1618) after Stradanus (Jan van der Straet) and Philipp Galle. Musikinstrumenten-Museum, Staatliches Institut für Musikforschung, Berlin/Bildarchiv Preussischer Kulturbesitz/ Art Resource, NY

"The distinction between sacrifice and sacrament in the mass of the waning middle ages [is] equivalent to a distinction between the Christian community considered as an assembly of distinct parts and that community considered as a transcendent whole." In short, the distinction between sacrifice and sacrament was as significant socially as it was theologically.

Bossy concluded his essay by listing two reasons that social unity—originally perceived as a liturgical or eucharistic task—was eventually secularized. First, the early fifteenth century saw the rise of "an asocial mysticism of frequent communion" that departed significantly from the medieval laity's earlier norm of an annual communion at Easter. The roots of this "mysticism of frequent communion" may be traced back to the Beguines of the early thirteenth century.[25] Second, Bossy pointed to "the tendency to transfer the socially integrative powers of the host away from the mass as such and into the feast of Corpus Christi, and by way of that feast to the rituals of monarchy and of secular community."[26]

There can be little doubt that the feast of Corpus Christi was one of the great liturgical success stories of the later Middle Ages. The Belgian city of Liège was the birthplace of the feast, and its origins owe much to the determination of one Juliana (c. 1193–1258), a devout woman and visionary who was part of the Beguine movement and whose work with lepers at a hospital run by the Premonstratensians at Mont Cornillon in Liège had become legendary. Juliana claimed that in a private vision, Christ had revealed to her his desire for a new feast, one that would focus on his body and blood, given to the faithful in the eucharist. Her campaign was taken up by the Dominicans, who had come to Liège in 1229, and in 1246 the city's bishop, Robert of Turotte, issued a pastoral letter (*Inter alia mira*) that established a eucharistic feast for his diocese. Eighteen years later, on 11 August 1264, Urban IV's encyclical *Transiturus de hoc mundo* introduced Corpus Christi to the whole Latin church, but Urban's death a scant two months later (2 October 1264) prevented *Transiturus* from taking hold, and it was not until 1317 that the Avignon pope, John XXII, reaffirmed Urban's letter and extended the feast's celebration to the whole Western Church. Bishop Robert's *Inter alia mira* had set the date for the feast as "feria quinta proxima post octavas Trinitatis," which, despite the Latin's ambiguity, referred to the first Thursday after Trinity Sunday, the date on which it was celebrated until the reforms of Vatican II (1962–1965). Thereafter, in some countries such as the United States, Corpus Christi (officially, "The Feast of the Most Holy Body and Blood of Christ") is celebrated on the Sunday following Trinity Sunday.

Throughout Europe, but especially in England, the feast emphasized social integration and unity as precisely eucharistic tasks. As popular enthusiasm for Corpus Christi grew, however, so did the emphasis on frequent communion. On the surface these two impulses seem quite compatible, but closer inspection tells a different story. As John Bossy argued, the feast of Corpus Christi was still largely "sociopetal"; its celebration (which included processions, pageants, and fairs as well as the liturgy itself) constituted a unified ritual display of all the important "orders" of medieval social life, from clerics and magistrates to guilds and peasants. At Corpus Christi every Christian citizen became an "insider," and this fact became a powerful, if implicit, critique of rigid arrangements that divided society into superiors and inferiors. In contrast, the late medieval "mysticism of frequent communion" moved in a different direction—away from unified social participation and toward religious isolation. All that Christians needed in order to "participate" fully in Corpus Christi's generous cycle of liturgies, plays, and fairs were their souls and bodies; but the mysticism of frequent communion implied a hierarchy of merit (some are more worthy to receive than others). As time went on, moreover, communicants were allowed to receive "before or after or outside Mass altogether."[27] Such communion "on demand" dissolved the sequence of ritual links within the Roman eucharist (eucharistic prayer, Lord's prayer, kiss of peace, communion). In short, the individual Christian could isolate the reception of communion, making it a devotional act independent from the liturgy itself.

It can be argued, then, that the Corpus Christi festival was the last firewall against the disintegrative forces that finally displaced the eucharistic liturgy as the preferred "social institution" for keeping communities whole and unified. Increasingly, during the late-medieval and early-modern eras, the "keepers of community" were not Christian liturgies but kings, courts, and constables. Moreover, the socially integrative powers of the host were drawn away from the rituals of mass as such—first, to the popular paraliturgies (processions, plays) of Corpus Christi itself and, later, to the royalist rituals of monarchies and secular communities. One may conclude that the late medieval mass lost power not only because of critiques by Reformers, but also because secular systems of "public order" gradually superseded local, religious ones (such as the parish Sunday eucharist).[28]

In sum, the late medieval eucharist was more important as a social institution than as a repository of theological ideas or doctrines (such as transubstantiation). It helped people find their place and negotiate their role in complex hierarchies that included the living and the dead, clerics and laity, church and state, work and leisure. As Bossy observes, "The medieval mass was a composite of two ritual traditions inherited from early Christianity and through it from the ritual corpus of antiquity: the tradition of the public worship practised by whole communities, and that of the private, family, domestic cult."[29] For the most part, medieval churchgoers did not view the eucharist as superstitious magic; it was, rather, the indispensable source that located them within the social body, as believers, villagers, family members, siblings, kin.

Protestant Critique and Liturgical Reform

1. **Eucharist: Luther (1483–1546).** Luther, too, appreciated the social significance of Sunday eucharist in the parish. Thus, his treatise *The Babylonian Captivity of the Church*—"which underlies all subsequent Protestant sacramental theology"[30]—denounced contemporary Roman liturgical practice but did not deny the fundamental importance of Christian worship and sacrament. Indeed, Luther's proposals for liturgical reform might be read as a commentary on the Thomist principle, *sacramenta propter homines* (sacraments exist for the sake of human beings). Luther could thus affirm that "Christ is truly present in the sacrament with his flesh and blood as it was born of Mary and hung on the holy cross," even as he protested the "tyranny of Rome" that denied layfolk access to the "complete sacrament" by withholding the cup.[31] He could affirm that baptism is truly a sacrament instituted by Christ, that it signifies "death and resurrection," that it should be administered to infants, while condemning those who "turn the sacrament into a command and faith into a work."[32] In short, though Luther disputed their number—holding for three sacraments or perhaps two, not seven—he did not deny their importance.[33] Indeed, in a beautiful passage on baptism in *The Babylonian Captivity*, he wrote:

> Although the ceremony itself is soon over, the thing it signifies continues until we die, yes, even until we rise on the last day. For as long as we live we are continually doing that which baptism signifies, that is, we die and rise again. We die, not only mentally and spiritually by renouncing the sins and vanities of this world, but in very truth we begin to leave this bodily life and to lay hold on the life to come.[34]

For this reason, many scholars see Luther's liturgical reforms as fundamentally conservative in nature.[35] In his *Formula Missae* of 1523, he insisted that "masses and the communion of bread and wine are a rite divinely instituted by Christ," and went on to furnish a rather mildly purged version of the Latin eucharist at which the minister could elevate the species and wear vestments, provided "pomp and the excess of splendor be absent."[36] Three years later, in his more radically revised vernacular *Deutsche Messe* (1526), Luther provided for a complete cycle of Sunday services, from matins (morning prayer, c. 5 o'clock or 6 o'clock), to mass (c. 8 o'clock or 9 o'clock), to vespers. At all three services there was to be preaching based on "the customary Epistles and Gospels."[37] Luther did not envision the *Deutsche Messe* as a replacement of his earlier *Formula*. In fact he felt the latter "ought to be used occasionally, if only to exercise the youth in the Latin language," just as he wished to retain the elevation while encouraging freedom in the matter of vestments, altars, and candles.[38]

But in all these proposals for the reform of public worship, Luther maintained his focus—*sacramenta propter homines*. One sees this principle at work in the second part of his *Formula Missae*, where he discusses the communion of the people. "It is most wrong," he notes, "if ministers make ready and adorn the common Supper of the Lord where there would be no guests who would eat and drink, and they alone, who ought to minister to others, would eat and drink at an empty table and in an empty sanctuary." Here one can see that Luther's primary complaint against "private masses" flowed from his conviction that the communion of the people is an essential part of the eucharist as it was instituted by Christ. One may also note Luther's recommendation that "private confession before communion," while "neither necessary nor to be demanded," is nevertheless "useful and not to be despised."

James White remarks that "the question of frequency of communion was the most problematic reform" linked to the eucharist, and that Luther's plan to have laypeople communicate frequently "was a radical step for people who had done so only at the very greatest festivals."[39] While true, this observation needs to be nuanced in light of the late medieval history sketched earlier in this chapter. The once-a-year communion at Easter was indeed a widespread medieval practice, if, at any rate, vernacular sermons from late medieval England are to be believed. An English Eastertide homily from about 1400, for instance, is devoted primarily to instruction about "the Sacrament on the awtur."[40] It begins as follows: "Good men and wymmen, now is passed the holytyme of Ester, and iche man and wymman is shryven and houseled, so that they have forsaken the devell and all is werkes and been turned to God and to is seruys."[41] The preacher's introduction reveals not only that Easter is *the* "communion Sunday" for medieval laypeople, but also that catechesis about the sacrament was not limited to doctrinal matters (real presence, transubstantiation); it stressed, as well, the moral consequences of holy communion for daily life. Preachers thus affirmed that "the same body that died on the Crosse and this day rose verry God and man, the same bodie is on the Sacrament on the awtur in forme of brede"; but they also urged the houseled Christian to build a house worthy of the Lord—a house whose ground is faith, whose wall is hope, and whose roof is love:

> The roff of thin howse must be large, and that must be charite. For Seynte Poule seith, "Si distribuero omnes facultates meas, et si tradedero [corpus] meum ut ardeam, caritatem autem non habuero, nichil mihi prodest." And therefore, good men, ye that haue made louedayes, be-ware that it be not Iudas loueday, that spake fayre to Crist, and yitt he betrayed hym.[42]

There was, in the mind of this medieval preacher, a close connection between holy communion and the practical practice of charity. Moreover, as indicated earlier in this chapter, there was already a notable trend within late medieval Catholicism toward "frequent communion," even though the essential connections between communion, the liturgy, and public life began to erode after "social unity" became a political rather than a religious (liturgical, eucharistic) goal. Even in an age of infrequent communion, the mass still served to establish social and spiritual solidarity among God, the Church, and the lay community. Thus, Virginia Reinburg contends that in late medieval liturgy, the effects that modern theologians may attribute solely to communion were seen as accruing to lay participants through other means: chiefly, the elevation, the passing of the *pax* board, and the distribution of blessed bread after mass.[43]

Pre-Reformation Christians thus assigned meanings to the liturgical rites quite different from those assigned by the clergy, a fact that is instantly clear if one compares the texts and rubrics of medieval missals (written for clergy) with the interpretations offered in vernacular expositions of the mass. In effect, medieval lay folk had redefined the ritual of communion so that it no longer meant—only or primarily—an eating and drinking of the consecrated elements (that was the priest's job); it embraced all those other acts by which the laity claimed the eucharist for themselves and extended its benefits into their daily lives (through secular rituals of charity and social exchange). Eamon Duffy has summarized this point well:

> The language of Eucharistic belief and devotion was saturated with communitarian and corporate imagery. The unitive theme was not simply a device in the process of the establishment of community or the validation of power structures. It was a deeply felt element in the eucharistic piety of the individual Christian too. . . . [T]he Host was the source simultaneously of individual and of corporate renewal and unity. . . . The Host, then, was far more than the object of individual devotion, a means of forgiveness and sanctification: it was the source of human community.[44]

Ironically, the impulse toward more frequent communion—already at work in late medieval Catholicism and promoted by Reformers like Luther—may have supported, not "communitarian and corporate" unity and renewal, but a potentially divisive individualism.[45]

Returning now to Luther's mass reforms of 1523 and 1526, one sees a desire to maintain the old medieval emphasis on eucharist as intrinsically "communitarian and corporate" (especially in the act of holy communion) while cleansing the rite of sacrificial language and interpretation. Indeed, in his 1521 treatise *On the Misuse of the Mass*, Luther had insisted that "to sacrifice to God and to be consumed by us are not compatible ideas." In short, sacrifice threatens communion. "'Eat and drink,'" Luther comments, "'That is all that we are to do with the sacrament. . . . But what we eat and drink we do not sacrifice; we keep it for ourselves and consume it.'"[46] Even in Israel's religion, Luther

Luther "preaches Christ crucified." Predella from the altarpiece by Lucas Cranach the Elder (1472-1553) in the Marienkirche at Wittenberg. FOTO MARBURG/ART RESOURCE, NY

further argued, the people did not "sacrifice" God's testament (the Law); rather, they received it. Neither, then, can "the New Testament, instituted by Christ himself, be a sacrifice, because it is a word of promise and grace, which is not sacrificed, but perfected and confirmed by the sacrifice of Christ on the cross." The new covenant between God and humanity is, therefore, not a sacrifice; it is the gospel itself:

> For if you ask: what is the gospel? you can give no better answer than these words of the New Testament, namely, that Christ gave his body and poured out his blood for us for the forgiveness of sins. This alone is to be preached to Christians, instilled into their hearts, and at all times faithfully commended to their memories. . . .
>
> Therefore these words, as a short summary of the whole gospel, are to be taught and instilled into every Christian's heart, so that he may contemplate them continuously and without ceasing, and with them, exercise, strengthen, and sustain his faith in Christ, especially when he goes to the sacrament. And that is what the minister is indicating when he elevates the host and the cup. He is not referring to any sacrifice. . . .
>
> It may well signify, however, that just as this pledge of the promise of Christ is elevated in order that the people may thereby be inspired to faith, so the Word should be preached publicly to the people in order that everyone may hear the testament and see the pledge, and through both be attracted and aroused to faith and strengthened in it.[47]

In my view this passage is crucial for understanding how Luther viewed the eucharist and what motivated his liturgical proposals of 1523 and 1526. The Christian "offering" is not a sacrifice, but a call to faith and obedience in the Word epitomized by the gospels' command to "take and eat, take and drink." Not surprisingly, then, the eucharistic prayers of both the *Formula Missae* and the *Deutsche Messe* highlight the *verba Christi* (the consecration), to the exclusion of almost everything else.[48] The Word—summarized in the eucharistic words of Jesus, and proclaimed and preached at every liturgical service—becomes the true center of authentic Christian worship. "The new Mass is drawn up with a mind to instruct the faithful and to excite their faith; it is a public call to faith and Christianity."[49]

By reducing the eucharistic prayer primarily to the *verba Christi*, Luther had "concluded the whole medieval trajectory since Ambrose (c. 339–397)."[50] If, as Ambrose argued, the bread and wine are changed into Christ's body and blood by the words of the Word—and if, as Luther insisted, those words are a "summary of the gospel" commanding us to eat and drink—then little more is required in the way of eucharistic praying.[51] As James White notes, "If . . . the words of institution alone are efficacious, could not the rest be eliminated? Luther had simply brought medieval thinking to its logical conclusion."[52]

In sum, just as Luther wanted to retain Lent, Palm Sunday, and Holy Week (though not their obligatory fasts and ceremonial "trickery"), so he wanted all liturgy to "center in the Word and Sacrament."[53] The services of Lent and Holy Week permitted daily preaching on the gospel accounts of Christ's cross and passion. And for Luther the ultimate gospel—the "summary of the gospel"—is contained in eucharistic consecration and communion, where believers take to themselves Christ's undying word and promise.

2. Eucharist: Calvin (1509–1564). The eucharistic theology and reforms of John Calvin are complex, and here it is possible to offer only the barest outline of them. Like Luther, Calvin maintained that the eucharist offered Christians a participation in the body and blood of Christ that is true, real, and effective. Indeed, in his treatise *De vera participatione Christi in coena*, Calvin wrote:

> It was fitting for Christ really and efficaciously to fulfill whatever the analogy of "sign" and "thing signified" demands. And therefore, there is truly offered to us in the Supper a communion with his body and blood—or (what amounts to the same thing) there is set

before us a pledge, under the bread and wine, which makes us participants in the body
and blood of Christ.[54]

It is important to note that while both Luther and Calvin agreed on the eucharist as a
real participation in Christ's body and blood, they arrived at this conclusion from different directions. Luther's starting-point for eucharistic reform seems to have been his
twin convictions that the *verba Christi* constitute a "summary of the gospel" (and hence
are the ultimate proclamation of God's gracious word of promise), and that the people's
communion is integral to the sacramental action as instituted by Christ. Calvin's premier eucharistic "preoccupation," however, was the unconditional sovereignty of God,
God's absolute freedom, divinity, and choice of election.[55] Any theory of sacrament that
would limit God's utter sovereignty must therefore be dismissed as idolatrous.

For this reason, too, Calvin's doctrines of Church and sacrament do not begin with
a theology of Christ's Incarnation (Christ as sacrament of God, the Church as sacrament of Christ, sacraments as actions of God-in-Christ acting through the efficacious
ministry of the church), but with an emphasis on God's sovereign, unconditional power
of election and predestination.[56] Calvin viewed sacraments as real and effective through
the power of the Holy Spirit who unites believers to Christ, but he was hesitant to
consider the Spirit a permanent endowment immanent within ecclesial life, since this
might seem either to compromise God's unconditioned freedom or to divinize the
church as the locus of God's activity and power.

For these reasons, among others, Reformed theology did not regard sacraments as
useless or unprofitable for the Christian. Thus, for example, two years after Calvin's
death, article 21 of the "Second Helvetic Confession" (1566), carefully distinguished
between three kinds of eating in the eucharist:

> There is *corporal* eating whereby food is taken into the mouth, is chewed with the teeth,
> and swallowed. . . . There is also a *spiritual* eating of Christ's body . . . whereby the body
> and blood of the Lord, while remaining in their own essence and property, are spiritu-
> ally communicated to us, certainly not in a corporal but in a spiritual way, by the Holy
> Spirit. . . . Besides the high spiritual eating there is also a *sacramental* eating of the body
> of the Lord by which not only spiritually and internally the believer truly participates in
> the true body and blood of the Lord, but also, by coming to the Table of the Lord,
> outwardly receives the visible sacrament of the body and blood of the Lord.[57]

What this article states seems to conform with what Calvin himself affirmed: that
Christ is really present to participants in the eucharist, and thus that the reception of
communion brings a real benefit to the believer. Still, Calvin did not wish to diminish
God's freedom or to make the Spirit "captive" to the Church's sacraments or to confine Christ locally within the species of bread and wine (since the risen, ascended
Lord sits at God's right in heaven). Whatever is affirmed about Christ's presence in
the eucharist must, Calvin argued, be subject to strict christological limits:

> We must establish such a presence of Christ in the Supper as may neither fasten him to
> the element of bread, nor enclose him in bread, nor circumscribe him in any way. . . . Let
> us never (I say) allow these two limitations to be taken away from us: (1) Let nothing be
> withdrawn from Christ's heavenly glory—as happens when he is brought under the cor-
> ruptible elements of this world, or bound to any earthly creatures. (2) Let nothing inap-
> propriate to human nature be ascribed to his body, as happens when it is said either to be
> infinite or to be put in a number of places at once.[58]

Calvin's "christological limits" were also clear in his treatise *De vera participatione*:

> When I say that the flesh and blood of Christ are substantially offered and exhibited to
> us in the Supper, I at the same time explain the mode, namely, that the flesh of Christ
> becomes vivifying to us, inasmuch as Christ, by the incomprehensible virtue of his Spirit,

transfuses his own proper life into us from the substance of his flesh, so that he himself lives in us and his life is common to us.[59]

For Calvin, then, all sacraments (including the eucharist) "have the same office as the Word of God: to offer and set forth Christ to us, and in him the treasures of heavenly grace."[60] The offering is effective only through faith, since faith is the Spirit's gift, and it is "the Holy Spirit who makes us partakers in Christ"—in the sacraments as in all other areas of Christian life.[61] It would thus be difficult to argue that eucharistic eating bestows on Christians any distinctive gift beyond what is already granted through faith. As Kilian McDonnell notes, Calvin believed that although "we have a real communion with the glorified Lord, with his body and blood . . . through the power of the Spirit," eating is not a uniquely eucharistic act "limited to altar and cup. . . . For Calvin, as for Luther, there is no specific eucharistic gift, no object, person, effect, or grace given in the Eucharist which is not given in faith outside of the Eucharist."[62] In Calvin's view, eucharistic eating and drinking are one moment within a much larger pattern, the perpetual eating of Christ's true body and blood through faith under the power of the Holy Spirit. This does not mean that Calvin belittled the importance of eucharist in Christian life. On the contrary, he affirmed that "baptism should be . . . an entry into the church, and an initiation into faith; but the Supper should be a sort of continual food on which Christ spiritually feeds the household of his believers."[63] It is clear, moreover, that Calvin wanted weekly celebration of the Lord's supper to be the norm among Reformed communities.[64]

What disturbed Calvin most about the late-medieval mass was its neglect of the Word. "The Sacrament cannot stand apart from the Word," Calvin declared. "For whatever benefit may come to us from the Supper requires the Word: whether we are to be confirmed in faith, or exercised in confession, or aroused to duty, there is need of preaching. Therefore, nothing more preposterous could happen in the Supper than for it to be turned into a silent action."[65] Calvin's principle—that the Word of God is what makes sacraments become sacraments—is clearly evident in *The Form of Church Prayers* (Geneva, Switzerland, 1542; Strasbourg, 1545).[66] The place of scripture reading and preaching is, of course, prominent, but perhaps more interesting is the way Calvin understands the relation between word and sacrament as these unite in the liturgy of the supper. The Roman priests, Calvin complained in an early version of the *Institutes*, prance about like sorcerers, "in pomps, ceremonies, and gesticulations. But there is not so much as a mention, an allusion, to the Word of God, without which sacraments themselves cannot be sacraments. Thus the Supper is buried, when it is turned into the Mass."[67]

In Calvin's view, what is required "to season the sacrament is not an 'incantation' over the bread and wine, but a 'lively preaching,' addressed to the *people*, setting forth the promises of Christ, which are antecedent to the Lord's supper and which supply meaning and reality to its signs." The lively preaching required by sacrament is accomplished through the sermon, of course, but especially through the words of Christ, which provide the promise and warrant for the Church's action in the supper, determine the ritual manner in which the supper is to be celebrated, and render efficacious what is exhibited in the sacrament.[68] Thus, the "eucharistic prayer" in Calvin's *Form of Church Prayers* becomes another sermon; it is preaching addressed to the people, rather than a request for God to "transform the gifts" or "accept the sacrifice" (as was the case in the old Roman canon).[69] The language of the words of institution is thus exhortatory rather than euchological or consecratory. The supper is an invitation to "lift our spirits and hearts on high where Jesus Christ is in the glory of His Father," rather than a consecratory act aimed at changing bread and wine into something else. After the *verba Christi* are ended, the minister invites the people to communion in the bread and cup, and brings the rite to a conclusion with a short "Thanksgiving after the Supper."

Calvin did not ignore the connection between eucharist and ethics. With their medieval forebears, the Reformers shared the notion that "Christian societies were sacred and had to be constituted around a sacred center." That center was not, however, located in symbols of immanence (such as the eucharist, in medieval Catholic piety) but in symbols of free and transcendent divine power. Christopher Elwood writes:

> The Reformed social idea was the communion of the saints, which the eucharist was supposed to achieve. . . . Like the ecclesiastical and political leaders of medieval communities, Calvin and his Reformed contemporaries hoped to extend this spirit of social integration and ordering beyond the churches where the sacrament was celebrated so as to influence the ordering of the social body.[70]

The ethical integrity (indeed, the moral rigor) demanded of believers—as revealed, for instance, by the records of the Geneva Consistory in Calvin's time—set them apart from all others and was a formative factor in the construction of a "Reformed identity."[71] The unique bond between eucharist (symbol of the transcendent God, who calls together the "communion of saints") and ethical integrity (social sign of the predestined elect) permitted the Reformed community "to maintain itself as a society of the saints" while also allowing it to keep "the social symbol of the eucharist as the table of Christ" and to use "persuasive and coercive techniques centered about this symbol to achieve that end."[72]

Not only, then, did Calvin reject the idea that the mass is a human work that "obligates" God to reward communicants, he also insisted that the Word that makes sacrament possible be intelligibly preached to the people (above all, in the words of institution). Lay participation that was "less than intellectually engaged" was to be avoided in Christian worship, and indeed, as Calvin stated in his preface to the Genevan Psalter, "Saying that we should have devotion, whether in prayer or in ceremony, while understanding nothing, is a great mockery. . . . The heart requires understanding."[73] In short, at public worship, "the congregation must understand every word or gesture of the minister." By insisting on "doctrinally informed lay participation," Calvin would eventually be joined by the Roman bishops at the Council of Trent, who also argued for the need of a sound grasp of the liturgy's meaning by participants at mass.[74]

3. Eucharist: Zwingli (1484–1531). This theme, that the people must have a clear understanding of the mass and its meaning, is especially prominent in the liturgical reforms of Ulrich Zwingli, for whom the primary purpose of the Lord's supper is "to recall Christ's passion and death, to accept it in faith and to partake of the symbolic species as a sign of profession."[75] Unlike Luther, who represented "the old learning and piety," Zwingli espoused "the new learning and a new kind of piety."[76] Their differences, especially in the matter of eucharistic theology, came to the fore at the Marburg Colloquy held in October 1529. At that meeting, the meaning of the phrase "This is my body" was vigorously debated, with Luther focusing on the literal meaning of the words and Zwingli contending that *is* means "signifies." Luther's (traditional) question was, "What happens to the elements?," whereas Zwingli's (new) question was, "What happens to the celebrating community?" As James White notes, "For Zwingli, the center of attention was not 'this is' but 'do this': what the community does in the Lord's Supper. . . . What Luther did not appreciate was that Zwingli was stating in a new way the reality of Christ's presence as a transubstantiation of the congregation rather than of the elements."[77]

It is sometimes assumed by modern writers that Zwingli interpreted the eucharist as a "merely" symbolic act, a "memorial" (not a sacrifice) that simply served to remind believers of the great benefits bestowed on them through Christ's passion and death.[78] But Zwingli, who had been a very popular Catholic pastor in Zürich, Switzerland, was not a symbolist in any modern sense; on the contrary, he affirmed, in language reminiscent of Calvin and Luther, that "the bread and wine become the body and blood of Christ to those who partake of them in faith."[79] Such a statement hardly sounds like someone who considers the elements nothing more than "bare tokens." Moreover, James White is surely right to note that modern interpreters view Zwingli from the other side of the Enlightenment, during which the universe was radically "desacralized." Zwingli himself "worked within a sacralized universe [and] certainly believed in the presence and activity of God in that world. . . . The world of Zwingli saw God, far from being absent, as *intervening* in the midst of the worshipping congregation."[80]

It is in this light that we need to read Zwingli's earliest effort at reforming the liturgy, the *De canone missae epicheiresis*, which appeared in the same year as Luther's *Formula Missae* (1523).[81] Perhaps the most striking feature of Zwingli's proposal was its Latin eucharistic prayer, a new creation of his own, which consisted of the traditional preface and Sanctus, followed by four prayers leading up to the words of institution. (The communion of the people immediately followed the institution account.) The first of Zwingli's four prayers praises God for creating humanity and redeeming it in Christ, who taught us to pray "Our Father. . . ." The second focuses on God as provident Provider who nourishes the hungry, quickens them with the Spirit, and enlightens them by the Word. The third prayer highlights the redemptive work of Christ, the Restorer of the divine likeness lost in Adam, the Lamb of God, Forgiver of sin and gracious Host (in prayer four) who "on the night on which he was betrayed . . . took bread."

Ironically, then, it was Zwingli the "symbolist" who, uniquely among the Reformers examined thus far, preserved the eucharistic prayer tradition familiar to Catholics. Indeed, taken together (as they were meant to be), Zwingli's four prayers created a strikingly good anaphora resembling classic models such as the Liturgy of Saint James. Moreover, in his *Epicheiresis*, Zwingli, like Luther, was willing to allow great freedom in "indifferent" (*adiaphora*) matters (for example, the use of vestments). In Zwingli's later and more radical reforms, however—for example, the *Action or Use of the Lord's Supper* (1525)—the eucharistic prayer of the *Epicheiresis* disappears, and the eucharist itself was no longer the "ordinary" Sunday service. Instead, the supper became a quarterly event (Easter, Pentecost, autumn, Christmas), with the usual Sunday service organized around scripture and sermon. In its more radical incarnation the Zwinglian eucharist became, in Bard Thompson's words, "a contemplative experience of the goodness of God manifest on the Cross of Christ—so vivid to the man of faith that he could 'grasp the thing itself.'" To that end, a simple communion table replaced the altar, for the site of celebration was "not a place where man offered to God, but where God gave to man; . . . it was not the precinct of priests, but a congregational table for the new family of God."[82]

4. Eucharist: Cranmer (1489–1556). Liturgical reforms on the European continent had been underway for more than two decades before a window of opportunity opened for the English Reformers. A few tentative steps had been taken after Henry VIII's break with Rome; for example, in 1539 the Great Bible appeared; in 1543, Convocation required that the English scriptures be read in course at morning and evening prayer on Sundays and feasts; in 1544 the English Litany was issued.[83] But more thoroughgoing reforms of public worship had to wait until after Henry's death in January 1547. Even after Edward VI's accession, Thomas Cranmer (who had become archbishop of Canterbury in 1533) used a cautious, "go-slow" approach to liturgical reform. His first move was to seek improvement in the quality of preaching in English parishes by issuing a *Book of Homilies* and by replacing the Latin Bible readings at mass with English ones (the rest of the ceremonial remaining undisturbed).[84] He also issued, as an English supplement to the Latin missal, an interim *Order of the Communion* (1548) in two parts: the first, an exhortation, to be delivered to the people a week before the eucharist was to be celebrated, admonishing them to prepare themselves for communion; the second, a form for administering communion to be inserted into the existing Latin mass.[85]

Here one can discern a common thread uniting the reforms of Luther, Calvin, Zwingli, and Cranmer: all four churchmen believed strongly that the communion of the people is, by dominical institution, absolutely integral to the eucharist—just as they believed that there can be no sacrament without the "lively preaching" of the Word. And although in the first *Book of Common Prayer* (1549) Cranmer retained the traditional form of a eucharistic anaphora for use during "The Supper of the Lorde, and The Holy Communion, Commonly Called the Masse," he carefully noted in the rubrics that "agreable to the usage of the primitive Church," the minister "shall alwaies have some [others] to communicate with him," and that he "shall forbeare to celebrate the Communion, except he have some that will communicate with him."[86] If, for Luther, eucharistic real presence was, essentially, "the presence of Christ's sacrifice," for Cranmer—already in 1549, but especially in the 1552 Prayer Book—the fundamental act of eucharist is to receive communion.[87] Indeed, for Cranmer, as Aidan Kavanagh notes,

> the act of Christian worship was receptive. This liturgical receptivity was characteristic of the nature of Christian life itself, which was subjective, affective, and mnemonic. He thus concentrated the whole sacramental economy into reception—of the Word, of the seal and certificate of baptism, and of the signs of bread and wine in the Supper of the Lord. Growth in faith was not by sacramental grace, but more by knowledge and feeling. ... [Thus] the Eucharist is ordered as a mnemonic ceremony. It culminates in the reception of bread and wine in place of the traditional anaphora's anamnesis, and with the words, "Take and eate this, in remembraunce that Christ dyed for thee, and feede on him in thy hearte by faythe, with thankesgeuing."[88]

Still, the exact nature of Cranmer's eucharistic theology has remained a topic of heated debate among scholars. James White concludes that "Cranmer . . . favored Zwingli, though he placed a high value on the sacrament."[89] One thing is clear: Cranmer's views on eucharistic presence evolved over time. This evolution has been studied by Peter N. Brooks, who writes of Cranmer's mature view of Christ's presence in the supper: "To Cranmer, . . . Christ is really, carnally and corporally absent from his Supper, for when he is locally circumscribed at God's right hand in heaven, the Lord's presence at the Eucharist is after a 'True' and 'spiritual' manner."[90] In other words, the eucharistic presence of Christ is a spiritual one "wrought within us invisibly by the omnipotent power of God."[91] It is in this light that the communicant's eating and drinking of Christ's body and blood in the supper are to be understood:

> [T]he true eating and drinking of the . . . body and blood of Christ, is with a constant and lively faith to believe, that Christ gave his body and shed his blood upon the cross for us, and that he doth so join and incorporate himself to us, that he is our head, and we his members, and flesh of his flesh, and bone of his bones, having him dwelling in us, and we in him. And herein standeth the whole effect and strength of this sacrament. And this faith God worketh inwardly in our hearts by his Holy Spirit, and confirmeth the same outwardly to our ears by hearing of his word, and to our other senses by eating and drinking of the sacramental bread and wine in his holy Supper.[92]

Such a spiritual presence does not, however, make the consecrated bread and wine empty signs. As Cranmer himself put it, "the sacramental bread and wine be not bare and naked figures, but so pithy and effectuous, that whosoever worthily eateth them, eateth spiritually Christ's flesh and blood, and hath by them everlasting life."[93] The faith-filled communicant does indeed participate in Christ at the supper, but does so in a manner that is not carnal: "For as Christ is a spiritual meat, so is he spiritually eaten and digested with the spiritual part of us, and giveth us spiritual and eternal life, and is not eaten, swallowed, and digested with our teeth, tongues, throats, and bellies."[94] In sum, Cranmer came to believe that Christ's real presence in the eucharist is not "in the sacramental elements as such, but in the heart of the receiver."[95]

This point is key to understanding Cranmer's liturgical reforms of the eucharist in the Prayer Books of 1549 and 1552. Because Christ's "one oblacion once offered" constituted a "full, perfect, and sufficient sacrifyce, oblacion, and satysfaccyon, for the sinnes of the whole worlde" (1549), there could be no question of the mass itself being a sacrifice in any propitiatory or reiterative sense. The only sacrifice Christians can offer is a "sacrifice of praise and thankes geuing" (1549 and 1552). Thus the eucharist can in no way alter, edit, repeat, or improve what God has already done for humanity in the cross of Christ. The key to understanding what happens in the eucharist is thus not the sacramental elements themselves, but "man's sacramental receptivity . . . concentrated in the ceremonial act of receiving creatures of bread and wine in the remembrance that Christ had died for him. . . . This was . . . the fundamental insight which Cranmer sought to translate into liturgical reality."[96]

Hence, it was not carelessness or imprecision that caused Cranmer to call the rite "commonly called the Masse" the "Holy Communion." For him the eucharist was precisely that—receiving communion. "Take and eate this, in remembraunce that Christ dyed for thee, and feede on him in thy hearte by faythe, with thankesgeuing. Drink this in remembraunce that Christ's bloude was shed for thee, and be thankefull" (1552). These words of administration constitute a concise epitome of Cranmer's eucharistic theology, as well as his liturgical revisions.

Another common thread runs through all these sixteenth-century reforms: the way in which laypersons participated in (and so experienced) the mass was to be transformed, and this transformation was to take shape as ritual intelligibility, as cognitive access to the meaning(s) of the Church's services. The goal, in short, was "well-informed lay participation," a clear understanding by every communicant of "every word and gesture of the minister." The old medieval modes of lay participation in the eucharist were to be abandoned. As Eamon Duffy writes concerning the situation in England after the launching of Cranmer's reforms in 1549 and 1552, "almost everything that had till then been central to lay Eucharistic piety" was to be eliminated: "the parish procession, the elevation at the sacring, the pax, the sharing of holy bread."[97] Even where old practices were retained (for example, vestments and the elevation in Luther's rites), they were reinterpreted in light of a new preoccupation: the communion of the people as the essential eucharistic act.

5. Baptism. I turn now to a brief discussion of Protestant proposals for revising the Church's other sacraments and services. Despite their emphasis on faith, "cognitive access," and ritual intelligibility, the Reformers for the most part retained and defended the practice of infant baptism, although they were critical of the medieval Roman rite.[98] "The way many churches signified becoming a Christian," writes James White, "was probably the least changed of all worship practices in this period. . . . The trajectory of medieval developments proved to be irreversible. No one in the Reformation seriously challenged the withholding of communion from baptized infants. . . . Except for Anabaptists and Quakers, infant baptism remained the normal practice."[99]

Luther's *Taufbüchlein* of 1523 (revised 1526) provides the earliest surviving Reformation ritual for baptism.[100] Like the *Formula Missae*, Luther's order for the celebration of baptism retains many elements that would have been familiar to medieval Catholics. At the beginning of the rite, for example, "the officiant shall blow three times under the child's eyes and shall say: 'Depart thou unclean spirit and give room to the Holy Spirit.' Then he shall sign him with a cross on his forehead and breast and shall say: 'Receive the sign of the holy cross on both thy forehead and thy breast.'" Exorcisms and signings would have been wholly familiar to any medieval parents bringing their baby to the parish church for baptism. And while Luther's rubrics do not directly call any part of the rite an "exorcism," the prayer that follows the signing with the cross asks God to "drive away all blindness" from the child's heart and to "break all the snares of the devil with which he is bound." Other traditional ceremonies—the giving of salt, the use of spittle in the "effeta," the renunciation of Satan, the prebaptismal anointing, the christening robe, the lighted candle—are all retained.[101] "For the time being," Luther explained, "I did not want to make any marked changes in the order of baptism. But I would not mind if it could be improved. Its framers were careless men who did not sufficiently appreciate the glory of baptism. However, in order to spare the weak consciences, I am leaving it unchanged, lest they complain that I want to institute a new baptism." By 1526 Luther had overcome his hesitations, and several of the medieval rite's ceremonies were dropped.

Late medieval practice (reflected still in the post-Tridentine *Rituale Romanum* of 1614) involved dipping the child with a triune immersion into the water, taking due precautions for the baby's safety. Luther's rites maintained this practice, as did the English Prayer Books of 1549 and 1552: "Then the priest shall take the child in his handes, and aske the name. And naming the childe, shall dyppe it in the water thryse." The usual trinitarian formula, "N., I baptize thee in the name of the father, and of the sonne, and of the holy gost. Amen," accompanied the immersion. Calvin's rite of 1542 also used a trinitarian formula in baptism, though he considered the mode of "washing" a matter of indifference.[102]

Leaving aside the Anabaptist position, it can be said that most sixteenth-century Reformers affirmed (as did the medieval church) that baptism was necessary to becoming a Christian; that the rite involved the use of water, accompanied by a trinitarian formula; and that the ceremony was not to be repeated. But what did the rite mean? Did it signify, and effect, the person's regeneration (rebirth)? Did it offer an actual forgiveness of sins, especially the "sin of Adam" ("original sin")? Or was it simply an enrollment in the church community? Luther's "Flood Prayer" spoke of the sanctified water's power to effect a "rich and full washing away of sins," and it prayed further that "by means of this saving flood all that has been born in him from Adam and which he himself has added thereto may be drowned in him and engulfed."[103] This sounds very much like an affirmation of baptism as the "remission of original sin," without actually using that controversial formula.

The Reformers were of course well aware of the complex historical controversies surrounding the *peccatum Adae*, but they were reluctant to reject the notion. When Adam lost "the gifts received," wrote Calvin, he "lost them not only for himself but for us all." Hence, "Original sin . . . seems to be a hereditary depravity and corruption of our nature, diffused into all parts of the soul, which first makes us liable to God's wrath, then also brings forth in us those works which Scripture calls 'works of the flesh.'"[104] But does baptism have any connection to Adam's sin? Certainly, in the view of a Reformed theologian like Calvin, baptism is a serious sacrament, something much more than "a token and mark by which we confess our religion before men."[105] Indeed, Calvin describes baptism as "the sign of the initiation by which we are received into the society of the church, in order that, engrafted in Christ, we may be reckoned among God's children." Baptism is thus a divine gift, but its power arises, not from the element of water, but from the Word. "Water contains in itself [no] power to cleanse, regenerate, and renew; . . . Paul joins together the Word of life and the baptism of water." So baptism is effective as "a token and proof of our cleansing; . . . it is like a sealed document to confirm to us that all our sins are so abolished, remitted, and effaced that they can never come to [the Lord's] sight, be recalled, or charged against us."[106]

Thus, while most of the Reformers maintained the necessity and appropriateness of baptism, they did not reconnect it, liturgically, to the Easter vigil or Pentecost. That ancient connection—still recognized in late medieval sources, though not generally observed—was not wisely restored until the twentieth century.[107] As for that second postbaptismal chrismation, which the medieval church knew as "the sacrament of confirmation," its fate varied according to the tradition. "By and large, it was recast as a graduation ceremony for those of sufficient maturity to know the catechism";[108] perhaps the rite closest to the medieval Catholic one is to be found in the 1549 *Book of Common Prayer*, which follows the Sarum rite in many particulars (replacing chrismation with a laying on of hands) and retains the bishop as ordinary minister. It can be noted, finally, that as the custom of immersion eroded (among both Catholics and Protestants), the size, shape, and location of baptismal fonts changed. Calvin, linking water and Word, insisted that the font should be near the pulpit, but "with remarkable tenacity, Roman Catholics and Anglicans clung to having the font situated near the main entrance [of the church]."[109]

6. Daily Prayer. It is often assumed that in the medieval church daily public prayer, the divine office ("liturgy of the hours"), was celebrated only in religious houses (for example, monasteries) or in larger collegiate or cathedral churches—in short, that the hours had become a matter of private recitation by clergy and were quite unfamiliar to lay Christians. That this was *not* so can perhaps be seen from the Reformers themselves. In his short work *Concerning the Order of Public Worship* (1523), Luther began by noting, "The *service now in common use everywhere* goes back to genuine Christian beginnings, as does the office of preaching. But as the latter has been perverted by the spiritual tyrants, so the former has been corrupted by the hypocrites." Luther's complaint was not that public prayer (the hours) and preaching had ceased, but that they had been abused. The Word had been silenced or surrounded by unscriptural legends and fables, whereas the services themselves had been "performed as a work whereby God's grace and salvation might be won."[110] A similar lament appeared in the preface of the 1549 *Book of Common Prayer*, which begins with these famous words: "There was never any thing by the wit of man so well devised, or so surely established, which (in continuance of time) hath not been corrupted: as (among other thinges) it may plainly appere by the common prayers in the Church, commonlye called divine service." Again, the charge is not that the services were never celebrated or that the laity was excluded from them, but that their language, music, form, and content needed reforming.

Implicitly, then, the sixteenth-century Reformers affirmed "the basic pattern of [late medieval] parochial worship, matins, Mass, and evensong."[111] Thus, in three of his earliest proposals—*Concerning the Order of Public Worship, Formula Missae*, and *Deutsche Messe*—Luther made provision for daily morning and evening prayer. Although he wanted the weekday masses discontinued, he was willing to compromise:

"[I]f any should desire the sacrament during the week, let mass be held as inclination and time dictate; for in this matter one cannot make hard and fast rules."[112]

In Strasbourg, under the leadership of Martin Bucer (1491–1551, formerly a Dominican friar), "The Reformed Church . . . inherited from the Middle Ages an elaborate discipline of daily prayer," morning and evening.[113] Calvin's *Form of Church Prayers* also presumed that there would be a non-eucharistic service of prayer and preaching on all weekdays ("working days"), with the supper added on Sundays.[114] Similarly, the 1549 *Book of Common Prayer* set about not to introduce something "new" that had been missing, but to "redress" the problems and "inconveniences" associated with the old Latin daily office. To that end, the Prayer Book's preface

> ordeyned nothyng to be read, but the very pure worde of God, the holy scriptures, or
> that whiche is evidently grounded upon the same; and that in such a language and order,
> as is most easy and plain for the understandyng, bothe of the readers and hearers. . . .
> Furthermore, by this ordre, the curates shal nede none other bookes for the publique
> service, but this boke and the Bible; by the meanes wherof, the people shall not be at so
> great charge for bookes, as in tyme past they have been.

But simplicity and economy were not, finally, the Reformers' principal contributions to the Christian tradition of daily public prayer; far more significant was their restoration of the Psalter as a congregational hymnal. As long as the Psalms were known primarily through prose translations, it was difficult to set the text to familiar folk melodies that people could easily sing. But by the early sixteenth century, French metrical translations of the Psalms—from, of all places, the French court—began to appear. Some of these metrical versions made their way into the Genevan Psalter, on which Calvin, after serving a stint as a spiritual leader in Strasbourg, began working in 1541.[115] The result was *La forme des prières et chants ecclésiastiques* (1542), which included a collection of thirty-nine psalms, canticles, and prayers for congregational use. In 1551 a fuller version of the psalms appeared; it "set the standard for the musical character of the Genevan Psalter, to which later additions . . . were made to conform."[116] It would be difficult to overemphasize the liturgical legacy of this psalter. In effect, as Barbara Douglas comments, "it returned the psalms to the people, giving positive, corporate shape to their congregational and private prayer."[117]

In sum,

> the Reformers very clearly committed themselves to continuing a discipline of daily
> prayer services as an integral part of the life of the Church. Just as they continued to
> celebrate the service for the Lord's Day, so they continued to celebrate daily prayer.
> These daily prayer services were considered a normative part of the regular worship of
> the Church, just as preaching, or the celebration of baptism or the Lord's Supper.[118]

Further, the Reformers did not fail to see the connection between public worship and social justice. Before they left the church at the end of morning or evening prayer, for example, worshipers at Strasbourg were reminded to give alms to the needy, and to that end "a great chest was put at the door of each church to receive alms and the money was used by the deacons to support the diaconal ministry of the Church."[119]

7. Other Pastoral Rites. Before considering the Catholic response to these Protestant initiatives, a few comments may be made about the Reformers' rites for marriage, penance (reconciliation, confession), pastoral care of the sick and dying, and ordination.

Marriage. The Reformers recognized that marriage was simultaneously a sacred and a secular reality, created by God but established, too, as part of social life governed by civil law. In his 1529 *Order of Marriage: For Simple Pastors*, Luther conservatively

Katharina Schütz Zell

Elsie Anne McKee

Katharina Schütz Zell (1498–1562) of Strasbourg, in present-day France, was one of the most articulate and gifted of the first-generation Protestant lay reformers. Devout from childhood, Katharina dedicated her life to God but was never able to feel assured of God's acceptance until she heard the new preaching of Luther's ideas through Matthäus Zell, Strasbourg's first Protestant priest. In December 1523 Katharina and Matthäus were married, establishing a remarkable partnership in ministry. Katharina shared Matthäus's work until his death in 1548 and continued her vocation as "church mother" and colleague of the clergy for the rest of her life.

Schütz Zell's experience of the preaching of the gospel—Christ as sole Savior, justification by faith and grace alone, the Bible as sole authority—was the great turning point of her Christian life. Worship had always been important to her, but now it took new forms. She welcomed liturgy purified of its many extra ceremonies and now actively engaging the gathered people, with down-to-earth biblical teaching in their own language. Preaching of the Word became central to Schütz Zell's piety, but a reformed understanding of the sacraments was also critical. Both Zells rejected emergency baptism and mechanical grace. They continued, however, to honor and use the sacrament of infant baptism as a significant part of public worship, although they objected to the practice of having godparents. Both also highly valued the Lord's supper, which Schütz Zell continued to explain in the more general terms of the early 1520s even after later theological arguments produced confessional distinctions, which she never adopted. Her sacramental views fall within the spectrum of the Reformed tradition, but since she refused to make precise definitions, it is not clear exactly how she understood particular points. What is clear is that she strongly rejected the developed Gnesio-Lutheran teaching (the strict interpretation of the Augsburg Confession of 1530) on both sacraments—which was becoming dominant in Strasbourg in the 1550s—as a reintroduction of Roman doctrine.

Schütz Zell was a strong supporter of the Protestant practice of congregational singing, and happy to include biblical hymns as well as psalms. She also understood this singing as a vital part of daily devotional life, not just public worship, and considered parents and householders responsible for the "lay preaching" of instructing their dependents in the gospel through good biblical songs. Christian education was an important part of parental duty, though Schütz Zell regarded her exposition on the Lord's prayer (1532) not only as catechesis but also as a means of pastoral counsel for troubled souls. In times of trial, however, it was particularly the Psalms to which she herself turned and to which she directed those who sought her aid. Scripture, understood through the Apostles' Creed and interpreted by the best writers (the early Protestant reformers), was her source for liturgy and living piety.

A remarkably prolific writer, Schütz Zell covered many genres of texts in her literary corpus, which conveyed how a lay reformer thoughtfully appropriated and clearly taught basic Protestant theology. Her appreciation for scriptural preaching and teaching is evident throughout her works, although she also advocated personal Bible study using the aid of theologians like Martin Luther, Matthäus Zell, Kaspar Schwenckfeld von Ossig, Martin Bucer, Heinrich Bullinger, and others. Her first booklet was a letter full of scriptural comfort "To the Women of

Kentzingen" persecuted for their faith (1524). At Matthäus's burial in 1548, Schütz Zell even delivered an exhortation (*Klag red*) to his congregation herself, which friends considered important enough to preserve. Her positive understanding of the sacraments is particularly clear in her exposition of the Lord's prayer. Her views on what was wrong in the doctrine of the sacraments, the practice of ceremonies, and work of authoritarian church leaders are found in polemical works addressed to Roman Catholics (*Entschuldigung*, 1524), Gnesio-Lutherans (*Ein Brieff*, 1557), and even her friend Schwenckfeld (letter, 1553). In 1534–1536 Schütz Zell published an edition of the Bohemian Brethren hymnbook with her own preface, which expresses her convictions about music, the priesthood of the laity, and "lay preaching." Her last work was a devotional collection that included her earlier exposition on the Lord's prayer, several very personal meditations on Psalms 51 and 130 (c. 1550), and a moving pastoral letter to a man of high rank afflicted with leprosy (*Den Psalmen Miserere*, 1558).

An unusual woman, outspoken and confident of God's call to be an instrument of the Gospel in her own right, Katharina Schütz Zell articulated a thoughtful picture of women's—and lay—leadership in the church. Constrained by Pauline teaching, she did not support the ordination of women, but she developed three different cases for "speaking out" by those who were not ordained clergy. One argument is based on the belief that anyone who sees the clergy repeatedly failing in their duty must rebuke them, as Judith did the elders of Israel, and Balaam's donkey the prophet. Another case involves the conviction that anyone who hears lies must refute them and set the record straight, out of duty to the truth and love for her neighbors, both the deceived and the deceivers; a complex series of biblical texts supports this argument. Schütz Zell's third case for unofficial preachers "speaking out" arises from her conviction that anyone, male or female, who is learned in the Scripture is qualified to teach in appropriate circumstances, especially where there is not an ordained minister willing or able to serve. This call is grounded not on inspiration but on education in the faith, both intellectual learning and practical piety of life; the key model for this vocation is Anna (Luke 2:36–38), not texts such as Joel 2:28. Schütz Zell took very seriously the importance of a learned ministry, but she did not confine it to the pulpit or ordained men; the latter are the usual means for preaching from the pulpit, but others who are qualified may and should preach and teach in the appropriate contexts.

References

McKee, Elsie Anne. *Katharina Schütz Zell: The Life and Thought of a Sixteenth-Century Reformer*, vol. 1. Studies in Medieval and Reformation Thought 69:1; *The Writings: A Critical Edition*, vol. 2. SMRT 69:2. Leiden, Netherlands: Brill, 1999.

McKee, Elsie Anne. *Reforming Popular Piety in Sixteenth-Century Strasbourg: Katharina Schütz Zell and Her Hymnbook*. Studies in Reformed Theology and History 2 (Fall 1994). Princeton, N.J.: Princeton Theological Seminary, 1994.

revised the medieval rite, retaining many familiar elements (such as the publication of banns, the consent, the giving of rings, the joining of hands, the "nuptial blessing"). Although marriage is not called a sacrament in this rite, it does typify—so the pastor's concluding blessing asserts—"the sacramental union of thy dear Son, the Lord Jesus Christ, and the church, his bride."[120] This assertion is repeated in the familiar opening address to the congregation in the marriage service found in the *Book of Common Prayer*, 1549 and 1552:

> Deerely beloved frendes, we are gathered together here in the syght of God, and in the face of his congregacion, to joyne together this man and this woman in holy matrimonie, which is an honorable estate instituted of God in paradise, in the time of mannes innocencie, signifying unto us the misticall union that is betwixte Christe and his Churche.

Like Luther, Cranmer conservatively revised a medieval model (the Sarum rite), though he kept one feature that Luther seems to have abandoned: the participation of the couple in the eucharist on the day of their marriage. The concluding rubric of both the 1549 and 1552 versions of the Prayer Book state: "The newe maried persones (the same daye of their marriage) must receive the holy communion."[121] Calvin, too, appears to have envisioned celebrations of marriage during the Sunday liturgy of the supper.

These variations in the marriage service are no cause for surprise. As Luther remarked in the prefatory section of his 1529 rite, "Many lands, many customs . . . Since marriage and the married estate are worldly matters, it behooves us pastors or ministers of the church not to attempt to order or govern anything connected with it, but to permit every city and land to continue its own use and custom in this connection."[122] Ironically, about thirty-five years later the Council of Trent's twenty-fourth session (11 November 1563) essentially adopted Luther's position about ritual variation in the celebration of weddings: "If any provinces have in this matter [of marriage] other laudable customs and ceremonies . . . the holy council wishes earnestly that they be by all means retained."[123]

Penance. Even though Luther had a high regard for penance, possibly considering it a sacrament, he deplored the fact that for many medieval Christians the confession of sins had become a compulsory "burden, instead of a privilege."[124] Although he provided a *Short Order of Confession before the Priest for the Common Man*, he clearly did not think of fruitful confession as a "clericalized affair."[125] Zwingli went even further, insisting that there was "no need of any priest" at all when a Christian sought God's forgiveness.[126] More important, perhaps, the Reformers took seriously the "penitential rite" at eucharist (the "Confiteor" of the medieval rite). Indeed, many of the reformed liturgies expanded the opening rites of confession and reconciliation. Calvin's *Form of Church Prayers* opens with a lengthy prayer of confession said by the minister, who invites the people to "follow my words in [their] hearts."[127] Calvin's rite also included recitation of the Decalogue, a feature found at the beginning of the eucharist in the 1552 *Book of Common Prayer*, where, after each commandment recited by the minister, the people reply "Lord, have mercye upon us, and encline our heartes to kepe this lawe."

Ministry to the Sick and Dying. Many of the Reformers seem to have regarded ministry to the sick and dying as acts of pastoral care rather than opportunities for ritual response. Though they recognized the value of prayer for the sick and dying, they had scant regard for medieval Catholicism's "extreme unction."[128] Both recensions of the *Book of Common Prayer*, however, retained distinctive rites for visiting the sick, administering communion to them, and burying the dead. The 1549 Prayer Book even retained the custom of anointing the sick, though this was dropped from the 1552 recension. Again, the 1549 book links the ministry to the sick and dying with eucharist, indicating that if the priest visits the sick on a day when the holy communion is not being celebrated, he "shal there [in the sick person's house] celebrate the holy communion after such forme and sorte as herafter is appoynted." The 1552 book maintains the connection between ministry to the sick and reception of communion, but insists there must be "a good nombre to receyve the communion wyth the sycke personne."

Ordination. Obviously, questions of ministry and priesthood in the sixteenth century could not be separated from larger questions about sacrament and sacrifice (eucharist). Perhaps the distance between Luther and the late medieval church is nowhere more evident than in that reformer's 1539 rite of *Ordination of Ministers of the Word.* Gone are the complex medieval rituals for ordaining priests (with their litanies, prostrations, anointings, *porrectio* of chalice and paten, vesture, and so on); in their place is a relatively brief liturgy that retains the laying on of hands but replaces the long medieval prayers of ordination (or consecration) with the Lord's prayer.[129] The rite thus reflects Luther's view that baptism is the "true sacrament of ordination" that makes every Christian a priest.[130] Calvin was well aware of the significance Catholics attached to the ceremonies of presbyteral ordination (especially the *porrectio instrumentorum* and the anointing of hands), and although he was inclined to "put it [presbyteral ordination] as number three among the sacraments," he declined to do so because "it is not ordinary or common with all believers, but is a special rite for a particular office."[131]

In England, Cranmer kept the orders of deacon, priest, and bishop, while eliminating the medieval church's "minor orders." One might assume, therefore, that his revisions of the ordination liturgy (such as his reform of the marriage rite, based on Sarum) would be quite conservative. But that is not the case. The Ordinal published in March of 1550 (*The forme and maner of makyng and consecratyng of Archebishoppes, Bishoppes, Priests and Deacons*), although it makes some use of medieval Latin sources, was far more profoundly influenced by the work of Martin Bucer.[132] Unlike Thomas Aquinas, who believed that handing over (*porrectio*) the "chalice with wine and the paten with bread" conferred on priests the "power of consecrating the body and blood of Christ," Cranmer believed that the most important parts of the ordination rite were "the litany, with its suffrage and collect, and the imposition of hands."[133] Paul Bradshaw remarks:

> The reason for Cranmer's close dependence on Bucer and almost total rejection of the wording of the medieval rites, in contrast to his usual use of sources in compiling the Prayer Book, is almost certainly to be found in his denial of the popular view of the sacrifice of the Mass and of the sacrificial priesthood. The medieval ordination rites were so full of sacrificial language that there was little which he could have adopted as it stood without implying ideas about the ordained ministry which he no longer held.[134]

By the time the Council of Trent began meeting in 1545, therefore, Reformed views of eucharist, ministry, sacraments, and worship had been evolving for several decades, and significant Protestant liturgical reform had been under way for a generation. The Catholic bishops thus found themselves in a reactive, rather than a proactive, position. By the time Trent's reform of the eucharistic liturgy appeared (*Missale Romanum,* 1570), Zwingli (d. 1531), Luther (d. 1546), Bucer (d. 1551), Cranmer (d. 1556), and Calvin (d. 1564) had all passed on. And by the time the final Tridentine liturgical book was published (*Rituale Romanum*), nearly a century had passed since the young Luther had nailed his ninety-five theses to the church door in Wittenberg.

Catholic Response: From the Council of Trent to the *Rituale Romanum* of 1614

Although we commonly speak of "the Council of Trent," the phrase is somewhat inaccurate. "Trent" describes, in fact, a complex series of meetings (not all of them in the city of Trent) held sporadically over a period of nearly twenty years (1545–1563).

Indeed, at its opening session on 15 December 1545, there were present only twenty-one bishops, four archbishops, one cardinal, three papal legates, and five generals of religious orders—thirty-four people in all, a rather small assembly for an "ecumenical council."[135] Trent's work was divided into three periods: Sessions 1–8 (1545–1547); Sessions 9–14 (1551–1552); and Sessions 15–25 (1562–1563). Sacraments and worship (including the mass and eucharistic theology) were debated during all three periods.[136] The first revised liturgical book of the Catholic Counter-Reformation did not appear until 1568 (the *Roman Breviary*); further reforms followed in 1570 (the *Roman Missal*), 1584 (the *Roman Martyrology*), 1596 (the *Roman Pontifical*), 1600 (the bishops' *Ceremonial*), and 1614 (the *Roman Ritual*).

Trent and the Eucharist

Trent's discussion of the mass in all its dimensions (sacramental, sacrificial, ceremonial) took place over a period of some fifteen years, from August 1547 to 17 September 1562;[137] its decisions were promulgated in three major decrees: those of 11 October 1551 (session 13), 16 July 1562 (session 21), and 17 September 1562 (session 22).

1. *Decretum de sanctissimo Eucharistiae sacramento,* 11 **October 1551.** It is indicative of the Tridentine bishops' frame of mind that the first eucharistic topics they chose to deal with were "real presence" and "transubstantiation," rather the mass as a corporate act of public worship. The opening words of the 1551 decree touch the heart of the matter as the bishops understood it: "First of all, the holy council teaches and openly and plainly professes that after the consecration of bread and wine, our Lord Jesus Christ, true God and true man, is truly, really and substantially contained in the august sacrament of the Holy Eucharist under the appearance of those sensible things."[138] The decree also affirmed that this "change . . . of the whole substance of the bread into the substance of the body of Christ . . . and of the whole substance of the wine into the substance of His blood" is "properly and appropriately" called by the Church "transubstantiation."[139]

Trent's first order of business was thus not to "reform the liturgy" but, rather, to defend the dual doctrines of transubstantiation and Christ's real presence against Reformers whose positions had been discussed in detail by theologians and prelates at previous working sessions during September and early October 1551.[140] The bishops also wanted to reaffirm the legitimacy of reserving the eucharist and offering it adoration: "There is . . . no room for doubt that all the faithful of Christ may . . . give to this most holy sacrament . . . the worship of *latria*, which is due to the true God."[141] These points were reiterated in a sermon given to the Council on 11 October 1551 by Archbishop Salvator Salapusius. "O truly stupendous miracle," he exclaimed, " . . . incomprehensible sacrament of sacraments . . . for the sanctifying power of every other sacrament is a preparation

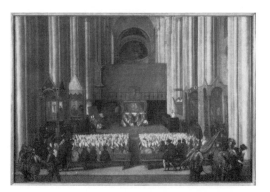

The Council of Trent. The nineteenth ecumenical council was convoked by Pope Paul III and held between 1545 and 1563. The council made important decisions concerning the doctrine and practice of Christian worship, especially the sacraments. Painting by Titian (Tiziano Vecelli, c. 1488–1576). MUSÉE DU LOUVRE, PARIS/GIRAUDON/ ART RESOURCE, NY

either for consecrating the eucharist or for receiving it! . . . This lavish table is prepared for us against all who afflict us. Let us eat therefore, fathers, let us adore."[142]

Still, despite the temper of the time and their rock-ribbed defense of traditional doctrine, the bishops at Trent showed a degree of conciliation by inviting Protestants to participate in conciliar deliberations. They granted safe-conduct to "each and all persons throughout the whole of Germany, whether ecclesiastics or seculars, of whatever rank, station, condition and circumstances . . . who may wish to come to this ecumenical and general council . . . that they may and shall enjoy full liberty to confer, make proposals, and discuss those things that are to be discussed in the council."[143] The bishops had hoped, early in 1552, to take up the question of liturgical ceremonies in the mass, but as noted in point 3 below, action had to be deferred. A full decade passed before Trent resumed its debates about the eucharist.

2. *Decretum de communione sub utraque specie et parvulorum*, 16 July 1562. Earlier in this chapter I noted that frequency of communion was a central concern in the Reformers' reaction to late medieval liturgical practice. Protestants insisted that communion, in both kinds, be restored to the people at every celebration of the eucharist. Trent began discussing this matter on 6 June 1562 and issued its decree on holy communion at the twenty-first session, 16 July 1562. Actually, of course, the debate about whether lay communicants could or should receive from the cup had been raging for nearly a century and a half by the time Trent acted. It was one of the issues that led to Jan Hus's execution at the Council of Constance in 1415.[144] Communion from the cup had, in fact, been conceded to lay Christians in Bohemia by the Council of Basel in 1433, but this decision failed ultimately to receive papal ratification and was subsequently revoked by Pope Pius II on 9 April 1462.[145]

A century later, the Council of Trent found itself discussing the matter anew. Its reactions were predictable. Reaffirming the doctrine of "concomitance"—that after the consecration, Christ is present whole and entire in either the bread or cup—the bishops insisted that, *salva illorum substantia*, the Church has the power to "change whatever she may judge most expedient for the benefit of those receiving . . . the sacraments."[146] Thus, the bishops reasoned, although "Christ the Lord at the last supper instituted and delivered to the Apostles this venerable sacrament under the forms of bread and wine, yet [this does] . . . not signify that all the faithful are [bound] by an enactment of the Lord to receive under both forms."[147] The real issue, as Trent saw it, was neither Christ's intention in instituting the supper nor the integrity of the sacramental action (communion of the people in both kinds as *essential* to the eucharist), but whether the Church (that is, its leadership) has power to alter modes of sacramental celebration "so long as their substance is preserved." Trent also denied that little children, already baptized, are "by any necessity bound to the sacramental communion of the Eucharist," although it conceded that such was the practice in antiquity.[148] Nevertheless, the council left open whether "the use of the chalice [is] to be conceded to a person, nation or kingdom."[149]

3. *Decretum de sacrificio missae*, 17 September 1562. Still, the bishops at Trent had not decided on a strategy for reforming the liturgical rites of the mass. Discussions about such a reform had been under way among Catholic *periti* (the bishops' theological advisers) since August 1547. These *periti* had already debated a number of points excerpted from the Reformers' critiques of the Roman liturgy before the bishops began their formal deliberations about the mass in December 1551. Among the points already debated by theologians had been this one attributed to Luther's

Babylonian Captivity: "In the celebration of Masses all ceremonies, vestments and external signs are provocations to impiety rather than duties of piety. And as Christ's Mass was extremely simple, therefore, the more the Mass is similar to and resembles the first of all Masses, the more Christian it is."[150] As noted earlier, however, Luther did not condemn additional rites and ceremonies as such; he objected, rather, to their addition without faith; so the "excerpt" prepared for the bishops' debate did not express Luther's "exact and complete thought."[151]

As this example shows, the bishops at Trent did not always possess accurate accounts of Protestant views. Nor were they always of one mind on matters such as the "primitive simplicity" of the eucharist or the wisdom of using the vernacular in its celebration.[152] Nonetheless, by January 1552 the bishops were ready to issue a decree about the eucharist as a real sacrifice instituted by Christ (chapter one), about the relation between the mass and the cross (chapter two), about the fruits of the mass (chapter three), and about its rites and ceremonies (chapter four).[153] In the final chapter of this decree, the bishops admitted that the Last Supper itself was "altogether simple and devoid of external symbols and decorations" because they were not needed at that time and place; still, they argued, "the same Spirit which incited Christ to sacrifice in that manner has instructed the Church to append becoming and religious ceremonies in due consideration of the times."[154] Note that the council's response differed substantially from the issue raised by the Reformers. The latter were asking: "What did Christ do at the Supper? What do scripture and history tell us?" Trent was asking, "What discretionary power does the Church have over sacraments and worship?"

The Council intended to promulgate its *Decretum de sacrificio missae* in a solemn session on 25 January 1552, but political circumstances changed that plan.[155] Initially, the bishops opted for a brief delay, but the outbreak of the Second War of Smalkald forced them to disband and flee. On 28 April 1552 the council suspended its activities. Although it intended to reconvene within two years, a decade passed before it could resume its work.[156] Trent's first and second periods had thus ended without the bishops having reached any decision about liturgical reform of the mass. When the council reconvened in 1562, it turned first not to reform of the mass but to questions about holy communion.[157] After that, on 17 September, the bishops revisited their decree concerning the mass as sacrifice, reaffirming traditional doctrine that "in this divine sacrifice . . . is contained and immolated in an unbloody manner the same Christ who once offered Himself in a bloody manner on the altar of the cross." For this reason, the bishops concluded, mass is "rightly offered not only for the sins, punishments, satisfactions and other necessities of the faithful who are living, but also for those departed in Christ but not yet fully purified."[158]

Trent's language about the mass as sacrifice was standard Catholic boilerplate; more interesting was what it finally began to say about mass as a liturgy. For it was at this 1562 session that the bishops (conceding perhaps far more than they knew to the Reformers) commanded pastors and "all who have the care of souls" to "explain frequently during the celebration of the mass some of the things read during the mass, and that among other things they explain some mystery of this most holy sacrifice, especially on Sundays and festival days."[159] In short, the council was "insisting on doctrinally informed lay participation" by telling pastors to instruct the people regularly during public worship.[160]

By now, however, the council's work was headed beyond pastoral exhortation. A commission had been established to assemble a list of major abuses in the celebration of the eucharist; its draft report (revised and shortened) formed the basis of Trent's disciplinary "Decree concerning the things to be observed and avoided in the celebration of

Mass," also passed on 17 September 1562.[161] In this decree the bishops admitted, first, that in the course of time—through "indifference and corruption"—things "have crept in that are foreign to the dignity of so great a sacrifice."[162] All such aberrations were to be banished from the liturgy: for example, celebrations led by "wandering or unknown priest[s]," music that "contains things that are lascivious or impure, . . . worldly conduct, vain and profane conversations, wandering around, noise and clamor, so that the house of God may be seen to be and may be truly called a house of prayer."[163]

Still, Trent did nothing about reforming the missal, breviary, or other liturgical books; it reacted to Protestant initiatives by "correcting" their doctrine, not by critiquing their liturgies or proposing Catholic alternatives to them. Thus, Trent's final (twenty-fifth) session on 3–4 December 1563 simply remanded reform of the liturgical books to the pope.[164]

Reform of the Roman Missal (1570)

Trent's failure to act did not result from inattention to worship and sacraments.[165] On the contrary, since at least 1 March 1546, bishops had been complaining about the "sheer quantity of rubbish" contained in the missal and breviary (the two places where the clergy, at least, encountered God's Word daily).[166] Sixteen years later, on 9 March 1562, the council was still being petitioned "to reform the Missal and breviary and cleanse them of spurious material."[167] So, despite their inaction, the Tridentine bishops had not lost sight of the goal of liturgical reform. Nor did it take long for Pius IV to act on Trent's decision to remand reform to the pope.[168] By 1564 he had established a liturgical reform commission that was subsequently enlarged by his successor, Pius V. Unfortunately for historians, we possess no detailed reports of who the members of this commission were or precisely what they did.[169]

The tasks facing this commission were formidable. Some of the demands to purify the mass liturgy could be met by reforming the calendar, revising or eliminating faulty texts (such as prefaces and sequences), and suppressing votive masses of doubtful merit.[170] Other tasks, especially those touching the liturgical ceremonies themselves, were more involved. It had been suggested, while the council was still in session, that "regional differences in the Roman Mass and the episcopal right to regulate them be left unrestricted."[171] But the papal commission chose another course, and the result was a new *Missale Romanum*, promulgated by a papal bull of 14 July 1570 and binding on the whole Western Church; however, rites in existence for more than two hundred years (for example, the Dominicans' rite, the Mozarabic rite) were permitted to continue in use. An effort was made to reconcile the new missal's calendar, collects, and gospel texts with the revised *Breviarum Romanum*, which had appeared two years earlier (1568). Overall, however, the *Missale Romanum* of 1570 (sometimes called the *Missale Pianum* or "Missal of Pius V") was based on late-medieval editions of the *Missale secundum consuetudinem Romanae Curiae*, which reflected usages of the papal court and was already popular throughout Europe. The rubrics governing ceremonial "were taken almost bodily from the *Ordo Missae* of the papal master of ceremonies, John Burchard of Strassburg, a work which appeared in 1502 and had meanwhile circulated widely."[172]

The principles that guided the liturgical commission in its work of reform are evident in the papal bull *Quo primum*, which introduced the new missal.[173] Five cardinal principles are announced. First, a single rite for mass and office is to be used throughout the Latin church.[174] Second, the antiquity, quality, and probity of the missal's contents are to be guaranteed by the work of scholars.[175] Third, the commission's primary goal is to restore the mass to the "pristine norm of the ancient Fathers."[176] Fourth, this patristic norm will be strictly interpreted by papal authority, for the regulation of liturgical practice in the Western Church belongs to the pope and is contained in the official books (*editiones typicae*) he approves and promulgates. Fifth, nothing may be added or subtracted either from the rites and rubrics found in the missal or from the bull *Quo primum*, except by direction of the pope.[177] In short, the Roman rite was redefined as a papal rite—papal in its origins (the liturgy of the papal court), papal in form and norm, and papal in its promulgation and regulation. By remanding reform of the liturgical library to the pope in its final session, Trent had (perhaps unwittingly) created a new liturgical universe, a style of reform based on political principles that would later serve the emerging "nation states" of early modern Europe.[178] In sum, the *Missale Pianum* of 1570 redefined the art of politics in matters liturgical. In the medieval world such politics had been local, with responsibility for worship in the hands of the local ordinary (the bishop); in the post-Tridentine world, liturgical politics became global, international, with final responsibility vested in the pope.

These were, of course, quite "modern" principles that reflected influences from both the new technology of the time (printing) and enlightened humanist scholarship. The pope blatantly admitted that the missal was the work of a professional class—liturgical "experts," scholarly librarians combing through "ancient manuscripts contained in our Vatican Library," not pastors responding to the needs of their people. He assumed, further, that the model of "historical repristination"—the "return to the sources" (which the Reformers themselves also esteemed)—was the proper one for such scholarly work.[179] Moreover, despite warnings against "lasciviousness" in church music, both Trent and the post-Tridentine reform actually embraced many modern ("secular") innovations in art, literature, architecture, and music.[180] On many levels, Trent's reform of Catholic worship, which took the form of purging late medieval rites of their disturbing "muddle" and "rubbish," represented Renaissance humanism's love for "clean, unadulterated forms."[181] One is not surprised, then, to read, in *Quod a nobis*, the papal bull which promulgated the reformed *Breviarium Romanum*, that Pius V lamented "divini cultus perturbatio" and wished to rid public worship of "orandi varietas."[182] To achieve such goals it was necessary to remove liturgy from the turgid flow of daily life and to make of it a kind of "political performance"—the "official cult" of the church as a public institution, rather than living worship by a holy community whose every member contributes to the action.[183]

Meanwhile, as work on the reformed liturgical books began, it was also necessary to settle the question of communion from the cup, another issue that Trent had remanded to the pope. After intense behind-the-scenes negotiations, Pope Pius IV authorized communion in both species for Germany (16 April 1564).[184] In effect, the question of communion in both kinds had become a political football, for Ferdinand I, the Holy Roman emperor, refused to authorize closure of the Council of Trent (a goal ardently sought by the pope) unless certain concessions were made, and the cup was one of them. The papal concession was extremely controversial (it was opposed, for example, by King Philip II of Spain and by several cardinals), and Pius IV had to defend his decision in a consistory held on 14 July 1564, a few days before Emperor Ferdinand's death (on July 25).[185] Eventually, permission to use the cup was extended to other parts of Europe as well—Bavaria, Austria, Bohemia, Moravia, and Hungary—but by 1621 all these concessions had been revoked.[186] Clergy who continued the practice of communicating laypeople in both kinds were severely censured, as witness a sentence imposed by Archbishop John Lohelius against John Locica, a pastor in Prague (April 1622):

> Like a dog returning to its vomit, he has fallen again into his former errors, . . . and following his own wishes, . . . has rejected the papal mandate, . . . viz., that neither he nor

any other pastor should give any lay person communion in both kinds. . . . Therefore we declare John Locica excommunicate . . . and we deprive him of his pastorate and of all ecclesiastical benefices.[187]

Other Post-Tridentine Liturgical Reforms

The tone of Archbishop Lohelius's judgment against one of his own pastors reflects, in many respects, the fate of liturgical reform in the Post-Tridentine era. The Roman liturgical library produced after Trent did little to alter the basic structure of sacramental celebrations as these had developed by the late medieval period, but it did—following the principles of Renaissance humanism—provide texts and rubrics that were "leaner and cleaner," purged of clutter.[188] The goal announced by Pius V in *Quod a nobis* became, in fact, Counter-Reformation Catholicism's liturgical motto: "uni deo, una & eadem formula, preces, & laudes adhibendi" (to one God, with one and the same formula, let prayers and praise be addressed).[189] This principle, asserted in the first of the reformed books (*Breviarium Romanum*, 1568), was reasserted in the last book to be reformed (*Rituale Romanum*, 1614):

> In order to restore observance of the sacred rites . . . and, at the same time, to provide the Catholic Church, gathered in unity of faith under *one visible head*, the Roman Pontiff, the successor of blessed Peter, with *one single order* of praying and singing, our predecessor of happy memory, Pope Pius V—mindful of the office that was then his and is now ours—decreed, with pastoral providence, that new editions of the *Breviary* [1568] and the *Roman Missal* [1570] be prepared. . . . Our predecessor Pope Clement VIII then . . . issued an accurately restored *Pontifical* [1596] and bishops' *Ceremonial* [1600]. All this accomplished, it remained to bring together *in one volume*, the holy (and now purified) rites of the Catholic Church which must be observed in the administration of the sacraments . . . by those who have the care of souls. . . . In this way, among such a multitude of Rituals, they may fulfill their ministry *according to a strict and public norm*.[190]

Once more, the principle is clear: in a global Church united under one visible head, there should be but one approved book that follows a strict, public norm and provides one order of service for all the sacraments. Despite such language, however, the concluding exhortation of *Apostolicae Sedi* hinted that although a single official book was being offered for the "public good of the Church of God," pastors might actually continue to use locally produced (diocesan) rituals, even if the Roman church, by its authority as "mother and teacher [*mater et magistra*] of all," urged them to use this book for all "sacred functions."[191] In short, the *Rituale* was not, to use Balthasar Fischer's words, a "global book," but a "model book."[192] Unlike Clement VIII's brief that accompanied the *Pontificale* of 1596—and explicitly "suppressed and abolished" all other versions[193]—*Apostolicae Sedi* used the vocabulary of persuasion to convince pastors to follow the new *Rituale*: "Hortamur in Domino" (We urge [you] in the Lord).[194] As Fischer notes, if this language of persuasion had been honored, it might have made an enormous difference to missionaries who needed to translate and adapt the contents of the *Rituale* to cultures vastly different from those of Europe.[195]

When one reviews the Roman liturgical library as it was reformed after Trent, one might think the Reformation had never happened, for the Catholic rites reveal scant willingness to learn from decades of Protestant liturgical reform and innovation. After all, nearly a hundred years separated Luther's *Formula Missae* and *Order of Baptism* (1523) and the revised *Rituale Romanum* (1614); yet one finds no concessions to Reformation worship and theology in the sacramental celebrations proposed by Paul V's model book. Baptism is spoken of as the "threshold of the Christian religion and of eternal life"; it occupies "first place among the sacraments of the New Law instituted by Christ," and its liturgy (for both children and adults) includes a full complement of exorcisms, exsufflations, signings, and anointings (pre- and postbaptismal). If an adult to be baptized was previously a Jew, a Muslim, or member of a Protestant communion, he or she is asked to renounce and "spit out" (the Latin verbs used are *horrescere* and *respuere*) the "Hebrew superstition" or the "Mohammedan perfidy" or the "heretical depravity and nefarious sects of the impious."[196]

Similarly, penance is described as "a sacrament instituted by Christ to restore those who lapse after baptism to grace," and the confessor's role is simultaneously that of judge and physician. Penitents must confess all their sins in number, species, and circumstance, and the absolution is given in the first person singular, "Ego te absolvo."[197] A similar first-person formula follows the declaration of consent by bride and groom in the liturgy of marriage, when the priest pronounces, "Ego conjungo vos"—"I join you in matrimony, in the name of the Father, and of the Son, and of the Holy Spirit." The concluding prayer of the ceremony succinctly summarizes the Church's view of this sacrament's purpose: "Look down, O Lord, ... upon these your servants, and assist with your gracious care the institution you ordained for the propagation of the human race."[198] Finally, the *Rituale* declares that "extreme unction" is also "a sacrament instituted by Christ," a "heavenly medicine not only for the soul but also for the healing of the body."

Unlike the terse, sober *Ordination of Ministers of the Word* provided by Luther in 1539, the Roman rites of ordaining men to minor (tonsure, porter, exorcist, acolyte, lector) and major (subdeacon, deacon, priest, bishop) orders remained complex and lengthy.[199] The rites made it abundantly clear that the Catholic priest was no mere preacher of the Word, but a person in whose consecrated hands there was placed the "power to offer sacrifice to God and to celebrate Mass for the living and the dead."[200]

In sum, the post-Tridentine liturgical books of the Roman church embodied two basic impulses: the impulse of Renaissance humanism, with its love of "clean, unadulterated forms" based on "classical models"; and the impulse of centralization, reflected in the phrase "uni deo, una & eadem formula, preces, & laudes adhibendi" and in the exertion of papal (not local or episcopal) control over the liturgy for "the good of the universal church."

Conclusions

I began this chapter with a discussion of *The Burning of a Heretic*, Sassetta's early-fifteenth-century painting, with its macabre scene of the eucharist being celebrated at the site of an execution. I conclude by inviting readers to meditate on another church-commissioned painting, Caravaggio's *Martyrdom of St. Matthew*, created for the Contarelli chapel in Rome's church of San Luigi dei Francesi in 1599–1600. This painting also pairs eucharist and execution, for Matthew is celebrating mass when his assailant strikes him with a sword, knocking him, bleeding, to the altar steps. Though these two altar paintings are separated by nearly two hundred years, and though they represent two different moments in the history of Western art, both confront us with brutal depictions of religion's troubling relation to violence. Caravaggio's painting hangs on the right wall of the Contarelli chapel and is lit from the left, as if from a window behind the altar. What makes the painting particularly disturbing is the artist's focus on the murderer's moment. This is a painting about a killing, not about "the triumph of virtue." Caravaggio's assassin is a Herculean youth, armed and dangerous, hacking a bearded old man who is still vested in alb and chasuble. Although Matthew props himself up on one hand, the gesture is obviously futile. The murderer's furious face tells us who will win this contest. Toward the "back" of the painting one catches a glimpse of Caravaggio himself, a departing onlooker whose face is lit and turned over his shoulder toward the drama he has created. Meanwhile, a young acolyte flees the altar, his mouth hanging open in a horrified scream.

Caravaggio was, of course, "a painter brilliantly gifted in rethinking the iconography of scriptural scenes."[201] His gritty naturalism, realism, and use of brilliant color and movement (all of which heighten his paintings' drama) suggest, as Helen Langdon notes, "the influence of sixteenth-century meditative techniques, which encourage the participant to visualize" biblical or religious scenes with as much intensity as possible.[202] But there is another dimension to Caravaggio's work that also deserves attention, because it tells us much about the period just reviewed in this chapter. The 1590s were a "sudden boom time" in Rome; the city was being rebuilt as a glittering monument to papal Catholicism; the "building and decorating trades were on a roll"; and any artist (painter, sculptor, architect, stonemason) who sought success and notoriety came to the "Eternal City."[203] Rome

The Martyrdom of Saint Matthew. Painting by Michelangelo Merisi da Caravaggio (c. 1573–1610). As the alb- and chasuble-wearing victim falls, an angel hovering over the altar hands him a martyr's palm leaf. CHURCH OF SAN LUIGI DEI FRANCESI, ROME/SCALA/ART RESOURCE, NY

as "symbol of a reformed Catholicism," Rome as rebuilder and redecorator on a monumental scale, Rome as "the world's great image factory," Rome as home to the "greatest church in Christendom" (the final stone in the cupola of Saint Peter's was laid in 1590)—all of this served as visible propaganda for the Counter-Reformation. As Peter Robb comments, "The church needed public art, rigorously policed and ideologically correct, to project itself afresh into the hearts and minds of the people and promote its own greater glory."[204]

For the most part, Caravaggio's paintings failed the test of "ideological purity" and outraged Rome's religious establishment, but it was against such a background of intense creative activity that the post-Tridentine reform of the Catholic liturgical library took place. *Roma resurgens* became the heart of an increasingly international Catholicism (the Church was sending missionaries to the far-flung regions of India, China, Japan, Canada, and California) managed by a strong, centralized papal government that could play political hardball when it had to. Indeed, heretics were still being executed to the accompaniment of the eucharist. While the Cenci family was being executed in 1599, Pope Clement VIII celebrated "a low mass for their souls a short distance away."[205] Despite the "hit" it had taken during the Reformation, the RomanChurch had, by the beginning of the seventeenth century, both the methods and the machinery to impose "the new papal order" on both friends and foes.[206] Ironically, the liturgy itself (through use of the "confessional" in the sacrament of penance) became one of Counter-Reformation Catholicism's most effective tools for enforcing what historians refer to as a "collective morality" supported by both the "culture of suspicion" and the monopoly of information.[207] (Recall that another of the items remanded to the pope by the Council of Trent was reform of the *Index of Forbidden Books*.)

Edward Muir has suggested that the Reformation can be viewed as "a revolution in ritual theory."[208] He argues that late-medieval lay Catholics based their religious practice on three assumptions: that ritual words, deeds, and objects (relics, the sacred host) created a real, physical bond between themselves and the Holy; that interaction with sacred objects was sensual and aesthetic, not primarily cognitive and "rational"; and that divine presence was perceived in strongly physical terms.

> Late medieval Christians expected to find the sacred manifest itself in material objects that could be seen, touched, smelled, tasted, and ingested. As the codification of a ritual system, the official sacraments and semi-official sacramentals depended upon the assumption that divine and saintly beings would make themselves present in material objects in response to the supplications of humans. These contractual, aesthetic, and sensual characteristics meant that Christian ritual demanded the presence of human and divine bodies to work its wonders.

The eucharist (as both sacramental action and sacred object) epitomized these lay views about ritual power. And while medieval lay participants experienced a mass liturgy monopolized by the clergy, they did not, it appears, feel "alienated from the orchestrated ritual of the altar"; indeed they were willing to pay for "ever more elaborate Corpus Christi processions and plays . . . more sumptuous altar cloths, more elaborate architectural frames for the mystic ritual." Thus, as Muir argues: "On the eve of the Reformation, Eucharistic piety composed one of the great pillars of the Christian ritual system, a pillar that held up in a straightforward, material way a vast edifice of incarnation theology and spiritual mystery." Although erudite dissenters (such as Wyclif and Hus) had already begun to challenge this eucharistic piety in the fourteenth and fifteenth centuries, a full-blown "crisis of the communal, performative sign" finally erupted in sixteenth-century Europe. In the Reformers' view, the medieval reliance on ritual was a "diversion from true spiritual concerns," and hence they sought to create "a new theological metaphysics by drawing precise boundaries between the spiritual and material worlds, breaking the deeply mysterious connections between the two made evident in traditional rituals." As a result, Reformation worship focused much more intently upon "cognitive access" to the mystery of Christ, upon informed intellectual participation nurtured by meditation on the Word purely proclaimed and preached in the language of the people. Ironically, Trent embraced a similar modernity, arguing, as noted earlier, that the mass contains much "instruction for the faithful," and that pastors should therefore "explain frequently during the celebration of the Mass some of the things read during the Mass." In short, Trent also saw the eucharist as a catechetical opportunity, though its postconciliar commission wound up creating "an obsessive ritual rigidity" that stifled the vibrant liturgical pluriformity of the late Middle Ages. The result was unintended irony on both sides of this sixteenth-century debate about the value of communal, performative signs. Protestants found they could not totally escape "the hold of collective rituals on religious practice," while Catholics created a universally obligatory "papal liturgy" that required constant control and interpretation by "properly trained clergy." Counter-Reformation Catholicism moved away from being a church that defined its doctrine by its worship to being a church that defined its worship by its doctrine (especially the doctrines of eucharistic real presence and transubstantiation).

Meanwhile art and architecture continued to reshape not only the spaces where mass was celebrated but also to reinterpret the stories that defined eucharistic doctrine. Biblical scenes such as the meal at Emmaus (Luke 24:13–32) became, in the hands of painters like Caravaggio, something quite different from comic-book illustrations of "real presence" or "transubstantiation." Caravaggio's earlier painting of this scene (c. 1601) sees the Risen Christ not as some remote, ghostly apparition, but as a sensual, youthful figure, "a contemporary figure, from the ordinary working world." Raised in blessing, Christ's hand thrusts energetically outward, almost breaking the painting's plane, into the viewer's own world. Caravaggio has "reread" this eucharistic story, suggesting by light and gesture that the body of Christ is present "throughout the created world, and the richness of the fruits [in a basket at the table's edge] suggests the beauty of this world, through contemplation of which the mind ascends to God."[209] By painting a biblical scene as though it were drawn directly from ordinary life, Caravaggio has purged the story of its familiar "visual rhetoric" and "transcendental messages," providing the viewer immediate access to meanings not mediated by the church's officials or the liturgy's "handlers."[210]

In sum, neither the Protestant Reformers nor the Catholic Counter-Reformers got their way when it came to the liturgy. Although Christians may have grown more intellectually "engaged" and "better prepared" for ritual, the miracle of a more active, informed participation in the liturgy did not necessarily happen for either group. The Reformation may indeed have been a "ritual process," but the process did not eliminate the "old-time religion." What emerged from the sixteenth century was a dual system of ritual languages, Protestant and Catholic, that became "persistent antagonists."[211] Far from dying out, moreover, eucharistic cult expanded and intensified among Catholics during the Counter-Reformation. "It became a synecdoche—the part that stood for the whole—of the community, strengthened by a reinvigorated, bishop-controlled, parish-based reformation of worship."[212]

Notes

[1]See Keith Christiansen, "The Arte Della Lana Altarpiece," in *Painting in Renaissance Siena 1420–1500*, ed. K. Christiansen, L. B. Kanter and C. B. Strehlke (New York: Metropolitan Museum of Art; New York: Harry Abrams, 1988) 64, 73–77. In 1448 Pope Nicholas V transferred the celebration of Corpus Christi in Siena from the Carmine to the cathedral church.

[2]See Enzo Carli, *Sassetta et le Maître de l'Osservanza* (Milan: A. Martello, 1957) 10. All three panels depicting the eucharist survive, although they are now located in different museums. The *Last Supper* (or *Institution of the Eucharist*) is in Siena at the Pinacoteca Nazionale; the *Miracle of the Holy Sacrament* is in the Bowes Museum, Barnard Castle, Durham, England; the *Burning of a Heretic* is at the National Gallery of Victoria in Melbourne, Australia.

[3]See 3.76.8. Aquinas was careful to note that the body and blood of Christ were really present in the sacramental species of bread and wine, but that this presence was not a "natural" one based on the local, physical ("quantitative," measurable) dimensions of Christ's body. Thus, Aquinas concluded that in these "miraculous appearances," Christ's "natural form" was not seen.

[4]These words are cited in translation from da Travale's chronicles in Christiansen, 77.

[5]See the "professio fidei in Eucharistiam Berengario praescripta" in H. Denziger and A. Schönmetzer, eds., *Enchiridion Symbolorum*, 33rd ed. (Rome: Herder, 1965), 690 (note that numbers refer to paragraphs, not pages). Hereafter this work is abbreviated DS, followed by the paragraph number. Berengarius was required to affirm that Christ is "sensually, not merely sacramentally" (*sensualiter, non solum sacramento*) present in the eucharistic species, and that when the faithful receive the sacrament, they truly break and tear Christ's body with their teeth (*corpus et sanguinem Domini nostri Iesu Christi esse . . . et frangi et fidelium dentibus atteri*).

[6]Miri Rubin, *Corpus Christi: The Eucharist in Late Medieval Culture* (New York: Cambridge University Press, 1991) 9.

[7]Rubin, 13.

[8]Woodburn O. Ross, ed., *Middle English Sermons*, Early English Text Society, no. 209 (New York: Oxford University Press, 1940; reprint, 1960) 127. This sermon probably dates from the late-fourteenth or early fifteenth century.

[9]This is a phrase found in one of Luther's early attacks on Roman eucharistic practice, *The Abomination of the Secret Mass* (1525). See A. R. Wentz, ed. *Luther's Works*, vol. 36 (Philadelphia: Fortress, 1959) 311; hereafter, LW 36.

[10]See Luther's 1523 treatise *The Adoration of the Sacrament* in LW 36:291.

[11]Trent was the first General Council to use the Latin noun *transsubstantiatio* in a formal decree. See the excerpts of the *Decretum de ss. Eucharistia* (from Session 13 of the Council, held on 11 October 1551), in DS, 1635-1661. Speaking of the "conversion" of the eucharistic bread and wine into Christ's body and blood, Trent affirmed "Quae conversio convenienter et proprie a sancta catholica Ecclesia transubstantiatio est appellata." It might be noted that Trent did not, technically, "define" transubstantiation as a Catholic dogma; rather, it affirmed that this term is "properly [*proprie*] and aptly" (*convenienter*, or, in Canon 2 appended to the Decree, *aptissime*) applied to the change of bread and wine into Christ's body and blood.

[12]I have discussed the rise of eucharistic confraternities and religious congregations of women and men in my *Cult and Controversy: The Worship of the Eucharist outside Mass* (Collegeville, Minn.: Liturgical Press, 1982) 206-210.

[13]See Virginia Reinburg, "Liturgy and the Laity in Late Medieval and Reformation France," *Sixteenth Century Journal* 33 (1992) 527. The rest of this paragraph and the next are drawn from this essay (pp. 527-542).

[14]On medieval lay participation at mass, see also Eamon Duffy, *The Stripping of the Altars: Traditional Religion in England 1400–1580* (New Haven, Conn.: Yale University Press, 1992) 91-130, 295-298.

[15]*The Canons and Decrees of the Council of Trent*, trans. H. J. Schroeder (St. Louis, Mo., and London: B. Herder, 1941; reprint, Rockford, Ill.: Tan Books, 1978) 148, emphasis added. For the Latin text of this canon, see DS, 1749.

[16]This would have been true whether the participants were wealthy and literate or poor and illiterate. As E. Duffy notes (p. 121), the difference between literate and illiterate experiences of religion have been exaggerated. Commenting on the kinds of devotional material found in medieval primers and Horae, he writes: "The world reflected in these Horae prayers and devotions, [is one] in which religion was a single but multifaceted and resonant symbolic house, within which rich and poor, simple and sophisticate could kneel side by side, using the same prayers and sharing the same hopes."

[17]Malcolm Lambert, *Medieval Heresy: Popular Movements from the Gregorian Reform to the Reformation*, 2nd ed. (Oxford: Blackwell, 1992) 85.

[18]Lambert, 87. For modern editions of important Catharist texts, see Christine Thouzellier, ed., *Livre des Deux Principes*, Sources chrétiennes 198 (Paris:

Cerf, 1973), and *Rituel Cathare*, Sources chrétiennes 236 (Paris: Cerf, 1977).

[19]Lambert, 146, 171.

[20]Lambert, 233.

[21]For the errors of Wyclif condemned at Constance, see DS, 1151-95. One of the denounced propositions reads "Christus non est in eodem sacramento identice et realiter in propria praesentia corporali" (Christ is not in this sacrament [that is, the eucharist] identically and really in his own proper bodily presence).

[22]James F. White, *A Brief History of Christian Worship* (Nashville, Tenn.: Abingdon, 1993) 105-106.

[23]White, 105.

[24]John Bossy, "The Mass as a Social Institution 1200-1700," *Past and Present* 100 (1983) 29-61. This essay originally appeared in French as "Essai de sociographie de la messe, 1200-1700," *Annales, Économies, Sociétés, Civilisations* 36 (1981) 44-70. Bossy's English version revises the earlier French article.

[25]I have discussed this point in greater detail in my essay "The Struggle of Religious Women for Eucharist," *Benedictines* 52 (1999) 12-25. Among the Beguines, however, the hunger for frequent communion cannot be characterized as "asocial."

[26]Bossy, 59.

[27]Bossy, 59.

[28]Bossy, 53.

[29]Bossy, 51.

[30]White, 107.

[31]Martin Luther, *The Adoration of the Sacrament* (LW 36:275) and *The Babylonian Captivity of the Church* (LW 36:27).

[32]Luther, *Babylonian Captivity*, LW 36:67.

[33]LW 36:18. Luther's opinions about the sacramentality of penance were ambiguous. James F. White notes that Luther, in writing *The Babylonian Captivity*, appeared to feel that the original meaning of penance had been forgotten in the medieval church, and that he "finally convinces himself that, lacking a material sign, it is not to be numbered among the dominical sacraments even though John 20:22-23 contains words of promise" (*Protestant Worship: Traditions in Transition* [Louisville, Ky.: Westminster John Knox, 1984] 39). The whole question of whether Luther viewed penance as a sacrament has been studied by Beverley Nitschke, "The Third Sacrament? Confession and Forgiveness in the *Lutheran Book of Worship*" (Ph.D. diss., University of Notre Dame, 1988).

³⁴LW 36:69.

³⁵See, for example, Bard Thompson, *Liturgies of the Western Church* (Cleveland, Ohio: World Publishing, 1961) 100.

³⁶Luther, *Formula Missae*, in Thompson, 106–122. Later citations of the *Formula Missae* are from this source.

³⁷Luther, *Deutsche Messe*, in Thompson, 123–137. Later citations of the *Deutsche Messe* are from this source.

³⁸Thompson, 103.

³⁹White, *Brief History*, 122.

⁴⁰For the phrase "Sacrament on the awtur," see the Easter sermon (22) in Ross, 127.

⁴¹Ross, 133 (sermon 23).

⁴²Ross, 126–127, 132 (sermon 22). In Middle English, to "housell" meant to administer the eucharist to a communicant. The Latin text is from 1 Corinthians 13:3: "If I give away everything I own, and if I hand my body over to burn, yet have not love, it profits me nothing." The "loueday" was "a day appointed for an attempt at settlement of a dispute" (p. 389).

⁴³Reinburg, 539–542.

⁴⁴Duffy, 92–93.

⁴⁵Duffy, 93. Duffy notes that frequent communion "was the prerogative of the few," and that frequent communicants—Margery Kempe, for example—were resented by their neighbors because they seemed to claim a "particular holiness of life" that separated them from other ("lesser") Christians.

⁴⁶Martin Luther, *The Misuse of the Mass*, LW 36:173.

⁴⁷LW 36:182–183.

⁴⁸The *Formula Missae* retains a short preface and recommends that the Consecration be followed by the singing of the Sanctus and the Benedictus, during which the consecrated species are elevated. The minister may "consecrate both bread and wine consecutively before he receives the bread; or between the consecration of the bread and wine he may communicate with the bread both himself and as many as desire it, and thereupon consecrate the wine and at length give to all to drink of it." The *Deutsche Messe* seems to eliminate the preface before the Consecration, while retaining the (German) Sanctus and elevation. Luther's preference in the *Deutsche Messe* is to consecrate the bread and then administer it to the people, then to consecrate the wine and administer the cup to the people.

⁴⁹Reinold (Jerome) Theisen, *Mass Liturgy and the Council of Trent* (Collegeville, Minn.: St. John's University Press, 1965) 7–8.

⁵⁰White, *Protestant Worship*, 42.

⁵¹See Ambrose, On the Sacraments, 4.14: "sermo Christi hoc conficit sacramentum"; Latin text in Bernard Botte, ed., *Ambroise de Milan: Des sacrements, des mystères*, Sources chrétiennes 25 bis (Paris: Cerf, 1961) 108–110. See discussion in Mitchell, *Cult and Controversy*, 56, 74, 146–147.

⁵²White, *Protestant Worship*, 42.

⁵³Luther, *Deutsche Messe*, in Thompson, 136–137.

⁵⁴Latin text in H. W. Baum et al., eds., *Ioannis Calvini opera quae supersunt omnia*, Corpus Reformatorum, vols. 29–87 (Braunschweig: A. Schwentschke, 1863–1900) 9:519: "Convenit etiam Christum re ipsa et efficaciter implere quidquid analogia signi et rei signatae postulat; ideoque vere nobis in Coena offerri communicationem cum eius corpore et sanguine, vel (quod idem valet) nobis arrham sub pane et vino proponi, quae nos faciat corporis et sanguinis Christi participes."

⁵⁵See Kilian McDonnell, *John Calvin, the Church, and the Eucharist* (Princeton, N.J.: Princeton University Press, 1967) 160–169.

⁵⁶McDonnell, 35. This is also one reason that Calvin opposed any notion of "secondary causality" in the sacraments; see pp. 167–169.

⁵⁷Translated in Arthur Cochrane, *Reformed Confessions of the Sixteenth Century* (London: SCM Press, 1966) 285–286; emphasis added. Distinctions among the kinds of eucharistic eating were common in medieval theology. Thus, for example, Aquinas distinguished spiritual from sacramental eating (see *Summa Theologiae*, 3.80.1). Likewise, Aquinas rejected a literal, natural, carnal eating of the Lord's body by communicants, insisting that *ipsum corpus Christi non frangitur* (the natural body of Christ is not broken) in the sacrament (3.77.7, ad 3).

⁵⁸*Institutes of the Christian Religion*, 4.17.19; English translation in *John Calvin: The Institutes of the Christian Religion*, ed. John T. McNeill, trans. Ford Lewis Battles, Library of Christian Classics, vols. 20–21 (Philadelphia: Westminster, 1960) 2:1381–1382. Note that in this passage Calvin seeks to eliminate both defective Roman views of local presence (Christ locally confined to bread and wine) and a certain Lutheran view that stressed the ubiquity of Christ's glorified body. *Institutes* is hereafter cited from this edition.

⁵⁹Translation by J. K. S. Reid in *John Calvin: Theological Treatises*, Library of Christian Classics 22 (Philadelphia: Westminster, 1954) 267.

⁶⁰Calvin, *Institutes*, 4.14.17; 2:1292.

⁶¹Calvin, *Institutes*, 4.14.16; 2:1292.

⁶²McDonnell, 178–179.

[63]Calvin, *Institutes*, 4.18.19; 2:1446.

[64]See Geddes MacGregor, *Corpus Christi. The Nature of the Church according to the Reformed Tradition* (Philadelphia: Westminster, 1958) 58, note 1, where the evidence from Calvin's works is assembled.

[65]Calvin, *Institutes*, 4.17.39; 2:1416.

[66]A collated and annotated translation of these texts may be found in Thompson, 197–210.

[67]Latin text in Peter Barth, ed., *Joannis Calvini Opera Selecta*, vol. 1 (Munich: Kaiser, 1926) 160.

[68]Thompson, 192.

[69]See text in Thompson, 205–208.

[70]Christopher Elwood, *The Body Broken: The Calvinist Doctrine of the Eucharist and the Symbolization of Power in Sixteenth-Century France* (New York: Oxford University Press, 1999) 147–148.

[71]See Elwood, 151–156. See also *Registers of the Consistory of Geneva in the Time of Calvin*, ed. Robert Kingdon et al., trans. M. Wallace McDonald (Grand Rapids, Mich.: Eerdmans; H. H. Meeter Center for Calvin Studies, 2000).

[72]Elwood, 151. For the connection between eucharist and ethics, see also Brian A. Gerrish, *Grace and Gratitude: The Eucharistic Theology of John Calvin* (Minneapolis, Minn.: Fortress, 1993).

[73]Translated from Calvin's 1551 preface by Reinburg, 545, note 37.

[74]Reinburg, 545.

[75]Theisen, 10.

[76]White, *Protestant Worship*, 58

[77]White, *Protestant Worship*, 59. White observes that the word *is* would probably not have been expressed "in the Aramaic spoken at the Last Supper."

[78]For example, Theisen (p. 14) speaks of an evolution in Zwingli's thought that caused him to abandon an "essential feature of the [Roman] Mass, the real presence."

[79]From Zwingli's *Attack on the Canon of the Mass*; trans. in Thompson, 142.

[80]White, *Protestant Worship*, 60.

[81]A convenient English translation of portions of Zwingli's *Epicheiresis* may be found in R. C. D. Jasper and G. J. Cuming, *Prayers of the Eucharist: Early and Reformed*, 3rd rev. ed. (New York: Pueblo, 1987) 183–186.

[82]Thompson, 143, 145.

[83]On these early efforts, see F. E. Brightman, *The English Rite*, 2 vols. (London: Rivingtons, 1915) 1:xlix–lxviii.

[84]Thompson, 228.

[85]Brightman, 1:lxxii–lxxvi. Brightman discusses the sources of this new communion rite in detail. Most of the text may be found in 2:650–652, 652–658, 696–700, 710.

[86]See *The First and Second Prayer Books of Edward VI*, intro. Douglas Harrison, Everyman's Library (London: Dent, 1910) 212. Citations from the 1549 and 1552 Prayer Books come from this source. For a brief history of Cranmer's two versions of the Prayer Book, see Brightman, 1:lxxviii–clxv.

[87]Gustav Aulen, *Christus Victor*, trans. A. G. Hebert (London: SPCK, 1931) 101; and Aidan Kavanagh, *The Concept of Eucharistic Memorial in the Canon Revisions of Thomas Cranmer, Archbishop of Canterbury, 1533–1556* (St. Meinrad, Ind.: Abbey Press, 1964) 203. For the eucharistic theology that undergirded Cranmer's 1552 revisions, see Kavanagh, 158–168.

[88]Kavanagh, 168, 170. The formula "Take and eate" is found for the administration of communion in the 1552 book.

[89]White, *Brief History*, 125. Kavanagh (p. 218) remarks that "Cranmer was basically 'Swiss' in his eucharistic outlook," and explains such in pages 129–148.

[90]Peter Newman Brooks, *Thomas Cranmer's Doctrine of the Eucharist: An Essay in Historical Development*, 2nd ed. (London: Macmillan, 1992) 107.

[91]John E. Cox, ed., *Writings and Disputations of Thomas Cranmer, Archbishop of Canterbury, Martyr, 1556, Relative to the Sacrament of the Lord's Supper*, Parker Society, vol. 15 (Cambridge: Cambridge University Press, 1844) 271.

[92]Thomas Cranmer, *A Defence of the True and Catholic Doctrine of the Sacrament of the Body and Blood of our Saviour Christ*, in *Archbishop Cranmer on the True and Catholic Doctrine and Use of the Sacrament of the Lord's Supper*, ed. Charles H. H. Wright (London: Chas. J. Thynne, 1907) 1.16; 25.

[93]Cranmer, *Defence*, 3.15; 195.

[94]Cranmer, *Defence*, 4.3; 202.

[95]Kavanagh, 135.

[96]Kavanagh, 217.

[97]Duffy, 464. As Duffy notes, Cranmer's emphasis on communion meant that "the priest was to celebrate communion afresh in the sick person's house, always provided that there was 'a goode nombre to receyve the communion' with them. The [prayer] book did not flinch from one inevitable consequence of this provision, that lonely people with no close neighbours would be unable to receive communion on their deathbeds. To these, as to any dying person who for one reason or another could not re-

ceive their last housel, the curate was to explain that true repentance, firm faith, and hearty thanks for the benefits of Christ would be just as profitable to their soul's health, 'althoughe he doe not recyve the Sacrament with his mouth.' The one exception allowed for in the prayer-book was in time of plague, 'when none of the parysh or neighbours can be gotten to communicate wyth the syck in theyr houses.' At such a time the priest alone might communicate with the dying person" (p. 474).

98For a succinct synopsis of the Reformers' critique of medieval practice and their defense of infant baptism, see J. D. C. Fisher, "Lutheran, Anglican, and Reformed Rites [of Initiation]," in *The Study of Liturgy*, ed. C. Jones et al., rev. ed. (New York: Oxford University Press, 1992) 154–155. A convenient summary of the rites of baptism in the churches of the Reformation may be found under "Baptism" (pp. 41–52) in Paul Bradshaw, ed., *The New Westminster Dictionary of Liturgy and Worship* (Louisville, Ky.: Westminster John Knox, 2002). See also Hans Hillerbrand, ed., *Encyclopedia of Protestantism* (New York: Routledge, 2003), "Baptism," by Geoffrey Wainwright.

99White, *Brief History*, 109. On the Anabaptists, see pp. 112–114; and, in this book, chapter 19.

100For translations, see Ulrich S. Leupold, ed., *Luther's Works*, vol. 53 (Philadelphia: Fortress, 1965) 95–109. J. D. C. Fisher, "Lutheran Anglican and Reformed Rites," 155 observes that Luther's 1523 rite is notable for its "Flood Prayer," which treats the biblical stories of flood and exodus as types of Christian baptism.

101Typically, in medieval rites, the "effeta" was done by the priest touching the baby's sense organs (nose, ears) with saliva and so declaring the child "opened" to the "odor of sweetness." See the rite of the Sarum Manual printed in J. D. C. Fisher, *Christian Initiation: Baptism in the Medieval West*, Alcuin Club Collections, no. 47 (London: SPCK, 1965) 164.

102For Calvin's rite, see J. D. C. Fisher, *Christian Initiation: The Reformation Period*, Alcuin Club Collections, no. 51 (London: SPCK, 1970) 112–117. The English editor of Luther's 1523 rite notes that three modes of baptizing were practiced in the late-medieval and Reformation period: *immersio*, *superfusio* (the child is held over the font while water is poured over him or her profusely), and *infusio* (the child's head is dipped into the water). See LW 53:100. *Affusio* (pouring of water onto the baby's head, sometimes in the form of a cross) was also practiced.

103LW 53:97 (1523); 53:107–108 (1526).

104See Calvin, *Institutes*, 2.1.5–8; 1:246–251.

105Calvin, *Institutes*, 4.15.1; 2:1304. Here Calvin was implicitly criticizing Zwingli, who seemed to regard baptism as nothing more than an external initiatory ceremony devoid of any real internal significance.

106Calvin, *Institutes*, 4.15.1–2; 2:1303–1304. The scriptural reference is to Ephesians 5:26.

107See the rubrics of the Sarum Manual in Fisher, *Christian Initiation: Baptism in the Medieval West*, 169, 171, 177.

108White, *Brief History*, 111.

109Calvin, "Draft Ecclesiastical Ordinances, 1541," in *John Calvin: Theological Treatises*, 66; and White, *Brief History*, 111.

110LW 53:11.

111Duffy, 464.

112LW 53:13; cf. 37–38.

113See Hughes Oliphant Old, "Daily Prayer in the Reformed Church of Strasbourg, 1525–1530," *Worship* 52 (1978) 121.

114See the initial rubrics in Thompson, 197.

115Barbara Jo Douglas, "Prayers Made with Song: The Genevan Psalter, 1562–1994," in *Pledges of Jubilee: Essays on the Arts and Culture, in Honor of Calvin G. Seerveld*, ed. Lambert Zuidervaart and Henry Luttikhuizen (Grand Rapids, Mich.: Eerdmans, 1995) 293–294.

116Douglas, 294. Douglas is quoting Walter Blankenburg, "Church Music in Reformed Europe," in *Protestant Church Music: A History*, ed. F. Blume (London: Gollancz, 1975) 520.

117Douglas, 305.

118Old, 137.

119Old, 136.

120LW 53:115. The biblical echo is to Ephesians 5:32.

121One may note that the Prayer Book services retained the couple's exchange of vows, in the famous words: "I N. take thee N. to my wedded wife, to haue and to hold from thys daye forwarde, for better, for wurse, for richer, for poorer, in sickenesse, and in health, to loue & to cherishe, till death vs departe: according to Gods holy ordeinaunce: And therto I plight thee my trouth." Luther's 1529 rite requires the couple to voice publicly their consent, but they do not "exchange vows."

122LW 53:111.

123Schroeder, 185.

124Editor's comments in LW 53:116. On the matter of Luther's ambivalent attitude toward the sacramentality of penance, see note 33 above.

[125]LW 53:117–118. See also Luther's *How One Should Teach Common Folk to Shrive Themselves* (1531); LW 53:119–121.

[126]See White, *Brief History*, 129. It should be noted that even within early medieval Catholicism, ways of confessing and seeking forgiveness existed that did not always involve clerical mediation. See Cyrille Vogel, *Le pécheur et la pénitence au Moyen-Âge* (Paris: Cerf, 1969) 15–35.

[127]Thompson, 197–198.

[128]On the way medieval English laity viewed the "last rites," see Duffy, 313–327.

[129]LW 53:125. An optional prayer, which the ordinator may say "if he desires or time permits," is also provided; see p. 126.

[130]See editor's comments in LW 53:122.

[131]Calvin, *Institutes*, 4.19.28; 2:1475–1476.

[132]For the text of the 1550 Ordinal, see Brightman, 2:928–1017. For Bucer as a primary source for the Ordinal, see Paul F. Bradshaw, *The Anglican Ordinal*, Alcuin Club Collections, no. 53 (London: SPCK, 1971) 18–36.

[133]*Summa Theologiae*, 3, supp. 37.2; and Bradshaw, 29. The question of what constituted the precise "matter" of holy orders continued to vex Catholic theology until the twentieth century. Finally, in *Sacramentum Ordinis* (1948), Pius XII declared the matter closed by asserting that the "matter" of ordination is the imposition of hands by the bishop.

[134]Bradshaw, 24.

[135]The first ecumenical council, at Nicaea, in 325, involved probably 250 bishops (though the traditional number given is 318).

[136]See Theisen, 29–85. The Second Vatican Council (1962–1965) published its constitution on the liturgy (*Sacrosanctum Concilium*) on 4 December 1963, four centuries to the day after the closing of the Council of Trent (4 December 1563).

[137]See A. Duval, *Des sacrements au Concile de Trente* (Paris: Cerf, 1985) 73. The opening debate took place at Bologna, Italy, from 29 July to 22 August 1547.

[138]Schroeder, 73. Latin text in *Concilium Tridentium Diariorum, Actorum, Epistularum, Tractatuum Nova Collectio*, ed. Goerres Society, 13 vols. (Freiburg: Herder, 1901–1964) 7, pt. 1, 200, lines 30–33. For records of discussions that took place concerning various parts of this decree and its accompanying canons, see 7, pt. 2, 95–236. Hereafter this work will be cited as CT.

[139]Schroeder, 75; CT 7, pt. 1, 201, lines 42–45. Although the participial adjective *transsubstantiatis* had

been used at the Fourth Council of the Lateran in 1215, Trent's decree marks the first appearance of the noun *transsubstantiatio* in a conciliar document.

[140]For the views discussed by the theologians, see CT 7, pt. 1, 111–193.

[141]Schroeder, 76; CT 7, pt. 1, 202, lines 2–4.

[142]CT 7, pt. 1, 227, lines 42–45; 228, lines 46–47; my translation.

[143]Schroeder, 87; CT 7, pt. 1, 207, lines 33–45. It might be noted that a small number of Lutherans ("Protestantes seu Lutherani") were in fact present during sessions of Trent's second period in 1551–1552. For their names, see CT 7, pt. 1, 542, lines 30–40.

[144]Hus himself may not have been pressing the issue of communion from the cup, but some of his moderate followers—known as "Calixtines"—contended that the laity should receive communion in both kinds.

[145]For the text of this papal revocation, see G. Constant, *Concession à l'Allemagne de la Communion sous les deux espèces*, 2 vols. (Paris: E. de Boccard, 1923) 2:771–772.

[146]Schroeder, 133; DS, 1728. On the history of the theory of eucharistic concomitance in the West, see James J. Megivern, *Concomitance and Communion: A Study in Eucharistic Doctrine and Practice*, Studia Friburgensia, n.s. 33 (Fribourg, Switzerland: University Press, 1963).

[147]Schroeder, 132–133; DS, 1727.

[148]Schroeder, 134; DS, 1730.

[149]Schroeder, 135; Latin text in *Canones et Decreta Sacrosancti Oecumenici Concilii Tridentini* (Rome: Sacred Congregation for the Propagation of the Faith, 1845) 112. Eventually, in 1562, the Council left the question of whether to grant use of the cup to the discretion of the pope. See Schroeder, 159; *Canones et Decreta Tridentini*, 133.

[150]Translation in Theisen, 134, note 59; CT 7, pt. 1, 377, lines 9–12.

[151]Theisen, 40–41.

[152]Bishop Francis Manrique of Orense, for example, was inclined to favor a reshaping of the mass to "bring it into closer resemblance to Christ's Mass," and he felt that vernacular languages should be permitted in the celebration of the eucharist. See Theisen, 45.

[153]The Latin text of this proposed decree ("*Doctrina de sacrificio missae proposita examinanda patribus 20. Ianuarii 1552, sed non conclusa neque firmata*") is printed in CT 7, pt. 1, 475, line 5 to 485, line 14.

[154]Theisen, 47; CT 7, pt. 1, 482, lines 27–31.

[155]These circumstances are discussed in Theisen, 51–52.

[156]Theisen, 52.

[157]Specifically 16 July 1562; the significance of this material on holy communion will be discussed below.

[158]Schroeder, 145–46; *Canones et Decreta Tridentini*, 121.

[159]Schroeder, 148; *Canones et Decreta Tridentini*, 123–124.

[160]Reinburg, 545.

[161]Schroeder, 150–152; *Canones et Decreta Tridentini*, 125–127; and Josef Jungmann, *The Mass of the Roman Rite*, trans. F. A. Brunner, 2 vols. (New York: Benziger, 1951; reprint, Westminster, Md.: Christian Classics, 1992) 1:133–134. For the work of this commission, which provided a comprehensive collection of reform ideas, see CT 8, 916–921.

[162]Schroeder, 150; *Canones et Decreta Tridentini*, 125.

[163]Schroeder, 151; *Canones et Decreta Tridentini*, 126.

[164]See Schroeder, 154–155; *Canones et Decreta Tridentini*, 222. See also H. Jedin, "Das Konzil von Trient und die Reform des Römischen Messbuches," *Liturgisches Leben* 6, nos. 1–2 (1939) 51. Jedin notes that as the council drew to a close, participants despaired of tackling a project as comprehensive as liturgical reform.

[165]In the first conciliar period, Trent published its decree on the sacraments in general and on baptism and confirmation specifically (3 March 1547); in the second period appeared the decree on the eucharist discussed earlier in this chapter (11 October 1551), as well as decrees on penance and "extreme unction" (25 November 1551); in the final period the bishops published decrees on communion (16 July 1562), the mass as sacrifice (17 September 1562), holy orders (15 July 1563), and marriage (11 November 1563). As I have noted, however, the thrust of all these decrees was theological, canonical, and disciplinary, rather than liturgical.

[166]See the comments of the bishop of Sinigaglia, CT 1, 502, lines 23–26. See also Jedin, 33. Ecclesiastics of the time recognized, too, that with the advent of print technology, it would be possible to "clean up" these books and create more uniform editions.

[167]See CT 13, 610; cf. Jedin, 37.

[168]Jungmann, 1:135, notes that the pope had begun preparing a reform in 1564.

[169]Jungmann, 1:135. Jedin (pp. 52–54) gathers together some hints about who was doing what on the papal commission.

[170]See Jedin, 52.

[171]Jungmann, 1:135.

[172]Jungmann, 1:135.

[173]Latin text in M. Sodi and A. M. Triacca, eds., *Missale Romanum. Editio Princeps (1570)* (Vatican City: Libreria Editrice Vaticana, 1998) 3–4. The text of this bull was printed as part of the "front matter" in all subsequent editions of the missal until 1970.

[174]"unum in Ecclesia Dei psallendi modum, unum Missae celebrandae ritum esse maxime deceat" (*Missale Romanum*, 3).

[175]"eruditis delectis viris onus hoc demandandum duximus, qui quidem diligenter collatis omnibus cum vetustis nostrae Vaticanae Bibliothecae aliisque undique conquisitis, emendatis atque incorruptis codicibus, necnon veterum consultis ac probatorum auctorum scriptis, qui de sacro eorundem rituum instituto monumenta nobis reliquerunt" (*Missale Romanum*, 3).

[176]"ad pristinam . . . Patrum normam ac ritum restituerunt" (*Missale Romanum*, 3).

[177]*Missale Romanum*, 3–4.

[178]On this point, see Edward Muir, *Ritual in Early Modern Europe* (New York: Cambridge University Press, 1997) 155–262.

[179]As Jungmann notes (1:137), "the self-evident idea, that the development which had taken place meanwhile, separating the present from the *pristina sanctorum Patrum norma* should not be put aside as long as it did not disturb the groundplan but rather unfolded it," never seems to have occurred to the pope or his commission.

[180]See Anton Mayer, "Renaissance, Humanismus, und Liturgie," *Jahrbuch für Liturgiewissenschaft* 14 (1934) 123–171.

[181]Mayer, 158.

[182]See M. Sodi and A.M. Triacca, eds., *Breviarium Romanum. Editio Princeps (1568)* (Vatican City: Libreria Editrice Vaticana, 2000) 3. The pope also sounded another of Trent's reformist themes—specifically, the need to overcome clerical ignorance about the church's rites and ceremonies.

[183]*Breviarium Romanum*, 170–171.

[184]See Constant, 1:416–531, for a detailed account of the events leading up to the papal decision.

[185]See Constant, 1:530–531, note 1, for an account of this consistory. The imperial party apparently felt (as perhaps Pius IV did as well) that Germany could be "brought back into the Catholic fold" if the cup were granted. Emperor Ferdinand was eventually succeeded by Maximillian II.

[186]The suppression of communion *sub utraque specie* happened over a period of several decades: first in Bavaria (1571), then in Austria (1584), Hungary (1604), and Bohemia (1621–1622). In some places in Austria, the cup continued to be used, although the practice was combated by Rome. See Constant, 1:687–769.

[187]For the Latin text, see Constant, 2:1042–1043; my translation.

[188]There was a limit to the liturgical housecleaning that popes after Trent were willing to accept. Thus, Pius V complained about those who had "fled" to the breviary of Cardinal Francisco de Quiñones, which restored a weekly reading of the Psalter, greatly shortened and simplified the daily offices, and ran to more than a hundred editions after it appeared in 1535 until it was suppressed in 1568. See *Breviarum Romanum 1568*, 3. See also White, *Brief History*, 118.

[189]*Breviarum Romanum 1568*, 3 (my translation).

[190]Pope Paul V, "Apostolicae Sedi," the apostolic constitution introducing the *Rituale Romanum* (1614), as reprinted in *Rituale Romanum* (Ratisbon: F. Pustet, 1929) vi; my translation. The 1614 *Rituale* was largely the work of the learned Cardinal Julius Santorio, who had labored on the book under five different popes, from 1570 until his death in 1602. See Balthasar Fischer, "Das Rituale Romanum (1614–1964): Die Schicksale eines liturgischen Buches," *Trierer Theologische Zeitschrift* 73 (1964) 257.

[191]*Rituale Romanum 1614*, vi–vii.

[192]Fischer, "Das Rituale Romanum," 262.

[193]See A. Ward and C. Johnson, eds., *Pontificale Romanum*, Ephemerides Liturgicae Subsidia, 103 (Rome: C.L.V.–Edizioni Liturgiche, 1999) 8: "omissis, quae sic suppressimus et abolevium, ceteris omnibus Pontificalibus." Ward and Johnson have edited the Pontifical according to the *editio typica* of 1962, although they note that the book remained substantially the same as it had been in 1596 until Pius XII established a commission for reform of the liturgy (p. xxiv). The principal changes introduced by the Commissio Piana affect the rites for Holy Week and the Easter vigil (which had been restored in 1951 and 1956) and the rituals for the dedication of a church.

[194]*Rituale Romanum 1614*, vii.

[195]Fischer ("Das Rituale Romanum," 264) notes the well-known controversy over the "Chinese rites," but also calls attention to a local ritual published in Nagasaki, Japan, in 1605 by the Portuguese Jesuit missionary Luis de Cerqueira.

[196]*Rituale Romanum 1614*, 5–65, esp. 49.

[197]*Rituale Romanum 1614*, 67–75.

[198]*Rituale Romanum 1614*, 226; my translation.

[199]See *Pontificale Romanum*, 316–359.

[200]*Pontificale Romanum*, 340.

[201]Helen Langdon, *Caravaggio: A Life* (New York: Farrar, Straus and Giroux, 1998) 5.

[202]Langdon, 234–235.

[203]Peter Robb, *M: The Man Who Became Caravaggio* (New York: Henry Holt, 1999) 31.

[204]Robb, 32–33.

[205]Robb, 87.

[206]Robb, 246–251.

[207]Robb, 147.

[208]Muir, 155–181, from which the following passages are cited.

[209]Landon, 231.

[210]Robb, 128.

[211]Muir, 198.

[212]Muir, 212. See also Muir's analysis of how Catholic ritual reform after Trent took root in parishes (pp. 204–212).

9

The Age of Revolutions

CONRAD L. DONAKOWSKI

"How can we have religion amid these caricatures?" asked the believing but enlightened archbishop of Vienna in 1783 as he looked about his ornate cathedral during a
sermon. In the crypt of a nearby church, the plain tomb of the archbishop's sovereign,
the enlightened despot Emperor Joseph II, stands beside the baroque sarcophagus of
his pious mother, Empress Maria Theresa. The rationalist son still seems to be asking
his traditionalist mother the same question.

Minds, Hearts, and Nations

Churches today still debate the issues defined during the Age of Reason and Revolutions, yet this era has been relatively overlooked by liturgical historians. Compared to
the privileged definitions of the patristic era, the labyrinthine syntheses of the Middle
Ages, or the schisms during the Renaissance and Reformation, the intellectual and
affective as well as the industrial and political revolutions of the modern world may
seem merely temporal matters. Actually, they are often applications of attitudes taught
through Christian religious practices.

Concerning worship, Christianity began a three-sided debate following the 1648
Peace of Westphalia whereby secular rulers put an end to the wars of religion. (In
Britain, the equivalent date was 1660, when the monarchy was restored.) The first
party to the debate was the party of the mind. Tired of the violence of the Reformation era, many thoughtful leaders now sought to make Christianity reasonable. According to these rationalistic reformers, worship should be reformed not only to revive
the supposed simplicity of the Early Church, but also to make Christianity more useful by minimizing distractions from its ethical teachings. Thereby many Christian
leaders were agents of the Age of Reason, the Enlightenment.

The second party was of the heart. They were "enthusiasts" in the strict sense of
the word. As in the original Greek meaning of this theological term, they sought the
indwelling of God through religious experience beyond verbal definition. Often they
favored a style of worship centered on small gatherings where individuals could speak
up and pour out their feelings. Sometimes pious reasons of the heart complemented
Enlightenment elitism and sometimes they reinforced communal folk traditions.
Though sometimes starting, like the Wesleys (the founders of Methodism, discussed
below), from zeal to invigorate established churches, enthusiasts always yearned for
the heartfelt personality of Jesus' church. Whether rebelling against the high-and-dry

Imperial tombs. The tomb of Emperor Joseph II in front of the tomb of Empress Maria Theresa in the Kapuzinergruft, Vienna. PHOTOGRAPH © CONRAD L. DONAKOWSKI

preaching of some Protestant denominations or the arid rubricism of much Roman Catholicism, all aimed at intensity of religious experience.[1] Despite the conflicting theological distinctions that separated them, the partisans of the heart included Pietists, Quakers, the Moravian Brethren, the Methodists, and many other new Protestant movements. Baroque Roman Catholics, too, psychologically all-embracing within their triumphalist liturgies or worldwide syncretic devotional practices, may be included among the enthusiasts because of their emotionally intense retreats, devotions, and artistic—even theatrical—practices. Among enthusiasts, the charismatic roles of personal (including communal), poetic (including oratorical), and artistic (particularly musical) incarnations of the Word in worship were a key to their strong appeal, though often the despair of theologians preoccupied with doctrinal distinctions.

The third party to the debate was the nascent nation–state, which sought to control religious ritual as a means of achieving national unity. In the medieval past, ecclesiastical leaders had often bested secular rulers in contests such as the Investiture Controversy between Pope Gregory VII (Hildebrand, risen from low estate; reigned 1073–1085) and Holy Roman Emperor Henry IV (reigned 1056–1106). A similar collision in Britain led to the martyrdom of Thomas à Becket (c. 1118–1170) that boomeranged against Henry II of England (reigned 1154–1189). Later, however, nationalistic champions such as the Anglican Henry VIII (reigned 1509–1547) and the Gallicans Henry IV (reigned 1589–1610) and Louis XIV (reigned 1643–1715) and Tsar Peter the Great of Russia (reigned 1689–1725) began to turn the tables by employing religious practices as tools to insinuate the divine right of kings. By the end of the eighteenth century, political and commercial-industrial revolutions worked to enhance the cult of the nation–state.

In the nineteenth century, the three-way debate continued. According to the liberal heirs of the Enlightenment, the achievements of science, technology, and capitalism seemed to require that religious worship be pared down. Perhaps it should be limited to discussion of useful social issues. Worship might be supported as a cultural amenity, like a museum. Or it might continue to serve as emblem of social cohesion. On the contrary, argued the Romantic cultural critics, coldhearted modern industrial society needed even more to celebrate inscrutable tradition and incomprehensible feelings as avenues to realities that transcend earthly empires. Meanwhile the national state emerged as the most powerful cultural force wherever Western civilization reached. Reasons of the mind, the heart, and the nation conspired to form, reflect, and communicate a complex cultural system expressed in public worship.[2]

Enlightenment Rationalism and Counter-Reformation Catholicism

"Since there is nothing man can give God, there is no particular duty we owe God," wrote the premier modern philosopher, Immanuel Kant (1724–1804), concerning worship.[3] This dictum epitomizes the critical humanism at work even within the churches during the eighteenth-century Age of Reason, the Enlightenment. The urge to revise Christian worship was linked to an impulse that would impel the French Revolutionaries to end it. However different in various countries and situations, sharp criticism was everywhere aimed against apparently irrational traditions, claims of special privilege, and closed canons that seemed no longer to serve any useful purpose.

Although the Enlightenment is sometimes pictured as the assassin of Christian civilization, it was actually a logical outgrowth of an intellectual tradition handed down by the Christian Church in the West, ever seeking to explain the unexplainable. The foundational philosopher of the Enlightenment, Sir Isaac Newton (1642–1727), was seeking not to undermine faith but to "justify the ways of God to men" (to use the poet John Milton's phrase). Few philosophers and theologians of the day questioned the ancient Platonic paradigm whereby religious ritual ought not to be left to mere artisans. Religious authorities still insisted on a psychological hierarchy of intellect over emotions in human nature, an artistic hierarchy of text over tone in music, an ecclesiological hierarchy of clerical over lay, male over female, and rubrics over imagination.

Debate was sharpest over Catholic worship because rationalistic critics found so much to criticize in the Roman Catholicism of the baroque and rococo eras. To be sure, the core of Catholic teaching and practice after the Council of Trent (1545–1563) emphasized the essentials of the sacramental system centered on the real presence of Jesus Christ in the eucharist, "body, blood, soul, and divinity," brought to earth through the mediation of his ordained priest. The liturgical panoply associated with the Catholic tradition appealed to sight, sound, smell, taste, touch, and every aspect of the imagination. Yet this artistic apparatus was always ancillary. The fixed rubrics that controlled every word and movement of the priest were not open to new modes of interpretation that might diminish priestly powers as the Protestants had done.

On the periphery of the liturgy, however, there flourished a dense network of activities by confraternities, sodalities, and religious communities that blended the pope-to-priest hierarchical system with popular religion and artistic creativity around the globe. The relationship between the strictly controlled priestly liturgy and its ancillary activities was often strained. This led to the ironic situation whereby, for example, the musicians who breathed life into the petrified rubrics of the Tridentine ceremonial find themselves reproached for "sins of the choir," as though a servant class, composers, conspired to prevent congregational singing of the official liturgy.

Baroque visual artists and their rococo successors, too, have been roundly condemned for overactive imaginations that sculpted far too many distracting stucco saints squirming in ecstasy. Like the gaudy gothic figures of the Middle Ages, baroque art and architecture has the reputation of bad taste among classically oriented critics who overlook the fact that the idealized ancient buildings often taken for models were actually in their own day brightly painted and decorated all over. By combining *l'esprit géométrique* of the Enlightenment with a prudish Platonic paradigm common among academic liturgists, though not among the Catholic peoples of the world, it has come to pass that the liturgies and music of the seventeenth through nineteenth centuries are reputed "disasters."[4]

In fact, baroque art and music may have saved the Counter-Reformation Roman Church and its liturgy from marginalization to the fringes of Western civilization. From a more holistic, anthropological perspective, what really happened is that the people were communicating—actively participating—through media beyond words, "riting beyond writing."[5] As Latin had been a primary means of maintaining church unity in the feudal centrifuge, it remained so in the face of the nation–state. Preelectronic acoustics, majority illiteracy in a society as yet unable to provide books for everyone, and churches without furniture for the congregation to sit still in and listen required a liturgy that depended on media other than the literal or oratorical. Few liturgical critics, who are always serious men of letters, were willing to grant that so playful a trinket as, for example, Italianate operatic masses could contain of themselves anything morally instructive or liturgically worthy. Yet, the composers were speaking through music of the Christian, as well as humanistic, dignity of men and women. By presenting the best music in church and appealing frankly to the emotions of the laity, as well as to the intellect of experts, composers and performers were revitalizing a humanizing tendency in Western myth and ritual. They were composing in the tradition of apostolic Pentecostal glossolalia (Acts 2:1-13), patristic mystagogia, medieval mystery/morality plays, and renaissance/reformed biblical vigor—each in its own way alive to an essential aspect of human spirituality.

Ordinary listeners could understand this concert style—with its clear melodic line and homophonic, dance-like accompaniment—more easily than the labyrinths that composers had constructed based on the rules of counterpoint. Classical music was, therefore, originally in part a folk style that said "Sursum corda" to the drama-and procession-loving Catholics of Europe. Missionaries overseas found that such a psychologically all-embracing style of worship appealed to the peoples of the globe.[6] This "lift up your hearts" may have been among the first romanticisms, that is, an affective revolution against the Platonic hierarchy of abstraction over experience. In those lands where literature was closely censored, humanism was usually more evident in music. In this case, as in others, the Roman Church knew how to absorb a heterodox element.

In *Amadeus*, the twentieth-century play, later film, by Peter Schafer, the title character representing Wolfgang Amadeus Mozart (1756–1791) obscenely insults His Excellency the Archbishop of Salzburg, who dislikes Amadeus's church music. In another scene—probably more true—Emperor Joseph II says that the composer's music has "too many notes." Despite the musician's bad manners, today's sympathies probably lie with the upstart. For he was asserting the rights of the underdog. Liturgically, he was proclaiming the value of imagination against narrow-minded literalism. Yet, the bishop and emperor were modernizers (*Aufklärer* in German) trying to streamline religious practices in order to communicate the Enlightenment to the populace through

Vierzehnheiligen. Nave of the Vierzehnheiligen church, near Banz in Franconia, Germany. Built by Balthasar Neumann (1687–1753), the pilgrimage church is dedicated to the fourteen "auxiliary saints," who are invoked in aid of various human needs. ERICH LESSING/ART RESOURCE, NY

the liturgy, the only mass medium that reached every social class and every village.[7] "Josephinism" and its cognates in other lands, trying to modernize, influenced subsequent liturgical reforms.[8]

The Enlightenment proposed a systematic revision of Christian worship. According to the humanistic principles found in Kant and applied to the reform of eighteenth-century liturgy, the goal of a cult should be found on earth, in the education and edification of humanity. Because specific ritual forms are not essentials of religion but accidents, the best rites would be formed not by tradition or divine mandate, but by reasoned investigation. Such investigation was the explicit purpose of many periodicals and books published in the late eighteenth century. In 1784 the initial article in *Seilers Liturgisches Magazin* (published at Erlangen in northern Bavaria) stated that it would circulate all opinions about religious rites because public debate would be good for liturgical studies. Though most of the articles in this and similar German periodicals were by and for Lutherans, the *Magazin* included articles on Catholic, Reformed, and Jewish rites. Although only eight issues of Seiler's quarterly were published, other periodicals soon took up the same study.[9] By the turn into the nineteenth century, there were periodicals by and for musicians, as well theological journals, debating issues of liturgical reform. Soon Germans of every ideological—not just religious—persuasion were offering suggestions about how public rites, festivals, and schools might help to transform the still-feudal German principalities into a unified nation capable of standing up to the French.

Judging from the number of published proposals suggesting improvement in the liturgies of various German religious groups, the year 1811 was the climax of the controversy over liturgical reform, coinciding with the War of Liberation against Napoleon's invading French armies bent on subordinating religious worship to imperial propaganda. Around that pivotal year, liturgical reform agendas turned Romantic. They began to look to national folk cultures as weapons wherewith to repel, rather than imitate, the Enlightenment.

In the contest between the Enlightenment and baroque Catholicism, the German lands lay culturally midway between the skeptical French intelligentsia and the solidly Counter-Reformation lands to the east and south. Catholicism used every conceivable means to fill the people's minds with lively images calculated to make them loyal children of Holy Mother the Church. This symbolic system extended prayer from the altar into every situation and place. The crucifix or saintly image placed not only in churches but in a corner of every room (taverns included), on every street corner, and in every farmer's field became a barrier more to the *Aufklärung* than to Protestantism. Surrounding the liturgy itself were such paraliturgical activities as processions, pilgrimages, and passion plays [see color plates 17 and 18]. Yet, such a pageantry might seem excessive.

A good example of the critical—even satirical—spirit abroad among educated Catholic clergy during the Enlightenment were parodies of Good Friday Passion plays like the one still performed every ten years in Oberammergau, Germany. Every Catholic town once had such pageantry, intended to involve the entire populace in the acting-out of Christ's passion and death. *A Bavarian Delight: Consisting of Worldly and Spiritual Comedies, Examples, and Satires*, published in 1782 by the disillusioned Benedictine, Anton von Bucher, included a "Sketch for a rural Good Friday Procession, together with a lively and spiritual prologue to the Passion Play."[10] Bucher's piece caricatured the ubiquitous Catholic paraliturgical devotions. In the procession, following the guilds and fraternities in their regalia, came a slapstick vignette of ancient Roman history mocking popular Christian notions with an absurdly pompous mounted emperor; then came a rampaging devil—always a crowd-pleaser. Next came Jews who insult the Lord, but are confounded by a preposterous miracle in reply. The parade was punctuated with interpolated irrelevant musical numbers; each episode was to be labeled with placards of misquotations from scripture supposedly commenting on the action. Although Protestants might view such iconoclastic burlesquing of ecclesiastical imagery as merely an extension of their own satires of popery during the Reformation, in Catholic lands such criticism struck at the very foundation of the Old Regime.

The argument over religious traditions and celebrations was keenest over music and everything that it represented. According to the classical aesthetic hierarchy, music was the language of the passions and therefore irrational. In the social hierarchy of the day, musicians were lumped with actors and prostitutes at the bottom of the ladder. Those professions seemed to pursue mere sensuality. Nevertheless, cloisters and ecclesiastical courts supported an astonishing musical establishment, resulting in hundreds of "Amadeuses" composing, singing, and playing to make the liturgy more spectacular than an opera house.[11] In fact, opera imitated the liturgy by applying to the stage many of the theatrical techniques developed for sacred oratorios and later applied to the liturgy itself. In the late eighteenth century, however, secular philosophers and enlightened Christians both believed that music—indeed all art—when employed in public celebrations ought directly to assist the teaching of ethics and the training of good citizens. Such a classically Platonic paradigm dictates that the arts and their makers as such offer scant moral nourishment. They might at best season biblical, moralistic, or civic texts in order to make them palatable. Music and art that took a congregation's mind off these objectives should be eliminated. For continental critics, England was a model of cultural reform along such lines. The congruence between English Protestant and Enlightenment attitudes was exemplified in the first regular newspaper in England, *The Spectator* (1711–1712). The voluble editors, Joseph Addison and Richard Steele, mocked Handel's imported operas for their elaborate stage machinery, visual and auditory trumperies, and florid language.[12] English Protestant culture, less musical and more literary because more biblical, was proudly judged to be "classical." By applying to the liturgy, the divine opera (the opus dei[13]), the same criteria that the classically minded critics applied to secular opera, ecclesiastical leaders pronounced melismatic (in which several notes may be assigned to a single syllable), Latinate music reprehensible. Whether it was in the fashionable Italian operatic style or in ancient Gregorian chant, it was worse than useless! In the words of even Catholic critics, "Let this expensive musical apparatus be turned to more touching songs and prayers which people can understand. If only aphrodisial sopranos and touchy castrati were replaced as singers by respectable persons and clergy, what could be achieved by worship to transform the hearts and souls of a wholesome people!" Thus wrote the relatively moderate Ernst Xaver Turin (1738–1810), the editor of the most used and copied German Catholic prayer and hymn book during the Enlightenment, the "Mainz Hymnal" (*Mainzer Gesangbuch*, c. 1787).[14]

Aufklärer warned that Jesus' church had "no mission to produce art critics, because the more artistic music becomes, the fewer it reaches." Less elaborate music—that is with fewer notes, as urged by Mozart's bishop and emperor—would give the Word a better chance to reach everyone. As with the neopagans outside the churches, so too within them, rededication to a useful and beloved antiquity seemed the way to modernity. Some Christians welcomed this trend because it seemed to promise a return to the classical age not so much of pagan Rome but of primitive Christianity. Their efforts were contemporary with the ritual style of propaganda on the part of the revolutionary leaders in France who desired to control every aspect of human behavior down to the details of dress and demeanor in order to replace Catholic manners.[15] In a double dose of neoclassicism, liturgical reformers combined admiration for the simplicity of the Christian Apostolic Age with secular aesthetic canons derived from pagan Aristotelian dramatic theories and Cartesian rationalism. In order to recover the model simplicity of Christianity's "classical" period, theologians proposed to revise their liturgies according to the unities of classical drama derived from Aristotle's *Poetics*. According to such dicta, good taste demanded that unities of action, place, and text be imposed on the ramified Roman rite that had evolved haphazardly over the centuries. *Unity of text* required that each service have a "theme," often moralistic. Readings and music would be selected specifically to enhance this theme. *Unity of action* meant that only one action should occur at a time and this should be in a language intelligible to the people. *Unity of place* demanded that the architecture should focus attention on the unified action, meaning that distracting windows, statuary, paintings, and competing altars ought to be removed. Such reforms seemed to conflict with venerable Catholic practices such as praying the rosary, looking at the windows or decor, moving about the church, listening to music, or thinking that mere physical presence sufficed while the priest recited the required Latin prayers. Even if the choir might interpret the Latin texts musically at a sung mass, the priest still had to recite every word, because, according to Tridentine regulations, only his prayer represented the church officially.

"In order to win the emotions for the intellect," as Kant phrased it, liturgical editors published experimental services built around a single didactic theme. These experiments sometimes began with an introductory essay tying the proposed reforms to the systematic theology of the day. Catholic proposals stated belief both in a vernacular, didactic Catholic liturgy and in papal primacy. Although Ernst Xaver Turin would later curse the "atheistical French" for singing *La Marseillaise* in German churches, he was nonetheless a German influenced by French thought.[16] Catholic theologians who hoped to improve their liturgy were hampered by a clerical and hierarchical liturgical tradition whose elaborate music and pomp seemed to reinforce a retrograde division of the Christian community into clerical professionals and lay outsiders. It seemed that if Catholicism were ever to regain a pristine community of love, its rites and music should follow the Protestant lead and hearken back to primitive Christianity. Protestant *Aufklärer* were better able to rationalize their liturgical tradition without contradicting it. "Preaching the Word," witnessing to personal religious experience, and explaining natural theology (theodicy) suited the rationalistic, nationalistic, and democratic trends of the eighteenth century even more than they had suited the Reformers of the sixteenth. Theologians of both centuries idealized the same golden age, the Christianity of the first three centuries. Enlightened authors reasoned that Christians must abandon the "pagan and Hebrew" notion of God as an Eastern potentate, and must instead emphasize the Christian image of a father, whose family we are, and whose rite, the eucharist, symbolizes a meal of the family of man, not the supine awe of subjects for a "king of kings."

An important mode of participation in the supposed simplicity of the Early Church was its presumably plain congregational singing. Catholic critics also wished to reform the existing "imperial" rites by editing hymnals and service books so that the tunes, as well as the texts, both obeyed and therefore taught rational rules, the better to inculcate rational mentality by smoothing the irregular rhythms of old Gregorian chant and chorales to the regular meter typical of the eighteenth century's neoclassical poetry and music. When enlightened rulers began to make education a state concern, they usually eliminated the choir schools, whose exclusively Latin and musical curriculum seemed to serve only the clergy, who were the secular rulers' competitors.[17] Simplified chorale tunes were to become the backbone of a congregationally sung Catholic worship. These tunes were rationalized according to the canons of neoclassical prosody. Regular meter, evenly scanned lines, and didactic texts became the rule. The old chorales lacked those attributes that neoclassicists wanted to impose on lyrics and music: four eight-measure phrases setting rhymed couplets. So, the classicizers stretched archaic patterns of speech to fit common grammatical paradigms, cut or padded tunes to fit regular meters, and replaced imagery with logic. To ensure that no one would drift into meditation or day-dreaming, reformers speeded up the tunes by translating the semibreves and minims into eighths and sixteenths. So, paradoxically, while the liturgiologists were expelling dance- and opera-inspired music from the temple, they made church music obey the rhythmic conventions of the entertainment music they banned. The entente between rationalism and liturgical reform that began in the eighteenth century flourished until the French excesses under Napoleon and the rebelliousness manifested in 1817 at the tercentennial Wartburg celebrations of Luther frightened the ruling classes. Metternich's Catholic and Hapsburg Vienna celebrated the three-hundredth anniversary of the Reformation in company with the Protestant Germanies. At the celebration, the notes of Luther's straightforward "Ein' feste Burg ist unser Gott" were chopped in half to fit a wordy new text.

These reforms imposed from the top sometimes collided with beloved popular religious traditions. When in 1791 the duke of Württemberg, a relatively liberal place bordering France, introduced in his domains a "corrected" hymnal for Protestants, they complained that it would "make them Catholics," because it included some hymns by Catholic authors. Christmas carolers found that if they used the new books, their tips were small indeed. Conversely, the Catholics worried about the protestantizing danger of the "corrected" hymnals given them. In Protestant Halle, the *Liturgisches Journal* for 1806, in treating the question of how one ought to introduce enlightened hymnals and prayer books to congregations, recommended that preachers proceed "according to the intelligence of their congregations." Yet, above all, the clergy must do their duty by *requiring* the spread of Enlightenment and morality.

By disposing of accretions to Christianity since its first centuries, the Enlightenment wished to make the message of the Gospels stand out. To "make Christianity relevant in all situations for all types of people" meant to avoid "dulling repetition of mechanical devotions which are the essence of priestcraft, for morality and religion cannot be taught '*ex opere operato*.'" [18] Catholic classicists worked to end the "aimless repetition" in the Roman missal, wherein a few masses from the Common of the Saints sufficed for most days not Sundays or major festivals. Critics now condemned the Gregorian liturgical books "which bear the name of a pope and teach ultramontanism to the younger clergy."[19] Enlightened priests argued that the Common of the Saints, which contained generalized liturgical prayers for various categories of saints such as widow, martyr, virgin, virgin-martyr, confessor, confessor-bishop, doctor of the church, and so forth, had no reference to the actual life of the particular person whose sanctity was being celebrated. This seemed to teach superstition, "for there is no proof that most of those names published by the Curia did anything worth admiring; indeed, monastic saints, even the authentic ones, are useless examples for modern people."[20] The prayers and readings from the Common spoke in general terms about "loving justice and hating iniquity" or declared, "The souls of the just are in the hands of God." The reformers wished that such "vague repetition" would yield to more pointed propers with lessons on specific ethical and theological themes.[21]

Among the festivals that the Catholic *Aufklärer* wanted to add to the liturgical year were some that the contemporary French revolutionaries like Maximilien de

Robespierre would make major festivals in the civic cult. These were celebrations to honor the state, peace, and education, or to explain ideas from natural religion, such as "The Unity of God" and "The Rational Order of the Universe." Even the inflexible canon of the mass was to be loosened in favor of allowing variations suited to various congregations or educational topics. In every mass, the climax of popular participation was to be a *Hauptlied*—a hymn following the theme of the mass—sung by the congregation in place of the preface and its response the Sanctus. There would be no occasion for any of Palestrina's—and certainly not for Mozart's or Franz Joseph Haydn's—masses!

Some reformers desired that congregational songs with lessons for everyday life replace the old poetical or generalized texts that had been bound to the yearly liturgical cycle. One proposed hymn encouraged workers to do their best so that hard currency would remain in their homeland. Another warned mothers that uneducated lads grow up to be vagrants. Reformers in the various Christian churches tailored baptismal rites to every conceivable type of candidate: infant, sickly infant, illegitimate infant (none of whom would be asked any ritual questions); peasant, noble, old, young, male, female.

Other authors combined ethics lessons with personal religious experience like those stressed in the German variety of personalist and enthusiastic religion, Pietism, which was both competitor and complement to the Enlightenment. One such combination of the personal with the rationalistic was "Jesus, Our Example" (*Jesus, Unser Vorbild*) by the radical reformer Benedict Maria Werkmeister (1745–1823). It had scant precedent in Jewish or Christian ritual:

> A Christian's joy and duty it is,
> Always and without conceit,
> To show love for one's neighbor.
> Whoever he may be,
> A Moslem, Jew or Heathen,
> He is a man like me,
> And often better still than many a Christian.[22]

This *Toleranzlied* reminds one of the contemporary drama of Gotthold Ephraim Lessing (1729–1781), *Nathan der Weise*.

In a book he edited, Werkmeister also included a civic hymn to exhort respect for oaths taken before the law and another to instill willingness to serve. The same book even included an animal rights anthem as well as two others warning against superstition. One of these ran:

> Too much credence neighbor Martin gives
> To sorcery and witchcraft and such things;
> He paints three crosses on the wall
> To banish evil spirits, thus he thinks.
> Who would not laugh at that?[23]

The fifth stanza of the second hymn spoke of apparitions:

> No one, once Death has taken him away,
> Has been allowed to reappear on earth.
> Scripture and reason tell us: No![24]

Werkmeister hoped that students would help to spread his ideas by making and distributing copies of hymns by him and other authors with the same ideals. Their hopes for Christian Enlightenment are summed up in a change proposed for the Litany of the Saints, which is part of the liturgy for the Resurrection (then celebrated on Holy Saturday morning) and some other solemn days of the church year: the Latin invocation "That you may bring low the enemies of Holy Church" should become "that you may give us the grace to love our enemies."[25]

Other Enlightenment hymns offered "advice for the practical life"—something like the *Farmer's Almanac*. A Catholic prayer book of 1791 included recommendations about what to do in a storm or fire and precautions to help preserve one's health or alleviate pains and toothaches, reminding us that the Enlightenment approach to religious ritual was related to its call for universal secular elementary education.

To popularize the Enlightenment, eighteenth-century theologians sometimes combined the pietistic first-person singular anthropomorphic style of address to God with Newtonesque, academic, and Latin-root German in mixed metaphors such as this:

> My Jesus knows how to
> Add and multiply,
> Even where
> There are only zeroes.[26]

The marriage between rationalism and popular piety was not always comfortable.

Paradoxically, the intended recovery of the classic simplicity of pre-Constantinian Christianity became an alliance with the new Constantines who were modernizing and centralizing the secular state. Christian rationalists often acquired the freedom to counsel a return to primitive Christianity by preaching support of enlightened despots such as Emperor Joseph II or Elector Maximilian III of Bavaria. These rulers wanted religion to foster vernacular culture and the loyalty of citizens equal before the law in a rationally organized state. Uniform religious practices were mass media being exploited to teach statism to the mass of people just emerging from feudalism.

Protestant Affinities for the Enlightenment and Pietism

The outwardly austere character of much Protestant worship and its architectural environment inculcated a mentality that was receptive both to the Enlightenment and its antipode, the celebration of an inner light as validator of the faith. Worship in the vernacular aided the rise of the nation–state as the dominant cultural power in Western civilization. The emphasis on preaching complemented the emphasis on scripture, implying that worshipers become literate and even sit still in pews to listen or study (see Chapter 12, "The Reformed Tradition in Continental Europe"). On the other hand, the insistence on a direct personal relationship with God might orient believers away from words toward the Word manifested in movement, music, and emotional outpourings.

"Four walls and a sermon" was all that John Calvin (1509–1564), the paradigmatic Reformed theologian, had required of the worship service. He thought that human awe before an incomprehensible God and the message of the Gospel had been obscured by the Roman Church's accretion of so many rites and ceremonies and works of music and art that amounted to pagan idolatry.[27] Protestant orientation away from mystagogic ceremonies to Bible study and preaching had been facilitated by the invention of movable-type printing, which allowed families of relatively modest means to own a Bible. By reading scripture, individuals might receive divine revelation directly, without the intervention of a priest or the sacramental system. Such individualism suited the middle classes, rising from peasant subordination. They were predisposed against the barrage of signs and symbols that advertised feudal aristocracy and ecclesiastical hierarchy.

The reductionist tendencies in Protestant worship, particularly on the Reformed side, also had an affinity to the neopagan classicism of Enlightenment thinkers, who tended to equate elaborate religious ceremony with superstition. The rationalist view of an original impersonal monotheism was put well in a letter by the Deist John Toland:

> The most ancient Egyptians, Persians, and Romans, the first Patriarchs of the Hebrews . . . had no sacred images or statues, no peculiar places or costly fashions of worship, the plain easiness of their religion being most agreeable to the simplicity of the divine nature, as indifference of place and time were the best expressions of infinite power and omnipresence.[28]

The concatenation of Protestant and Enlightenment-Deist thinking can be seen in the preference for plain churches proportioned along the lines of ancient Greek or Roman temples. The Old South Church in Boston documents the religious trends of the Age of Reason. Its simple design with a balcony to bring all present within hearing of the pulpit is intended to facilitate the hearing and consideration of the *word*, rather than mystical *ceremonies*.

The legacy of the ancient synaxis found expression in other ways in Protestant worship, where the preaching service became the norm. For the sermon, by virtue of its placement in the liturgy and sheer length, became the climax toward which the rest of worship moved.[29] Whereas Lutherans and Anglicans retained a structure of calendar and lectionary, the Reformed tradition virtually abandoned any connection between sermon and the old medieval liturgical year. In Calvin's Geneva, the preacher expounded the running texts of the books of Scripture, both Old Testament and New (*lectio continua*).[30] Under this understanding of worship, all liturgy is shaped or determined by the biblical text being proclaimed, since the primary task of the worship leader is to interpret the Word. At its best, Reformed worship aims to emphasize the prophetic aspect of preaching. The utterance of the preacher is a supernatural act in which God again addresses humanity. At its worst, the service may function to manipulate the congregation into a receptive, agreeable frame of mind for the preacher's personal agenda. The pulpit is central; the preacher's chair dominates; baptismal font and altar table are lower and smaller. In all, absence of space for congregational movement indicates that the role of the laity is in fact limited and prescribed. In some cases, these factors combine to foster an understanding among laity of worship as something produced by the preacher rather than being the work of the Christian community, as intended by Reformation theology.

Yet, despite the lionizing of preachers, there were democratic lessons implicit in Protestant worship. For its most memorable experience might be the actions of individuals giving testimony or singing together. Over the centuries, the volumes of printed sermons lie silent on dusty shelves, yet the hymnals are worn out with use every decade. If the Word and the Word alone is the vehicle of grace, and if placing the congregation's response to the Word lies in the singing of the chorale rather than in the liturgical action, then the sacraments appear almost as a confirmatory appendage to the sermon. Therefore, analogous to the Catholic or Orthodox liturgies, the most heartfelt aspect of hearing the Word again became less verbal and more musical.

The British Isles in the Eighteenth Century

After the restoration of the English monarchy, annual communion in the Established Church became from 1673 a political test used for determining eligibility for the privilege of holding public office, and this remained the case until 1829. (Similar tests were enforced in most European countries.) The liturgy itself remained a compromise: in outline a mass in English, yet theologically a Protestant Lord's supper. Some scholars favor the view that "the strength of the Anglican reaction of 1660 lay not exclusively, or even principally, in the response of a gentry who craved the return of a hierarchical Church which would shore up a hierarchical government and society, but in the popularity of traditional religious forms at all levels of society."[31] Under the Commonwealth, Presbyterians had favored a more strictly Protestant service of preaching and teaching in a plain hall stripped of distractions. Ceremonial would be minimal and music restricted to metrical psalm singing. Aristocrats and, it appears, many common folk liked a liturgy that appealed to diverse human faculties, differentiated from common speech, and employing elevated media such as artistic music in surroundings replete with signs and symbols.

Compared with the elaborate rubrics of the pre-Reformation Old Sarum liturgy, which spelled out the correct music for each feast in detail, the 1662 *Book of Common Prayer* hardly touches on this matter. Even so, custom continued to dictate the observance of holy days and singular occasions with special ceremony and traditional musical adornment. The Sunday morning worship was commonly called "Divine Service." It included the Order for Morning Prayer; the Litany of confession, petition, and intercessions; and the ante-communion. In most churches, the service went on to communion itself only a few times per year. The intention was to highlight worship as an act of the community, not only of the priest, and to keep communion for special occasions.

Beside that mainstream many alternatives flourished. After the "Glorious Revolution" of 1688 drove out the Catholic Stuart family, those clergy who refused to swear allegiance to the new Protestant dynasty became "Non-Jurors." They produced their own liturgies along more "catholic" lines, even separating matins and lauds from the Divine Service. Following a number of compromises among the various factions, their 1718 liturgy resembled that of the compromise reached after the death of Henry VIII back in 1547. Further controversies erupted over significant details that signaled the political and cultural wars of the day. "Usagers" wanted a further return to pre-Reformation practice of a "mixed chalice," wherein water was added to the wine, and the liturgy included prayers for the dead. "Non-usagers" avoided such "papist" remnants in favor of Protestant theology but were loyal to the Scottish Stuart dynasty that continued to offer pretenders to the throne until and beyond their final military defeat in 1746.[32]

The revival of plainsong was critical to continuity in liturgical tradition. Precise musical practice, such as accompaniment of certain chants by the organ, was a matter of the tradition, not spelled out in the Prayer Book or rubrics, but presumed among persons who knew the traditions of the craft of music. Choral services resumed in Saint Paul's Cathedral in London in the 1690s.

In the eighteenth century, evangelical movements in the Church of England favored liturgical simplification, eschewing anything that resembled the sacramental system of the Roman Church. They emphasized the acceptance of Christ as personal Savior and deemphasized the role of the church as mediator. In the performance of the liturgy they favored a greater role overall for the congregation, including responses by them, rather than the choir. Despite the "low church" taste of the Evangelicals, their emotional intensity could lead to the artistic enhancement favored by some of the later Oxford Movement men, such as John Henry Newman (1801–1890), who was raised as an Evangelical.

Worship in the Church of England had become sermon-centered, clearing the way for the rationalistic discourses favored as centerpieces of the service during the Age of Reason. Controversies over the form of the Sunday service reflected the political contests between parliamentary and monarchical parties. The former tended to see religious worship as an occasion for instruction, affecting a Lockean behavioralist psychology and contract political theory. The latter desired contact with the incomprehensible sublime, reflecting either a desire for intense personal religious experience or organic continuity with hallowed tradition. In the interests of edification, the ceremonies and music were reduced to serve intelligibility of the text. Still setting the standard for music was John Merbecke's adaptation of the plainchant for the 1549 Prayer Book: for each syllable, only one note![33]

The latitudinarianism persisting into the Georgian era avoided liturgical extremes that might lead to civil discord and thus upset the pursuit of power and wealth by leaders of the industrial revolution at home and in the growing empire overseas. Within the church, economic factors such as changes in the value of money allowed niggardly old salaries to prevent full attention to the job of singer. Salaries in the capital were a multiple of those in provincial cathedrals, where, in consequence, performances were miserable.

Parallel to the eighteenth-century tendency for hymn tunes to adopt a regular meter and simpler melody line, Anglican chants were also smoothed out, leaving few of the grace notes or passing tones that had once been used by professionals. Differentiations became evident between cathedrals and parish churches as well as between "catholic" and "protestant" tendencies in the liturgy. The extent of the decline of musical quality in the cathedrals is hard to discern. During the course of the eighteenth century, cathedral practices tended to become the norm for parishes. In the early nineteenth century, romanticism led to the exploration of the older Latin liturgy as a way of rebelling against an increasingly commercially oriented and secular society, some of whose leaders favored disestablishment, especially in Ireland. Rising economic resources in London and market towns allowed the support of trained musical leadership. The psalmodist or precentor, who led the musical part of the Reformed church service, became an advocate of musical literacy among the general populace. In colonial America the composer William Billings (1746–1800) was a leader of the "singing school" movement that began in New England but persists today mainly in the rural South through shape-note singing, sometimes called after its best-known songbook, *The Sacred Harp*. The controversy over whether "regular singing" from musical notation usurps congregational participation continues to the present day.

Liturgical issues in the small Episcopal Church in Scotland, where the Established Church was Calvinist, were influenced by disputes between juring clergy, who swore allegiance to the Hanoverians, and the nonjuring, who were loyal to the Stuarts, governed by the successors of a remnant of bishops. Juring clergy were allowed to worship publicly in qualified chapels, but belonged to no episcopal jurisdiction. In parishes, liturgical practice of the juring faction approximated that in England, that is, services were chanted. After repeal of penal laws against Non-Jurors in 1792, reconciliation began in 1803. Liturgical and musical practices followed those in juring parishes. The

Plate 11. A medieval preacher. Saint Bernardino preaches in the Piazza del Campo, Siena. [See chapter 6.] MUSEO DELL'OPERA METROPOLITANA, SIENA, ITALY/SCALA/ART RESOURCE

Plate 12. Funeral. Office of the dead, from the book of hours of Catherine of Cleves, Utrecht, c. 1435. [See chapter 6.] THE PIERPONT MORGAN LIBRARY, NEW YORK, M.94/ ART RESOURCE, NY

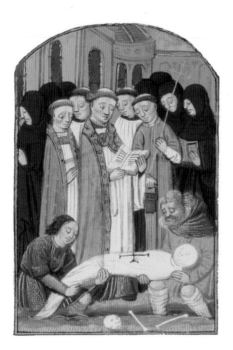

Plate 13. Burial of the dead. From the Playfair Book of Hours, a late fifteenth-century book of hours from Rouen. [See chapter 6.] VICTORIA & ALBERT MUSEUM, LONDON, MS. L. 475-1918, FOL. 125R/ART RESOURCE

Plate 14. Palm Sunday, 1212. The bishop of Assisi hands a palm to the young woman who would become Saint Clare; c. 1360. Saint Francis stands at the left, behind the altar. The dramatic commemoration of Christ's Entry into Jerusalem (Matt. 21:1–11; John 12:12–19) dates from the fourth century, as Egeria's *Travel Diary* records (31). In the Middle Ages the Palm Sunday reenactment spread throughout western Europe. Specimens still exist in Germany of the wheeled wooden donkey (*Palmesel*) on which a figure of Christ was seated. In recent generations, the Palm Sunday procession has been introduced in churches which otherwise have little use for such observances. A favorite processional hymn is "Gloria, laus, et honor" by the ninth-century Theodulph of Orleans, translated by John Mason Neale: "All glory, laud and honour / To thee, Redeemer, King, / To whom the lips of children / Made sweet hosannas ring." THE METROPOLITAN MUSEUM OF ART, THE CLOISTERS COLLECTION, 1984 (1984.343), PHOTOGRAPH © 1987 THE METROPOLITAN MUSEUM OF ART

Plate 15. The Holy Trinity. Icon (c. 1410) by Andrei Rublev (c. 1360/70–c.1430). The story of the three heavenly visitors to Abraham and Sarah in Genesis 18 is taken to allow the indirect representation of the Three Persons of the Godhead. The chalice evokes the eucharist and thus the Lamb slain from the foundation of the world (Rev. 13:8). The nearest equivalent in the medieval Western tradition is the composition of the *Gnadenstuhl* or Mercy-Seat, in which the Father is depicted supporting the crucified Christ and the two are linked by the Holy Spirit in the shape of a dove. Christian worship is essentially trinitarian in its grouping and practice. Christian worship is essentially trinitarian in grounding and practice. [See chapters 1 and 7.] TRETYAKOV GALLERY, MOSCOW/SCALA/ART RESOURCE, NY

Plate 16. Virgin and Child. Mosaic from the apse of Hagia Sophia,
Istanbul, shortly after 834. [See chapters 3 and 7.] ERICH LESSING/ART
RESOURCE, NY

Non-Jurors were influenced by the drier style of the established Presbyterian Church, whose music was metrical psalms.

The Toleration Act of 1712 had secured the right of Episcopalians in Scotland to follow Anglican forms in spite of the Presbytery. Scottish Episcopalians were proud of their unique heritage, not wishing to be considered a type of heathen Anglican. An English visitor to Saint Paul's Church in Aberdeen about 1730 reported that when the (Hanoverian) king was prayed for, "men and women set themselves about some trivial action, as taking snuff, &c. to show their dislike, and signify to each other they were all of one mind," and despite loud responses of the congregation to the rest of the liturgy, not a single voice was heard in response to that bidding.[34] There were organs, choirs, precentors, and pay for musicians from the merchant class, as in England, whereas the Presbyterians abhorred such "popery" in their services.

The Anglican Church in the colonies that became the United States was in a position analogous to that of the Scottish Episcopalians. It followed English parish practice, omitting reference to specifically British festivals, eventually replacing them with American celebrations, such as Thanksgiving. In prosperous coastal cities such as Boston, New York, Philadelphia, and Charleston, there was some familiarity with English cathedral practice. The first musicians and organs came from England to a situation with less choral singing, more reading, and simple chanting. The repertory was eclectic, drawing in part from other North American denominations, including the Moravian Brethren and Roman Catholics. The first bishop of the Episcopal Church was ordained by the bishop of Aberdeen, Scotland.

During the late eighteenth century, a movement toward more frequent communion arose with the Evangelicals and was in the next century vigorously pursued by the Tractarians. At first these Oxford Movement men were staunch defenders of the Prayer Book as it stood, but liturgical alteration soon flourished. It became common to publish the Prayer Book rite of Holy Communion with interpolations and additions from the Roman Missal in English. Demands from Anglo-Catholics for revision became louder in the light of controversies and even litigation over

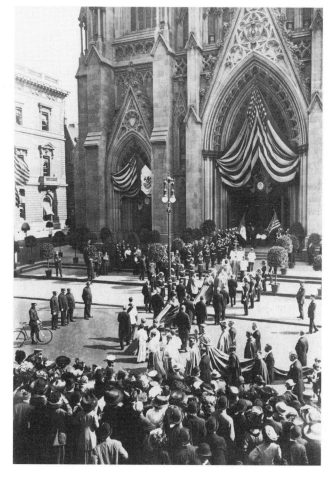

Saint Patrick's Cathedral.
Procession into the cathedral, on New York's Fifth Avenue, early twentieth century. PRINTS AND PHOTOGRAPHS DIVISON, LIBRARY OF CONGRESS

ritual. The issues of ecclesiastical discipline and liturgical revision thus became almost inextricably interwoven. The Erastian—state controlled—ideal of uniform public worship saw it as the glue that held civil society together. Alleged incidents of indiscipline in public worship signaled the depth of feelings involved, particularly when the question of disestablishment was raised, beginning with the Church of Ireland, a publicly supported member of the Anglican communion in an overwhelmingly Roman Catholic country. Issues deriving from that dispute are still alive, particularly among English-speaking Roman Catholics in America, who have tended to pattern their attitudes toward worship by ideas derived from the artistically and musically silent liturgy of the very political and verbal Irish Roman Catholics.[35] As they saw it, even their rightful heritage of ancient churches had been confiscated or destroyed to support an alien cult.[36] When freed from the trammels of the old country, Irish Americans soon sought to demonstrate their faith and civic presence by constructing some of the nation's most magnificent church buildings. Saint Patrick's Cathedral in New York, perhaps the best example, was intended to be the most magnificent building in the city, which it was until the age of modern skyscrapers. It was commissioned in 1853 as a witness against the tidal wave of anti-Catholic prejudice, laid on the drawing board just after the peak of penniless peasant immigration from Ireland. It remains a gothic assertion of the supernatural set against the rationalistic styles favored for the towering temples of mammon that later surrounded it.

Reasons of the Heart

The most important revolution in worship can be expressed in one word: intensity. As we have noticed, the Deistic Enlightenment, which viewed God as an impersonal engineer, was complemented by its apparent opposite, an "Inner Light" theology that pursued the experience of Jesus Christ as personal Savior. Both frequently—though not always—objected to elaborate ceremonies and clerical authority. The difference lay in their worship style as much as in their theology. Dissatisfied with the dry Deism of natural religion and the bureaucratic routine of established state churches, alternative leaders arose intending to reach a sense of intimacy with the person of Jesus Christ. Baptists and Evangelicals everywhere, Pietists among Lutherans, Methodists among Anglicans, and diverse free-church groups all shared a continuing Protestant antipathy to "popish" ceremonial in favor of an attempt to recover the simple agape (love feast) of early Christians.

The Roman Church had its analogous movements. Successors of Jansenism and Quietism continued to question the tendency toward a religion of works encouraged by the Jesuits. Yet, these, too, used every conceivable approach in their efforts to touch the human heart through education that appealed to every human faculty or retreats intended to facilitate life-changing experience like Ignatius Loyola's experience at Manresa. Impressive celebrations were calculated to envelop the worshipers with a sense of divine presence that outrivaled courtly pomp. Meanwhile, devotion to the Sacred Heart and saints, so repugnant to Jansenists, also encouraged worshipers to feel a personal relationship with their Savior. Although these many and diverse movements usually intended to revitalize the established churches, they sometimes wound up challenging their authority.

"Inner light" is a synonym for "enthusiasm," the literal indwelling of God that was the goal of many Protestant movements of the seventeenth and eighteenth centuries.

Plate 19. Sami Lutherans. A Lutheran service with Sami ("reindeer people") participants from Finland, Norway, Russia, and Sweden, at Jokkmokk, Sweden, in June 2004. [See chapter 11.] PHOTOGRAPH COURTESY OF NILS-HENRIK NILSSON

Facing page, top

Plate 17. Corpus Christi. Procession of the Feast of Corpus Christi in Naples. Watercolor by James Duffield Harding (1798–1863). [See chapter 9.] BOLTON MUSEUM AND ART GALLERY, LANCASHIRE, U.K./BRIDGEMAN ART LIBRARY

Facing page, bottom

Plate 18. Corpus Christi. A Corpus Christi procession in Naples in the eighteenth century. Public adoration of the eucharist blends with popular nonliturgical devotions in which the devout cleanse the path of the sacrament with their tongues. [See chapter 9.] MUSEO DEL FOLKLORE, ROME/PHOTOGRAPH © CONRAD L. DONAKOWSKI

Plate 20. The Christening. The Reverend Dr. William Ferdinand Morgan administers the sacrament of baptism at Grace Church in New York City. Painting (1868) by William DeHartburn Washington (1833–1870). [See chapters 16 and 22.] COLLECTION OF CHRIS AND DAVE KNOKE, MARIETTA, GEORGIA

Yet, it was sometimes hurled as a reproach, as though their worship was abandoning divinely sanctioned order for capricious chaos. "Inner light" churches may at first glance seem to be unstructured in their worship, but their ritual does follow a pattern, although the allocation of time to its various components may vary considerably from service to service. The sacrament, an outward sign of inward grace, is taken to be an individual spiritual experience or sharing of fellow feeling among those who have known that experience, rather than the prescribed reception of elements through the mediation of a specially ordained priest.[37]

A pattern for worship applicable across denominational boundaries may be found in the Isaiah passage where the actual felt presence of the Almighty overpowered those at prayer in the Temple. In the gathering there was an expectation of immanent direct divine revelation to worshipers (6:1–4); penitence and confession of unworthiness (6:5); assurance of cleansing and forgiveness (6:6–8); new receptivity to the voice of God (6:8); and the human response (6:9b) of turning one's life over to the Lord, "Here I am; send me."[38] Of course, "high church" worshipers find the same immanence in their elaborate liturgies. Hence, although dogma may divide, reasons of the heart are common to all people seeking to express the ineffable. In order to carry on the charisma of the initial encounter, the leaders have always developed forms of worship that seek to make an occasion for that "charism," "inner light," "enthusiasm," "ecstasy," or "rapture" to be widely and permanently available. High culture, especially music, aims to expand the scope and extend the durability of such intensity. In short, the Christian Church in its liturgies may be seen as aiming to institutionalize reasons of the heart. Hence the habitual distinction between "high" and "low" churches may be only a presumption inherited from theological tradition. For example, John Henry Newman was brought up an Evangelical in the Church of England, was taunted as "that Methodist" in his thirties because of his spellbinding pulpit oratory, passed through high church Anglicanism, and eventually became a Roman Catholic cardinal who spoke of doctrine as his first principle. Although his biographers have been zealous to preserve him from the label "Romantic," which colors the Victorian era, Newman, who was a fine musician, chose for his prelatial coat of arms the motto *Cor ad cor loquitur*—"Heart speaks to heart."[39]

Indeed, the institutionalization of personal experience is often problematic. For example, the Puritans in North America originally insisted on individual conversion as a test for church membership. When, however, mere church membership became itself a test for citizenship in a large and diverse secular political order, the Puritans found themselves in the dilemma of the Church of England, whose rites they had scorned as empty tokens of a political regime that they despised. The First Great Awakening that began in eighteenth-century New England was an effort to recover the conversion experience. Yet, intense preaching and public conversion is only one way to maintain a sense of contact with the divine. Such transcendence of ordinary experience may be the austere silence of the Quakers or glossolalia of Pentecostals. Successful institutionalization of contact with the divine presence usually requires a combination of poetic words, skilled rhetoric, and music. Central European Pietism, which began as private Bible study and prayer in groups active within the evangelical (Lutheran) state church, flourished publicly in hymns by writers such as Matthias Claudius (1740–1815). He wrote the lyrics for popular chorales that expressed a quasi-physical sharing in Jesus' bloody wounds. Also influenced were products by local craftsmen, such as statues by Polish woodcarvers or music by German *Kantoren* such as Johann Sebastian Bach (1685–1750). Bach's cantatas grew out of the Lutheran propers sung between the scripture readings for a particular Sunday of the liturgical year. Florid arias setting pietistic texts about "Jesus and me" give the recitative of a biblical passage an expanded emotional response. Thereby the composer converted the dramatic impact of neopagan operatic theater to Christian interior religious experience.[40]

Pietism influenced the Moravian Brethren, a communal settlement that developed a complex liturgy with appropriate music for each service, analogous to the medieval monastic office. The Moravians exerted enormous influence through their hymnody and the experiences of visitors to the estates of Count Nikolaus von Zinzendorf (1700–1760). He insisted on sharing the members' personal lives in a microcosm of the Christianities, an "ecclesiola" drawn from many denominations regardless of doctrinal detail but dependent on a sense of personal intimacy with the Lord. The purpose of the community was to establish a foretaste of heaven on earth by demonstrating a community of love among representatives of all Christianities. Educated visitors sometimes scoffed at the mawkish sentimentality of Moravian hymnody, full of "hideous repetition" of references to Jesus as a "little lambkin," in whose "pierced side it is our only wish to dwell as in the womb of our mothers." Sophisticates found the Moravians a curious mixture of repression and expression. Unusual among Protestants, they employed vivid pictures, equivalent in style to Roman Catholic holy pictures in baroque churches. The Moravians' religion was the opposite of rationalistic. They refused to pray to the Father as too remote a figure without the specific mediation of a living human person, his Son, with whom a human being could identify.[41]

Stifling as the Moravians' communal life may have seemed to some observers, they pointed in a new direction not only among central European Protestants, but also for some of the most sophisticated representatives of Western civilization. Theologies of the heart had ready affinity with the secular philosophical teachings of Jean-Jacques Rousseau (1712–1778) in the French-speaking world. The great German *Sturm und Drang* poet and literary leader of the reaction against rationalism, Friedrich Schiller (1759–1805), was raised a Pietist. As an adult, he translated his heartfelt religion into a plea that education, indeed society itself, should recognize that the feelings are as necessary as the senses and the intellect to the attainment of full humanity.[42] He became a virtual prophet who channeled the communal practices of Pietism into the most important cultural revolution of modern times, Romanticism. The greatest Romantic theologian, Friedrich Schleiermacher (1768–1834), was also raised a Pietist. His insights about religion as more than a set of theological propositions converted Romanticism into a weapon on behalf of religious culture that commanded respect from the intellectual class.

River baptism. Baptism at Berg on the Neckar river in the presence of pastor Johann Gerhard Onken on 14 October 1838. Color lithograph. Photograph by Ruth Schacht/ Bildarchiv Presussischer Kulturbesitz/Art Resource, NY

The Moravians also influenced a zealous Anglican priest, John Wesley (1703–1791) during his missionary voyage to America. Returning to England he yearned to foster a more intense sacramental life in his church. In London he frequented meetings of a "religious society" which included both earnest Anglicans and Moravian Brethren organized in bands who celebrated a version of the early Christian agape or love feast. Wesley's *Journal* for 24 May 1738 records this: "In the evening I went very unwillingly to a society in Aldersgate Street, where one was reading Luther's Preface to the Epistle to the Romans. About a quarter before nine, while he was describing the change which God works in the heart through faith in Christ, I felt my heart strangely warmed. I felt I did trust in Christ, Christ alone for salvation, and an assurance was given me that he had taken away *my* sins, even *mine*, and saved *me* from the law of sin and death." [43] Through fervent preaching and hymns, Wesley spread an invitation for others to share this experience, intending to enlarge the appeal of the Church of England. Like all places of worship outside the Established Church, Methodist preaching houses could not be called churches, only chapels, even though the building and congregation might be larger than those of the parish church in the same town. By 1791 Methodism became effectively separate from its parent denomination, abandoning the attempt to remodel Anglicanism and retaining a style of worship marked by vigorous congregational singing. The essence of Wesleyan Methodism seems to be avoidance of the sort of smug routine religiosity so repugnant in the likes of Mr. Collins in Jane Austen's *Pride and Prejudice* (1813). He was "attentive and conciliatory towards everybody, especially toward those to whom he owes his preferment."

Perennial controversy surrounds the social effect of active churchgoing. Some critics see worship as an opiate of the people diverting energies that might otherwise become a revolutionary explosion. Others take the celebration of Jesus' life as participation in his proactive compassion. Did Wesleyan sermonizing and hymn singing among newly industrialized populations keep their minds off the need for social reform? Robert R. Palmer writes:

> The effects of Methodism, however, were by no means conservative. Men taught to read in Methodist Sunday Schools, or to speak up in Wesleyan meetings, often figured as leaders in radical clubs. Home missions, Bible reading, and itinerant preaching, in both England and Scotland, offered a competing program to that of the French Revolution calling the established order into question. [44]

Prime Minister William Pitt is said to have feared the effect of the Methodist teaching and worship more than the blunt propaganda of outright rebels. A similar continuing controversy in America concerns the role of Christian worship—generally evangelical—in the life of slaves. Did all that singing and preaching of humility serve to create docile "happy darkies," or was Christianity an impregnable hope, where "getting happy" in church amounted to a rehearsal for personal assertiveness, and the lyrics of Negro spirituals sometimes gave the actual code words of Underground Railway escape routes? [45]

In the nineteenth century, the Tractarians and the Oxford Movement would make a fresh attempt to reinvigorate the Church of England. Like Wesley, they intended to apply the enthusiasm of their evangelical backgrounds to the revitalization of an Established Church that sometimes seemed more of a political formality than an instrument of worship. John Henry Newman made intensity of preaching and worship a badge of faith. John Keble (1792–1866) spoke of the liturgy in erotic language as the locus of thoughts that could not be expressed otherwise. Anglo-Catholicism was at first hardly attractive to the social and political elite, who counted religion a routine. With the increasing adoption of "catholic practices," an effort was made to share the beauty of the restored liturgy to reconnect with the lower classes, who led dreary lives in the new industrial cities. The neomedieval architect Augustus Welby Pugin (1812–1852) published a book of paired facing pictures, *Contrasts*.[46] Its tenor resembled a religious version of a novel by Charles Dickens (1812–1870). Pugin's engravings argued that urban public space and inspiring buildings dedicated to Christian worship and social service had formerly been common property for all people to share and enjoy. Now, the tradition of worship and service was being abandoned, and the built heritage allowed to decay. Profiteers rule, and the people's patrimony is squandered. Under industrial capitalism the finer things in life were available only to those with money to buy them. The later Arts and Crafts movement also intended the spiritual benefit of bringing less sermonizing and more imaginative riches to the populace of Victorian England.[47] The Oxford Movement is often reckoned a prop of the Tory political order; its inspiration, however, amounted to a revolution driven by energies similar to those driving the revolutions on the Continent, where socialists adapted attitudes ingrained through ages of Christian religious practices to serve a new earthly agenda.[48]

Meanwhile, John Henry Newman and the successive generations of Anglo-Catholics developed their enthusiasm into a scholarly quest for an organic link to the past that they discerned in Roman Catholic liturgical traditions. Newman himself passed beyond neomedievalism through emulation of Saint Philip Neri. After an ecstatic conversion experience Neri had inaugurated the sixteenth-century equivalent of entertainment evangelism in the form of the oratorio as a supplement to the Catholic liturgy in Rome. Neri's outreach methods in the Oratory, the church-like auditorium where sacred musical theater named after the place were staged, became a pattern for the popular appeal of the baroque Catholicism. In Newman's case, the somewhat spare hall-like Oratory in industrial Birmingham became the setting for his preaching and liturgical reform. In London, the baroque, even Byzantine, splendor and fine music of the Brompton Oratory incarnates this eminent Victorian's enthusiasm for a spiritual reality anterior to the religion of the monarchy. Similarly, the family descendants of John and Charles Wesley turned to the high art of liturgical splendor. Samuel Sebastian Wesley (1810–1876) was reckoned the finest British composer and organist of his time.[49]

In the American South, where John Wesley had experienced failure as an Anglican pastor, an important mass movement of heartfelt religious worship was the First Great Awakening, which had begun in New England in the 1740s. The founding preachers, Jonathan Edwards (1703–1758) and Wesley's colleague George Whitefield (1714–1770), discouraged dramatic preaching, bodily excitement, and groaning. Yet, there was always an expectation of an outward sign of inward grace, different from the decorum expected in established churches, where even in the American colonies worship had slipped into the servitude of being merely a token of secular citizenship or social respectability. Soon the Great Awakening spread to the South, where it continues to have a dramatic impact, not only on southern Protestantism, but also on American culture and therefore on the world. The American mutations of Protestantism might be compared to the inculturation of Roman Catholic religious practices during the European Middle Ages or the Iberian colonies in Central and South America.

English settlers in the American South had at first tried to repeat the Anglican establishment that eventually became the Protestant Episcopal Church in the United

States of America. However, there was no resident bishop to ordain or confirm. Outside Virginia, in the Carolinas and Georgia, the South was sparsely settled. So there were gaps in the parish coverage, leaving the field open to itinerant preachers, who presented a challenge to the authority of the Anglican Church. Baptists and later Methodists called one another brother and sister and might include slaves in their religious family, offering an alternative to the hierarchical social system favored by the planter families. Many southerners also believed that faith and learning were in conflict. This was far cry from the New England Puritans, who established Harvard College just a few years after arrival. Southerners concentrated on issues of personal holiness, often condemning dancing and drinking, attacking obvious evils rather than analyzing profound issues. Preaching was extemporaneous and colloquial. Sometimes even a church building was lacking. There might be only a temporary gathering whose atmosphere could be all the more fervent through the pressure of a unique, fleeting opportunity proffered to people forced otherwise to live a difficult life virtually alone. So, despite the outward simplicity of church organization and leadership, the emotional life of the church was intense. The sacraments became religious drama. There were river baptisms and communal celebrations of the Lord's supper. Worship featured emotional release encouraged by enthusiastic singing and the joyful tears of conversion experiences.

Outsiders could easily misunderstand all of this. Pastor Charles Woodmason, a traveling Anglican pastor working in the Carolina backcountry in the eighteenth century, looked down on these American nonconformists, saying:

> The reason my congregation here is not larger, I am told, is because there are a gang of Baptists or "new lights" across the river, to whom many on that side resort. And on Swift's creek, ten miles below, a Methodist has set up to read and preach every Sunday. Both of them are low and exceedingly ignorant persons. Yet, the lower class chooses to resort to them rather than to hear a well-connected discourse. All this obliges me to repeat the liturgy by heart and to use no prayerbook but the Bible when I read the lessons. I have all the services and the whole office at my fingers ends. I also give an extempore prayer before sermon, but cannot yet venture to give extempore discourses, though certainly could perform beyond any of these poor fools.[50]

The new religious style of the eighteenth-century Great Awakening transformed the encounter between America's black and white races because social as well as religious differences were disparaged in a system that placed all Christians on the same level. Evangelical Christianity often welcomed all kinds and conditions of people, including African American preachers, who sometimes became leaders of Baptist and Methodist religious communities. On-the-spot conversion to Christianity replaced the long process of instruction that previously had been required of slaves. And literacy was not required for evangelical conversion. Many evangelicals were opposed to slavery itself. In the early nineteenth century, however, American white evangelicals would largely back away from antislavery positions and African American evangelicals essentially went on a separate track. They would understandably have little interest in a God who approved of slavery. In the nineteenth century, American Protestants continued their gradual proportional move away from the "liturgical" churches when a new wave of awakening brought forth hundreds of intentional communities, some of whom became the Latter Day Saints (Mormons), Adventists, and Disciples of Christ. These small sects grew into major forms of American religion. Although by 1850 the single largest church body in the United States was Roman Catholicism,

the enthusiasm-based Methodists and Baptists were the largest Protestant denominations, with the Baptists outstripping the Methodists in the twentieth century. The
latter had by now dispensed with Wesley's expectations of regular Morning Prayer
and Holy Communion as provided for in his *Sunday Service of the Methodists* (1784); a
more freely constructed preaching service took over, even though the less frequent
celebrations of the Lord's supper might go by the book. Religious freedom and absence of established churches in the United States encouraged an entrepreneurial spirit
of competition, revivalism, and organization for specific moral issues. The new religious style of the nineteenth century seemed increasingly based on democratic values,
which the Methodists and Baptists possessed in their church polity, often along with
an opportunity for individuals to speak up within the worship service. In their ministers, they wanted enthusiastic preachers more than erudition.

A new burst of activity in the first third of the nineteenth century was amplified by
Methodist circuit riders who brought together families on the lonely frontier in "revival meetings" that were a rare opportunity for sociability afforded to frontier people,
including young people seeking a spouse. An older contemporary of Abraham Lincoln in the backwoods of the new Midwest and the upper South was Peter Cartwright
(1785–1872). He was a Methodist circuit rider whose autobiography reports a revival
in Kentucky:

> A shed was erected that might shelter 5,000 people from wind and rain. Ten, twenty,
> and sometimes thirty ministers of different denominations would come together and
> preach night and day, sometimes for four or five days together. And indeed, I have known
> these camp meetings to last three or four weeks. And great good resulted from them. I
> have seen more than a hundred sinners fall like dead men under one powerful sermon.
> And I have seen and heard more than five hundred Christians all shouting aloud the high
> praises of God at once. Some sinners mocked. Some of the old, dry professors opposed.
> Some of the old Presbyterians preached against this exercise. But still the work went on
> and spread in almost every direction, gathering additional force until our country seemed
> all coming home to God.[51]

In the age of Andrew Jackson, a self-made man and first president from west of the
Appalachians, as the United States moved both westward and toward an urban-indus-
trial society, American evangelical Protestantism found a populist model in Charles
Grandison Finney (1792–1875). Initially apprenticed to become a lawyer, he defined
modern high-pressure evangelism, which values academic learning less than the effective manipulation of the emotions. An immensely important man in American history by any standard, his revivals were a powerful force in the rising antislavery
movement and in the growth of urban evangelism.[52]

Finney organized protracted meetings that ran for several weeks. Advance teams
publicized the coming revival and set up prayer meetings, sometimes exclusively for
women. His meeting featured an "anxious bench." Anyone concerned about the state
of his or her soul could come to a front pew where he or she would be addressed
personally and become the subject of public prayer. In the spirit of Methodist
Arminianism, Finney believed that a successful revival was not only a miracle of God's
grace but also depended on the right use of the appropriate opportunities. Innovative
worship techniques were needed in order to keep the message before the world.

Finney developed his methods in the raw cities along the new Erie Canal that
connected the Midwest with New York City. This area of New York State was soon
nicknamed the "burned-over district" because it became the center of a firestorm of

new religious movements that reached Midwestern cities like Detroit and Cleveland; back east to Boston, New York, and Philadelphia; and overseas to the industrial suburbs of Birmingham and Manchester. Parallel utopian and millenarian movements included the Adventists, some of whom settled along waterways in Michigan, or the Latter Day Saints, who emigrated to the farthest frontier.

Using language that uneducated listeners could "understand without the use of a dictionary," Finney offered direct and forceful preaching. Sensing the plasticity of modern urban culture, he declared that it would be impossible for the church to gain the attention of the world without exciting preaching and sufficient novelty to get the public ear. He advocated persuading sinners the way a shrewd attorney approaches a jury of ordinary folk making a life-or-death decision.[53]

Among Finney's auditors in upstate New York was a precocious girl, Elizabeth Cady (1815–1902)—later married to a judge Stanton. She became a leading abolitionist, temperance advocate, and a founder of modern feminism. Herself used to commanding an audience, she recalled Finney as

> a pulpit orator who, as a terrifier of human souls, has proved almost the equal of Savanarola. I can see him now, his great eyes rolling round the congregation, and his arms flying in the air like a windmill. One evening he described Hell and Devil so vividly that the picture glowed before my eyes in the dark for months afterwards. On another occasion, when describing the damned as wandering in the Inferno, and inquiring their way through its avenues, he suddenly pointed with his finger, exclaiming, "There! Do you not see them?" and I actually jumped up in church and looked around.[54]

Ever full of himself, Finney took possibly justifiable credit for influencing revivalism even among Roman Catholics, whose practices he thought delusory. One of his converts from 1838, Clarence A. Walworth (1820–1900), passed through Episcopalianism, eventually becoming a priest of the Redemptorist Order.[55] The Redemptorists specialized in missionary work, parish missions, and retreats—all characterized by vivid preaching. In 1858 with Isaac T. Hecker, formerly a keen Methodist and now also a Redemptorist, Walworth broke off to found a new American missionary order, the Paulists. This first generation of American Catholic intellectuals sought stratagems for outflanking the Yankee Protestants and their pretensions to reach down to ignorant slaves while these same Protestants were contemning Catholic immigrants as witless dupes in a game of sacramental hocus-pocus.[56]

Similar to contemporary Oxford Movement men in Britain, the Paulists sought to complement homiletic strength by the panoply of the Roman liturgy as a conduit of truth and beauty, the necessary path received from our fathers as the way to full life lived in God's grace. Meanwhile, some of the best and brightest young Protestant Americans were going abroad to Continental consulates, universities, or conservatories and returning to prove the value of their overseas experience. European-educated composers wrote music such as John Knowles Paine's grandiose, Latin-text *Mass in D* (1867) so that Boston brahmins might be edified by spiritual encounters in concert halls, new temples of bourgeois Protestantism. Museums and concert halls were similar to the permanent institutions built around the sites of encampments, manifestations of Inner Light spilling over into public good.

Hecker and the Paulists strove to turn the tables. They argued that Protestant theology, being based on the presumption of human depravity, was unworthy of a free people seeking transcendental achievement. Even the invitation to human cooperation in the work of salvation, as in the Arminian spin that Methodism put on Calvinism, was viewed as inferior to Catholicism, which was declared superior not only in numerical plurality among denominations, but in quality of culture. For example, as prominent Protestant churches filled great gothic-style edifices with the finest professionally led sacred music, the Paulist Choir of men and boys in New York worked to demonstrate that the true locus of human achievement apt to a meritocracy was derived from the Roman Catholic liturgy. In short, all major denominations adapted their worship to the burgeoning American marketplace that its best observer, Alexis de Tocqueville, found so healthy.[57]

Finney's rivals and successors worked to keep the fire glowing. Their enthusiasm was enshrined in all aspects of church life, which became the center of American communities. Moments of conversion in a temporary meeting spilled over into permanent opportunities.

The evangelicals logically encouraged lay participation in all aspects of the work, including preaching. Some of the temporary encampments became permanent institutions that offered opportunities for ongoing study of all aspects of the Bible and the development of every human faculty. Such development of the whole person naturally evolved beyond unsophisticated forms of praise to embrace theological, literary, artistic, and musical excellence. Some of these educational efforts, aimed at both the increase of personal holiness and the amplification of ecstatic preaching to the world, turned into colleges and universities as well as centers of religiously based leisure, education, and entertainment such as those founded by Methodists at Chautauqua, New York, and Bay View, Michigan. These and other encampments became permanent settlements and evolved into communities of permanent buildings devoted to study and practice of the intellectual disciplines and artistry related to preaching and singing. The earnest zeal and hungry sociability of the original campground worship services spilled over into voluntary extensions of worship that have endured longer than the chapel attendance originally required at the dozens of denominational colleges such as Oberlin and Otterbein in Ohio, or Carleton in Minnesota.

Hence there was a long-term trend toward enrichment of worship in denominations that had seemed most opposed to grand buildings, elaborate ceremonies, and sophisticated music, but did have a respect for the priesthood of each individual Christian. This belief entailed respect for all talents as vocations, whether ecclesiastically ordained or not. As a result, Protestant denominations that had originally eschewed outward splendor lest it interfere with the Inner Light now erected impressive worship spaces. Their congregations might also develop excellent public church music as an outward sign of divine indwelling. Thus the worship programs of even "nonliturgical" Protestant churches in America often became centers of intense musical activities, mounting high-quality productions of concert music even in isolated towns, whereas the Catholics even in a metropolis were often satisfied with a perfunctory performance of a fixed ritual. Ironically, opera, that offspring of Counter-Reformation "papist" culture, flourishes in the early 2000s at the fundamentalist Bob Jones University. Although women seem always to form the majority of active members in any church, they were not often able to become Protestant leaders of worship, despite the egalitarian implications of Inner Light theology. Yet many spoke out against slavery, for temperance, or claimed the right to preach. Though excluded from politics and commerce, women might more often define themselves in religious terms than did men.

Hymnody

In the churches of the Reformation, congregational singing remained the principal way in which the people participated in the service.[58] Hymn singing bloomed in Lutheran Germany, where a distinctive tradition of church music was already in place. The relatively conservative nature of Lutheran liturgical revision facilitated the use of new hymns because there were already texts in the inherited liturgy that were not excerpts from scripture. In general, the Lutheran Sunday morning service, like that of the Church of England, consisted of the ante-communion that corresponded to the Roman Catholic mass up to the offertory. Since the Lutheran Sunday service retained the pre-Reformation selection of epistles and gospel, the chorales, cantatas, and voluntaries tended to be selected in relation to those readings, thus becoming "proper" to particular Sundays or festivals. Luther, who loved the Latin liturgy and its music, desired to retain much of this heritage while developing vernacular congregational participation. He saw no conflict between high arts and popular participation. Based on "the example of prophets and kings in the Old Testament, who praised God with singing and playing, with hymns and the sound of all manner of stringed instruments," he favored the use of all kinds of instruments in church.[59] His theology facilitated the integral development of congregational chorales and art music such as the organ preludes or cantatas composed on chorales by the town *Kantor*, the best known of whom was Johann Sebastian Bach. Many of Bach's most astounding compositions are based on the congregational chorales of the evangelical (Lutheran) Church that were derived from Gregorian chant and have remained in Lutheran hymnals to the present day. Interpolated with liturgical and biblical texts, Bach often employed sentimental pietistic lyrics that personalize theological concepts derived from the scripture. Both the roots in Roman Catholic liturgical tradition and empathy with heartfelt common experience are evident in his cantatas, such as "Come Now, Healer of Us Heathens" (*Nun komm der Heiden Heiland*) for Advent and "Christ Lay Shackled in Death's Prison" (*Christ lag in Todesbanden*) for Easter.[60]

The Lutheran exploitation of the possibilities of chorale tunes was analogous to the medieval development of polyphony out of cantus firmi excerpted from Gregorian chant or popular melodies of the day such as "L'homme armé." Despite Bach's being bullied by his clerical employers, Lutheran acceptance of high-quality hometown musical craftsmen invites comparison with the enduring Roman Catholic division into lay and clerical classes, wherein professional musicians tend to be defined either as lay poachers on clerical turf or as mere substitutes for congregational singing.

In the Reformed churches derived from Calvin's Geneva, liturgical change had been radical. All sung texts were to be strictly biblical, generally the Psalms. No new hymns were composed to fit the liturgical year because it, like the annual cycle of prescribed epistles and gospels, tended to disappear. Connections with irreligious music were eliminated, as were perceived rivals to the word such as professional musicians, choirs, and organs. Following the French-language example, the Psalms were translated into vernacular tongues using a few poetic meters sung to a few simple tunes that functioned like the psalm-tone formulas of the old Roman liturgy. This utilitarian music, rather than Lutheran-style through-composed chorales, characterized the Congregationalist, Presbyterian, and other Reformed churches. In Scotland, the *Forme of Prayers* by John Knox (1513–1572) had ordered the singing of psalms "in a playne tune"—not plainsong. The texts of sacred scripture were not to be used during mere music rehearsals. Hence arose the use of "practice verses" for learning the tunes

before singing them to the biblical text during the actual service. This custom resulted in memory slips that occasioned the lining out of a naughty ballad during at
least one inspired performance.[61]

The services set forth in the Church of England's *Book of Common Prayer* contained
occasions for congregational involvement, but in times of widespread illiteracy it was
the metrical psalms "lined out" by the clerk that gave worshipers their best chance for
active participation. These became a regular and expected ingredient of worship, sung
before and after the sermon. After the restoration of the monarchy in 1660, metrical
psalms took their place alongside choral anthems, instrumental voluntaries, and settings of canticles. Eventually bound together with the Prayer Book, they thereby attained a quasi-official status and were widely used as an appendix to the liturgy. The
Reformation-era literal translation in Thomas Sternhold's and John Hopkins's *Whole
Book of Psalms* (1562)—the "Old Version"—was superseded at the turn of the eighteenth century by a "New Version" (1696) written by two clerical literati, Nahum
Tate (1652–1715) and Nicholas Brady (1659–1726). Their versification, which bent
biblical bluntness to the classical suavity of the Augustan Age, remained in print until
the nineteenth century. Their turn from the strict letter of scripture toward rhetorical
paraphrase, the taste of the time, or personal appeal marks the beginning of the modern English-language hymn.[62] While preaching in the established churches during
the Age of Reason may have been a "high and dry" exercise for the mind, hymn writers consciously strove to connect with the heart.

An eighteenth-century "flowering of English hymnody" extended from the *Hymns
and Spiritual Songs* (1707) of the Independent pastor Isaac Watts through the compositions of John and Charles Wesley in the middle years to John Newton and William
Cowper's *Olney Hymns* (1779) and the writings of Thomas Kelly and James Mont-
gomery beyond century's end. Though not immediately incorporated into the liturgy
of the Church of England, they represented a new enthusiasm for hymns and the
recovery of some ancient purposes under fresh guises. Two famous prefaces make the
points. That of Isaac Watts to his *Psalms of David Imitated in the Language of the New
Testament* (1718) was concerned that the Old Testament be interpreted in the light of
the New Testament, and that the Psalms in particular be sung as the church's praise:
David should be made to "speak like a Christian." Thus Psalm 72 becomes "Christ's
Kingdom among the Gentiles":

> *Jesus* shall reign where'er the sun
> Doth his successive journeys run. . . .

Watts's tunes may have been limited to a few standard meters already in use for singing; for the texts, however, he found a new fluency, and deployed literary skills that
did not spoil their simplicity. The sometimes stilted phrasing of Tate and Brady was
replaced by a combination of vigor and elegance that has stood the test of time, as in
Watts's version of Psalm 90:

> Our God, our help in ages past,
> Our hope for years to come,
> Our shelter from the stormy blast,
> And our eternal home. . . .

In addition to Watts's paraphrases of psalms, his lyrics on divine subjects make him a
hymn writer in the modern sense. He may indeed be best remembered for his redemptive fusion of the personal, the cosmic, and the divine in his communion hymn

based on Galatians 6:14: "When I survey the wondrous Cross." On the other hand, much of his work has passed into oblivion, as, for example, his verses for November 5th on "papist idolatry reproved," to commemorate the foiling of Guy Fawkes's plot in 1605 to blow up Parliament.

John Wesley's preface to *A Collection of Hymns for the Use of the People called Methodists* (1780) describes how he organized the hymns "according to the experience of real Christians," claiming that "no such hymnbook as this has yet been published in the English language." Not only that, but the book contained "all the important truths of our most holy religion, whether speculative or practical." The piety of John Wesley (1703–1791) and his brother Charles (1707–1788) was grounded in the classic dogmas and the liturgical life of the Church of England. Yet, as may be seen also in their publications for the great festivals and their eucharistic hymns, they use intimate first-person forms even when rephrasing the doctrines of redemption or invoking the coming of Christ into the worship assembly. Take the Passion hymn originally found in *Hymns and Sacred Poems* (1742):

> O Love divine! what hast Thou done?
> The immortal God hath died for me!
> The Father's co-eternal Son
> Bore all my sins upon the tree;
> The immortal God for me hath died!
> My Lord, my Love is crucified.

Or the text from *Hymns on the Lord's Supper* (1745) that develops the Resurrection story from Luke 24:13–35:

> O Thou who this mysterious Bread
> Didst in Emmaus break,
> Return herewith our souls to feed,
> And to Thy followers speak.
> Unseal the volume of Thy grace,
> Apply the gospel word,
> Open our eyes to see Thy face,
> Our hearts to know the Lord. . . .

A prolific poet, Charles Wesley was able to use a much greater variety of meters than Watts; and John Wesley, who also translated hymns from the German, insisted editorially on poetic excellence for inclusion in the books intended for use in worship.[63] According to Bernard Manning, the Wesleys' 1780 *Collection* "ranks in Christian literature with the Psalms, the Book of Common Prayer, and the Canon of the Mass. In its own way, it is elemental in its perfection."[64]

This growth in hymnody made for a new way of using hymns in all churches of the dissenting tradition, with which Methodism was by the end of the eighteenth century aligned. As Manning put it, hymns became "for Dissenters what the liturgy is for the Anglican. They are the framework, the setting, the conventional, the traditional part of divine service as we use it. They are, to adopt the language of the liturgiologists, the Dissenting Use."[65] Thus there was a sharp distinction between the liturgically limited use of hymns in the Church of England and their use in churches with less fixed liturgies. But, as Alan Dunstan observes, the distinction became "much less marked with the growth of more set liturgical forms in the Free Churches" combined with "a more flexible approach to liturgy in the Church of England."[66]

The diverse denominational efforts to make orthodox Christianity more attractive to the sentiments of modern worshipers often influenced one another, even when their defined dogmas might be at odds. The writing of hymns that may seem today merely sentimental testifies to a quest for heartfelt appeal that was at one with the Bible and traditions of the church. Pietistic Moravians in Lutheran lands, French Rousseauvian reformers on the eve of the Revolution, and repeated Evangelical revivals in Britain and America all addressed the hearts of worshipers who were facing the possibility of choice among competing codes of life.

In the nineteenth century, interaction among partisans of the head, heart, and nation became particularly vivid. As England, in particular, became more urban, industrial, and secular, Liberal politicians considered disestablishing the state church, beginning in Ireland, where the preponderance of the population was Roman Catholic anyway. Faced with this prospect, the defenders of the Church of England turned to traditions older than the state. Prior to secular government they saw a Christian culture out of which the nation had evolved. So, for example, while retaining evangelical-style hymns that made Christianity subjective, the men of the Oxford Movement wanted to revivify an "objective" liturgical tradition that extended back to the patristic era when some Church Fathers had found that the original imperial support of Christianity under Constantine presented difficult problems. Hence historical restoration in modern secular states had a political agenda.

More profound was the yearning for the sublime. Repelled by the surfeit and squalor of the modern industrial metropolis, the eclectic and postrationalistic cultural movement called Romanticism embraced everything except simplistic definitions. From mass appeal to effete detail, every mode of religious idea was available. Hence the hymnals of the nineteenth century, like its buildings, music, and rubrics, are easy to praise or condemn according to one's taste. The devout Tory Tractarian John Keble was opposed to political freedom, but was nonetheless an apostle of psychological freedom. The Oxford Movement's measure of religiosity was its intensity, not mere rubricism. Among their models were the revivalistic evangelicals of the Whitefield-Wesley century. According to Keble, all the arts and poetry, especially religious traditions that have survived the centuries, speak the ineffable. They liberate repressed feelings.[67]

Scholarly historicism and personal appeal also blended in the largest and most widespread ecclesiastical body, Roman Catholicism. Sentimental songs associated with reputed apparitions of the Sacred Heart in the seventeenth century or the Blessed Virgin Mary at Lourdes in the mid-nineteenth flourished alongside meticulous research into Gregorian chants of the monastic office. Among Roman Catholics, there is a mistaken belief that only since Vatican II have congregational hymns been sung regularly at mass. This is an oversimplification of a complex question. In Europe, concessions to vernacular in the liturgy were used during the Counter-Reformation campaign to recover central Europe from Protestantism. In German-speaking countries the *Hochamt* (High Mass) regularly included a *Hauptlied*, a principal song, not just to frame the sermon, as in Protestant worship, but as the musical banner of the eucharistic prayer in place of the Latin Sanctus. This compromise, like the all-German *Singmesse*, would continue through the church-versus-state Kulturkampf of the later nineteenth century and provide some of the impetus toward the vernacularizing reforms of Vatican II. The combination of Roman liturgy with vernacular language allowed the members of the Roman Catholic Church to claim that they were both *Deutsch und Katholik*.

Roadside Jesus, Poland.
PHOTOGRAPH © CONRAD L.
DONAKOWSKI

In submerged nationalities ruled by foreign governments, such as the Prussian Germanization in Poland, loyalty to the Latin language would seem nationalistic because the Catholic Church tended to avoid accepting the secular government's definition of vernacular. From the partitions in the late eighteenth century down to the extreme situation of the Nazi occupation during the youth of Pope John Paul II, Polish leaders sought to evade German influence. A mixture of their home vernacular for informal worship combined with unswerving loyalty to Roman Latin for the liturgy seemed the right mix. If the liturgy itself had been in the official, legal, and established language of the region, the Poles might have been required to celebrate mass in German. By the beginning of the twentieth century, the vernacular-versus-Latin question came to America with the various Catholic immigrant groups. Some highly educated Germans had arrived among the refugees from the failed revolutions of 1848. They became cultural, political, and liturgical leaders in new cities such as Cincinnati, Chicago, and Detroit. Other central European ethnic groups might be less educated but they had similar practices. Vernacular songs were employed alongside Latin even during High Mass and were normal during Low Mass, as had been conceded in Europe during the Counter-Reformation. Slavic Americans addressed their parish music director by the honorific title of professor, and many a parish of miners and laborers supported a full-time organist and choir director. This seemed odd to many of the Irish American leaders for whom the liturgy had better not be in the vernacular nor too public, and certainly not sung too well; for the Catholic Irish had surrendered their aboriginal tongue even while conquering modern English literature. Mass in the vernacular—especially if accompanied by professionally directed music—would have meant the mass in English and implied submission to the Anglican Church of Ireland whose practices the English oppressors wanted to impose.[68] On the other hand, to central-European immigrants such suspicion of the craft of music made the Irish Americans seem like WASP killjoys who wanted to take the fun out of church. Whereas Protestants might be perceived as different, the Irish-dominated hierarchy could be perceived as dangerous. The differences were institutionalized in several Catholic parishes, such the Sweetest Heart of Mary Church, a Polish-American assembly in Detroit, Michigan, where a magnificent edifice was erected, but never turned over to the ownership of the bishop, as required by canon law. Instead, a congregational style of parish government persists to this day, whereby the pastor, although the bishop's appointee, cannot spend any money without the approval of an elected board of lay trustees. Similar controversies in other places led to the creation of the Polish National Catholic Church, now headquartered in Doylestown, Pennsylvania.

Well before Vatican II, it had in fact become normal for Catholic congregations to sing vernacular hymns at all Sunday masses. But the liturgical renewal was beginning to show signs of a split partly because of different ethnic heritages and partly on account of different tastes, as between the partisans of popular music styles and that prescribed by the then-existing documents on the liturgy, which set up Gregorian chant and Renaissance polyphony as models.

Relations with Civil Religion

During the nineteenth century, civic ritual designed to inculcate patriotism spread in the wake of the French Revolution. The new statist cult owed much to Christian practice and would in turn influence modern religion. Like secularized festivals such as Mardi Gras in Latin countries, the celebrations of the Revolution kept a flavor related to manifestations of popular religion in Catholic countries. The form of the message also owed much to the behavioralist psychology of leading eighteenth-century thinkers. Following John Locke (1632–1704), they believed that human nature is malleable and that virtues can be inculcated by associating them with pleasant sensations such as music, dance, and spectacle. The leaders of these spectacles were conscripted largely from the ranks of church musicians, such as the music director at Notre Dame de Paris, Jean-François Lesueur (1760–1837). Even before the Revolution he was experimenting with massive compositional effects in the cathedral. He applied these grandiose gestures to music composed for the fêtes of the Revolution. Eventually he passed his massive approach to ceremonial music on to his student Hector Berlioz (1803–1869). The Lockean behavioralist psychology was reinforced through its relation to the classic debate over the balance between reason and emotion, which had become part of Christian liturgical theory.[69]

Mediation of the new consciousness sought by the cult of the nation–state was deliberately planned after the recommendations of Jean-Jacques Rousseau, whose prolix writings on community-building as antidote to the Enlightenment demolition of tradition had been summarized in his recommendations to a submerged—Polish—nation trying to survive. Use rites, rituals, songs, and stories to create a community, he says. Maintain traditions and institute practices that regulate even the most intimate aspects of life, as Moses had done among the Hebrews or Lycurgus among the Spartans, because "a fortress built in the heart is impregnable."[70] Since then, Rousseau's blend of conformity and compassion has influenced virtually every reform movement in Western civilization from the liturgical movement to radical socialism.

When analyzing the relationship between the cult of the Revolution in France and traditional Catholicism, historians have tended to concentrate on startling innovations such as the Cult of Reason or the great celebrations such as that of the Deist Festival of Supreme Being in Paris in June 1794. These were artificial creations of the revolutionary government and as such have little to do with the spontaneous evolution of civic religious practices derived from Catholicism. When radical dechristianization got under way in 1793–1794, it was under the direction of bourgeois ideologues who concocted imagery borrowed from their secular classical education. Not so among the true sansculotte masses in the cities or peasants in the countryside, who still perceived reality in terms of imagery derived from their Catholic upbringing. Although the doctrinal anti-Christian aspects of the civic rites was essentially political propaganda for the new regime, the sentiments of the people changed their attachments from the old to the new dispensation only little by little, if at all. The fervent and mostly female crowds came less for a philosophy lesson and more to venerate the latest revolutionary saints who demonstrated God's miraculous providence for his people.[71]

Religious imagery borrowed from familiar songs such as the Easter carol "O filii et filiae" (O sons and daughters) promised a new life, a resurrection under a new political regime. New lyrics to the ancient tune seem both eschatological and related to the theology of the eucharist:

> The vine that we thought dead
> A new crop of grapes had bred;
> What a miracle. Alleluia, alleluia, alleluia.[72]

Gradually the civic cult moved away from Catholicism. The fall of the Bastille on 14 July 1789 was celebrated by a Te Deum sung in Notre Dame. The following year witnessed sermons by patriot-priests who said that it was the aristocracy that crucified Christ and therefore the sacrifices made at the Bastille were like Christ's sacrifice. This implies that dead patriots were Christian martyrs and were therefore saints in heaven. The year wore on with numerous Blessings of Banners for the National Guard, a citizen, rather than royal, army. Solemn oaths in imitation of ancient pagan Roman ceremonies joined Christian prayers. A year later, the first Bastille Day saw a Catholic mass concelebrated by three hundred priests wearing tricolor red, white, and blue cinctures. This Festival of Federation was intended to reconcile all factions in France. As it turned out, however, this was the end of public unity between the civic and Catholic liturgies for the next decade. Meanwhile a bishop withdrew from the Catholic Church, addressing the Convention about Holy Equality; a Reformed pastor declared that "Henceforth I shall have no other gospel than the Republican

The Festival of Federation. *La Fête de la Fédération*, folk painting of the first Bastille Day celebration, which was a mass, on 14 July 1790. Photograph © Conrad L. Donakowski

Constitution"; and new songs, such as "La Marseillaise," sang of holy nature and the sacred love of country. "Le jour de gloire est arrivé" was proclaimed with all the eschatological overtones that such phrases still aroused among the general population.

Most delegates to the Estates General that had been called to reform France's problems back in 1789 assumed that the Christian cult was the clergy's business. So, the juring clergy, who swore allegiance to the new regime in 1791, discussed the improvement of worship in the Gallican church. Yet by the time the juring bishops got around to decreeing substantive changes in the liturgy, the Revolution was bent on destroying, not changing, Christianity. Moreover these Constitutional Clergy—loyal to the spirit of Henry IV, for whom "Paris was worth a mass," and regardless of their personal opinions—as a whole hesitated to go the way of the Protestants with their tendency to divide the church into competing sects. Loyal Gallicans to the end, these successors of the nation-building cardinals Mazarin and Richelieu wished to avoid disrupting the consolidation of the French state that had taken a thousand years from the days of Clovis's conversion to the religion of his wife, Saint Clotilde.

As the Revolution sped on, progressives departed the upper ranks of even the Constitutional Clergy. Some vernacular Catholic liturgies may have been performed in a few parishes, but one cannot be sure that the mass was ever said in French during the decade of Revolution. The refractory, nonjuring clergy who remained loyal to the Roman church concentrated on maintaining church unity, declaring—rather like the Irish during the English occupation—that in such times it was sufficient for the priest to understand the Latin rites and the people to attend. The liturgical policy of the Republic was officially to follow Jean-Jacques Rousseau's advice to "turn the spectators into the spectacle" with rites designed to be performed by and for the people, not in confining buildings but under the open sky. The Revolutionary "pageant masters" conscripted musicians and published a *Magasin* that was a resource book of music for an annual round of rituals intended to replace the Catholic liturgical year with civic festivals such as those honoring the Supreme Being, Natural Law, and Love of Country. Wherever the revolution spread it replaced old habits with new, such as the metric system, even temporarily expunging the seven-day week with a ten-day *decade*.[73]

Napoleon's Concordat with the papacy officially settled the conflict between the two competing cults in 1801 by returning the church to the liturgical status quo ante. After the persecutions suffered during the Revolution, the Catholic Church in romance-language countries tended to be dominated by an internal-émigré mentality that estranged it from modern civilization. There remained no concessions to the vernacular except in paraliturgical devotions or hymns that might be used during the liturgy but were technically not part of it. During the remainder of the nineteenth century there was a clear split in France between Catholic and civic ritual, such as the requirement that all couples be married before a town magistrate, thus making the sacrament of matrimony unnecessary in the eyes of the state. Nevertheless the full separation between church and state did not come until 1905–1906.

Romanticism: The Culture of Bourgeois Democracy

The Enlightenment had encouraged the European elite to criticize reason itself. Furthermore, by the end of the eighteenth century, reform and revolution had proven insufficient guides to the pursuit of happiness. The expansion of intellectual horizons led to an expansion of affective insights whereby the Enlightenment itself was judged insufficient by a new cultural movement, Romanticism. Because of its respect for those realities that are beyond reason, Romanticism was open to religion. Because one of those realities is tradition, Romanticism was usually friendly toward religious heritage. Fearing that social capital was being destroyed by cutthroat capitalism, Romanticism was often communitarian and therefore respectful of communal rituals, though not always reverent toward churches. Romanticism included solicitude for endangered species of belief and practice. These included the lost innocence of childlike aspirations, traditions of communities, unique events, and incomprehensible mysteries that they named "The Sublime" (*das Erhabene*).

By insisting that reality includes many things that are beyond scientific explanation, the Romantics tended to subvert the traditional intellectualist hierarchy of the "higher" and "lower" human faculties, much as the democratic and industrial revolutions had subverted feudal presumptions about "higher" and "lower" classes of humanity. This subversion had many dimensions in cultural matters. Among them was a psychological reorientation from the objective outside world to the subjective world of imagination and feelings within; a social reorientation from idealization of the privileged to idealization of the people; a geographical reorientation away from the classical culture lately borne by the French to indigenous cultures wherever found; a gender reorientation away from a masculine to an androgynous ideal; from the adult to the child; from the urbane sophisticate to the simple peasant. All of these changes marked a fresh emphasis on themes continuous in the Western cultural tradition but inseparable from the industrial and political revolutions of the same years. Romanticism, which recognized organic links with the past, was often historicist and therefore conservative. It could also be liberal in its search for democratic culture, in which self-esteemed "reasonable men" must come to terms with the unreasonableness of mass feeling often expressed in popular religions. In short, where classically minded Rationalism sought rules, Romanticism valued variety.

While proceeding to new creation in this spirit, the Romantics usually thought it necessary simultaneously to reestablish contact with living or viable traditions where emotion or imagination had flourished. The part of the human past that most fascinated them was that which lay psychically anterior to calculation and historically prior to civilization and its discontents. There the function of ritual was to give a healing outlet for secret emotions, to speak the unspeakable and to communicate the ineffable.

Ultimately, the zeal to conserve past religious experience came to support the belief that artistic imagination is the key to future religion and therefore to future civilization. Speaking of the artistic playfulness of the liturgy, Romano Guardini, much the student of the Romantics, contrasted the apparent purposeless of the liturgy with didactic syllabi like Ignatius of Loyola's *Spiritual Exercises*:

> The difference resembles that which exists between a gymnasium, in which every detail of the apparatus and every exercise aims at a calculated effect, and the open wood and fields. In the first, everything is consciously directed towards discipline and development; in the second, life is lived with Nature, and internal growth takes place in her.[74]

In those places where traditional ritual and music survived through the eighteenth into the nineteenth centuries, their use was like the churches they served, often more a habit than a conviction. Still, there was no lack of leaders who hoped to revive the liturgy. In part the roots of the return to liturgical integrity are in the Enlightenment, not only in its Protestant-like critique of distracting accretions to the liturgy but also in its desire that human behavior be in accordance with the laws of social and psychological nature, which may be discerned but are too complex to be defined. Like so many things, the restoration of the liturgy owes something to Jean-Jacques Rousseau, philosopher of the natural impulse who despised sophisticated urbanity. His theories, perhaps the most influential of modern times, appeal to the heart or tradition but can be dangerous allies for religionists. For Rousseau religious expression may be necessary, but theologies and church authority are not. Most of his works deal obliquely with the question of the need for worship and what form this might take. His *Dictionnaire de musique* became an often-unacknowledged handbook. Besides disseminating some of the first scholarly information on folk and non-Western music, it gives a clue to his attitude toward religious worship as an evolutionary phenomenon that is both a product and a measure of the total culture. He believed that the good things in Christian worship, like Gregorian chant, "were a noble relic of classical Greek culture . . . preferable to the theatrical [read "operatic"] music usually heard in churches, which was merely a display of vocal technique, whereas Chant clothed the text and thus expressed it better for the listeners."[75] His ideas were exploited both by those who wished to repristinate Christian worship and those who desired to replace it with a new cult.[76]

Another pioneer of liturgical reform was Martin Gerbert (1720–1793), abbot of Saint Blasien, who collected and published the then-known writings of earlier ecclesiastical authors concerning liturgical music. Like Rousseau, his thesis was that modern music was too proud to serve the liturgy. His nostalgia for the liturgy of earlier days was tempered with vernacularist teaching that Latin hymns "are of no use to a peasant," who should have the opportunity to sing in his native tongue for the sake both of edification and of piety, as "he did in the old Germanic liturgy."[77] The theological tradition that teaches that civilization has run downhill from some ideal antiquity derives from Plato, who speaks of music as the most potent art and warns of its dangers when insubordinate. Prior to the age of Rousseau and Mozart, there was scant published information about the actual craft of music, which was reckoned the purview of ignorant artists. Christian scholars abhorred the arrival of not just hymn lyricists but of professional musicians into liturgical leadership. The rise of music in the estimation of the Romantics from last to first in the aesthetic hierarchy connoted a profound cultural revolution—Romanticism—that toppled Western civilization's Platonic presumptions inherited through the Church.[78]

Johann Michael Sailer and Prosper Guéranger

The paradigm of Roman Catholic liturgical reform and ecumenism in more modern times is Johann Michael Sailer (1751–1832), who rose from the peasantry to become bishop of Regensburg.[79] He is important for many reasons. First, his ideas combine the Protestant and Enlightenment critique of Catholic worship with those of nascent Romanticism. Second, his pastoral application of these ideas made him a prophet both of progressive Catholicism and of liturgical revival based on historical research. He was the patron both of a program to restore old music and of popular participation in the liturgy. Through his students, among them King Ludwig I of Bavaria, he was also a forerunner of the German Center Party mixture of Catholicism and nationalism. Ironically, the work of Sailer, who appreciated non-Catholic and non-Christian culture, led to the Caecilian Society, which was defensively ultramontane.

Sailer's biographers consider him the most important religious leader of his time. Having lived and died within the Roman Catholic Church, he has attracted no liberal historians, unlike the famous apostate Felicité de Lamennais (1782–1854). Since ecclesiastical enemies questioned Sailer's orthodoxy, his promotion to bishop was delayed until he was eighty and his cause neglected thereafter. Comparable to Rousseau among the French philosophes and the folklorist Johann Gottfried von Herder (1744–1803) among Protestant Germans in his wide embrace, Sailer's influence was in part responsible for the ideas eventually enshrined in the Second Vatican Council.

Sailer was the first Catholic theologian to recognize the importance of Romanticism. He appreciated the music of Ludwig von Beethoven (1770–1827) as a document of the possibilities of genius freed from artificial social restrictions and was in turn admired by the composer. Sailer's via media between Erastian statism and ultramontane devotionalism foreshadowed John Henry Newman's later attempt to synthesize an evolutionary view of history with the doctrines and practice of Christianity. Both Sailer and Newman saw the doctrines and liturgy of the Church as organic parts of an all-embracing, though locally adaptable, continuum wherein diverse forces were reconciled.

Sailer argued that the development of every human faculty is necessary in the formation of a complete individual, just as the development of all human types is necessary in the formation of a good society. Hence, simple piety or musical sensitivity is as human as abstract philosophy or political cunning. Noteworthy among the thirty-three volumes of his published works is *The Union of Religion and Art* [Bund der Religion und Kunst] (1808), which balances devotion to the institutional Church with sensitivity to the simple Inner Light stressed by the "enthusiasts." He combines appreciation for past heritage with need to update its expressions. Sailer was regarded most highly as a pastor and mentor of young priests. The ideas handed down for 150 years through students of his students are preserved in the *Constitution on the Sacred Liturgy* of the Second Vatican Council.

Along with the Bavarian polymath Sailer, the French Benedictine Dom Prosper Guéranger (1805–1875) shares honors for beginning the chain of events that led to the liturgical reforms of the twentieth century.[80] In his youth Guéranger was the disciple of Felicité de Lamennais, who was at that time a firebrand Catholic apologist.[81] Guéranger believed that Enlightenment rationalism was not only insufficient but also dangerous, as evidenced by the destructive excesses of the French Revolution. According to him, the modern world needed communitarian spiritual priorities higher than political power founded on selfish capitalistic greed. Only the Roman Catholic Church, led by the pope, could provide true freedom, which would include independence of any secular regime. Revival of the ancient liturgical life of Benedictine monasticism was believed seminal for Roman Catholic revival in much the same way as the Pietist Nikolaus Ludwig Zinzendorf and his Protestant commune had believed they were the pilots for Lutheran regeneration. According to Dom Guéranger, who later achieved the reputation of having begun the restoration of an ancient continuous utopian community, the congregation need not even understand, let alone directly participate in, the ceremonies of the church. The liturgical chant functioned *ex opere operato*. Nevertheless, with his mind on his beloved ages of faith, he insisted that "plain chant is the sung prayer of the people": "its prosody bears the people's accent, its modes are natural scales, the people's."[82] Like many other exemplars of the complex nineteenth-century cultural revolution called Romanticism, Guéranger combined right-wing theology with left-wing sociology. As the Wesleys and revivalists had tried to rejuvenate churches in the changing Anglophone world, so did Continental liturgical reformers attempt to recreate an imagined Christian community that had been ruined by internecine nationalism and selfish materialism. By restoring the liturgy and its music Guéranger believed that he could save the world. If he could only return to the people their stolen heritage of chanted worship, a community of love would follow under the guidance of the Holy Spirit. He began the restoration in the 1830s, the same decade depicted in Victor Hugo's *Les misérables* (1862), which portrayed common ground between the rituals of revolutionary camaraderie and Christian agape.

In 1833 Dom Guéranger began the reintroduction of monasticism into France. At the Priory of Solesmes they again lived Saint Benedict's Rule in a combination of "prayer and work" (*ora et labora*). They hoped to be a model for a confused modern society as Benedict had hoped his communities would build Christian civilization amid the chaotic dark ages that followed the fall of the Roman Empire.[83]

Benedictine monasticism is a communitarian total environment, the heart of which is the chanting of the liturgy. The aim is that the ritual engage all the senses with its view, colors, light, and darkness; its texture; its incense; its kinesthesia; and its sound. The sounds were monophonic chant. In the age of industry and its chief critic, Karl Marx (1818–1883), the oldest communism extant in Western civilization seemed to many idealists no longer "the denial of humanity" that the Enlightenment had spoken of, but "the art of arts," as Romano Guardini would call it. Part of the rationale for dissolving the cloisters in the eighteenth century—as for Henry VIII in the sixteenth— had been to transfer their resources and loyalties to the state. On the Continent, the revival of the monastic way of life aimed to reverse this process while providing a refuge against materialism.

When Guéranger and his associates dedicated themselves to the restoration of the "art of arts," it was almost inevitable that Solesmes would become concerned with music, the art most thoroughly integrated with the day-to-day performance of the *opus Dei*, the liturgy of the hours. At first, the medieval music seemed the most easily accessible affect because it appeared to depend only on authentic manuscripts and competent performers. Yet music proved to be both the emblem of unity and the sign of contradiction within the liturgical restoration.

With one hand Guéranger fought the religious rationalism that would delete everything nonbiblical—that is, everything medieval—from the Roman rites and even replace its first-person plurals with singulars. With the other, he fought Gallican traditions that were concessions to local custom. These were anathema to the followers of Lamennais because they suggested that the cosmic authority of Christianity depended on local bishops, who were now state employees. So, Guéranger worked to destroy all trace of non-Roman missals. Only by being handwritten were some Gallican rites preserved. Most were so efficiently proscribed and destroyed by the Romanizers that much music and text that had equal claim to be preserved by the church has been lost. Researchers today have difficulty even learning about the existence of these rites.

To an ultramontane like Guéranger, Parisian and other Gallican missals and service books were nothing but "an unhappy amalgam of Roman chants and parodies of miscellaneous ancient pieces." For many others, however, it was an honest difficulty to choose among all the versions that presented themselves as authentic Roman chant. The Gallicans insisted that an arbitrarily uniform version would confound rather than edify the faithful, who may have sung their particular Gallican chants for generations. To Guéranger's party, however, community meant uniformity, just as it would to the papal party at the First Vatican Council in 1870. The right to publish the official service books for the entire Roman Catholic Church was, of course, a financial prize. Desclée in Belgium published the Solesmes version; its major competitor was the Ratisbon version, published by Pustet in Regensburg, where the patriarch of the nonultramontane reformers had been Johann Michael Sailer.

The contest for the hearts of the French people was waged by the nineteenth-century church and state in monumental ways. One of the most visible was the construction of the church of Sacré-Coeur on the highest hill overlooking Paris. Its curvaceous towers contradict the straight-edged neoclassical style favored by the Enlightenment, Revolution, and the financial institutions of economic liberalism. Although the great churches of the capital of European culture, Paris, were now national property, Sacré-Coeur was not. It was built with the contributions of Catholics to apologize to God for the Commune of 1871 and, implicitly, for the sins of modernity. The Blessed Sacrament is exposed there in perpetual adoration.

A Century of Secular and Religious Tensions

During the course of the nineteenth century, forms of Christian worship evolved in active dialogue with ideals derived from Enlightenment liberalism. With the lifting of legal sanctions against nonattendance at church services in western Europe and North America, religious practice now seemed a matter of personal commitment and patriotic outreach of European states through their empires. Western civilization circled the globe in both directions, as testified by the Catholic cathedrals built from Algiers to Saigon, the onion domes of Orthodox churches planted down the western coast of America, Anglican bishoprics spreading from Cape Town to Shanghai, and the singing of Methodist hymns virtually everywhere in virtually every language. The most secularist national empires were eager to support overseas conversion to the homeland denominations of Christianity in order to color maps abroad after the mother country.

The United States of America presents a special case. Though the constitution is secular, territorial expansion marched on a proudly Protestant pilgrim liturgy of manifest destiny. In every town, edifices arose to house Christian worship. The journey past the frontier, whether to build a Shakertown, an Oneida, or a Temple in the wilderness for the Latter Day Saints, seemed to reinstitute God's covenant as his Chosen People claimed a promised land. Progress, personal fulfillment, and national destiny seemed to be at one with the Christian paradigm. To journey beyond the Old Law became as salvific a ritual action as the medieval walk to Canterbury or Muslim pilgrimage to Mecca. The rationales of enlightened progress, personal encounter with the Ultimate, and reasons of state were at one in the revised myth and ritual of the redeemer nation.[84] Yet the full implications of such mythic journeys were not to be seen until righteous America ruled the globe.

At home in Europe and in the old colonies of Iberia, however, the situation of Christian worship as emblem of a Christian nation grew problematic. Although the cultural treasures of liturgical art, music, and architecture were being restored, theology became embattled. By the end of the nineteenth century, energies that once made the practice of Christianity the center of Western culture were being transferred to secular myths that grew out of the Judeo-Christian impetus. Socialist celebrations, originally utopian versions of Christian ritual and contemporary with new religions like Mormonism in America, turned to effect a scientific antireligiosity. In romance-language countries, the aggressive legacy of the Revolutionary and Napoleonic eras

The Dream of a Universal Democratic and Social Brotherhood. Painting (1848) by Frédéric Sorrieu (b. 1807). An eclectic utopian vision in which Liberal democracies progress together to worship the risen Christ at the altar of Liberty. Below the motto of brotherhood, the nations of the world are marching toward the statue of Human Rights. Musée Carnavalet, Paris/Bildarchiv Preussischer Kulturbesitz/Art Resource, NY

made the state and church enemies, with the state seeking either to end religious worship or to use it—through its sweeping social and geographical reach—as a vehicle to consolidate the state's own position. In France, while the monks of Solesmes were laboring over new editions of Gregorian chant, the government was preparing laws meant to assert the final dissolution of monastic communities whose liturgies had for centuries provided the ideal for Catholicism.[85]

The hymns of Protestant worship seemed to match the old liturgical chant and polyphony in diversity and durability as vehicles for popular participation and inspiration for art music. Choral music by professional choirs of men and boys returned not only to the cathedrals of the Church of England but to larger parishes as well.[86] A converted Jewish composer, Felix Mendelssohn (1809–1847), had revived the *St. Matthew Passion* of Bach in 1829 at Berlin, the putative capital of the Germanies. In 1846 he premiered *Elijah* in industrial Birmingham, while concert-hall temples of Romantic art religion were being constructed to celebrate Christian civilization worldwide. Choral singing, usually of religious texts, became the most widespread leisure and educational activity of the century, giving the patina of religious worship to public communal cultural life. In Cincinnati, Ohio, by the 1880s both a cathedral and a concert hall of European proportions were complete in a city that fifty years before had been on the frontier. By the turn into the twentieth century, new North American industrial cities such as Chicago were spreading vast skylines punctuated by magnificent churches of every conceivable ethnic group and denomination, often supported by poor laborers in joyful imitation of their best memories of the homeland.

Proud as Germans were of their cultural heritage expressed in their legacy of music, it often became a sign of contradiction. Centered in Sailer's Regensburg, Catholics resisting the German chancellor Otto von Bismarck's Kulturkampf dug in liturgically much as the Benedictines did in France.[87] The Roman Catholic Caecilians wanted to sustain a Latin-language liturgy that would indicate the priority of church over state. Leaders of Protestant background, including Johannes Brahms (1833–1897) flourishing in Catholic Vienna, produced vernacular pieces like his *Deutsches Requiem* (1868–1872), which was the acme of a choral movement that was equally education, heartfelt religion, and national propaganda. To politically submerged neighboring nations such as Poland, however, German material, even though biblical, was a threat to be avoided. To the East in the tsarist empire the legacy of completely sung liturgy as center of the church reinforced the position of the national Orthodox churches derived from Byzantium rather than Rome. Russian choral music testifies to the strength of that tradition and the care lavished on its cultivation. Russian Romantic religious worship balanced western techniques with a sense of unbroken tradition.

At the turn into the twentieth century, each Christian denomination had a liturgy whose form would be readily recognizable. Seeking to insulate Roman Catholicism from modernist tinkering, in 1903 Pope Pius X issued a *motu proprio* that offered guidelines for refurbishing liturgy in a way that might protect it from the assaults of secular culture. In many ways, this date marks the fruition of the Romantic dream of historical authenticity that reinvigorated all branches of Christianity. Whereas theological disputation with higher critics or state authorities might be losing battles, intense worship experience—whether in Protestant preaching and hymnody or Catholic sacramental life—seemed impregnable. As a Congregationalist convert to Anglo-Catholicism—W. C. Roberts—put it:

> The Mass and the confessional were bugbears to Protestant England; their reappearance in the National Church was viewed with horror and gave Dissenters further reason for separation from it. They were in fact the two things that I needed. The rather cultured Nonconformist church in which I was brought up gave me a picture of Christ as of someone long ago who told us the truth about God, bringing home his love, and strengthening us by His example, but it was a tale of long ago. I wanted Someone here and now. Catholicism taught the real Presence of Christ among us through the Apostolic Sacraments.[88]

Liberal Christian rituals offered no such comforts that could not be found equally well satisfied in social work or cultural endeavors with similar high-minded people. So insisted the Unitarian minister Henry Gow:

> The old unreasoning habit of Public Worship which took our forefathers to church or chapel has been broken down. There is a tendency for good men to care for Practice without Prayer, to believe in morals without religion.[89]

Seen from this light, the branches of Christianity most likely to survive eventually proved to be those whose practices, if not their intellectual self-analysis, were farthest from liberalism. These are Roman Catholicism and evangelical fundamentalism. The latter had its own version of the real presence in the public acceptance of Jesus as a personal savior.

On the theoretical and historical level, liturgical scholars tend to be officially suspicious of Romanticism as "liberalism in art" or mere sentimentalism. The core of Romanticism is that the most reasonable assessment of ultimate reality is that it lies beyond the limits of reason alone. Christian worship at the turn into the twentieth century owed much to Romanticism.

Bibliography

Davies, Horton. *Worship and Theology in England*. Vol. 3: *From Watts and Wesley to Maurice*, 1690–1850. Princeton, N.J.: Princeton University Press, 1961; Vol. 4: *From Newman to Martineau, 1850–1900* (1962); and Vol. 5: *The Ecumenical Century: 1900–1965* (1965).

Donakowski, Conrad L. *A Muse for the Masses: Ritual and Music in an Age of Democratic Revolution, 1770–1870*. Chicago: University of Chicago Press, 1977.

Notes

[1] The comprehensive, though unsympathetic, treatment in Ronald Knox's *Enthusiasm: A Chapter in the History of Religion with Special Reference to the Seventeenth and Eighteenth Centuries* (Oxford: Clarendon, 1950; repr. New York: Oxford University Press, 1961), demonstrates the essential consonance of many movements often viewed as conflicting.

[2] Clifford Geertz, "Religion as a Cultural System," in *Anthropological Approaches to the Study of Religion*, ed. Michael Banton (New York: Prager, 1966) 1–46.

[3] Immanuel Kant, *Die Religion innerhalb der Grenzen der blossen Vernunft* [Religion within the limits of reason alone], in *Immanuel Kants Werke*, vol. 6 (Berlin: Cassirer, 1923) 302.

[4] Note the critical tone in Josef Jungmann's sweeping characterizations of "liturgical life on the eve of the Reformation and in the Baroque period" in *Liturgisches Erbe und pastorale Gegenwart* (Innsbruck, Austria: Tyrolia, 1960) 87–119.

[5] Contrary to the neoplatonic interpretation in Catherine Pickstock, *After Writing: On the Liturgical Consummation of Philosophy* (Oxford: Blackwell, 1998).

[6] The film *The Mission* (1986) depicts this appeal sympathetically. The general cultural historian Kenneth Clark allows the Roman church's ability to create a sort of cultural democracy that shares good things with all citizens. "The Catholic revival was a popular movement, that . . . gave ordinary people a means of satisfying, through ritual, images and symbols, their deepest impulses" (Kenneth Clark, *Civilisation* [New York: Harper and Row, 1969] 167).

[7] Donakowski, *A Muse for the Masses*, offers a contextual view of the issues raised here. The classic work of Johan Huizinga still stands as definitive of ritual theory: *Homo Ludens* (Haarlem, Netherlands: Tjeenk Willink, 1938; Eng. trans. *Homo Ludens: A Study of the Play-Element in Culture*, London: Routledge and Kegan Paul, 1949). Modern theorists include Clifford Geertz (see note 2) and Claude Lévi-Strauss (*Structural Anthropology*, trans. Claire Jacobson and Brooke Grundfest Schoepf [New

York: Basic Books, 1963] 232–241). Among historical works on this period, still cogent is the synthesis in Robert R. Palmer, *The Age of Democratic Revolution*, 2 vols. (Princeton, N.J.: Princeton University Press, 1959–1964), see esp. 2:572. The impulse to reform Christian and Jewish cults resembled that which urged the French revolutionaries to liquidate the medieval symbolic system in favor of a civic religion.

[8] Hans Hollerweger, *Die Reform des Gottesdienstes zur Zeit des Josephinismus in Österreich*, Studien zur Pastoralliturgie 1 (Regensburg, Germany: Pustet, 1976); Albert Gerhards, "Die Synode von Pistoia 1786 und ihre Reform des Gottesdienstes" in ed. Martin Klöckener and Benedikt Kranemann, *Liturgiereformen: Historische Studien zu einem bleibenden Grundzug des christlichen Gottesdienstes*, Liturgiewissenschaftliche Quellen und Forschungen 88 (Münster, Germany: Aschendorff, 2002) 496–510.

[9] See Ottfried Jordahn, "Georg Friedrich Seiler—der Liturgiker der deutschen Auklärung," *Jahrbuch für Liturgik und Hymnologie* 14 (1969) 1–62.

[10] Anton von Bucher, "Entwurf einer landlichen Charfreytagsprocession samt einem gar lustigen und geistlichen Vorspiel," in *Bairische Sinnenlust bestehend in welt-und geistlichen Comödien, Exemplen, und Satiren, mit einem Nachwort herausgegeben von Reinhard Wittman* (1782) 17–37.

[11] A parallel secular dispute was the Buffoons' Quarrel, in which men of letters fulminated against Italian opera for the same reasons: that it was "irrational," "dominated by music," and even therefore "immoral." A humorous, though profound, fictional dramatization of the quarrel is found in Denis Diderot, *Le neveu de Rameau*, which has many English translations.

[12] *The Spectator*, Tuesday, 6 March 1711, cited from Oliver Strunk, ed., *Source Readings in Music History: The Baroque Era* (New York: Norton, 1965) 151–154.

[13] The Latin word *opus* is a singular whose plural *opera* is a synonym for the Greek *leitourgia*, whence derives the English word *liturgy*.

[14]Quoted from Ernst Xaver Turin's unpublished diaries in Rupert Giessler, *Die geistliche Lieddichtung der Katholiken im Zeitalter der Aufklärung*, Schriften zur deutschen Literatur für die Görresgesellschaft 10 [1928] (Augsburg, Germany: B. Filser, 1929) 156–172, here 164–165. Concerning hymns, songs, and liturgical theories from the *Aufklärung*, see Donakowski, *A Muse for the Masses*, 76–105. See also the bibliographical précis "Aufklärungszeit" in each number of the *Jahrbuch für Liturgiewissenschaft*.

[15]See Ian Germani and Robin Swales, eds., *Symbols, Myths, and Images of the French Revolution: Essays in Honour of James A. Leith* (Regina: Canadian Plains Research Center, University of Regina, 1998); and Donakowski, 33–75. Anthony Burgess's novel, *Napoleon Symphony* (1974), parodies the imperious regulation of every aspect of existence, an implicit counterpoint to the former Catholic culture.

[16]See Giessler, 167, again quoting from Turin's diaries.

[17]There was a practical reason for turning Continental church music into simple community singing. The secularization of church property, together with the advent of more secular and fewer ecclesiastical schools, meant that many religious institutions would no longer have the resources to support elaborate musical establishments. Hence, zeal for a didactic liturgy augmented an unwillingness or inability to train and support musicians who could perform music that required sophisticated skills such as the ability to decipher figured bass at sight. Beginning in the late eighteenth century, one written-out accompaniment sufficed for all verses, and tune books eschewed any hint of an instrumental interlude between verses. Note values were equalized throughout the hymn. In short, there was no longer any attempt musically to interpret the sentiment behind the words; the tune became a vehicle to carry the text, and no more. This simplification continued the convention found in many genres of *Gebrauchsmusik*, including folk and church music. Among examples of the same music serving seemingly conflicting texts is the familiar "O Sacred Head" (*O Haupt voll Blut und Wunden*) used repeatedly in Johann Sebastian Bach's setting of the *St. Matthew Passion*. The tune was originally a love song. After all, even the venerable Palestrina, like most liturgical composers, employed profane cantus firmi, sometimes disguised in Masses *sine nomine*. An eighteenth-century hymn writer, Ignaz Franz, uses the same tune for the sober "Von der Todesangst am Ölberg" (Agony on the Mount of Olives) and for a German version of the festive Te Deum text. The secularization of cloisters at the end of the eighteenth century dismantled much indigenous musical life.

[18]*Liturgisches Journal* 3 (1803) 16.

[19]Benedict Maria Werkmeister, *Beyträge zur Verbesserung der katholischen Liturgie in Deutschland* (Ulm: 1789) 396; Albert Vierbach, *Die liturgischen Anschauungen des Vitus Anton Winter* (Munich: Kösel and Pustet, 1929) 336.

[20]Burchard Thiel, *Die Liturgik der Aufklärungszeit in Deutschland: Ihre Grundlagen und die Ziele ihrer Vertreter* (Breslau, Germany: Nischkowsky, 1926), 8.

[21]Thiel, 29–35; Giessler, 108–116.

[22]Benedict von Werkmeister, *Einleitung zum Gebrauche des neuen Gesang- und Melodienbuches bey den Gottesverehrungen der Catholischen Kirche* (Tübingen, Germany: Jacob Heerbrandt, 1808) 50.

[23]Werkmeister, *Einleitung*, 63.

[24]Werkmeister, *Einleitung*, 63.

[25]The latter proposal came from Benedikt Peuger, the late-Enlightenment would-be reformer of Catholic worship. On Peuger, see Friedrich Zoepfl, *Benedikt Peuger: Ein Beitrag zur Geschichte der kirchlichen Aufklärung*, Münchener Studien zur historischen Theologie 11 (Munich: Kösel and Pustet, 1933).

[26]Mein Jesus kann addieren
und kann multiplizieren
selbst dort, wo lauter Nullen sind.
In Hans Joachim Moser, *Die evangelische Kirchenmusik in Deutschland* (Berlin: Merseburger, 1954) 221.

[27]*Institutes* 1.11–12. See John Calvin, *Institutes of the Christian Religion*, vol. 1, ed. John T. McNeill, trans. Ford Lewis Battles (Philadelphia: Westminster, 1960) 99–120.

[28]Burton Feldman and Robert D. Richardson, *The Rise of Modern Mythology, 1680–1860* (Bloomington: Indiana University Press, 1972) 27.

[29]Carol Norén, "The Word of God in Worship," in *The Study of Liturgy*, ed. Cheslyn Jones, Geoffrey Wainwright, Edward Yarnold, and Paul Bradshaw, rev. ed. (London: SPCK; New York: Oxford University Press, 1992) 43–44.

[30]Yngve Brilioth, *Landmarks in the History of Preaching* (London: SPCK, 1950), 27–28. For a detailed picture of the period, see Hughes Oliphant Old, *The Reading and Preaching of the Scriptures in the Worship of the Christian Church*, vol. 4: *The Age of the Reformation* (Grand Rapids, Mich.: Eerdmans, 2002).

[31]John Morrill, "The Church in England, 1642–9," in *Reactions to the English Civil War*, ed. John Morrill (London: Macmillan, 1982; New York: St. Martin's Press, 1983) 89–114, here 91. See also Ruth Mack Wilson, *Anglican Chant and Chanting in England, Scotland, and America, 1660 to 1820* (Oxford: Clarendon Press; New York: Oxford University, 1996).

[32]On the liturgies of the Non-Jurors, see W. Jardine Grisbrooke, *Anglican Liturgies of the Seventeenth and Eighteenth Centuries* (London: SPCK, 1958).

[33]R. T. Beckwith, "The Anglican Eucharist from the Reformation to the Restoration," in *The Study of Liturgy*, 310–311.

[34]Wilson, *Anglican Chant*, 194, quoting from Edward Burt, *Letters from a Gentleman in the North of Scotland to his Friend in London* (1754; 5th ed. 1822) 212.

[35]Accurate, though opinionated, is Thomas Day, "Divine Lunacy" and "The Green Mainstream" in *Why Catholics Can't Sing* (New York: Crossroad, 1991) 11–22. An exception to Irish Catholic suspicion of liturgical grandeur can be observed in James Joyce's *Ulysses* (published 1922), which alludes to a turn of the twentieth-century Dublin congregation's preference for Rossini's operatic music over the oratory of the noted preacher Father Bernard Vaughan.

[36]Alexis de Tocqueville, *Journeys to England and Ireland*, ed. J. P. Mayer, trans. George Lawrence and K. P. Mayer (London: Faber, 1958) 180; cf. 168–173.

[37]John Bishop, "The Form and Order of Public Worship in the Free Churches," in *Methodist Worship in Relation to Free Church Worship*, rev. ed. (n.p.: Scholars Studies Press, 1975) 1–63. See also Larry Ward, "Filled with the Spirit: The Musical Life of an Apostolic Pentecostal Church in Champaign-Urbana, Illinois" (Ph.D. diss., University of Illinois, 1997), who discusses the elastic but patterned format of worship in that congregation. In traditional black churches the shouting and holy dancing that may follow preaching are referred to as "getting happy." See E. Franklin Frazier, *The Negro Church in America* (New York: Schocken, 1963) 54; and W. E. B. Du Bois, "Faith of the Fathers," from *The Souls of Black Folk* (1903) quoted in Phil Zuckerman, ed., *Du Bois on Religion* (Walnut Creek, Calif.: Alta Mira, 2000) 47–56.

[38]Bishop, *Methodist Worship*, 4; Norén, "The Word of God in Worship," 45.

[39]On the permeability of ecclesiological boundaries see John Walsh, "Origins of the Evangelical Revival," in *Essays in Modern English Church History in Memory of Norman Sykes*, ed. G. V. Bennett and J. D. Walsh (London: Black; New York: Oxford University Press, 1966) 132–162. On Newman as a paradigm for psychological consistency despite denominational migration, see Donakowski, 270–302.

[40]Note the text, which does not speak of Christian doctrine so much as of a personal encounter with "my Jesus."

[41]Knox, 389–421. For a more appreciative account, see Wilhelm Bettermann, *Theologie und Sprache bei Zinzendorf* (Gotha: Klotz, 1935).

[42]Friedrich Schiller, *On the Aesthetic Education of Man, in a Series of Letters*, trans. Reginald Snell (London: Routledge and Kegan Paul, 1954).

[43]John Wesley, *The Works of John Wesley*, vol. 18, ed. W. Reginald Ward and Richard P. Heitzenrater (Nashville, Tenn.: Abingdon, 1988) 249–250.

[44]Palmer, 2:466. Bernard Semmel, *The Methodist Revolution* (New York: Basic Books, 1973), finds Methodism (and by inference all Evangelical-style denominations) implicitly democratic; the 1906 classic Elie Halévy, *The Birth of Methodism in England*, trans. and ed. Bernard Semmel (Chicago: University of Chicago Press, 1971), does not. The context for this issue, which is basic to American cultural history, is supplied by David Hempton, *The Religion of the People: Methodism and Popular Religion, c. 1750–1900* (London and New York: Routledge, 1996); by the masterful introduction to Sydney E. Ahlstrom, *A Religious History of the American People* (New Haven, Conn.: Yale University Press, 1972) 1–13, who, however, falters when in treating the twentieth century he does not recognize how assimilated Catholics have become to the perfervid nationalism of much American Evangelical Protestantism; by the classic Robert E. Riegel and Robert G. Athearn, *America Moves West*, 5th ed. (New York: Holt, 1971) 140–148; and by the definitive Palmer.

[45]Richard Crawford, *America's Musical Life* (New York: Norton, 2001) 407–423.

[46]Augustus Welby Pugin, *Contrasts, or a Parallel between the Noble Edifices of the Middle Ages and the Corresponding Buildings of the Present Day Showing the Present Decay of Taste* (London: 1845).

[47]Carole Silver, "Setting the Crooked Straight: The Work of William Morris," in *The Earthly Paradise: Arts and Crafts by William Morris and his Circle* (Toronto: Key Porter, 1993) 1–17.

[48]Donakowski, 173–187.

[49]William Olesson, "The Context of the Music of Samuel Sebastian Wesley," Lecture, University of Nottingham, Conference on the Life and Music of Samuel and Samuel Sebastian Wesley, December, 2003. See also Erik Routley, *The Musical Wesleys* (New York: Oxford University Press, 1968).

[50]Charles Woodmason, *The Carolina Backcountry on the Eve of the Revolution*, ed. Richard J. Hooker (Chapel Hill: University of North Carolina Press, 1953) 20.

[51]Peter Cartwright, *The Autobiography of Peter Cartwright: The Backwoods Preacher*, ed. W. P. Strickland (New York: Carlton and Porter, 1856) 46. See

also Karen B. Westerfield Tucker, *American Methodist Worship* (New York: Oxford University Press, 2001); Mark Noll, *A History of Christianity in the United States and Canada* (Grand Rapids, Mich.: Eerdmans, 1992); and Sydney Ahlstrom, *A Religious History of the American People*, chapters 26–29.

⁵²Ahlstrom, 461.

⁵³Charles Grandison Finney, *The Memoirs of Charles G. Finney: The Complete Restored Text*, ed. Garth M. Rosell and Richard A. G. Dupuis (Grand Rapids, Mich.: Zondervan/Academie Books, 1989) 85–96 and passim.

⁵⁴As reported in Theodore Tilton, editor of *The Independent*, "Elizabeth Cady Stanton," *Sanctum Sanctorum* (Indianapolis, Ind.: [no publisher], 1873) 260.

⁵⁵Finney, 136, 443–444; Jay P. Dolan, *Catholic Revivalism in the United States, 1830–1900* (Notre Dame, Ind.: University of Notre Dame Press, 1977), 69–70.

⁵⁶See, for example, Orvilla S. Belisle, *The Arch Bishop [sic] or Romanism in the United States*, 7th ed. (Philadelphia: Smith, 1855), a novel that virtually catalogues the Know-Nothing picture of Catholic practices.

⁵⁷Alexis de Tocqueville, "Principal Causes which Render Religion Powerful in America," *Democracy in America* [1835–1840], vol. 1, ed. Francis Bowen and Phillips Bradley, trans. Henry Reeve (New York: Knopf, 1945) 308–314.

⁵⁸For an account with strong emphasis on the English scene, see Alan Dunstan, "Hymnody in Christian Worship," in *The Study of Liturgy*, 507–519. See also Erik Routley, *Hymns and Human Life* (London: John Murray, 1952); and, for literary studies, Donald Davie, *The Eighteenth-Century Hymn in England* (Cambridge and New York: Cambridge University Press, 1993); J. Richard Watson, *The English Hymn: A Critical and Historical Study* (Oxford: Clarendon; New York: Oxford University Press, 1997); and his *Annotated Anthology of Hymns* (Oxford and New York: Oxford University Press, 2002).

⁵⁹Martin Luther, *Wittemberger Gesangbuch*, foreword to the first edition [1524], *Publikationen älterer und theoretischer Musikwerke*, 7 (Berlin: 1878), preceding p. 1, quoted in Oliver Strunk, ed., *Source Readings in Music History* (New York: Norton, 1950) 341. See also Paul Nettl, *Luther and Music*, trans. Frida Best and Ralph Wood (Philadelphia: Muhlenberg, 1948) 1–26 and passim.

⁶⁰Manfred F. Bukofzer, *Music in the Baroque Era: From Monteverdi to Bach* (New York: Norton, 1947) 291–300. See also Jaroslav Pelikan, *Bach among the Theologians* (Philadelphia: Fortress, 1986); and

Christoph Wolff, *Johann Sebastian Bach: The Learned Musician* (New York: Norton, 2000).

⁶¹See the amusing chapter on "practice verses" in Millar Patrick, *Four Centuries of Scottish Psalmody* (London: Oxford University Press, 1949) 164–178.

⁶²Louis F. Benson, *The English Hymn: Its Development and Use in Worship* (London: Hodder and Stoughton; New York: George H. Doran, 1915) 48–55.

⁶³See Frank Baker, *Representative Verse of Charles Wesley* (London: Epworth; New York and Nashville: Abingdon, 1962).

⁶⁴Bernard Lord Manning, *The Hymns of Wesley and Watts* (London: Epworth, 1942) 16.

⁶⁵Manning, 133.

⁶⁶Dunstan, 518.

⁶⁷*Keble's Lectures on Poetry 1832–1841*, vol. 1, ed. and trans. E. K. Francis (Oxford: Clarendon, 1912) 42–48; M. H. Abrams, *The Mirror and the Lamp: Romantic Theory and the Critical Tradition* (New York: Oxford University Press, 1953) 144–148; Horton Davies, 3:249–250.

⁶⁸See Day, *Why Catholics Can't Sing*, 18–22 ("The Irish Way: The Green Mainstream").

⁶⁹Donakowski, 137–138.

⁷⁰Jean-Jacques Rousseau, "Considérations sur le gouvernement de la Pologne," in *Œuvres*, 25 vols. (Paris: Dupont, 1823–1826) 5:264.

⁷¹Germani and Swales, *Myths, Images, and Symbols*, passim.

⁷²Cornwell B. Rogers, *The Spirit of Revolution in 1789: A Study of Public Opinion as Revealed in Political Songs and Other Popular Literature at the Beginning of the French Revolution* (Princeton, N.J.: Princeton University Press, 1949) 57–58 and passim.

⁷³Donakowski, 33–75.

⁷⁴Romano Guardini, *The Church and the Catholic, and The Spirit of the Liturgy*, trans. Ada Lane (New York: Sheed and Ward, 1935) 171–184, here 177.

⁷⁵Jean-Jacques Rousseau, *Dictionnaire de Musique* (Paris: Duchesne, 1768) 302–303 ("Motet"); 373–379 ("Plain-chant"); cf. *Œuvres*, 12:451 and 13:85.

⁷⁶Donakowski, 140–141.

⁷⁷Martin Gerbert, *De cantu et musica sacra a prima ecclesiae aetate usque ad praesens tempus*, vol. 2 (St. Blasien, Germany: 1774) 408–409.

⁷⁸For support of the present author's interpretation, see Donakowski, 305–312 and passim.

⁷⁹Donakowski, 166–172.

[80]See Cuthbert Johnson, *Prosper Guéranger (1805–1875): A Liturgical Theologian*, Studia Anselmiana 89 (Rome: 1984). A concise statement of Guéranger's developed liturgical principles can be found in the "general preface" to his multivolume *The Liturgical Year*, trans. Laurence Shepherd, vol. 1: *Advent* (Westminster, Md.: Newman, 1948) 1–19.

[81]Ernest Sevrin, *Dom Guéranger et Lammenais* (Paris: Librairie Philosophique, 1933).

[82]Hans Eckardt, *Die Musikanschauung der französischen Romantik* (Kassel, Germany: Bärenreiter, 1935) 41–42, citing a letter from Guéranger to A. Gontier.

[83]Katherine Bergeron, *Decadent Enchantments: The Revival of Gregorian Chant at Solesmes*, California Studies in Nineteenth-Century Music 10 (Berkeley: University of California Press, 1998) 1–24.

[84]Ernest Lee Tuveson, *Redeemer Nation: The Idea of America's Millennial Role* (Chicago: University of Chicago Press, 1968).

[85]Bergeron, 124–129.

[86]Bernarr Rainbow, *The Choral Revival in the Anglican Church 1839–1872* (London: Barrie and Jenkins, 1970). For "the renascence of Roman Catholic worship" in England in the nineteenth century, see Davies, 4:15–41.

[87]James Garratt, *Palestrina and the German Romantic Imagination: Interpreting Historicism in Nineteenth-Century Music* (Cambridge and New York: Cambridge University Press, 2002).

[88]Hugh McLeod, *Class and Religion in the Late Victorian City* (Hamden, Conn.: Archon, 1974) 248–249.

[89]McLeod, 250.

10

The Lutheran Tradition in the German Lands

HANS-CHRISTOPH SCHMIDT-LAUBER

According to the Augsburg Confession of 1530, the Church is "the congregation of saints in which the gospel is purely taught and the sacraments are rightly administered."[1] The Lutheran Reformation sees the Church as rooted in worship, or more precisely in baptism and the eucharist, as the place in which it receives its life and lives it. Only through the gospel preached and the sacraments distributed in the gathering of believers could the uncertainty be overcome that had burdened the West in late medieval times as to whether one's achievements and the additional merits of the saints sufficed to give one standing before the Eternal Judge. Thus the Reformation was first a reformation of worship, which as "the very heart of the church's life" had to be exposed to "judgment by the apostolic word."[2]

There were "without doubt good grounds in contemporary theory and practice" for the Reformers' criticism of the sacrifice of the mass as a work of human self-justification and an obfuscation of the once-for-all sacrifice of Christ that was made present in the eucharist for believers' appropriation. But the theory and practice of the time must not "simply be identified with the Catholic position as such."[3] Instead, the attack was mounted against the misuse and distortion of worship when compared to the standard of the Early Church. Luther was convinced that he had scripture and the Church Fathers on his side and that he was preserving the legitimate catholic tradition from which the Roman Church had deviated. He desired not to set up a new type of worship but rather to "cleanse the one in use, which is vitiated by the worst kind of accretions, and to demonstrate the proper use. For we cannot deny that the mass and communion in bread and wine are a rite divinely instituted by Christ" (*Formula missae et communionis / Formula of Mass and Communion* [FMC], 1523).[4] Thus the Augsburg Confession rejects the accusation that the Protestants "have abolished the mass. For, without boasting, it is obvious that the mass is observed among us with greater devotion and seriousness than among our opponents. . . . For since the mass among us is supported by the example of the church found in Scripture and the Fathers, we are confident that it cannot be condemned" (article 24).[5] But is this claim justified?

Luther and the Century of the Reformation

The sixteenth century is fundamental to worship in the churches of the Reformation. It begins with Luther's new understanding of the matter. This was developed in an exemplary manner in Wittenberg, though with no claim to detailed validity elsewhere. Thus the church orders that were created by the Reformers in the various geographical and political areas set the shape of worship in their particular regions. So the liturgical variety that marked the Western tradition until the Council of Trent was continued in the churches of the Protestant Reformation, whereas the Roman Catholic Church went over to a unified and even uniform liturgy with the 1570 Missal of Pope Pius V.

Theological Foundation: Luther's Understanding of Worship

The renewal of worship did not begin with new forms: Luther's conduct in the matter was decidedly conservative. His starting point was deeper, in that he acquired a new understanding of worship from the *articulus stantis et cadentis ecclesiae*, the evangelical message of the justification of the sinner by the grace of God through faith, without any merit on the sinner's part. He found at his disposal a concept in the Old High German vernacular that could replace the inherited designations of worship as *cultus Dei, officium, opus, servitus, obsequium*, and so on: worship is not, as in the medieval doctrine of the virtues, a "service" that humans owe to God, but primarily "God's service" to them through Christ, which makes their service to God possible and qualifies it as the response of faith. The word "Gottesdienst"—it was at first written as two words, "Gottes Dienst"[6]—included from the start both meanings: God's service to humans, and their service before God (a positive ambiguity also found in the English expression "divine service"). In his sermon at the dedication of the castle church in Torgau, the first newly built house of God in the Reformation, Luther expressed this new understanding of worship in the classic formulation that "this new house should be so ordered that nothing occurs in it but that our dear Lord himself speaks with us through his holy word and we in turn speak with him through prayer and praise" (WA 49:588). One of the moving events of the ecumenical twentieth century was that the Second Vatican Council should come to an almost identical definition in its *Constitution on the Sacred Liturgy* (*Sacrosanctum Concilium*, 33).

Luther's understanding of worship follows a pattern of address and response: the work of God elicits the answering work of faith. Divine service is God's work toward humans, by which faith is awakened, sustained, and deepened; it is God's gift (*beneficium, donum, testamentum*), not an independent human work (*sacrificium, opus bonum, meritum*). The medieval picture of an angry God whom human beings must placate is countered by a picture of God from the gospel, that of the merciful Father who in Christ seeks people out and reconciles them to himself. "For this is a right God, one who gives, not takes, who offers help, not asks for it . . . in short, who does and gives all things and needs no one, and who does everything freely, out of pure grace and without merit, for the unworthy and undeserving, yes, the lost and the damned. That is how he wishes to be acknowledged, confessed, and honored" (*Vermahnung zum Sakrament des Leibes und Blutes Christi / Admonition on the Sacrament of Christ's Body and Blood*, 1530; WA 30/II:603). Therefore the mass is "not a benefit God accepts but rather one that he gives; it is not a good deed that we do, but rather it does good to us" (*Ein Sermon von dem Neuen Testament, das ist von der heiligen messe / A Treatise on the New Testament, that is, the Holy Mass*, 1520; WA 6:364). The fight against the sacrifice of the mass is a fight against the antiscriptural understanding of the demanding judge, "who makes it necessary to have Mary and the departed saints as intercessors and to placate God by the sacrifice of the mass" (*Das 14. und 15. Kapitel Johannis / The Fourteenth and Fifteenth Chapters of St. John*, 1538; WA 45:524). According to the papists,

God is far removed from humankind and heaven is closed, while in truth it is humankind that has fallen away from God and is in rebellion against a loving and gracious creator. Thanksgiving is the only gift that Christians can bring to this God. "The sacrifice of thanksgiving is what affords Me My divine honor, what makes and keeps Me God, says God, whereas the sacrifice of works takes from God his divine honor and make him an idol and keeps him from being God" (*Vermahnung / Admonition*, 1530; WA 30/II: 602).

The character of worship as divine gift comes to expression also in the idea of testament. Luther already equates "testament" with "promise" in his first commentary on the Letter to the Galatians (1516–1517), expounding Galatians 3:14ff. (WA 2:519). With his institution of the eucharist, or more exactly with the words of institution, Christ has left us his "last will and testament," which has been brought into force by his death and includes the promises of both Old and New Testaments as well as the sacrament. The publication of this testament should "awaken and strengthen our faith."[7] Luther could also consider the elevation of the elements before communion as an expression of this testament that summons to faith in the gift (*Deutsche Messe / German Mass*, 1526; WA 19:99). This notion of the testament has been criticized as forcing the mass into "a legalistic metaphor that is incapable of capturing the meaning of Christ's sacrificial death."[8] But that misses the point, for Luther's explanation is "shaped by the idea of covenant as an expression of the righteousness of faith."[9] The entire gospel "is comprehended in the word 'testament'" (*De captivitate Babylonica / On the Babylonian Captivity of the Church*, 1520; WA 6:525), "for preaching should be nothing but the proclamation (*vorklerung*) of the words of Christ which he spoke in instituting the Mass, 'This is my body, this is my blood, etc.' What is the whole gospel but a *vorklerung* of the testament? Christ summed up the entire gospel in a nutshell with the words of this testament or sacrament" (*Ein Sermon von dem Neuen Testament / Treatise on the New Testament*, 1520; WA 6:374). All preaching is oriented to this "summary of the gospel"; that is, it is sacramentally related. That applies also to the preaching service.

For Luther the "for you" (*pro vobis*) of Christ's own words is decisive. This sums up the gracious turning of God's mercy toward humans that is experienced in God's service to them. The forgiveness of sins does more than remove the negative, "for where there is forgiveness of sins, there also is life and salvation" (*Small Catechism*, 1529; BELK, 520). Opposite that stands the "Do this" (*hoc facite*), which was emphasized in the Roman theology and employed as a basis for the priest's authority to consecrate and thus to turn the mass into a work of the Church. Luther expounds that phrase "not as a command to perform a human act before God but rather as the proclamation of Christ's action for us," and he opposes the scholastic notion of the *opus operatum* by that of an *opus operantis*.[10] He thereby corrects the notion that grace is effected through the mere performance of an act and replaces it with the notion of the right exercise of the gifts of God: Believe, and you have it!

Worship is, however, also an act of God-given faith. Salvation depends on trust in the concept "Christ for me" (*Christus pro me*). Such faith does not come by human power; God creates it in humans. Without personal faith the mass effects no grace; it is an expression of human righteousness of works. Vajta writes: "Luther does not think of grace as a supernatural power working independently of the human person. Grace is rather the fellowship which God establishes with human persons when he enters their lives and turns them from the life of unbelief to the life of faith."[11] Luther expresses this: "These two things go together, faith and God. What you set your heart

Altarpiece with baptism, Lord's supper, and confession. The altarpiece, by Lucas Cranach the Elder (1472–1553) is in the Stadtkirche in Wittenberg, Germany. Luther retained the practice of individual confession, but his position concerning its sacramental nature ("penance" in the medieval schema) was ambiguous. FOTO MARBURG/ART RESOURCE, NY

on and trust in is really your god" (*Large Catechism*, on the first commandment; BELK, 560). Human beings face alternatives: either God or idol, either faith or superstition, either the righteousness of faith or the righteousness of works.

If worship is God's action through word and sacrament toward the congregation of his people, then that entails the proclamation of the work of Christ and the administration of his sacraments as the responsibility of his congregation. But it remains Christ who acts and reconciles: "Ministry and sacrament are not ours but Christ's, for he has ordained things so and has bequeathed them to his Church, to be used and practiced until the end of the world, and he does not trick and deceive us. Therefore we cannot turn them into something else but must perform and keep them according to his command as an expression of this testament that summons to faith in the gift" (*Von der Winkelmesse und pfaffenweihe / On Hole-and-Corner Masses and the Consecration of Priests*, 1533; WA 38:240). In this connection Luther can even employ the notion of "cooperation": "God himself does everything, but through us" (*Genesisvorlesung / Lectures on Genesis*, 1545; WA 44:648).

Worship itself is faith: "What we call the chief and supreme worship in the true sense is Christian faith and love toward God through Christ" (*Kirchenpostille / Church Sermons*, 1522; WA 10/1:675). Consequently, the mass is a "public incitement to faith and to Christianity" (*Deutsche Messe / German Mass*, 1526; WA 19:75). In faith the Christian participates in the work of God but also in the unique priesthood of Christ: "We are all priests and kings in Christ, all of us who believe in Christ" (*De libertate christiana / On Christian Liberty*, 1520; WA 7:56), for Christ wishes to share everything with those who believe in him (1 Peter 2:9). "Being a priest with Christ" leads to "being a priest for the neighbor."[12] Despite his polemics against the sacrifice of the mass, Luther never denied that sacrifice belongs to the common priesthood of believers; it no longer belongs to the ordained ministry as such but is rather the task of the faith that receives God's gift, and it is performed in the sacrifice of praise and thanksgiving, in the sacrifice of prayer and "the surrender of your bodies as a living sacrifice" (cf. Romans 12:1): "Sacrifice is a living out of baptism. . . . The new man, the sacrificial man, is hidden under the putting to death of the old man."[13] This is where worship as a work of faith expands into everyday life and one's vocation in the world. Gustav Wingren has shown how closely Luther's teaching on vocation is connected with the dying of the old nature and the life of the new:[14] one's vocation is the work of faith, is worship in the secular realm.

The two sides of Luther's understanding of worship constitute a unity: "Worship as the work of God manifests itself as God's service to us, whereby in Christ he turns himself toward humanity. Worship as the work of faith shows itself as the service of the human believer, whereby in Christ he lives in faith before the face of God. In this unity, in Christ, of God and faith, the unity of the theology of worship can be preserved: Christ is God's service to us, and he is also our service to God in faith."[15]

Liturgical Practice at Wittenberg

In the matter of practical liturgics Luther spoke only hesitantly; he stressed time and again that he did not wish by his writings to issue any kind of binding prescriptions for worship by Protestant congregations. He did not circulate his report on Wittenberg usage in the *Deutsche Messe* of 1526 with the intention "of bossing anyone or imposing rules, but rather because pressure was coming from all quarters for a German mass and service of worship." He admonishes "all who wish to see or follow our order in worship, that they do not make it into an obligatory law or catch and ensnare anyone's conscience with it, but rather that, according to Christian freedom, they use it as they please, where, when, and for as long as circumstances suit and require it." Consequently, there are four criteria for the production and validity of orders of worship: (1) freedom, which admits no obligatory law; (2) love, which respects the neighbor and avoids scandal; (3) unity, within the geographical limits of a local church; and (4) order, which restrains arbitrariness and confusion. The fourth criterion does not carry equal weight with the other three, for "order is an external matter, and however good it may be, it can end in abuse. . . . Proper use is the life, value, power and virtue of all order; otherwise it is worth nothing and quite unfitting" (*Deutsche Messe*, 1526; WA 19:72f., 113).

In judging Luther's liturgics, one must take into account the particular conditions under which the reformation of worship in the sixteenth century took place. In the worship of the late medieval church, the action at the altar and the worship of the people were two quite separate processes: here the mass, there a popular devotion, running at best in parallel. Moreover, the canon was prayed silently by the priest, so that its words remained unfamiliar to the faithful, with only the ringing of the bell at the consecration to join the two.

The need for intelligibility and for the participation of the congregation was obvious. And the enormous need for remedial instruction (catechism) and the preaching of the gospel determined the first steps on the road to an evangelical service of worship that would uncover the sound kernel of the catholic inheritance.

In Luther's *Von ordenung gottis diensts ynn der gemeyne* (*On the Ordering of Worship in the Congregation*, 1523), it is less a question of the mass than of the daily prayers of the hours (matins and vespers), in which lessons from the Old and New Testaments were read in sequence (*lectio continua*) and expounded. Private masses and masses for the dead drop out, the mediatory role of the priest is rejected, and the sermon receives a firm place in the Sunday mass. "Worship as it is now conducted everywhere among us has a fine Christian pedigree, as has the office of preaching. . . . It is all a matter of God's word, that it may always get moving to raise and quicken souls, so that they grow not weary" (WA 12:35).

The *Formula missae et communionis*, published at the insistence of the Zwickau pastor Nikolaus Hausmann and with the approval of the prince elector of Saxony and the council of Wittenberg, describes the Latin mass as it was then celebrated at Wittenberg. Every reminder of sacrifice, work, and priestly prerogative has been excised; communion is distributed with both bread and cup; German hymns, of which there are admittedly yet few, allow the congregation to participate. At the "examination of faith"

Communion distributed under both kinds, with bread and cup. Woodcut by Lucas Cranach the Elder (1472–1553). John Hus is brought anachronistically into the story of Luther and prince elector Johann Friderich. BIBLIOTHÈQUE NATIONALE, PARIS/ SNARK/ART RESOURCE, NY

(*interrogatio seu exploratio de fide*)—which occurred only once a year, and only once in a lifetime for the well-educated—the point was to discover whether the communicant was in a position to "give an account of his faith"; but this was the start of what, in the history of Protestant worship, turned into the theologically problematic requirement of individual confession and absolution before the reception of communion in the Lord's supper.[16] In the liturgy of the Lord's supper, the eucharistic prayer is still present, but now pieced together from the introductory dialogue, the preface, the *verba testamenti* (grammatically linked to the preface by a relative pronoun: "through Christ our Lord, who on the eve of his suffering"), and (at this point) the Sanctus and Benedictus, during which the elevation of the elements takes place. This is followed by the Our Father and the peace (*pax*), as a "kind of public absolution of the communicants from their sins, . . . the sole and most worthy preparation for the Lord's table." The Agnus Dei is sung during communion. It is clear that Luther was seeking to follow the Western tradition in this formulation:

Introit	complete Psalm preferred
Kyrie and Gloria in excelsis	Gloria may be omitted
Collect, Epistle, Gradual, Alleluia	no proses or sequences
Gospel	candles and incense optional
Nicene Creed	
Sermon	may precede the entire liturgy
Preparation of the elements	during the Creed or after the sermon
Eucharistic dialogue and preface	
Qui pridie . . . verba testamenti	in prayer tone, like the Our Father
Sanctus + Benedictus	with elevation, "for the weaker brethren"
Lord's prayer and Peace	as confession and general absolution
Communion, with Agnus Dei	optional: prayer before communion; words at distribution; communion anthem
Post-communion prayer	two forms, omitting notions of sacrifice
"Let us bless the Lord"	instead of "Ite missa est"
Blessing	customary form, or replaced by Numbers 6:24-26 or Psalm 67:6b-7[17]

The *Deutsche Messe* of 1526, however, marks a clear break with the inherited tradition. The liturgy of the meal is reduced to the two "constitutive" components: recitation of the words of institution and communion. In order to underline the connection between consecration and distribution, Luther can even contemplate distributing the bread immediately after its consecration, and then doing the same with the cup. The Our Father is paraphrased into the form of an exhortation and located before the consecration. The exhortation does indeed take up features from the thanksgiving, but remarkably, a prayer has been turned into a sermon; thanksgiving to God has become an address to the congregation, and it may take a fixed form (*conceptis seu praescriptis verbis*) and be spoken from the pulpit rather than at the altar. Luther is here laboring under a late medieval misconception that took the "preface" in a temporal sense as "coming before" what really counted, whereas the *prae* in *praefatio* is properly to be understood in a spatial sense as the speaking of praise "before God."

The attempt has been made to interpret this extreme reduction of the liturgy as the special achievement of the Reformation, whereby Luther "rescued the biblically grounded meal of the congregation from the medieval mass as sacrifice and spectacle."[18] But exegesis and liturgical scholarship have shown this thesis to be untenable: the primitive eucharistic prayer is closely connected to the *birkat ha-mazon* of the Jewish meal liturgy and cannot be reduced to the institution narrative. The Protestant reformers mistakenly took a Roman misinterpretation—that the words of institution alone constituted the moment of consecration—for original and absolutized it, whereas the Roman canon had been spared from that reduction by virtue of the conservative force of the liturgy that kept the entire prayer intact. The *Deutsche Messe* of 1526 bears the following structure:

Introit	
Threefold Kyrie	hymn or German psalm in the first tone
Collect	the Gloria is not mentioned
Epistle	
Hymn	sung in the eighth tone
Gospel	e.g., "Nun bitten wir den heiligen Geist"
Creed	sung in the fifth tone
Sermon	Luther's "Wir glauben all an einen Gott"
Paraphrased Lord's prayer and Exhortation	on the Gospel of the day
"The Office and Consecration":	
Verba testamenti	
the bread, with elevation;	sung in the first gospel tone while the German Sanctus or "Gelobt sei Gott" or "Jesus Christus, unser
the chalice, with elevation	Heiland" are sung while the other hymns or the German
distribution	Agnus Dei are sung
Post-communion thanksgiving collect	
Aaronic Blessing[19]	

In his *Deutsche Messe* of 1526, Luther in fact mentions three different forms of the mass: the Latin, the German, and a third intended for those who "are serious about being Christians" (WA 19:75), though the last remained an unfulfilled dream; and he envisions also a quantity of daily prayers for Sundays and weekdays as well as a comprehensive series of texts for preaching. There emerges here a thoroughgoing pedagogical impulse—"for the sake of young people and the simple, who shall and must be instructed and educated daily in the scriptures and in God's word" (WA 19:73; cf. 112). As the reports of parish visitations confirm, there was certainly a great need for catechizing in the face of popular ignorance, but Luther's "pedagogical and didactic emphasis has from time to time had a fateful effect in the history of Protestant worship."[20] "The whole tone of the service was altered in two respects: there was more of the scriptural and more of the instructional. . . . The church thus became not only the house of prayer and praise but also a classroom."[21] Geoffrey Wainwright makes the point more sharply yet: "Concern for the purity of worship led also to its impoverishment. Obsession with the preached word has imposed on Protestant worship a mostly dry, didactic character."[22]

In his *Small Catechism* of 1529, Luther included, between the sections on baptism and the sacrament of the altar, an order for individual confession, which he considered indispensable. He also appended orders for the marriage service and for the baptism of infants. The order for baptism consists of exorcisms, the "Flood-prayer" (which originated in the old Latin liturgy and had at that time been widely taken up in the Protestant world in the course of the rediscovery of the Easter vigil and its baptismal celebration), the so-called children's gospel (Mark 10:13–16), the Lord's prayer (with imposition of the hand on the infant's head), the baptismal interrogations (which "the child answers through its godparents"), the immersion in water, and a prayer that the child who has thus been born again by water and the Holy Spirit and had its sins forgiven may now be "strengthened by grace unto eternal life." Confirmation was reintroduced only after Luther's death—first in Pomerania in 1544—as the conclusion to the delayed catechumenate that awaited those baptized in infancy. In the wedding service, it is first announced from the pulpit that "Hans" and "Greta" seek God's blessing on their intended marriage. Then, at the church door, the couple exchange consent (and rings) and are pronounced joined in matrimony—both of which were originally secular procedures—with the pastor acting as *pater familias* or the representative of civil authority. The pastor then leads the bride and bridegroom to the altar and expounds to them the nature of marriage on the basis of verses from Genesis 1–3 and Ephesians 5:22–29. The final blessing refers to the state of matrimony as "the sacrament of [God's] dear Son and the Church" (Eph. 5:32).

In the theology of worship, Luther has exercised outstanding influence right down to the present day and the modern ecumenical movement, but he does not bear the same importance in the matter of liturgical practice. His reduction of the tradition without the compensation of a fresh and scripturally grounded creativity is to be explained, on the one hand, by the inadequate knowledge of liturgical history that he shared with most theologians of his day and, on the other hand, by his methodologically dubious idealization of "Christ's first mass" as the *usus primitivus* ("primitive practice"; *De captivitate Babylonica*, 1520; WA 6:512, and in many other passages). Substantially, he missed the eschatologically new character of Christ's institution; and ritually, he overlooked the way in which the oldest Christian liturgies then known already went beyond the bare outline of the Last Supper. True, Luther could judge positively many of the later "additions" (*FMC* 1523; WA 12:206f.), but the upper hand was gained by his skepticism toward the further "unfolding" of the *verba testamenti* that took place in the liturgical life of the early Christian congregations. Changing worship into pedagogy, turning the liturgy into a homily, linking the Lord's supper with penance: these are three tendencies by which Luther, against his own intentions, has had a crippling effect over long stretches of the history of Protestant worship. Historical honesty requires us to recognize that Luther found no congenial help in liturgical matters such as Thomas Cranmer provided for the English through the *Book of Common Prayer*. Much was thereby lost.

The Church Orders of the Sixteenth Century

Few German bishops took the side of the Reformation, and so authority in liturgical matters—the *ius liturgicum*—passed to the princes or the city councils as "emergency bishops," who issued comprehensive church orders and matching liturgies. The large number of these corresponds to the multiplicity of civil authorities in the German lands at the time; such diversity, however, was not unusual, since it was not until the Missal of Pius V in 1570 that uniformity replaced regional pluralism in the Roman rite. Luther's two liturgies, though not adopted without change by any of the various church orders, nevertheless influenced the formation of two distinct Lutheran liturgical families in the century of the Reformation. Roughly speaking, these were the "Bugenhagen" type and the "Brandenburg-Nuremberg" type. Their differences were most marked in the sacramental part of the service, though not only there. For the sacrament they ran thus:

BUGENHAGEN TYPE	BRANDENBURG-NUREMBERG TYPE
Congregational hymn	Exhortation to the Supper
Exhortation to the Supper	Words of institution
(which, in certain orders or at certain times, could be preceded, replaced, or followed by the Preface and Sanctus)	Sanctus, Lord's Prayer, Peace
	Distribution (with singing, including Agnus Dei)
Lord's Prayer	Post-communion collect of thanks
Words of institution	Benedicamus Domino
Distribution (with singing)	Blessing [23]
Agnus Dei	
Post-communion collect of thanks	
Blessing	

Many of the church orders of northern Germany were composed by Johannes Bugenhagen, the city pastor of Wittenberg, after the pattern of Luther's *Deutsche Messe* of 1526. They minimize the great eucharistic prayer, and they link the words of institution directly with the communion. This type can still be found into the twentieth century, as in Form A of the *Lutherische Agende I* (1955). However, the divided consecration and communion, first of the bread and then of the cup, with the congregation going up twice to the altar, was adopted only by a few (early) church orders (e.g., Brunswick, 1528), and on purely practical grounds it could not survive for long.[24]

The other group follows Luther's *Formula missae et communionis* of 1523. Its chief representative is the order composed in 1533 for the politically linked territories of Brandenburg and the city of Nuremberg; the principal authors were Andreas Osiander, pastor of St. Sebaldus in Nuremberg, and Johannes Brenz, pastor in Schwäbisch-Hall.[25] This type remains structurally open to a full eucharistic prayer. It spread in southern Germany and in the nineteenth century, by way of the Prussian *Agende*, even into the Evangelical Church of the Union (EKU), right up until the EKU *Agende I* (1959); and, by way of Form B of the Lutheran *Agende I* (1955), it offered a starting point for the restoration of the eucharistic prayer that was to take place in the last decades of the twentieth century.

The Lutheran churches in the sixteenth century stuck to the mass as the form of the principal Sunday service, whereas the churches in southwest Germany and the Reformed churches adopted rather the form of the locally popular late-medieval preaching service, the "prone." Nevertheless, even Lutheran cities such as Schwäbisch-Hall, Heilbronn and Frankfurt-am-Main adopted already in the early years of the Reformation the independent preaching service that in the later Middle Ages had sprung loose from the mass because the sermon with its own liturgy was gaining strength as a form of worship. It offered a particularly suitable forum for the Reformers' preoccupation with the preaching of the Word. Under Johannes Brenz the Lutheran church of Württemberg switched from the mass form in the church order of 1536 to the preaching service in the church order of 1553, showing that it was not a simple matter of the difference between Lutheran and Reformed. The Württemberg preaching service had the following structure:

Latin introit	sung by the school boys
German psalm-paraphrase	
Sermon on the Gospel	comprising introductory *votum*, invocation of divine grace, silent Our Father, reading of the scripture text, sermon, and announcements
Ten Commandments, Creed, Our Father	spoken aloud, with the congregation quietly joining in
General prayers of the church	
Our Father	
Psalm or hymn	
The Lord's supper could be appended:	
German creed	
Exhortation	
Confession of sin with absolution	"offene Schuld"
Prayer for right reception	
Our Father	
Words of institution	where possible spoken toward the congregation
Distribution, with singing	
Post-communion prayer of thanks	
Blessing	

Both the mass form and the preaching service were taken over from the pre-Reformation tradition, but the difference between them was lessened by the fact of popular reluctance to take communion, which had existed from the early Middle Ages and was not overcome until the twentieth century. Already the Brunswick church order of 1528 had to provide rules for cases when there were no intending communicants. The solitary communion of the priest was rejected and the service closed after the preface, Sanctus and Lord's prayer with the Agnus Dei, the Sunday collect, and the blessing; it was thus a mass without the supper. Whether because of the fear of sinning through unprepared reception of communion (without confession) or because of the special reverence for the sacrament which did not allow it to serve as the weekly high point of the life of faith, the Reformation did not recover what it knew to be the obvious unity of word and sacrament in the Early Church. A special place is occupied by the Hesse *Agende* of 1574, which includes the Lord's supper in the mass form but sets out the preaching service according to the southwest German pattern.

The potential range of the Lutheran liturgy may be seen by comparing the southwest German preaching service with Joachim I's 1540 church order from Electoral Brandenburg and its great openness to the liturgical tradition. Joachim says that he recognizes neither the "holy Roman Church" nor the "holy Wittenbergian Church" but only the "holy Catholic Church."[26]

The Lutheran church orders tried to open up the prayers of the hours—matins, vespers, and sometimes compline—to the congregation, using in particular the New Testament canticles, the Te Deum, scripture readings by *lectio continua*, and in principle an exposition of the scriptures. This practice continued into the eighteenth century, when it was replaced by Bible studies (first in Vienna in 1788) and catechetically oriented teaching. Even today, one can find vespers and matins on high feasts, especially Christmas, but in quite different forms.

The Lutherans—unlike the Reformed—took over the annual calendar of the church, with temporal propers and the sequence of epistle and gospel readings, and the reckoning of post-pentecostal Sundays as "after Trinity" (the most recent major feast, instituted in 1334). The German Lutheran churches still keep to that way of counting, not having adopted the new ordering of the church year issued from Rome in 1969, which resulted in the loss of many of the Sundays that were designated and marked by the appointed lessons from the Early Church. In the propers of the saints, many feast days have been retained by the Lutherans, including Marian feasts insofar as they are christologically oriented.

The old Protestant worship was able to hold the civil and ecclesial communities together for more than two hundred years. Admittedly, attendance at service was not voluntary, but catechism and catechetical preaching played an important role from the start, binding church, home, and school into a daily process of religious socialization. "By the guiding thread of the catechism and its chief items worship opened up an entire world, an interpretation of the whole of life."[27] The emphasis shifted from the bodily senses to the word, which soon had its effect even on the disposition of the liturgical space (the innovations of pews, orientation to the pulpit, and the combined pulpit-altar in the Baroque period). "There was a cultural move from seeing to hearing, from the external to the internal, from the vision of the holy to the communication of faith by word and music."[28] The strength of Lutheran worship resided in the chorale, which with the congregational responses of the liturgy secured active participation by the people.

The Break with Liturgical Tradition in Pietism and the Enlightenment

Paul Graff describes the development of worship from the seventeenth century to the Enlightenment as "the history of the dissolution of the old liturgical forms in the Protestant Church of Germany." The process that this book title perhaps formulates in a rather exaggerated fashion lasted for more than two centuries. It reached a first climax in the age of Lutheran orthodoxy, whose doctrinal didacticism was countered by the revivalistic and evangelistic style of Pietism. The Enlightenment and Rationalism then abandoned the inherited liturgical patterns in favor of spiritual edification and the cultivation of religious feeling.

The Period of Protestant Orthodoxy

This period is usually dated from 1655 to 1740, but in a certain sense the process started earlier. Soon after Luther's death, and at the latest by the time of the Formula of Concord in 1580, the didactic character of worship was strengthened by Lutheran orthodoxy, as it defined itself vis-à-vis Calvinism and dealt with the internal doctrinal disputes among Lutherans. Thus the old words of distribution inherited from the Early Church, "The body of Christ, given for you" and "The blood of Christ, shed for you," became overloaded with doctrinal and confessional freight as early as 1567: "Take and eat/drink, this is the *true* body/blood of our Lord Jesus Christ, given over to death for you/poured out for your sins: may it strengthen and preserve you in *true* faith for eternal life" (Magdeburg). Pastors who did not act in conformity with the confessions were disciplined on both sides, while loyalty to a confession could also lead to loss of position. The life story of Paul Gerhard (1606–1676), the most important German hymn writer after Luther, bears sad witness to that.

Lutheran Communion in the Minorites church, Augsburg, 1732. Engraving by C. Sperling. BIBLIOTHÈQUE DES ARTS DÉCORATIFS, PARIS/DAGLI ORTI/THE ART ARCHIVE

Worship services grew longer and longer, and in the seventeenth and eighteenth centuries they could last three hours or more: "One hour of entrance liturgy, with music, and sometimes a pastoral office; one hour of preaching, with hymns and prayers, as a kind of liturgy in miniature; followed by the prayers of the church, announcements, and public notices, and perhaps also more pastoral offices, the Lord's supper, or a closing liturgy."[29] No wonder that the members of the congregation were unable to last it out. From the middle of the seventeenth century one starts to hear complaints about a decline in attendance, and they have never stopped.

It would, however, be wrong to view this orthodoxy only in a negative way. Against such a judgment speak a rich literature of prayer, books of edification, and efforts at reform on the part of leading representatives of the spiritual renewal during the rebuilding of the land and its church after the Thirty Years' War. Above all, one must consider the blossoming of church music during this period: Heinrich Schütz (1585–1672) placed musical composition in the service of the word with his motets, spiritual songs, and choral pieces. Paul Gerhard, even during the turmoil of the Thirty Years' War, created hymns that remain immediately accessible to congregations today. The organ gained in importance through the provision of organ chorales for congregational singing and through its taking over of the sung parts of the mass. It was above all Johann Sebastian Bach (1685–1750) who brought Protestant

church music to its peak, especially as there were no time limits set for motets, oratorios, and organ music in the liturgy. Although the city of Leipzig had a population of
29,000 in Bach's time, almost 50,000 people presented themselves there for communion.[30] Later, the number of communicants in both towns and countryside dropped
rapidly: in Hamburg, with a population of 120,000, the number of communicants
sank from 63,000 in 1784 to 26,000 in 1816.[31] General attendance at worship reached
its earlier customary heights only when famous preachers were present.

Pietism

Philipp Jacob Spener (1635–1705), with his *Pia Desideria* (1675), helped to introduce
a new movement that arrived in the middle of the seventeenth century from England
by way of Holland and found a foothold first in the Reformed parishes of the Lower
Rhineland. He gave it the name "Pietism." Conversion, new birth, and sanctification
took the forefront, in the place previously occupied by right faith in Christ's saving
work. Admittedly, Spener did not consider the devotional meetings in the *collegia
pietatis* an alternative to congregational worship, but rather a supplement to it. Nevertheless, it was probably inevitable that this movement should gain a hold on public
worship and turn the congregation, insofar as it had not yet been "awakened," from
the role of responsible liturgical subject to that of an object of missionary activity, so
that the dominance of preaching was even further strengthened. The notion of "devotion" or "edification" became the basis for making freedom, variety, and flexibility
the criteria of good liturgy: "Whatever at this time and place most favors piety." Free
prayer, which had been lost to the Western tradition, was thereby introduced into
Protestant worship, although Spener meant by that not improvisation but personally
prepared texts. The eucharistic liturgy was unfamiliar to him, perhaps as a result of his
origins in southwest Germany. He had hardly any sense of church music, because its
art "was understood by very few"; he saw its task as simply the accompaniment of
congregational singing. The official service books necessarily lost authority.[32]

Pietism was no uniform phenomenon. Looking to primitive Christianity as the
ideal had begun earlier, even in Luther. The precursors of Pietism included Johann
Arndt (1555–1621), the writer of books on "True Christianity" (*Vom Wahren
Christentum*, 1605–1610) and "Paradise Garden" (*Paradies-Gärtlein*, 1612). These are
reckoned among the classics of mystical piety and devotional literature in Lutheranism,
and they helped to create a new language for prayer. From Arndt's kind of piety came
the work of August Hermann Franke (1663–1727), the founder of the Pietism of
Halle, with its emphasis on a definite moment of conversion, a strict separation between the children of God and the children of the world, and an understanding of
theology as knowledge of the Bible with Christ as "the heart of Scripture." The Danish king Frederick IV in 1705 put Franke in charge of missions in the Danish colonies,
which resulted in the sending of Bartholomew Ziegenbalg to Tranquebar, India. The
Institutum Judaicum—for the mission to Jews—was also a product of Halle Pietism.
After Franke's death, the piety of the orphanage at Halle that had shaped so many
theologians lost its attraction. Its decline passed by way of Siegmund Jakob Baumgarten
(1706–1757) through the reception of the philosophy of Christian von Wolff (1679–
1754) and into the Enlightenment theology of Johann Salomo Semler (1725–1791)—
a case in which quite divergent theologies actually bear a close relationship.

In contrast, the Moravian Community (*Brüdergemeine*) established at Herrnhut by
count Nikolaus Ludwig von Zinzendorf (1700–1760) was able to combine an
unsectarian piety that was both revivalist and churchly with a deep understanding of

liturgy. "The sacred rites have the inherent value of furthering true devotion" (23 April 1746), for "if ever the liturgy is neglected, one must certainly be prepared for a spiritual decline" (11 September 1758)[33]. Zinzendorf's liturgical creativity is displayed in various practices: the Herrnhut litany, which was said and sung before the preaching service;[34] the monthly celebration of the Lord's supper, held in conjunction with a love feast and without preparatory confession; and the *Singstunde* or "hymn-sing," which often turned into a "hymn-sermon." Zinzendorf valued short sermons, congregational singing, and the treasury of traditional prayers (he translated into German the Anglican *Book of Common Prayer*).

The Enlightenment and Rationalism

Unlike the case in England and in France, the Enlightenment in Germany bore a theological character; it was not until the advent of Rationalism that the connection with scripture was lost and reason allowed to decide over faith. This explains the escalating criticism of traditional worship toward the end of the eighteenth century, but also the efforts to correct and improve it that were expressed in numerous liturgical pamphlets, magazines, and even privately composed *Agenden* or service books; this activity has been seen by some as an early form of the Liturgical Movement. The Enlightenment turned the congregation into a "public" that the preacher "addressed" from the pulpit with a "useful" message; in the view of Rationalism, it even became simply a matter of the instruction and moral improvement of the people by the "teacher of religion."

Unrestrained subjectivism demolished the bridges to the past and made enlightenment, social pacification, and individual betterment the purposes of worship, which should convey a sense of reverence and cultivate the religious sentiment. Worship was shaped as a thematic unity around the sermon. Music's job was to create a dignified celebration and inspire pious feelings. Just how far the pedagogical ideas of the Enlightenment could penetrate the liturgy is shown by the grotesque sermon titles for the First Sunday of Advent, "On Stealing Wood" (referring to the cutting of palm branches in Matthew 21:8, from the gospel of the day); for Christmas, "On the Use of Stall Fodder"; for Easter, "On the Danger of Being Buried Alive"; for Pentecost, "How We Should Behave Piously and Prudently during Thunder Storms." And, without specified biblical texts, there were sermon themes such as "Health," "Vaccination against Cow Pox," "The Growing of Potatoes," "The Three-Field System of Agriculture," and so on. The Lord's supper was transformed from a congregational event into the private communion of the several social conditions and classes. Even the words of distribution at communion show the spirit of the Enlightenment: "Taste this bread: may the spirit of devotion rest upon you with its fullest blessing! Taste a little wine: the power of virtue resides not in this wine but rather in you, in divine doctrine, and in God!"[35]

Even the Roman Catholic Church was not spared such tendencies in the German-speaking countries. Thus Veit Anton Winter (1750–1814), professor of theology at Ingolstadt, described the "sublime purposes" of worship as the moral and religious illumination of the understanding, the betterment of the heart, and the growth of human brotherhood. Catholics borrowed from the Protestant reforms and hymn books and demanded "national liturgies" for themselves.

Thus the Enlightenment sought to improve upon the old traditions of worship, but it did not succeed everywhere or for long. In the year 1778 one could still find in the Enlightened city of Berlin, in the church of Sankt Nicolai, a Lutheran order of worship that ran thus:

Morning hymn ("Allein Gott in der Höh sei Ehr")
Greeting and a prayer for the beginning of the day
Epistle of the day, followed by the principal hymn
Gospel of the day, followed by a hymn of faith
Sermon, preceded by an exordium and the pastor's silent Our Father
General confession, with absolution and sometimes prayers of intercession
Luther's Sanctus-hymn, as candles are lit and the pastor vests for mass
Prayer to Jesus, Lord's prayer, and institution narrative sung by the minister, or else the
    congregation sings the Sanctus and the Agnus Dei during the consecration
Hymn-verse ("Jesu, wahres Brot des Lebens")
"May the peace of the Lord be with you, so that you may worthily eat and drink
    the Lord's supper"
Communion, with the old Lutheran words of distribution and a communion hymn
Concluding "Gott sei gelobt"

In many *Agenden*, however, the preaching service could shrink to a morning hymn, a general prayer, the principal hymn, the sermon, and the hymn after the sermon.

Liturgical Renewal in the Nineteenth and Twentieth Centuries

After the extensive evacuation of the tradition in the previous centuries, the Protestant churches of Germany in the nineteenth century began to experience a fundamental renewal of worship through two parallel but by no means concordant developments in theology and liturgical reform. It must be borne in mind that Lutheran worship set the pattern for the new churches of the Prussian Union, and that there was an increasing convergence between Lutheran and Reformed worship, which in fact had already been adumbrated in the coexistence of the mass form with the preaching service. Moreover, besides the more innovative efforts, there were also regions, such as Bavaria, in which the more traditional liturgies had been retained.

Schleiermacher and Neo-Protestantism

The Berlin theologian Friedrich Ernst Daniel Schleiermacher (1768–1834) is considered "both the heir and the conqueror" of the Enlightenment[36] and the founder of the "cultural Protestantism" that prevailed in Germany until the First World War. He is the real originator of the science of liturgics among Protestants.

Schleiermacher's theory of "the cult" (his preferred term for worship) assumes and deepens the anthropological approach of the Enlightenment. The cult effects nothing that was not already present in the believers. It is "an action that depicts or portrays" (*darstellendes Handeln*), it is "essentially the common religious life," and its purpose is "the circulation of the religious interest." It is not a matter of "instructing or improving the individual," or of catechizing the youth, for in that case it would be "an educational tool," "merely an institution for human improvement" (*Praktische Theologie*, 1850, 65–76, 130). Schleiermacher's conception of worship rejects any idea of directly "effective action" (*wirksames Handeln*), whether with the purpose of "purifying and restoring" or of "disseminating," as was the case with doctrinal instruction in Protestant orthodoxy, conversion in Pietism, and moral perfection in the Enlightenment (*Christliche Sitte*, 1843, 50f., 97, 291). Yet worship does not remain without some effect, for by virtue of "depictive communication" a "higher religious consciousness" is achieved and the congregation is edified, above all by the preaching (*Praktische Theologie*, 1850, 71f.): "The efficacy of the Christian cult to edify rests principally on the communication of the pious self-consciousness that here reaches conceptual form" (*Kurze Darstellung*, 1830, § 280).

The cult finds its place in the "pauses between effective action" in everyday existence, which is "worship in the broader sense that extends through the whole of life"; the cult "stands out as a festival or celebration," and "its echoes resound throughout life and there achieve their effect." For the shaping of the cult, as for all the theological disciplines, the "rules of the art" are to be drawn up, which is the business of liturgics (*Christliche Sitte*, 1843, 530, 536; *Praktische Theologie*, 1850, 44f., 131; cf. *Kurze Darstellung*, 1830, § 5 and passim).

Schleiermacher shows great reserve toward the notion of *Gottesdienst*. In this matter, "only the upward movement comes into sight" (*Christliche Sitte*, 1843, 525). The Reformers' downward approach by way of the word of God and the means of grace—seeing worship as a saving event—clearly recedes in importance for Schleiermacher. Yet it would be wrong to accuse him of a purely subjective, anthropocentric approach, because pious self-consciousness as "the first work of divine grace" arises from the activity of the Holy Spirit and remains bound to Christ, especially since "everything needed by the fellowship of believers for its own existence proceeds from him" (*Christlicher Glaube*, 1821/22 ed., §§ 126, 133). Perhaps one can find in Schleiermacher an elliptical continuum, its two poles being "the human consciousness of absolute dependence" and "the person of Christ as the revealer of God."[37] Already in his work there are elements that help to overcome the theological reductionism that accompanies the focus on religious experience. Thus, in his doctrine of the Lord's supper, "Its whole efficacy proceeds directly and undividedly from the word of institution, which both depicts and conveys the redemptive love of Christ that also creates communion" (*Christlicher Glaube*, 1821/22 ed., § 156). Again, he defines worship as "the content of all actions by which we represent ourselves as, by God's Spirit, the instruments of God"; even if "effective action" is directly excluded from "depictive action" and occurs there only *per accidens*—for effective action is "that whereby we as God's instruments actually produce something, rather than merely showing ourselves to be such"—nevertheless there is a bridge here toward understanding worship as a saving event (*Christliche Sitte*, 1843, 525f.).

Schleiermacher's conception of the cult as a feast or festival made its way into the practical theologies of Neo-Protestant writers and found its liturgical concretion in the Strasbourg founders of the so-called First Liturgical Movement, Julius Smend (1857–1930) and Friedrich Spitta (1852–1924), as well as in the three-volume private *Agende* of the *Evangelisches Kirchenbuch* of Karl Arper and Alfred Zillesen (1917, 7th ed. 1940). It has been taken up again among supporters of "contemporary" or "experiential" worship.

Reform of the Service Books in the Nineteenth Century and Neo-Lutheranism

The same period saw the beginning of reform of the official service books in light of historical research and the recovery of Reformation theology, and this has continued into the present. A start was made by the Prussian king Frederick William III (1770–1840), who, as a Hohenzollern, belonged ecclesiastically to the Reformed minority;

he sought to reinvigorate worship in his territory and to bring Protestants of both the Lutheran and the Reformed confessions into union on the occasion of the three-hundredth anniversary of the Reformation in 1817. On the basis of his own considerable studies in the history of liturgy and of the Reformation, he composed an *Agende* (1816, Preliminary Remarks; 1817, Draft; 1821, *Agende* for the Military; 1822, *Agende* for the Court Church and Cathedral). Its introduction into general practice by order of the king's cabinet (1829–1834, editions for the provinces; 1856, first revised edition) set off a fierce liturgical battle. In 1895, the general synod finally passed the *Service Book for the Protestant Church of Prussia* (*Agende für die evangelische Landeskirche Preussens*).[38] The principal service on Sundays and festivals follows the mass form; it highlights the Kyrie by way of a preceding prayer of confession and a subsequent word of grace; it gives the eucharistic dialogue, preface, and Sanctus a place in the preaching service when there is to be no sacramental celebration; and it uses words at the distribution of the elements that were later to become controversial. In outline:

> Entrance hymn
> "In the name of the Father . . . ."
> "Our help is in the name of the Lord . . . ."
> Opening sentence from Scripture
> "Glory be to the Father . . . ."
> Confession of sin, Kyrie, and word of grace
> "Glory be to God in the highest . . ." (on feast days only)
> "The Lord be with you . . . ."
> Collect
> Epistle
> Hallelujah
> Gospel (with "Praise be to you, O Christ" and "Glory be to you, O Lord")
> Apostles' creed (or Luther's hymn "Wir glauben all an einen Gott")
> Hymn before the sermon
> Greeting from the pulpit
> Sermon
> Verse of a hymn
> Requests for prayer and announcements
> Blessing from the pulpit
> Verse of a hymn
> [If there is to be no communion, the dialogue, preface, and Sanctus nevertheless
>   may be said at this point]
> Prayers of intercessions
> If there is no communion: conclusion with Lord's prayer, Aaronic blessing,
>   Amen, and a closing hymn-verse
>
> If communion:
> Verse of a hymn for the Lord's supper
> "The Lord be with you. . . ."
> Communion exhortation (unless there has been preparatory confession and
>   absolution directly before the main service)
> Eucharistic prayer: dialogue, preface, Sanctus, prayer for fruitful communion
> Lord's prayer (here, or after the words of institution, where customary)
> "Kneel and hear" the words of institution
> Agnus Dei

Peace
Prayer to Christ for forgiveness of sins and faithful obedience
Invitation (Matthew 11:28 or Psalm 34:8a)
Communion ("Take and eat/drink," based again on the words of institution)
Post-communion prayer of thanks
Aaronic blessing, Amen, and a closing hymn-verse

The "Other Form of the Principal Service" abbreviates the preaching service, makes a second scripture reading optional, and follows Reformed usage in the celebration of the supper.

During this period, almost all the German *Landeskirchen* acquired new *Agenden*.[39] Liturgical science bloomed in Neo-Lutheranism with the cathedral preacher at Schwerin, Theodor Kliefoth (1810–1895), as well as Johann Friedrich Wilhelm Höfling (1802–1853), Adolf von Harless (1806–1879), and Gerhard von Zezschwitz (1825–1886), all three of Erlangen, and above all Theodosius Harnack (1817–1889). The last named took up Schleiermacher's experiential, anthropological approach as the "subjective factor" but subordinated it to the history of salvation as the "objective factor" (*Praktische Theologie I*, Erlangen 1877, 267–282). The practical theologian at Leipzig, Georg Rietschl (1842–1915), authored the first Protestant textbook in liturgics (*Lehrbuch der Liturgik*, two vols., Berlin 1900/1909), in which he understood worship as both the adoration of God and the edification of the congregation, being in both aspects "the work of the people" (I, 63). Wilhelm Löhe (1808–1872), the pastor of Neuendettelsau, likened the liturgy of the principal Sunday service—which he also called *Communio*—to "a twin-peaked mountain such as Horeb and Sinai, where one peak is slightly lower than the other. The first peak is the sermon, the second is the sacrament of the altar, without which I cannot conceive a full service of worship on earth." In the service book that he composed for the congregations of Lutheran emigrants to America—*Agende für christliche Gemeinden des lutherischen Bekenntnisses* (1844)—he describes worship in terms of drama, with stage directions for place, singing, and gestures; nor does he fail to call attention to the anaphora of the Eastern Orthodox Church, with the people's acclamations after the institution narrative.[40] This last is now a feature of the missal of Paul VI (1970) and of other liturgies, including the *Evangelisches Gottesdienstbuch* of 1999.

In the liturgics of Neo-Lutheranism there was a comprehensive reconception of worship that drew on a notable rediscovery of liturgical history and showed the first tendencies toward ecumenical exchange and the unity of a life lived before God. Cornehl writes: "It was the achievement of Neo-Lutheranism, by its restoration of the classic ordinary of the mass, to have rescued from disappearance an essential element of liturgical continuity and confessional identity, and to have secured the substance of the liturgical tradition against the Enlightenment. Confessional theology showed its strength, moreover, in the discovery of the character of worship as action. . . . The interpretation of the Lutheran pattern of word and response in terms of theater or drama opened up dimensions of the liturgical action that had previously been captured neither by the purely dogmatical nor by the purely depictive interpretation."[41]

Liturgical Reform in the Twentieth Century

The decline of cultural Protestantism and the ending of the link between throne and altar in Germany was followed in the 1920s by a new theological orientation. Karl Barth's theology of the word of God—in the face of both Neo-Protestant modernism and Catholic "sacramentalism"—concentrated on the content and authority of preaching. During the Church's struggle against Nazism in the 1930s, Barthian theology turned to worship in both theory and practice (Barmen Declaration 1934, third thesis; Hans Asmussen; Joachim Beckmann). At the same time, the Luther renaissance awakened a new interest in the doctrine and practice of worship at the time of the Reformation (Paul Althaus, Otto Dietz, Theodor Knolle). The new Liturgical Movement in Lutheranism was itself a complex phenomenon. It sought access to the heritage of both the Reformation and the Early Church; for example, under Friedrich Buchholz (1900–1967) at Alpirsbach, they used the Gregorian chant in the principal Sunday service and in the prayer of the hours in order to serve the word by bringing the text to clear expression. The movement also had a broader ecumenical dimension; for instance, Friedrich Heiler (1892–1967), and the High Church Movement looked for an "evangelical catholicity" in encounters with the Swedish and English churches, the Orthodox liturgy, and the mass liturgy of the early Catholic West. It connected also with the youth movement, which pressed for a comprehensive renewal and re-shaping of the Church; thus Wilhelm Stählin (1883–1975), Karl Bernhard Ritter (1890–1968), and the Brotherhood of Saint Michael (*Michaelsbruderschaft*) gathered around Berneuchen, with their order of mass, prayer of the hours, confession, and the creation of a modern language for prayer. Finally, the Liturgical Movement drew, through Oskar Söhngen (1900–1983), on the *Singbewegung* or "singing movement," which favored the Reformation chorales, congregational hymnody, and new church music.

After the Second World War, in the context of the rebuilding of church structures, the various *Landeskirchen*, on the Lutheran side, were united into the Vereinigte Evangelische-Lutherische Kirche Deutschlands (VELKD); more broadly, for certain purposes the Lutheran, Reformed and United (EKU) churches formed the Evangelische Kirche Deutschlands (EKD). In this new setting, the several complex movements just mentioned paved the way for a comprehensive reform of the liturgy in two phases. The first phase, in the 1950s, produced *Agende I* for the principal Sunday service and further *Agenden* for all other services and pastoral acts; the second phase, at the end of the twentieth century, produced the *Evangelisches Gottesdienstbuch* as the first common *Agende* for the greater part of German-speaking Protestant churches in Europe (officially introduced in the VELKD, the EKU, and the Evangelical Church of the Augsburg Confession in Austria, and further used in other churches and countries).

The Heidelberg dogmatician Peter Brunner (1900–1981) supplied the theological foundation for the post-World War II reform in his "Lehre vom Gottesdienst der im Namen Jesu versammelten Gemeinde" (1953), the very title of which—"The Doctrine of Worship in the Congregation That Assembles in the Name of Jesus"—provided an important programmatic motto derived from an analysis of the New Testament terminology. The Church's worship has a threefold location: a theological locus within God's universal economy of salvation; an anthropological locus in the existence of the individual Christian; and a cosmological locus between the praise of God by the other earthly creatures and that offered by the angels. By the power of the Holy Spirit, the congregation's worship thus acquires, in the proclamation of the word and in the sacramental supper, the character of a saving event. The first and fundamental preaching of the gospel brings people across the baptismal boundary into the church; the other task of preaching is then continually to reinforce the existing congregation through remembrance and renewal. In preaching occurs the anamnesis of Christ, which also, in conjunction with the sacramental action as the effective *representatio* of the Christ-event and the *antecipatio* of what is still to come, constitutes the essence of the Lord's supper. Brunner interprets the consecration with the help of Ernst Lohmeyer's concept of *Identitätsverknüpfung*: the association which Jesus' words create between the bread and his body, the wine and his blood, is not one of analogy but one of identity (Brunner, 233; cf. ET 173). Fundamental to the consecration—in line with the Early Church's understanding and practice—is obedience to the word by which Christ instituted the supper, or more precisely the prayer of blessing spoken over the bread and the wine (*eulogia*). This prayer includes more than the recitation of the Lord's own words of institution, though these are its foundation. Last, Brunner turns to the concrete shape of worship and grounds it dogmatically: the inescapability of forms as well as the allowance of eschatological liberty; the attachment to the divine word; the character of liturgical signs; the historicity of the liturgy; its subjection to the criterion of love. He examines the factors that give it a tangible shape, including the arts; and he offers the draft of a *eulogia* for the Lord's supper, including an anamnesis (memorial of Christ's saving work) and an epiclesis (invocation of the Holy Spirit). For the use and reform of service books, Brunner assumes the appropriateness of signs as vehicles of the Holy Spirit.

Soon after the introduction of *Agende I*, however, strongly critical voices could be heard lamenting its allegedly rigid forms, its antiquated language, its presumed inflexibility, and its lack of contemporary themes. The German Lutheran Liturgical Conference, which had done the work for the *Agende*, quickly took note of the new situation. It developed the idea of a new kind of *Agende* and in 1974 issued a "structure paper" in the form of a study document under the title "Versammelte Gemeinde. Struktur und Elemente des Gottesdienstes. Zur Reform des Gottesdienstes und der Agende."[42] But what had first been envisaged as simply an aid to the understanding and more flexible use of the current *Agenden* became in fact the first step toward a new reform of the *Agenden*. The bipolar concept of a stable and recognizable "basic structure" and a multiplicity of "practical variations" was an attempt to mediate between tradition and innovation. In the five elements of "opening, invocation, proclamation of the word and confession of faith, supper, and dismissal" the basic structure "calls to mind the attachment of Christian worship to its origins and thereby its continuity and its self-identity," while "the practical variations show the pliancy of the liturgy." The study paper thereby makes the point: "Worship is a job that needs fresh work every time; it is not a program to be mechanically run" (p. 9).

In 1980 the church authorities of the EKU and the VELKD set up a working group to prepare a new *Agende*. The group presented its draft text—*Erneuerte Agende*—in 1990. In 1999 the definitive version, produced by a second working group, was approved and introduced. The change in title to *Evangelisches Gottesdienstbuch / Protestant Worship Book* was not accidental but programmatic. This book no longer contains fixed orders in the style of an *Agende*; rather, it is a workbook to help in constructing services suitable to a particular place and situation. Thus, Part I for "Worship on Sundays and Feast Days" begins not with regular orders of service but with "basic forms." Only then come two "Complete Liturgies," with a short appendix for baptisms in the main congregational service. Part I concludes with "other services" such as some for smaller groups or domestic gatherings, a Lord's supper at table, a service for Good Friday or on days of penitence, and "free-form" services within a basic structure, including family services, a "eucharistic fellowship meal" in "contemporary" style (the *Feierabendmahl* popularized by the Nuremberg *Kirchentag* of 1979), and "more interactive" types of service. The term *Feierabendmahl* depends on a wordplay in Ger-

Liturgy in Wittenberg. "Peace and the care for creation are good goals, but they do not form the content of Christian hope," said Hans Christian Knuth, presiding bishop of the Lutheran Church in Germany, preaching on Hebrews 10:35–11.1 in the Stadtkirche at Wittenberg, Germany, on 15 September 2002. The altarpiece, the work of Lucas Cranach the Elder, portrays Luther's understanding of the gospel as embodied in word and sacrament. © Lutheran World Federation/ Photograph by D. Zimmerman

man. *Abendmahl* is the usual word for "(Lord's) supper"; *Feierabend* is what one might call an "evening out" or even a "party." Part II of the book contains the propers for the church year and special occasions. Part III offers an anthology of texts for selective use. The book includes detailed explanations for each of the sections and for the individual liturgical items in order to promote practical competence, so that instead of merely "reading out from the book," the worship leader may become a "working liturgist" or even a "creative" one.[43] In 2002 a supplementary volume (*Ergänzungsband*) added yet more materials, ending with a list of the sources drawn on in the two books.

Seven "normative criteria" clarify the concept of *Evangelisches Gottesdienstbuch*. (1) Worship supposes—in terms similar to the *plena, conscia atque actuosa participatio* of chapter 14 in Vatican II's *Constitution on the Sacred Liturgy*—the "responsibility and involvement of the whole congregation." (2) It follows "a stable, recognizable basic structure that allows for various possible actuations." (3) Traditional and new texts are given equal value. (4) "Protestant worship stands in a living ecumenical relationship with the worship of the other churches." (5) An "inclusive language" is needed, in which "the community of men, women, youth and children and the various groups in the church can find their appropriate expression." (6) "Liturgical action and conduct engages the whole person, including the body and the senses." (7) "Christianity remains linked with Israel, the first-called people of God." The last two points were added after the 1990 draft and indicate the latest trends.

The *Gottesdienstbuch* of 1999 contains two "basic forms." The first, like the Lutheran Reformation, follows the Western mass type; the second adopts the tradition of the southwest German and Reformed preaching service, the "second form" of the EKU's *Agende I* of 1959. The decisive point, however, is that the second basic form in the book of 1999 is expanded by the addition of the Lord's supper, which did not originally belong with the preaching service. The result is a common basic structure shared between forms I and II, whose twin kernel of proclamation and meal is preceded by an introductory and gathering part and followed by a dismissal for mission in everyday life. It was thus the merit of the "structure paper" to have demonstrated the liturgical relationship between the two main types of worship tradition in German Protestantism and thereby to have opened the way to a common service book for all the Protestant churches.

The service book sets out parallel descriptions of the two "basic forms" in their four-part structure: (A) Opening and Invocation; (B) Proclamation of the Word and

Confession of Faith; (C) the Lord's supper; (D) Dismissal and Blessing. These can be described from the congregation's viewpoint as Gathering, Orientation, Communion, and Mission. The first basic form offers various alternative emphases for its structural parts. Part A (Opening and Invocation) may focus on (1) a psalm, or (2) the Kyrie or other invocations of Christ, or (3) the Greater Gloria or other acts of praise. Parts B and C may focus on (1) the sermon and supper "in close connection", or (2) general confession after the sermon, or (3) general confession as preparation for the supper, or (4) confession of faith and supper "in close connection." Part D (Dismissal and Blessing) may focus on (1) praise through the Greater Gloria or the Te Deum, or (2) the dismissal through announcements, intercessions, and a mission charge, or (3) the blessing, with expanded words, movements, and gestures.

The "Complete Liturgies" are practical examples of the two basic forms, intended only as guidance and aids, but no doubt they will nevertheless acquire considerable importance as they stand. The most important changes in the 1999 Liturgy I in comparison with *Agende I* of 1955 are these:

- "The Lord be with you" is moved from its connection with the collect to the beginning of the service.
- The scripture readings are expanded by the addition of an Old Testament lesson.
- The general confession (previously used only on Good Friday and days of penitence) is inserted between the sermon and the blessing from the pulpit.
- The confession of faith now occurs in response to the scripture readings *and* the sermon together.
- The announcements may be made at one of several places in the service or even divided up.
- The monetary offering and the preparation of the gifts may be verbally developed.
- A eucharistic prayer surrounding the words of institution now becomes the norm.
- In the eucharist, the Lord's prayer now usually occurs at a point after the *verba testamenti*.
- The peace that follows the Lord's prayer is now exchanged by both word and gesture.
- There are congregational acclamations in response to the scripture readings and in the eucharistic prayer.
- The intercessions can be linked with the prayer after communion.

The large array of texts proposed differs from those of the 1990 draft above all in four respects. (1) The feminist movement that arose during the development of the new book criticized the masculine and authoritarian image of God—Lord, Father, Almighty—and sought to replace the traditional address to God by a recovery of other biblical images; the integration of some of these concerns has removed the need for separate "women's liturgies." (2) The problem area of the relations of Christians and Jews led to acceptance of the abiding election of Israel and the deletion especially of any hint of mission to Jews. (3) The language of prayer took up modern trends to expressive, sometimes inventive, occasionally picturesque language, and no doubt generally short-lived forms, in evident contrast to the accumulated experience of prayer in the Church over the centuries. (4) Ecumenical openness receded somewhat as Protestantism made its distinctive voice more clearly heard.

Linguistic change—especially during the last decade of the twentieth century—was remarkable. In the daily prayers, the address to God is varied with many devices:

- adjectives such as "wonderful," "gracious," "loving," "rich," "merciful," but also "unfathomable," "incomprehensible," "vulnerable";
- appositional nouns in the genitive case so as to avoid the use of grammatically masculine adjectives applied to God: "God of salvation and justice," "God of all light, of peace and joy, of life";
- vocative appositions such as "You the Breath of Paradise," "the Ground of all joy," "the Source of knowledge, of light, of life, of grace," "the Protector of all who put their trust in You";
- entire clauses such as "God, you are our ground and our support," or descriptive nouns such as "God our Judge and our Savior, Liberator, Redeemer," or thematic qualifications such as "You, the God of Mary" (fourth Sunday in Advent);
- the simple use of "God" and "our God" and the corresponding omission of qualifying adjectives and predicates that might be exposed to criticism as patriarchal, exclusive, or authoritarian;
- the address to Christ as "Jesus" plus a vocative apposition such as "You Source of wisdom, You Gate of life, our Brother and our Friend."

In the processes of selection, alteration, and new formulation it is not only formal questions that are brought into play but also substantial changes which must be recognized and either accepted or corrected. In any case, it may be expected that very little of what is now spontaneously formulated will survive and be passed on to future generations, but this does not make it superfluous.

Along with the earlier opening to the eucharistic tradition of the wider Church there has been an increase in the frequency of celebrating the Lord's supper. Between 1963 and 1996 the number of celebrations per year in the EKD more than doubled, from 138,000 to 281,000, and the proportion of church members receiving communion at least once a year rose from 25 to 38 percent. Most striking is the rapid decline—from 62 to 8 percent—in the practice of annexing the Lord's supper as a separate service after the preaching service. The rediscovery of the Lord's supper as the center of the congregation's life has led to a "eucharistic movement" that found expression also in the "Feierabendmahl" celebrations at the Protestant *Kirchentage* of Nuremberg in 1979, Hamburg in 1981, and Hanover in 1983. The result is "an integrative model that mediates creatively between free-form worship and the classical mass form."[44] Individual sacramental piety is transformed into the experience of common worship.

The most striking characteristic of the new orders of service in terms of liturgical history is the recovery of the eucharistic prayer in a pattern rooted in the Jewish and primitive Christian thanksgiving over the gifts. Twelve such prayers are provided, drawing on the Early Church inheritance and on ecumenical resources. As is probably the case in all liturgical reforms of the late twentieth century, the most ancient source employed is the anaphora of the so-called *Apostolic Tradition* of Hippolytus (see Chapter 2 in this volume). The text printed here in the *Gottesdienstbuch* of 1999 (p. 645 f.) sticks closer to the original than does Eucharistic Prayer II of the 1970 *Missal* of Paul VI; it nevertheless avoids an oblation of the gifts and a direct invocation of the Holy Spirit on the elements:

> Thus we remember before you, our God, the death and resurrection of your Son. We thank you that you have called us to stand before you and to serve you. We ask you to send *to us* your Spirit and bless this meal; let all who receive the body and blood of Christ be made one in him; and strengthen our faith.

Another eucharistic prayer (p. 643f.) is taken from an American source, the *Lutheran Book of Worship* (1978); it is considerably shortened and in several places reworded, but the substance and sequence are preserved: in the post-Sanctus it mentions the covenant with Israel, and in the anamnesis of Christ his association with outcasts and sinners. The epiclesis refers to both the congregation and the elements ("Send your Holy Spirit. Join us and all who receive this bread and drink from this cup into fellowship with you") and ends with the eschatological prospect ("May we enter into the fullness of the heavenly kingdom and receive our inheritance with all the saints in light"). Yet another eucharistic prayer takes up the text of the Lima liturgy (see Chapter 28 sidebar) and again shortens it but retains its characteristic structure: preface, mentioning creation and Christ's place in salvation history; Sanctus; first epiclesis, recalling the work of the Spirit and allowing for a verse from a Pentecost hymn; the *verba testamenti*, with the acclamation "Your death, O Lord, we proclaim, and your resurrection we praise, until you come in glory"; anamnesis (of Christ's birth, life, baptism, last supper, death, descent to the realm of death, resurrection, exaltation, heavenly intercession, and expected return in glory); maranatha; second epiclesis (on the congregation); self-offering ("May we be a living sacrifice to the praise of your glory"); another maranatha; concluding doxology. Some of the changes betray conservative Lutheran influences: the introduction to the Sanctus carries the insertion "Therefore we *proclaim* and sing" and similarly with the anamnesis ("we *proclaim* his resurrection"), while the central notion of memorial is slanted in a psychological or even rationalistic direction toward "we remember."

The remaining nine eucharistic prayers take up earlier models, such as Form B of the Lutheran *Agende I* of 1955, the Kurhessen-Waldeck *Agende I* of 1996, and the confirmation *Agende* of the VELKD (draft 1995). They may also play fast and loose with traditional structures, distance themselves from the classical content of the anamnesis and the epiclesis, adopt a homiletical style, employ a feminine spirituality—so many evidences of a rapidly changing theological and linguistic situation.

The lengthy labors have been rewarded, and the *Evangelisches Gottesdienstbuch* has become a respectable *Agende*, supplying reliable help and guidance to the various traditions and contemporary trends and offering ample material for use in worship without the need for anyone to surrender his or her own position. But amid all these riches there occur some problems and theological tendencies that demand criticism and further work:

- The use of the three lessons from scripture is more the form than the rule.
- The theme of sacrifice has almost disappeared, in that Christ's *sacrifice* on the cross is never mentioned in the eucharistic texts, and the "redemption" which he there accomplished (p. 634) is expressed in such general concepts as "freedom" (p. 642), "liberation" (p. 654), "fullness of life" (p. 655), and "joy" (p. 663).
- The emphasis in "communion" is increasingly shifted from the divine gift we receive through Christ's body and blood to the human duty of passing on to others what we have ourselves shared.
- The concept of the eucharistic prayer remains unclear. The phrase "Words of Institution with Great Prayer of Thanksgiving (Eucharistic Prayer)" creates more confusion. The simple title "Eucharistic Prayer" would express better the unity of the prayer of thanksgiving over the gifts.
- A properly inclusive language has not yet been found; it has certainly not been achieved by the preference for "Jesus our brother" over the New Testament "Kyrios."

- A controversy that broke out in connection with the 1990 draft has had a constricting effect and needs further clarification: to the ecumenical and liturgical understanding of the Lord's supper as eucharist is opposed its interpretation as an act of proclamation that excludes a eucharistic prayer.[45]

Certainly the *Evangelisches Gottesdienstbuch* of 1999 is not the only *Agende* produced by contemporary German-speaking Lutheranism, but it is the most representative expression of "the worship of the congregation that assembles in the name of Jesus" in this linguistic area.[46]

Bibliography

Sources

Bekenntnisschriften der evangelisch-lutherischen Kirche. Göttingen: Vandenhoeck & Ruprecht, 1930. [BELK]

Evangelisches Gottesdienstbuch: Agende für die EKU und für die VELKD. Berlin: Evangelische Haupt-Bibelgesellschaft und von Cansteinsche Bibelanstalt; Bielefeld: Luther-Verlag; Hanover: Lutherisches Verlagshaus, 1999.

Herbst, Wolfgang, ed. *Evangelischer Gottesdienst: Quellen zu seiner Geschichte.* Rev. ed. Göttingen: Vandenhoeck & Ruprecht, 1992.

Luther, Martin. *Deudsche Messe und ordnung Gottis diensts,* WA 19:72–113. [DM 1526]

Luther, Martin. *Formula missae et communionis pro Ecclesia Vuitembergensi,* WA 12:205–220. [FMC 1523]

Secondary Literature

Brunner, Peter. "Zur Lehre vom Gottesdienst der im Namen Jesu versammelten Gemeinde." In *Leiturgia,* vol. 1, edited by Karl Ferdinand Müller and Walter Blankenburg, 83–364. Kassel: Stauda, 1954. English translation, *Worship in the Name of Jesus.* Translated by M. H. Bertram. St. Louis: Concordia, 1968.

Cornehl, Peter. "Gottesdienst. VIII." In *Theologische Realenzyklopädie,* vol. 14, 54–85. Berlin and New York: Walter de Gruyter, 1985.

Graff, Paul. *Geschichte der Auflösung der alten gottesdienstlichen Formen in der evangelischen Kirche Deutschlands.* Vol. 1: *Bis zum Eintritt der Aufklärung und des Rationalismus.* Göttingen: Vandenhoeck & Ruprecht, 1921, 1937. Vol. 2: *Die Zeit der Aufklärung und des Rationalismus.* Göttingen: Vandenhoeck & Ruprecht, 1939.

Lurz, Friedrich. "Die Einführung des Evangelischen Gottesdienstbuches—ein Ereignis ökumenischer Relevanz." *Theologische Literaturzeitung* 125 (2000) 231–50.

Messner, Reinhard. *Die Messreform Martin Luthers und die Eucharistie der Alten Kirche: Ein Beitrag zu einer systematischen Liturgiewissenschaft.* Innsbrucker theologische Studien, 25. Innsbruck: Tyrolia, 1989.

Nagel, Wilhelm. *Geschichte des christlichen Gottesdienstes.* Berlin: de Gruyter, 1970.

Niebergall, Alfred. "Agende." In *Theologische Realenzyklopädie,* vol. 1, 755–784, and 2, 1–91. Berlin and New York: Walter de Gruyter, 1977 and 1978.

Reed, Luther D. *The Lutheran Liturgy: A Study of the Common Liturgy of the Lutheran Church in America.* Rev. ed. Philadelphia: Muhlenberg, 1959.

Schmidt-Lauber, Hans-Christoph. *Die Eucharistie als Entfaltung der verba testamenti: Eine formgeschichtlich-systematische Einführung in die Probleme des lutherischen Gottesdienstes und seiner Liturgie.* Kassel: Stauda, 1957.

Senn, Frank C. *Christian Liturgy: Catholic and Evangelical*. Minneapolis, Minn.: Fortress, 1997.

Vajta, Vilmos. *Die Theologie des Gottesdienstes bei Luther*. Göttingen: Vandenhoeck & Ruprecht, 1952. Abridged English translation, *Luther on Worship: An Interpretation*. Translated by U. S. Leupold. Philadelphia: Muhlenberg, 1958.

Notes

[1] Confession of Augsburg, article 7, Latin version; in BELK, 60.

[2] Brunner, "Zur Lehre vom Gottesdienst," 115; English trans. [ET], 27.

[3] Karl Lehmann and Wolfhart Pannenberg, eds., *Lehrverurteilungen - kirchentrennend?*, vol. 1 Rechtfertigung, Sakramente und Amt im Zeitalter der Reformation und heute (Freiburg im Breisgau: Herder; Göttingen: Vandenhoeck & Ruprecht, 1986, 1988) 89–124—a document of the Ökumenischer Arbeitskreis evangelischer und katholischer Theologen; also Karl Lehmann and Edmund Schlink, eds., *Das Opfer Jesu Christi und seine Gegenwart in der Kirche - Klärungen zum Opfercharakter des Herrenmahls* (Freiburg im Breisgau: Herder; Göttingen: Vandenhoeck & Ruprecht, 1983, 1986), esp. 215–238.

[4] Text in WA 12:206. Translations into English in the present chapter are directly from the original languages. Translations of many of Luther's main writings on worship may also be found in the American edition of *Luther's Works* (Concordia and Fortress presses), particularly vols. 35–38 (1959–1971) on "Word and Sacrament," and volume 53 (1965) on "Liturgy and Hymns."

[5] BELK, 91 f., 95.

[6] "Von ordenung gottis diensts ynn der gemeyne" (1523), WA 12:35; "Deudsche Messe und ordnung Gottis diensts" (1526), WA 19:72. On the Luther Bible, cf. Grimm, *Deutsches Wörterbuch*, 8:1213ff.

[7] Cf. Schmidt-Lauber, 103–108.

[8] Yngve Brilioth, *Eucharistic Faith and Practice* (London: SPCK, 1953) 102.

[9] Vajta, *Die Theologie des Gottesdienstes*, 65; ET *Luther on Worship*, 41.

[10] Vajta, 73–87; cf. ET, 46–51.

[11] Vajta, 81; cf. ET, 49.

[12] Vajta, 272; cf. ET, 150.

[13] Vajta, 279–281; cf. ET, 154.

[14] Gustaf Wingren, *Luthers Lehre vom Beruf* (Munich: C. Kaiser, 1952).

[15] Vajta, 351; cf. ET, 187.

[16] Brunner, 337 f.; ET, 287 f.

[17] Text in Herbst, *Evangelischer Gottesdienst*, 16–49.

[18] Nagel, *Geschichte des christlichen Gottesdienstes*, 137. Cf. Bryan Spinks, *Luther's Liturgical Criteria and his Reform of the Canon of the Mass* (Bramcote, Notts. U.K.: Grove, 1982): "Luther believed that he had replaced the canon with the gospel. . . . He was in fact giving radical liturgical expression to justification by faith" (p. 37).

[19] Text in Herbst, 69–87.

[20] Nagel, 125.

[21] Roland Bainton, *Here I Stand: A Life of Martin Luther* (Nashville, Tenn. and New York: Abingdon-Cokesbury, 1950) 340.

[22] Geoffrey Wainwright, "Der Gottesdienst als 'Locus Theologicus', oder: Der Gottesdienst als Quelle und Thema der Theologie," *Kerygma und Dogma* 28 (1982) 252.

[23] Cf. Niebergall, "Agende," 2:13

[24] See Herbst, 88–93.

[25] See Herbst, 96–102.

[26] Cf. Schmidt-Lauber, 117 f., 218–220.

[27] Cornehl, "Gottesdienst. VIII," 57.

[28] Cornehl, 59.

[29] Cornehl, 58.

[30] Cf. Günther Stiller, *J. S. Bach und das Leipziger gottesdienstliche Leben seiner Zeit* (Kassel and Basel: Bärenreiter, 1970).

[31] Graff, *Geschichte der Auflösung*, 2:142.

[32] Nagel, 163f.

[33] Both quotations from Zinzendorf, see Nagel, 166.

[34] See Herbst, 149–152.

[35] Graff, 2:124–129, 156.

[36] Cornehl, 64.

[37] Christoph Albrecht, *Schleiermachers Liturgik* (Göttingen: Vandenhoeck & Ruprecht, 1963) 14.

[38]See Herbst, 172–185.

[39]See Niebergall, 2:55–66.

[40]Wilhelm Löhe's texts are reprinted in volume 7/1 of his *Gesammelte Werke* (Neudettelsau: Freimund-Verlag, 1953). For particular references, see pp. 13, 47–76, 83.

[41]Cornehl, 66.

[42]Available in Herwarth von Schade and Frieder Schulz, eds., *Gottesdienst als Gestaltungsaufgabe* (Hamburg: Lutherisches Verlagshaus, 1979).

[43]See Frieder Schulz, "Zukunftsperspektiven der Gottesdienstpraxis," *Pastoraltheologie* 71 (1982) 34.

[44]Cornehl, 80.

[45]See Dorothea Wendebourg, "Den falschen Weg Roms zu Ende gegangen? Zur gegenwärtigen Diskussion über Martin Luthers Gottesdienstreform und ihr Verhältnis zu den Traditionen der Alten Kirche," *Zeitschrift für Theologie und Kirche* 94 (1997) 437–467, and "Noch einmal: Den falschen Weg Roms zu Ende gegangen? Auseinandersetzung mit meinen Kritikern," *Zeitschrift für Theologie und Kirche* 99 (2002) 400–440; and, in refutation, Ulrich Kühn, "Der eucharistische Charakter des Herrenmahls," *Pastoraltheologie* 88 (1999) 255–268; Kerygma-Hans-Christoph Schmidt-Lauber and Frieder Schulz, "Kerygmatisches oder eucharistisches Abendmahlsverständnis?" *Liturgisches Jahrbuch* 49 (1999) 93–114; and Frieder Schulz, "Eingrenzung oder Ausstrahlungen? Liturgiewissenschaftliche Bemerkungen zu Dorothea Wendebourg" in *Liturgiewissenschaft und Kirche: Ökumenische Perspektiven*, ed. Michael Meyer-Blanck (Rheinbach: CMZ, 2003) 91–107.

[46]On the whole topic of the reform of the *Agende* see Frieder Schulz, *Agende—Erneuerte Agende—Gottesdienstbuch: Evangelische Agendenreform in der 2. Hälfte des 20. Jahrhunderts: Texte aus der VELKD* (Lutherisches Kirchenamt der VELKD, Postfach 510409, D-30634 Hanover); also the special issue of *Für den Gottesdienst*, no. 54, October 1999 (Arbeitsstelle für Gottesdienst und Kirchenmusik, Knochenauerstrasse 33, D-30159 Hanover). A detailed analysis of the eucharistic prayers in their historical context is found in the Rostock dissertation of Jörg Neijenhuis, *Das Eucharistiegebet—Struktur und Opferverständnis. Untersucht am Beispiel des Projekts der Erneuerten Agende* (Leipzig: Evangelische Verlagsanstalt, 1999).

11

The Lutheran Tradition in Scandinavia

NILS-HENRIK NILSSON

Liturgical developments in the Lutheran national churches in Scandinavia from the Reformation onward are intimately connected with the general history of these countries. Wars, periods of great power, the level of education in society at large, and independence movements among specific groups or entire parts of the country have influenced the status of the churches and developments of their life of worship.

The Scandinavian countries of the early twenty-first century are Denmark, Norway, Sweden, and Finland—three kingdoms and one republic. At the time of the Lutheran Reformation in Scandinavia, this part of Europe consisted of only two kingdoms: Denmark, to which Norway belonged, and Sweden, of which Finland was a part. In the Nordic countries, the Lutheran Reformation was closely linked to the wishes of the kings to gain financial and political independence from the Roman Catholic Church. The influences from the embryonic Lutheran activities in Germany during the 1520s were strengthened and supported by the efforts of the Nordic rulers to gain independence and greater influence within their own countries. It was only during the twentieth century that Norway (1905) and Finland (1917) became independent states with their own constitutions and their own heads of state. Another Nordic country, Iceland, has a similar history. For a period Iceland was part of Denmark, but it gained independence as a national state in 1918 and elected its first president in 1944.

The participation of the churches in the strivings of Norway, Finland, and Iceland to gain independence has contributed to securing for them and for their life of worship a more prominent position in society. The Lutheran churches took part as the people won the freedom they longed for. This has left its traces even in the early twenty-first century and is evident in the disposition to participate in worship and in the considerable public confidence placed in the church. By contrast, the visible status of the churches in Denmark and Sweden has been weakened, and attendance figures at worship in the early twenty-first century are among the lowest in Europe in terms of percentage of the population and also in terms of percentage of church membership figures.

In Denmark, Norway, and Finland the Lutheran national churches are still established with official public status within the law and the education system, whereas in Sweden the established state-church system was abolished at the end of the year 1999. Its status is now about the same as that of the Evangelical Lutheran Church of Finland, which had to be separated from the state during the Russian period (1809–1917), when Finland had a sovereign of Russian Orthodox belief.

In order to understand the liturgical life of these various national churches, it is important to recognize the differences in the historical developments of the respective countries. During certain periods, some new areas were incorporated into the country. That often sparked off some developments in the area of the liturgy in order for the new citizens to become integrated in the worship life of their new country. Periods of great power, based on military success or economic developments, have contributed to greater education and have often coincided with periods of increased hymn writing and attention to the artistic decoration of the churches.

The Reformation

Just as in Germany, the Lutheran Reformation had a prehistory in Scandinavia. The developments in the liturgy that took place had begun before the Reformation. The Renaissance sought to promote education in the humanities, to enhance classical studies, and to raise the general level of knowledge. This led to a reappraisal of the sermon, which gained increased significance in the Church. In many churches in Scandinavia pulpits date from as early as the late fifteenth century or early sixteenth century. At that time the sermon was, however, not a part of the service but a separate opportunity for teaching prior to the main service. Hymns for the primary purpose of education were also written and sung but were normally not used within the framework of the Sunday mass.

In Scandinavia the art of printing led to the gradual decrease in importance of the separate diocesan liturgical traditions. Extant missals and pontifical rites preserved in the research libraries show that several lines have been struck out in the earliest printed editions and the local tradition has been added by hand. The Lutheran Reformation continued the process of change toward a more nationally unanimous form of service. The efforts to harmonize the form of liturgy to ensure that services were celebrated in the same way across the entire country reached their peak during the seventeenth and eighteenth centuries.

It is significant for the Lutheran Reformation generally and in Scandinavia as well that the Reformation did not begin with changes to the worship. Its initial features

"Proper" worship. In a single scene a sermon is preached, an infant is baptized, and both the bread and the wine are received at communion. Painting (1561) from the front of the altar in the Torslunde Church, Denmark. NATIONALMUSEET COPENHAGEN DENMARK/ ART ARCHIVE

were the preaching of the gospel, closely linked to the publication of books about the Christian faith and to translations of the Bible into the vernacular. As a consequence, liturgical abuses were then removed; the congregations were given greater opportunities to participate when the liturgy was celebrated in the vernacular and as hymn singing became an increasingly significant part of the service.

The Bible Humanism and the need for biblical texts as the basis for preaching led to vernacular translations, first of the New Testament and later of the whole Bible. The translation of the New Testament was published in Denmark in 1524 and in Sweden in 1526; the New Testament was first available in Finnish in 1548. During the early history of the Reformation in Scandinavia, Lutheran pamphlets were spread quite widely through the trade channels, and this led to some questioning of parts of Catholic liturgical practice. This early period is therefore called "the period of the preachers." It was a time of Lutheran preaching, primarily outside the framework of the ordinary services. The bishop of Linköping in Sweden, Hans Brask, published a manifesto against Lutheran heresies at Easter 1525, but there are no mentions of any changes to the worship at that time. The attempts to celebrate services in the vernacular at that time were all in private. The first Lutheran mass celebrated in Swedish in Sweden may have been that held on 11 February 1525 at the marriage of the Swedish Reformer Olaus Petri (1493–1552). Evangelical hymns were probably used in Denmark, at the training seminary for priests at Haderslev, in the year 1526 as part of the recitation of the divine office. A year or so later the mass was celebrated in Danish. In Sweden too hymns were sung in Swedish at this time. In Norway the first evangelical mass was celebrated privately within the Carmelite College in 1526.

In Sweden the meeting of the Riksdag (Parliament) in Västerås in June 1527 and in Denmark the meeting at Odense in August of the same year proved significant for the future development of worship in these countries. These parliamentary meetings accorded the right to preach Lutheran sermons in the churches while waiting for a general church council that would settle the matter about the content of the teaching of the faith. Denmark provided legal protection for evangelical preachers. In Sweden the bishop would, as hitherto, continue to be responsible for the oversight of the teaching proffered by the priests and for the services they rendered, but from now on the king was accorded a much stronger position in relation to the bishops.

By this decision at Västerås, evangelical preaching became not only permitted but prescribed in Sweden, which led Olaus Petri, who had studied at Wittenberg, to publish anthologies of sermons both in 1528 and in 1530 to enable the priests to preach Lutheran doctrine. In Denmark many members of the clergy had been given an evangelical education since this country had such close connections with Germany, and their preaching was quickly spread. Hans Tausen became the most outstanding preacher of Lutheran doctrine in Denmark, and he also published hymnals. In November 1529 the so-called Malmö mass composed in Danish by Claus Mortensen was published in Malmö (then part of Denmark) in a volume that also contained hymns and other liturgical material. Before that an order of mass in Danish, which had found its inspiration in the Lutheran orders of service published in Germany, had been used at Haderslev.

At the church council at Örebro in Sweden in February 1529, the matter of worship was again discussed, and the differences were solved by a careful compromise. The worship should retain its outward format but should be translated into the vernacular and the content given a Lutheran interpretation. Only a few months later Olaus Petri published his first printed service book in Swedish. *Een handbock påå Swensko* contained orders of services for baptism, marriage, the churching of women, communion of the sick, commendation of the dead, funerals, and preparation for death for those sentenced to execution. The book corresponds to the medieval manual in that it contained orders for services led by a priest or a deacon other than the order of mass. Orders of services not included by Olaus Petri in his service book were, for example, various types of blessings for candles or food.

Of the outward rites, Olaus Petri retained many of the gestures and ceremonies from the Middle Ages. As before, the order of baptism, for example, included making the sign of the cross, exorcisms (of which Martin Luther had been particularly protective), placing salt on the tongue of the child, renunciation of evil, anointing with the oil of baptism, questions about the faith, chrismation, dressing with the baptismal white garment, and giving of the baptismal candle. The only obvious exclusion was the blessing of the salt, which Olaus Petri considered unnecessary. This order of baptism was not a translation of the text in the normal sense but a rewriting that made the content correspond to the views of the reformers. The prayer used at the anointing with the oil of baptism between the renunciation of evil and the affirmative questions about the Christian faith is an example. Here Olaus Petri directed that the following words should be used: "May God, who in his great mercy has called you to baptism, anoint you with the oil of gladness," whereas the medieval tradition from the manuals referred to the priest as the subject: "And I anoint you." Besides the Swedish medieval tradition, Olaus Petri also made use of the rites of baptism formulated by Luther. He adhered more closely to Luther's conservative *Taufbüchlein* from 1523 in preference to the more radical version from 1526. The order of baptism was so arranged that anyone who had not previously understood the service when baptism was celebrated in Latin would hardly notice any difference at all. The ministry to the sick retained the anointing [just as it did in the order of service composed by the Strasbourg Reformer Martin Bucer (1491-1551)], although with the directive that it could either be used or omitted.

In general Olaus Petri worked with great independence compared to developments in other countries, and his preference was to continue the Swedish liturgical traditions inherited from the Middle Ages. The service book was published in two further unaltered editions in 1533 and in 1537, which testifies to its usage. In 1541 a revised edition was published in which, for example, the salt and the anointings were omitted.

Olaus Petri's Swedish Mass from 1531 was a critical revision of the Swedish medieval order of mass. As a model he used Luther's *Formula Missae*, the Nuremberg mass from 1525, and to some extent Luther's *Deutsche Messe*. Petri's order of mass makes it clear that his purpose was to provide for a service in which the congregation (the "people" according to the text) would participate. The changes, compared to the tradition from the medieval missal, were greater here than in the service book. The purpose was to create a congregational service in the vernacular, in which the sermon, congregational hymn singing, and the distribution of communion to the people were firm parts. This evangelical reordering of the mass is particularly evident in the canon, which lacked any reference to the mass as a sacrifice.

In regard to the service book and to the mass in Swedish, it should be noted that both Olaus and his younger brother, Laurentius Petri (archbishop 1531–1572), were inspired, through their studies at Wittenberg, by early Lutheran criticism of liturgical abuses. However, in their work of creating a Swedish Lutheran life of worship, they took as their starting point the medieval traditions with which they were familiar from their own country and primarily those from Strängnäs and Uppsala. These they used as the foundation for their work, designed to preserve in the vernacular much of the old traditions but revised and purified from what they considered heretical.

Olaus Petri also collated a hymnal, which was first published as a small pamphlet in 1526 and was later extended in the editions of 1530 and 1536. (Only the last of these has been preserved.) The 1536 hymnal, *Swenske Songer eller Wisor*, contained forty-six hymns and an appendix with a few songs about the Antichrist. The hymnal itself included the New Testament canticles for the divine office—the Benedictus, the Magnificat and the Nunc Dimittis—as well as the Te Deum and nine paraphrases of psalms from the Psalter. All subsequent work on hymnals in Sweden at that time was based on the 1536 hymnal.

The official transition to reformed worship took somewhat varied forms in the Scandinavian countries. In Denmark two evangelical service books were published in 1535. One of them was published in Malmö and contained orders of services for both the mass and the occasional offices. The other was published in Copenhagen and contained only orders of service for the occasional offices. The prolegomena of the latter make it clear that it was designed to be used all over Denmark until a common church order for the entire country could be published. Johannes Bugenhagen, parish priest in Wittenberg, was invited to Denmark to participate in the work on the church order, which was published in Latin as *Ordinatio Ecclesiastica Regnorum Daniae et Norwegiae* in 1537. Following a revision and translation into Danish in 1539, it was then adopted for the whole country in 1542 as *Den rette ordinans for kirketjenesten i Danmark og Norge*. Thus the transition to Lutheran worship had been decided. This church order shows clear similarities to others Johannes Bugenhagen helped to compose. From the beginning, Lutheran worship in Denmark was more akin to the continental tradition compared to services in Sweden-Finland.

Worship, as prescribed by the Danish church order, was highly influenced by Bugenhagen and by the life of worship at Wittenberg. This has proved greatly significant for later Danish liturgical developments. There is a striking direction in this order that if no communicants are present, the service must end immediately after the intercessions with the Lord's prayer, the Aaronic blessing, and a hymn. Here already are hints of the development toward a main service without the celebration of communion. This would become the most common form of worship in the Lutheran national churches in Scandinavia following the period of the Reformation right up until modern times: a service dominated by Bible reading, preaching, and hymn singing.

In Sweden a church council at Uppsala took the decision to introduce the Swedish mass at all the cathedrals and in all the churches where this could suitably happen. There is evidence in Finland in the year 1537 that the mass was celebrated in both Swedish and Finnish. It was, however, not until 1540 that the Swedish king forced a total transition to Lutheran teaching and worship in the entire country. In 1541 the mass in Swedish was published as the officially prescribed order of service, which included the sermon as part of the order of mass itself. The 1541 editions of the service book and the missal were later reprinted in several editions without any significant alterations. In 1549 Michael Agricola (1512–1557), renowned as the Reformer of Finland, published the mass in Finnish.

Archbishop Laurentius Petri worked to enlist support for a proposal for a church order that would regulate and provide directions for church life and for worship. His first proposal in 1546 was rejected, even though it had been scrutinized by both the bishops and the aristocracy. His intention was to preserve as much as possible of the medieval inheritance by an evangelical interpretation. Only such alterations as were necessary with respect to doctrine should be made.

The Council of Uppsala in 1593 confirmed the *Swenska Kyrkeordningen* as proposed by Laurentius Petri in 1571 as the norm governing church life in Sweden. The confession and absolution now received its place before rather than as part of the mass, and the obligation to make confession prior to communion was laid down. Directions and orders were given for baptism, private confession, corporate confession, excommunication, mass, matrimony, ministry to the sick, funeral, ordination of priests, and consecration of bishops. These orders, however, assumed the availability of the service book and the missal, as not every part was written out in full. Laurentius Petri also gave many examples of exhortations or addresses that could be used during the services.

The church order stipulated that with regard to the celebration of mass there should be freedom to retain or to omit the use of the elevation, vestments, altar cloths, candles, and "whatever else befits these ceremonies." The Church Order also underlined the requirement that anyone wanting to receive communion should, as a matter of obligation, inform the priest of this intention the previous evening or, at the very latest, on the morning of the same day. A special chapter is devoted to the divine office, which Laurentius Petri wanted to keep, especially in the cities, where matins and evensong should be offered, including the singing of psalms in Latin but readings from the Bible in Swedish.

Hertig (Duke) Karl, the heir to the throne, had several reservations against this decision of the council and refused to sign the decision unless the exorcisms in the baptismal rite were removed. As a compromise the council permitted the omission of the exorcisms at celebrations of baptism by the congregation at the Royal Court, whereas the Lutheran tradition should apply in the rest of the country. In Denmark too a tension between Lutheran and Calvinist theology that affected the worship arose. In 1606 one of the daughters of King Christian IV was baptized without any exorcism as a result of a direct command by the king.

In the following century worship in the Scandinavian countries entered a period of consolidation, during which worship took on a more confessional mark and also became a more integral part of the law and order of society in general.

The Period of Lutheran Orthodoxy

The accomplishment of the Reformation in the Scandinavian countries left obvious marks on their worship throughout the subsequent centuries. All further editions of service books and hymnals build largely on the foundations laid during the reformation process and further develop directions already given in the first editions of the church orders. Thus worship in Denmark-Norway has focused on the sermon and on hymn singing. In Sweden-Finland too the sermon has been of great importance, but attention has also been given to the liturgical shape of the service and its interpretation, both in the course of church life and as an object of theological controversy.

In order to establish a norm for worship in Denmark, the king had in 1568 stipulated that the liturgical arrangements at the Church of Our Lady in Copenhagen should be considered the norm. The worship in this church should provide the pattern according to which the bishops ordered the worship in the other Danish dioceses.

At the beginning of the year 1604, the Norwegian bishops began working on a Norwegian church order. Once their proposal had been sent to Copenhagen for approval, a reworked church order was approved three years later. The Norwegian church order of 1607 (*En Kirkeordinans*) corresponds completely to the Danish one from 1537 but changes the word "Danish" to "Norwegian."

The period from 1537 until 1685 saw in Denmark-Norway a tug-of-war between the use of Latin prose and the use of Danish hymns at mass. From the very beginning the celebration of mass, and not only services of preaching, was considered the norm. Gradually the celebration of the mass with hymns in Danish took over completely, which meant that from 1685 onward the Latin introit was replaced by an entrance hymn, the Latin Kyrie by a kyrie hymn, the Greater Gloria by another hymn, and the credo by yet another hymn. Niels Jesperssøn, in his *Graduale* of 1573, had published texts and melodies arranged according to the *de tempore* principle.

During the seventeenth century a separate liturgical tradition emerged in Denmark and Norway, which, particularly in Denmark, has been preserved until modern times. In 1644 one of the Danish bishops published opening and concluding prayers in a pastoral letter. These prayers were to be led by the parish clerk, a layman. The inspiration behind these prayers came from German orders of service. The prayers quickly spread and were included in the church service rites published in 1685 for use in Denmark and Norway (*Danmarks og Norgis Kirke-Ritual*). In 1688 the orders of service were collated and published in an altar book, and in 1699 a new hymnal (*Kirke-Salmebog*) was published. The hymnal had been preceded by publications of hymns written by the Danish priest Thomas Kingo between 1674 and 1681. The hymnal published in 1699 included eighty-five of Kingo's hymns and is usually referred to as Kingo's Hymnal. Many of Kingo's hymns are still among those best loved and most frequently sung in Denmark.

In Iceland, Hallgrímur Pétursson's hymns on the Passion were published in 1666. These fifty hymns are meditations on the Passion of Christ and on his work of salvation, and they have earned their author the distinction of being considered one of the most outstanding hymn writers in Nordic church history. In the same period the Norwegian poet Petter Dass wrote several hymns that later were included in the hymnbooks in Norway and Denmark.

When the 1614 *Handbok* was published in Sweden, it was the first time that all the church's orders of services were collated within the same volume. The exorcisms in the baptismal rite had by then been shortened, but even so they were no less forceful. The criticism by Hertig Karl, later King Karl IX, of the service book could by then be left aside, and the decisions taken by the council at Uppsala in 1593 were fully applied. This service book took the Swedish tradition from Olaus Petri further, with regard to both the mass and other orders of service. In 1686 a church law was published in which the provision of services was also regulated. Some new provisions were introduced, among them an order for the dedication of a church, which had previously been rejected. The church law reinforced the requirement for uniformity in worship, which was a consequence of Lutheran orthodoxy and also of the fact that, through the peace treaties in 1645 and in 1658, Sweden had taken over sovereignty from Denmark for several major areas. In 1693 a new service book was published that was a revision of the previous one and was largely built on its foundation.

In Sweden too several prominent hymn writers appeared in this period. One of them was Jesper Swedberg. In 1691 Swedberg was appointed a member of a hymnbook committee, and he undertook most of the work himself. When the Swedbergian hymnal came off the printing press, it was carefully scrutinized from a doctrinal perspective, and the representatives of Lutheran orthodoxy found "major heresies" therein. Following a revision, this hymnal was published in 1695 in a shortened and partly reworked version. Copies of the rejected edition were sent to Swedes who had founded a colony known as New Sweden at the mouth of the Delaware River in North America, which indicates that the content was not so harmful that this book could not be put to good use. The hymnal of 1695, published in a Finnish translation in 1703, has proved significant for the life of worship in both Sweden and Finland. Several of Swedberg's hymns are still sung in the early twenty-first century.

The Enlightenment and Modernity

At the beginning of the eighteenth century, Lutheran orthodoxy held sway, and thanks to various earlier successful military campaigns, both Denmark and Sweden were major political powers. Trade connections and the emerging industrialism led these countries to make new contacts and to explore new theological thinking, which influenced the status and the worship of the churches. A high level of education among the upper levels of society led to the emergence of internationally renowned scientists and also to demands for raising and extending the general level of education among the population. A reform undertaken in Denmark and Norway in 1770 and in Sweden in 1772 is a sign of the transition from an agrarian to an industrialized society. Because of a reduction in the number of work-free days by about one-third, this reform has subsequently been called "the major demise of holidays." Among others, the keeping of the feast days of the apostles and the third day within the octaves of Christmas, Easter, and Pentecost were abolished as public holidays. Feast days that had hitherto been celebrated on a specific date were moved to the nearest Sunday.

In Denmark, Bishop Hans Adolph Brorson (1694–1764) was the most prominent Pietist hymn writer. Through the work of Hans Nielsen Hauge (1771–1824), a lay preacher with great impact on Norwegian spirituality, Brorson's hymns were brought into Norway at the beginning of the nineteenth century.

The bishop of the diocese of Zeeland in Denmark, Nikolai Edinger Balle, made an attempt in 1783 to abolish the use of exorcism in the rite of baptism. His commentary on evangelical Christian religion appears to be a typical contemporary expression of the current strand of rationalism prevalent in academic theology. The ethic of duty was at the center, and the sacraments were paid only passing attention. With Balle's encouragement and active participation, an evangelical Christian hymnal titled *Evangelisk-kristelig Psalmebog* was published in 1798. A major driving force behind his work was the intention to raise the general level of education among the public.

In 1811 the *Kyrko-Handbok* was adopted in Sweden. The prolegomena stated the ideals behind its orders of services: "to follow the increasing contemporary cultural level of thoughts and expressions." All the orders that had previously been found in the service book and in church law were now collated in this new service book, which in its entirety is marked by new theological thinking. The purpose of the service is not seen as primarily the worship by the congregation present. The primary purpose of the service is rather to provide teaching to raise the level of education among the general public. This new Swedish service book immediately became the object of intense criticism. Major groups within the country wrote to the king requesting permission to continue to use the old service book, but permission was refused. It was

Swedish communion. *Nattvardsgång* (1854) by Bengt Nordenberg portrays communion in a country church in Sweden. NATIONAL MUSEUM, STOCKHOLM

primarily the order of baptism that caused concern, since any reference to exorcism was altogether absent and the concept of sin was hardly mentioned at all. The complaints focused on the moralizing attitude of the order of baptism and its failure to point clearly to salvation and forgiveness. The opportunity for active participation by the congregation in the main Sunday service had been severely reduced in favor of the view that the congregation should primarily receive moral education. Many parishes in Sweden continued, in spite of the prohibition, to use the old service book.

A new hymnal, *Den swenska psalm-boken*, was published in 1819. The priest Johan Olof Wallin (later archbishop) was its major instigator and contributor. He had previously worked on the task of revising hymns, but he now took the step of writing new hymns. His contribution to the 1819 hymnal consists of about 130 of his own hymns, and it is therefore appropriately known as Wallin's Hymnal. Because of his frequent use of references to the Bible, although interpreted in the context of the moralist interpretations preferred by the Enlightenment, Wallin's Hymnal was able to fill a function as part of general public education for a considerable period.

The most exceptional person who influenced the life of worship in Scandinavia during this period was, however, the Danish priest Nicolai Frederik Severin Grundtvig (1783–1872). Through his preaching and writing, Danish hymn singing became inseparably linked to popular national traditions, which were thus brought alive and invested with a sense of urgency and significance. Published in 1899, *Psalmebog for kirke og hjem* contains many of Grundtvig's hymns for use in church and at home.

Following the 1808–1809 war between Russia and Sweden, Finland became part of Russia. For the Finnish Lutheran Church, this meant the continued use of the old service books and hymnals from the Swedish period. Thus when the 1811 service book and the 1819 hymnal were adopted for use in Sweden, the Finnish Lutheran Church continued to use the old books. The only alteration was a change of the petition for the king of Sweden and his council in the intercessions.

Work by the Finns aiming to achieve service books of their own was soon underway. Among the most prominent hymn writers working for a new hymnal were the poets Johan Ludvig Runeberg, whose name was among the authors behind a proposal for a new hymnal in 1857, and Zacharias Topelius. However, not until 1886 could a new book replace the old Swedish hymnal. In the same year the Finnish Church Assembly adopted a new service book for the Evangelical Lutheran Church in Finland. *Kirkko-Käsikirja* was largely based on the Swedish service book of 1693 with some influences from the service book of 1834 (in Swedish) and 1835 (in Finnish) for the Evangelical Lutheran parishes in Russia (mainly the Saint Petersburg area and Ingria). The service book of 1834–1835 in turn had been influenced by the Swedish service book of 1811.

By a peace treaty in 1814, Danish sovereignty ceased to apply to Norway. A union between Norway and Sweden was set up in its place, and Norway adopted its own constitution on 17 May 1814. A Norwegian hymnal was published in 1869, and a liturgy for high mass followed in 1887. The road toward these books is of interest, since it has something to say about developments that were underway also in Sweden and Finland. There are clear signs from the 1840s and the 1850s that many people were worried about decadence in the area of worship. Proposals for liturgical improvements were debated during clergy conferences, and books showing the historical background of the liturgy were published in Norwegian. In 1849 the study of liturgy had become a subject in its own right at the seminary for practical theology.

The priest and hymn writer Magnus Brostrup Landstad (1802–1880) was appointed to begin the work toward a new hymnal. The *Kirkesalmebog* was given official status in 1869. Kingo's hymnal provided a model for its structure: its parts followed the liturgical year and the order of the service and also included such hymns as were prescribed as definitive parts of the liturgical rite. The new 1887 order for high mass, the result of the work done by Gustav Margerth Jensen (1845–1922), was followed in 1889 by the *Alterbog* (altar book). Here the emerging liturgical research made a clear mark, and the tendencies to historical restoration are obvious. The hymn mass was now replaced with a prose mass following the medieval structure.

Recovery and Renewal

Work of restoration and renewal of both the form and the content of the worship marked the entire twentieth century in all the Scandinavian national churches. The emerging Liturgical Movement influenced developments particularly in Norway, Sweden, and Finland but also in Denmark, especially in the experimental orders of services that have been published there. Inspiration came both from the Reformation and from the Middle Ages, but gradually attention was directed more and more toward worship in the Early Church, which has become the primary source for new thinking about worship, as in many other churches.

Throughout the nineteenth century, Sweden experienced extensive debate about both the service book and the hymnal. This led to several proposals for a new service book. In 1858 the Riksdag took a decision to instigate a partial revision of the service book. Another reading was added to the order of high mass, the theme of salvation was strengthened in the order of baptism, and various alterations affected other services as well. This was, however, not sufficient to silence the critics. A committee was appointed to make a proposal for a new

Norwegian Pietism. Hans Nielsen Hauge, an evangelical preacher who is said to have never departed from Lutheran doctrine, is recognized as the founder of Norwegian Pietism. Because in Norway religious meetings were prohibited except under the supervision of a parish pastor, Hauge and his followers met clandestinely in private homes and other buildings, as depicted in *Haugianere* by Adolph Tidemand (1814–1876). NATIONAL MUSEUM OF ART, ARCHITECTURE AND DESIGN, OSLO/PHOTOGRAPH BY J. LATHION

service book. The *Handbok för svenska kyrkan* was adopted in 1894. The "de tempore" principle was applied, and prayers with variations according to the liturgical year underlined further the importance of an active worshiping congregation. The criticism of the removal of exorcism was reduced by the inclusion of the phrase "who alone sets us free from all evil" and the sentence reminiscent of exorcism "remove thee from the power of darkness." The 1894 service book was the basis for the 1917 Swedish service book that took the same title. The hymnal too had been the object of criticism. A proposal for a corrected and more orthodox version was published in 1849. That proposal was widely used among the Swedish immigrants to America, but it did not acquire any major importance in Sweden.

Following the dissolution of the union between Norway and Sweden, liturgical work was continued in Norway, largely inspired by the thought of the historical continuity of worship. A new altar book was published in 1920, and a revised version of Landstad's hymnal was introduced in 1926. The most obvious changes to Norwegian worship achieved by the worship books published in 1887, 1889, and 1920 were that holy communion became a normal part of the service of high mass and that this was now generally seen as the high point of Christian worship. Instead of the structure of the service being based on hymns, which had even replaced some of the ordinary parts of the mass, a return was made to the original structure of the mass, into which hymns were now inserted. There were still discussions on how the preface, the words of institution, and the Lord's prayer should be featured. A full eucharistic prayer had not yet emerged at that time. Work in progress aimed to abolish the introductory prayer led by the parish clerk. The content of the prayer gave, according to its critics, the impression that worship would only consist of listening to the sermon.

The Church of Norway adopted a new service book in 1992 (*Gudstjenestebok for den norske kirke*), which introduced many new liturgical features. Most of these were brought into use during the 1980s. In 1977 the Church of Norway got a new liturgy for high mass, including a new lectionary with readings from the Old Testament every Sunday. In the service book the introduction stipulates which liturgical colors should be used on Sundays and holy days throughout the liturgical year and how various kinds of processions should be performed. There is also an explanation of their meanings. The eucharistic part of the mass begins with the greeting and the Sursum corda, followed by the preface, the Sanctus, either of the Eucharistic Prayers A or B, the Lord's prayer, the words of institution, and the Agnus Dei. Echoing the *Didache*, both eucharistic prayers mention as the fruits of communion the engrafting of the faithful into the True Vine and their gathering into God's Kingdom. Eucharistic Prayer B includes an anamnesis immediately after the words of institution. The position of the Lord's prayer before the words of institution in both eucharistic prayers indicates its kinship to the Danish liturgical tradition. The hymnal adopted in 1985 may be used in worship following a decision by the local parish. The book is characterized by a broad range of texts and music from different traditions.

Compared to the situations in the other countries, Danish worship had not in any equal measure been open to influence from the Liturgical Movement. There was certainly work in progress in parishes and other organizations to make proposals about the restoration and the renewal of the services. This work focused particularly on how the eucharist could become a normal part of the life of worship, so it would no longer be a case of the communicants gathering for a special celebration after the preaching service had finished. A new altar book was published in 1901, and new orders for baptism and holy communion were published by the bishops in 1912. In these services the sacrament is seen as an integral part and the theological high point of a complete mass. From the 1920s onward the Liturgical Movement became more evident in Danish church life. The experimental services published in 1963 are obviously influenced by the attempts to restore the structure of the service. The order of service used in the Danish national church dates from 1992. Here some careful attempts have been made to draw near to general liturgical developments. The prayer led by the parish clerk is still an important part of Danish tradition. In the eucharistic part of the mass, the offertory hymn is followed by one of three alternatives: the first is a short address, the second is a prayer, and the third is the Sursum corda and a preface. A short prayer is followed by the Lord's prayer, the words of institution, and the Sanctus. As an alternative, a prayer of anamnesis may be offered after the Sanctus. *Den danske salmebog*, published in 1953, contains 754 hymns, many written by Grundtvig. Several editions have been published, and in 2000 a proposal for a new hymnal caused extensive debate. In 2002 a new *Den danske salmebog* was approved by the queen and published.

The Evangelical Lutheran Church in Finland adopted a new service book in 1913: *Kirkkokäsikirja Suomen Evankelis-luterilaiselle Kirkolle Hyväksytty Suomen seitsemännessä Yleisessä Kirkolliskokoukessa*. In the eucharistic part the Sanctus was inserted between the preface and the words of institution. Following the confession of sins, a so-called assurance of grace built on a reference to John 3:16 was introduced. In 1933 a minor revision of the service book was undertaken following the independence of Finland. In 1969 a service book was adopted in which the services are obviously structured in accordance with the ideals of the Liturgical Movement but retain Finnish tradition. Particularly remarkable are the introduction of an epiclesis immediately before the words of institution and the direction that the peace may now be exchanged between the priest and the congregation. Hymnals were published in 1939, 1948, and 1986. The classical structure of the mass is clear in the service book (*Suomen evankelis-luterilaisen kirkon kirkkokäsikirja I Jumalanpalvelusten kirja*) adopted in 2000. The lectionary, which was adopted the same year, specifies the liturgical color for each Sunday and holy day. Immediately before the order of the mass there are preparatory prayers to be used by the priest while vesting and also prayers to be used by priests and assistants in the sacristy before and after the mass. In the eucharistic part of the service the offertory hymn is followed by the Sursum corda, the preface, the Sanctus, and five different prayers that all include the words of institution. All these eucharistic prayers also include an anamnesis and an epiclesis for the benefit of communion. A consecratory epiclesis upon the elements is found in one of them. The service book also includes orders for the divine office.

The Evangelical Lutheran Church of Iceland adopted its order of service (*Handbók íslensku kirkjunnar*) in 1981 and hymnal (*Sálmabók íslensku kirkjunnar*) in 1997. In the early twenty-first century the Icelandic order of service is also clearly influenced by the Liturgical Movement and follows the classical structure of the mass. After the offertory hymn comes the Sursum corda, the preface, the Sanctus, and one of three alternative eucharistic prayers. A prayer of anamnesis is included.

Liturgical work in Sweden continued in the spirit of the Liturgical Movement, inspired by the thinking of the emerging Ecumenical Movement and its thoughts about "evangelical catholicity," a desire to let the service show that we all belong together in one universal Christian community. Thanks to his contacts with liturgical developments in other countries and also because of his own work of research, the bishop and scholar Yngve Brilioth (1891–1959) had a significant influence. The service book adopted in 1942 was in many aspects marked by his views, although he did not gain acceptance for all his proposals. In the 1942 *Den svenska kyrkohandboken* the structure of the mass is restored in accordance with medieval ideals. The eucharistic part was, however, still the object of concern. Following the Sursum corda and the preface came the Sanctus and then a prayer referring to John 3:16 and including a communion epiclesis but no anamnesis. The prayer was followed by the words of institution.

In 1937 the Riksdag and the Church Assembly adopted *Den svenska psalmboken*, which testifies to another development in worship. The intention was not only restoration but also a desire to make the service seem relevant for worshipers by the use of images and ways of expression normally found in contemporary everyday life rather than based on an agrarian culture, which most people had long since left behind. The hymn writer Anders Frostenson (born 1906) contributed his own hymns during a great part of the twentieth century and also made hymns from other countries and traditions available through translations. Through his hymnological work he is well known in all Scandinavian churches. In 1986 a new *Den svenska psalmboken* was adopted for the Church of Sweden. The first 325 hymns are common to most churches and denominations in Sweden, including the Roman Catholic Church. In the same year the Church adopted *Den svenska kyrkohandboken*, which, among other things, provides eight fully developed eucharistic prayers, one of which is used in common with several free churches.

In 1995 an order of the divine office was published based on the *Liturgia Horarum*, the Roman Catholic divine office as reformed by the Second Vatican Council, but revised and complemented by material from the Swedish tradition of the offices to suit Swedish circumstances. Its prolegomena commends it for use in the parishes jointly by the Roman Catholic bishop, the archbishop of the Church of Sweden, and the leader of the Swedish Covenant Church. This too is an important indication of the desire for fellowship in worship that exists among many Christians in Sweden.

Finally, it could be added that in the northernmost parts of the Scandinavian countries a Sami indigenous population exists for whom the Bible, the orders of service, and the hymnals have over the centuries been translated into their own languages. In the last few years of the twentieth century their own hymn writing was included in some editions of hymnals [see color plate 19].

History continues to influence people's views, so even in the early twenty-first century theologians and musicians in the Scandinavian countries have to some extent different thoughts about what worship actually is. The developments and debates of the past still give the presumptions for the everyday conversations in the Scandinavian churches. Anyone visiting Denmark and expressing an interest in liturgy will soon enough become involved in a lively debate about Grundtvig's hymns, whereas the same sentiments expressed in Sweden might equally quickly bring involvement in conversations about the suitability or otherwise of some particular liturgical action.

Translated from the Swedish by Gerd Swensson

Bibliography

Brilioth, Yngve. *Eucharistic Faith and Practice: Evangelical and Catholic.* London: SPCK, 1930.

Brinth, Ole, Helle Christiansen, et al. *Højmessen i Den Danske Folkekirke: En liturgisk håndbog.* Frederiksberg: Anis, 2000.

Den svenska kyrkeordningen 1571. Edited by Sven Kjöllerström. Lund: Håkan Ohlssons Förlag, 1971.

Fæhn, Helge. *Gudstjenestelivet i den norske kirke*. Oslo: Universitetsforlaget, 1994.

Handbok för svenska kyrkan. Lund: C. W. K. Gleerups Förlag, 1899.

Johansson, Hilding. *Hemsjömanualet*. Stockholm: Svenska kyrkans diakonistyrelses bokförlag, 1950.

Martling, Carl-Henrik. *Svensk Liturgihistoria*. Stockholm: Verbum, 1993.

Martola, Yngvill. *Worship Renewal in the Evangelical Lutheran Church of Finland*. Publication No. 50. Tampere: Research Institute of the Evangelical Lutheran Church of Finland, 2001.

Martola, Yngvill. "Worship Renewal in the Evangelical-Lutheran Church of Finland." *Studia Liturgica* 31 (2001) 83–91.

Nilsson, Nils-Henrik. "The Church of Sweden Service Book." *Studia Liturgica* 31 (2001) 92–100.

Nilsson, Nils-Henrik. "Eucharistic Prayer and Lutherans: A Swedish perspective." *Studia Liturgica* 27 (1997) 176–199.

Nilsson, Nils-Henrik. *Gudstjänst i Svenska kyrkan*. Stockholm: Svenska kyrkan Mitt i församlingen, 1994.

Nilsson, Nils-Henrick. "The Principles Behind the New Sunday Lectionary for the Church of Sweden." *Studia Liturgica* 34 (2004) 240–250.

Olaus Petris Samlade Skrifter. Part II. Uppsala: Sveriges Krisliga Studentrörelses Förlag, 1915.

Senn, Frank C. *Christian Liturgy*. Minneapolis, Minn.: Fortress, 1997.

12

The Reformed Tradition in Continental Europe

Switzerland, France, and Germany

BRUNO BÜRKI

Medieval Roots—Catholic and Critical

It would be a serious mistake, and in several respects even an insult, to consider the worship of the Reformed or Presbyterian family of churches an invention of the sixteenth century. In the first place, this worship is simply a branch of the liturgy of the apostolic Church, which across the centuries has celebrated at the two tables of word and sacrament the mystery of Christ *semper et ubique* (to borrow a famous formula).[1] The more immediate roots of Reformed worship are found in the Middle Ages in the regions of the Rhône and the Rhine. They are of two kinds: on the one hand, Catholic; on the other, those critical of the institutional church. This distinction is highly significant for the future of the worship tradition that was later called Reformed.

On the critical side must be mentioned the merchant and layman Waldo of Lyons, who came to attention upon his conversion around the year 1170. He was accused of preaching in the streets and in public places to a considerable audience, attracting both men and women—especially the latter—to a faith and life of evangelical simplicity. His movement was a ministry of laypeople. No details are known about the forms of such preaching by "the Poor Men of Lyons," which was no doubt accompanied by prayers, but it must have been very dynamic and spontaneous. It was carried across several countries of Europe before finally withdrawing into the Alpine Valleys. The Waldensians, followers of Waldo, came to the side of the Protestant Reformation in 1532.

Within the Catholic Church, one must mention as precursors Master Eckhart (died c. 1327) and his disciple John Tauler (died 1361), both of them Dominicans and promoters of Rhenish mysticism. They were active chiefly in the region of Strasbourg, in present-day France, although Eckhart also went to Cologne, Germany, where he died during his trial for heresy. Master Eckhart forged links between his mystical and very personal preaching, on the one hand, and the instituted liturgy of the Church, on the other. The liturgy gives shape to the preaching; the preaching, in turn, preserves the liturgy from rigid ritualism. In the end, everything depends on the action of God. God is above and beyond all the human forms by which he is worshiped. Besides the mystics, priests who had received a scholastic training also took up preaching. Preaching was very popular in the last two centuries of the Middle Ages, in particular in the cities along the Rhine.

In the Middle Ages a special term existed for the service of the word conducted by the preacher: *pronaus* was derived from the French *prône*, which in the fifteenth century designated either the screen separating the choir from the nave or else the pulpit. From there the priest could address the faithful during mass. The Latin root of *pronaus* and *prône* is the term *praeconium*, synonymous with *praedicatio*. The preaching service took place also outside of mass. Sometimes well-to-do families preferred to create positions for preachers rather than to endow chantries for mass. Unfortunately, researchers do not have the necessary historical resources to decide how widespread the movement was. On the eve of the Reformation, preaching outside the mass could, in certain places, occur daily. The phenomenon belonged essentially to the cities, in which the middle classes were already affected by the humanist spirit. It was more widespread in the region of the Rhine than elsewhere.

In this context must be mentioned the parish priest (*Leutpriester*) of the Church of Saint Theodore in Basel, Johann Ulrich Surgant (c. 1450–1503).[2] The future reformer Huldriech Zwingli, while still a student, knew him and heard him preach. In 1503 Surgant published his *Manuale Curatorum*, a manual for parish priests, giving an example in the second part of how *pronaus*, or the Sunday preaching service, was celebrated in the Basel parish of which Surgant had charge (though the parish in Klein-Basel belonged to the diocese of Constance). At that time, the practice on Sundays was to rehearse from the pulpit the text of the Our Father, the Ave Maria, the Apostles' Creed, and the Decalogue—knowledge of them being required for admission to communion. To these were added at the time of preaching the general confession of sin (*offene Schuld*) and the intercessions. There could be a long list of parish notices concerning feast and fast days, indulgences, marriage banns, and deaths. Obviously, that all took place in the vernacular, as indeed had already long been the case for the parts of the liturgy that were directly addressed to the faithful. Surgant is particularly interesting because he dealt in an informed way with homiletical and liturgical questions, drawing his teaching from his own experience. The first part of the *Manuale* is devoted to the art of preaching. This manual went through several editions in Germany—at Basel, Augsburg, Mainz, and Strasbourg—doubtless on account of its practical character. Surgant was not only a parish pastor but also a professor of canon law in the law faculty of the University of Basel. He served four times as rector of the university. He is to be reckoned with the humanists of his time and region; as a young man he had acquired a licentiate degree from the University of Paris.

It is generally recognized that the incalculable gain of the Reformation was the discovery of the Word of God freshly alive and evangelical. At the end of the fifteenth century, preaching was generally in a decadent state. It had lost contact with the Word of God; it was drowning in hagiographical tales and moral recommendations and took delight in artificial scholastic distinctions. In this matter, even the honest efforts of a Surgant or the appeals of an Erasmus did not really change the situation. Both of them remained indebted to the medieval theory and art of preaching. In contrast, the evangelical sermons of Luther and the biblical homilies of Calvin, along with the scriptural and spiritual preaching of other reformers, prepared the way for a new style of worship.

In the matter of liturgical customs, both communal and personal, the Reformation nevertheless started from the given situation. Naturally, the abolition of the mass and the removal of images and statues were major decisions, but the reformers were less interested in creating new rites than in cleaning up what was there. The reduction in the number of clergy deputed to cultic functions also helped to alter the scene, but in the area of ritual as in other areas, the reformers did not wish to create a new church; rather, they sought to transform the church of their fathers in an evangelical direction. In any case, ritual change has never been easy, even when it has been attempted. Evangelical preaching was the prime concern of the reformers. The action of the living Word of God itself was at the heart of worship.

The cost of the reformers' choice—in particular the cost to those working in southern Germany and in the territories of the Swiss confederation or close to it— was the bracketing, if not the loss, of the sacramental dimension of worship. Worship became exclusively verbal, with a strongly catechetical orientation. The people had to progress in the knowledge of God. Salvation was not transmitted liturgically in the celebration of the mysteries. It was received by the faith born from the Word prior to being confirmed by the sacraments instituted by Christ. Before blaming the reformers for this frustrating restriction of the gift of God, one must recognize that the medieval manner of celebrating the divine mysteries—at a distance from the faithful and with more attention to form than to lively communication—had already long ago created a ditch between the clergy and the faithful. A separation between the sacred domain and everyday life seemed natural. The most awakened people (for example, bourgeois families in those cities that were to go over to the Reformation) had become accustomed to looking for their spiritual food elsewhere than at the mass, even if the mass was still considered necessary for the salvation of the living and the dead; it remained a mass performed at a distance from the people. The arrangement of the medieval church with its screen or grille separating the nave from the choir prefigured this break.

Huldriech Zwingli: Adaptor and Innovator

Zwingli (1484–1531), the Zürich reformer, has remained the leading figure of German-speaking Protestantism in the Swiss regions. He was undoubtedly the most striking ecclesiastical personality of his day. Dying an early death in the battle between the defenders of the traditional church and the innovators, he did not have the opportunity to oversee the development of church life in his city and beyond. But he has had an important and lasting influence on German-speaking Swiss Protestantism, in particular in the area of worship but also in social ethics. The link between liturgy and civil life has remained important in the Reformed world.

Zwingli had received in Vienna and in Basel a quite remarkable humanistic formation and a theological initiation in the line of the *via antiqua* of Thomist and Scotist realism. While profiting from the early writings of Luther, he nevertheless took another tack. The thought and action of Zwingli are dominated by his study of the Divine Word. The Word is living and active in the world and in the hearts of the faithful. It is by his Spirit that God acts internally in all who come to faith and constitute the community of God's elect (cf. John 6:63). The concepts of divine providence and the election of the people of God are fundamental to both the philosophical and the theological thought of Zwingli.

Thus, Zwingli was above all a preacher of the Word of God. After pastoral ministry in a country parish and a ministry to pilgrims at the Abbey of Einsiedeln, he came

Zwingli preaching. Mural painting (1900) by Carl von Haeberlin, Stein am Rhein, Switzerland. THE ART ARCHIVE

to Zürich on New Year's Day 1519 to devote himself to preaching. He began this ministry by preaching through the Gospel of Matthew from beginning to end, soon giving up his other pastoral functions in order to devote himself solely to the position of preacher (*Prädikant*) authorized by the city council. It is as a preacher that Zwingli led the city over to the Reformation, profiting from his long preparation in the scriptures and moved by the personal spiritual experience of being cured from the plague. In his "Prayer-hymn during the Plague" ("Gebetslied in der Pest"), he sees himself as an instrument in the hands of God. At the time, the preaching service followed the order of *pronaus* proposed by Surgant, though not without significant modifications.[3] According to the ecclesiastical constitution of Zürich, this order governed the divine service on Sundays and weekdays in the "cathedral church"—the *Grossmünster*—as well as in the parish churches of Zürich, both in the town and in the country. The biblical homily (a homily rather than a sermon) was preceded and followed by the usual catechetical items, prayers (especially the great intercession), the announcements of deaths and of marriages, and other parish notices.

On the days on which there was no communion, which was the case for most of the year, the preaching service thus formed an entity on its own. In 1525 the mass was suppressed by a decision of the civil powers, although the decision was long delayed and it passed by only a narrow majority. The mass was replaced by an evangelical holy supper, but since this was infrequently celebrated, only the preaching remained from the regular liturgical diet of the medieval church.

In Zürich there was no singing in this context. Singing would be allowed only later—and organ accompaniment later still—into this worship centered on the preaching. With the demise of clerical singing, which was apparently of poor quality by the end of the Middle Ages, Zwingli worked for the development of singing in civil life. He himself was a knowledgeable music lover and musician. By the seventeenth century the *collegia musica* would be flourishing in Zürich as in other cities.

The liturgy of the word was sustained by the institution of the *Prophezei*, a course intended for ministers and laity that nourished on a daily basis the biblical culture of both. The teaching was not simply "professorial" but depended on the contribution of several people; it was based on the biblical text in the original languages.

In the conflict with the Anabaptists, Zwingli and his Zürich collaborator Leo Jud were forced to create a baptismal ritual. At first that had not been a priority for the reformers. Zwingli himself, to begin with, shared the ideas of some who criticized the inherited understanding and practice of the sacrament of initiation. But now it seemed necessary not only to correct the Catholic sacrament but also to defend the practice of infant baptism itself against the demand for baptism upon personal profession of faith. The result was an *ordo* that—besides the usual questions addressed to the godparents and the reading of the "children's gospel" (Mark 10:13–16), as in the Catholic rituals of the time—consisted essentially in the baptismal act with the trinitarian formula and aspersion by water. This baptismal act was preceded by a blessing of the water, which was its only original feature, although it, too, was shared with Luther. Following the structure of a Jewish *berakah* (blessing), this "Flood Prayer" (*Sintflutgebet*) evokes the saving action of God toward Noah and his family and then prays for the light of faith for the new Christian.[4] In conclusion, the newly baptized is dressed in a white garment. This baptism of infants signified the child's integration into the church community. The symbolic action was likened to Jewish circumcision. It was not the transmission of salvation, but the confirmation of divine election. Faith would be the gift of God, and in this faith the newly baptized was called to a life of obedience.

What is the meaning of communion in this community? From Easter 1525 onward Zwingli aimed to offer to the faithful at the traditional seasons of communion an evangelical celebration of the Lord's supper. The supper was to take place four (or three) times a year, thus going beyond the obligatory annual communion of the medieval Church. The *Action oder Br(a)uch des Nachtmahls* is the most original liturgical disposition of the Zürich reformer.[5] The supper is integrated into the usual preaching service. It can in no way, however, become the ordinary Sunday celebration; rather, it represents the occasional symbolic repetition of the Last Supper of Jesus with his disciples. There cannot be a liturgical sacrifice like that of the abolished mass. There will be no consecration and transformation of the eucharistic elements. In place of all that, the assembled believers themselves become the body of Christ. Zwingli's service is more festive and celebratory than any other order of the period. It begins with the Greater Gloria proclaimed in the church. Then come the biblical readings that were used at the feast of Corpus Christi. The distribution of the elements is brought as close as possible to the recitation of the institution narrative. The farewell discourses of John's Gospel conclude this representation of the Lord's Last Supper. Behind this original liturgical proposal, one can still sense the "spiritual play" of the Middle Ages, except that here it is no longer "theater" but the committed action of a community of believers. As was said at the start, Zwingli believed firmly in the creative action of the Word of God and in the calling of a community of disciples chosen to live the faith. This community has become the body of Christ. As such, it is the bearer of the liturgical action.

Zwingli's liturgical forms took root only in the Reformed Church of Zürich and in some neighboring regions (Glaris and the Grisons). And even at Zürich, despite an apparent continuity of forms, the heritage of Zwingli was soon adjusted to a more common Reformed or Protestant concept. The words at the breaking of bread for the distribution become a substitute consecration outside the eucharistic prayer. Zwingli's troubled relation with sacramental communication, in connection with the Anabaptist conflict, weighs upon liturgical life here more than elsewhere. The double resistance— against institutionalism, on the one hand, and spiritualism, on the other—was doubtless necessary, and Zwingli must be respected for the courage with which he took up his duty as a watchman and guard. But the church of Zürich needed, and still needs, to move out from what were blind alleys for its liturgical and sacramental life. Owing to the work of Heinrich Bullinger in the next generation, agreement was reached on eucharistic doctrine with the Calvinists of French-speaking Switzerland in the *Consensus Tigurinus* of 1549 and the Second Helvetic Confession of 1566, but Zürich remains attached to the "sacramentarianism" of which Luther accused Zwingli.

The Strasbourg Crossroads

Located on the linguistic boundary between German speakers and French, Strasbourg is not a typically Reformed city in the way Zürich or Geneva or even Basel are. After its first contacts with Zürich, Strasbourg came closer to Lutheranism following the Diet of Augsburg (1530). By the end of the sixteenth century, the liturgy at Strasbourg had been conformed to Lutheran orthodoxy. After its annexation by Louis XIV in 1681, the city returned to being an episcopal see, and its cathedral was restored to Catholic worship. A partial and provisional restoration of Catholic worship had already taken place between 1549 and 1559 as a result of the promulgation of the Interim of 1548, which was meant to settle the confessional question in the German Empire. What is of interest here is the vocation or destiny of Strasbourg to be a crossroads on the liturgical and ecclesiastical map as well as in other areas. At the time of the Reformation, then, Strasbourg was a German city.

In the sixteenth century the liturgical developments at Strasbourg—after honorable pioneers such as Theobald Schwartz (or Theobald Nigri, c. 1484–1561) and Wolfgang Capito (1478–1541)—depend chiefly on Martin Bucer (1491–1551), the indefatigable reconciler amid an already divided Protestant world, particularly on the question of the sacraments. The Dominican theologian Bucer had been won for the Reformation by his meeting with Luther. At Strasbourg he found a field of action that was already strongly marked by evangelical forces. Later on, he became the principal teacher of John Calvin, who lived in Strasbourg between 1538 and 1541. Bucer merits attention as much for his conception of the sacramental life as for his ecclesiology. He tried to secure the reformation by setting up "house churches" within the larger church community, a measure that anticipated Pietism and some modern conceptions of pastoral practice. Toward the end of his career, Bucer was forced from Strasbourg into exile on account of interconfessional quarrels among the "Reformed," Catholics, and Lutherans. This gave Bucer the opportunity to play a part also in the Anglican liturgical reformation.

Strasbourg is interesting for the way in which it managed the passage from the medieval Catholic liturgical regime to Protestant orders of worship. There was no liturgical revolution such that the transition from Catholicism to Protestantism would have taken place at a single moment. Rather, Strasbourg experienced the slow evolution of old usages toward new forms of worship that appeared to correspond better to the Word of God. Thus, more than half a dozen liturgical orders were issued one after another. They began with the creation of a German mass and ended after 1525 with a Lord's supper that looked for conformity with the scriptural model. The name *Messe* was replaced by *Kirchenamt* or *Kirchenübung*.[6]

The disappearance of the mass and the prayer of the hours produced a vacuum in the Strasbourg churches. Bucer and his fellow workers labored to fill this in a manner that became typical of the Protestant churches, particularly in the Reformed domain: the establishment of a dense system of weekday—as well as, of course, Sunday—preaching. Timing of the services was adapted to the different social strata of the city. The population seems to have been quite assiduous in listening to the biblical message, the preaching easily lasting more than hour. The service of the word was linked with the office of prayers. On the other hand, attempts failed to reestablish, in the numerous conventual churches, a canonical office according to an evangelical conception of it.

The Strasbourg liturgical reform is remarkable also because of the place given to liturgical song. From the beginning, Bucer here took a different position from that of

Zwingli, who had banned congregational singing in worship. Bucer's choice was decisive for Calvin. According to Bucer's commentary on the Psalms, music was appreciated for its convergence with mysticism: music rendered the soul sensitive to the Word of God. So, in worship at Strasbourg, there was to be singing, not only traditional liturgical singing, especially for the ordinary of the liturgy, but also biblical psalms versified in the vernacular with new and simple tunes suitable for singing by the assembly. Other *geistliche Lieder* were used, too—traditional compositions, some of which had Gregorian melodies, as well as new songs. Several of Luther's hymns were much appreciated in Strasbourg. The organ did not accompany the singing of the assembly but rather came in as an aid to meditation. By the end of the sixteenth century, polyphonic singing would be used only after the conclusion of the official services.

Given the limited historical knowledge at their disposal, Bucer and his cohorts sacrificed both form and content of the ancient eucharistic prayer in favor of an evangelical Lord's supper deemed as close as possible to the biblical model. The preface and Sanctus progressively gave way to a long exhortation addressed to the faithful, who were thereby to remember Christ and his sacrifice. In a spiritual context marked by personal piety surrounding communion, the liturgical solemnity of a eucharistic preface was no longer fitting. *Vermahnung*—didactic and parenetic exhortation—was in the air. The *memento* prayers in the traditional Roman canon perhaps suggested the idea of placing the universal or intercessory prayer, together with a prayer of preparation for communion, in the framework of the supper. Any idea of a sacrifice or of a meritorious celebration of mass had to be excluded. To the universal prayer was joined an epicletic invocation upon the faithful and an anamnetic evocation of Christ. The Our Father was placed by Bucer after this prayer rather than at the moment of communion, in order to bring communion as close as possible to the institution narrative. Restored to strict scriptural wording, the biblical narrative of the institution was considered an essential element of the supper, since it contained the words of Christ himself. That, in fact, is not too different from the high value placed on the words of consecration in the medieval mass; but here the function of the institution is solely kerygmatic. Naturally, communion was given under both kinds from the beginning of the Reformation. The service was concluded by a final prayer—the first note of thanksgiving to be struck in the whole of this—and by the benediction.

With the suppression of the weekday masses, a theologically correct attempt was made at Strasbourg to celebrate the Lord's supper on every Lord's day. But doubtless on account of the paucity of communicants, the reformers had to be content, as far as the various parish churches of the city were concerned, with a rotating system of eucharistic celebrations every fourth Sunday. At the cathedral the supper was celebrated every Sunday. In the country districts the frequency was once a month or once every two months. Quite different from Zürich then, the idea of frequent communion and the relation in principle between the Lord's day and the Lord's supper were held in honor at Strasbourg.

As for eucharistic doctrine, Strasbourg theologians at the beginning were, like Zwingli, influenced by a spiritualist current: the presence of Christ is spiritual for believers. But then Bucer, coming closer to Luther and adopting the Wittenberg Concord of 1536, allowed the notion of a sacramental union between the bread and the body of Christ. For him this union must always be sealed by the faith of the communicant. Calvin's eucharistic doctrine will find its roots here.

So then Calvin was influenced by Bucer. The liturgy of Geneva, which will also become the liturgy of the French Reformed, has its roots in Strasbourg. Moreover, Bucer was called upon by the prince elector Philip of Hesse to help in the organiza-

The Paradise Church in Lyons.
After the wars of religion, which
included the Saint Bartholomew's Day
Massacre of 1572, French Protestants
were given extensive rights under the
Edict of Nantes, signed by Henry IV,
himself a former Protestant, in 1598.
The edict was revoked by Louis XIV
in 1685. Painting, 1564. Bibliothèque
Publique et Universitaire, Lyon,
France/Erich Lessing/Art
Resource, NY

tion of the Hessian church as well
as that of Kassel, where the prince
resided. Of course, it was not a case
of simply transposing the Strasbourg rites into a different context.
Nevertheless, for both Geneva and
Hesse, the Strasbourg genealogy is
clear and important. Thus, Strasbourg is a cradle of the Reformed liturgy for both the German-speaking
and the French-speaking churches.

The Calvinist Model:
"Prières et chants ecclésiastiques"

At first blush, Calvin is not to be reckoned among the great figures in the history of
the Christian liturgy—those of the stature of Luther, Thomas Cranmer, or Gregory
the Great. Yet, without having sought it, Calvin has his place, owing to the Genevan
liturgy, *La Forme des prières et chants ecclésiastiques*, the durable model of worship for
one of the great Christian families: the Reformed churches.[7]

John Calvin was, above all, a Bible reader in both testaments, and from the biblical
witness he transmits a sound and clearly articulated doctrine. In a still exploratory
way, he drafted at Basel in 1536 the first version of his magisterial work *The Institutes
of the Christian Religion*. This first edition already contains the section on worship that
will keep its place in the systematic presentation of the Christian faith by the reformer
(see the 1559 *Institutes*, 4.17.43). In this context Calvin appeals to apostolic usage
described in Acts 2:42. The liturgy of the word is followed by the administration of
the Lord's supper according to the biblical instructions; the reformer always pleaded
for a frequent celebration of the supper. Bread and wine having been placed on the
table, the minister recalls the institution of the supper and the promises linked with it.
The table is fenced, for one does not communicate without discernment. The Lord is
prayed to, to make the supplicants worthy of receiving with faith and thanksgiving the
food that he gives. The faithful sing psalms and receive both bread and the cup. That,
then, is the essential structure of Reformed Sunday worship.

While living in Strasbourg, Calvin had charge of a community of French-speaking
refugees, and he engaged in stimulating and fruitful dialogue with Martin Bucer. He

benefited from the ecclesiastical and liturgical experience of the church in this city. Theologically he received the stamp of Bucer. This all prepared him to become the future moderator of the church of Geneva, the monitor of all who came to seek refuge, advice, or formation in this city that became the beacon of Reformed Protestantism. The second generation of reformers is now at hand. And it is less a matter of original creations than of putting into place a viable practice for the church. It is impossible to overemphasize the spirit of openness and care for the coherence of the faith and its practice that marked the persons involved in this reformation. Their openness was exemplified in a large network of correspondence and fraternal links that, as of this writing, remain characteristic of the Reformed and Presbyterian world.

The preaching of the Divine Word is at the heart of the Reformed service. God himself addresses the Church in the scriptures read and expounded, in order by the Holy Spirit to arouse the faith of all the elect. Conscious of the scope of such preaching—revelation of God and edification of the Church—Calvin devoted himself assiduously to it in Geneva. On Sunday mornings the homily treated the New Testament;

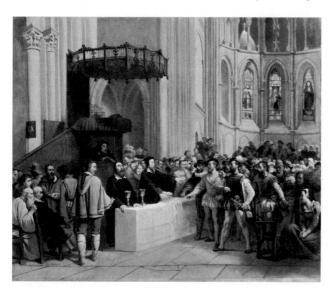

John Calvin refusing holy communion to libertines in Saint Peter's cathedral, Geneva. Location: Bibliothèque Universitaire, Geneva. THE ART ARCHIVE/UNIVERSITY LIBRARY GENEVA/DAGLI ORTI

in the afternoon, the Psalms; and on weekdays, the Old Testament in *lectio continua*. The assembly received instruction and exhortation; doctrine had to be realized in life. Calvin's preaching was neither rhetorical nor allegorical; biblical typology was put directly into the service of daily Christian life.

There are three features characteristic of worship in Calvin's style: prayer as the foundation of the celebration (a prayer whose liturgical use nevertheless raises several problems); the active participation of all the faithful in the celebration, especially in the singing of psalms; and consecration to God and the appeal to the Holy Spirit for the disciples of Christ in the whole of the lives of the faithful, as well as at worship.

Calvin's prayer flowed from his familiarity with scripture.[8] The greater part of his prayers was based on the biblical text from which he preached and taught. Transmitted and adapted, Calvin's prayers have remained alive—still consistent, demanding, but too dense for today's liturgical sense. It is useful to recall, in particular, the famous prayer that opens a Reformed service, which is more a vigorous profession of the trinitarian faith of the community than simply a confession of sin. Nevertheless, it is as such that the text is presented:

> O Lord God, eternal and almighty Father, we confess and acknowledge unfeignedly before Your holy majesty that we are poor sinners. . . . O Lord, we are grieved that we have offended You; and we condemn ourselves and our sins with true repentance, beseeching Your grace to relieve our distress.

> O God and Father most gracious and full of compassion, have mercy upon us in the name of Your Son, our Lord Jesus Christ. And as You blot our sins and stains, magnify and increase in us day by day the grace of Your Holy Spirit.[9]

When the Lord's supper was to be celebrated, Calvin placed a further long prayer after the prayers of intercession and the paraphrase of the Lord's prayer. The text represents a transcription of the corresponding Strasbourg prayers as these had come to slow maturity through the different phases of the reform of worship in Strasbourg. There, too, the tone is essentially that of confessing the faith: Christ communicates to humanity his body and his blood, which were offered in sacrifice on the cross. His spiritual and heavenly food causes humankind to live a holy life in him. It is the meal of the covenant, celebrated with thanksgiving. At the supper itself the reading of the institution according to 1 Corinthians 11:23–29 is followed by a long exhortation that culminates in the summons to "lift our hearts on high," where Christ lives and reigns with the Father and waits to feed us with his very own substance. Then the bread and the cup are distributed as the "visible signs" of his bounty.[10]

The great attention that Calvin gave to the participation of the assembly in the liturgy appears clearly in the letter to the reader that precedes the *Forme des prières et chants ecclésiastiques* in the standard version published in Geneva in 1542.[11] This book is not a liturgical book for the officiant—Calvin never bothered to publish such a book—but rather the manual for each of the believers. Thus, the latter are motivated and rendered responsible. The preface assumes that all members of the church must know and understand what happens in the assembly. Calvin's purpose is neither formal nor intellectual but spiritual: the Holy Spirit active in the hearts of the believers will give them to understand what takes place. Their participation is a matter of having their hearts enlightened by the very Spirit of God. The different elements of worship evoked by Calvin here are preaching, public and solemn prayers, and the administration of the sacraments. The sacramental consecration is effected by the word of faith that is received by the faithful; one catches here the polemic against the abuses in Catholic practice at the time, but also the pastoral concern for an authentic participation by all. In his letter, Calvin ends with the singing of psalms, which he presents as one of the forms of public prayer engaged in by the faithful. In a later addition to the text, Calvin will follow Saint Augustine in declaring that the singing of the biblical psalms is preferable to any other song, whether in the assembly or at home or anywhere else that spiritual singing could be practiced; the point is that God, by the psalms, puts into worshipers' mouths the words that are to be sung. God sings in humankind! Reformed worship is therefore a worship to inspire all participants in all its parts.

Thus, it can be understood how for Calvin worship is a consecration of all and of everything to the glory of God. The reformer's lack of interest in the church year and sacred space is not intended sacrilegiously; rather he wants the whole of life and the world in its entirety to be consecrated to the Lord. Worship is not a matter for certain special days but for every day, just as it is a duty for all the people rather than a few clerics. In his full humanity, Jesus Christ draws the life of every person into his own complete consecration. To avoid any misunderstanding, one has to be aware how fundamental, for the reformer, is the fact that this consecration to God could not be the result of human effort, whether in the religious or in the secular sphere. It is the Spirit of God that alone consecrates men and women and all creation to make of them a liturgy that renders thanks to God and glorifies God for the divine work of salvation.

The sacraments of baptism and the Lord's supper are real means of grace with which God acts. The sacraments are not distant, symbolic signs. The Sacrament is the channel through which the Spirit of God works, just like the revealed Word (the key word for Calvin is *with* the bread and the wine, Lutherans say *in, mit, und unter*). For Calvin the liturgy of the word is preceded by an epiclesis, or invocation of the Holy Spirit, whose form is left to the discretion of the minister. Word and sacraments are thus sacramental, if by that one understands the saving and mysterious presence and action of God in the world for believers.

Sunday, as the Lord's day, becomes the great and marvelous eschatological sign of the fact that everything comes from God and everything awaits the final intervention by God.[12] Everything else, whether in life or in liturgy, is but the obedience of disciples and the thanksgiving of the children of God. All this finds its support in the daily services of worship at Geneva and in the other Reformed cities as well as domestic worship in more isolated circumstances.

Practice in Basel and Bern: The Preaching Service

Turning to Basel and Bern, one comes back in fact to a period whose beginnings in the Reformation antedate the activity of Calvin. The proof is to be found in Guillaume Farel (1489–1565, a native of the French Dauphiné): it was he who in 1536 kept Calvin in Geneva and who, in the service of Bern, already had at that time to his credit a career as a reformer in the French-speaking regions of present-day Switzerland. With his *Manière et Fasson*, an adaptation of a German-speaking model from Bern, Farel created as early as 1533 the first Reformed liturgy in French. It is a directory for the components of worship rather than, strictly speaking, a liturgical book; it is an apologia for the work of this traveling reformer who often found himself in the midst of turbulence.[13] Later, as a pastor in Neuchâtel, Farel served the extension of Calvin's reformation.

In Basel the Reformation was the fruit of evangelical preaching patiently developed over several years by ministers whose first concern was neither polemical nor moral—even though criticisms of abusive Catholic practices and an ethical emphasis after the style of Erasmus were known—but evangelical in the full sense of the term. The biblical foundation and appeal to scripture was of prime importance to this preaching, both when criticisms were being made and when positive affirmations were being advanced. Several of the preachers sermonized on entire books of the Bible read *in continuo*. The spread of the printed book was an effective support for the preached word. John Oecolampadius (1482–1531), who was to become the principal reformer of Basel, had received a first-class training in the humanities and in the Bible in southern Germany, a region particularly favorable to the development of new thought. For long seeking his way, as a priest and briefly a monk, Oecolampadius was both professor and preacher in one, traveling extensively and finally settling in Basel, where he contributed to the foundation of a piety and culture that were durably marked by the biblical spirit. The Word of revelation is both food for the soul and rule for life; the Christ of whom the Gospels speak is the one and only way. Preaching becomes the proclamation and transmission of salvation, in place of the mass. Of first importance is the correspondence of worship with the true faith. In the celebration of worship, faith finds its expression. The form is given by the biblical message in contrast to the sacrifice of the mass, ecclesiastical institutions, or the mediation of saints.

Well before the final break with the traditional church, Oecolampadius had stopped saying mass in his church of Saint Martin at Basel. This duty was yielded to chaplains. Already in 1525 the reformer, for his part, was thinking about a service of communion for the hearers of the Word. Giving up even the name of the mass, he developed the *Form und Gestalt wie des Herren Nachtmahl etc. zu Basel gebraucht und gehalten werden.*[14] This ordo, moreover, contains also the service of baptism and the communion of the sick. The communion of the faithful is organically linked to preaching, being prepared for by an appeal to trust in the forgiveness that would be given in the supper. The long list of the excommunicated—its proclamation is a peculiarity of the Basel celebration of the supper, although it had antecedents in the *pronaus*—is opened by an address to those who despise the body of Christ, the Word of God, and the two sacraments (this latter is a swipe at the Anabaptists or Spiritualists). The capital sin is a lack of faith, which makes a mockery of God, "for God will have a holy and bold people." The minister moves from the pulpit to the table only for the institution narrative. Before communion there are long scripture readings, and especially the narrative of Christ's Passion. The word of scripture takes the place of the prayers of the canon. Apart from the institution narrative, the order of communion is totally removed from the structure and content of the mass. In both composition and style, one recognizes an authentic pastoral act. The community is directed back to the event of Christ's death in order to be exhorted to a life of holiness. The weakness of the Basel ordo is inherited, doubtless unwittingly, from the liturgical habits of the Middle Ages; the communion of the faithful is detached from any eucharistic consecration of the elements. The communion, and nothing more, follows on the preaching of the gospel.

In the introduction of the Reformation as in the celebration of worship, the faithful of Basel took an important and active part. On several occasions the decisions were carried by popular vote. Liturgically, the people of Basel participated by the singing of the Psalms in German versification, unlike what was possible and allowed at Zürich. The people even began to sing spontaneously. It was during the communion that the popular singing of psalms was first heard. One may guess that this singing found a place also in the preaching service. The first psalter for singing by the faithful appeared at Basel in 1581, taking over from the previous spontaneous and improvised usages.

Despite the similarity between Protestant worship at Basel and at Bern, an essential difference must be noted: in Bern, it is not a devout people seeking to give to worship a form corresponding to their spiritual aspirations (as was the case in Basel); rather, it is the political authorities of the land who, at the instigation of a few cultivated and far-sighted personalities, attempt to renew and transform the ecclesiastical institutions. Worship is part of that, without being the cornerstone of the Bernese reformation. The matter of relics and indulgences, for example, was more important. Decrees of the city council in 1523 and especially in 1528 instituted the reform of the church. Two liturgical and ecclesiastical documents of Bern deserve special mention: the *Cancel und Agend Büchlin der Kilchen zu Bärn* (1529) and the *Berner Synodus* (1532). The former takes its cue from the liturgical practices of Zürich for the preaching service, baptism, and the commemoration of the departed, and then from the Basel liturgy for communion.[15] Here the supper (as already with Oecolampadius) is "our mystery," and the tone—both for exclusion from communion (at Bern this takes place in the conscience of the individual) and for the invitation to communion—becomes truly pastoral, or *seelsorgerlich*. The *Berner Synodus* presumes that baptism will be celebrated in the assembly of the faithful. For the eucharist the service seeks a pastoral presentation of the mystery and of brotherly communion, not delving much into doctrinal questions, but keeping in general a middle way between Luther and Zwingli in anticipation of later Calvinism. Wafers are used for the bread.

Looking around the Reformed churches of the sixteenth century, especially in Switzerland, one notices the various possibilities of adaptation according to the particular and varied situations, but also the limits of a liturgy exclusively organized by the local church. At that time, the Roman Catholic Church—especially through the creation of the post-Tridentine liturgical books—undertook to coordinate the usages of the several missals and rituals from one local church to another. In 1531 the delegates of the Reformed churches deliberated at Basel over the possibility of unifying the rites and ceremonies in the churches of the Swiss Confederation. The question seemed to be premature, but it was taken up again on several occasions in the sixteenth century. Unity in the confession of faith was more important than the question of a common liturgy.

The birth and development and then, in the seventeenth century, the rigidifying of confessional orthodoxy had not only doctrinal consequences but also liturgical implications. In Basel, Lutheran tendencies made themselves felt in the second half of the sixteenth century. Attempts were made at a more solemn type of worship, using organ music and the kneeling of ministers during the Lord's supper. The future, however, belonged to Calvinism. At the Synod of Dort, which in 1618–1619 gathered representatives from all the Reformed churches, Calvinist orthodoxy—with the Swiss and the French as principal supporters—crystallized around the doctrine of the predestination of the individual faithful. On the liturgical front, Calvinist orthodoxy emphasized what were apparently minor points: the use of ordinary bread rather than the wafers that had been used in most of the Swiss churches, and the confession of sins in Calvin's formulation instead of the *offene Schuld* of the medieval type. Calvin himself had considered the use of leavened or unleavened bread, as well as of red or white wine, among the indifferent matters (*Institutes* 4.17.43).

Johann Jakob Grynäus (1540–1617), the Antistes who fulfilled episcopal functions in Basel, was an important precursor of Calvinist orthodoxy in the German-speaking churches. His opposition was no longer as much directed against Catholicism as against Lutheranism. In 1642 Basel rejoiced at the "Einführung des Brotbrechens," the liturgical gesture of the "fraction" and the use of ordinary bread; this was an important feature of Calvinist identity to which even an "ideological" sense was attached. A generation later Calvin's confession of sins was the only prayer to precede the sermon in the Basel liturgy. The church of Zürich, with its Antistes Johann Jakob Breitinger (1575–1645), increased the number of prayers adopted from the Reformation period, including a prayer for funeral services that attracted much attention. In the time of confessional orthodoxy, the treatment of the liturgy was more conservative than creative. It limited itself to minor adjustments, but also highlighted signs that had become identity markers of a church that was by now in its own way traditional.

The Palatinate Option: A *Kirchenordnung*

In the first half of the sixteenth century, the Rhineland-Palatinate, in Germany, experienced a troubled ecclesiastical history marked by diverse liturgical influences. First these were of a Lutheran kind coming from Württemberg, but then also emanating from Strasbourg. Moreover, the Swiss Reformation was in the neighborhood, and particularly the forceful personality of Zwingli. With the accession to power of the prince elector Frederick III, Calvinist influence became decisive. The prince appealed to the theologians trained in Calvin's school, in particular Zacharius Ursinus and Caspar Olevianus. With the aid of his theologians at Heidelberg, the prince involved himself in the introduction of the "church order" of 1563, and he received a nickname that suited him well—Frederick the Pious. The *Kirchenordnung* of 1563, in fact, was not only put into force in the Palatinate, but also it exercised a broad and most durable influence elsewhere.

The *Kirchenordnung* is a complex work. Besides some regulations of a disciplinary kind—as is to be expected from its general title—the collection contains, though in a sequence that is not very obvious, liturgical items for different ecclesiastical acts and particularly the liturgy of the holy supper. If the details of the composition are not simple, the theological intention is quite fundamental: the celebration of worship and the confession of faith must match each other closely in a well-instructed community of the faithful. One might evoke the adage *lex orandi, lex credendi* (mindful that in the Reformation tradition the priority resides with the *lex credendi*, which must then be expressed in prayer). In the middle of the *Kirchenordnung*, inserted between the liturgy of baptism and the liturgy of the Lord's supper, figures the famous Heidelberg Catechism. It is preceded by instructions concerning catechesis and followed by a summary suitable for use at the proposed admission of catechumens to the supper. The liturgical use of the catechism is a major purpose of the whole enterprise. The catechism was to be taught in the Sunday worship services, morning and afternoon. Its material is distributed over fifty-two Sundays, with no consideration given to the different liturgical seasons—which corresponds well with Calvin's view of things.

The organization of the catechism is original, and constitutes an important theological step. The opening question is entirely christological: "What is your sole comfort in living and in dying?" It is Christ and his work of salvation. Then follow the three parts of the catechism: "of the misery of mankind"; "of the redemption of mankind" (a long section of almost thirty Sundays, concluding with the doctrines of baptism and the Lord's supper); and "of gratitude" (the ethical part of Christian teaching including the Ten Commandments, which are expounded here rather than being treated at the beginning of the catechism). The last eight Sundays are devoted to prayer, and in particular to the Our Father. The final question, entirely liturgical and spiritual, asks what is the meaning of the little word *Amen*.

Question Eighty of the catechism, in a very sharp and polemical way, opposes to "the Catholic mass" the celebration of the Lord's supper as a witness to full redemption through the sacrifice of Christ. The daily sacrifice of the mass constitutes "a negation of the one sacrifice of Christ." It is idolatry.

Prayers are proposed for the different services of the community, both Sunday and weekdays. They share the tonality of the ample and well-furnished prayers of the Calvinist tradition. The first of the prayers intended for opening worship contains a faithful transcription of Calvin's prayer for the confession of sins, which is followed by reminders that are more catechetical than liturgical, and by the Lord's prayer. In the *Kirchenordnung* there are no precise instructions concerning the sequence of the ordinary service of worship. One may guess that the liturgical order was that of the preaching service customary elsewhere in southern Germany and in Switzerland.

Apart from the catechism the most remarkable part of the *Kirchenordnung* is the ordo for the celebration of the supper.[16] Its influence radiated more or less directly throughout German-speaking areas and even as far as the Netherlands. It became and has remained in these regions the Reformed liturgy of the Lord's supper par excellence. The order for baptism, which is found at the beginning of the *Kirchenordnung*, is taken literally from Calvin's Geneva liturgy. For the celebration of the supper, one confronts a pattern that partially reflects Calvin's, but that is inspired by the transformation this received from John à Lasco, a minister of Polish origin active in the Reformed communities of London, Lower Saxony, and Poland. Then, too, certain parts of the earlier local Lutheran tradition are recognizable, as well as borrowings from Strasbourg. The whole constitutes a compilation that is not just a patchwork but rather brings together different affirmations in an attempt at a unified theology and practice of the Lord's supper.

The exhortation to the communicants (the *Abendmahlsvermahnung*, an obligatory element in traditional Protestant orders for the supper) constitutes the theologically richest part. The institution narrative is, as with Calvin, placed before this exhortation. It is transmitted according to a single and exclusively biblical text (1 Cor. 11, as far as verse 29), not in the composite form traditional in the church's liturgical formulations. The exhortation evokes and organizes a certain number of essential themes for the doctrine and the celebration of the Lord's supper. The prominent themes in the Palatinate service at this point are self-examination, fencing of the table, the encouragement of the timid, the memorial of Christ's saving work, application of the words of institution (adding now the forgiveness of sins from Matthew's Gospel), and communion with Christ and fellow members of his Body; and a brief prayer asks that God will work by the Holy Spirit in the hearts of the recipients. As is generally the case in Protestant orders, the exhortation says in kerygmatic mode what traditional eucharistic prayers say in euchological mode.[17] While the formulation in this case is particularly rich and elaborate, drawing on the Heidelberg Catechism, the limitation of this enterprise remains the rather uncelebratory character of the whole. The fact that the address is an exhortation to human beings rather than a glorification of God for his benefits makes it difficult to catch the liturgical spirit. This is doubtless a question of style and of context. In the background there is probably also a problem of theological conception, even of attitude toward God. It is therefore welcome that subsequent Reformed liturgies dared to go further in the celebration of the mystery. From the start, the elements of a fuller theology of the liturgy were present and ready for later development. Moreover, the road was open for adaptations to a changing context.

Both in town and in the country, the observance of the supper in the Palatinate was relatively rather frequent, compared with what was found elsewhere. The importance given by the *Kirchenordnung* to preparation, both communal and individual, for the celebration must be underlined. There is an admirable theological solidity as well as a serious personal disposition about what is required for the celebration of the sacrament. As is regularly the case with the Reformed, worship appears as an eminently important center of the Christian life, and the Christian life, in order to bear witness to a true gratitude toward God, must match up to the high calling that God addresses to the faithful.

Liturgical Reforms in the Enlightenment and in Pietism: J.-F. Ostervald at Neuchâtel, and Eugène Bersier in Paris

In the eighteenth century and again in the nineteenth, certain ministers—and then laypeople—in the French-speaking Reformed churches became aware that the heritage received from John Calvin did not meet all needs in the area of worship. The principal bearers of these new liturgical aspirations were, first, Jean-Frédéric Ostervald (1663–1747), pastor in Neuchâtel (a city at the foot of the Jura and its surrounding area that today belongs to Switzerland), and then, a century later, the Parisian pastor Eugène Bersier (1831–1889). Certain philosophical presuppositions, a renewed spirituality, and the changing place of the church in society all prompted these men to expand their options.[18] They nevertheless appealed to the theological and ecclesial heritage of the Reformation. The last point is particularly important for Bersier. In both cases contact with other churches was decisive. This openness on their part leads one to regard these men as precocious precursors of ecumenism. Henceforth it becomes clear that worship is not simply the worship of the Reformed church; any particular church is indebted in this area to various others. At the time, the Roman Catholic Church was hardly to be reckoned as supplying a model at the liturgical level. Rather, these men turned their gaze to communities stemming from the Reformation. For Ostervald the model was unquestionably the Anglican Church. Bersier found his inspiration in the liturgy of a marginal Protestant church, likewise British in origin, namely the Catholic Apostolic Church, or the Irvingites (so named after its Scottish founder, A. E. Irving, 1792–1834). He was, moreover, familiar with texts in the wider liturgical tradition, including Anglicanism.

Ostervald belonged to the early Enlightenment, whereas Bersier's worldview was indebted to Romanticism. If Ostervald desired to bring together all the forces of Protestantism between Berlin and London, Bersier, as the product of the Evangelical revival in the nineteenth century, hoped rather for the restoration of unity between the branches of the Reformed church in France. Both of the men felt that the worship life of the parish and the churches to which they belonged should constitute a lever for renewal and unity, which in their eyes was the prime condition for an authentic Christian life on the part of all. Beyond the differences of time and place, this new awareness of the fundamental role of liturgically ordered worship—dependent on the liturgical tradition of the whole Church—was a new feature in Protestantism, at least in Protestantism of the Reformed type. Hitherto the question of rite or ceremonies had been considered secondary, to be settled according to circumstances.

As a very young pastor, Ostervald was rapidly recognized for the mission he undertook in the Neuchâtel church, and he labored over a decade for the introduction of a new liturgy in the parishes of his land parallel to other reforming measures intended to elevate the faith and life of the people. He himself composed a catechism, insisting of religious duty, although it met with opposition from the heirs of Calvinism. As for worship, the very sober regulations dating from the time of the Reformation made a total reexamination necessary. Ostervald was particularly keen on the reading of Holy Scripture during weekday services, following a lectionary that distributed the chapters of the New and the Old Testaments through the course of the Christian year. Honor was restored to the liturgical year and its principal festivals. From the Church of England's *Book of Common Prayer*, Ostervald borrowed the prayers or collects appointed for the different Sundays and seasons. He composed hymns to be recited while still awaiting the possibility of having them sung in addition to the Psalms that were familiar in the churches of Calvinist tradition. The ordo of the Lord's supper is borrowed from the Anglican liturgy, including especially the eucharistic prayer. Following the traditionally Reformed exhortation to the communicants, there is the prayer of the preface in the Western tradition, followed by the Sanctus (recited simply by the officiant). Then, after the prayer of intercession and the confession of our sins, the "consecration" is performed at the table. At the very end, before a final exhortation, there is the recitation of the Greater Gloria.

The ceremony of confirmation, when children instructed in the faith are called on to ratify and confirm the vow of their baptism, was significant for the church of Ostervald. Upon their promise, and in the hope that it will be "religiously kept," the catechumens are admitted to "the holy sacrament of the supper." All the ceremonies and texts for public worship are included in *La liturgie*, an impressive book when compared with Calvin's *Forme des prières et chants ecclésiastiques*. Yet it has to be admitted that, for all the great religious devotion, there is little sense of sacramental uplift or of the operation of the Holy Spirit to feed the faithful on the substance of Christ in glory (to take up the terms of Calvin). There is more of morality than of divine mystery.

Bersier, too, created a *Liturgie à l'usage des Églises réformées*, for which he drew on the missal and ritual of the Catholic Apostolic Church (the Irvingites).[19] The ritualist controversies going on in the Church of England at the time also made Bersier aware of the importance of liturgical gestures and symbols.

Bersier's liturgy was conceived for the Reformed parish of the Étoile in Paris, whose church was expressly built for the celebration ordained by its pastor. Here, as with Ostervald, the liturgically ordered reading of Holy Scripture is important. Bersier rewrote the texts of the traditional prayers in the declamatory and sometimes sumptuous style of the period. He rediscovered for Protestantism the elements that give liturgy its identity, such as doxologies or litanies. Seeking to promote worship as adoration, Bersier also recovered the liturgical memorial, and he wished to give the Lord's supper a significant role. His communion liturgy contains a eucharistic prayer in the tradition of the Roman canon, although including an epiclesis before the institution narrative (an avant-garde move that was already found in the Catholic Apostolic liturgy).

To allow the participation of the faithful in the liturgical action proper, rather than reducing his parishioners to the singing hymns added to the liturgical performance, Bersier created liturgical responses. His sister-in-law, the musician Henriette Hollard, was a valuable help here. These responses became the most widely imitated part of this participatory liturgy; they represented a new development in Reformed worship. But the liturgical initiative was not simply of a formal kind. It matched Bersier's communion ecclesiology. The "communion of the saints" was for him a fundamental notion, with Christ's redeemed forming a worshiping community, which would gather together for eternity. The community consciousness could arise in the fraternal climate of the Evangelical revival. It became an element of challenge and enrichment in the Reformed churches, where the faithful originally kept themselves much more distant from one another.

With numerous revisions and new editions, Ostervald's liturgy long remained the official liturgy of the Reformed church of Neuchâtel. Bersier's liturgy was adopted by two Reformed parishes in Paris. But the principal benefit of the liturgical reforms of Ostervald and Bersier was to have created in Reformed circles an authentically liturgical sensitivity and to have awakened a readiness for the celebration of worship in communion with the entire Church. What were at first the two locally limited initiatives found an echo in other churches of the Calvinist Reformation: Ostervald's influence was felt among the Reformed in Germany, just as Bersier's responses became common property in the parishes of Switzerland and France. By different routes a more catholic form of celebration had been recovered. The confession of the Reformed faith was not incompatible with a liturgical order recognizable in the universal

Church. A similar experience occurred in the Presbyterian churches of the English-speaking world, and (as will be seen) much later and more timidly in the German-speaking Reformed communities. In the French-speaking Reformed churches of the twenty-first century, one can observe particularly welcome signs of openness to the common liturgy. Nevertheless, the celebration of Christ's paschal mystery in the Church remains to be fully recovered in practice and integrated into theological thought.

The Contemporary Situation in French-Speaking Switzerland and in France: Tradition at Grips with Modernity

The French-speaking Reformed churches benefited from what may be called a providential preparation for liturgical renewal. If one agrees on the limitations of the changes made in the Calvinist reformation in the area of worship, one must, on the other hand, acknowledge the prophetic importance of the liturgical projects of an Ostervald and a Bersier in the eighteenth and nineteenth centuries. Raising the sensitivity of the faithful—at least in a part of the Reformed church—to the significance and beauty of cultic forms was just as valuable as their disposition toward a renewal of worship according to the common liturgical tradition of the church. These new liturgical insights were in perfect harmony with the heritage of the Huguenot psalms and the attention to the entirety of the Holy Scriptures that had been characteristic of Calvin's preaching. In the first half of the twentieth century, the pioneers and then the bearers of the modern Liturgical Movement were able to take up the suggestions of the previous generations. Particularly important were Jules Amiguet (1867–1946), the pastor of Saint-Jean in Lausanne, and Richard Paquier (1905–1985), another pastor in the canton of Vaud and founder of the "Église et Liturgie" movement.[20] The former set in place in his city church in Lausanne a celebration that was remarkable for its rootage in, above all, the Eastern tradition; the latter assembled elements from the living traditions of Rome and of Canterbury, England, but also of Syria, and thus provided for a liturgical renewal among the French-speaking Reformed that honored the contemporary ecumenical challenge. Everything bespoke the future in the work of Paquier—from the daily office to the restoration of the eucharistic prayer to the

Church at Chêne-Pâquier. Exterior and interior of the Reformed church at Chêne-Pâquier, Vaud, Switzerland. Built in 1667, the church was the first to be constructed in the region since the Reformation. The canton of Vaud has always occupied a significant place in the Protestantism of western Switzerland. PHOTOGRAPH BY BRUNO BÜRKI

rooting of the liturgy in a theological concept of evangelical catholicity. The boldness of this enterprise provoked criticism within Protestantism, and indeed certain of his rather traditionalist options were open to criticism.

On these foundations there developed in the second half of the twentieth century an astonishingly rich liturgical creation that not only drew on the treasures of the tradition but was also open to new theological challenges, both ecumenical and Reformed. The influential teaching of Jean-Jacques von Allmen at the University of Neuchâtel helpfully provided this evolution with an imaginative and critical accompaniment.[21] Then there were those who called into question these achievements and developed a different kind of creativity. In relation to these two successive and sometimes simultaneous waves, one may speak of a Reformed liturgy in which tradition is at grips with modernity.

First, one can admire the creation of a *Liturgy* for the Reformed Church of France (ERF), which itself was constituted by the merger of four unions of churches in 1938. Its synod brought together the traditional Reformed and the Evangelicals, and it developed a common *Discipline* in which liturgical questions have their importance. By stages there developed by 1963 the so-called *Liturgie verte* (so designated because of its green binding), a solid book for Sunday worship and the celebration of the pastoral offices. This *Liturgie* of the ERF was original among the Reformed in providing a liturgical ordo in which the celebration of the Lord's supper is an integral part of Sunday worship. Moreover, the eucharistic prayer is at the heart of the celebration of the supper; its structure was inspired by the proposals of "Église et Liturgie," and it therefore bears the marks of the Liturgical Movement. Bersier's responses stud the service, but also the Huguenot psalms are sung with renewed vigor. Intercessions occupy a prominent place in a church aware of its responsibility in the world. The ERF is a committed church, even militant, as may be sensed in its liturgy.

Two decades later, there appeared the so-called *Liturgie blanche*—two large and beautiful volumes bound in white—"for use by the Reformed Churches of French-speaking Switzerland." This *Liturgie* was the fruit of long labors by the working group of the cantonal liturgical commissions. Pastor Jean-Louis Bonjour (1920–2001) had been able to impose the demands of an elevated liturgical style and a concept of theology and liturgical history rigorously thought out in the school of Karl Barth and other Reformed theologians. The result is not too distant from the liturgical reforms in the Roman Catholic Church, although care was taken to give the book its own specific features. At the heart of this liturgy is the paschal mystery. The great Easter vigil itself is celebrated with scriptural readings and the renewal of baptismal vows, and it includes the Exsultet proclaimed by a deacon. Prayers and other texts are proposed for every Sunday in the church year, whose structure in fact is taken up from the post–Vatican II Catholic liturgical reform. The three-year biblical lectionary with three readings for every Sunday and feast day is slightly different from the *ordo lectionum* of the Roman Missal. The prayers remain recognizably Reformed by virtue of their theological density and also their length.

The working group produced liturgies for baptism and the various stages of Christian initiation, for marriage, and for other ecclesiastical acts. It was involved also in establishing the collection *Psaumes et cantiques*, the songbook that brings together the best French Protestant hymns with a good number of translated German (Lutheran) hymns. The liturgy was published between 1979 and 1986, and *Psaumes et cantiques* in 1976.

Yet that is not the end of the matter. Don't forget the youth! From the late 1960s onward, the younger generations have presented new demands in liturgy as in other things. In language the classic style and the pastoral tone became unbearable and soon incomprehensible. The adjective "light"—even "lite"—would soon be used for worship, too. The most striking feature was the importance assumed by improvisation, whereby people try to show their spontaneity. The old practice of "free prayer"— specially valued in Pietist or Evangelical circles, where it is counted as a sign of true piety—is transformed into written and rewritten personal texts, printed on loose leaves and soon gathered into binders. The Reformed Church of the canton of Vaud has officially taken up this practice; it has published, even in several editions, big binders for worship containing several hundred pages or index cards. In other places, too, index cards and binders, official or personal, for sale or free, have found a place. Copyright questions have arisen. Now the exchange of information by internet or e-mail has become a significant resource in the preparation of worship. Remarkable texts appear but are then just as quickly lost; the ephemeral has taken over from the habitual and the traditional. Naturally, it is very difficult to come to a real appreciation of what is being said. In church as elsewhere, the catchy is favored over the correct. To secure a common expression of liturgical prayer, all that remains is a schematic ordo with a few suggestions as to content. There has been a rapid movement away— not only in the Reformed world, but in that world particularly—from referring to a durable and recognized text even for the eucharistic prayer.

Amid all this ferment, the French Reformed *Liturgy* that was adopted at the national synod in Mazamet, France, in 1996 as a new common liturgy for the entire church constitutes a point of reference that, if not stable, is at least tangible. It offers texts and rubrics for the various services of the church beginning with Sunday worship. For each type of celebration a booklet has been prepared of modest dimensions and attractive presentation, the whole being gathered under the title *Liturgie de l'Eglise Réformée de France*. To take account of the very dispersed and largely minority situation of the Reformed communities in France, the orders of worship are simpler than the preceding liturgy. The language is accessible, familiar in tone rather than liturgically elevated. It is largely a lay work in various senses of that term. For the worship by the whole community, it will quickly seem flat. Theologically, the line taken is generally Reformed or Protestant, although ecumenical gains are in general respected. Henceforth one may expect that the central prayer of the Lord's supper will contain an anamnesis of the work of Christ and an epiclesis. The celebration of the supper is without doubt more frequent than it used to be, and it is above all better integrated into the common practice of the church than was true previously. But in France the weekly eucharistic celebration has not yet prevailed, perhaps in some cases to ensure a distinction from the Catholic church. Elsewhere, particularly in French-speaking Switzerland, a service with preaching and eucharist has in many places become the ordinary and habitual Sunday worship.

To complete the picture, one must mention the "States General of Protestant Worship," organized in the summer of 2000 by the Pastoral Institute of French-speaking Switzerland at Crêt-Bérard in the canton of Vaud. It included a significant French Reformed participation as well. The title, borrowed from the history of France before the Revolution, was rather pompous, and the subtitle a riddle: "Do We Still Believe in Worship?" More pertinent than that question is probably that of the cohesion and concordance of a worship life swarming with particular initiatives that need to be brought together.

Significant in a different way was the publication in 1994 of a book of daily prayers[22] for the use of groups or individuals: *Le coq* (a rooster, the herald of dawn, is printed on the binding) is the last in a series of books of the hours for the daily office that appeared throughout the twentieth century in French-speaking Reformed Protestantism. The prayer life of such communities as the sisters of Grandchamp (near Neuchâtel) have inspired them.

The Options of the Reformed Alliance in Germany: Limitations and Openness of a Confessional Tradition

Today a Reformed Alliance (*Reformierter Bund*) exists in Germany, constituted by the Evangelisch-reformierte Kirche (a synod of Reformed churches in Bavaria and northwest Germany), the Church of Lippe in Westphalia and Lower Saxony, and parishes of the Reformed confession dispersed throughout Germany. Its leadership is called the *Moderamen*. Its parishes and synodical churches house the specifically Reformed German tradition originating in the *Kirchenordnung* of the Palatinate. In the Nazi period these Reformed churches played a pioneering role in the Church struggle (*Kirchenkampf*), wherein the Barmen Theological Declaration took its stand against the heretical ideology of a racial Christianity propagated by the so-called German Christians. Since the end of the Second World War, the Reformed Alliance has been involved, at the liturgical level, in the maintenance and renewal of the Reformed tradition of worship. Its spirituality is solidly biblical, with respect for the liturgical orders stemming from the sixteenth-century Reformation and the prayer of John Calvin that still nourishes the engagement of Reformed Christians in the contemporary world. The psalms also continue to play their part in the liturgy. A *Kirchenbuch* (Book of Church Orders), which first appeared already in 1941 and then was reworked in postwar editions of 1951 and 1956, bears witness to this Reformed rootage of worship, which is without equal at least in the European world. In the edition dating from the 1980s (1983–1990), a reform of the tradition was undertaken in order to meet the expectations and needs of a new epoch; it embodied openings toward a modernized and more spontaneous cultic practice, without however reneging on the traditional heritage. For four decades, pastor Karl Halaski (1908–1996) was the principal guide along the liturgical path for the German-speaking Reformed communities. Moreover, the churches of the Reformed Alliance belong to the EKD, the Evangelische Kirche in Deutschland.

The Reformed communities of Germany demonstrate that the tradition cannot be maintained and renewed except by way of an opening to new challenges. For without that, it will choke and produce perverse effects, especially in the liturgical domain. Awareness of this is now more alive than in the past, and work was resumed at the turn of the millennium. The question is now openly advanced: Does a specific and explicitly Reformed liturgy really make sense in the church of today? What can be the particular mission of the Reformed churches in Germany and on the ecumenical scene beyond?[23] Concretely, it was a matter for the Reformed Alliance of Germany to relate itself to the broad and common enterprise of the *Erneuerte Agende* of the Lutheran and United churches of Germany that was produced and published in the last decade of the twentieth century. For its part, this large and new German Protestant liturgy— which became the *Evangelisches Gottesdienstbuch* (1999)—has not ignored the orders and texts of the Reformed tradition. This tradition has been drawn on for important elements in the variety of material offered. However, the Reformed theologians and faithful of Germany have not felt able simply to adopt the *Evangelisches Gottesdienstbuch*,

whose primary inspiration remains Lutheran. That struck them as being too con-
formist and lacking in fidelity to a specifically Reformed vocation in the liturgical
domain as elsewhere. They have therefore, on the basis of their earlier *Kirchenbücher*,
created and brought into use, also in 1999, the *Reformierte Liturgie*, which became
common to all the Reformed confessional family in Germany. Such widespread adoption is a novelty, even though the varying degrees of its official character in the different communities depend on complex reasons well known in confessional history and
especially in liturgical history.

The principal characteristic of the *Reformierte Liturgie* is indicated by its subtitle,
which the new liturgy shares with its predecessors: *Gebete und Ordnungen für die unter
dem Wort versammelte Gemeinde* (Prayers and Orders for the Congregation Assembled
under the Word). The insistence on maintaining this fundamental liturgical program
is not without meaning: the Reformed are concerned that church life be characterized
by a discipline of prayer rather than a discipline of rites and gestures. The Word of
God, on the one hand, and the community gathered "under" that Word, on the other,
are the indispensable elements in constituting Reformed worship.

It should not be a surprise that the care taken over both the form and the content
of prayer is amply but also carefully nourished by the Word. One cannot have as one's
spiritual masters such praying preachers as John Calvin and Karl Barth without its
leaving a permanent mark on liturgy as the worship of the Church of God responding
to divine revelation. For the Reformed in the twenty-first century, as in the past,
public worship is "an event in which God himself is present to serve those who gather
in his name" ("ein Geschehen, in dem Gott selbst den in seinem Namen Versammelten
dienend gegenwärtig ist"), a place in which divine revelation is received by an ecclesial
community.

This relation between the Word of revelation and the word of worship is the theological soil in which the typically Reformed link between liturgy and catechesis is
rooted. It makes good liturgical sense that the attribution of the parts of the catechism
to Sunday worship no longer mechanically follows the sequence of the questions in
the catechism (still that of Heidelberg, 1563). Rather, it now responds to the content
of the Sunday or the feast celebrated, although such a correspondence is not always
easy to establish. In my opinion, even more significant is the considerable attempt at
liturgical instruction addressed to the body of the faithful as much as to the officiants,
thus honoring the concept of the conscious participation of all in the liturgy; it is a
kind of mystagogical procedure.[24] Ecumenically welcome is the appearance of a liturgical calendar and lectionary with certain specifically Reformed items. These are all
ways in which the structure of the liturgy is supported.

The proclamation and preaching of the Word remains the principal objective of
worship according to the *Reformierte Liturgie*; the celebration of the Lord's supper,
which is becoming more important and more frequent, is integrated into the liturgy
without constituting its climax. Thus, the order is principally that of the traditional
form of the preaching service and not the order of the mass, but the eucharistic celebration incorporated into this preaching service is not simply an addition. The old
practice of the instructions and the exhortations related to the administration of the
sacraments is here, in the case of the Lord's supper, rendered liturgically more acceptable by virtue of the link made to a somewhat more fully developed eucharistic
prayer. Certain questions remain unresolved from the viewpoint of sacramental structure and the underlying sacramental theology, but a rapprochement with the Lutheran

and Catholic churches has been deliberately sought in the eucharistic celebration. Therein resides the promise of a fuller conception of liturgy and sacraments.

One must note several characteristics of this Reformed liturgy that are signs of openness and are closely connected with the path followed by the Reformed churches in Germany while the liturgy was being developed. Without being politically partial—which always runs the risk of harming the liturgy by making it an instrument of external ends—the German Reformed Liturgy is open to questions of the day and of public life. In its worship the church here is ready to assume its responsibilities in the contemporary world. The *Reformierte Liturgie* is also the first liturgy of any among French- and German-speaking areas to take into account the importance of a liturgically inclusive language. It is not content with a few scattered concessions to the women, in the form of timid adjustments or additions; instead, the whole question is faced as an important element in the celebration within the present-day context. Excesses are avoided. Similarly, one also notes the respectful attention given to the relation between the Christian liturgy and the Jewish tradition; this is shown, for example, in the introduction to the cycle of feasts, which both explains the Church's own calendar and also teaches the laity to pay attention to that of others, in particular the people of the first covenant in the midst of which Jesus was born. There, too, is a wise moderation.

To this must be added that in creating the *Reformierte Liturgie*, care was taken to offer to the church a full Sunday liturgy as well as the pastoral offices in a book that yet remains portable. Thus, the liturgical explosion that affects several churches has been at least moderated if not altogether avoided. In this sense, it is hopeful that reformed liturgy recognizes its limits: confessional, cultural, or others.

The Reformed Churches in German-Speaking Switzerland Today: Diverse or Arbitrary?

Ever since the time of the Reformation, the Reformed churches of German-speaking Switzerland have been different from any other churches. Moreover, they differ among themselves; Zürich and Basel have never lived the same reality. That is true also of their liturgical life, despite some obvious similarities between them. All the Swiss churches have preserved their particularities. In the decades after the First World War, their worship practice followed the liturgical books and usages proper to each cantonal church. There was a Zürich liturgy and a Bernese, and yet a third for the German-speaking parishes of the Grisons (*Graubünden*), and so on. Later in the twentieth century the attempt was made to find a greater concordance among them and also on a wider plane. A contribution was made by the ecumenical movement. The history of the liturgy mirrors the general evolution of the country.

Contrary to the French-speaking Reformed churches or the English-speaking Presbyterian churches, the German-speaking Reformed churches shared hardly at all in the Liturgical Movement of the first half of the twentieth century. The Zürich liturgy had been a little marked by the earlier movement of Julius Smend and Friedrich Spitta, whose theological inspiration was liberal. The few Swiss members of the Protestant Brotherhood of Saint Michael (*Evangelische Michaelsbruderschaft*) or the Berneuchen movement from Lutheran Germany cut rather isolated figures; their liturgical initiatives remained eccentric and were easily considered excessive. The theological renewal initiated by Karl Barth, and more widely the growing interest in the tradition of the Reformation, exercised a notable influence on worship. That is not immediately evident because it was preaching and not the instituted liturgy that counted for Barth and his disciples. Barth could make fun of the "liturgical movement," and yet his preaching called for a regular Sunday celebration of the eucharist.

Since the Second World War an interest has developed in celebrating worship in ways that owe less to the conventions of the nineteenth century or even to Pietism and the Enlightenment. The confessions and church orders of the sixteenth century have been rediscovered. At the same time, contemporary theological debate has helped to give new life to preaching and liturgical prayer, which by no means remain confined to closed circles. The liturgist and hymnologist Markus Jenny (1924–2001) is a good example of this evolution. He did not hesitate to emphasize the value of the traditional church orders for the celebration of the sacraments. Psalm singing acquired meaning as it related Christians to Jews. At the same time, an appreciation started to be shown for certain elements in the early liturgy, for the universally sung elements in the ordinary of the eucharistic celebration, and for features indispensable in a full Christian liturgy, such as the anamnesis, or memorial of the work of Christ, and the epiclesis of the Holy Spirit. Even if these liturgical elements were sometimes put into strange relationships with one another and scattered about in a celebration that was not truly ordered, yet the link to the universal Church was, as it were, reestablished.[25]

In 1956 the Swiss Reformed began to create a liturgy for all their German-speaking churches, which was a novelty for the dozen or so cantonal churches that had, and still have, as of this writing, their own autonomous synods. The common liturgy was to entail several volumes. But the undertaking was too much a compilation. The first volumes, which included prayers for ordinary Sundays and for the Christian festivals, were anthologies of texts from every quarter and tradition proposed for the free choice of the officiant or, rather, of the preacher. Even the volume devoted to the celebration of the Lord's supper gathers together a considerable number of divergent orders. The texts of the Reformers stand alongside the scarcely modified order of mass from the Roman Missal of 1970, together with much later compositions. The liturgical book reflects, in fact, the way many ministers of worship function. Their celebrations are occasional compositions. The liturgical commissions stressed the indispensable need for a common liturgical reflection in the church and for regulations that would, if respected, allow the active participation of the assembly. The liturgical freedom that is often highlighted by modern Reformed Christians is incapable of ensuring a communal and churchly worship.

In the 1960s the church of Zürich created a liturgy that was an alternative, even a conflicting alternative, to the common German-speaking liturgy; and in this context new expectations were raised. It was the same with the more or less unofficial synodical gatherings of the second half of the twentieth century—first the Swiss Protestant Synod (Schweizerische Evangelische Synode), and then the Zürich "Disputation" of 1984. These expectations concern the language of worship, where the desire is to become simpler, contemporary rather than classic. There is also the demand for an inclusive language, which poses a new series of questions. Not only the words, but also the images and names of God require reformulation. New symbolic expressions are looked for. "Woman churches," which are often ecumenical in their composition, have developed their own liturgical practices. To that must be added contemporary musical researches and creations. Worship usages that had long remained traditional and almost frozen, except in marginal circles, are undergoing a transformation. One can be surprised, sometimes pleasantly, sometimes less so.

On all sides, liturgical life can be threatened by the arbitrary. Consequently, at stake in the near future will chiefly be the development of certain broadly acceptable criteria for common worship in the Reformed community—worship open to new cultural challenges but also faithful to the biblical revelation and recognizable in the fellowship of Christ's disciples. If the apostle said that everything is possible in the communion of the Church but not everything is edifying for the faith of the community, that is especially true in the area of worship. Reformed worship must avoid the arbitrary in order to remain faithful and to permit communication with others, whether other churches or the society in the midst of which the Church resides is called to bear unequivocal witness to Christ.

Here Reformed Christians are rejoining a concern that had already been that of their predecessors in the sixteenth century. The classical Reformation differed from the radical reformation, partly by virtue of its appreciation for common order in the church. The writers and editors of the first volume of the German-speaking liturgy from the 1960s included a reflective introduction offering advice for the use of traditionally Reformed orders of worship with or without the Lord's supper. According to the volume *Abendmahl* (1983), the order of mass from the Roman Missal could make sense for the Reformed, given a few adjustments. More innovative was the step taken by the Zürich liturgy of the 1960s that developed the notion of worship as a journey (*Wegcharakter*): gathering, praise, preaching, intercession, dismissal. Unlike the French-speaking Reformed and the English-speaking Presbyterians, the German-speaking Reformed churches have not paid much attention to developing a eucharistic prayer that would always include an anamnesis and an epiclesis. They remain attached to the order of the south German preaching service (*oberdeutscher Predigtgottesdienst*). Yet the ecumenical debate is not yet closed as to what would be the constitutive parts of a Sunday celebration that was normally eucharistic. Faith and Order's Lima text of 1982 had introduced this idea in its day (*Baptism, Eucharist and Ministry*, E27).

A happy event was the production of a new hymnal, the *Gesangbuch der Evangelisch-Reformierten Kirchen der deutschsprachigen Schweiz*, which came into force in 1998, simultaneously with a similar book on the Roman Catholic side; the two were the fruit of a largely common and concerted preparation. A worthy successor to the Geneva Psalter from Calvin's day, the new *Gesangbuch* has quickly been accepted in the parishes, and it appears capable of helping the churches to find a common and clearly oriented path for their worship. It will help in the preparation of services and the edification of the faithful. This expectation is allowed not only by the psalms and traditional hymns, but also by texts that have been more recently adopted. Aid is offered, too, by the liturgical catechesis that is given in the same book. Carefully conceived introductions help ministers and faithful in the preparation and performance of the celebration.[26] This is true for the main service, which in principle is conceived as a liturgy of the word and of the Lord's supper, as well as for the daily prayers to be said by a group or individually, and also for the occasional services or pastoral offices. In sum, this is a true Prayer Book, or Psalter, so that the liturgy of the Reformed may strike the right note in the future.

Bibliography

Sources

"La forme des prières et chants ecclésiastiques." In *Joannis Calvini Opera selecta*, vol. 2, 1–58. Munich: 1952. English translation in *Tracts and Treatises on the Doctrine and*

Worship of the Church. Translated by Henry Beveridge, 100–128. Grand Rapids, Mich.: Eerdmans, 1958.

Gesangbuch der Evangelisch-reformierten Kirchen der deutschsprachigen Schweiz. Basel: Friedrich Reinhardt Verlag; Zürich: Theologischer Verlag, 1998.

Liturgie à l'usage des Églises réformées de la Suisse romande. 2 vols. Lausanne: AREC, 1979–1986.

La liturgie ou la manière de céeléebrer le Service Divin; qui est établie dans les Églises de la Principauté de Neufchâtel et Vallangin. Basel: Jean Pistorius, 1713.

Pahl, Irmgard, ed. *Coena Domini I: Die Abendmahlsliturgien der Reformationskirchen im 16./17 Jahrhundert*. Freiburg in der Schweiz: Universitätsverlag, 1986.

Reformierte Liturgie: Gebete und Ordnungen für die unter dem Wort versammelte Gemeinde. Im Auftrag des Moderamens des Reformierten Bundes, Deutschland. Wuppertal: Neukirchen-Vluyn, 1999.

Studies

Allmen, Jean-Jacques von. *Célébrer le salut: Doctrine et pratique du culte chrétien*. Geneva: Labor et Fides; Paris: Éditions du Cerf, 1984.

Allmen, Jean-Jacques von. *Worship: Its Theology and Practice*. London: Lutterworth, 1965; New York: Oxford University Press, 1965.

Bornert, René. *La réforme protestante du culte à Strasbourg au 16e siècle*. Leiden: Brill, 1981.

Bürki, Bruno. *Cène du Seigneur—eucharistie de l'Église: Le cheminement des Églises réformées romandes et françaises depuis le XVIIIe siècle, d'après leurs textes liturgiques*. 2 vols. Fribourg: Éditions Universitaires, 1985.

Ehrensperger, Alfred. *Gottesdienst: Visionen–Erfahrungen–Schmerzstellen*. Zürich: Theologischer Verlag, 1988.

Gagnebin, Laurent. *Le culte à choeur ouvert: Introduction à la liturgie du culte réformé*. Paris: Les Bergers et les Mages; Geneva: Labor et Fides, 1992.

Kunz, Ralph. *Gottesdienst evangelisch reformiert: Liturgik und Liturgie in der Kirche Zwinglis*. Zürich: Pano Verlag, 2001.

Vischer, Lukas, ed. *Christian Worship in Reformed Churches Past and Present*. Grand Rapids, Mich.: Eerdmans, 2003.

Notes

[1] See Hughes Oliphant Old, *The Patristic Roots of Reformed Worship* (Zürich: Theologischer Verlag, 1975).

[2] See Dorothea Roth, *Die mittelalterliche Predigttheorie und das "Manuale curatorum" des Johann Ulrich Surgant* (Basel: Helbing & Lichtenhahn, 1956).

[3] See Markus Jenny, *Die Einheit des Abendmahlsgottesdienstes bei den elsässischen und schweizerischen Reformatoren* (Zürich: Zwingli Verlag, 1968); cf. Ralph Kunz, *Gottesdienst evangelisch reformiert. Liturgik und Liturgie in der Kirche Zwinglis* (Zürich: Pano Verlag, 2001).

[4] Cf. Luther's "Flood Prayer," which was an important source for Zwingli's own formulation of the prayer.

[5] For the text, see Pahl, 1:182–184, 189–198.

[6] For the texts, see Pahl, 1:299–329.

[7] See Bruno Bürki, "Jean Calvin, avait-il le sens liturgique?" in *Communio Sanctorum: Mélanges Jean-Jacques von Allmen* (Geneva: Labor et Fides, 1982) 157–172; and Elsie Anne McKee, "Context, Contours, Contents: Towards a Description of Calvin's Understanding of Worship," in *Calvin Society Study Papers, 1995, 1997*, ed. D. Foxgrover (Grand Rapids, Mich.: CRC Product Services, 1998) 66–92.

[8] See Hans Scholl, *Der Dienst des Gebetes nach Johannes Calvin* (Zürich: Zwingli Verlag, 1968); and Bruno Bürki, "Teneur d'une prière liturgique

réformée d'origine calviniste," in *La prière liturgique: Conférences Saint-Serge Paris 2000*, ed. A. M. Triacca and A. Pistoia (Rome: Edizioni Liturgiche, 2001) 91–107.

[9]Cited from Elsie Anne McKee, *John Calvin: Writings on Pastoral Piety*, The Classics of Western Spirituality (New York and Mahwah, N.J.: Paulist, 2001) 111–112.

[10]For the texts of Calvin's service of the Lord's supper, see Pahl, 1:347–351, 355–362.

[11]See *Der Genfer Psalter*, ed. P. E. Bernoulli and F. Furler (Zürich: Theologischer Verlag, 2001).

[12]See Bruno Bürki, "Der Sonntag—ein Abschnitt reformierter Theologie" in *Der Sonntag. FS Jakob Baumgartner*, ed. A. M. Altermatt and Th. A. Schnitker (Würzburg: Echer Verlag; Freiburg in der Schweiz: Universitätsverlag, 1986) 197–212.

[13]For the texts concerning the Lord's supper, see Pahl, 1:339–346.

[14]Pahl, 1:199–215.

[15]Pahl, 1:227–236.

[16]Pahl., 1:495–523.

[17]See Frieder Schulz, "Eucharistiegebet und Abendmahlsvermahnung," in *Sursum corda. FS Philipp Harnoncourt*, ed. E. Renhart and A. Schnider (Graz: Akademischer Druck und Verlag, 1991) 147–158; and Friedrich Lurz, *Die Feier des Abendmahls nach der kurpfälzizischen Kirchenordnung von 1563* (Stuttgart: Kohlhammer), 1998.

[18]See Pierre Barthel, *Jean-Frédéric Ostervald l'Européen (1663–1747): Novateur neuchâtelois* (Geneva: Slatkine, 2001; and Stuart Ludbrook, "La liturgie de Bersier et le culte réformé en France: "ritualisme" et renouveau liturgique" (doctoral thesis, Université de Paris Sorbonne/Institut catholique de Paris, 1999).

[19]See John Bate Cardale, *Readings in the Liturgy and the Divine Offices of the Church*, 2 vols. (London: Thomas Bosworth, 1874–1875); and Kenneth W. Stevenson, "The Catholic Apostolic Church: Its

History and Eucharist," *Studia Liturgica* 13 (1977) 21–45.

[20]Richard Paquier's *Traité de liturgique: essai sur le fondement et la structure du culte* (Neuchâtel: Delachaux & Niestlé, 1954) was, for its time, a remarkable manual.

[21]Besides his manuals (listed in the bibliography of this chapter), von Allmen was the author of a magisterial study for Faith and Order concerning the eucharist: *The Lord's Supper*, Ecumenical Studies in Worship (London: Lutterworth Press; Richmond, Va.: John Knox Press, 1968) 19.

[22]*Le livre de la prière quotidienne* (Lausanne: Éditions Librairie de l'Ae, 1994).

[23]For this matter, note particularly the meetings organized for several years at the Foyer John Knox in Geneva by the World Alliance of Reformed Churches, and especially the papers contained in *Christian Worship in Reformed Churches Past and Present*.

[24]The "*liturgiedidaktische Hinweise*" gives explanations about the various features of the liturgy, practical advice for choosing among the elements proposed, and hints toward the preparation and conduct of the service. In this they go well beyond the traditional function of rubrics and resemble, rather, the pastoral introductions in the Roman Catholic liturgical books produced after Vatican II.

[25]Concerning the participation of the Swiss Churches in the Liturgical Movement, see my contribution "La vie liturgique des Eglises protestantes d'Europe occidentale au 20e siècle" in *Conférences Saint-Serge: 50e Semaine d'études liturgiques, Paris 2003* (Rome: Edizioni Liturgiche, 2004) 35 - 57; also Karl-Heinrich Bieritz, "Liturgische Bewegungen im deutschen Protestantismus" in *Liturgiereformen: Historische Studien zu einem bleibenden Grundzug des christlichen Gottesdienstes*, ed. M. Klöckener and B. Kranemann, vol. 2 (Münster: Aschendorff, 2002) 711–748.

[26]Cf. what was already said in note 24 concerning the German Reformed *Liturgie* of 1999.

13

The Reformed Tradition in the Netherlands

HARRY KLAASSENS

The cradle of Dutch Calvinism lies in congregations of Dutch refugees in exile in England and Germany. During the sixteenth century many Dutch Protestants fled abroad because the policy of the authorities made it impossible to worship in public. King Edward VI of England (reigned 1547–1553) offered them hospitality; "Austin Friars" at London, a former church of Augustinians, still belonged to a Dutch community in the early 2000s. It was founded in 1550 as the first Dutch Protestant Church. There the French-speaking section of the Flemish refugees used a liturgy that Valerand Pullain drew up (*Liturgia Sacra*, 1551), which was based on the liturgy he had learned from Martin Bucer in Strasbourg, where Pullain had been an elder. Pullain intended to inform the intelligentsia of the Reformed liturgy. The Flemish or Dutch-speaking section, under the leadership of the ministers Marten Micron (1523–1559) and Wouter Delenus (1500–1563), used a Dutch liturgy drawn up by their superintendent John à Lasco, who came from Germany in 1549. The text was published when he again went to Emden (*Forma ac Ratio*, 1555) but Marten Micron edited a Dutch translation and abbreviation (*Christlicke Ordinancien der Nederlantser Ghemeinten te London*) in 1554 in Frankfurt, where the Dutch congregation, together with many English Protestants, had fled because of the hostile policy of Mary Tudor (reigned 1553–1558) after the death of King Edward VI. In the town of Norden, on the East Frisian coast, a congregation was started in 1553, guided by Marten Micron.

STRUCTURE OF MICRON'S REFORMED LITURGY FOR SUNDAY MORNING

1. Prayer for the sermon, closed with the Lord's prayer
2. Singing of a psalm
3. Reading of the scripture
4. Sermon
5. Announcements
6. Prayer after the sermon
7. Ten Commandments (the so-called Lord's Law)
8. Confession of sins
9. Absolution
10. Reading of the creed
11. Prayer of intercession and supplication
(*Here can be celebrated baptism, eucharist, the marriage ceremony*)
12. Singing of a psalm

13. Exhortation to be merciful to the poor and to pray for each other
14. Blessing (Num. 6:24)

In London, the French-speaking section celebrated the Lord's supper every other week; the congregation of Micron once a month. No member could refuse to participate unless he had a very good reason. In order to celebrate peacefully, the community sat at tables, like Christ and his disciples. The service on Sunday afternoon was didactic, with an explanation of the catechism. Every Thursday evening there was a meeting where people could ask questions.

A third congregation that fled from London to Germany, guided by Peter Datheen (1531–1588), went in 1562 to Frankenthal near Worms, where Frederick III of the

Palatinate (reigned 1559–1576) offered them hospitality. The prince was devoted to the Calvinistic reformation and supported the foundation of a German Calvinistic theology, published in the Heidelberg Catechism, developed in the University of Heidelberg by Zacharias Ursinus (1493-1539) and Caspar Olevianus (1536-1587). The person and the work of Peter Datheen had an enormous influence on the developments in the Dutch Reformed liturgy. He was a great organizer and published a church book that contained his translation of the metrical psalms of Clément Marot (c.1496–1544), the Heidelberg Catechism, and several liturgical forms and texts in Dutch. In 1566 he printed it in many thousands of copies, and consequently it was soon available also beyond his own congregation. He drafted no new texts but made available what he had learned when he came to

Reformation and iconoclasm. In 1566 Calvinists in the Netherlands destroyed statues, stained glass, works of art, and relics in an effort to rid the churches of "idolatrous" worship. Engraving by Hogenberg. FOTO MARBURG/ART RESOURCE, NY

Frankenthal. The liturgy of the Lord's supper that was used in the Palatinate had apparently undergone influence from at least three directions. First, Geneva: Ursinus and Olevianus had a busy correspondence with John Calvin (1509–1564). Second: the Heidelberg theologians knew the liturgies of both Micron and à Lasco in a German translation. Third: the Lutheran Württemberg church order (1553) still influenced the Palatinate, which had been Lutheran until Frederick III switched to the Reformed tradition. The texts of the Dutch Reformed liturgy are therefore not exclusively of Calvinistic origin.

Translations of the Psalter in Dutch were also drafted by Willem van Zuylen van Nyevelt (died in 1543), Souterliederkens (died 1540), Lucas d'Heere (1543-1584), Jan Utenhove (1520-1566), and Marnix of Saint Aldegond (1540-1598), but the psalms of Datheen were the best known and most used. The church book that Datheen edited contained, among other things: forms for baptism, marriage, and the Lord's supper;

morning and evening prayer; prayer for the sick; prayer at a funeral; and prayers to open and close church council meetings. The form for the eucharist is didactic in style, based on 1 Corinthians 11. The ritual part includes a prayer, a creed, an exhortation and a summons not to pay attention to the earthly bread and wine but to lift up hearts to Christ, the heavenly Priest and Intercessor. The communion is distributed with the words of Paul in 1 Corinthians 10:16–17.

The National Synods of the Sixteenth Century

Peter Datheen presided at the Synods of Wesel (1568), Dordrecht (regional, 1574), and Dordrecht (national, 1578). The use of the Psalter in Datheen's version was first recommended (1568) and later mandated (1574, 1578). The singing of hymns was allowed. Articles 27–31 from the Synod of Wesel show that the main service of the week consisted of scripture reading, sermon, confession of sins, intercession, and singing of psalms. The Synod of Dordrecht (1574), the first one on Dutch territory, gives some details from which we can construct the order.

STRUCTURE OF THE SERVICE IN THE REFORMED CHURCHES
IN THE NETHERLANDS IN THE SIXTEENTH CENTURY

1. Scripture reading and the singing of a psalm
2. Votum (Ps. 124:8)
3. Prayer
4. Singing
5. Sermon
6. Prayer
7. Reading of the creed
8. Singing
9. Blessing (Num. 6:24)

This order remained almost the same into the twenty-first century, save that the creed was replaced by the Ten Commandments and moved to the afternoon service. The Lord's supper was celebrated every other month. The Dordrecht Synod of 1574 decreed that 1 Corinthians 10 had to be extended with the words: "Take part, eat, remember and believe that the precious body/blood of our Lord Jesus Christ was given as a complete satisfaction for all our sins." This text is found in the liturgy of à Lasco/Micron and therefore they called it "the London appendix."

Our Lord in the Attic. After 1578, Dutch Catholics were not permitted to worship in public. A merchant in Amsterdam, in the years 1661–1663, converted the upper story of his family dwelling into a clandestine space for worship, which served a parish until 1887. MUSEUM AMSTELKRING, AMSTERDAM/PHOTOGRAPH BY KAREN WESTERFIELD TUCKER

The National Synod of 1578, also in Dordrecht, took several decisions on liturgy. The reading of the gospel from the *Missale Romanum* was replaced by a *lectio continua* of the New Testament and, when the local church council decided, also of the Old Testament. There was to be no evening prayer on weekdays: Sunday had to remain central. Since a funeral service might suggest honor to the dead instead of God, following a death there was only to be preaching. Baptism was to be administered in the midst of the community on Sundays, in the presence of at least the father of the child. Before the celebration of the Lord's supper, a *censura morum* (that is, a moral investigation of the parishioners' behavior) was to be held among the ministers, deacons, and elders. Furthermore the members of the community would be visited in the week before the celebration. The Lord's supper could only be celebrated in the community; a communion for the sick at home was not possible. Only Datheen's psalms were to be sung during the service. The Synods of Middelburg (1581) and The Hague (1586) dealt with the church year. Sunday was central. Middelburg did not allow a celebration of Christmas but decreed a commemoration of the birth of Christ on the Sunday before 25 December. The Hague Synod, however, ordered a sober celebration on Christmas, New Year's Day, and other holidays, in order to prevent idleness. The Middelburg Synod also decided that no explicit absolution should be given, since the preaching of the Gospel itself contains the forgiveness of sins.

There was never an official edition of the forms and prayers. Revisers sometimes examined the text and provided a new edition, which, however, was not approved by any general synod. The Synod of The Hague (1586) added to the forms of Datheen's church book four more: (1) for the ordination of ministers; (2) for the ordination of elders and deacons; and (3) and (4) for the excommunication and receiving of members of the church. The National Synod of Dordrecht, 1618–1619, was ordered by the government of the Netherlands because the Reformed Church had become the national church. This synod consolidated the decrees of former synods and officially adopted Datheen's liturgy. A form for the baptism of an adult and several prayers for church council meetings and meetings of the deacons were added. Concerning the celebration of the Lord's supper, the Dordrecht Synod decreed that communion should be held every other month. Sitting at tables, standing, or coming to the table were all equally permitted. Organ playing was not allowed and the singing of hymns during the service was forbidden. A very important result of this National Synod was the decision to set up a Dutch Bible translation. This translation, the so-called "*Statenvertaling*," was published in 1637 and played a very important role in the development of the Dutch language.

Church Life in the Seventeenth and Eighteenth Century

In the seventeenth century the few "liturgical" elements—such as reading of the scriptures, the Ten Commandments, the creed, and the didactic forms for baptism and eucharist—all took place in a sort of pre-service. The main Sunday morning service opened with the reading of the scriptures by a lector in order to quiet the congregation. It was only then that the minister entered the church, said a prayer, and started to preach. Datheen's psalms were—badly—sung, usually to begin and end the service. The long prayer before the sermon consisted of confession of sins, illumination with the Holy Spirit, and intercessions; and another long prayer summarized the sermon just delivered. Because of liturgical freedom the set prayers of the liturgy were no longer observed and were replaced by free prayers. Sometimes people left the church immediately after the sermon. Although local authorities imposed a fine on preaching too long, the sermon was regarded as the central element of the service. The homilies most of the time displayed the learning of the ministers. The intention was to celebrate the eucharist six times a year; however, liturgical freedom led in some cases to an even lower frequency, sometimes only once a year. The congregation members came to church dressed in black clothes. It was meant to be a celebration, but it looked more like a funeral service. Even during the reading of the form the minister remained at the pulpit. The elders and the deacons together with the ministers constituted the church council and were equal in position. The council members were mostly taken from the upper classes.

In the seventeenth century the status of Sunday caused conflicts. The orthodox observed the Sunday as a Sabbath on which no work but also no recreation was allowed. Others went to church but used Sunday also as a time for relief.

During the Sundays of Lent the seven words of Jesus on the Cross were read. Maundy Thursday and Good Friday were not observed; at Easter one celebrated the Lord's supper in a sober way to emphasize the death of Christ. Easter Monday, however, was a feast day. People dressed in new clothes, and fires were lighted on every "hill" (the so-called *Paasberg*). Because of the low quality of the singing, numerous church councils ordered the playing of the organ to support congregational song. Others still considered the organ to be pagan. After 1640, however, many churches built new organs and used them during the services. Another vexed question was the text of the psalms. Datheen's texts were still sung, but poets such as Constantijn Huygens, Pieter Corneliszoon Hooft, Joost van Den Vondel, and Jacob Revius, and musicians and theologians protested against the quality of the rhyme. Eventually, the government ordered a church commission, which presented in 1773 a new translation of the Psalter. Only after much quarreling did it come into use. The singing of hymns was still not allowed. In pietistic groups, however, hymns and spiritual songs in Dutch were part of the meeting. The hymns of the German Pietist poets and the English Methodists were translated. And when the 1773 Psalter was inaugurated, the advocates of the singing of hymns in the service saw new possibilities. Eventually, in 1807 the first church hymn book was presented, the *Evangelisch Gezangboek*.

The Nineteenth Century

In 1817 another national synod dealt with the liturgy. Because of the resistance against "Datheen's" forms of the sixteenth century, and the fact that there were not many ministers who used them, the synod decreed that the use of the forms was optional. Liturgical freedom was complete. The use of set forms of prayers was regarded as a sign of weakness. Those who used them would show that they were not inspired by the Holy Spirit. Concerning the preparation of the celebration of the Lord's supper, the synod dictated four questions that were to be put to the community on the preceding Sunday. Synods of the Dutch Reformed Church recommended the observance of Good Friday with a celebration of the Lord's supper. Furthermore, directions were given on the vestments of the ministers: the black gown. The singing of a hymn during the Sunday service was now obligatory. It came to a discussion between the orthodox and the liberals and caused the first schism in the Dutch Reformed Church: the Christian Reformed Church was founded in 1834. They intended to use the "old liturgy of the Fathers of Dordrecht."

Because of the liberal atmosphere in the Dutch Reformed Church, in 1886 some congregations separated from the Dutch Reformed Church (the Nederlandse Hervormde Kerk) and united themselves as the "Reformed Churches in the Netherlands" (the Gereformeerde Kerken in Nederland).

Liturgical Renewal in the Twentieth Century

In 1911 Abraham Kuyper (1837-1920), an important leader of the Gereformeerde Kerken, published a book on liturgy entitled *Onze Eredienst* (Our Liturgy), whereas Johan Hermannus Gunning JHzn (1858-1940) wrote in 1890 a study of liturgy with the same title on behalf of the Dutch Reformed. In 1920 other such pioneers as E. F. Kruyf, H. H. Meulenbelt, B. J. H. Gerretsen, and H. W. Creutzberg founded a group for liturgical study and renewal, the so-called *Liturgische Kring* (Liturgical Circle), under the chairmanship of the famous minister and professor Gerardus van der Leeuw (1890–1950). They published from 1923 a series of *Liturgische Handboekjes* (liturgical booklets), and in 1934 edited a *Handboek voor den Eeredienst in de Nederlandsche Hervormde Kerk* (Handbook for Divine Service in the Dutch Reformed Church). In 1938 the Dutch Reformed Church published a new hymnary, *Psalmen en Gezangen voor de Eeredienst der Nederlandsche Hervormde Kerk* (Psalms and Hymns for the Divine Service in the Dutch Reformed Church), that included the complete Psalter in rhyme and 306 hymns. The fundamental principles were set forth in van der Leeuw's *Liturgiek* published in 1940 and reprinted in 1947.

The Dutch Reformed Church in 1946 set up a Council on Church and Liturgy, which published a periodical entitled *Kerk en Eredienst* (Church and Worship). Between 1960–1968, a *Jaarboek voor de Eredienst* (Yearbook for the Liturgy) appeared annually. A very important moment was the appearance in 1955 of a new service book, the *Dienstboek in ontwerp* (Service Book: A Draft). This consisted of all classical formularies of the sixteenth century in contemporary Dutch, but also some sort of Reformed-ecumenical order, although universal prayers were screened and censored. In the Gereformeerde Kerken, a liturgical group called the Gereformeerde Werkgroep voor Liturgie was started in 1956 by a number of ministers. The synods of 1965 and 1967 dealt with the liturgy. The first professor of liturgy in the Gereformeerde Kerken, Gerrit Nicolaas Lammens, played an important role.

In the period that followed, liturgical renewal became more and more a case of the church members themselves. Many experimen-

Sunday worship in a Reformed Church in the Netherlands. KERK IN ACTIE/PKN, THE NETHERLANDS

tal congregations were started. A foundation for the encounter of liturgy and arts came into being: the Prof. Dr. G. van der Leeuw Stichting. It published an ecumenical ordinarium in 1978 under the title *Onze Hulp* (Our Help) that included a lectionary based on the *Missale Romanum*, church music, and an important collection of liturgical prayers *(Liturgische Handreiking)* in three volumes (1967, 1975, 1977).

Liturgical renewal brought many churches together. In 1973 the two main Protestant churches together with three other churches—the Dutch Lutherans, the *Doopsgezinden* (Mennonites) and the Remonstrants—published a new hymnary, *Liedboek voor de Kerken* (Songbook for the Churches). In 1984 a new council of the two Reformed churches was set up by their synods, the Samenwerkingsorgaan voor de Eredienst (Council for Cooperation in Liturgy). In the 1970s the Nederlandse Hervormde Kerk together with the Gereformeerde Kerken in Nederland and the Evangelisch-Lutherse Kerk in het Koninkrijk der Nederlanden (Evangelical Lutheran Church in the Kingdom of the Netherlands) began the process of reuniting. The joint commission on liturgy published parts of a new service book in draft, consisting of (I) liturgies for funerals (1987), (II) liturgies for ordination (1989), and (III) liturgies for baptism and confirmation (1993). The first volume of the service book was published in 1998: *Dienstboek—een proeve: Schrift, Maaltijd, Gebed* (Service Book—A Draft: Scripture, Meal, Prayer). It deals with the Sunday services and the liturgy of the hours and contains, among other things, a complete set of propers for each Sunday and holiday; eucharistic prayers; orders for word services and for services of word and sacrament; newly composed liturgical music; several lectionaries; prayers for weekdays and various occasions; orders for morning and evening prayer; and a selection of psalms in the responsorial style. Remarkable in this book is the possibility for alternative tracks through many of the orders, not simply as the juxtaposition of different materials, but as a deliberate liturgical and theological statement. In the service book there is only one basic pattern of worship: the Holy Scriptures and the Lord's supper. The first order therefore is the order for a full service of word and eucharist. The second order consists of an order for a word service; in fact it is the same order as the first, but communion is not celebrated. The third order is the Reformed rite for a teaching service or instructional gathering where one of the catechisms may be studied. The last order, the fourth, is for a church service without the leadership of an ordained pastor. To serve the whole of the plural Reformed tradition in the Netherlands, one of two tracks may be followed in the first part of the service, either "A" or "B." Below, the Sunday morning service, in the Service Book of 1998.

THE SERVICE FOR "HOLY SCRIPTURE AND
THE LORD'S MEAL" IN THE 1998 SERVICE BOOK

Permanent Elements	Variable Elements
THE GATHERING	
	prayers at home, in the church
bell ringing	
practice of liturgical music	
welcome	

lighting of candles
silence

INTRODUCTION—A

(apostolic) greeting

votum (Ps. 124:8)

prayer of approach

psalm or hymn
Kyrie

Gloria in excelsis

collect or prayer for illumination

INTRODUCTION—B

(apostolic) greeting

votum (Ps. 124:8)

prayer of approach

psalm or hymn

prayer of humiliation
Ten Commandments

collect or prayer for illumination

THE HOLY SCRIPTURE

lessons

Old Testament
Psalm
Epistle
hallelujah, psalm, canticle, or hymn
Gospel
acclamations

sermon

creed, hymn

THE LORD'S MEAL—A

the pastoral prayer:
   thanksgiving and intercessions

invitation
(greeting of peace)
offering

hymn, music
prayer of dedication

table prayer:
   preface

Sanctus, Benedictus

   anamnesis
   words of institution
   acclamation
   epiclesis
Lord's prayer

(greeting of peace)
sharing of bread and wine

Agnus Dei
hymns, anthems, music

post-communion prayer

THE LORD'S MEAL—B
_____

invitation to, and instruction on the
  Lord's meal
offering and prayer of dedication
words of institution
prayers over the bread and wine
Lord's prayer   hymn
sharing of the bread and cup
prayer after communion

DISMISSAL AND BLESSING
_____

                                hymn
dismissal
blessing

                                hymn
                                postlude

The first track begins with prayers of repentance and approach, a scriptural greeting, and a calling for mercy in the Kyrie, followed by the Gloria in excelsis. The other—which is closer to the traditional Reformed pattern—includes a prayer of humiliation and the reading of the Ten Commandments as the expression of God's merciful admittance in the covenant. Both tracks conclude the introduction with a collect or a prayer for illumination by the Holy Spirit. The second part of the service always consists of the reading of the Holy Scriptures and preaching, with the singing of psalms and hymns. The confession of faith concludes this section. The third part is called intercessions and gifts.

In many congregations the Lord's supper is now celebrated eight to ten times a year, in some even more, although orthodox communities celebrate it four times a year. The first order for the eucharist follows a pattern that is ecumenically recognizable through the Liturgical Movement. The second order takes up the Lord's supper service of John Calvin (1542) in which a significant component is the self-examination, which follows after the admonition of sinners.

In the *Dienstboek* of 1998, the set elements are few and there are possibilities for variety. A wide range of prayers and texts are offered that allow alternatives and invite creativity. The existence of a basic structure permits other appropriate and new texts to be placed in the liturgy. Seven newly composed services are provided, 153 liturgical texts are edited with music. Special attention is paid to a characteristic element of Calvinistic Protestantism: the Ten Commandments. There are new formulations and there is newly composed liturgical music for the Decalogue. New also is the offering of several lectionaries. This service book of the Reformed and Lutheran churches in the Netherlands, by following the suggestions of the World Council of Churches' *Baptism, Eucharist and Ministry*, thus participates in the liturgical renewal found in churches all over the world.

In 2004 a new and extended version was published: *Dienstboek—een proeve: Leven, Zegen, Gemeenschap* (Service Book—A Draft: Life, Blessing, Community). It contains new liturgies for eucharist with the sick, reconciliation, blessings of all kinds, and a celebration of marriage and other relationships.

Bibliography

Dienstboek—een proeve. Vol. 1: *Schrift, Maaltijd, Gebed* (1998). Vol. 2: *Leven, Zegen, Gemeenschap* (2004). Zoetermeer: Boekencentrum, 1998, 2004.

Rutgers, F. L. *Acta van de Nederlandsche Synoden der zestiende eeuw*. Dordrecht: J.P. van den Tol, 1980. Reprint from the original edition of 1899.

Schotel, G. D. J. *De openbare eredienst der Nederlandse Hervormde Kerk in de zestiende, zeventiende en achttiende eeuw*. Leiden: A.W. Sijthoff, 1870; repr. ed. H.C. Rogge, 1906.

van der Schoot, B. *Hervormde Eredienst. De liturgische ontwikkeling van de Nederlandse Hervormde Kerk*. The Hague: Boekencentrum, 1950.

Vrijlandt, M. A. *Liturgiek*. The Hague: Meinema, 1987.

14

The Reformed Tradition in Scotland

DUNCAN B. FORRESTER

A Radical Reform

The Reformation in Scotland was among the most radical and thoroughgoing of the Calvinist reformations in Europe. In relation to worship, doctrine, and other matters as well there was a strong sense of discontinuity, of sweeping away a sullied past, of making a new start with a return to the purity, integrity, and simplicity of the worship of the Early Church. The Bible, and the Bible alone, was to be normative for authentic Christian worship. All else was idolatry, a dangerous distortion of the worship of the triune God. Images and statues, stained glass windows, relics, pilgrimages, the cult of the saints, special feasts and festivals, and indeed the whole Christian year save for Sunday and Easter were to be swept away. In order that "Christ Jesus be truly preached and his holy sacraments rightly ministered," idolatry and the centers in which it had flourished were "to be utterly suppressed in all bounds and places of this Realme." By idolatry was understood "the Masse, invocation of Saints, adoration of images and the keeping and retaining of the same. And finally, all honouring of God not contained in his holy word."[1]

A clean sweep, a radical break with the past, and a new beginning were the intention, and the worship of the medieval Church was denounced in its entirety as "idolatrie." Inevitably, though, there was a good deal of continuity. The same church buildings were used for congregational worship, although with major modifications in their layout. Many priests and monks conformed to the Reformation and were made readers or ministers. Some of them eagerly and intelligently embraced the new understanding of the faith; others were time-servers and continued quietly with many old practices and customs. Popular feeling in many parts of lowland Scotland was inflamed against Romanism, and it was urban mobs that destroyed many friaries, shrines, and images, and removed altars and the instruments of "idolatrie."

But sometimes the very same people were strongly attached to old practices that the leaders of the Reformation discountenanced, such as the celebration of saints' days, especially when associated with fairs or seasonal festivities; and funeral and birth rituals continued to fulfill an important role in society. Popular prejudices against, for instance, the frequent reception of communion died hard and triumphed over the Reformers' intentions and their theology of the Lord's supper.

Such continuities are, by the nature of things, hard to demonstrate or document in detail. Even harder is to substantiate the suggestion, which goes back at least as far as the Reformation humanist George Buchanan (1506–1582), that the Scottish Reformation restored the purity and the practices that had been characteristic of the ancient Celtic church before it was subordinated to Rome. Most of the specific suggestions—that Scottish Reformed worship inherited from the Eastern churches via the Celtic church the so-called Great Entrance at the offertory in the Lord's supper, or the emphasis on the epiclesis—are no more than romantic fancies of the nineteenth or twentieth century.

Granted the fact that people in general are more conservative in matters of worship than in almost anything else, it would be surprising had there not been some carryover of worship practices from the medieval Church. What is surprising is that religious change so radical became generally accepted. In most of Scotland the old ways were laid aside with remarkably little resistance, and new worship practices found a fairly ready acceptance, perhaps because the corruption of the late medieval Church had encouraged the development of widespread anticlericalism.

Whatever continuities there may have been with the more immediate Roman tradition or the more remote Celtic religious past of Scotland, it is abundantly clear that the patterns of worship established in the Reformation period were greatly influenced by outside forces. These may be summed up under three headings, in ascending order of significance: German Lutheranism, the English Reformation, and Calvinism.

German Lutheranism

Early Scots Reformers such as Patrick Hamilton (martyred 1528) and George Wishart (martyred 1546) were deeply influenced by the German Reformation and brought distinctively Lutheran doctrines with them. We may assume that they also imported Lutheran understanding and practices of worship. However, evidence that distinctively Lutheran worship ever took roots in Scotland is virtually nonexistent. What is clear is that the Reformation in Scotland, as in Germany, was born in song, and much of this song at the beginning came from German Lutheran sources. This is especially true of *The Gude and Godlie Ballates* compiled by the Wedderburn brothers, James, John, and Robert, merchants from Dundee. This collection was published in some form between 1542 and 1546 (no copy of the original edition is extant) and became immensely popular, being published in edition after edition until 1621.[2] It includes many metrical psalms, metrical versions of the creed and the Lord's prayer, a catechism in meter, ballads and popular spiritual songs set to ballad tunes, Christmas carols, and hymns. Many of these were translations from the German, and the doctrine of the catechism was distinctly Lutheran. It is not clear how far this book was used in public worship, and how much in the family circle. The fact that it included numerous examples of what can only be called "taunt songs" against the Roman Catholics suggests that it was a popular rather than an officially sanctioned book for worship. In *The Gude and Godlie Ballatis* there is sublime devotion:

> Our Saviour Christ, King of grace,
> With God the Father maid our peace;
> And with his bludie woundis fell,
> Hes us redemit from the Hell.

> And he, that we suld not foryet,
> Gave us his body for to eit

> In forme of breid, and gave us syne
> His blude to drink in forme of wyne.[3]

And, at the other extreme, a lively attack on the pope in the form of a folk song:

> The Paip, that pagane full of pryde,
> He hes us blindit lang;
> For where the blind the blind dois gyde,
> Na wonder baith ga wrang:
> Lyke prince and king he led the ring
> Of all iniquitie:
> Hay trix, tryme go trix,
> Under the greenwood tree.[4]

English Influence

The English and Scottish reformations interacted closely with each other. The Reformation party in Scotland constantly sought an alliance with England. There was much movement of people, especially ministers, between the two countries. John Knox himself (c. 1513–1572), the principal reformer, spent much of his ministry in England. He was a court chaplain to Edward VI and played some part in the production of the Second Prayer Book of 1552. He was prepared "to think well of the Book" and advised his congregation in Berwick to use it. There is evidence that this prayer book was widely used in Scotland, and it continued to be used there and among the Marian exiles long after it was abolished on Queen Mary's accession in England. In 1557 the Protestant nobles of Scotland enjoined its use in every parish of the land. Only after 1560 did more radically Calvinist forms of worship gradually displace the second English *Book of Common Prayer*.

Calvinist Worship

By the late 1550s, it seemed to many people that the Reformation movement was getting out of control. *The First Book of Discipline* suggests that some treated the ordinances of religion with contempt; one of its sections is headed "For punishment of those that Profane the Sacraments and contemne the Word of God and dare to presume to minister them not being thereto lawfully called."[5] In Saint Andrews a man informed one of the Deacons, "I shall buy a pint of wine and a loaf and I shall have as good a sacrament as the best of them all shall have."[6] The *Book of Discipline* calls for drastic punishment for "idolaters"—that is, Roman Catholics—and also for "those who despise the Sacrament."

By 1560, there was a pressing need widely felt to bring order to the worship of the Reformed Kirk (Scots for "church"). It was Calvinism that gave this order, principally by way of two documents, both promulgated in 1560: *The Scots Confession* and *The First Book of Discipline*. In traditional Calvinist style, the *Confession* puts as the first two "marks of the true Kirk" the faithful preaching of the Word of God, and the right administration of the sacraments of Jesus Christ, "quhilk man [which must] be annexed unto the Word and promise of God, to seale and confirme the same in our hearts."[7] Word and sacrament together are the vital and essential components of Reformed worship. Word without sacrament lacks demonstrative power; sacrament without word is in danger of becoming magic or idolatry.

There is evidence that John Knox insisted on frequent celebrations of the Lord's supper and its centrality in worship from the earliest days of the Scottish Reformation.[8] The sacramental doctrine of the movement is clearly set out in the *Scots Confession*. Sacraments are not simply "naked and bare signs." Through the sacraments we are joined to Christ: "be Baptisme we ar ingrafted in Jesus Christ, to be made partakers of his justice, be quilk our sins are covered and remitted. And alswa, that in the Supper richtlie used, Christ Jesus is so joined with us, that hee becummis very nurishment and fude of our saules."[9] Transubstantiation is explicitly excluded, but through the working of the Holy Spirit who enables Christians to share now in the heavenly banquet, "the faithful . . . do so eat the bodie and drink the blude of the Lord Jesus, that he remaines in them and they in him."[10] The real presence of Christ is conveyed to worshipers in the elements of the Lord's supper. As Robert Bruce suggested in his remarkable sermons on the Lord's supper delivered in the High Kirk of Edinburgh in 1586, the supper is a *verbum visibile*, the Word made visible. It "exhibits and delivers the thing that it signifies to the soul and heart, as soon as the sign is delivered to the mouth."[11] In and through the supper, the Lord gives himself to the faithful.

Knox's Liturgy

The actual practice of worship in the early years of the Reformation may be found in the *First Book of Discipline* and in the service book which quickly displaced the Anglican *Book of Common Prayer*, and was largely derived from Geneva, where Knox and others had been in exile. This first *Book of Common Order*, popularly known as "Knox's Liturgy," was authorized in Scotland in 1564. The Lord's supper is "commonly used once a month, or as oft as the Congregation shall think convenient."[12] The practice of Jesus is to be followed as closely as possible. Accordingly, communicants are to receive communion sitting at the table, not on their knees before an altar. The communion service follows the usual Sunday service of prayers, psalm singing, Bible reading, and preaching. After the reading of the institution from 1 Corinthians 11 comes an exhortation that excludes all unrepentant sinners from the table and calls on the congregation to "consider, then, that this Sacrament is a singular medicine for all poor sick creatures, a comfortable help to weak souls, and that our Lord requireth no other worthiness on our part, but that we unfeignedly acknowledge our naughtiness and imperfection."[13] The minister then, standing at the table, takes bread and gives thanks in words such as these:

> At the commandment of Jesus Christ our Lord, we present ourselves to this His Table, which he has left to be used in remembrance of His death until His coming again, to declare and witness before the world, that by Him alone we have received liberty and life, that by Him alone Thou dost acknowledge us Thy children and heirs, that by Him alone we have entrance to the throne of Thy grace, that by Him alone we are possessed in our spiritual Kingdom, to eat and drink at His Table, with whom we have our conversation presently in heaven, and by whom our bodies shall be raised up again from the dust, and shall be placed with Him in that endless joy, which Thou, O Father of mercy, hast prepared for Thine Elect before the foundation of the world was laid.[14]

After the prayer of thanksgiving, often called in Scotland the "Action Prayer," the minister breaks the bread, and the people divide and distribute the elements among themselves. Then follow a prayer of thanksgiving for communion, the singing of a psalm, and the blessing. The *Book of Common Order* was much more than a directory, but it was not a book for the people, nor was the wording of its prayers mandatory. Its use was authorized and usual in Scotland until it was replaced in 1645 by the *Westminster Directory of Public Worship*.

From *The Government and Order of the Church of Scotland*, 1641

Alexander Henderson

The Sacrament of the Lords Supper, is more frequently ministred in some Congregations, then in other, according to the number of the Communicants, and Proficiency of the People in the way of Christ; and in some places upon one Sabbath, in other places upon two, or three Sabbaths, as it may be done most conveniently, which is determined by the Minister, and Eldership of the Church.

None are admitted, to the Lords Supper, but such as upon examination are found to have a competent measure of knowledge in the grounds of Christian Religion, and the doctrine of the Sacraments; and are able according to the Apostles Commandements, and professe themselves willing, to examine themselves, and to renew their Covenant made with God in Baptisme, promising to walk as beseemeth Christians, and to submit themselves to all the Ordinances of Christ. The ignorant, the Scandalous, the obstinate, and such as are under Censure, or publike admonition in the way to censure, are not admitted; Neither are strangers received, but upon sufficient testimony, or otherwise be very well known.

The Sabbath day next before the Communion shall be celebrated, publike warning thereof is made by the Pastor, and of the doctrine of preparation, to be taught the last day of the week, or at least toward the end of the week; That the Communicants may be the better prepared, by the use of the means, both in private and publike.

Upon the day of the Communion (notice being given after the doctrine of preparation, of the houres of meeting, which useth to be before the ordinary time observed other Sabbaths) a large Table decently covered, is so placed, as that the Communicants may best sit about it, and the whole Congregation, may both hear and behold.

The Preface, prayers, and preaching of that day, are all framed to the present matter of the Sacrament, and the duties of the receivers; after Sermon immediatly the Pastor useth an exhortation, and debarreth from the Table all ignorant, prophane, and scandalous persons, which being done, he goeth from the Pulpit, and sitteth down with the people at the Table, where the bread standing before him in great Basins, fitly prepared for breaking and distribution, and the wine in large Cups in like manner, he first readeth, and shortly expoundeth the words of Institution, shewing the nature, use, and end of the Sacrament, and the duties of the Communicants; next he useth a prayer, wherein he both giveth thanks, especially for the Inestimable benefit of Redemption, and for the means of the Word and Sacraments, particularly of this Sacrament, and prayeth earnestly to God for his powerfull presence, and effectuall working, to accompany his own Ordinance, to the comfort of his people now to communicate.

The Westminster Standards

From as early as 1615 there was steady pressure from the crown to reintroduce into Scottish worship practices that had been abandoned in Scotland but had been retained in England, or reintroduced under archbishop William Laud. Charles I and Laud initially wanted Scotland to adopt the English prayer book. This met deep-seated opposition in Scotland, and the next effort, to introduce in 1637 a substantially altered Scottish prayer book, led to riots in Edinburgh and elsewhere. The crown's attempts to reform the worship of Scotland were overtaken by the Civil War, and in practice abandoned without having any significant effect on what actually happened in most churches. The Westminster Assembly of Divines was convened by the English Parliament in 1643 to reform the Church of England and its practices and, in the view of the Scots commissioners at least, to unite the two great churches of Britain "in one forme of Kirk Government, one Confession of Faith, one Catechism, and one Directorie for the Worship of God." This directory was intended, in the words of Robert Baillie, one of the Scots commissioners, "to abolish the great Idol of England, the Service Book, and to erect in all the parts of worship a full conformitie to Scotland in all things worthie to be spoken of." In 1645, the English Parliament ordered that the *Westminster Directory* be observed throughout England, Ireland, and Scotland, and in the same year, reflecting the different constitutional position, it was enacted by the General Assembly and approved by the Scottish Parliament.

Objection to the Prayer Book. Riot took place in Saint Giles' Cathedral, Edinburgh, on the reading of the new prayer book, 23 July 1637. Anonymous engraving, seventeenth century. Bridgeman Art Library

The *Westminster Directory of Public Worship* should be read alongside the other documents of the Westminster Assembly. One the one hand, the Confession, the Larger and Shorter Catechisms, and the Form of Church Government outline the relatively new federal Calvinism which was now the orthodoxy of Presbyterian Scotland and which deeply shaped the understanding of worship and the sacraments in the *Directory*. On the other hand, the General Assembly moved quickly to introduce, in 1647, the *Directory for Family Worship*, a reminder that "the secret worship of each person alone, and private worship of families" should take place during the week; on the Lord's Day, the congregation gathered for public worship in the church.

The *Westminster Directory* starts with a quaint, and revealing, account of how the people should behave in times of worship. Apart from psalm singing, the people's part is very passive. They are not to read in church, and they should abstain from "all private whisperings, conferences, salutations . . . as also from all gazing, sleeping and other indecent behaviour." Normal Sunday worship is centered on Bible reading and the sermon. All the canonical books are to be read in order. What was called the "lecture"—an exposition of the passages read—was allowed in addition to the sermon. Preaching was given a preeminent place, and the *Directory*'s section on preaching is a classic account of biblical preaching: "Preaching of the Word, being the power of God unto salvation, and one of the greatest and most excellent works belonging to the ministers of the Gospel, should be so performed that the workman need not be ashamed, but may save himself and those that hear him." Thus the preacher should do his work "painfully, . . . plainly, . . . faithfully, . . . wisely, . . . gravely, . . . with loving affection, . . . as taught of God, and persuaded in his own heart, that all that he teacheth is the truth of Christ; and walking before his flock as an example to them in it." A model of a long prayer before the sermon and a shorter prayer afterwards is offered, and after a final psalm the people are dismissed with a blessing.

Baptism is assumed to be baptism of infants into the covenant. It should be in public, usually as part of the ordinary Sunday service—and it should not be in "popish fonts"! The Lord's supper is "frequently to be celebrated," although how often is not specified. It should take place after the sermon, the reading of scripture, and the prayers; it starts with an exhortation which is both an invitation and a "fencing of the table," excluding notorious and unrepentant sinners from communion. There is to be no altar, but a table "decently covered" and so placed that the communicants may "orderly sit about it or at it." This provision represented a compromise between the Scots and the English. The Scots believed that biblical precedent required that communicants sit at long tables, as for a meal, while the English at the time were accustomed to tables set lengthways in the chancel, with the minister at the center of the north side and the people gathered around. The minister begins the "Action" "with sanctifying and blessing the Elements of Bread and Wine set before him . . . having first in a few words showed that these Elements, otherwise Common, are now set apart and sanctified to this holy use by the Word of Institution and Prayer." After this "Taking" and the reading of the narrative from 1 Corinthians 11:23–27, the "Prayer, Thanksgiving, or Blessing" is outlined in some detail. After thanksgiving for all God's goodness, there is a strong echo of Knox's Liturgy's christological emphasis: "There is no other name under heaven by which we can be saved, but the name of Jesus Christ, by whom alone we receive liberty and life, have access to the throne of grace, are admitted to eat and drink at his own table, and are sealed up by his Spirit to an assurance of happiness and eternal life." There is a more explicit consecration, praying to God

> to vouchsafe his gracious presence and the effectual working of his Spirit in us, and so to sanctify these elements, both of bread and wine, and to bless his own ordinance, that we may receive by faith the body and blood of Jesus Christ, crucified for us, and so . . . feed upon him, that he may be one with us, and we one with him; that he may live in us, and we in him, and to him who hath loved us, and given himself for us.

After this prayer, the minister breaks the bread and gives to the people. The mode of distribution was left unspecified. The Scots wanted communicants to pass the elements from hand to hand, each serving and being served by neighbors within the royal priesthood; the English wished to permit a variety of practices. After a brief post-communion prayer, the service concludes.

The *Westminster Directory* certainly influenced the worship of Presbyterian Scotland very profoundly, and only in modern times has it been effectively replaced with the various *Books of Common Order* and their like. Some later periods of history left their mark on the worship of Scotland, most notably the struggles between the Covenanters and the "prelatists," supported by the government. Powerful and evocative stories of Covenanters worshiping in the open air and celebrating the Lord's supper in the hills, with sentries in place to warn of coming dragoons, were etched deeply in the Presbyterian psyche, and they contributed to the shape of worship after the firm establishment of Presbyterianism in 1688.

The Communion Season

Although in many Scottish parishes communion was celebrated infrequently, commonly once a year, from the seventeenth century "the communion season" was a great festival, attracting in some cases thousands of people for services over a period of nearly a week and climaxing in the great celebration of communion on the Sunday. Robert Burns wrote a poem titled "The Holy Fair," and at his time the communion was just that—not simply a liturgical activity but a great social occasion, attracting thieves, drunkards, and whores as well as the devout:

> How mony hearts this day converts,
>   O' sinners and o' lasses!
> Their hearts o' stane, gin night, are gane, as saft as any flesh is:
>   There's some are fou o' love divine;
> There's some are fou o' brandy.

The crowds were so large that services frequently spilled out of the church building into the surrounding fields, with hundreds of communicants taking seats at long trestle tables for each of the successive sittings. In the country areas the communions were fixed at times in the summer when there was not much activity on the farms and when travel was easy. Teams of ministers led the various services, and the devout would travel a circuit of such events in the course of the summer, thus receiving communion frequently. The communion season was exported to America and for a time played a major part in the spirituality of its camp meetings.

Except in the western highlands, where the communion season survives, the Lord's supper is celebrated today in most parishes quarterly, and in an increasing number monthly or even weekly. The latest service book of the Church of Scotland, *Common Order* (1994), offers several orders for the Lord's supper, ranging from one that is derived from Knox's Liturgy to modern ones influenced by the Iona Community and the modern interest in Celtic Christianity.

Church Music

The Scottish Reformation was hostile to accompanied singing in church. Medieval organs were destroyed or removed. Despite the rich diversity represented by *The Gude and Godlie Ballatis*, the steady practice from the early days was that only psalms should be sung in church and in family worship. Each family was expected to have, for church and family use, a Bible and a psalmbook. The latter often contained, in addition to psalms, metrical versions of the creed and a number of prayers. The tunes should be "plain tunes" so that the people could take a full part in this, their central role in worship. At the beginning, many of these tunes were imported from Geneva, but gradually a magnificent diversity of psalm tunes was composed. There were few choirs to assist the singing, but each church had a precentor to lead it, often using the prac-

Worship at Iona Abbey. Clergy and laity carry the eucharistic elements to the table at a service held on 6 August 1955. The Rev. George MacLeod, a parish minister in Glasgow, founded the ecumenical Iona Community in part to restore the ruined abbey that had been founded in 563 by Saint Columba. The community today is a center for worship, spirituality, and social change, and publishes its own liturgical resources. PHOTOGRAPH BY MAURICE AMBLER/HULTON ARCHIVE/ GETTY IMAGES

tice of "lining," whereby the precentor sings each line alone and the congregation then repeats it—a practice probably dating from the time when many in a congregation were illiterate.

Successive versions of the metrical psalter were authorized by the General Assembly, the most recent in 1929. Some Scottish metrical psalms have passed into the treasury of the universal church, such as Psalm 23, "The Lord's my shepherd," Psalm 100, "All people that on earth do dwell," and Psalm 121, "I to the hills will lift mine eyes." The authorization, in 1781, of certain paraphrases of scripture passages other than psalms caused much controversy; but a few of the paraphrases have become classics—for example:

> I'm not ashamed to own my Lord,
> or to defend his cause,
> Maintain the glory of his cross,
> and honour all his laws.

Hymns were introduced later in the nineteenth century, and the Scottish Presbyterian tradition has produced a number of distinguished hymn writers, among whom John Bell of the Iona Community is preeminent today.

Church Buildings

From the time of the Reformation, churches have been regarded in Scotland not as shrines but rather as meeting places for God's people when they come to worship God together. During the Reformation, most of the monastic chapels and chantries, and even the cathedral in a city like Saint Andrews, were destroyed or left to decay, stripped of their furnishings and ornaments. It was quite different with parish churches and college chapels, which had to be adapted for the use of a Reformed congregation. Big city churches, after they had had altars and all the instruments of the old forms of worship removed, were often divided into two, three, or even four churches for different congregations, often with galleries and a high pulpit so that everyone could hear the preacher.

Scotland being a poor country, there were relatively few splendid country kirks; most were very simple rectangular affairs, easily adapted to Reformed worship by putting the pulpit halfway along the long wall. If expansion became necessary, an aisle and gallery could be added opposite the pulpit, thus giving the common T-shaped church design. The pulpit, with the precentor's desk beneath it, and often seats for the elders within an enclosure around the pulpit, was the commonest plan. A baptismal bowl was often attached to the pulpit, but there was normally no fixed communion table; for communion, trestle tables were erected in the center of the church, or perhaps outside if the congregation was large. When pews became common, many churches had an ingenious arrangement, still to be seen in some places, whereby the pews could be adjusted so that they made long, narrow tables with seats at both sides.

City churches built in the eighteenth and nineteenth centuries tended to be designed as auditoriums, with huge pulpits, often in front of a display of organ pipes, and galleries around three sides. The Scoto-Catholic movement encouraged building churches in Gothic style, although favor was also shown to churches of the Romanesque basilican type with the communion table in the apse so that minister and elders could sit behind it. There are a number of interesting modern churches, but on the whole little attention has been given for some time to the requirements for a church building to house contemporary Reformed worship.

Bibliography

Burnet, George B. *The Holy Communion in the Reformed Church of Scotland, 1560–1960.* Edinburgh: Oliver and Boyd, 1960.

Forrester, Duncan, and Douglas Murray, eds. *Studies in the History of Worship in Scotland.* 2nd ed. Edinburgh: T. & T. Clark, 1996.

Hay, George. *The Architecture of Scottish Post-Reformation Churches.* Oxford: Oxford University Press, 1957.

Maxwell, William D. *A History of Worship in the Church of Scotland.* Oxford: Oxford University Press, 1955.

McMillan, William. *The Worship of the Scottish Reformed Church, 1550–1638.* London: James Clark, 1931.

Patrick, Millar. *Four Centuries of Scottish Psalmody.* Oxford: Oxford University Press, 1949.

Schmidt, Leigh Eric. *Holy Fairs: Scottish Communions and American Revivals in the Early Modern Period.* Princeton, N.J.: Princeton University Press, 1989.

Notes

[1] James K. Cameron, ed., *The First Book of Discipline* (Edinburgh: St. Andrew Press, 1972) 94–95.

[2] Modern editions are David Laing, ed., *A Compendious Book of Psalms and Spiritual Songs, commonly known as "The Gude and Godlie Ballates,"* reprinted from the edition of 1578 (Edinburgh: W. Paterson, 1868); and Iain Ross, ed., *The Gude and Godlie Ballatis* (Edinburgh: Oliver and Boyd, 1939), a selection.

[3] Ross, 17.

[4] Ross, 60.

[5] *The First Book of Discipline,* 204.

[6] Cited in William McMillan, *The Worship of the Scottish Reformed Church, 1550–1638,* 40.

[7] G. D. Henderson, ed., *Scots Confession 1560 and Negative Confession 1581* (Edinburgh: Church of Scotland, 1937) Article 18 (p. 75).

[8] James S. McEwan, *The Faith of John Knox* (London: Lutterworth, 1961) 56–59.

[9] *Scots Confession,* Article 21 (pp. 83–85).

[10] *Scots Confession,* p. 85.

[11]Robert Bruce, *The Mystery of the Lord's Supper*, trans. and ed. T. F. Torrance (London: James Clark, 1958).

[12]The *First Book of Discipline* judges four times a year to be "sufficient."

[13]George W. Sprott and Thomas Leishman, eds., *The Book of Common Order of the Church of Scotland and the Directory for the Public Worship of God* (Edinburgh: Blackwood, 1868) 125.

[14]Sprott and Leishman, 126.

15

The Reformed Tradition
in Korea

SEUNG-JOONG JOO and
KYEONG-JIN KIM

The Reformed tradition was introduced into Korea in the nineteenth century by Presbyterian missionaries from Scotland and the United States. The long journey in time and space means that Presbyterian worship in Korea is not the same as that of Geneva in the sixteenth century. To what extent then can Korean Presbyterian worship be called Reformed? To describe the worship of the Korean Presbyterian Church, three questions are asked: (1) What liturgical traditions did Presbyterian missionaries introduce into Korea in the late nineteenth century and early twentieth century? (2) How did the early Korean Presbyterian liturgies develop? (3) What are the present features of Korean Presbyterian worship?

The Bible and the Early Korean Faith Community in Manchuria

The history of the Presbyterian Church in Korea began in the fall of 1884, when the first resident Presbyterian missionary came to Korea.[1] However, the beginning of the Korean Presbyterian Church could be traced back to 1879 in terms of liturgy because the first Presbyterian baptism of Koreans was performed in Manchuria in 1879 by the Reverend John MacIntyre (1837–1905), a Scottish Presbyterian missionary.[2] This means that Scottish missionaries in Manchuria started the primitive Korean Christian communities and worship for Koreans before the American missionaries arrived in Korea.

In 1876 in Manchuria, John MacIntyre and John Ross (1842–1915), another Scottish Presbyterian missionary, sought a way to evangelize Korea. They invited young Korean intellectuals to help them translate the Chinese Bible into Korean. The first Korean Bible extracts, the Gospels of Luke and John, were published in 1882. Ross and MacIntyre finally published the Korean version of the whole New Testament, *Yesu Syonggyo Chonso*, in 1887. Thus the first Korean Christians were mostly connected with the literary works regarding the Bible translation in Manchuria. From the outset, the Bible was placed in the center of Korean Presbyterian worship as it was in sixteenth-century Reformed worship.

The Early Presbyterian Worship Brought by American Missionaries

Even though the Korean Presbyterian communities and their worship trace their origins back to Manchuria in 1879, the organized Protestant mission work in Korea commenced later in 1884. The arrival of the first resident Presbyterian missionary and physician, Horace N. Allen (1858–1932), marked the beginning of the mission. He was then followed by many American missionaries. Thus the Korean mission was mainly conducted by American missionaries, not by the Scottish missionaries. For more than one hundred years the Korean Church worshiped according to the forms and traditions introduced by the American missionaries. What, then, were the liturgies that resident missionaries to Korea introduced and developed?

The worship forms that were introduced to Korea by American missionaries reflected the "non-liturgical" or "Puritan" pattern that prevailed in the Presbyterian churches in the United States at the end of the nineteenth century. Of all the teachings of the Puritans, none was more important than that of *sola scriptura*. The Puritans insisted that scripture alone was sufficient to guide all aspects of life and faith. They also moved away from the highly ritualized worship of the Church of England toward simpler forms of worship, which eventually led to a complete revision of that liturgical tradition. In addition, some more radical (Scottish) Puritans even opposed the traditional elements of Christian worship, such as singing of a doxology, the use of the Lord's prayer in public worship, and public reading of scripture.[3] This "Puritanized" service was what the Presbyterians in America inherited, and such Puritan tradition was applied in Korean worship. For instance, the missionaries in Manchuria strongly believed in the Puritan tradition of focusing on the Bible. Ross and MacIntyre conducted Bible studies at least twice a day for the baptized members or catechumens. In addition, the missionaries in Manchuria used a very simple order of worship, which consisted of only three elements: hymn singing, Bible reading (study), and prayer. Even such liturgical elements as the Lord's prayer, the Apostles' Creed, doxologies, or the confession of sin were not used as a part of their worship.

Along with Puritan traditions, Pietism and revivalism influenced the shaping of the Korean Presbyterian liturgies. The American Puritans were influenced by the Great Awakenings that originated from Pietism. Pietism greatly affected two Great Awakening movements (eighteenth century and nineteenth century) in North America in a characteristically evangelical, emotionally intense, individualistic, and anti-intellectual fashion.

Another development that took place along with the Great Awakenings was the emergence of "frontier" worship, of which the camp meeting was one manifestation. It is significant that frontier worship was specifically designed to make converts. Thus these revivals generated a new style or order of worship that came to dominate American Protestant worship. Characteristically, its normal Sunday service had three parts: a song service or praise service sometimes caricatured as "preliminaries," a sermon, and a harvest of new converts.[4] As a result Methodists, Baptists, Presbyterians, Disciples of Christ, and many other denominations made this three-part form their basic order of worship.[5]

Both revivalistic and puritan features characterized the liturgies that the American missionaries introduced into Korea. From the beginning, American missionaries started "prayer meetings" and "week of prayers" with other simple, regular worship services and Bible studies. Since evangelistic work was unlawful in Korea, the early missionaries had to content themselves with weekly English-language services limited to foreigners at the missionary house. Sooner or later, however, Koreans attended the English services. Evidence indicates that Koreans might have participated in the English-language worship as early as January 1886.[6]

In addition to weekly Sunday worship, another form of English-language worship service called "week of prayer" was observed. In 1886 H. G. Underwood, a Presbyterian missionary, started the week of prayer, a liturgy familiarized by all missionaries through the American mission movement. According to a letter Underwood wrote to a Dr. Ellinwood, several Koreans also participated in this week of prayer liturgy.[7] Other forms of English services appeared as well, some of which included the "regular morning prayer" and "noon prayer" services. These forms of worship service were the first examples of revivalistic liturgy that the early missionaries brought into Korea. Because these were the first forms of worship available, Koreans naturally copied these revivalistic liturgies as their own when they started worshiping in their native language.

Perhaps the best example of the atmosphere of a revival liturgy in Korea can be illustrated from the Great Revival of Korea, which took place during 1903–1910. This revival started through the prayer meeting and week of prayer. The Great Revival of Korea was characterized by the emotional outpouring of Korean Christians. Koreans expressed themselves through various forms of prayer, such as the audible prayer, mountain prayer, and dawn prayer.[8] Those who expressed themselves through

Dawn prayer. "Dawn prayer" at Myungsung Presbyterian Church in Seoul, South Korea, on 9 June 2005. Services are held with large congregations at 4, 5, 6, and 7 AM. The 7 AM service, a half an hour in length, follows the structure of Apostles' Creed, hymn, spontaneous prayer spoken out loud by the congregation ("tongsung kido"), scripture reading, responsive psalm, sermon, pastoral prayer, and the Lord's prayer (in unison); it concludes with private prayers. PHOTOGRAPH BY KAREN WESTERFIELD TUCKER

tongsong kido (audible prayer) prayed freely and fervently to God in a loud, outpouring unison. Such methods of prayer further intensified the emotions of those attending the revival. These Great Revivals became more commonplace, and the Korean Church began regularly organizing revival meetings once or twice a year. These meetings were called *puhunghoe* (revival meeting) and have their origins in the *sagyonghoe* (Bible classes). With a history of revivals dating back to the nineteenth century, the meetings have become a characteristic in Korean Presbyterian worship.

The Influence of the Nevius *Method* on the Early Presbyterian Worship in Korea

In 1886 the Reverend John L. Nevius, a Presbyterian missionary to China, published a book, *Method of Mission Work*.[9] Nevius's book caught the eyes of many young Presbyterian missionaries in Korea and planted in their hearts a new concept of mission principles for Korea. In 1891, based on the Nevius *Method*, the Presbyterian Mission (Northern) officially adopted *The Presbyterian Northern Mission and By-Laws*. Since then the Nevius *Method* has become the backbone of Korean mission policies.

The Nevius plan, which emphasized self-support, self-propagation, and self-government, maximized the participation of the native people in the mission work and their church life. The Nevius *Method* also had a profound effect on the liturgies and practices of Korean Presbyterian churches. The liturgical instructions of the Nevius *Method* included: (1) liturgical initiatives of native people, (2) teaching rather than preaching in worship services, (3) simplified worship services, (4) the need for a time of probationary membership, (5) the Bible class system, and (6) union worship services. From the Nevius *Method*, the Korean Church developed unique Korean liturgies, such as the liturgy of *haksup* (learner) and of *sagyonghoe* (Bible classes).

Nevius published his *Manual for Enquirers* in order to propagate his mission methods. This book was originally designed for enquirers themselves, but the real purpose was to aid the native leaders and helpers so they could preside or lead congregations. In 1895 H. A. Moffett, a Presbyterian missionary, prepared *Wi wonip kyoin kyujo* (Manual for Catechumens), which may have been directly translated from *Manual for Enquirers*. The translated manual played a monumental role in the development of the liturgy of the Korean Presbyterian Church because it has forms of prayer with the Lord's prayer, an order for church service, an essay on the sacraments and offerings, and a selection of common hymns.

Especially the order of worship service described in the *Manual* was meant for settings without helpers or pastors. This worship order was designed for the native leaders or elders who conducted their own congregations or for small gatherings of worship, such as family worship. The order was described as follows:

(1) Hymn singing
(2) Prayer
(3) Scripture reading
(4) Prayers of the congregation (one or two among the congregation may pray)
(5) Hymn singing
(6) Teaching from the Bible
(7) Prayer
(8) Offering
(9) Hymn singing[10]

Since no pastor was expected in the service, the benediction was omitted, and worship concluded with hymns. Again, for the same reason as above, the teaching of the Bible was held instead of preaching. The *Manual* also included a short description of sacraments, a few Bible passages on the sacraments, and hymns. Through all of these, the Nevius *Method* had a great influence on the early Korean Presbyterian liturgy.

The Establishment of the Korean Presbyterian Church and the Shaping of the Official Liturgies

With the establishment of the Presbyterian Church of Korea and the ordination of Korean pastors (1907), the liturgical context changed. Newly ordained Korean pastors were now able to run these churches and consequently weakened the role lay leaders had played in previous worship services. And the newly established Presbyterian Church of Korea needed a constitution. Thus the new Korean Church of 1907 adopted the Confession of Faith that had been prepared by the Council of Presbyterian Mission. Five years after the organization of the first Korean presbytery, the first General Assembly of the Presbyterian Church of Korea (*Chosen*) took place in Pyongyang in 1912.[11] The Korean Presbyterian Church that started with seven Korean pastors in 1907 had fifty-five pastors by 1912. Along with the increase in their number, the role of Korean pastors in the church became greater as well. The Korean pastors were now expected to exercise jurisdiction and discipline and administered baptism and the Lord's supper as the missionaries had done before. Gradually, as more responsibilities were thrust upon them, the newly ordained Korean pastors felt the need to standardize the form of worship to be used on various occasions.

Thus during the formative period of the Korean Presbyterian liturgy, between 1907 and 1934, the church adopted official liturgies, such as the *Directory of Worship of the Presbyterian Church of Chosen* (1922) and the *Honsang yesikso* (Forms of Marriage and Burial, 1924). Other publications of liturgical instructions, such as *Kangdo yoryong* (Homiletic Lectures, 1910), *Moksa chibop* (Pastoral Theology, 1919), and *Yebae chopkyong* (Aids for Public Worship, 1934) also came out.

In 1921 the general assembly adopted the Constitution of the Presbyterian Church of Korea (Chosen) and published it for the public in 1922. The constitution consisted of five parts: (1) the Confession of Faith as in 1907, (2) the Westminster Shorter Catechism, (3) a Form of Government, which was modeled after that of the American churches, (4) a Book of Discipline, which was basically the book of the American Presbyterian church (Northern) with a few modifications, and (5) a Directory of Worship, which was the same as that of the American church (Southern) save for a few modifications.

Liturgical Renewal Movement in the 1920s

In the meantime some missionaries began to put their efforts into introducing more traditional forms of worship to replace the simple form of worship first introduced to the Korean Presbyterian Church. As was discussed, the early missionaries adopted the Nevius *Method* and followed liturgical strategies congruent with the methods. But some of the early missionaries considered the simplified worship service only a temporary necessity even though they actively used it in the mission field. They expected that Korean Christians would eventually have more formal services in the future.

For instance, Charles Allen Clark, a professor of Pyongyang Presbyterian Theological Seminary, thought these simple forms of worship derived from the Nevius *Method* were no longer suitable for the Korean churches. Thus he published *Kangdo yoryong* (*Homiletic Lecture*) in 1910 and insisted that pastors should prepare well-organized sermons for their worship services. Nine years later Clark introduced Reformed liturgies in his book *Moksa chibop* (*Pastoral Theology*, 1919) and suggested the inclusion of the confession of sins, the continuous reading of the Bible, and the reading of the Psalms, which are characteristic of John Calvin's liturgy. Clark also included the Ten Commandments in the beginning part of the worship service with other options, such as the Apostles' Creed. This inclusion of the Decalogue reflected Calvin's theology of worship. In the Strasbourg liturgy, Calvin appointed the Decalogue to be sung with the Kyrie eleison after each law.[12] Like Clark, many missionaries appealed to the Korean pastors and to the other missionaries to stress that the Korean Presbyterian liturgy should recover the Reformed tradition, especially of John Calvin, marked by decorum and solemnity.

Unfortunately, however, the liturgy of the Korean Presbyterian Church had already started taking its shape. Because of the initial influences of revivalism in Korea, the Korean churches began adopting the liturgies of revivals. Even though many missionaries successfully made available official liturgies, like the *Directory of Worship* and *Forms of Marriage and Burial*, and published liturgical instructions, many Korean pastors did not want to give up the revival liturgies that were already familiar to them. For example, the order for Sunday worship (1932) of the Saemunan Presbyterian Church,[13] which was the first Presbyterian local church in Korea, does not reflect Clark's liturgy in *Moksa chibop* at all. Instead, the liturgy of the Saemunan Church strongly reflects Moffett's liturgy introduced in *Wi wonip kyoin kyujo* (1895). Moffett's liturgy was designed for the native leader or elder who conducted his or her own congregation or for small gatherings of worship, such as family worship. This liturgical tradition, shaped by Puritanism and revivalism, continued into the late 1970s in most Korean Presbyterian churches, until liturgical renewal movements began in the early 1980s. It is ironic that this temporary order of worship became the standard for regular Sunday worship services in the Korean Presbyterian churches for so long. Even though it was not accepted by Korean churches, the renewal of Korean Presbyterian worship was actually started by those early missionaries in the 1920s, long before liturgical scholars put forth their proposals in the 1980s and 1990s.

The Liturgical Movement in the Presbyterian Church of Korea since 1980

As described, until the 1980s the worship of Korean Presbyterian churches did not have a strong liturgical or sacramental character. Like most Christians in the Reformed tradition, Presbyterians have been predominantly "People of the Word." The Lord's supper in most churches has been confined to celebrations two to four times a year. Although the Reformed churches of the United States and Scotland showed signs of remarkable liturgical revival in the last several decades of the twentieth century, the Presbyterian churches in Korea remained very conservative in the matter of liturgical renewal.

However, since 1980 traditional Korean Protestant worship has been informed by the "liturgical movement" in Korea led by some liturgical scholars and pastors.[14] Their efforts can be summarized in three ways: (1) recovery of the specifically Reformed or Calvinist tradition, as distinct from the Puritan tradition, such as including the Lord's supper more frequently in the Sunday worship service and the introduction of a lectionary system for preaching; (2) interest in ecumenical worship as exemplified by the Lima Liturgy and production of creative liturgies; and (3) concern for the contextualization of Christian worship, including the Christian acceptance of certain forms of traditional ancestor veneration and incorporation of Korean festivals into the church calendar.

When the Liturgical Movement arose among Presbyterian churches in Korea, the Presbyterian Church of Korea (*Tonghap*) was the leading exponent of the movement.[15] When Chang-Bok Chung introduced the liturgical movement into Korean churches, the Presbyterian Church of Korea (Tonghap) joined the movement of the Reformed churches throughout the world and restored many elements in the Reformed worship that had been lost. Following is the order of the Lord's day service, including the Lord's table:[16]

> Gathering
>> Prelude, Call to Worship, Choral Response, Sentences of Scripture, Prayer of the Day or Opening Prayer
> Praise and Confession
>> Hymn of Praise, Prayer of Confession, Silent Prayer, Assurance of Pardon, Gloria Patri (Doxology)
> Time of Intercession
>> Prayer, the Lord's Prayer
> Proclamation of the Word
>> First Reading of Old Testament, Second Reading of Epistles, Anthem (Hymn, Psalm), Gospel Reading, Prayer for Illumination, Sermon, Ministerial Prayer
> Offering
>> (It is a part of the eucharist when it is celebrated)
> Eucharist
>> Affirmation of Faith, Hymn (Canticle, Psalm, or Spiritual), Invitation to the Lord's Table, Epiclesis, Breaking of Bread, Receiving Cup, Communion, Prayer of Thanksgiving, Hymn (Spiritual, Canticle, or Psalm)
> Sending
>> Charge, Benediction, Postlude

Looking at this order, it is apparent that the worship order of the Korean Presbyterian Church is in accordance with the Reformed churches that pursue the Liturgical Movement. Of course not every Presbyterian church in Korea follows this kind of worship form, yet the Korean Presbyterian churches are in the process of renewing their worship and are trying to catch up with the liturgical features of the Reformed churches in the world.

Churches Following a "Non-Liturgical" Trend

A new trend of worship in the Korean Church is the "seekers' service," which is called "open worship." This non-liturgical, revival style of worship has spread quickly among big, interdenominational churches. Open worship has not been clear in concept and content, leading to confusion. It is, however, known that the goal of open worship is to modify the formal worship style and make it a large, celebrating worship focused on young people. The music is taken from contemporary Christian music, and liturgical dance is involved in praise and worship. The form of the sermon is also taken from the forms of drama and testimonial sermons. In the early twenty-first century a majority in the Presbyterian Church in Korea takes a defensive and negative stance toward open worship.

Bibliography

Chung, Chang-Bok. *Theology of Worship*. Seoul: Presbyterian College and Theological Seminary Press, 1999.

Joo, Seung Joong. "The Christian Year and Lectionary Preaching: A Liturgical Contextualization for the Presbyterian Church of Korea (*Tonghap*)." Th.D. diss., Boston University School of Theology, 1997.

Kim, Kyeong Jin. "The Formation of Presbyterian Worship in Korea 1879–1934." Th.D. diss., Boston University School of Theology, 1999.

Park, Keun-Won. *Theory of Worship for Today*. Seoul: CLSK, 1992.

Presbyterian Church of Korea. *The Book of Common Worship*. Seoul: Publishing House PCK, 1997.

Notes

[1] Allen D. Clark, *A History of the Church in Korea* (Seoul: Christian Literature Society of Korea, 1971) 88.

[2] J. Ross, "China-Manchuria Mission," *United Presbyterian Missionary Records* (1 October 1880) 333–334.

[3] Hugh Thompson Kerr, "The Story of the *Book of Common Worship*," *Journal of the Presbyterian Historical Society* 29 (1951) 206.

[4] James F. White, *Protestant Worship* (Louisville, Ky.: Westminster/John Knox Press, 1989) 177.

[5] James F. White, *Protestant Worship*, 177–178.

[6] H. G. Underwood, letter to Dr. Ellinwood, 20 January 1886, in *Correspondence and Reports, 1884–1911*.

[7] H. G. Underwood, letter to Dr. Ellinwood, 20 January 1886.

[8] The Korean Church has been known for its emphasis on prayer. Every church has a daily dawn prayer meeting (usually 5:00 AM) that consists of two parts: a pastor's exposition of scripture for twenty to thirty minutes and private prayer. Mountain prayer is popular and plays an important part in devotional life. On Fridays many Korean Christians go to "prayer mountains" (or prayer retreat centers), where they listen to messages, give testimonies, and pray all night.

[9] John L. Nevius, *Method of Mission Work* (Shanghai: Presbyterian Mission Press, 1886).

[10] H. A. Moffett, *Wi wonip kyoin kyujo* (Seoul: Korean Religious Tract Society, 1913) 13–14.

[11] The Presbyterian Church of Korea (Chosen) is the first official name of the Presbyterian Church of Korea.

[12] William D. Maxwell, *An Outline of Christian Worship: Its Development and Forms* (London: Oxford University Press, 1936) 114.

[13] Saemunan Presbyterian Church, *Saemunan Kyohoe Paengnyonsa, 1887—1987* (Centennial History of Saemunan Presbyterian Church, 1887–1987) 239.

[14] Among them Dr. Chang-Bok Chung, a professor of practical theology at Presbyterian College and Theological Seminary, and Dr. Keun-Won Park, a professor at Hanshin University, are leading figures.

[15] The Presbyterian Church of Korea consists of four groups divided by theological conviction and not region: Tonghap, Hapdong, Koshin, and Kijang. The Presbyterian Church of Korea (Tonghap) is the largest of the four groups.

[16] Presbyterian Church of Korea, *The Book of Common Worship*, 61–74.

16

Anglicans and Dissenters

BRYAN D. SPINKS

The liturgical traditions, official and unofficial, stemming from the English Reformation have their beginnings in the later years of the reign of King Henry VIII in the 1530s. Until 1689 it is technically incorrect to speak of Anglicans and Dissenters. In the sixteenth and seventeenth centuries there were, on the one hand, official, authorized legal forms of worship and, on the other hand, unofficial, unauthorized, and illegal liturgical practices. Much of the latter was the work of disaffected clergy and laity of the Church of England, and only in exceptional cases until the mid-seventeenth century did such people secede from the national church to become "Separatists." This was to change in 1689 with the passing of the Toleration Act, when, as John Spurr has noted, the national church became an established church, and others who refused to conform became legally tolerated Dissenters.[1]

The Period 1529–1553

Henry VIII, unable to persuade the pope to grant an annulment of his marriage to Catherine of Aragon, directed the English Parliament to enact legislation that legally separated the church in England from any jurisdiction of the bishop of Rome. The result was that by 1536 the English church was an independent Catholic church. The only immediate liturgical reforms were the omission of mention of the pope in church prayers, and the abolition of the feast of Saint Thomas à Becket, the archbishop of Canterbury who had championed the jurisdiction of Rome over Henry II. Henry VIII was no Protestant and had, with the help of Bishop John Fisher, authored a book against Martin Luther that had earned him from the pope the title "Defender of the Faith." During his reign, however, liturgical reforms of a Protestant nature appeared in editions of primers, or books of hours, intended for educated lay use.[2] These indicate not only a desire in some quarters to promote a more Protestant spirituality but also a lay clientele for such material. Thus, George Joye's *Hortulus Animae*, 1529, included the hours in English, the penitential psalms and the commendations, but also a number of prayers of Lutheran origin. This primer was reprinted in 1534 by William Marshall, with some alterations, including two sermons by Martin Luther. A second edition followed, and this included Luther's Litany, disguised by the addition of a number of saints. John Hilsey's primer was issued with authority in 1539; in this, in the rite for the departed (*Dirige*), the Old Testament lessons of lament were replaced by New Testament readings of assurance.

Although these changes were unofficial, and modest, there was a far more visible sign of change afoot, and this was the gradual dismantling of the cult of the saints and pilgrimage. The visitation of the smaller monasteries as a prelude to their suppression in 1536 led to the exposure of many false relics, such as combs belonging to Mary Magdalene and the chains that had imprisoned Saint Peter. Also in that year, certain holy days were abolished as public holidays. Then in 1537 a book of doctrine, known as the Bishops' Book, was published. It included an attack on images, and it prohibited the lighting of candles before saints' images. Injunctions issued in 1538 ended the practice of pilgrimage and effected the destruction of the tomb of Becket at Canterbury and the destruction of the Shrine of our Lady of Walsingham. A contemporary ode, possibly by Philip, Earl of Arundel, lamented the latter:

> Toads and serpents hold their dens
> Where the palmers did throng.
> Weep, Weep, O Walsingham,
> Whose Days are nights,
> Blessings turned to blasphemies,
> Holy Deeds to despites.
> Sin is where our Lady sat,
> Heaven turned is to hell.
> Satan sits where Our Lord did sway;
> Walsingham, O farewell.

Many who were unable to commit themselves in verse almost certainly shared these sentiments, and custom died hard. In 1547 more injunctions were issued, among which was the condemnation of "wandering to pilgrimages." Masses for the departed and chantries were suppressed, as were the *Salve Regina* and office of the Blessed Virgin Mary. In the same year Archbishop Thomas Cranmer issued the "Homily on Good Works," in which he listed those parts of the Catholic cultus that were being swept away:

> And briefly to pass over the ungodly and counterfeit religion, let us rehearse some other kinds of Papistical superstitions and abuses, as of Beads, of Lady Psalters, and Rosaries, of Fifteen Oes, of Saint Bernard's Verses, of Saint Agathe's Letters, of purgatory, of masses satisfactory, of stations and jubilees, of feigned relicks, of hallowed beads, bells,

A reformer preaches. Hugh Latimer (c. 1485–1555) preaches before King Edward VI (reigned 1547–1553) at Westminster in 1547. Latimer was popular as a court preacher and as an advocate of social and ecclesiastical reform. After the accession of Mary he was examined, excommunicated, and burnt at the stake. Woodcut from "Acts and Monuments" by John Foxe (1516–1587). PRIVATE COLLECTION/ BRIDGEMAN ART LIBRARY

bread, water, palms, candles, fire, and such other; of superstitious fastings, of fraterni-ties, or brotherhoods, of pardons, with such like merchandize; which were so esteemed and abused to the great prejudice of God's glory and commandments, . . .Thus was the people, through ignorance, so blinded with the goodly shew and appearance of those things, that they thought the keeping of them to be a more holiness, a more perfect service and honouring of God, and more pleasing to God, than the keeping of God's commandments.[3]

Here the reforming archbishop outlined the final phases of a process, begun in 1536, of abolishing popular devotional practices. Yet until the death of Henry VIII, the Latin Catholic rites remained the norm of public worship in the English church.

The official revision of the rites for public worship was the work, or at least the inspiration, of Archbishop Cranmer, who had succeeded to the see of Canterbury in 1533. Skilled in diplomacy under Cardinal Wolsey, Cranmer had spent some time in Germany where he acquired both a knowledge of Lutheran worship and a German wife.[4] Although Henry allowed no drastic changes in English public worship, he ap-pointed a number of men with Protestant sympathies to key positions. It is known from Manuscript Royal 7B IV in the British Library that Cranmer had already started experimenting with liturgical revision as early as 1538. This manuscript contains two attempts at, or two versions of, reform of the divine office, and the first version is more radical than the second. Here Cranmer drew on ideas from the Lutheran re-forms, as well as from the semiofficial Roman Catholic reform of the breviary carried out by Cardinal Quiñones at papal request. In 1543 a Royal Injunction required les-sons at matins and evensong to be read in English. In 1544 Cranmer published the litany in English, which took the place of all other litanies in the processional. If he was working on other revisions, no documentary evidence has survived. Only with Henry's death in 1547, and the succession of his young son Edward VI with a Protes-tant regency council, was the way open for official liturgical reform. In 1548 the *Order of the Communion* was issued with a Royal Proclamation. This order was a communion devotion or preparation, in English, which was to be inserted in the Latin mass just before the communion. Some of the material was taken from the *Consultation* drawn up by Martin Bucer and Philipp Melanchthon for Archbishop Hermann von Wied of Cologne, although in such devotional prayers such as "We do not presume to come to this thy table" (later known as the "Prayer of Humble Access"), one can see Cranmer at work weaving together material from older collects and biblical imagery to provide a fine new composition. The *Order* consisted of exhortations, a confession and abso-lution, "comfortable words of scripture," and directions for administration of the com-munion in both bread and wine. Much of the material would reappear in various versions of the *Book of Common Prayer*.

The Proclamation that accompanied this devotion requested that it be received quietly, and that such reception by those who wished to run afore would encourage those in authority "further to travail for the Reformation and setting forth of such godly orders." A rubric explained that this order would stand only "until other or-der shall be provided." "Godly orders" here suggests that this was but the first in a series of planned measures. Indeed, one year later, taking effect on Pentecost Sun-day, 9 June 1549, a *Book of Common Prayer* was issued that, by an Act of Uniformity, replaced all the Latin Catholic rites. Already in April of that year, however, Martin Bucer had written to friends in Strasbourg, indicating that this was merely an in-terim order:

We hear that some concessions have been made both to a respect for antiquity and to the infirmity of the present age; such, for instance, as the vestments, commonly used in the sacrament of the Eucharist, and the use of candles; so also in regard to the commemoration of the dead and the use of chrism; for we know not to what extent or in what sort it prevails. They . . . affirm that there is no superstition in these things, and *that they are only to be retained for a time*, lest the people, not having yet learned Christ, should be deterred by too extensive innovations from embracing his religion, and rather that they may be won over.[5]

Whether it was part of Cranmer's plan all along or due to pressure from more extreme Protestant politicians and immigrant churchmen, on All Saints' Day, 1552, a second *Book of Common Prayer* with a new Act of Uniformity replaced that of 1549.[6]

For a good many people, the 1549 *Book of Common Prayer* may have seemed nothing more than the old services rendered into English; indeed, with regard to services such as confirmation and the churching of women after childbirth, they were more or less just that. Although the book made no provision for items mentioned in Cranmer's homily of 1547, such as palm crosses and the Easter new fire, it did retain a certain amount of ceremonial and vesture, which reinforced such a view. Nonetheless, there were certain important changes of a devotional and doctrinal nature. First, all services were in the English language. Next, as an extension of Cranmer's earlier experimentation with the divine office, only two daily services were provided, matins, or morning prayer, and evensong, or evening prayer. The former used versicles and responses and canticles from the old Catholic matins, lauds, and prime; and the latter drew on vespers and compline. The service of the holy communion, commonly called the mass, suppressed the old private preparation of the priest, retaining only what came to be known as the Collect for Purity, which, with the Lord's prayer, opened the service. Collects for the King were provided, but gone were the gradual, sequence, alleluia, and tract. Retained were the collect of the day (but with new compositions), epistle, and gospel. All mention of sacrifice associated with the mass was omitted, and the old "little canon," or offertory prayers of the Roman mass, which had anticipated the offering of the canon of the mass, were removed and replaced by scriptural sentences referring to the giving of alms. Indeed, the concept of sacrifice was limited in understanding to the sacrifice of Calvary then, and the offering of the worshipers' alms, souls, and bodies, and prayers and praises now. The old Roman canon was replaced by a new English composition, with Sursum corda, preface and proper preface, and Sanctus with Benedictus, followed by a lengthy intercession for the Church, godly rulers, and the faithful, including the departed. The prayer resumed with an emphasis on the single offering of Christ on the cross, and included a petition for consecrating the elements: "And with thy holy spirite and worde, vouchsafe to bl+esse and sanc+tifie these thy gyftes, and creatures of bread and wyne, that they maie be unto us the bodye and bloude of thy moste derely belouved sonne Jesus Christe."

Some commentators, aware that Cranmer had access to the Eastern liturgies of Saint Basil and Saint John Chrysostom (and that Henry VIII had a copy of the Liturgy of Saint James), have suggested that here he "restored" an epiclesis to the eucharistic prayer. Nowhere else, however, did Cranmer draw on the Eastern rites (the collect of Saint John Chrysostom in morning prayer was from a Latin translation), and far better parallels can be adduced in medieval pontifical blessings, as well as in the teaching of Peter Martyr Vermigli, who lodged with Cranmer while the 1549 book was being compiled.[7] The recital of the words of institution followed, but a rubric forbade any elevation of the elements. Whereas the old canon had then offered the "bread of eternal life and the cup of everlasting salvation," the 1549 prayer celebrated and made "the memoryall whyche thy sonne hath wylled us to make," once again removing any idea of the sacrifice of the mass. What is offered is our souls and bodies as a reasonable, holy, and lively sacrifice. After the Lord's prayer and the Peace, parts of the 1548 communion devotion appeared—exhortation to confession, confession, absolution, "comfortable words," and the prayer "We do not presume." Communion followed, and the "clerks" could sing the Agnus Dei. Sentences of scripture, a prayer of thanksgiving, and the blessing concluded the rite. Although much of it was consistent with the old mass, the canon had been skillfully transposed into a more Protestant key.

In the service of baptism one finds simplification. The exorcism of salt, the *ephphathata*, signing of the hand, anointing of the breast, and the giving of the candle were all discarded, together with a number of prayers. A prayer from Luther—the "Flood Prayer"—was introduced into the English rite, and the gospel reading was taken from Mark 10 (Jesus' blessing of the children). The marriage rite included a new exhortation, but otherwise it followed the Sarum rite fairly closely, except that various prayers associated with the nuptial mass were now brought forward to a place before the mass. Although a mass could follow, no propers were provided; however, since in the old Sarum rite, it would have been a votive mass of the Trinity, it was possibly assumed that the propers provided for Trinity Sunday would be used. The lengthy medieval funeral rite was considerably shortened, although the old prayer for the departed was retained.

A number of methods were employed in formulating these new services. Cranmer used the old Sarum Latin—the use of Salisbury—as a base. He drew on Lutheran and contemporary Catholic liturgical reform, and incorporated phraseology from existing English-language devotions; for example, the primers provided much of the language for morning and evening prayer. Cranmer also used theological language already found in a book of doctrine of 1543, the King's Book, which was a revised version of the Bishops' Book.[8] Yet, as good a liturgist and theologian as Cranmer may have been, he was not a musician, and music was left in an ambiguous situation. Since the Latin rites were outlawed, the music and settings became obsolete. Furthermore, the rubrics of the *Book of Common Prayer* were vague, and it was not clear to musicians how much of the service should be sung, and to what music, and in what manner. In 1544 Cranmer had expressed his private view that there should be a single note to a syllable, and this was certainly endorsed in the injunctions for York Minster issued by Archbishop Holgate:

The choir of Salisbury Cathedral. Thomas Cranmer drew heavily upon the liturgy used at Salisbury—the Sarum rite—for his *Book of Common Prayer*. LONDON STEREOSCOPIC COMPANY, 1950/HULTON ARCHIVE/GETTY IMAGES

> *Also*, we will and command that there be none other note sung or used in the said church at any service there to be had, saving square note plain, so that every syllable may be

plainly and distinctly pronounced, and without any reports or repeatings which may induce any obscureness to the hearers.[9]

Some difficulties were resolved by the appearance of John Merbecke's *The booke of Common praier noted* in 1550. Peter Le Huray comments:

> In his *booke of Common praier noted* he supplied simple plainsong-style music for all sections of morning, communion and evening prayer, and for some of the more important occasional offices as well. His book probably represents the kind of solution that would have been acceptable to radical though not extreme churchmen at that time.[10]

It would seem that some parishes and some circles were eager for reform. Experiments with the liturgy in English seem to have been taking place in the Chapels Royal, and at Saint Paul's Cathedral, where the dean, William May, was an advocate of Protestant reform. Charles Wriothesley recorded in his "Chronicle" of 1549 that

> at this session of Perliamente one uniforme booke was sett fourth of one sort of service with the ministration of the holie communion and other sacramentes to be used in this realme of Englande and other the Kinges dominions whatsoever. To be observed after the feast of Pentecost next coming, as by an Act of Perliament against the transgressors of the same doeth appeare. Howbeit Poules quire, with divers parishes in London and other places in England, begane the use after the said booke in the beginning of Lent, and putt downe the private masses as by the acte is ordayned.[11]

And two weeks after the book had come into force, Wriothesley recorded that Cranmer came to Saint Paul's Cathedral to celebrate communion, and he vested in a cope and alb, rather than the traditional vestments.[12] At Easter in 1551, Bishop Nicholas Ridley

> altered the Lordes table that stoode where the high aulter was, and he removed the table beneth the steepps into the middes of the upper quire in Poules, and sett the endes east and west, the priest standing in the middest at the communion on the south side of the bord, and after the creed song he caused the vaile to be drawen, that no person shoulde see but those that receaved, and he closed the iron grates of the quire on the north and sowth side with bricke and plaister, that non might remaine in at the quire.[13]

But if some wished to give these rites an obvious Protestant interpretation, Bishop Stephen Gardiner, confined to the Tower of London, pronounced the communion rite "not distant from the catholic faith."[14] It seems clear that many parish priests did indeed carry on celebrating the rites, as far as possible, in the manner in which the Latin services had been. John Hooper, whose objections to episcopal vesture landed him in prison, complained in 1549 to Heinrich Bullinger of Zürich:

> The public celebration of the Lord's supper is very far from the order and institution of our Lord. Although it is administered in both kinds, yet in some places the supper is celebrated three times a day.... They still retain their vestments and the candles before the altars; in the churches they always chant the *hours* and other hymns relating to the Lord's supper, but in our language. And that popery may not be lost, the mass-priests, although they are compelled to discontinue the use of the Latin language, yet most carefully observe the same tone and manner of chanting to which they were heretofore accustomed in the papacy.[15]

But such diversity was to change in 1552, with the issue of a new *Book of Common Prayer*, to take effect on All Saints' Day.

The 1552 book moved public worship in an unmistakably Protestant direction. Now the traditional eucharistic vestments retained in 1549 were to be discarded, and in their place surplice, tippet, and academic hood were to be worn for all services. The old altar with its candles was to be removed, and a wooden table set in its place. Wriothesley commented:

> This day all copes and vestments were put downe through all England. . . . After the feast of All Saintes, the upper quire in St. Pawles Church, in London, where the high aulter stoode, was broken downe and all the quire thereabout, and the table of the communion was set in the lower quire where the preistes singe.[16]

The services themselves were further reformed. The services for morning and evening prayer were now prefaced by sentences of scripture, an exhortation to repentance, confession, and a declaration that God forgives those who repent. The communion service was remodeled in such a way that neither Bishop Gardiner nor anyone else would be able to pronounce it as "not distant from the catholic faith." The 1549 canon was rearranged, with the intercessory part now placed before the offertory sentences; the devotional prayer "We do not presume" was shorn of the reference to the body and blood of Christ "in these holy mysteries," and now placed immediately after the Sanctus, from which the Benedictus had been removed. The petition for consecration by Spirit and Word was removed, and replaced by a more "receptionist" petition. The Agnus Dei disappeared, along with the Peace, and communion followed immediately after the recital of the words of institution. The words of administration, "Take and eat this in remembrance that Christ died for thee, and feed on him in thy heart by faith with thanksgiving," and "Drink this in remembrance that Christ's blood was shed for thee, and be thankful," contained no reference to the elements of bread and wine being in any way the body and blood of Christ. What had been the final part of the 1549 canon now came after the communion as an alternative thanksgiving. The Gloria in excelsis was removed from the beginning of the service to the conclusion, just before the blessing. What Cranmer had done was to remove any intercession from the vicinity of the taking and eating the elements, and he had removed anything that suggested some link between the elements and Christ's body and blood. Furthermore, only the Sanctus and Gloria in excelsis remained of the sung propers, rendering most of Merbecke's setting useless. The so-called Black Rubric was added, which explained that, although communicants were to kneel for reception of the elements, this was not to be interpreted as adoration of any physical presence of Christ in the bread and wine.

In baptism the whole service now took place at the font. Exorcism, unction, and the chrisom robe were discarded, and there was no blessing of the water. The marriage rite was further simplified, the tokens of espousal of 1549 now disappearing. In the funeral rite any hint of prayer for the departed person was removed.

How popular these new services were is difficult to judge. The argument of revisionist scholars such as Christopher Haigh and Eamon Duffy that the English Reformation and liturgical reform were imposed by a few in power on a reluctant majority has been challenged by Diarmaid MacCulloch. Much depended on geography, and MacCulloch has shown that in many southern areas the Reformation had popular support. The liturgical reforms of 1552, however, were short lived. Edward VI died on 6 July 1553, the Protestant council collapsed, and Mary Tudor, a staunch Catholic, was proclaimed queen. Wriothesley recorded:

> Thursdaye, the 24 of August and St. Bartholomews daye, the olde service in the Lattin tongue with the masse was begun and sunge in Powles in the Shrowdes, now St. Faythes parishe. And lykewise it was begun in 4 or 5 other parishes within the Cittie of London, not by commaundement but of the peoples devotion.[17]

Religious Settlement, Unofficial Reforms, and Separatist Worship, 1559–1603

The reign of Mary was spent attempting to undo the Reformation and to restore religious practices in England to what they had been in 1536. Mary was not a popular monarch. Her Spanish marriage was regarded by many with suspicion, and the martyrdom of ordinary laity alongside the leading Protestant bishops did not endear her to her subjects. Although many were happy to see altars, rood screens, and vestments restored, bearing the cost of these revisions was another matter. But with Mary's death in 1558, the succession of her half-sister Elizabeth to the throne brought an end to the papal restoration. Again Wriothesley was to record: "The 14 of May, beinge Whitsonday, the service began in English in divers parishes in London, after the last booke of service of Common Prayer used in the tyme of King Edward the VI."[18]

Once more Saint Paul's Cathedral was a precursor, with the newly restored altar and rood screen being taken down on 12 August. In that same month many London churches had their roods, images, and vestments confiscated and burnt.[19] Whatever religious settlement Elizabeth might have liked, she had to limit herself to the restoration of the 1552 *Book of Common Prayer*, with minor alterations, and the issue of injunctions that distinguished between the usage of cathedrals and the royal chapels, on the one hand, and parish worship, on the other. Apart from adding the name of the monarch in the collects, the changes in the 1559 *Book of Common Prayer* were three.

In the first place, a rubric was inserted before morning prayer, allowing chancels and vesture to accord with what was prescribed in the second year of Edward VI. Technically this allowed eucharistic vestments as well as altars and candles, but the injunctions insisted that eucharistic vestments must be surrendered and were not to be used, and most parishes removed the stone altars and replaced them with a wooden table. The table stood in the old altar position when not in use, but when used for a communion service, it was moved into the chancel and usually oriented east-west, with communicants kneeling around the table. Furthermore, most clergy wore only a surplice for services, although, as will be noted, a good many wore only a black gown.

The second change was that the 1549 words of administration in communion were restored and prefixed to those of 1552. This provided an indication that perhaps the elements were in some sense the body and blood of Christ.

Thirdly, the rubric added in 1552 explaining that kneeling for reception of communion was for reverence, but did not signify any real or essential presence in the elements themselves, was removed. In Elizabeth's Royal Chapel there was a table in altar position with candles. The injunctions required copes to be worn in cathedrals. Cathedrals and Chapels Royal retained choirs that developed their own repertoire for singing the new services. Most parish churches, however, simply used metrical psalmody. The result was a varied performance of the prescribed rites, as attested in a manuscript dated 14 February 1564, transcribed by John Strype, which explained as follows:

> Some say the service and prayers in the chancel; others in the body of the church. Some say the same in a seat made in the church; some in the pulpit, with their faces to the people. Some keep precisely the order of the book; others intermeddle Psalms in metre. Some say with a surplice; others without a surplice. The table standeth in the body of the church in some places; in others it standeth in the chancel.
>
> Some with surplice and cap; some with surplice alone, others none. Some with chalice; some with a Communion cup; others with a common cup. Some with unleavened bread, and some with leavened.

> Some receive kneeling, others standing, others sitting.
>   Some with a square cap; some with a round cap; some with a button cap; some with a
> hat; Some in scholar's clothes, some in others.[20]

Although for Catholics the Church of England was a Protestant church, for some English Protestants it was still too close to the Roman Church for comfort. It retained the Roman Catholic structure of ministry—bishop, priest, and deacon—and had canons and archdeacons. It still retained most of the medieval canon law. Although it had shed eucharistic vestments, it still shared the surplice with Roman clergy. Furthermore, the *Book of Common Prayer* looked very different from continental Reformed service books, retaining versicles and responses, sung canticles, the sign of the cross in baptism, confirmation by bishops, and the ring in marriage—all of which most Reformed churches had jettisoned. Those who regarded these things as a disgraceful hand-me-down from popery wished for further reforms. Already in 1550 an English translation of John Calvin's liturgy had been made, in a format that suggested it was intended for use, albeit unofficially. Furthermore, during Mary's reign, a good number of English churchfolk had sought refuge on the continent, particularly at Frankfurt, Strasbourg, Zürich, and Geneva. The English congregation that settled in Frankfurt felt compelled to carry out emendations to the 1552 Prayer Book to bring it more into conformity with the Reformed worship of the city. This is known as the *Liturgy of Compromise* (1555). Among other things, it abandoned the surplice and omitted versicles and responses. Those who had journeyed on to Geneva, such as William Whittingham, later the dean of Durham, helped author the *Genevan Form of Prayers*, which combined some of Cranmer's material with Calvin's rite, and the 1550 Berwick-on-Tweed rite that John Knox had compiled. The *Genevan Form of Prayers* had the following structure for the Sunday morning service:

> A Confession of sins, from Daniel 9,
>   or, Another Confession "for all states and times"
> Psalm
> Prayer of illumination
> (Lection)
> Sermon
> A Prayer for the whole State of Christ's Church
> Lord's prayer
> Creed
> Psalm
> Aaronic Blessing

The Lord's supper, when it was celebrated, followed the creed and Psalm of the morning service and consisted of the following:

> Institution Narrative
> Exhortation with excommunication of the unworthy
> Eucharistic Prayer
> Fraction and Delivery; reading scripture during delivery
> Thanksgiving
> Psalm 103 or a similar psalm
> Blessing (from the Morning Service)

This was rather different from the *Book of Common Prayer;* gone were versicles and responses as well as familiar songs and canticles such as the Gloria in excelsis, Sanctus, Magnificat, and Nunc dimittis.

The *Genevan Form of Prayers* was to be adopted by the Church of Scotland in 1564; however, English clergy and laity who returned to England when Elizabeth came to the throne hoped that a Prayer Book like the *Liturgy of Compromise* or the *Genevan Form of Prayers* would be introduced into the English church. Some of the leading Marian exiles immediately refused to wear the restored surplice, and this vestarian nonconformity came to be a recurring feature in the Elizabethan and Jacobean church.

Those clergy who regarded the Church of England and its worship as being in need of further reform tended to have a strict regard for scriptural authority. It was not sufficient for something to be an adiaphoron, a matter of indifference. If a thing was adiaphoron, then it should not be enforced. Only if something was mandated in scripture was it absolutely necessary. Thus, bread and wine were essential to the holy communion. But no vesture is prescribed in scripture; hence, the surplice should not be enforced. The concerns of these ministers (called "puritan" in the older histories but referred to in much later scholarship as "the godly") were articulated in the *Admonition to the Parliament*, 1572. Contrasting practice at that time to what they believed to have been the case in the Early Church, the authors, John Field and Thomas Wilcox, wrote:

> They ministred the Sacrament plainely. We pompously, with singing, pypyng, surplesse and cope wearyng. They simply as they receeved it from the Lorde. We, sinfullye, mixed with mannes inventions and devises. And as for Baptisme, it was enough with them, if they had water, and the partie to be baptised faith, and the minister to preach the word and minister the sacraments.
>
> Nowe, we must have surplesses devised by Pope Adrian, interrogatories ministred to the infant, godfathers and godmothers brought in by Higinus, holy fonts invented by Pope Pius, crossing and suche like peces of poperie, which the church of God in the Apostles times never knew (and therfore not to be used), nay (which we are sure of), were and are mannes devises, broght in long after the puritie of the primative church. . . .
>
> We speake not of ringing when Mattens is don and other abuses incident. Bicause we shalbe answered, that by the boke they are not maintained; only we desire to have a booke to reforme it. As for organes and curious singing, thoughe they be proper to popishe dennes, I meane to Cathedrall churches, yet some others also must have them. The queenes chappell, and these churches must be paternes and presidents to the people, of all superstitions.[21]

Other objections included the use of the sign of the cross in the rite of baptism and the use of a ring in the marriage ceremony. Many of these clergy made their own emendations and reforms to ceremonies and liturgies. Some, like Richard Greenham of Dry Drayton, Cambridgeshire, had permission from the bishop to dispense with the surplice, the cross in baptism, and the ring in marriage.[22] Others did so with the connivance of their congregation; still others were less lucky, or more outspoken—such as Arthur Hildersham—and were prosecuted in the church courts and suspended. As far as textual reform is concerned, the following is found:

1. Ad hoc emendations. The minister simply omitted certain parts, such as versicles and responses. John Elliston admitted that he left out the epistle and gospel from the ante-communion (the first part of the communion service), and it was reputed that Richard Bowler, rector of Leverington, Ely, "addeth and diminisheth at his pleasure in the use of the book."[23] Eusibius Paget admitted to the Court of High Commission that he omitted parts of the liturgy that offended his conscience.[24]

2. Emended editions of the *Book of Common Prayer*. Although Patrick Collinson was of the opinion that these were simply versions of the Prayer Book for domestic use, A. E. Peaston argued convincingly that these were "puritan" editions, with minor, but significant changes, which could go undetected. The rubrics and services that were omitted were all ones to which the godly objected.[25]

3. Use of the *Genevan Form of Prayers*. Already in 1567 and 1568 there were semiprivate congregations in London using the *Genevan Form of Prayers*. It is hard to gauge how widespread its use was in England, but in 1583 Stephen Beamund of Easthorpe was brought before the assizes because he neither wore a surplice nor used the *Book of Common Prayer*, but celebrated other services—which probably referred to this rite. In 1584 and again in 1587, attempts were made to introduce bills into Parliament to replace the *Book of Common Prayer* with the editions of the *Genevan Form of Prayers*.

4. In 1572 there had been an attempt to allow those "of tender conscience," who had scruples about some of the ceremonies of the *Book of Common Prayer*, to use the liturgies of the so-called Stranger Churches. These were the French, Dutch, and Italian congregations in London and in other British towns—Canterbury, Norwich, and Glastonbury. During Edward VI's reign, these churches had been placed under the supervision of John à Lasco and were allowed to use their own Reformed rites. Under Elizabeth they were placed under the titular authority of the bishop of London, but continued the right to use their own liturgies—the *Forma ac Ratio* by John à Lasco, its adaptation by Marten Micron, and Valerand Poullain's version of Calvin's Strasbourg liturgy. Collinson aptly comments that "they played the part of a Trojan horse, bringing Reformed worship and discipline fully armed into the midst of the Anglican camp."[26]

The authors and promoters of these liturgies for the most part remained within the Church of England, even though the more extreme and persistent were deprived of their livings. Their aim was to further reform the national church. By the 1580s, however, some of the more ardent gave up all hopes of further reform, and concluded that the Church of England was too flawed to be regarded as a true church. But they also believed that Reformed churches were far from perfect. These "Separatists," though not Congregationalists, certainly operated with a congregational polity, and were in many ways precursors of the later Independents, or Congregationalists. These groups believed that public prayer was a gift of the Holy Spirit and part of ministerial charisma, and they eschewed all printed liturgies, "for thuse of set or stynted praier (as they terme it), this they teach that all stynted praiers and redd service is but babling in the Lorde's sight."[27]

Two of the most prominent of these groups were the Brownists and the Barrowists. Robert Browne graduated from Cambridge in 1572 and was influenced by the writings of Thomas Cartwright, which called for further reformation in the English church. By the 1580s he had set up his own church, which he later removed to the Netherlands. According to *The Brownists Synagogue*, 1641, the normal worship of this congregation consisted of prayer, lasting half an hour, and including a petition that God would be pleased to turn the hearts of those who had come to laugh and scoff, and a sermon lasting an hour, followed by comments. Browne himself described the service as including prayer, thanksgiving, reading of scripture, exhortation, and edifying.[28] For the communion, he advises:

> The preacher must take breade and blesse and geve thankes, and then must he breake it and pronounce it to be the body of Christ, which was broken for them, that by fayth they might feede theron spirituallie & growe into one spiritual bodie of Christ, and so he eating thereof himselfe, must bidd them take and eate it among them, & feede on Christ in their consciences.

Likewise also must he take the cuppe and blesse and geve thankes, and so pronounce it to be the bloud of Christ in the newe Testament, which was shedd for remission of sinnes, that by fayth we might drinke it spirituallie, and so be nourished in one spirituall bodie of Christ, all sinne being clensed away, and then he drinking thereof himselfe must bydd them drinke thereof likewise and divide it among them, and feede on Christe in their consciences.[29]

Browne later returned to the Church of England, whereas the leaders of the Barrowists—Henry Barrow, John Penry, and John Greenwood—preferred martyrdom to conformity, and were executed for sedition. A little information about their worship can be gleaned from depositions made before the magistrates. Meetings took place in private houses and secluded spots. From a certain Clement Gamble one learns that in summer they met in fields outside London and sat down for exposition of the Bible. In winter they met in a house for prayer and exposition. After a meal they took up a collection to pay the expenses, and any that remained was taken to their members who were in prison. One John Dove described their worship: "In there praier one speketh and the rest doe grone, or sob, or sigh, as if they wold wringe out teares, but saie not after hime that praieth, there praier is extemporall."[30] From the deposition of Daniel Bucke, at the Barrowist church led by Francis Johnson in Kampen and Norden in the Netherlands, comes the following:

They had neither god fathers nor godmothers, and he tooke water and washed the faces of them that were baptised: the Children that were there baptised were the Children of Mr Studley Mr Lee with others beinge of severall yeres of age, sayinge onely in th'administracion of this sacrament I doe Baptise thee in the name of the father of the sonne and of the holy gost withoute usinge any other cerimony therin as is now usually observed according to the booke of Common praier.[31]

Of the communion, Bucke said:

Fyve whight loves or more were sett uppon the table and that the pastor did breake the bread and then delivered yt unto some of them, and the deacons delivered to the rest, some of the said congregacion sittinge and some standinge aboute the table and that the pastor delivered the cupp unto one and he to an other, and soe from one to another till they had all dronken usinge the words at the deliverye therof according as it is sett downe in the eleventh of the Corinthes the xxiiiith verse.[32]

And of marriage, Bucke commented that "marriage in a howse without a mynister by Consent of the parties and frends is sufficient."[33]

On the whole, Separatism was not a large movement in Elizabeth's reign, though the clandestine nature of their meetings suggests that it may have been more widespread than has been recorded for posterity. What they bequeathed was a radical view of worship. No set forms were used, but prayer "in the Spirit." Certain ordinances, such as marriage, but possibly funerals too, were not regarded as belonging to Christian worship at all.

The Jacobean and Caroline Church, 1603–1640

At the death of Elizabeth I in 1603, the throne passed to James VI of Scotland, linking the fortunes of two nations and two churches. Since Scotland was by this time Presbyterian in church government, and used John Knox's *Genevan Form of Prayers* under the title the *Book of Common Order*, many of the "godly" in England hoped that James would conform the Church of England to the pattern and standards of Scotland. On his route from Edinburgh to London, James was presented with the Millenary Petition (supposedly signed by a thousand godly clergy) asking for liturgical and organizational changes. The petitioners asked the following:

> 1. In the church service: that the cross in baptism, interrogatories ministered to infants, confirmations, as superfluous, may be taken away: baptism not to be ministered by women, and so explained: the cap and surplice not urged: that examination may go before the communion: that it be ministered with a sermon: that divers terms of priests and absolution and some other used, with the ring in marriage, and other such like in the book, may be corrected: the longsomeness of service abridged: church songs and music moderated to better edification: that the Lord's day be not profaned: the rest upon holydays not so strictly urged; that there may be an uniformity of doctrine prescribed: no popish opinion to be any more taught or defended: no ministers charged to teach their people to bow at the name of Jesus: that the canonical scriptures only be read in the church.[34]

James' response was to call a conference at Hampton Court, where a small number of representatives of the "godly" met with a larger number of bishops and deans who debated possible reforms. The outcome was the 1604 *Book of Common Prayer*, which in fact conceded little to the petitioners. The main concession was a rubric forbidding baptism by midwives and laypeople, and the catechism was expanded to include teaching on the sacraments. As a result, other pamphlets were written criticizing the enacted liturgy, attacking, among other things, the concept of baptismal regeneration and kneeling for reception of communion.

Although James warmed to the idea of some conformity between the churches in England and Scotland, his intention was to bring the Church of Scotland into greater conformity with that of England, which was unfortunate for the "godly." Thus, no further official changes were allowed in England, and James attempted to enforce conformity to the rubrics, particularly over vesture. In practice, it seems that it was generally sufficient for a minister to promise to consider the matter and to promise occasional conformity.

In Scotland James reintroduced bishops, and through the Five Articles of Perth, 1618, attempted to impose certain liturgical observances on the whole of the Scottish Church. Furthermore, between 1616 and 1619, a new liturgy was drafted for Scotland. Three drafts have survived. The first was concerned just with the Sunday morning service. The two later drafts provided for other occasions, including the sacraments, and these were the work of Bishop William Cowper. The Five Articles alone, however, met with considerable opposition and hostility, and so plans for the new liturgy were shelved.[35]

James's policy toward the English church for the major part of his reign was to balance power so as to reflect the prevailing "Calvinist consensus." Most English clerics followed broadly the prevailing Reformed theology, which was a synthesis of teachings of Calvin, Beza, Bullinger, Vermigli, Musculus, Zanchius and Ursinus, to name but a few. Most clerics viewed the Church of England as Reformed, though having its own distinct polity. Among the staunch conformists of the church, however, were those who viewed the Church of England as being quite distinct from the Reformed churches as well as the Roman Church. From among the ranks of the strict conformists there emerged a group that felt too much had been jettisoned by the Reformation, and that some things which were "indifferent" might conveniently be recovered. These divines tended to stress order and decency in worship, and place sacraments above preaching. They also saw the episcopal polity of the English Church not as a popish leftover but as a divine virtue.

A leading figure in this minority group was Lancelot Andrewes, one of James's favorite preachers. Andrewes, who was to become bishop of Winchester, had a high regard for the patristic era and a knowledge of the Eastern liturgies. In his "Notes" on the *Book of Common Prayer*, he gave meticulous instructions such as washing the hands immediately before what he called the "Prayer of Consecration" (not so entitled in England until 1662), on the use of wafer bread, and on wine in a barrel on a cradle with four feet, which are offered in the name of the whole congregation upon the altar.[36] The notes also reveal that Andrewes supplemented the Prayer Book text, demonstrating that the "nonconformity" of some of the "godly" was not the only type of nonconformity!

A description of the furnishings of Andrewes's Chapel at Winchester House in London has survived. The description includes a plan of the chapel, which included an "altar-wise" communion table, on a dais at the east end, with communion rail, and two candlesticks with tapers on the altar. The chalice had engravings, including a depiction of Christ with a lost sheep on his shoulders. The chapel had wall hangings depicting Old Testament events, and was equipped with a thurible (censer).[37]

As dean of the Chapel Royal and bishop of Winchester, Andrewes had some influence, and among his protégés was Richard Neile, later to be the bishop of Durham and then the archbishop of York. Neile, when bishop of Durham, collected together a group of his own protégés, known as the Durham House group. This group was intent on restoring some of the ceremonial and grandeur of worship, which they felt had been lost at the Reformation, including an altar decently furnished and railed in, the use of copes, and good music. Among the group were John Cosin and William Laud, the future archbishop of Canterbury. The ethos and piety of this group, often known as "Laudianism," was expressed in a sermon by John Cosin at the consecration of Francis White as bishop of Carlisle:

> Now to make men observe and do what the Church teaches them is, or should be, in the Bishop's hands. We suffer scandal from them of the Church of Rome in many things, in nothing more than this, that we are sent to preach sermons to the people, as men that had some pretty commodities to sell them which, if they liked, they might buy or use; if not, they might let them alone; that we talk of devotion but live like the careless; that we have a service, but no servants at it; that we have churches, but keep them not like the houses of God; that we have sacraments, but few to frequent them; Confession, but few to practise it; finally, that we have all religious duties (for they cannot deny it), but seldom observed; all good laws and canons of the Church, but few or none kept; the people are made to do nothing; the old discipline is neglected, and men do what they list. It should be otherwise, and our Church intends it otherwise.[38]

Quite a number of this group gained preferment in the later years of James's reign, and further preferment under his son, Charles I, when Laud had become archbishop of Canterbury. Moves toward a more "decent and orderly" worship can be seen at Durham Cathedral, where Neile had been bishop, and Cosin and some others of the group prebendaries. Ceremonial was introduced, including bowing toward the altar, copes were worn more frequently, and Dean Hunt installed a stone altar. Sackbuts and cornets were used with the organ to accompany the choir. Cosin was also invited to draw up a book of private devotions, modeled on the old primers, which had long fallen into desuetude and replaced by a different lay spirituality.[39] Neile, followed by Bishop Wren, and eventually Laud, began insisting that the communion table should be placed where the old altar had stood, and be railed in so that communicants could kneel in an orderly fashion around the table. According to Laud's first biographer, by 1635,

> many things had been done at *Cambridge* . . . as beautifying their Chappels, furnishing them with Organs, advancing the Communion Table to the place of the Altar, adorning it with Plate and other Utensils for the Holy sacrament, defending it with a decent Rail from all prophanations, and using lowly Reverence and Adorations, both in their coming to those Chappels, and their going out.[40]

Furthermore, this refurbishing of churches was accompanied by an aggressive attempt to impose conformity and to punish nonconformity. The result was twofold. First, this type of churchmanship became more and more despised by the "godly"; and second, the more extreme of the "godly" chose to emigrate rather than use what they deemed to be "popish" ceremonies.

The Emigrant Separatism and the Rise of Independency

A number of the more extreme "godly" ministers found some relief and freedom in the service of the English Merchant Adventurers, who had a monopoly on trade with the Low Countries, and who had their own chaplains. Scottish regiments in the Low Countries also had their own chaplains. Some of the Separatists, as in the case of the Barrowists, found refuge in Holland. Stephen Goffe, a "Laudian" chaplain, reported the following liturgical uses in 1633:

> It is to be observed that of those Engl: Minister which use not the Englishe forme:
>
> 1. Some use the Dutch translate, as Mr. Paine. but yet that mended much left out, and some things added, as may appear by Mr. Paines booke.
> 2. Some use none at all as Mr. Forbes. but every time they administer the sacraments a new. they doe not stand to one of their owne.
> 3. Some use another English forme putt out at Midleborough 1586. This Mr. Goodyer saith he useth at Leyden. and Mr. Peters saied to me that was the forme he found in his consistory. But whether he use it or no I cannot tell, I beleive he goes the Forbesian way.
> 4. Some use our English forme in the sacraments but mangle them Leaving out and putting in whole sentences.[41]

Thus, some English ministers in Holland used the Dutch Reformed rite, the *Genevan Form of Prayers*, or even their own extempore forms.

For Separatist groups, extempore prayer was the rule, with much emphasis on preaching and exposition of scripture. John Smyth, one of the first English Baptists, who gathered a believers' baptism church at Amsterdam, described the manner of service as follows:

> The order of the worshippe and government of oure church is 1. we begynne with a prayer, after reade some one or two chapters of the bible, gyve the sence thereof, and confer upon the same, that done we lay aside oure bookes, and after a solemne prayer made by the 1. speaker, he propoundeth some text out of the Scripture, and propheciett owt of the same, by the space of one hower, or three Quarters of an hower. After him standeth up a 2. speaker and propheciett owt of the said text the like time and space, some tyme more some tyme lesse. After him the 3. the 4. the 5.&c as the tyme will geve leave, Then the 1. speaker concludeth with prayer as he began with prayer, with an exhortation to contribute to the poore, wch collection being made is also concluded with

prayer. This morning exercise begynes at eight of the clocke and continueth unto twelve of the clocke the like unto 5. or 6. of the Clocke. last of all the execution of the government of the church is handled.[42]

The following account of worship at this Amsterdam congregation was given by Richard Clayton in 1612:

1. Prayer and giving of thanks by the pastor or teacher.
2. The Scriptures are read, two or three chapters, as time serves, with a brief explanation of their meaning.
3. The pastor or teacher then takes some passage of Scripture, and expounds and enforces it.
4. The sacraments are administered.
5. Some of the Psalms of David are sung by the whole congregation, both before and after the exercise of the Word.
6. Collection is then made, as each one is able, for the support of the officers and the poor.[43]

Another Baptist, John Robinson, gave similar advice on worship for his Leiden congregation, and this form was transported by the Plymouth Separatists to America.

At a later date John Cotton left his parish in Boston Lincolnshire in 1633 to escape the Laudian persecution, and with others he established Independent churches in New England. Cotton insisted that he was not a Separatist and was not separating from the Church of England. Rather, he held that the churches of New England were examples of what the English church should be. A form of worship was developed there, however, which was akin to that of the Plymouth Separatists. Indeed, Doug Adams has established the direct link, in a letter of Edward Winslow in 1646:

> Some of the chiefs of them advised with us (coming over to be freed from the burden-some ceremonies they imposed in England) how they should do to fall upon a right platform of worship, and desired to that end since God had honored us to lay the foundation of a Commonweale, and to settle a Church in it, to show them whereupon our practice was grounded.
>
> We accordingly showed them the primitive practice for our warrant, taken out of the Acts of the Apostles and the Epistles . . . together with the commandments of Christ, and for every particular we did from the book of God. They set not the Church at Plymouth before them for example, but the Primitive Churches were and are their and our mutual patterns and examples, which are only worthy to be followed.[44]

Adams comments:

> When one examines worship practices and their justifications, one sees that the Bay Colony reliance on Robinson's Leyden [Leiden] and Plymouth church models was substantial. In a Separatist Leyden church and not in Puritan English churches were the roots of the distinctive elements in early American worship (strong lay participation in shaping prayer, prophesying through exhortation and question, and admitting and casting out members during the worship).[45]

John Cotton gave the following description of Independent, or Congregationalist, worship in New England:

> First then when wee come together in the Church, according to the Apostles directions, 1 *Tim* 2:1, wee make prayers and intercessions and thanksgivings for our selves and for all men, not in any *prescribed* forme of prayer, or *studied Liturgie*, but in such manner, as the Spirit of grace and of prayer (who teacheth all the people of God, what and how to

pray, *Rom* 8:26, 27) helpeth our infirmities, wee having respect therein to the necessities of the people, the estate of the times, and the worke of Christ in our hands.

After prayer, either the *Pastor* or *Teacher*, readeth a Chapter in the Bible, and *expoundeth* it, giving the *sense, to cause the people to understand the reading*, according to Neh.8.8. And in sundry Churches the other (whether *Pastor* or *Teacher*) who *expoundeth* not, he *preacheth* the Word, and in the afternoone the other who *preached* in the morning doth usually (if there be time) *reade* and *preach*, and he that *expounded* in the morning *preacheth* after him.

Before Sermon, and many times after, wee sing a Psalme, and because the former translation of the Psalmes, doth in many things vary from the originall, and many times paraphraseth rather then translateth; besides divers other defects (which we cover in silence) wee have endeavoured a new translation of the Psalmes into *English meetre*, as neere the originall as wee could expresse it in our *English* tongue, so farre as for the present the Lord hath been pleased to helpe us, and those Psalmes wee sing, both in our publick Churches, and in private.

The seales of the Covenant (to wit, the Sacrament of Baptisme and the Lords Supper) are administred, either by the *Pastor* or by the *Teacher*. . . . Both the Sacraments wee dispense . . . [t]he Lord's Supper to such as neither want *knowledge* nor *grace* to *examine and judge themselves* before the Lord. Such as lie under any offence publickly known, doe first remove the offence, before they present themselves to the Lords Table; according to *Mat.* 5.23, 24. The members of any Church, if any be present, who bring Letters testimoniall with them to our Churches, wee admit them to *the Lords Table* with us. . . . The prayers wee use at the administration of the seales, are not any *set formes* prescribed to us, but conceived by the Minister, according to the present occasion, and the nature of the dutie in hand. . . .

In the time of *solemnization* of the Supper, the Minister having taken, blessed, and broken the bread, and commanded all the people to take and eate it, as the body of Christ broken for them, he taketh it himselfe, and giveth it to all that sit at Table with him, and from the Table it is reached by the *Deacons* to the people sitting in the next seats about them, the Minister sitting in his place at the Table.

After thay have all partaked in the bread, he taketh the cup in like manner, and *giveth thanks anew* (blesseth it), according to the example of Christ in the Evangelist, who describes the institution *Mat.* 26.27, *Mark* 14.23, *Luke* 22.17. All of them in such a way as setteth forth the Elements, not blessed *together*, but either of them *apart*; the bread first by itselfe, and afterwards the wine by itselfe; for what reason the Lord himselfe best knoweth, and wee cannot be ignorant, that a received solemne blessing, expressly performed by himselfe, doth apparently call upon the whole assembly to look againe for a supernaturall and speciall blessing in the same Element also as well as in the former; for which the Lord will be againe sought to doe it for us.[46]

Cotton and his fellow Independents would play a decisive role in the reformulation of worship in England in the 1640s.

Liturgical Changes, 1637–1660

Although in England the Durham House, or Laudian, liturgical ideals were confined to church furnishings and ceremonial, they were to have an explosive effect in Scotland. Charles I continued the policy of his father to conform the Church of Scotland to that of England, although Scottish bishops in James's reign never had the authority that English bishops enjoyed. The Caroline Scottish bishops attempted to increase their status, and showed considerable sympathy for the Durham House ethos. The liturgical revision of 1618–1619 was revived by Bishops Maxwell and Wedderburn and, by orders of Charles, in consultation with Archbishop William Laud. Although

Laud would have preferred that the Scottish church simply use the English book, the Scottish bishops asserted their independence and took the opportunity to write a liturgy drawing on the 1549 Prayer Book. There were certainly Scottish elements— Pasch for Easter, Yule for Christmas, and *presbyter* rather than *priest*; however, the text and rubrics expressed some of the theology and ceremonies espoused by the Laudian school. Thus, in the "Flood Prayer" in baptism, which Cranmer had borrowed from Luther, a petition for sanctifying the water was inserted. A rubric directed the following:

> The holy Table, having at the Communion time a carpet and a fair white linen cloth upon it, with other decent furniture meet for the high mysteries there to be celebrated, shall stand at the uppermost part of the Chancel or Church, where the Presbyter, standing at the north side one end thereof, shall say the Lord's Prayer with the Collect following for due preparation.

A rubric directed the preparation of the bread and wine with these words: "And the Presbyter shall then offer up and place the bread and wine prepared for the sacrament upon the Lord's Table, that it may be ready for that service." The Sursum corda and preface were linked with the prayer containing the words of institution, now called "The Prayer of Consecration," into which was restored a petition for the Word and Holy Spirit, modified from the 1549 book. The words of administration were those of the 1549 book.

There was a carefully orchestrated revolt against the introduction of this 1637 book for Scotland. It was seen partly as an episcopal ploy, and partly as an English work, tainted by popery and Arminianism. Its introduction also, however, coincided with the emergence of a radical party in the Scottish church, represented by Samuel Rutherford and George Gillespie, who—in kindred spirit with the English Separatists and New England Independents—rejected all set forms of worship, including their own *Book of Common Order* by John Knox.[47] The whole protest gathered momentum, resulting in the National Covenant of 1638, the abolition of episcopacy, and the invasion of England by a Scottish army. Events snow-balled, resulting in the calling of the Long Parliament, civil war, the execution of the king, the Commonwealth and Protectorate, and the two nations being theoretically linked through the Solemn League and Covenant. The English Long Parliament of 1640 put the blame for ecclesiastical unrest on the English bishops, and particularly the Laudians. Discussions on the reduction of episcopacy gave way to its abolition, and the Westminster Assembly of Divines was called to work out a Reformed polity and confession of faith for the Church of England.

One result was the issue of Ordinances in 1641 and 1643 for removal of the Laudian furnishings of churches, together with the destruction of many medieval images and glass windows that still pointed to Roman superstition, the defacing of carvings on fonts, and the removal of copes and surplices. William Dowsing was commissioned in 1643 to implement the Ordinances in the English towns of Cambridgeshire and Suffolk, and he recorded his legal iconoclasm in his journal. On 21 December 1643 he recorded that at Peterhouse, Cambridge,

> we pulled down two mighty great angells, with wings, and divers other angells, and the 4 Evangelists, and Peter, with his keies on the chappell door (see Ezek.viii.36, 37 and ix.6; Isa.xxvii.9 and xxx.22) and about a hundred chirubims and angells, and divers superstitious letters in gold.
>
> And at the upper-end of the chancell, these words were written as followeth: *Hic locus est domus Dei, nil aliud, & porta coeli.*[48]

At Sotterley in Suffolk, on 6 April 1644, he recorded:

> There was divers superstitious pictures painted, which they promised to take down; and I gave order to levell the steps; and to break in pieces the rayles, which I have seen done; and to take off a cross on the church.[49]

As far as forms of worship were concerned, the Westminster Assembly was charged with drawing up suitable forms to replace the *Book of Common Prayer*. The discussions on polity, however, were thrown into turmoil by the arrival and participation of a small but vocal group of Independents, who rejected a presbyterian polity as much as they rejected an episcopal polity. Like Cotton, they also objected to set forms of worship. A subcommittee was appointed under the chairmanship of Stephen Marshall, vicar of Finchingfield, Essex, and a prominent "godly" preacher. The subcommittee consisted of Charles Herle, Herbert Palmer, and Thomas Young, with four Scottish commissioners, Robert Baillie, George Gillespie, Samuel Rutherford, and Alexander Henderson, together with the English Independent Thomas Goodwin, who co-opted another Independent, Philip Nye. Of these, Rutherford and Gillespie were against set forms, as were Goodwin and Nye, and Charles Herle often sided with the Independents. In other words, half the subcommittee was against authoring a set form of worship. It is little wonder that the result was *A Directory of Public Worship*, which was completed by 12 November 1644, and, by an Ordinance of 17 April 1645, replaced the *Book of Common Prayer*.

The *Directory*, for use in the Church of England and the Church of Scotland, was a compilation of rubrics for various rites and occasions, with a summary of what the various prayers, confessions, and exhortations might say. This allowed the more Presbyterian-minded ministers to use prayers from the *Genevan Form of Prayers*, and from other sources, as well as using extempore prayer. It allowed Independents to use entirely free prayer, the substance of the *Directory* being merely a guide; and it also allowed moderate episcopalian clergy who remained in active parochial ministry in the Parliamentarian church to recite from memory suitably disguised Prayer Book material.

The *Directory* made provision for Sunday public worship, requiring people to enter in a "grave and seemly manner," but without adoration and bowing. The minister was to pray a prayer expressing the majesty of God and the vileness of the people, and ask for pardon and assistance, particularly to hear scripture. The reading of scripture was given to the "Pastors and Teacher," and they chose the lection and its length. Only canonical scripture was to be read. Then provision was made for a psalm, along with the prayer before the sermon. This prayer again recalled humankind's sinful nature, asked God to hear the people's intercessions and give them comfort and grace through the Holy Spirit, and then petitioned for all sorts and conditions of people and society. A long section entitled "Of the Preaching of the Word" was the work of Stephen Marshall, and advocated what has come to be known as the "Puritan plain-style" of sermon (which was anything but plain in structure) rather than the "metaphysical" style associated with Lancelot Andrewes and John Donne. A prayer of thanksgiving followed the sermon, and the Lord's prayer was recommended. The service concluded with the singing of a psalm and a solemn blessing.

The provision for baptism stressed that its celebration should take place at public worship and that the old fonts were not to be used. Before baptism the minister was to give an instruction on the nature, use, and ends of the sacrament, and then admonish all to repent. He then was to exhort the parents in their duties. After a prayer for the privileges of this ordinance, the child was baptized with the triune formula, without further ceremony. In the celebration of the Lord's supper, after an opening exhortation warning about unworthy eating, and an invitation, the minister was to come to the table, which "being before decently covered, and so conveniently placed, that the Communicants may orderly sit about it, or at it," and then begin "the action with sanctifying and blessing the elements of Bread and Wine set before him." The permission for sitting at the table, or about it, was intended to allow for both the preferred Scottish usage of successive tables of communicants and the Independent practice as outlined by Cotton. Sanctification of the elements was performed by reciting the institution narrative with a prayer of thanksgiving and blessing, which included a petition for God to work his Spirit in the congregation, and so to sanctify the elements. There followed a fraction and giving of the bread and the cup. After a postcommunion word on the grace of God, the minister was to give a solemn thanksgiving, followed by a collection for the poor.

Provision was also given for marriage, visitation of the sick, burial of the dead, public fast days and days of thanksgiving, and a note on psalm singing. The provisions for marriage were brief, with a prayer, an exhortation, and a solemn exchange of vows. Later, however, Parliament also made provision for civil marriage before a justice of the peace. The burial rite was stark and to the point; the dead body was to be interred without ceremony, prayer, reading, or singing.

It is extremely difficult to gauge how far the *Directory* was used. Judith Maltby has shown how much moderate opinion in England was quite content with the *Book of Common Prayer*, even if not with its Laudian choreography.[50] The researches of Paul Seaver, Ronald Hutton, and John Morrill show that the Prayer Book, though illegal, remained in use more widely than was once thought, and it became more common under Cromwell's Protectorate. Nonetheless, if the use was too obvious, arrest was possible. The diarist John Evelyn recorded how a Christmas celebration in 1657 was rudely interrupted:

> I went with my wife &c: to *Lond*: to celebrate *Christmas* day. Mr. *Gunning* preaching in *Excester* Chapell on 7: *Micha* 2. Sermon Ended, as he was giving us the holy Sacrament, The Chapell was surrounded with Souldiers: All the Communicants and Assembly surpriz'd & kept Prisoners by them, some in the house, others carried away.[51]

As it became clear, however, that the army, which contained a large number of Independents and sectarians, would not allow a presbyterian polity to be implemented, other more radical dissenting groups began to emerge. Among these were the Friends, or Quakers, who eventually repudiated the use of sacraments. George Fox taught his followers to trust in the inner light and promptings of the spirit. There was place neither for Prayer Book nor *Directory*. Francis Higginson, a Cumberland clergyman, described his attendance at a Quaker gathering:

> The places of their Meetings are for the most part, such private houses as are most solitary and remote from Neighbours . . . their Speakers . . . standing . . . with his hat on, his countenance severe, his face downward, his eyes fixed mostly towards the earth, his hands & fingers expanded, continually striking gently on his breast . . . If . . . their chiefe Speaker be . . . absent, any of them speak that will pretend a revelation; sometimes girles are vocal. . . . Sometimes . . . there is not a whisper among them for an houre or two together.[52]

One Baptist described Quaker meetings and worship as "a company of worshippers, in great confusion, praying and singing, or teaching and singing, all or many

ASSEMBLÉE des QUAQUERS à Londres
A. Quaqueresse qui prêche.

A Quaker meeting in London, 1736. Engraving by Bernard Picart. PRIVATE COLLECTION/ARCHIVES CHARMET/BRIDGEMAN ART LIBRARY

together with loud voices," and another complained of their "humming, blowing, and hollow sighing."[53] More positively, the Quaker William Penn explained that the Quaker

silently waits to feel the Heavenly Substance brought into his Soul, by the Immediate Hand of the Lord, for it is not fetching in this Thought, or remembring the other Passage in Scripture, or calling to Mind what has been formerly known, *but every Immediate Word that proceeds from out of the Mouth of God, that can satisfie him.*[54]

Quakers objected to singing the psalms in rhyme and meter because David's words had been altered and they were not sung in the Spirit. Singing induced by the Spirit, however, was approved by George Fox, and early Friends sang psalms and hymns in their meetings and elsewhere. They objected to "steeple houses" as places for worship, marriage, and burial. The Quaker marriage ceremony was performed in the home of Friends, with other Friends to act as witnesses. Friends sometimes bought land for burial rather than have to allow the parish minister to conduct the funeral in the church with burial in the churchyard.

Akin to the Friends in terms of stressing the inner Spirit, but antedating them, was the Family of Love, which followed the teachings of the Dutch mystic Hendrick Niclaes. Much of the activities and beliefs of this sect remain shrouded in mystery, since the Family mixed openly with late Elizabethan and then Stuart society, some members holding posts such as churchwarden, yet keeping their "extra" religious affiliation a secret. The sect focused on inner unity with the Divine, and perfection, although it certainly did not renounce set forms of prayer. Indeed, set forms for morning and evening family worship, as well as for grace at meals, were provided in the *Exhortatio I*, and domestic sacred songs were published in the *Cantica*.[55]

If the *Westminster Directory* represented the direction of "official" liturgical provision, its permissive rubrics, which gave freedom to Independents, also gave a loophole to the Royalist Episcopal divines who wanted to use set forms of prayer. Jeremy Taylor, as a private chaplain, authored a *Collection of Offices*, providing for morning and evening prayer, baptism, and communion. The communion rite drew heavily upon the Greek version of Saint Basil's Liturgy, and the Syriac version of the Liturgy of Saint James, illustrating the fruits of what might be regarded as the beginnings of Anglican liturgical research and scholarship.

Official Liturgy and Lawful Dissent: The Restoration Church

With the death of Oliver Cromwell in 1658 and the reluctance of his son Richard to take over as Protector, the way was opened for prominent members of the army to negotiate the restoration of the monarchy with Charles II. In 1660, having met with representatives of the Presbyterian Anglican party, as well as with Royalist Episcopal divines, Charles issued the Declaration of Breda, promising liberty and some toleration toward those "of tender conscience." On his return to the throne, however, the once prominent Presbyterian party began to lose power, and found themselves on the defensive. Charles eventually called a conference at the Savoy to deliberate on liturgy. This was of little help to the Presbyterian cause, for the Episcopal divines announced that they were happy with the *Book of Common Prayer*, placing the onus upon the Presbyterian Anglicans to say what was wrong with the book. Their list, known as the Exceptions, repeated many of the objections of the "godly" first articulated in the 1570s.

One of their number, however, Richard Baxter, did produce an alternative liturgy, to stand alongside the *Book of Common Prayer*. Here material from the Prayer Book and material from the *Westminster Directory* were combined with scriptural texts and Baxter's own, rather long-winded explications into a "godly" set liturgy. This rather verbose rite deserves more attention than it has received, since it represents the type of set liturgy many of the "godly" clergy would have been content to use, as well as giving an insight into seventeenth-century English sacramental theology. Nevertheless, the Savoy conference was to break up without consensus, and Baxter's liturgy was relegated to the history of "what might have been if only."

Meanwhile, some survivors of the Durham House group—Matthew Wren (released from a long imprisonment in the Tower) and John Cosin (returned from exile in France)—set to work to try to incorporate some of the material from the 1637 and

Seventeenth-century liturgical practices. Two occasional offices: confirmation (left) and the churching of women. From *Eniautos: or, A Course of Catechizing*, 2nd ed. (London: Printed by J. C. for Fra. Kirkman, 1674).

1549 tradition into the Restoration *Book of Common Prayer*. Cosin's work, copied by his chaplain, William Sancroft, is found in a 1619 edition of the *Book of Common Prayer*. The newly returned Cavalier Parliament, however, was in no mood to appease any party that they deemed responsible for the turmoil of the two previous decades, and the liturgical agendas of both the Presbyterian Anglicans and the Durham House group were on the whole ignored. The task of drawing up a new liturgy was given to Convocation. With some 600 changes made to the previous liturgy, mainly in rubrics, modernizing, and tidying up language, and the addition of some new material, the Cranmerian *Book of Common Prayer* in its 1662 format was issued with a new Act of Uniformity. Not only were all incumbents to use the new set liturgy, but all had to be in episcopal orders, and those not so would have to submit to further ordination before being allowed to continue in their benefice. This compliance had to be fulfilled by Saint Bartholomew's Day, 1662. Some 2,000 ministers, including Richard Baxter, chose nonconformity. Though initially no nonconformity was to be allowed and severe legal restrictions and penalties were enacted in the 1660s, the Toleration Act of 1689 recognized the permanent and separate existence of English Protestant dissent.

How did the 1662 book affect Anglican worship? The changes were in one sense minimal. The word *priest* was substituted for *minister* in some places. In the Ordinal it was made clear that bishops were ordained to a distinct order, and the scriptural readings used made it less easy to argue that bishops and presbyters were originally one order. For the rite of baptism, provision was made for the blessing of the water and a new rite was provided for the baptism of those "of riper years." The rite for funerals was remodeled, with the first part of the service held in the church, the congregation moving only afterward to the graveyard for the committal. The marriage rite remained practically unchanged, except that communion was now recommended but could be postponed until "an opportune time." For the Lord's supper the people were directed to stand for the gospel and creed. The book included directions to place bread and wine on the table. It entitled the prayer containing the words of institution the "Prayer of Consecration" and mandated manual acts during the recital of the institution narrative. The book provided for the consecration of fresh elements if one or both failed, and any remaining elements were to be covered and consumed. The Black Rubric, dropped in 1559, was now restored, but whereas the rite of 1552 had rejected "real and essential" presence, that of 1662 rejected "corporal" presence, which in seventeenth-century sacramental theology was contrasted with "real," "spiritual" and "sacramental" presence.[56] The surplice was enjoined, and in general usage the communion table was to be placed in a Laudian position, railed in with altar rails. In cathedrals, copes were reintroduced, and organs and choirs flourished once more. As John Spurr noted, however, some clergy undertook to conform, but immediately continued the older "godly" practice of omitting parts of the liturgy, and wearing a preaching gown throughout the service.

On account of the political and religious threat to Protestantism under James II, who was a Roman Catholic and who gave toleration to Catholics, the need for a united Protestant opposition prompted some Anglicans to make overtures to certain Presbyterians with suggested emendations to the liturgy. This proposal of 1689 is known as the "Liturgy of Comprehension."[57] It included the provision of the Beatitudes as an alternative to the Ten Commandments at the beginning of the communion service—as proposed in Jeremy Taylor's *Collection of Offices*. There was also provision for renewal of baptismal vows at confirmation. The surplice, sign of the cross in baptism, the ring in marriage, and kneeling for communion were to be made optional, and the language of baptismal regeneration was toned down. The Liturgy also suggested use of the litany and ante-communion as separate services and replaced the term *presbyter*

Comments on worship by engraver William Hogarth (1697–1674). The "Sleepy Congregation" (1736) (right) mocks dull worship, whereas "Credulity, Superstition, and Fanaticism. A Medley" (1762) (left) offers a critique of Evangelical approaches. PRINT COLLECTION, MIRIAM AND IRA D. WALLACE DIVISION OF ART, PRINTS AND PHOTOGRAPHS, NEW YORK PUBLIC LIBRARY, ASTOR, LENOX, AND TILDEN FOUNDATIONS

with *priest*. But nothing came of the proposals, and when James was deposed, and the succession passed to William of Orange, and the Toleration Act of 1689 was passed, the comprehension was not pursued.

Dissenting Worship in the Seventeenth and Eighteenth Centuries

Once freed from the Established Church, Presbyterians joined Independents and Baptists in having no printed form of liturgy. Thus, as with the Separatist groups of the sixteenth century, researchers have to rely on contemporary accounts for information about their worship. A Scottish minister, Robert Kirk, visited London in 1689 or 1690 and in a commonplace book recorded the worship he attended. There are also an account of morning worship at Angel Street Chapel, Worcester; the details of services at Rothwell Independent Meeting, Northampton, around 1700; as well as and account of Isaac Watts's morning service and communion at Bury Street about 1723.

According to Kirk the morning service of the Independent Mr. Cockain and the Presbyterian William Bates consisted of prayer, sermon, and prayer. Kirk also attended a service conducted by Richard Baxter—by then a dissenting Presbyterian minister—which was recorded in more detail. There was a psalm, extempore prayer, a psalm reading as well as Old and New Testament readings, prayer, the sermon, a long prayer, and the Lord's prayer, with (probably) a psalm and blessing.[58] At Richard Davis's church in Rothwell, according to an account:

when the Congregation is assembled, the Preacher (whether Pastor or Elder) begins with Prayer, the People generally standing, (they look upon those as lazy who sit and will not suffer any Man to be covered): When Prayer is ended, they cover their Heads, and sit or stand, as they please, during the Sermon. This is the whole of their Behaviour and Service, unless they Sing an Hymn, which they ordinarily do.[59]

At Bury Street, Isaac Watts followed the order of psalm, short prayer, exposition, psalm or hymn, long prayer, sermon, psalm or hymn, short prayer, and blessing.[60] At Rothwell baptism was described as follows:

They Baptize both Children and Adult, in the Name of the Father, Son, and Holy Ghost, without the Sign of the Cross, Praying before and after. None Pray on this occasion but the Pastor, and none but he may Baptize, and that only the Members, or Children of the Members of his own Congregation.[61]

The account of the celebration of the Lord's supper in this church continues:

Every Member is required to receive the Sacrament as often as it is administred. The Table stands in the midst of the Congregation, near the Pulpit. The Pastor sits in his Chair near the Table, and the Receivers on Forms round about it; the People, as Spectators, at some small distance behind them.

The Pastor Prays (all standing) and craves a Blessing on the Bread; then sets it apart in almost the same Words which the Church of *England* uses; then breaks it into small pieces and puts them on divers Plates, saying whilse he is breaking, *Thus was our Lord's Body torn, mangled, broken, &c.* The Bread thus broken is carried in the Plates, by the Deacons, to the several Receivers. The Pastor sits in his Chair Eating with the rest.

As soon as the Bread is Eaten, the Pastor Prays; then pours out the Wine, saying, *Behold the Blood of Christ poured out for thee, and for me, and for all of us, &c. Drink ye all of this, drink large draughts of the Love of Christ, &c.* as he thinks most proper to express himself. Then he drinks and gives to the Deacons. When all have drunk, the Pastor Prays, an Hymn is Sung, and the Assembly is dismissed.[62]

The order of service at the church of Isaac Watts was similar. What is noticeable is that the Independents had separate blessings over the bread and wine, whereas the Presbyterian practice was normally to have a single blessing over both the bread and the wine.

Baptists emerged as four distinct groups: General Baptists; Calvinist Baptists; Particular Baptists; and Seventh Day Baptists. The latter group chose Saturday as the day of Christian worship, but the pattern of worship services was not too distinct from that of the other Baptist groups, and similar in many respects to that of the Independents. The compact agreed on for Paul's Alley, Barbican Baptist Meeting, London, asserted

that the publick Worship in the Congregation on the Lord's day be thus performed, viz. In the morning about half an hour after nine, some Brother be apointed to begin the Exercise in reading a Psalm, & then to spend some time in Prayer; & after yt to read some other Portion of H. Scripture, till the Minister comes into the Pulpit; and after Preaching & Prayer to conclude with singing a Psalm. The afternoon exercise to begin abt half an hour after one, & to be carried on & concluded as in the forenoon.[63]

The General Baptist Thomas Grantham (1634–1692) recorded details of a Baptist wedding ceremony:

The parties to be married . . . call together a competent number of their relations and friends; and, having usually some of our ministry present with them, the parties concerned declare their contract formerly made between themselves, and the advice of their friends, if occasion require it; and then taking each other by the hand, declare, That they from that day forward, during their natural lives together, do enter into the state of marriage, using the words of marriage in the service book, acknowledging the words to be very fit for that purpose. And then a writing is signed by the parties married, to keep in memory the contract and covenant of their marriage. . . . After these things some suitable counsel or instruction is given to the parties, and then prayer is made to God for his blessing upon the parties married, &c.[64]

What is interesting here is that the wording of the *Book of Common Prayer* seems to have been used for the marriage at this General Baptist church.

The account of Independent worship at Rothwell mentions hymns, and the pastor, Richard Davis, composed hymns. Although sacred songs and poems were not unknown in the English church, the general practice of the Church of England, and of the early Independent churches, was to sing metrical psalmody. The Church of England had the versions of Thomas Sternhold and John Hopkins, and, later, Nahum Tate and Nicholas Brady. The attempt by George Wither in 1623 to publish hymns came to grief when, despite having royal approval, the Stationers' Company declared them unfit to keep company with the psalms of David.[65] Many Independents, such as John Cotton, condemned singing nonscriptural songs but promoted psalm singing. It was among the Baptists, with Benjamin Keech, that one finds the first collection of scripturally inspired songs for regular inclusion in public worship. Davis was also a pioneer in this enterprise. The first collection of hymns made available to supplement the singing in dissenting worship, however, was Isaac Watts's *Hymns and Spiritual Songs*, 1707, a collection that became popular.[66]

The Eighteenth Century: Unitarians, Nonjurors, Methodists, and the American Prayer Book

The older view that the Church of England in the eighteenth century was entirely dreary, Latitudinarian, and in need of reform has been exposed by more recent scholarship as a distorted picture. It is certainly true that some clergy made worship tedious,

Eucharistic theology visualized. The congregation kneels before the altar rail at the east end of the church. The celebrant, wearing surplice, hood, and scarf, stands at the north end of the table upon which rest two flagons, two chalices, two patens, and a Prayer Book. In the clouds above the table a parallel action occurs. Beneath the heavenly altar are the words "Rev. VIII.3.4." Standing to the left is Christ, the great High Priest, robed in an alb, his arms upraised in prayer. Around his head is written "Heb. IX.11,23; VII.26." The entire engraving bears the caption "Matth. XVIII.19.20; I Cor. XI.23.24.25.26." From the frontispiece of Charles Wheatly's *A Rational Illustration of the Book of Common Prayer of the Church of England* (1720).

although that is true of all ages. The normal Sunday morning worship was morning prayer, litany, ante-communion, and sermon. In many churches a three-decker pulpit—housing desks for the clerk and minister, with the highest platform for the sermon—obscured the communion table. The service was sometimes read in a dull manner, and it was certainly also a prevailing custom of some clergy (Jane Austen's father being an example) to read the printed sermons of others rather than preach afresh. It is true as well that in many parishes the music was led by the parish band and a west gallery choir, with metrical psalms and carols being sung to popular, secular folk tunes. But in other churches and cathedrals worship was livelier and more dignified. César de Saussure, visiting from France, wrote in 1729:

> I have told you that several Roman Catholic ceremonies have been preserved, and are in use in the Anglican services at the present time. The Book of Common Prayer, which is the liturgy, is almost a missal, if you cut off the prayers addressed to the Holy Virgin and to the saints, and those for the dead. The priests and choristers all wear long white surplices when they celebrate divine service, but the preachers take them off before stepping into the pulpit. In the royal chapels, the cathedrals, and collegiate churches the services are chanted in a tone resembling that used by the Roman Catholics in their services.[67]

And at the end of the century a future succentor of York Minster wrote:

> In my return through York I strayed into the Minster. The evening service was then performed by candlelight. I had never before been in the Minster but in the middle of a summer's day. The gloom of the evening, the rows of candles fixed upon the pillars in the nave and transept, the lighting of the chancel, the two distant candles glimmering like stars at a distance upon the altar, the sound of the organ, the voices of the choir raised up with the pealing organ in the chaunts, service, and anthem had an amazing effect upon my spirits as I walked to and from in the nave. The varied tones, sometimes low, sometimes swelling into a great volume of harmonious sound, seemed to anticipate the songs of the blessed and the chorus of praise round the Throne of God and the Lamb. I was greatly affected.[68]

Though some parishes had communion only quarterly, others had it monthly. Robert Cornwall has demonstrated that confirmation also was taken seriously. William Wake, then bishop of Lincoln, in 1709 confirmed 12,800 candidates in twenty-four centers.[69] Indeed, far from existing in a period of stagnation, the eighteenth-century English church produced some lively movements. One trend was a questioning of the doctrine of the Trinity, and the espousal of a unitarian position, a debate in which the *Apostolic Constitutions* figured prominently.

The *Apostolic Constitutions* is a document that modern scholars date to around 380 in the region of Antioch. It appears to be the work of a semi-Arian or at least someone whose christology was sub-Nicene. This church order had been published in the sixteenth century in the hope of discrediting some of the Reformation attacks on the mass. Purported to be the work of Clement of Rome, it fascinated a number of eighteenth-century churchmen. Its low christology proved attractive to William Whiston, the Lucasian Professor of Mathematics at Cambridge, who made no secret of his neo-Arian, or unitarian, views. In 1711 he published an *Essay on the Apostolic Constitutions*, defending its authenticity, and drawing certain conclusions from his work. In chapter 2 of Book 8 he wrote:

> The *Liturgies*, and Forms of publick Devotions and Administration of Baptism and the Eucharist here Extant, for their Piety, Simplicity, Zeal, fulness of Matter, and close Ad-

herence to the Scripture Methods and Language, are exceeding admirable: Nay, far beyond the Composures of all the latter Ages; and highly worthy of the Apostles themselves.[70]

Although he was answered by the Oxford scholar and convert from German Lutheranism, Dr. Johannes Grabe, who demonstrated that the work was fourth century, Whiston was not to be deterred, even though his heterodoxy cost him his chair at Cambridge. In 1713 he published *The Liturgy of the Church of England reduc'd nearer to the Primitive Standard. Humbly propos'ed to Publick Consideration*. Here Whiston attempted to bring the Church of England liturgy into line with *Apostolic Constitutions*.

Another Church of England cleric, John Henley, who befriended Whiston and some of the Non-Jurors (of whom more will be said), eventually set up his own Oratory in London, and used a version of *Apostolic Constitutions* for his services. Other eighteenth-century English clerics shared Whiston's anti-trinitarian stance, although not his love of *Apostolic Constitutions*. Dr. Samuel Clarke, the rector of Saint James, Westminster, published a book that seriously questioned the doctrine of the Trinity. He made his own private revision of the Prayer Book in which the Nicene Creed was replaced by a psalm, and all trinitarian formulae were modified or removed. John Jones, the vicar of Alconbury, voiced similar demands in his *Free and Candid Disquisitions relating to the Church of England, and the means of advancing religion therein*, 1749.

Theophilus Lindsey, the vicar of Catterick, also argued for a church without subscription to creeds and articles. Lindsey became a Presbyterian, and most English Presbyterian congregations became Unitarian. Lindsey had access to Clarke's proposals, and developed these in the liturgy he published in 1774. Not only was it unitarian, but the absolution at morning and evening prayer was replaced by the Collect for Purity, and many of the canticles were dropped. Although only a few ministers of the Church of England followed Lindsey's example in quitting the church, a considerable number were in sympathy with his views, and saw his reforms as a modernizing of the liturgy. It is perhaps no accident that in America, King's Chapel, Boston, would issue its own Prayer Book, which was unitarian; the congregation half expected that this path would be followed by other Anglican congregations in America. In England between 1792 and 1854, fifteen liturgies were published based on the *Book of Common Prayer*, but with "modernization" in a unitarian direction. A. Elliott Peaston remarked that "in general these liturgies are remarkable for the rationality of their thought, and the tediousness of their expression. They would seem indeed to have been in the tradition of John Locke."[71]

On the accession of William of Orange to the English and Scottish thrones in 1689, a number of Church of England clergy, including the archbishop of Canterbury, felt unable to take an oath of allegiance to William, since they had already taken a binding oath to the deposed James II. Their refusal resulted in their being deprived of office, and they became known as the Non-Jurors. In Scotland negotiations resulted in the removal of episcopacy; the bishops, and those who went out of the church with them, were also technically Non-Jurors. The worship of the latter was at first no different from what it had been prior to 1689, being based loosely on the *Westminster Directory*. At a later date, through contact between the Scottish Episcopalians and the English Non-Jurors, some changes in worship took place.

Once released from the confines of the Act of Uniformity, some of the second-generation Non-Jurors began to develop certain ceremonies as obligatory and to agitate for liturgical reform. A split occurred between what have come to be called the "usagers" and the "non-usagers," and a bitter pamphlet war broke out between the two groups.[72] The usagers placed a high premium on liturgical tradition and regarded the 1552, 1559, and 1662 Prayer Books as a concession to Calvin. They looked back to 1549 and to the ancient liturgies. They insisted that the wine in the chalice should be mixed with water, that an invocation of the Holy Spirit should be added to the prayer of consecration, that the prayer of oblation should follow the consecration, and that the departed should be prayed for. The non-usagers saw all these things as adiaphora and tried to remain loyal to the 1662 Prayer Book as the true and lawful successor to 1552 and 1559. In 1718 three leading usagers issued a service book containing offices for communion, confirmation, and the visitation of the sick. The communion office showed clear influence of the 1549 *Book of Common Prayer*, but the compilers also drew on the Roman mass and the liturgies of the Eastern churches— Saint Basil, Saint James, and *Apostolic Constitutions*. The latter served as the catalyst for the 1734 liturgy of the usagers published by Thomas Deacon. Contacts with the Scottish bishops resulted in the publication of the "wee bookies," based on the abortive 1637 communion service. One of the Scottish bishops, Thomas Rattray, was to publish a liturgy based on that of Saint James, and Bishop William Falconar undertook a further revision of the 1637 rite in 1755. What becomes evident is a deliberate attempt to revive the eucharistic pattern and theology of the 1549 and 1637 books, resulting in two strains of eucharistic liturgy within Anglicanism.[73]

A rather different piety was evident in the liturgical work of John Wesley. As an Oxford student and tutor, Wesley was a regular communicant, and he read the works on the eucharist of Daniel Brevint. This particular influence is to be seen in the hymns that John and his brother Charles composed for the eucharist; they are largely Brevint turned into meter and song. Wesley's experience in America brought him into contact with Moravians, as well as the more spartan resources in the colonies, compared

Old Orthodox. Caricature of John Wesley, 1777. Wesley holds a book inscribed with "Hymns to be sung or said standing, sitting or lying, mornings or evenings"—a mocking reference to the Methodist production and zealous use of hymns. With permission of Duke University Rare Book and Special Collections Library

with those of Oxford collegiate chapels. His own evangelical conversion at Aldersgate in 1738, and his familiarity with the Oxford University sermon and its brief liturgical structure, would influence the structure of the Methodist preaching services.[74] He was also aware of the Non-Jurors' work and the Exceptions of the Presbyterian Anglicans at the Savoy conference. He was also probably familiar with some of the more rationalistically inspired ideas for Prayer Book revision, some of which appealed to him for pastoral and pragmatic reasons.

Both the Wesleys and their sometime colleague George Whitefield remained Church of England clergy throughout their lives, even if at odds with the mainstream church and its authority. Wesley saw his own preaching services as augmenting those of the parish church, and he advised and expected Methodists to attend their parish churches (and press for communion) in addition to Methodist preaching services. Many of his followers and his lay preachers, however, saw no reason to supplement what they did as Methodists with worship at the Established Church, and thus the preaching service format became for many their only act of public worship. This was particularly true in the American colonies, where services of a more informal nature quickly developed.[75]

In 1784 Wesley issued the *Sunday Service of the Methodists* for use by Methodists in America, and a version in 1786 for use in "His Majesty's Dominions." American Methodists politely accepted the 1784 book, but it was probably never widely used and, after Wesley's death, was employed primarily as a resource for the sacramental rites. James White has observed that this was a service book rather than a Book of Common Prayer, saying, "Wesley prunes away all the paraphernalia of an established national church."[76] The word *priest* was replaced by *minister*, extempore prayer was permitted in the communion service, and services such as confirmation and the churching of women were removed. Morning prayer was shortened, and could stand on its own without the litany and ante-communion. In evening prayer the Magnificat and Nunc dimittis were removed. The ring in marriage disappeared. The psalter was also abbreviated, removing psalms that Wesley deemed unsuitable for Christian worship. White comments:

> Every page of the *Sunday Service* bears marks, not of a casual reviser, but of one who had read or heard the prayer book daily throughout eight decades, and who is determined to retain all that wore well and to discard only that which proved inadequate in his own experience.[77]

Be that as it may, English Methodists split among themselves, and the *Sunday Service* faded in practical importance as many congregations adopted forms of service akin to that of Independents. It was the same with George Whitefield and the Countess of Huntingdon's Connexion; when Lady Selena's Proprietary Chapels were deemed not legal as private Anglican chapels, her ministers had to secede from the Church of England, and although the *Book of Common Prayer*, with ad hoc emendmendations, was enjoined, ministers quickly went to freer forms of worship.

Evangelicals within the Church of England, such as Charles Simeon, held a very high view of sacraments and encouraged frequent reception of holy communion. Simeon "believed that the service is a medium of communion with Christ actually present with his disciples hosting them with bread and wine as the Giver of Grace."[78] To young clergymen, Simeon's advice was this:

> "Pray the prayers, and don't read them only; adhere sacredly to the directions of the Rubric, except where they have become obsolete, and the resumption of them would

clearly do harm." "The finest sight short of heaven," he once declared, "would be a whole congregation using the prayers of the Liturgy in the true spirit of them."[79]

Wesley's work was, of course, a development from Anglicanism, but one that took his movement out of Anglicanism. Rather more significant for Anglican development was the making of the American Prayer Book. The War of Independence put the Church of England in a difficult position, since the services contained prayers for the monarch and bishops were appointed by the monarch and Parliament. Once the war was over, it became clear that the Anglicans in America had to survive without being part of the Church of England. Moves for a new Prayer Book resulted in a draft book in 1786, which showed many similarities with Wesley's *Sunday Service* and reflected some of the rationalistic objections of the time. The word *priest* was removed; the Athanasian Creed was removed, as were the Magnificat and Nunc dimittis in evening prayer; and only a selection of psalms were included. Since there were still no bishops for America, however, the proposed book remained on the table. Eventually Samuel Seabury of Connecticut was consecrated bishop in Scotland by the Scottish bishops, and he undertook to use the Scottish communion service rather than that of 1662; indeed, he issued an edition of the Scottish rite for use in Connecticut. But the way was soon cleared for bishops for America to be consecrated in England, and three more bishops were consecrated. Deliberations continued through to 1789, with some states adopting the proposed book of 1786. Eventually the bishops and deputies of the General Convention made a fresh revision, restoring many things omitted in the 1786 proposal. Nevertheless, the revision still omitted the Magnificat and Nunc dimittis as well as the Athanasian Creed, still had a selected psalter, and breathed a Latitudinarian spirit. The one exception was in the communion office, where the Scottish petition for consecration (derived from 1549 and 1637) was used. More significant, however, was the fact that now Anglicanism was no longer the Church of England at home and abroad worshiping with the 1662 rite. Anglicanism was now larger than the Church of England, and Anglicans abroad could adapt and author their own liturgy. The Protestant Episcopal Church would undertake further revision in 1892.

The Nineteenth Century

The nineteenth century witnessed the rise of the Romantic movement and with it a sense of nostalgia for things medieval. Already apparent at the beginning of the nineteenth century are moves toward the revival of plainsong in Anglican worship, more common use of the organ, and the introduction of a surpliced choir to replace the west gallery singers. There was a trend toward refurbishing churches to make the communion table the focal point,[80] which accelerated with the gothic revival style of ecclesiastical architecture, promoted as being the only genuinely Christian style. Both plainsong and the gothic style were championed by the Ecclesiological Society at Cambridge. Then, in the 1840s, the rise of Tractarianism heightened the sense of ecclesiology and decency in worship in the Anglican Church. The second- and third-generation Tractarian clergy—or "Anglo-Catholic," as they came to be called—reintroduced much of the old, discarded Catholic ceremonial. At first this meant candles and a cross on the altar, the use of a credence table, and the wearing of the surplice during the sermon, rather than replacing it with the black gown. As modest as these practices were, they often sparked controversy. At Saint Nicholas Witham in Essex, not noted as a center of Tractarianism, the Reverend John Bramston caused controversy in 1845:

> Upwards of 20 objections were presented to the reverend gentlemen including the preaching in a surplice, the offertory, the cross erected at the altar, the credence or side table for the elements of the holy communion, the placing of the alms basin on the altar at All Saints Church, the manner of singing in the morning service, the minister turning from the people during prayer, the performance of baptism in the congregation, the application of the alms for other purposes than those of the poor of the parish and other points.[81]

Later Tractarians expanded the modest ceremonial to include eucharistic vestments outlawed since the Elizabethan Visitations, incense, and holy water. Since some of the ceremonial existed for rites not found in the *Book of Common Prayer*, the Anglo-Catholic groups began to publish service books in which the Anglican rites were supplemented, usually with texts from the Roman Church. A "ritual" war broke out, with bishops seemingly powerless to curb ceremonial excesses. The Public Worship Regulation Act of 1874 resulted in some Anglo-Catholic clergy being imprisoned, and in the end the Act was allowed to fall into abeyance. A study by Nigel Yates has shown that the number of churches adopting a full Catholic ceremonial and vestments prior to the twentieth century was relatively small. Yates has also challenged the belief that the movement was more popular among working-class parishes; the truth is that it was the most successful among the middle class.[82] Nevertheless, the combined impact would change the face of Anglican worship. Churches tended to be reordered, regardless of churchmanship, with candles and a cross on the altar. Even if eucharistic vestments were not worn, the colored stole over the surplice became common, and even most Evangelical clergy abandoned the black gown for the sermon, wearing the surplice throughout.

The nineteenth century also established the organ as the instrument of Anglican worship. In Anglo-Catholic parishes a sung eucharist or high mass came to be the main Sunday morning worship. Reforms in 1872 made legal the separation of morning prayer, litany, and ante-communion, and the main Sunday morning service in most parishes became choral morning prayer with sermon.

The 1872 Act also allowed for a "Third Service," which could be used after morning and evening prayer. It was often scheduled for six o'clock or six thirty and was more evangelistic in nature. This tried to provide an "Anglican" form for the more informal evangelistic and missionary services that certain Evangelical Anglican clergy had been pioneering.[83]

Another important trend in the nineteenth century was the Anglican Church's adoption of hymns and hymnals. Hitherto, hymn singing had been associated with dissenting worship. But in the nineteenth century the metrical psalms gave way to hymns and a new industry of published hymnals, the most famous perhaps being *Hymns Ancient and Modern*.[84]

Wesleyan Methodists published versions of Wesley's *Sunday Service* in the nineteenth century, but other Methodist groups preferred to follow a free prayer pattern of worship, although they published manuals for the ministers to use at baptisms, marriages, and funerals. Yet it was within Congregationalism that the most remarkable development was to be found. The tradition had originally repudiated set forms of worship. But, having introduced hymns, which were a type of set worship form, some Congregationalists in the nineteenth century began to consider printed forms as a possible option. Tracts and books arguing for or against set forms were published, as well as a number of liturgies for optional use.

The latter tended to fall into three categories. First were "biblical liturgies." These were really centos of scriptural material put together in a manner suitable for incorporation in a worship service. An example of this type was *A Biblical Liturgy* by David Thomas (1855), which went through several editions. A second type was the unabashed emendation and adaptation of the *Book of Common Prayer*. Examples of this type include *The Book of Common Prayer Adapted for the Use of the Congregational Church, Finchley Common* (1864); *Free Church Service Book* (1867); and *Let us Pray* (1897). A third type was the compilation of a genuinely new liturgical work, and this was associated with Dr. John Hunter, minister of the King's Weigh House Chapel, London, though part of his earlier ministry was spent in Scotland. The first edition of his *Devotional Services* was published in 1880. It went through six different editions, and the final edition remained in print until 1943. In this work Hunter provided Congregationalists with a full, dignified worship book that was independent of the *Book of Common Prayer*. His famous communion invitation, "Come to this sacred Table, not because you must, but because you may," passed into many other free church service books, and crossed the Atlantic to the American Protestant churches.

Why this liturgical revival? It was not unconnected to the Romantic movement, for Congregational meetinghouses were now replaced with gothic-style buildings. But it was also linked with the social, economic, and political position of many of its members. Some of the books and tracts speak about the need not to repel "refined" and cultured people by long-winded prayers of the minister. The denomination also saw the introduction of organs and choirs—a long way down the road from the sentiments of John Cotton. Still, the type of service recorded at Rothwell in the eighteenth century did not entirely fade away, especially in more rural areas.

Most of the liturgies were concerned with Sunday morning and evening worship. The communion service tended to be celebrated in much the same way that it had been in the previous century. Such a service was described in *The Christian World* in 1890. It consisted of: silent prayer; the hymn "Come let us join our cheerful songs" (Isaac Watts); a prayer ("It is the tender pleading of one who feels the goodness of God, the splendid manhood, the saving brotherhood of Christ; that he would come with us and dwell with us, and make us like Himself—loving, gentle, strong to do God's will, and very patient with each other. All the problems of life are brought to the Cross, and grace is asked that in the light which streams therefrom they may be solved in God's time."); 1 Corinthians 11; distribution of the bread in silence, words over the cup, and distribution of the wine in silence; collection; a sung doxology; and a benediction.[85] One change that did begin to take place in many free churches—Congregationalist, Baptist, and Methodist—was linked with their embrace of the temperance movement. Wine at communion was replaced by grape juice. Juice, however, lacked the antiseptic properties of alcohol, and this reality, combined with nineteenth-century concerns about hygiene, led to the traditional common cup being replaced by individual communion cups on trays.

Mention must also be made of the Irvingite, or Catholic Apostolic, Church, founded in the 1840s. It originated as a charismatic or pentecostal occurrence in a London Church of Scotland congregation, but spread and was reorganized as a distinct church, stressing gifts of the Spirit as a sign of the final age. It appointed twelve "Apostles," who ordained a threefold ministry. The Apostles also authored an elaborate liturgy, compiled after careful study of the Roman Catholic, Eastern and Anglican rites. It was celebrated with a Catholic ritual including vestments, incense, lamps, and candles, all combined with an evangelical piety. Though its ritual was frowned upon by other

Protestant denominations, the texts of the liturgy were influential among some free churches in England as well as in the German Reformed Church in the United States, and in the Church of Scotland.

The Twentieth Century

The ritual controversies in the Church of England resulted in the appointment of a Royal Commission, which reported in 1906 that the current provisions for worship were too narrow. Discussions began on revision of the *Book of Common Prayer* but were prolonged by the Great War. The experience of many chaplains during the war pointed to the urgent need for a liturgy sensitive to the spiritual hunger and alienation from the Church which that generation felt. The liturgical scholars and ecclesiastical factions each argued their own agenda, however, and the resulting book of 1927, known as the *Deposited Book*, was basically Cranmer's text but enriched with services such as compline, a petition for consecration by the Holy Spirit inserted into the prayer of consecration in the eucharist, and modest provision for prayers for the dead. Even so, it was not Catholic enough for Anglo-Catholics, who refused to be bound by it, and it was too Catholic for many Evangelicals. This unholy alliance, combined with free church prejudice in Parliament, resulted in the book failing to gain Parliamentary assent. It was revised and presented again, in 1928, and although it had 72 percent support in the Church Assembly, it once more failed to gain a majority in Parliament. The archbishops of Canterbury and York arranged for the 1928 Prayer Book to be printed and issued a statement saying that its use would not be regarded as inconsistent with loyalty to the principles of the Church of England.

Christmastide liturgy. A choir of men and boys sings at a war-time service in Ely Cathedral on 26 December 1942. Anglican choral music centers on the service–settings of the liturgy, including the psalms–and the anthem. PHOTOGRAPH BY BILL BRANDT/ HULTON ARCHIVE/GETTY IMAGES

Meanwhile two other developments were taking place. Already in the nineteenth century, certain parishes, usually having some link with the Christian socialism movement, began pioneering a parish communion as the main Sunday service. This was quite distinct from the Anglo-Catholic solemn high mass (at which the people did not communicate) and the more common choral morning prayer. This trend began to be more widely copied from the 1930s onward, advocated by such exponents as Gabriel Hebert of the Society of the Sacred Mission (Kelham). Second, other Anglican provinces began to publish more revisions of the Prayer Book: Canada in 1918, the United States in 1928, South Africa in 1929, and Scotland in 1929. While there was certainly overlap with the discussions in England and development of the 1928 English Prayer Book, each of these new books represented an independent adaptation and development of the inherited Anglican liturgical tradition.

In British Methodism a number of the separate groups came together in union in 1932, and the resulting Methodist Church produced the *Book of Offices* in 1936. Among other things, it contained an order of morning prayer modeled on the Anglican form and a communion service that showed influence of the 1928 book. The English Congregational Union produced an official service book in 1920, heavily dependent on Anglican forms, in which separate prayers of blessing over the bread and wine were abandoned in favor of a single prayer. During the 1920s, however, many of the younger Congregational ministers became influenced by the liberal Protestant theologies, and this prevailing liberalism came to the fore in the 1936 *A Manual for Ministers*. In this book one of the communion rites described the communion as being a "holy custom of the church"; liberal theology was uncertain that it had been instituted by Jesus, feeling it was probably the invention of Saint Paul copied from the mystery cults. But as the book appeared, a more orthodox group of younger ministers, many being influenced by neo-orthodoxy, sharply criticized the liberalism of many of the established ecclesiastical bureaucrats of the Congregational Union. In 1948 this younger group produced a much more orthodox and dignified liturgy for use in the denomination, published by Oxford University Press under the title *A Book of Public Worship*.

The churches of the post–Second World War period were faced generally with the crises of an increasingly technological culture, an increasingly affluent society, and secularism, which in the 1960s exploded in a radical questioning of many traditional values and practices. Calls for liturgical revision to meet the needs of the twentieth century were fused with the ideas that stemmed from the Roman Catholic liturgical movement. The latter stressed the need for active participation in the liturgy by the laity, combined with a vision derived from the liturgy of Christian action in the world. It was believed that liturgy and life should be inseparably linked. Mention has already been made of Gabriel Hebert. His views were taken up in the "Parish and People" movement, which tried to apply the lessons of the Liturgical Movement at parish level. But often the text of the liturgy did not make the desired links with life. The ultimate implication of the Liturgical Movement—in both the Roman Catholic and other churches—was that the liturgies needed to be reformulated.

Already in 1954 the Church of England had appointed a liturgical commission to consider certain aspects for liturgical revision. At the 1958 Lambeth Conference the subject was the *Book of Common Prayer* as a center of Anglican unity. What emerged from the conference was that different Anglican provinces had already taken divergent paths, depending on whether they followed the 1552 and 1662 paradigm, or the 1549 and 1637 paradigm, and the divergences were continuing. Anglican liturgical scholars were in touch with one another and shared similar scholarly insights. But it was the calling of the Second Vatican Council, and the publication of the *Constitution on the Sacred Liturgy*—leading to the complete revision of the Roman Catholic liturgies—that acted as an instant catalyst in sparking unprecedented liturgical experimentation and revision throughout Anglicanism and in most major Protestant churches.

In the Church of England, experimental services of the 1960s and 1970s (called Series 1, 2, and 3) resulted in the 1980 *Alternative Service Book* (*ASB*), available for use alongside the 1662 *Book of Common Prayer*, and actually displacing the latter for most services in most English parishes. Hallmarks of the new services, shared in common across the denominations, were the use of contemporary English, a return to the patristic era for inspiration in structures and texts, and a more relaxed, informal manner of celebrating the services. One example of the patristic influence was a return to fourth-century or "classical" patterns for the eucharistic prayer, by the late 1990s called that rather than "prayer of consecration." Particularly influential was the theory advanced by Dom Gregory Dix of Nashdom Abbey that the eucharist centered on a four-action shape, which was reflected in the 1980 rite: taking of bread and wine; giving thanks; breaking the bread; and communion. The modern-language communion service gave a choice of eucharistic prayers. A major inspiration was a eucharistic prayer from the *Apostolic Tradition*, which scholars of the 1960s and 1970s were prepared to attribute to Hippolytus and date around AD 215. In 1985 a book entitled *Lent, Holy Week, and Easter* was produced by the liturgical commission, and commended by the archbishops. In this work the Church of England made official provision for the services of the Easter Triduum, abolished in 1549.

The Episcopal Church of the United States of America (having dropped the word *Protestant* from its title) had published a number of *Prayer Book Studies*, which consisted of discussions about possible revision of the 1928 book, with experimental services. These were to culminate in the 1979 *Book of Common Prayer*. Meanwhile the Church in Australia had produced a new book in 1978, and Ireland would do so in 1984, Canada in 1985, and South Africa and New Zealand in 1989. Many other provinces revised parts of their liturgy or issued experimental books.

By the 1990s the Church of England's new liturgical commission, appointed in 1986, had taken stock of the situation. The general consensus among its members was that the language of the 1980 *ASB* was too flat, too much like reading the *Daily Telegraph* newspaper, and that better, more resonant language was needed. They also perceived a need to recycle some of the more traditional *Book of Common Prayer* material and to cater to the increasing popularity of "Family Services." These were usually some form of morning prayer, but often so metamorphosed and interpolated with home-authored material as to be hardly recognizable as Anglican services at all. Some of these services reviewed by the liturgical commission had liturgical merit; most had serious doctrinal flaws and displayed an appalling banality.

The 1980 *ASB* baptismal rite had introduced a new element into Anglican baptismal liturgy (as had the American Prayer Book of 1979 and also the Canadian book), in which the parents and godparents undertook promises before the actual baptism of an infant. By the 1990s the English commission had diagnosed this as reflecting an undiscussed covenant theology of the Reformed tradition, suggesting that an infant's right to baptism rested on the ecclesial engagement and level of faith of the parents, which was at best semi-Pelagian. The service was structured with promise of parents (conditions) coming first, and then baptism (grace subsequent to conditions).

Furthermore, the 1980 revision of the daily office and morning and evening prayer for Sundays had been a rushed job and was merely "Cranmer" in modern English, with a richer provision of canticles. The commission felt that the more thorough knowledge of the history of the office now available should facilitate a richer and more radical revision. In addition, the popular paradigm in the communion service, from the *Apostolic Tradition*, was being assessed more and more by scholars as a later composite text, far less representative of the early patristic era than the previous generation of scholars had uncritically judged it to be.

The result of the stock taking was, first of all, *Patterns for Worship*, 1995, which provided material for those constructing their own "Family Services" or word services. Then, replacing the 1980 *ASB*, from Advent Sunday 2000 and on, came new services entitled *Common Worship*, although some of the new services, such as those for festivals and ordination, are still in progress. The language in *Common Worship* is noticeably richer and more resonant than that of the 1980 book. The rites are written in inclusive language for humanity, but a firm decision was taken by the commission that, although biblically based feminine imagery for God might be used ("as a mother tenderly gathers her children"), it was not doctrinally acceptable to impose feminine names for the divine ("God our Mother"). A new daily office has been provided, with a different structure than Cranmer's. The initiation rites provide for stages through faith, and in the rite for infant baptism, the covenant theology has been severely re-shaped to give a theological structure of ecclesial context (faith of the Church), baptism (grace), and then Christian obligations (response to free grace). The modern English communion rite includes eight eucharistic prayers, and some have congregational responses. The funeral rite is also structured in stages, providing for prayers in the home after a death and a vigil as well as the actual funeral rite. The marriage service has been enriched with the addition of alternative blessings for the rings, nuptial blessings, and intercessions, and suggestions that the shape of the rite should be that of the ante-communion or synaxis, with the scripture readings and homily coming before the exchange of marriage vows. A rubric, which attracted some media attention, also suggests an alternative to the deep-seated English custom of the bride being escorted into church by her father and being "given away"; it allows the almost universal Eastern and European continental custom of bride and groom processing into church together as two equal parties in their marriage.

Alongside the new book there are also a few signs of a move to a more dignified, less informal manner of celebration of the rites, with a new appreciation for symbolism and a move away from the functionalism of the 1960s and 1970s. Most parishes have the eucharist as the main Sunday service, and the cassock-alb with stole is a common vestment across the older churchmanship divides. A nave altar, with celebration facing the people, has been prevalent since the 1970s. High mass vestments are quite common in English cathedrals, and the chasuble is a fairly usual garment.

In contrast to this, however, many Church of England churches of the Evangelical tradition have been influenced by the megachurch and seeker service style of worship from the United States, where the television chat show host seems to be the model, and worship is seen as entertainment for the congregation. Saint Aldate's Church, Oxford, is an example of this trend. The church underwent extensive refurbishing in 2000. The worship space is oriented so that the south side of the nave is the focal point, and has a stage that houses the band. There is a central music and sound center, from which words of choruses are projected on monitor screens hanging from the ceiling. Ecclesiastical vesture has been abandoned. Technically, this is a new form of nonconformity and raises the question of whether the Church of England still has "common prayer."

Other Anglican provinces have also continued to revise services. For example, in 1995 both Australia and the province of the West Indies published new and distinctive Prayer Books. In India and in African countries, there has been encouragement to "inculturate" the liturgy—that is, to develop rites that are characteristically Indian or African Anglican, rather than Indian and African Anglicans using a British liturgy. Inculturation most obviously displays itself in architecture and music, but Indian cultural gestures, for example, have been utilized, and in the new Kenyan rite, traditional African concepts of the divine that do not contradict scripture have been incorporated into the prayers. *A New Zealand Prayer Book* 1989 included material expressing the Maori culture. But some Anglican provinces in developing countries find liturgical revision an expensive undertaking and, where there is widespread illiteracy, an unhelpful exercise.

In the United States, under the title of "Expansive Language," experimental services have been issued that have trod where the Church of England deemed it unacceptable to go; specifically, these services provide prayers that consciously avoid calling God "Father," "Lord," or "King"; in which the names of the persons of the Trinity, "Father, Son, and Holy Spirit," are taken as male metaphors that can be interchanged with other terms; and in which Jesus is addressed as "our Mother." It may be that such developments reflect one particularly vocal subcultural trend of American society. These issues, together with the variety of new Anglican liturgies, have resulted in increased divergence. In an effort to give some overall guidance, the International Anglican Liturgical Consultation meets every four years to discuss liturgical topics, and it issues reports that it is hoped will give some guides for common patterns.

Among the free churches in England the same recovery of the classical period is in evidence. The Baptist Union produced a book for ministers, *Patterns and Prayers for Christian Worship*, 1992. The Methodist Church published *The Methodist Service Book*, 1975, which was pioneering when it appeared but quickly seemed out of date and conservative as other denominations produced their new liturgies. It was in modern English and promoted the communion as the main Sunday service, although only one eucharistic prayer was provided. Several years in gestation, *The Methodist Worship Book* finally appeared in 1999, providing a much wider choice. It includes a controversial eucharistic prayer, approved at the eleventh hour, which addresses God as "our Father and our Mother."

The Congregational Union, which became the Congregational Church, produced experimental liturgies in the 1960s. It united, however, with the Presbyterian Church of England (originating with Scottish émigrés) in 1972 to form the United Reformed Church. A new *Book of Services* was published in 1980, with a communion service based on the classical rites, and alternative eucharistic prayers (one prayer, not separate blessings over bread and wine), including one by the Roman Catholic priest-poet, Huub Oosterhuis. Then, after a further union took place, with the Churches of Christ, yet another new worship book appeared, in 1989, the *Service Book*. It reflected the liturgical usage of the Churches of Christ by incorporating a form of baptism for believers and a communion service that gave separate blessings over the bread and wine. There was a certain irony here that it was the Churches of Christ influence which restored the older Independent practice to the service book. The United Reformed Church has more recently revised its forms of worship again. These books, like those of the Methodist and Baptist, are not compulsory liturgies and are simply provided for the minister's use if he or she so desires. Like some of the Anglican evangelical churches, some of the free church congregations and ministers have adapted the seeker service style for their worship.

Mention should be made of the Joint Liturgical Group (JLG), which is an ecumenical liturgical group representing churches in England, Scotland, Wales, and Ireland, founded in 1964. In its early years, when ecumenism was more in vogue, the JLG produced material that was utilized by the member churches and that was regarded as breaking new ground. These included a form of daily office and a two-year lectionary that was widely adopted by the churches. In years leading up to the twenty-first century, the JLG's work became less well received, and its lectionary has on the whole been replaced by the Revised Common Lectionary. Nevertheless, it remains a useful forum where representatives of the various churches can exchange ideas and update one another on the progress of worship provisions in their respective churches.

Bibliography

Adelmann, Dale. *The Contribution of Cambridge Ecclesiologists to the Revival of Anglican Choral Worship*. Aldershot, Hants.; Brookfield, Vt.: Ashgate, 1997.

Bowmer, J. C. *The Sacrament of the Lord's Supper in Early Methodism*. London: Dacre Press 1951.

Buchanan, Colin O., ed. *Latest Anglican Liturgies, 1976–1984*. London: Alcuin Club and SPCK, 1985.

Burdon, Adrian. *The Preaching Service—The Glory of the Methodists*. Alcuin/GROW Liturgical Study 17. Bramcote, Notts.: Grove, 1991.

Cuming, G. J. *The Godly Order*. London: Alcuin Club; SPCK, 1983.

Cuming, G. J. *A History of Anglican Liturgy*. Rev. ed. London: Macmillan, 1982.

Davies, Horton. *Worship and Theology in England*. 5 vols. Princeton, N.J.: Princeton University Press, 1961–1975; vol. 6, Grand Rapids, Mich.: Eerdmans, 1996; combined edition in 3 vols., Grand Rapids, Mich.: Eerdmans, 1996. [reference here made to the combined edition]

Fenwick, John, and Bryan D. Spinks. *Worship in Transition. The Liturgical Movement in the Twentieth Century*. New York: Continuum, 1995.

Grisbrooke, W. J. *Anglican Liturgies of the Seventeenth and Eighteenth Centuries*. London: SPCK, 1958.

Hatchett, Marion. *The Making of the First American Book of Common Prayer*. New York: Seabury, 1982.

Peaston, A. E. *The Prayer Book Reform Movement in the XVIIIth Century*. Oxford: Blackwell, 1940.

Spinks, Bryan D. *Freedom or Order? The Eucharistic Liturgy in English Congregationalism, 1645–1980*. Alison Park, Pa.: Pickwick, 1984.

Spinks, Bryan D. *From the Lord and "The Best Reformed Churches": A Study of the Eucharistic Liturgy in the English Puritan and Separatist Traditions*. Rome: C.L.V.–Edizioni Liturgiche, 1984.

Spinks, Bryan D. *Sacraments, Ceremonies, and the Stuart Divines. Sacramental Theology and Liturgy in England and Scotland, 1603–1662*. Aldershot, Hants.; Burlington, Vt.: Ashgate, 2002.

Varcoe, Gilian, ed. *A Prayer Book for Australia: A Practical Commentary*. Alexandria, NSW: Dwyer, 1997.

Watson, J. R. *The English Hymn*. Oxford: Clarendon, 1997.

Yates, W. Nigel. *Anglican Ritualism in Victorian Britain, 1830–1910*. Oxford: Oxford University Press, 1999.

Yates, W. Nigel. *Buildings, Faith, and Worship: The Liturgical Arrangement of Anglican Churches, 1600–1900*. Oxford: Clarendon, 1991

Notes

[1] John Spurr, *The Restoration Church of England* (New Haven, Conn., and London: Yale University Press, 1991) 104.

[2] C. C. Butterworth, *The English Primers, 1529–1545* (Philadelphia: University of Pennsylvania Press, 1953).

[3] *Certain Sermons or Homilies* (London: SPCK, 1938) 60.

[4] See Diarmaid MacCulloch, *Thomas Cranmer* (New Haven, Conn., and London: Yale University Press, 1996).

[5] *Original Letters relative to the English Reformation* (Cambridge: University Press, 1846) 535–536; quoted in A. H. Couratin, "The Holy Communion 1549," *Church Quarterly Review* 164 (1963) 148–159; my italics.

[6]For divergent views that date at least as far back as the eighteenth century, see A. H. Couratin, "The Holy Communion 1549," and his "The Service of Holy Communion 1552–1662," *Church Quarterly Review* 163 (1962) 431–442; and Basil Hall, "Cranmer, the Eucharist, and the Foreign Divines in the Reign of Edward VI," in *Thomas Cranmer: Churchman and Scholar*, ed. Paul Ayris and David Selwyn (New York: Boydell, 1993) 217–258.

[7]See Bryan D. Spinks, "'And with thy Holy Spirite and Worde': Further Thoughts on the Source of Cranmer's Petition for Sanctification in the 1549 Communion Service," in *Thomas Cranmer*, ed. Margot Johnson (Durham: Turnstone Ventures, 1990) 94–102.

[8]See Cuming, *The Godly Order*; and Bryan D. Spinks, "Treasures Old and New: A Look at Some of Thomas Cranmer's Methods of Liturgical Composition," in Ayris and Selwyn, 175–188.

[9]Quoted from Peter Le Huray, *Music and the Reformation in England, 1549–1660* (New York: Oxford University Press, 1967) 25.

[10]Le Huray, 22.

[11]W. D. Hamilton, ed., *A Chronicle of England during the reigns of the Tudors from A.D. 1485 to 1559 by Charles Wriothesley*, 2 vols. (London: Camden Society, 1875) 2:9.

[12]Hamilton, 2:16–17.

[13]Hamilton, 2:47.

[14]Thomas Cranmer, *The Works of Thomas Cranmer*, 2 vols. (Cambridge: Cambridge University Press, 1844) 1:92.

[15]*Original Letters*, 75 (27 December 1549).

[16]Hamilton, 2:78–79.

[17]Hamilton, 2:101.

[18]Hamilton, 2:145.

[19]Hamilton, 2:146.

[20]John Strype, *The Life and Acts of Matthew Parker*, vol. 1 (Oxford: Clarendon, 1821) 302; cited in S. C. Carpenter, *The Church of England, 597–1688* (London: John Murray, 1954) 330.

[21]W. H. Frere and C. E. Douglas, *Puritan Manifestoes* (London: SPCK, 1907) 14, 29–30.

[22]See Kenneth L. Parker and Eric J. Carlson, *"Practical Divinity": The Works and Life of Revd. Richard Greenham* (Aldershot, Hants.: Ashgate, 1998).

[23]"A seconde parte of a register"; cited in Patrick Collison, *The Elizabethan Puritan Movement* (London: Jonathan Cape, 1967) 365.

[24]L. J. Trinterud, ed., *Elizabethan Puritanism* (New York: Oxford University Press, 1971) 380–383.

[25]See Collison; also A. E. Peaston, *The Prayer Book Tradition in the Free Churches* (London: James Clarke, 1964) 16–32.

[26]Patrick Collison, "The Elizabethan Puritans and the Foreign Reformed Churches in London," *Proceedings of the Huguenot Society of London* 20 (1958–1964) 528–555, esp. 529.

[27]Leland Carlson, *The Writings of John Greenwood, 1587–1590* (London: Allen and Unwin, 1962) 295.

[28]*The Brownists Synagogue* (London: n.p., 1641) 5ff.; Robert Browne, "A true and short declaration," in *The Writings of Robert Harrison and Robert Browne*, ed. Albert Peel and Leland Carlson (London: Allen and Unwin, 1953) 422.

[29]Robert Browne, "A Booke which sheweth the life and manners of all true Christians" in Peel and Carlson, 284.

[30]Carlson, 295.

[31]Champlin Burrage, *The Early English Dissenters*, 2 vols. (Cambridge: Cambridge University Press, 1912) 1:143.

[32]Leland Carlson, *The Writings of John Greenwood and Henry Barrow, 1591–1593* (London: Allen and Unwin, 1962) 307.

[33]Burrage, 1:144.

[34]Edward Cardwell, *A History of Conferences* (Oxford: Oxford University Press, 1860) 131–132.

[35]For further details, see Spinks, *Sacraments, Ceremonies, and the Stuart Divines*.

[36]See notes in *Two Answers to Cardinal Perron, and Other Miscellaneous Works of Lancelot Andrewes* (Oxford: John Henry Parker, 1854) 153, 156.

[37]Reprinted in William Prynne, *Canterburies Doome* (London: John Macock, 1646) 121–124.

[38]*The Works of the Rt. Rev. Father in God John Cosin, Lord Bishop of Durham*, 5 vols. (Oxford: John Henry Parker, 1843–1855) 1:97.

[39]See Bryan D. Spinks, "What Was Wrong with Mr. Cosin's Couzening Devotions? Deconstructing an Episode in Seventeenth-Century Anglican 'Liturgical Hagiography,'" *Worship* 74 (2000) 308–329.

[40]Peter Heylyn, *Cyprianus Anglicus* (London: Printed for A. Seile, 1668) 314–315.

[41]Burrage, 2:274.

[42]Cited in Davies, *Worship and Theology in England*, 1:500–501.

[43]Robert Ashton, ed., *The Works of John Robinson*, 3 vols. (Boston: Doctrinal Tract and Book Society, 1851) 3:485.

[44]Cited in Doug Adams, *Meeting House to Camp Meeting* (Austin, Tex.: Sharing Company, 1984) 65.

[45]Adams, 65.

[46]John Cotton, *The Way of the Churches of Christ in New-England* (London: Printed by Matthew Simmons, 1645) 66–69.

[47]Samuel Rutherford was to declare of Knox's liturgy: "We will not owne this liturgy. Nor are we tyed unto it." Manuscript. Minutes of the Westminster Assembly, Dr. Williams's Library, London, 2:492. See further in Spinks, *Sacraments*.

[48]Trevor Cooper, *The Journal of William Dowsing* (Woodbridge, Suffolk: Boydell, 2001), 155–156.

[49]Cooper, 292.

[50]Judith Maltby, *Prayer Book and People in Elizabethan and Early Stuart England* (Cambridge: Cambridge University Press, 1998). For the book's devotional influence, see Ramie Targoff, *Common Prayer: The Language of Public Devotion in Early Modern England* (Chicago: University of Chicago Press, 2001).

[51]*The Diary of John Evelyn*, ed. E. S. De Beer (Oxford: Oxford University Press, 1959) 383.

[52]Francis Higginson, *A Brief Relation of the Irreligion of the Northern Quakers* (London: n.p., 1653) 12–14; quoted in Adrian Davies, *The Quakers in English Society, 1655–1725* (Oxford: Clarendon, 2000) 77.

[53]John Wigan, *Antichrist's Strongest Hold Overturned* (London: n.p., 1665) 49, and Joseph Wright, *A Testimony* (London: n.p., 1661) 164; quoted in T. L. Underwood, *Primitivism, Radicalism, and the Lamb's War* (Oxford: Oxford University Press, 1997) 94.

[54]William Penn, *The Christian-Quaker* (London: Andrew Stow, 1674) 127.

[55]See Christopher W. Marsh, *The Family of Love in English Society, 1550–1630* (Cambridge: Cambridge University Press, 1994).

[56]See Spinks, *Sacraments*.

[57]Timothy Fawcett, ed., *The Liturgy of Comprehension, 1689* (Southend-on-Sea, Essex: Alcuin Club; Mayhew-McCrimmon, 1973).

[58]Quoted in Donald Maclean, *London at Worship: 1689–1690* (Manchester: Presbyterian Historical Society, 1928).

[59]*Account of the Doctrine and Discipline of Mr. Richard Davis of Rothwell in the County of Northampton, and those of his separation* (London: n.p., 1700) 20–21.

[60]"From the Bury Street Records," *Congregational Historical Society Transactions* 6 (1915) 333–342.

[61]*Account of the Doctrine and Discipline*.

[62]*Account of the Doctrine and Discipline*.

[63]Cited in Davies, 2:127–128.

[64]Cited in *Transactions of the Baptist Historical Society* 1 (1908–1909) 122–123.

[65]See Watson, *The English Hymn*.

[66]Watson, *The English Hymn*.

[67]César de Saussure, *A Foreign View of England in the Reign of George I and George II* (London: J. Murray, 1902) 318–319.

[68]G. E. Aylmer and R. Cant, *A History of York Minster* (Oxford: Clarendon, 1977) 263.

[69]Robert Cornwall, "The Rite of Confirmation in Anglican Thought during the Eighteenth Century," *Church History* 68 (1999) 359–372.

[70]William Whiston, *Essay on the Apostolic Constitutions* (London: n.p., 1711) chap. 1, xxiii.

[71]Peaston, *The Prayer Book Reform Movement*, 20.

[72]See Leonel L. Mitchell, "The Influence of the Rediscovery of the Liturgy of Apostolic Constitutions on the Nonjurors," *Ecclesia Orans* 13 (1996) 207–221; James David Smith, *The Eucharistic Doctrine of the Later Nonjurors*, Alcuin/GROW Liturgical Study 46 (Cambridge: Grove, 2000); and Stuart Hall, "Patristics and Reform: Thomas Rattray and the Ancient Liturgy of the Church of Jerusalem," in *Continuity and Change in Christian Worship*, ed. R. N. Swanson, Studies in Church History 35 (Woodbridge, Suffolk: Boydell, 1999) 240–260.

[73]See Mitchell, "Influence."

[74]Burdon, *Preaching Service*.

[75]For the United States, see Lester Ruth, *A Little Heaven Below: Worship at Early Methodist Quarterly Meetings* (Nashville, Tenn.: Kingswood, 2000); and Karen B. Westerfield Tucker, *American Methodist Worship* (New York: Oxford University Press, 2001).

[76]James F. White, *John Wesley's Prayer Book: The Sunday Service of the Methodists in North America* (Akron, Ohio: OSL Publications, 1995) 1.

[77]White, *John Wesley's Prayer Book*, 3.

[78]Arthur Bennet, "Charles Simeon: Prince of Evangelicals," *Churchman* 102 (1988) 130.

[79]Charles Smyth, *Simeon and Church Order: A Study of the Origins of the Evangelical Revival in Cambridge in the Eighteenth Century* (Cambridge: Cambridge University Press, 1940) 291.

[80]See Adelmann, *The Contribution of Cambridge Ecclesiologists*; and Yates, *Building, Faith and Worship.*

[81]Reported in the *Essex Standard*, 21 February 1845. The Parish Church did not use eucharistic vestments until the late 1960s, when they were introduced with the consent of the congregation by Canon John Derrett.

[82]Yates, *Anglican Ritualism in Victorian Britain.*

[83]Bryan D. Spinks, "Not so Common Prayer: The Third Service," in *The Renewal of Common Prayer*, ed. Michael Perham (London: SPCK; Church House, 1993) 55–67.

[84]See Watson; also Ian Bradley, *Abide with Me: The World of Victorian Hymns* (London: SCM, 1997).

[85]*The Christian World* (25 September 1890) 763–764.

17

The Church of South India

SAMSON PRABHAKAR

The liturgy of the Lord's supper in the Church of South India is, under God, a creative expression of faith coming out of a long and prayerful grappling of people who dreamed of and labored for the birth of a unified body of Christ in the southern part of the Indian subcontinent. No wonder, then, that the Church of South India, and particularly its liturgy, from the start motivated churches in the other parts of the world both to reflect on the call to Christian unity and to take a fresh look at their own liturgies. In the second half of the twentieth century, this South Indian liturgy took root in local soil as well as standing as a prime example of worship ordered according to the principles of the ecumenical Liturgical Movement.

After decades of negotiation, the Church of South India (CSI) was inaugurated in Saint George's Cathedral, Madras (Chennai), on 27 September 1947, six weeks after the passage of India to independence from the British crown. The CSI resulted from an organic union, in an episcopally ordered body, of churches springing initially from missionary work in the Anglican, Methodist, Presbyterian, and Congregationalist traditions. The tenth chapter of its founding constitution listed nine elements that should be included in every service of holy communion, demonstrating the intention to be authentically Christian according to Scripture and the Tradition of the universal Church:

(i) *Introductory Prayers*.

(ii) *The Ministry of the Word*, including readings from the scriptures, which may be accompanied by preaching.

(iii) *The Preparation of the Communicants* by confession of their sins, and the declaration of God's mercy to penitent sinners, whether in the form of an absolution or otherwise, and such a prayer as the "Prayer of Humble Access."

(iv) *The Offering to God of the gifts of the people*.

(v) *The Thanksgiving* for God's glory and goodness and the redemptive work of Christ in His birth, life, death, resurrection and ascension, leading to a reference to His institution of the Sacrament, in which His own words are rehearsed, and the setting apart of the bread and wine to be used for the purpose of the Sacrament with prayer that we may receive that which our Lord intends to give us in this Sacrament.

(vi) *An Intercession for the whole Church*, for whom and with whom we ask God's mercy and goodness through the merits of the death of His Son.

(vii) *The Lord's Prayer*, as the central act of prayer, in which we unite with the whole Church of Christ to pray for the fulfilment of God's gracious purposes and to present our needs before the throne of grace.

(viii) *The Administration of the Communion*, with words conformable to Scripture indicating the nature of the action.

(ix)   *A Thanksgiving for the Grace received in the Communion*, with which should be joined the offering and dedication of ourselves to God, unless this has been included earlier in the service. This Thanksgiving may be accompanied by an appropriate hymn.

In March 1948 the Synod of the CSI met in Madurai and appointed its first liturgical committee. While it was expected that forms of service from the constituent traditions would continue in local use, "it soon became clear," in the words of the convenor of the liturgical committee,

> that a new Communion Service was most desirable, if not absolutely necessary, for use on occasions when members of a diocese drawn from several different traditions met together. The Church very rapidly became conscious of itself as a united body and wished for some expression in its worship of the unity which was transcending the differences of tradition within it.[1]

Disclaiming technical expertise on their own part, the members of the committee did their homework and also consulted by letter with liturgical scholars in other parts of the world. A new Order for the Lord's Supper was prepared in time for use at the next Synod meeting at Madras in 1950. After the experience of use in Tamil, Malayam, Telugu, and Kannada, as well as in English, and further international consultation, the service was slightly revised and then "approved by Synod, January 1954, for general use wherever it is desired." It became integrated with other services into the Church of South India's *Book of Common Worship* (1962–1963).

The Order provides an opportunity for a devotion before the Lord's supper that is recommended for use on the night before or at an earlier time on the day of the communion. In light of the reading of 1 Corinthians 11:23–29 (which functioned as a "warrant" in the Reformed tradition) and the Ten Commandments or "our Lord's Summary of the Law and the Prophets," an Exhortation summons worshipers to self-examination and penitence with a view to receiving the benefits of the sacrament. In practice, this has not been much employed.

The Liturgy of the Eucharist proper begins with a section entitled "Preparation," consisting of a hymn or psalm; an entrance procession carrying the Bible; the collect for purity from the Anglican tradition ("Almighty God, unto whom all hearts be open . . . "); the Gloria in excelsis, or the "Holy God, Holy and Mighty, Holy and Immortal, have mercy on us" from the Orthodox tradition, or the Litany of the Lamb based on the Book of Revelation; and a simple form of confession of sin, followed by words of assurance and a prayer for forgiveness or absolution.

The Ministry of the Word of God, after the opening greeting and the collect of the day or other short prayer, includes three readings from the Bible (Old Testament, Epistle, and Gospel, thus restoring an ancient triple practice that many churches had lost), a sermon, one of the two ancient creeds (normally the Nicene Creed), and intercessory prayers. A first benediction then allows those who do not and cannot partake in the holy communion to leave the place of worship.

The Breaking of the Bread begins with biblical sentences—Psalm 133:1, 1 Corinthians 10:17, Psalm 27:6—that prepare for the exchange of the Peace and the presentation of the Offertory, which includes what has been collected as well as the bread and wine. The eucharistic prayer begins with the Sursum corda dialogue between minister and people, and the Preface celebrates God's work in the creating of the heavens and the earth, the making of humankind in the divine image, and the redemption of fallen humanity to be "the first fruits of a new creation." The Sanctus and the Benedictus qui venit flow into a blessing of God for Christ's saving work that is strongly reminiscent of the Prayer of Consecration in the Anglican tradition. The recital of the Lord's institution of the sacrament is followed by a congregational acclamation (in Syrian-Indian style) and an anamnesis that commemorate Christ's passion and death, his resurrection and ascension, and look forward to his second coming. An epiclesis asks the Father to "sanctify with thy Holy Spirit, us and these thine own gifts of bread and wine, that the bread which we break may be the communion of the body of Christ, and the cup which we bless the communion of the blood of Christ." The eucharistic prayer concludes with a trinitarian ascription of praise and the congregation's Amen.

The Lord's prayer and the Prayer of Humble Access ("We do not presume to come to this Thy table, O merciful Lord, trusting in our own righteousness, but in Thy manifold and great mercies . . . ") precede the Fraction (which may be accompanied by words from the Orthodox liturgy ("The things of God for the people of God") and the distribution of communion (when the Agnus Dei or another hymn may be sung). The recommended words of administration are "The Body of our Lord Jesus Christ, the Bread of Life" and "The Blood of our Lord Jesus Christ, the True Vine."

Communion is followed by one of two prayers of thanksgiving and self-oblation that each draw on scriptural language (Rom. 12:1–2) and phraseology from the Anglican *Book of Common Prayer*. The second benediction may be followed by a hymn, or part of Psalm 103, or the Nunc dimittis.

One of its authors judged the CSI liturgy to be

> a happy blend of contributions from the different heritages. At the same time these varying contributions have been transcended, and a mere miscellany of existing practices avoided, by our aim of reappropriating the great classical tradition of Christian worship, as found in the ancient liturgies, while subjecting it to the critical insights of the Reformation.[2]

Another of its authors staked for the CSI liturgy the claim that it is "a graceful and natural combination of Scripture and tradition, of ancient and modern, of evangelical and catholic, of East and West. It can be, and is, used in a service of great simplicity or to the accompaniment of stately ceremonial. It satisfies the needs of the humble villager and of the ecumenical theologian."[3]

Apart from the ecumenical features already noted, several more may be mentioned. It is recommended that the celebrant preside from "behind the Table, facing the people"; this stance was already familiar in the Reformed tradition and has since been recovered as "the basilican position" among Roman Catholics, Anglicans, and others. One of the forms proposed for the prayers of intercession is derived from a litany in the Syrian-Indian Liturgy of Saint James. The exchange of the peace had been preserved among the Thomas Christians, passed from the ministers to the people and then throughout the congregation in the form of a social greeting familiar in South India ("The giver places his right palm against the right palm of the receiver, and each closes his left palm over the other's right hand"). In adopting that form, the CSI set an example for many churches in the West. A prayer at the offertory is said to "echo the prayer of the veil in the Liturgy of St. James,"[4] and its theme of Christ as the "new and living way to the throne of grace" (Heb. 10:19–20) was present in the Church of Scotland's 1940 *Book of Common Order*. A second prayer leading into the anaphora takes up the *Adesto* of the Mozarabic liturgy and appends a verse from the Emmaus story (Luke 24:35): "Be present, be present, O Jesus, thou good High Priest, as thou wast in the midst of thy disciples, and make thyself known to us in the breaking of the bread. . . ." The CSI was a pioneer in the recovery of a fully developed eucharistic prayer among churches that benefited from the Liturgical Movement.

Eclectic as it may appear in its sources, the CSI liturgy was quickly experienced as a harmonious whole. It met with great appreciation from liturgical scholars overseas. According to R. C. D. Jasper, it "marked a kind of watershed in the history of liturgical revision; it colored the thinking of would-be revisers; and its influence, whether direct or indirect, was undeniable."[5] In his encyclopedic collections of Anglican liturgies, Colin Buchanan considers the CSI to have left such a mark on the shape and contents of several of them that one may speak of its having engendered a "family" of rites.[6] Scottish scholars ranked the CSI eucharist among "the most interesting and influential of the new wave of liturgies."[7] The Roman Catholic Louis Bouyer esteemed it highly, considering it "much more satisfactory than any other liturgy that emanated from the Reformation," though regretting the absence of the Blessed Virgin, the saints, and the faithful departed.[8]

The Lord's Supper, or the Holy Eucharist was published in a further revised version in 1972. It shows no changes in basic structure, although the Prayer of Humble Access has unaccountably been dropped. In place of the former post-communion prayers, a new short text prays God to "direct our minds, so that we do what you want and not what the world wants us to do. Help us to obey you on earth and to rejoice with all your saints in heaven." This prayer, in fact, gives a clue to the principal type of change throughout the revision, also where the longer prayers are retained: the language has been simplified through the elimination of archaic terminology and phrases that Indian celebrants found difficult; the English text has been shifted from "Thou" to "you." The final benediction has been fused with a dismissal for mission: "Go out into the world as witnesses and servants of Christ, and the blessing of God Almighty, the Father, the Son, and the Holy Spirit be with you always."

A few points may be made about local practice. From the start, the framers of the CSI liturgy desired it to be "the corporate act of the whole congregation."[9] In rural areas, one can see worshipers seated on the floor, singing Indian music to the accompaniment of Indian instruments such as the tabla, the vina, or the thamburu; even illiterate congregations sing the set pieces of the liturgy and the acclamations and responses by heart. Two points of engagement for the congregation are the announcements and the offertory. Normally, the announcements follow the recital of the creed: here is a convergence of church and world, of spiritual life with common life; at this perhaps painful point of word becoming flesh, concerns are voiced that can be presented to God in the intercessory prayers. At the offertory lay people may bring the bread and wine to the altar, and also other "products of human labor: the first fruits of the plaintain trees in the garden, the first egg that a pullet has laid, the first measure of milk from a newly purchased cow."[10]

Regarding the collection of alms, T. S. Garrett further noticed a growing practice of placing at the door of the church "a *chembu* or plain brass pot, such as can be bought by anyone from the brassmonger in the bazaar, identical in pattern and quality with the one that a woman uses to pour water on her child when giving him a bath beside the village well or to serve *rasam* (curried soup) to her hungry family"; and he commented that "this manner of collection . . . can be a more prayerful and self-dedicatory action than the handing around of a bag with or without the accompaniment of a hymn."[11] In many of the regional language congregations, the practice of having all people come forward and place their special offerings at the altar, where the pastors holds a tray, is in line with the cultural practices of India. Those of other faiths, particularly Hindu, go to the temple where they either put their offering in a vessel at the entrance or place it at the feet of their god and offer it to the *poojari* while sacred music is playing. The CSI liturgy provides space for various ways of giving offertory that the pastors should adapt according to the local culture and ethos. Since "giving" itself is religious act, a theology of giving should be developed from Indian perspective.

The CSI liturgy was meant from the beginning to be "Indian in character."[12] Indian Christian lyrics were encouraged from the start, flowing from "poetic creativity in the tradition of the great *bhakti* poets of Hinduism."[13] Several borrowings have already been noted from the Syrian-Indian Orthodox tradition as well as the adoption of some practices from social and local religious life. The litany in the baptismal rite contains an echo of the oft-quoted prayer from the Upanishads:

> [From the unknown lead us to the known,]
> From darkness lead us to light,
> From death lead us to life.

With biblical resonances to Ephesians 5:14 and 1 Peter 2:9–10 and awareness of the patristic designation of initiation as *phôtismos*, the implication may be that the "age-long desire of the soul of India finds its true fulfilment in Christian Baptism."[14] In marriage services it has become a widely accepted practice in the CSI to use *tali* (originally a thread dipped in turmeric tied by the bridegroom around the neck of the bride and considered auspicious) and also the "seven steps" (*saptapadha*) both of which are genuinely Indian. Some pastors have adopted saffron dye—a sacred color in Indian religions—for their robes or stoles.

This demonstrates a facility for assimilating foreign elements into the culture while still remaining Indian in essence. Worship takes place in church buildings that are mostly gothic in architecture, but the worship offered in them is rooted in India. "Somehow, an Indian atmosphere always succeeds in asserting

Baptism near Chennai. An infant is baptized in the Church of the Good Shepherd on the outskirts of Chennai (Madras). PHOTOGRAPH BY PETER WILLIAMS/WORLD COUNCIL OF CHURCHES

itself."[15] This is certainly the case with the liturgy of the CSI in its first half-century of use, where elements for the most part alien to India nevertheless became rooted in ways that allow kinship with the cultural heritage to be expressed.

In rural areas, where most people are illiterate, there is perhaps more openness to changes and the inclusion of indigenous elements in the worship; what matters is coming together, singing together, saying together, and being together. In congregations where there are a large number of members coming originally from the so-called free traditions, changes in the liturgy are appreciated for the freshness of experience and spontaneity that is regarded as the sign of the working of the Spirit.

From early days, however, there were critics—at first mainly perhaps from overseas but then also within the CSI—who looked for a much more deliberate Indianization of worship. In 1985–1986 the synod authorized for experimental use an Alternative Liturgy of the Holy Eucharist. It was greatly influenced by the experimental services conducted at United Theological College, Bangalore, under the leadership of Eric J. Lott and Christopher Duraisingh.[16] The stated aim was "to express an understanding of worship that is more Indian than our traditional Christian worship form," with an encouragement "to conduct the service in an authentic Indian style as far as possible, and . . . to adapt the service to fit local conditions and customs."[17] The Alternative Liturgy became "popular in the theological colleges";[18] and a version of it was employed in a service at the Lambeth Conference in 1998, when CSI bishops were welcomed for the first time as full members in the Anglican Communion.[19] But it has failed to make its way into the pews, for reasons that one of its principal authors describes as "complex, involving the political, ideological, and communal tensions within the Church of South India's hierarchy as much as the innate conservatism of the congregations, and the general lack of concern for dynamic liturgical reform."[20]

Occasional, unauthorized experimentation sometimes takes place, moving in the directions of secularization or sanskritization. Some are ill prepared to distinguish the wind of the Spirit from the "gale of the time." On one occasion an eco-conscious group visiting a college in Bangalore decorated the pine tree on the lawn and performed other acts in the name of secularizing the worship. On another occasion an activist led a "worship" without any reference to God or any deity in an attempt to make worship atheistic. There are also instances of worship made so brahmanic that it becomes very difficult for common people either to understand or to derive any meaning from them. Moreover, the contemporary zeitgeist encourages an individualistic piety that mars a genuine Christian spirituality and disrupts the corporate character of Christian worship.

The CSI liturgy, especially that of the Lord's supper, has a rich tradition that creates a distinctive yet ecumenical identity for the church. Albeit in multiform ways and in accordance with the regional culture, the CSI liturgy is deeply rooted in most of the congregations. It has itself become an icon: people are gathered around the table by and through this liturgy; it occupies a place next only to the Bible. It is a work of art, allowing worship to be theologically profound, authentically Christian, and culturally relevant.

Notes

[1] Leslie W. Brown, "The Making of a Liturgy," *Scottish Journal of Theology* 4 (1951) 55–63. Inside accounts by other members of the liturgy committee are: Marcus Ward, *The Pilgrim Church: An Account of the First Five Years in the Life of the Church of South India* (London: Epworth, 1953) 127–148; T. S. Garrett, *Worship in the Church of South India* (London: Lutterworth; Richmond, Va.: John Knox, 1958; 2nd ed. 1965). See also the thesis of Michael J. Hill, *The Formative Factors in the Compilation of the Eucharistic Liturgy of the Church of South India between 1949 and 1954* (Bangalore: United Theological College, 1978).

[2] Garrett, 8; 2nd ed., 10.

[3] Ward, 134–135.

[4] Garrett, 29, 2nd ed., 35.

[5] R. C. D. Jasper, *The Development of Anglican Liturgy, 1662–1980* (London: SPCK, 1989) 206.

[6] C. O. Buchanan, *Modern Anglican Liturgies, 1958–1968* (London: Oxford University Press, 1968), 5; and his *Further Anglican Liturgies, 1968–1975* (Bramcote, Notts: Grove, 1975) 15, 279–288, 416.

[7]Duncan Forrester, James I. H. McDonald, Gian Tellini, *Encounter with God* (Edinburgh: Clark, 1983) 124.

[8]Louis Bouyer, "A Roman Catholic View of the Church of South India," *Theology* 54 (1956) 3–11; cf. his *Eucharistie: Théologie et spiritualité de la prière eucharistique* (Tournai: Desclée, 1966) 420–423.

[9]Ward, 135.

[10]Garrett, 5; 2nd ed., 7.

[11]Garrett, 5, 25; 2nd ed., 7, 31.

[12]Ward, 135–136.

[13]Garrett, 9; 2nd ed., 11.

[14]Garrett, 41; 2nd ed., 50.

[15]Garrett, 9; 2nd ed., 11.

[16]See *Worship in an Indian Context: Eight Inter-Cultural Liturgies* (Bangalore: United Theological College, 1986); and Eric J. Lott, "Faith and Culture in Interaction: The Alternative CSI Liturgy," in *Reflections* [Festschrift for the Rt. Revd. Sundar Clark, Bishop in Madras], ed. Sathianathan Clarke (Madras: Poompuhar Pathipagam, 1987) 120–140

[17]*Church of South India Liturgy: The Holy Eucharist* (Madras: CLS, 1985) 1.

[18]Israel Selvanayagam, "With the Cross and the Lotus: The Church of South India in Fifty Years," *Epworth Review* 25 (1998) 107–114.

[19]See *Lambeth Prayer: Daily Worship for the Conference 1998* (London: Anglican Consultative Council and SPCK, 1998) 18–27.

[20]Eric J. Lott, "Historic Tradition, Local Culture: Tensions and Fusions in the Liturgy of the Church of South India," in *The Sunday Service of the Methodists: Twentieth-Century Worship in Worldwide Methodism*, ed. Karen B. Westerfield Tucker (Nashville, Tenn.: Kingswood Books, 1996) 66. Some description of the 1985 liturgy and adaptive language and symbolization can be found in Thomas Samuel Jr., "Some Reflections on the Church of South India Liturgy since 1961," *Studia Liturgica* 30 (2000) 143–150.

18

The Uniting Church in Australia

ROBERT W. GRIBBEN

The Uniting Church in Australia was formed in 1977 by the union of the Methodist Church with the majority of Australian Presbyterian and Congregationalist churches. The failure of an earlier proposal to form a concordat with the Church of South India, and indeed to take a "reformed episcopacy" from that church, meant the forfeiture of a possible source of liturgical enrichment. The liturgical books of the previous denominations, variations on their British counterparts, remained important guides at union, though the secularist and modernizing mood of the 1960s meant that many "experimental" orders of worship, not least for youth gatherings, were already supplanting liturgies marked by solemnity and archaic language.

There was soon a clamor for liturgies that represented the new united situation. Largely by chance, an ecumenical hymnal—the *Australian Hymn Book*—appeared in the year of union and was enthusiastically adopted as its own by the Uniting Church. A series of draft liturgies began to appear in 1980. The booklet *Holy Communion* (1980) contains three orders, roughly representing the Methodist (Anglican) and the Presbyterian/Congregationalist forms, but reflecting more recent scholarship and practice (e.g., modern English is used). Each order provides for a single Sunday service of word and sacrament, indicating a major shift from recent tradition. Where there were divergent customs (e.g., for distributing communion, the use of wine or grape juice, the role of lay elders), the National Commission on Liturgy urged experimentation and local decision.

After a further decade of life, the church was ready to authorize a new resource, *Uniting in Worship* (Melbourne: 1988) which appeared in two handsome volumes. The *People's Book* contains the structure of all main services, together with common responses and texts (generally adopting those of the English Language Liturgical Consultation) to maximize the congregation's verbal participation, a liturgical psalter (without music), and an anthology of responsive prayers and litanies that might also serve as a resource for private and family prayer. The *Leader's Book* is much larger, containing many alternative resources for each service. In the event, the idea of putting a book into the hands of the worshipers failed, perhaps because of fears of its formality, or perhaps because of the increased use of photocopied service sheets for Sundays. There is, however, evidence of the widespread use of the *Leader's Book* in the preparation of Sunday services.

The new book was both ahead of its time and consciously conservative of the constituent denominations' histories. The baptism and related services reflect the recovered view that confirmation is a "reaffirmation of baptism"; the book encourages a more generous use of water as symbol, including immersion; it adopts the use of a candle for the newly baptized, but places its presentation in the dismissal rite to underline the missionary significance of baptism. Concerns arising from charismatic renewal and internal debates over infant baptism show in the provision of services for the repeated reaffirmation of baptism by individuals and congregations; the status of baptism was being revalued through liturgical experience. One such liturgy is a form of the Methodist Covenant Service, recast to heighten the baptismal reference. In the marriage service, nuptial blessings appear for the first time. Services of healing and of (personal) reconciliation give clear permission for these pastoral tools. The funeral service provides a rich resource for local adaptation, and liturgies for perinatal deaths are now added.

Of writing ordinals there has seemed no end, as the Uniting Church has struggled to articulate its theology and forms of ministry. In 1991 it fulfilled a promise made at union to inaugurate a distinct "permanent" diaconate in addition to the presbyterate. The two ministries are barely distinguishable by function, both including presidency of the eucharist, and the ordination services are probably too similar. In time, practice may clarify this further, not least if the ministry of the *pastor pastorum* (usually a role of the presbytery minister) is further defined. Both diaconate and presbyterate are open to women as well as men.

At the eucharist, the influence of Gregory Dix's theory of the fourfold "shape" of primitive Christian worship (see Chapter 2) is plain to see; this has the effect of purging the liturgy of some traditional notes; though the Reformed tradition of reading the institution narrative as a "warrant" remains a choice. There is a newly composed Great Prayer of Thanksgiving, which sounds an Australian note in the preface with "In time beyond our dreaming, you brought forth life out of darkness," allowing an imaginative connection with the Aboriginal notion of the dreamtime but drawing also on the biblical significance of dreams; similarly, in the christological section, Ephesians 2 is paraphrased, thus ending with the tag loved by the Reformers and Wesley, "for by grace we are saved, through faith." Little else is characteristic of Australian or denominational insights. The former aspect is being explored in popular liturgical writing and in songs. There are eight alternative Great Thanksgivings drawn from sources as wide as the United Church of Canada and Prayer IV of the 1970 *Roman Missal*.

These extensive and ecumenically supported resources were, however, innovations for many ministers and people. The generation since union knew neither Calvin nor Wesley, nor the ways of the churches they founded, nor realized how much in common practice was owed to the

Invermay Chapel. Located near the gold town of Ballarat, Victoria, the now Uniting Church chapel is a good example of the nineteenth-century rural Protestant chapel or church found in Australia and elsewhere. PHOTOGRAPH BY KAREN WESTERFIELD TUCKER

nineteenth and early twentieth centuries. Revivalism and neo-evangelicalism were as formative as the discoveries of the liturgical or ecumenical movements. Not only rural congregations found the use of a book strange, and old prejudices against Rome and Anglicanism provoked resistance as much as a dislike of change. Australians pride themselves on an informal and democratic spirit; they do not place their clergy on a pedestal; they hold their own opinions over against "authorities," and they do not like dressing up either literally or linguistically. Ministers and lay preachers have felt free (with the liberty allowed by the free church tradition) to alter and adapt the official books and a wide range of other resources. The rule is that such variations may be made provided theological integrity is maintained. This is not easily achieved when liturgies are made with scissors and paste, or when prayer is offered extempore. In any case, there is a wide range of opinion and practice within the Uniting churches. It will be a major issue in the next round of liturgical revision as to how such integrity is maintained at all since material will be provided on the Internet and on CD-ROM, from which much is already borrowed with little regard to provenance. In many ways, this reflects the present individualism and fragmentation in other parts of Western culture.

The rapid growth of churches in the colonial period meant a surplus of buildings after union, and rationalization has been overtaken by dire necessity as numbers of worshipers diminish. There was a spate of new building in the 1950s and 1960s, reflecting the first phase of the liturgical movement in making the table central and moving the pulpit to the side. A less formal phase of alteration has followed in which the pulpit is largely ignored and ministers pray and preach from ill-adapted lecterns closer to the people. Sermons are briefer and more conversational; many preachers continue to follow the recommended Revised Common Lectionary. Banners are popular, and the use of liturgical colors in church and in vestments has changed the mood of many formerly austere places. Guidelines for these have largely prevented the visual cacophony of some Protestant experimentation; some ministers, of course, choose to wear secular dress; older ministers still wear the black gown of former times, but alb and stole or scarf are now common.

A new worship resource—*Uniting in Worship 2*—was published in 2005. The need to demonstrate faithfulness to Methodist or Calvinist ancestors has largely gone, but it is not yet clear what criteria define the Uniting Church's theology of worship. What does it mean to be an "ecumenical" church? Is there now permission to revisit old theological disputes and revise practices in the light of new perspectives? To what extent should "Old Europe," the colonial Australian myths, or the "latest from the United States" affect "New Australia"? "Multicultural Australia" should certainly be easier to observe in the Uniting Church's worship than it is. Are the results of recent theological convergence too fluid to guide liturgical decisions? Twenty-five years of union is a short time in church and cultural history, and the Uniting Church will need to bring out all its treasures, both old and new, to fund its future.

Bibliography

Gribben, Robert W. *A Guide to Uniting in Worship*. Melbourne: Uniting Church Press, 1990.

Gribben, Robert W. "*Uniting in Worship*: The Uniting Church in Australia." In *The Sunday Service of the Methodists: Twentieth-Century Worship in Worldwide Methodism*, ed. Karen B. Westerfield Tucker, 67–79. Nashville, Tenn.: Abingdon, 1996.

Wood, H. D'Arcy. "Text and Context in a Newly United Denomination: The Liturgical Experience in Australia." In *The Sunday Service of the Methodists*, ed. Karen Westerfield Tucker, 81–93. Nashville, Tenn.: Abingdon, 1996.

19

Mennonites

JOHN REMPEL

Anabaptism, the sixteenth-century movement from which Mennonites, Hutterites, and Amish emerged, began in a liturgical act. Radical followers of the Zurich reformer Ulrich Zwingli became convinced that the ultimate goal of renewal must be the restoration of the Church as a community of believers outside the sphere of the state. Baptism upon profession of faith was for them the act by which one entered a Church of believers in contrast with infant baptism, which initiated everyone into a Christianized social order. Similarly the Lord's supper was the event by means of which believers were united with Christ and one another in personal relationships. Both of these actions were spontaneously carried out in a farm kitchen near Zurich in January 1525 and constitute the beginning of what was to become the Mennonite Church.[1]

Introduction

For Anabaptists the Church was a visible community constituted by outward signs. It is worth noting that their ecclesiology distinguished the Anabaptists from both the Spiritualists (such as Kaspar Schwenckfeld) and the Magisterial Reformers (Martin Luther, Zwingli, John Calvin, Thomas Cranmer) who, in different ways, held to an invisible Church of the elect. Although the Anabaptists, like members of movements of the Reformation as a whole, were marked by the spiritualistic impulse of late medieval theology, they were sacramental in their conviction that the body of Christ on earth was a visible, historical entity. This helps to explain two matters. One of them is the Anabaptists' preoccupation with discipline: if those gathered in the name of Jesus are his body, then they must appear "without spot or wrinkle" (Eph. 5:27). The other matter is the this-worldly nature of Anabaptist worship: the Spirit was present in everyday life and activity rather than in a special religious sphere. Therefore worship needed no symbols pointing to a beyond. For most Anabaptists, visible signs, such as baptism, the Lord's supper, and foot washing, were essential to the life of the Church. The symbolic weight lay more on the human response than the divine initiative, but it was, for example, through the act of water baptism that a believer was admitted to the universal Church and a particular congregation. So central was this conviction about the outward nature of the body of Christ on earth that its protagonists were willing to suffer imprisonment and martyrdom rather than retreat from the world into a spiritualistic conventicle. Unlike the Spiritualists, the Anabaptists were unwilling to make peace with the world by giving up believers' baptism: an outward rite of initiation was indispensable to an outward community. This Church was to be a charismatic society whose members, individually and collectively, were bearers of the Holy Spirit. When they gathered for worship, Bible study, and decision making, believers relied on the immediate promptings of the Spirit in any member to reveal truth from God.[2]

A tension between inward and outward, letter and spirit, order and inspiration, characterizes every religious collective, but usually one side of the tension is allowed to dominate. This was certainly the case with individual Anabaptist fellowships, but in the movement as a whole the goal remained to hold the outwardness of the Church's existence in the world and the inwardness of the Spirit's work together. This is illustrated by the work of the most liturgical of first-generation Anabaptist leaders, Balthasar Hubmaier. In his "A Form for Christ's Supper" he severely alters but retains the form of the Roman mass. Within this form he provides, after the sermon, for any worshiper with insight into the preaching text to contribute it, after the manner of 1 Corinthians 14.[3]

Anabaptist vitality became routinized in the course of the second and third generations because of persecution and exhaustion. With the exception of Hubmaier, only fragmentary attempts were made to fashion worship forms out of pre-Reformation tradition. At the same time ancient habits were engraved on the people's souls. For example, the enquiry by the priest into the holiness of life of Easter communicants at a late medieval preparatory service during Holy Week is carried over with little change into Mennonite eucharistic practice.[4] For the most part, liturgy emerged from below: prayers that a presider had led extemporaneously became normative as they were repeated by himself and others and then were set down in manuscript. At the same time, there is a pattern of evidence that these orders were altered and even discarded from one generation to the next. In many Mennonite communities across the centuries, order and inspiration were reconciled by having members, and especially leaders, internalize concepts and turns of phrase so that a predictable liturgical vocabulary was established. Yet because these were not written down, the fiction was preserved that worship was extemporaneous.

Anabaptism never became an established social institution. In the early generations, it was persecuted. Where it survived, it remained marginalized. It did not become a church by means of a political or theological declaration but through a liturgical act, baptism. Its most trenchant criticism of the existing theological and social order was not a document but a ceremony, baptism. Therefore published records were scant; there were no official orders of service established by law. At the same time, prayers for use in church and home were collected, published, and used across a broad range of Mennonite communities. A few exceptions aside, orders for occasional services (for example, communion, ordination) were hand copied, and their use was limited to the area of origin and migrations therefrom. The order of service for an ordinary Sunday was usually predictable but not written down, even in the minister's manuals that came into being after 1800.

Much of the story of Mennonite worship is told by diary entries and the perseverance of ancient customs. In the North German stream, for instance, it was customary to bring along a fine white cloth in which to hold the bread on communion Sundays. Among the Amish there persisted the practice of bending one knee when taking the communion cup.

Because of their emphasis on the congregation as the normative (but not only) manifestation of Church and a resistance to central authority, Mennonites have re-

Mexican Mennonites. A community in Cuauhtémoc, Mexico, worships with the sexes separated. Women and girls cover their heads; the men's and boys' hats hang in orderly fashion on beams suspended from the ceiling. PHOTOGRAPH BY MICHEL SETBOUN, 2000/CORBIS

mained an astonishingly diverse body from the time of their origins. It has often been said, and not without justification, that factionalism is the chronic Mennonite illness. Historically, after the dispersal brought about by persecution, there were two geographic centers of Mennonite life. The "Northern" one stretched from the Netherlands, across northern Germany, and then down to southern Russia. The "Southern" one stretched across the Alsace, southern Germany, and northern Switzerland. In brief, there are now three tendencies in historic Mennonitism in North America. The majority is moderates, who try to marry tradition and innovation in worship as well as in theology and lifestyle; in worship they borrow cautiously from evangelical, charismatic, and liturgical sources. The minority at one end is "old order" movements, which arose at the close of the seventeenth century and again at the close of the nineteenth to preserve old ways. The form of their worship comes from Mennonite practice of the eighteenth century and early nineteenth century but continues to change slowly. The growing minority at the other end tends toward independent evangelicalism, increasingly charismatic in nature; the form of their worship is a mixture of revivalistic and contemporary Christian styles.

Apart from the old order groups, the face of Mennonitism has changed markedly in the course of the twentieth century. Between 1850 and 1900 most Mennonite bodies in Europe and North America experienced revival and with it the recovery of a missionary vision they had lost in the seventeenth century. Often the tension between tradition and innovation burst the bounds of communal life, and new Mennonite bodies came into being. Missionary activity led to the encounter with other cultures, both in the North Atlantic world and beyond it. Direct reliance on the Holy Spirit in worship and the long-standing marginality to mainstream culture should have helped Mennonites inculturate their faith and life in other societies. It was, in fact, the evangelical rather than the Anabaptist impulse that inspired Mennonites to sit lightly to their historical forms of worship in missionary settings. Sometimes the translation never moved beyond the transitional phase of western generic evangelicalism.

But gradually new Mennonite churches around the world have taken ownership of their lives and created worship forms that express their soul. Written worship resources in these settings are limited to the informal copying of resources passed on from congregation to congregation. The ecstatic dimension of many societies of color has drawn them to passages like 1 Corinthians 14, much as it drew the Anabaptists. At the same time these cultures are also more at home with elaborate ritual than is rationalistic white, Protestant culture in the West. This richness of expression leads to elaborate services in which many gifts of the Spirit are exercised. Third world Mennonite communities borrow music from their own and popular Western culture as well as composing their own songs. The hymnals produced for the Mennonite World Conferences of 1978 and 1997 illustrate how widely this is the case.[5]

In North America home missions among Native Americans, blacks, Hispanics, and immigrants from around the world have led to similar inculturation. During the last thirty years of the twentieth century, the moderate white Mennonite majority worked prodigiously to renew worship by the judicious borrowing of musical form and style from three sources: church growth/charismatic worship, the Liturgical Movement (especially Taizé), and African worship (especially western and southern). As to the spoken parts of worship, the conferences have sought to recast the riches of the liturgical movement for a Mennonite ecclesiology. An abundance of pamphlets, many based on the church year and the Revised Common Lectionary, hymnals, and the 1998 *Minister's Manual* of the new Mennonite Church USA/Canada have been issued in the hope of preserving the best prayers and hymns of the tradition and blending them with the fruits of liturgical reform in the larger Christian Church. Along with that has been an encouragement to improvise on basic historic patterns in ways that make these resources accessible to people who lift up the charismatic dimension of worship.[6]

Probably one-third of mainstream Mennonites have a blended worship style. But most go one way or the other: there the liturgical and charismatic movements exist like two solitudes. As congregations break out of old conventions, they look in opposite directions for inspiration. There are fewer and fewer common ways of acting out the root symbols and memories of the community. This is a time of testing for Mennonite community in North America. Will the center hold? Worship in which people of diverse backgrounds and convictions share a common passion and recognize a common core is being lost. New forms of worship that shape and unify a people are not yet in reach.

Worship on the Lord's Day

Order

The central rhythm of Anabaptist communities was their gathering to worship and their dispersal to announce and demonstrate "a new humanity" (Eph. 2:15) as a sign of the coming kingdom. When they met, the heart of the matter was interpreting the scriptures and building one another up for mission. Singing, preaching, praying, and prophesying according to the pattern of 1 Corinthians 14 provided an organic pattern for worship.[7]

Proclamation of biblical texts by preachers, and initially by all with a gift of prophesy, was central to worship but was not set in opposition to the Lord's supper. Because Anabaptists did not have formally trained clergy, the service focused less on a single leader and a single act of proclamation. The guiding thought was the fellowship of believers; the ideal was apostolic church life in Jerusalem and Corinth. In this scheme of things word and sacrament were not opposites but complements.

Gradually worship assemblies took on the form they were to retain in most settings until the mid-twentieth century. Fixed texts, like the Aaronic blessing, were more common in the Northern than in the Southern stream of Mennonitism. Although there were regional variations on the theme, the progression was a variation of what follows:

> Congregational singing
> Greeting ("Peace be unto us")
> Opening reflection on a biblical text

Opening prayer (kneeling; often in silence)
Scripture reading
Sermon (often begun with "Grace be unto us and peace")
Pastoral prayer (kneeling; the Lord's prayer in unison often concluded this prayer
      or it was offered by the presider alone just before the blessing)
(Communion, baptism, or a wedding would come here)
Hymn
Blessing (usually "The Lord bless us" or "The grace of our Lord Jesus Christ")

As part of the routinization, roles were formally assigned in the worship assembly: the unsung parts were more and more reserved to the elder or bishop (preaching and presiding at ceremonies), minister (preaching), and deacon (reading and praying). Inspired commentary on the proclamation became confined to these leaders.

As with Protestantism in general, bringing the Bible close to the people through preaching was central to Mennonite worship. After the short-lived first generation of theologically astute leaders, preaching was carried out by people who made their living as farmers or craftspeople. Later, as Mennonites pursued higher education, in the Netherlands it became common to choose medical doctors as ministers, and in Russia teachers were favored.

In a traditional service there would be at least two preachers. In the Southern stream they would be chosen as all the ordained met only moments before the service began. The first proclamation would be a brief devotional reflection on a text to open the service and set its tone. The second proclamation was a major discourse whose theme was often the ways of God with humanity—lessons of God's interventions in Old and New Testament times or the challenges of discipleship. In the Southern stream there was a second distinctive. After the main sermon any of the ordained present were invited to "give witness." This meant that they could add affirmation or insight to the preacher's words. In the course of the twentieth century in the Mennonite mainstream, with more and more educated and full-time clergy, there is usually a single sermon presented on the basis of a manuscript or at least notes.

With the modern addition of instruments, choirs, and liturgical responses, these were given a place in worship but seldom a role. In other words, they were not integrated into the action in a way that allowed them to carry worship forward. In the early twenty-first century the dominant trends have a recognizable order. In liturgically influenced worship, care is taken to sew each act of worship into a common garment. In charismatically shaped worship, there tends to be a half-hour sequence of

Young Mennonites. Children at the West Union Mennonite Church in Parnell, Iowa hear a message during Sunday morning worship. PHOTOGRAPH BY LAURIE L. OSWALD, MENNONITE CHURCH USA NEWS SERVICE

songs interspersed with short prayers and biblical citations and followed by a half-hour sermon and then a closing hymn and prayer.

Music

Congregational singing was and is the most profound form of self-expression for the congregation.[8] But in the first congregations in the canton of Zurich, this was not yet the case. Taking their lead from Zwingli, leaders such as Conrad Grebel forbade singing. Garside's study of liturgical life in sixteenth-century Zurich sheds light on this extreme reaction. Apparently the Fraumünster was notorious for liturgical extravagance. Because of the musical complexity of mass settings and anthems and their confinement to Latin texts, the Zurich reformers concluded that church music was inaccessible to the congregation and of no value in worship.[9]

This judgment was not shared by Anabaptism at large.[10] Two widely used hymnals were issued in Dutch and two in German in the 1560s alone. The texts were a mixture of ones borrowed from Catholic and Protestant tradition and ones written by Anabaptists. They included psalms, a few patristic texts, and their own contemporary martyr ballads. Their separatism notwithstanding, this uninhibited and voracious borrowing of musical materials has characterized Mennonite worship ever since. In fact few hymn tunes or texts have been written by Mennonites since the sixteenth century. Psalmody slowly lost ground to the German chorale tradition, which in turn was augmented by the more heartfelt texts and tunes of German Pietism and later English free church hymnody. Thereafter American gospel music, often in German translation, entered the field. A combination of these strands characterizes Mennonite hymn collections of the twentieth century; they were carried along into missionary settings. Of late a certain reciprocity exists in which third world compositions are being sung in the United States.[11]

Since the congregation was to be the only human actor in worship, a choir was not needed to sing on its behalf. The same logic was used to banish instruments from worship. But the medieval office of cantor took root in Anabaptist assemblies. Usually there were two or three song leaders who led the congregation with their voices. The first innovation on this pattern came in urban Dutch congregations in the late eighteenth century when, in imitation of the major churches, organs were introduced. Choirs in worship first arose in Russia in the 1870s as an extension of the development of more sophisticated music instruction in the Mennonite school system there. North American Mennonites of Swiss background resisted both innovations until the 1960s. But no sooner had Mennonites' habits assimilated into the middlebrow patterns of mainline Protestantism than the charismatic renewal burst upon the scene with a host of different instruments, ensembles, and singing styles.

Architecture

The break with medieval tradition is the most pronounced in relation to houses of worship and their furnishing. Since the Anabaptists were lawbreakers, they were often on the run; even when they were not, they were often forbidden to own real estate. To what extent was necessity turned into a virtue? To what extent were Anabaptists opposed to traditional church buildings because they were driven from them? Clearly their circumstances played a role. Yet the Anabaptist concentration on the gathered assembly as the sine qua non of worship seems to make the setting quite secondary.

In the first generation, and in some areas in the second, Anabaptists met for worship wherever they could safely do so—in houses, barns, and forests. Thereafter some of them, notably the Amish, continued to meet in houses or barns as a matter of principle. Even where this was not the case, house or barn often remained the setting for weddings and, to a lesser extent, funerals until the mid-twentieth century. Gradually the Mennonites in Europe were permitted to build houses of worship. They were almost always an adaptation of the Dutch Reformed design of a nearly square rectangular church with worshipers on three sides and presiders on the other, without a choir, apse, or long aisle; but in the Northern pattern there was often a three-sided balcony. The early-seventeenth-century Singel Kirk in Amsterdam is the prototype of this style of meetinghouse. The pulpit was a long, slightly elevated table built in front of the presiders' bench. In some places the Lord's table stood permanently before that bench; in others it was brought in only on communion Sundays.

Both the law and fear of intimidation made sure that meetinghouses were so plain on the outside that no one could identify one as a church.[12] Such vessels as were used for baptism, the breaking of bread, and foot washing were brought to church only for the occasion. No permanent symbols, such as the cross, were displayed.[13]

As spiritual and cultural assimilation proceeded, architecture followed suit. In the late nineteenth century, simple adaptations of neo-Romanesque and neo-Gothic structures were attempted. The long aisle that made the whole congregation face the preacher rather than one another worked against fellowship as the central reality of the assembly. With this change in architecture, the custom arose of painting a verse of scripture, such as "Christ the power and wisdom of God" (1 Cor. 1:24). Later a large, plain cross was often mounted on the front wall of the church. In its successive borrowings there has been a singular lack of originality in Mennonite church architecture; most designs are derivative and betray a lack of awareness of the history of Christian symbolism. Ironically the ecumenical trend to place the Lord's table in the midst of the assembly—a gesture that fits perfectly with Mennonite theology—has been resisted for two reasons. One reason is that it goes against the pattern of church design that was borrowed a century ago. The other is that in churches recently built on the pattern of a theater, the stage for musicians is so dominant that other symbols become insignificant.

The Lord's Supper

The eucharistic controversies of the sixteenth century were among the most impassioned of that passionate age. This was so because in the breaking of bread everything is at stake: eating and drinking with Jesus is the primal act of the Church. The following can be said, by way of summary, of Anabaptist views of the supper. There were iconoclasts among them with extreme anticlerical and antisacramental views. There was never a single voice setting down a systematic eucharistic theology. One aspect of teaching that received special emphasis was the sacramental body of Christ as the Church and the mystical body as the eucharist, though the early Anabaptists would not have used such language. The Anabaptists emphasized that in the breaking of bread the gathered church is re-created; the transformation which takes place is that of people, not of things.[14] For the most part Anabaptist views resisted the conclusions (if not always the logic) of Spiritualism. In a lingering ambivalence, Mennonite sacramental language has always remained guarded. It holds that grace is given in sacraments only to faith; bread and wine are signs of Christ's presence by the power of the Spirit. The movement's foremost sacramental thinker, Pilgram Marpeck, emphasized the function rather than the nature of the elements. In an examination of 1 Corinthians 10 and 11, he writes:

> Damnation, therefore, is not dependent upon what the bread and the wine are in the Lord's Supper, but rather on the correct use of the bread and wine, and upon the condition of the heart in which the bread and wine are taken. Whoever is worthy to eat of this bread and drink of this cup experiences a participation in the flesh and blood of Jesus Christ, as Paul testifies.[15]

How did these claims come to expression in worship? From the beginning there are records indicating that the assembly for worship often climaxed in the breaking of bread. In late-medieval Catholicism the priest communicated without a congregation; in sixteenth-century Anabaptism the congregation communicated without a priest. The whole priesthood of believers was to be the actor in the service of the word and of the table. Ordinary vessels were to be used. Because early Anabaptists were regularly persecuted or engaged in missionary journeys, the Lord's supper was usually a gathering of utter simplicity for ease of understanding by converts. But there is an exception to this pattern in Hubmaier's "A Form of Christ's Supper" of 1527:[16]

> Confession of sin
> Reading and expositing of scripture so that the congregation, "may be set afire in fervent meditation of Christ's bitter suffering and death in contemplation, love, and thanksgiving"
> Response by the congregation with the hymn, "Stay with us, O Christ"
> Further teaching on the preaching text, "from one to whom something is revealed"
> Self-examination according to 1 Corinthians 11
> Silence
> Lord's prayer
> Pledge of love
> Prayer of thanks
> Breaking and distribution of bread as the words of institution are spoken
> Exclamation of thanks
> Passing of the cup as the words of institution are spoken
> Call to live out the baptismal covenant
> Blessing

The form of the Lord's supper varied from region to region, but by the beginning of the seventeenth century it exhibited a recognizable pattern. Like other Christians—Protestant and Catholic—Mennonites were unable to overcome the medieval dread of unworthy communion and so, as their life became routinized, they lapsed into the practice of communicating once or twice a year. Confession, often called *Umfrage* (inquiry), happened the week before communion. At the supper the sermon set forth the suffering and sacrifice of Christ. This theme was continued in a general communion prayer. In some prayers the Spirit was invoked to make the breaking of bread into a "communion of the body and blood of Christ." This phrase from 1 Corinthians 10:17 as well as the words of institution from that epistle were preferred to the language of the Synoptic Gospels. Interestingly language derived from John 6 was common, although its interpretation was more mystical than realist. The prayers of thanks Jesus offered before the bread and cup, as recorded in the Synoptics, were imitated (without knowledge of their Jewish character or their evolution in the Early Church into the eucharistic prayer) as simple acts of gratitude for his body and blood before each of the elements was received.[17] A prayer of thanksgiving followed. Gradually the rite of foot washing became the normative conclusion to the service. In sum, the breaking of bread was an act of covenant renewal, in which believers pledged to lay down their lives for others as Christ had laid down his life for them. As the missionary fire subsided and congregations lived generation after generation in confined rural settings, the door to the Lord's table became conformity to community norms more than sanctity of life.

This pattern continued for two centuries. Then in Germany a church moving out from its isolation renewed itself by the extensive borrowing of liturgical and devotional prayers from Lutheran sources.[18] Half a century later in Russia, the borrowing of a reform movement—the Mennonite Brethren—turned to Baptist sources. It simplified the service, emphasized grace and assurance of salvation to counter the dread of unworthy communion, and instituted a monthly celebration. A similar approach gradually took root across the Mennonite mainstream. In the early twenty-first century in North America this approach is being taken in two directions. One of them is typified by the 1998 *Minister's Manual* that seeks to enrich the traditional Mennonite eucharistic pattern with resources from the Liturgical Movement. The other trend is toward improvisation with a prayer of thanks for the work of Christ and the act of eating and drinking as the only core.

Baptism

Baptism is to be offered to people, according to the Schleitheim Confession of 1527, "who have been taught repentance and the amendment of life and believe truly that their sins are taken away through Christ and to all those who desire to walk in the resurrection."[19] Initially baptisms took place wherever believers met, in private homes, at village wells, in forests. As settled congregations developed, baptism was preceded by instruction (initially based on the Apostles' Creed, later on articles of faith, such as the Dordrecht Confession of 1632, as these were composed). In some cases a personal testimony of faith as well as a willingness to give and receive counsel in the congregation were asked for in addition to a confession of Christ as savior and assent to trinitarian doctrine. For Mennonites baptism has always been initiation into the body of Christ universal, enacted by means of entry into a local congregation. These characteristics have found expression in a variety of baptismal formulations. A contemporary one and an adaptation of an eighteenth-century order are illustrative:

CONTEMPORARY
> Do you renounce the evil powers of this world and turn to Jesus Christ as your savior? Do put your trust in his grace and love and promise to obey him as your lord?
> Do you believe in God the Father Almighty, maker of heaven and earth; in Jesus Christ, God's Son, our Lord; and in the Holy Spirit, the giver of life?
> Do you accept the Word of God as guide and authority for your life?
> Are you willing to give and receive counsel in the congregation?
> Are you ready to participate in the mission of the church?[20]

EIGHTEENTH CENTURY
> Are you sorry for your sins?
> Do you believe in God the Father, in Jesus Christ the Son, and in the Holy Spirit the Giver of Life?

> Do you promise, by God's grace, to follow Jesus the Lamb, all the days of your
> life, ready to love your enemies and suffer wrong nonresistantly?
> Do you accept the way of life set forth in our confession of faith?[21]

What is a Mennonite baptismal service like? Baptism is the centerpiece and the theme of the readings and preaching. Until the act of initiation itself, the service follows the normal pattern, though usually more festive in spirit. A short description is given of the meaning of baptism. If they have not done so in a previous service, the candidates will usually give a testimony of faith and express their desire to be part of the Church. Questions like those above will be asked and answers given. Then the trinitarian formula is spoken as water is added. Often a prayer for the Holy Spirit follows immediately. The candidates are received into the congregation. After the service, members informally congratulate them and express a willingness to give and receive counsel with them.

Surprisingly the form of baptism seems simply to have followed traditional local practice. Sprinkling and pouring, once or three times, were most common, but immersion was also practiced. The form of baptism did not become a matter of polemics until renewal movements among Mennonites in the seventeenth and nineteenth centuries (Dompelaars in Germany and Mennonite Brethren in Russia) associated immersion with a crisis conversion and an intensity of faith lacking in the Mennonite Church of the day. Baptism was and remains a highlight of Mennonite church life in all branches; the service often culminates in the celebration of the Lord's supper.

What happens, as Mennonites understand it, in baptism? All would agree that the event acts out the preceding response of faith to grace (commonly described as dying and rising with Christ, as in Rom. 6:3–4) and the grafting of the believer into the body of Christ. Some would place the primary weight in baptism on the human response: it is the initial act of obedience which the Christian renders to Christ. Others would also emphasize baptism as the seal of the Holy Spirit (God's act) and a vouching for the faith of the candidate (the church's act).[22]

Other Ceremonies

Ordinances

Although the Lord's supper and baptism were always held up as the central actions of the Church, there were various lists of additional ordinances among Anabaptists in the sixteenth century. The most elaborate one is by Dirk Philips. As marks of the Church, he lists and describes ordination, sacraments (communion and baptism as a single mark), foot washing, discipline, love, commandment keeping, suffering.[23] Other lists appear across the centuries; their common characteristic is the bringing together of ritual acts and moral acts as marks of the Church, binding together its worship and mission.

Discipline

Church discipline was thought of as the necessary complement to baptism: one entered the Church with a promise to live a holy life; one was excommunicated if one persistently violated that promise. Matthew 18:15–22 was held up as the model of charitable admonition. Although the motivation was to be one of mutual correction, the process often descended into self-righteousness. There was usually a public declaration of excommunication. Some formularies include a rite for the reception of penitents.[24]

Ordination

Conversion and baptism made women and men equal as heirs of grace, as set forth in parts of Paul's ecclesiology. Both possessed the Spirit, so both were called to witness to Christ at home and work. Almost as many women as men endured martyrdom. In some settings witnessing by women led to their role as interpreters of biblical texts.[25] As congregations braced themselves for battle with the world, the setting apart of leaders became more formalized. Only men were chosen for these roles, which generally perpetuated the threefold ministry on the basis of biblical precedent. Initially provision was made for prophets who received a direct call from God and had only to be acknowledged by the congregation. Mention of this role ceases after the second generation.

Otherwise choosing leaders seems to have happened by congregational or regional church discernment or by lot. The use of the lot (Acts 1:21–26) was widespread, especially where more than one name for an officeholder had been put forth by members of the congregation. The only formal criterion was evidence of the Holy Spirit's work in the man's life. The names would be announced and a day of prayer and fasting declared. On the ordination day identical Bibles or hymnals would be given to each candidate; in one of them a slip of paper would be placed. There was a moment of breathtaking drama as each candidate opened his book and one of them discovered the slip of paper. Ordination followed immediately.

In the Southern stream of Mennonites all leaders were ordained. In the Northern stream elders or bishops were always ordained, ministers usually, and deacons often not. Because of the importance of singing, song leaders were elected by the congregation. All of this changed in the latter half of the twentieth century. In the mainstream few district conferences call bishops. Some have overseers for a smaller number of congregations than traditionally constituted a bishop district. Others appoint conference ministers for that role. Deacons have been replaced or, in some cases, complemented by "elders" in the Reformed understanding of that role. In 1915 the Dutch Mennonites ordained their first woman minister. This shift happened in North America in the two largest conferences in the late 1960s. Now most of their regional conferences have women at all levels of leadership. The smaller groups range from ordaining women only as assistant ministers to reserving all appointed ministries for men. Of all the Mennonite groups, only the Dutch ordain homosexuals in a partnership.

The spiritual and theological formation of ministers happened without educational institutions for most of Mennonite history. New leaders would be taught preaching and presiding by older ones. They would rely on books of sermons as exemplars and, in some settings, as texts that they reread word for word in the Sunday assembly.[26]

Marriage

Such limited records of wedding services as there are tell us that into the nineteenth century the vows were most often celebrated as an appendix to the regular Sunday assembly. The couple came forward to sit in chairs set out for them in order to hear an admonition by the minister concerning the joys and pitfalls of conjugal life. His text was often Tobit 8. The vows for the woman and the man were usually identical. Later on weddings were more and more often solemnized domestically in a separate service in the bride's home or (elaborately decorated) barn. In the course of the twentieth century church weddings became the norm in mainstream Mennonitism. Of all the rituals Mennonites celebrate, their marriage rite differs least from those of other denominations.

Funerals

There is sparse documentation of funeral practices until the nineteenth century, when collections of funeral sermons appear. According to oral tradition, congregational singing accompanied the service and the cortege as well as the burial. The order was that of a regular preaching service, with prayers for the occasion. In some records the weight of the sermon was placed on gratitude for the work of grace in the deceased's life; in others it was an occasion to warn mourners against the wrath to come. There was and is a wariness of a eulogy since it was thought to place the focus on the achievements of the deceased; instead, the weight was to be placed on God's provision. Along with Christian circles at large, Mennonites have moved from a predominant emphasis on judgment to one on resurrection. In mainstream Mennonitism there is a place for memorial services, cremation, and acts of committal for miscarriages and stillbirths.

Anointing

Anointing for healing is but rarely mentioned in early Mennonite lore.[27] It is not often part of prayer formularies or ministers' manuals until the twentieth century, but it has a firm basis in oral tradition: everyone assumes it has always been done. The traditional practice was for a minister, a deacon, and representatives of the congregation to visit a member privately at his or her sickbed. In the early twenty-first century anointing is increasingly practiced on an occasional basis in public worship not only for physical illness but for healing of relationships.[28]

Celibacy

Like anointing, celibacy is rarely mentioned but is provided for as an honorable estate. By common prejudice, marriage was the preferred state, but in some settings older women of stature were set aside as deaconesses. With the institutionalization of church life in the nineteenth century, celibate women were permitted to undertake missionary service at home and abroad, and a few deaconess orders, whose ministry was nursing, emerged. There is a "Blessing of a Life of Celibacy" in one of the early twenty-first century worship formularies.[29]

The Church Year

Aside from the Lord's day there is scant reference in Anabaptism to the church year and the lectionary. Formally they were discarded by Anabaptists as part and parcel of their rejection of clericalism and, in their view, religion imprisoned by its outer forms. But informally the use of seasonal scripture readings is in evidence. Much was made of Sunday as the day of worship and of rest. Gradually anecdotal references appear, for example, to the breaking of bread on Good Friday, meeting for worship on Ascension day, celebrating baptism on Pentecost. Bit by bit the liturgical calendar from Advent through Pentecost makes its way into Mennonite custom. In the 1767 Prussian hymnal, for example, the Lutheran lectionary is included. New Year's eve and day were almost universally observed. In the early nineteenth century Eternity Sunday, a European Protestant alternative to All Saints' and All Souls' days held on the last Sunday of the church year, was taken up in some circles. In settings influenced by revivalism in the early twentieth century and by charismatic renewal in the early twenty-first century, little is made of the church year.

Plate 21. Last Supper. Painting by Marcos Zapata (eighteenth century) in Cuzco, Peru, Cathedral. The replacement of the paschal lamb with a local guinea pig is a gesture toward inculturation. [See chapters 24 and 25.] CATHEDRAL OF CUZCO, PERU/TONY AND MARION MORRISON/SOUTH AMERICAN PICTURES

Plate 24. Women in worship. The nuns of the monastery of Port-Royal-des-Champs in choir. Anonymous gouache after an engraving by Madeleine Hortemels, eighteenth century. [See chapter 29.] Musée des Granges de Port-Royal, France, MV 6009/Réunion des Musées Nationaux/Art Resource, NY

Facing page, top

Plate 22. Mass in the early twentieth century. Painting by Jose Arnosa y Gallegos (1859–1917). [See chapter 27.] Weber Gallery, Great Britain/Fine Art Photographic Library, London/Art Resource, NY

Facing page, bottom

Plate 23. Christian initiation. Archbishop Alexander Brunett invites the elect to make their baptismal promises at the paschal vigil in St. James Catholic Cathedral, Seattle, Washington, 2005. [See chapter 27.] Photograph by Randy Redford, St. James' Cathedral, Seattle

Plate 25. Baptism in North Africa. A sixth-century quadrilobe font from Kélibia (ancient Clupea), Tunisia. Mosaic decorations symbolize baptism and the abundant life of paradise. Originally located in a baptistery attached to the Church of Felix in Kélibia, the font is now installed in the Bardo Museum in Tunis. [See chapter 31, sidebar "Baptismal Fonts."] Reproduced with permission of S. Anita Stauffer

Plate 26. The Last Supper. Tao Fong Shan Porcelain Workshop, Hong Kong. [See chapter 32, sidebar "The Visual Arts in Africa, East Asia, and the Pacific."] Photograph courtesy of Geoffrey Wainwright

Plate 27A. Christ in majesty.
Altarpiece in the chapel of
Libermann College, Douala,
Cameroon, by Engelbert Mveng
(1930–1995). [See chapter 32,
sidebar "The Visual Arts in
Africa, East Asia, and the
Pacific."] PHOTOGRAPH COURTESY
OF GEOFFREY WAINWRIGHT

Plate 27B. Christ crucified.
Batik painting by the Indonesian
artist Bagong Kussudiardja
(1928–2004). [See chapter 32,
sidebar "The Visual Arts in
Africa, East Asia, and the
Pacific."] PHOTOGRAPH COURTESY
OF GEOFFREY WAINWRIGHT

Plate 27C. The Virgin enthroned. Central panel from the altarpiece by Duccio di
Buoninsegna (c. 1260–1319) at Siena. [See chapter 32.] MUSEO DELL'OPERA METROPOLITANA,
SIENA, ITALY/SCALA/ART RESOURCE, NY

Plate 28. Saint Peter baptizing the new converts. Fresco by Masaccio (1401–1428) in the Brancacci Chapel, Santa Maria del Carmine, Florence. [See chapter 32.] SCALA/ ART RESOURCE, NY

Conclusions

One of the distinctive features of Anabaptism was its early attempts to marry freedom and order, charismatic utterance and read prayer. An aspect of this synthesis has been preserved among the Amish, but only for the ordained. They have a simple but invariable order of service. At the same time it is left until immediately before the service to decide who will preach. The assumption is that God will direct the thoughts of those chosen on a given Lord's day as they speak.

For the most part Mennonite worship has veered unevenly between the two poles of freedom and order. Memorized habits of speech and ritual, both from pre-Reformation usage and immediate experience, were written down. But as if by instinct there have been groups in every century that have broken the pattern, made room for spontaneous expression, and created new forms or borrowed them from other traditions. As this cycle moved farther and farther away from the sixteenth century, the structures of classical worship receded from the Mennonite mind.

There is a second tension in Mennonite worship. On the one hand, its missionary vision led to the creation of simple, inviting forms of praise that were accessible to new converts. On the other hand, Mennonite congregations tended to become private meetings of initiates. Worship forms ceased having an evangelistic flexibility. The assembly's chief function was to strengthen the covenant of obedience—and conformity. This struggle for balance in worship and congregational life between accessibility and accountability has been taken up in many congregations in the early twenty-first century. There is still not a strong sense of "public" worship as an open event with a recognizable structure in which newcomers can join. Worship planners and leaders still tend to create public worship based on small group or individual religious experience.

In sum, Mennonite worship has at least three traits. First, it is improvisional in constantly holding together form and freedom. Second, it is created locally and does not have a single, normative form. Third, it seeks to make worship and obedience inseparable: the gathered and the scattered Church are to be a seamless garment. Of the free churches, Mennonites have the strongest sense of liturgical order and tradition. At the same time they were a charismatic, missionary community in the sixteenth century. In the early twenty-first century many churches seek to combine tradition, charisma, and mission. It is more in their attempts to hold these three together than in their creation of profound forms of worship that Mennonites have an ecumenical contribution to make. The loftiest liturgical striving of Mennonites is to hold themselves accountable at work on Monday to the words they spoke in worship on Sunday.

Bibliography

Finger, Thomas N. *Christian Theology: An Eschatological Approach*. Vol. 2. Scottdale, Pa.: Herald, 1989.
Jeschke, Marlin. *Believers Baptism for Children of the Church*. Scottdale, Pa.: Herald, 1983.
Kreider, Eleanor. *Communion Shapes Character*. Scottdale, Pa.: Herald, 1997.
Neufeld, Bernie, ed. *Music in Worship*. Scottdale, Pa.: Herald, 1998.
Rempel, John, ed. *Minister's Manual*. Scottdale, Pa.: Herald, 1998.

Snyder, C. Arnold. *Anabaptist History and Theology.* Kitchener, Ont.: Pandora, 2002.
Stoffer, Dale R., ed. *The Lord's Supper: Believers Church Perspectives.* Scottdale, Pa.: Herald, 1997.

Notes

[1]Fritz Blanke, *Brothers in Christ* (Scottdale, Pa.: Herald Press, 1966) 21–27. For a succinct introduction to the Anabaptist movement, see Walter Klaassen, *Anabaptism: Neither Catholic nor Protestant* (Waterloo, Ont.: Conrad, 1973). For an extensive bibliography on Mennonite worship, see John D. Rempel, *The Lord's Supper in Anabaptism* (Scottdale, Pa.: Herald, 1993) 254–260. For a summary of current worship practices, see *The Mennonite Encyclopedia*, vol. 5 (Hillsboro, Kan.: Mennonite Brethren Publishing House, 1990) 943–948.

[2]The most trenchant apology for this unity of inner and outer in the sixteenth century was that of the South German Anabaptist theologian Pilgram Marpeck. For a compendium of his work, see *The Writings of Pilgram Marpeck*, ed. William Klassen and Walter Klaassen (Scottdale, Pa.: Herald, 1978). For selections from his sacramental theology, see *Later Writings by Pilgram Marpeck and His Circle*, vol. 1, trans. Walter Klaassen, Werner Packull, and John Rempel (Kitchener, Ont.: Pandora, 1999).

[3]*Balthasar Hubmaier, Theologian of Anabaptism*, ed. H. Wayne Pipkin and John H. Yoder (Scottdale, Pa.: Herald, 1989) 395–396. The whole service, which is a mixture of rubrics, the theological rationale for them, and the actual liturgy, is on pages 393–408.

[4]Eamon Duffy's description in *The Stripping of the Altars* (New Haven, Conn.: Yale University Press, 1992) 93—96, is remarkably like that of traditional Mennonite communities in the early twenty-first century and as the practice is recorded in Valentin Dahlem, *Allgemeines und Vollständiges Formularbuch* (Neuwied, Germany: J. T. Haupt, 1807) 299–301.

[5]*International Songbook* (Lombard, Ill.: Mennonite World Conference, 1978); *International Songbook: India 1997* (Calcutta: Mennonite World Conference, 1997); and *International Songbook: Africa 2003* (Kitchener, Ont.: Mennonite World Conference, 2003). See also Ross Bender, "Glimpses of Mennonite Worship on Five Continents," *Courier* 6 (1991) 5.

[6]Two worship formularies encouraging improvisation on historic patterns were issued at the same time. The Dutch Mennonite Conference published *De Gemeente komt samen*, ed. W. Bakker and G. G. Hoekema (Amsterdam: Algemene Doopsgezinde

Sociëteit, 1998). The Mennonite Church USA and Canada published *Minister's Manual*, ed. John Rempel, in 1998. The former prints rubrics and themes but no actual prayers, while the latter has a wide range of historic and contemporary Mennonite and ecumenical prayers.

[7]Shem Peachey and Paul Peachey, "Answer of Some Who Are Called (Ana)Baptists: Why They Do Not Attend the Churches," *Mennonite Quarterly Review* 45 (1971) 5—32, contains one of the few extant descriptions of a mid-sixteenth-century service.

[8]Neufeld, *Music in Worship.*

[9]Charles Garside, *Zwingli and the Arts* (New Haven, Conn.: Yale University, 1966) 17ff.

[10]In fact a volume of interviews and reflections on the meaning of congregational singing for Mennonites in worship concludes that congregational song is the Mennonite "sacrament." See Marlene Kropf and Kenneth Nafziger, *Singing: A Mennonite Voice* (Scottdale, Pa.: Herald, 2001).

[11]*Worship Together* (Winnipeg: General Conference of Mennonite Brethren Churches, 1995).

[12]Illustrations of three worship settings in three eras are in Alister Hamilton et al., eds., *From Martyr to Muppie* (Amsterdam: Amsterdam University Press, 1994) 12, 27, 144.

[13]In response to this practice, see Rodney Sawatsky, "A Call for the Recovery of the Visual Arts in Worship," in *Music and the Arts in Christian Worship*, ed. Robert E. Webber, book 2 (Nashville, Tenn.: Star Song, 1994) 516–518.

[14]See Rempel, *The Lord's Supper*, esp. 197–226.

[15]Rempel, *The Lord's Supper*, 269; see also 129, 263–267 passim. Analogous language is used in Article 12, "The Lord's Supper," in *Confession of Faith in a Mennonite Perspective* (Scottdale, Pa.: Herald, 1995) 50–54.

[16]*Balthasar Hubmaier*, 395–396. The service is a list of rubrics and acts that are not separate from each other.

[17]Leenaerdt Clock, a minister at the beginning of the seventeenth century, wrote a much-prized set of eighteen prayers that went through many editions as part of a beloved volume of devotional writ-

Plate 29. Korean icon. Icon of Christ by Song Shin-Ae, 2005. [See chapter 32, sidebar "The Visual Arts in Africa, East Asia, and the Pacific."] PHOTOGRAPH BY KAREN WESTERFIELD TUCKER

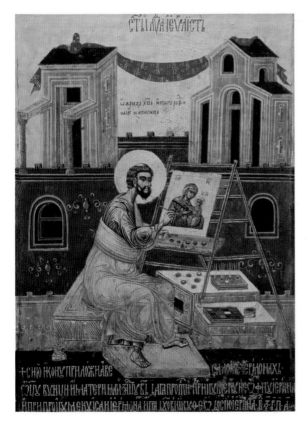

Plate 30. Saint Luke painting the Virgin and Child. Icon (c. 1672–1673) by Master Abesalom Vujicic. Christian iconography is theologically grounded in the fact and doctrine of the Incarnation. Some artistic traditions themselves display this grounding pictorially. Other examples apart from Saint Luke as painter entail the Holy Face, as taken from the imprinted cloth sent by Christ to king Abgar of Edessa or from the veil of Veronica used to wipe Christ's face while he was carrying the Cross. [See chapters 7 and 32.] SNARK/ART RESOURCE, NY

Plate 31. Immersion baptism. In keeping with tradition, a child is immersed face down at the Church of All Saints in Akademgorok/Novosibirsk, Russia. [See chapter 7.] © 2004 PETER WILLIAMS

ings. It is preserved in a new translation, *An Earnest Christian's Handbook*, ed. and trans. Leonard Gross (Scottdale, Pa.: Herald, 1996). Clock's contemporary, Hans de Ries, left collections of sermons, prayers, and orders of service behind. Some of his work is preserved in *Minister's Manual* (1998), 28, 30, 82–87.

[18]Dahlem, *Allgemeines und Vollständiges Formularbuch*.

[19]Walter Klaassen, ed., *Anabaptism in Outline* (Scottdale, Pa.: Herald, 1981) 168.

[20]*Minister's Manual* (1998), 48.

[21]*Minister's Manual* (1998), 50–51.

[22] See Marlin Jeschke, *Believers Baptism for Children of the Church*, esp. 42–49.

[23]Dirk Philips, *The Writings of Dirk Philips, 1504–1568*, trans. and ed. Cornelius J. Dyck, William E. Keeney, and Alvin J. Beachey (Scottdale, Pa.: Herald, 1992) 363–374.

[24]An attempt has been made to reclaim binding and loosing in *Minister's Manual* (1998), 225–231.

[25]See C. Arnold Snyder and Linda Hecht, eds., *Profiles in Anabaptist Women*, Studies in Women and Religion, vol. 3 (Waterloo, Ont.: Wilfred Laurier University Press, 1996).

[26]From the mid-seventeenth century to the late nineteenth century the publishing of Mennonite sermons was a flourishing trade, e.g., J. Gerrits, *Vijf Stichelijche Predikaten* (Amsterdam: Gerrit van Goedesbergh, 1650), and R. Rahusen, *Predigten und Reden* (Bremen: G. L. Foerster, 1784). One of the rare books on homiletics itself is Russell L. Mast, *Preach the Word* (Newton, Kans.: Faith and Life, 1968).

[27]"Glaubensbekenntnis als auch Formular der Taufbedienung … bei Schwetz," 1787, Ms., p. 8, Bethel College Historical Library, Newton, Kans.

[28]In *Minister's Manual* (1998), 213–214, for example, there is a rite for anointing after divorce.

[29]*Minister's Manual* (1998), 129–132.

20

Baptists in Britain

CHRISTOPHER ELLIS

Baptists stand within the free church and evangelical traditions. They represent a worldwide community of more than 100 million, with a baptized membership of nearly half that number. Baptists baptize only those who profess personal faith and they also give high priority to evangelism. Although there is some variety around the world, the main features of Baptist worship developed in Britain. Until the latter half of the twentieth century, the development of Baptist worship had been gradual, so that a distinguished Baptist, E. A. Payne, was able to write in 1952: "The general pattern of church services has remained the same from the 17th century to the present day: scripture, prayer and sermon, interspersed with hymns."[1] This generalization can be defended, though it needs considerable qualification with regard to both the evolving shape of services and the shifts of emphasis within them. However, it is important to recognize from the outset that Baptist worship originated as a direct challenge to the liturgical worship of the Church of England and the Roman Catholic Church. Suspicious of historical accretions and therefore of the tradition of the church, Baptists through the years have attempted to restore Christian worship to what they believed to be the pattern of the New Testament church. In reality, this has meant a stripping of worship to the bare essentials, allowing only those practices which have been perceived to have either biblical precedent or biblical command (called "ordinances"). Until the nineteenth century their places of worship tended to be called "meeting houses," with more emphasis put on the gathering of the congregation for worship than on a sense of a holy place. Holiness has been located in people rather than things, whether buildings or the media of worship. From the beginning Baptists have valued spontaneity in prayer, instruction and challenge in preaching, and a devotional commitment on the part of the congregation that eventually led to the development of congregational hymn singing.

British Baptists trace their origins as a distinct community to the early part of the seventeenth century and the emergence of two groups, the General (Arminian) Baptists and the Particular (Calvinistic) Baptists. Both developed from the diverse Separatist congregations that refused to remain within the established Church of England. Similar in theology to the Puritans, they argued that the Church should comprise only believers and that the state should have no authority over the faith and life of the Church.

General Baptist Worship

The first General Baptist congregation in England was in Spitalfields, London. A group of Lincolnshire Separatists under the leadership of John Smyth and Thomas

Helwys had, in search of religious freedom, emigrated in 1608 to Amsterdam, where they came into contact with Mennonites. Smyth and some of the group eventually joined the Mennonites, while others, together with Helwys, returned to England and established the London congregation in 1612.

While they were meeting in an Amsterdam bakehouse, their worship had consisted of several extempore sermons based on a common scripture text. A letter written to a relative at home in 1609 describes their pattern of worship at this early stage of development (see sidebar). There were two Sunday services, each three or four hours long. The account simply states "we begin with prayer," which is followed by the reading of scripture, together with its interpretation, and a discussion. After this period of preparation, all books, including scripture, are put aside and the first speaker "propheseys" on a text, followed by several other speakers on the same text. This period of inspired proclamation was brought to a close by the first speaker, who "concludeth with prayer as he began with prayer." After exhorting to give to the poor, and a collection having been taken for that purpose, the same speaker concluded with prayer.

Early English Baptist Observances

Around 1609 an English couple, Hughe and Anne Bromheade, wrote a letter from the Netherlands to their cousin in London. Prominent among the reasons the exiles give for their separation from the Church of England is their desire for worship strictly according to the Scriptures. Interspersed among their complaints against the liturgy of the Established Church are positive statements concerning their own understanding of worship. Finally the Bromheades describe the Lord's day practices of Pastor John Smyth's English congregation in Amsterdam.

These churches ar ruled by and remayne in subiection und[er] an Antichristian, and ungodly goverment, contrarie to the institution of oure Saviour Christe. [(?)] For the better confirmation of these [four previous charges] we have thought good to add certayne argumentes .1. no Apocrypha must be brought into the publick assemblies, for there [?] only godes word and the lyvely voice of his owne graces must be heard in the publique assemblies. But mens writinges and the reading them over for prayer ar apocrypha, therfore may not be brought into the publique assemblies[.] .2. argument. we must do nothing in the worshippe of god w^th^ow^t^ warrant of his worde. but re^a^dd prayers have no warrant in his worde. Therfore re^a^dd prayers ar not to be used in the worshippe of god. .3. argument we may not in the worshippe of god receyve any tradition wch bringeth oure libertie into bondage: Therfore readd prayer &c. .4. argument because true prayer must be of faith uttered wth hearte and lyvely voyce, It is presumptuous Ignorance to bring A booke to speake for us unto god &c. .5. Argument to worshippe the true god after an other maner then he hath taught, is Idolatrie. but god commaundeth us to come unto him heavy loaden [?] wth contrite hartes to cry unto him for oure wantes &c Therfore we may not stand reading A dead letter in steade of powring foorth [?] oure petitions. .6. argument we must stryve in prayer wth continuance &c but we cannot stryve in prayer and be importunate wth continuance reading upon A booke, Therfore we must not reade when we should praye. .7. argument we must pray as necessi[tie?] requireth but stinted prayers cannot be as necessitie requireth, Therfore stinted prayer is unlawfull. .8. Argument read prayers were devised by Antichrist and Maynteyne superstition and an Idoll Ministerie. therfore read prayers and such stinted service ar intollerable &c. .9. argument the prayers of such C[hristian?]s and people as stand under a false goverment are not acceptable, not only because they aske [?ami]sse, but because they kepe not his commaundements. The prayers of such ministers and people as be [s]u[bie?]ct to antichrist ar abhominable. Th[o?]s[e?] ministers and people w[ch] [?] stand subiect [?] to the [?Bisho]ppes and the Courtes [?] ar subiect to antichrist &c therfore the prayers &c / [?] . . . .

The order of the worshippe and goverment of oure church is .1. we begynne wth A prayer, after reade some one or two chapters of the bible gyve the sence therof, and conferr upon the same, that done we lay aside oure bookes, and after a solemne prayer made by the .1. speaker, he propoundeth some text ow[t] of the Scripture, and prophecieth ow[t] of the same, by the space of one hower, or thre Quarters of an hower. After him standeth up A .2. speaker and prophecieth ow[t] of the said text the like tyme and space some tyme more some tyme lesse. After him the .3. the .4. the .5. &c as the tyme will geve leave, Then the .1. speaker concludeth w[th] prayer as he began w[th] prayer, w[th] an exhortatation to contribution to the poore, w[ch] collection being made is also concluded w[th] prayer. This Morning exercise begynes at eight of the clock[e?] and continueth unto twelve of the clocke the like course of exercise is observed in the aft[er]n[o]wne from .2. of the clock unto .5. or .6. of the clocke. last of all the execution of the g[over]ment of the church is handled / . . . .

Yours [?] In the lorde at all tymes to use.
Hughe and Anne Bromheade[1]

* * * *

There seems to have been a clear break between what was seen as the preparation for worship, including the initial reading of scripture and its exegesis, and the service itself. Between these sections, we are told that all books, including the Bible, were laid aside. Most of the remaining time was spent by different members of the congregation expounding and applying scripture, quoting it from memory. There seems to be an assumption that true worship occurs under spontaneous divine inspiration rather than through any written media, even scripture. It is not surprising that half a century later, some of the early Quakers emerged from these General Baptist groups.

The developing life of General Baptist congregations flowed from this beginning, though the reading of scripture *within* worship did become firmly established. During the years of the Civil War and the persecution of 1660–1688, the General Baptists tended not to build many meeting houses, preferring to meet in farmhouses, barns, and forest clearings. However, the toleration that followed 1688 led to some building, and by the end of the century worship probably looked like this:

Eighteenth-century accounts of baptism and the Lord's supper are found in the church records of Baptist congregations in East Anglia.

> This day the two churches of Walden and Cambridge met by mutual consent at Whittlesford to administer the ordinance of baptism. This church some-times administers baptism in public (as now) in the presence of many hundreds of spectators; so John the Baptist administered it: sometimes in private; so S. Paul administered it to the jailor, though never in the night, because we are not only not persecuted, but we are protected by law. Circumstances must determine when a private, or when a public baptism is proper. Previous to this, twenty-five persons had professed their faith and repentance to the church at Walden; and twenty-one had done the same at Cambridge; and all had desired baptism by immersion. Dr Gifford, at ten o'clock, mounted a move-able pulpit near the river in Mr Hollick's yard, and, after singing and prayer, preached a suitable sermon on the occasion from Psalm cxix.57. After ser-mon, the men retired to one room, the women, to two others, and the bap-tizer, Mr Gwennap, to another, to prepare for the administration. After about half an hour, Mr Gwennap, dressed as usual (except a coat, which was sup-plied by a black gown made like a bachelor's) came down to the water-side. He was followed by the men, two and two, dressed as usual, only, instead of a coat, each had on a long white baize gown, tied round the waist with a piece of worstead-binding, and leaded at bottom that they might sink: they had on their heads white linen caps. The women followed, two and two, dressed as usual, only all had white gowns, holland or dimity. Their upper-coats were tacked to their stockings, and their gowns leaded, lest their clothes should float. Mr Gwennap sang an hymn at the water-side, spoke about 10 minutes on the subject, and then taking the oldest man of the company by the hand, led him to a convenient depth in the river. Then pronouncing the words, I baptize thee in the name of the Father, and of the Son, and of the Holy Ghost, he immersed the person once in the river. Robinson stood in a boat, and, with other assistants, led the rest in, and, having wiped their faces after their baptism, led them out. Mr Gwennap added a few words more after the administration at the water-side, and concluded with the usual blessing.
>
> Church Book, Stone Yard Meeting, Cambridge
> 10 April 1767[2]

Led by an appointed member of the congregation:

Psalm	*Read from the Bible*
Prayer	*Extempore*
Scripture Reading	

Led by the minister from the pulpit:

Sermon	
Prayer	
Psalm	*Solo led by member of congregation*

As soon as the afternoon public service was concluded, such as chose to go home went. Such as chose to be spectators went up the galleries. The outer gate was fastened for the avoiding interruption; always hurtful in public worship, particularly so in the Lord's-supper-time. Mary Morris, the servant of the church, covered the table with a clean linen cloth, and sat thereon bread in a basket, the crust being taken off: two borrowed silver cups: and three pints of red port wine. The pastor took his seat at the upper end of the table. The deacons next him, two on each hand. The elder men-members at the table. The younger in the pews on the pastor's right hand. The women in pews at his left. The pastor began with a short discourse on the occasion, nature, benefits, etc. of this ordinance.

Then he read I.Cor.xi.23. till he came at the words '*took bread*', then, taking the bread in his hand, he read, '*and when he had given thanks*' and said, 'Let us do likewise', on which, the congregation rising, he gave thanks. This ended, and the church sat down again, he added, '*When he had given thanks, he brake it*': and broke the bread. During which he spoke of the sufferings of Christ, etc. Then, delivering the plates of bread to the deacons, he said, '*Take eat; this is my body, which is broken for you: do this in remembrance of me*'. The deacons then carried the bread round to the members: during which the pastor and all the church sat silent. The deacons at their return took bread and ate: the pastor last of all because the servant of all. After he had eaten the bread he rose again and added, taking the cup into his hands, '*After the same manner also he took the cup*'. The congregation rising again he gave thanks again. Then he poured the wine from the bottles into the cups, discoursing as while he broke the bread. The deacons rising at the close, he gave them the cups, saying '*This cup*' and so on the end of the 26th verse. After the deacons returned, and were seated, they drank, and last the pastor: all sitting silent from the delivery of the cup to the deacons. The pastor rising subjoined, Our Saviour and his disciples '*sang a hymn and went out*', let us do likewise. An hymn or psalm was then sung: after which a collection for the poor was made: the blessing added: and the assembly dismissed. The whole time was about three quarters of an hour.

The Stone Yard Meeting House, Cambridge
28 June 1761[3]

Sources

[1]Champlin Burrage, *The Early English Dissenters in the Light of Recent Research (1550–1641)*, vol. 2 (Cambridge: Cambridge University Press, 1912) 172–177.

[2]*Church Book: St. Andrew's Street Baptist Church, Cambridge 1720–1832*, English Baptist Records, vol. 2, edited by L. E. Addicott and L. G. Champion (Didcot: Baptist Historical Society, 1991) 41–42.

[3]*Church Book: St. Andrew's Street Baptist Church, Cambridge 1720–1832*, 27–28.

These Baptists were radical in their belief that every worship practice needed scriptural justification. Their concern was for spiritual integrity, and although they permitted spontaneous solo singing, they resisted congregational singing—even the communal singing of psalms. This radical conservatism contrasted with their general theology, which—influenced by the growing intellectual climate of rationalism—in time became increasingly Unitarian. By the end of the eighteenth century, most General Baptist churches in England had in fact become Unitarian, apart from a largely new group that emerged from the Evangelical revival. The latter, called General Baptists of the New Connexion, embraced congregational singing, an important element in that revival and the evangelicalism that emerged from it.

Tewkesbury Baptist meeting house. The Baptist church in Tewkesbury, Gloucestershire, was well established by the middle of the seventeenth century. Its building was adapted from a fifteenth-century house. Note the central pulpit, the communion table, and the baptistery, which would have normally been covered, as here, except when in use. PHOTO-GRAPH COURTESY OF CHRISTOPHER J. ELLIS

Particular Baptists

Particular Baptists represented the larger strand within the developing British Baptist community. They began as a distinct community when, in a Separatist congregation that was eventually to become Independent or Congregationalist, a group of church members separated and formed a Particular Baptist congregation. The disagreement resulted from their growing conviction that baptism should be restricted to believers. The separation was reasonably amicable; indeed, Particular Baptists remained in close association with Congregationalists and shared a common theology and similar worship. We have no contemporary accounts of their early services, though we do have certain clues; we can assume that their worship resembled that of the Independents, later known as Congregationalists, right through into the twentieth century. We can reasonably speculate that early eighteenth century Particular Baptist worship followed this pattern on Sunday mornings:

Psalm	*Metricated version sung by the congregation*
Short prayer	*Invocation asking for the Divine presence in all the following parts of worship.*
Exposition of Scripture	*About half an hour*
Prayer	*Petition for various blessings, spiritual and temporal, for the whole congregation; confession of sins; thanksgiving for mercies; petitions for the whole world, for the churches of Christ, for the nation, for all rulers and governors, together with any particular cases represented. Requests of the congregation were usually written on pieces of paper and passed to the minister in the pulpit.*
Sermon	*Delivered from the pulpit*

Hymn by Anne Steele

Anne Steele (1716-1778), who wrote under the pen name "Theodosia," was a prolific British Baptist hymn writer whose hymns were included (and still appear) in English-language hymnbooks of various denominations around the world. This hymn is subtitled, "Hymn for the Lord's Day Morning."

Great God, this sacred day of thine,
　　Demands our souls' collected powers:
May we employ in work divine,
　　These solemn, these devoted hours!
O may our souls adoring own,
The grace which calls us to thy throne!

Hence, ye vain cares and trifles fly,
　　Where God resides appear no more,
Omniscient God, thy piercing eye
　　Can every secret thought explore.
O may thy grace our hearts refine,
And fix our thoughts on things divine.

The word of life dispens'd to day,
　　Invites us to a heavenly feast;
May every ear the call obey,
　　Be every heart a humble guest!
O bid the wretched sons of need,
On soul-reviving dainties feed!

Thy spirit's powerful aid impart,
　　O may thy word with life divine
Engage the ear, and warm the heart;
　　Then shall the day indeed be thine:
Then shall our souls adoring own,
The grace which calls us to thy throne.

From Anne Steele, *Hymns, Psalms, and Poems* (London: Daniel Sedgwick, 1863) 151-152.

| Psalm or Hymn | *This was the usual place for the second item of sung praise though, for local reasons, it was sometimes placed before the sermon. This was either a metricated psalm or, as the century developed, it might have been a hymn—especially one of these written by Isaac Watts and in wide circulation in the Baptist community.* |

Short Prayer
Benediction

The rationalist intellectual climate of the eighteenth century led to a theological shift by which many churches, especially in the London area, became high Calvinist, with a consequent restraint in the conduct of worship. However, a more open and evangelical Calvinism continued in other parts of the country, and this was inevitably strengthened by the Evangelical revival with its emphasis on religious experience. The results were evangelistic preaching, continued exhortations to the devotional life, and an increasing place for congregational song. These changes were slow, perhaps reflecting the internal tensions of a community that was both Calvinistic and Evangelical. It was probably well into the nineteenth century before the hymns of Charles Wesley were widely sung by Particular Baptists, and by mid-century the number of hymns in a service had only increased to three. Indeed, in 1845 Baptist worship in Norwich was described by William Brock as following this pattern, still with only two hymns:

Prayer for the Holy Spirit	*to guide the day*
Song of praise	*A hymn of joy or thanksgiving*
Scripture reading	
Prayer: supplications and intercessions, with thanksgiving	*"for all men, especially the household of faith"*
Song of praise	
Exposition	or *"discourse intended to build you up on your most holy faith, and to open the Scriptures to the understanding of the people, that they may become wise unto salvation by faith in Jesus Christ"*
Dismissal and Blessing	

Baptist Worship in the Twentieth Century

By the twentieth century, the evangelical General Baptists of the New Connexion had formally united with most of the Particular Baptists. Worship in most places had developed into what is often termed "the hymn sandwich," representative of most free churches, though it was only from the later nineteenth century that this included four or more hymns. In this pattern the whole service was usually led from the pulpit by the same person who also preached.

Invitation to worship	*Sometimes omitted, this might include an informal greeting and the reading of verses of scripture*
Hymn	*The congregation would usually sing these hymns to organ accompaniment. The hymns texts would be printed in a single hymnbook, usually one published by the Baptist denomination.*
Bible reading	*This would often be a single passage that was chosen by the preacher and would not usually relate to any calendar or lectionary.*
Hymn	

Prayer	*Sometimes called "the big prayer" this would be a compendium of praise, confession, thanksgiving, intercession and petition.*
Notices	*Usually undertaken by the Church Secretary, this item, at its best, linked worship to the ongoing life and mission of the congregation.*
Offering	*This included the collection of people's money offerings and a dedicatory prayer.*
Hymn	
Sermon	
Hymn	*While this hymn might offer a mechanism for response to the sermon, the other hymns would often only link tangentially to the theme of the service.*
Benediction	

In this pattern we see little rationale except for a movement toward the climax of the sermon. There was infrequently an attempt to provide thematic cohesion between different parts of the service, and the hymns were often chosen by the organist rather than the preacher.

The period since 1950 has seen the greatest and most rapid development in worship. The influence of the Liturgical Movement has produced change in response to its concerns in some Baptist churches. A concern for the overall shape and flow of the service has led to a restructuring of the components in worship and their expansion. An increased emphasis on the church as the people of God and the congregation as active participants in worship has led to the increased use of written material to be spoken by the congregation. In addition, a series of manuals has been produced for ministers and others leading worship, and there has been use of ecumenical resources.

The charismatic renewal has had an even wider impact, though often in different churches from those influenced by ecumenical and liturgical developments. It has led to extended periods of singing and prayer, a concern with engaging the religious affections, and the opportunity for the exercise of "spiritual gifts" by members of the congregation. A pattern of such worship might look like this:

Block of worship songs	*These may be thematically connected and will sometimes be linked with scripture verses and short prayers. They will usually be led by someone other than the preacher, and each will usually be repeated.*
Prayers of petition	*Sometimes led by a member of the congregation, this may be placed before the reading or after the sermon.*
Offering	
Reading	*This will usually be read by the preacher and may only include a few verses.*
Sermon	
Song	
Ministry Time	*An opportunity for individuals to come forward for prayer or for open worship.*

In 1997, a survey of Baptist churches in England and some in Wales indicated that about 10 percent of churches followed this pattern on a weekly basis, while half of the churches used this pattern at least monthly, or incorporated some elements, such as the block of worship songs, into a pattern that fused them with more traditional material.

British Baptists have been open to both ecumenical and charismatic influences, and both are reflected in the present diversity of their worship. It could be argued that the importance of the sermon has been reduced in both these movements. Although there may be other factors at work, such as the erosion of religious certainty, the liturgical approach to preaching has placed the sermon as the servant of the read word and subservient to the celebration of the eucharist.[2] In charismatic worship the place of preaching remains, though often as an explanation of, or preparation for, the experience of the Holy Spirit in prayer and "ministry." There are often complaints about the lack of scripture reading in such worship, which is reminiscent of the Quaker-Baptist disputes of the mid-seventeenth century, circling around issues of experience or objectivity, freedom or subservience to the Word. From this evolving and diverse pattern we may perhaps deduce that if the primary focus of expectation for the encounter with God tends to be placed as the climax of worship, then that climax may be found in sermon, Lord's supper, or ministry time. This diversity of worship reflects a diversity of theology and spirituality.

Evangelical Identity

Tracing the developing pattern of Baptist worship does not, however, communicate all that needs to be said. Baptist worship is to be seen primarily as representative of the evangelical free church tradition. The most widely accepted modern account of evangelicalism identifies a number of characteristics:

> There are the four qualities that have been the special marks of Evangelical religion: *conversionism*, the belief that lives need to be changed; *activism*, the expression of the gospel in effort; *biblicism*, a particular regard for the Bible; and what may be called *crucicentrism*, a stress on the sacrifice of Christ on the cross. Together they form a quadrilateral of priorities that is the basis of Evangelicalism.[3]

Broadly speaking, evangelicalism emerged from Puritan devotion and was renewed and established by the eighteenth-century revival with its concern for conversion. It expanded in the nineteenth-century enthusiasm for organization and has been diversified by various movements in the twentieth century. Baptists and their worship reflect all these movements. This evolving evangelical identity provides an explanation for and integration of various features in Baptist worship.

The Spirituality of Baptist Worship

The spiritual bases of Baptist worship reflect both continuity and divergence in the wider history of Christian practice. The following sections discuss particular features related to the sacraments, employment of scripture, freedom or diversity, community, congregational song and mission.

Sacraments

The patterns of worship outlined above demonstrate that the usual Baptist Sunday service is not eucharistic. The Lord's supper has normally been celebrated on a monthly basis and, though significant for the spirituality of the congregation, it does not determine the logic of most services, which are services of the word, as the quotation from Ernest Payne in the introduction of this chapter makes clear. Baptists have tended to use the word "ordinance" rather than "sacrament," though they used both words in the seventeenth century, and in recent times a number of Baptist writers have attempted to develop a sacramental theology in dialogue with other parts of the Christian Church.

The word "ordinance" implies obedience to a dominical command and historically has not only included the Lord's supper and baptism but also has embraced all aspects of worship. This concern to be "biblical" has meant that praise and preaching have been regarded as ordinances; for the General Baptists of the seventeenth century, foot washing was so regarded as well.

However, both baptism and the Lord's supper focus the Baptist understanding of the Church as a "fellowship of believers." At the Lord's supper, believers gather to sit around a table rather than stand before an altar. The simple service re-enacts the events of the upper room, though the transition from *Last* Supper to *Lord's* supper is acknowledged. It is an expression of the gathering of the church to remember what God has done in Christ and to meet with the risen Lord. Bread and wine tend to be understood as "symbols," and the divine activity is believed to center on the relationship of the believers to God and to one another.

The baptism of believers makes clear that those who enter the Church do so trusting in the redemption of Christ and the regeneration of the Holy Spirit. Practical evidence of discipleship is expected prior to baptism because it is the baptism of those who are already believers. This is both an expression of the Baptist view of the Church and a means whereby that view is maintained. It centers the church in gospel proclamation and the call to discipleship. Children are brought for a service of infant presentation in which the parents and the congregation give thanks for the gift of new life, make promises concerning the Christian nurture of the children, and offer a prayer of blessing for the child.

Scripture

Born out of the "radical reformation" in which the Bible was placed in the hands of all Christians, Baptist spirituality needs to be understood within the polarity of scripture and experience. The reading of scripture has been the source of Baptist worship practices but is also central to the content of worship. In particular, preaching has tended to dominate the other elements of worship, and even the most famous Baptist preacher, C. H. Spurgeon (1834–1892), urged his students not to demote the rest of the service in favor of the sermon. This dominance displays both a desire for instruction in the faith and a concern to proclaim the gospel challenge so that new people may come to faith. Preaching can provide an integration of the Christian faith and the daily experience of the congregation and should be seen as an event in which the Holy Spirit is at work in both preacher and hearer. Although Baptists do not gather for a weekly eucharistic celebration, there is a sense in which evangelistic preaching has a similar function in rehearsing the story of salvation and applying it to the lives of the congregation. Some will find it helpful to see here a sacramental understanding of preaching, with the Spirit working through the personality of the preacher and the exposition of scripture.

Personal Faith and Devotion

In Baptist writings about worship, the primary concern has been not so much about the ordering of worship as about a concern for the integrity of the worshipers. From the celebration of faith and discipleship in the baptism of believers to the prizing of extempore prayer, Baptists are concerned more about sincerity and the "spiritual" aspect of worship than about the way in which certain activities in worship might be undertaken. What they call "simple" worship is often "abstract," with a focus on intellect and interior feelings; recognition of the importance of the devotional dimension is essential to understanding Baptist worship. John 4:24 has been regarded as a crucial text: "God is spirit, and those who worship him must worship him in spirit and in truth."

Freedom

Since Thomas Helwys, Baptists have been champions of religious liberty. Their worship also displays this concern: each congregation is free under God to design its own worship services. The closing decades of the twentieth century saw some increased use of written prayer material, but most prayer is still offered by someone speaking spontaneously on behalf of the congregation. This is regarded both as an expression of that person's devotion, and therefore sincere, and as a dependence on the Holy Spirit and therefore Spirit-filled.

Most Baptist worship is, then, relatively informal and flexible. There is a lack of distinction between public worship and personal devotion at a number of levels, and gathering with others is very important. Worship is a social event, in the sense that the community gathers, as well as an opportunity for personal devotion. Indeed, the notion of fellowship combines these elements so that communion is understood both horizontally (among the congregants) and vertically (between congregation and God).

Community

Although they have always held the office of minister in high regard, Baptists believe strongly in the doctrine of the priesthood of all believers. The ministerial role is relatively well defined, though there is, in practice, nothing a minister does that cannot in certain circumstances be undertaken by a lay person. For example, a minister normally presides at the Lord's supper, but a church without a minister may well invite whoever is leading worship on a particular day, whether ordained or not, to lead the communion service. Increasingly, the leadership of services in Baptist churches is shared between ministers and other members of the congregation.

Congregational Singing

Perhaps the best expression of community in worship and congregational devotion is to be found in the singing of hymns and songs. Particular Baptists were the first congregations in England to sing hymns, as distinct from psalms. In the later decades of the seventeenth century, Benjamin Keach introduced a congregational hymn at the monthly Lord's supper and eventually after the sermon each week. The practice grew, though not without controversy, and the hymns of Isaac Watts were widely sung by Particular Baptists until they were supplemented by the *Bristol Collection* of Ash and Evans (1769) and especially the various editions of John Rippon's *Selection* (1791). The nineteenth and twentieth centuries were the age of the denominational hymnbook, which provided a cohesive element of common worship among congregations as well as allowing a congregation to sing together. The widespread use of books saw the demise of "lining out," in which each line was sung twice, first by a precentor and then by the congregation. More intricate tunes and more stirring singing became possible as hymns increasingly provided an opportunity for corporate devotional expression.

As has been seen, the number of hymns in each service has increased, though the "hymn sandwich" with at least four hymns is probably not much more than a century old. This trend has accelerated with the spread of the charismatic culture, with its blocks of songs. Given also a modest use of responsive readings and prayers, the proportion of the service in which the congregation actively participates has increased considerably. There are clearly contemporary cultural reasons for this greater involvement, but in addition, participation on the part of the congregation is a more appropriate expression of Baptist ecclesiology than worship in which most words are uttered by one person.

Mission

The commitment to a "believer church" ecclesiology, which is embodied in their restricting baptism to believers, has given Baptists a theological focus which nurtures both the devotional warmth referred to above and a concern for mission. Especially since the eighteenth century, evangelism has become a significant priority and the influence of revivalism has ensured that much Baptist worship includes evangelistic preaching and an invitation to congregants to respond to the proclamation of the gospel. This mission concern also sometimes expresses an effort to make the worship accessible to outsiders or "seeker sensitive."

Future Developments

Baptists in worship display a clear resemblance to other evangelical groups. In other parts of the world inculturation is beginning to challenge the dominant North American revivalist culture, while in Britain charismatic and ecumenical influences, coupled with a commitment to mission, continue to modify traditional worship. Yet an awareness of Baptist spirituality, with its concern for devotional warmth, relevant preaching, and freedom in community, will need to offer a critique of future developments as Baptists continue to prize relevance in worship as a priority for missionary congregations.

Bibliography

Cross, Anthony R. *Baptism and the Baptists: Theology and Practice in Twentieth Century Britain*. Carlisle, Cumbria: Paternoster Press, 2000.

Cupit, Tony. *Baptists in Worship; Report of an International Baptist Conference on Worship in Berlin, Germany*. Falls Church, Va.: Baptist World Alliance, 1998.

Ellis, Christopher J. "Duty and Delight: Baptist Worship and Identity." *Review and Expositor* 100 (2003) 329–349.

Ellis, Christopher J. *Gathering: Spirituality and Theology in Free Church Worship*. London: SCM, 2004.

Ellis, Christopher J., and Myra Blyth. *Gathering for Worship: Patterns and Prayers for the Community of Disciples*. Norwich: Canterbury Press and the Baptist Union of Great Britain, 2005.

McKibben, Thomas R. "Our Baptist Heritage in Worship." *Review and Expositor* 80 (1983) 53–69.

Patterns and Prayers for Christian Worship. Oxford: Oxford University Press and Baptist Union of Great Britain, 1991.

Skoglund, John. "Free Prayer." *Studia Liturgica* 4 (1974) 151–66.
Walker, Michael J. *Baptists at the Table*. Didcot: Baptist Historical Society, 1992.

Notes

[1] E. A. Payne, *The Fellowship of Believers: Baptist Thought and Practice Yesterday and Today*, enlarged ed. (London: Carey Kingsgate, 1952) 96.

[2] This sweeping statement would need to be examined, though the concept of "liturgical preaching" and the increased centrality of the eucharist certainly support it. However, to what extent either of these concepts may be significant in *Baptist* churches may be another matter.

[3] D. W. Bebbington, *Evangelicalism in Modern Britain: A History from the 1730s to the 1980s* (London: Unwin Hyman, 1989) 2–3. Bebbington argues that evangelicalism was a new phenomenon of the eighteenth century, though he concedes "there was much continuity with earlier Protestant traditions" (p. 2).

21

Pentecostal and Charismatic Worship

TELFORD WORK

The liturgy of Pentecostal churches and charismatic communities is deeply indebted to the nineteenth-century American Wesleyan Holiness tradition that focused on a "second blessing" of sanctifying grace upon believers. Because of Pentecostalism's origins in Holiness Christianity and its decades of cultural isolation, often but not always self-imposed, Pentecostal and charismatic worship for much of the twentieth century remained relatively unaffected by the fundamentalist-modernist controversy that was formative for American Protestant liberals and evangelicals. Despite Pentecostalism's partial assimilation into evangelicalism since the 1970s and charismatic Christianity's partial assimilation into the Protestant and Catholic mainstream since the 1960s, the tradition has remained a vital third force in American spirituality, and an explosive force in Christian spirituality throughout the world.

The Pentecostal Movement

Pentecostals have usually narrated their revival as beginning in Midwestern Holiness circles at the turn of the twentieth century through the career of Charles Fox Parham, and maturing at William J. Seymour's revival meetings at the Azusa Street Mission in Los Angeles in 1906. However, since the 1950s revisionist histories have suggested an older history reaching back into the nineteenth century. At any rate, it was at the Apostolic Faith Mission in Los Angeles that the movement gained the synthesis of features that continues to characterize it: "restorationism, revivalism, divine healing, sanctified holy living or a 'higher life,' and millenarianism"[1] The movement drew substantially from both black and white lower-class American church traditions, though racism, cultural inertia, and "upward mobility" have often kept Pentecostal denominations ethnically segregated.

While its most famous practice has been glossolalia or "speaking in tongues," in fact glossolalia predates the Pentecostal revival (e.g., in some nineteenth-century Wesleyan Holiness circles), and Pentecostalism has many distinctive features beyond this one. These are rooted in various strands of Protestantism. Pentecostalism reproduces specific Wesleyan convictions regarding Jesus Christ as savior, healer, baptizer with the Holy Spirit, and coming king, as well as the Wesleyan Holiness movement's vocabulary of baptism in the Holy Spirit and its dual focus on cleansing and power as two effects of the Spirit's work following justification and regeneration. Pentecostalism also draws on Reformed and Keswick convictions about atonement and sanctification (the latter emphasizing the strengthening of surrender to God, the filling with the Spirit it invites, and continued dependence on Christ for moral power), Pietist practices of prayer and faith-healing, restorationist primitivism, and Dispensational eschatology, as well as the black-church practices of its Azusa Street origins. However, even if the individual features of Pentecostal spirituality are precedented, its chroniclers contend that the combination is new.

More recent historical continuities notwithstanding, in Pentecostal remembrance the decisive historical influence has been the original apostolic church, particularly as depicted in the book of Acts. From their beginnings Pentecostals have idealized and imitated the Early Church as "Christ-centered, Spirit-dominated, and Word-based."[2] The movement took its name from a widespread conviction that its founding experience was an eschatological restoration of the presence of the Spirit of the original apostolic church that was increasingly lost in later centuries. Its signs and wonders and distinctive liturgical forms reflect that conviction. The charism of tongues is prominent in the movement not as an end in itself but as evidence of the baptism in the Holy Spirit promised in Peter's Pentecost sermon (Acts 2:38) and subsequently delivered to the ends of the earth (Acts 8:17, 10:4–45, 19:6).

Charismatic

At first Pentecostals formed strong sectarian communities, not least because of ostracism, although some, such as Foursquare Pentecostals, were ecumenically friendly. In the later charismatic revival (sometimes called the "second wave") Pentecostal practices crossed over into other communities and adapted to practically every Christian liturgical tradition. This history is conventionally dated to 1960, when Dennis Bennett, an Episcopal rector, announced his "baptism in the Holy Spirit" to his Los Angeles congregation. The church's subsequent trauma made national headlines.

In infiltrating non-Pentecostal communities, Pentecostal liturgical practices have both transformed and supplemented liturgical forms. Many charismatics (not all) report greater appreciation not only for Pentecostal practices, but for the traditional practices of their traditions. Charismatic movements have met with mixed receptions, the coolest from Southern Baptists and Missouri Synod Lutherans, the warmest from nondenominational independents.

A recent and influential movement in the tradition has found evidence of the Spirit's eschatological outpouring beyond Seymour's "baptism in the Holy Spirit with the necessary evidence of tongues." The Vineyard Christian Fellowship, founded by John Wimber, represents this "third wave" of Pentecostal spirituality, which focuses on "signs and wonders" of divine power—healing, prophecy, mercy, exorcism, and ecstasy—as manifestations of the immanent Kingdom of God.

Thus, while "little distinguishes Pentecostalism other than its spirituality,"[3] the special quality of Pentecostal spirituality has not only been decisive for the ecclesiastical traditions that formed around it, but has been transformative for adherents of nearly every ecclesiastical tradition of the church catholic. Far from being merely an existential movement or modern revival of mysticism, "the charismatic renewal is a prophetic renewal movement,"[4] calling all Christians to a whole way of faith and order, life and work. Its forcefulness has generated both division in local churches and denominations, especially early on, and ecumenical convergence among long estranged traditions and local fellowships, especially over time.

Pentecostal Liturgical Features

The variety of Pentecostal ceremonial forms makes description of "the typical Pentecostal liturgy" all but impossible, but many features of its distinct liturgies are widespread across the tradition.

The daily liturgy is a typical evangelical Protestant pattern of extemporaneous family prayer and personal, Bible-centered devotional. The weekly liturgy features midweek meetings for Bible study, prayer, fellowship, and healing, a family evening event, and one or more distinctive Sunday services. In churches too large to accommodate all worshipers on Sunday morning, the traditional Sunday morning service may also be held Saturday or Sunday evening. The annual liturgy is sparse. Christmas and Easter are taken seriously, civil holidays are observed casually, and other Christian feasts and fasts (including Pentecost!) are usually neglected.[5] In the United States, Halloween is increasingly stripped of its occult features and celebrated as a harvest festival if at all. A Pentecostal's "lifetime liturgy" from birth to death centers on conversion in both typically Wesleyan and distinctly Pentecostal ways.

Sunday Corporate Worship

On the one hand, the whole service emphasizes the sovereign power, spontaneous presence, and personal mystical experience of Christ in the Holy Spirit. On the other hand, in part because of its premillennialism,[6] it recognizes the continued power of God's defeated enemies, Satan in particular, whom the worshiping church battles in spiritual warfare. Pentecostal worship thus secures and celebrates the healing—supernatural and natural, spiritual, social, psychological, and bodily—that God effects in the present dispensation. Key biblical texts for communicating the sense of Pentecostal worship are 2 Corinthians 3:17, "where the Spirit of the Lord is, there is freedom," and Galatians 5:1, "for freedom Christ has set us free."

While Pentecostals have well-defined liturgical forms and routinized services, they are suspicious of liturgical "ritualism." (Indeed, the ritualistic connotations of the word "liturgy" cause many Pentecostals to prefer the equivalent word "ceremony.") By ritualism Pentecostals usually mean loyalty to liturgical forms that are alien to the spirit of Pentecostal worship, seem to operate independently of personal faith, fail to support Pentecostal practices, resist creativity and experimentation, prove inflexible to adapting spontaneously during the worship event, promote congregational passivity, or divorce the physical from the spiritual.

Pentecostal liturgy is thoroughly social as well as thoroughly personal. It stresses full congregational participation by the widespread charismatic empowering of the Holy Spirit, an empowering that breaks down boundaries among ethnicities, the genders, social classes, and clergy and laity. Yet while Pentecostals and charismatics have a reputation for disorder (and partly because the early reputation was sometimes well deserved), in fact church authorities typically exercise strong and even authoritarian pastoral and liturgical leadership to maintain communal order while encouraging congregational participation. The charisma of leadership is taken as seriously as the charismata of all the worshiping faithful. Where the pastor's role in noncharismatic traditions might be likened to a conductor (and in less happy cases, a soloist), in Pentecostal and charismatic liturgy it is closer to the leader of a jazz band. While men may dominate in political and liturgical leadership, women have also been prominent, especially in the movement's early days. In many Pentecostal polities all roles are formally open to women.

Architecture varies widely, not least because Pentecostals have a strong conviction that a church is people rather than buildings and prioritize building budgets accordingly. Nevertheless Pentecostal architecture tends to appropriate from Reformed and Baptist styles. Congregations often avoid traditional churchly language (preferring "lobby" to "narthex," "platform" and "stage" to "chancel"). Congregational attention focuses on a central lectern or pulpit, with the communion table in front or to one side, backed by a choir or praise band. The table may be removed during weeks without the Lord's supper. Where space permits there is often room between the pulpit and the first rows of pews or seats for prayer and healing with respondents to altar calls. Iconography is sparse or absent, though a cross or Bible verse may be prominent. Dress and conduct can be sacral (liturgical robes), formal (dresses and business suits in the West), or casual.

Yet verbal imagery and bodily movement suggest rich awareness of sacred space. Hands are often raised during times of praise, held when a congregation prays, and laid on or extended toward the objects of prayer. Worshipers experience the eschatological presence of God and God's cloud of witnesses as the Spirit fuses temporal and spatial horizons. God's presence transforms a primitive storefront church sanctuary into the heavenly throne room into which the nations are gathered and from which prophets and apostles are sent to proclaim the good news.

The Bible is formally and materially central as the living voice of God and the congregation's canonical authority. Even in services where biblical practice is less explicit, for instance where preaching is topical rather than expository, the Word norms the message. Likewise, where congregational prophesying, tongues, words of knowledge, and wisdom are prominent, all these things are tested with the canon that alone governs the universal church.

A typical Pentecostal service has three phases: "worship," sermon, and response. Services begin with neither silence, a prelude, nor a processional, but with conversation among the congregation interrupted by the call to worship. In the first phase, a

Preaching at a Pentecostal Church. Worship at a Cambria, Illinois, Pentecostal church in 1939. PRINTS AND PHOTOGRAPHS DIVISION, LIBRARY OF CONGRESS/ PHOTOGRAPH BY LEE RUSSELL

"worship leader" leads the congregation in an extended introductory time of singing and participatory praise by introducing songs, inviting response, and leading in spontaneous prayer. Participants may rely on hymnals, overheads, slides, or often memory alone. Though an outline is generally developed in advance, the leader adjusts the liturgy to the demands and opportunities of the moment. He or she may call attention to particular themes and lyrics, repeat stanzas and choruses, initiate unplanned songs, pause for congregational prayer, call for applause or spoken praise to the Lord (sometimes in tongues), or interrupt to invite or offer prophetic words of knowledge. This part of the service may last anywhere from minutes to hours, lengthening especially outside the West.

The leader and congregation direct exuberant worship toward God. Worshipers may express themselves with raised hands, applause, laughter, cheering, open displays of emotion, calls and responses reminiscent of the black church tradition, and standing and moving individually and corporately during times of praise and prayer. These acts may be spontaneous or directed. So long as they seem to edify worshipers personally or collectively and do not become disruptive to congregational order, they are understood as movements of the Holy Spirit.

The sung liturgy ends with a pastoral welcome (the pastor's first official act), a meditation and prayer rather like a collect that draws together the time just passed and points forward to the sermon, a call to greeting, intercessory prayer as a body or in small groups, announcements, and an offering.

Either within the "worship time" (that is, the sung liturgy; the charismatic renewal seems responsible for defining worship in terms of music) or soon afterward often comes an interval of ecstatic charismatic "utterances": praying and sometimes singing in tongues, speaking in tongues, interpretation, and intercession. Pentecostals distinguish between "praying in tongues" and "speaking in tongues." Both are regulated by Paul's call to the Corinthians that "all things be done decently and in order" (1 Cor. 14:40), but in different ways. The former is devotional in nature, the latter prophetic.

Prayer in tongues is directed to God alone. It may be private or public, individual or corporate, spoken or sung. It need not be accompanied by interpretation, but it must not be disruptive (for instance, interrupting a sermon).

Speaking in tongues happens individually, but it is directed to the whole gathering. One worshiper speaks with the gift of tongues, rarely in a human tongue unknown to him or her (for instance, a Chinese speaking Hebrew) or more commonly in an "angelic" tongue unknown to anyone. Then the congregation waits until another, with the gift of interpretation, rises to interpret the word in the language of the congregation. All, particularly those with the spiritual gift of discernment, then weigh the message to confirm its prophetic content and thus its authority. It must be materially biblical, authored by the Holy Spirit, spoken in the Holy Spirit, and/or acknowledged as such by those with discernment. The whole process is a harmonious interplay of spiritual gifts (1 Cor. 12–14) aimed at edifying the body of Christ.

In the second phase, a long and dynamic sermon follows the time of praise and prayer. Strong doctrines of both inspiration and illumination guide both the preacher and the congregation in their biblical interpretation, both in prior study and in delivery. Whether the message is focused exegetically, morally, or topically, the goals are evangelism, edification, and revival. A Pentecostal preacher "does not make a speech, but presents a challenge."[7] Vibrant congregational responses, in changed lives even if not in visibly enthusiastic reception, confirm homiletical success. Messages may be punctuated with applause, songs, and other practices.

The liturgical consummation of a service is a call to commitment or recommitment, often delivered as the conclusion of the sermon. This third phase serves the goals of personal and congregational repentance and revival. Pentecostals adapt the classical evangelical "altar call" as a time for people to come forward who need not just salvation, but also baptism in the Holy Spirit, deliverance and liberation, healing, and intercessory prayer. Some Pentecostals practice foot washing as a sign of humble recommitment to all others.[8] Pentecostals also adapt the Lord's supper as a time of rededication to Christ. Practiced occasionally, it often uses crackers and grape juice (at least in the West) and is accompanied by congregational singing. Habits vary widely. An "open table" that invites all to participate is typical. Pentecostals may have either a "Zwinglian" theology that takes the Lord's supper as a mere commemoration of Christ's atoning death or a more sacramental account of eucharist.[9] Either way, they understand the rite as a means of powerful divine presence and saving work.

Whether or not the ministry that follows these times of recommitment is still considered part of the service, it too may last anywhere from minutes to hours. It is an intense time to begin what Orthodox Christians call "the liturgy after the liturgy," in which disciples immediately take up the service's divine power, word, and gifts in ministry. The formal liturgy signifies and empowers congregational ministry around the altar and beyond the sanctuary throughout the coming week. "Going" in mission and mercy ministry is taken as seriously as "gathering" in worship.

Small Group Worship

Midweek gatherings of small groups are important in Pentecostal and charismatic communities. They may meet in homes or church classrooms. They are structured similarly to Sunday liturgies, but with briefer and more intimate introductory singing, "teaching" (usually Bible study) rather than "preaching," extended intercessory prayer and spiritual warfare (prayer and prophecy against powers and principalities and the devil, sometimes including exorcism), accountability and recovery, and general fellowship. Like the Sunday liturgy, they express the essentially social as well as personal character of Pentecostal life.

The Liturgical Lifetime

Worship services, children's catechesis, retreats, and small group activities all aim to take, remember, and build on the basic steps in Pentecostal life passages. Like evangelical Wesleyans, Pentecostals center their stories on the personal experience of conversion, also called salvation or new birth. This is signified but not accomplished by baptism, which is administered to new believers rather than infants or young children, often but not necessarily in the context of Sunday worship services. (Pentecostals refer to "water baptism" in

Laying on of hands. A worship service of the Elim Pentecostal Church. The Elim movement began in 1915 in the United Kingdom but quickly spread abroad. The largest church in the movement is Kensington Temple in London. PHOTOGRAPH BY DAVID BUTCHER/ ART DIRECTORS AND TRIP

order to distinguish it from "Spirit baptism.") Like "Second Blessing" Holiness Christians, Pentecostals understand conversion to be only the first of several decisive steps of transformation. The second most significant step is a "baptism in the Holy Spirit," an "openness to the presence and power of the Spirit" that empowers full Pentecostal spirituality.[10] Spirit baptism is accompanied and evidenced by the gift of tongues, which are then practiced in personal devotion, intercession, spiritual warfare, and assembled worship. But Spirit baptism is understood to yield further fruit in sanctification, assurance, other gifts, and spiritual maturity. In "third wave" communities Spirit baptism is less prominent than spiritual gifting in general, and tongues less prominent than signs and wonders in general.

Though Pentecostals often reject the formal category of sacrament, the various spiritual and liturgical practices of Pentecostal life demonstrate a conviction that God works powerfully in physical events. This lends a sacramental sensibility to the tradition and to its rites of baby dedication, intercessory prayer, healing, exorcism, confession and conversion, communion, water baptism, Spirit baptism, ordination, foot washing, renewal, and marriage. All these are outward signs of inward grace, by which God bestows salvation.

Charismatic Liturgical Features

Charismatic renewal has entered and found some acceptance in practically every liturgical tradition. Its characteristic themes match the themes of Pentecostalism: hunger for and acknowledgement of Christ's presence in the Holy Spirit, signs of God's redemptive power, and joyful praise.

The renewal is legitimately labeled charismatic in understanding itself as a Spirit-driven prophetic movement aimed at renewing churches by restoring neglected gifts to their rightful places in community life. Yet in this context the label has the unfortunate connotation of describing only "enthusiastic" practices as gifts of the Holy Spirit, seemingly relegating traditional practices of word and sacraments, and even the church itself, to the "uncharismatic." Identifying charism with enthusiasm plays precisely into the kinds of abuses—abuses by both enthusiasts and antienthusiasts—that Paul's charismatic theology opposes.

Because the charismatic renewal came to fellowships that already had established liturgies, it presented a challenge to church order in ways Pentecostalism had not. Broadly speaking, charismatic liturgy reflects a synthesis of Pentecostal practices and other communities' liturgical practices. The combination is not merely an incorporation of the one into the other, because Pentecostal practices are rooted in a Wesleyan Holiness tradition that may be foreign or even hostile to other traditions. For instance, Lutheran and (North American) Baptist communities appropriate Pentecostal practices much more critically than Methodist, Presbyterian, Anglican, Catholic, and Orthodox communities. Which Pentecostal practices are appropriated, how they are redefined and appropriated, and what practices they displace are matters negotiated in each tradition.

Charismatic liturgical patterns generally honor the basic framework of the sponsoring traditions, modifying and supplementing them rather than replacing them. Charismatics have exerted the most pressure for modifying prior liturgical traditions in several ways.

First, charismatic stress on personal conversion as a decisive moment in one's liturgical lifetime pressures Augustinian sacramental practices. First, it highlights discrepancies between God's supposed work in the sacraments and its existential and ethical appropriation in the believer's life. Second, "Spirit baptism" suggests a moment of transformation after conversion that does not yet clearly have a sacramental sign. (The closest analogue would seem to be ordination, not water baptism nor confirmation.) Positive consequences of this pressure include renewal of faith, hope, and love among those who describe their former lives as "cold" or "dead," checks on formalism, greater zeal for evangelism, and a rediscovery of the roles of laity in the life of their communities. Negative consequences include charges and fears of elitism among charismatics, insecurity among noncharismatics, and privileging of existential over sacramental speech.

A related challenge concerns charismatic leadership. Charismatic renewal can build spiritual hierarchies that may interfere with or even contradict formal hierarchies. If Spirit baptism is an anointing to service and leadership that comes sovereignly irrespective of ordination, then it presses liturgies that have long restricted rites of healing, exorcism, ordination, proclamation, or eucharistic presidency to ordained clergy.

Second, charismatics have reconciled the spiritual, local ecumenism of classical Pentecostalism with the formal, structural ecumenism of the ecumenical movement, to which Pentecostals have generally been hostile. Cooperation, friendship, and community among charismatics of different traditions have broken down barriers to visible unity, and this has softened liturgical as well as doctrinal and political battle lines at both the local and global levels. This has not always mollified ecumenists who regard charismatic convergence as a surrender to spiritualism and experientialism. Yet it has reinforced the trend of liturgical appropriation and cooperation across traditions that has characterized liturgical reform over the last half century.

Third, charismatics press traditional liturgies with their habits of spontaneous and expressive praise. (In Latin America, for instance, charismatics are sometimes known pejoratively as "alleluias.") On the one hand, both charismatic inroads and the inculturation of Orthodox, Catholic, and Protestant liturgies in African, Latin American, and Asian contexts have demonstrated that the charismatic worship style is profoundly compatible with most traditional liturgical structures. On the other hand, charismatic styles may be much more threatening to the cultures of local congregations, both Western and non-Western.

Thus it is not so surprising that traditions loyal to a universal, fixed liturgy have reportedly been more successful at incorporating charismatic practices, for instance in the eucharist and in litanies of specific intercession, than churches with "free" liturgies habituated to the local culture. Charismatic renewal demonstrates that locally free liturgies may be constrictive as well as liberating, and denominationally fixed liturgies may be liberating as well as constrictive.

Still, in the decades since the charismatic renewal began, initial disruptions, early confrontations, and splits in many congregations have gradually given way to toleration and even welcome of a contingent of members who raise hands, applaud the Lord, whisper in tongues, stand spontaneously, prefer choruses to formal hymns, and speak of baptism by the Holy Spirit. Their presence spreads other habits of expression, participation, and informality throughout their congregations. This is true in both free and fixed liturgical traditions.

At supplementary gatherings, charismatic worship patterns are more pronounced and distinctively Pentecostal. These take forms such as midweek small group meetings, charismatic worship services, Sunday school classes, revival meetings and harvest festivals, and chapels in charismatic institutions and covenanted communities. There worshipers raise hands, speak in tongues, pray for healing, preach forcefully, prophesy, and wage spiritual warfare. Other charismatic liturgy takes place at the personal level, such as devotional Bible reading, private prayer in tongues, and witnessing in the workplace and marketplace.

Reliance on supplementary liturgies has the advantage of offering more opportunities for profound liturgical participation among laity accustomed to passive roles or token participation on Sundays. However, along with this comes the danger of marginalizing the congregational Sunday service and its special practices, which some charismatics may see as unimportant to the work of the Spirit. Since sacramental practices have long been concentrated in Sunday liturgies and practiced by the clergy, this raises the further problems of sundering churches' charismatic and sacramental life and divorcing the rites of the clergy from the work of the laity, and effectively withholding some spiritual gifts from other members of the body.

Bibliography

Albrecht, Daniel E. *Rites in the Spirit: A Ritual Approach to Pentecostal/Charismatic Spirituality*. Sheffield: Sheffield Academic Press, 1999.

Anderson, Robert. *Vision of the Disinherited: The Making of American Pentecostalism*. New York: Oxford University Press, 1979.

Blumhofer, Edith L., Russell P. Spittler, and Grant A. Wacker, eds. *Pentecostal Currents in American Protestantism*. Urbana: University of Illinois Press, 1999.

Burgess, Stanley M., and Gary B. McGee, eds. *Dictionary of Pentecostal and Charismatic Movements*. Grand Rapids, Mich.: Regency Reference Library, 1988.

Dayton, Donald W. *Theological Roots of Pentecostalism*. Metuchen, N.J.: Scarecrow, 1987.

du Plessis, David. *Simple and Profound*. Orleans, Mass.: Paraclete, 1986.

Knight, Cecil B., ed. *Pentecostal Worship*. Cleveland, Tenn.: Pathway, 1974.

MacRobert, Iain. *The Black Roots and White Racism of Early Pentecostalism in the USA*. New York: St. Martin's, 1988.

McDonnell, Kilian, ed. *Presence, Power, Praise: Documents on the Charismatic Renewal*. 3 vols. Collegeville, Minn.: Liturgical Press, 1980.

Notes

[1] Daniel Albrecht, *Rites in the Spirit*, 35.

[2] Burgess and McGee, eds., *Dictionary of Pentecostal and Charismatic Movements*, "Preaching, a Pentecostal Perspective," by R. H. Hughes.

[3] Albrecht, 23–24.

[4] Kilian McDonnell, *Presence, Power, Praise*, 1:xix.

[5] Albrecht, 124.

[6] Donald Dayton, *Theological Roots of Pentecostalism*, 165.

[7] Roberto McAlister, from *A esperiência Pentecostal—A base bíblica e teológica do Pentecostalismo*, cited in Richard Schaull and Waldo Cesar, *Pentecostalism and the Future of the Christian Churches: Promises, Limitations, Challenges* (Grand Rapids, Mich.: Eerdmans, 2000), 53.

[8] Burgess and McGee, *Dictionary*, "Ordinances, Pentecostal," by H. D. Hunter.

[9] Hunter, "Ordinances, Pentecostal."

[10] Albrecht, 125.

Pentecostal Worshipers on Their Services

A British Pentecostal youth describes the communion service at his church:

> Our church has a Pastor. He has been specially trained at Bible College, and although he does tend to lead the services, often other people do, or they share something they have learnt about God. The Pastor doesn't wear special clothes, and is very relaxed and friendly. We believe that everyone has something important they can do to help others in the church, and many people have special jobs, including the Elders who help the Pastor, and the Deacons who help organise more practical things. We have a band which leads the songs with a keyboard, drums and electric guitar. . . .
>
> We normally have communion in the morning service, although sometimes in the evening too. We read from the Bible about how Jesus had some bread and wine with his disciples, and told us to think of him. We will pray, and then share the bread and wine. Sometimes some music is played, but at other times it is quiet, so we can talk to God ourselves and thank him for sending Jesus so we can be forgiven, and know him today. We stay sitting in our seats while the bread and wine are passed around. Anyone who loves Jesus, and wants to, can share the wine and bread. The wine is usually in special tiny glasses, so that everyone gets one each, but the bread is a broken up loaf that you break a small piece off.
>
> http://www.request.org.uk/main/churches/pentecostal/pentecostal02.htm

Charity Dell describes African-American eucharistic practices, which have been influential on Pentecostalism especially in Latin America and Africa:

> Holy Communion in African-American churches tends to be accompanied by vigorous singing, and in Pentecostal churches, can be filled with dancing and shouting. Communion typically has a more "festal" feel, in contrast to some Euro-American churches which observe Communion more as a "solemn" event. Music is sung and played throughout the service, except for spoken scripture and prayers. However, black Christians usually hum, moan or chant while prayer is being rendered. It is understood in the black Christian community that all visitors are equally welcome to any Communion rituals observed during worship, and this includes their children.
>
> http://www.fni.com/worship/200201/msg00193.html

A tract offers biblical justifications for charismatic worship practices:

> We pray together aloud because in the Bible we read, "They lifted up their voice to God with one accord" (Acts 4:24). We lift our hands in praise because in the Bible we read, "Lift up your hands in the sanctuary, and bless the Lord" (Psalm 134:2). We sing with all our hearts because in the Bible we read, "Make a joyful noise unto the LORD, all the earth: make a loud noise, and rejoice, and sing praise" (Psalm 98:4). We play musical instruments because in the Bible we read, "And all the house of Israel played before the

LORD on all manner of instruments" (2 Samuel 6:5). We clap and shout unto God because in the Bible we read, "O clap your hands, all ye people; shout unto God with the voice of triumph" (Psalm 47:1). We dance before the LORD because in the Bible we read, "Praise Him with the timbrel and dance: praise Him with stringed instruments and organs" (Psalm 150:4). We testify publicly because in the Bible we read, "I will declare thy name unto my brethren; in the midst of the congregation will I praise thee" (Psalm 22:22). We anoint with oil for divine healing because in the Bible we read, "Is any sick among you? Let him call for the elders of the church; and let them pray over him, anointing him with oil in the name of the Lord" (James 5:14). We allow the operation of the spiritual gifts because in the Bible we read, "When ye come together, every one of you hath a psalm, hath a doctrine, hath a tongue, hath a revelation, hath an interpretation" (1 Corinthians 14:26).

(From the Word Aflame Press tract "The Way We Worship," #6602.)
http://www.meta-religion.com/World_Religions/Christianity/Denomina-
tions/way_we_worship.htm

A Neo-Pentecostal Service in Kenya

Geoff Morgan

The service described here took place at the Chrisco Fellowship in Nakuru Town, Kenya, on 29 February 1996. Chrisco was founded by a man named Harridas in the 1980s. It is an indigenous, interdenominational mission church, and many midweek supporters at this meeting also went to other churches.

The lunchtime service took place in a hired public meeting hall in the town center. An arrangement of benches in rows faced the front of the hall. Posters declaring that "Jesus Christ is enthroned in this place," and notifying of revival meetings adorned the walls.

A worship ensemble consisting of singers, a keyboard player, bass and lead guitars and drums was set up in front of the benches. Before the service began, many gathered in the worship space and bowed their heads in devotion. A lead singer with a roving microphone led the singing, which modulated into expository and "rap"-style prayer, and prayer in tongues, each one praying on his or her own. The prayer was in English and called for revival and for the blessing of bishops and leaders; it was addressed to God, using such calls as "Wrap us in Your Spirit, Lord." This continued for five minutes.

There was then a mass rendition of the English hymn "There Is Power in the Blood," which lasted two minutes, followed by more mass intercessory prayer, singing in tongues, and prayers for the "President, the Vice-President, for Provisional, Divisional, District Officers, Chiefs, and Sub-chiefs, and for the fear of the Lord to come upon them."

The hymn *Asante sana Yesus* (translated from the English "Thank you, thank you, Jesus") was sung in Kiswahili for about five minutes, and then the congregation was encouraged "to shout praises out loud to the Lord." This lasted another five minutes. After another Kiswahili version of an Anglo-American hymn, the pastor welcomed the congregation and announced that the collection would be taken during the next hymn, which was also Anglo-American.

Another period of public prayer followed in which the visiting preacher, using bilingual English and Kiswahili, commanded every ear to hear and receive the word. There were prayers for those who had requested them, announcement of some "words of knowledge," and prophetic utterances directed at some specific people or needs.

The sermon followed, in which the preacher opened with the question: "Why do some situations come upon us?" The emphases were eschatological, on the sanctification of the faithful and the coming revival. The congregants were exhorted to wave if they understood what he was saying; for example:

> We are all on our way to the promised land . . . I used to sometimes take a long route home from school for fun and to parental disapproval; God took the children of Israel on a long route to Canaan because he wanted to spend time with them. When there is no problem we are full of hallelujah, but when problems come our testimony evaporates. The people came to the Red Sea, Egypt was behind them and there was no going back (nods from congregation); they complained, "Is this what you call Deliverance?" Remember where, how, and when God visited you. You have your holy ground, your burning bush; there is hope for you when you pass through the waters, when in financial crisis, or hopeless. The other day I met a woman who had marriage problems, who had attempted suicide, and she accepted Jesus, praise God . . . .

This sermon lasted thirty minutes and was to be continued the next day.

Most people left rapidly to get back to work. In personal conversation, the pastor was concerned to stress that revival was already present in their group, and that "we (Chrisco) are here to bring individuals to Jesus, not communities."

Reference

Morgan, Geoff. "An Analytical, Critical and Comparative Study of Anglican Mission in the Dioceses of Nakuru and Mount Kenya East, Kenya, from 1975." Dissertation, Open University/Oxford Centre for Mission Studies, 1997. This excerpt is reprinted in Graham Kings and Geoff Morgan, *Offerings from Kenya to Anglicanism*, Joint Liturgical Studies 50 (Cambridge: Grove, 2001) 38–39.

22

North America

KAREN B. WESTERFIELD TUCKER

In the fifteenth and sixteenth centuries, the search for new economic resources brought Catholic Spain to the southern regions of the North American continent, while Catholic France principally explored Newfoundland and northern areas along the Saint Lawrence River to the Mississippi River. Newly Protestant England focused its expeditions on the east coast, and the Dutch established themselves in the West Indies and (in the 1620s) in the areas around the Hudson River. Thus ecclesiastical—and liturgical—diversity characterized North America from the very beginnings of its colonizing by Europeans. As the "New World" became known as a place for religious freedom, liturgical expressions of the Christian faith multiplied. By 2005, 217 distinct church traditions were identifiable in Canada and the United States, with some groups themselves characterized by liturgical pluriformity.[1]

Because of the complexity of the North American situation, only a few churchly traditions may be highlighted as the liturgical picture is painted on a large canvas. Attention in this chapter focuses upon Christian liturgy in the United States and Canada, since Mexico and Central America are discussed elsewhere.

Transplantation and Adaptation

Roman Catholic and Anglican Worship

A year after taking possession for Spain of what he called San Salvador, Cristóbal Colón sailed in 1493 to Hispaniola (now Haiti and the Dominican Republic) with a contingent of seventeen ships and at least five priests for the purpose of establishing a colony and spreading Christianity to the natives. Spanish Catholic missionaries were more successful in the Caribbean than in Florida, but even these endeavors paled in comparison with the large-scale implantation of the Christian faith in the Southwest. Missioners to the area north of the Rio Grande in the early sixteenth century—principally Franciscans who had been granted special authority in 1521 by Pope Leo X—brought with them the mass and sacramental formularies used by their Order and later the liturgical texts authorized by the Council of Trent. They also came with a willingness to connect Christian practices with the indigenous religion for the sake of evangelism and instruction. Franciscans living with the Pueblo Indians of New Mexico readily linked the native katsina cult (of Cloud Spirits or the ancestors) with the Christian saints and associated annual Pueblo ceremonies with the Christian liturgical year, conflating Christmas, for example, with winter solstice celebrations.[2] These early

Roman Catholic burial in early California. A priest is carried on a litter to a roughly made church topped with a cross. "Burial of the Abbé Chappe d'Auteroche in California, 1767," drawing by Alexandre J. Noel (1752–1834). MUSÉE DU LOUVRE, PARIS/RÉUNION DES MUSÉES NATIONAUX/ART RESOURCE, NY

paraliturgical adaptations are, in some cases, the origin of certain modern devotional practices of Hispanic Catholics.

In what is now Canada, the first recorded eucharist according to the rite of the Church of England was celebrated in 1578 by Robert Wolfall, chaplain to Martin Frobisher's expedition, at what is now Frobisher Bay; today the event is commemorated in early September by Canadian Anglicans. Regular worship from the *Book of Common Prayer* in Newfoundland probably took place in 1583 at the unsuccessful settlement sponsored by Humphrey Gilbert and was certainly present from 1612 at the colony of Ferryland under the guidance of the clergyman Erasmus Stourton. Formal Roman Catholic worship may have occurred in Canada in the late sixteenth century if a priest was part of a French expedition. By 1610 two priests had arrived and baptized dozens of First Nations peoples. Soon the Jesuits came to lead in missionizing efforts and in the pastoral work of the growing French communities at Quebec and Montreal, and their labors were carefully recorded. The *Jesuit Relations* for 1645 describes the jubilee held following the election of Pope Innocent X in 1644 with participation by the French in Quebec and by the members of the Montagnais tribe in the nearby Jesuit-founded village of Saint Joseph:

> The Christians of St. Joseph, who had not yet heard mention of this devotion [that is, the jubilee and its plenary indulgence], prepared for it with most extraordinary affection. They were told that the preparations for obtaining this pardon were fasting, alms, and prayer or orisons.
>
> As for fasting, they observed it very easily, for they had not many things to eat at that time. ...
>
> As for alms, they had more difficulty; for they knew not what to give. Gold and silver have no currency among these peoples, and their poverty easily dispensed them from being wasteful. ...
>
> As for the prayers, they failed not to perform their Stations. And all, besides [took part] in a somewhat arduous and difficult procession, which they made from Saint Joseph even to Quebec—the distance is about a league and a half. It was held on the day of Saint Stephen, the day after Christmas, in extremely cold weather; they all walked, two by two, in fine order; the children wished to be of the company. The cross and the banner marched before; the Fathers who have charge of that little church led their flock.
>
> They intoned hymns on issuing from the church; they continued their procession, reciting their rosaries, and offering other prayers. Arriving at Quebec, they delighted the French; their first station was in the church of the Ursuline Mothers; having there

prayed to God, and sung some spiritual songs, they moved straight to the parish church, where the blessed sacrament was exposed. They were received [by the French] with motets full of piety, which were sung in honor of him whom they came to adore; when he [that is, Christ] had given them his blessing, by the hands of the priest, they proceeded to the third station, which was at the hospital, where likewise they prayed for the [intentions specified by the pope], being continually led and directed by their pastors. Upon departing thence, they returned fasting—two by two, as they had come—concluding the last act of the jubilee in their own church.[3]

Worship according to the Church of England's *Book of Common Prayer* was also held at English settlements established farther south, such as in the second colony planted on Roanoke Island (off the North Carolina coast) in 1587. There two baptisms are recorded to have taken place soon after arrival: of Manteo, a native, on August 13, and of Virginia Dare on the Sunday after her birth on August 18. Chaplain Robert Hunt, who accompanied the settlers to Jamestown, Virginia, in 1607, celebrated the Lord's supper immediately after the first landing. Soon thereafter a simple structure was built to house the celebration of that sacrament and the church's other rites; the fifth church building constructed at Jamestown (1647) seems to have conformed to medieval English parish designs.[4] Eventually the Church of England became the established church in the colony of Virginia, with first the Elizabethan 1559 Prayer Book and then the Prayer Book of 1662 the official liturgical texts. However, because of the large area covered by a single parish, liturgical adjustments were sometimes necessary. For instance, because it was sometimes impossible on account of distance for a new mother to receive "churching" after childbirth in the parish church, the Prayer Book rite was on occasion performed in the woman's home. Virginia was the only colony to enforce conformity to the Church of England, yet that position was officially softened with the 1689 English Act of Toleration, allowing the Society of Friends (Quakers) and others who had already settled in the colony the freedom to worship in their own way. Quakers preferred to wait silently upon God without formal orders of service or designated preachers.

In the case of Roman Catholics and Anglicans, existing liturgical formularies were brought to the New World, and some allowances (approved and unapproved) were made for adaptation to local circumstances. The practices of the early settlements in New England expressed a different way of thinking. Worship came not from a humanly contrived prayer book believed to be prohibited by the second Commandment but from scripture itself, following a principle of *Quod non jubet, vetat* (What [God] does not command, he forbids). At first European models for worship were followed, but gradually new approaches—theological, liturgical, and practical—began to emerge.

Puritan and Congregational Worship

The Plymouth Colony established near Cape Cod, Massachusetts, in 1620 consisted of Separatists, who did not conform to the Church of England and its *Book of Common Prayer* and chose instead a simple form of worship focused upon prayer and the reading and exposition of the Word of God. In 1628 the Salem Colony farther to the north was settled principally by persons self-identified as non-Separatists, who regarded themselves as part of the Church of England yet desired to reorient the church and its worship in a more scriptural and Protestant direction. The second paragraph of the Salem Church covenant (1629), stretching the definition of non-Separatist, asserts:

> Wee give our selves to the Lord Jesus Christ, and the word of his grace, fore the teaching, ruleing and sanctifyeing of us in matters of worship, and conversation resolveing to cleave to him alone for life and glorie; and oppose all contrarie wayes, cannons and constitutions of men in his worship.[5]

A "great migration" of "non-Separatists" arrived in the early 1630s as part of the Massachusetts Bay Colony; by the early 1640s there were more than twenty thousand persons in New England. The royal charter that the Massachusetts Bay colonists carried with them did not indicate the place from which governance would occur, accidentally (it seems) allowing for the possibility of self-governance, which was then actively pursued in the development of the "holy commonwealth." For the New England settlers, the new land offered an opportunity for worship according to conscience as a fulfillment of covenant obligations and an occasion for the raising of a pure Christian society.

The keeping of the Sabbath in obedience to the fourth Commandment, but understood in the Christian dispensation to refer to the first day of the week, was essential for spiritual edification as well as for social and moral order: "Take away a Sabbath," posited Thomas Shepard, pastor of the Cambridge, Massachusetts, congregation, "who can defend us from Atheisme, Barbarisme, and all manner of Devilisme and prophanesse?"[6] Under the "holy commonwealth," the law reinforced compulsory worship attendance and rest from physical labor, and so the populace was expected to gather, both in the morning and in the afternoon, at the meetinghouse (not the "church," since that term referred to the community of believers itself). Descriptions of Christian Sabbath worship practices in early New England are in the Anglican (and anti-Puritan) Thomas Lechford's *Plain Dealing; or, News from New England* (1642) (see "The Publique Worship")[7] and in *The Way of the Churches of Christ in New England* (1645) by the Puritan John Cotton (see Chapter 16 "Anglicans and Dissenters"). Morning services on the Lord's day began around 9 AM and generally took this shape:

> Prayer (including intercessions and thanksgivings)
> Reading of a chapter from the Bible
> Exposition of the reading
> Psalm singing
> Sermon
> [Exhortation]
> [Psalm singing]
> Prayer
> Blessing

Afternoon services followed a similar structure.

Lechford notes that the "solemn prayer" at the start of the service was about fifteen minutes in length, which suggests this was the longer of the two prayers (some congregations located the longer prayer after the sermon). If so, this prayer was of short duration compared to other reports of Lord's day prayer. The Dutch Labadist Jasper Danckaerts, writing in his journal in 1680 about Sunday worship in Boston, comments that the prayer before the sermon lasted one hour; two days before, at a special service of fasting and prayer not atypical for New England congregations, he had observed that the "minister made a prayer in the pulpit of full two hours in length."[8] Prayers were most often spontaneous, in obedience to the scriptural dicta that Christians are to pray with and in the Spirit (cf. Rom. 8:26–27; Eph. 6:18). Following this

The Publique Worship

The publique worship is in as faire a *meeting house* as they can provide, wherein, in most places, they have beene at great charges. Every Sabbath or Lords day, they come together at *Boston*, by wringing of a bell, about nine of the clock or before. The Pastor begins with solemn prayer continuing about a quarter of an houre. The Teacher then readeth and expoundeth a Chapter; Then a Psalme is sung, which ever one of the ruling Elders dictates. After that the Pastor preacheth a Sermon, and sometimes *ex tempore* exhorts. Then the Teacher concludes with prayer, and a blessing.

Once a moneth is a Sacrament of the Lords Supper, whereof notice is given usually a fortnight before, and then all others departing save the Church, which is a great deale lesse in number then those that goe away, they receive the Sacrament, the Ministers and ruling Elders sitting at the Table, the rest in their seats, or upon forms: All cannot see the Minister consecrating, unlesse they stand up, and make a narrow shift. The one of the teaching Elders prayes before, and blesseth, and consecrates the Bread and Wine, according to the words of Institution; the other prays after the receiving of all the members: and next Communion, they changes turnes; he that began at that, ends at this: and the Ministers deliver the Bread in a Charger to some of the chiefe, and peradventure gives to a few the Bread into their hands, and they deliver the Charger from one to another, till all have eaten; in like manner the cup, till all have dranke, goes from one to another. Then a Psalme is sung, and with a short blessing the congregation is dismissed. Any one, though not of the Church, may, in *Boston*, come in, and see the Sacrament administered, if he will: But none of any Church in the Country may receive the Sacrament there, without leave of the congregation, for which purpose he comes to one of the ruling Elders, who propounds his name to the congregation, before they goe to the Sacrament.

About two in the after-noone, they repaire to the meeting-house againe; and then the Pastor begins, as before noone, and a Psalme being sung, the Teacher makes a Sermon. He was wont, when I came first, to reade and expound a Chapter also before his Sermon in the afternoon. After and before his Sermon, he prayeth.

After that ensues Baptisme, if there be any, which is done, by either Pastor or Teacher, in the Deacons seate, the most eminent place in the Church, next

line of reasoning, and because it was regarded as a "vain repetition" (cf. Matt. 6:7), the Lord's prayer was determined to be a model for prayer and not a precise text for liturgical usage, though by the beginning of the eighteenth century it came to be repeated more frequently in Sunday worship.

As Cotton and Lechford mention, congregations were often served by a pastor and a teacher whose offices sometimes overlapped, though it was the teacher who principally took the responsibility in worship of providing detailed commentary on the scripture reading. Toward the end of the century, when churches struggled to maintain the separate teaching office, the option was sometimes taken to drop the separate scripture reading rather than omit the explication, thus avoiding the "dumb reading" practiced by Anglicans. Eventually the reading of scripture was returned, without interpolation of commentary.[9] The pastor, usually robed in a black academic gown,

under the Elders seate. The Pastor most commonly makes a speech or exhortation to the Church, and parents concerning Baptisme, and then prayeth before and after. It is done by washing or sprinkling. One of the parents being of the Church, the childe may be baptized, and the Baptisme is into the name of the *Father*, and of the *Sonne*, and of the *holy Ghost*. No sureties are required.

Which ended, follows the contribution, one of the Deacons saying, Brethren of the congregation, now there is time left for contribution, wherefore as God hath prospered you, so freely offer. Upon some extraordinary occasions, as building and repairing of Churches or meeting-houses, or other necessities, the Ministers presse a liberall contribution, with effectuall exhortations out of Scripture. The Magistrates and chiefe Gentlemen first, and then the Elders, and all the congregation of men, and most of them that are not of the Church, all single persons, widows, and women in absence of their husbands, come up one after another one way, and bring their offerings to the Deacon at his seate, and put it into a box of wood for the purpose, if it bee money or papers; if it be any other chattle, they set it or lay it downe before the Deacons, and so passe another way to their seats againe. This contribution is of money, or papers, promising so much money: I have seene a faire gilt cup with a cover, offered there by one, which is still used at the Communion. Which moneys, and goods the Deacons dispose towards the maintenance of the Ministers, and the poore of the Church, and the Churches occasions, without making account, ordinarily.

But in *Salem* Church, those onely that are of the Church, offer in publique; the rest are required to give to the Ministerie, by collection, at their houses. At some other places they make a rate upon every man, as well within, as not of the Church, residing with them, toward the Churches occasions; and others are beholding, now and then, to the generall Court, to study wayes to enforce the maintenance of the Ministerie.

This done, then followes admission of members, or hearing matters of offence, or other things, sometimes till it be very late. If they have time, after this, is sung a Psalme, and then the Pastor concludeth with a Prayer and a blessing.

Reference

Thomas Lechford, "Plain Dealing; or, News from New England," in *New-Englands Advice to Old-England* (n.p.: 1644) 16–19.

engaged in mostly expository preaching aimed at instruction, conversion, and edification. The learned "plain style" was preferred in order to persuade both the uneducated and the reluctant. The sermon rarely lasted less than an hour.[10]

Psalms in the English metrical verse of Sternhold and Hopkins (1562) and Henry Ainsworth (1612) were used prior to the introduction of *The Whole Booke of Psalmes* or the *Bay Psalm Book* (1640), the first book published in America. The preface to this work, believed to have been written by John Cotton, contends that in translating the Hebrew into English, "wee have respected rather a plaine translation, then to smooth our verses with the sweetnes of any paraphrase," it being "part of our religious care and faithfull indeavour, to keep close to the originall text." Thus the psalms, while not in elegant language, were carefully crafted in order to offer "the Lords songs of prayse according to his owne will":

> The Lord to mee a shepheard is,
>   want therefore shall not I.
> Hee in the folds of tender-grasse,
>   doth cause mee downe to lie:
> To waters calme me gently leads
>   Restore my soule doth hee:
> he doth in paths of righteousnes:
>   for his names sake leade mee.[11]

Singing the Psalms was a "gospel ordinance" and a "holy duty," following the expectations stated in scripture (notably Eph. 5:19, Col. 3:16, and James 5:13).[12] Two methods were used for the selection on a given day: *lectio continua*, or the following of Psalms in their given biblical sequence; or pastoral choice, according to the subjects and emphases to be addressed. Psalms were rendered without instrumental accompaniment since such was not explicitly commanded by God. A cappella singing was often disorderly, and when "lining out" by a precentor was introduced (the reading of a line followed by the singing of that same line), the system aided participation but disrupted the flow of the text. In the eighteenth century new approaches to congregational singing were gradually accepted: organs were installed to assist the congregation, and in company with the more literal versions of the Psalms were sung the psalm paraphrases of the English Congregationalist Isaac Watts, whose first American edition was Benjamin Franklin's 1729 printing of *Psalms of David*.

The first "seal of the covenant," the sacrament of baptism, was, according to Lechford, observed on the Lord's day afternoon following the sermon, along with (when necessary) special contributions of money and other goods, admission of members to the church, and acts of penance and discipline. The baptismal rite itself was simple: exhortation, prayer, baptism in the triune Name by "washing or sprinkling," and prayer. No "sureties"—sponsors—were required since older candidates could speak for themselves, and parents who had "owned the covenant" and professed a personal experience of regeneration, thus becoming full church members, were expected to take on the spiritual nurture of their "seed" who received the sign of saving grace. The simplicity of the rite stands in stark contrast to the increasing complexity of baptismal praxis: namely, when the baptized "seed" sought the baptism of their own children, though they themselves had not yet offered evidence of conversion. These parents were professing Christians but were regarded as being only in the "external" covenant that made them ineligible for admission to the Lord's table and the baptism of offspring. The solution reached in 1662 was the "Half-Way Covenant" that allowed such persons, as long as they assented to the church's doctrine and had not lived immoral lives, to present their children for baptism. The parents, however, were still not admitted to the supper. Opinion was divided on this compromise, for it was recognized that the fundamental definition of the Church as a pure community of "visible saints" had been essentially altered.[13]

In early American Congregationalism, only the regenerate of the local congregation and those outsiders with written verification of their spiritual status or with local approval were welcomed to the second seal—and renewal—of the covenant, the Lord's supper. The record of a Salem Church meeting in 1665 discloses this process:

> [Mrs. Sherman] submitted to the Examination of the Pastor and publikely professed her assent to the doctrine of Faith, and her consent to the Covenant and her subjection to discipline and so had her child baptized and staying here to the Lords Day after, she having been with the Pastor the day before, who examining of her declared unto the

Church that he did observe her as able to examine herselfe and discern the Lords body and so she was admitted to partake of the Lords Supper.[14]

However, by the 1670s questions were raised about restricting the sacrament to the converted, notably by Solomon Stoddard, who saw the sacrament itself as a "converting ordinance." In the eighteenth century admission was often opened to adult baptized Christians of sound belief and behavior. Communicants were expected to engage in a period of preparation and self-examination before the day of reception—a practice shared with other denominations. Lechford indicates that prior to the rite at the Lord's day morning service, many non-communicants left the meetinghouse—the majority of persons in attendance—in effect creating a distinct two-part Sunday service.

Lechford and Cotton describe a service at which bread and wine are blessed apart in two distinct actions (following, says Cotton, Christ's own institution) and minister and elders sit at table to receive while the rest of the congregation partakes in the seats, served by the laity. No "set forms" are used, claims Cotton. Yet eighty years later a similar shape of the Congregational liturgy is set out, but more fully, in *Ratio Disciplinae Fratrum Nov-Anglorum* (1726) by Cotton Mather.[15] After the pastor "descends from the Pulpit unto the Table" and reads the names of members from other churches desiring to attend, he exhorts the communicants. A "short Passage equivalent unto the *Sursum Corda* of the Ancients" is spoken, followed by the reading of the institution of the supper in toto from Luke (Luke 22:19–20) or Paul (1 Cor. 11:23–26), or else divided according to the respective action with the bread and the cup. In either case the pastor then performs the actions related in the institution narrative, invoking again the scriptural account. At the reference to Christ taking bread, the pastor touches the bread on the table before him. With the words "And HE BLESSED it," he offers a prayer with the communicants standing, "filled with the Acknowledgements of the *Evangelical Truths*, which this Institution invites us to think upon; and Supplication for the Divine *Blessing*, upon that Part of the *Sacrament*, now before them, and upon themselves in the Receiving of it." When the prayer is concluded, the communicants sit, and the pastor breaks the bread into "convenient Parcels" accompanied by a "*Sentence* of the sacred Scriptures, or of their own Pathetic Thoughts." Once the bread is broken, "he says to this Effect":

> Our Lord *JESUS CHRIST*, having broken the Bread, He *GAVE IT* unto His Disciples, saying, This is my Body which is broken for you, take it, and eat of it, and do it in Remembrance of me. Wherefore in the Name of that Glorious Lord, I now invite you, to *TAKE*, and *EAT* hereof; and to do it in Remembrance of Him.

The pastor serves himself and then gives the dishes to the deacons for distribution to the seated congregation. When the deacons return, the pastor inquires if all have received (this suggesting a large attendance), and then the deacons are seated and partake. When it comes to the second element, the pastor, standing, "*takes* a *Cup* of the *Wine* that is now in the *Flagons* and the *Tankards* on the Holy Table." At the words "And He *GAVE THANKS*," the communicants stand and the pastor "pours out a Prayer, of the like Importance, the like Tendency, with the former." Then "filling out the *Wine* from the *Flagons* into the *Cups*," the pastor speaks to similar effect as with the bread, making appropriate substitutions. The process of reception is repeated with the cups, and after inquiry as to whether all have been served, the deacons receive. A Psalm follows, and then the pastor offers a third prayer, "consisting of the most Raised *Thanksgiving* to GOD, and *Assurance* of the Blessings in the *New Covenant*, sealed by this Ordinance." Money is collected to relieve the poor and "defray the Charges of *Eucharist*," and the assembly is dismissed with a blessing.

Besides the Lord's supper, another service defined explicitly as covenant renewal was also practiced, accompanied with fasting, repentance, and prayer; the content and shape of such a service was determined by the local community and its own church covenant. This was a simple service, though as the years progressed it sometimes was enlarged. Such shifts toward liturgical expansion are evident for other services. Burials at first were simple interments with no prayer, scripture reading, or sermon; gradually these components were added along with extravagant (and disputed) funerary accoutrements. Although ministers preached sermons at public marital engagements, weddings were conducted by magistrates in the home, and if a minister was present, he might be invited to give one of the prayers. By the time Cotton Mather wrote his *Ratio*, the minister had assumed a key role, offering prayer, setting out the marriage covenant to the couple and soliciting their consent, and declaring their marriage "according to the Laws of GOD, and of this Province."[16]

The meetinghouse, where many of these services of worship took place, was at first a simple wooden structure, square or elongated, with a central and dominant pulpit set opposite the main entrance, which made a visual statement about worship as principally engagement with the Word of God. Galleries provided extra seating on as many as three sides and brought upper-floor worshipers closer to the pulpit. Large windows facilitated lighting for the congregation seated on simple benches or in enclosed box pews that granted additional warmth in the often-unheated building. A small, freestanding table might be placed in front of the pulpit for the Lord's supper; or as at the "Old Ship" in Hingham, Massachusetts, the only surviving (though restored) seventeenth-century meetinghouse (1681), the table was attached by hinges to the elders' and deacons' pew just below the pulpit and could be folded out of the way when not in use.[17] A baptismal basin was placed on the table as needed. Only minimal

"Old Ship" Church, Hingham, Massachusetts. The oldest surviving meetinghouse (1681) is still used for weekly Sunday worship. PHOTOGRAPH BY KAREN WESTERFIELD TUCKER

Hinged communion table, folded down. In the "Old Ship" Church, Hingham, Massachusetts. PHOTOGRAPH BY STUART R. TUCKER

decoration enhanced the space, lest the listeners be distracted. Authoress Harriet Beecher Stowe, daughter of the famed preacher Lyman Beecher, was impressed as a child by the simplicity and solemnity of the meetinghouse she attended in Litchfield, Connecticut, in the early 1800s:

> To my childish eyes our old meeting-house was an awe-inspiring place. To me it seemed fashioned very nearly on the model of Noah's ark and Solomon's Temple, as set forth in the pictures of my scripture catechism—pictures which I did not doubt were authentic copies; and what more respectable and venerable architectural precedent could any one desire? Its double rows of windows of which I knew the number by heart, its doors with great wooden curls over them, its belfry projecting out of the east end, its steeple and bell, all inspired as much sense of the sublime in me as Strasburg Cathedral itself; and the inside was not a whit less imposing. How magnificent to my eye seemed the turnip-like canopy that hung over the minister's head, hooked by a long iron rod to the wall above! How apprehensively did I consider the question, what would become of him if it should fall. With what amazement I gazed on the panels on either side of the pulpit, in each of which was carved and painted a flaming red tulip, bolt upright, with its leaves projecting out at right angles. Then there was a grapevine, basso-relievo in front, with its exactly triangular bunches of grapes, alternating at exact intervals with exactly triangular leaves.
>
> To me it was a faultless representation of how grapevines ought to look, if they would only be straight and regular, instead of curling and scrambling, and twisting themselves into all sorts of uncanny shapes.[18]

The Worship of Other Church Traditions

Early immigrants typically brought with them strong connections to their homeland church, its worship practices, and when they existed, its liturgical books.[19] The Dutch Reformed and German Reformed brought Reformation-era liturgies and psalmbooks, the latter typically using the "Palatinate Liturgy" of 1563 composed under the supervision of the prince elector Frederick III. The French Reformed (Huguenots) who settled in South Carolina, New York, and Canada worshiped when possible in a manner derived from John Calvin's *La forme des prières et des chants ecclésiastiques* (1542). Because of their small numbers, they were sometimes assimilated with the Dutch in the North and the Anglicans in the South. A Huguenot congregation in Charleston, South Carolina, still worshiping together in the twenty-first century, drew its orders of service from the liturgy of the Swiss churches of Neuchâtel and Vallangin that had borrowed liturgical material from the Church of England.[20] Swedish Lutherans, who settled along the Delaware River, and Dutch and German Lutherans brought their church orders or agendas, psalmbooks, and hymnals. Mennonites were unencumbered with prayer books but carried hymnals to aid their singing, offered in conjunction with preaching, praying, and prophesying. Presbyterians relied upon the metrical psalter popular for their community and turned to John Knox's *Forme of Prayers* or the *Directory for Public Worship* (1645) for guidance; the first presbytery was formed in 1706 by Irish and English Presbyterians and ministers from the Church of Scotland. Although they might not have understood themselves as "immigrants," monks from Valaamo, Russia, including one later known as "Saint Herman of Alaska," brought with them the Orthodox faith and its rites to Kodiak Island in 1797.

As well as Baptists arriving from overseas, there were other persons who became Baptist while in North America as the result of dissent from the practices and government of the "holy commonwealth" or from theological conviction. Rhode Island became a center for Baptist activity, welcoming those who found scriptural difficulties with infant baptism or the mode of sprinkling, experienced rigidity and formality in Congregational worship, and questioned the purity of the church in light of what was perceived as increasing laxity.

Piety and Reason

Throughout the eighteenth century and beyond, Christian worship in North America (as elsewhere in the West) was influenced by two movements that had developed in Europe in the seventeenth century: Pietism and Rationalism. The former, first emerging within German Lutheranism, called for greater attention to the use of scripture in public and in private, accountability in the personal faith and religious practices of the individual, and a stronger sense of Christian community. An emphasis on the "religion of the heart" encouraged fervent and emotional preaching, extemporary prayer even in set liturgies, and hymnody that not only extolled the mighty works of God but also addressed the spiritual state of the singer. The First Great Awakening, experienced in New England and mid-Atlantic areas and intensified by the preaching of George Whitefield, was shaped by this movement, as also were new groups who emigrated from Europe during the eighteenth century. Vocal and instrumental music was an integral component of Moravian (*Unitas Fratrum*) worship, especially at the love feast or fellowship meal, with songs often utilizing the lyrics of their leader Count Nikolaus Ludwig von Zinzendorf. Prayer was usually not extempore in public but rather was offered in the form of a long "litany." A distinctive custom was an Easter service at dawn in the burial ground during which those who died during the preceding year were named. The Brethren were believer baptists who anointed the sick (cf. James 5:14) and used triple submersion at baptism, the latter earning them the nickname "Dunkers." Love feast and foot washing as acts of reconciliation often came before the Lord's supper, which then concluded with a "holy kiss of charity" and the right hand of fellowship. The worship of Shakers (United Society of Believers in Christ's Second Appearing) was brought to North America by "Mother" Ann Lee and was carried out in elegantly simple meetinghouses with separate doors and seating for men and women. Persuaded that it was a "gift to be simple," the celibate Shakers engaged in ecstatic worship (hence their epithet) and danced communally to the accompaniment of nonsensical syllables or songs that sometimes portrayed the divine in feminine images.

Brethren wash feet. Curious onlookers watch while the Brethren men engage in the ancient practice of foot washing. Illustration by G. L. Croome from Peter Nead's *Theological Writings* (1850). COURTESY OF THE BRETHREN HISTORICAL LIBRARY AND ARCHIVES.

The second movement, Rationalism, in which human intellect and reason were exalted, cast doubt upon the reliability of biblical revelation and the plausibility of divine intervention in the world. The Christian faith was accountable to reasonableness; hence those things unexplainable were questioned, such as the grace offered and divine presence found in the sacraments. From a rationalist perspective, worship's task was to instruct and edify: repetitions or lengthy liturgical texts risked disengagement; the Lord's supper was viewed as incomprehensible, though it was retained in obedience to the biblical command. Preaching was the main task of worship, inviting hearers to a moral life, and to meet that purpose, worship spaces were designed first and foremost to accommodate public speaking. Rationalism and Pietism thus shared some striking commonalities—especially the stress on the individual and the importance of edifying preaching—though the underlying intentions were quite different.

Shaker worship near Lebanon, New York. Dances and marches, with persons separated by gender, were accompanied with songs and hymns. Nineteenth-century lithograph by Currier and Ives. PRINTS AND PHOTOGRAPHS DIVISION, LIBRARY OF CONGRESS

In the American colonies of the eighteenth century, Enlightenment philosophies undergirded the bid for independence from England with the watchwords of "freedom" and "individual liberty"; rationalism permeated the environment. Newly (re)emerging Unitarianism therefore readily found a home in the colonies in the 1700s and flourished in the century following. Ralph Waldo Emerson, a Unitarian minister and later transcendentalist, on 9 September 1832 preached the sermon "The Lord's Supper," in which he offered his resignation as pastor of a Boston congregation because, on the basis of reasoned study, he could no longer in good conscience administer that sacrament. "Jesus did not intend to establish an institution for perpetual observance when he ate the Passover with his disciples," he stated, adding, "we ought to be cautious in taking even the best ascertained opinions and practices of the primitive church for our own." Besides, "we are not accustomed to express our thoughts or emotions by symbolical actions. Most men find the bread and wine no aid to devotion, and to some it is a painful impediment. To eat bread is one thing; to love the precepts of Christ and resolve to obey them is quite another." While "forms are as essential as bodies ... to exalt particular forms, to adhere to one form a moment after it is outgrown, is unreasonable, and it is alien to the spirit of Christ."[21]

Early Lutheran and Reformed Liturgical Documents

During the eighteenth century, liturgical materials were composed and published in a milieu in which Pietism, Rationalism, and interest in liturgical orthodoxy coexisted. One of the first American liturgies to appear was written by a Lutheran, Henry Melchior Muhlenberg, who apparently used for his work the printed German Lutheran order of Saint Mary's at Savoy in the Strand, London—which had been adapted from the so-called Antwerp *Agende* of 1567—as well as German regional liturgies with which he was familiar. Although he was a Pietist, Muhlenberg's *Agende* remained consistent with historic German and Scandinavian Lutheran liturgies. The mainly German-language work contains five chapters: "The Order of Public Worship," "Baptism," "Marriage," "Confession and the Lord's Supper," and "Burial"; baptism and marriage texts appear in English and are derived from the 1662 *Book of Common Prayer*. There are incomplete texts for collects, epistles, and gospels; these were supplied in the Marburg hymnal that was widely used in the colonies and printed in an American edition in 1762. The regular service followed this sequence:

> Hymn of invocation of the Holy Spirit
> Confession of sins: Exhortation, Confession, farsed (expanded, paraphrased)
>   Kyrie
> Gloria in Excelsis, in metrical form: "Allein Gott in der Höh"
> Salutation with Collect for the Day
> Epistle
> Hymn
> Gospel
> Nicene Creed: "Wir glauben all an einen Gott" (the Gospel and creed were
>   omitted on occasion of baptism since the baptismal liturgy supplied those
>   texts)
> Hymn
> Sermon (the Gospel is read a second time, the people standing)
> General Prayer, with intercessions, or Litany
> Lord's Prayer
> Announcements
> *Votum*: "The peace of God which passes all understanding"
> Hymn
> Salutation and Closing Collect
> Aaronic benediction (Num. 6:24–26) with invocation of the Trinity

Holy Communion, at the minimum, would have been celebrated at Christmas, Easter, and Pentecost using this order beginning after the sermon:

> Preface and abbreviated Sanctus
> Exhortation (from Martin Luther's *Deutsche Messe* of 1526)
> Lord's Prayer
> Words of Institution
> Invitation to communion (from the Saint Mary's liturgy)
> Distribution
> Versicle and Post-Communion Collect (from *Deutsche Messe*)
> Aaronic benediction with invocation of the Trinity

Muhlenberg's liturgy was adopted in 1748 by the Ministerium of Pennsylvania, the first Lutheran synodical body in America. The text was never printed and was used for approximately forty years in handwritten copies.[22] In 1786 Muhlenberg took a central role in the issuing of *Erbauliche Liedersammlung*, the first Lutheran hymnal published in America, which closely followed the arrangement of the Halle hymnal of J. A. Freylinghausen. Muhlenberg noted in the preface the advantage of a single German-language hymnbook to unify the congregations that had been using different collections brought from their homelands. The first English-language Lutheran hymnal, John Christopher Kunze's *A Hymn and Prayer-Book* (1795), contained hymns originally written in English and translations of German hymns as well as an English version of a revision of Muhlenberg's liturgy produced in 1786 (*Kirchen-Agende der evangelisch-lutherischen vereinigten Gemeinen in Nord-America*).[23]

Several branches of the Reformed family during this period formally organized themselves and produced as norms for public prayer liturgical books or worship directories. The Consistory of the Dutch Reformed Church in New York printed in 1767 an English translation of the liturgy brought from the Netherlands that became the basis of the liturgy used by the Dutch Reformed Church in North America (incorporated in 1819 as the Reformed Protestant Dutch Church and in 1867 renamed the Reformed Church in America). The 1767 publication included set prayers for before and after the sermon on the Lord's day; forms of baptism for "infants of believers" and adults; forms for excommunication and the "confirmation of marriage before the Church"; and a liturgy for the Lord's supper arranged with a long exhortation containing the words of institution, prayer, the Apostles' Creed, an invitation to "lift [hearts] up on high in Heaven" (echoing Calvin on the sacrament), communion with Psalm singing or scripture reading (e.g., Isa. 53; a section from John 13–18), excerpts from Psalm 103, and a final prayer.[24] There was no set order supplied for a Sunday morning service of the word, as was also the case for congregations affiliated with the Presbyterian Church in the United States of America whose *Directory for Worship* was authorized in 1788. This *Directory* contained no precise liturgical texts (though in baptism the minister was to use the triune Name) but rather rubrics, suggestions for the content of prayers, and model prayers.[25] Nevertheless it is possible to glean from the *Directory* a likely sequence of components for a Sunday morning Presbyterian service—including, significantly, hymn singing;[26] and from eyewitness records colonial Sunday morning worship for a Dutch Reformed congregation may be reconstructed, taking into account the activity of the lay *voorlezer* (forereader), who assisted with reading and the singing.[27] In both denominations it was advised that preachers avoid overly long sermons, a recommendation that apparently was regularly ignored.

Dutch Reformed	*Presbyterian*
	Prayer
	of adoration, confession, invocation, and preparation
Scripture reading	[Scripture reading
lectio continua by the voorlezer	at least one chapter by the
as the people gather	minister or teacher located here or elsewhere]
The Decalogue	
read by the voorlezer	
Psalm	Psalm or hymn
by the congregation;	
entrance of the minister	
Votum (invocation) and Salutation	
Exordium remotum	
(introduction to the sermon)	
Prayer	Prayer
	may include adoration, thanksgiving, confession, supplication, petitions, and intercession
[Psalm]	
Sermon	Sermon
"Long" Prayer	Prayer
including supplications	

Lord's Prayer
   by the minister, the congregation
   silently

[Offering
   here or elsewhere]
	[Offering
	   here or elsewhere,
	   preceded or followed by prayer]

Psalm Benediction	Benediction

Both denominations were indebted to Calvin. Yet the liturgical manifestations of that interpreted theology—set in the American context and influenced by external movements—took different forms; and even within the single denomination there were variations, with scripture reading, exposition of scripture, prayer, and singing remaining the stable core.

A Baptist Order

Although not a liturgical book per se, *Customs of Primitive Churches* (1768) by the Baptist pastor Morgan Edwards of Philadelphia documents in detail and with careful explanation Baptist worship practices familiar to him, thereby wittingly or unwittingly providing a paradigm for other Baptist communities.[28] Edwards summarizes the essentials required for each liturgical event and supplies a sample of how that event might be performed. For public worship—"at least of evening worship"—he provides an order in which preaching and the Lord's supper are central, with prayer also commanding an important place. The sequence he puts forward bears strong similarities to what Lechford and Cotton described more than a century earlier for New England Congregationalism. Not surprisingly absent are formulas such as a creed, the Decalogue, and the Lord's prayer found in other worship orders of the period since their liturgical use lacks scriptural warrant; and there is no explicitly stated prayer of confession, although in fact one of the prayers could carry confessional overtones:

> A short prayer suitably prefaced
> Reading a portion of scripture
> A longer prayer
> Singing
> Preaching
> A third prayer
> Singing a second time
> Administering the Lord's supper
> Collecting for the necessities of saints
> A benediction

Edwards's stipulation that this order is appropriate for evening worship is made clear by his comments in the section on the Lord's supper: not only did Christ institute the meal at the end of the day, "the name of the ordinance viz. *supper* requires it should be kept in the evening." The meal is to be held every Lord's day evening, administered by a minister with the people sitting; the "frame of mind" is to be "serious and examinatory." A single loaf and red wine are used, and "implements" include a table, a dish, "a cup or more if needs be," and candles. In giving the outline of the service, Edwards notes that "all the parts of the solemnity are significant." Here, as with Congregational custom, the actions with the bread and the cup are distinct and separated:

> A suitable exordium
> Taking the bread, blessing it and giving thanks

> Breaking it
> Giving it to the people
> Uttering the words of distribution
> Taking and eating
> Likewise taking the wine, blessing it, and giving thanks
> Pouring the wine
> Giving it to the people
> Uttering the words of distribution
> Taking and drinking the wine
> Singing a hymn (as at the conclusion of the Last Supper)

In the section on baptism, Edwards presents a succinct theological declaration that furnishes brief indications regarding performance:

> Baptism is a rite of divine institution and perpetual obligation. The subjects of it are, such as credibly profess regeneration; repentance; faith; and subjection to the gospel. The administrators are only those of the sacred character. The principal ends of it are, encouraging hope of pardon, sanctification, and salvation; putting on christianity; binding the party to observe its laws; having a right of admission into a visible church; and confirming the doctrine of the resurrection. The manner of performing it is, once dipping a person in the name of the father, son, and holy ghost. The attendant rites are prayer, imposition of hands, &c.

A portion of his fuller description of liturgical practice supplements the basic statement and gives evidence of a procedure also employed by Baptists of later years: causing the candidate to go backward into the water as a stronger indicator of the Christian's dying and rising with Christ (Rom. 6:4):

> Then the minister took the candidate by the hand to the water, repeating these words as they went (Acts 8:36, 38). When far enough in the water, the minister, with his right hand took hold of the thumbs of the candidate; and with his left, the neck of his garment behind, and dipped him once (backward) after uttering these words: "In the name of the Lord Jesus, and by the authority of our office, we baptize you in the name of the father, in the name of the son, and in the name of the holy ghost. Amen." When baptism was over, the parties dressed and met again, the minister addressed him ... prayed, and laid hands on him. ... Then gave him the right hand of fellowship and kiss of charity.

Edwards also gives attention to the love feast, which has as its defined purpose "promoting brotherly love and relieving the poor." "Any eatables and drinkables" are suitable, he says, but his sequencing of the rite—prayers, singing, washing feet ("with a form of words expressive of the ends of the rite"), kiss of charity, and right hand of fellowship—gives no mention of where sharing of food and drink might be located. In his "sample" of the love feast, he invites the singing of a hymn by Isaac Watts, thereby integrating a new and humanly composed text into an ancient event. But the rite is clearly specified for the home and not the church's building.

Revisions of the *1662* Book of Common Prayer

With the creation of an independent United States at the end of the eighteenth century, antipathy toward the Church of England reached a peak, resulting in the flight of some Anglican Loyalists to Canada, where that Church would persist until 1893, when the autonomous Church of England in the Dominion of Canada was formed. No bishop had been resident in the colonies, which meant no confirmations or ordinations. After the American Revolution, the absence of a bishop in America, an insufficient number of Anglican clergy, and reactions to formulations in the Prayer Book about the monarch and the royal family (priests were bound by their ordinations to offer prayers for the king) prompted the leaders of two groups to take steps that ultimately resulted in published revisions of the 1662 *Book of Common Prayer* and two nascent denominations.

Methodism had come to the colonies in the 1760s and was spread by means of male and female lay leadership and by Anglican clergy receptive to this evangelical movement within the Church of England. Methodists, who were organized as "societies," held services for prayer and preaching in addition to watch nights (from approximately 8 PM to past midnight) and love feasts, all accompanied by the singing of hymn texts that had flowed from the pens of the founders and Anglican priests John Wesley and Charles Wesley. Discouraged from holding their services during "church hours," Methodists were expected to attend the Anglican parish church on Sunday and to receive the sacraments there. When it became clear that the Americans wanted to receive the sacraments from the hands of their own Methodist clergy, John Wesley in England took the irregular actions of ordaining three men for the work in America and emending the Prayer Book mostly by deletion (see "Comparative Outlines of Orders"). Using language characteristic of Rationalism, he conceded that because of their new political freedom, Methodists could become a separate ecclesiastical body and were "at full liberty, simply to follow the scriptures and the primitive church." In conformity to apostolic practice as well as Reformation-era preference, Methodists were advised to celebrate the Lord's supper on every Lord's day.[29] The Prayer Book revision, which John Wesley believed was closer to a primitive standard, was printed in 1784 under the title *The Sunday Service of the Methodists in North America* and supplied the Methodist Episcopal Church founded in that same year with texts for morning and evening prayer (for Sunday use only), the Lord's supper, infant and adult baptism (no rite of confirmation was included), marriage, burial, and ordination. Although attempts were made in urban centers to adhere to the advice of weekly eucharist, it proved impossible to execute. Eight years after the American Methodists adopted the *Sunday Service* and one year after John Wesley's death, the stated services again went through a revision and in 1792 were put into the denomination's book of *Discipline* rather than in a separate worship book. Morning and evening prayer disappeared and were replaced with rubrics instructing that Sunday morning worship consist of "singing, prayer, the reading of a chapter out of the Old Testament, and another out of the New, and preaching." The other services remained mostly unchanged, though the ante-communion was dropped from the order for the Lord's supper. Methodists for almost one hundred years thereafter found it better at the Sunday morning service of the word to pray with their eyes closed than with their eyes open (i.e., according to a prayer book); communion was held at least quarterly.

Anglicans in the new United States were faced with the need for episcopal leadership and a *Book of Common Prayer* appropriate to the changed situation. Samuel Seabury of Connecticut, at the request of area clergy, petitioned for and in November 1784 received consecration from nonjuring bishops in Scotland because consecration as bishop in England was contingent upon an oath of allegiance to the Crown. In exchange the nonjuring bishops secured Seabury's promise that he would attempt to introduce for American usage their communion office of 1764, which had affinities with the 1637 Scottish Prayer Book and the 1549 *Book of Common Prayer*. Three years later, aided by an enabling act from the English Parliament, William White and Samuel Provoost were consecrated as bishops. All the while various state conventions and

Comparative Outlines of Orders for Morning Prayer and Holy Communion

Church of England, *Book of Common Prayer*, 1662	*Sunday Service of the Methodists in North America*, 1784	Protestant Episcopal Church in the United States of America, *Book of Common Prayer*, 1789
	Morning Prayer	
Morning Prayer (daily)	(Lord's Day only)	Morning Prayer (daily)
Scripture Sentences	Scripture Sentences (abbreviated)	Scripture Sentences (expanded)
Call to Confession	Call to Confession (abbreviated)	Call to Confession
General Confession	General Confession	General Confession
Absolution	Prayer for Pardon	Absolution or Prayer for Pardon
Lord's Prayer	Lord's Prayer	Lord's Prayer
Versicles	Versicles	Versicles (abbreviated)
Gloria Patri	Gloria Patri	Gloria Patri
Praise ye the Lord ...	Praise ye the Lord...	Praise ye the Lord...
Venite (Psalm 95) or Anthems		Venite or Anthems
Appointed Psalms with Gloria Patri	Appointed Psalms with Gloria Patri	Psalms with Gloria Patri or Gloria in Excelsis
First Lesson—Old Testament	First Lesson—Old Testament	First Lesson—Old Testament
Te Deum or Benedicte with Gloria Patri	Te Deum (said only)	Te Deum or Benedicte
Second Lesson— New Testament	Second Lesson— New Testament	Second Lesson— New Testament
Benedictus or Jubilate (Psalm 100)	Jubilate (said only) with Gloria Patri	Jubilate or Benedictus
Creed (Apostles' or Athanasian)	Creed (Apostles')	Creed (Apostles' or Nicene)
Salutation	Salutation	Salutation
Kyrie	Kyrie	
Lord's Prayer and Suffrages		Suffrages (abbreviated)
Collect for the Day (the same as for Communion)	Collect for the Day (the same as for Communion)	Collect for the Day (except when Communion follows)
Collect for Peace	Collect for Peace	Collect for Peace
Collect for Grace	Collect for Grace	Collect for Grace
Anthem		
Prayer for the King's Majesty	Prayer for the Supreme Rulers	Prayer for the President of the United States, and all in in Civil Authority

local congregations set forward proposals for an American prayer book, many of which drew upon unauthorized revisions of the period, including that by John Wesley.[30] A rather conservative Proposed Book was printed in 1786, the same year Seabury published his Scottish-influenced *Communion-Office* for the Connecticut clergy, but additional changes and compromises were required before final approval at the General Convention of 1789. Some adjustments to the Morning Prayer in the 1789 book are similar to Wesley's, such as the dropping of repetitious material and the recasting of the prayers for the sovereign (see "Comparative Outlines of Orders"). The communion rite

Prayer for the Royal Family		
Prayer for Clergy and People		Prayer for Clergy and People (edited)
Prayer for All Conditions	Prayer for All Conditions (optional)	Prayer for All Conditions
General Thanksgiving	General Thanksgiving	General Thanksgiving
Prayer of Saint John Chrysostom	Prayer of Saint John Chrysostom	Prayer of Saint John Chrysostom
Apostolic Benediction	Apostolic Benediction	Apostolic Benediction
(Litany on Sunday, Wednesday, Friday)	(Litany on Wednesday, Friday)	(Litany on Sunday, Wednesday, Friday)
Holy Communion	Holy Communion (every Lord's Day)	Holy Communion
Introductory directions	Introductory directions	Introductory directions
Lord's Prayer (priest)	Lord's Prayer (minister)	Lord's Prayer (optional)
Collect for Purity	Collect for Purity	Collect for Purity
Decalogue with response	Decalogue with response	Decalogue with response
		Summary of the Law
		Kyrie (if no Decalogue)
Two Collects for the King	Collect for Supreme Rulers	Collect
Collect of the Day	Collect of the Day	Collect of the Day
Epistle Lesson	Epistle Lesson	Epistle Lesson
Gospel Lesson	Gospel Lesson	Gospel Lesson
Nicene Creed		Apostles' or Nicene Creed (unless done previously)
Notices	Notices	
Sermon or standard Homily	Sermon	Sermon
Offertory Sentences with Collection of Alms	Offertory Sentences (abbreviated) with Collection of Alms	Offertory Sentences (expanded) with Collection of Alms
Rubric for presentation of bread and wine		Rubric for presentation of bread and wine
Prayer for Christ's Church Militant	Prayer for Christ's Church Militant	Prayer for Christ's Church Militant (edited)
Warning and exhortations		Warning and exhortations

adds the option of the Summary of the Law popular among Non-Jurors and latitudinarian groups, allows for either the Apostles' or the Nicene Creed and for the omission of the creed if one had been used immediately before in Morning Prayer, and most significantly, includes a Scottish-derived eucharistic prayer with an invocation or epiclesis:

> And we most humbly beseech thee, O merciful Father, to hear us; and of thy almighty goodness, vouchsafe to bless and sanctify, with thy Word and Holy Spirit, these thy gifts and creatures of bread and wine; that we, receiving according to thy Son our Saviour Jesus Christ's holy institution, in remembrance of his death and passion, may be partakers of his most blessed Body and Blood.

Thus in a strange twist the communion liturgy used by Methodists in North America (into the twenty-first century in some African American Methodist denominations) remained closer to that of the Church of England than the one approved by the Protestant Episcopal Church in the United States. Additional revisions to the Protestant Episcopal Church's Prayer Book followed in 1892, 1928, and 1979.[31]

Invitation	Invitation	Invitation
General Confession	General Confession	General Confession
Absolution	Prayer for Pardon	Absolution
Comfortable words	Comfortable words	Comfortable words
Sursum corda	Sursum corda	Sursum corda
Common preface (priest facing table)	Common preface (no rubric for location)	Common preface (priest facing table)
Proper preface	Proper preface (optional)	Proper preface
Sanctus	Sanctus	Sanctus
Prayer of Humble Access	Prayer of Humble Access	Prayer of Humble Access
Prayer of Consecration (with manual acts)	Prayer of Consecration (manual acts?)	Prayer of Consecration (with manual acts)
		Oblation
		Invocation
		Prayer of Thanksgiving (first prayer from 1662 Prayer Book)
		Hymn
Distribution, clergy first	Distribution, clergy first	Distribution, clergy first
Lord's Prayer	Lord's Prayer	
Prayer of Thanksgiving (two)	Prayer of Thanksgiving (one)	Prayer of Thanksgiving (second prayer from 1662 Prayer Book)
Gloria in Excelsis	Gloria in Excelsis	Gloria in Excelsis
	Rubric for extempore prayer	
Benediction	Benediction	Benediction

Revival, Reaction, and Reform

Revival

The enthusiasm generated by the Great Awakening had slackened by the 1760s. But at the end of that century and into the next, spiritual fires were kindled in New England, Canada, the southern United States, and the still-expanding western regions. Heartfelt preaching was heard at the Gaspar River Church in southwestern Kentucky under the leadership of the Presbyterian minister James McGready and also from the pulpit at Yale College in the educated discourse of its president, Timothy Dwight. Revivalism particularly took hold in the American South and was intensified across the nation by days-long meetings in the open air with hundreds of participants and dozens of conversions. The setting for worship that became known as the camp meeting was not new; its antecedents were outdoor preaching services by Methodists and certain Baptist groups and also the eucharistic "sacramental seasons" and "holy fairs" brought by Scottish Presbyterians.[32] Camp meetings were not only religious gatherings; they were important social events, particularly in sparsely settled areas.

The earliest sites for camp meetings were situated near sources of water, wood, and pasturage where participants created a temporary home with wagons or tents. A platform or wagon provided the elevation needed for a pulpit or pulpits; the congregation sat on the ground or upon rough-hewn benches. Often natural amphitheaters were chosen to amplify the voice. As the camp meeting increased in popularity, some campgrounds constructed multiple and permanent pulpit stands in front of which were enclosed areas covered in straw or sawdust referred to in some places as the "altar."

Here those seeking redemption found "mourners benches" or "anxious benches" as well as spiritual encouragement. Printed manuals circulated to assist in the organization and maintenance of these assemblies.[33]

The camp meeting quickly evolved into a four-day scheme, beginning on a Thursday night with the format typical for evening services—singing and exhortation, not preaching (preachers "took a text")—intended to improve receptivity. The songs might come from denominational hymnals or out of camp meeting songsters produced by denominational editors and by independent compilers that stressed themes of repentance, judgment, and the benefits of heaven. Spontaneous songs or choruses could also erupt that might be repeated at future meetings, and an independent and new refrain could be added to a well-known existing hymn text, such as one by Isaac Watts or Charles Wesley. Songs were also an integral component of small-group and family worship at the campground, the corporate early morning prayer service, the preaching services scattered throughout the day, and the Lord's supper service held as the last event on Sunday. Many of the early camp meetings mixed denominations (principally Baptists, Methodists, and certain Presbyterians), language groups, and races, though theology and racism usually meant that Baptists, native peoples, and persons of African descent celebrated the Lord's supper separately. Methodists and Presbyterians early in the nineteenth century limited admission to the table, with access only by a ticket or token certifying spiritual qualification.[34] Baptist "closed communion" was claimed to rest upon scriptural and historical foundations and upon the premise that communicants ought to be those who were baptized by personal profession, exhibited moral and disciplined living, and had been spiritually prepared and examined prior to reception. As part of the Landmark movement in the southern United States during the second half of the nineteenth century, the founder J. R. Graves took closure a step farther by limiting the ordinance to the local congregation and its members in good standing.[35]

The presence at the camp meeting of persons of different ethnic and racial backgrounds provided an occasion for the sharing and mingling of musical forms, influencing the development, for example, of white and black spirituals. The camp in effect was a nursery for the gospel style of church song that became widespread in the late nineteenth century. Singing was an integral component of worship in black communities from the outset and was regarded as a medium of prayer, spiritual empowerment, and proclamation but also as a vehicle for inveighing against human injustices

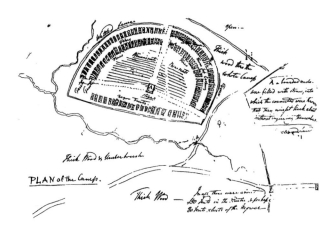

Camp meeting plan, 1806. Drawn by the architect Benjamin Henry Latrobe. Latrobe notes that "wattled fences" separated the camp from the thick woods. Fires were scattered throughout the two horseshoe-shaped rows of tents—the "white camp"—with the fires on the right identified for cooking. The "negro tents" stretched in a line behind the stage and "altar" (A). Women's seating was on the left, the men's on the right. From Talbot Hamlin, *Benjamin Henry Latrobe* (1955).

A camp meeting. Lithograph by
Edward Williams Clay from an
engraving by Henry R. Robinson,
1836. © New York Historical
Society/Bridgeman Art Library

before God. The song could take the
characteristically African form of
call and response ("Have you got
good religion? Certainly, Lord";
"Have you been baptized? Certainly, Lord"), inviting easy partici-
pation. Certain songs functioned as code during slavery: singers and listeners might
be advised that assistance (a "sweet chariot") was at hand ("swing low") to "carry them
home" to a place without slavery.

The rural camp meeting as a distinct form persisted, surviving even into the twenty-
first century, nurtured largely by Holiness and other evangelical denominations. In
urban settings the style of camp worship was duplicated in "protracted meetings" or
multiday revivals that, during the second half of the nineteenth century, met in large,
acoustically sound, auditorium-style church buildings designed for an unobstructed
view of the pulpit or speaker's desk. Direct descendants of the urban revival worship
form and its venue in the twentieth and twenty-first centuries were the evangelistic
crusades of Billy Graham and others and the megachurch buildings that could seat
thousands. Urbanization of the camp meeting was stimulated by the Presbyterian
turned Congregationalist Charles Grandison Finney, who in the 1830s applauded the
"new measures" that had arisen out of these revivals. Over the objections that these
innovations lacked biblical justification, Finney countered that

> when Christ came, the ceremonial or typical dispensation was abrogated, because the
> design of those forms was fulfilled, and therefore themselves of no further use. ... The
> Gospel was then preached as the appointed means of promoting religion; and it was left
> to the discretion of the church to determine, from time to time, what *measures* shall be
> adopted, and what *forms* pursued, in giving the gospel its power.

The purpose of measures and forms is "to make known the gospel in the *most effectual*
way, to make the truth stand out strikingly, so as to obtain the attention and secure
the obedience of the greatest number possible."[36] Finney's approach of liturgical prag-
matism evaluated by "effectiveness," which combined pietistic and rationalistic streams
in a unique way, would prove quite influential and long-lasting within North American Protestantism.

Reaction

The response to the camp meeting revivals and Finney's new measures was, however,
mixed. Churches that adopted the measures grew rapidly, the Methodists and Baptists among them. Many Presbyterian groups disassociated themselves from the camp
meeting and its methods, leading eventually to a denominational split sparked by "old
school" and "new school" sensibilities. The Presbyterian leaders of what would become in 1832 a "brotherhood" of Disciples of Christ and "Christians" were sympathetic to the underlying purposes of revivalism but were equally troubled by a number

of theological claims of Presbyterianism and the departure from what were judged to be biblical and apostolic practices. In the Christian/Disciples' aim of restoration, there was to be faithful observance of the Lord's day as a community, no creed in worship, baptism by immersion given to believers, and a weekly Lord's supper—presided over by senior laity without benefit of a liturgical text; the clergy had responsibility for preaching, in some congregations after the "great ordinance of the day of the Resurrection" had already been served.[37]

A scathing reaction came from the German Reformed theologian John Williamson Nevin of that denomination's seminary in Mercersburg, Pennsylvania. In his critical work *The Anxious Bench* (1843), Nevin denounced the "heresy" of the new measures because they promoted Pelagianism, overlooked God's ongoing work of sanctification, and hindered true and vital godliness. Faith nurtured by the study of the catechism, claimed Nevin, was far preferable to the coarseness of the "bench." Soon after the book's publication, Nevin was joined on the faculty by the theologian and historian Philip Schaff, and together they teamed to develop the so-called "Mercersburg theology" centered upon ecclesiology and christology and sympathetic to a more "catholic" view of the church. In 1846 Nevin brought out *The Mystical Presence: A Vindication of the Reformed or Calvinistic Doctrine of the Holy Eucharist*, wherein he reexamined Calvin's doctrine of the church and theology of the sacrament. He concluded, contrary to the position of most Reformed in the mid-nineteenth century, that "the Eucharist forms the very heart of the whole Christian worship" and that in the action of eating and drinking, the Holy Spirit unites the faithful with Christ in his human and divine natures.[38] In answer to objections from the Princeton professor Charles Hodge and others, Nevin bolstered his claims by referring to historic Reformed documents in his long essay "The Doctrine of the Reformed Church on the Lord's Supper" (*Mercersburg Review*, 1850) and thereby effectively silenced his critics.

The synod of the German Reformed Church had adopted a liturgy in 1840, but there had been much dissatisfaction with it. A recommendation came in 1847 that the old Palatinate Liturgy be reprinted or a new liturgy be prepared, to which assent was given in 1848. The next years were characterized by liturgical study and political wrangling, during which time a significant historical study of the Reformed liturgy was released by the Presbyterian Charles Baird. Baird determined in *Eutaxia* (literally, Good order) that "example abundantly warrants the use of liturgical forms in the Presbyterian Church," and he approved the efforts of those ecclesiastical bodies, including the German Reformed Church, that had begun "to take action upon the revival of their ancient forms of worship, hitherto regarded with indifference."[39] In the end a minority of the committee charged with preparing a liturgical text, led by John H. A. Bomberger, preferred a revision of the old Palatinate Liturgy that focused upon prayer and preaching. The majority, including Nevin and Schaff, sought essentially a liturgical expression of the Mercersburg theology. A Provisional Liturgy, approved and printed in 1857, was composed under Schaff's guidance and utilized as sources quotations from scripture, original contributions, liturgies of the Early Church and the Reformation (especially the Palatinate Liturgy and the Church of England's *Book of Common Prayer*), and the liturgy of the Catholic Apostolic Church (the "Irvingites"). The Irvingite Liturgy first appeared in print in 1842; Schaff in 1854 had worshiped with them in London.[40] Four forms, from complex to quite simple, were provided in the Provisional Liturgy for Lord's day use. The Holy Communion service was structurally a conflation of the *Book of Common Prayer* and Irvingite liturgies but also with unique characteristics, such as the reading of scripture sentences following the Collect for Purity—a prayer that combines Prayer Book, Irvingite, and original material (see "The Holy Communion, German Reformed Church"). The exhortation blended original composition with occasional quotation from scripture, the result being a succinct articulation of the "mystical presence" and other classical Reformed emphases advocated by Nevin. The first part of the eucharistic prayer (Thanksgiving) joined original work to Irvingite contributions. The entirely original epiclesis invoked the "mystical presence." The oblation contained material from scripture, the Prayer Book, and the Irvingite Liturgy.

The Holy Communion, German Reformed Church

Provisional Liturgy (1857)	Order of Worship (1866)
Greeting	Greeting
	Call to Confession
	Confession
	(essentially as in the Provisional Liturgy)
	Declaration of Pardon
	Nicene Creed
	Versicle
Collect for Purity	
Almighty and everlasting God, who by the blood of Thy dear Son hast consecrated for us a new and living way into the holiest of all; cleanse our minds, we beseech Thee, by the inspiration of Thy Holy Spirit, that we, Thy redeemed people, drawing near unto Thee in these holy mysteries, with a true heart and undefiled conscience, in full assurance of faith, may offer unto Thee an acceptable sacrifice in righteousness, and worthily magnify Thy great and glorious name: through Jesus Christ our Lord. Amen.	
Scripture Sentences	
(Isa. 53:4–7; John 1:29–34; John 3:14–17; 1 John 1:5–9; 1 John 4:9–10; John 15:4–5; John 6:51–58)	
Gloria in Excelsis; or Te Deum, Canticle or Hymn	Gloria in Excelsis
Gospel	Gospel
Epistle	Epistle
	Gloria Patri
	Salutation (The Lord be with you ...)
Collect of the Day	Collect of the Day
Festival Prayer for the Season	Festival Prayer
	Psalm or Hymn
Sermon or Homily	Sermon or a brief Gospel reading recounting Christ's passion and death
Nicene Creed (Athanasian Creed at the last communion in the church year)	[located above]

Offertory (Alms and Communion Elements)

Offertory (Alms and Communion Elements)

Collect (opening collect from the
  Provisional Liturgy)

Scripture Sentences (selections from the
  Provisional Liturgy)

Exhortation

Dearly Beloved in the Lord: Our blessed
Saviour Jesus Christ, when He was about to
finish the work of our redemption by making
Himself a sacrifice for our sins upon the cross,
solemnly instituted the Holy Sacrament of His
own Body and Blood; that it might be the abiding
memorial of His precious death; the seal of His
perpetual presence in the Church by the Holy
Ghost; the mystical exhibition of His one offering
of Himself made once, but of force always, to put
away sin; the pledge of His undying love to His
people; and the bond of His living union and
fellowship with them to the end of time. From all
this we may understand how great and glorious
the Sacrament is, and with what just reason it hath
ever been regarded in the Church as that act of
worship, the which men are brought most near to
God, and, as it were, into the innermost sanctuary
of His presence, the holiest of all, where more than
in any other service it is fit that their adoration
should be joined with sacred reverence and awe.
We have to do here, in a mystery, not with the
shadows and types only of heavenly things, but
with the very realities themselves of that true
spiritual word in which Christ, now risen from the
dead, continually lives and reigns. See, then, as
many of you as have it in mind to take part in this
service, that ye be properly clothed for the
occasion with the spirit of humility, self-
recollection, penitence, and prayer. Examine
yourselves, whether ye be in the faith; prove your
own selves. Renew inwardly your baptismal
engagements and vows. Renounce all sin both in
your lives and in your hearts. Be in perfect charity
with all men. Christ our Passover is sacrificed for
us; therefore let us keep the feast, not with old
leaven, neither with the leaven of malice and

The Provisional Liturgy received use but also protest, much of it spearheaded by Bomberger. A revised version was published in 1866 as *An Order of Worship for the Reformed Church*, with omissions, additions, and changes in the structure of some services (see sidebar for comparison). In the communion order, for example, a more Reformed shape is taken for the service overall, the exhortation is eliminated, and the oblation is reduced in length, but even so the eucharistic prayer remains largely intact. Bomberger and others were still not satisfied. Bomberger continued to rail against his church's "ritualistic" movement and put his complaints to print in *Reformed, Not Ritualistic, Apostolic, Not Patristic* (1867). Agitations within the denomination persisted until the authorization of a *Directory of Worship* in 1884.

wickedness, but with the unleavened bread of sincerity and truth. Present yourselves on the altar of the Gospel, in union with His glorious merits, a living sacrifice, holy, acceptable unto God, which is your reasonable service; giving thanks unto the Father, which hath made us meet to be partakers of the inheritance of the saints in light; who hath delivered us from the power of darkness, and translated us into the kingdom of His dear Son: in whom we have redemption through His blood, even the forgiveness of sins. And now that we may be able so to compass God's holy altar with righteousness and joy, let us first of all bow down before Him, and make humble confession of our sins, that we may obtain forgiveness of the same through His infinite goodness and mercy.

Confession	[located above]
Declaration of Pardon	[located above]
Introductory Dialogue	Introductory Dialogue
Sursum Corda, etc.	Sursum Corda, etc.
Thanksgiving	Thanksgiving (essentially the same as the Provisional Liturgy)

Before the mountains were brought forth, or ever Thou hadst formed the earth and the world, even from everlasting to everlasting, Thou art God. Thou didst in the beginning create all things for Thyself. By Thy word were the heavens made, and all the host of them by the breath of Thy mouth. The armies of the invisible world, angels and archangels, thrones, dominions, principalities, and powers; the glorious firmament on high, sun, moon and stars; the earth and the fulness thereof; all are the work of Thy hands, and all are upheld by Thee continually in their being, as they stand by Thee, likewise, in their appointed order and course.

Thou also at the first didst make man in Thine own image, and after Thine own likeness, and didst set him over the works of Thy hands, endowing him with the excellent gift of righteousness, and forming him for immortality. And when afterwards, through the fraud and malice of Satan, he fell by transgression from that first estate, Thou didst not leave him still to perish

Reform

The controversial "Mercersburg Liturgy" that derived from theological reflection and historical investigation was intended to be simultaneously Reformed and catholic. Its production was but one example of the move in several ecclesiastical communities toward the recovery of historic liturgical forms and practices that been distorted by pietistic and rationalistic tendencies, although ironically this Romantic quest benefited from methods of scholarly inquiry advanced by the Enlightenment. Within the Church of England, the Oxford (or Tractarian) and Cambridge movements took shape around 1833–1834 and stressed a reexamination of ecclesiology and with it a reassertion

utterly in his fall, but wast pleased to raise him up
again and to restore him to the joyful hope of
everlasting life, by the promise of redemption
through Jesus Christ; who, being God of God,
very God of very God, dwelling in the bosom of
the Father with unspeakable blessedness from all
eternity, at last when the fulness of time was come,
came down from heaven, and became man, for us
men and for our salvation.

For all Thy mercies and favors, known to us and
unknown, we give Thee thanks. But most of all,
we praise Thee, the Father everlasting, for the gift
of Thine adorable, true, and only Son, our Saviour
Jesus Christ, who by His appearing hath abolished
death and brought life and immortality to light
through the gospel. We bless Thee for His holy
incarnation; for His life on earth; for His precious
sufferings and death upon the cross; for His
resurrection from the dead; and for His glorious
ascension to Thy right hand. We bless Thee for
the giving of the Holy Ghost; for the institution of
the Church; for the means of grace; for the hope of
everlasting life; and for the glory which shall be
brought unto us at the coming, and in the kingdom,
of Thy dear Son.
(continues with introduction to the Sanctus)

Sanctus	Sanctus (from the Provisional Liturgy)
Words of Institution (Fraction and Elevation)	Words of Institution (Fraction and Elevation) (from the Provisional Liturgy)
Epiclesis	Epiclesis (from the Provisional Liturgy)

Almighty God, our heavenly Father, send down,
we beseech Thee, the powerful benediction of Thy
Holy Spirit upon these elements of bread and wine,
that being set apart now from a common to a sacred
and mystical use, they may exhibit and represent to
us with true effect the Body and Blood of Thy Son,
Jesus Christ; so that in the use of them we may be
made, through the power of the Holy Ghost, to
partake really and truly of His blessed life, whereby
only we can be saved from death, and raised to
immortality at the last day.
R. Amen.

Oblation	Oblation
And be pleased now, O most merciful Father, graciously to receive at our hands this memorial of the blessed sacrifice of Thy Son, which we, Thy servants, thus bring before Thy divine Majesty,	And be pleased now, O most merciful Father, graciously to receive at our hands this memorial of the blessed sacrifice of Thy Son;

of classical Anglican (and catholic) sacramental theology. Alongside these theological agendas was placed a reclamation of older (i.e., Catholic and medieval) forms for church architecture, the arrangement and decoration of liturgical space, ceremonials, vestments, and music. For Anglicans in Canada and the United States influenced by these "Anglo-Catholic" movements, there was interest, for example, in retrieving a theology of baptismal regeneration that had in many quarters been questioned on account of its suspected conflict with justification. The baptismal rites in Wesley's *Sunday*

according to His own appointment and command; showing forth His passion and death; rejoicing in His glorious resurrection and ascension; and waiting for the blessed hope of His appearing and coming again. We are not worthy in ourselves to offer unto Thee any worship or service. Wherewith shall we, sinners of the dust, come before the Lord, or bow ourselves before the most high God? We bring unto Thee, O holy and righteous Father, the infinite merits of Jesus Christ, Thine adorable, true, and only Son, in whom Thou hast declared Thyself to be well pleased, and through the offering of whose body once for all, full satisfaction has been made for the sins of the world. Have respect unto this glorious sacrifice, we beseech Thee, in union with which we here offer and present unto Thee, at the same time, O Lord, the reasonable sacrifice of our own persons; consecrating ourselves, on the altar of the gospel, in soul and body, property and life, to Thy most blessed service and praise. Look upon us through the mediation of our great High Priest. Make us accepted in the Beloved; and let His name be as a pure and holy incense, through which all our worship may come up before Thee, as the odour of a sweet smell, a sacrifice acceptable, well pleasing to God.

R. Amen.

Intercessions

Lord's Prayer

Benedictions

Peace

Communion

Benediction

Post-Communion Prayer

Te Deum [if not used earlier]

Benediction

in union with which we here offer and present unto Thee, O Lord, the reasonable sacrifice of our own persons; consecrating ourselves, on the altar of the Gospel, in soul and body, property and life, to Thy most blessed service and praise. Look upon us through the mediation of our great High Priest. Make us accepted in the Beloved; and let His name be as a pure and holy incense, through which all our worship may come up before Thee, as the odor of a sweet smell, a sacrifice acceptable, well pleasing to God.

R. Amen.

Intercessions (from the Provisional Liturgy)

Lord's Prayer

Peace

Communion (from the Provisional Liturgy)

Benedictions (from the Provisional Liturgy)

Post-Communion Prayer (from the Provisional Liturgy)

Te Deum

Benediction (from the Provisional Liturgy)

The text of the Provisional Liturgy was taken from *A Liturgy: or, Order of Christian Worship. Prepared and Published by the Direction and for the Use of The German Reformed Church in the United States of America* (Philadelphia: Lindsay and Blakiston, 1859) 190–202. The outline of the 1866 liturgy follows *An Order of Worship for the Reformed Church* (Philadelphia: S.R. Fisher, 1867) 171-187.

Service had omitted some references to regeneration, and American Methodists in the following generations took the purging even further. Altar-centered gothic-revival became a preferred style for the construction or renovation of Anglican buildings throughout the nineteenth century and beyond. The translations of Latin and Greek hymns by John Mason Neale found a place in the Protestant Episcopal Church's official hymnbooks.

Roman Catholicism and Lutheranism likewise experienced recoveries, the former by investigations into the performance practice of Gregorian chant taken up first at the Benedictine monastery of Solesmes in France. Wilhelm Löhe of Neuendettelsau in northern Bavaria produced a Lutheran *Agende für christliche Gemeinden* (1844) as the outcome of a reexamination of Reformation and older materials along with personal commitments to frequent confession and communion. Löhe exported the liturgy for use by pastors in the Lutheran communities settled in the midwestern United States, and it was used for a time. But its more important role was as a resource in the creation of a Lutheran "Common Service" in 1888 because of its reliance on Reformation and pre-Reformation materials. The recovery of older methods of musical performance was also of interest to Lutherans, especially those in Missouri, who endeavored during the mid-nineteenth century to reverse the trend of equalizing irregular rhythms in order to restore early German chorales and Genevan psalter tunes to their original configurations.[41]

Ready participants in revivalism also joined in this reclamation of the past, though to a much more limited degree. Baptist Landmarkism may be understood in this vein. Methodists, always seeking to recover the evangelical fervor of the founders (and splitting into new denominations if the perceived spiritual ideal and liturgical simplicity was not being achieved), had not reprinted Wesley's *Sunday Service* since it was laid aside in 1792. In response to a request from an Alabama congregation, the Methodist Episcopal Church, South published in 1867 Wesley's orders for morning and evening prayer in combination with that denomination's own revisions of the other rites (e.g., baptism and Lord's supper). There was no real interest in implementing Wesley's advice for weekly communion, thus continuing for Methodists—as for most congregations that were not Roman Catholic, Orthodox, or Christian Church–Disciples of Christ—a normative Sunday practice of prayer, scripture reading, preaching, and singing, with occasional observance of the eucharist (ranging from annual to monthly).

Identity and Change

Tensions in Liturgical Revision

In the final decades of the nineteenth century, however, many of the "free" denominations started to witness a move from a simple to a more complex Sunday morning practice, sometimes codified by an outline or formalized with a text. On this matter, the partial republication in 1867 of Wesley's *Sunday Service* is a significant historical marker for denominations in the American Methodist family. In a stated attempt to establish uniformity in public worship on the Lord's day, the Methodist Episcopal Church in 1888 expanded in its *Discipline* the rubrics that had guided Sunday worship since 1792. Eight years later the suggested order was enlarged in the 1896 *Discipline*:

1888	*1896*
	[items in brackets may be omitted]
	[Voluntary]
Singing	Singing
a hymn from "our" hymnbook	from the hymnal
the people standing	the people standing
	[The Apostles' Creed]
Prayer	Prayer
minister and people kneeling	minister and people kneeling
Lord's Prayer	Lord's Prayer
said by all	said by all
	[Anthem]
Old Testament Lesson	Old Testament Lesson
may be read responsively	if from Psalms, may be read responsively
	[Gloria Patri]

New Testament Lesson	New Testament Lesson
may be read responsively	
Collection	Collection and Notices
Singing	Singing
one of "our" hymns	from the hymnal
the people sitting	the people standing
Preaching	Sermon
Short prayer	Short prayer
for a blessing on the word	for a blessing on the word
Singing	Singing
closing with a doxology	closing with the Doxology
the people standing	the people standing
Apostolic Benediction	Apostolic Benediction

The orders are essentially the same, but the changes—some subtle—are significant. Two musical additions are made to the 1896 service: a voluntary or organ prelude and an anthem by a choir. Methodists, like many Baptists and Reformed, had objected to an organ for solo offerings and the accompaniment of congregational singing, finding it scripturally unwarranted and more of a distraction (and expense) than an aid. Great debates had ensued within the various denominations about the propriety of musical instruments in public worship, yet by the end of the nineteenth century, most had accepted organs. Primitive Baptists, "noninstrumental" congregations of Disciples, and others did not; they continue to worship in the twenty-first century without instruments, the former Disciples as (since 1906) the Churches of Christ (Non-Instrumental).[42] Choirs were equally problematic for many Protestants because they deprived the congregation of their duty of song making, but by 1900 they too had mostly become standard. Musically the 1896 order also hints that a single doxology had been settled upon, most probably the stanza by Thomas Ken increasingly preferred by Methodists and other denominations, even though the denomination's 1878 hymnal included multiple options. The 1896 order officially returned to Methodists three components lost when Prayer Book–style morning prayer was jettisoned—the Apostles' Creed, the Gloria Patri, and the (responsive) reading of the Psalms—though Methodists tended to regard them more as "enrichments" than as liturgical recoveries. It is also notable that "preaching" was redesignated the "sermon," a term that, by comparison, suggests a greater formality, erudition, and social respectability befitting a denomination that had become, in the course of one hundred years, large, middle class, and influential. When a sister denomination, the African Methodist Episcopal Church, printed a similar Sunday order in the 1890s, it included a component from Wesley's (and the Prayer Book's) ante-communion: the rehearsal of the Decalogue. The printing of formal orders and the stated desire of uniformity notwithstanding, Methodists were not required or even expected to frame worship "by the book," and in local congregations an altar call or time of commitment would often have been added following the sermon.

The printing of a simple order for worship in 1888 and its slight elaboration in 1896 drew the ire of many in the denomination who bemoaned the increasing liturgical formalism as a distancing from Methodism's origins and as a concession to a "ritualism" they saw evident in Episcopal churches influenced by the Oxford Movement and among newly immigrant Roman Catholics. For them, the printing of a liturgical order not only limited the liberty to worship as the Spirit moved, it also risked deadening the spirit entirely. This contrasting of liturgical forms and spiritual freedoms

A Southern baptism. A freshwater baptism at Aiken, South Carolina in the first decade of the twentieth century. NEW YORK PUBLIC LIBRARY, HUMANITIES AND SOCIAL SCIENCES LIBRARY/PHOTOGRAPHY COLLECTION, MIRIAM AND IRA D. WALLACH DIVISION OF ART, PRINTS AND PHOTOGRAPHS

was not unique to the Methodist Episcopal Church. Other ecclesiastical bodies in Canada and the United States experienced similar reactions—as well as other concerns—as they engaged in the work of liturgical revision, the printing of worship resources, or the creation of a denomination's first liturgical book during the late nineteenth and early twentieth centuries.[43] In a nod to this issue, the (northern) Presbyterian Church in the United States of America testified in the preface of its first *Book of Common Worship* (1906) that while "Liberty of Worship has been esteemed a most precious privilege and inheritance" and Presbyterians have been "both fearless and faithful to uphold it against the intrusion of superstitious and burdensome ceremonies," they have also been "diligent to seek, in the Public Services of Religion, the golden mean between a too great laxity and a tyrannical uniformity."[44] To allay apprehensions, the cover page of the book carried the words, "For Voluntary Use."

Unresolved disputes on the subject of a denomination's worship sometimes contributed to the formation of new denominations within the confessional family; such fractures also accompanied liturgical revisions throughout the twentieth century. Liturgical dissatisfaction may have contributed—along with the winds of a new spiritual awakening—to the emergence of Pentecostalism and charismatic worship in the early 1900s. At the heart of the matter were questions about how to define a denomination's liturgical identity—an identity that could be linked to broadly confessional origins or to a particular founder, to various stages in an ongoing evolution, to a desire for apostolicity and catholicity (however determined), to evangelistic concerns, or to projections of future directions. Committees appointed to consider liturgical revision were faced with untangling the web that was liturgical identity, and as was the case with the Mercersburg Liturgy, internal politics were inevitably involved. Beginning in the early nineteenth century and continuing into the next century, with more intensity in certain decades, a key part of the discussion in most processes of revision was the study of the liturgical history and theology of the particular denomination as well as the broader Christian tradition.

Worship and Social Issues

The concerns of the region and the nation figured regularly in the prayers of most communities in Sunday morning and evening services and, where available, in the worship of Sunday schools and also in the corporate worship services and prayer meetings held on other days of the week. At times of crisis, national leaders requested the prayers of the churches; interdenominational fasts often accompanied these prayers. Particular

Civil war mass in the field. Mass celebrated in the field on Easter Sunday, 1864, by Rev. P. P. Cooney, C.S.C., chaplain general of the Indiana troops, Army of the Cumberland, during the Atlanta campaign. Chromolithograph, 1877. PRINTS AND PHOTOGRAPHS DIVISION, LIBRARY OF CONGRESS

social issues inspired additional resources for worship, and changes in technology brought controversial but lasting adjustments to liturgical practice in certain communities. Shifting perceptions of society and its structures sometimes prompted the nuancing of extant liturgical texts or the formulation of new ones.

Thematic hymnbooks edited by denominations, activist groups, and individuals supplied a quickly published means for addressing emergent social concerns. Antislavery hymnals used at rallies and at interdenominational and congregational services of worship circulated in Canada and the United States in the early nineteenth century. Similarly employed and located temperance songbooks with texts (many by women) warning of the evils of alcohol proliferated in the second half of the nineteenth century and into the twentieth. During the American Civil War (1861–1865), troops of the North and South received special hymnals, some books also containing prose devotional materials and selections from the Bible. Whether compiled by Baptist, Episcopalian, Presbyterian, or Methodist hands for their military, these hymnals were intended as a resource for public and private worship in the field and as an evangelistic tool for those who might soon meet their Maker. Between 1890 and 1930 hymn collections were produced expressing the theological emphases of the Social Gospel movement. Representative hymns were placed into denominationally authorized hymnals for Sunday worship in that and later generations, among them "O Holy City, Seen of John," written by the Episcopal priest and Union Theological Seminary professor Walter Russell Bowie and published in *Hymns of the Kingdom of God* (1910); the fourth and final stanzas summarize well the focus of the movement:

> Give us, O God, the strength to build
>   The city that hath stood
> Too long a dream, whose laws are love,
>   Whose ways are brotherhood,
> And where the sun that shineth is
>   God's grace for human good.
>
> Already in the mind of God
>   That city riseth fair:
> Lo, how its splendor challenges
>   The souls that greatly dare—
> Yea, bids us seize the whole of life
>   And build its glory there.[45]

Hymns and hymnals advocating temperance were not the only liturgical means of addressing the subject. From the early nineteenth century onward, concerns had been expressed across several denominations about the type of liquid poured into the communion chalice and its unintended condoning of alcohol use. In *Scriptural View of the Wine-Question* (1848), the Congregationalist Moses Stuart attempted to prove by biblical and historical evidence that a nonalcoholic drink had been on the table at the Last Supper. Leon C. Field, a Methodist, posited in *Oinos: A Discussion of the Bible Wine Question* (1883) that unfermented wine had been present both at Cana and in the upper room and that Jesus himself had neither imbibed nor commended alcoholic drink. The commercial marketing in the 1870s of Dr. Welch's Unfermented Wine made available an alternative to alcohol but subsequently provoked lasting debate about Christ's own example and sacramental practice within and between denominations.

Questions about the communion cup were not limited to its contents. With the discovery that germs caused illness and disease, physicians and church members in the late 1880s wondered if a "poisoned chalice" at the sacrament could spread contagion. Alternative methods of reception were proposed: the use of siphons or straws; individual spoons; individual cups; and intinction, or the dipping of a piece of bread into the cup, though it did not replicate the distinct actions of eating and drinking commanded in the words of institution. Individual cups seemed to many a viable option, supported by the line of reasoning that Jesus had neither mandated a common cup nor specified a number of cups and that many congregations already used several chalices at a single event, including different chalices for men and women. Arguments against included the unsuitability of a "saloon" method, the departure from historic and traditional practice, and the destruction of the symbolism of unity evoked by a common cup. Like the subject of wine versus grape juice, the common cup versus individual cups was a contentious issue. Nonetheless Methodists and certain Baptists were using individual cups by the turn into the twentieth century, and it was generally acceptable to Lutheran groups by the 1930s.[46]

Advances in technology had altered the way some congregations received the sacrament of the table. Another innovation in the 1880s had a wider impact still: the duplication of paper copies by inked stencils in a process called mimeograph invented by A. B. Dick that allowed local congregations to print orders of service in a Sunday bulletin and pastors to supply textual adjustments as needed. Among other technological developments that had liturgical ramifications were embalming of the dead, a technique employed during the American Civil War that became popular afterward, and in the early twentieth century, moving pictures and public mass transportation, which were seen as threats to the sanctity of the Sabbath and worship attendance.

Adjustments to liturgical practices were also triggered by changing social and theological perceptions of human beings and their institutions. These modifications are readily noticed in printed orders for the pastoral offices or Christian rites of passage. In the case of marriage rites, motivation for some denominations to rework their texts came from challenges by women's groups along with theological reflection on the nature of Christian marriage and an awareness of emerging societal definitions of women's roles and the family. In the period from the mid-nineteenth to the early twentieth century, certain denominations removed "obey" and "serve" (or similar words) from the woman's declaration of intention and added to her words roles present in the man's statement, such as "comforter." The two declarations were brought into parity with both promising to "love, comfort, honor, and keep." In the early twentieth century, liturgical texts caught up with the increasingly common practice of the double wedding ring: the exchange of rings between both partners rather than a single ring given to the woman that was traditionally in the West a sign of her bride-price. The presence of rings at Methodist, Congregationalist, and Presbyterian weddings shows a capitulation to the prevalent custom, since those groups historically disapproved of rings as superstitious and superfluous ornaments that had no justification in scripture.

The inclusion of a separate funeral rite or specific funeral resources for the death of a child in new liturgical books published during the first decades of the twentieth century was an acknowledgement of the changing views of children and childhood extant in the larger society. These services were also possible because of a shift that had already occurred in approaches to death in many of the churches, clearly visible in the distribution of hymns under the headings "funeral/burial" or "death" in the succession of official denominational hymnals: away from judgment and warning and toward hope and consolation. The prayers for a child's funeral concede the full humanity of the child but sometimes also suggest the absence of the long-assumed taint of original sin. A collect from the 1928 Protestant Episcopal *Book of Common Prayer* offers a good example of this different theological mood:

> Almighty and merciful Father, who dost grant to children an abundant entrance into thy kingdom; Grant us grace so to conform our lives to their innocency and perfect faith, that at length, united with them, we may stand in thy presence in fulness of joy; through Jesus Christ our Lord.

The Theory and "Spirit" of Worship

In his Merrick Lectures given at Ohio Wesleyan University in 1926, G. A. Johnston Ross declared that within the "nonliturgical" churches only rarely did public prayer "assist to expression the instinct of reverence" and, because of that neglect, there was a "yearning for beauty, a desire for orderliness, dignity, impressiveness."[47] Not simply a variant on the question of liberty versus liturgical forms, Ross's comment pointed to a perceived gap left both by Sunday worship focused more on the preacher than on God and by the theological stress upon divine immanence and human positivism characteristic of the social gospel. What was lacking was an emphasis upon the transcendence and mystery of God (already reasserted by Rudolf Otto and others) and the "spiritual" aspect of worship. Into this breach stepped two writers whose work was quite influential in the 1920s and throughout the 1930s among mainline Protestants. In the writing of the Congregationalist turned Unitarian Von Ogden Vogt, beauty and worship are virtually similar. Vogt insisted that gothic architecture best inspired true worship because its verticality evoked both emotion and mystery; other aspects of the past might also be borrowed if they were not "burdened with abandoned concepts."[48] Willard L. Sperry, a Congregationalist who was dean of Harvard Divinity School, was concerned in *Reality in Worship* (1925) with the "objective" in worship and with how the outer form of worship expressed inner experience or personal religion. Although both Vogt and Sperry suggested principles for the ordering of public worship, neither gave serious attention to the sacraments in their writing and were apparently ignorant of the "mystery theology" (*Mysterientheologie*; from Odo Casel's *Die Liturgie als Mysterienfeier*, 1922) and "spirit" of liturgy (Romano Guardini, *Vom Geist der Liturgie*, 1918) being cultivated at the time under Roman Catholic theologians and liturgical scholars in Europe and filtering into North America. In spite of their omissions, the focus of Vogt and Sperry upon the spirituality of worship had an effect on liturgical revisions, the design of liturgical space, and liturgical arts during that time and gave rise to psychological, anthropological, and aesthetic studies on the theory and practice of worship.

One of the beneficiaries of Vogt's and Sperry's writing was the Federal Council of the Churches of Christ in America, founded in 1908 and vital to the progress of the Social Gospel movement. Roman Catholics and Orthodox were not represented on the Council, but various Episcopalians, Baptists, Lutherans, Methodists, and Reformed were as well as the Society of Friends, Moravians, and others. By the end of the 1920s the Council's attention turned toward the subject of worship, and in 1932 a committee was constituted for special work, such as the compilation of a worship bibliography and the creation of a worship research library. To foster the spirit and practice of worship across the churches, the Committee on Worship in 1936 printed "Seven Principles of Public Worship," which was circulated in conjunction with that year's National Preaching Mission. The following year, *The Christian Year* was published to introduce the Christian calendar, especially to those churches ignorant or suspicious of it, and to "revitalize" the traditional calendar with contemporary expressions. A christological framework governed liturgical, civil, social (e.g., Race Relations Sunday), and ecumenical (e.g., Christian Unity Sunday) days and seasons. In the Council's 1937 annual report, the Committee on Worship explained its rationale, using language reminiscent of the social gospel and the writings of Sperry and Vogt:

> The calendar as published ... follows the historical pattern by making the events in the life of our Lord the basis of the calendar from the Advent season to Pentecost (Whitsunday), slight modifications of traditional usages being suggested from time to time. For the period between Pentecost and Advent a new season is introduced, known as Kingdomtide, paralleling the recognized seasons like Advent and Eastertide. During Kingdomtide the center of interest is the bringing of the message and influence of Christ to bear upon the contemporary life of the world. This approach makes it possible to incorporate the more important modern "days"—such as Labor Day and World Peace Day—effectively into the calendar. The comments already made concerning the calendar encourage the Committee to believe that it has succeeded in combining the historic approach with an approach based upon present-day needs of the individual and society.[49]

The Federal Council's *Christian Year* influenced the liturgical awareness and practices of several denominations who officially adopted a filled-out liturgical calendar (more than Christmas and Easter) for the first time. Methodists were particularly enamored of Kingdomtide, and despite official moves away from that designation in the 1980s, the term still appeared in Methodist worship bulletins decades later.

Convergence, Renewal, and Continuity

Early Ecumenism and Worship

Throughout the nineteenth century denominations were cognizant of each other's liturgical practices and polity, using that information positively for Christian fellowship and for the framing or reevaluation of liturgical texts, or negatively out of the intention to claim over against others the most scriptural and apostolic practice. The formation of the Federal Council in 1908 bore witness to serious and constructive ecumenical engagement, with the sharing of liturgical resources an important consequence. During the 1930s orders of service were printed intentionally for use across denominational lines. One collection was the *Book of Common Worship for Use in the Several Communions of the Church of Christ* (1932, 1936), edited by the Methodist bishop

Wilbur Thirkield and Oliver Huckel, a Congregational minister. As chairperson of the Federal Council's Committee on Worship, Thirkield had overseen the preparations of the committee's 1936 and 1937 liturgical publications. The foreword states that the book was produced because of deepening interest in the "spirit and form of worship" and the desire for "more adequate services of worship" on the part of churches with no prayer book; it was compiled from historic prayers as a "fresh and grateful realization of our common heritage" and from modern sources since "every age has its own need and must speak in its own tongue."[50] Similar patterns of worship were regarded as one means of furthering the ecumenical agenda.

The 1930s saw the reuniting of some denominations that had split over liturgical, political, or social issues, and with union came the creation of new liturgical texts consonant with the rites and practices of the joining groups. Mergers that had begun in the 1910s from among the twenty or more Lutheran church bodies present in the United States continued again in the 1930s, mostly as before along lines of linguistic and national origin; here too liturgical amalgamation needed to be considered. In 1932 the *Book of Common Order* was published by the United Church of Canada, newly formed in 1925 by the union of churches with different origins and histories: the Methodist Church, Canada; the Congregational Union of Canada; the General Council of Union Churches; and 70 percent of the Presbyterian Church in Canada. Unlike the other mergers, this one liturgically not only required a blending of texts but also the compromise of different underlying theologies and traditions of worship, even though liturgical distinctions tended to fall more by location (urban versus rural) than by confession and all the groups shared a conviction for "ordered liberty in common worship." The new denomination perpetuated that principle in declaring in the book's preface two fundamental ideals: a congregation should be able to "follow the leading of the Spirit of Christ in their midst," and "the experience of many ages of devotion" should be preserved.[51]

The new United Church of Canada services for the Lord's day essentially took three principal forms. Under the heading "The Public Worship of God" were two forms—directories—each with two derivative orders of worship that offered suggested prayers (see "The Public Worship of God, The United Church of Canada, 1932"). Although Methodists generally did not employ the term "directory," the format of a bare outline with rubrics would have been familiar. The first Directory, which indicated two possible sequences in the section labeled "Introduction," had strong affinities with the contributing Presbyterian order and older Presbyterian services as well but also approximated common Methodist and Congregational practices. The tripartite second Directory intentionally restored the shape of the Reformed ante-communion. The third form was an order for the Lord's supper created from the blending of recent Reformed and Methodist rites with historic practices from the broader Christian tradition. The result was a single, unified service of word and sacrament that departed from the long-standing practice in the three major predecessor denominations of tacking the sacramental service to the conclusion of a service of the word (a separate order for the Lord's supper was provided in the United Church book for that purpose). The entire service followed a Reformed structure but utilized prayers taken from Methodist (i.e., English *Book of Common Prayer*) and ecumenical sources. Taking a shape that would become common in decades following, the communion liturgy begins with the preparation of bread and wine at the offertory, and the breaking of the bread (fraction) occurs after the eucharistic prayer instead of during the words of institution said during the course of the prayer. The formulators of the United Church

---

The Public Worship of God
The United Church of Canada, 1932

DIRECTORY 1		DIRECTORY 2
THE INTRODUCTION		THE INTRODUCTION
Call to worship		
Prayer of Invocation		
Psalm or Hymn	Psalm or Hymn	Psalm or Hymn
Prayers of Confession and Supplication	Prayers of Invocation, Confession and Supplication	Prayers of Confession, Thanksgiving, and Supplication
Lord's Prayer		Lord's Prayer

THE PSALMS	THE WORD OF GOD
Psalms (one or more)	
Gloria Patri	
THE LESSONS	
Old Testament Lesson or New Testament Lesson other than Gospel	Old Testament Lesson or New Testament Lesson other than Gospel
Canticle, Psalm, or Hymn	Psalm
New Testament Lesson	Gospel Lesson
THE PRAYERS	
Prayers of praise and thanksgiving of entreaty of intercession for the Church, the nation, the human family, the conditions of humankind of thanksgiving for the faithful departed	
Lord's Prayer (if not said before)	
Offering (located here or after the sermon)	
Anthem	
THE SERMON	
Hymn	Hymn
Announcements	Announcements (or before the hymn)

---

liturgy, for the Lord's supper rite, took advantage of current liturgical scholarship—Protestant, Anglican, and Catholic—that was reexamining and starting to appropriate Early Church theology and practices.[52] Yet such attention was lacking (or church politics prevailed) in regard to the service for the baptism of "innocent" children wherein no mention is made of sin or baptismal regeneration: baptism is portrayed as a dedication, an entry into fellowship and discipleship, a reception of heavenly grace, a token and badge of God's love, and an anticipation of the "liberty" of God's kingdom.

New Appropriations of the Liturgical and Theological Past

During the nineteenth and early twentieth centuries, interest in the renewal of the liturgy among Catholics had received direction and voice particularly within the Benedictine communities of western Europe. In North America this process was now

Sermon	Sermon
	Offering
	Psalm, Hymn, or Anthem
	THE FELLOWSHIP OF PRAYER
Prayers	Prayers
of thanksgiving for the Word of God	of praise and thanksgiving
for perseverance in the divine grace	of entreaty
of remembrance of the whole Church	of intercession for the Church, the
of Christ	nation, the human family,
	the conditions of humankind
	of thanksgiving for the faithful
	departed
	Lord's Prayer
Psalm or Hymn	Psalm or Hymn
Benediction	Benediction

The Book of Common Order of the United Church of Canada (Toronto: United Church Publishing House, 1932) 1–2, 9.

stimulated and expanded by Virgil Michel, a monk of Saint John's Abbey in Collegeville, Minnesota. While in Europe to study philosophy, Michel had visited the important monastic centers for liturgy and received from Lambert Beauduin, a leader in the growing Liturgical Movement, instruction in the doctrine of the mystical body of Christ. Michel returned from Europe in 1925 committed to restoring to the church a greater awareness of its identity as Christ's living body. To that end several concerns permeated his thinking and writing, among them the necessity of the informed and active participation of all the people in worship; the recovery of an understanding of community and the common good that stood in stark contrast to the individualism rampant in the West; and the inseparable connection between worship and work for social justice. In order to accomplish his goal, the dissemination of information was critical. Under Michel's leadership the Liturgical Press was created to publish a Popular Liturgical Library and other resources and the periodical *Orate Frates* was introduced (1926), renamed *Worship* twenty-five years later. Michel was not alone in this sometimes controversial "liturgical apostolate." Numbered among the co-workers and educators in the early days were William Busch, (Abbot) Alcuin Deutsch, Martin Hellriegel, and Gerald Ellard.[53]

In the 1940s the efforts of liturgical renewal in the Catholic Church received new momentum with the establishment of the Liturgical Conference and the cooperation of other organizations, such as the Grail, which had been founded as a laywomen's movement.[54] The national liturgical days for education and encouragement that had gathered committed crowds in the late 1920s and throughout the 1930s were now expanded to national liturgical "weeks": almost thirteen hundred people attended the first event in Chicago in 1940; over twenty thousand met at Saint Louis in 1964. The dream of a renewed Catholic liturgy described by H. A. Reinhold as one of his "Timely Tracts" in *Orate Fratres* was held by many:

> My parish was gathered in a small church, built out of good, but local and inexpensive material, in no particular historical style, but such that it would serve one essential purpose: the

liturgy of the parish. It was quadrangular in shape, so that my people would be close to the altar, lined up in fan formation with the altar as the center. ... The priest stood behind it facing his flock. ...

No pews immobilized my dream congregation and made my church look like a school room. ...

The priest and the assistants vested in the sacristy, which was in the back of the church, alongside of the baptistery and the confession chapel. While vesting they recited the prayers which we used to say at the foot of the altar. Then the procession was formed: a father of a family carrying the altar cross on a long shaft flanked by six young men carrying the altar candles, the censer bearer, one man bearing the missal and another one carrying the beautiful and costly gospel book. Also the schola was in the procession. Then came the subdeacon, deacon and priest. When they entered the rear of the church the schola sang a beautiful antiphon, adapted from the Gregorian, and intoned a psalm. Mind you, the whole thing was in English. Imagine my surprise, when I suddenly heard the whole populace respond with a short verse. This happened after every psalm verse. Many of the people were so enthusiastic that they sang the whole psalm with the schola. The priest and his assistants joined in too.

[The essay goes on to describe various aspects of the "dream" mass, including offerings that were given "for the support of the church, the clergy, and the poor who lived in the parish hospice next door."]

All during the offertory the schola sang one of the old offertory verses. ... The people took up short responses. I was told by my neighbor that the priest's offertory prayers were in Latin and that the whole sacrificial part would be in this sacred language of the Mystery. The only change would be that the people would sing the whole *Sanctus*. ...

The sacred banquet started with the Our Father, again in English. The deacon recited the Communion prayers with the faithful, after the triple "Lamb of God." ... While the priest and deacon gave holy Communion, schola and people alternated communion verse and a psalm in an adapted Gregorian melody in English. It made the reception for those who heard the tune and sang the words so concrete and vital that everybody seem to be quite himself on a higher level. Nothing of a forced attitude was visible. It all looked like a family meal and the priest like the father of the house. ...

I was wondering if my "dream" congregation with its singings, processions, listening, its open eyes and ears, was really so much more "distracted" and so much less inwardly assisting at Mass than my "real" congregation, which supposedly is all in a more sublime, more spiritual, more juridical and more acquiescent state of mind. I liked my dream in spite of its uncanonical rubrics. But, nevertheless, thank God that it was a dream only! Where would I be if it had happened in reality?"[55]

Several aspects of Reinhold's dream would become reality with the Second Vatican Council's reforms of the liturgy. But some Catholics could not wait for that unforeseen day when changes would occur, leading some within parishes and religious communities to experiment with textual adjustments to the mass and other rites and to say or sing portions of the liturgy in the vernacular. Some use of English was officially permissible with approval of Pope Pius XII in 1954.

By the 1940s many Protestants were aware—first- and secondhand—of the liturgical ferment taking place among Catholics and were deeply engaged in renewal work of their own. Some of the points raised by Catholics seeking reform in the twentieth century were ones that had been set out by the Reformers in the sixteenth—liturgy in the vernacular, full and faithful preaching of the Word of God, active participation of the congregation in (frequent) communion and congregational singing. But these were also hallmarks of the liturgy of the early Christian communities as study of the docu-

Holy Communion. Holy communion celebrated in an unidentified Methodist Church in the 1950s using individual cups. PHOTOGRAPH BY ROY SMYRES/REPRODUCED WITH PERMISSION OF THE GENERAL COMMISSION ON ARCHIVES AND HISTORY, THE UNITED METHODIST CHURCH

ments and church orders from the first four centuries, such as the so-called Apostolic Tradition of Hippolytus, had shown. For Protestants, participation in the wider liturgical renewal underway offered an opportunity to assert the catholicity of their Reformation roots and reclaim, in part for ecumenical reasons, the early Church heritage that belonged to all Christians. Societies and organizations emerged to support the application of liturgical research and reflection to local church practices and potentially to the revision of liturgical texts. The Methodist Church's Brotherhood of Saint Luke (1946; in 1948 renamed Order of Saint Luke) had as a prime goal the frequent and informed performance of the sacraments. Also founded on the heels of the Second World War, the Associated Parishes for Liturgy and Mission was legally incorporated in 1946 by members of the Episcopal Church who too wanted to restore the centrality of the eucharist to parish life and to link sacrament with societal issues. Inspiration for Associated Parishes and the reformation of worship came from William Palmer Ladd of Berkeley Divinity School (New Haven, Connecticut), who, in his *Prayer Book Interleaves* (1942) and elsewhere, advocated an adaptation of inherited worship for modern generations. Ladd's person and work influenced Massey Shepherd, Jr., one of the founders of Associated Parishes and himself a leader for liturgical renewal within and outside the Episcopal Church. Shepherd served as a member of the Episcopal Church's Standing Liturgical Commission for thirty years, assisting with sixteen *Prayer Book Studies* produced from 1950 to 1963 and the preparation of trial services that culminated in the 1979 Prayer Book.[56] Shortly after Vatican II, in 1966, Shepherd was appointed an observer to the Roman Catholic Consilium for the Implementation of the *Constitution on the Sacred Liturgy* and to membership in the Worship Commission of the Consultation on Church Union (COCU).

The liturgical reform that came as a consequence of the Second Vatican Council thus was not limited to Roman Catholics. In the forty years after Vatican II , most major Anglican and Protestant groups authorized liturgical revisions that took into account the issues discussed at Rome and the liturgical formulations that developed from them, but also reflected the content of early Christian liturgical documents and the work of an ecumenical range of liturgical scholars and worship committees. Because the liturgical revisions drew upon common sources, texts and orders of worship bore similarities across the churches. For many denominations, a normative and unified pattern for Sunday worship of word and sacrament was approved—even when weekly celebration of the eucharist on Sunday was not likely in view of the strong custom of a preaching service as the main event. Textual revisions were usually preceded by a period of experimental or trial services, which reveal clues about the rationale of the final, approved text. New resources introduced during this time included the Evangelical Lutheran Church in America's *Lutheran Book of Worship* (1978); *The Book of Alternative Services* of the Anglican Church of Canada (1985); the *United Methodist Book of Worship* (1992); the *Book of Common Worship* (1993) of the Presbyterian Church (U.S.A.) and the Cumberland Presbyterian Church; *Chalice Worship* (1997) of the Christian Church (Disciples of Christ); and the United Church of Canada's *Celebrate God's Presence* (2000).

The Roman Catholic Church's promulgation of a Rite of Christian Initiation of Adults (RCIA) in 1972 (English, 1974) came at a time when many churches in North America recognized the urgent need for new strategies to deal with the increasing numbers of adults who had not heard or responded to the Christian gospel. RCIA's models were the catechumenal processes employed in the first centuries of the Church that focused upon spiritual formation, liturgical participation, and Christian ethical living as preparation for the sacrament of baptism and ongoing response afterward. While Catholics struggled with and rejoiced at the implementation of the RCIA (the North American Forum on the Catechumenate was later formed to assist in such endeavors), non-Catholics engaged informally and formally in conversations with them and with each other on the subject of the catechumenate. One such venue was the scholarly North American Academy of Liturgy founded in 1975. By the end of the twentieth century, organized processes for the catechumenate were available in several churches (e.g., the Evangelical Lutheran Church in Canada, Mennonite Church USA and Mennonite Church Canada, and the Christian Reformed Church), and the ecumenical North American Association for the Catechumenate had been established.

The liturgical commonalities that were recognized and realized, particularly in the years following Vatican II, contributed to the opening of doors for more formal ecumenical dialogues and held out a greater hope for eucharistic fellowship across the churches. The Consultation on Church Union, founded in 1962, published an experimental *Order of Worship for the Proclamation of the Word of God and the Celebration of the Lord's Supper* in 1968 that had some usage in ecumenical gatherings, theological seminaries, and university chapels. *Guidelines for Interim Eucharistic Fellowship* followed in 1973. More concrete progress was made, however, in bilateral dialogues. Full communion was established between the Evangelical Lutheran Church in Canada and the Anglican Church of Canada by the joint Waterloo Declaration of 2001; and in May 2003 "Guidelines for Common Worship for Lutherans and Anglicans in Canada" were approved.[57] While confirming that it was most appropriate to use the extant eucharistic liturgy of either of the churches for joint celebrations, the document conceded that some occasions warranted the development of a common rite "based on existing liturgical forms" that followed a "traditional structure":

> Gathering
>> Greeting
>> [Hymn of Praise]
>> Prayer of the Day
> The Word of God
>> [Old Testament Reading]
>> [Psalm]
>> [New Testament Reading]
>> Gospel
>> Homily

> [Apostles' or Nicene Creed]
> Intercessions, Thanksgiving, Petitions
> The Exchange of the Peace
> The Holy Communion (Meal)
> Preparation of the Table
> The Great Thanksgiving
> The Lord's Prayer
> Breaking of the Bread
> Communion
> Commissioning (Sending)
> Thanksgiving for Communion and Prayer for Mission
> [Blessing]
> Dismissal

This "traditional structure" was the general structure in use by many churches across North America at the end of the twentieth century and into the twenty-first.

Continuity and Innovation

While the influences of the Liturgical Movement and Vatican II made a mark upon the liturgical texts and life of Catholics and many North American Protestant denominations, not all groups were as receptive. The "freer" of the "free" church denominations continued as if almost oblivious, although interests were piqued for some about the Christian year. A few Baptist groups began to explore the addition of a season of Lent as akin to the already well-rehearsed seasons of revival. Adjustments to familiar worship practices, when they came, were often the result of the introduction of new musical styles accompanied by previously unused or disallowed musical instruments. For example, Sunday worship at Saint John Progressive Baptist Church in Austin, Texas, with an average attendance of fifty persons, carried on in the style of charismatic black worship of previous generations:

> "Take your time," Pastor Pearson says, turning around in his high-backed chair to address the choir. "Make it pretty, now." Not until their third selection does the choir show its virtuosity in a fast, contemporary song. The snare drum and organ begin, followed by piano, until the choir joins in singing the song's title, "I'll Be with You, That's What He Said." The third time they reach the refrain the repetition of the words, "Said it, that settles it," adds to the musical tension created by the instruments. Piano and

The evangelist Billy Graham. Billy Graham addresses an estimated eight thousand students at the Greek Theater, University of California at Berkeley, on 27 January 1967. Graham first aired his "Hour of Decision" radio broadcast on 5 November 1950, providing sermons and an opportunity of worship for persons unable to leave their homes for the community church. AP WORLDWIDE

organ have become as percussive as drum and cymbals. One soprano swoons in a faint, while surrounding choir members try to prop her up.

   Their attempts are useless in the face of the continuing music. Another singer begins to shriek, jumping up and down, tearing the constraining robe off her shoulders. Closing her eyes while singing the refrain, soloist JoCarole Bradshaw can no longer hold herself back from the descending Holy Spirit. Concerned that her jerking movements are moving her precariously close to the edge of the dais, the ushers hurry to prevent her from tripping and falling. Sister Rosie, vigorously tapping her stiletto heels against the floor, yells out, "Let her go! She can't hurt herself in the Spirit." ...

   With the instruments' pulsations, shouting spreads from the choir to the congregation. Several members stand up and wave their uplifted palms, a joy that usually precedes trance. ...

   "Let Him have His way!" someone says, referring to the free movement of the Holy Spirit among the congregation. ...

   Waving cardboard fans bearing colorful lithographs of Christ, Martin Luther King, Jr., or Mahalia Jackson, the congregation settles down for the continuation of the service. A congregant, not yet calmed, sporadically shouts, "Hallelujah! Thank you Jesus!" The pastor, rising slowly from his high-backed chair, comes to the pulpit. The ritual has reached its focal point: the sermon. In a reassuring, calm voice that contrasts with the preceding shouting, Pastor Pearson requests that the congregation sing "Must Jesus Bear the Cross Alone?"—composed in the seventeenth century—as he lines out the verses from the pulpit.[58]

Certain Pentecostal groups toward the end of the twentieth century chose to take up more formal liturgies based upon Roman Catholic, Orthodox, or Anglican models, but this borrowing may have been motivated by factors other than an influence from the Liturgical Movement.

   During the second half of the twentieth century, the practices of the Early Church were but one source for liturgical reform put forward in order to revitalize the churches and to address the circumstances of modern life. From the 1960s onward, additional approaches to liturgical change were proffered on the basis of certain facets of societal need, and these were taken into account in different ways by the churches. A mounting concern for the environment led to the development of hymns, songs, and nondenominational liturgical resources on ecological themes, which were sometimes taken up into denominational materials; the preface in some eucharistic prayers shows this interest. Theological and liturgical reflection by feminists led to questions about the language for human beings and God used in worship, emendations in the formulation of hymns, songs, and ritual texts, the reexamination of leadership roles and levels of participation, and the creation of entirely new materials for women's worship as well as for gender-mixed communities. Movements for civil rights and new appreciation for the limitlessness of God's love prompted a greater attention to ethnic and racial diversity in worship, inclusive of native peoples, long-standing residents of African and European ancestry, and new immigrants from

Hymn singing in Choctaw. Members of five historic Native American United Methodist congregations from around Oklahoma City gather for worship and fellowship in 2002. PHOTOGRAPH BY MIKE DUBOSE/UNITED METHODIST NEWS SERVICE

Asia and elsewhere. Multicultural and multilingual worship resources appeared for use within and across denominations with translations of older material and the offering of new.

Catechumenal processes, such as the one recommended by the RCIA, presented one model for dealing with the unchurched in North America. Another that emerged in the 1980s borrowed from the methodologies of business and marketing and reappropriated the tactics of the "new measures" promoted by Finney. The church growth movement encouraged the development of worship practices based on the perceived needs of those who had consciously rejected the church and its worship (bored by pre–Vatican II styles and confused by post–Vatican II forms) or who were spiritual "seekers." The style of worship that emerged

Worship with a praise band. Sunday worship at Calvin Christian Reformed Church in Ottawa, Canada. CALVIN INSTITUTE OF CHRISTIAN WORSHIP

drew heavily upon the current culture with lively music and drama as well as employment of constantly developing electronic technology. Churches such as Willow Creek Community Church in South Barrington, Illinois, cultivated this form, which, though deceptively simple, required the advanced preparation and coordination of a team of worship planners. A worship order might take this shape:

> Music (by the band)
> Soloist
> Chorus ("Hold to God's Unchanging Hand"), congregational song
> Dramatic skit
> Comments on the skit
> Song (by singers and the band)
> Message
> Music[59]

Willow Creek's music-driven worship service served as a model for nondenominational and denominational congregations, with some local churches opting to hold two or more styles of worship service on a given Sunday. From the 1980s into the twenty-first century, other new formats for worship were promoted as effective in encouraging worship attendance and faithful disciples. In some instances new technology and currently popular music were combined with recovered practices of the Early Church to yield what was believed to be a style of worship suitable to postmodern people.

Bibliography

Black, Kathy. *Worship Across Cultures: A Handbook*. Nashville, Tenn.: Abingdon, 1998.

Costen, Melva Wilson. *African American Christian Worship*. Nashville, Tenn.: Abingdon, 1993.

Davies, Horton. *The Worship of the American Puritans, 1629–1730*. New York: P. Lang, 1990; repr. ed. Morgan, Pa.: Soli Deo Gloria Publications, 1999.

Hatchett, Marion J. *Commentary on the American Prayer Book*. New York: Seabury, 1981; repr. ed. San Francisco: HarperSanFrancisco, 1995.

Melton, Julius. *Presbyterian Worship in America: Changing Patterns since 1787*. Richmond, Va.: John Knox, 1967.

Pecklers, Keith F. *The Unread Vision: The Liturgical Movement in the United States of America; 1926–1955*. Collegeville, Minn.: Liturgical Press, 1998.

Reed, Luther D. *The Lutheran Liturgy*. Rev. ed. Philadelphia: Fortress, 1947; repr. ed. Philadelphia: Muhlenberg, 1959.

Rohr, John von. *The Shaping of American Congregationalism, 1620–1957*. Cleveland, Ohio: Pilgrim Press, 1992.

Westerfield Tucker, Karen B. *American Methodist Worship*. New York: Oxford University Press, 2001.

White, James F. *Christian Worship in North America, a Retrospective: 1955–1995*. Collegeville, Minn.: Liturgical Press, 1997.

Notes

[1] Eileen W. Lindner, ed., *Yearbook of American & Canadian Churches 2005* (New York: National Council of the Churches of Christ, 2005) 61.

[2] Ramón A. Gutiérrez, *When Jesus Came, the Corn Mothers Went Away: Marriage, Sexuality, and Power in New Mexico: 1500–1846* (Stanford, Calif.: Stanford University Press, 1991) 82–85.

[3] J. Frank Henderson, "Jubilee, Liturgy, and the Early History of Canada [New France, Quebec]," June 1999, http://www.compusmart.ab.ca/fhenders/pdf/JUBILEE.PDF.

[4] James F. White, *Protestant Worship and Church Architecture: Theological and Historical Considerations* (New York: Oxford University Press, 1964) 99–100.

[5] *The Records of the First Church in Salem, Massachusetts, 1629–1736*, ed. Richard D. Pierce (Salem, Mass.: Essex Institute, 1974) 3.

[6] Thomas Shepard, *Theses Sabbaticae; or, The Doctrine of the Sabbath* (London: Printed by T. R. and E. M. for John Rothwell, 1650) 26; see also *Theses Sabbaticae: The Second Part* (London: Printed for John Rothwell, 1650) 3. For a comprehensive study of Puritan Sabbath theology and practice, see Winton U. Solberg, *Redeem the Time: The Puritan Sabbath in Early America* (Cambridge, Mass., and London: Harvard University Press, 1977).

[7] *Plain Dealing*, first published in 1642, was later included as part of Lechford's *New-Englands Advice to Old-England* (n.p.: 1644).

[8] Jaspar Danckaerts, *Journal of Jasper Danckaerts, 1679–1680*, ed. Bartlett Burleigh James and J. Franklin Jameson (New York: Charles Scribner's Sons, 1913) 261–262.

[9] See Cotton Mather, *Ratio Disciplinae Fratrum Nov-Anglorum. A Faithful Account of the Discipline Professed and Practiced; in the Churches of New-England. With Interspersed and Instructive Reflections on the Discipline of the Primitive Churches* (Boston: Printed for S. Gerrish, 1726) 63–68.

[10] On Puritan sermons, see Davies, *The Worship of the American Puritans*, 79–123.

[11] From Psalm 23, *The Bay Psalm Book: A Facsimile Reprint of the First Edition of 1640* (Chicago: University of Chicago Press, 1956) n.p.

[12] John Cotton, *Singing of Psalmes a Gospel-Ordinance* (London: Printed by M. S. for Hannah Allen, 1647).

[13] On the "Half-Way Covenant," see Williston Walker, *The Creeds and Platforms of Congregationalism* (Boston: Pilgrim Press, 1960) 238–339; and E. Brooks Holifield, *The Covenant Sealed: The Development of Puritan Sacramental Theology in Old and New England, 1570–1720* (New Haven, Conn., and London: Yale University Press, 1974), esp. 139–196.

[14] *The Records of the First Church in Salem, Massachusetts*, 107.

[15] Mather, *Ratio Disciplinae Fratrum Nov-Anglorum*, 94–102.

[16] Mather, *Ratio Disciplinae Fratrum Nov-Anglorum*, 111–117; see also Davies, 215–245.

[17] Marian Card Donnelly, *The New England Meeting Houses of the Seventeenth Century* (Middletown, Conn.: Wesleyan University Press, 1968) 72–77 and related figures.

[18] Charles Edward Stowe and Lyman Beecher Stowe, *Harriet Beecher Stowe: The Story of Her Life* (Boston and New York: Houghton Mifflin, 1911) 28–30.

[19] See other chapters in this book for details of the "homeland" practices implanted in North America.

[20]*The Liturgy;, or, Forms of Divine Service, of the French Protestant Church, of Charleston, S.C., Translated from the Liturgy of the Churches of Neufchatel and Vallangin: Editions of 1737 and 1772. With Some Additional Prayers, Carefully Selected. The Whole Adapted to Public Worship in the United States of America*, 5th ed. (n.p.: 1853).

[21]Ralph Waldo Emerson, *Miscellanies* (Boston and New York: Houghton Mifflin, 1876, 1911) 3–25.

[22]Reed, *The Lutheran Liturgy* (1947), 163–168.

[23]Carl F. Schalk, *Source Documents in American Lutheran Hymnody* (Saint Louis, Mo.: Concordia, 1996) 11–16, 29–33; Reed, 170.

[24]For the text and an analysis of the 1767 formulation published as *The Psalms of David, with Hymns and Spiritual Songs, Also the Catechism, Confession of Faith, Liturgy, &c.*, see Daniel James Meeter, *"Bless the Lord, O My Soul": The New-York Liturgy of the Dutch Reformed Church, 1767*, Drew University Studies in Liturgy 6 (Lanham, Md., and London: Scarecrow, 1998).

[25]For a thorough examination of various Presbyterian directories in America from the *Westminster Directory* to the Presbyterian Church (U.S.A.) Directory of 1989, see Stanley R. Hall, "The American Presbyterian Directory for Worship: History of a Liturgical Strategy" (Ph.D. diss., University of Notre Dame, 1990).

[26]The Presbyterian order is derived from material in Hall, "The American Presbyterian Directory" and *The Constitution of the Presbyterian Church in the United States of America, Containing the Confession of Faith, the Catechisms, and the Directory for the Worship of God ... and as Amended in the Years 1805–1888* (Philadelphia: Presbyterian Board of Publication, n.d.) 499–503.

[27]The order is extracted from the description in Gerald F. De Jong, *The Dutch Reformed Church in the American Colonies*, Historical Series of the Reformed Church in America 5 (Grand Rapids, Mich.: Eerdmans, 1978) 129–133.

[28]Morgan Edwards, *Customs of Primitive Churches; or, A set of Propositions Relative to the Name, Matterials, Constitution, Power, Officers, Ordinances, Rites, Business, Worship, Discipline, Government &c. of a Church* (Philadelphia: Printed by Andrew Steuart, 1768), esp. 79–101.

[29]John Wesley, Letter to "Our Brethren in America," 10 September 1784, in *The Letters of the Rev. John Wesley, A.M.*, vol. 7, ed. John Telford (London: Epworth Press, 1931) 238–239.

[30]For the full story of this process and the results, see Marion J. Hatchett, *The Making of the First American Book of Common Prayer, 1776–1789* (New York: Seabury, 1982).

[31]For the ritual texts of these Prayer Books compared in columns, see Paul V. Marshall, *Prayer Book Parallels*, 2 vols. (New York: Church Hymnal Corporation, 1989–1990). For various documents related to the production of the 1789 book, including the text of Seabury's *Communion-Office*, see 2:485–527.

[32]On the rituals of the sacramental seasons, see Leigh Eric Schmidt, *Holy Fairs: Scottish Communions and American Revivals in the Early Modern Period* (Princeton, N.J.: Princeton University Press, 1989).

[33]For example, B. W. Gorham, *Camp Meeting Manual: A Practical Book for the Camp Ground; in Two Parts* (Boston: H. V. Degen, 1854).

[34]On the use of metal tokens, see George A. MacLennan, *The Story of the Old Communion Service and Worship; also the Metallic Communion Token of the Presbyterian Church in Canada, 1772–* (Montreal: MacLennan, 1924).

[35]James R. Graves, *Intercommunion Inconsistent, Unscriptural, and Productive of Evil*, 2nd ed. (Memphis, Tenn.: Baptist Book House, 1882) 164–184.

[36]From the lecture "Measures to Promote Revivals," cited in Charles Grandison Finney, *Lectures on Revivals of Religion*, ed. William G. McLoughlin (Cambridge, Mass.: Belknap Press of Harvard University Press, 1960) 251.

[37]Colbert S. Cartwright, *Candles of Grace: Disciples Worship in Perspective* (Saint Louis, Mo.: Chalice, 1992), esp. 22.

[38]John W. Nevin, *The Mystical Presence: A Vindication of the Reformed or Calvinistic Doctrine of the Holy Eucharist* (Philadelphia: J. B. Lippincott, 1846) 3, 221–236.

[39]Charles W. Baird, *Eutaxia; or, The Presbyterian Liturgies: Historical Sketches, by a Minister of the Presbyterian Church* (New York: M. W. Dodd, 1855; repr. Grand Rapids, Mich.: Baker, 1957) 254, 257.

[40]The process before and after the creation of the "Mercersburg Liturgy" is chronicled in Jack Martin Maxwell, *Worship and Reformed Theology: The Liturgical Lessons of Mercersburg*, Pittsburgh Theological Monograph Series 10 (Pittsburgh, Pa.: Pickwick Press, 1976). Maxwell also includes a color coding of source materials for the rites of holy communion and ordination and extensive commentary on these as well as the regular Lord's day services.

[41]Fred L. Precht, "Worship Resources in Missouri Synod's History," in *Lutheran Worship: History and Practice*, ed. Fred L. Precht (Saint Louis, Mo.: Concordia, 1993) 88–92.

[42]On the absence of instruments in the worship of some small Baptist denominations—and on the style and content of their worship—see Howard Dorgan, *Giving Glory to God in Appalachia: Worship Practices of Six Baptist Subdenominations* (Knoxville: University of Tennessee Press, 1987).

[43]For a survey of the worship books, directories, and hymnals produced by the major Episcopal, Lutheran, Methodist, and Presbyterian bodies in the United States from their founding to the late twentieth century, see "Sources for the Study of Protestant Worship in America," in White, *Christian Worship in North America*, 75–92.

[44]*The Book of Common Worship. Prepared by the Committee of the General Assembly of the Presbyterian Church in the United States of America* (Philadelphia: Presbyterian Board of Publication and Sabbath-School Work, 1912) iii.

[45]Cited from Henry Sloane Coffin, ed., *Hymns of the Kingdom of God* (New York: A. S. Barnes, 1910) no. 187.

[46]Fred W. Meuser, "Facing the Twentieth Century: 1900–1930," in *The Lutherans in North America*, ed. E. Clifford Nelson (Philadelphia: Fortress, 1975) 425. For Methodist responses to the issues of grape juice and individual cups, see Westerfield Tucker, *American Methodist Worship*, 150–154.

[47]G. A. Johnston Ross, *Christian Worship and Its Future* (New York and Cincinnati, Ohio: Abingdon, 1927) 8–9.

[48]Von Ogden Vogt, *Art & Religion* (New Haven, Conn.: Yale University Press, 1921) 187–189; and *Modern Worship* (New Haven, Conn.: Yale University Press, 1927) 3–104.

[49]Federal Council of the Churches of Christ in America, *Annual Report, 1937* (New York: Federal Council of the Churches of Christ in America, 1937) 57; and Fred Winslow Adams, *The Christian Year: A Suggestive Guide for the Worship of the Church* (New York: Federal Council of the Churches of Christ in America, 1937; rev. ed. 1940). The number of Sundays in Kingdomtide is reduced in the revised edition.

[50]*Book of Common Worship for Use in the Several Communions of the Church of Christ*, 2nd ed. (New York: E.P. Dutton, 1936) v.

[51]*Book of Common Order of the United Church of Canada* (Toronto: The United Church Publishing House, 1932) n.p.

[52]On the worship practices of the groups prior to merger, see Thomas R. Harding, *Presbyterian, Methodist, and Congregational Worship in Canada prior to 1925* (Toronto: n.p., 1995); and on United Church Sunday worship from its founding, see Harding, "Ordered Liberty: Sunday Worship in the United Church of Canada," in *The Sunday Service of the Methodists: Twentieth-Century Worship in Worldwide Methodism*, ed. Karen B. Westerfield Tucker (Nashville, Tenn.: Kingswood, 1996) 95–116.

[53]Two volumes briefly identify the contributions of men and women, Roman Catholic and not, to the various stages of the Liturgical Movement: Kathleen Hughes, ed., *How Firm a Foundation: Voices of the Early Liturgical Movement* (Chicago: Liturgy Training Publications, 1990); and Robert L. Tuzik, ed., *How Firm a Foundation: Leaders of the Liturgical Movement* (Chicago: Liturgy Training Publications, 1990).

[54]On the relation of Catholic social movements, including the Catholic Worker, to the Liturgical Movement, see Pecklers, *The Unread Vision*, 97–124.

[55]H. A. Reinhold, "Timely Tracts: My Dream Mass," *Orate Fratres* 14 (1940) 265–270.

[56]For a history of Associated Parishes and the process leading to the 1979 Prayer Book, see Michael Moriarty, *The Liturgical Revolution: Prayer Book Revision and Associated Parishes; A Generation of Change in the Episcopal Church* (New York: Church Hymnal Corporation, 1996).

[57]The "Guidelines" are available at the Web sites of both denominations; see, for example, National Church Council of the Evangelical Lutheran Church in Canada and the Council of General Synod of the Anglican Church of Canada, "Guidelines for Common Worship for Lutherans and Anglicans in Canada," Spring 2003. www.anglican.ca/faith/worship/common-worship.htm.

[58]Walter F. Pitts, *Old Ship of Zion: The Afro-Baptist Ritual in the African Diaspora* (New York: Oxford University Press, 1993) 20–21. On the spirituality of black worship, see in particular James H. Cone, "Sanctification, Liberation, and Black Worship," *Theology Today* 35 (1978–1979) 139–152.

[59]This was Willow Creek's order for the Sunday morning "seeker" service on 10 June 1995 as observed by the author.

23

Roman Catholics in Hispanic America

JAIME LARA

The topic of Catholic liturgy among the nineteen Spanish-speaking countries of the Americas—of which the United States is the fourth largest at the beginning of the twenty-first century—is a formidable task. This chapter therefore paints with broad strokes and is confined for the most part to the paradigmatic experience of the ecclesial communities on the American mainland.

First Contacts

The first Christian worship in the New World took place on 6 January 1494, when Christopher Columbus had his chaplain sing a solemn mass on the feast of the Epiphany at La Isabela, the ill-fated colony that the explorer founded on the north coast of Hispañola (present-day Haiti and Dominican Republic). The feast day had a special importance for the celebrants, not only because it was the feast of revelation to the gentile and pagan world in which they had just landed, but also because Columbus was certain that one of the Magi had come from that island. Little else is known about early Christian worship on the Caribbean islands of the West Indies.

Much more is available by way of chronicles and documentation about the liturgical practices of the mendicant friars—the Franciscans, Dominicans, and Augustinians—in New Spain (Mexico), the land of the great civilizations of the Maya and the Mexica (commonly known as the Aztecs). The evangelization of the American continent began in 1524 with the arrival of the "twelve Franciscan apostles," as they have become known. They appear to have had millennial expectations, believing that the discovery and evangelization of the "New World"—itself an eschatological term—was a sign of an approaching golden age of the Holy Spirit when the universal Church would be renewed in holy poverty and a way of life similar to that shared by the nascent church in the apostolic period. This eschatology was a backdrop to their missionary efforts and is frequently glimpsed even in liturgical and artistic matters.[1]

In 1524, when the first friars arrived, there were approximately 20 million Amerindians in Mesoamerica: a ratio of one missionary-liturgist to about 2 million souls. Although the task of evangelizing was initially chaotic, the friars soon realized the need to learn indigenous languages, to catechize by creative, visual, and nontextual means, and to take advantage of the popularity of music, dance, and drama that were

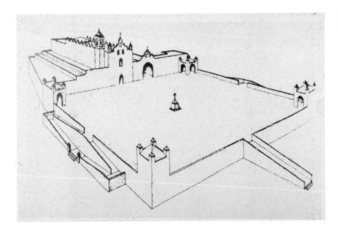

Franciscan conversion center at Izamal, Yucatan, Mexico. The drawing shows the center as it would have appeared in the mid-sixteenth century with an atrium, open chapel, four posa chapels, atrial cross, and single-nave church with attached friary. DRAWING BY JAIME LARA

hallmarks of pre-Christian religious observance. In their zeal to eradicate what they considered satanic idolatry (*cultus sangrientis*), they dismantled the Amerindian worship spaces—monumental atria with pyramid-temples for human sacrifice—but then used the same locales, stones, and selected symbols for their new catechetical centers. Christianity was both literally and figuratively built on top of the old religion.[2]

The catechetical complexes constructed by this partnership of neophytes and friars are worthy of note as the "stage sets" for conversion by Christian liturgy, music, and sacramentals. They were designed for outdoor Christian worship en masse and appear to have been based loosely on medieval plans of the temple of Jerusalem.[3] They consist of a huge atrium with open-air apse, altar, and pulpit for eucharist and the liturgy of the hours. Initially, before the construction of pseudo-gothic churches, there were outdoor stone baptismal fonts that easily accommodated the immersion of infants and dunking the heads of adults, as the rites prescribed. Furthermore, the atrium sheltered four chapels (*posas*) in its corners for the stational processions that were perhaps the most appealing aspect of Christian worship to the Native Americans, and similar to part of their ancient rites. The conversion complex was completed with a monumental stone cross at the atrium's center, a stone-vaulted church, and a friary with cloister garth. All the elements of the complex functioned for public worship with processions and communal dancing, as well as for education, community organization, social gathering, and health needs.

Pre-Tridentine Period

In order to put into effect their evangelizing program, the friars experimented with novel forms of communication such as pictographic catechisms, liturgical drama, and pantomime. They also created an indigenous college on the outskirts of Mexico City to train the young men of the Mexica nobility and to collect ethnological information about the old religion, customs, and mores. Within a decade, the school had produced trilingual and quadrilingual Native Americans who translated religious materials from Latin and Spanish into indigenous languages, often with great freedom and poetic license. Even in liturgical texts, they created startling metaphors borrowed from the old religion; they recycled for Christ, the saints, and the sacraments metaphors employing the sun, feathers, flowers, maize, music, and dance, precious jewelry and body ornaments, even tortillas. Other native translators, working under the guidance of friars like Bernardino de Sahagún (1499–1590), created dictionaries, catechisms, model sermon books, confessional manuals, translations of the divine office, private prayer books, and lectionaries in Nahuatl, the language of the Mexica which became the lingua franca of the missionary enterprise throughout central Mexico. Sadly, few of these documents have survived to this day, and we know of most through secondary sources. One that has survived is the *Psalmodia Christiana* (c.1558). More of a kinesthetic hymn book than a true psalter, it allowed the Mexica Christians to sing the catechism and biblical paraphrases for every Sunday and major feast of the liturgical year, all the while dancing to ancient Mesoamerican melodies. The dancing and singing took place in the atrium around the monumental stone cross and, where possible, the congregation moved through the four *posa* chapels, in one door and out the other.

Knowledge of the sacred scriptures reached a high degree of dissemination and sophistication among the natives, as is proved by the records of the publication of biblical selections in indigenous languages and, sadly, by the later repeal of such permission and the confiscation of such liturgical and biblical material by the Inquisition.[4] (Latin American children are still baptized with the names of every biblical personage found in the Old and New Testaments, even the most obscure of the Hebrew prophets, royalty, and heroes.) An example of biblical devotional literature in Nahuatl is the *Daily Spiritual Exercises* composed around the mid-sixteenth century; it also reveals much about personal liturgical piety among the neophytes.[5] These texts remain to be translated and studied by liturgists.

Early liturgy in the New World was typically medieval, lacking uniformity in texts and rubrics. Even in the Old World a movement had begun at the close of the fifteenth century toward including some vernacular elements in the mass for the sake of the converts from Islam and Judaism, and we hear of ritual books, such as lectionaries and psalters, in Arabic. But even in Latin the late medieval liturgy was highly kinesthetic and colorful as, for example, the feast of Corpus Christi and its procession demonstrate; and this was its appeal to the new Christians of America. A visual source will help to appreciate liturgical practice in the nascent Amerindian church. In 1579 the Franciscan friar Diego Valedés published a work on preaching and evangelistic communication entitled *Rhetorica Christiana ad concionandi et orandi usum accommodata utriusque facultatis exemplis suo loco insertis: quae quidem ex Indorum maxime de prompta sunt historiis. Unde, praeter doctrinam summa quoque delectatio comparabitur* (Christian Rhetoric for the purpose of speaking and praying in public, with examples of both actions chiefly taken from the histories of the Indies, inserted in their place; besides doctrine, supreme delight will be drawn from it. By the very reverend father Didacus Valedés.).[6] Valedés was a mestizo, half Spanish and half Indian, and had labored with the first generation of Franciscans in Mexico. His text is a gold mine of information about liturgical practice, and it contains an engraving of an idealized evangelization center in which each activity—identified by a letter corresponding to the commentary—is depicted as occurring simultaneously.

"Baptismus" is the word that appears in the lower center at a vignette of a fountain with living water. The friar, in surplice and stole, is assisted by three servers, one of whom holds the oils.[7] The first and most important sacrament in this New World of new Christians was, of course, baptism. An examination of the sources reveals that among the books that the friars had brought with them was the *Liber Sacerdotalis* (Priest's Handbook) of the Dominican Alberto Castellani (or da Castello).[8] It had been first printed in Venice in 1523 for the conversion of Muslims and Jews in southern Europe, and thus was well suited to be used for similar conversions on the other side of the Atlantic. In his preface, the author states that he did his research in the

Sixteenth-century conversion center. The plan of the center was depicted in Diego Valadés' *Rhetorica Christiana* (1579). REPRODUCTION COURTESY OF THE BEINECKE RARE BOOK AND MANUSCRIPT LIBRARY, YALE UNIVERSITY

Vatican Library, where he had found manuscripts of the "ancient and venerable customs and rites of the Western church." The rites were perfectly adaptable to the new situation of mass conversions of adult Aztecs, Mayas, and Incas.

At the beginning of Castellani's baptismal ritual is a short admonition to the minister that, if the candidate is an adult, he or she should first receive catechesis and the exorcisms (scrutinies).[9] The rite is fairly standard in terms of medieval baptismal liturgies in the greeting and reception at the church door. After the exorcism over the salt and its placement on the tongue, there follows a long series of scrutinies, or exorcisms, taken from ancient patristic sources that Castellani had found in the Vatican Library. Then the candidates are led into the middle of the nave, where they are instructed:

> Enter the church of God and be careful to avoid the snares of death. Reject the horrors of idolatry, flee from falsehood, and fear God the Father Almighty and Jesus Christ his Son with the Holy Spirit, who is to come to judge the living and the dead by fire. Amen.[10]

Baptism by immersion is indicated as the best means, although other forms were permitted. This was to be followed by anointing with chrism and placing a white cloth on the head, and finally the giving of a lit candle, with the words:

> Accept this burning lamp, guard your baptism, obey the commands of God, that with the Lord and all the saints you may come to the wedding feast in the banquet hall of heaven, possessing eternal life forever and ever. Amen. Go now in peace, and the Lord be with you.[11]

The rite was drastically reduced because of the sheer numbers to be baptized: everything not absolutely necessary to the valid reception of the sacrament was eliminated, while the rest was reserved for later instruction. This caused such great dissension among the three religious orders in the 1530s that legislation and uniformity in practice needed to be enacted. It was also realized that the bare rite of the *Liber* needed to be acculturated to the Mesoamerican ethos. It lacked the warmth, welcoming, and communal aspect that the missionaries had observed in their initial encounter with pre-Hispanic culture. Therefore, the bishops and leaders of the three missionary orders commissioned Vasco de Quiroga, a civil lawyer and bishop of Michoacán, to draw up a new book or manual for the baptism and marriage of adult Indians. In 1540 he published the *Manual de Adultos* (Manual for Adults), one of the first books to be printed in the New World. It was used until the reforms of the Council of Trent and the more conservative days of the 1560s.

Tragically, not one copy of the *Manual* survives today. Its section on baptism is known through two secondary sources that appear to quote the original text, rubrics, and pastoral notes.[12] The admonitions are filled with references to Saint Ambrose's *De Consecratione* and other classical sources. The catechumenate begins at mid-Lent (or mid-Eastertide when baptism is administered at Pentecost) with the scrutinies/exorcisms and dismissal rite, but it delays the anointing with the oil of catechumens until the actual day of baptism. The parts directed to the candidates were to be translated into the many languages and dialects of Mexico. The text opens with an admonition to the minister:

> If a native comes to you requesting baptism, receive him [or her] in a friendly manner, and with great warmth say: *What do you wish, my friend?* If he says, "I want to be a Christian," answer: *You are most welcome, friend. You ask for an excellent thing because to be a Christian is to be an adorer of God and his servant, and even more so, to be a friend and child of*

God. Have courage then that I may teach you what you have to learn. To be a Christian you
ought to believe in God and I shall instruct you in these things so that you may know them.

Then followed several weeks of group catechesis, during which time the natives
were to attend mass but be dismissed after the sermon. The exorcisms were performed
twenty days before Easter (or Pentecost). The day of baptism was a public holiday,
with several Indian towns assembling for a communal celebration. Some of the secondary rites, such as the giving of the candle and the white vesture, were suppressed,
or only performed on a representative few, because it was not uncommon to baptize
hundreds or thousands on one day. The trinitarian formula was used with a triple
immersion of the head. Men were to strip to the waist for the immersion, while women
need only remove their headgear. The kiss of peace terminated the ceremony, which,
like other liturgical events, was adorned with festive vesture for all, the participation
of native orchestras and choirs, communal dancing, and banqueting.

Sadly, the *Manual de Adultos* and its adult catechumenate were short-lived. The
book was succeeded by the *Manuale Sacramentorum secundum ecclesiae Mexicanae*, also
known as the *Mexicaniensis*, printed in 1560, three years before the Council of Trent
addressed liturgical issues and 54 years before the *Roman Ritual* of Paul V (1614)
would appear.[13] Its compiler, Cristobal de San Martín, was a Latinist and secular priest
of Mexico City who appears to have had little pastoral experience with the natives or
knowledge of their languages. His method was eclectic, picking something here, adding something there, always seeking to curtail lengthy texts and eliminate what he
considered superfluous.[14] Lamentably, he removed all references to the catechumenate
and to the welcoming of candidates (the *dulcissima receptio . . . et cum maxima caritate*,
"kindest reception . . . and with the greatest charity") for the sacrament. It is certain
that adult baptism was becoming rarer in the New World by the time San Martín was
writing, and legal regulations and disciplinary discussions occupied more of his attention.[15] The *Mexicaniensis* was adopted by other episcopal regions of the Caribbean,
Peru, and the Philippines; it was also a model for the early Japanese liturgical manual.[16]
Lest one think that the New World contributed nothing to liturgical history, one
should note the fact that the baptism rite of the *Mexicaniensis* became a model for the
universal *Roman Ritual* of 1614, which accepted verbatim its shortened form of the
consecration of the water.[17]

Neither confirmation nor holy orders appear in Valadés's idealized atrium. We are
very badly informed about the administration of the former. A brief of Leo X had
authorized the religious to confirm in the absence of a bishop. The friars did not avail
themselves of this privilege, however, but only prepared the natives to receive the
sacrament.[18] In 1548 bishop Zumárraga stated that he had been confirming for four
days without a pause, and that the numbers exceeded 400,000.[19] He died a few days
later, no doubt from exhaustion.

"*Discunt Paenitentiam*," "*Discunt Confiteri*," and "*Confessiones*" illustrate the sacrament of penance. The Aztecs had a form of public confession that, in some sense,
prepared them for the Christian sacrament. However, there was no sense among them
of personal responsibility or moral guilt for action.[20] Nevertheless, the sacrament of
penance became immensely popular with the Indians, and the chroniclers relate stories about confessions extending into the small hours of the morning. The doctrinal
preparation was received in a group, and we are shown the natives crouched before a
portable wooden pulpit from which the friar discourses on the "norms required for
the sacrament, and he incites in them a hated for their past life . . . so that they might

repent of their sins and confess in an orderly manner."[21] The mendicants were very conscious of the idolatry that persisted among the natives and the cultural practices that the friars saw as demonic. The presence of Satan in the Americas is a constantly recurring theme in the chronicles and in the preaching of the missionaries.[22]

It appears that after the general instruction on sin and the horrors of punishment in hell (which Valadés addresses at length and gruesomely illustrates), the neophytes passed to a more proximate preparation of the sacramental rite itself. There they recited the Confiteor in their own language or dialect. The Decalogue was then read while each penitent used pebbles or grains of corn to count out the number of particular sins or drew some image to explain the gravity and circumstances of his particular sins.[23]

The three Indians, two men and a woman, are waiting their turn to confess. As Valadés explains, they have tickets or badges in their hands that indicate their readiness.[24] Such a practice was common in the Middle Ages. The ticket would be stamped or marked by the confessor as proof that the penitent was now spiritually able to receive communion.

The portico on the lower left displays the confessor seated on a simple high-backed chair while the Indian confessing kneels before him. This too was common practice until the innovation of the confessional with screen was introduced in the latter half of the sixteenth century. However, several Mexican establishments did have confessionals built into the walls either of the church or of the convent entranceway, thus anticipating the European practice by several decades.

"*Examen Matrimonii*," "*Scribunt Nomina*," and "*Matrimonium*" introduce us to the problematic area of monogamous Christian marriage among a people accustomed to polygamy.[25] The first vignette shows the friar seated in his teaching chair and using a pointer to explain consanguinity (the rules governing marriage between blood relatives) on a special tree arranged for this purpose. We must suppose that the couple had already received doctrinal instruction in the sacrament, "*Discunt Doctrinam*."[26] They pass to the notary where their names are recorded, together with those of their parents and witnesses. Finally the wedding ceremony, without mass, takes place. First the priest offers a short sermon regarding the meaning and efficacy of the sacrament and an exhortation to mutual love and fidelity. There follows a general confession and absolution, whereupon the priest unites the couple's hands:[27]

> They wash their hands with great care, adorn their heads with crowns of flowers, and carry wax candles in their hands. With great composure they enter the church (*templum*) reciting prayers (*preces*) after having been sprinkled with holy water. Because of the great numbers being married the Mass is deferred to the following day. During this time the spouses abstain from conjugal relations out of reverence for the sacrament.[28]

The *Mexicaniensis* of 1560 preserved the marriage ritual of the Mozarabic rite that was probably contained in the now-lost section of the *Manual de Adultos*. [For the text of the Mozarabic rite, see Chapter 5 in this book.] The new ritual still followed the separation of the exchange of consent and the matrimonial consecration. It also preserved the Iberian practice of the giving of the *arras*, the solemn handing over of the bride, and the veiling of the couple immediately after the elevation of the consecrated host.[29]

"*Mortuus*" and "*Cantores*" present us with a burial scene. The body of a deceased woman is being carried into the atrium on a bier. According to Valadés, her body would be covered with a precious cloth adorned with the sign of the cross and with ribbons. Burials were conducted in the morning after mass and in the afternoon after vespers. The *Liber sacerdotalis* (and probably the *Manual de Adultos*) included a beautiful series of Easter psalm songs for the funeral liturgy, songs that still existed in the Mozarabic rite. Sadly, the *Mexicaniensis* of 1560, in its tendency to shorten, eliminated the joyful paschal psalms and prescribed instead five Our Fathers in the vernacular.[30]

"*Communio*," "*Missa*," and "*Extrema Unction*" balance the open-air confessionals on the opposite side of the portico or *portería*. Valadés simply states that "here the holy sacrifice of the Mass is celebrated and there are administered likewise Communion and Extreme Unction, with the veneration and solemnity that is due them."[31] Notice that, because extreme unction involves the receiving of viaticum, it is placed here together with mass.[32] Note also that communion appears to be separated from the celebration of the eucharistic action. It is not surprising that at a time when the most pious Spaniards only rarely received communion, the administration of the eucharist to the Indians should have been viewed with many doubts and misgivings. Some religious were of the opinion that the neophytes could not be admitted to the communion table, that they had been too recently converted, that they were incapable of knowing the value and grandeur of the sacrament, and that it should be denied them lest they fall into frequent sacrilege. Others thought that it was impossible to make a general and sweeping decision, that this was a theological question, and that it was reasonable to give communion to the Indians who asked for it. The Franciscans made communion a penitential sacrament. They created a Sodality of the Holy Sacrament in which the Indians took communion during Lent. There were villages in which as many as five thousand persons were seen at communion in Lent, but in the course of the year it was rarely administered, except to the sick. This may have to do with the facts that Lent was a time of confessions, and that the Indians were not admitted to communion without the sacrament of reconciliation.

The Dominicans divided their converts into two categories: the first, receiving permission to take communion whenever they wished, were the "graduados" or "communiotlacatl"; the second took communion only at Easter or when gravely ill, and then only with the consent of their confessors.[33]

The Augustinians chose those deemed ready for communion a week in advance of reception. On the communion day itself, the Indians had to arrive at seven in the morning, dressed as for a wedding, and remain silent up to the moment of communion, which they received with great piety, some of them crawling to the altar on their knees. Before communion they recited Nahuatl translations of the prayer of Thomas Aquinas, *Omnipotens sempiterne Deus*, and later his thanksgiving after mass, *Gratias tibi ago, Domine*.[34]

Early Inculturation

It was in the realm of baptism and the secondary elements of liturgical ritual, such as processions, blessings, and exorcisms, where the greatest inculturation was accomplished. Although the texts of the late medieval eucharistic rite remained in Latin, it too was celebrated in a uniquely Mesoamerican manner. The celebration of the mass on Sundays represented one of the most important religious practices of the Amerindian neophytes. The night before, the church stewards reminded their subordinates in the *barrio* (the Indian settlement surrounding the mission church) to go to bed early because they woke the faithful up at three in the morning. After a head count, all went in procession to the evangelization complex, singing their catechism along the way. When they arrived at the atrium, they knelt down and paid homage to the sacrament within the church. The open-air liturgical space had been decorated with tapestries, which were also hung from the church battlements, while the floor was carpeted with aromatic plants. While the Indians were seated on the ground in the atrium, they received religious instruction and continued to sing the catechism or the Little Hours of the Virgin in the vernacular. This was followed by announcements from the friar and a sermon in one or more languages. Combined with the high mass, the Sunday service lasted three to six hours. The quasi-monastic service in the early hours of the morning also continued the practices of pre-Hispanic times, when many ceremonies occurred throughout the night. When there was no priest present, a specially designated member of the laity conducted an assembly for prayer, the liturgical office of matins.[35]

As they shaped the church year in the New World, the mendicants made a concerted effort to give the Indians, used to the pomp and ceremony of the Aztec religion, an equivalent replacement in number and extravagance. The liturgical year provided the most suitable framework for a new lifestyle. The first vespers of a feast began with the ringing of bells, with songs and the sounding of musical instruments from the roofs or parapets of the church. Early in the morning, around two or three o'clock, the *mitote* dances began "in the old tradition." They were interrupted only by high mass, which was followed by a procession through the *posa* chapels. Christmas, Epiphany, and Candlemas had special solemnity—Epiphany especially, because the natives identified with the Magi, who were not European or necessarily white. Lent, which was underscored on the one hand by the scrutinies and exorcisms of the catechumens, and on the other by penance, confession, and communion, culminated not so much in Easter as in the celebration of the suffering of Christ. Eastertide was effectively extended into May with the feast of the Finding of the True Cross, wherein every available cross was decorated with flowers.

The Indians enjoyed Palm Sunday because of its mimetic drama and the chance to improvise on the story. A "liturgical realism" of the gospel text was achieved:

> On Palm Sunday . . . (it) is a marvel to see the different devices into which they (Indians) fashion their palms. Over the palm, many place crosses made of flowers, and these appear in a thousand shapes and in as many colors. Since the palms are green and they carry them aloft in their hands, it looks like a forest. Along the road they erect large trees, while in some places the trees occupy their natural site. Up these trees boys climb, some cutting off branches and strewing along the road when the crosses pass by; others, perched in the tree, are singing, while below many others cover the road with their mantles and blankets, which are so numerous that the cross-bearers and the ministers are almost constantly treading on blankets.[36]

Equally impressive were the following days of Passiontide and their daily processions and self-flagellation, which moved the Indians more than anything else. Blood had been a sacred element in pre-Hispanic religion, and self-bleeding was an honored part of the religious cult; victims of human sacrifice were revered as heroes and gods. The Indians fasted and disciplined themselves with a scourge during Lent, often drawing blood. Even at the end of the sixteenth century, when the masochistic pre-Christian rites had been forgotten, the natives still held "penitential orgies" in the atria at night, by turns scourging one another while praying or chanting.[37]

The foot washing on Holy Thursday was combined with a banquet given for the poor of the town and the construction of the Easter sepulchre, into which a puppet-like

Christ would be deposited—a relict of the medieval *Quem Queritis* tropes and rubrics that Castellani had incorporated into his *Liber Sacerdotalis*. On Holy Thursday, the Indians participated by donating foodstuffs or live animals—another continuation of medieval custom. Other offerings were embroidered cloths used as the *portapaz*, or pax tablet, for the liturgical kiss of peace. Holy Week also saw the use of the liturgical dragon-on-a-pole (*draco*), a quasi-theatrical prop representing Satan defeated, and common in the processions of the great European cathedrals.[38] But of all the celebrations, Corpus Christi—the "apex of the liturgical year"—with its costumed cast of characters portraying all of salvation history from Genesis to Apocalypse, and with its music and pageantry, enjoyed the greatest degree of popularity.[39] The militarization of Corpus Christi was a unique feature of Iberian spirituality, and this continued in the New World with the dances dramatizing battles between Moors and Christians (or devils and angels) that accompanied the sacramental processions.

These liturgical celebrations of the church year were supplemented by events and practices of a more popular nature, which nevertheless had the task of gradually permeating the life of the new communities with a new Christian identity. These practices included, among others, a flourishing veneration of the saints, various talismanic prayers to the Name of Jesus and to the Holy Cross, and the late medieval innovations of the Stations of the Cross and the rosary. A new structure was given to Amerindian time and space by the peal of bells, the recitation of the Angelus, frequent use of holy water, christological greetings and leave-takings, family blessings and table prayers, home recitation of compline in the vernacular at bedtime, and, of course, the cult of images.

The friars knew how to enlist the participation of the native population, especially when it came to music, liturgical drama, and dance. There hardly was ever a service without singing, which seems natural considering the rich musical tradition of pre-Hispanic times. The fact that the faithful participated in the singing (hymns, part-singing, and native tunes with religious lyrics), recruiting large choirs, playing local and European instruments—not to mention the fact that dance was made an integral part of the service—demonstrates the excitement and joy of the new Mexica Christians in public worship. The appeal of worship was not limited to eucharist but included matins and vespers. Assistance at Sunday vespers was the rule rather than the exception. There the people sang along, imitated the posture of the celebrants, and carried lit candles during the singing of the Magnificat. Outside of the communal celebration of the hours sung in Latin, the Indians, individually or in groups, were encouraged to recite the Little Hours of the Virgin, which had been translated and printed in several languages. On ferial days (weekdays on which no feast fell), vespers was followed immediately by sung compline. Among the sung prayers and hymns that the Indians commonly knew both in Latin and in their own languages can be numbered the Hail Mary, Our Father, Creed, *Pange Lingua*, *Ave Maris Stella*, *Veni Sancte Spiritus*, *Salve Regina*, Magnificat, Benedictus, *Christus factus est*, *Miserere mei Deus* (Ps. 50), and more. The *Te Deum Laudamus* became, effectively, the national hymn of the Indian church.[40]

Before leaving the topic of mass, a comment on the popularity of the "dry masses" is appropriate. The term "dry mass" denotes a truncated rite that retained from the "sacramental" part of the service the Our Father, *Agnus Dei*, kiss of peace, and postcommunion prayers, but always omitted the consecration and communion. Such ceremonies were common aboard ships as a way of satisfying devotion when the celebration of eucharist was prohibited for fear of spilling the elements. Columbus, for example, had had dry masses said every morning on shipboard.[41] The definitive character of the dry mass was given by the papal master of ceremonies John Burkhard in his *Ordo Missae* of 1502, a text that was incorporated into Castellani's *Liber Sacerdotalis*.

We know that at least one friar in Mexico had instructed his Indian boys in how to preside at such a service in the absence of a priest.[42] And it is certain that two Mexican councils of bishops (1555 and 1565) had to prohibit repeatedly what one chronicler describes in praising the devotion of his Amerindian flock:

> And on this theme [of the dry Mass] I will recount something that I saw which filled me both with laughter and admiration. Arriving one day at a church far from our friary, I discovered that the whole town had been called together. They had just rung the bells as for Mass; they had sung their Christian doctrine, and afterwards their Our Father and Hail Mary. Then [the native musicians] played an Offertory song while everyone prayed in silence. When they sang the *Sanctus* everyone struck their breasts. Then the Indian leader-of-prayer put on the priest's vestments, ascended to the altar and celebrated a dry Mass, elevating a cross in place of the Eucharistic host. They told me that they had heard Mass with their souls and with the greatest desire, because they had no priest to say it for them.[43]

It is noteworthy that the sung recitation of the catechism acted as a substitute for a liturgy of the word, while the most important part of the ritual was deemed to be the need to adore the elevated Christ of the crucifix. Communion was, of course, unnecessary in an age when, even at a real mass, few of the faithful communicated.

This early period of Latin American religious history has been called the American Middle Ages, and with good reason. The appeal of the new religion of the interlopers resided precisely in the pomp and circumstance and the kinesthetic beauty of the late medieval liturgy brought to the New World. In an age when liturgical uniformity was still unknown, the friars took ingenious liberties with the way official worship was performed, perhaps more in its elaboration and ephemeral details than in its texts. For example, it was common practice to perform pantomimed homilies, or to halt the celebration of mass to insert an instructive and festive drama with elaborate cast, costumes, and sets. Real baptisms were performed on catechumens who happened to be acting the roles of converted Moors or Jews in a performance of the eschatological drama *The Final Conquest of Jerusalem*, or during a representation the life of Saint John the Baptist. And as mentioned above, selected elements of the Mexica religion—such as sacred geography, architecture, metaphors, and divine attributes—were consciously reworked to accommodate them to a new notion of human sacrifice: Christ as the center of a new sacred time and space. Anthropologists call this process one of "guided syncretism" or "synthetization," but it is evident that it was not the one-sided work of the mendicant friars.[44] The resultant acculturated Catholicism was evidently accomplished with the input, prodding, and guidance of the Amerindian neophytes, especially the native scholar-elite, many of whom had been priests or scribes in the old religion.

Tridentine Period

Although liturgical reforms were dealt with in the last session of the Council of Trent (1563), they did not reach the American shores immediately. There were more pressing and explosive questions for the American church, particularly that of the power and authority of the episcopacy over the mendicant friars and the newer missionary orders, such as the Jesuits. The *Roman Breviary* appeared in 1568 and the *Missal* of Pius V in 1570, but it would not be until 1614 that the new *Roman Ritual* would be imposed and Castellani's manual banned. Even then, there is indication that some resistance to the new Tridentine liturgy existed. The earlier and much more popular breviary of 1535—that of the Spanish cardinal Francisco de los Ángeles de Quiñones (a member of the Franciscan millennialist group that sent the first "twelve apostles")— had been well received in the New World. Its shorter form made it ideal for busy missionary friars; sadly, Trent condemned it. In New Spain, the Holy Office of the Inquisition had to collect and burn earlier missals, the *Liber Sacerdotalis* and the *Manual de Adultos*, not because of questions of unorthodox doctrine but because of resistance to the new and novel.

Noteworthy in this Tridentine period was the interest in the ancient Iberian form of worship known as the Mozarabic rite. It had been the liturgy of Spain until 1088, when, through the reforms and hegemony of Cluniac monks in Iberia, the Roman liturgy was imposed against the will of the people. As a concession to the Peninsula— which had recently been liberated from the Moors in 1492—Pope Alexander VI (a Spaniard, reigned 1492–1503) permitted its revival in several select locales, notably Toledo, where it is still celebrated today. In eighteenth-century New Spain, Francisco Antonio Lorenzana, former canon of Toledo and then archbishop of Mexico City, published a new edition of the *Missa gothica seu mozarábica et officium gothicum* in 1770. Lorenzana was a cultured bibliophile and a prolific writer; and his interest in the Mozarabic office and eucharistic rite appears to have been more antiquarian than practical. The work was published by the seminary press of the neighboring diocese of Puebla, with introductory explanations by the local archbishop, Francisco Fabián y Fuero.[45]

Spain and its Latin American colonies had always retained some elements of the ancient liturgy, especially in the rite of matrimony. In 1795, the Benedictine abbot of Monserrate published a new edition of the *Roman Ritual* with Mozarabic chant and an appendix containing selections from the *Manual* of Toledo.[46] Copies are known to have existed in several colonial libraries in Mexico. Its most popular element, even until the present day, has been precisely the rite of marriage, because it prescribes the customary giving of the *arras*, the binding together of the couple with a cord, and their veiling.[47] Ceremonial books, especially the ritual manuals of Toledo and Seville, were frequent imports from Europe.[48]

Other members of the episcopacy contributed to liturgical renewal and the devotion of the laity. Devotion to the Virgin Mary and the saints was intimately connected with participation in eucharistic devotion and the sacraments. Saint Toribio of Mogrovejo (d. 1606), archbishop of Lima, Peru, composed the litanies of the *In Laudem Beatae Mariae Virginis* (which included expressions of Amerindian piety) prior to the appearance of the Roman *Litany of the Virgin*.[49]

The Tridentine period corresponded to what historians call the Baroque era, but the Baroque was more than an art form in Latin America; it can be said to have been a way of life, a *modus vivendi* and *operandi* that accompanied a society totally immersed in a world view formed and dominated by the Catholic Church. This is seen in the sheer number of religious holidays—sometimes several in one week—whose typical manifestation was the liturgical procession that included every stratum of society, particularly the guilds and confraternities. Although a similar externalization of the faith was evident in coeval southern Europe, nothing there could compare with the grandeur and mass participation of natives, creoles, Africans, and Iberians in colonial Spanish America's musical and theatrical religious spectacles. This is particularly evident in the eucharistic feast of Corpus Christi. In Spain, the feast had become "militarized" as a harbinger of the victory of the Christian cross over the Muslim crescent, and as an apotropaic event against incipient Protestantism. In America those connotations continued, with the addition of triumph over idolatry and human sacrifice. The feast was used as a catechetical moment to rehearse all of salvation history, with costumed actors portraying scenes from the Creation to the Last Judgment. The dance of Moors and Christians, still performed by Amerindian descendants today, was transmuted into a battle of angels against devils in a moralizing display. The extroverted liturgy of Corpus Christ, with its eucharistic bread in a sunburst monstrance, allowed a symbiotic bridge between the old sun worship of the Aztecs and Incas and the new Christian worship of Christ, the Sun of Justice. The fact that, in the Andes, the feast coincided with the Inca feast of the Inti Rami, the divine sun god, solidified its acceptance and popularity among native peoples. Men and women of letters in the Baroque period, such as Sor Juan Inés de la Cruz, composed florid poetry and theatrical pieces to celebrate the solar sacrament, and painters portrayed the procession of the eucharistic cart and monstrance crushing under its wheels heretics such as Calvin and Luther. An adequate exposition of the spirituality and worship life of Baroque America would have to deal with the superbly operatic and melodramatic nature of its art and architecture.

Another factor needs to be considered in speaking of Baroque liturgy: personal devotion and pious literature. In this regard, the records of colonial booksellers bear witness to a vast interest in the spirituality of worship. For example, the inventory of one Lima book dealer indicates that, in the year 1606, he sold 153 copies of *Reflections on the Gospels for the Whole Year*, 13 copies of *Outlines for Sunday and Feastday Sermons from December until Quadragesima*, 33 copies of *Gospels and Epistles read in Church during the Whole Year*, 28 copies of *Lenten Sermons*, 4 copies of *Lenten and Eastertide Sermons*, and 9 copies of an *Instruction on How to Hear Mass*, as well as copies of *The Ceremony and General Rubics for the Order of Mass*, and *Discourses for Preaching on the Ceremonies and Mystery of the Mass.*[50] Some of the texts were evidently directed to clergy, while others were primarily for the use by the literate laity. During the seventeenth, eighteenth, and nineteenth centuries, liturgical texts continued to be published in native languages throughout the Americas, mainly preaching and confessional manuals for priests but also devotional literature for Amerindians.[51]

This Tridentine-Baroque period of liturgical history witnessed much greater and more active participation of the laity in the eucharist and sacraments than occurred in the later Independence period (mid-nineteenth century), which was marked by strong anticlerical and anti-ecclesiastical feelings. Nevertheless, civil reforms and the expropriation of church property did not abolish public liturgical events nor lay participation. Taking church buildings away from the clergy, as was done in Mexico, and putting them in the hands of elected lay corporations effectively guaranteed that externalized worship and religiosity in the streets would continue on the popular level. Indeed, the level of lay liturgical devotion, as witnessed by Spanish-language publications and by the multiplicity of feast days, far outshone what was occurring in the nascent United States and the English-speaking world. Latin America never suffered from the relatively low level of lay Catholic participation in liturgical events seen in pre-Vatican II North America.

Twentieth Century

The effects of the liturgical legislation of Vatican II in Latin America are comparable with what happened in Europe and North America, with the exception that Hispanic popular religiosity has continued, in some cases in opposition to liturgical renewal. This is true because popular religion and its public externalization was, in large measure, a lay movement. As in colonial times, it falls to the town officials and parochial lay stewards to finance and execute the feasts and processions, and hence this is an inherently conservative phenomenon. Recently these "archaic" ceremonies have proven to be lucrative tourist attractions, beneficial for local businesses.

Liturgical music in Latin America suffered in parallel with that in other parts of the Christian world. By the late nineteenth century and early twentieth, a saccharine hymnody had crept in. After Vatican II, Latin America quickly adapted folkloric elements, especially music, into the liturgy, with the same ambivalent results as the adoption of the folk music mass in United States. The great tradition of polyphonic music, much of which had been composed by native musicians, was quickly eclipsed by guitar-accompanied hymns with simple melodies. In the 1970s the bishop of Cuernavaca,

Mexico, instituted a "Mariachi Mass" that later became widely popular, especially in the southwestern United States. Under the influence of the social movements of the later twentieth century and "liberation theology," many of the hymn texts were social commentaries reflecting a "preferential option for the poor." These were themes articulated by the meetings of the Catholic bishops of Latin America (Consejo Episcopal Latinoamericano, CELAM) in Medellín, Colombia, in 1968, and in Puebla, Mexico, in 1979, which also urged liturgical renewal and a reintegration of popular religiosity into the church's worship. CELAM established a Department for Liturgy in 1969, first at Medellín and later at Bogotá.[52] Its purpose was to coordinate translations of ritual books and to provide education for clergy.

Michaelmas. Festal procession on the feast of Saint Michael the Archangel in the atrium of the Franciscan conversion center at Huejotzingo, Puebla, Mexico, which dates from the mid-sixteenth century. PHOTOGRAPH BY JAIME LARA

Unlike the English-speaking world, Latin America never created the equivalent International Committee on English in the Liturgy (ICEL) with uniform translations of the lectionary. Only when the *Texto Único* (the ordinary parts of the mass) was imposed in the 1990s was there anything like verbal uniformity. Lectionaries tend to vary from country to country depending on what Bible translation the particular bishops' conference chooses to use.

In popular belief the guitar is the typical musical instrument of Latin America, but the reality is that the pipe organ and the harp had been the liturgical instruments in the earlier years of evangelization. The Guaraní Indians of Paraguay, for example, had manufactured and exported harps, harpsichords, and small organs to Europe in the eighteenth century. Only recently are colonial organs beginning to be repaired and used in the parishes, and a few professionally trained musicians are recuperating the great Latin American polyphony of earlier centuries. In spite of the fact that Latin American cathedrals still have canons who sing the divine office, it is still rare that the liturgy of the hours is celebrated in the vernacular or with communal participation. Once priests leave the seminary, they seldom have the opportunity to engage in further study in worship, perhaps because liturgy is still a relatively low priority in developing countries. National liturgical offices in Latin America have had varying success, in part because of limited funding and the level of interest of the nation's bishops. One of the more productive offices is that of Mexico and its publishing house, La Obra Nacional de la Buena Prensa. Its bimonthly journal, *Actualidad Liturgica*, uses innovative elements like cartoons and comic anecdotes to teach clergy about planning and presiding. It also provides attractive visual bulletin inserts for the laity, and homily notes.

Perhaps some of the greatest liturgical creativity has occurred in the United States because of its enormous population of immigrants from south of the border. In 1973 the National Hispanic Institute of Liturgy (IHL) was formed by bilingual musicians, clergy and lay leaders. The IHL has provided translations of liturgical documents and texts, the Spanish-language lectionary for the United States, ritual books, and commentaries. It has also fostered the composition and publication of choral and congregational music in missalettes and hymnals, drawing on a variety of liturgical music from Spain and all the Latin American countries. The IHL organizes nationwide conferences and symposia every two years on topics related to worship, the liturgical arts, and Hispanic popular religiosity.

Future Prospects

At the start of the twenty-first century, Latin America continues to live liturgically in the light of the Second Vatican Council. A nostalgic desire to return to the pre-Tridentine Latin liturgy, which has become such a controversial topic in Europe and North America, is not an issue in Spanish-speaking countries. Recently the renewed liturgy has been allied to the "new evangelization" of the continent that Pope John Paul II called for during 1992, which the Catholic Church celebrated as the quincentennial year of the beginning of the first evangelization. One of the major themes among episcopal conferences and liturgical commissions has been that of "inculturation," which was articulated officially by Pope Paul VI's *Evangelii Nuntiandi* (1975) and which has resonated with every Latin America country in spite of recent attempts by Vatican officials to dilute it. Some understand the process as an adaptation of the traditional liturgy to the cultural models of local communities, while others prefer to see it as the incorporation into worship of selected elements of diverse cultures in regard both to the rites and to the language of symbols.

Recent liturgical guidelines of CELAM insist that Catholic worship should facilitate a living encounter with Jesus Christ and have a visible effect on the lives of believers. Also emphasized is the fact that lively and participatory worship cannot be achieved without attention to personal and communal spirituality. Hispanic popular religiosity, so rich in its expressions and in its emphasis on the festive and communal, should properly serve conversion to the gospel rather than being an end in itself. In line with the theologies of liberation that have captured the Hispanic imagination, worship is seen as the ideal place for the proclamation of human freedom, and as a foretaste of a world more fraternal and just.

In the realm of liturgical music, there are abundant folkloric creations and hymns with profound biblical and social content. But there is a need to evangelize all the contemporary cultural expressions—music, art, dance—and imbue them with the spirit of the gospel. Moreover, there is growing awareness of the need to diversify cultural expressions beyond the merely folkloric and ethnic, and to raise the general level of musical composition and performance for the liturgy. Church documents also speak of the need for a liturgical and spiritual formation (not just education) of all ministers, both lay and ordained; and this will be a practical challenge for parishes and diocesan liturgical commissions.

Until recently, Latin American dioceses have shown little interest in the *Rite for the Christian Initiation of Adults*, probably because in earlier times all Catholics had been baptized as infants. Now, however, there is a growing concern to incorporate the adult rites into parish life as part of a larger re-evangelization program, made especially necessary by the increasing number of adolescents and adults who have been neither baptized nor catechized. The new interest in the *Rite* and its use should also be seen against the background of the rise of pentecostal and evangelical churches in Latin America, and as a countermeasure to the growth of those groups. Whether or not the Church's liturgy can accomplish all this remains to be seen. Certainly, it seems that, as part of a more total concern for a new evangelization of the continent and for a true inculturation of faith and worship according to the gospel, the liturgy will have a uniquely Hispanic flavor and sound.

Bibliography

Baumgartner, Jakob. *Mission und Liturgie in Mexiko*. 2 vols. Neue Zeitschrift für Missionswissenschaft, Supplementa 18 and 19. Schöneck/Beckenried: Administration der Neuen Zeitschrift für Missionswissenschaft, 1971–1972.

Guarda, Gabriel. *Los Laicos en la Cristianización de América*. Santiago: Ediciones Universidad Católica de Chile, 1987.

Lara, Jaime. *City, Temple, Stage: Eschatological Architecture and Liturgical Theatrics in New Spain*. Notre Dame, Ind.: University of Notre Dame Press, 2004.

Pardo, Osvaldo. *The Origins of Mexican Catholicism: Nahua Rituals and Christian Sacraments in Sixteenth-Century Mexico*. Ann Arbor: University of Michigan Press, 2004.

Ricard, Robert. *The Spiritual Conquest of Mexico*. Translated by Lesley Byrd Simpson. Berkeley: University of California Press, 1966.

Notes

[1] Francisco López de Gómara, *La Conquista de México* (1552): "The greatest thing since the creation of the world, save the Incarnation and death of Him who created it, is the discovery of the Indies that are thus called the New World." See Jaime Lara, *City, Temple, Stage: Eschatological Architecture and Liturgical Theatrics in New Spain*, chap. 2.

[2] Lara, passim.

[3] Lara, chap. 4.

[4] Jakob Baumgartner, *Mission und Liturgie in Mexiko*, 1: 421. The Inquisition was particularly severe on those possessing copies of the Epistle or Gospel pericopes in the vernacular—an indication that they may have been used in lay-presided "dry masses." See below.

[5] See Bernardino de Sahagún, *Adiciones, Apéndice a la Postilla y Ejercicio Cotidiano*, Facsimile ed. Arthur Anderson (Mexico: Universidad Nacional Autónoma de México, 1993) 145–203.

[6] Diego Valadés, *Rhetorica Christiana* (Perugia: 1579).

[7] Valadés, 108, B.

[8] The *Liber Sacerdotalis* was also known as the *Sacerdotale ad consuetudinem S. Romanae Ecclesiae.*

[9] Alberto Castellani, *Liber Sacerdotalis* (Venice: 1523) folio 13r. All translations, unless otherwise noted, are those of this author.

[10] Castellani, folio 16r.

[11] Castellani, folio 16v.

[12] "Códice Franciscano," in *Nueva Colección de Documentos para la Historia de México*, ed. Joaquín García Icazbalceta (Mexico: Chavez Hayhoe, 1941) 75–85; and Juan Focher, *Itinerarium catholicum profisciscentium ad infideles convertendos . . .* (Seville: 1574), introduction and notes Antonio Eguiluz (Madrid: Libreria General Victoriano Suarez, 1960) 107–212. The section on marriage, which may have had some adaptation to pre-Columbian pagan practice, is completely lost.

[13] The *Mexicaniensis* was implemented under the second archbishop of Mexico City, the no-nonsense Dominican Montúfar, who had been an inquisitor for the Holy Office.

[14] See Baumgartner, 2: 294–378. San Martín made use of the previously mentioned books as well as rituals from Toledo and Salamanca.

[15] Baumgartner, 2: 316.

[16] For Peru, see the *Rituale seu manuale Peruanum, et forma brevis administrandi apud Indos* (Naples: 1607).

Also see Raoul de La Grasserie, *Langue puquina; textes puquina contenus dans le Rituale seu manuale peruanum* (Leipzig: K. F. Koehler, 1894) and Baumgartner, 2: 379. For the islands of the Pacific, see Luis Balquiedra, "The Liturgical Principles used by Missionaries and the Missionary Background to the Christianization of the Philippines," *Philippiniana Sacra* 30 (1995) 5–79.

[17] Baumgartner, 2: 291.

[18] Baumgartner, 1: 222–225.

[19] Robert Ricard, *The Spiritual Conquest of Mexico*, 126.

[20] Baumgartner, 1: 265–268.

[21] Valadés, 108.

[22] Witness the work of fray Andrés de Olmos, *Tratado de Hechicherías y Sortilegios* [1553], ed. Georges Baudot (Mexico: Universidad Nacional Autónoma de México, 1990).

[23] Valadés, 213.

[24] Ricard, 124.

[25] For the many problems regarding the attempt to impose monogamous marriage, see Ricard, 110–116, and Baumgartner, 293 ff.

[26] Baumgartner, 1: 303

[27] Baumgartner, 1: 315–321.

[28] Valadés, 221.

[29] Baumgartner, 1: 411–422. The *arras* were small gold coins that the groom placed into the hands of the bride, thereby entrusting her with the economic charge of the new household. Today this is accompanied with a statement about the mutual sharing of material goods.

[30] Baumgartner, 2: 291.

[31] Valadés, 219, I.

[32] Baumgartner, 1: 259–263.

[33] Ricard, 122–125.

[34] Baumgartner, 1: 256.

[35] Baumgartner, 1: 231 ff., 419.

[36] Toribio de Benevente Motolinía, *Motolinia's History of the Indians of New Spain*, trans. Francis Borgia Steck (Washington, D.C.: Academy of American Franciscan History, 1951) 143.

[37] Toribio de Benevente Motolinía, *Memoriales: libro de oro*, ed. Nancy Joe Dyer (Mexico: El Colegio de México, 1996) 95, 110; and Juan de Torquemada, *Monarquía Indiana*, 7 vols. (Mexico: Universidad Nacional Autónoma de México, 1983) 3: 223.

[38]*Liber Sacerdotalis*, 23; and Carlos Duarte, "Las fiestas de Corpus Christi en la Caracas Hispánica (tarasca, gigantes y diablitos)," *Archivo Español de Arte* 255 (1991) 337–347.

[39]Baumgartner, 1: 420.

[40]Ricard, 178.

[41]Dry masses were also celebrated on land where a priest was required to celebrate more than one mass per day but could not maintain the eucharistic fast, or by priests who found themselves hostages of Muslims, who would not permit them to have wine.

[42]Rafael García Granados, "Simulacros de misa," *Excelsior*, Mexico City, 8 Dec. 1931, relates a letter of fray Pedro dated 27 June 1529 in which he states that he has taught the Indian boys "to read, write, sing, preach and celebrate the divine office in imitation of the priests."

[43]Motolinia, *Memoriales*, chap. 34.

[44]Hugo Nutini and Betty Bell consider syncretism as equivalent to religious acculturation and the creation of hybridity: "When two religious systems meet (in a variety of contexts which may include voluntary interaction, forced acceptance, social and political pressures, and the like) the resultant religious system is different from the two original interacting systems because of mutual, albeit often unequal, borrowings and lendings, which are internalized and interpreted in a process of action and reaction" (*Ritual Kinship: The Structure and Historical Development of the Compadrazgo System in Rural Tlaxcala*, 2 vols. [Princeton, N.J.: Princeton University Press, 1980] 1: 291). Some prefer the term "selective synthesis" or "synthesization," a form of religious meshing which does not contaminate the orthodox content of the faith. See Jaime Vidal, "Towards an Understanding of Synthesis in Iberian and Hispanic American Popular Religiosity," in *An Enduring Flame: Studies on Latino Popular Religiosity*, ed. Anthony Stevens-Arroyo and Ana María Díaz-Stevens (New York: Bildern Center for Western Hemisphere Studies, 1994) 69–95.

[45]*Missa Gothica seu Mozarábica, Facsímil de la primera edición de 1770*, introduction by Manuel Olimón Nolasco (Mexico: Comisión Nacional de Arte Sacro, 1996).

[46]*Rituale Romanum Pauli V. Pont. Maximi jussu editum, cum cantu Toletano, & Appendice ex Manuali Toletano* (Matrini: Typus Societatis, 1795).

[47]See *Don y Promesa, Costumbres y Tradiciones en los Ritos Matrimoniales Hispanos; Gift and Promise, Customs and Traditions in Hispanic Rites of Marriage*, ed. Raul Gomez, Heliodoro Lucatero, and Sylvia Sánchez (Portland: Oregon Catholic Press, 1997).

[48]Antonio Ybot León, *La Iglesia y los eclesiásticos españoles en la empresa de Indias*, 2 vols. (Barcelona: Salvat, 1954–1963) 1: 396f. A popular text in the eighteenth-century New World appears to have been Bartolomé de Olalla y Aragón, *Ceremonial de las misas solemnes cantadas, con diaconos o sin ellos* (Madrid: Juan Garcia Insanzon, 1707).

[49]Gabriel Guarda, *Los Laicos en la Cristianización de América*, 90.

[50]Irving Leonard, *Books of the Brave* (Berkeley: University of California Press, 1992) 337-403; and Guarda, 85–93. Also see the discussion of Dominican, Franciscan, and Jesuit rituals in Balquiedra, 24 f.

[51]See, for example, *A Guide to Confession Large and Small in the Mexican Language, 1634 by Bartolomé de Alva*, ed. Barry Sell and John Frederick Schwaller (Norman: University of Oklahoma Press, 1990).

[52]See www.celam.org for CELAM, its documents, and its Department for Liturgy.

24

Mainline Protestants in Latin America

WILHELM WACHHOLZ

The Types of Latin American Protestantism in Their Contexts

From the time of the Spanish and Portuguese invasion in the late fifteenth century up until the beginning of the nineteenth century, Christian worship in Latin America was basically that of pre-Tridentine Roman Catholicism, transported from the Iberian Peninsula and adapted to the realities of the New World. To this were added some elements of indigenous and African origin.

In the sixteenth and seventeenth centuries some attempts were made to break the Catholic hegemony in Latin America. The first occurred when French Calvinists established themselves in the Bay of Guanabarra (Rio de Janeiro), which they reached on 10 November 1555, under the leadership of Vice Admiral Nicolas Durand de Villegagnon. In this joint project France was seeking new territories for colonization, and the Huguenots were looking for mission fields. A second expedition, consisting of around three hundred people, arrived on 7 March 1557. Of these immigrants, fourteen were Huguenots, two of them pastors. Three days after their arrival, Peter Richier and William Chartier celebrated the first Protestant worship on Brazilian soil and on 21 March the first Lord's supper according to the Calvinist rite. However, bad planning and internal theological disputes about the supper so weakened the project that the French ended up being totally expelled in 1567.[1]

In the seventeenth century the French set up at São Luís do Maranhão in Brazil (1612–1615), in Haiti, in Guadeloupe, in Martinique, and in French Guyana. The French influence on worship in these contexts still needs to be investigated.

The efforts of the Dutch to establish themselves in Latin America were more significant. In 1624, while the Netherlands were at war with Spain, some Dutchmen landed in Bahia (Brazil), though they remained there only a year. Between 1630 and 1654, however, the Dutch settled in the northeast of Brazil, where they founded the city of Recife. They included forty pastors and eight missionaries to work among the Indians. But weakened by the Netherlands' war against Spain and England and soon also against France, the Dutch agreed to withdraw from Brazil.[2] The stamp of Dutch Calvinism on worship in Brazil disappeared with the recovery of Portuguese Catholic hegemony. On the other hand, on some Caribbean islands and in Surinam, Dutch Calvinism influenced local worship in a permanent way.

The military defeat of France at the beginning of the nineteenth century resulted in the subjection of Spain and Portugal to British commercial power. Influenced by Enlightenment ideals, Britain decided to support the emancipation of the Latin American states. On the one hand, the Latin American governments wanted to maintain relations with Rome, yet on the other, they were obliged to tolerate non-Catholic populations. This gave rise to a "Josephinist" policy in Brazil, Argentina, Uruguay, and Chile: the non-Catholic religion could be professed only in private houses, which could not bear the outward appearance of a church with a cross, towers, or bells.[3] The Brazilian imperial constitution of 1824 clearly stipulated that "the catholic and apostolic Roman religion will continue to be the religion of the Empire. All other religions will be permitted to practice domestic or private worship in houses intended for it, without any external form of a church."

The British influence in Latin America opened the continent to liberal capitalism and turned the area into a market for British industrial products.[4] This led to the establishment of British businesses in the principal cities of Latin America and to the founding of a certain number of Anglican communities. Thus Protestantism arose as a "by-product" of capitalism. Moreover British pressure, aiming to put an end to the slave trade, forced the Latin American governments to allow the immigration of people from non-Catholic European countries. From the 1820s this new workforce began the "whitening" of the populace, accompanied by the elimination of the indigenous peoples, the exploitation of the land, and the creation of a middle class.[5] In this way Latin America acquired Protestant populations who constituted immigrant or "transplanted" communities and churches, especially Anglicans from England and Lutherans, Reformed, and United from German-speaking countries in Europe (but also Missouri Synod Lutherans). A particular case was the Waldensians from the Alpine valleys.

In the second half of the nineteenth century, another type of Protestantism penetrated more strongly into Latin America. This came by way of missionaries from churches in the United States: Methodist, Presbyterian, Episcopalian, Congregationalist, and Baptist.[6] As a result, Protestant worship in Latin America can be characterized according to its two origins, either European and immigrant or North American and missionary.

Three more types of church, less traditionally "Protestant," deserve to be mentioned, although they will not be analyzed here. These are the Pentecostals, the neo-Pentecostals, and the transconfessional groups that have resulted from the breaking down of denominational walls.[7]

Worship in the Immigrant Churches

Anglicanism

Anglicanism was introduced quite early into Jamaica (1665) and the Bahamas (1731). Later, as a result of increased commerce with Britain, the presence of English Anglicans spread through practically the entire southern continent. These Anglicans set about preparing buildings for the celebration of their worship. On 12 August 1819 the foundation stone was laid in Rio de Janeiro for the first, so far as is known, Protestant place of worship in Latin America.[8] The English Anglicans brought with them the *Book of Common Prayer* that was used for worship both on the British ships anchored in port and at house services or, later on, in their churches. In 1861 the prayer book was in part translated into Portuguese by Richard Holden.[9] After the official installation of

Baptism in Jamaica. Baptism of 135 people near Brawns Town, Jamaica, c. 1842.
Victoria & Albert Museum, London/Art Resource, NY

the Anglican Church in Brazil (1890), a fuller translation was made from the prayer book of the Protestant Episcopal Church in the USA (1893). Only in 1930, however, was the first complete *Book of Common Prayer* produced in Brazil. A new version was published in 1984, which remains in use. The *Hinário Episcopal* was published in 1962.[10]

In the early twenty-first century there is no liturgical uniformity among Anglican congregations in Brazil or in Latin America more generally. In southern Brazil, Anglo-Catholic influence brings rituals and symbolism more into prominence: chasubles, candles, images, tabernacles, and so forth. In the northeastern regions, where Protestant influences are stronger, the congregations do not follow cultic forms and symbols so strictly. In the center of the country, congregations adopt both Protestant and Anglo-Catholic elements. Similar features can be observed in other Latin American contexts. In central Argentina and Uruguay, for example, congregations are more Anglo-Catholic in style and have adopted the *Book of Common Prayer* of the Episcopal Church in the USA, translated into Spanish. In northern Argentina, Paraguay, Bolivia, and Chile the tendency is anti-Catholic, and the congregations use an adapted form of the English Prayer Book of 1662.

The Lutheran, Calvinist, and United Churches

The Lutheran, Reformed, and United churches in Latin America were formed in the nineteenth century by the immigration especially of German-speaking people from Germany itself, Austria, Switzerland, and the Volga region of Russia. Settlement took place chiefly in Brazil, Argentina, Chile, Uruguay, and Paraguay. In the other countries it was rather the resident business communities who constituted these churches.[11] Because of confessional diversity, most of the first synods founded in Latin America opted for the broader name of "Evangelical" rather than Lutheran, Reformed, or

United. This diversity was reflected in the patterns and styles of worship, with the use of different service books, catechisms, hymnals, and vestments, and the presence or absence of liturgical objects, such as the crucifix, candles, paraments, and flowers on the altar.[12]

The book that found most acceptance and exercised a force for unity in worship was the *Kirchenagenda für die Hof- und Domkirche in Berlin* (1822).[13] Originally formulated for the court and cathedral in Berlin, this church order was introduced especially into those areas where the Church of the Prussian Union assumed direct or indirect responsibility for sending pastors and support of congregations in Latin America. This applied particularly to the immigrant churches: the Evangelical Church of the Lutheran Confession in Brazil (IECLB); the Evangelical Church of the River Plate (IERP), that is, Argentina, Uruguay, and Paraguay; and the Evangelical Lutheran Church of Chile (IELCH). In the IECLB the Prussian service book of 1822 was officially adopted. In 1930 it was translated into Portuguese under the title *Manual do Culto para uso nas Comunidades da Igreja Evangélica de Confissão Lutherana no Brasil.*[14]

In the Spanish-speaking context, a book was produced in 1964 with the title *Culto Cristiano* that contains orders of worship, prayers, psalms, and hymns. This book went into use not only in congregations of the IERP and the IELCH but also in the great majority of Spanish-speaking Lutheran churches in Latin America. In the IERP use is made also of a complete version of the Prussian book of 1822, a Spanish translation of which was begun in 1967 and finished in 1979. Its title respects its origin in the Church of the Prussian Union: *Manual de Cultos de la Iglesia Evangélica de la Unión.*[15]

More recently, under the inspiration of the movement for liturgical renewal that crossed confessional boundaries, there have also arisen a number of worship books of a provisional character. In the IECLB these include *Celebrações Litúrgicas* and *Celebrações do Povo de Deus* (1986 and 1991) and in the IERP *Pequeño Manual de Liturgia* (2000).

The great variety of hymnals brought by the German-speaking immigrants from their different countries and provinces frequently presented problems for the choice of hymns in worship. In the IECLB the synods aimed to establish some degree of liturgical uniformity, especially in hymnody, and in this connection the late nineteenth century and early twentieth century saw the introduction of such hymnals as the *Evangelisches Gesangbuch für Rheinland und Westfalen*, the *Gesangbuch für die evangelisch-lutherische Kirche in Bayern*, or the *Evangelisches Hausbuch für Deutsche im Ausland*. From around 1924 the *Deutsches Evangelisches Gesangbuch für die Schutzgebiete und das Ausland* (DEG, 1915) gradually found an increasingly wide acceptance. This book was replaced in 1949 by the *Evangelisches Gesangbuch* (new edition, 1994). The prohibition of the German language at the height of the First and Second World Wars stimulated the translation and publication of hymnals in Portuguese. *Hymnos da Igreja Lutherana* was published in 1939, and this hymnal, from the second edition onward under the title *Hinos da Igreja Evangélica*, remained in use for about twenty years. The *Hinário da Igreja Evangélica de Confissão Lutherana* was published in 1964, and it retained the status of official hymnal until it was replaced as such in 1981 by the *Hinos do Povo de Deus* (HPD, 1981). HPD was criticized for its extensive dependence on decontextualized hymns, and the quest for more indigenous hymns led to the production of HPD-II in 2001.[16]

Prussian influence was felt also in the adoption by pastors of the *talar* or black robe that had been authorized by Frederick William III in 1811. This vestment served the cause of uniformity in worship until the late twentieth century, but its exclusive use was broken, for example, by the authorization of the beige robe in the IERP in 1983.

The same vestment was authorized in the IECLB in 1990, followed by the alb and stole in 1994.[17]

In sum, the German, and particularly the Prussian, influence on this "immigrant" type of Protestant worship in Latin America is historically very strong.

The Missouri Synod Lutherans

Missouri Synod Lutherans have been present in Latin America since 1900. In some regions (Cuba, Mexico, El Salvador, Panama) they came for mission work, but in other places (Guatemala, Venezuela, Chile, Uruguay, Paraguay, Argentina, Brazil) they profited rather from crises within the immigrant Protestant communities.[18]

In Argentina this type of Lutheranism is represented by the Evangelical Lutheran Church of Argentina (IELA) and in Brazil by the Evangelical Lutheran Church of Brazil (IELB). At first the IELB attracted the same type of members and communities as the IECLB, namely German immigrants and their descendents. As with the IECLB, the great variety of catechisms, hymnals, and liturgical practices reflected the geographical and confessional variety of the IELB's members. Their churches were generally simple, without towers or bells. Their pastors wore the black Prussian robe. Except for the final years of the First World War (1917–1918), German was the predominant language in worship until 1942, when during the Second World War it was again prohibited. Between 1900 and 1920 the Missouri Synod churches used—though not without some resistance among the congregations—the Missouri Synod's *Kirchen-Agende* and the *Kirchen-Gesangbuch für Evangelisch-Lutherische Gemeinden ungeänderter Augsburgischer Confession*. The Portuguese-language *Hinos e Orações* was published in 1920, replaced in 1938 by the *Hinário Luterano*, which itself was published in enlarged editions in 1949, 1976, and 1986. All these hymnals included also orders of worship. The first of these were heavily dependent on the *Kirchen-Agende*. But from 1947 the liturgy employed was a literal translation from the North American *Lutheran Liturgy* (Missouri Synod, 1943). This order was maintained in 1986 but has been increasingly overtaken by one similar to that in the North American *Lutheran Worship* (Missouri Synod, 1982).[19]

In Central America the Fellowship of Lutheran Churches (CILCA) published a *Manual de Oficios* (Costa Rica, CILCA, 1995). This manual is based on North American Lutheran models and, to a lesser degree, on *Culto Cristiano*. It aims an "adaptation to the uses and customs of the region."

Worship in the Missionary Churches[20]

Congregationalism

Congregationalists began work in Jamaica in 1837, in Brazil in 1855, and in other countries later still. In Brazil they had no official service book, and their style of worship resembled that of the Baptists. Their main contribution came by way of hymnology. Especially notable were Robert Reid Kalley (1809–1888) and Sarah Poulton Kalley (1825–1907).[21] The hymnal produced by this married couple, *Salmos e Hinos*, containing translations from various authors as well as compositions by the Kalleys themselves, served to a greater or lesser degree as the hymnbook of the Protestant churches of missionary origin and indeed still does so. Moreover the immigrant churches, particularly in Brazil, also borrowed many of the hymns from *Salmos e Hinos*. These hymns are predominantly of a revivalist and individualist kind. The first edition came out in

1861 and included eighteen psalms and thirty-two hymns. The second edition, in 1868, had seventy-six hymns. Successive editions contained an ever-increasing number of hymns. Robert Kalley's influence was felt also through the institution of lay preaching in services conducted in homes for families.

Presbyterianism

The Presbyterians came to Jamaica in 1800, to Chile in 1845, to Colombia in 1856, to Brazil in 1859, to Mexico in 1872, to Guatemala in 1882, and to Trindad in 1886. In Brazil, Presbyterian worship is characterized by "liturgical improvisation," a style inherited from the "domestic worship" introduced by the Kalleys. The *Manual de Culto*, first published in 1874, was never declared to be the official, let alone the exclusive, service book of the Presbyterians. Pastors continued to conduct worship as they wished. Perhaps the *Manual de Culto* was not used much by them but was rather intended for use by lay people when they led worship.[22]

Methodism

The beginning of Methodist missionary activity dates from 1760 in Antigua, 1789 in Jamaica, 1809 in Trinidad, 1867 in Argentina and Uruguay, 1873 in Mexico, 1888 in Peru, and finally from the very end of the nineteenth century in Costa Rica, Panama, and Bolivia. As far as Brazil is concerned, the Methodist Episcopal Church, South, in 1876 sent the Reverend J. J. Ransom from the United States to scout the territory. Finding groups of people who had been reading the Holy Scriptures for themselves, he prepared a book that would help them conduct Sunday worship together. Published in Rio de Janeiro in 1878, *O Culto Dominical* contained orders for morning and evening prayer taken from the services John Wesley had adapted from the English *Book of Common Prayer*. North American Methodism itself, however, had long since abandoned for its regular worship the *Sunday Service* of John Wesley; and when more sustained missionary work was introduced into Brazil from 1886, the dominant pattern became that of a more loosely structured preaching service there also. As in the United States, however, the orders for baptism and the Lord's supper followed the prescribed ritual. In hymnody Methodism adopted much of the inheritance from the Kalleys. Methodism exercised a strong influence on the successive editions of the *Hinário Evangélico com Antífonas e Orações* produced by the Confederação Evangélica in 1945, 1953, and 1962. Although it was officially adopted only by the Methodists, this book recommended an order of worship that became very popular in several Brazilian denominations:

1. Approach to God: Adoration
2. Confession of Sins before God: Confession
3. Exaltation of the Power of God: Praise
4. Hearing the Word of God: Edification
5. Resolve to Follow God: Dedication.

The new edition of the *Hinário Evangélico* in 1964 provided also a complete service for the Lord's supper according to the same fivefold structure, again employing many elements from the Methodist rite.[23]

Baptists

The presence of Baptists in Jamaica dates from 1814, in Brazil from 1881, in Bolivia from 1898, and in other Latin American countries from later still. The first Baptist worship book in Brazil, *Manual das Igrejas*, was published in 1926. Similarly to that of the Presbyterians, Baptist worship is marked more by "spontaneity" than by orders from a book.[24] This is due to the Baptist ecclesiology, in which each local congregation is autonomous; theologically the style is strongly individualist, aiming at conversion. In Brazil the Baptists used *Salmos e Hinos* until 1924, when their own hymnal was published under the title *Cantor Cristão*. This was followed by the *Hinário para o Culto Cristão* in 1991.[25]

Analysis of Protestant Orders of Worship in Latin America

The churches of missionary origin can be divided into those that have worship manuals (Presbyterians and Methodists) and those that do not (Baptists and Congregationalists).[26] All of these may be considered "non-liturgical" churches, compared with the "liturgical" Lutheran and Anglican churches, but this distinction is not rigid.[27] Churches that place a strong theological emphasis on God's immediate and direct communication to every person tend to lack liturgical or symbolic forms as mediating instruments.

In the "liturgical" churches, rites such as the eucharist, baptism, confirmation, ordination, and marriage occupy a prominent place in worship. The prayers are normally fixed in writing. Special care is taken over the posture and gestures of the officiants and their assistants. Candles, flowers, a cross, and a Bible are placed on the altar, and the paraments change color with the liturgical calendar. Pulpit, lectern, and font are normally integrated into the liturgical space. The officiant wears a robe or an alb.[28] On the other hand, worship in the "liturgical" churches is not without its problems. Although ritual may be valued, it quite often happens that the sermon is exalted over the other features of the liturgy. With regard to the eucharist, there could exist, up until the 1980s, a veritable "breach" between the service of the word and the sacramental supper. Pastors pronounced a benediction at the end of the service of the word so that people who did not wish to take part in communion could nevertheless leave with a blessing. Under Prussian influence the sacrament had clearly acquired the status of an "appendix" to worship.

Influenced by Puritanism, Pietism, and revivalism and seeking also to differentiate their worship from the Catholic mass, the "non-liturgical" churches more or less renounced the use of fixed cultic formulas, rites, and procedures. Focusing worship on the sermon, they almost turn the altar into a pulpit. Prayers are extempory. Hymns have an individualist and conversionist appeal. The preacher wears a suit and tie (though robes may sometimes be worn among Presbyterians and Methodists). The sacrament, when indeed administered, figures as an appendix to worship. For most of the "non-liturgical" churches, baptism is no more than an outward sign of what has already taken place in the heart, namely conversion.[29]

An informal style of worship was transferred from the North American "frontier" to the missionary churches in Latin America and affected even the immigrant churches. Its characteristic expression was found in the preaching and in the singing. As representatives of the "American way of life," the missionaries understood themselves as "frontline troops" whose "job" was to "convert" individuals and then report on the number of the converts. Worship was aimed at conversion and rededication. The individualism can be seen in the numerous first-person-singular hymns of *Salmos e*

Hinos—often translated from English and (especially) North American sources—that not only were sung in the missionary churches but also were included in the hymnals of the immigrant churches (such as the HPD of the IECLB). In the missionary churches the condemnation of idleness, coupled with the pragmatist spirit and the ambiguous translation of the English word "service," led to the understanding of worship as "work," with the aim of social transformation. Moreover the perceived need to bring people into the way of "truth" and keep them there, especially in the face of the "error" of Roman Catholicism or "syncretism," gave to the ecclesiastical buildings more and more the character of "lecture halls."[30]

Two points of resistance to liturgical renewal are to be noted, particularly in the context of the missionary churches. The first is related to the hymnological tradition inherited from North American revivalism, which is maintained with vigor. Nevertheless there are examples of a renewed hymnology in Argentinean Methodism (prompted in part by opposition to military dictatorship) as well as in Brazilian Methodism.[31] The second point of resistance is connected with the presumption that the Bible is the exclusive property of Protestants, while the entire liturgical tradition belongs to the Roman Catholic Church. Thus resistance to liturgical renewal is nourished more by anti-Catholic sentiment than by a properly theological reflection on worship.[32]

In the "liturgical churches" there is also strong resistance to the use and development of liturgical orders in places that have been influenced by missionary Protestantism and, more recently, neo-Pentecostalism and the charismatic movement. Here a certain biblicism, claiming Luther's *sola scriptura*, is allied with an emotionalism aroused by "praise bands" (drums, guitars, vocalists) or the raised voice of the preacher. Such worship services are basically composed of three "liturgical elements": singing, prayer, and preaching.

Especially in the "liturgical churches," however, there are more concrete signs of liturgical renewal, stimulated in the late twentieth century by the effects of the Second Vatican Council. The evidence is found in scholarly research and publications but also in practical efforts at liturgies that, on the one hand, take the origins of Christian worship into account, valuing especially the eucharist, and on the other hand, are contextualized and call for the active participation of the community.[33]

To this end the Twenty-second Council of the IECLB in the year 2000 framed a landmark definition of the order of worship:

(1) Liturgy of Gathering: bells, prelude, entrance hymn, greeting (apostolic or trinitarian), confession of sins, Kyrie eleison (as a lament for the sorrows of the world), Gloria in excelsis (praise), prayer of the day.

(2) Liturgy of the Word: scripture readings, interspersed hymns, sermon, confession of faith, communication of needs and concerns, the general prayer of the church.

(3) Liturgy of the Eucharist: preparation of the table and offertory (the monetary offering is collected and the bread and wine are placed on the altar), offertory prayer, eucharistic prayer, the Our Father, the peace gesture, the fraction (breaking of the bread), the Agnus Dei, communion, post-communion prayer.

(4) Liturgy of Departure: community notices, blessing, dismissal, hymn.

Signs of liturgical renewal can also be seen in hymnody. An example is the following, taken from HPD-II. It stands opposed to the individualist and conversionist tradition, aiming rather at Latin American contextualization. Authored by Ernesto B. Cardoso, it is a summons to the celebration of Christian hope and liberation:

1. Deus chama a gente pr'um momento novo
de caminhar junto com seu povo.
É hora de transformar o que não dá mais;
Sozinho, isolado ninguém é capaz
(*Estribilho*):
Por isso vem!
Entra na roda com a gente,
também você é muito importante.
Vem!

2. Não é possível crer que tudo é fácil.
Há muita força que produz a morte,
gerando dor, tristeza e desolação.
É necessário unir o cordão

3. A força que hoje faz brotar a vida
atua em nós pela sua graça
É Deus quem nos convida p'ra trabalhar,
o amor repartir e as forças juntar.

In sum, we observe a very diversified worship practice among the Protestant churches in Latin America. If there still exists a certain disdain for liturgical elaboration, nevertheless there are clear signs of the desire for liturgical renewal.

Bibliography

Dreher, Martin N. *A Igreja Latino-Americana no Contexto Mundial.* São Leopoldo: Sinodal, 1999.

Hahn, Carl Joseph. *História do culto protestante no Brasil.* São Paulo: Associação de Seminários Teológicos Evangélicos, 1989.

Mendonça, Antônio Gouvêa. "Crise de culto protestante no Brasil: diagnóstico et alternatives." In *Introdução ao Protestantismo no Brasil.* Edited by Antônio Gouvêa Mendonça and Procóro Velasques Filho, 171–204. São Paulo: Loyola, 1990.

Prien, Hans-Jürgen. *Formação da Igreja Evangélica no Brasil.* Petrópolis, Brazil: Vozes; São Leopoldo: Sinodal, 2001.

Prien, Hans-Jürgen. *La Historia del Christianismo en América Latina.* Salamanca, Mexico: Sígueme; São Leopoldo, Brazil: Sinodal, 1985.

Notes

[1] See Hahn, *História do Culto Protestante no Brasil*, 59–62.

[2] Hahn, *História do Culto Protestante no Brasil*, 40, 62–63.

[3] Martin N. Dreher, *A Igreja Latino-Americana no Contexto Mundial*, 161–164.

[4] See Hans-Jürgen Prien, *Formação da Igreja Evangélica no Brasil*, 32f.

[5] Hans-Jürgen Prien, *Formação da Igreja Evangélica no Brasil*, 32ff.

[6] Hans-Jürgen Prien, *La Historia del Cristianismo en América Latina*, 407–408.

[7] Dreher, *A Igreja Latino-Americana no Contexto Mundial*, 220–221, 230–236.

[8] Hahn, *História do Culto Protestante no Brasil*, 70–72; Prien, *La Historia del Cristianismo en América Latina*, 717.

[9] Hahn, *História do Culto Protestante no Brasil*, 72, 84.

[10] See Francisco de Assis da Silva, *Liturgia Anglicana: Evolução, diversidade, e espiritualidade* (Porto Alegre, Brazil: Metrópole, 1999).

[11]Prien, *La Historia*, 718–719, 722.

[12]Martin N. Dreher, "Protestantismo de Imigração no Brasil," in *Imigrações e História da Igreja no Brasil*, ed. Martin N. Dreher (São Paulo: Santuário, 1993) 109–131, here 120–122.

[13]See Chapter 10 by Hans-Christoph Schmidt-Lauber in the present volume.

[14]See Prien, *La Historia*, 725, 743, 749ff.; and Silvio Tesche, *Vestes Litúrgica: Elementos de prodigialidade ou dominação*, Escola Superior de Teologia, Instituto Ecumênico de Pós-Graduacão, Teses e Dissertações, 5 (São Leopoldo: Sinodal, 1995), 8.

[15]*Culto Cristiano* (New York: El Escudo, 1964); and *Manual de Cultos de la Iglesia Evangélica de la Unión* (Buenos Aires: Iglesia Evangélica del Río de la Plata, 1979).

[16]See Leonhard F. Creutzberg, *Estou Pronto para Cantar* (São Leopoldo: Sinodal, 2001) 17–132; Denise Cordeiro de Souza Frederico, *Cantos para o Culto Cristão: Critéros de seleção a partir da tensão entre tradição e contemporaneidade*, Escola Superior de Teologia, Instituto Ecumênico de Pós-Graduacão, Teses e Dissertações, 16 (São Leopoldo: Sinodal, 2001), 32–33; and Jochen Eber, "Hinos do Povo de Deus (HPD): Auxílios pastorais," in *Estudos Teológicos*, 38 (1998) 273–281.

[17]Tesche, *Vestes Litúrgica*, 7–10, 130.

[18]See Prien, *La Historia*, 735.

[19]See Paulo Gerhard Pietzsch, *A Eucaristia na Igreja Evangélica Luterana do Brasil à Luz das Origens do Culto Cristão* (São Leopoldo: Escola Superior de Teologia, Instituto Ecumênico de Pós-Graduacão, Dissertação de Mestrado, 2002) 89–107; and Frederico, *Cantos para o Culto Cristão*, 284, 290.

[20]Antônio G. Mendonça, Crise do Culto Protestante no Brasil, 171-204

[21]On this couple—the husband Scottish, the wife English—see Hahn, *História do Culto Protestante no Brasil*, 133–153, 311–312. Robert was a medical doctor and an ordained pastor; Sarah was a linguist,

poet, and musician and an enthusiast for Sunday schools. They worked as missionaries in Brazil in 1855–1876. See also Frederico, *Cantos para o Culto Cristão*, 280–281; Antônio Gouvêa Mendonça, *O Celeste Porvir: A inserção do protestantismo no Brasil*, Estudos e Debates Latino-Americanos, 10 (São Paulo: Paulinas, 1984) 185–186.

[22]See Hahn, *História do Culto Protestante no Brasil*, 312–323.

[23]See Hahn, *História do Culto Protestante no Brasil*, 123, 243–244, 324–331; also Simei Ferreira de Barros Monteiro, "Singing a New Song: Developing Methodist Worship in Latin America," in *The Sunday Service of the Methodists: Twentieth-Century Worship in Worldwide Methodism*, ed. Karen B. Westerfield Tucker (Nashville, Tenn.: Kingswood Books, 1996), esp. 265–270.

[24]See Hahn, *História do Culto Protestante no Brasil*, 331–333.

[25]See Frederico, *Cantos para o Culto Cristão*, 35, 283.

[26]Antônio Gouvêa Mendonça, "Crise de culto protestante no Brasil: Diagnóstico e alternativas," 194.

[27]Prócoro Velasques Filho, "Protestantismo no Brasil: Da teologia à liturgia," in *Introdução*, ed. Mendonça and Velasques, 145–170, here 155–157.

[28]Velasques, "Protestantismo," 155; and Frederico, *Cantos para o Culto Cristão*, 275.

[29]Velasques, "Protestantismo," 155–156; Mendonça, "Crise," 177–182; and Frederico, *Cantos para o Culto Cristão*, 275.

[30]Mendonça, "Crise," 175, 182–190.

[31]See Monteiro, "Singing a New Song," esp. 271–282.

[32]Mendonça, "Crise," 200ff.

[33]See Maucyr Gibin, *Liturgia para a América Latina: Documentos e estudos*, Igreja-Eucaristia, 5 (São Paulo: Paulinas, 1977) 5–6.

25

Mission and Inculturation: East Asia and the Pacific

ANSCAR J. CHUPUNGCO, O.S.B.

"Liturgical inculturation" refers to the process of inserting the texts and rites of the liturgy into the framework of the local culture as a result of which the texts and rites assimilate the people's thought, language, values, ritual, symbolic, and artistic pattern. In Asia this process is as complex as Asia itself, which is an amalgam of cultural traditions, religious affiliations, and political history, not to speak of thousands of languages across the continent and the adjacent islands. Although we can formulate principles of liturgical inculturation that are applicable to the churches in Asia, we admit that there are no fast rules, because of diversity not only in culture but also in the worship tradition and discipline of the churches themselves.

This chapter has two parts. The first deals with the principles of liturgical inculturation in the context of Asia and the difficulties they entail for the Christian churches. The second part gives some examples of inculturation in those parts of Asia where Christianity has been present for a long period of time and in one island country in the South Pacific.

Principles of Liturgical Inculturation

Christian liturgy and local culture are the protagonists of liturgical inculturation. This sounds obvious. However, the implications are not always obvious. History and recent experiences show that inculturation has brought about a diversity in the forms of worship and consequently a certain cultural-liturgical distancing among churches in various parts of the globe. More seriously, inculturation has diversified the shape of the liturgy not only among different confessional churches but also within the same church.

Unity in Diversity Through Inculturation

One of the many things that have bound together mainstream Christian churches is the liturgical culture they share despite their differences in some beliefs and discipline. In the West, for example, they still share the common layers of cultural tradition they inherited from Judaism, the Greco-Roman world, the Franco-Germanic people, and medieval Europe. When the great Reformers of the sixteenth century set out to correct the abuses that had crept into the medieval church, they did not abandon the cultural and liturgical heritage of the Western Church. Reformed ways of celebrating baptism and the Lord's supper were introduced, but many of the underlying cultural elements in these forms of worship remained. The prayer formulas continued to be hieratic in style, which is typical of Greco-Roman orations. In several churches the institutions and symbols originating from the Franco-Germanic era have been retained. A good number of the Jewish roots of the liturgy of the word, baptism, and the Lord's supper have remained intact.

The question that arises is this: if inculturation causes cultural expressions in the liturgy to become diversified according to the culture of the local church, will it not adversely affect the cultural unity that still binds the various Christian churches across confessional differences? When people speak of the liturgy of the Roman Catholic Church, the Anglican Communion, or the Protestant churches, they normally refer to those worship celebrations, however vaguely similar in form, that hold them together as Christian churches of the West. In the case of each of these churches, it has been the normal practice that the founding church from Europe or North America brought its liturgy, which is identifiably Western, to the daughter church in Asia. Thus both mother and daughter churches share the same cultural tradition in worship. But what happens when a daughter church in Asia inculturates the liturgy? Will unity with the mother church not become less evident?

The liturgy is an action of a particular ecclesial community living in a particular cultural milieu. In this sense the liturgy, like the community that celebrates it, is also a cultural reality. The language, rites, and symbols of Christian worship cannot be extricated from the culture of the people. It is not possible to celebrate the liturgy outside a cultural context or in a cultural vacuum. No church, after all, lives in a cultural vacuum. Liturgical history attests to the integration of cultural elements drawn from the different peoples with which the church came into contact in the course of several centuries. This explains the existence of different layers of culture in Christian worship.

Indian Last Supper. Painting by Angelo Da Fonseca. The representation of the Last Supper under dress styles and meal customs local to an artist is a hint towards inculturation, even when actual liturgical practice does not reach so far. PHOTOGRAPH COURTESY OF GEOFFREY WAINWRIGHT

The interplay between Christian worship and local culture raises a basic question. May everything and anything cultural, provided it is not diametrically opposed to the gospel message, be integrated into the liturgy? It has happened that in the name of liturgical inculturation some elements of culture with no relation to worship are simply juxtaposed with the liturgy. The liturgy has its own requirements that ultimately determine the limits of inculturation. Culture, on the other hand, has its own laws that should be respected in the process of integrating its elements into the liturgy.

Some Theological and Cultural Criteria

In light of the search for unity in diversity through inculturation, it is timely to review three important principles of liturgical inculturation in order to set the stage for the inculturation of the liturgy in Asia and the South Pacific. First, inculturation as a dialogue between liturgy and culture is marked by the spirit of respect for what is honest, beautiful, and noble in human culture. Early Christian writers such as Justin Martyr, Hippolytus of Rome, and Tertullian minced no words in condemning the moral decadence of the Greco-Roman world. However, they accepted the introduction of suitable cultural elements into church worship. Second, inculturation means that the cultural elements adopted by the church for liturgical use are properly integrated into the texts and rites of worship. Inculturation is not a juxtaposition of unintegrated elements; inculturation requires integration, not mere juxtaposition. When there is no integration, the uninitiated faithful even among the westernized sectors of Asia have great difficulty understanding those elements of the Christian liturgy that have been borrowed from the Jewish, Greco-Roman, Franco-Germanic, and late medieval European cultures. Third, inculturation fosters mutual enrichment. Culture is evangelized when it comes in contact with the gospel message that the church proclaims during worship. Evangelization results from the critique of culture made by the gospel, a critique that implies correction of defective values or perhaps the rejection of ideas and practices that by their nature are incompatible with the gospel message. Thus inculturation has a counter-cultural role: the eucharistic assembly stands as a critique, for instance, of the loss of family and community values in many societies today. In turn, however, Christian worship itself is enriched by the culture it embraces, as the liturgies of the Eastern and Western Churches attest. Churches have yet to discover the wealth of culture that the Asian continent is able to offer for the enrichment of their celebration of divine worship.

Two considerations will shed further light on the principles of liturgical inculturation. From a theological point of view we may regard inculturation as a consequence of the mystery of the Incarnation. The Incarnation of the Son of God is the paradigm or model of inculturation. Just as Christ became human in all things, save sin, and bound himself to the culture and traditions of his people, so the church has the mission to make the mystery of Christ's incarnation a continuing reality in our world. The Church accomplishes this by integrating suitable components of human culture into its preaching, worship, and works of service to humankind. The mystery of the incarnation refers to both head and body, that is, to Christ and the Church. The Church extends the mystery of Christ's incarnation in time and space when it "incarnates" itself among the nations. The incarnation of the Church means that, in imitation of Christ, it shares the history, culture, and traditions of its people. The measure in which the Church is "incarnated" is the measure in which Christ and his gospel are incarnated today in our world. Liturgical inculturation is the Church's most visible and effective means of prolonging in time and space the great mystery of the incarnation.

From an anthropological point of view we may regard liturgical inculturation as a dialogue between Christian worship and culture. While Christianity has successfully dialogued with the Western culture, it has hardly begun the dialogue with the civilizations of Asia. Dialogue between Christian worship and local culture is carried out in the context of the three components of culture, namely values, patterns, and institutions. These components should be closely examined by those who engage in the work of inculturation. Values are principles that influence and direct the life of a community. They form the community's basic behavior toward religious, political, and ethical realities. Some notable human values that dialogue with Christian worship are family or community spirit, leadership, and hospitality. These are values that are likewise found in liturgical celebrations. Cultural patterns, on the other hand, are the typical and hence predictable way members of a society form concepts, express themselves in language and arts, and celebrate various events of life together. Lastly, institutions are the traditional rites that families and communities celebrate to mark the passage of persons from birth to death. Initiatory rites, the rites of marriage and parenthood, and rites connected with sickness, death, and funerals fall under this category.

Limits

The Asian continent possesses ancient cultural traditions and is the home of great world religions. These enviable traits might lead some people to forget the limits of liturgical inculturation. What are these limits? First, inculturation is based on the living and received liturgical *ordo* of the Church. Its starting point is actual praxis or tradition. Inculturation does not and should not produce alternative liturgies that are not backed by tradition or praxis. The practical implication of this is that the work of inculturation should be preceded by a careful study of the Church's received tradition or its existing ordo.

Second, while what is good, beautiful, and noble in every culture should be respected, not everything found good in it should be integrated into the liturgy. Cultural elements should not only be beyond doctrinal or moral reproach, they should harmonize with the meaning and purpose of Christian worship. Furthermore the greatest care should be taken not to impose on the liturgy such cultural values, patterns, and institutions as will obscure the Church's received tradition and actual ordo. By "ordo" we mean the accepted components and pattern of celebrating a liturgical rite. Again, the cultural components must be integrated into Christian worship and not remain as alien bodies that have nothing to do with the liturgy.

Third, the Christian liturgy itself sets the limits to what may be integrated into it. There are principles that must be complied with in order to keep the meaning and purpose of Christian worship. One such principle is the central position of Christ in the liturgy as priest and mediator. Asians, like other people in the world, have mythical stories and legends in abundance. They are proud of their political history and yearly celebrate their nature festivals with abandon. There is much opportunity here for inculturation. The caution is that such elements should become part of Christian worship only after they have been purified and integrated, not merely juxtaposed, with the mystery of Christ. In short, the liturgy celebrates Christ in the context of the Asian people's culture, history, and traditions.

A second principle is that the liturgy is the assembly of the priestly people who respond in faith to God's gratuitous call. The liturgy should therefore mirror the universality of the Church, a universality that knows no barriers, no social division based on class, race, or nation. The liturgical assembly should project the value of hospitality; it should become a critique of sociocultural systems that deny human equality between men and women and the dignity of those who belong to the lower ranks of society. Asia has still some of the poorest nations in the world today, and Christian assemblies should be the paragon of socioeconomic equality.

A third principle is that the inculturation of the liturgy should not cause the fragmentation of the community. The aim of inculturation is to allow diversity of cultural expressions while preserving universal liturgical traditions. In this way mother churches will continue to be one with their daughter churches in the essentials of belief and worship, though different in how the essentials are culturally expressed. Lastly, the Holy Scripture should not be replaced by any other text, no matter how venerable it may be. The temptation to do so is felt strongly in India, which is in possession of sacred writings that are not canonically recognized by Christian churches. Nevertheless, it should be feasible to assimilate some of these sacred writings into the Christian liturgy by way of integrating their style and suitable content into prayer formulas and songs.

The Asian Experience of Inculturation

At the end of the twentieth century the total population of Asia was estimated at 3,563,000,000. China had the largest population of 1,275,000,000, while India had 1,000,000,000, followed by Indonesia and Bangladesh, which had 209,000,000 and 130,000,000 respectively. Japan ranks next with a population of 126,800,000. Of the three billion and a half Asians, there are only approximately 160,000,000 Christians. Oceania, a large group of islands in the South Pacific including Melanesia, Micronesia, and Polynesia, on the other hand, which had a total population of 29,155,000, counted as many as 23,000,000 Christians.

The disturbing question often raised is why the number of Christians is so small in the most populous continent of Asia. In the course of two thousand years Christianity has deeply penetrated Europe and the Americas and set itself up in much of Africa. Christians, however, remain a relatively small minority group in Asia, except in the Philippines, East Timor, and possibly in the next century also in South Korea. How do we explain this Asian phenomenon? One possible reason is this: when Christian missionaries came successively to Asia, the other great religions had already taken root in the continent. Hinduism, Buddhism, Shintoism, and Islam were firmly established among the peoples of India, China, Thailand, Japan, and Southeast Asia. Conversion from these religions, especially Islam and to a degree also Hinduism, was and still is a herculean task. Added to this is the perception in Asia—a perception that is, alas, based on political experience—that Christianity being a Western religion is an instrument of colonial domination. On the other hand, in the sixteenth century, when the Spanish missionaries arrived in the Philippines, the inhabitants of these over seven thousand islands were animists. The formation of the Philippine islands into a nation went hand in hand with the work of evangelization, following the formula adopted by the Conquistadors: the cross and the sword. The natives of the Philippines fought battles against them, but they did not have great difficulty embracing the Christian faith brought by the missionaries. In fact the majority remained faithful to the Roman Catholic faith even when they proclaimed independence from Spain and despite the presence of Christian fundamentalists in the last thirty years.

One of the recurring topics in the agenda of the Federation of Asian Catholic Bishops' Conferences and of the yearly meeting of the Southeast Asian Liturgy Forum is how to present Christianity and its worship as an Asian religion with an Asian identity. Asians realize that Christianity is Asian in origin, yet they find it difficult to identify with it because it has embraced Western thought and political structures. This is often the reason why native Christians are considered alien and their own families disown those who convert to Christianity. The problem thus boils down to the question of inculturation. Are Christians willing to integrate suitable Asian cultural and religious elements into their way of life and worship, without of course sacrificing their gospel and moral values? Can their form of worship be consonant with Asian traditions of worship in terms of language and rites? If such inculturation is possible, will Asian Muslims and Hindus not regard it with suspicion as attempts at backdoor proselytism? They disapprove the attempts of some Christians to assimilate the symbols (e.g., architecture for worship) and ritual language (e.g., "Allah") of other Asian religions. Lastly, will the Christians themselves not experience a sense of betrayal when their form of worship is no longer neatly distinguishable from the religious ceremonies they renounced at baptism? This in fact was the objection of Catholic Indians to the inculturated mass for India. In Thailand, on the other hand, Roman

Catholics feel uncomfortable with new Western practices such as hand clapping, hand raising, and loud music during liturgical celebration.

The answer to these questions will most likely depend on two things, namely the openness of the Christian churches to embrace Asian culture and religious patterns and their relationship with the predominant religion of the country. In the Asian continent inculturation is a very complex problem because we are dealing with ancient culture, deeply rooted religious traditions, and centuries of biases against the West. Principles and criteria of inculturation are not easy to formulate and much less apply to the multireligious situation of Asia. What is acceptable to Buddhists—who are, generally, more open to other religions and at times given to syncretism—might not be acceptable to Muslims. It also happens that totalitarian states take the initiative to impose local customs on Christians for the sake of nationalism and religious control. The government of China has established the patriotic society to monitor Christian churches. In this matter the Roman Catholic Church is probably at a greater disadvantage than several of the Protestant churches because of centralized government, numerous dogmatic definitions, and specific liturgical norms.

The following examples record how Christian worship, especially the Roman Catholic, has interacted with some of the great civilizations of Asia and with those of the South Pacific. The examples are limited to a few because of the unavailability of written materials from countries where the Christian religion is still a minority or inculturation is regarded with caution or even suspicion not only by church authorities but also by the faithful. The former case is exemplified by Japan, where the growth of Christianity is almost at a standstill. The latter case is verified in South Korea, one half of whose population is Christian, but where the Church is quite reluctant to engage in the project of liturgical inculturation. Nonetheless the examples given below should offer a reasonably clear picture of the Asian situation with respect to the question of liturgical inculturation.

India

According to the tradition of the Christians in Kerala, Saint Thomas the Apostle preached the gospel in South India toward the year 52, converted the high-caste Hindus, and established seven churches. They were named Thomas Christians. It is claimed that Saint Thomas introduced the use of rice for the celebration of the eucharist. Christianity thrived because of the pervading Buddhist principle of mutual religious respect and the similarity between the Christian and the native systems of family and social life. Christianity was admitted into the Hindu caste system and was considered one of the religions of the people. This era offers one model of inculturation in Asia.

In the fourth century, Christians from Persia migrated to India to escape persecutions by King Sapor II. They brought with them the traditions of their church and developed the Malabar rite, a form of the East Syrian liturgy with some Hindu practices, such as the use of the *thali*, a braided cord, in the marriage rite.

The arrival of the Portuguese missionaries in the sixteenth century was a turning point in the history of the Thomas Christians. To purge the Malabar rite of its "Nestorian" elements, the Catholic archbishop of Goa with the help of the Jesuit missionaries imposed Latin liturgical usages on the Thomas Christians. Only the Syriac language and the shape of the divine office were retained (in the 1960s Syriac was supplanted by Malayalam). Unleavened bread was prescribed and only communion under one species was allowed. The manuscripts of the ancient Malabar rite were destroyed to prevent their use, and "Nestorian" saints were removed from the calendar. The Thomas Christians who refused the Latinization of their liturgy placed themselves under the jurisdiction of the patriarch of the Syrian Orthodox church, adopting the West Syrian liturgy in the process. This liturgy is used both by the Syrian Orthodox and by the Malankara Roman Catholics.

In 1969 the Vatican approved for India the so-called "Twelve Points" concerning especially gestures and postures that might be used at mass in adaptation from Hindu forms of worship and social ceremonials.[1] After work in the All-India Liturgical Meetings and in the Episcopal Conference of India's Commission for Liturgy, in 1974 the National Biblical, Catechetical, and Liturgical Centre in Bangalore published two new Orders of Mass for India for careful experimental use. These drew inspiration from the Agamic tradition of temple worship with such elements as washing with water, offering of flowers and incense, the waving of light (*arati*) in front of the temple image, the gesture of prostration (*panchanga pranam*, which consists of touching the floor with the forehead), and the use of mantra. Based on the theology that the "seed of God's Word" is present in Indian scriptures, the Order of Mass included a reading from them. The main eucharistic prayer made allusion to the presence of divine revelation in the various religious traditions and communities on the subcontinent.

PLAN OF THE FIRST ORDER OF MASS

1. *Introductory Rite.* This consists of reception and welcome (washing of feet and hands before entering the church, imposition of sandal paste on the forehead, welcoming of the presider with the *arati*, and the greeting: "Fullness there, fullness here, from fullness fullness proceeds; once fullness has proceeded from fullness, fullness remains"); rite of purification (sprinkling with water, prostration by the celebrant, and sign of peace); and the lighting of the lamp (hymn to light, touching the flame with the tips of the fingers, and placing the fingers on one's eyes).

2. *Liturgy of the Word.* This includes the following elements: honoring of the sacred books with the *arati*; proclamation of four readings (the Indian Scripture, Old Testament, New Testament letter, and Gospel; the reading from the Indian Scripture is followed by the hymn: "From the unreal lead me to the real, from darkness lead me to light, from death lead me to immortality"); and the homily by the presider who holds the hands in the gesture of *upadesha mudra* (joining the tips of the forefinger and thumb of both hands in front of the breast with the left palm facing the heart and the right palm facing the assembly).

3. *Liturgy of the Eucharist.* This has the following parts: preparation of the gifts (gifts for the poor, bread and wine, eight flowers on a tray symbolizing eight attributes of Christ, and general intercessions); the eucharistic prayer (long and short forms ending with the Great Amen: "Amen. You are the Fullness of Reality, One without a second, Being, Knowledge, Bliss! Om, Tat, Sat!"); communion rite followed by a mantra and silence.

4. *Concluding Rite.* This includes some parting words and the blessing of the assembly by the presider who lifts right hand with palm toward the assembly and the left hand toward the ground.

At the Fourth All-India Liturgical Meeting in 1973 it had been decided to adopt a second form on an experimental basis for use in the Catholic Church in the whole of India including both the Latin and the Oriental rites. The underpinning theology is that of sacrifice, whose principal aim is to sustain the universe in integrity and fullness. Some of the significant elements of the rite follow:

PLAN OF THE SECOND ORDER OF MASS

1. *Preparation of the Altar.* An Indian lamp and flowers decorate the altar; the Bible and a crucifix are placed at the center of the altar; people face the East (for those who belong to

the Oriental tradition); and people bring to the altar the eucharistic gifts of bread and wine and other offerings.

2. *Interior Preparation*. This consists of the lighting of the Indian lamp (symbolic of Christ, the Eternal Priest and Mediator), act of repentance, and exchange of the sign of peace.

3. *Liturgy of the Word*. The presider blesses the assembly with the Bible in the form of a cross, incenses it, and touches it with his forehead.

4. *Eucharistic Prayer*. At the end of the eucharistic prayer the presider raises the bread and wine, while triple *arati* with lamp, incense, and flowers is performed. The assembly sings a hymn.

5. *Final Blessing*. After receiving the blessing the assembly chants: "Now and for ever. Om! We adore you, the Uncreated Being! Om! We adore you, the God-Man. Om! We adore you, the Holy Spirit! Om! Shanti! Shanti! Shanti!" The song is meant to produce inner peace, which is the result of worship.

In 1975 a letter from the cardinal prefect of the Roman Congregation for Divine Worship "called a stop to unauthorized experimentation and liberties," citing especially "the use of the Indian Anaphora and the use of Non-Biblical Scriptures in the liturgy."[2] The "Twelve Points of Liturgical Adaptation," however, were never revoked, and they are still practiced on special occasions.

China

The Buddhist and Confucian traditions of the Chinese would have made them sympathetic toward Christianity. But the Roman Catholic Church's doctrinal stand on ancestral veneration and the animosity among the religious orders that worked in China obstructed evangelization. It can be said that the Church's mission in China received a traumatic blow from the Chinese rites controversy that raged for over a hundred years.[3] The controversy, which was connected with worship, started after the death in 1610 of the Jesuit missionary Matteo Ricci and was not resolved until 1742. The controversy involved three religious orders in China: the Dominicans and Franciscans, on the one hand, and the Jesuits, on the other. Five popes intervened: Innocent X, Alexander VII, Clement IX, Clement XI, and Benedict XIV. The controversy was marked by two features. The first revolved around the Jesuit missionaries' use of Chinese words to express Christian belief. The second comprised the permission they granted to their converts to perform, with certain restrictions, the Chinese rites in honor of Confucius and their ancestors. Unlike the missionaries in the Philippines who simply foisted Spanish words, like *Dios*, *gracia*, *santo*, *sacramento*, *bautismo*, *santa Misa*, and *iglesia* on the natives, the Jesuits sought Chinese words that approximated Christian concepts such as God and heaven. But the major issue in the controversy concerned the ancestral rites that the Chinese considered an essential element of their culture. There were two types. The first was in honor of the ancestors. The rite expressed filial devotion, a virtue that every Chinese valued above all else. To wooden tablets bearing the ancestors' names the Chinese directed gestures of reverence and offered food, flowers, and incense. The rite was similar to the ancient Roman festival of *cara cognatio* and reflected the early Christian practice of *refrigerium*. [*Cara cognatio* was a family banquet held in conclusion of the *parentalia* (the annual commemoration of the deceased ancestors marked by decorating a chair or *cathedra* in honor of the dead). It was a pagan feast celebrated on February 22 and was the origin of the Christian feast of the Chair of Saint Peter (and Saint Paul) who was regarded by the Christians of Rome as one such ancestor. *Refrigerium* was a funerary meal, a banquet celebrated in memory of the deceased especially on the anniversary of their death.

Baptism in China.
Baptism on Christmas Day 1946 by Alfred Bosshardt in the river at Chang-Sao, China. Bosshardt, a Swiss evangelical free-church missionary, who had been taken prisoner in the Long March in 1934–1935.
PRIVATE COLLECTION/ BRIDGEMAN ART LIBRARY

It was also of pagan origin but the early Christians remained attached to the practice. They held *refrigeria* on the death anniversary of the martyrs.] Unfortunately the Franciscans and Dominicans must have forgotten these historical data. The other rite was in honor of Confucius. To the Great Teacher ordinary Chinese directed a rite similar to that of the ancestors, but the philosophers performed a solemn rite that displayed, according to the Dominican missionaries, traces of idolatry. This type of Confucian rite the Jesuits actually forbade.

Likewise the Jesuits forbade direct petitions to the ancestors and the burning of paper money as part of ancestral veneration. Furthermore they instructed their converts to reject the belief that the ancestral spirits resided in the tablets and drew sustenance from food offerings. The Jesuits also made adaptations in the ancestral tablets by inserting the sign of the cross with the words: "Worship the true Lord, Creator of heaven, earth, and all things, and show filial piety to ancestors and parents." Missionaries from Manila, who saw the converts perform the ancestral rites, denounced the Jesuits for this act of idolatry. The Roman decision on toleration or outright prohibition depended on who was pope. Thus in 1659 the Roman Congregation Propaganda Fide wrote to the vicars apostolic to China about the absurdity of implanting France, Spain, Italy, or any part of Europe in China: "Rather, bring the faith, which does not repudiate nor destroy the rites and customs of any nation, provided they are not perverse, but rather keeps them whole and intact." Unfortunately the significance of this letter was lost at the height of the controversy until 1939 when Pope Pius XII through Propaganda Fide permitted the Chinese Christians to take active part in the ancestral rites, provided these were regarded as mere social conventions devoid of any cultic significance. The permission, however, came too late, for soon China fell to communist rule.

Perhaps it is correct to say that the difficulty the Chinese had with embracing Christianity stemmed from the prohibition of ancestral rites. Chinese converts could not easily be persuaded to abandon the rites that they considered the bedrock of their civilization. This was probably a case where inculturation could have mattered in the Church's mission of rooting the gospel in Asia. Nevertheless it is not out of place to muse whether the Chinese would in fact have accepted Christianity had the ancestral worship been allowed, and whether Christian worship would have been subjected to syncretism.

The Philippines

According to the census of the year 2000 the Philippines had a total population of 75,800,000. Roman Catholics formed 84 percent of the population. Other Christians comprised ten percent, while Muslims made up five percent and other religions one percent. Filipinos have been described as a people who lived for 377 years in the Spanish convent and for 43 years in American Hollywood. The independence of Mexico from Spain in 1821 and the propagation of the ideals of the French Revolution gave birth to Filipino nationalism that led to Philippine independence from Spain (though under U.S. rule) in 1898. The last years of the nineteenth century marked the transition from Spanish to American rule. It is amazing that the cultural and religious effects of Spanish colonization did not vanish with the arrival of the Americans.

The global political turmoil of the nineteenth century and the social discontent with the Spanish rulers and friars did not cause the Filipinos to abandon the Catholic faith and religious practices. Swept by the tide of nationalism, the priest Gregorio Aglipay proclaimed in 1902 a church independent from Rome. This church was the first to celebrate the liturgy in the vernacular for fuller participation of the assembly. Later on, the arrival of American Protestants, many of whom were schoolteachers called Thomasites, helped to set the stage for the Filipino Catholics to welcome the use of the vernacular in the mass.

Until the early twentieth century the Catholic faithful attended Sunday mass in traditional Latin. But as written records show, the heat and the length of the celebration made the faithful restless and even caused them to fall asleep. More attractive to them were the processions with sacred images held around the town after the solemn mass on feasts of their patron saints. The mass was celebrated in the style of the baroque period, with choir and orchestra on special feasts and the ringing of church bells at the consecration. Holy communion by the faithful was infrequent, if not totally absent. The focus of the mass was the elevation of the consecrated species when the church bells were rung, the Spanish anthem was played outside the church, and firecrackers sounded. By tradition dating from the sixteenth century, the sermon was in the vernacular because it was meant to be moralizing and catechetical. Men usually left the church during the homily that was probably intended for them and returned for the consecration. The Sunday assembly was sometimes described as the church of women and children. Many left before the rite of holy communion.

The Liturgical Movement that started among Catholics in Belgium in 1909 reached the Philippine shores through the European missionaries. By the late 1950s translations of liturgical prayers and readings for the use of the faithful existed in some of the vernacular languages. But active participation in responses and songs and the lay liturgical ministry of adult men and women did not come about until after the reforms of Vatican II. The great majority of Filipino Catholics accepted the changes coming from Rome, even if it took the older ones some time to break with their devotional practices during the mass, such as praying the rosary or reciting novenas in honor of saints. The shift to the vernacular was welcomed, the altar facing the people became a normal sight, and the assembly sang the mass without difficulty.

The liturgical euphoria brought by Vatican II's liturgical reform expressed itself in the celebration of experimental masses, especially in schools, religious houses, and seminaries. However, parish masses on Sunday usually observed the published norms. In line with contextualization—which is an arm of inculturation—nonbiblical readings were used during mass in the 1970s and popular songs having no connection with the liturgy were sung as entrance, offertory, and communion songs. This situation improved with the popularization of songs for mass based on Filipino colonial music and the introduction of more liturgical songs in English from the United States. Desire to inculturate made some priests daring: in the late 1960s and early 1970s a few introduced native foodstuff and drink (bread and wine were considered foreign). During the same decade, under the rule of martial law, student masses were politically oriented: antigovernment slogans, protest gestures, and red banners became part of the sacred rite.

There are two major attempts at liturgical inculturation in the Philippines on the part of Roman Catholics, namely the Order of Mass, which was completed in 1975, and the marriage rite, which was approved by Rome in 1983. The outline of both rites is presented here for reference.

The Mass of the Filipino People

1. *Entrance Rite.* This follows the Roman rite, consisting of procession to the sanctuary, penitential rite or sprinkling of holy water, Gloria, and the opening prayer. Two ritual elements have been incorporated here, namely the veneration of the cross and the sign of peace.
2. *Proclamation of God's Word.* This consists of the usual three biblical readings (Old Testament, epistle, gospel), responsorial psalm, gospel acclamation, homily, and general intercessions. Two new elements have been added: the veneration of the Book of Gospels at the beginning of the Liturgy of the Word and the blessing of the readers.
3. *Celebration of the Lord's Supper.* This includes the offertory procession, the eucharistic prayer (in long and short forms), and the communion rite. A dialogue between the offerers and the presider stresses the value of generosity. To heighten the solemnity of the eucharistic prayer, altar candles are lighted and the church bells are rung before the prayer is said.
4. *Concluding Rite.* The short rite of dismissal is elaborated with new elements: parting words of the presider, blessing with the cross, and veneration of the cross.

A number of liturgical criteria guided the formation of the Filipino Order of Mass. First, the texts, where appropriate, must clearly express the Church's doctrine on the mass as sacrament of Christ's sacrifice on the cross and make reference to the Last Supper. Second, the texts and rites should project Filipino values, idioms, proverbs, and images drawn from the experience of the people. Third, without forgetting the needs of the universal Church, the texts should include such local concerns as social justice, peace and development, and lay leadership. Fourth, when proclaimed, the texts of the prayers should be clear, dignified, and prayerful. Fifth, there should be several occasions during mass when the assembly can participate actively and prayerfully through postures, gestures, songs, and responses. Lastly, an atmosphere of prayer and reverence should be encouraged amidst the Filipino pattern of festive or baroque-like celebration.

The use of the cross is peculiar to the Filipino mass. At the start and end of the mass people are blessed with a large cross, which is afterward venerated with a song of praise. The veneration of the cross stems from Filipino Catholics' great devotion to the cross. They venerate crucifixes at home or carry them around. Indeed they make the sign of the cross at every significant moment of their day to ask for divine guidance, blessing, or protection. The veneration of the cross is a distinct Filipino way of calling attention to the doctrine that the mass is the sacrament of Christ's sacrifice on the Cross.

As the liturgy of the word begins, the gospel book is raised for the veneration of the assembly, which acclaims the Word with a song in praise of God, whose word reveals his will and teaching and guides the people on the path of life. The readers make the gesture of *mano po* to the presider and receive his blessing. *Mano po* is performed by placing the right hand of the elder person on one's forehead. It is the gesture whereby Filipinos ask for the elder's blessing before they perform a special task or it is simply a sign of respect. At the general intercessions the people kneel. Standing is the traditional Roman posture for the general intercessions. Filipinos, however, associate kneeling with urgent petitions.

A Filipino cultural tradition, which is quite transcultural in Asia, has found a worthy place in the Filipino mass. It is a canon of Filipino hospitality that the head of the family or the host eats last, that is, after serving or entertaining the guests. Parents feed their children before they themselves partake of food. In the Filipino mass the presider receives holy communion after distributing it to the assembly. It expresses the Filipino values of leadership, hospitality, and parental concern. Incorporated into the mass, this practice alludes to the saying of Christ that the first should be the last and the servant of all (Matt. 20:26–28).

As regards the language used in the Filipino mass, much effort was made, including several consultations with the National Commission on Filipino Language and with Tagalog experts, in order to ensure that the texts, when proclaimed or sung, are clear, dignified, and prayerful. To foster the solemnity of the eucharistic celebration, the composers of the texts adopted the type of Tagalog that is slightly poetic and often observes terminal as well as internal rhyme. In solemn speeches Filipinos have a predilection for sentences that rhyme. Likewise they value rhythmic cadence and the use of idiomatic speech. The committee that worked on the texts of the Filipino mass paid careful attention to these linguistic preferences of Tagalog speakers. On several occasions the Filipino mass employs words and phrases that express Filipino values. For example, at the penitential rite the Filipino attitude that combines humility, unworthiness, and embarrassment is integrated into the text recited by the assembly. At collection time the presider reminds the assembly of the popular proverb: "God blesses those who give with open hands," that is, generously.

THE FILIPINO RITE OF MARRIAGE

1. *Presentation of the Couple by the Parents.* After the homily the parents or guardians present the couple to the assembly to ask for their acceptance into the Christian community as a married couple.

2. *Marriage Covenant.* This consists of the scrutiny, exchange of consent, prayer recited by the couple, and the act of witnessing on the part of the godparents and the presiding minister.

3. *Blessing of Arrhae and Rings.* After the giving of the *arrhae* (usually coins to symbolize mutual support) and rings, the newly married couple kiss, while the assembly applauds. The nuptial blessing is recited after the Lord's prayer.

4. *Imposition of the Veil and the Cord.* This rite, which is borrowed from the marriage rite of Toledo, Spain, is done after the offertory procession. A white veil is placed on the head of the bride and around the shoulder of the groom. A white cord in the form of the number eight is placed over the veil. [For the Mozarabic marriage rite, see the sidebar in Chapter 5 of this book.]

The Vatican approved this inculturated form of marriage rite in 1983 for the use of the Tagalog-speaking faithful. It was composed in response to a popular request that

Christian wedding, Manila, Philippines.
Photograph by Peter Teanor/Art Directors and
TRIP

the celebration of church marriage be enriched with
meaningful texts and symbols. To do this the composers of the rite integrated into it pertinent Filipino cultural patterns, symbols, and linguistic
expressions connected with marriage. Even during
the Second Vatican Council bishops complained
that the church ceremony of marriage was too sober, too legalistic, and too short (it was over in five
minutes) to convey the Christian doctrine on marriage. Indeed the Roman rite did not capture this
romantic and memorable event in the life of couple.

The Filipino marriage rite underlines the role
of parents in the life of their sons and daughters.
Parents present the couple to the assembled community at the start of the marriage celebration.
Below is an English translation of the Tagalog text:

> Brothers and sisters,
> we are pleased to present to you N. and N.
> Receive them into our community
> as a married couple
> now and always.

The rite employs elegant, romantic, and poetic language that is adopted from the
treasury of popular proverbs and idioms on marriage. For example, the formula for
the exchange of consent incorporates the Filipino maxim that the spouse is the extension of one's life:

> N., before God and the people
> I enter into covenant with you as my wife (husband).
> You alone shall I love and regard
> as the extension of my life
> now and always.

At the exchange of rings the newly married couple promise fidelity to each other.
The Tagalog text, with its startling opening line, is an attempt to give dramatic impact to the sobriety of the Roman formulary:

> N., I shall never betray you.
> Wear this ring
> as a pledge of my love and fidelity.

While the bridegroom gives the *arrhae* to his bride, he recites these endearing
words:

> N., I shall never forsake you.
> I entrust to you these *arrhae*
> as a sign that I value your well-being
> and that of our offspring.

Liturgy and Filipino Popular Religiosity

Liturgical inculturation in the Philippines would be unthinkable without reference to popular religiosity or extra-liturgical devotions. In some sense, popular religiosity can be considered the bedrock of Filipino Catholicism. Perhaps there is truth to such claim. At a time when the official liturgy of the Roman Church was far removed from the culture of the people, their faith was often sustained by popular piety. Because of the Filipino Catholics' attachment to their processions, sacred images, and devotions to saints, fundamentalist groups do not easily make headway in conversion. In some instances Filipino popular religiosity has influenced the liturgy, become part of it, and offered to it materials for inculturation.

The following manifestations of popular religiosity merit special attention because they are widespread inside and outside the country wherever Filipinos form large groups. These are *Simbang Gabi*, *Panuluyan*, and *Encuentro*. All three are Filipino forms of Marian devotion, and do justice to the Filipino claim of being a Marian people.

In the Philippines Christmas starts on 16 December with the novena masses called *Simbang Gabi*. It is also called, in Spanish, *Misa de Gallo*, because it is celebrated at early dawn or at cockcrow. We are told that the Spanish missionaries kept this early schedule in order not to delay the farmers' work in the fields. Some also call it *Misa de Aguinaldo* to evoke the spirit of gift giving at Christmas time. For nine consecutive dawns before the feast of the Nativity itself, the faithful throughout the country flock to the churches in a festive mood. The mass itself is anything but sober, as one would normally expect during the season of Advent. The Gloria, which is omitted from the Roman Advent liturgy, is sung daily, white vestments are used, flowers decorate the sanctuary, and musical instruments are played. Church bells are rung festively before mass begins and in some places a band of musicians goes around town.

Panuluyan is a street drama held on the evening of 24 December before midnight mass. Performed in the manner of a street procession, it dramatizes Mary and Joseph's search for an inn at Bethlehem. The images of Mary and Joseph, the same that will

Black Nazarene, Manila, Philippines. The Black Nazarene is a statue of Christ carrying his Cross, so called because of the color of the image which was brought from Mexico by the Augustinian Recollects some 150 years ago. It is venerated by devotees every Friday. Thousands attend the procession on Good Friday and 9 January (the day when the image was transferred from the Recollects to the parish church of Quiapo in the heart of Manila). Devotees include men and women from all walks of life, but especially from the poorer sectors of Philippine society, attracted to it because of the image of suffering. Many join the procession as an act of petition or thanksgiving for answered prayers. Together with the Child Jesus (Santo Niño), the Black Nazarene is the most popular devotion of Filipinos to Christ. PHOTOGRAPH BY PETER TREANOR/ART DIRECTORS AND TRIP

be placed in the church's crib, are carried in procession in front of designated houses. The group carrying the images sings verses expressing the couple's request for hospitality. In rude manner they are told to search elsewhere. The procession ends in church in time for the midnight mass. This Marian piety gives strong accent to the value of hospitality that every Filipino cherishes. It warns people that the stranger looking for assistance could be none other than Mary herself.

Holy Week in the Philippines is a happy combination of liturgical celebrations and popular religious practices. Religious processions are held along streets on Wednesday and Good Friday after church service. The images borne on decorated carriages are personages of the passion: the apostle Peter with the rooster, Veronica, Mary Magdalene, the apostle John, Christ being flagellated, the *Ecce homo* (a depiction of Jesus wearing the crown of thorns), the crucified Christ, and the *Santo entierro* or entombment of Christ (on Good Friday), and finally the Blessed Virgin, the *Mater dolorosa*. The images can include other personages or scenes, and the number of carriages can vary from seven to about a hundred. Some carriages may represent the whole scene of the Last Supper (Christ, the apostles, and the women in waiting). But the central image is always that of the sorrowful mother clad in mourning. As the carriage passes, people make the sign of the cross or genuflect in veneration. As they march before Mary's image, devotees recite the rosary and sing hymns.

Encuentro is the apogee of Marian piety in the Philippines. It is a form of popular devotion that can be described as both procession and drama. It is held at early dawn on Easter Sunday to commemorate the meeting between Mary and her risen son. There are two sets of procession that meet at the town square: one is of women accompanying the image of Mary totally veiled in black, and the other of men carrying the image of the risen Christ. On an elevated stage the two images are placed facing each other. A little girl dressed like an angel is slowly lowered from the roof of the canopy, while she sings in Latin the *Regina caeli*. Upon reaching the image of Mary, the girl gradually unveils it. Then by some mechanism the two images are made to bow to each other as a sign of greeting. In some places a young girl, carrying a white banner, dances in front of the images and recites or sings verses of Easter greeting to Mary. The images are then carried in procession to the church for the Easter dawn mass. No Easter celebration in parishes is complete without the *encuentro*. In 1971 the Vatican allowed this dramatic representation to replace the entrance rite of the mass. This is a rare case when a popular religious practice becomes part of the Roman liturgy.

The South Pacific

The population of the island republic of Western Samoa is divided equally between Presbyterians and Roman Catholics. Sunday is strictly observed by both and almost in the same manner. Sunday service is held in the morning. Presbyterians and Roman Catholics don their white native dress (*lava-lava*). They carry their personal Bibles to church as part of the Sunday apparatus. After the service, families share a festive meal where the traditional drink called *kava* is served, especially when there are guests. Because of the discipline of Sunday rest, families cook the food for Sunday on Saturday. Shops are closed for the day, and it is unusual for people to stay out of their homes, except for the services in church. In the evening they return to church for another worship service.

Baptism in the Solomon Islands. Baptism in the Anglican Church of the Province of Melanesia at Honiara, Solomon Islands, November 1999. PHOTOGRAPH BY PETER WILLIAMS

Inculturation is generally confined to the external aspects of the liturgy. Worship presiders wear the traditional *lava-lava*. Flower garlands are used to honor special persons. Vessels for the eucharist are of local inspiration. Liturgical songs are patterned after native melodies and accompanied by native musical instruments. On solemn occasions the Roman Catholics decorate the altar with a lei of flowers to honor the consecrated species. Although these examples are on the external side, they create an atmosphere suitable for the celebration of the local church. They are a good starting point for a more profound type of inculturation, which involves liturgical texts.

Conclusion

Liturgical inculturation in Asia and the adjacent islands is not an entirely new project. Thomas the Apostle, as held by tradition, introduced rice for the eucharist. The Spanish friars in the Philippines translated the Lord's prayer in Tagalog, substituting for bread a word that suggests rice. The Jesuits, who understood the role of ancestors in the life of the Chinese, permitted the rite of ancestral veneration.

Yet despite all the efforts of churches to evangelize Asia, Christianity is like a mere drop of water in the ocean. This essay has discussed some of the possible reasons that explain the phenomenon. Reasons range from attachment to native culture and religion to the Asian bias against the West with which Christianity is, for good or ill, identified. With the advent of globalization perhaps attitudes will change.

Churches in Asia will likely continue to take the challenge of inculturating their forms of worship. A number of churches have responded to the challenge. Liturgical inculturation aims to present a Christ and a church that have Asian identity. It is an effective means of extending in time and space the great mystery of the incarnation of Christ, the Son of God.

Bibliography

Chupungco, Anscar. "Liturgical Inculturation and the Search for Unity." In *So We Believe, So We Pray: Towards Koinonia in Worship*, edited by Thomas F. Best and Dagmar Heller, 55–64. Geneva: WCC Publications, 1995.

Chupungco, Anscar. "Liturgy and Inculturation." In *Handbook for Liturgical Studies*, edited by Anscar Chupungco, vol. 2, 337–375. Collegeville, Minn., Liturgical Press, 1998.

Eilers, F.-J. *For All the People of Asia*. Vol. 2. Quezon City, The Philippines: Federation of Asian Bishops' Conferences, 1997.

Federation of Asian Bishops' Conferences. *Asian Worship in Spirit and Truth*. Madras, India: 1995.

National Biblical, Catechetical, and Liturgical Centre. *New Orders of the Mass for India*. Bangalore, India: 1974.

Paul VI Institute of Liturgy. *Supplement to the Roman Sacramentary*. Pasay City, The Philippines: 1999.

Pastoral Institute of Korea. *Process and Perspectives of the Asian Church's Inculturation*. Seoul: 2000.

Rosales, G., and C. Arevalo, eds. *For All the Peoples of Asia*. Vol. 1. Quezon City, The Philippines: Federation of Asian Bishops' Conferences, 1997.

Notes

[1] See J. A. G. Gerwin van Leeuwen, *Fully Indian— Authentically Christian: A Study of the First Fifteen Years of the NBCLC (1967–1982), Bangalore, India, in the Light of the Theology of Its Founder, D. S. Amalorparadass* (Kampen: Kok, 1990) 95–96.

[2] van Leeuwen, 79–80. In the eucharistic prayer, the "cosmic covenant with all men" was applied to the Indian context through successive allusions to animistic religions (with their worship of God as power present in nature), Hindu religion (with its three paths to salvation: *karma, jnana, bhakti*), Buddhism and Jainism together, and finally Islam:

> God of the nations,
> You are the desire and hope
> of all who search for you with a sincere heart.

You are the power almighty
adored as Presence hidden in nature.
You reveal yourself
to the seers in their quest for knowledge,
to the devout who seek you through sacrifice
and detachment,
to every man approaching you by the path of
love.
You enlighten the hearts that long for release
by conquest of desire and universal kindness.
You show mercy to those who submit
to your inscrutable decrees.

[3] See François Bontinck, *La lutte autour de la liturgie chinoise aux XVIIe et XVIIIe siècles* (Louvain: Nauwelaerts, 1962).

26

Mission and Inculturation: Africa

NWAKA CHRIS EGBULEM

A Foreign or Authentic African Church?

During my childhood in a small West African village, my earliest notion of the Church and its celebrations was woven around the missionary pastor who ministered there. An Irish Catholic priest, he spoke English, celebrated in Latin, owned a car, and ate eggs for breakfast. Although we considered him kind and hard-working, he did not seem to like African drums and definitely could not keep rhythm. He dressed differently from us and used every opportunity to condemn the village masquerades. When he preached, the village catechist attempted interpretation. When he presided at the eucharist, he turned his back to the people and then bowed again and again—a gesture that was considered an insult to the villagers, who were accustomed to bow low for dogs to clean them up after they had relieved themselves in the forest. The priest would pour some wine in a cup and, in front of everyone, dilute it with water. That, according to some elders, was not a good habit either. Worse still, when the time came, the priest drank the wine all alone, neither sharing with the elders present nor pouring libations to the ancestors. That pastor seemed to have his own set of values; he left no room for anyone to question him, not even the local chief and elders. I was initiated into the Christian faith by such missionariess, and later taught in seminary school by several of them. As my childhood innocence expired, I continued to admire the zeal of these people who came from far away to share the Gospel, while at the same time questioning the methods their mission employed. Would this missionary pastor in my village bow with his back to the people if he knew how they interpreted it? Catholic missionary theology during those years did not have much room for dialogue and did not give much respect to the wisdom of traditional peoples.

Much has changed since those early years in the village, and yet much remains the same in how the Christian faith is lived there. Both the great efforts and the omissions made by missionaries and by Africans attempting to generate authentic Christian worship in Africa must be acknowledged. Identifying traditional African values lays a solid ground for constructive engagement in the process of liturgical inculturation. It must also be asked why the inculturation movement in Africa, especially in the institutional missionary churches, has been dwarfed by concerns unrelated to Africa's religious wellbeing and progress.

SOCIÉTÉ FRANÇAISE POUR L'ABOLITION DE L'ESCLAVAGE.

Vigneron, Del. & Lith.   Lith. de A. Jourdan.

M.ʳ L'ABBÉ MOUSSA DU SÉNÉGAL (A.D.)

Officiant à l'Autel portatif qui lui a été donné pour ses Missions

PAR S.M. MARIE AMÉLIE REINE DES FRANÇAIS.

An African priest in Latin vestments. The abbé Moussa saying mass at a portable altar in Senegal, c. 1840. Lithograph by Pierre Roch Vigneron (1789–1872). Bibliothèque des Arts Décoratifs, Paris/Archives Charmet/Bridgeman Art Library

In Celebration of African Shrines

To appreciate the impact of Christian presence on traditional African life, one must begin by recalling what traditional African life was like, particularly the ritual life of the people. Even today there exist family and village shrines. My grandfather's shrine, right outside his home, was a place for constant prayers and offerings, libations and commendations, a place where the living embraced the ancestors and sought to maintain communion with them. The elders did not drink wine without first pouring some to the ancestors; they also shared their food with them. In return, the ancestors kept watch over their own people and were said to become reincarnated regularly in newborn babies of their families. The birth of a baby called for village celebrations, for an ancestor was said to have come back to life. The naming ceremony soon followed, and the umbilical cord was ceremonially buried, often at the foot of a palm tree, signifying that the child had claimed membership in the family and would begin to share in its riches. There were various rites of passage through life (adulthood, marriage), and finally the passage into eternity with the ancestors. Traditional marriage was celebrated over many months and sometimes years. All of life was regularly punctuated with celebrations and festivities. Even death became a ceremonial event, especially that of an elder. In some African cultures, such as the Igbo of Nigeria, an elder's funeral extended for months and was repeated in several consecutive years.

Apart from celebrations that reflect the rhythms of human life, there are also sacred moments that Africans regularly celebrate. The new moon, the beginning of planting season, the harvest season, and the new yam festival are a few of the many reasons people celebrate in the course of the year.

What are the pillars of African life that should have some form of expression in liturgical celebration? In the years following independence in many sub-Saharan African countries, there was a continental movement toward "authenticity." Theologians and liturgists were not the only ones eager to get back to their true African roots in order to see how to enrich the Church with Africa's blessings; social scientists and ethnologists also inquired into the once-forsaken values of traditional African life.[1] The results of their inquiries would motivate theologians in Africa, and the consequent reawakening of these experts to their duty helped to instill new courage and strength in embracing authentic African values. By the early 1970s, it was already an accepted position in Africa that for any liturgy to be called African, it ought to reflect in a visible way its sensitivity to traditional African values.[2]

There are eight value themes to be discussed briefly. The first is the African notion of *the active presence of the Creator God in the world*. African spirituality gives a most prominent place to the Creator. This God is father and mother. God is present, alive, active, and remains in direct communication and collaboration with creation. Although here with us, God is higher than we are. God is the beginning without an end. All that exists has its origin and meaning in God and will terminate in God. In a special way, African spirituality sees the glory of God made manifest in humanity. Across the middle-belt region of Africa, names given at traditional naming ceremonies ordinarily have spiritual references to God or other religious connotations.

Second is the African *unified sense of reality*. For the African, divinity and humanity are not seen apart. The sacred and the so-called profane interact, and just as body is united to soul, divinity is indwelling in our world. The visible and the invisible worlds interpenetrate. All the beings in the universe and beyond exercise influence over one another. The world of the spirits participates in the human world. Spiritual needs are as important to the body as bodily needs are to the soul. All are part of human experience, just as life and death are. The human body is like a capsule, an integral whole, incorporating blood, water, fire, air, soil, and all other symbols of life. In short, dualism has little or no place in African thought.

Third is the African notion of *life as the ultimate gift*. African spirituality identifies life as the prime act of donation from Creator to creature. On the human plane, life is the starting point. It is to be received, sustained, enhanced, and safeguarded. Life at all levels is sacred. It is for this reason that marriage and procreation play central roles in the social and religious rites of African peoples, as do rituals of initiation. Between birth and death, rituals of healing occupy an important place as efforts to regenerate and sustain life when threatened by illness or a hostile environment. Traditional African healers occupy a prominent place in the life of the village. Through the power of the spoken word, incantations, divinations, prayers, sacrifices, and offerings, and the use of roots, herbs, and other natural substances, the healing ministry continues to be promoted in traditional African life.

Fourth is the concept of *the family and community as the place to be born, live, and die*. African spirituality discerns a vital link between a person and the members of his or her family, clan, or community. Being born into a family plunges one into a kind of current, and it is one's ability to be identified within that family and community that will determine one's nature of existence and survival. The life of the individual is therefore lived in participation with others in the community. This is true for both men and women. The kinship system, which reinforces the traditional notion of the extended family, is what has kept the predominant African family structure alive today. The African is incomplete when alone. The unique African style of hospitality remains a big attraction today, especially to foreigners; it must be seen from the point of view of its origin in the system of the extended family and community. This too translates into the moral order, in the strict demand for the practice of social justice, and in the promotion of life and the wellbeing of others.

Fifth is the African concept of *the nature and role of ancestors*. The African world actively extends beyond the visible world. The ancestors, sometimes called "the living dead," are those members of the family or community whose lives left a great heritage and honor to the living, and who continue to influence their families through their legacy. Their memory is invoked in various ceremonies and rituals. They are called on as intermediaries between God and the people, in continuation of their earthly function combining heading their families with ritual leadership. This is the context in which special respect and place are accorded to old people. The elderly are believed to be in special communion with ancestors, both by the fact of their having lived and worked for such a long time under the inspiration of the ancestors, and by the fact of their proximity to joining their company. Old age is usually associated with wisdom, dignity, and respect.

Sixth is the place of *oral tradition* in African life. African spirituality accords a great potency to the spoken word, for three reasons. First, the spoken word derives from the divine presence in the world. The sounds of nature (thunder and lightening, for example) are ways in which God's voice is actualized. Second, the spoken word proceeds immediately from the most privileged part of creation: the human person. Words used to bless or to curse are believed to possess effective power. Third, the word is not just sound; it names, identifies, and describes a subject. It is what makes history real. The word in African thought encompasses the entire system of communication. This is what is generally referred to as oral tradition in African life, which includes communication in music, song, dance, poetry, proverbs, storytelling, and rituals.

Seventh is the African notion of *the sanctity of nature and environment*. Africans see the presence of the divine in creation. The environment is like the writing board of the Creator. The moon and the stars, rivers and seas, hills and mountains, fish and animals, human beings: all carry the message of God's presence. Created nature and the human environment (visible and invisible) bear the mark of goodness and godliness. This is the first premise in the African notion of the environment. It is for this reason that human activities are generally considered from the religious point of view. All space is sacred. Although there may be designated locations for worship and sacrifices, the one who is on the way to worship is considered as already in the act of worship. The fruits of the earth coming from the labor of men and women are seen as worthy elements for offerings and sacrifices to God. In this context, we must also note the importance placed on the land itself. The land that we stand on is a prime inheritance and has much to do with wealth and happiness; on it, homes will be built and farms will be cultivated. Ownership of land in one way or another thus becomes an important aspect of belonging to the community.

Eighth is Africa's notion of *time*. What is important is ritual time, not clock time. Although people have come to regulate activities with the aid of the movement of the sun, the moon and stars, or the cock crowing, events tend to follow a rhythm of their own. A village assembly would remain in session as long as the issue at hand needed to be discussed. A dance exhibition at the village square would continue as long as the dancers were extraordinary; if it did not entertain, it ended sooner. Time, in essence, is life celebrated.

The eight values described above form the core of the African worldview, or African spirituality. How these may be expressed in the diverse cultures of the African continent may differ in their details but not in their substance. There may be some isolated discrepancies; for instance, the Nuer of the Sudan do not have a cult of ancestors. Nevertheless, there exist sufficient grounds for holding to what has been called "a common Africanness" or a basic worldview among Africans. This is true especially for sub-Saharan Africa, and more specifically for middle-belt Africa.

Having identified the central values of African life, our task is to examine in what ways (if any) these have found expression in the emergent Christian liturgies in Africa. A value need not be directly expressed; it may be the symbolic expressions of these values that make their appearance in celebration.

The Notion of Liturgical Inculturation

Pedro Arrupe's definition of inculturation following the thirty-second General Assembly of the Society of Jesus in 1978 states:

> Inculturation is the incarnation of the Christian life and message in a concrete cultural situation, in such a way that not only is this experience expressed with elements typical of the culture in question (otherwise it would only be a superficial adaptation), but also that this same experience transforms itself into a principle of inspiration, being both a norm and a unifying force, transforming and recreating this culture, thus being at the origin of a new "creation."[3]

In this definition, neither the Gospel nor the culture is independent of the other. Both interact at a deep level of mutual give and take. In the process, a new creation is made. Every genuine attempt in church history to have the message and life of the Gospel appropriated into the lived experience of a given culture can be said to have been inspired by the spirit of inculturation.

Liturgical inculturation pertains to the incarnation of Christian liturgical experience in a local worshiping community. Anscar Chupungco has described liturgical inculturation as

> the process whereby the texts and rituals used in worship by the local Church are so inserted in the framework of culture, that they absorb its thought, language, and ritual patterns. Liturgical inculturation operates according to the dynamics of insertion in a given culture and interior assimilation of cultural elements. From a purely anthropological point of view, inculturation means that the people are made to experience in liturgical celebrations a "cultural event," whose language and ritual they are able to identify as elements of their culture.[4]

Liturgical inculturation not only makes established liturgical rites meaningful in a given local situation but also develops new dimensions in the church's worship patterns, thus bringing some new yet authentic experiences of worship into the church. This would happen at the level of the sensitive and inspired translation of liturgical texts and the creation of entirely new ones, or the transmission of rituals and the creation of new ones according to local needs. Thus the challenge of liturgical inculturation lies not in either explaining away or squeezing in foreign missionary worship models in an African locality, but in celebrating the Christian mystery in such a way as to exhibit both the true sense of the saving action and the authentic cultic sense of a given African people.

The Challenge of Liturgical Inculturation in Africa

Institutional Christian churches present in Africa, such as the Catholics and Anglicans, faced a dilemma in accomplishing creative liturgical inculturation. First, the missionaries had to write home to request permission from their superiors, most of whom knew little or nothing about Africa. The missionaries themselves were still striving to comprehend the native peoples. Even those who had persevered in learning to speak the local language were at a loss in decoding the idioms and proverbial codes for which African languages are known. It did not take long for them to sense that good will was not enough. In their urgency, many of the missionaries concluded that they had to erase the people's liturgical practices altogether and replace them with those they had imported.

There was another difficulty. Even for the missionaries and for the African church leaders who were open to embracing African culture as they should, there was some tension. African culture, like all other cultures, is not static but evolving. The search for the genius of African culture runs the risk of invading the present-day church with aspects of past African life which may impede progress, or which have by their nature become obsolete. Discernment is needed. The Gospel itself can challenge traditional cultural practices.

By the nature of Christian worship, the cultural elements and values to be incarnated in the liturgy will have to undergo critical evaluation. According to Vatican II's *Constitution on the Sacred Liturgy*, 37, nothing should be admitted that is indissolubly bound up with superstition and error. Instead, the features of the local culture should be harmonized with the true and authentic spirit of the liturgy. For example, that some ancient African tribes sacrificed human beings during religious ceremonies is a fact that neither the Gospel nor today's African life wishes to reinstate in Christian worship. Therefore, when we talk about African heritage, we must do so in the context of evolution and growth. This is a fundamental concern for inculturation.

The third problem is equally acute. Official church documents tend to give prominence to the primacy of the Gospel in such a way that the carrier of that gospel, the Church, is presented as having been fully made already. Everything in the Church's way of life is seen as part of the authentic mystery of the Christ. The Church thus claims to be the judge of culture, using itself as the standard (regardless of its cultural accretions through history). Certain traits of a given local culture then become condemned because they do not immediately fit the vision of the Church as perceived by the evangelizer.

Authentic inculturation needs to respect the pillars of a culture. Inculturation brings the Church and the culture into mutual dialogue and sharing, and introduces an experience of bonding. The end result, a "creation," will bear the mark of authentic Christianity and authentic Africanness. According to Elochukwu Uzukwu:

> If we insist that inculturation involves the meeting between the heart of the Gospel and the heart of African culture so that the Christ becomes the principle of animation to generate a new creation, then we must insist that conversion and on-going renewals are

requisites. If a new African reality is presupposed in this experience, its experience in the eucharistic rite would embody commitment to the dead-risen Jesus who animates his African assembly convoked in joy to celebrate his mystery in the meal ritual.[5]

For there to be real Christian liturgical inculturation, the heart of the local situation must encounter the Christ, an encounter which takes ritual embodiment. At the same time, the Church's message will have to be "converted" into a mode assimilable to the culture and expressible in its language patterns. "Language" here means not just words but the entire process of re-presenting the message of the gospel in a concrete way.

Why do we insist on the double aspect (Gospel and culture), or, for clarity, the triple aspect of inculturation (Gospel, culture of the evangelized, culture of the missionary)? We do not possess a pure Christian gospel devoid of cultural traits. For this reason, inculturation will allow the Gospel as transmitted to be challenged and transformed with the view of liberating it from the cultural accretions of other peoples. This "confrontation" is important. Liturgical inculturation is not based simply on what the Gospel does with culture; it is about what the Gospel and culture do with each other in the continuous process of encounter and mutual embrace. Chupungco puts it thus:

> There must be reciprocity and mutual respect between liturgy and culture. Culture has also its categories, dynamics and intrinsic laws. Liturgy must not impose on culture a meaning or bearing that is intrinsically alien to its nature. Authentic inculturation respects the process of trans-culturation whereby both liturgy and culture are able to evolve through mutual insertion and absorption without damage to the identity of each.[6]

There are certain aspects of culture that by their nature witness to the highest realities of the Gospel. Chupungco refers to this concurrence of meaning as "connaturalness." This was how Christian liturgy adopted and maintains the use of bread and wine, water, oil, incense, candles, genuflection, immersion, laying on of hands, anointing, and so on. In all these, different cultures retain and expand their traditional expressions and vitality.

Altar-table. Altar-table at the Benedictine monastery of Christ the Word, Macheke, Zimbabwe, designed by the Art Workshop, Driefontein Mission, Mvuma, Zimbabwe. Artistic carving in the traditional medium of wood is brought into the service of the central mystery of the Christian faith. [For a detail of the base, see the sidebar in chapter 32.] PHOTOGRAPH BY ALBAN CROSSLEY, O.S.B.

Therefore, four positions may be identified at this time. First, some cultural values, by their condition of connaturalness with the gospel values, can and should have expression in the liturgy. Second, certain cultural characteristics may need to be purged of certain meanings before they can truly bear an evangelical character. The theologian of inculturation, inspired by the Gospel, should liberate such values from images contrary to the truth. Third, what is evidently and wholly contrary to the Gospel must not be admitted into the liturgy. Finally, there may be unique aspects of a culture that could enrich the Gospel, and these could be admitted into worship.

What is said here about cultural values applies already to the inherited liturgy. Much has been accumulated into the Christian liturgy from the various cultures of the world. While certain aspects of the liturgy today may have their references in scripture, some do not. Even when scripture and tradition promote the use of a particular element in the liturgy, it is possible to find a cultural situation where that element bears a negative meaning. Chupungco raises the question without offering an answer:

> Among some peoples, the drinking of wine and the laying on of hands rank high among the religious and cultural prohibitions. Since the use of wine for the Eucharist and the laying of hands for ordination are of biblical origin and are essential to these sacraments, can the dynamics of transculturation in these cases be dispensed with? Can catechesis dissipate the religious and cultural objections against them? Or should the Church look into the possibility of adopting some other elements which can equivalently express the meaning of the sacraments?[7]

If the dynamics of culture are to be respected in such cases, it would be inconsistent with the nature of inculturation to attempt to impose such foreign and "ungodly" elements on a people. Evangelical, pastoral, and missionary prudence would require seeking out and assimilating other practices and elements that bear the marks of both authenticity and gospel spirit.

No group has been more insistent on living out the ideals of liturgical inculturation in Africa than the indigenous African Christian churches.[8] Credit must be given to leaders among several churches that evolved around African charismatics. Former members of institutional Protestant churches, these leaders broke away because they

---

Cherubim and Seraphim

One of the African Initiated Churches and an "Aladura" community (a Yoruba word meaning "prayer people"), the Cherubim and Seraphim Society began in Nigeria in 1925 as a prayer group within Anglicanism, but by 1928 it had become independent. Founded by Moses Orimolade ("Baba Aladura" or "Praying Father") and Christiana Abiodun Akinsowon, the Seraphim practice healing and regular fasting, and they believe that God speaks to the faithful in visions and dreams. Members are recognizable by their white robes modeled on Western clerical vestments. For more about them, see Elizabeth Isichei, *A History of Christianity in Africa* (Grand Rapids, Mich.: Eerdmans, 1995) 281–282.

Worship Services

The following orders of worship are published in *Explanatory Notes to the "Order" Pamphlet of the Eternal Sacred Order of Cherubim and Seraphim* (Lagos: Eternal Sacred Order of Cherubim and Seraphim, 1958) 3–5. The instructions for the Wednesday watchnight state: "This is strictly for young men only. Elders may attend if they wish. Outsiders without prayer gowns are allowed. No sisters must attend." A note to item 9 adds: "Water should be provided in a bucket before the beginning of this prayer and should be consecrated by all present at the end of the circle prayer for spiritual power. This should be given to the members by the most senior elder or leader present according to seniority of members in descending order."

WEDNESDAY MID-NIGHT PRAYER

1. Any two songs and then Holy, Holy, Holy.
2. Confession: Psalms 51, 130 & 24 and opening prayer.
3. A song.
4. Three members prayer:
   Subject: prayer for visioners, dreamers, and workers in the vineyard.
5. A song.
6. A circle prayer. Members present will enter the circle in turns and receive prayers.
7. After the prayers members take seat.
8. Followed by a short address by the member who leads the prayer.
9. Taking of the water.
10. Closing Hymn
11. Closing prayer and grace

SATURDAY MID-NIGHT PRAYER – 12 MIDNIGHT TO 2 OR 3 A.M.

Before starting this prayer, as a rule, we must light four candles, one at each of the four corners of the House of prayer and deputise one man each (in prayer gown) to stand by each of the candles. And then 3 or 7 candles to be lighted on the altar.

1. Singing of any two Songs and then the 3rd to be "Holy, Holy, Holy, Lord God Almighty"
2. Confession: Reading of Psalms 51, 130 and 24 followed by opening prayer
3. Singing of 3 songs
4. 3 Members prayer after reading a Psalm or any Bible portion.
5. Visions and Dreams
6. Repeat prayer as in 3 and 4 as many times as possible until 3 A.M.
7. Consecration of the church
   Proceed to the four corners already lighted with candles.
   (i)   4 candles to be lighted at the 4 corners
   (ii)   7 candles at the altar
   (iii) A bucket of water with palm leaves in it
   (iv)   Four Elders will be posted to the four corners of the church
   (v)   Four elders will recite Psalm 24 one after the other starting from the North, ending in the east.
          North (Holy Uriel), South (Holy Rapheal), West (Holy Gabrial), East (Holy Micheal).
          After reading of Psalm 24, the elders will request the presence of the angels to assist in the prayer.
   (vi)   3 candles lighted at the centre of the church
   (vii) Three elders will stand at the centre of the church with the most senior at the middle. Each of them will read Psalm 24 one after the other. (With this reading, Psalm 24 should have been read 7 times). The most senior elder will then direct for a joint prayer to be said by the four elders at the corners. Thereafter the 2 elders standing with the most senior elder will also pray for the consecration. The most senior elder then prays similarly and thoroughly sanctions the prayer.
8. Grace by the most Senior Elder

saw a large gap between what the missionaries preached and how their people lived and felt. Their mother congregations, founded mostly in Europe, were opening up to traditional cultures, but the process tended to be slow and timid. These African church leaders were women and men who were deeply religious and wanted to implant the faith in African soil much faster and more securely. Many of them did not have much formal theological training, but they were spirited preachers and leaders. They assumed titles such as prophet, evangelist, or bishop. Not having to go abroad to seek permission to praise God in their native land, these founders led the way in seeking a balance between Gospel and life. Thus began the formation of small Christian communities that were able to incorporate aspects of the traditional life of African peoples in an eclectic way. The Cherubim and Seraphim Church and the Christ Apostolic Church, both in Nigeria, are examples of this movement. These efforts and initiatives, most of which began long before political independence in their nations, would be the first attempts at inculturating Christian worship in Africa.

Creative Worship of the Indigenous African Christian Churches

An important aspect of the worship experience promoted in the indigenous African Christian churches is healing. Many leaders in these churches did not share in the teachings of the missionary churches (such as the Catholics) who tended initially to reserve anointing of the sick for the final stage of life. The African churches, on the contrary, saw healing as accompanying the entire life journey. The role of the medicine man or woman in the village was important not only in daily life but also in the spiritual experiences of the people. The search for healing is ultimately a search for wholeness. In this process, there is no body/soul dichotomy. It is the total person who needs to be saved.

These groups lay so much emphasis on the active presence and participation of the community that they regard the congregation more as family. Every church member is a brother or sister. If a member needs food or a job, or is seeking a partner in marriage, it is mentioned during worship, and the community prays for results. And when the prayers are answered, the community shares its testimonies. Bearing witness to everyday miracles is an important aspect of living the Word. Whoever in the community has a special gift for healing, preaching, testifying to the faith, caring for children, proclaiming the Word, or other capacities is prayed with and commissioned by the community to exercise that gift for all. In this way, leadership in all ministries is open to women and men. Certain ministries, such as singing and praying, are the concerns of all. When the people worship, music, song, dance, and body movement are important. They can be loud, and it is all about praising God the best one can. It is a common practice to invoke the memory and intercession of the ancestors in the community gathering. These ancestors, they pray, will guide them along their path of pilgrimage in life as they present their needs to God in heaven.

Many of these communities adapted traditional initiation rites for the Christian sacraments, using symbolic elements of the naming ceremony and the important roles of parents as ministers for the initiation of members. In general, their celebration of the Word far exceeds their attention to other rituals. Although they have ritual meals, the eucharist has not formed a major focus of some of these communities.

Some Catholic Liturgical Projects

The question of inculturation, with special reference to the liturgy, has also been a central issue for the Roman Catholic Church on the African continent since the late 1960s. Following inspiration drawn from the Second Vatican Council and statements made about Africa under the pontificate of Paul VI (and later by John Paul II), theologians in Africa have continued to reflect together on how best to help Christian life be incarnated among the people of that huge continent. Scholars began to refer to much earlier documents that encouraged evangelical sensitivity and respect to local cultures, such as a document sent from the Propaganda Fide to missionaries in China in 1659, as well as directives from Francis Mary Libermann to missionaries of the Holy Ghost Congregation. These documents asked people going into missions not to impose foreign cultural elements on the people to whom they were sent. Later, especially following the Second Vatican Council, a shift was being made in Africa. There came a call for Africans to become their own missionaries, clearly expressed in addresses made by Paul VI.[9]

Over the years there were marginal initiatives in Nigeria, Ghana, South Africa, and almost everywhere else on the continent. The renewed rites for Christian initiation of adults in today's Catholic world were inspired in part by West African mission initiatives. The GABA Institute in East Africa went further and offered liturgical conferences and workshops and produced new initiatives for worship. Out of their dedication and service came several prayer compositions, including the All-Africa Eucharistic Prayer.[10] Most of these texts, however, remained at the academic level.

The Congolese Liturgical Project

The church in the Democratic Republic of Congo (then Zaïre) was particularly courageous. Even before the Second Vatican Council, the Catholic Bishops' Conference there had encouraged the development of Christian African philosophy and theology. With institutions dedicated to the study of African theology and African philosophy and well-informed national and diocesan liturgical commissions, the Bishops' Conference launched ecclesiastical projects that have grown to prominence not only locally but also around the world. Early on, they promulgated the *Missa Luba*, which employs African music. Then they began the project of the *Rite Zaïrois* for the eucharistic celebration, which Cardinal Malula of Kinshasa called a living example and result of the liturgical movement and inculturation program in the Congolese church.

The bishops of the Congo who assembled in 1961 knew that there was a problem with the liturgy they celebrated and they were determined to change it. From the beginning, their special liturgical commission worked its way through consultations at various levels of church life: parish and diocesan liturgical commissions, a committee of bishops, and constant dialogue and correspondence with Roman congregations. Using the *Roman Ordo* as a starting point, the commission reflected on how the role of a village chief in a traditional assembly could be associated with the Christian celebration of the eucharist. At that time, it was understood that the role of the presider at the eucharist would mirror the role of the chief in the village assembly. As time went on, the emphasis on the role of the presider was modified to include the whole assembly. In the development of this rite, therefore, three models were merged: that of the *Roman Ordo*, that of the chief-presider, and that of the gathered assembly.

Elochukwu Uzukwu, a Nigerian theologian and an influential liturgist in Central Africa during the 1980s, kept challenging the Congolese liturgical commission to go deeper in its efforts to evolve a eucharistic liturgy that is truly African and truly Christian. Such an effort would include not only cultic sensitivity but also the experience of the liberation movement in Africa.

It took approximately twenty years for the Vatican to approve the final text of the new liturgy, which came at that time to be known as the *Zairean Rite of the Eucharist*. The official title chosen by Rome was *Missel romain pour les diocèses du Zaïre* or *Roman Missal for the Dioceses of Zaire*.[11] (The present writer has made a full presentation of this liturgical celebration elsewhere.[12]) The enthusiasm that marked the beginning of that liturgical project seemed to subside during the long period while Vatican approval was being sought.

In the end, however, the celebration itself became more important than the text: the former remains full of spirit and life, while the latter is rigid. At the celebrations, the people participate actively and remain very lively. Music, song, and dance are accepted aspects of the celebration. Even where the text does not permit the presider to participate in the dance, he almost always does. Time is ritual time, not clock time. The sense of community is very strong. Word and proclamation are important. The Congolese liturgical experience is the first to incorporate a memorial of African ancestors in Catholic worship, albeit in a timid way. Traditional African musical instruments and local art patterns play essential roles. Much of what characterizes African life is reflected in a liturgy which holds hopes and promises.

There are, however, aspects of traditional African life that seem to have eluded serious consideration in the evolution of the Congolese liturgy. First, the centrality and primacy of life could have been better articulated if there were some ritual of healing in this liturgy, since healing rituals are among the most central in traditional life on a continent menaced by all sorts of challenges to human life and survival. Second, the question of adopting local sacramental elements for the eucharist was not really addressed by the liturgical commission in the Congo. It is a matter of the sanctity of the environment, and the fact that God has blessed the African soil with nutritional elements holy enough for eucharistic worship. Although the people bring the produce of their farms for offertory gifts, foreign elements are still used for the eucharistic elements. What is wrong with palm wine and millet bread? The importation of wines from Portugal, Spain, or the United States, as well as white wafers, are aspects of the foreign domination of Christianity that ought to be challenged and eliminated in the spirit of inculturation. There are religious and spiritual reasons to rescind this practice, and increasingly there are economic reasons too. The third major omission in the Congolese liturgy is the question of gender and presidency at the celebration. This is important not only for the matriarchal and matrilineal communities in Africa but for the world Church as well. Liturgical inculturation is not a cosmetic adventure; it may and should touch on the structure itself of Christian organization. Liturgical leadership in the indigenous African Christian churches can become an inspiration in this regard. Prophetesses in these churches have continued spiritually to energize their communities and to lead them toward excellence in liturgical celebrations. Another issue is that this liturgy depends greatly on imported prayer books and foreign prayer styles, suppressing spontaneity and other aspects of oral tradition. This spells insensitivity to the rich prayer traditions of Africa. In spite of these and other handicaps, however, the Congolese liturgy is usually cited as the clearest result of the Catholic inculturation movement in Africa.

The Eucharistic Prayer from the
Roman Catholic "Rite Zaïrois"

Priest: The Lord be with you.
Assembly: And with your spirit.
P: Let us raise our heart.
A: We turn our heart to the Lord.
P: Let us give thanks to the Lord our God.
A: Truly, it is right (to do so).

P: Truly, Lord,
        it is good that we give you thanks,
        that we glorify you,
        you, our God,
        you, our Father,
        you, the sun we cannot fix our eyes on,
        you, sight itself,
        you, the master of all peoples,
        you, the master of all things.
        We give you thanks
        through your Son Jesus Christ, our mediator.
A: Yes, he is our mediator.

P: Holy Father,
        we praise you through your Son
        Jesus Christ our mediator.
        He is your Word who gives life.
        Through him you created heaven and earth.
        Through him you created the streams of the world, the rivers,
        the lakes, and all the fish that dwell in them.
        Through him you created the forests, the plains, the savannahs,
        the mountains, and all the animals that inhabit them.
        Through him you created all the things that we see
        and those that we do not see.
A: Yes, through him you created all things.
P: You made him master of all things.
        You sent him among us
        that he may become our Redeemer and Savior.
        He is God made man.
        By the Holy Spirit,
        he took flesh from the Virgin Mary.
        We believe it to be so.
A: We believe it to be so.
P: You sent him
        that he may gather all men (and women)
        that they may form one single people.
        He obeyed,
        he died on the cross,
        he conquered death,
        he rose from the dead.

A: He rose from the dead,
he conquered death.
P: That is why
with all the angels,
with all the saints,
with all the dead who are with you,
we say (sing): You are holy.
A: Holy! Holy! Holy!
Lord, God of the universe,
heaven and earth are filled with your glory.
Hosanna in the highest heavens.
Blessed is he who comes in the name of the Lord.
Hosanna in the highest heavens.

P: (and the concelebrants):
Lord our God, you are holy.
Your only Son, our Lord Jesus Christ, is holy.
Your Spirit, the Paraclete, is holy.
You are holy, almighty God.
We pray you, listen to us.

Look at this bread.
Look at this wine.
Look at them;
sanctify them.
May the Holy Spirit descend on these offerings
which we bring before you.
May they become for us
the body and blood of our Lord Jesus Christ.

The same night that he was arrested,
he took bread.
He praised you.
He implored you.
He gave you thanks.
He broke the bread
and gave it to his disciples, saying:
Take and eat, all of you,
this is my body,
I deliver it for you.

So also at the end of the meal,
he took the cup.
He praised you.
He implored you.
He gave you thanks.
He gave it to his disciples, saying:
Take and drink, all of you,
for this is the cup of my blood,
the blood of the new and everlasting covenant.
It will be for you and for all people

the remission of sins.
Do this for my remembrance.

P: It is great, the mystery of faith.
A: You have died;
we believe it.
You have risen;
we believe it.
You will return in glory;
we believe it.

P: (and concelebrants):
Lord our God,
we remember the death and resurrection of your Son.
We offer to you the bread of life.
We offer to you the cup of salvation.
We thank you for making us your chosen ones
worthy to serve in your presence.

Lord God of mercy,
behold, we shall eat the body of Christ.
We shall drink the blood of Christ.
We therefore ask you:
Have mercy on us.
Send your Spirit upon us.
May your Spirit gather us together.
May we become one.

A: Lord, may your Spirit gather us together.
May we become one.

P: Lord, remember your Church;
its presence is felt all over the world.
May all Christians love one another, as you love us.
Remember the Pope . . . .
Remember our bishop . . . .
Remember those who are faithfully guarding over the apostolic faith.
Remember those who govern the nations.
A: Lord, remember all of them.
P: Lord, remember our brothers (and sisters)
who have died in the hope of resurrection or of salvation.
Remember them all.
Remember all those who have left this earth
whose hearts you know.
Remember all of them.
Receive them in your presence.
May they behold your face.
A: Lord, remember all of them.
P: Lord, we pray you,
Remember all of us.

May we be received in your presence some day
where you dwell with the blessed Virgin Mary, mother of God,
the Apostles, and the saints of all ages,
all those whom you love, and who have loved you.
May we then be in your presence
to praise and glorify you
through your Son, Jesus Christ, our Lord.

P: Lord, may we glorify your name!
A: Yes.
P: Your name!
A: Yes.
P: Very honorable!
A: Yes.
P: Father!
A: Yes.
P: Son!
A: Yes.
P: Holy Spirit!
A: Yes.
P: May we glorify it!
A: Yes.
P: Today!
A: Yes.
P: Tomorrow!
A: Yes.
P: For ever and ever!
A: Yes.

The text in English translation is taken from Chris Nwaka Egbulem, "The 'Rite Zaïrois' in the Context of Liturgical Inculturation in Middle-Belt Africa Since the Second Vatican Council" (S.T.D. diss., The Catholic University of America, 1989) 368-373.

A New Millennium of Hope?

When institutionalized apartheid ended in South Africa, many churches removed the symbolic chains placed on their sanctuaries. Central Africans then joined their friends down south to dance freedom with legs lifted higher up; they turned in the air and stamped into the earth with energy. Sunday liturgies for a while incorporated hope for total human revival in Africa. But victory was brief. Today the continent continues to face devastating experiences: the HIV/AIDS crisis, droughts and floods, the decay of economic and political infrastructure in some countries, and growing poverty. African worship must address the current issues of justice and peace on the continent. Young people now being ordained to the priesthood will preside over far more funerals than baptisms in their lifetime unless a dramatic and miraculous intervention can be made against the AIDS pandemic. What does Easter mean in this environment? Will the community ever again gather in joy, or has Job become the patron saint of

An African Initiated Church. Members of the Holy Spirit
Church of East Africa marching to their place of worship in
Bul Bul, Kenya, April 2004. © 2004 BY PETER WILLIAMS

the survivors? What kind of hope is the Gospel proposing to Africans today? How long
will a people truly dance to the drum music of praise when their hearts are so heavy with
thoughts of their sick and dead? Let the healers and miracle workers now rise.

Some years ago, Archbishop Emmanuel Milingo of Lusaka, Zambia, was assigned
to live in Rome, not in recognition of his outstanding healing ministry in Africa but so
that his ministry might cease.[13] Now more than ever, Africa needs all its healers to
return home and call down the power of God. At the beginning of the third Christian
millennium, healing liturgies are needed to form the center of liturgical life in Africa.
The struggle to live and be well is intrinsically tied up with our understanding of the
Gospel of Jesus Christ. In this struggle, all believers who plan to be at the banquet
should prepare themselves by cleaning the wounds of the afflicted.

When the process of liturgical inculturation began in Africa, some thought that it
was enough just to replace the imported piano or organ with the native drums. Others
simply translated Latin texts into the vernacular. These and other cosmetic exercises
played their parts. Today, however, theological and liturgical honesty calls for a much
deeper engagement of the Gospel with African life. No preacher is needed to remind
people to praise God when the eucharist truly announces healing and hope. Perhaps
the expression of common Africanness indicated earlier in this chapter centers now
on the enduring tension and pain that African people have experienced over the centuries. The celebration of the sacraments must therefore embody a deep sense of
liberation and freedom, a reminder that the paschal mystery is a journey from passion
and death to resurrection. As is so often heard in the testimony of African Americans
in their struggles, let there be an announcement that "joy comes in the morning."

Bibliography

Egbulem, Nwaka Chris. *The Power of Africentric Celebrations.* New York: Crossroad,
    1996.
Uzukwu, E. E. *Worship as Body Language: An African Orientation.* Collegeville, Minn.:
    Liturgical Press, 1997.

Notes

[1] See John Mbiti, *African Religions and Philosophy* (New York: Frederick A. Praeger, 1969).

[2] A fuller treatment of this subject appears in Egbulem, *The Power of Africentric Celebrations*, 77–111.

[3] Pedro Arrupe, "Lettre sur l'inculturation," 14 May 1978, quoted in Bruno Chenu, "Glissements progressifs d'un agir missionaire," *Lumière et vie* 33 (1984) 75. My translation.

[4] Anscar Chupungco, "A Definition of Liturgical Inculturation," *Ecclesia Orans* 5 (1988) 17.

[5] Elochukwu Uzukwu, "Inculturation of Eucharistic Celebration in Africa Today," *CHIEA: African Christian Studies* 1 (1985) 17.

[6] Chupungco, 19.

[7] Chupungco, 20.

[8] See Kofi Appiah-Kubi, "Indigenous African Christian Churches: Signs of Authenticity," *Bulletin of African Theology* 1 (1979) 241–249.

[9] Paul VI, "Closing Discourse to All-African Symposium," *Gaba Pastoral Papers* no. 7 (1969) 50–51.

[10] See Aylward Shorter, "An African Eucharistic Prayer," *African Ecclesial Review* 12 (1970) 143–148.

[11] See Jean Évenou, "Le Missel romain pour les diocèses du Zaïre," *Notitiae* no. 264 (1988).

[12] See Egbulem, *The Power of Africentric Celebrations*.

[13] Many reactions have been expressed with regard to the Milingo story, but it is certain that Africa needs healing ministries. See E. Milingo, *The World In-Between: Christian Healing and the Struggle for Spiritual Survival* (Maryknoll: Orbis, 1984).

27

The Liturgical Movement and Catholic Ritual Revision

ANDRÉ HAQUIN

The modern Liturgical Movement in the Roman Catholic Church does not represent an absolutely new start.[1] History shows that the liturgy never ceased to be "in movement," that rites changed in the course of time in the different churches and even in the Latin Church after the Council of Trent, though in limited fashion. From the outset, however, we need to distinguish between "liturgical movement" and "liturgical reform" in order better to perceive the differences and complementarity.

The Liturgical Movement refers essentially to pastoral initiatives and efforts undertaken by groups and individuals to rediscover the meaning of the Church and the liturgy, and the place of the liturgy in the Christian life, in order to encourage "the active participation" of all the baptized and improve the quality of the celebrations; for liturgy is neither the monopoly of the clergy nor a private matter but the celebration of the whole Church. Thus the Liturgical Movement or renewal belongs at the level of pastoral action. Its proponents have no authority to introduce changes or to alter liturgical rules, even if their research and their initiatives lead them to desire eventual reforms and to prepare the Christian communities to accept them. On the other hand, liturgical reform, whether partial or general, belongs to the competent authority, concretely between Trent and Vatican II, the Holy See: the pope himself and the Sacred Congregation of Rites founded in 1588.[2] Once achieved, the restructuring of the rites and the new rules for celebration have the force of law for all the Christian communities of the Latin rite that depend on the Holy See. However, the latter has the responsibility of furthering a better understanding of the liturgy and participation in it, which is the purpose of the liturgical reforms it undertakes. The Liturgical Movement and the liturgical reform of the twentieth century are contemporaneous and, in the best cases, mutually supportive: without a public opinion favorable to the reforms, the reforms risk remaining a dead letter or, as is nowadays said, they "lack reception"; on the other hand, without decision of the competent authority, liturgical renewal cannot achieve a full participation and a renewal of the Christian life. Take, for example, various objectives, such as ministries entrusted to lay people, the use of vernaculars, and the place of the Word of God in worship.

Should one speak of a single liturgical movement or rather of several in the modern period? There may be a risk in speaking of a single movement in the case of a multiform action spread out over a century (1833–1963) and freely developed in different countries. It is only after the event that historians, struck by the many convergences and connections, sketch a history of "the" Liturgical Movement. Nevertheless, taking into account the family resemblances between the convictions and initiatives of the actors in the movement, it is permitted to use the word in the singular, as long as one does not lose sight of the particular marks of each period and the diverse sociocultural and ecclesial contexts.

There is another danger awaiting the history of the Liturgical Movement, which is to consider the movement by and for itself, whereas in fact it belongs at the heart of the multisided life of the church. The modern Liturgical Movement will meet along its road the "eucharistic movement," whose objectives do not coincide exactly with its own. Likewise, it will have to take account of the achievements in the area of sacred music and singing, the existence of various spiritualities that are distinctively modern, and then other developments, such as Catholic Action and the birth of ecumenism. Finally, contemporary historians are sensitive to the place of the Liturgical Movement in the entire politico-religious project of the Catholic Church in the different periods of its history.[3]

Unlike some other authors, I will sketch in a single sweep the development of the Liturgical Movement and the liturgical reform from the initiatives of the Abbey of Solesmes (1833) until Vatican II (1962–1965) and the post-conciliar liturgical reform.[4]

Liturgical Restoration of the Nineteenth Century

The modern Liturgical Movement is rooted in European monastic life in the nineteenth century following on the French Revolution and especially in the Abbey of Solesmes, refounded in 1833 by Dom Prosper Guéranger (1805–1875). At that time various European countries were experiencing a renewal of Christian life characterized by the desire to connect again with the great Tradition of the Church, following on the rationalism of the eighteenth century and the spirit of the Enlightenment. In Germany the famous theologians Johann Adam Möhler (1796–1838) and Matthias Scheeben (1835–1888) renewed ecclesiology, especially by a return to the Fathers of the Church; thus they prepared a receptive ground for the liturgical renewal, in which the Abbey of Beuron was one of the principal agents from its foundation in 1863. In England, by their work on church history and patristics, the first Tractarians and the Oxford Movement contributed to a certain re-Christianization in society and culture; with Augustus Welby Pugin, in the artistic domain, the neo-gothic style attempted to re-create a medieval climate favorable to grand celebrations. Italy is notable for its interest in sacred music and Gregorian chant (Monsignor Lorenzo Perosi, 1872–1956) in reaction against the secular styles of music that had invaded the churches. Pope Pius X approved of this movement and expanded it at the beginning of the twentieth century.

Dom Proper Guéranger and the Abbey of Solemes (1833)

For a while the young diocesan priest Guéranger adhered to the traditionalism of Felicité de Lamennais, but then he undertook the restoration of Benedictine life in France.[5] He bought back the Priory of Solesmes and became its first abbot in 1837. By founding the religious life of Solesmes on the liturgy, which he considered "the chief vehicle of the Tradition of the Church," Dom Guéranger became one of the most luminous representatives of the Restoration. He wished to reconnect with the past and to come as close as possible to Roman doctrine and liturgy from before the times of

Gallicanism and Jansenism; he fought effectively in favor of abandoning "neo-Gallican" liturgies and the return of the French dioceses to the pure Roman liturgy. He planned to write a liturgical and dogmatic summa as well as a treatise on canon law and ecclesiastical institutions. Only four volumes of his *Institutions liturgiques* (1841–1866) were published. To encourage a liturgical and ecclesial spirituality, he edited a small encyclopedia commenting on the seasons and festivals titled *L'année liturgique* (9 volumes, 1841–1866, and 6 posthumous volumes, 1878–1901). Guéranger may even have been the first to use the term "liturgical movement."[6] Solesmes devoted itself also to the scientific study and spread of Gregorian chant.

The Abbey of Beuron (1863)

The monastic influence of Solesmes was considerable. After the foundations of Ligugé and Marseilles in France, Solesmes contributed to the restoration of the Abbey of Beuron in Germany under the brothers Placid and Maur Wolter. Dom Maur Wolter, the first abbot of Beuron, is known for his commentary on the rule *Praecipua Ordinis Monastici Elementa* (1880) and on the psalms *Psallite Sapienter* (5 volumes, 1871–1890). Inspired by the liturgical spirit of Solesmes, Beuron likewise found fame through its research into Gregorian chant and the practice of sacred art.

The Abbey of Maredsous (1872)

Escaping from the Kulturkampf under Bismarck, the monks of Beuron fled to Belgium and founded the Abbey of Maredsous with the help of the Desclée family of Tournai; Dom Maur Wolter became its first abbot. Several initiatives of the young abbey served the liturgical renewal and, in the very first place, the creation of the Abbey School, founded by Dom Gérard van Caloen (1881). Caloen began there the practice of dialogue masses for the pupils at a time when liturgical law reserved to acolytes alone the dialogue with the priest. In 1882 he published the bilingual *Missel des fidèles* in Latin and in French. His Beuron confrere, Dom Anselm Schott, who had

Pietà, or Vesperbild. An example of Beuron sacred art, on the west wall of the nave in the chapel of the Convent of St. Gabriel, Prague, from the 1890s. The concept was that of the monk Desiderius Lenz (1832–1927). PHOTOGRAPH COURTESY OF GEOFFREY WAINWRIGHT

resided at Maredsous, did the same for German in 1883. At the Eucharistic Congress of Liège in 1883, Caloen presented a well-documented report titled *La communion des fidèles pendant la messe*. The liturgists rejoiced in the fact that, thanks to the eucharistic movement, the faithful were starting to receive communion again, but they regretted that communion was rarely received at its proper place within the eucharistic liturgy. Maredsous also distinguished itself through its researches in the biblical and liturgical fields and its school for ecclesiastical arts and crafts. With the publication of the *Revue bénédictine* from 1894 onward, the participation of Maredsous in the renewal took place chiefly through works of scholarship.

The Liturgical Movement at the Beginning of the Twentieth Century

In 1899 the Abbey of Maredsous founded the monastery of Mont César in Louvain, which, with Dom Lambert Beauduin (1873–1960), began the contemporary phase of the Liturgical Movement. For his part Pope Pius X gave a new stimulus to chant and sacred music (*Tra le sollecitudini*, 1903), opened the way to more frequent communion by the laity (*Sacra Tridentina*, 1905), and invited children to communion from a young age (*Quam singulari*, 1910). He undertook a long-term liturgical reform: by his apostolic constitution *Divino afflatu* (1911), he restored the weekly recitation of the psalter in the divine office and gave back to Sunday its precedence over the feasts of saints that had often displaced it. With the *motu proprio, Abhinc duos annos* (1913), the pope envisaged a reform of the calendar and of the biblical and patristic lectionary in the divine office. His death in 1914 prevented this plan from being followed.

Dom Lambert Beauduin and the Abbey of Mont César (1909–1914)

Having been a diocesan priest and workers' chaplain in the line of Leo XIII's social encyclical *Rerum Novarum* (1891), Octave Beauduin became a monk of Mont César in 1906 and discovered the riches of the Church's liturgy, which he then desired to share with all the faithful.[7] The Liturgical Movement of Mont César, less elitist than that of Solesmes, was frankly pastoral and even parochial. "The liturgy must be democratized," its promoter said. Finding support in a little-noticed sentence in *Tra le sollecitudini* according to which the "active participation" in the liturgy is "the prime and indispensable source" of the true Christian spirit, Dom Lambert Beauduin seized the opportunity given him by the Congress of Catholic Works at Malines to present the liturgy as *La vraie prière de l'Eglise* (23 September 1909) and to suggest different paths of action with the approval of Cardinal Mercier. This was the prelude to liturgical action: a popular monthly *Missel-revue* started to appear at the end of 1909, accompanied by a *Supplément* intended for the clergy, which by 1910 became the review *Questions liturgiques*. Liturgical weeks and retreats in French and in Flemish were organized at Mont César for the supporters of liturgical action; a notable participant was the future bishop of Chartres, Monsignor Harscouët. The foundation of an *École liturgique* at Mont César was envisaged in 1910 and 1912; unfortunately this plan was never realized, but in 1956 the French Centre de Pastorale Liturgique (CPL) and the Abbey of Mont César combined to found the Institut Supérieur de Liturgie in Paris. The encounter with various spiritualities was not always easy. Different religious orders favoring personal prayer, retreats, and the Spiritual Exercises of Saint Ignatius became worried by the progress of the Liturgical Movement and certain writings, such as Dom Maurice Festugière's *La liturgie catholique* (1913). Showing that the liturgy is an authentic religious experience, he at the same time refuted the individualism that, according to him, marked the Spiritual Exercises and modern spiritualities. The polemics were ended by a serene text from Dom Beauduin on the nature of the liturgy and what was at stake in the renewal, titled *La Piété de l'Eglise* (1914), the "basso-ostinato" of the Liturgical Movement before the First World War.

Biographical Sketch of Dom Lambert Beauduin (1873–1960)

Born into a landowning family of Catholic tradition and liberal politics, Octave Beauduin was ordained a priest in the diocese of Liège in 1897. At the major seminary he had taken courses in moral theology under Father Antoine Pottier, who was heavily engaged in social action along the line of the encyclical *Rerum Novarum* (1891). In 1899 Beauduin entered a society of priests who took care of young workers otherwise left to themselves. In 1906 Beauduin joined the Benedictines at Mont César, Louvain, where he discovered with Dom Columba Marmion the riches of the Christian liturgy and of a churchly spirituality based in the teaching of the apostle Paul and above the mystery of the Church. Wishing to allow the whole of the Christian people to live the liturgy, he began a liturgical movement in the parishes with the help especially of Cardinal Mercier. The Congress of Catholic Works at Malines (September 1909), at which he presented his report *La vraie prière de l'Église*, is regarded by historians as the birth date of the modern Liturgical Movement. Various other measures followed: numerous publications, including a *Missel-revue* (1909) and a revue *Questions liturgiques* (1910); liturgical weeks and retreats in French and in Flemish; and the failed project of a liturgical school at Mont César (1910, 1912). The encounter between liturgy and modern spiritualities was a source of polemics, but Beauduin stayed above the fray in publishing *La piété de l'Église* (1914), a veritable charter of the Liturgical Movement. After spending the war years in the resistance, and in search of a renewed monasticism (Edermine, Ireland), Beauduin came back and became a professor in Rome, where he got to know Christians of other rites who were interested in the questions of uniatism. In response to the letter *Equidem verba* (1924) of Pius XI, Beauduin founded the monastery of Amay (1926), which was transferred in 1939 to Chevetogne. At the fourth of the Malines conversations (1925), Cardinal Mercier read a programmatic text titled *L'Église anglicane unie, non absorbée*, which had been written by Beauduin. Numerous difficulties led Father Lambert away from his monastery and his country for twenty years (1932–1951); during his residence in France, he exercised the ministry of a preacher, developed ecumenical contacts, and shared in the foundation of the CPL in Paris (1943) and in the creation of the liturgical weeks at the Orthodox Institute of Saint Sergius (1953). The final years of his life were spent peacefully in Chevetogne, where he was surrounded by his confreres and his friends and honored by the highest authorities for his liturgical and ecumenical activities. Liturgy and the unity of the Church of Christ are the key words in this very full life, to which one might add social concern, the reform of monastic life, and the search for an authentic spirituality.

The Abbey of Maria Laach and German-Speaking Regions

Already before the First World War various European countries, particularly Germany, were sensitized to the liturgical renewal. In 1913 the Abbey of Maria Laach invited young university students to live there during Holy Week and to explore the riches of the liturgy. Abbot Ildefons Herwegen, Dom Kunibert Mohlberg, and Dom Odo Casel, the "theologian of the mysteries," stamped their marks on the German liturgical movement. As early as 1918 three collections started to appear at Maria Laach, *Ecclesia Orans*, *Liturgiegeschichtliche Quellen*, and *Liturgiegeschichtliche Forschungen*, and in 1921 the review *Jahrbuch für Liturgie*, which is in the early twenty-first century titled *Archiv für Liturgiewissenschaft*. Pastoral action developed in parallel in the Katholischer Akademiker-Verbund, in the movement of young students at Quickborn with Romano Guardini, and in the association of young people directed by Monsignor Wolker.

The Abbey of Maria Laach in the German Rhineland. Vanni/Art Resource, NY

Austria joined in at the level of parochial animation, with Pius Parsch and the Canons Regular of Klosterneuburg; the Bible and the liturgy were at the heart of their popular apostolate. Likewise the Oratorians of Leipzig, Munich, and Frankfurt made an effective contribution to the liturgical renewal of the parishes.

The Spread of the Movement

Many European countries were active in the liturgical renewal between the world wars: the Netherlands, Italy, Portugal, and Spain but also Brazil, England, and the United States, not to mention Poland with the young priest Michel Kordel (1892–1936). Clearly a full history of the modern Liturgical Movement remains to be written. Monasteries played a leading role in many places. Belgium was less to the fore, but Mont César, particularly with Dom Bernard Capelle, Dom Bernard Botte, Dom Joseph Kreps, and Dom Eugène Moeller, and the Abbey of Afflighem hold an important place. Similarly the Abbey of Saint-André in Brugge, Belgium, followed suit thanks in the first place to the dynamism of Dom Gaspar Lefebvre, famous for his missal that became a veritable international best seller and for his numerous publications. In the wake of Louis Duchesne, France distinguished itself by the works of its historians Pierre Batiffol, Victor-Martial Leroquais, Fernand Cabrol, Henri Leclercq, and others and by the animation of student circles, thanks particularly to the Jesuit Father Doncoeur and his work among the Scouts and Father Paris among his university students.

The Liturgical Movement in England and Ireland[8]

In England the completion of the building of Westminster Cathedral in 1903 gave to English Catholics a taste for a solemn liturgy and participation, especially by congregational singing. The creation in 1929 of the Society of Saint Gregory by Dom Bernard McElligott of Ampleforth Abbey played a capital role in the development of the Liturgical Movement and formation of Catholics in liturgy. At the beginning of the century low masses were the custom in the parishes, even on Sundays; the liturgy was lived in an individual manner, and devotions were sometimes more highly regarded than liturgical celebrations. A task of persuasion was necessary and, to that end, formation and information. That was the special role of the society. In its early years it applied itself above all to the diffusion of Gregorian chant; from 1942 onward it devoted itself more and more to liturgical formation in the parishes. The evolution of the review published by the society and its name changes testify to its successive interests: *Music and Liturgy* (1929–1943) became *Liturgy* (1944–1969) and then *Life and Worship* (1970–1974). The Cambridge Summer Schools likewise assumed a favorable role in liturgical formation. From 1962 onward regular sessions were organized for pastors by the Conference of Practical Liturgy. Among the pioneers must be mentioned Monsignor James D. Crichton (1907–2001), whose numerous publications have awakened many to the true meaning of the Christian liturgy. Nor must we forget the role of the great scholars in the Church of England and their publications, particularly in the Henry Bradshaw Society.

In Ireland the liturgical action was centered after the Second World War on the Abbey of Glenstal. Characteristic too is the *Collectio rituum* (1960) that displays a firm resolve in favor of the language of the country and the recognition of national peculiarities.

The Liturgical Movement in the United States of America[9]

The liturgical action in the United States took place in the particular context of a relatively unstructured Catholic Church that included numerous immigrants of different cultures needing to be brought together. The big theme of the Liturgical Movement was that of the mystical body of Christ to which the liturgy gives access by the active participation of all, laity and clergy, men and women, rich and poor, recent immigrants and established citizens. The depression of the 1930s that followed on the industrial explosion explains in part the affinities of the Liturgical Movement with social action.

The father of the Liturgical Movement was Dom Virgil Michel (1890–1938), a Benedictine of Saint John's Abbey in Collegeville, Minnesota, and of German ancestry, like many of his confreres. As a student at the Abbey of Saint Anselmo in Rome, he took classes in ecclesiology from Dom Lambert Beauduin, whose *La Piété de l'Église* he would later translate. Thanks to Beauduin, Michel came in touch with the Liturgical Movement in various European countries and especially in Germany. The mystery of the Church and its liturgy presented itself to him as a meeting place for Christians in all their diversity and the nodal point at which the various aspects of the Church's mission converge. Returning to the United States in 1926, he led an extremely busy life in his remaining years, interesting himself in philosophy, music and the arts, social questions, and above all the liturgy, whose principal center Saint John's Abbey became. He started the review *Orate fratres* that in 1952 became *Worship*, a veritable "bible of the Liturgical Movement," and created Liturgical Press for the sake of popular education. He was succeeded by Dom Godfrey Diekmann (1908–2002), equally charismatic, thanks to whom the liturgy penetrated deeply into the primary and secondary schools operated by the Catholic Church. Other American liturgists to be mentioned are Gerald Ellard; Michael Mathis, who founded in 1947 the summer school program in liturgy at the University of Notre Dame; H. A. Reinhold; Reynold Hillenbrand; and William Busch. Like Catholicism itself in the United States, the American Liturgical Movement bears a popular and pragmatic character and gives importance to liturgical formation. Its success is due to its vision of an integrated liturgy, that is to say inscribed into the concrete life and linked to the various aspects of the Church's mission, and more especially to the social movement that was so useful in its time. This gave credibility to the liturgy and its message while in turn the liturgy gave a foundation and spiritual orientation to the Christian social movement.

The 1950s

In a prophetic sign of the new period, French and German liturgists began to fraternize and to collaborate before the end of the Second World War. Together they got the Liturgical Movement going again and brought it toward maturity.

Germany

The Catholic Church in Germany went through a crisis in the Second World War. Driven to take refuge in the churches in order to live their faith, Catholics accorded a major place to their participation in the liturgy. Pastors could rely on the strong musical and liturgical tradition of the Church in the matter of *Gemeinschaftsmessen* (dialogue masses), *Singmessen* (sung masses), *Betsingmessen* (sung masses with congregational chants, readings, and prayers in the vernacular), and finally, the *Deutsches Amt* (mass sung in the vernacular by the community and the choir).

If the Liturgical Movement spread and gathered force at the doctrinal, spiritual, and pastoral levels, it also aroused opposition on the part of certain spiritualities and certain ecclesiastical authorities. Max Kassiepe put a match to the powder with his book *Irrwege und Umwege im Frömmigkeitsleben der Gegenwart* (1939; 2nd ed., 1940); in turn August Dörner reinforced the prejudices against the Liturgical Movement in his *Sentire cum ecclesia* (1941). In the other direction, Romano Guardini staked all his credit on his remarkable apology for the Liturgical Movement, *Ein Wort zur Liturgischen Frage*. At that point the German bishops took the Liturgical Movement into their hands by first setting up a liturgical group in the episcopal conference and then an authentic liturgical commission with representatives from the various German and Austrian liturgical centers. Nevertheless matters were far from settled: Archbishop Gröber of Freiburg im Breisgau also expressed his unease in his *Beunruhigungen*. In 1943 the papal nuncio transmitted to the German bishops' conference a memo from a commission of cardinals worried about the evolution of the Liturgical Movement both at the level of faith and at the level of the unity of the Church and ecclesiastical discipline. This document asked the bishops to exercise discernment and to send a report to the Holy See. The response was written by Cardinal Bertram of Breslau in the form of a defense of the Liturgical Movement. Pope Pius XII himself stepped in with two encyclical letters, one devoted to the Church, *Mystici Corporis* (1943), and the other to the liturgy, *Mediator Dei et hominum* (1947). The latter recognized the value of the Liturgical Movement but also formulated some concerns and some reproaches; it remained the charter of the Liturgical Movement and inspired the writers of Vatican II's *Constitution on the Sacred Liturgy*. The Liturgical Institute of Trier, founded by the bishops in 1947, became the center of study for the movement; as early as 1950 it organized the first national liturgical congress at Frankfurt.

France

The situations experienced by French Catholics during the war, especially in the camps, stimulated aspirations for a more simple and profound liturgy. Similarly the discovery of de-Christianization, highlighted by Henri Godin's *La France, pays de mission?* (1943), raised radical questions about the awakening and formation of faith. Faced by that situation, the Dominicans Pie Duployé and Aimon-Marie Roguet, soon joined by Father Aimé-Georges Martimort, founded the Centre de Pastoral Liturgique in Paris in 1943. As soon as the war ended, French liturgists, especially in bilingual Alsace, entered into contact with German liturgists. The review *La Maison-Dieu* was started in 1945 and has in the early twenty-first century become the principal organ of research in the French-speaking world in the area of liturgy and sacraments. Formation and research—these two axes of work in the CPL—have allowed both the welding of a multidisciplinary work group (especially in the Vanves sessions) and the diffusion of research results in the Versailles sessions and the national congresses. The collaboration of the CPL with the French bishops expanded in the 1950s, and in 1964 the Centre National de Pastorale Liturgique (CNPL) succeeded the CPL. The Institut Supérieur de Liturgie was set up in 1956 for the purpose of forming researchers, teachers, and pastoral leaders.

Internationalization of the Movement

The years 1951–1960 were decisive particularly because of the international congresses of liturgy, where in the first place French and German liturgists met and then many others and especially those from the overseas missions.[10] At these meetings an ever-broader consensus developed concerning the most desirable liturgical changes. The international congress at Assisi in 1956, with the presence of a delegate from the Holy See and a papal audience in Rome, constituted a historic turning point: henceforth the alliance was sealed between the Liturgical Movement and the liturgical reform. Moreover those who attended the congress could not but be pleased at the general project of liturgical reform announced in 1948 by Pope Pius XII. The restoration of the paschal vigil in 1952 and then of Holy Week in 1955 were the first fruits. The authorization of evening masses (1947), partial use of vernaculars for the biblical readings at mass and for singing, bilingual rituals in Latin and French and in Latin and German (1947), the simplification of rubrics (1955 and 1960), the relaxation of the eucharistic fast (1953, 1957, 1964), and the encyclical *Musicae sacrae disciplinae* (1955) show that the movement by now was well underway.

Paschal vigil. Lighting the Easter fire at St. Joseph's Catholic Church, Roehampton, Surrey, England. One of the earliest signs of the transition from "Liturgical Movement" to official ritual revision occurred between 1951 and 1955, when Pope Pius XII restored the paschal vigil to the evening hour on Holy Saturday, brought order into the scripture readings, and introduced a renewal of baptismal vows for the whole congregation. PHOTOGRAPH BY HÉLÈNE ROGERS/ART DIRECTORS AND TRIP

The Conciliar Reform of Vatican II

The Second Vatican Council

On the eve of the council, liturgists were convinced of four things: the fundamentally pastoral character of liturgy; the importance of liturgy in the overseas missions and the young churches and indeed in the "missionary" situation of the West; the necessity of adopting living languages in the liturgy; and the desire for concelebration. In line with the general aggiornamento of the Church set by John XXIII as the aim of the council, the Constitution on the Liturgy *Sacrosanctum Concilium*,[11] passed on 4 December 1963, had as its objective the reform (*instaurare*) and promotion (*fovere*) of the liturgy (SC 1). The preparatory commission on liturgy, created in 1960 with Cardinal Cicognani as president and Annibale Bugnini as secretary, contained thirteen subcommissions and completed its work on the draft in 1962. In the course of the fifteen general sessions of the council treating the Constitution on the Liturgy, difficulties were raised concerning above all the language of the liturgy, the communion of lay people from the chalice, and the divine office. At the final vote of the fathers on the text of the constitution, a very broad consensus emerged: 1,992 in favor, 180 in favor with reservations, 11 against, and 5 invalid ballots. Pope Paul VI promulgated the constitution on 4 December 1963, thus opening a new period in the history of liturgy and harvesting the fruit of the long labors of the Liturgical Movements.

The Work of the Consilium (1964–1969)

The Consilium ad exsequendam Constitutionem de Sacra Liturgia, founded in January 1964 with Cardinal G. Lercaro as president and Annibale Bugnini as secretary, was succeeded by the Congregation for Divine Worship (1969–1975). The work of these bodies was to compose new "typical" liturgical books in Latin that the different countries would translate and adapt according to the needs of their people and also to formulate various liturgical norms. The consilium numbered more than two hundred experts from all countries who were divided into various working groups (*coetus*).

The most important liturgical books were promulgated between 1968 and 1977: in 1968 the first four eucharistic prayers and the ritual for ordaining bishops, priests, and deacons; in 1969 the rites for marriage, the baptism of infants, and funerals; in 1970 the missal of Paul VI, the rituals for religious profession, the blessing of abbots and abbesses, and the consecration of virgins; in 1971–1972 the divine office (*Liturgia horarum*); in 1971 the rite for confirmation; in 1972 the rites for the Christian initiation of adults and for the anointing of the sick as well as the rite for instituting lectors and acolytes; in 1974 the rite of penance and reconciliation; in 1977 the rite for dedicating a church and the altar. In 1984 appeared the book of blessings and the ceremonial of bishops. The new code of canon law in 1983 included the norms for the celebration of the sacraments as formulated by the various rituals. At the level of adaptation to pastoral situations must be mentioned also the instruction on masses for particular groups (1969), the directory for children's masses (1974), and the directory for Sunday assemblies in the absence of a priest (1988).

In general the liturgical reform was favorably received apart from the reactions of a few groups of traditionalist Catholics.[12] On the other hand, certain uncontrolled experiments, especially with the composition of eucharistic prayers, provoked lively reactions in Rome. Some people made Monsignor Annibale Bugnini the scapegoat for this situation; he was disgraced and became apostolic nuncio in Tehran.[13]

The Future of the Liturgy

Can one consider the liturgical reform concluded? If one is thinking of the production of new liturgical books, then it can be said that the Roman phase of the reform is practically complete. But the various countries are far from having at their disposal all the liturgical books in the 350 languages that are at present officially recognized.

"Liturgical adaptation" (SC 37–40), for which the early twenty-first century's preferable term is the "inculturation" of the liturgy, is a particular concern in Africa and in Asia. The mass rite approved for Zaire (1988) is a quite successful example. By contrast, the secularization and the crisis in sacramental practice and in the faith that are in the early twenty-first century characteristic of Western Europe and the economically developed countries make a new initiation necessary, without which Christians will not be able to participate actively—that is, as authentic believers—in the liturgy of the Church. The magisterium has to show itself as the "guardian" and "promoter" of liturgy and to assist in an authentic inculturation even in the countries of old Christendom.

Is the time of the Liturgical Movement past? Certainly one essential phase has been completed. On the other hand, the need now is for a deeper appreciation, especially of the Word of God that is now read in its fullness, and for a true liturgical spirituality and a better articulation between the liturgy and the other moments in the mission of the Church. The liturgy is a treasure of the Church: for years it has been at the heart of ecumenical dialogues.[14] Is the eucharist not the "source and summit" of all the Church's activity? (SC 14, 19, 21). In the West the Roman Catholic Church and the Protestant churches, so long opposed to one another on justification by faith, the relation between faith and reason, and the relation between word and sacrament, are learning again to listen to one another and to bring back together things that had been separated.

First communion. The children of St. Francis of Assisi Church, Raleigh, North Carolina, gather with the priest before the altar. The baptismal font, reminding them of their baptisms, stands at their left. PHOTOGRAPH COURTESY OF ST. FRANCIS OF ASSISI CHURCH, RALEIGH, NORTH CAROLINA

The Missal of Paul VI: Eucharistic Prayers II and IV

Eucharistic Prayer II was inspired by the anaphora found in the early church order that was widely connected in twentieth-century scholarship with the *Apostolic Tradition* of Hippolytus of Rome (see the chapter in this book by Maxwell Johnson), a prayer that was also drawn on by liturgical writers in other churches in the third quarter of the twentieth century. Eucharistic Prayer IV is the new Roman composition that most nearly follows the West Syrian or Antiochene-

Byzantine pattern of an anaphora; it met with admiration among professional liturgists and was adapted for inclusion in service books of other denominations. Accounts of the new Roman eucharistic prayers from scholars of the generation that produced them can be found in *The New Liturgy: A Comprehensive Introduction*, edited by Lancelot Sheppard (London: Darton, Longman & Todd, 1970). Studies in greater detail are offered by Enrico Mazza in *The Eucharistic Prayers of the Roman Rite* (translated by Matthew J. O'Connell, New York: Pueblo, 1986). The Roman prayers are set within the broader context of anaphoral compositions of the period in the symposium edited by Frank C. Senn, *New Eucharistic Prayers: An Ecumenical Study of their Development and Structure* (New York: Paulist Press, 1987).

Eucharistic Prayer II

Priest:　The Lord be with you.
People:　And also with you.
Priest:　Lift up your hearts.
People:　We lift them up to the Lord.
Priest:　Let us give thanks to the Lord our God.
People:　It is right to give him thanks and praise.

> Father, it is our duty and our salvation
> always and everywhere
> to give you thanks
> through your beloved Son, Jesus Christ.
> He is the Word through whom you made the universe,
> the Savior you sent to redeem us.
> By the power of the Holy Spirit
> he took flesh and was born of the Virgin Mary.
> For our sake he opened his arms on the cross;
> he put an end to death
> and revealed the resurrection.
> In this he fulfilled your will
> and won for you a holy people.
> And so we join the angels and the saints
> in proclaiming your glory
> as we say:

> Holy, holy, holy Lord, God of power and might,
> heaven and earth are full of your glory.
> Hosanna in the highest.
> Blessed is he who comes in the name of the Lord.
> Hosanna in the highest.

The priest, with hands extended, says:
> Lord, you are holy indeed,
> the fountain of all holiness.

He joins his hands and holding them outstretched over the offerings, says with concelebrants:

> Let your Spirit come upon these gifts to make them holy,
> so that they may become for us

He joins his hands and, making the sign of the cross once over both bread and chalice, says:

> the body + and blood of our Lord, Jesus Christ.

He joins his hands. The words of the Lord in the following formulas should be spoken clearly and distinctly, as their meaning demands.

> Before he was given up to death,
> a death he freely accepted,

He takes the bread and, raising it a little above the altar, continues:

> he took bread and gave you thanks.
> He broke the bread, gave it to his disciples,
> and said:

He bows slightly.

> Take this, all of you,
> and eat it:
> this is my body
> which will be given up for you.

He shows the consecrated host to the people, places it on the paten, and genuflects in adoration. Then he continues:

> When supper was ended, he took the cup.

He takes the chalice and, raising it a little above the altar, continues:

> Again he gave thanks and praise, gave the cup to his disciples, and said:

He bows slightly.

> Take this all of you, and drink from it:
> this is the cup of my blood,
> the blood of the new and everlasting covenant.
> It will be shed for you and for all
> so that sins may be forgiven.
> Do this in memory of me.

He shows the chalice to the people, places it on the corporal and genuflects in adoration. Then he sings or says:

> Let us proclaim the mystery of faith.

People with celebrant and concelebrants:

> Christ has died, Christ is risen, Christ will come again.

Then, with hands extended, the priest says:
> In memory of his death and resurrection,
> we offer you, Father, this life-giving bread,
> this saving cup.
>
> We thank you for counting us worthy
> to stand in your presence and serve you.
> May all of us who share in the body and blood of Christ
> be brought together in unity by the Holy Spirit.
>
> Lord, remember your Church throughout the world;
> make us grow in love,
> together with N. our Pope, N. our bishop, and all the clergy.
>
> Remember our brothers and sisters
> who have gone to their rest
> in the hope of rising again;
> bring them and all the departed
> into the light of your presence.
> Have mercy on us all;
> make us worthy to share eternal life
> with Mary, the virgin Mother of God,
> with the apostles, and with all the saints
> who have done your will throughout the ages.
> May we praise you in union with them,
> and give you glory

He joins his hands.
> through your Son, Jesus Christ.

He takes the chalice and the paten with the host and, lifting them up, sings or says:
> Through him,
> with him,
> in him,
> in the unity of the Holy Spirit,
> all glory and honor is yours,
> almighty Father,
> for ever and ever.

The people respond:
> Amen.

Used with kind permission of International Commission on English in the Liturgy, Washington, D.C.

Eucharistic Prayer IV

Priest: The Lord be with you.
People: And also with you.
Priest: Lift up your hearts.
People: We lift them up to the Lord.
Priest: Let us give thanks to the Lord our God.
People: It is right to give him thanks and praise.

Father in heaven,
it is right that we should give you thanks and glory:
you alone are God, living and true.
Through all eternity you live in unapproachable light.
Source of life and goodness,
you have created all things,
to fill your creatures with every blessing
and lead all men to the joyful vision of your light.
Countless hosts of angels stand before you to do your will;
they look upon your splendor and praise you, night and day.
United with them,
and in the name of every creature under heaven,
we too praise your glory as we say:

Holy, holy, holy Lord, God of power and might,
heaven and earth are full of your glory.
Hosanna in the highest.
Blessed is he who comes in the name of the Lord.
Hosanna in the highest.

The priest, with hands extended, says:
Father, we acknowledge your greatness:
show your wisdom and love.
You formed man in your own likeness
and set him over the whole world
to serve you, his creator,
and to rule over all creatures.

Even when he disobeyed you and lost your friendship
you did not abandon him to the power of death,
but helped all men to seek and find you.
Again and again you offered a covenant to man,
and through the prophets taught him to hope for salvation.
Father, you so loved the world
that in the fullness of time you sent your only Son to be our Savior.

He was conceived through the power of the Holy Spirit,
and born of the Virgin Mary,

a man like us in all things but sin.
To the poor he proclaimed the good news of salvation,
to prisoners, freedom,
and to those in sorrow, joy.
In fulfillment of your will
he gave himself up to death;
but by rising from the dead,
he destroyed death and restored life.
And that we might live no longer for ourselves but for him,
he sent the Holy Spirit from you, Father,
as his first gift to those who believe,
to complete his work on earth
and bring us the fullness of race.

He joins his hands and, holding them outstretched over the offerings, says with concelebrants:
Father, may this Holy Spirit sanctify these offerings.

He joins his hands and, making the sign of the cross once over both bread and chalice, says:
Let them become the body + and blood of Jesus Christ our Lord

He joins his hands.
as we celebrate the great mystery which he left us as an everlasting covenant.

The words of the Lord in the following formulas should be spoken clearly and distinctly, as their meaning demands.
He always loved those who were his own in the world.

When the time came for him to be glorified by you,
his heavenly Father,
he showed the depth of his love.

While they were at supper,

He takes the bread and, raising it a little above the altar, continues:
he took bread,
said the blessing,
broke the bread, and gave it to his disciples, saying:

He bows slightly.
Take this, all of you, and eat it:
this is my body which will be given up for you.

He shows the consecrated host to the people, places it on the paten, and genuflects in adoration. Then he continues:
In the same way, he took the cup, filled with wine.

He takes the chalice and, raising it a little above the altar, continues:
He gave you thanks, and giving the cup to his disciples, said:

He bows slightly.

> Take this, all of you,
> and drink from it:
> this is the cup of my blood,
> the blood of the new and everlasting covenant.
>
> It will be shed for you and for all
> so that sins may be forgiven.
> Do this in memory of me.

He shows the chalice to the people, places it on the corporal, and genuflects in adoration. Then he sings or says:

> Let us proclaim the mystery of faith.

Concelebrants and people:

> Christ has died, Christ is risen, Christ will come again.

Then, with hands extended, the priest says:

> Father, we now celebrate this memorial of our redemption.
> We recall Christ's death,
> his descent among the dead, his resurrection,
> and his ascension to your right hand;
> and, looking forward to his coming in glory,
> we offer you his body and blood,
> the acceptable sacrifice which brings salvation to the whole world.
>
> Lord, look upon this sacrifice
> which you have given to your Church;
> and by your Holy Spirit,
> gather all who share this bread and wine
> into the one body of Christ,
> a living sacrifice of praise.
>
> Lord, remember those for whom we offer this sacrifice,
> especially N. our Pope, N. our bishop,
> and bishops and clergy everywhere.
> Remember those who take part in this offering,
> those here present and all your people,
> and all who seek you with a sincere heart.
> Remember those who have died in the peace of Christ
> and all the dead whose faith is known to you alone.
>
> Father, in your mercy grant also to us, your children,
> to enter into our heavenly inheritance
> in the company of the Virgin Mary, the Mother of God,
> and your apostles and saints.

Then, in your kingdom,
    freed from the corruption of sin and death,
    we shall sing your glory with every creature
    through Christ our Lord,

He joins his hands:
    through whom you give us everything that is good.

He takes the chalice and the paten with the host and, lifting them up, sings or says:
    Through him,
    with him,
    in him,
    in the unity of the Holy Spirit,
    all glory and honor is yours,
    almighty Father,
    for ever and ever.

The people respond:
    Amen.

Used with kind permission of International Commission on English in the Liturgy, Washington, D.C.

Description of the Solemn Parish Mass

At the Beginning of the Twentieth Century

Mass is celebrated according to the missal of Pius V though with a few changes introduced after Pius X's *Divino Afflatu* (1911). It unfolds in two parts, which the missals of the faithful called the "fore-mass" or "mass of the catechumens" and the "mass of the faithful," which begins at the offertory. The texts of the Ordinary (*Ordo missae*) are for the most part sung in plainsong by the choir and the assembly (Kyrie, Gloria, Credo, Sanctus, and Agnus Dei). The other parts are sung by the choir alone; they change with each celebration because they belong to the proper of the season or the proper or common of the saints, not to mention votive masses or masses of devotion that were employed on weekdays.

After a private preparation of the priest in the sacristy, the procession moves forward singing the introit; the priest performs the aspersion with holy water, then recites prayers at the foot of the altar and censes the altar; after the Kyrie (and the Gloria), he chants the collect. Then come the biblical readings: the Epistle (or a text from the Old Testament), sung by the subdeacon or the priest, is followed by the singing of the gradual Psalm and the Alleluia (or, during Lent, the tract) and, lastly, by the singing of the Gospel by the deacon. The sermon in the language of the people is the task of the priest; it is systematic in kind (on the Commandments or on the Creed), sometimes replaced by the reading of a pastoral letter from the bishop. The sermon is followed by the announcements of parish matters. After the singing of the creed comes the offertory and the beginning of the sacrificial part, that is to say the canon of the mass, a single eucharistic prayer of which some parts are variable, namely the preface, the *communicantes*, and the *hanc igitur*. The acolyte rings the bell at the Sanctus, at the elevation of the host and of the chalice, and at the concluding *per ipsum*. The Paternoster is chanted by the priest alone. After the Agnus Dei and the fraction comes the moment of communion, first of the priest and then of the faithful (under one kind only), at least for those still rare people who do receive. After the communion anthem, the priest chants the final prayer (post-communion prayer) and blesses the assembly. *Ite missa est!* The "Last Gospel" (John 1:1–14) is read. The faithful, or at least the more pious among them, continue to offer thanks in silence, which the priest also does using, if he wishes, ad hoc prayers.

This type of eucharistic liturgy is celebrated according to the missal of Pius V (1570), slightly modified and expanded in the course of the centuries, particularly in the sanctorale. One could characterize it as "an aesthetic liturgy" addressed to the five senses (music, colors, flowers, light, scents at the triple censing) celebrated under the sign of "mystery" (physical distance between the faithful and the clergy, who are in the choir; cultural distance of the Latin language; the priest with his back to the people) [see color plate 22].

The Church favors the use of Gregorian chant, with the people singing in alternation with the choir. On certain feast days the chant gives way to "musical masses" or modern polyphony, though still in Latin. Frequent communion is encouraged by Pope Pius X. The proper masses of Sunday regain their place over the numerous feasts of the saints that had intervened. The Liturgical Movement publishes missals with translation into the language of the country and initiates the faithful into the meaning of the rites and their relevance to the Christian life.

The 1950s

Latin is still in use, particularly for the chanting of solemn masses, while at weekday masses, especially at dialogue masses, singing in the vernacular is starting to take hold (for example, the chants of Joseph Gelineau). Sometimes a "commentator" accompanies the eucharistic rite, explaining to the assembly the meaning of the various parts. In French-speaking countries a French lectionary (published by Mame, 1960) is offered to the parishes on the basis of an authorization from the Holy Office in 1956. After the Epistle and the Gospel have been read or sung in Latin, they may read again in the vernacular.

It cannot be said that the eucharistic ritual has undergone any change of structure, but there is a clear desire for better understanding and involvement, thanks to the efforts of the Liturgical Movement and the participation of laypeople in the life of the Church.

The two characteristics already mentioned, beauty and mystery, have not disappeared, but they are experienced in a different way. Aesthetically there is doubtless a preference for simplicity in liturgical vestments, in flower arrangements, and in the use of candles and incense; the work of historians of the liturgy has contributed to this since they have demonstrated how the liturgy in the course of the centuries has been amplified and even overloaded. As to mystery, this dimension is not neglected but is again differently conceived: proximity overtakes distance, the interiority of faith overtakes decorum, the communal act of celebration overtakes the practices of individual piety, the sobriety of the rite overtakes the multiplication of gestures and prayers. Preoccupation with the exact following of rubrics yields to the search for meaning and greater attention to the pastoral and spiritual import of the liturgy as a celebration of the believing community called together by the Lord of the covenant.

This is the moment at which the so-called "sense of the liturgy" develops. Some have it; others less so. This sense is more than precise knowledge of liturgical rules and rubrics and respect for them. It consists in an intelligent awareness of the liturgy in its essence and of the eucharistic celebration in particular. This "liturgical sense" is acquired by contact with history, with an educated faith, with an authentic pastoral sensitivity, and a certain conception of the Church as the communion of all the faithful. The biblical, liturgical, and pastoral movements have combined to favor the discovery of the soul of the liturgy or "the spirit of the liturgy" (Romano Guardini).

The Eucharist according to the Missal of Paul VI (1970)

The document introducing the missal, *Institutio generalis missalis romani*, describes the new eucharistic celebration and sets out its theology. Henceforth the mass includes two principal parts, the liturgy of the word and the eucharistic liturgy, framed by an opening rite and a concluding rite. The opening rite includes the entrance song, the penitential act (three options), the Glory Be to God on High, and the first prayer. These days, in masses where the majority are children, it can be simplified to contain only two elements: the first prayer preceded by one of the others. The liturgy of the word gains major status as a dialogue between God and his people. For Sunday eucharists the biblical lectionary contains three readings (Old Testament, apostolic writing, Gospel), which are spread over a three-year cycle; between them are sung the psalm and the Alleluia. The homily emphasizes the word of the day, intended to nourish Christian faith and daily life; it is followed by the creed, either the Apostles' Creed or the Nicaean-Constantinopolitan Creed. The universal prayer or prayer of the faithful closes the liturgy of the word.

The eucharistic liturgy properly so-called contains a shorter "presentation of gifts" than the old "offertory." That introduces the major eucharistic act: the great blessing or eucharistic prayer is proclaimed aloud throughout and is punctuated by various interventions of the assembly. The slightly simplified Roman canon is no longer the sole eucharistic prayer. Since 1968 three other texts have been available. Besides these four permanent eucharistic prayers, certain others were soon authorized: two prayers for reconciliation and two for masses with children and also a eucharistic prayer for large gatherings (with four sets of variable items).

The kiss of peace has become common again in the assemblies; eucharistic communion can now be received by all under both elements of bread and wine. The opportunity for silent thanksgiving is now included in the eucharistic rite itself. Moreover eucharistic concelebration is allowed again. Thus the eucharist is experienced in a more communal way; its structure stands out more clearly, and its celebration is generally quicker, but the biblical readings, the eucharistic prayer, liturgical song, and the celebratory space show that the eucharistic liturgy of Vatican II is not an insubstantial rite or lacking in solemnity, at least on certain days.

The active participation of all, especially through singing, silent

Communion at St. Joseph's Catholic Church, Roehampton, Surrey, England. Photograph by Helene Rogers/Art Directors and TRIP

prayer, listening to the Word, the universal prayer, the acclamations of the eucharistic prayer, the kiss of peace, and eucharistic communion, is a priority of the Vatican II reform, where the liturgy is presented as the source and summit of the action and life of the Church. Another element to emphasize is the redistribution of liturgical acts among various ministries, even lay ministries, such as that of the reader, the precentor, and the extraordinary minister of communion. As was the case before the year 1000, the missal has again become a "sacramentary," that is to say, the book of the president of the assembly, leaving room for other liturgical books for the readings and for singing.

The terminology of the Church as assembly (*ecclesia*) or communion, so precious to Vatican II, finds its most beautiful illustration in the physical and spiritual gathering of Christians around the altar, the place of the sacrificial meal and the paschal memorial. Simplification of church building and the disposition of space, of liturgical vestments, and of iconography aims at emphasizing the mystery of "the Church in prayer," the Christian community gathered to encounter its Lord.

The most obvious changes in the new celebration concern the general use of the language of the people, the quality and quantity of new biblical lectionaries (Sundays, weekdays, feasts of the saints, and days of the sacraments), the richness of the new eucharistic prayers, the kiss of peace, communion under two kinds, the renewal of preaching, the creation of new repertories of liturgical song, the use of new musical instruments, and the appearance of contemporary art in the building. But these new elements assume "reception" on the part of the Christian communities, a reception both in sensibility and in practice and, even more, in understanding and faith, in other words, a living and integral participation of each and of all. Such a reception will not be achieved without a slow and permanent initiation affecting the sensibility and spirituality of the people of God and its daily living of the Gospel.

Time will be needed to attain a new level of participation in the liturgy, to create a new repertory of liturgical songs and a new climate in the celebration. The twentieth-century Liturgical Movement has something to teach us even after Vatican II.

The Rite of Christian Initiation of Adults (Ordo initiationis christianae adultorum)

In the early twenty-first century there are three baptismal rituals in use: the rite for the Christian initiation of adults, the baptism of school-age children, and the baptism of infants. Whereas at the time of Vatican II the adult catechumenate scarcely existed anymore except in mission countries, in the decades afterward all the local churches are discovering it. This institution is of capital importance: What would evangelization be if no adult person discovered Christ and was converted to the Gospel? Catechumenate teams take in charge not only groups of the unbaptized but also the baptized who are not confirmed, communicant, or even evangelized. These last categories cannot be called catechumens in the precise sense of the term but rather "those starting over" (Henri Bourgeois). There can be no question for these of rebaptism but rather of rediscovering their baptismal status and entering upon an active and conscious Christian life.

The characteristic feature of the Rite of Christian Initiation of Adults (RCIA) is that it encompasses a long catechumenal road culminating in the reception in a single celebration of the three sacraments of the one Christian initiation: water bath, con-

Scrutinies. The scrutinies administered in Lent before an Easter baptism at St. James' Catholic Cathedral, Seattle, Washington. PHOTOGRAPH BY M. LAUGHLIN, ST. JAMES CATHEDRAL, SEATTLE

firmation, and eucharist. The unity of the three sacraments of Christian initiation and the links between them thus appear plainly. After a first approach comes the entry into the catechumenate proper: the inquirer is presented to the Christian community by a sponsor (future godparent); he or she discovers in this way both the face of God and the face of the Church, the body of Christ. At this point a liturgy of the word and the rite of signation take place; henceforth the one to be baptized is put in relation with Christ and his paschal mystery. The catechumenate may last two or three years; together with their sponsors and other catechumens, those to be baptized progress in the discovery of Christ and of the Church, learning the ways of the Church and the demands of Christian life, in prayer and in celebrations. To the catechumen is delivered (*traditio*) the creed and the Our Father.

During the Lent preceding their baptisms, they receive the final preparation. The decisive call takes place on the first Sunday, and the names of the "elect" are written into a register. On the third, fourth, and fifth Sundays, which have baptismal gospel readings, the scrutinies and exorcisms take place: the Church is asking God's strength for those to be baptized. On Holy Saturday the final preparatory rites take place, the return of the creed (*redditio*), the effeta, and anointing with the oil of catechumens.

The paschal vigil was the high point for baptisms in the Early Church and now is also for Christian communities who are to receive adults in baptism [see color plate 23]. The celebration of Christ's Passover is also the moment of the great passage from death to new life for the whole Church and for the baptized. After the famous biblical readings of Easter night[15] comes baptism itself (blessing of the water, renunciation of evil and profession of faith, triple immersion or ablution, putting on the white garment, giving the lighted candle). Confirmation follows immediately, celebrated by the priest if the bishop is not present; it "confirms" or completes the baptism by the full gift of the Holy Spirit (prayer, imposition of hands, anointing with holy chrism using the Byzantine formula employed since antiquity: "The seal of the gift of the Holy Spirit"). The liturgy culminates in the Easter eucharist; received at the family table for the first time, sharing the body and blood of Christ, the newly baptized are henceforth "initiated" or constituted Christians. They can live the life of the Gospel in its various dimensions (confessing the faith, celebrating, being an active witness) and become joined to the Christian community, which is "in some way a sacrament of union with God and unity of the whole human race" (*Lumen Gentium* 1). The initial formation nevertheless has to continue, their Christian experiences have to be deepened (mystagogy), and they have to find their places gradually in concrete ecclesial communities.

The Liturgy of the Hours

Long neglected by Catholic communities, the liturgy of praise has been brought to the fore again by the reform of Vatican II. The aim of this liturgy is to sanctify time (night and day), human life, and the whole of history. As an essential dimension of the Christian faith, the praise of God develops in Christians their capacity for eucharistic action.

Reorganization of the Divine Office

The liturgy reform kept seven moments of the office, clarifying the importance of each one; it abandoned the office of prime that was a doublet of lauds. The two symmetrical and most significant moments of the day are lauds (morning prayer) and vespers (evening prayer); they match the fundamental cosmic rhythms (morning and evening) and evoke the great moments in the history of salvation (on the one hand creation and resurrection, on the other the passion of the Lord and the expectation of his final advent). These two celebrations bear a similar structure.

The office of readings (matins) that is celebrated at night in the monasteries can now be placed at any moment of the day for other Christians; it is the time of the *lectio divina*, the reading both of the scriptures and of writings by the Fathers and other Christian authors.

The intermediate hours, terce, sext, and none, are celebrated in choir; where there is no communal celebration, one may choose to say one of these three offices (prayer in the middle of the day). Finally, compline is the bedtime prayer in which Christians are invited to acknowledge the faults they have committed during the day.

Simplification and Enrichment

The reform wished to take into account contemporary forms of living, especially for priests engaged in parochial ministry, as will be understood from what has already been said. It was decided to spread the 150 Psalms over four weeks and not just over one as previously. Moreover each office including matins now only has three psalms.

The theology of the office is set out in a remarkable way in the *General Instruction on the Liturgy of the Hours*. The office appears as the prayer of Christ and of the Church, the prayer of the local community, and the prayer of the individual Christian. Special attention is given to the meaning of the psalms and to the way Christians can pray them in relation to Christ, the sole savior.

The office is enriched by a fair number of hymns, often directly written in the national languages, and by biblical and nonbiblical readings as well as by intentions for praise at lauds and vespers, like the intentions for intercession in the prayer of the people at mass.

Lastly, the liturgical books allow the office and eucharist to be said successively or the integration of the office into the eucharist, which can be the case especially with morning prayer or evening prayer. In those cases the hymn and the psalms of the office are followed by the opening prayer and the biblical readings of the mass; the prayer intentions of the office take the place of the universal prayer at mass; the Benedictus in the morning and the Magnificat in the evening may be sung after communion.

The Divine Office in the Parishes

The great tradition of evensong in the English-speaking world shows the capacity of the Christian people for entering into the liturgical praise of the Church. Previously the Catholic communities of the European continent celebrated Sunday vespers. In the early twenty-first century all this has to be thought through again, because the mobility of modern life does not make pastoral action easy in this area. Certain experiments have been made; for example, in some cathedrals the Sunday mass is preceded by the singing of morning prayer, with all the faithful joining in the singing of the psalms. More often the office of vespers is celebrated every Sunday with the Christian community. On weekdays certain parishes insert the singing of a psalm before evening mass. Other parishes in city centers have created a little office in the middle of the day. Some publishers include in their monthly missalettes an abbreviated daily office for morning and evening. The shortened office in French, *Prière du temps présent*, was a best seller in the 1970s.

Bibliography

Haquin, André. *Dom Lambert Beauduin et le renouveau liturgique*. Gembloux, Belgium: Duculot, 1970.

International Commission on English in the Liturgy. *Documents on the Liturgy, 1963–1979: Conciliar, Papal, and Curial Texts*. Edited and translated by Thomas C. O'Brien. Collegeville, Minn.: Liturgical Press, 1982.

Johnson, Cuthbert. *Prosper Guéranger, 1805–1875: A Liturgical Theologian; An Introduction to His Liturgical Writings and Work*. Studia Anselmiana 89. Rome: Pontificio Ateneo S. Anselmo, 1984.

Loonbeek, Raymond, and Jacques Mortiau. *Un pionnier Dom Lambert Beauduin, 1873–1960: Liturgie et Unité des chrétiens*. 2 vols. Louvain-la-Neuve: Collège Erasme, Editions de Chevetogne, 2001.

Pecklers, Keith F. *The Unread Vision: The Liturgical Movement in the United States of America, 1926–1955*. Collegeville, Minn.: Liturgical Press, 1998.

Notes

[1]See Waldemar Trapp, *Vorgeschichte und Ursprung der liturgischen Bewegung* (Regensburg: 1940; 2nd ed. Münster: 1979); Olivier Rousseau, *Histoire du mouvement liturgique: Esquisse historique depuis le début du XIXe siècle jusqu'au pontificat de Pie X* (Paris: Éditions du Cerf, 1945); Ernest Benjamin Koenker, *The Liturgical Renaissance in the Roman Catholic Church* (Chicago: University of Chicago Press, 1954); Ferdinand Kolbe, *Die liturgische Bewegung* (Aschaffenburg, Germany: P. Pattloch, 1964); and Bernard Botte, *Le mouvement liturgique: Témoignage et souvenirs* Paris: Desclée, 1973).

[2]For the official texts of the liturgical reform in the twentieth century before Vatican II, see Annibale Bugnini, *Documenta pontificia ad instaurationem liturgicam spectantia*, Bibliotheca Ephemerides Liturgicae, vol. 1: 1903–1953 (Rome: Edizioni liturgiche, 1953), and vol. 2: 1953–1959 (Rome: Edizioni liturgiche, 1959).

[3]See Marià Paiano, *Liturgia e società nel novocento: Percorsi del movimento liturgico di fronte ai processi di secolarizzazione* (Rome: Edizioni di Storia e Letteratura, 2000); Jean-Yves Hameline, "Le son de l'histoire: Chant et musique dans la restauration catholique," *La Maison-Dieu* 131 (1977) 5–47, and "Liturgie, eglise, société," *La Maison-Dieu* 208 (1996) 7–46.

[4]Various encyclopedias contain articles on the Liturgical Movement and provide bibliographies: *Liturgisch Woordenboek*, vol. 2 (Roermond, Netherlands: J. J. Romen, 1965–1968), "Liturgische Bewegung," by Lukas Brinkhoff; *New Catholic Encyclopedia*, vol. 8 (New York: McGraw-Hill, 1967), "Liturgical Movement, Catholic," by L. C. Sheppard; Domenico Sartore and Achille M. Triacca, eds., *Nuovo Dizionario di Liturgia*, vol. 1 (Rome: Edizioni Paoline, 1984), "Movimento liturgico," by Burkhard Neunheuser, and "Riforma liturgica," by

Gottardo Pasqualetti; Gerhard Müller, ed., *Theologische Realenzyklopädie*, vol. 21 (Berlin and New York: De Gruyter, 1991), "Liturgische Bewegungen," by Hans-Christoph Schmidt-Lauber; and Walter Kasper, ed., *Lexikon für Theologie und Kirche*, vol. 6, 3rd ed. (Freiburg in Breisgau: Herder, 1997), "Liturgische Bewegung," by Hans J. Limburg.

⁵For studies on Guéranger, see Louis Soltner, *Solesmes et Dom Guéranger, 1805–1878* (Sablé-sur-Sarthe: Abbaye Saint-Pierre de Solesmes, 1974); Johnson, *Prosper Guéranger*; and André Gillet, ed., *Dom Guéranger et le renouveau liturgique: Une introduction à son oeuvre liturgique* (Paris: Téqui, 1988).

⁶Johnson, *Prosper Guéranger*, 13–14.

⁷The indispensable work of reference now is the compendious collection by Raymond Loonbeek and Jacques Mortiau, *Un pionnier: Dom Lambert Beauduin*, which, on the basis of numerous sets of archives, offers both a historical and a theological presentation of the work of the Belgian pioneer. One may also consult earlier works, such as Sonya A. Quitslund, *Beauduin: A Prophet Vindicated* (New York and Toronto: Newman, 1973); Haquin, *Dom Lambert Beauduin et le renouveau liturgique*; J.-J. von Allmen, R. Aubert, and N. Egender, *Veilleur avant l'aurore: Colloque Lambert Beauduin* (Chevetogne, Belgium: Editions de Chevetogne, 1978); *Mélanges liturgiques recueillis parmi les oeuvres de Dom Lambert Beauduin, o.s.b. à l'occasion de ses 80 ans, 1873–1953* (Louvain: Abbaye du Mont César, 1954).

⁸See J. D. Crichton, H. E. Winstone, and J. R. Ainslie, *English Catholic Worship: Liturgical Renewal in England since 1900* (London: Geoffrey Chapman, 1979); also James D. Crichton, *Understanding the Mass* (1993) and *Lights in Darkness: Forerunners of the Liturgical Movement* (Collegeville, Minn.: Liturgical Press, 1996).

⁹For the United States, see Pecklers, *The Unread Vision*; Paul B. Marx, *The Life and Work of Virgil Michel* (Washington, D.C.: Catholic University of America Press, 1957); and Kathleen Hughes, *The Monk's Tale: A Biography of Godfrey Diekmann, OSB* (Collegeville, Minn.: Liturgical Press, 1991).

¹⁰See Siegfried Schmitt, *Die internationalen liturgischen Studientreffen 1951—1960: Zur Vorgeschichte der Liturgiekonstitution* (Trier: Paulinus-Verlag, 1992).

¹¹For the text of the Conciliar Constitution *Sacrosanctum Concilium* of Vatican II, see *Acta Apostolicae Sedis* 56 (1964) 97–134. An English translation is in the International Commission on English in the Liturgy, *Documents on the Liturgy*, 4–27. Earlier drafts of the text are in *La Maison-Dieu* 155 (1983) and 156 (1983). The full history of the council is G.

Alberigo, ed., *Histoire du Concile Vatican II, 1959–1965*, vol. 1: *Le Catholicisme vers une nouvelle époque: L'annonce et la préparation* (Paris: Cerf-Peeters, 1997), esp. chap. 3, "Le combat pour le concile durant la préparation," by J. A. Komonchak; and vol. 2: *La formation de la conscience conciliaire* (Paris: Cerf-Peeters, 1998), esp. chap. 3, "Le débat sur la liturgie," by Matthijs Lamberigts. See also the thesis by Marià Paiano, "'Sacrosanctum concilium': La costituione sulla liturgia nella preparazione e nello svolgimento del Vatican II. Continuità o rottura?" (Th.D. Thesis, Institute of Theological Studies of Bologna, 1995–1996).

¹²Criticisms were addressed particularly to the *Ordo Missae* of 1969 and the missal of Paul VI (1970) on the grounds that they had been infiltrated by Protestant ideas about the eucharistic sacrifice, the real presence, and the priesthood of all believers. On this subject, see Adrien Nocent, *La célébration eucharistique avant et après s. Pie V* (Paris: Beauchesne, 1977); and especially the well-documented article by Aimé-Georges Martimort, "La réforme liturgique incomprise," *La Maison-Dieu* 192 (1992) 79–119.

¹³For the official documents from the post-conciliar period, see Reiner Kaczynski, *Enchiridion documentorum instaurationis liturgicae*, vol. 1: 1963–1973 (Turin: Marietti, 1976), vol. 2: 12 April 1973–12 April 1983 (Rome: CLV, Edizioni Liturgiche, 1988); vol. 3: 12 April 1983–12 April 1993 (Rome: CLV, Edizioni Liturgiche, 1997). English versions of texts as far as 1979 are in the collections *Documents on the Liturgy* mentioned in note 11. The memoirs of the secretary of the consilium, who had already been secretary of the Commissio Piana of 1948, are in Annibale Bugnini, *The Reform of the Liturgy, 1948–1975*, trans. Matthew J. O'Connell (Collegeville, Minn.: Liturgical Press, 1990). See also the official review of the consilium and of the congregation, *Notitiae: Commentarii ad nuntia et studia de re liturgica; Congregatio pro cultu divino et disciplina sacramentorum; Congregatio ad exsequendam constitutionem de sacra liturgica*, 36 vols. (Rome: Libreria Editrice Vaticana, 1965–2000).

¹⁴The ecumenical importance of the liturgy is apparent from numerous articles in the *Dictionary of the Ecumenical Movement* (Geneva: WCC Publications, 2002) as well as from the review *Studia Liturgica* of the Societas Liturgica, the ecumenical and international society for the study of liturgy.

¹⁵The older series of twelve Old Testament readings has been reduced to seven: Genesis 1:1–2:2; Genesis 22:1–18; Exodus 14:15–15:1; Isaiah 54:5–14; Isaiah 55:1–11; Baruch 3:9–15, 32–34:4; Ezekiel 36:16–28. The typological stories of Noah, Jonah, and Daniel are no longer read.

28

Ecumenical Convergences

GEOFFREY WAINWRIGHT

Two Movements, One Source

Church life in the twentieth century was often described, by observers and participants alike, in terms of "movements" that stretched over several decades. Probably the strongest and most comprehensive of these were the Ecumenical Movement and the Liturgical Movement. After diverse beginnings, the ecumenical and the liturgical streams flowed in some places quite closely together, and certainly for much of the second half of the century their currents intermingled. Indeed the Second Vatican Council, in session between 1962 and 1965, by that time attributed them to a common source: the Holy Spirit. The conciliar decree on "the restoration of unity among all Christians" used liturgical tones in its opening sketch of ecumenism:

> In recent times more than ever before [the Lord of the Ages] has been rousing divided
> Christians to remorse over their divisions and to a longing for unity. Everywhere large
> numbers have felt the impulse of this grace, and among our separated brethren also
> there increases from day to day a movement, fostered by the grace of the Holy Spirit, for
> the restoration of unity among all Christians. This movement toward unity is called
> "ecumenical." Those belong to it who invoke the Triune God and confess Jesus as Lord
> and Savior, doing this not merely as individuals but also as corporate bodies. For almost
> everyone regards the body in which he has heard the Gospel as his Church and indeed,
> God's Church. All however, though in different ways, long for the one visible Church of
> God, a Church truly universal and sent forth into the world that the world may be con-
> verted to the Gospel and so be saved, to the glory of God." (*Unitatis Redintegratio*, 1)

For its part, Vatican II's Constitution on the Sacred Liturgy declared that "zeal for the promotion and restoration of the liturgy is rightly held to be a sign of the providential dispositions of God in our time, a movement of the Holy Spirit in his Church" (*Sacrosanctum Concilium* [*SC*], 43); and, while having the Catholic Church principally in view, that very first document to be promulgated from the Council saw liturgical renewal as serving causes that were widely shared in the modern ecumenical movement which the Roman Catholic Church was now somewhat belatedly joining:

> This Sacred Council has several aims in view: it desires to impart an ever increasing
> vigor to the Christian life of the faithful; to adapt more suitably to the needs of our own
> times those institutions that are subject to change; to foster whatever can promote union
> among all who believe in Christ; to strengthen whatever can help to call the whole of
> humanity into the household of the Church. The Council therefore sees particularly
> cogent reasons for undertaking the reform and promotion of the liturgy. (*SC*, 1)

The closing session of the Second Vatican Council, 8 December 1965. The texts on the liturgy and on ecumenism rank among the most important documents of the council, authorizing Catholic ritual revision along the lines proposed by the Liturgical Movement and further stimulating Catholic participation in the wider endeavor to recover the full visible unity of Christ's Church. PHOTOGRAPH BY CARLO BAVAGNOLI/ TIME LIFE PICTURES/GETTY IMAGES

That complex statement of purpose for liturgical renewal matches well the broader cluster of concerns that had marked the ecumenical movement as it had been developing largely among Protestants, and to some degree the Orthodox, from the early part of the twentieth century: "faith and order," "life and work" (*praktisches Christentum*), "mission and evangelism."

The overlap between the Liturgical and Ecumenical Movements should hardly be surprising, for the worship assembly of the Church is the point at which all the facets of its life converge. There the Gospel is read, proclaimed, and taught—so that both what unites Christians and what divides them is heard (matters of faith or doctrine). There the congregation's characteristic social structures and operative functions are embodied in institutionally variable ways (matters of order and ministry). From everyday existence the worshipers bring their personal, professional and political concerns in thanksgiving and intercession and seek insight and strength for service (matters of life and work). It is from the worship assembly that Christians proceed to evangelize by word and deed, but how shall they bear a common witness if they are not united among themselves? And to which of the rival gatherings shall converts be invited for the glory of God?

Anticipations and Beginnings

If the Roman Catholic Church was slow off the mark in the Ecumenical Movement (in 1928 Pope Pius XI by the encyclical *Mortalium animos* forbade participation for fear of doctrinal indifferentism), the twentieth-century Liturgical Movement owes its initial thrust to figures in the Catholic Church, and liturgical scholars and practitioners in other churches have usually kept at least an eye on developments in Catholicism and have often—at first warily but then perhaps increasingly—drawn direct inspiration from them.

Some precursors of the twentieth-century Liturgical Movement have already been mentioned at earlier points in this book. Most prominent on the Catholic side was Dom Prosper Guéranger (1805–1875), who may indeed have coined the phrase "le mouvement liturgique." From the Abbey of Solesmes in northern France, which he had refounded in the 1830s, his influence spread widely, and it is not accidental that the Benedictine order later housed many centers of liturgical renewal in both scholarship and practice. The most signal achievement of Solesmes was the recovery of plainchant as a more intelligible rendition of the texts than polyphony and yet still acoustically pleasing. While the ultramontane Guéranger was himself hardly an ecumenist *avant la lettre*, Benedictine communities have often proved ecumenically hospitable, and it is there that other Christians have been introduced to dignified celebrations of the Catholic eucharist and daily office as well as finding collaborators in historical and theological research. The first official notice from the highest Roman authority of what would become the principal pastoral concerns of the Liturgical Movement came from Pope Pius X, who in *Tra le sollecitudini* of 1903 encouraged the use of plainchant as part now of what he called "the active participation of the faithful in the holy mysteries and in the public and solemn prayer of the church." The same pontiff in a series of later pronouncements urged more frequent communion on the part of the laity. The principle of "active participation" in worship and the furtherance of eucharistic practice became fundamental to liturgical renewal right across the ecumenical board.

In the churches of the Reformation, the liturgical work of the Lutheran Wilhelm Löhe in the mid-nineteenth century at Neudettelsau has been noted, with its twin peaks of word and sacrament in the Sunday service and the notion of worship as drama that he exported to Lutheran settlers in America (see Chapter 10 "The Lutheran Tradition in the German Lands"). Among the Reformed, attention has been called to Jean-Frédéric Ostervald at Neuchâtel, with his interest in the English *Book of Common Prayer* already in the eighteenth century, and to Eugène Bersier at the influential Parisian parish of the Étoile in the nineteenth, where the liturgy drew inspiration from the Catholic Apostolic Church of the Irvingites (see Chapter 12 "The Reformed Tradition in Continental Europe"). In Presbyterian Scotland, the Church Service Society was founded in 1865 "to study the liturgies—ancient and modern—of the Christian Church, with a view to the preparation and publication of forms of Prayer for Public Worship and services for the Administration of the Sacraments," and from 1867 it provided such materials in successive editions of the *Euchologion*. Among Anglicans: following the ecclesiological and sacramental recovery initiated by the Oxford Movement of the 1830s and 1840s, the later generations of Anglo-Catholics devoted more attention to matters of symbol and ceremonial, and the second half of the nineteenth century witnessed "ritualist" controversies that went as far as the ecclesiastical and civil courts in a number of cases. While the more domestically inclined tried to stay within the rubrics and canons of the Church of England as "Prayer Book Catholics," those oriented to Rome borrowed accoutrements and even texts from that exotic source. Socially concerned Anglo-Catholics located their more colorful practices as part of their ministry amid the laboring classes and in the urban slums.

Given these various adumbrations, the Liturgical Movement proper is almost universally dated by historians from the Congress of Catholic Works at Malines in 1909 (and even more specifically the address by Dom Lambert Beauduin on "The True Prayer of the Church"), rather in the way that the Ecumenical Movement is conventionally dated from the World Missionary Conference at Edinburgh in 1910, which not only strategized about global evangelism but also aroused in some an awareness that went beyond cooperation among the existing confessions to an imperative for the recovery of ecclesial unity in faith and order. Just as the historically and aesthetically interested "Gothic Revival" of worship in the second half of the nineteenth century can be seen culturally as a late flowering of Romanticism in face of the intellectual, industrial, and political revolutions of modernity, so the twentieth-century Liturgical Movement needs from the start to be seen against the background of an incipient dechristianization of the European homelands and a simultaneous spread of "overseas missions" and the growth of Christianity in Africa, the Pacific, and some parts of Asia. It will be part of what came to be the perceived need for a "re-evangelization" of Western Christendom as well as the blossoming of Christianity among newly converted peoples.

The ecumenical history of liturgical renewal in the twentieth century may be traced by way of scholarly and pastoral writings, significant meetings and events, official institutions and voluntary associations, and (last but not least) the production, content, and use of service books. Service books do not tell the whole story, but—to degrees that vary with ecclesiastical and cultural circumstances—they both reflect and regulate what actually occurs in the worship life of the people of God. However, given the impossibility of detailed description of so many rites, and the fact that some account is given in other parts of this book of their twentieth-century history in the various confessional traditions, the emphasis here will fall on the principles, doctrinal and practical, that have been perceived and proposed to govern Christian worship and its liturgical celebration insofar as the attainment of Church unity in faith, life, and mission and its embodiment before God are affected.

The Early Phases: 1910–1945

Between (let us say) 1910 and 1945 efforts at liturgical renewal showed some similarities on the Protestant and Catholic sides of the ecclesiastical divide, but interaction was hampered by prohibition and ignorance on the Catholic side and by suspicion and independence on the Protestant side (despite the fascination that "Rome" exerted on some "high-churchmen"). The similarities may be chiefly accounted for as responses to common challenges and opportunities and as a gradual reversion to common resources. That convergent steps in matters of worship occurred a little more quickly among Protestant bodies themselves is due to the earlier start of the Ecumenical Movement in their midst, with its concerns for the restoration of unity both in faith and order and in mission and evangelism. From the Second World War onward, however, increasing intellectual collaboration in biblical and patristic studies as well as among scholars in the history and theology of worship helped to create the conditions in which the Roman Catholic Church felt able to enter officially on the ecumenical scene; and from then on, in the 1960s through the 1980s, the widespread doctrinal and practical agreements among professional liturgical scholars allowed for remarkable harmonies in the new and revised service books that the various churches were producing. For half a century the World Council of Churches—in process of formation from 1938 and established in 1948—provided the main framework for multilateral ecumenism, and a way for reading liturgical history during that time runs from the comparative study "Ways of Worship" prepared for the World Conference on Faith and Order at Lund in 1952 to the Lima text "Baptism, Eucharist, and Ministry" of 1982 and the churches' responses to it. Since the Second Vatican Council, however, most of the "world confessional families" or "Christian world communions" have also engaged in bilateral dialogues with the Roman Catholic Church, which has thereby become in its own way a center of ecumenism and—correspondingly—a touchstone for liturgical work.

Beauduin (1873–1960)—baptismally Octave and monastically Lambert—came from parish ministry and industrial chaplaincy to the Benedictine order. His key insight and argument, both in the address to the Belgian pastoral conference of 1909 and in the little book of 1914, "The Piety of the Church," was that the gathering for worship was the principal site for the formation of Christian faith and life and the shaping of the Christian community. This principle found increasing acceptance across the churches, in theory and in practice.

At Klosterneuburg in Austria, Pius Parsch (1884–1954) and the canons regular made the reading and understanding of the Bible important to their liturgical apostolate. Their periodical *Bibel und Liturgie* was an emblem of that, and Parsch's *Das Jahr des Heiles* further contributed to the recovery of "salvation history" as a crucial category in worship and preaching. Klosterneuburg thus prepared the way for a rapprochement with scripture studies and dogmatics in contemporary Protestantism and finally affected lectionary use across a wide ecumenical range.

At the Abbey of Maria Laach in the Rhineland, under Ildefons Herwegen (abbot 1913–1946), historical research and theological reflection among the Benedictines in the 1920 and 1930s concentrated attention on the patristic and early medieval period: the historical results were published in the series *Liturgiewissenschaftliche Quellen und Forschungen*, and other studies came in the *Jahrbuch für Liturgiewissenschaft* (later *Archiv für Liturgiewissenschaft*). The most prominent theological contribution came in the writings of Odo Casel (1886–1948). The latter's works—*Die Liturgie als Mysterienfeier* (1922) and *Das christliche Kultmysterium* (1932)—remained under suspicion for exaggerating the influence of the pagan mystery religions on early Christian worship, but there is no question that, in a chastened form, his notion of the liturgy as the "making present" of the "mysteries" of Christ's incarnation, death, resurrection, and ascension exercised very great influence on official revisions of service books across the broad ecumenical front in the second half of the twentieth century, where particularly participation in the "paschal mystery" of the Savior's death and resurrection became a dominant category in both baptism and eucharist.[1] Casel himself passed away after the acclamation of the "Lumen Christi" during the Easter vigil 1948.[2]

In a more popular vein, the Abbey of Maria Laach also published a series of theological studies in the series *Ecclesia Orans*. The first of these, and probably the most lasting in its influence, was *Vom Geist der Liturgie* (1918) by Romano Guardini (1885–1968), translated into English as *The Spirit of the Liturgy* (1930). Inspired by the psalm-verse from the priest's approach to the altar at mass ("I will go to the altar of God, to the God who rejoices my youth"), it introduced the notion of the "playfulness" of the liturgy. In conjunction with Johan Huizinga's *Homo Ludens* (1938; Eng. trans. 1949), an anthropological light was thereby cast on worship, the reflections of which eventually ranged from the Swiss Reformed Jean-Jacques von Allmen's serious description of Christian worship as "an eschatological game" to the wilder experiments in "balloon liturgies" among the hippier Protestants in the late 1960s and early 1970s—although neither Guardini nor von Allmen is to be blamed for the latter.[3]

At the practical level, Maria Laach was significant in the interwar period for the educative value of its "crypt masses," where the priest faced the people across the altar and the congregation voiced their responses in dialogue fashion.[4] After World War II the German Catholic bishops established a Liturgical Institute at Trier, where scholarship was put to pastoral service; the Institute's literary outlet was *Liturgisches Jahrbuch*. The pastoral concerns that had motivated Lambert Beauduin from the beginning were carried by him from Mont César in Belgium to France, where he founded the Centre de Pastorale Liturgique in Paris in 1943. The Belgian *Questions Liturgiques et Paroissiales* was matched by the Parisian periodical *La Maison-Dieu*, in which history and theology continue to be applied to matters of current interest in liturgy, with an increasingly ecumenical band of contributors. Before Vatican II, the left-bank parish of Saint-Séverin pioneered many moves toward the active participation of the people in the liturgy. In the United States, the social activism of Dom Virgil Michel (1890–1938) ensured that the liturgical movement radiating from Saint John's Abbey in Collegeville, Minnesota, shared certain interests with the "life and work" stream of the broader ecumenical movement.

Important historical work in patristics was accomplished from the 1930s by the Belgian Dom Bernard Botte (1893–1980), whose edition of *La tradition apostolique* (1963) would help to mediate the influence of that ancient church order on Catholic liturgical revision after Vatican II as well as in other churches. Botte became the first director of the Institut Supérieur de Liturgie in the Catholic Faculty of Theology at Paris (1956). The Tyrolese Jesuit Josef A. Jungmann (1889–1975), in his patristic study *The Place of Christ in Liturgical Prayer* (*Die Stellung Christi im liturgischen Gebet*, 1925, 2nd ed. 1962; Eng. trans. 1965), clarified for the benefit of liturgical theologians and revisers the fundamental structure of worship in a way that was fully trinitarian while respecting the mediatorial role of the incarnate Son. His full-scale history of the Roman rite, *Missarum sollemnia: Eine genetische Erklärung der römischen Messe* (1946 and later editions; abridged Eng. trans. 1959) made it possible to distinguish the wood from the trees and thus cleared the way to responsible revision in line with the best of the tradition. Jungmann's *Early Liturgy to the Time of Gregory the Great* (1959), arising from summer-school teaching at the University of Notre Dame, placed worship firmly within its social, cultural, and even political setting. In this way, as well as more directly in his *Liturgisches Erbe und Pastorale Gegenwart* (1960; Eng. trans., *Pastoral Liturgy*, 1962), he contributed to discussions of liturgical inculturation and contextualization in the arena of mission and evangelism.[5]

In the Church of England, much of the historical study in the service of renewal has been undertaken in association with the Alcuin Club, or at least by members of that organism.[6] The Alcuin Club was founded in 1897 to "promote the study of the history and use of the Book of Common Prayer." In the background were the ritualist controversies of the later nineteenth century; in prospect, the revision of the *Book of Common Prayer* (in 1906 a royal commission concluded that "the law of public worship in the Church of England is too narrow for the religious life of the present generation"). In Alcuin Club publications the historical investigation in fact went behind the sixteenth-century Reformation and, where occasion demanded, reached back into the earliest centuries in a style that was thoroughly in line with the traditional patristic interests and claims of Anglicanism. W. H. Frere studied medieval pontificals and earlier sacramentaries; F. E. Warren published *The Sarum Missal in English* (1913); and the temporal and geographical sweep was broad in E. G. C. F. Atchley's *History of the Use of Incense in Divine Worship* (1909) and *On the Epiclesis of the Eucharistic Liturgy and in the Consecration of the Font* (1935), in W. H. Freestone's *The Sacrament Reserved*

(1917), and in J. W. Tyrer's *Historical Survey of Holy Week: Its Services and Ceremonial* (1932). F. E. Brightman had already published with Oxford University Press in 1896 a volume of his announced *Liturgies Eastern and Western* (in fact, only the first volume ever appeared, devoted to the eucharistic rites of the East), and his *English Rite: Being A Synopsis of the Sources and Revisions of the Book of Common Prayer* appeared with Rivingtons in 1915. Darwell Stone's two-volume *History of the Doctrine of the Holy Eucharist* (Longmans, Green, 1909) magisterially surveyed both East and West from the apostolic age to its own time.

In the run-up to the expected revision of the *Book of Common Prayer*, in which a number of party interests were at stake, the purpose of such scholars as those just mentioned—in 1911 Frere published *Some Principles of Liturgical Reform*—was to safe-guard and stress the first element in the Church of England's self-understanding as "both catholic and reformed"; they may perhaps be seen, liturgically though not con-stitutionally, as prolonging the line of the Non-Jurors.[7] The Book proposed by the Church for parliamentary approval included beside the services of 1662 some "alter-native orders." That "For the Administration of Holy Communion" introduced ex-plicit prayer for the faithful departed in its "intercession" for "the whole state of Christ's Church" ("grant them everlasting light and peace").[8] Its prayer of "consecration" ex-tended beyond the words of institution into an anamnesis-oblation and epiclesis:

> Wherefore, O Lord and heavenly Father, we thy humble servants, having in remem-brance the precious death and passion of thy dear Son, his mighty resurrection and glo-rious ascension, according to his holy institution do celebrate and set forth before thy divine Majesty with these thy holy gifts, the memorial which he hath willed us to make, rendering unto thee most hearty thanks for the innumerable benefits which he hath procured unto us.

> Hear us, O Merciful Father, we most humbly beseech thee, and with thy Holy and Life-giving Spirit vouchsafe to bless and sanctify both us and these thy gifts of Bread and Wine, that they may be unto us the Body and Blood of thy Son, our saviour, Jesus Christ, to the end that, receiving the same, we may be strengthened and refreshed both in body and soul.

The "Alternative Order for the Communion of the Sick" allowed for extended reser-vation of the consecrated elements after the public celebration, but stipulated that "the Sacrament so reserved shall not be brought into connexion with any service or ceremony, nor shall it be exposed or removed except in order to be received in Com-munion." A proposed rubric forbade any "private" insertions by the priest into these services (a protection against "catholicizers" who wanted to go further); but all this was already too much for the evangelical wing of the Church of England, which stood by "1662" against any reversion to "1549," let alone more distant parts of Western or Eastern liturgical history. "Protestant" opposition—in which Free Churchmen joined—twice ensured the rejection of the "Deposited Book" by Parliament, in 1927 and 1928; its use was nevertheless subsequently permitted by the English Primates. While this side of liturgical revision doubtless seemed to some to involve mere technicalities, its importance cannot be denied for a church that sees its "beliefs" exhibited in its "prayers," as the frequent appeal to a principle of *lex orandi, lex credendi* implies. Hence the continuing significance of official liturgical composition in the ecumenical search for unity in faith and order.

Liturgical renewal in the Church of England during the interwar period certainly had its more pastoral and social side. Chaplains in the First World War had observed both the spiritual aspirations and the institutional alienation of the soldiers in the trenches, and in reflection on their experiences a report asserted that "it is reality and not High Church bias that makes men prefer the Lord's Supper to a service invented 300 years ago. The meal of the brotherhood of Jesus is more to them than a choir office."[9] These sentiments chimed with the mood of Christian Socialism from the previous generation, whose incarnational theology—inherited from F. D. Maurice and exemplified in Charles Gore—in fact prompted Donald Gray to dub its proponents "the sacramental socialists."

The intellectual basis for the widespread transfer of these notions into parochial practice awaited the 1930s, and the writings of two men in particular: Henry de Candole (1895–1971) and Gabriel Hebert (1886–1963). Two short books by the former, both published in 1935, indicate his themes: *The Church's Offering: A Brief Study of Eucharistic Worship*, and *The Sacraments and the Church: A Study in the Corporate Nature of Christianity* . In a capsule statement elsewhere, de Candole employs the characteristic ecumenical phrase "life and work," while the ecclesiological concern for "faith and order" and the witnessing power of worship for "mission and evangelism" are not far away:

> Christian worship is the Christian community offering its life and work to God through our Lord. Liturgy means the activity of the people of God, which is primarily a corporate common activity of the whole fellowship. That action is one of offering, and most clearly set forth and illustrated in the Eucharist, which is the heart of Christian worship.[10]

A. G. Hebert, of the Society of the Sacred Mission (Kelham), was an international figure who had already served in South Africa and would later go to Australia. By the 1930s he had contacts both with the Lutherans in Sweden, having translated Yngve Brilioth's *Natvarden i evangeliskt gudstjänstliv* (1926) as *Eucharistic Faith and Practice: Catholic and Evangelical* (1930), and with the Benedictines of Maria Laach. Hebert's own epoch-making book was *Liturgy and Society* (1935). In it he presented the church organically as the mystical body of Christ, sustained by scriptural and creedal faith, and having a mission to the modern world in face of its material and spiritual degradation. His practical proposal to make "The Parish Communion" the central service of Sunday was further advanced—again with insistent theological support—in a symposium published in 1937 under that title and under Hebert's editorship. Concretely, that meant a "parish eucharist . . . celebrated every Sunday at or about 9 a.m." (instead of the more frequent pattern of an "early service" followed by the "main service" at eleven in the shape of "morning prayer" or, according to churchmanship, "high mass"). "Liturgical preaching" was encouraged (a sermon based on the propers of the day). One ingredient in a strong concept of sacrifice was the "offertory procession," whereby lay members of the congregation would bring the bread and wine to the altar as representative of their daily lives. The sense of fellowship would be carried from the holy communion into a "family breakfast" following the liturgical service.

Interrupted by the Second World War, the implementation of this program owed much to the Parish and People movement, founded in 1949. An explanatory pamphlet of 1960 expounded its aims in terms that were ecumenical in both theme and range:

> The object of the Parish and People Movement is to help members of the Church of England and its sister Churches in and beyond the Anglican Communion to understand better:
>
> (a) THE BIBLE, in particular what it makes known about God and His people, the Church;

(b) WORSHIP, especially as it is corporately offered by the People of God in Holy Communion;

(c) CHRISTIAN ACTION, as the People of God are sent to live in the world in order to transform the world.[11]

Certainly, parallel movements were afoot in other parts of Anglicanism (for instance, Associated Parishes in the Episcopal Church in the United States) and in other denominations, whether directly influenced by the English example or not. But we have jumped ahead of ourselves. Before retracing our steps, however, let us at least glimpse how a prominent member of Parish and People could concretize its ideas in the "house churches" that he—Ernest Southcott—set up on the public housing estate in his industrial parish of Halton in the city of Leeds:

> Early on weekday mornings there are house-church meetings with celebrations of Holy Communion in some of the small houses of the Halton Moor Estate. The lights of the houses break through the cold and blackness outside and testify to the gathering of Christians within for the breaking of bread together—a very effective form of communication, one is told by certain men and women who first observed the goings on from outside, across the street or way, and who are now inside the fold taking part. The kitchen table is set up within the living room in one of the compact, slum-clearance dwellings. Used candles from the altar of the parish church are placed upon the table that becomes the altar. . . . Home-made bread, the same bread that the family had eaten for tea the night before, is used for the service. The Bible and last evening's newspaper are close together; and they will shortly be in the same conversation, too.[12]

Meanwhile other churches beside the Roman Catholic and Anglican had also been engaging—in their own fashions and without necessarily using the term—in a "liturgical movement" that brought together historical, theological, and pastoral interests. Among German Lutherans, there was the "High Church Movement" around Friedrich Heiler (1892–1967), the Alpirsbach practice of the daily office and Gregorian chant around Friedrich Buchholz (1900–1967), the "Berneuchner Bewegung" and the Evangelische Michaelsbruderschaft around Wilhelm Stählin (1883–1975) and Karl Bernhard Ritter (1890–1968) (see Chapter 10 "The Lutheran Tradition in the German Lands"). In the United States, Lutherans of varied ethnic origin and theological bent had since 1888 agreed on a "Common Service," which received a historically learned and ecumenically sensitive commentary in the late classic of Luther D. Reed (1873–1972), *The Lutheran Liturgy* (1947; rev. 1959). In the Reformed family of churches, William D. Maxwell (1901–1971) accomplished pioneering historical work with *John Knox's Genevan Service Book 1556* (1931) and located the practices of the Reformation churches within the deeper and broader tradition of both East and West in his *Outline of Christian Worship: Its Development and Forms* (1936). Theologically, the great Karl Barth (1886–1968) expounded preaching and the Lord's supper on the basis of the Scots Confession of 1560 in his Gifford Lectures, *The Knowledge of God and the Service of God* (1938). Historico-theological studies followed at intervals in the shape of Ronald Wallace's *Calvin's Doctrine of the Word and Sacrament* (1953), Hughes Oliphant Old's *The Patristic Roots of Reformed Worship* (1975) and *The Shaping of the Reformed Baptismal Rite in the Sixteenth Century* (1992), and Brian A. Gerrish's *Grace and Gratitude: The Eucharistic Theology of John Calvin* (1993). In Scottish Presbyterianism, liturgical thinking in the interwar years was instanced by H. J. Wotherspoon's *Religious Values in the Sacraments* (1928) and D. H. Hislop's *Our Heritage in Public Worship*

(1935). Following the union between the Free Kirk and the Auld Kirk in 1929, a new *Book of Common Order* was published in 1940, with "model" rather than "prescribed" services for morning and evening and an Order for the Lord's Supper of which W. D. Maxwell could say that it "represents a long tradition brought to a high perfection, indigenously Scottish and Reformed and essentially Catholic. In its dignity of action, centrality of content, and felicity of expression, it provides a vehicle for worship entitling it to a place among the great rites of Christendom, and is rapidly being recognized as such."[13]

The reunion in 1932 of the branches of British Methodism into the Methodist Church of Great Britain was marked by a new hymnal, *The Methodist Hymn Book* (1933), and a new service book, *The Book of Offices* (1936). The latter stuck to the pattern of Cranmer and Wesley in its order for morning prayer and its first order for the Lord's supper, although by far the most familiar form of worship was in point of fact a more freely constructed "preaching service." Methodists still saw the Wesleyan hymns as their main treasure (the "*MHB*" contained over 250 such at the heart of its ecumenically expanded total of almost a thousand), and these were expounded in such studies as *The Hymns of Methodism in Their Literary Relations* by Henry Bett (1913; 3rd ed. 1945), *The Evangelical Doctrines of Charles Wesley's Hymns* and *The Eucharistic Hymns of John and Charles Wesley* by J. Ernest Rattenbury (1941 and 1948 respectively), and *The Hymns of Charles Wesley* (1952) by Robert Newton Flew, who was a leading figure in the international Faith and Order movement. The wider liturgical interests of J. E. Rattenbury (1870–1963) found published expression in his *Vital Elements of Public Worship* (1936) and in four books of meditations on the prayers and scriptures for seasons, festivals, and saints' days. Having already in 1903 helped to create the Wesleyan Methodist Union for Social Service, Rattenbury in 1935 founded the Methodist Sacramental Fellowship to "reaffirm the Catholic faith" based on scripture and the Nicene Creed, "to restore to Methodism the sacramental worship of the Universal Church and in particular the centrality of the Eucharist," and "to work and pray for the restoration of Catholic unity in Christ's Church." A similar combination of sacramental and social passion characterized also Rattenbury's successor in the West London Mission at Kingsway Hall: Donald Soper (1903–1998) practiced a weekly eucharist, engaged in open-air apologetics on Tower Hill, and actively supported the Labour Party in politics.

During the same period, worship in mainstream American Methodism was characterized first by a desire for the "beauty of holiness" (an aesthetic interest in architecture, ornamentation, and vestments), and then, perhaps a little later, by a concern for greater historical depth. On the *Methodist Hymnal* of 1935, the contemporary form of the "social gospel" left its mark, while the number of classic compositions by John and Charles Wesley sank to 63 from the figure of 140 in the *Hymnal* of 1905. In comparison with the *Book of Worship* of 1945, the *Book of Worship* of 1965 represented something of a Wesleyan recovery in the matter of rites, and the *Hymnal* of the same year raised the number of hymns by the Wesleys to 88. In 1946, the Brotherhood of St. Luke was founded (since 1948: the Order), with a view to studying the worship of the Early Church and improving sacramental practice in Methodism.

Hitherto account has been given of the informal ecumenical connections and range of liturgical renewal in the various confessional churches, such as the story largely was up until the Second World War. Now the time has come to relate liturgical thought and practice to institutional ecumenism as this developed from that point on.

Changi Mural

A mural of the institution of the Lord's supper was painted by the British soldier Stanley Warren (1917-1992) in the Chapel of St. Luke, built by the prisoners in the Changi camp during the Japanese occupation of Singapore in World War II. Both the construction and the art were accomplished with makeshift materials. Wartime conditions sometimes stimulated Christians in an ecumenical direction in both practical and liturgical areas. Anglicans, Methodists, and Presbyterians in the circumstances of Changi constituted a single worshiping community. Another painting by Warren took the theme, "Father, forgive them, for they know not what they do."

Wartime Ecumenism. "This Is My Blood of the New Testament Which Is Shed for Many" by Stanley Warren; Changi Chapel, Singapore. PHOTOGRAPH COURTESY OF GEOFFREY WAINWRIGHT

Ways of Worship: 1945–1965

"Faith and Order," as a continuing component in the Ecumenical Movement, is concerned with matters of doctrine and institutional structure that have divided the various communities claiming to be "Church" and now seeking to recover unity among themselves. Many of their differences show themselves in worship, and especially in the sacraments, and so it is natural that liturgical questions should have figured on the agenda of Faith and Order from the start. Participation in Faith and Order bodies characteristically depends on nomination or approval by the various confessional churches, which gives the members' work a certain official status, although the reports of Faith and Order conferences and commissions carry no authority short of adoption by the sponsoring churches.

The first World Conference on Faith and Order, comprising representatives from many churches of the Reformation and some Orthodox churches, took place at Lausanne, Switzerland, in 1927. According to its final report, there was agreement "that sacraments are of divine appointment and that the Church ought thankfully to observe them as divine gifts," as "means of grace through which God works invisibly in us." More precisely:

> We believe that in baptism administered with water in the name of the Father, the Son, and the Holy Spirit, for the remission of sins, we are baptized into one body. . . .
>
> We believe that in the holy communion our Lord is present, that we have fellowship with God our Father in Jesus Christ his Son, our living Lord, who is our one Bread, given for the life of the world, sustaining the life of all his people, and that we are in fellowship with all others who are united to him. We agree that the sacrament of the Lord's supper is the Church's most sacred act of worship, in which the Lord's atoning death is commemorated and proclaimed, and that it is a sacrifice of praise and thanksgiving and an act of solemn self-oblation.

Regarding baptism, existing differences in "conception, interpretation, and mode" are not further specified. Regarding the eucharist, the report mentions "divergent views, especially as to (1) the mode and manner of the presence of our Lord; (2) the conception of the commemoration and the sacrifice; (3) the relation of the elements to the grace conveyed; and (4) the relation between the minister of this sacrament and the validity and efficacy of the rite." The report concluded: "We are aware that the reality of the divine presence and gift in this sacrament cannot be adequately apprehended by human thought or expressed in human language. We close this statement with the prayer that the differences which prevent full communion at the present time may be removed."[14]

The Second World Conference on Faith and Order was held in Edinburgh in 1937. It was able to develop somewhat its points of agreement on the eucharist, introducing the pneumatological and eschatological dimensions:

> We are throughout in the realm of the Spirit. It is through the Holy Spirit that the blessing and the gift are given. The presence, which we do not try to define, is a spiritual presence. We begin from the historical fact of the Incarnation in the power of the Holy Spirit, and we are already moving forward to the complete spiritual reality of the coming of the Lord and the life of the heavenly city.

Nevertheless, much of the section on ministry and sacraments in the final report is given over to the stating of differences, the rejection of some potential misunderstandings, and to footnotes in which particular churches and traditions make their own additions or disclaimers.[15]

As Professor Leonard Hodgson of Oxford, then secretary of Faith and Order, would later put it, it had become clear that "many, if not most, of the issues on which Christians are divided have their roots in different conceptions of the nature of the Church"; and the suggestion came that "besides a direct examination of this doctrinal question, a study of the ways of worship characteristic of different Churches might be a profitable undertaking"; this in turn led to pressure for "a discussion of what in his Conference sermon Archbishop William Temple had called 'the greatest of all scandals in the face of the world,' the maintenance of barriers against completeness of union at the Table of the Lord." As part of Faith and Order's contribution to the World Council of Churches "in process of formation," three international study commissions were set up, which eventually produced their reports under the titles of "The Nature of the

Church," "Ways of Worship," and "Intercommunion." These were presented to the Third World Conference on Faith and Order at Lund, Sweden, in 1952, following on the inaugural Assembly of the World Council of Churches at Amsterdam in 1948. It is the second of these reports that is of most interest to our subject. Like the other two, *Ways of Worship* was compiled under difficult wartime and postwar conditions. The chairman of that commission was the Dutch Reformed philosopher and theologian—and indeed cabinet minister—Gerardus van der Leeuw (1890–1950), who had published his own *Liturgiek* (1940).[16]

The commission's members—Orthodox, Lutheran, Reformed, Anglican, Congregationalist, Methodist, Old Catholic—were to expound their "ways of worship" from within their own traditions; Roman Catholics and Quakers also supplied information. The writers' work was largely descriptive, though some degree of self-evaluation was not excluded. Their principal terms of reference are instructive, especially in view of some issues that we have already seen emerging and others that will recur in respect of both the doctrine and the practical conduct of worship—indeed as far as today:

I. How far are the following expressive of Means and Ends in worship?

    (A) THE WORD OF GOD
        (i)   Reading of the Bible
        (ii) The sermon
        (iii) Instruction
        (iv) Liturgical forms

    (B) SACRAMENTAL WORSHIP
        (i)   The Eucharist
        (ii) Baptism
        (iii) Other Sacraments

    (C) WHAT IS THE RELATION BETWEEN THESE TWO ELEMENTS?

II. How far should worship provide for:
        (i)   Thanksgiving
        (ii) Penitence and Absolution
        (iii) Adoration
        (iv) Petition and Intercession for living and dead
        (v)   Oblation or offering

III. How far should worship make use of free prayer as well as of set forms of prayer?

IV. What is the relation between
        (i)   The worship of the local congregation
        (ii) The worship of the Church Universal
        (iii) The worship of the Church in Heaven?

V. Are there other elements which should be included?

VI. How are these elements provided in the customary worship of the writer's Church?

VII. Are they held to be of equal importance, or should some be given special emphasis?

VIII. Is there any right sequence in which they should occur in a complete act of worship?[17]

Given our interest in the relation between the Liturgical and the Ecumenical Movements, some conclusions drawn by the editors of *Ways of Worship* are particularly pertinent:

> One outstanding fact to which our evidence directs attention is the widespread growth, however tentative in some parts of the Church, of a Liturgical return. It should not be overlooked that the new understanding of liturgical values has been fostered by exegetical, historical and theological study within the separate communions, widened after the war by the renewed possibility of international contacts. The development is further due to the experience of ecumenical thinking and personal contacts during a growing series of ecumenical gatherings, both large and small. We may also feel that the values of the *grande tradition* had worked silently, and were now beginning to come into their own in places where such renewal might have seemed least likely, even if long desired. Under these various influences the contrast between Word and Sacrament has become at least a carefully studied comparison, and at best a new realisation of a needed integration in our total worship of God in the wholeness of His Church.[18]

The Lund Conference's "report to the churches" registered several fundamental agreements in the matter of worship:

> We worship one God, Father, Son and Holy Spirit, by whose Spirit all true worship is inspired and unto whom all Christian worship is offered. . . .
>
> God's encounter with us, and the response to Him in worship, involves the whole man. It is made in worship, in witness, and in Christian obedience and service. . . .
>
> Word and Sacrament are both the gifts of God. In the reading and the preaching of the Word and the administration of the sacraments, God offers us His grace, imparts saving knowledge of Himself and draws us into communion with Himself. . . .
>
> All worship is by and within the family of God's people, alike in heaven and on earth. . . .
>
> The worship of the congregation is both the basis of all private prayer and devotion, and a powerful and essential Christian witness to the world.

"Unsolved problems" include "varying stresses upon the importance of preaching and the sacraments"; "different emphases on the place in worship of things we can touch and see"; difficulties "between Churches having a set liturgy and those allowing more freedom to the individual minister"; the relationship between ordained ministry and the priesthood of all believers in the leadership of worship; the understanding of Christ's presence and the sacrificial character of the eucharist; and the status of the Virgin Mary, the saints, and indeed all the departed in Christian worship.

It is suggested that many of the differences in ways of worship are bound up less with "irreconcilable dogmatic differences" than with "non-theological factors" of various social, cultural, and psychological kinds. The churches on earth "are involved at every level in the tensions and conflicts of history." Expressions in a language "gather a whole fabric of associations" that color their use in worship. "Habits of worship differ from country to country." Archaisms may carry with them "the accidents of their worldly history rather than the vital substance of the faith." There are often "great differences of idiom between congregations recruited from different social classes." Such factors "operate not merely to postpone re-union, but frequently contribute to hinder evangelism and to damage the internal life of individual Churches." Moreover, temperamental differences come into play in the face of ritual:

> There are many both learned and simple who find their imaginations stimulated by such symbolism; others mistrust what seems to them to savour of trickery and an assault on their emotions. Here the puritan and the man of science are at one in their reactions; both show a single-minded repudiation of what seems to them obscure, unreal and artificial.

Recommendations to the churches included "the promotion of an analysis, psychological, historical and theological, both of origin and development, of particular traditions of Christian faith and worship" and "a more detailed exploration, theological, metaphysical and psychological, of *mystery* in relation to worship." The more classical ecumenical questions to be pursued included reflection on how far "varieties in forms of worship within the same communions make it possible to conceive of a similar rich variety within a united Church" and "study of the liturgical movements going on in various parts of the world, coupled with study of the roots of modern antagonism to Christian worship in all its forms."[19]

Future doctrinal work in Faith and Order was to be transmuted by an important advance in methodology on the part of the Third World Conference:

> We have seen clearly that we can make no real advance toward unity if we only compare our several conceptions of the nature of the Church and the traditions in which they are embodied. But once again it has proved true that as we seek to draw closer to Christ we draw closer to one another. We need, therefore, to penetrate behind our divisions to a deeper and richer understanding of the mystery of the God-given union of Christ with his Church. We need increasingly to realise that the separate histories of our churches find their full meaning only if seen in the perspective of God's dealings with his whole people.[20]

Instead of talking to one another around the circumference of a circle, the churches were henceforth to move in toward its center. The 1950s were the heyday of "biblical theology," of the "salvation history" perspective in dogmatics, of the Barthian "christological concentration." An outstanding example of scriptural, historical, and theological scholarship impinging on Christian worship was the Jesuit Jean Daniélou's *Bible et Liturgie* (1951, Eng. trans. 1956), where the Old Testament figures and their New Testament fulfillments were shown to form the basis of the early Fathers' expositions of the rites and feasts of the Church.[21]

Before pursuing the doctrinal work of Faith and Order on worship, however, we need to note some intervening developments in practical liturgy. First is the impact that was to be made on liturgical composition over the next twenty-five years by the book of Gregory Dix (1901–1952), *The Shape of the Liturgy* (1945). The Anglican Benedictine there expounded a thesis he had adumbrated in the chapter he contributed to *The Parish Communion*. He

Gregory Dix. Gregory Dix (1901–1952), an Anglican Benedictine of Nashdom Abbey, England. Speculative historian and brilliant writer, he was the author of the extremely influential volume *The Shape of the Liturgy* (1945). COURTESY OF SAINT GREGORY'S ABBEY, THREE RIVERS, MICHIGAN

discerned in the eucharist a "four-action shape." The seven table-actions of Jesus at the Last Supper—first he took, blessed, broke, and distributed the bread, and at the end he took, blessed, and circulated the cup—had been "telescoped" by the primitive church, through the bringing together of the bread and the wine, into four. These set the ritual structure of the sacramental meal: to the "taking" corresponded "the offertory"; to the "blessing," the "great eucharistic prayer"; to the "breaking," the "fraction"; to the "giving of the bread and the cup," the "communion." This "shape" fascinated an entire generation of liturgiographers, particularly in the English-speaking world, although it was eventually criticized for exaggerating the first and third items: the utilitarian "taking" of the bread and wine became seen as a somewhat slender basis for processional and other elaborations around the offertory, which indeed some accused of Pelagianism; and the "breaking," though it had been a focus of symbolic attention especially in the Orthodox and the Reformed traditions, reverted to a lesser status as necessary preparation for the communion itself.[22]

Next we note from the 1950s two newly composed liturgies that may be considered the first fruits of the Liturgical Movement in its ecumenical range, stemming from the Church of South India and from the Taizé community. The South India story merits its own telling elsewhere in the present book (see Chapter 17 "The Church of South India"). Coming from the 1947 church union that brought together the missionary labors of Anglicans, Presbyterians, Congregationalists and Methodists, *The Holy Eucharist* in its 1954 version served as an inspiring model for many in those traditions elsewhere in the world, and it became tangibly evident on the international scene when it was celebrated at global ecumenical occasions under the presidency of a young and energetic bishop of that church: Lesslie Newbigin (1909–1998).[23] The Taizé community was founded by two young Swiss Reformed theologians in wartime Burgundy, Roger Schutz and Max Thurian; as it grew, it gradually developed a characteristic liturgical life, with Brother Max (1921–1996) as the principal writer of texts. *Eucharistie à Taizé* was published in 1959 (Eng. trans. 1962). Its ritual structure—which is explained in a substantial introduction—may be described as a clarified version of the dominant classical rite of the West (and thus, coming remarkably from the Reformed side, an anticipation of the post–Vatican II reforms in the Roman Catholic Church); an appendix prints the eucharistic prayer of the Church of South India, "en signe de communion et d'espérance oecuméniques." The *Office de Taizé*, first published in 1961, has introduced many visitors to the daily and seasonal rounds of prayer, and Jacques Berthier's chants have had a wide diffusion, proving particularly attractive to young Christians. Also arising within the Reformed tradition, based in Scotland but allowing for a more widespread active membership, was the Iona Community, which has contributed much to the daily prayer of Christians and, especially through the compositions of John Bell, to their hymnody.

Faith and Order's doctrinal work on worship was conducted in the decade before the Fourth World Conference, to be held at Montreal in 1963, by a theological commission that operated in three geographical sections: European, East Asian, and North American.[24] At one level, the Europeans of "old Christendom" saw themselves in "the tension between a disappearing christianized world, with its specific style of life, and a 'new' modern world with its allegedly non-Christian or 'purely secular' style of life"; yet it would be truer to the New Testament to formulate the issue as that between the Church and "a world which worships other gods":

> The very tenacious medieval outlook which still to a large degree determines the thought-habits of European theologians deeply affects our way of acting and thinking in worship

and may hinder us from grasping the deep, genuinely "worldly" (or "world-concerned") attitude of New Testament worship. There is a constant temptation, in Europe as elsewhere, to cultic introversion, to make God and his worship serve the pious people in the Church instead of calling the members of the Church to serve the world in and through their worship of the one true God.

The more suitable theological framework proposed was trinitarian in basis, cosmic in scope, and salvation-historical in sequence: "creation and worship," "redemption and worship," "new creation and worship." Special attention is accorded to Sunday as, since pre-Nicene times, "the day when the people of God gathered for that corporate worship of which the Eucharist, the meal instituted by Christ, was the centre." In relation to Sunday as the Constantinian and now post-Constantinian day of rest and leisure, corporate worship on the Lord's day should be treated as "the centre of all life (*Gottesdienst*), comprehending all forms of corporate and individual worship and the whole of daily life as well, both its work and its recreation."

The East Asian section operated within the same trinitarian, christological, and ecclesiological framework. While insisting that "indigenization" is not just a question for the churches in Asia but is "a principle inherent in the Christian doctrines of Creation and Redemption, and the Incarnation of the Word of God," this group remarked on certain features of its cultural context. Whereas "worship in Asian religions is individualistic or, at most, collective," Christian worship is properly "corporate." Moreover, attempts at liturgical indigenization will remain artificial unless Asian Christians engage evangelically with the common problems of ordinary life on their terrain. Quoting the Japanese Masao Takenaka:

> From the struggling of this rhythmic life rooted both in Christ and in Asian soil there will come a spontaneous expression in songs and art forms of joy and thankfulness for his suffering yet victorious ministry. Indigenization will arise from within, from the process of the wrestling participation of God's people in the present concretely reality of Asian society.

The North American section located its report firmly within American religious and political history and experience. It studied the scriptural "matrix" and "vocabulary" of worship, emphasizing the "interaction" of "kerygma," "cultus," and "ethical obedience" and drew the discussion toward "worship, intelligibilty, and contemporary culture." Given their "Christian particularity and history within the generality of worship," "acknowledgment" and "responsibility" are the correlative categories that need revival not only for regular church-goers but for the "secularists," whether "casual" or "serene," who regard "the kingdom of man founded on the sciences" as the only plausible end of human existence.

At the Montreal World Conference itself, the section on "Worship and the Oneness of Christ's Church" was able to register agreement on the fundamental character of Christian worship:

> In Christian worship, God comes to us in Christ through the Holy Spirit, sustains us through his grace, establishes us in fellowship with him and with one another, and empowers us for his service in the world. In worship, we come to God in Christ, the True Worshipper. . . . In him, truly God, we have access to the Father; in him, truly Man, we are restored to our true nature as worshippers of God. Christian worship is, therefore, a service to God the Father by men redeemed by his Son, who are continually finding new life in the power of the Holy Spirit.

> Christian worship, as a participation in Christ's own self-offering, is an act formative of Christian community—an act, moreover, which is conducted within the context of the whole Church, and which represents the one, catholic Church. Ecclesiastical division among our churches, personal estrangement, and social division based upon class, race or nation contradict true worship, because they represent a failure fully to carry out the common ministry of reconciliation to which we are all called in Christ. . . .
>
> Christian worship is at once remembrance, communion and expectation. It points beyond the present moment to the tasks of Christian witness which lie before us, as we join in Christ's ministry to the world, and as we look to the consummation of God's kingdom; for this side of that kingdom all our doings in the Church are but partial anticipation of the glory which is to come.

Keenly aware of "the essential connection between the worship of the Church and its missionary task," the Montreal report sharpens the permanent question of the relation between Church and world into contemporary shape:

> In her worship the Church rejoices that God is Lord of both the Church and the world. . . . In worship Christians accept the world as the sphere of their obedience to God. They do so in the strength of their renewed life in Christ.
>
> The worship of the churches is today celebrated within a world at once brilliant in technological achievement and deeply troubled. In both perennial and new forms, our world presents a face opposed or indifferent to Christian worship, or insensible to the good news of Christ. Sometimes heedless and apparently disdainful of any transcendent human destiny, men often affect a resolute endurance of meaninglessness when earthly preoccupations fade or measurable securities fail.
>
> In the face of this situation, the worship of the churches warrants examination. The churches should ask themselves whether the liturgical language, images and symbols used are adequately intelligible to the modern mind. . . . [I]t is the function of the Christian teacher to use with discrimination the language of the day to interpret what is enshrined in the liturgy. . . . The timely illumination of the biblical symbolism is part of the witness of the churches.

Those considerations seem largely aimed at the modern West, yet that culture is not exempt from the remarks on "indigenization" that are more usually addressed to places of the Gospel's new or more recent arrival. In each case, worship is to function in critical transformation:

> Just as faith finds its own ways of expression in worship, so the Church's mission involves indigenization, a process of becoming rooted in the culture of the people. This process occurs normally, and most authentically, where Christian faith and worship possess the maturity and vitality to appropriate and convert prevailing cultural forms for the service of Christ. In this way Christian worship not only takes root in the culture but converts it to Christ, and so shares in the reconciliation of the whole creation to God. We ought not to be so much concerned with adapting worship to the local culture that we forget that the culture itself is to be transformed. Indigenization, we believe, is more nearly conversion than accommodation. The indigenization of Christian worship, required in every time and place, is the offering of the created order back to God, but converted and transfigured by the redemption that is in Christ.

Montreal's report on worship took up again the themes of baptism and eucharist, which had figured on the Faith and Order agenda ever since Lausanne 1927, and began in a more concentrated way the process that would eventually lead to the most widely received text in Faith and Order history, namely the Lima document of 1982, *Baptism, Eucharist, and Ministry.* Another section of the Montreal conference produced a report, "Scripture, Tradition and traditions," that proved methodologically important in this latter work.[25] However, we are once more jumping ahead of ourselves, and some tensions affecting ecumenical work on worship in the 1960s and beyond must first be described.

The "Secular Sixties"

In the Ecumenical Movement, we have noted three strands—"faith and order," "life and work" (or "church and society," as it came to be called), and—located perhaps somewhere between the other two—"mission and evangelism." These three should be mutually complementary rather than contradictory, but in fact there are often tensions among them, and worship sometimes has to bear those tensions. At the Second Vatican Council, a Roman Catholic version of these interests was exemplified in several concilar documents: "Dei Verbum" on revelation and "Lumen Gentium" on ecclesiology correspond to Faith and Order; "Gaudium et Spes" on the Church in the modern world, to Life and Work, or Church and Society; "Ad Gentes," to Mission and Evangelism. As I suggested at the start of this chapter, all were adumbrated in *Sacrosanctum Concilium* (1963), the constitution on the liturgy, and set in an ecumenical context by the decree "Unitatis Redintegratio."

In the 1960s, some "church and society" interests gained a new prominence, and with a particular slant. We have already noticed, in connection with worship, some concerns about "secularization." This was a category much employed by sociologists in their analysis and description of contemporary Western culture, which they saw as having a global reach. Some theologians, particularly those of a liberal Protestant stripe, took this process as something to be endorsed, typified by Paul Van Buren's *The Secular Meaning of the Gospel* (1963) and Harvey Cox's *The Secular City* (1965). Adopting, and perhaps twisting, notions from the wartime writings of Dietrich Bonhoeffer about "mankind come of age," the "secular theologians" spoke about living in the world "as though God were not" (*etsi Deus non daretur*). Frankly, living "without God in the world" does not seem to have much to commend itself biblically (cf. Eph. 2:12); and it appears on the face of it downright disabling to Christian worship, which is addressed to the God who is both active in history and also transcends the world as its creator, redeemer and consummator. Pure immanence finds its cultic expression in idolatry, the worship of the creature instead of the worship of God (Rom. 1:18–32).

A section at the Fourth Assembly of the World Council of Churches, held at Uppsala in Sweden in 1968, was faced with a preparatory draft emanating from the Council's staff under the title "Worship in a Secular Age" and marked by what David L. Edwards called a "secularizing trend." The same observer noted in the discussions within the section a severe tension between "the secularizing radicals and the heavenly conservatives." Its final report was a compromise. On the one hand, it acknowledged that "worship needs no more justification than does love. It acknowledges the deep mystery which surrounds human life. For those who believe in the God who is revealed in Jesus Christ, fundamentally worship is a privilege more than a problem, for it enables man to share in the joy, the peace and the love of God." On the other hand, "the churches, while wishing to affirm the reality of God in the world, often do so at the expense of the reality of man and the world, thus provoking a denial of the reality of God"—and it is "secularization" that "can recall us to true worship which affirms the reality of God, of man and of the world." Jean-Jacques von Allmen was deeply disappointed by the Uppsala report on worship, having himself tried to retrieve the more classical perspectives of Faith and Order. Anecdotal confirmation of the dominant mood at Uppsala may be found in the rapturous ovation given by the ecclesiastical *soixante-huitards* to Pete Seeger's singing of the satirical rendition of the gospel as "There'll be pie in the sky when you die."[26] The tensions from Uppsala continued into a WCC consultation on "Worship in a Secular Age" held in Geneva in 1969. The Orthodox bishop Anthony Bloom acknowledged that Christians participated in a "secular" society in the sense that it had "lost the sense of God" and therefore also the sense of the world's sacred "depth," its "vocation" and its "destiny"; the acute—and ecumenical—responsibility of Christians and their communities now was to allow *God* to be the celebrant of their liturgies, which would then become a "challenge" to "what is evil, godless, blind, opaque in the secular approach" and a stage on the way toward the day when God will be all in all.[27] A valuable ecumenical impulse would come from the side of Orthodoxy with the notion of "the liturgy after the Liturgy": the eucharistic celebration prepares the faithful to share the bread of life in evangelism and service.[28]

Secularization eventually fell out of fashion, both among the sociologists who had proposed it as fact and theory, and among the theologians who had endorsed it, but not before it had led some liturgical theory and practice into blind alleys. This is not to say that the issues involved in the ambivalent status of "the world" in scriptural perspective simply disappeared, or indeed those connected with the status of "religion."

The Uppsala report itself was honest enough to acknowledge that behind the "crisis of worship" lay "a widespread crisis of faith." The ecumenical statesman Lesslie Newbigin argued at the time that such a crisis of faith lay also behind "the crisis in mission" that affected the modern Western world and wherever its tentacles reached. Again, there are ramifications for worship. The late 1950s and the 1960s were the high point of political decolonization. Talk began about the need, for instance, for (an) "African theology," and debates developed as to whether this should relate more to the inherited "culture" or to the current "context." In matters of worship, the younger missionaries were sometimes, on Protestant terrain at least, more enthusiastic for "africanization" than the African Christians. A pioneering attempt at "A Liturgy for Africa" was made in the early 1960s around Leslie Brown, then Anglican Archbishop of Uganda, who had earlier participated in the South Indian union and the formation of the liturgy of the Church of South India; but this was overtaken, at least in part of the continent, by the drafting of an "East Africa United Liturgy" in the context of (finally unsuccessful) church union consultations that were taking place among Anglicans, Presbyterians, Methodists, Lutherans, and Moravians.[29] A generation or so later, in 1993, a continent-wide consultation on "African Culture and Anglican Liturgy" would be convened at Kanamai near Mombasa by the Kenyan bishop David Gitari.[30] The Anglican Church of Kenya has consistently taken a lead in official liturgical revision.[31] A characteristically African theme in *Our Modern Services* (2002) from that church is the concern for the ancestors, as in the post-communion prayer:

> O God of our ancestors, God of our people, before whose face the human generations pass away: We thank you that in you we are kept safe for ever, and that the broken fragments of our history are gathered up in the redeeming act of your dear Son, remembered in this holy sacrament of bread and wine. Help us to walk daily in the Communion of saints, declaring our faith in the forgiveness of sins and the resurrection of the body. Now send us out in the power of your Spirit to live and work for your praise and glory. Amen.

On the Catholic side, a highly significant "international study week on mission and liturgy" took place in the Netherlands in 1959, in the conviction that "the problems, difficulties, and needs confronting liturgical renewal," both "at home" and "in the mission territories," were "most typically exemplified in the mission field where *mutatis mutandis* they could also be most easily and effectively realized." The papers of the Nijmegen symposium were published under title *Liturgy and the Missions* (ed. Johannes Hofinger, New York: P. J. Kenedy & Sons, 1960). These matters would very soon be taken up by the Second Vatican Council in its *Constitution on the Sacred Liturgy*, which, besides contemplating extension of the use of the vernacular (*SC*, 36), set out some "norms for adapting the liturgy to the culture and traditions of peoples" (37–40). The technical terminology soon shifted from indigenization and adaptation to inculturation and acculturation. The theoretical debates and practical efforts are recounted for Asia and Africa elsewhere in this book (see Chapter 25 "Mission and Inculturation: East Asia and the Pacific" and Chapter 26 "Mission and Inculturation: Africa"). In parts of the world where the traditional and ambient culture is shot through with religion, the theological question concerns the evaluation of pre-Christian and extra-Christian religions, and the liturgical form of that question concerns the adoption or rejection of religiously fraught features of the culture, their assimilation or critical integration into Christian worship or their dismissal from it—all with an eye also to their possible longer-term effects not only on the Church but also, contrariwise, on the culture. These questions affect all the churches, although the approach to them may differ in confessionally characteristic ways.

Liturgical Revisions: 1965–1980

In the midst of the various crises, steady work continued to be done by a band of liturgical scholars and practitioners who were certainly not unaware of questions— both perennial and contemporary—relating to the Church, its worship, and the human story. Rather than seek dramatic solutions to contemporary problems, however, they looked for more modest revisions of the churches' current rites in continuity with the Christian tradition and in light of the best of it. A kind of ecumenical fellowship developed among many of them. A vital role was played here by Wiebe Vos (1921–2004), a Dutch pastor who had been a pupil of Gerardus van der Leeuw and secretary of the theological commission on Ways of Worship. Vos conceived the triple project of a journal, a society, and a study center, all to be international, ecumenical, and in the service of liturgical research and renewal. *Studia Liturgica* made its first appearance in 1962 as a quarterly under his editorship; Societas Liturgica was founded under his inspiration in 1967, and it has since met biennially in congress under the presidency of such figures as Ronald Jasper (chairman of the Church of England's Liturgical Commission), Jean-Jacques von Allmen (Reformed, Switzerland), Balthasar Fischer (Liturgisches Institut, Trier), Pierre-Marie Gy (Centre de Pastorale Liturgique, Paris), Hans-Christoph Schmidt-Lauber (Lutheran, Vienna), Robert Taft (Pontifical Oriental Institute, Rome), Bruno Bürki (Reformed, Switzerland), Irmgard Pahl (Catholic, Germany), Jacob Velian (Catholic, India), and Paul De Clerck (Institut Supérieur de Liturgie, Paris). Membership in Societas Liturgica reached a figure of five hundred. Regional organizations with similar aims are the North American Academy of Liturgy (founded in 1975), the British Society for the Study of Liturgy (1978), and the Australian Academy of Liturgy (1982). Other results of ecumenical scholarly cooperation were the *Dictionary of Liturgy and Worship*, edited by J. G. Davies (1972; revised 1986; and replaced in 2002 by a thoroughly reworked edition under the editorship of Paul Bradshaw), and what became the standard textbook in seminaries, *The Study of Liturgy* (eds. Cheslyn Jones, Geoffrey Wainwright, and Edward Yarnold, 1978; rev. 1992).

Many Protestant churches in the Western world produced revised or newly composed rites in the 1960s that were used for trial periods and then, after further work, figured in more complete service books in the 1970s or 1980s. Following Vatican II, the work of the Roman consilium for the revision of the liturgy was accompanied by observers on behalf of the World Council of Churches (Raymond George, British Methodist), the Anglican Communion (Ronald Jasper from England and Massey Shepherd from the United States), and the Lutheran World Federation (Eugene Brand from the United States), themselves leading figures in the liturgical commissions of their churches. The outstanding achievements of the Missal of Paul VI (1969–1970) and the *Rite for the Christian Initiation of Adults* (1972) in some ways paralleled work that was already being accomplished in other churches, and in other ways inspired other churches in their own process of liturgical revision. Many churches now possess rites that in various manners view Christian initiation as a single coherent, though complex, ritual which, after evangelization and catechumenate, includes baptism, confirmation, and first communion after the pattern that RCIA relearned from the patristic period. Several churches now own eucharistic prayers closely based, like the Roman Eucharistic Prayer II, on the anaphora of the so-called *Apostolic Tradition* of Hippolytus and other prayers, like Roman Eucharistic Prayer IV, in the Eastern mode of Saint Basil (see sidebars "Eucharistic Prayer II" and "Eucharistic Prayer IV" in Chapter 27 "The Liturgical Movement and Catholic Ritual Revision"). The return to the patristic pattern of word and table has meant that the homily has once more become for Roman Catholics "a part of the liturgy itself" (*SC*, 35 and 52), whereas Protestants for their part have moved toward more frequent observance of the Lord's supper. Overall, the awareness has grown of Christian liturgy as the celebration of the paschal mystery, an anamnesis of Christ's death and resurrection, including the adoption of an annual Easter vigil by several Protestant churches under the inspiration of the Roman Catholic rite that underwent restoration and renewal already in the 1950s. The ecumenical upshot of all this has been orders of worship that converge with regard to both structure and even wording. This has been achieved by means of mutual borrowings and critiques as the rites were being produced, and, above all, by dint of a common return to the freshly investigated and interpreted texts of the early centuries.

Great Britain provides, in its Joint Liturgical Group (JLG), a strong example of a semiofficial body of liturgical scholars who were all active in the practical work of their own churches and whose collaborative publications exercised great influence throughout the British Isles. In particular, their two-year Sunday lectionary—owing much to Allan McArthur's *Evolution of the Christian Year* (1953) and prepared before the new Roman three-year *Ordo lectionum missae* (1969)—found its way into the service books of Methodist, Reformed, and Anglican churches. The JLG also contributed significantly to the International Consultation on English Texts (ICET, later reborn as the English Language Liturgical Consultation, ELLC), which composed standard translations of ancient and classical texts, including the Lord's prayer, the Apostles' and Nicene Creeds, the Kyrie, the Gloria in excelsis, Sursum corda, Sanctus and Benedictus qui venit, Agnus Dei, Gloria Patri, Te Deum, Benedictus, Magnificat, and Nunc dimittis.[32]

Another semiofficial ecumenical group of liturgical scholars has been the North American Consultation on Common Texts. Its *Common Lectionary* (1983; revised 1992) is based on the Roman *Ordo lectionum missae* but differs chiefly by allowing, in the "ordinary" Sundays after Pentecost, for a semicontinuous reading of the Old Testament in which readings from the Pentateuch are matched with Matthew in his gospel year, from the Davidic narratives with Mark in his year, and from the Prophets with Luke in his.[33] This lectionary has found widespread acceptance in Protestant churches throughout the English-speaking world, and finally in Britain also. Requests to have Rome readopt its own lectionary in revised form—a move not without precedent in liturgical history—have not so far met with success. The pastoral aim of the lectionaries is to immerse the hearers of the word into the entire history of salvation to which they belong and thereby equip them to become also "doers of the word" in order to prolong that history by their witness.

A further area in which liturgy has taken an ecumenical turn is the commemoration of the saints. On account of what they perceived as abuses in the medieval cult of the saints, the Reformers either greatly reduced the *sanctorale* (as with Anglicans and Lutherans) or practically abandoned all liturgical mention of conspicuous Christians from the past (as with the Reformed). Allowing once more, however, for a modest commemoration of the saints (though rarely the invocation of their prayers), even churches having no formal process of canonization have begun to introduce or expand calendars in their official service books. These calendars often include figures from before the schisms of the eleventh and sixteenth centuries, especially the martyrs of the early centuries, the missionaries to the nations, and the great patristic doctors of both the Greek and the Latin churches. From the times after the schisms the new calendars include figures not only from their own side but also from "the other party." The Uniting Church in Australia names Ignatius Loyola, the North American *Lutheran Book of Worship* mentions Calvin (though not Zwingli!), and the Church of King Henry VIII dares to list for 6 July "Thomas More, martyr, 1535." The Catholic and Anglican martyrs of nineteenth-century Uganda are all commemorated on 3 June, which is kept as a national holiday, and pilgrimage is undertaken to the sites at Namugongo. The recognition that, in the words of a Russian proverb, "the walls of separation do not reach up to heaven" may prove a significant step toward the attainment of ecclesial unity on earth.[34]

"Baptism, Eucharist and Ministry": Lima 1982 and Beyond

The subjects of baptism, eucharist, and ministry had been on the Faith and Order agenda from its beginnings at Lausanne in 1927, but it was only with the post-Lund shift in method that a sustained and comprehensive statement of agreement on the topics could be attempted.[35] A report on "The Meaning of Baptism," published as part of *One Lord, One Baptism* (1961), was commended by the World Conference at Montreal in 1963. The meeting of the Faith and Order Commission at Aarhus, Denmark, in 1964 took up seriously again the theme of the eucharist and commissioned from Jean-Jacques von Allmen a study that later appeared as *Essai sur le Repas du Seigneur* (1966; Eng. trans. *The Lord's Supper*, 1969). Work on "the special ministry of the ordained" at first stressed its location "in today's world" and suggested the need for "more flexible forms of ministry," but the churches were suspicious of any attempt to bypass long-standing questions about the validity of orders and the proper sacramental structure of the ordained ministry. A tripartite draft text was presented to the Faith and Order Commission at Accra, Ghana, in 1974 under the title *One Baptism, One Eucharist, and a Mutually Recognized Ministry*. Much of the early composition, making use of previous ecumenical texts, had been accomplished by Max Thurian, himself the author of an influential study, *L'eucharistie: Mémorial du Seigneur, sacrifice d'action de grâce et d'intercession* (1959, Eng. trans. *The Eucharistic Memorial*, 1960–1961). Scripture, read in the light of early Tradition, lay at the heart of the document—particularly in its sections on baptism and eucharist—as the attempt was made to find a common basis on which the confessionally divided traditions could agree. From Accra the text was sent around the globe to churches and theologians for comment, and 150 replies were received at the WCC offices in Geneva. Detailed consideration of these allowed a near-final version to be brought to the Faith and Order Commission at Lima, Peru, in 1982. There it was further polished and finally approved with unanimity as "mature" for transmission to the churches with a request for "official response" at "the highest appropriate level of authority" as to "the extent to which your church can recognize in this text the faith of the Church through the ages; the consequences your church can draw from this text for its relations and dialogues with other churches; the guidance your church can take from this text for its worship, educational, ethical, and spiritual life and witness." The Lima text—*Baptism, Eucharist and Ministry*, rapidly dubbed "BEM"—elicited an unprecedented measure of interest worldwide, being translated into some forty languages and ultimately, in its English original alone, being reprinted three dozen times.[36]

Baptism, which "initiates the reality of the new life given in the midst of the present world," is "a sign and seal of our common discipleship"; it is "both God's gift and our human response to that gift." In light of the fact that baptisms always "take place in the Church as the community of faith," the suggestion is made to "regard as equivalent alternatives for entry into the Church both a pattern whereby baptism in infancy is followed by later profession of faith and a pattern whereby believers' baptism follows upon a presentation and blessing in infancy." The subsequent responses to BEM were taken as "a hopeful sign" that the churches were "coming to an understanding of initiation as a unitary and comprehensive process, even if its elements are spread over a period of time. The total process vividly embodies the coherence of God's gracious initiative in eliciting our faith."[37] Ecumenical advances have certainly been achieved in the mutual recognition of baptism, but interconfessional debates continue on unresolved ecclesiological questions concerning the proper subjects of baptism and the authority of the particular communities to administer it.[38]

Concerning the Lord's supper, it is affirmed in BEM that "in accordance with Christ's promise, each baptized member of the body of Christ receives in the eucharist the assurance of the forgiveness of sins (Matt. 26:28) and the pledge of eternal life (John 6:51–58)." The meaning of the eucharist is expounded as thanksgiving to the Father, memorial of Christ, invocation of the Spirit, communion of the faithful, and meal of the kingdom. The churches welcomed the confession of "Christ's real, living and active presence," yet their responses continued to ask, from various directions, for precision concerning the relation between that presence and the signs of bread and wine. As the celebration of Christ's Resurrection, the eucharist was particularly associated with Sunday, and since it is "the new sacramental meal of the people of God, every Christian should be encouraged to receive communion frequently." BEM observed that "the liturgical reform movement has brought the churches closer together in the manner of the Lord's Supper. However, a certain liturgical diversity compat-

ible with our common eucharistic faith is recognized as a healthy and enriching fact."
Properly embracing "both word and sacrament," the eucharistic liturgy is "essentially
a single whole, consisting historically of the following elements in varying sequence
and of diverse importance":

—hymns of praise;
—acts of repentance;
—declaration of pardon;
—proclamation of the Word of God, in various forms;
—confession of faith (creed);
—intercession for the whole Church and for the world;
—preparation of the bread and wine;
—thanksgiving to the Father for the marvels of creation, redemption, and sanctification;
—the words of Christ's institution of the sacrament according to the New Testament tradition;
—the anamnesis or memorial of the great acts of redemption, passion, death, resurrection,
    ascension, and Pentecost, which brought the Church into being;
—the invocation of the Holy Spirit (*epiklesis*) on the community, and the elements of bread
    and wine (either before the words of institution or after the memorial, or both; or some
    other reference to the Holy Spirit which adequately expresses the "epikletic" character of
    the eucharist);
—consecration of the faithful to God;
—reference to the communion of saints;
—prayer for the return of the Lord and the definitive manifestation of his Kingdom;
—the Amen of the whole community;
—sign of reconciliation and peace;
—the breaking of the bread;
—eating and drinking in communion with Christ and with each member of the Church;
—final act of praise;
—blessing and sending.[39]

Regarding ministry: the churches on the whole welcomed the idea of BEM that the
presiding presence of ordained ministers "reminds the community of the divine initiative, and of the dependence of the Church on Jesus Christ, who is the source of its
mission and the foundation of its unity" (M 12). Perhaps the most controversial notion was that of "episcopal succession as a sign, though not a guarantee, of the continuity and unity of the Church" (M 38). For some churches this went too far, for
others not far enough.

BEM both reflected and supported much of the work done by churches in revising
their service books in the 1960s and 1970s, and its influence was felt among the late-
comers to liturgical revision (for example, the German-speaking Lutheran *Erneuerte
Agende*, 1990, and *Evangelisches Gottesdienstbuch*, 1999). Its principles continued to find
respect in the next generation of service books, such as the Church of Scotland's *Book
of Common Order* of 1994 coming after that of 1979, the British *Methodist Worship Book*
of 1999 after the *Methodist Service Book* of 1975, and the Church of England's *Common
Worship* of 2000 after the *Alternative Services Book* of 1980; and in the United States,
the Presbyterian *Book of Common Worship* of 1993 following the *Worshipbook* of 1970,
and the *United Methodist Book of Worship* of 1992 following various partial texts from
the 1970s.

The success, above all, of BEM's section on the eucharist may have been fur-
thered by the so-called Lima Liturgy. Principally drafted by Max Thurian, this order of service was first used for the eucharist at the close of the meeting of the Faith

Lima Liturgy. Robert Runcie, then archbishop of Canterbury, presiding at the celebration of the Lima Liturgy during the Sixth Assembly of the World Council of Churches at Vancouver, Canada, 1983. The familiar ecumenical logo of the boat is here shaped toward a traditional local culture. PHOTOGRAPH COURTESY OF WORLD COUNCIL OF CHURCHES

and Order Commission from which the final text of BEM came, although it was not formally adopted in the same way as the doctrinal text. On that occasion at Lima in January 1982, the liturgy was presided over by Robert Wright, of the Episcopal Church in the USA, with the widest ecumenical range of concelebrants canonically allowed; the Catholic and Orthodox members of the Commission, by their own church discipline and to their expressed sorrow, did not receive communion. The heavy stress on the themes of baptism, eucharist, and ministry, suitable to the original occasion, was modified in later celebrations of the Lima Liturgy, as when it was employed in the Ecumenical Centre Chapel in Geneva during the meeting of the WCC Central Committee in July 1982, with General Secretary Philip Potter as the presiding minister, and again at the Sixth Assembly of the WCC at Vancouver in 1983, under the presidency of Robert Runcie, Archbishop of Canterbury. Following such examples, the Lima Liturgy became adopted and adapted for many local ecumenical events around the world, and its popular reception is at least an indication of the felt need for an instrument whereby a common faith can be confessed, celebrated, proclaimed, and taught together.[40]

The unprecedented intensity of liturgical encounters at the Fifth World Conference on Faith and Order, held at Santiago de Compostela in 1993, resulted in calls for further attention to be given to worship "on the way to fuller koinonia" or fellowship among the churches.[41] A first response came in a geographically representative consultation held under the hospitality of a women's community at Ditchingham in Norfolk, England, in 1994. There the emergence was noted of a "common ordering" in both ritual and temporal structures (daily, weekly, annual) of "the most primary elements of Christian worship":

> Many churches, in pursuing their own process of liturgical renewal, have discovered a convergence towards fundamental patterns of Christian worship. Such a resource—rooted in the New Testament, witnessed to in the sources of the ancient church, practised increasingly, and with more conscious intention, among more and more churches today, and capable of wide variations in local practice—can be a powerful inspiration for unity. It provides a basis for Christians and the churches, while exploring new possibilities in worship, to remain accountable to the experience of Christians through the ages. By offering a touchstone, it helps the churches to appreciate each other's distinctive gifts and emphases in worship.[42]

A follow-up consultation, held at the Ecumenical Institute of Bossey, near Geneva, in 1995, was devoted to "eucharistic worship in ecumenical contexts." While the original Lima Liturgy continued to be appreciated (and examples were offered of its regional adaptation), encouragement was given to local gatherings to create their own occasional texts with considerably greater freedom, though with the recommendation that they observe the following "fundamental pattern (*ordo*) of the eucharistic service":

GATHERING of the assembly into the grace, love and koinonia of the triune God

WORD-SERVICE
Reading of the scriptures of the Old and New Testaments
Proclaiming Jesus Christ crucified and risen as the ground of our hope
(and confessing and singing our faith)
and so *interceding* for all in need and for unity
(sharing the peace to seal our prayers and prepare for the table)

TABLE-SERVICE
Giving thanks over bread and cup
Eating and drinking the holy gifts of Christ's presence
(collecting for all in need)
and so

BEING SENT (DISMISSAL) in mission in the world.[43]

Given the current canonical impossibility of a fully common celebration, however, the Eighth Assembly of the World Council of Churches, at Harare, Zimbabwe, in 1998, did not include any eucharistic service on its official program of worship. Instead, a service of penitence was held in recognition of continuing divisions, and various local Zimbabwean congregations representing the Orthodox, Reformation, and Catholic streams of Christianity hosted WCC delegates at their respective celebrations of a Sunday eucharist, in the understanding that existing protocol be observed.

The Lima Liturgy

The Lima Liturgy is the name acquired by the rite that was first celebrated at the conclusion of the meeting of the World Council of Churches, Faith and Order Commission at Lima, Peru, in January 1982, when the final text of *Baptism, Eucharist and Ministry* was established. The liturgy came largely from the hand of Brother Max Thurian of the Taizé Community. Its original form—together with an account of its structure—can be found in Thurian and Wainwright (1983). At the Lima meeting, the themes of baptism, eucharist and ministry were particularly prominent, but that emphasis was modified when the Lima Liturgy came to be used on other occasions. Here it is given in the form adapted for the Sixth Assembly of the World Council of Churches at Vancouver in 1983, where the general theme was "Jesus Christ, the Life of the World," and the eucharist was celebrated as "the Feast of Life." Presiding at the service was Robert Runcie, then archbishop of Canterbury. The rite has often been adapted since for other occasions, a sign of the widespread desire for a common eucharistic liturgy that can be employed when doctrinal and ecclesiological circumstances permit.

THE FEAST OF LIFE

Singing
Prelude
Welcome and Call to Worship

Liturgy of Entrance:

Opening Hymn ("Praise to the Lord, the Almighty, the King of Creation")
Greeting (2 Cor. 13:13)
Confession of Sin
Absolution
Kyrie Litany
Gloria in Excelsis

Liturgy of the Word:

Collect ("O Lord our God: You have brought all spiritual and rational powers into being for the sake of obeying your will. We beseech you to accept the hymns which we, in unison with all your creatures, sing to your glory. Reward us with the overflowing graces of your bounty, for every creature in heaven, on earth, and below the earth bows down before you, and every creature sings of your ineffable glory. You are the only true and all-merciful God, and all the powers of heaven praise you, and we glorify You —Father, Son, and Holy Spirit—now and ever, and forever. *Amen.*")

Reading of Deuteronomy 16:1–3, 8 ("The Feast of Liberation")
"Holy God, Holy Mighty, Holy Immortal! Have mercy on us."

Reading of Isaiah 55:1–3 ("The Feast of Hope")
"Holy God, Holy Mighty, Holy Immortal! Have mercy on us."

Reading from the Acts of the Apostles 2:42–47 ("The Feast of Communion")

Alleluias

Reading from the Gospel of Saint John 6:47–51, in various languages ("The Feast of Life")

Homily

Silence for Reflection

Hymn ("Worship the Lord, Worship the Father, the Spirit, the Son")

Nicene-Constantinopolitan Creed

Intercessions (*"Lord, have mercy. Christ, have mercy. Lord, have mercy"*)

Free Prayers, and a concluding prayer

Liturgy of the Eucharist:

Prayers of Preparation

> Blessed are you, Lord God of the universe, you are the giver of this bread / this wine.... As the grain once scattered in the fields and the grapes once

dispersed on the hillside are now reunited on this table in bread and wine, so, Lord, may your whole Church soon be gathered together from the corners of the earth into your Kingdom."

Maranatha! Aleluya!
Lord, come soon! Aleluya!

Eucharistic Prayer:

> The Lord be with you.
> *And also with you.*
> Lift up your hearts.
> *We lift them to the Lord.*
> Let us give thanks to the Lord our God.
> *It is right to give him thanks and praise.*

Truly it is right and good to glorify you, at all times and in all places, O Lord, Holy Father, Almighty and Everlasting God. Through your living Word you created all things, and pronounced them good. You made human beings in your own image, to share your life and reflect your glory. When the time had fully come, you gave Christ to us as the Life of the World. He accepted baptism and consecration as your Servant to announce the good news to the poor. At the last supper, Christ bequeathed to us the eucharist, that we should celebrate the memorial of the Cross and Resurrection, and receive his presence as the Bread of Life. Wherefore, Lord, with the angels and all the saints, we proclaim and sing your glory:

Sanctus, Sanctus, Sanctus Dominus Deus Sabaoth.
Holy, holy, holy Lord God of Sabaoth.

O God, Lord of the universe, you are holy and your glory is beyond measure. Upon our eucharist send the life-giving Spirit, who spoke by Moses and the prophets, who overshadowed the Virgin Mary with grace, who descended upon Jesus in the river Jordan and upon the apostles on the day of Pentecost. May the outpouring of this Spirit of Fire transfigure this thanksgiving meal, that this bread and wine may become for us the body and blood of Christ.

O Holy Spirit, come to us. Fill us with your gift of grace.

May this Creator Spirit accomplish the words of your beloved Son, who, in the night in which he was betrayed, took bread, and when he had given thanks to you, broke it and gave it to his disciples, saying: Take, eat: this is my body, which is given for you; do this for the remembrance of me. After supper he took the cup, and when he had given thanks, he gave it to them and said: Drink this, all of you: this is my blood of the new covenant, which is shed for you and for many for the forgiveness of sins; do this for the remembrance of me.

Great is the mystery of faith.
Your death, Lord Jesus, we proclaim!
Your resurrection we celebrate!
Your coming in glory we await!

Wherefore, Lord, we celebrate today the memorial of our redemption: we celebrate the birth and life of your Son among us, his baptism by John, his last meal with the apostles, his death and descent to the abode of the dead. We proclaim Christ's resurrection and ascension in glory, where as our Great High Priest he ever intercedes for all people; and we look for his coming at the last. United in Christ's priesthood, we present to you this memorial: Remember the sacrifice of your Son and grant to people everywhere the benefits of Christ's redemptive work:

Maranatha, Aleluya!

Behold, Lord, this eucharist which you yourself gave to the Church and graciously receive it, as you accept the offering of your Son whereby we are reinstated in your Covenant. As we partake of Christ's body and blood, fill us with the Holy Spirit that we may be one single body and one single spirit in Christ, a living sacrifice to the praise of your glory:

O Holy Spirit, come to us.
Fill us with your gift of grace.

Guide us to the joyful feast prepared for all peoples in your presence, with the blessed Virgin Mary, with the patriarchs and prophets, the apostles and martyrs … and all the saints for whom your friendship was life. With all these we sing your praise and await the happiness of your Kingdom where with the whole creation, finally delivered from sin and death, we shall be enabled to glorify you through Christ our Lord:

Maranatha! Aleluya!

Through Christ, with Christ, in Christ, all honour and glory is yours, Almighty God and Father, in the unity of the Holy Spirit, now and for ever:

Amen.

The Lord's Prayer

The Peace

The Breaking of the Bread

Agnus Dei

Communion (with singing of hymns)

Prayer after Communion:

We give you thanks, most gracious God, for the beauty of earth and sea;
for the richness of mountains, plains, and rivers; for the songs of birds and the

loveliness of flowers. We praise you for these good gifts, and pray that we may safeguard them for our posterity. Grant that we may continue to grow in our grateful enjoyment of your abundant creation. Now that we have tasted of the banquet you have prepared for us in the world to come, may we all one day share together the inheritance of the saints in the life of your heavenly city, through Jesus Christ, your Son, our Lord, who lives and reigns with you in the unity of the Holy Spirit, ever one God, world without end. Amen.

Closing Hymn ("A toi la gloire, o Ressuscité")

Word of Mission

Blessing

Postlude

Singing

Reference

Thurian, Max, and Geoffrey Wainwright, eds. *Baptism and Eucharist: Ecumenical Convergence in Celebration*. Geneva: World Council of Churches, and Grand Rapids, Mich.: Eerdmans, 1983, pp. 241–255.

Achievements, Limitations, and Prospects

The achievements of the century-long Ecumenical and Liturgical Movements have been considerable, but much remains to be done. Following such pioneering steps as the annual Women's World Day of Prayer and the Week of Prayer for Christian Unity, Christians of different denominations have learned to pray together, but this has either stopped short of sharing communion at the Lord's table or has been limited to the occasional practice of "eucharistic hospitality" toward individual members of the divided churches. Theological dialogues have registered wide-ranging convergences in understanding, but these have rarely been consolidated into a doctrinal consensus that could be built into the official teaching of the respective churches (a welcome exception was the adoption by Catholics and Lutherans in 1999 of a Joint Declaration on the Doctrine of Justification), and several major dogmatic topics remain at issue even on such "liturgical" matters as the sacraments, ministerial order, and the communion of the saints. Even where churches of different traditions have attained mutual recognition and "full communion," there have been relatively few examples of structural union across the historic confessional lines such as was notably achieved in the Church of South India (1947) and the Church of North India (1970). The eleventh-century schism between East and West remains unhealed, and the divide between "Catholic" and "Protestant" remains in Western Christianity.

To judge by their service books produced in the second half of the twentieth century, many churches of the West have done a fair job in putting their own liturgical house in order, but most places in "old Christendom" have undergone a sharp decline in church allegiance and attendance. To cite only statistics from the established Church of England: between 1950 and 2000, the rate of infant baptisms for every thousand live births in the nation fell steadily and steeply from 670 to 190, while the absolute number of baptisms of persons over the age of 12 rose only to 8,000 annually; and average Sunday attendance at Anglican services in 2000 ran to 1.06 million, and Easter communicants to 1.16m. (1.36m. at Christmas), in a population of 49 million. While secularization may have faded as a thesis and perhaps as a fact, current signs of "spirituality" or "religiosity" often have little to do with historic or institutional Christianity, and there is talk of "the new paganism." Pope John Paul II called for the "re-evangelization of Europe"; and even in the United States, where the public practice of Christianity remains much more prominent, proposals for the creation or restoration of an "adult catechumenate," whether initiatory or remedial, find favor among "mainline" churches; and there are ecumenical calls for a "baptismal spirituality," whereby the whole of the Christian life would be treated as living from, or into, one's baptism in the midst of a baptismally aware community, sustained by the preached word and the Lord's meal.

On the global scene, the structures of the World Council of Churches are no longer adequate to the Ecumenical Movement. There is talk of a wider "forum," in which the WCC would have a part along with the Christian World Communions and perhaps other international organizations. The big question concerns the role and place of the Roman Catholic Church, which accounts for half of the world's Christians. The Roman Church never undertook membership in the WCC, but in the wake of the Second Vatican Council it has conducted bilateral dialogues with other churches and confessional families, has had official representatives on Faith and Order since 1968, and has had its "irrevocable commitment" to the cause of Christian unity reaffirmed by John Paul II in his encyclical *Ut unum sint* (1995). In that same letter the pope asked whether "the real but imperfect communion existing between us" might persuade other "church leaders and their theologians" to engage with him in "a patient and fraternal dialogue" in order to "find a way of exercising the primacy which, while in no way renouncing what is essential to its mission, is nonetheless open to a new situation." What are the prospects for a "Petrine ministry" in the universal service of truth and love for the sake of an authentic witness to the Gospel before the world? Could such a primacy constitute the lynch-pin in a conciliar and synodical structure that would accommodate a basic unity in faith, mission, life, and worship, while allowing for a historically and geographically conditioned variety that was enriching rather than divisive?

The question is complicated by two further factors. The first is the evident southward shift in the demographics and energy of Christianity. What Philip Jenkins has envisaged in *The Next Christendom: The Coming of Global Christianity* (Oxford University Press, 2002) is likely to bear a rather "Pentecostal" complexion, and the dialogue in which the Roman Catholic Church has already engaged with "some Pentecostal churches and some participants in the Charismatic Movement"—which has included worship among its themes—could prove to have been a portent.[44] The other factor is the increasing urgency of dealing with "the world religions." While many theologians are looking for a "theology of religions" that will allow the most favorable view of others compatible with the Christian faith, most would hold that the necessary respect to adherents and dialogue with them should not detract from the obligation to authentic evangelization (as distinct from coercive proselytism). And in the geopolitical realm, it may be that humankind is facing, on some sort of quasi-religious base, a "clash of civilizations" whose outcome is unforeseeable.

Bibliography

Crichton, James D. *Lights in Darkness: Forerunners of the Liturgical Movement*. Dublin: Columba Press; Collegeville, Minn.: Liturgical Press, 1996.

Davies, Horton. *Bread of Life and Cup of Joy: Newer Ecumenical Perspectives on the Eucharist.* Grand Rapids, Mich.: Eerdmans; Leominster, Heref. and Worcs.: Gracewing, 1993.

Davies, Horton. *Worship and Theology in England.* Vol. 3. Grand Rapids, Mich.: Eerdmans, 1996. See part 5: "The Ecumenical Century, 1900–1965"; part 6: "Crisis and Creativity 1965–Present".

Fenwick, John R. K., and Bryan D. Spinks. *Worship in Transition: The Liturgical Movement in the Twentieth Century.* Edinburgh: Clark; New York: Continuum, 1995.

Irvine, Christopher. *They Shaped Our Worship: Essays on Anglican Liturgists.* Alcuin Club Collections 75. London: SPCK, 1998.

Wainwright, Geoffrey. *Worship with One Accord: Where Liturgy and Ecumenism Embrace.* New York and Oxford: Oxford University Press, 1997.

Notes

[1]See Irmgard Pahl, "The Paschal Mystery in Its Meaning for the Shape of Christian Liturgy," *Studia Liturgica* 26 (1996) 16–38.

[2]See the preface to the fourth edition of Odo Casel's *Das christliche Kultmysterium*, ed. Burkhard Neunheuser (Regensburg: Pustet, 1960) 5.

[3]To gain an idea of the shenanigans of that time, see John Killinger's *Leave It to the Spirit: Commitment and Freedom in the New Liturgy* (New York: Harper and Row, 1971). For Jean-Jacques von Allmen (1917–1994) on Christian worship as "un jeu eschatologique," see his *Prophétisme sacramentel* (Neuchâtel: Delachaux & Niestlé, 1964) 287–311, and "Worship and the Holy Spirit," *Studia Liturgica* 2 (1963) 124–135.

[4]See B. Neunheuser, "Towards a History of Maria Laach between the Wars, 1918–1939," *Monastic Studies* 13 (1982) 217–226.

[5]Less easily accessible is a brilliant set of essays, written by Anton L. Mayer from the 1920s through the 1950s, locating the liturgy in the periods of European intellectual and cultural history: *Die Liturgie in der europäischen Geistesgeschichte*, ed. Emmanuel von Severus (Darmstadt: Wissenschaftliche Buchgesellschaft, 1971).

[6]Peter J. Jagger, *The Alcuin Club and Its Publications, 1897–1987: An Annotated Bibliography* (Norwich, Norfolk: Hymns Ancient and Modern, on behalf of the Alcuin Club, 1986).

[7]See "Anglicans and Dissenters" in this book. W. J. Grisbrooke's *Anglican Liturgies of the Seventeenth and Eighteenth Centuries* was an Alcuin Club publication, though admittedly not before 1958.

[8]The heavy loss of life in the First World War had led to wider sympathy toward prayer for the dead, but the memory of medieval abuses sustained Protestant opposition to this ancient practice; see

G. K. A. Bell, *Randall Davidson: Archbishop of Canterbury* (London: OUP 1935; 3rd ed. 1952) 828–831, cf. 440–441. More recently, see Geoffrey Wainwright, "The Saints and the Departed: Confessional Controversy and Ecumenical Convergence," *Studia Liturgica* 34 (2004) 65–91, in particular 76–77.

[9]Donald Gray, *Earth and Altar* (Norwich: Canterbury Press for the Alcuin Club, 1986) 181–182.

[10]Peter J. Jagger, *Bishop Henry de Candole: His Life and Times (1895–1971)* (Leighton Buzzard, Beds.: Faith Press, 1975), 119.

[11]Quoted in Fenwick and Spinks, *Worship in Transition*, 47.

[12]Malcolm Boyd, *Crisis in Communication* (Garden City, N.Y.: Doubleday, 1957) 83. See also Ernest W. Southcott's own *The Parish Comes Alive* (London: Mowbray, 1956), esp. 43, 67–74 for domestic eucharists.

[13]Maxwell's "not entirely unprejudiced view" is cited from his *History of Worship in the Church of Scotland* ([London: Oxford University Press, 1955] 183) by Duncan Forrester in *Studies in the History of Worship in Scotland*, ed. Duncan Forrester and Douglas Murray, 2nd ed. (Edinburgh: Clark, 1996) 180.

[14]See *Faith and Order: Proceedings of the World Conference, Lausanne, August 3–21, 1927*, ed. H. N. Bate (London: SCM, 1927) 466–473.

[15]See *The Second World Conference on Faith and Order, Held at Edinburgh, August 3–18, 1937*, ed. Leonard Hodgson (London: SCM, 1938), esp. 219–269.

[16]See *Ways of Worship: The Report of a Theological Commission of Faith and Order*, ed. Pehr Edwall, Eric Hayman, and William D. Maxwell (London: SCM, 1951). The remarks of Leonard Hodgson quoted earlier are taken from his general preface to that volume, p. 5.

[17]*Ways of Worship*, 44.

[18]*Ways of Worship*, 11.

[19]For the part of the Conference's "report to the churches" that concerned "ways of worship" see *The Third World Conference on Faith and Order, Held at Lund, August 15th to 28th, 1952*, ed. Oliver S. Tomkins (London: SCM, 1953) 39–48.

[20]See *The Third World Conference on Faith and Order*, 15.

[21]See Geoffrey Wainwright, "'Bible et Liturgie': Daniélou's Work Revisited," *Studia Liturgica* 22 (1992) 154–162.

[22]See Kenneth Stevenson, *Gregory Dix: Twenty-Five Years On*, Grove Liturgical Study 10 (Bramcote, Notts: Grove Books, 1977); and B. Spinks, "Mis-Shapen: Gregory Dix and the Four-Action Shape of the Liturgy," *Lutheran Quarterly* 4 (1990) 161–177.

[23]See Geoffrey Wainwright, *Lesslie Newbigin: A Theological Life* (New York and Oxford: Oxford University Press, 2000) 270–279.

[24]See *Report of the Theological Commission on Worship*, Faith and Order Paper 39 (Geneva: World Council of Churches, 1963).

[25]See *The Fourth World Conference on Faith and Order: The Report from Montreal 1963*, Faith and Order Paper 42, ed. P. C. Rodger and L. Vischer (London: SCM Press, 1964) 69–80 for "Worship and the Oneness of Christ's Church," and 50–61 for "Scripture, Tradition and traditions."

[26]For the report itself, the observations of David Edwards, and the judgment of von Allmen, as well as some Orthodox reflections by Emilianos Timiadis, see *Studia Liturgica* 6, no. 2 (1969).

[27]See *Worship and Secularization*, ed. W. Vos, a special issue of *Studia Liturgica* 7, nos. 2–3 (1970).

[28]See Emmanuel Clapsis, "The Eucharist as Missionary Event in a Suffering World," in *Your Will Be Done: Orthodoxy in Mission*, ed. G. Lemopoulos (Geneva: WCC, 1989) 161–171; and Ion Bria, *The Liturgy after the Liturgy: Mission and Witness from an Orthodox Perspective* (Geneva: WCC, 1996).

[29]See L. W. Brown, *Relevant Liturgy* (New York: Oxford University Press, 1965). The texts of *A Liturgy for Africa* and *The East Africa United Liturgy* are reprinted, with their history, in *Modern Anglican Liturgies 1958–1968*, ed. Colin O. Buchanan (London: Oxford University Press, 1968) 48–89.

[30]*Anglican Liturgical Inculturation in Africa: The Kanamai Statement "African Culture and Anglican Liturgy"*, ed. David Gitari, Alcuin/GROW Liturgical Study 28 (Bramcote, Notts: Grove Books, 1994).

[31]See *Offerings from Kenya to Anglicanism: Liturgical Texts and Contexts including "A Kenyan Service of Holy Communion"*, ed. Graham Kings and Geoff Morgan, Joint Liturgical Studies 50 (Cambridge: Grove Books, 2001).

[32]See ICET, *Prayers We Have in Common* (1970; 2nd ed. 1975); ELLC, *Praying Together* (1988).

[33]See Horace T. Allen and J. Russell, *On Common Ground: The Story of the Revised Common Lectionary* (Norwich, Norfolk: Canterbury Press, 1998).

[34]See Wainwright, "The Saints and the Departed."

[35]See Geoffrey Wainwright, *Worship with One Accord*, 65–83 ("The Lima Text in the History of Faith and Order").

[36]For the original text: *Baptism, Eucharist and Ministry*, Faith and Order Paper 111 (Geneva: WCC, 1982).

[37]See *Baptism, Eucharist and Ministry, 1982–1990: Report on the Process and Responses*, Faith and Order Paper 149 (Geneva: WCC, 1990) 112. Almost two hundred official responses from the churches were collected in six volumes under Max Thurian's editorship, *Churches Respond to BEM* (1986–1988).

[38]See *Baptism and the Unity of the Church*, ed. Michael Root and Risto Saarinen (Grand Rapids, Mich.: Eerdmans, 1998).

[39]For analysis of the official evaluations pronounced on the eucharistic section of BEM, see Geoffrey Wainwright, "Word and Sacrament in the Churches' Responses to the Lima Text" in *One in Christ* 24 (1988) 304–327; and "The Eucharist in the Churches' Responses to the Lima Text" in *One in Christ* 25 (1989) 53–74.

[40]The original text of the Lima Liturgy can be found, with commentary, in *Baptism and Eucharist: Ecumenical Convergence in Celebration*, ed. Max Thurian and Geoffrey Wainwright (Geneva: WCC; Grand Rapids, Mich.: Eerdmans, 1983) 241–255.

[41]See *On the Way to Fuller Koinonia: Official Report of the Fifth World Conference on Faith and Order*, Faith and Order Paper 166, ed. Thomas F. Best and Günther Gassmann (Geneva: WCC, 1994), in summary pp. xv–xvi, 306.

[42]*So We Believe, So We Pray: Towards Koinonia in Worship*, Faith and Order Paper 171, ed. Thomas F. Best and Dagmar Heller (Geneva: WCC, 1995) xi.

[43]*Eucharistic Worship in Ecumenical Contexts: The Lima Liturgy—and Beyond*, ed. Thomas F. Best and Dagmar Heller (Geneva: WCC, 1998) 29–35.

[44]See Geoffrey Wainwright, "The One Hope of Your Calling? The Ecumenical and Pentecostal Movements after a Century," *Pneuma: The Journal of the Society for Pentecostal Studies* 25 (2003) 7–28.

29

Women in Worship

TERESA BERGER

Women have been liturgical practitioners through the ages, though often neither in their own right nor in their own rite. Unfortunately, no liturgical history available to date renders women's ways of worship visible in a historically continuous manner. Liturgical "facts" continue to be configured as gender-blind or gender-neutral, with little recognition that what comes to be counted as "fact" is always theory-specific.[1] As feminist research has shown again and again, a theory oblivious to gender as a fundamental marker of cultural formations will, first, present seemingly ungendered facts; second, it will thereby occlude a crucial shaper of historical practices; and third, it will therefore offer few guidelines for a world where traditional gender systems are in crisis. For a feminist reconfiguration of liturgical historiography the task is clear: to begin to write gender back into the "facts" of liturgical history. Such work is not about discarding what has come to be authorized as "liturgical tradition," but about uncentering its "malestream" constructions. Obviously this is a massive task which demands sustained collaborative effort by diverse scholars in the years to come.

In the present chapter, I illustrate the claims made above in three parts. The first part sketches the conceptual framework and interpretive strategies of a gender-attentive approach to liturgical historiography against the backdrop of more traditional ways of conceiving this task. I then turn to the material contours of a gender-attentive form of writing the history of worship. Because of both the magnitude of the project and the poverty of documentation, I proceed with radical selectivity—or more accurately, with fragments.[2] The four fragments I have chosen come from distinct time periods and highlight different liturgical practices, each illustrating larger theoretical and practical issues. I conclude with some thoughts on the politics of writing the past of women's rites. I claim that such history writing is part of a struggle over the meaning of liturgical practice for today and tomorrow.

The End of Liturgical History (As We Knew It)

Writing women (back) into the history of worship is a recent scholarly endeavor that brings the tools of feminist theory to the discipline of liturgical historiography. This scholarly endeavor centers on two tasks. One can be termed the task of deconstruction, or, less technically and more dramatically, the end of liturgical history as we knew it.[3] Here, the traditional interpretive strategies that have informed the writing of the history of worship become the subject of critical analysis. Questions are raised about

A nun lights the perpetual candle on an altar dedicated to the Virgin Mary. From an Austrian-Bohemian illuminated manuscript, c. 1430, parchment. INV. MIN. 12834. PHOTOGRAPH BY JOERG P. ANDERS. BILDARCHIV PREUSSISCHER KULTURBESITZ/ ART RESOURCE, NY

traditional liturgical historiography and its explanatory power: If what comes to be authorized as fact is always theory-specific, what is occluded in this history writing? What assumptions about gender (or the unimportance of gender) are written into the liturgical record as we know it? How have women's absences shaped that liturgical record? Josef Andreas Jungmann's thousand-page *The Mass of the Roman Rite*, to take one example, lets women surface (as women) only just over ten times, and in passages that narrate women's liturgical presence and agency as problematic, marginal, or nonexistent. Feminist historiography renders visible such traditional, seemingly ungendered histories of the liturgy as quite particular representations of past liturgical practices. These histories are, for the most part, event-centered institutional histories, and histories of elites and of their scholarly productions. Such histories bypass liturgical sites that are not shaped according to the accepted scholarly paradigm. In this way, traditional liturgical historiography projects onto the object studied what its own interpretive strategies and investigative procedures require: a liturgy untouched by gender. The fact that these interpretive strategies functioned with only limited success already points to gender as not only a fundamental but also a powerful marker of cultural formations, including liturgical practices. Indeed, as some older studies especially demonstrate, the historical narrative of the liturgy was shaped by, and itself shaped, performances of gender, gender divisions, and symbolic meanings associated with femininity and masculinity.[4] Traditional histories of worship do speak the power of gender, albeit unwittingly. However, in traditional liturgical historiography, gender is clearly—if only through silence—marked as marginal to that which is deemed central to the history of worship: the development of rites and institutions. Moreover, where gender does surface, traditional liturgical history presents it to be natural, essential, and binary.

The time has come to acknowledge the end of liturgical history as we knew it—or at least of its explanatory power. Such a claim is not about discarding the past; it is about uncentering traditional ways of representing the past. This brings me to the second task of restoring women to the history of worship. If deconstructing the traditional narrative is the first task, then the second is that of (re-)construction. What would a gender-attentive historical narrative of the liturgy look like? The question points well beyond a simple unified "history of women at worship," as helpful as an attempt at constructing such a history might initially seem to be.[5] But such history writing too often still assumes the viability of an "add-women-and-stir" approach. Seeking, however, to include women in liturgical history by focusing on women's participation in the established master narrative is a problematic enterprise. Women will remain marginal and particularized subjects because their inclusion does not challenge the foundational making of the master narrative.

There are two reasons why constructing a gender-attentive historical narrative of the liturgy is of some urgency. First, the field of feminist historiography, although "wonderfully unwieldy,"[6] has produced sustained challenges to traditional forms of historiography,[7] of which liturgical historiography clearly is one. Liturgical historiography ignores to its own detriment these theoretical challenges. Second, the fields of women's studies and of feminist history writing have by now produced a great deal of material on women's lives. Again, liturgical historiography ignores at its own peril the wealth of data available for understanding the actual lives of those who worshiped. It is high time to bring together the two separate versions of the past originating from the writing of liturgical history, on the one hand, and the writing of women's history, on the other. Bringing these two separate historical narratives together would enable us, for example, to understand Christian liturgy within the deeply gendered social contexts in which this liturgy was formed and celebrated.[8] These cultural contexts were marked by myriad forms of marginalization and legislated inferiority of women, but also by women-specific power structures, networks, and sites of women-centered agency. The development of Christian liturgy occurred within these contexts and has to be displayed as such. A feminist historiography of the liturgy in turn could contribute to broadening and deepening the field of feminist historiography, which continues to be weak in sustained engagement with the religious lives of women.

The writing of women's liturgical history today can bypass two earlier interpretive strategies of feminist historiography. Although important within the history of the discipline, these earlier attempts have been supplanted by more sophisticated approaches. I have already mentioned the key problem with one such attempt, an "add-women-and-stir" approach. This approach's weakness is its adherence to the traditional master narrative. A second problematic approach represents women primarily as victims within the master narrative—that is, as mere objects of patriarchal oppression. This renders invisible the multiple sites of women's agency and engagement in liturgical practices. Moreover, it does not do justice to how cultural materials, including liturgical materials, actually circulate among dispossessed groups. Dispossessed groups, in this case women, are not devoid of agency. They never simply receive, but also transform. A more fruitful approach to writing women (back) into the history of worship thus begins with the assumption that gender has shaped liturgical practices in a multitude of ways, and it examines how gendered differences themselves are constitutive of the historical narrative of the liturgy. Proceeding from that, one can ask how gender as a marker of difference affected women's liturgical lives in particular ways.

It will be clear by now that I assume the category "women" to be unstable, a variable rather than a constant. The category never stands by itself, but is inflected by other markers of difference, such as age, ethnicity, and ecclesial affiliation, to name but three. Similarly, gender is coded differently in different historical contexts. In fact, for much of the history of the liturgy the dominant marker of difference might be said to be ascribed status (combining gender and class), rather than gender alone. In restoring women to the history of worship, one thus must assume multiplicity in the cultural and liturgical constructions and performances of gender, in gender divisions, and in the symbolic meanings associated with femininity and masculinity. My attempt to write women back into the history of the liturgy primarily is an attempt to historicize, not to essentialize, gender differentiations in worship. Having elsewhere proposed thirteen interpretive strategies for reconstructing women's ways of worship,[9] I will assume these interpretive strategies to be in place in the following, second part of this essay.

Material Contours

Fragment 1. Biblical Roots: Prayers of Women

A look at the scriptures offers a first glimpse at the problems and possibilities of reconstructing women's ways of worship. I will focus on women's practices of prayer here. As far back as the early parts of the Hebrew scriptures, songs and prayers are put in the mouths of women—but only about ten of the nearly three hundred instances of recorded prayers or allusions to prayer in the Hebrew scriptures purport to be those of women.[10] If we look for biblical traces of women's prayers, then, the stark and gender-specific asymmetry in the amount of evidence is striking. The content of the prayer traditions also speaks to the power of gender in shaping prayer and devotion, ritual and worship. The majority of prayers put in women's mouths in the Hebrew scriptures are related to women's reproductive and maternal roles. There is Hagar's desperate plea in face of her dying child (Gen. 21:16 f.); Leah's praise of God at the birth of her son (Gen. 29:35); the blessing over Naomi by her women friends on the occasion of Ruth's marriage to Boaz (Ruth 4:14); and Hannah's agonizing prayer for a son (1 Sam. 1:10), followed by her exuberant praise when the prayer is answered (1 Sam. 2:1–10). Disproportionately, women's prayers, as represented in scripture, are shaped by women's reproductive and maternal roles (which, to be sure, were coded differently from today: much more broadly). That these roles exhaust neither women's lives nor women's prayers becomes visible in two powerfully prophetic voices of prayer and praise in the Hebrew scriptures: Miriam's triumphant song after the crossing of the Red Sea (Exod. 15:21), which is part of a larger women-centered ritual under Miriam's leadership, and the mighty song of Deborah (Judg. 5:1–31) after Jael's killing of Sisera. In the Apocryphal/Deuterocanonical books, indeed, prayer "often undergirds female actions that are courageous, unconventional, and subversive."[11]

Looking to the New Testament, we find two prayers put in the mouths of women that became part of the liturgical tradition of the Church. Mary's song of praise at her encounter with Elizabeth (Luke 1:46–55), known by its Latin opening word "Magnificat," has its place in the

Annunciation and Visitation. Sixth-century Coptic textile. VICTORIA AND ALBERT MUSEUM, LONDON, UNITED KINGDOM

daily prayer of the church. Elizabeth's prophetic blessing of Mary, "Blessed are you among women, and blessed is the fruit of your womb" (Luke 1:42), is part of the prayer known as the Hail Mary and recited again and again as a key part of the rosary (surely making Elizabeth the most frequently quoted woman in the Christian tradition, at least in its Catholic embodiment). These two songs of praise, like their counterparts from the Hebrew scriptures, are situated within women's reproductive and maternal roles. Beyond the powerful voices of these two pregnant women, however, the other women described in the New Testament as praying and praising God remain speechless in the recorded testimony, from the prophet Anna (Luke 2:38), to "certain women" devoting themselves to prayer with the other disciples of Jesus after the Ascension (Acts 1:14), to the four nameless daughters of Philip who prophesy (Acts 21:9).

The uneven witness of the scriptures to the prayer practices of women continues in the Christian tradition. Two thousand years of women's ways of worship remain largely hidden. Where women's prayers and practices do surface, they are often related to women's bodily and reproductive functions. The implications of these observations for a (re-)construction of women's ways of worship are sobering. Where earlier feminists might have celebrated, in the prayers of biblical women, the devotional voices of our foremothers, feminist historians today increasingly confront questions of textual representation.[12] The past of women's ritual practices, after all, is accessible only through multiple mediations, especially the mediation of (always gender-specific) texts, and the politics of documentation that made these texts, rather than others, accessible. Whether "real" women and their liturgical practices can be uncovered in the midst of these mediations is a real question.

Last but not least, there is the narrator of the past whose mediation develops our image of the past. The decisive role of the narrator's mediation is illustrated by a look at a second fragment of women's ways of worship. The texts and documentation for the reconstruction of this particular fragment have been available, for the most part, for centuries. However, the traditional narrators of the past, almost all of them male clerics, read these materials with particular interpretive strategies that precluded a sustained interest in what these texts might reveal about women's ways of worship.

Fragment 2. The Fourth Century: Women and Liturgical "Publicity"

Given that much of women's liturgical presence is in their absence as far as documentation is concerned, the task of rereading the traditional sources with new interpretive strategies takes on added urgency. The fourth century provides a case in point. In traditional liturgical historiography, this time period is marked as a watershed of liturgical development: with the so-called Constantinian revolution, Christian liturgy became a *cultus publicus* and grew into an elaborate public event that provided the ritual focus of the increasingly Christian society. With this ascendancy of liturgy to the rank of *cultus publicus* came a number of significant shifts in the liturgical lives of women—shifts that were problematic, and gender-specifically so. I take the topic of liturgical "publicity" as a case in point.

"Domesticity was the female role," Gillian Clark claims in her study *Women in Late Antiquity*—and then goes on to show how domestic life and work might include all kinds of buying, selling, and trading, how the domestic sphere was intertwined with public life, and how we know relatively little about the actual layout of houses and women-specific spheres within them.[13] These reminders that Greco-Roman households were not the private sphere of, say, pious Victorian women are important when focusing on these households as sites of early Christian worship. Here, after all, Christian women gathered the community, formed new churches, and took on specific leadership functions.[14] The existence of the particular form of the private "household workshop"—that is, extended households which could include shops, some of them the workplaces of women (wool dressing, embroidery, hairdressing, beautification, gold-leaf, ivory work, etc.)—aided this development. With the fourth century, however, sacred space came to be located in the public political arena (e.g., basilicas). This space was not immediately hospitable to women. If the fourth century indeed is a watershed for liturgical development, it has to be displayed as problematic for women worshipers who found themselves in a cultural matrix that put considerable constraints on most women's public presence. This problematic development is manifest, for example, in the ways in which gender-specific constraints on public appearance intensified during the fourth century. As the examples below show, the public presence of women at worship was increasingly "policed" by detailed regulations concerning women's clothing, coiffure, makeup, and jewelry. These regulations point to liturgical gender divisions, divisions that women had to embody and perform. It was women who constantly had their presence put under liturgical constraints by being admonished what to wear, how to do their hair, and how to comport themselves. If these admonitions were effective, there were clear constraints on the kind of presence and the kind of bodies women could bring to worship. However, rather than simply accepting these prescriptions as descriptions and therefore as "facts," a more convincing interpretive strategy will read these admonitions as pointers to contested practices. That is, in these admonitions we catch glimpses of how women's bodies might have been present at worship as sites of liturgical contestation. These glimpses appear in a number of different sources that prove suggestive when seen side by side, even if it is impossible to create a composite picture. These sources help us to imagine, however, what might have shaped the liturgical lives of the many Christian women of the fourth century. And even if these stipulations reveal more about their authors than about real women's liturgical lives, they do reveal a distinct pattern: the negative association between women's bodies and women's liturgical presence and agency. All of those— women's bodies, presence, and agency—had to be controlled in a variety of ways.

The early-third-century *Traditio Apostolica* (ch. 21) already stipulates that women have to remove all gold jewelry and open their hair at the point of their baptism. The third-century Syrian *Didascalia Apostolorum* (ch. 3) enjoins women to receive the eucharist with their heads covered. The fourth-century Egyptian *Canones Hippolyti* (Can. 17; special material) prescribe that women attending worship come without jewelry, do not wear their hair open, do not receive the eucharist with their hair artificially curled, and refrain from talking and laughing during worship. Ambrose of Milan (died 397) warned virgins against sighing, clearing their throats, coughing, and laughing during the liturgy (*De virginitate* 3.3, 13). He addressed a similar request to women neophytes (*De sacramentis* 6.3, 15 and 17). In the same vein, Cyril of Jerusalem (died 386) admonished women catechumens to pray silently, that is, merely to move their lips in public prayer (*Procatechesis* 14). And repeatedly, early Christian sources encourage women to come to worship veiled. Since there were different ways of veiling, it is often unclear which form a particular author wanted to encourage or prescribe (see, for example, the discussion in Tertullian, *De virginibus velandis* 16). As far as women's actual ways of attending worship are concerned, early Christian sources provide some interesting glimpses into that reality. From the letters of Jerome (died 420), for example, we know that Roman aristocratic women toward the end of the fourth century might come to worship accompanied by their eunuchs (*Epistolae* 22,

32) and have their own footstools at church (*Epistolae* 22, 27). This show of status and wealth within the liturgical assembly naturally attracted the sharp criticism of Jerome. Similarly, Jerome's contemporary Chrysostom (died 407) lamented that *virgines subintroductae* are received at the door and guided into church by the men with whom they cohabit (and who in thus accompanying the virgins into church fulfill the tasks of eunuchs).[15] From non-Christian sources we know that affluent women were used to attending religious festivals in festive dress, arriving at the place of worship in their own carriages and accompanied by many household slaves.[16]

The public, mixed-gender nature of the liturgical assembly could make worship a dangerous space for women. As one historian of women in antiquity puts it: "the usual setting for rape was a festival crowd (and Christian martyr-feasts . . . were not much better). Going out was asking for trouble."[17] The Byzantine historian Sozomen, in his ecclesiastical history written in the fifth century, mentioned a woman in Constantinople who accused a deacon of having raped her in church during her penitential exercises (*Historia Ecclesiastica* 7.16). Jerome warned that a daughter should stay close to her mother during vigils, and not visit churches and the martyrs' graves on her own (*Epistolae* 22, 17; 107, 9; 130, 19). Funerals and night vigils, in particular, came to be marked as dangerous liturgical sites for women.[18] Jerome praised the Roman aristocrat Marcella, who frequently visited the martyrs' graves privately but shunned public assemblies (*Epistolae* 127, 4; cf. 128, 4). Some of the latter prescriptions are certainly based on the topos of an ascetic renunciation of the world. They continue the trend, though, of associating women's liturgical presence and agency with trouble.

The association of women's bodies with liturgical trouble has been a powerful script throughout much of liturgical history. Since much of that writing was done by male authors, it gives us little indication of how women themselves lived and reflected on the liturgy. Only in late medieval and early modern times do we get more than rudimentary reflections by women writers themselves on worship.

Fragment 3. The Beginnings of Modernity: Writing Women on/at Worship

Communities of religious women provide for a specific interplay between women and worship, and of reflection on that interplay. Many convents were privileged sites of female literacy, not least because religious women were enjoined to recite the divine office.[19] Teresa of Avila (1515–1582) is one example of the many religious women who not only lived lives of daily liturgical practice but who also wrote on fundamentals of this practice, and whose writings, moreover, are both extant and readable today (countless religious women's writings remain in manuscript form in archives). Teresa stands in a tradition of writing women, but she was also on the cusp of new developments. Her lifetime saw the final breakup of Western Christendom with the Reformation, the conquest of the Americas, the global expansion of Christian mission, and the formation

Portrait of Teresa of Avila, age 61. Painted by Fray Juan de la Miseria in the convent of San José, Seville, 1576. Erich Lessing/Art Resource, NY

of Tridentine Catholicism, which shaped the Roman Catholic Church well into the twentieth century.

In Teresa's writings, liturgy is no subject matter of its own.[20] As a woman of the sixteenth century (and as a Christian of Jewish descent), Teresa was in no position to intervene in liturgical developments, champion liturgical reforms, or shape liturgical laws and practices, at least not beyond the confines of her own convents. Nevertheless, Teresa, as a monastic reformer responsible for the lives of her sisters and as a woman writing on the life of prayer, does afford us glimpses into how liturgy shaped her life and that of her communities. Teresa's world offered her a conflictual context for her reflections. Religious renewal movements advocated interior prayer and mystic contemplation, and a critical indifference vis-à-vis liturgical forms, vocal prayer, and popular devotional practices. Women experimented with new forms of living and praying, elite women exercised profound influence on religious life through patronage,[21] and writing women flourished.[22] Not surprisingly, many of these movements, inspired both by Erasmian and by Pietist ideals, attracted the sustained suspicion of the Spanish Inquisition. Teresa lived and wrote in this context.[23]

With male confessors and the Inquisition looking over her shoulder, and with male clerics and theologians insisting that contemplative prayer was dangerous particularly for women, Teresa knew well the objections to her chosen lifestyle: "it's not for women, for they will be susceptible to illusions"; "it's better they stick to their sewing"; "the Our Father and the Hail Mary are sufficient" (*Way of Perfection* 21:2).[24] Teresa herself did not deny the importance of formal liturgical prayer (although that prayer came in a language in which she most likely was phonetically literate only; cf. *Book of Her Life* 26:5). Teresa insistently wove formal liturgical and contemplative prayer together by depicting formal prayer as open to, indeed as embedded within, contemplative prayer (e.g., *Way of Perfection* 22; 24; 25; 30). At the same time, she acknowledged her early lack of interest and skill in liturgical and musical practice, as well as her lack of interest in the more extravagant popular devotions, which she depicted as particularly attractive to women (*Book of Her Life* 31:23; 6:6). At one point, Teresa included the recitation of the divine office in a list of monastic trials and tribulations (*Way of Perfection* 12:1). Her description of the problems with the recitation of the divine office in the convent in Villanueva de la Jara provides a good illustration of these trials: only one of the sisters was able to read well, and the sisters used different breviaries, including old Roman ones handed down to them from clergy. As Teresa put it: "God must have accepted their good intention and effort, for they must have said little that was correct" (*Book of Her Foundations* 28:42). Teresa also recounted the Devil tempting her to be satisfied with the recitation of the divine office, like all the other nuns, and not to aspire to deeper ways of praying (*Book of Her Life* 19:10). Not surprisingly, according to the *Constitutions*, the four offices of prime, terce, sext, and none on non-feast days are to be recited in one at 6 o'clock in the morning (2 f.). The offices, moreover, and daily mass are to be spoken, not chanted.[25] Teresa claimed efficiency as her reason, writing that the sisters would have more time to earn their livelihood if they said, rather than chanted, the liturgy.

On the other hand, Teresa's writings are filled with references to frequent confessions, devotion to the saints, feast days, penances, novenas, and all the other forms of devotion to be expected from a sixteenth-century nun. She wrote poems and songs for liturgical occasions, and urged her sisters not to neglect the divine office, since it renders them available to hear God's call (*Way of Perfection* 18:4). Aspirants for the novitiate should not only be healthy and intelligent, but also "able to recite the Divine

Office and assist in choir" (*Constitutions* 21). And there is at least one passage in Teresa's writings that conveys a clear sense of pleasure in the description of a liturgical event: a procession with the blessed sacrament into the church of a new convent (*Book of Her Foundations* 28:37).

Furthermore, Teresa developed her theology of prayer through an interpretation of formal prayer, namely the Lord's prayer (*The Way of Perfection* 27–42)—after insisting, with strategic humility, that she only reflected on minor details of the life of prayer, leaving a real theology of prayer to learned men.[26] Teresa's spirituality is also deeply material: devotional objects, images, statues of the suffering Christ, the crucifix, the rosary, holy water, the sign of the cross—these all have their place in her spirituality. Moreover, there are numerous passages in Teresa's writings that link formal prayer or liturgical moments with mystical experiences. Her first ecstatic experience occurred when intoning the hymn "Veni Creator" (*Book of Her Life* 24:5–7). Praying the rosary brought her to the heights of mystical experience, and while reciting the office she heard the Lord audibly speak to her (*Book of Her Life* 38:1; 19:7). During a festive mass she received a vision of redeemed humanity, during another mass an ecstatic experience of being clothed in a white vestment—an experience that rendered her unable to see the elevation of the host and to follow the rest of the liturgy (*Book of Her Life* 33:14). The Virgin Mary appeared to Teresa in choir after compline, and Teresa had visions during funeral services and during matins (*Book of Her Life* 36:24; 38:24f; 40:14). Worship also figured repeatedly as an entry point for experiences of the demonic. One All Souls' Night, for example, Teresa struggled with the Devil alighting on her prayer book to prevent her from finishing her prayers (*Book of Her Life* 31:10, cf. 38:23). Of all liturgical moments, receiving communion was especially important to her: God's presence became tangible as nowhere else, and she described an almost unspeakable desire to receive the eucharist (*Book of Her Life* 39:22). Quite a number of her mystical experiences occurred at this point. Going to communion on the feast day of Saint Clare, for example, Teresa had a vision of the Franciscan saint promising to support her (*Book of Her Life* 33:13). The reservation of the blessed sacrament held special importance for Teresa and was one of the key reasons for her horror of the "Lutherans" (*Book of Her Foundations* 3:10).

In summary, Teresa lived and reflected an oscillating liturgical spirituality. Clearly, the liturgy was a fundamental part of her daily life. Equally clearly, liturgical celebrations were often the gateway for Teresa's mystical experiences. But these mystical experiences could transcend any liturgical event or be connected with other than liturgical celebrations. What can a gender-attentive form of liturgical history writing learn from women such as Teresa of Avila? I suggest the following: although Teresa accepted the liturgy as a site of encounter with the Holy One, she also relativized that site. As a woman of her time, she could intervene in the construction and performance of liturgical life only within her own limited sphere. Teresa was aware of some of these limitations. She hinted at not having the freedom, as a woman, to preach and hear confession, but instead had to be satisfied with decorating images (*Book of Her Life* 30:20f)—a stark analysis of gendered liturgical power relations. Yet from Teresa's marginalized subject-position grew a particular insight: the insistence that the ultimate point of liturgy lies beyond liturgy is a crucial corrective to a tradition which linked grace strongly to the performance of particular rites (many of which continued to be gendered to the disadvantage of women). Ultimately, Teresa reassigned the place of the liturgy in the lives of women by placing it within broader possibilities of the mediation of divine presence: "the Lord walks among the pots and pans," that is,

God is present in the menial domestic work usually assigned to women (*Foundations* 5:8). The everyday lives of women, so often trivialized, and the liturgical practices of the Church both are sites of encounter with God.

If such a sentence will meet with little resistance today, this is due not only to women like Teresa of Avila, but even more to the cultural and ecclesial shifts that occurred in the twentieth century. The fourth and last fragment attends to these shifts.

Fragment 4. The Twentieth Century: The Struggle for Women's Rites

The twentieth century profoundly reshaped women's liturgical lives. At the beginning of the century, the majority of Christian women still worshiped in a starkly gendered world. In most churches, liturgical leadership was in the hands of men; women themselves seldom took a public liturgical role. Some liturgical rites excluded women by virtue of their gender (such as various ordinations), and others focused on women because of their gender (the blessing of the bride, the "churching" of women after childbirth). Liturgical space was divided by gender, and women were all but excluded from the sanctuary. In the Roman Catholic Church, women's singing, where it was possible at all, was defined as nonliturgical. Most Catholics did not understand the language of the liturgy (learning Latin was the prerogative of an educated elite, a group which, for the most part, still excluded women). And last but not least, women continued to be subjected to detailed regulations of their dress code and appearance.

The renewal movement known as the Liturgical Movement, which emerged in the first half of the twentieth century, did not challenge the basic gender divisions and performances of gender in worship. The movement nevertheless offered women a vision of worship that enabled them to claim this "wonderful world of the liturgy"[27] for themselves in new ways. In that sense, the Liturgical Movement served as a midwife of the feminist liturgical movement that erupted in the second half of the twentieth century. Together, these liturgical renewal movements spawned a redefinition of women's ways of worship unimaginable in preceding centuries.

The classical Liturgical Movement at its heart was a rediscovery of the communal celebration of the liturgy as *the* fundamental act of being Church. The movement thus signaled a break with an understanding of liturgy that centered on a conglomeration of individual rites and rubrics. The rediscovery of the local assembly as the subject of the liturgy included the recognition of women as liturgical agents. This was no mere theoretical recognition. Women liturgical activists in the movement gained space for their own liturgical experience, work, and leadership—something generally not accessible to women at the time, at least not in the more "catholic" Churches. Despite its conservative woman-script, the Liturgical Movement thus could prove quite "liberating" for women, especially for educated and professional women. They were the ones who had gained decisively from the first wave of the women's movement and who claimed the Liturgical Movement's liberating potential for themselves. These women were products of major cultural shifts at the turn of the twentieth century: they began to enter secondary and higher education, and professional and semiprofessional careers. They fought for an end to their legal inferiority and for the right to vote. Not surprisingly, they began to draw on the liturgy not to support but to critique the traditional woman-script. But it needed more than the Liturgical Movement had to offer and more than the first wave of the women's movement achieved to challenge the deep-seated gender divisions in liturgical life.

A feminist liturgical movement emerged in the wake of the second-wave women's movement and of ecclesial shifts in the 1960s (e.g., the move to women's ordination in several Protestant churches, and the Second Vatican Council in the Roman Catholic Church). The decade also marked a period of major cultural shifts in women's lives, such as the rise of new reproductive technologies, changing sexual practices, diversifying family patterns, and an increasing awareness of women's marginalization. The liturgical reforms begun in the 1960s for the most part remained untouched by these concurrent shifts in women's lives. It took years before many Protestant churches had opened all ministries to women, before women presiders, preachers, liturgists, ushers, readers, eucharistic ministers, and hymn-writers were no longer the exception, and before the numbers of women bishops began to rise. Throughout these years, women also continued to be a strong, albeit clearly self-disciplining presence in more traditional Christian communities and their worship services.

As part of a liturgical movement of women, women-identified prayers, songs, creeds, blessings, and liturgies have multiplied. Liturgy, indeed, has become a crucial site of women's activism within the church, and women have rendered visible the liturgy as a site for what, arguably, it has always been: the negotiation of faith and women's lives. This has involved recognition both of the regulatory power of the traditional liturgy and of worship as a potential site of alternative liturgical practices.[28] By now, there is a recognizable feminist liturgical tradition that circulates globally. Women-identified liturgies are celebrated in such diverse places as Peru and the United States, Australia and Iceland, Korea and Canada, Chile and Sweden, the Philippines, Germany, and southern Africa.[29] What might this feminist liturgical movement mean within the overall history writing of the liturgy?

Making Liturgical History

History writing never simply was about "*wie es eigentlich gewesen*" ("what really was") although the nineteenth-century historian Leopold von Ranke did shape generations of historians with that claim. Rather, the activity of making history is a situated and interested mode of knowing that selects, orders, and interprets.[30] The role of the narrator of the past is crucial for the making of any history. To put it in the context of the present essay, my historical narrative, like all others, orders the past in relation to the present and the future, in this case that of women's ways of worship. What comes to be authorized as liturgical tradition, then, is the product of an ongoing contest over liturgical practices and interpretations today. Writing liturgical history can be seen as one site of struggle over symbolic resources and as an always selective, never stable site of the production of meaning. Tradition, here, is not a fixed and unified block of material, which is merely passed on and received; rather, tradition is seen as constructed in the here and now in an ongoing struggle over a diversity of practices and interpretations. What comes to be designated as tradition is, first, highly selective, but second, rather unstable, open to redesignation.[31]

Interpretive strategies such as these are helpful in understanding the contemporary surge of women-identified liturgical practices. Rather than designating these practices as a decisive break with and the very undoing of "the Liturgical Tradition," women-identified liturgical practices can instead be seen as part and parcel of the continuous construction and reconstruction of liturgical tradition in the life of the church. In the past, women have remained largely invisible as the ever-present though marginalized agents in this construction and reconstruction of liturgical tradition. Today, from normal parish liturgies to feminist rituals, from convent liturgies to base ecclesial communities, from charismatic healing services to Pentecostal revivals, the more than one billion Christian women worldwide[32] have become visible as never before. The future of the liturgy is in their children's hands.

Acknowledgments

I am deeply grateful to colleagues who read and commented on drafts of this essay, especially Elizabeth A. Clark, Gisela Muschiol, Angela Berlis, and Susan Thorne.

Bibliography

Berger, Teresa. *Women's Ways of Worship: Gender Analysis and Liturgical History*. Collegeville, Minn.: Liturgical Press, 1999.

Bynum, Caroline Walker. "Women Mystics and Eucharistic Devotion in the Thirteenth Century." In *Fragmentation and Redemption: Essays on Gender and the Human Body in Medieval Religion*, 119–150. 3rd ed. New York: Zone, 1994.

Clark, Elizabeth A. "Women, Gender, and the Study of Christian History." *Church History* 70 (2001) 395–426.

Muschiol, Gisela. *Famula Dei: Zur Liturgie in merowingischen Frauenklöstern*. Beiträge zur Geschichte des alten Mönchtums und des Benediktinerordens 41. Münster: Aschendorff, 1994.

Procter-Smith, Marjorie, and Janet Walton, eds. *Women at Worship: Interpretations of North American Diversity*. Louisville, Ky.: Westminster/John Knox, 1993.

Taft, Robert F. "Women at Church in Byzantium; Where, When—and Why?" *Dumbarton Oaks Papers* 52 (1998) 27–87.

Notes

[1] This concise formulation is Linda McDowell's in *Gender, Identity and Place: Understanding Feminist Geographies* (Minneapolis: University of Minnesota Press, 1999) 227.

[2] Cf. Caroline Walker Bynum, "In Praise of Fragments: History in the Comic Mode," in *Fragmentation and Redemption*, 3rd ed. (New York: Zone, 1994) 11–26, esp. 14.

[3] I borrow this expression from J. K. Gibson-Graham, *The End of Capitalism (As We Knew It): A Feminist Critique of Political Economy* (Cambridge: Blackwell, 1996).

[4] This is especially clear in studies dealing with other than "central" liturgical rites, e.g. Adolf Franz, *Die Kirchlichen Benediktionen im Mittelalter*, 2 vols. (Freiburg im Breisgau: Herder, 1909; repr. Graz: Akademische Druck- und Verlagsanstalt, 1960).

[5] For a detailed critique of Susan J. White's *A History of Women in Christian Worship* (Cleveland: Pilgrim, 2003), see Teresa Berger's review in *Worship* 78 (2004) 367-369.

[6] Pamela Cox, "Futures of Feminist Histories," *Gender and History* 11 (1999) 164.

[7] For good introductions to this field, see especially these three collections: Ann-Louise Shapiro, ed., *Feminists Revision History* (New Brunswick: Rutgers University Press, 1994); Joan Wallach Scott, ed., *Feminism and History* (New York: Oxford University Press, 1996); Barbara Laslett, et al., eds., *History and Theory: Feminist Research, Debates, Contestations* (Chicago: University of Chicago Press, 1997); and the two journals *Gender and History* and *Journal of Women's History*.

[8] Michael P. Penn's work on the ritual kiss is a powerful illustration of this point. See his "'With a Chaste and Closed Mouth': Kissing, Social Boundaries, and Early Christian Communities" (Ph.D. diss., Duke University, 1999).

⁹See Berger, *Women's Ways of Worship*, 5–26.

¹⁰Cf. Patrick D. Miller, "Things Too Wonderful: Prayers of Women in the Old Testament," in *Biblische Theologie und gesellschaftlicher Wandel*, ed. Georg Braulik, et al. (Freiburg im Breisgau: Herder, 1993) 237.

¹¹Toni Craven, "'From Where Will my Help Come?': Women and Prayer in the Apocryphal/Deuterocanonical Books," in *Worship and the Hebrew Bible*, ed. M. Patrick Graham, et al., Journal for the Study of the Old Testament, Supplement Series 284 (Sheffield: Sheffield Academic Press, 1999) 99.

¹²See, for example, Elizabeth A. Clark, "The Lady Vanishes: Dilemmas of a Feminist Historian after the 'Linguistic Turn,'" *Church History* 67 (1998) 1–31, and "Rewriting Early Christian History," in *Theology and the New Histories*, ed. Gary Macy, Annual Publication of the College Theology Society 44 (Maryknoll, N.Y.: Orbis, 1999) 89–111.

¹³Gillian Clark, *Women in Late Antiquity: Pagan and Christian Life-Styles* (New York: Oxford University Press, 1993) 94.

¹⁴For a good overview, see Francine Cardman, "Women, Ministry, and Church Order in Early Christianity," in *Women and Christian Origins*, ed. Ross Shepard Kraemer and Mary Rose D'Angelo (New York: Oxford University Press, 1999) 300–329.

¹⁵*Adversus eos qui apud se habent subintroductas virgines.* I thank Elizabeth A. Clark for pointing me to this passage. Chrysostom's text is available in English translation in Elizabeth A. Clark, *Jerome, Chrysostom, and Friends: Essays and Translations*, Studies in Women and Religion 2 (New York: Edwin Mellen, 1979). The paragraph in question can be found on p. 194.

¹⁶For more, see Deborah F. Sawyer, *Women and Religion in the First Christian Centuries*, Religion in the First Christian Centuries (New York: Routledge, 1996).

¹⁷Gillian Clark, *Women in the Ancient World*, Greece and Rome: New Surveys in the Classics 21 (New York: Oxford University Press, 1989) 17.

¹⁸See Taft, "Women at Church in Byzantium," 72f., and Berger, *Women's Ways of Worship*, 50–54 for more details.

¹⁹See Anne Bagnall Yardley, "'Ful weel she soong the service dyvyne': The Cloistered Musician in the Middle Ages," in *Women Making Music: The Western Art Tradition, 1150–1950*, ed. Jane Bowers and Judith Tick (Urbana: University of Illinois Press, 1987) 17–19.

²⁰I owe my interest in this topic to Gemma Hinricher, "Gott erfahren: Zum Liturgieverständnis Teresas von Avila," in *Liturgie und Frauenfrage: Ein Beitrag zur Frauenforschung aus liturgiewissenschaftlicher Sicht*, ed. Teresa Berger and Albert Gerhards, Pietas Liturgica 7 (St. Ottilien: EOS-Verlag, 1990) 211–227.

²¹Patronage is a way in which (elite) women exercised profound liturgical influence, but women's liturgical patronage is hardly studied to date. For background, see Elizabeth A. Clark, "Patrons, Not Priests: Gender and Power in Late Ancient Christianity," *Gender and History* 2 (1990) 253–373. How some women of Teresa's time used patronage to influence religious life can be seen in Jodi Bilinkoff, *The Avila of Saint Teresa: Religious Reform in a Sixteenth-Century City* (Ithaca: Cornell University Press, 1989) 35–52.

²²See Ronald E. Surtz, *Writing Women in Late Medieval and Early Modern Spain: The Mothers of Saint Teresa of Avila*, Middle Ages Series (Philadelphia: University of Pennsylvania Press, 1995). Cf. Lesley Smith, "Scriba, Femina: Medieval Depictions of Women Writing," in *Women and the Book: Assessing the Visual Evidence*, ed. Jane H. M. Taylor and Lesley Smith, British Library Studies in Medieval Culture (Toronto: University of Toronto Press, 1997) 21–44.

²³For more, see Gillian T. W. Ahlgren, *Teresa of Avila and the Politics of Sanctity* (Ithaca: Cornell University Press, 1996).

²⁴All quotations are from the three volumes of *The Collected Works of St. Teresa of Avila*, trans. Kieran Kavanaugh and Otilio Rodriguez (Washington, D.C.: Institute of Carmelite Studies, 1976–1985).

²⁵In manuscripts from the Carmelite convent of the Incarnation in Avila, where Teresa spent the first two decades of her religious life, the divine offices are notated, suggesting that they were chanted. See James Boyce, *Praising God in Carmel: Studies in Carmelite Liturgy* (Washington, D.C.: Carmelite Institute, 1999) 17.

²⁶For more on Teresa's rhetorical strategies, see Alison Weber, *Teresa of Avila and the Rhetoric of Femininity* (Princeton, N.J.: Princeton University Press, 1990).

²⁷The quotation is from an author identified only as Lina M., "Wie ich zur Liturgie kam," *Bibel und Liturgie* 5 (1930/31) 324.

²⁸For more, see, for example, the work of Marjorie Procter-Smith, especially *In Her Own Rite: Constructing Feminist Liturgical Tradition* (Nashville, Tenn.: Abingdon, 1990; repr. Akron, Ohio: OSL Publications, 2000).

²⁹Cf. Teresa Berger, ed., *Dissident Daughters: Feminist Liturgies in Global Context* (Louisville, Ky.: Westminster/John Knox, 2001).

[30]Cf. Susan Stanford Friedman, *Mappings: Feminism and the Cultural Geographies of Encounter* (Princeton, N.J.: Princeton University Press, 1998) 200 f.

[31]I rely here on the insights of Kathryn Tanner. For a more detailed account, see Kathryn Tanner, *Theories of Culture: A New Agenda for Theology*, Guides to Theological Inquiry Series (Minneapolis: Fortress, 1997) 128–138.

[32]Cf. David Barrett, et al., eds., *World Christian Encyclopedia*, 2nd ed. (New York: Oxford University Press, 2000).

30

Liturgical Music

WILLIAM T. FLYNN

The huge diversity of forms, styles, and functions in the music used for Christian worship (both historically and today) makes it difficult to define a category of liturgical music. Indeed many writers have rejected the term altogether.[1] Nevertheless it draws attention to an important distinction between music used in Christian worship and other uses of music. At all times and places there seems to have been a perception that music used in Christian worship ought to be subordinated in some way to the larger aim of the liturgy; that is, it ought to support the public and corporate worship of God. On the other hand, churches have developed many different means of supporting public worship with music. This diversity of musical practice and changes to the music of a rite over time reveal underlying diversity in how the participants have interpreted the worship service; they also reveal the processes by which musicians have attempted to integrate new forms of expression into their inherited views of worship. Thus the history of liturgical music illustrates a history of an ongoing critical evaluation of the worship service itself: both diversity and changes in the practice of liturgical music reflect various underlying theological issues.

There are three issues that so often underlie the patterns of change in liturgical music that they may be considered systematic (or at least perennial). First, musical roles have been distributed in different ways in different rites. For example, within the Roman rite, one can trace a change from chant performed by a lector with a congregational response to chant performed by a schola and a largely silent congregation; and in some of the churches of the Protestant Reformation, a unique musical role for the minister disappeared. Second, musical styles and forms arise in a complex interaction with the liturgy, in which a style may be favored or rejected or a form may be adapted to a new liturgical function. For example, the use of polyphonic music, cultivated in Western churches, may be contrasted with its absence from most Byzantine rites and compared with the different polyphonic forms that emerged in that rite in Russian Orthodox use. Third, there is a complex dynamic between liturgical and musical change. Liturgical changes may spur musical change, but it is also the case that musical changes have spawned liturgical innovations. Some musical genres, such as late-medieval vernacular carols and the congregational *Leisen* that arose outside official rites, may later become incorporated in them. This essay will address each of these issues in turn, examining representative examples from the history of liturgical music in order to focus more closely on their musical and theological ramifications.

Musical Roles

The proper distribution of musical roles has been a perennial issue for the Church. Part of the reason for this is that the matter is caught up with wider questions of lay and ordained ministry and the Church's models for worship. However, even though many studies of the origins of several of these musical roles have appeared, no synthetic history has yet been attempted. The short sketch that follows is therefore overly simplified, and much more research is needed to fill in the outline. Nevertheless it will cover some of the key developments of the first fourteen centuries, when each of the roles that are still present in many liturgies emerged.

Surprisingly, solo singing by musically gifted members of the gathered church is the most clearly attested musical role during the first three centuries. The earliest reports from the New Testament and from the second and third centuries suggest that singing was most common at meals, whether eucharist or agape.[2] Among the very slender evidence, Paul's first letter to the troublesome Corinthians (1 Cor. 11–14, especially 14:26–27) stands out for its description of urban worship in the first century.[3] He lists singing among a number of worship practices (including teaching, prophesying, speaking in tongues, and interpreting) that individuals spontaneously offered to the assembly during the course of worship.[4] In a passage from the early third century, Tertullian (c.170–225) describes similar practices at the agape: "After the washing of hands and the lighting of lamps, each is urged to come into the middle and sing to God, either from sacred scriptures or from his own invention (*de proprio ingenio*)."[5]

One may also infer that two other important roles emerged during the first four centuries (although there is not sufficient evidence to be certain). First, it is likely that there were some forms of ministerial chant, since the public "reading" of scripture and prayers may have had a musical element (declamation stylized into cantillation). Second, if such chant were sung, it would no doubt have been answered by congregational acclamations such as "Amen," "Maranatha," and "Alleluia." Evidence of the congregational singing of hymns is either nonexistent or controversial for the period.

The literary evidence is much more abundant from the late-fourth century through the fifth century. The Constantinian Settlement (313) provided the opportunity for much larger assemblies to meet, with consequent changes to the ordering and content of services, and the rise of desert and (especially) urban monasticism provided a renewed focus on the reciting and singing of biblical Psalms that became a regular feature of eucharistic services.[6] For much of the fourth century the psalm was still considered to be a reading, but it changed from a lightly inflected reading into a more melodic chanting. This led to two differences in the distribution of musical roles. One difference was the creation of a musical role for the lector, which during the course of the century led to the creation of the new musical office of *psaltes* or cantor. The lector, often a youth, was appointed to sing the verses of the psalm among the readings in the eucharistic liturgy of the word.[7] In response to each verse, the congregation sang a melodic refrain. The many references mentioning the importance of the congregation's response suggest that that body's singing melodies in unison was a new practice.

Another difference was the rise of group singing, principally of monks and nuns but also of the laity, including groups of children. During the late-fourth century through the sixth century, such practices can be traced mainly in the divine office rather than in eucharistic liturgies, and there is no doubt that groups of urban monks and nuns led the way. However, groups of laity leading a quasi-monastic existence often joined them or even held their own services.[8] The reports show a wide variety of solo and choral practices: the familiar responsorial psalm, the singing of *antiphona* (possibly nonbiblical refrains) with psalms and without psalms, and hymn singing by congregations, by choirs and soloists, and occasionally by two choirs singing in alternation.

The evidence of musical roles during the sixth through the seventh century is particularly sparse because of the cycle of invasions of Germanic tribes in the West and doctrinal and political conflict in the East and the consequent instability of Christian institutions in the former Roman empire.[9] The fifth-century practices seem to have continued, especially in monasteries that survived the invasions. In spite of the slender evidence, three new trends can be discerned. First, in churches the deacon seems often to have replaced the lector as the soloist for the psalm in the eucharist—a practice criticized in Rome by Pope Gregory I in 595, who put lectors back in charge of this part of the rite. Second, possibly as an unintended consequence of Gregory's reform (at least in Rome), groups of clerics (not monks or nuns) began to form scholas, where singing later became a principal focus. As Joseph Dyer has argued, a group of clerics specifically assigned to sing at papal liturgies was founded during the second half of the seventh century.[10] According to James McKinnon, this group, the Roman schola cantorum, was responsible in large part for creating the entire Proper of the Roman mass.[11] By the end of the century this schola is well attested at Rome and figures prominently in all of *Ordo Romanus I* (c. 700), which describes services largely composed of ministerial and choral singing. Third, wherever clerical scholas developed, the responsorial singing of the congregation at the eucharist seems to have been largely replaced by choral singing. However, the congregation was not entirely silent, as there are reports of them singing the Sanctus until the twelfth century.[12] Simple responses such as amens and greetings do not tend to be reported, but it is unlikely that an expectation of unison response at such points died out immediately if at all. The creation of clerical scholas had the consequence of nearly silencing women in parish and cathedral churches; however, women did continue to participate fully in monastic scholas, filling all musical roles (except that of the celebrant at eucharistic liturgies), contributing their own compositions, and developing their own musical traditions.

Only during the high and late Middle Ages (1100–1450) did any instrumental musicians gain a significant liturgical role. Organists, in particular, acquired a firm liturgical role, but only in the West. During this period organs gradually became

Organ. Toward the end of the first millennium in the West, organs began to appear in churches, especially monastic communities, but were not used regularly in the church's sung liturgy until the end of the thirteenth century. By the time of J. S. Bach in the early eighteenth century, the organ had become an integral component of the liturgical performance. The organ in the Thomaskirche, Leipzig, was installed in 1590 by Johann Lange and repaired in 1721–1722 by Johann Scheibe. The present instrument dates from the late-nineteenth century. FOTO MARBURG/ART RESOURCE, NY

a normal furnishing in many large monastic houses and large churches. Toward the end of the period (possibly as early as the late thirteenth century) some form of playing the organ *in alternatim* with the clerical or monastic choir developed.[13] In the thirteenth and fourteenth centuries specific injunctions against playing any instruments other than the organ begin to appear, showing that they also were occasionally used. Thus by the end of the fourteenth century or beginning of the fifteenth century, the full range of musical roles that is in use in the early-twenty-first century had emerged in the liturgy; these comprised discrete roles for ministers, the congregation, cantors, choirs, organists, and occasionally other instrumentalists. However, it is also clear that after the High Middle Ages there was only the most rudimentary role for lay congregations.

The emergence of discrete musical roles and the changes in balance among them is theologically significant, because the ordering of the worship service may be considered to be a social performance of the gathered community's relationship to God and to each other. The distribution of liturgical roles may therefore be considered to reflect a church's governing images of worship and its ecclesiology. Two of these images are of particular importance, since they encapsulate the dual command of right relationship with God and neighbor, which lies at the heart of the Gospel. They are often found in traditional descriptions of the eucharist, conceived as (1) a foretaste of the heavenly banquet, that is, a participation in eschatological worship; and as (2) a communal celebration of the remembrance and presence of Christ. Indeed scripture offers support for both models of ideal worship: the rich musical descriptions of the Temple in the Old Testament and even more important New Testament passages reporting choirs of angels and martyrs (e.g., Rev. 4–5) support an eschatological model, whereas Paul's descriptions of first-century household worship supports a communal model.

It is important to note that neither of these two images need exclude the other. Moreover it would be a gross oversimplification to speak of the first as suggesting an exclusively "vertical" (doxological) organization and the second as suggesting an exclusively "horizontal" (sanctifying) organization; both images are rich enough to organize both sets of relationships. The eschatological image emphasizes the role of the Church as a vivid sign of the continuing presence of Christ to the world, and therefore it can incorporate the Church's kerygmatic and diaconal functions. As Avery Dulles has argued, it may heighten a community's sense that it must be the hearers and preachers and doers of the Word.[14] The communal image may also support such sacramental functions, since the community gathers in celebration and anamnesis of Christ. It also incorporates kerygmatic and diaconal functions, heightening the sense that the community is charged to be God's people for the sake of the world. Indeed both the eschatological and the communal images are implicit in Paul's metaphor of the Church as the body of Christ. Since either image may incorporate features of the other, each may be used to construct an adequate ecclesiology. For this reason churches have tended to emphasize one or the other according to the specific needs of the historical situation and culture that they serve. For example (although there was considerable overlap among medieval institutions), the communal model was particularly developed by cenobitic monasticism, whereas the eschatological model was particularly developed in secular churches.

The musical practice of a church is particularly significant in negotiating the relationships between these images, since music's own core metaphors clearly express them.[15] Commentators from the fourth century onward mention unison singing as expressing *symphonia* (sounding together, i.e., acclamatory agreement) and the distribution of musical roles and the structure of music itself were considered to express *harmonia* (the right relationship of parts to a whole).[16] As stated by Clement of Alexandria, the whole Church could be characterized as being in harmony with Christ: "The union of many, which the divine harmony has called forth out of a medley of sounds and division, becomes one symphony, following the one leader of the choir and teacher, the Word, resting in the same truth and crying out: 'Abba, Father.'"[17]

These core musical metaphors were also used to reflect on existing musical practices in order to demonstrate how they supported the proper organization of the Church's ministry. From this perspective, the early church's charismatic solo song, which seems to have emerged as a way of expressing the uniqueness of the new faith, needed to be properly integrated into the service. As Paul's letter to the Corinthians makes clear, such offerings needed to be "edifying" in order to be in the correct relationship (harmony) with the church. The fourth- and fifth-century emergence of lector chant with congregational response seems to have signified a particularly important balance, since the unison singing of the response could be interpreted as expressing the unity of the Church and the invocation of that response by the solo singing of the lector could be interpreted as ordering both soloist and congregation into a musical harmony centered upon listening and responding to scripture. Ambrose, preaching on the story of the prodigal son, explained why the music (*symphonia*) that the Father ordered to be played to welcome his lost child home was a fitting symbol of the restoration of their relationship: "For this is a symphony (*symphonia*), when there resounds in the church a united concord of differing ages and abilities as if of diverse strings; the psalm is responded to, the amen is said."[18] For Ambrose the psalm's *symphonia* "joins those with differences, unites those at odds and reconciles those who have been offended, for who will not concede to him with whom one sings to God in one voice?"[19] Moreover by the late-fourth century the sense of community expressed by these images was considered to extend to the Church invisible. This is particularly noticeable in commentaries on the Sanctus, where the congregation is considered to be singing the words along with the "superterrestrial hosts."[20]

Singers. Detail from *Saint Benedict Excommunicating Two Nuns and Absolving Them after Their Deaths* by Giovanni Antonio Bazzi (1477–1549; also known as Il Sodoma). Abbey of Monte Oliveto Maggiore, Italy. SCALA/ART RESOURCE, NY

The change from lector chant to schola chant and the subsequent (if not necessarily consequent) reduction in the musical role of the congregation marked a major shift in the church's musical practice. However, it would be wrong to suggest that this shift produced a distortion of a communal nature of the liturgy. There is little evidence to support any notion that the laity was chronically disaffected or disengaged from the rite and much evidence to the contrary. The shift may be more accurately described as a shift toward a conception of the worship service as an anticipation of heavenly worship that required a richly articulated symbolic representation. Part of the reason for this must have been the need to find more effective ways for the Church to communicate with societies that had only recently experienced any form of written language and whose structures and institutions were still largely traditional. In such societies culturally agreed symbolic action is considered more binding than written formulations, and for this reason the specific words of a religious rite are emphasized less than their symbolically negotiated meanings that are mediated by vernacular preaching and catechesis. Thus it is not surprising that allegorical interpretations of the actions of the liturgy, such as that written by Amalarius of Metz in the ninth century, became particularly popular (especially in the Germanic-speaking parts of the former Western Empire).[21] Within this context, the music of the liturgy was interpreted as reflecting heavenly joy and binding the congregation to God and to each other through moving them to devotion. These themes can be seen clearly in the eleventh-century liturgical commentary of John of Avranches, *De officiis ecclesiasticis*: "At feasts, the cantor gives the water covered with a linen cloth to the deacon, which the deacon mixes with wine: for by the sweet music (*odulatione*) of the cantor, the people are inflamed with pious devotion and divine love, and thus run to the Lord, and one body in Christ is made."[22]

Moreover in the late Middle Ages the endowments of altars in the naves (i.e., the lay portion of the church) of both monasteries and secular cathedrals often made provision for polyphonic music specifically to foster such devotion.[23] The underlying image of heavenly worship and the role of music in forming the devotion of the laity continued throughout the late Middle Ages and was most eloquently invoked during the 1540s by a few English bishops unfavorable to the iconoclastic excesses of some of the reformers; thus in the unpublished book "Ceremonies to Be Used in the Church of England":

The sober, discreet and devout singing, music, and playing with organs used in church for the service of God, are ordained to move and stir the people to the sweetness of God's Word, the which is there sung and not understood, and by that sweet harmony both excite them to prayers and devotions and also to put them in remembrance of the heavenly triumphant Church, where there is everlasting joy with continual laud and praise to God.[24]

Thus the burgeoning of clerical and monastic musical roles cannot be seen to be disconnected from a concern with liturgical harmonia. Rather, the powerful aural symbols created by musical harmonia were often developed precisely to foster liturgical harmony and unity.

Musical Styles and Forms

Neumes. Musical notation on a leaf from a Dominican antiphonary. Flanders, c. 1300. VICTORIA AND ALBERT MUSEUM, LONDON, Ms. 8997.A SCALA/ART RESOURCE, NY

The symbolic systems of the liturgy, which include gesture, art, environment, words, and music, are interlocking, and any meaning that emerges from the rite emerges from their interplay. However, it is also clear that the interplay between these systems must make the goal of the liturgy clear to the congregants, otherwise one or another element may seem to be out of balance and destructive to the rite. In the history of liturgical music, this need to balance the tensions between musical and other symbolic systems has become most apparent when music interacts with the words and actions of the rite.

For example, from the fourth century to the early-fifth century, the new melodic style of singing the eucharistic psalm (described above) caused some church figures (most notably Athanasius) to outlaw the practice. However, the style was welcomed in Milan by Ambrose and grudgingly accepted by Augustine. In his famous reflection on the new style, Augustine confessed that he was prone to be moved more by the melody than the words of the scriptural texts that were sung and therefore sometimes considered that it would be safer if the church adopted Athanasius's practice of having the "reader of the psalm" inflect it so little that it was closer to speaking than to singing. Nevertheless in the end he accepted the style because of its ability to "elevate weaker souls to devotion."[25] Augustine's critique of liturgical music is, in part, based on his neo-Platonic aesthetic. For Augustine, earthly music is a reflection of heavenly music (conceived as number and order), but its arousal of the passions challenges its ability to lead to the more abstract contemplation of divine order. Thus whereas the goal of music is contemplation of God's harmonia, Augustine is enough of a realist to concede that such contemplation has an eschatological goal that needs the crutch of sounding music in order to attract weaker souls with a more concrete symbol of God's order.[26]

Moreover even though this passage is often quoted as identifying a systematic tension between music and text, it would be more precise (in analyzing its liturgical importance) to say that it is discussing a tension between music and scripture. In other words, it describes a liturgical situation where the "reader of the psalm" is not reading but singing melodiously. For Athanasius, the "psalm" was intended to be one of several biblical readings, but for Augustine it was no longer clear whether the "psalm" was intended to be a biblical reading or a "song." Augustine's struggle with the melodious singing of the psalm reflects the fact that during his lifetime the liturgical function of the "psalm" was being transformed. As readings, psalms were chosen for their appropriateness to the celebration. However, there is no evidence that they were subordinated to other readings of the rite or that they functioned as a meditative reflection upon the other readings, as would be appropriate for a "song." As James McKinnon has pointed out, lectionaries (in which the psalm was subordinated to the other readings) emerged shortly after this controversy had been settled, effecting the transformation of the former biblical reading into a gradual psalm.[27] The new musical style was accepted because the interaction between music, text, and liturgical placement created this new liturgical function that ensured that the gradual psalm would support the readings in the liturgy.

Another example of how music, texts, and actions interact in the liturgy can be traced in the histories of the use of tropes, sequences, and polyphony in the West.[28] The reason for grouping tropes (textual and musical interpolations into existing songs of the rite), sequences (prose or verse texts for the *pneumae sequentiae* of the Alleluia), and polyphony together is that ecclesiastical centers that cultivated one genre usually cultivated the others, and all three seem to have had the liturgical function of festal embellishments of the rite. The three forms display subtly differing ways of increasing the solemnity of feasts. Tropes (especially cultivated by composers from the ninth century through the eleventh century) consist of one or two lines of prose or verse. Although they were interpolated into most of the proper and ordinary items of the festal eucharist, they were never incorporated into the most musically developed songs of the mass (the Gradual or the Alleluia) but instead were reserved for chants that had a mixture of one to five notes per syllable. Sequences, although often related to the improvised melodic extensions of the last melisma of the Alleluia, came to have a separate identity as a largely syllabic poem that commented on the Alleluia and introduced the reading of the Gospel. During the ninth century through the thirteenth century, polyphony was cultivated especially within the Gradual and the Alleluia. The development of polyphony and the sequence also intersect, and numerous settings of sequences with alternate polyphonic verses survive; such polyphonic settings restore a sense of musical embellishment to the sequence, evoking its connection with the Alleluia.

A similarity among these three developments is a tendency toward greater and greater rhythmic organization: tropes show a distinct increase in the cultivation of accentual and hexameter verse during the period they were in vogue. Sequences show a change from rhetorical cursus to partially rhymed or assonant verse and finally to fully rhymed, fully accentual verse in regular stanzas. Similarly the increasing rhythmic organization of polyphony and its notation was one of the most important musical developments of the twelfth to fifteenth centuries. All of these developments support a neo-Platonic interpretation of the function of music in the liturgy, in which the lavish attention to the rhythmic and harmonic organization of musical structure could be experienced as a mystical vision of God's ordering of creation.

Interpreting polyphony in this manner may also have been a factor in ensuring that the organ (and other instruments) came to be accepted in the liturgy. The early history of the organ is plagued by the lack of unambiguous evidence concerning its placement in churches, the details of its construction, and its uses, if any, in the liturgy. Nevertheless it is most likely that the earliest liturgical use of the organ was as a signaling device, calling people to the rite or marking various points of the liturgy in a fashion similar to the uses of bells. The fact that the Te Deum and the sequence attracted polyphonic embellishment during the eleventh century suggests that the organ may also have been used (perhaps playing *in alternatim*).[29] Nevertheless, as noted above, clear evidence of such practices emerges only during the late thirteenth century. By the fourteenth century it is clear that the organ was regularly played on feast days, and it would not be unreasonable to speculate that alternatim playing in those parts of the services that were most musically embellished was already a common practice. By the early fifteenth century the *Codex Faenza* (the earliest extensive source of liturgical keyboard music) demonstrates that alternatim playing of the Kyrie and Gloria on feasts, as well as the alternatim embellishment of the festal office blessing and (possibly) of the festal Marian office hymn, was an established practice in part of Italy.[30]

The reason tensions can arise between the various symbolic systems in the liturgy stems from their relative autonomy from each other. In the first example given above, it is clear that the controversy over musical style developed in part because the music influenced how the text of the psalm was to be performed and understood. It did this by punctuating the text through melodic formulas and cadences; by emphasizing certain words through melisma, or repetition; and by reorganizing the length and balance of the psalm, changing a rite of scripture reading into a rite of reading and sung response. In the second example, the rite was embellished through the addition of words that were structured by musical rhythm and through the harmonic embellishment of chant melodies. In the third example, instrumentally embellished chant came to be substituted for sung chant, dispensing with the words but not with the melodies associated with them. Underlying such musical changes is a notion that the embellishment of the liturgy signifies a greater festivity (solemnity) of the rite, and it is not surprising that this notion would also easily support the changes in a core metaphor of worship toward signifying eschatological joy that was noted in the first section of this chapter. The medieval term used to describe this embellishment was *ornatus*.

The cultural and theological meanings of ornatus were established by two key texts: the first Creation story in Genesis 1–2:2 and the extended reflection upon the creation in Wisdom 9–11. Genesis 2:1 introduces the seventh day of creation: "Thus, the heavens and the earth were completed, and all of their *ornatus*." Here ornatus refers to everything that is created in heaven and earth, that is, the heavens, the earth *and the fullness thereof*. Wisdom 11:21 concludes an extended reflection on creation with the words: "you [God] ordered all things in measure, number, and weight." Measure (*mensura*), number (*numerus*), and weight (*pondus*) would have reminded any medieval clerical or monastic musician of discussions of harmonia found in music and rhetorical theory, and as Umberto Eco has pointed out, these two scriptural texts were frequently quoted by medieval theologians to justify artistic creation and to relate it to God's creation.[31]

Because of the equation of embellishment with the fullness of creation and God's harmonious disposition of it, music (and the musically ordered words of poetry) came to be considered especially tied to the core feasts of the liturgy. Such feasts celebrated the renewal of the created order implicit in the Incarnation and were intended to lead to a vision of the new creation implicit in the Resurrection: the closer the feasts were tied to narratives of the redemption of creation, the more likely they would attract musical ornatus.[32] Writers like Augustine (as shown above) were concerned that the sensuous qualities of the arts could lead to idolatrous worship of the creation rather than to the proper worship of the Creator and therefore stressed the ascetic side of Christian mysticism. Nevertheless the goal of such asceticism was a control of the senses that enabled the mystic to contemplate God's creation in its essential goodness.[33] Music, because of its ability to provide order and proportion to the words of scripture, came to be considered as having a particular power to reorder the liturgy and its participants toward a more perfect Christian devotion.

Liturgical and Musical Change

Readers of this chapter may have been struck by the lack of references to the musical and liturgical developments within the churches of the Protestant Reformation. The reason for this is that I have been discussing music within the context of "organic" changes in liturgical traditions, in which certain liturgical and musical features remain relatively stable and new elements are adapted to them. In "organic" traditions the lushness of a new growth may obscure, and even overwhelm, old features, but its goal is to sustain an existing tradition through a process of continual change. I will return to the idea of "organic" change in the last part of this section but will now turn to "reformative" change, which Geoffrey Wainwright summarizes under the heading of "Revision":

> Revision is called for when existing forms of worship are felt to be inadequate, but the sense of inadequacy may arise in two distinct ways. On the one hand, a gap may be perceived between a degenerate current practice and the practice of an earlier and clas-

sical period. In that case, the demand will be for a return to the sources. If degeneration has lain in impoverishment, a restoration of the pristine fullness will be required. If the degeneration has lain in adulteration, it is the former purity which will need to be restored. On the other hand, the gap may emerge between inherited or imported forms of worship and the requirements of worshippers in a changed cultural situation. In that case, the demand will be for updating or adaptation: updating, where the cultural shift has been temporal; adaptation, where the cultural shift has been geographical.[34]

All of these strategies of reform may be traced in reformations of liturgy and music within Roman and Orthodox Catholicism as well as in the early modern Reformation and Counter-Reformation. For example, the strategy of "return to the sources" was a feature of the twelfth-century reforms advocated by the Cistercians.[35] Bernard believed that the Church had lost sight of the need for ascetic discipline and contended that the rites of the Church had become excessively adorned not to enhance prayer but to enhance profits. In his attack on Cluniac monasticism he wrote: "Everything is covered with gold, gorging the eyes and opening the purse-strings. Some Saint or other is depicted as a figure of beauty, as if in the belief that the more highly colored a thing is, the holier it is. . . . People run to kiss them, and are invited to give donations."[36]

For the Cistercians, the return to the sources meant first a return to a strict interpretation of the *Rule of Saint Benedict*. The office was purged of psalms, litanies, and prayers that were not prescribed by the rule. Traditions of long standing were discarded: the singing of five antiphons at lauds was reduced to one, and office hymnody was limited to only those hymns the reformers believed were written by Saint Ambrose; this meant that only one hymn meter (iambic tetrameter, which is analogous to common meter) was retained. Moreover polyphonic performance was generally banned as well as singing in falsetto and improvising additional ornaments to the notated chant. Since they also believed their local chant tradition had become corrupted over the years, the Cistercians sent a team of scribes to Metz, a center they correctly identified as having musical traditions of great antiquity. However, what they found must have disappointed them, as it was a tradition of equal complexity to their own. Nevertheless they sang the Metz versions of chant until the late 1140s, when it was decided that the chant needed to be adapted to their local tradition. At the same time they updated a small amount of the music, bringing some particularly wide-ranging melodies into line with current theoretical ideas about the ambitus of modes. Newly composed or adapted hymn texts and tunes were introduced, but the Cistercians also reclaimed some of the hymn repertory they had rejected in the first stage of the reform.

The strategy of "return to the sources" also featured strongly in the series of reforms that led to the modern Liturgical Movement. Although this was a multiconfessional and multinational phenomenon, I will concentrate particularly on its manifestation in the Anglican Church of the second third of the nineteenth century. The Anglican Tractarians sensed that the church had become unpopular and irrelevant to a newly industrialized, urbanized, and revolutionary society. According to John Julian, John Henry Newman's famous hymn "Lead Kindly Light amid the Encircling Gloom" was "the impassioned and pathetic prayer . . . one of the birthpangs . . . of the Oxford Movement."[37] The Tractarians' sense of deficiency centered on what they considered an inability of the church to speak theologically, because in the cozy relationship between state and church the clergy acted "as ministers of the government rather than ministers of the Gospel."[38]

The notion that the clergy had lost its sense of vocation and spirituality was a powerful motivating force for the Tractarians, and whereas their theological sources were largely the Latin authors of the first five centuries, their spirituality was based upon the Romantic notion of the Middle Ages as the great Age of Faith. For this reason their liturgical "return to the sources" was motivated by restoring a medieval "fullness" of ceremonial. The liturgical details were worked out by the Cambridge Camden Society (later the Ecclesiological Society) under the leadership of the young John Mason Neale. As Nicholas Temperley points out:

> The aesthetic of the Tractarians was not closely tied to their theology. They were eclectic in their choice of past traditions for revival. . . . Their architectural ideal was the Decorated Gothic . . . of the fourteenth century. Their liturgy was, perforce, of the sixteenth century. Their musical models were the Gregorian chant, believed to date from early Christian times, and the harmonic and contrapuntal style of the Renaissance. Many of their vestments and ceremonial customs dated from the later middle ages. With the help of creative imagination and passionate advocacy, this conglomeration soon assumed a strong integrity, recognized by friends and foes as the outward form of the Oxford movement.[39]

Indeed so far as the restoration of Gregorian chant was concerned, the Cambridge ecclesiologists creatively misread the historical evidence, believing that congregations (led by robed and surpliced choirs) had spontaneously joined in singing chant during the Middle Ages. Furthermore being obliged to accept the *Book of Common Prayer*, they became particularly interested in the Reformation experiments in adapting plainchant to English (such as John Merbecke's *The Book of Common Praier Noted*, 1550). Unlike previous "high" churchmen, they participated in the popular movement to include hymns (as opposed to metrical psalms) in services, but their hymnody came to be based on their translations of the hymns of the Roman and other Latin Breviaries, together with their chant tunes. At first this appropriation was uncritical, but Neale's *Hymnal Noted* (1851, 1854) was a turning point for the reappropriation of Latin hymnody. (Greek hymnody became the focus of the Oxford Movement slightly later.) Finally, there were concerted efforts to introduce congregational chanted psalmody, the more successful of which were based on the Gregorian tones (e.g., Thomas Helmore's *The Psalter Noted*, 1849). Although the "musicology" of the Cambridge Ecclesiologists was historically flawed, it would be a mistake to consider all of their liturgical innovations romantically naive. The Merbecke adaptation of Gregorian chant for the Ordinary (now accompanied by organ) remained in many congregations' repertories until revisions of the language of the *Book of Common Prayer* in the 1970s and 1980s displaced it. The revival of Latin texts and tunes and of Greek texts became a central feature of English hymnody. Even the notion of congregational chanted psalmody was not misguided: as the Tractarians' parallel revival of monasticism had shown, small communities committed to a common devotional life found it to be an important liturgical practice. In the few places where these prerequisites for its introduction were in place, Gregorian psalmody (in English) flourished and is still practiced in the early twenty-first century.

The reforms of the early modern Reformation displayed all four strategies of liturgical revision. Certain practices were considered degenerate and corrupt (e.g., multiple masses, indulgences) and required a return to an earlier and classical form of Christian practice largely dictated by the witness of the New Testament. Moreover many of these practices were thought to be aggravated and reinforced by the cultural gap of language. The Reformers (all educated and completely capable of understanding the Latin Bible and fully participating in the Latin liturgy) wished the unlettered (as Martin Luther says, the "simple layman") to put aside their traditional practices. Luther objected to these practices principally upon the grounds that they were tied to a problematic "works-righteousness," whereas John Calvin and the more radical reformers considered them to be "idolatrous." Moreover because of the success of late-medieval catechesis, such ideas appealed greatly to the not-so-simple laypeople in the university towns where the Reformation first took hold.

The Lutheran and Calvinist Reformations both had a deep pedagogical urgency, and it is this that shaped much of the strategy for reforming the rites. Luther's preface to his *Deudsche Messe* (1526) is particularly revealing. Here he first justifies liturgy largely because of its pedagogical utility:

> [Liturgical orders] are needed, most of all, for the sake of the simple minded and the youth, who shall and must be drilled and trained in the Scriptures and God's Word every day so that they may become familiar with the Scriptures, apt, well-versed and learned in them, enabled to defend their faith and in due time may teach others and help to increase the Kingdom of Christ. For their sake we must read, sing, preach, write and compose, and if it would help the matter along, I would have all the bells pealing, and all the organs playing, and let everything chime that has a clapper.[40]

Next Luther describes three kinds of service, which can be used to summarize Reformation strategies of liturgical and musical reform. For Luther, two of them served pedagogical aims, and the third had to be reserved only for the more spiritually advanced, whom he called "real Christians." The first order of service was his revision of the Latin Mass (*Formula Missae*, 1523). Luther thought the Latin Mass was particularly useful for the "youth": "For I would in no wise banish the Latin tongue entirely from the Service, for the youth is my chiefest concern. If I could bring it to pass and Greek and Hebrew were as familiar to us as the Latin, and offered as much good music and song, we would hold mass, sing and read on successive Sundays in all four languages, German, Latin, Greek and Hebrew."[41]

Luther's second order is specifically directed to the unlettered: "The German Mass . . . should be introduced for the sake of the simple laymen. . . . For among them are many who do not believe and are not yet Christians."[42] As the next passage makes clear, Luther is not denying that the unlettered laity is baptized and confirmed, nor would he ever advocate rebaptism; rather, he believed it to be enmeshed in liturgical and devotional practices that had lost their pedagogical orientation:

> For this is the damnable thing in the papal services, that they have been changed into laws, works and merits to the utter destruction of faith. Nor did they use them to educate the youth and the simple minded, to drill them in the Scriptures and God's Word, but became so enmeshed in them as to regard them as themselves useful and necessary for salvation. . . . The ancients did not institute nor order them with such intentions.[43]

It is not at all clear whether Luther actually believes his third order is practical, since he holds to his doctrine of *simul justus et peccator*, but he does describe a service that harks back to the Pauline domestic model described at the beginning of this chapter. According to Luther, this form of worship was to be used only by the spiritually elite, and although it invokes New Testament practices, it is also close to the rhetoric of monasticism:

> The third kind of Service which a truly evangelical church order should have, would not be held in a public place for all sorts of people, but for those who mean to be real Christians and profess the Gospel with hand and mouth. They would record their names on a

list and meet by themselves in some house in order to pray, read, baptize, receive the Sacrament and do other Christian works. . . . The many and elaborate chants would be unnecessary. There could be a short, appropriate Order for Baptism and the Sacrament and everything centered on the Word and Prayer and Love. . . . But as yet I neither can nor desire to begin, or to make rules for, such a congregation or assembly.[44]

The emphasis on pedagogy shows that the high-medieval idea that liturgical ceremony could lead to contemplation of God had not died out but had instead been transformed from its roots in neo-Platonic theology to a newer belief in the power of the spoken and printed Word of God. Therefore it should not be surprising that music (and the other arts) was similarly transformed. The most telling example of this transformation is the change from medieval to early modern strategies of text setting, in which music was used not simply as a vehicle for the expressive *delivery* of the text but instead was used to imitate the *meaning* of the text. The most simplistic form of this is melodic "word painting," such as an ascending line on the word *ascendit* (he arose), but a more subtle and pervasive use of controlled harmonic dissonance also supported the trend to attempt to express the meaning of the text through musical analogies. Luther's favorite composer, Josquin des Prez (c.1440–1521), was a master of this new style. For a music theorist of the High Middle Ages, all music, whether it set joyful or sorrowful words, had expressed the goodness of the created order that culminated in a sense of eschatological joy. But for a theorist of the early modern period, it was possible to speak of joyful or sorrowful *music* because of the association of specific musical strategies with specific texts. However, prior to the Reformation, music based on the new strategies of text setting had been used principally at the margins of the official liturgy. It was more common in motets than in masses and in votive anthems rather than in office antiphons and had been particularly prominent in pre-Reformation traditions of vernacular religious song, such as the carol, the *lauda* and the *Ruf.* As mentioned at the beginning of this chapter, repertories of vernacular religious song had been used at the margins of the official liturgy; however, they were sometimes associated with vernacular preaching and were well established in confraternities and guilds and their public ceremonial as well as in the households of the educated classes.[45]

The varied strategies of Lutheran reformers toward music indicate a concentration on the first two of Luther's three model orders of service discussed above. Because of the well-established tradition of vernacular religious song in Germany, its popular melodies and

Music in Leipzig. The Saint Thomas Church and Johann Sebastian Bach's music school, c. 1729. Bach composed church cantatas and larger works that required different combinations of instruments, from small chamber groups to a substantial orchestra. Engraving, eighteenth century. MUSÉE DES ARTS DÉCORATIFS, PARIS; GIRAUDON/ART RESOURCE, NY

texts could be adapted for official use in vernacular services for the "simple laymen." These could be supplemented with translations of the texts and adaptations of the tunes of the Latin liturgy; gaps in the repertory could be filled with new hymns. Luther's own hymn production centered on providing a core liturgical repertory, initially focused on parts of the mass Ordinary. (For this, he already had the model of the *Leisen* which may have been derived from troped Kyries.) He was also keenly conscious of the need for a mass Proper and stated that services for principal feasts had to be conducted in Latin "until enough German hymns become available."[46] Luther also carefully adapted ministerial chant to German, and in creating formulas suitable to its patterns of syllabification and accentuation, he eventually arrived at a hybrid chant style that interacted well with the new musical rhetoric of the hymns. Because both of Luther's first two orders were essentially geared at reorientation of already existing practices, they tended to be amalgamated into a macaronic service that persisted in university towns as long as Latin held sway as the principal literary language of the educated classes.[47]

Perhaps because he was not a member of the clergy and therefore had less of an investment in the old rites, Calvin tended to classify all late-medieval ceremonial as idolatrous. Unlike Luther, who considered that such ceremonial features could be freed of works righteousness if their true meanings were understood, Calvin considered the mass to consist of "magical mumblings" and the people to be full of "stupid amazement."[48] For Calvin, only a pattern such as that advocated in Luther's third order would suffice, because only such a pattern had sufficient warrants in a literal rather than allegorical interpretation of scripture. A key text, in addition to Paul's letters, is the "rule of Christ" described in Matthew 18. In line with humanistic interpretations of scripture, other models of worship, such as those found the Old Testament or the book of Revelation, were rejected, since they could not be used literally but would require an allegorical adaptation to fit them for practical use.

Calvin's Geneva order (1542) suggests the singing of one psalm before the lesson and sermon and other psalms during the distribution of the Lord's supper.[49] The Strasbourg order (1545) shows a more nuanced use of music: the singing of the "first table of commandments" is a response to the general confession and follows the absolution. The "second table" is a response to a prayer seeking continual growth in grace and leads to the lesson and sermon. During distribution, the metrical version of Psalm 138 (*Louange et grâce*) is specified, and a metrical version of the biblical canticle of Simeon (*Maintenant Seigneur Dieu*) follows the after-supper prayer of thanksgiving. Services without the Lord's supper substitute an appropriate metrical psalm for the canticle, and the rite concludes with a blessing and dismissal.

This rite used a new style of music developed from courtly song and ballad similar in essence to earlier forms of vernacular devotional song developed by the religious confraternities known as *puy*.[50] Thus in the French-speaking forms of Calvinistic worship, a strong musical component was retained because of the variety in the metrical organization of words and the consequent metrical variety (and complexity) of the melodies. Even though the singing was restricted to biblical texts and polyphony was allowed only for household and not for public worship, the texts and tunes displayed a wide variety of rhythms, accents, and meters.

Calvin's order of service was for the spiritually "elect" but could be transmitted and maintained through corporate confession (including a reflection on the Decalogue), preaching and extended exhortation, and if necessary, through excommunication. Therefore he did not consider it inaccessible to the laity. Calvin's strategy is reminiscent of adaptations of the cenobitic forms of fourth-century desert monasticism (which had started as a lay movement) to urban contexts. The Calvinist focus on a sober style of service, and an exclusive use of biblical canticles and psalms supported by a melodic style of singing is as reminiscent of fourth- and fifth-century models as it is of the New Testament. The scholarly Calvin would have encountered numerous descriptions of the virtues of psalm singing in his close reading of the Latin Fathers, and one may speculate that he was directly, even if unconsciously, influenced by them. The principal characteristic in these examples of "reformative change" is the sense that the inherited traditions had become unintelligible, corrupt, or otherwise deficient. The tendency was to adopt the strategy of removing those elements of the rite that were deemed deficient and to incorporate them with new musical forms, which were often borrowed from the repertories cultivated by the literate classes in lay confraternities and in elite households.

Because change can also be interpreted as "organic," as a natural growth from existing practices, some repertories of liturgical music have come to be considered "classics." Since they have been mediators of a strong sense of the presence of God to a church, the tendency is to build upon them (either refining or elaborating their structures) rather than to rebuild from the ground up. Even whole repertories may be considered relatively indispensable, as can be seen from the transfer of the Byzantine liturgy, including its chant, to Slavonic-speaking territories. This necessitated a careful and ingenious adaptation of the melodies that all Orthodox accept as being essential. Moreover to a certain extent chant may serve as a literal or model structure upon which to build, as is seen in the incorporation of Slavonic chant in the polyphony of the Russian Orthodox Church. The Roman rite showed a greater tendency toward elaboration, but even developments that obscured or replaced the chant (such as Renaissance polyphony) retained strong connections with it, either by borrowing its melodic clichés or by retaining its modal structures. Moreover in the Lutheran Church the hymn became just such an "organic" repertory and acquired various forms of elaboration in polychoral motets, organ music, and cantatas.

The later changes to hymnody in churches of the Protestant Reformation may be seen as organic as well. Although the liturgical practice of the whole congregation

Congregational singing. An accordion accompanies singing at a Pentecostal community in Zimbabwe. PHOTOGRAPH BY DAVID BUTCHER/ART DIRECTORS AND TRIP

United in Song?

Geoffrey Wainwright

Congregational singing has been particularly characteristic of worship in the Protestant churches. Roughly speaking, the production of psalters and hymnals has historically passed through three phases, which indeed overlap. First, a church confines itself to material generated in its own ranks. Second, a church expands its repertoire by drawing on congenial outside sources, whether the borrowings occur across time or across space; indigenous productions, whether past or contemporary, nevertheless retain a favored spot. Third and much later, hymnals have been deliberately composed by ecumenical agencies and with an ecumenical range that is not only cross-confessional but cross-cultural; sometimes these have displaced "denominational" hymnals, but only perhaps where the cultural spread of the items is not very wide or prominent, for excessive stylistic and linguistic complexity militates against use in most local congregations, where indeed positive value is attached to the preservation of a particular tradition.

In the Reformed churches, the principle lasted for several centuries of singing directly scriptural songs, at least in translation. Thus the precisely named *Psautier Genevois* consisted of the biblical Psalms, together with the Decalogue and the Nunc dimittis, all in the verse translations of Clément Marot (c.1497–1544) and Théodore de Bèze (1519–1605), accompanied by the tunes of Louis Bourgeois (c.1510–c.1561). The Church of Scotland long kept itself to the "metrical psalms" (first in a version from the 1560s and then the Scottish psalter, *The Psalms of David in Meeter*, of 1650), joined later by the *Translations and Paraphrases in Verse of Several Passages of Sacred Scripture* (1781); and again these remained prominent in the unofficial hymnbooks compiled by nineteenth-century parish ministers and in the official *Church Hymnary* when it first appeared in 1898. The Church of England had the metrical psalms of Sternhold and Hopkins

singing together instilled a sense of praise and a harmony of purpose, this sense could only be maintained in tension with changed devotional emphases. For example, Isaac Watts's innovative restoration of the christological interpretation of the Psalms in the early eighteenth century led eventually to an acceptance of nonbiblical hymns in most reformed rites; this practice is ironically more in line with the New Testament than is the use of psalms alone. The hymnody of the later-eighteenth-century Evangelical revival emphasized tropological (moral and inspirational) themes to express a renewed sense of the need for a closer connection between worship and Christian discipleship. These changes did not influence the basic musical structure of hymns, but they did affect the way they were performed. Centers of the revival rejected the "old" practice of "lining out" psalms, gradually replacing it with a "regular" (and rhythmically lively) practice of singing from a book.[51] As a result of this, by the mid-nineteenth century whole congregations embraced the singing of music in parts, in effect becoming a polyphonic choir and elaborating the sense of harmony with actual musical harmony. All of these changes in hymns are broadly analogous to the changes in the Gregorian office and mass from the ninth century through the twelfth century: the christological interpretation of its largely psalm-based texts was reinforced with new poetry that was also intended to support a tropological interpretation of the inherited texts, high-

(the "Old Version," 1562) and of Tate and Brady (the "New Version," 1696).

However, a shift began (more or less) with the Independent pastor Isaac Watts (1674–1748). His explicitly christological interpretations of the Psalms represented a return to earlier hermeneutics, where the Psalms were understood as Christ himself speaking (*vox Christi*), or as addressed to Christ (*ad Christum*), or as telling about Christ (*de Christo*). Watts's other great step—again entirely traditional in the deeper sense—was to compose his own hymns on doctrinal and spiritual themes. This latter mode eventually came to dominate Protestant congregational singing.

The Methodists went that way from the start, whether within their own gatherings or when Methodist sympathizers uncanonically introduced hymns into Anglican services. The Wesley brothers in 1745–1746 published collections of hymns for the Lord's Nativity, Resurrection, and Ascension and for Pentecost and other great festivals as well as *Hymns on the Lord's Supper*. Even more characteristic was the type and range of hymns—very largely from Charles Wesley's pen or translated by John Wesley from the German—gathered in the climactic *Collection of Hymns for the Use of the People Called Methodists* (1780), where the texts were ordered in an experiential soteriology according to "the experience of real Christians."

In other denominations too hymnals gained enormously in popularity in the nineteenth century, with or without acquiring official status. Anglican bishops tried their hand at verse: thus Reginald Heber's trinitarian "Holy, Holy, Holy, Lord God Almighty," Christopher Wordsworth's, "See the Conqueror Mounts in Triumph," William Walsham How's "For All the Saints Who from Their Labours Rest," Phillips Brooks's "O Little Town of Bethlehem," and so on. The Church of England's claim to historical continuity was captured by the standard, though unofficial, *Hymns Ancient and Modern*, whose first edition in 1861 contained 123 translations from the Latin, both office hymns for times and seasons and also texts of a more devotional character. The rival *English Hymnal*

lighting the active appropriation of the scripture. Later the cultivation of polyphony brought out anagogical (eschatological) themes. Moreover all of these practices had their births in the early medieval monastic choir that had achieved, for a few, what the reformers desired for the many. It took about the same amount of time (two hundred years) for similar changes of textual emphasis and musical practice to develop in vernacular hymn singing.[52]

Pressing the analogy between the medieval choir and the modern congregation a little further, one may conceive of the technological breakthroughs of the early twentieth century, whereby one may purchase professional performances of practically any kind of music on sound recordings, as extending the possibility of having one's own household or "court" music to those of comparatively modest means.[53] The widespread availability of professional models of musical performance has been followed by a decline in group singing at both secular and sacred rituals in many western countries, and part of the difficulty in encouraging singing in communities where it was not already established may be related to this phenomenon. Even if "professional" music making in church may be criticized if it overshadows or eliminates all corporate song, a church that rejects all forms of "professional" music making is likely to be depriving a congregation extremely well-trained in listening of a powerful form of

(1906), favored by adherents of the "branch theory" of the Church as "Eastern, Western, British," contained also a significant number of translations by John Mason Neale (1818–1866) from the great Byzantine tradition of dogmatic hymnology. Catherine Winkworth (1827–1878), the most brilliant of a bevy of women translators, turned to Evangelical Germany, where from the Reformation onward fresh compositions had complemented vernacular adaptations of the biblical Psalms and of some medieval Latin materials. Winkworth's guiding principle was that "any embodiment of Christian experience and devotion, whether in the form of hymn or prayer or meditation, or whatever shape art may give it, if it do but go to the heart of our common faith, becomes at once the rightful and most precious inheritance of the whole Christian Church"; and her reward has been the adoption of her texts by the English "free churches" and by Lutherans in North America and Australia (in the latter case, the *Lutheran Hymnal* employs eighty-three examples of her work).

Lutheran hymnals in North America have typically included also intra-confessional translations from the Scandinavian languages (N. F. S. Grundtvig, 1783–1873, was great among the Danes). At the global level the Lutheran World Federation has produced a multilingual *Laudamus* on the occasion of its successive assemblies. The basic core from German and Nordic sources was gradually expanded by some English-language originals and then by a few texts from Asia, Africa, and Latin America; its limited compass suffices for occasional international gatherings but makes the book inadequate for regular Sunday use. A rather

devotional practice. The music of the medieval cathedral and of the modern megachurch have a certain degree of similarity in that they both display the high "production" values expected by a musical public trained to listen to, rather than participate in, complex music. For this reason it may be important for churches to incorporate forms of music that are culturally identified as being "sacred" in the liturgy.[54]

To sum up, the model of "reformative change" emphasizes the recovery of an authoritative past tradition, whereas the model of "organic change" emphasizes the sustaining of a past tradition. As Nicholas Lash has observed, the authority of any tradition is constituted by "whatever truth and value have been perceived and achieved in the past, truth and value that can only be 're-covered' and sustained to the extent that we risk critically appropriating the past in the transformation of the

Choir. First Mennonite Church in Newton, Kansas. PHOTOGRAPH BY LAURIE L. OSWALD/MENNONITE CHURCH USA NEWS SERVICE

deliberate display of global awareness was made by the United Methodist Church in its *Hymnal* of 1989. While clearly produced in the United States, this book made efforts to include material generated in the United Methodist Church overseas as well as from more domestic sources of "our rich ethnic diversity": "More than 70 hymns are included to represent the African-American, Hispanic, Asian-American, and Native American heritages."

Geographical range is invoked by the German *Evangelisches Gesangbuch* of 1994, with an alphabetical index of exotic sources stretching from Belgium to Zimbabwe (paragraph 959), as testimony to the fact that "Christianity is a worldwide fellowship"; some of the hymns from abroad are printed in their original tongues in the body of the book. Inter-confessionally the same book lists 195 hymns for which an "ecumenical text" has been established by the "Arbeitsgemeinschaft für ökumenisches Liedgut," and 95 of these are indicated as shared with the Roman Catholic *Gotteslob* (1975). That Catholic hymnal remarkably took in Martin Luther's "anthem of the Reformation," "Ein' feste Burg," while the Protestant book finally adopted the translation of the Te Deum, "Grosser Gott, wir loben dich," by the Catholic priest Ignaz Franz (1719–1790) as well as the ubiquitous and mawkish product of Austrian Catholicism, "Stille Nacht, heilige Nacht." English-language Catholic hymnals in the last third of the twentieth century happily included favorites from the standard Protestant repertoire: the *New Catholic Hymnal* of 1971 contained four texts by George Herbert, six by Isaac Watts, and eight by Charles Wesley as well as six of Catherine Winkworth's translations from the German. Any current British or North American hymnal, of whatever confession or denomination, is likely to draw on such contemporary writers as Fred Kaan and Brian Wren (both United Reformed), Jeffrey Rowthorn and Carl Daw (both Episcopalian), Ruth Duck (United Church of Christ), Thomas Troger (Presbyterian), Fred Pratt Green (Methodist), Miriam Therese Winter (Roman Catholic), or Graham Kendrick (of the independent Ichthus Fellowship, London, and Make Way Music). In addition songs have made their wider way from religious communities of ecumenical composition or intent, such as Taizé or Iona.

With unofficial predecessors already in the songbooks compiled in the late-nineteenth century and the early-twentieth century in revivalist and holiness movements, the second half of the twentieth century saw the production of a number of hymnals either by an inter-confessional group of denominations for national use or by official ecumenical organizations at the regional or global level.

At the national level a significant example is *The Australian Hymn Book*, produced between 1968 and 1977 at a time when the Methodists, the Presbyterians, and the Congregationalists were on the way to forming the Uniting Church in Australia; and in the composition of the hymnbook they were joined by the Anglicans, even though the latter no longer envisaged being party to the union. The hymnal brings together the staples of native British hymnody, including texts by the Catholics John Henry Newman and Frederick William Faber, as well as translations from the ancient and medieval Church and from German Protestantism. In 1974 the Roman Catholic Archdiocese of Sydney "enquired into the possibility of using the Australian Hymnbook," and consequently the book was also issued "with Catholic Supplement," intended to "express more completely the beliefs and aspirations that Catholics profess in their worship" (notably more hymns for the mass as well as devotions to the Sacred Heart and to the Blessed Virgin). Not always under the same title, the Australian book also gained a favorable reception in some other places. In 1999 it was succeeded by *Together in Song: Australian Hymn Book II.*

Regional ecumenical production may be exemplified from East Asia. The *East Asia Christian Conference Hymnal* of 1963 began with a "general section" containing some ninety staple English-language hymns and paraphrases. This was followed by about a dozen spirituals from the black or African American tradition. The "Asian section" comprised almost one hundred texts by fifty-four authors (including twelve missionaries) identified not confessionally but geographically. Nevertheless the Ceylonese Methodist D. T. Niles (1908–1970), a prominent figure at the world level of the Ecumenical Movement, was the writer of forty-four of the texts. This pioneering work was succeeded by the Christian Conference of Asia's *Sound the Bamboo* (1990). Here the geographical, the cultural, the linguistic, and especially the authorial range was further expanded. In the later decades of the twentieth century, the main motivator behind the regional creativity was I-to Loh, who edited *Asian Songs of Worship* (1988) and indeed *African Songs of Worship* (1986). In Africa a leading figure was Patrick Matsikenyiri of Zimbabwe and the Africa Association for Liturgy, Music, and the Arts. In Latin America ecumenical collections of hymns and songs were produced in Buenos Aires under the leadership of Pablo Sosa at the Higher Evangelical Institute of Theological Studies, with its project of "an open songbook" (*Canconiera Abierto*), and in Brazil under the direction of Jaci Maraschin and Simei Monteiro (*A Canção do Senhor na Terra Brasileira*, 1982; *O Novo Canto da Terra*, 1987).

The outstanding example of a long-term hymnal produced by a global ecumenical organization is the World Student Christian Federation's *Cantate Domino.* The first edition, published in 1924, contained 64 hymns, the second (1930) 82, the fifth (1951) 95, and the sixth (1957) 120. Many of the originally English, German, or French hymns appeared in all three languages, whereas hymns from other languages were accompanied by a translation in at least one

present for the construction of our future."[55] The musical practices of the Christian Church in all of their contextual complexity and diversity present a fund of such provisional "achievements" that may substantially challenge, enrich, and renew our ongoing "constructions" of Christian worship.

Bibliography

Blume, Friedrich. *Protestant Church Music: A History.* New York: Norton, 1974.

Cavarnos, Constantine. *Byzantine Sacred Music.* Belmont, Mass.: Institute for Byzantine and Modern Greek Studies, 1974.

of the principal three (R. Birch Hoyle did a sterling job with the English versions). A completely new edition appeared, under the aegis of the World Council of Churches (WCC), in 1974. Its editor, Erik Routley, claimed "a much wider coverage of cultures, styles and languages" as well as "active participation in its editing from within the Roman Catholic and Orthodox Churches." The book was envisaged for use in "international gatherings, large or small," and as a "supplement" to parish or school hymnals.

Meanwhile the WCC itself was taking another track in the provision of hymnody for its meetings. Helped by the ease of producing printed material with electronic processes, the practice has developed of publishing a special booklet, including of course hymns, for most major gatherings. The advantage is "topicality," of both theme and time; the corresponding dangers are faddishness and ephemerality. Some account of these developments, and some samples, are in the spiral-bound *Worshipping Ecumenically*, edited by Per Harling (1995). The book's subtitle, *Orders of Service from Global Meetings with Suggestions for Local Use*, points in the direction of formalizing and expanding a procedure that in any case already occurs when participants in international ecumenical gatherings return home with the worship booklets that have been employed at the assembly.

In all these various ways, hymnody has played its part in the Ecumenical and Liturgical Movements. An "exchange of gifts" has increasingly taken place on both the confessional and the cultural grids. Eschatologically put, the earthly Church is thereby becoming assimilated to that gathering from "every tribe and tongue" that will, according to the book of Revelation, sing the praises of God and the Lamb. Ecclesiologically, the use of material across the boundaries of historic divisions seems to give some recognition to the presence of Christian faith and life in the separated communities within which the poets and composers were nourished and which were responsible for the mediation of their artists' work to the wider Christian Tradition. Thus may Christians come closer to "one voice" as they "glorify the God and Father of our Lord Jesus Christ" (Rom. 15:6), allowing for the "harmony" and "symphony" that Origen ascribes to the Church at the beginning of the fourteenth book of his *Commentary on Matthew*.

Fellerer, Karl Gustav. *The History of Catholic Church Music.* Translated by Francis A. Brunner. Baltimore: Helicon, 1961.

Le Huray, Peter. *Music and the Reformation in England, 1549–1660.* New York: Oxford University Press, 1967.

McKinnon, James, ed. *Music in Early Christian Literature.* New York: Cambridge University Press, 1987.

Oettinger, Rebecca Wagner. *Music as Propaganda in the German Reformation.* Aldershot, Hants.: Ashgate, 2001.

Reymond, Bernard. *Le protestantisme et la musique: Musicalités de la parole.* Geneva: Labor et Fides, 2002.

Routley, Erik. *Church Music and Theology.* Philadelphia: Fortress, 1965.

Schalk, Carl. *Music in Early Lutheranism: Shaping the Tradition (1524–1672)*. St. Louis, Mo.: Concordia Academic, 2001.

Temperley, Nicholas. *The Music of the English Parish Church*. Cambridge and New York: Cambridge University Press, 1979.

Williams, Peter F. *The King of Instruments: How Churches Came to Have Organs*. London: SPCK, 1993.

Wilson-Dickson, Andrew. *A Brief History of Christian Music: From Biblical Times to the Present*. 2nd ed. Oxford: Lion, 1997.

Notes

[1]For a discussion of the problem, see Robin A. Leaver, "What Is Liturgical Music?" in *Liturgy and Music: Lifetime Learning*, ed. Robin A. Leaver and Joyce Ann Zimmerman (Collegeville, Minn.: Liturgical Press, 1998) 211–219.

[2]For the first five centuries, see *The New Grove Dictionary of Music and Musicians*, 2nd ed., ed. Stanley Sadie and John Tyrell (London: McMillan, 2001), "Christian Church, Music of the Early," by James McKinnon. (References to this dictionary will hereafter be cited as *NGDMM*.)

[3]Wayne A. Meeks examines worship practices in the Pauline orbit in *The First Urban Christians* (New Haven, Conn.: Yale University Press, 1983) 14–63.

[4]The text says "each of you has a psalm," but since the terms "psalm," "hymn," and "ode" were interchangeable and the nature of the singing seems somewhat spontaneous, this passage could easily refer to newly composed or even improvised texts and melodies.

[5]Many passages from early Christian authors cited in this chapter are in James McKinnon, ed., *Music in Early Christian Literature*. For convenience, the original work will be cited first, followed by its item number in McKinnon's volume. For example, the citation for this passage is Tertullian, *Apologeticum* 39:17–18; McKinnon 74.

[6]See Joseph Dyer, "Monastic Psalmody of the Middle Ages," *Revue Bénédictine* 99 (1989) 41–74; and James McKinnon, "Desert Monasticism and the Later Fourth-Century Psalmodic Movement," *Music and Letters* 75 (1994) 505–521.

[7]See James McKinnon, "The Fourth-Century Origin of the Gradual," *Early Music History* 7 (1987) 91–106.

[8]See McKinnon numbers 114, 118, 126–128,139, 146, 152, 198, 223–224, 242, 253, 349, 351, 393. Egeria's description of the late-fourth-century Jerusalem liturgy (not covered in McKinnon) is also particularly full of descriptions of various groups of singers of office psalms and hymns; see *Itinerarium* 24.

[9]A particularly good discussion of this period is in James W. McKinnon's *The Advent Project: The Later-Seventh-Century Creation of the Roman Mass Proper* (Berkeley and Los Angeles: University of California Press, 2000) 60–98.

[10]Joseph Dyer, "The Schola Cantorum and Its Roman Milieu in the Early Middle Ages," in *De musica et cantu: Helmut Hucke zum 60. Geburtstag*, ed. P. Cahn and A.-K. Heimer (Hildesheim, Germany, and New York: G. Olms, 1993) 19–40.

[11]This is the thesis of McKinnon's *Advent Project*, and I am persuaded by his arguments.

[12]See Edward Foley, *From Age to Age: How Christians Celebrated the Eucharist* (Chicago: Liturgy Training Publications, 1992) 75, 102.

[13]*NGDMM*, "Organ," by Peter Williams and Barbara Owen. In *alternatim* practice, organ music replaces sections of a chanted piece. This means that only half of the text of the piece is actually sung, but the text is present in memory: the schola and organist certainly had standard texts memorized, and even the illiterati would have attended many nonfestal services where the whole text was chanted (instead of being embellished with polyphony or organ playing).

[14]Avery Dulles, *Models of the Church* (Garden City, N.Y.: Doubleday, 1974). Dulles argues that a "Sacramental" model, in which the Church is conceived as a symbol of Christ's presence, is the most adequate model; however, he may have distorted his model of "Communion" by focusing exclusively on its "Mystical" and hence invisible side.

[15]Core metaphors are metaphors that organize a person's or a community's practice. For a full discussion of the theory, see George Lakoff and Mark Johnson, *Metaphors We Live By* (Chicago and London: University of Chicago Press, 1980). George S. Worgul's *From Magic to Metaphor: A Validation of*

the *Christian Sacraments* (New York: Paulist Press, 1980) explores similar territory relating core metaphors to eucharistic theology.

[16]See William Flynn, "Liturgical Music as Liturgy," in *Liturgy and Music: Lifetime Learning*, ed. Robin A. Leaver and Joyce Ann Zimmerman (Collegeville, Minn.: Liturgical Press, 1998) 252–264.

[17]Clement of Alexandra, *Protrepticus* 9, as quoted in Johannes Quasten, *Music and Worship in Pagan and Christian Antiquity* (Washington, D.C.: National Association of Pastoral Musicians, 1983) 67, 102.

[18]Ambrose, *Expositio evangelii secundum Lucam* 7:238; McKinnon 284.

[19]Ambrose, *Explanatio psalmi* 19; McKinnon 276.

[20]See Cyril (or John) of Jerusalem, *Mystagogical Catechesis* 5:6; McKinnon 157. Kenneth Levy has made a convincing case that one surviving melody for the Sanctus (and indeed the music for the whole introductory dialogue and preface as well) dates from the fourth century and could be adapted for contemporary congregational use; see Levy, "The Byzantine Sanctus and Its Modal Tradition in East and West," *Annales musicologiques* 6 (1958–1963) 7–68.

[21]See William Flynn, *Medieval Music as Medieval Exegesis*, Studies in Liturgical Musicology 8 (Lanham, Md., and London: Scarecrow, 1999) 117–123.

[22]As cited in Flynn, *Medieval Music as Medieval Exegesis*, 126.

[23]See Frank L. Harrison, *Music in Medieval Britain*, 2nd ed. (London: Routledge and Paul, 1963) 218–219; and Eamon Duffy, *The Stripping of the Altars: Traditional Religion in England c.1400–c.1580* (New Haven, Conn., and London: Yale University Press, 1992) 91–154.

[24]As cited in Robin A. Leaver, introduction to *The Book of Common Praier Noted, 1550*, Courtenay Facsimile 3 (Abingdon, Oxon.: Sutton Courtenay Press, 1980) 18.

[25]Augustine, *Confessiones* 10:33; McKinnon 352.

[26]For a full discussion, see Augustine, *De musica*, book 6. Catherine Pickstock argues that such "metaphysical" views of music need to be recovered in order to construct a theological ontology, psychology, and politics. See her chapter "Music: Soul, City and Cosmos after Augustine," in *Radical Orthodoxy: A New Theology*, ed. John Milbank, Catherine Pickstock, and Graham Ward (London and New York: Routledge, 1999) 243–277.

[27]McKinnon, "Fourth-Century Origin of the Gradual," 185–186.

[28]The incorporation of the *Kanon* into the Byzantine *Orthros* during the seventh century through the ninth century is somewhat analogous. The literature on tropes and proses is enormous, but for a liturgical-theological view, see Flynn, *Medieval Music as Medieval Exegesis*. On the emergence of polyphony from a liturgical perspective, see Karl Fellerer, *The History of Catholic Church Music*.

[29]For a discussion of the early and high medieval organ, see Peter Williams, *The Organ in Western Culture 750–1250* (Cambridge: Cambridge University Press, 1993).

[30]The only office hymn setting in the *Codex Faenza* is of *Ave Maris Stella*, and since this consists of a single verset, it may be introductory rather than alternatim. It is just as likely, however, that the single verset represents a model and that the organist is expected to improvise the remainder. Both the mass setting (*Cunctipotens Genitor*) and the hymn are normally associated with feasts.

[31]Umberto Eco, *Art and Beauty in the Middle Ages* (New Haven, Conn.: Yale University Press, 1986). Eco's book was written as part of a survey of aesthetics in 1958, and his specific historical statements concerning music are often inaccurate. However, his insights into the relationships between "metaphysical theories and artistic production" and the broader trajectories of medieval aesthetics that he narrates are still reliable.

[32]Indeed not only music but also all the other arts participated in establishing liturgical solemnity, as can be seen from the festal use of icons, vestments, candles, incense, processions, etc.

[33]Eco, *Art and Beauty*, 6.

[34]Geoffrey Wainwright, *Doxology: The Praise of God in Worship, Doctrine, and Life* (New York: Oxford University Press, 1980) 324.

[35]For a comprehensive overview of the musical reforms of the Cistercians, see Claire Maître, *La réforme cistercienne du plain-chant: Étude d'un traité théorique* (Brecht, Belgium: Cîteaux, Commentarii Cistercienses, 1995).

[36]Bernard of Clairvaux, *Apologia ad Guillelum* 12; as cited in Eco, *Art and Beauty*, 7.

[37]John Julian, ed., *Dictionary of Hymnology, Setting Forth the Origin and History of the Christian Hymns of All Ages and Nations*, 2nd ed., vol. 1 (London: John Murray, 1907) 668.

[38]*The Black Book; or, Corruption Unmasked!* (1820), as quoted in Dikran Y. Hadidian, "A Bibliographical Epilogue: Before and after *Lux Mundi*," in *Keeping the Faith: Essays to Mark the Centenary of Lux Mundi*, ed. Geoffrey Wainwright (Philadelphia: Fortress Press; Allison Park, Pa.: Pickwick Publications, 1988) 376.

[39]Nicholas Temperley, *The Music of the English Parish Church*, vol. 1 (Cambridge: Cambridge University Press, 1979) 251.

[40]Martin Luther, *Deudsche Messe*, in *Liturgies of the Western Church*, ed. Bard Thompson (Philadelphia: Fortress Press, 1980) 124.

[41]Luther, *Deudsche Messe*, 124–125.

[42]Luther, *Deudsche Messe*, 125.

[43]Luther, *Deudsche Messe*, 124.

[44]Luther, *Deudsche Messe*, 125–126.

[45]The liturgical history of religious devotional song is still being written. The most complete studies concentrate on the *lauda*, which had its influence primarily on the liturgical music of the Counter-Reformation. The *Ruf* (e.g., *Leise*) was a congregational acclamation in the form of a hymn stanza, sung at the end of the vernacular sermon. The carol found occasional use as the last blessing of festival office liturgies and substantial use in guild plays. All three forms seem to have their origins in mendicant preaching and the consequent rise of popular devotional practices. See *NGDMM*, "Carol," "Lauda," "Leise," and "Ruf."

[46]Luther, *Deudsche Messe*, 136. For Luther's German hymns, see Markus Jenny, *Luther, Zwingli, Calvin in ihren Liedern* (Zurich: Theologischer Verlag, 1983) 13–171.

[47]See Günther Stiller, *Johann Sebastian Bach and Liturgical Life in Leipzig* (St. Louis, Mo.: Concordia Publishing House, 1984) 29–167.

[48]As quoted in Thompson, *Liturgies*, 185.

[49]For Calvin's contribution at both Geneva and Strasbourg, see Jenny, *Luther, Zwingli, Calvin in ihren Liedern*, 215–281.

[50]*NGDMM*, "Puy," by Elizabeth C. Teviotdale.

[51]Stephen A. Marini, "Rehearsal for Revival: Sacred Singing and the Great Awakening in America," in *Sacred Sound: Music in Religious Thought and Practice*, ed. Joyce Irwin, *Journal of the American Academy of Religion Thematic Studies* 50 (Chico, Calif.: Scholars Press, 1983) 71–91.

[52]For literary and theological appreciations of vernacular hymns, see Donald Davie, *The Eighteenth-Century Hymn in England* (New York: Cambridge University Press, 1993); and J. Richard Watson, *The English Hymn: A Critical and Historical Study* (Oxford: Clarendon; New York: Oxford University Press, 1997). Classic status is still enjoyed by Louis F. Benson, *The English Hymn: Its Development and Use in Worship* (New York: Hodder and Stoughton, 1915).

[53]Walter Benjamin explored the effects of technology on the arts, pointing to the positive aspects of the democratization of aesthetic experience and the negative aspects of its commodification, in his classic essay "The Work of Art in the Age of Mechanical Reproduction," in *Illuminations* (New York: Schocken, 1969) 217–251.

[54]In the developed West, particular attention might be paid to "minimalist music," "New Age music," music of world religions, including chant and various forms of "early music." Gerardus van der Leeuw pays particular attention to music in his *Sacred and Profane Beauty: The Holy in Art* (Nashville, Tenn.: Abingdon, 1963).

[55]Nicholas Lash, "What Authority Has Our Past?" in *Theology on the Way to Emmaus* (London: SCM, 1986) 61.

31

The Spatial Setting

JAMES F. WHITE

Christian worship and space are closely related to each other, even though Jesus makes it clear that true worship is independent of location (John 4:21). Twenty centuries of relationships between worship and space have produced an amazing array of possibilities but experimentation still continues. No permanent resolutions have been made. As worship changes, so do spatial needs; as architecture evolves, so do forms to accommodate worship.

When we look at church architecture historically, we see surviving buildings as documentation of worship needs at various times and places. Indeed, the built environment may sometimes be our only documentation as to how worship was performed. Existing baptismal fonts can tell us how baptisms were performed at the time when they were constructed, for the mode of baptism depends on the size and shape of the container for water. The retreat of the altar-table from proximity to the congregation tells us much about medieval developments in liturgy, perhaps even more than written documents. Thus space reveals what has happened in worship at any given time.

Equally, available space determines how worship will evolve. The ready availability of the civil basilica as a form for Christians to use when worship became public in the fourth century helped shape suitable ceremonial. The small meeting houses of English dissenters made congregational song a real possibility in the eighteenth century, while more grandiose churches delayed this practice for another century.

We shall examine services common to most Christian communities. After defining the liturgical spaces and liturgical centers (material foci) required for each, we shall move on to a quick survey of how space has been shaped to meet these needs. In some cases, different communities have resolved the same needs for space and centers in differing ways. But most of the worship needs that have had to be accommodated are similar.

That is because Christian worship has largely utilized five basic types of services. These are services of initiation revolving around baptism, the service of the word, the service of the table, daily public prayer, and occasional services that accompany life's journey and passages. Less dominant roles may be played by evangelistic services, sacred concerts, and observances of special days and commemorations, but these are not the main staples of Christian worship. The liturgical needs may seem simple, but the means that have been employed to fulfill these needs can be quite complicated. Obviously, we can notice here only the most significant landmarks.

Baptism

The services of Christian initiation revolve around a process that can include catechetics, baptism, first communion, and confirmation. It is baptism that needs the most specific liturgical center and space. The foremost of these is a container for water, a *font* or *baptistery*. At various times, outdoor locations have sufficed, such as rivers, lakes, or pools (Acts 8:36). This is still common in missionary situations. The size and design of the container will be determined by the mode of baptism preferred: immersion, pouring, or sprinkling. If virtually all candidates for baptism are infants, a smaller font may be adequate than when adults may also be immersed. The spatial requirements vary according to whether baptism is seen as a private affair (especially when done in the nude) or a public event. Space must be provided for the ministers, the candidates, the sponsors, and (perhaps) the whole community. Rooms to change clothes may be desirable. The location of the font or pool in relation to other liturgical centers and spaces will be an important consideration. But *baptismal space* remains an important need for this sacrament.

Our earliest reference in the history of baptismal space occurs in the *Didache*, probably written in the first century. It states a preference for running (literally "living") water that is cold. The inference is that immersion in a stream is most desirable but pouring may be the only possibility. In the mid-second century, Justin Martyr simply indicates "where there is water," which could be the Tiber but more likely a courtyard fountain. He repeatedly calls it "washing," so the quantity must be considerable. Tertullian speaks of being "thrice immersed," and the *Apostolic Tradition* speaks of the naked candidates descending "into the water" although it admits that the most desirable "flowing" water is not always available. The *Didascalia Apostolorum* also speaks of going "down into the water."

Our first physical evidence occurs with the font in Dura-Europos built between AD 232 and 256. This would seem to allow for immersion of babies but only pouring over the head of an adult, since it is just over two feet deep. Adult immersion would thus be unlikely but not impossible. Visually the font is directly adjacent to a wall painting of the three Marys and the empty tomb. This connection of baptism with death and resurrection (Rom. 6:3–5) came to have a prominent role, and Ambrose tells us that the font in Milan "is somewhat like a tomb in shape." Other early fonts survive as depressions in the floor level usually sunk two or three steps.[1] Ambrose speaks of the candidates being "plunged" and then "emerging," but many of the earliest surviving fonts seem better suited for the candidates to stand in while water is poured over their heads.

A tradition developed of baptisteries as separate buildings containing the font at the center of liturgical space. These were built in a variety of shapes: square, circular, hexagonal, or octagonal. Mausoleums were frequently the models for these structures, with the font substituted for the tomb of the family patriarch. Most of the examples of freestanding baptisteries are in Italian cathedral cities but they were not unknown in France.

The eventual christianization of northern Europe rendered such buildings with large pools for adult baptisms unnecessary, since only infants were left to baptize. Infant baptism became normative as the *Roman Ritual* of 1614 presumes (with only a brief addendum for the "Baptism of Adults"). Baptism became a parish activity rather than an episcopal affair at the cathedral.

The consequence of this was the multiplication of baptismal fonts and spaces. In most instances, baptism began in the church porch and then the infant was carried inside to a font that stood near the west end of the church. Thus there were two baptismal spaces: the church porch for the opening ceremonies; then "when they have entered the church," the remainder of the rite at the font. Medieval fonts tended to be of lead or stone, large enough for dipping the infant.[2] Increasingly, square or circular fonts gave way to octagonal, which in some places had images of the seven sacraments and a cross on the sides.[3] The font was often surmounted by a font cover that could be locked to prevent theft of blessed water. Locations near the door were most common.

Change was underway in the late Middle Ages, as pouring or sprinkling became acceptable alternatives to dipping the infant.[4] Thus Martin Luther is clearly conservative in stating a strong preference for baptism of infants by immersion. For John Calvin, other factors predominated, particularly in making baptism a public act before the gathered community "at the time of Sermon," so the "font is to be near the pulpit." In Reformed churches, this often meant a metal basin either on a table or on a metal hoop on the pulpit. For the Anabaptists, pouring was the normal mode, and Balthasar Hubmaier used an ordinary milk pail. Anglicans generally retained the position of the font by the west door but the size diminished as Anglicans (despite the Prayer Book rubrics) abandoned the practice of dipping infants.

A similar situation prevailed among Roman Catholics with many new fonts too small for a baby. The opposite direction was taken by English Baptists beginning in the 1640s. In distinction from the Anabaptists, they began to argue for immersion of adult believers. The immersion debates were fought all through the nineteenth century,

Saint Francis of Assisi Catholic Church, Raleigh, North Carolina. One of the last churches for which the liturgical designer Frank Kacmarcik served as a consultant. To the left and front of the freestanding altar is a font adequate for adult immersion. PHOTOGRAPH COURTESY OF SAINT FRANCIS OF ASSISI CATHOLIC CHURCH, RALEIGH, NORTH CAROLINA

Baptismal Fonts

S. Anita Stauffer

When investigating the meaning and practice of holy baptism in history, much can be learned through the sizes, shapes, and decorations of baptismal fonts. It is especially the shapes that will be considered here, drawing on the author's own site work, mostly in fourth- through eighth-century sites, and largely in France, Italy, and Tunisia.[1] Much decoration (mosaic facings, sculpture, and frescoes) disappeared as the early churches and their baptisteries were destroyed when the Arabs invaded North Africa in the seventh century. The fonts largely survived by their location as pools in the ground, and now only need careful excavation and conservation. Examples are the beautifully restored Kélibia font in the Bardo Museum in Tunis [see color plate 25] and the Vitalis font at Sbeitla, also in Tunisia.[2] The most common shapes, depending on time and place, were rectangular, circular, octagonal, cruciform, and various forms of rectilinear and polylobe. One complicating factor regarding shapes is that fonts were often renovated or overbuilt; for example, in Aosta, Italy, the first font, dating from the fifth century, was octagonal, but in the sixth century it was transformed into a somewhat smaller circular pool. Another important issue is the relationship between the shape of the font and that of its enclosing baptistery.

The shape of a font is usually interpreted to refer to one meaning or another—paschal imagery (death/resurrection) or birth imagery, and so forth. However, Richard Krautheimer warned against overinterpretation of baptistery shapes:

> the symbolical significance is something which merely accompanied the particular form which was chosen for the structure. It accompanied it as a more or less uncertain connotation which was only dimly visible and whose specific interpretation was not necessarily agreed upon. Yet as a connotation it was nearly always coupled with the pattern which had been chosen. Its very vagueness explains the variety of interpretations given to one and the same form either by one or by different authors.[3]

Baptismal pool. At Trinity Methodist Church in Singapore, the outdoor font doubles as a cooling fountain. PHOTOGRAPH COURTESY OF ALPHONSUS LOH AND PHILIP LIM

with Baptists and others insisting that only immersion of adults was biblical. Frequently such baptisms were performed in rivers and lakes and still are in some places. But this mode of baptizing believers led to a hundred thousand tank baptisteries or baptismal pools in churches of Baptists, Disciples of Christ, Churches of Christ, Mormons, Adventists, and many others. Usually such tanks are four or five steps deep, allowing baptism by lowering the person baptized backward into the water. Changing

Rectangular Fonts

The oldest font discovered thus far by archaeologists (Dura Europos, Syria, the only Eastern font to be considered here) was a rectangle in shape. It dates from the early third century, and was probably part of a house church. The font itself was seemingly without decoration, but the walls of the baptistery were covered with frescoes of biblical scenes related to the meanings of baptism. Roman and early Christian sarcophagi were rectangular, so that fonts in that shape may perhaps point to the meaning of the sacrament as burial with Christ (Rom. 6:4). However, many bathing pools were also rectangular, which might suggest baptism as cleansing.

The third-century San Ponziano Catacomb in Rome included a rectangular pool that was undoubtedly used as a font. It was likely the only catacomb font in Rome. It is fed by a spring, and flooding waters have done heavy damage to the font and the frescoes above it.[4] Once surmounting the water was a large fresco cross; in the next register above is a lovely scene of the Baptism of Christ surrounded by an angel and a hart (Ps. 42).

Circular Fonts

Round fonts, which seem to have originated in fourth-century Rome, were more common in the East than the West, and within the West, there were probably more in what is now Algeria than what is now Tunisia. Various interpretations of the circle (such as in the round Lateran Baptistery in Rome) have occurred in early Christianity, but it may simply have derived from the cold circular basins (*frigidaria*) in Roman baths that were common in Rome and Pompeii. Some have suggested that the womb language of this font's inscription implies birth symbolism (see John 3:3–8; Titus 3:5; 1 Peter 1:3), but the water language is too multivalent to limit it to one meaning.[5]

An outstanding circular font, small but still large enough for adult submersion, is the one found—probably restored—at Mustis, Tunisia. Its location is nearly unique: the baptistery is along the wall of the apse. This font resembles a public frigidarium at Pompeii.

rooms are usually adjacent. The baptistery most frequently is on the main axis of the church, behind the pulpit, and often concealed by a curtain when not in use. Folk art paintings of the River Jordan abound.

Ironically, in recent years pedobaptists (those baptizing infants) have sometimes been persuaded that immersion at whatever age is the most desirable for the fullness of the sign of cleansing and death and resurrection. A number of Roman Catholic churches in recent years have introduced baptismal pools for the immersion of infants and adults alike.[5] At the same time, the location of the font has been the object of various experiments whereby the font is sometimes closely linked in space to pulpit and altar-table, a location long favored by Lutherans.

It is safe to say that the fonts have become larger and more prominent in many Protestant churches, especially Anglican or Lutheran. This shows a greater concern

Octagonal Fonts

The eight-sided form is one of the most ancient in the West for both fonts and baptisteries. Scholars debate whether the eight sides were intentional or whether it was just simpler to construct an octagon than a circle.

Dating to the early fourth century, the octagon has been one of the most common shapes for fonts and baptisteries, especially in Italy and France. (They are not known in Tunisia.) Usually the symbolism is that of resurrection, or that of the Eighth Day, the day of Christ's Resurrection as the eschatological dawning of the new age, which is entered in the waters of holy baptism.[6]

The most notable octagonal font is that of the Milanese baptistery officially known as San Giovanni alle Fonti, probably constructed in about AD 379–381 while Ambrose was bishop of Milan. Most scholars believe this is the site of Ambrose's baptism of Augustine at the Easter vigil on 24 April 387. The Ambrosian baptistery, as it is usually called, was almost certainly modeled after the octagonal imperial mausoleum (third century) within the fortress of San Vittore al Corso in Milan. It resembles the extant mausoleum of Sant'Aquilino attached to the imperial basilica of San Lorenzo in present-day Milan.[7] At least some of the interior walls of the Ambrosian baptistery were polychromed, and there was a gold and multicolored dome mosaic, but the designs can no longer be discerned. An eight-distich inscription (now preserved only in a ninth-century codex), probably from around the bottom of the dome, is famous for its emphasis on the octagonal baptistery and font, and thus of the primary paschal (octagonal) meaning of baptism.[8] The understanding of the sacrament in terms of both burial and resurrection with Christ and cleansing from sin and guilt is reflected also in the baptismal homilies of Ambrose (e.g., *De sacramentis*, 1:12;

about the importance of the first sacrament and a desire to increase congregational participation and the fullness of the sign. Undoubtedly, baptismal fonts and space will continue to evolve as practices change.

The Service of the Word

We move now to the service of the word. Whether as the first half of the eucharist or as a free-standing preaching service, it affirms the centrality of God's Word read, preached, and sung in Christian worship. Only small groups such as Quakers can dispense with it by substituting direct dependence on the Spirit (itself the author of the word).

Though it can and frequently does take place in the out-of-doors, for convenience the service of the word is normally celebrated in a building. Evangelistic preaching services have adapted to whatever circumstances were available, whether it be Paul's hired lecture hall in Ephesus (Acts 19:9) or John Wesley's field preaching. But certain liturgical centers and spaces have come to be regarded as most convenient.

Since the service focuses on a book, it is not surprising that some place for the Bible or lectionary is the most important liturgical center just as the ark is for the

2:20, 23; 3:2; *De mysteriis*, 20–21). It is significant that Ambrose spoke of the font as a grave and a tomb; perhaps he was thinking of the imperial mausoleum after which the baptistery may have been modeled. The font in the Ambrosian baptistery was not quite the largest of its time, but it was among the largest and probably the most important; it has been well excavated and preserved. The Lateran font in Rome was also greatly important, but excavations leave it nearly impossible to see. There were many differences in the baptismal ritual between Rome and Milan. Rome's round Lateran font contrasts with Milan's octagonal pool; it is not known whether that difference is significant, either theologically or liturgically.

Another important octagonal font (fourth or early-fifth century) is that in Fréjus, in southern France. It is a much smaller pool than Milan or Rome. It is octagonal at the top of the pool, but circular at the bottom; the walls of the font were revetted in grey or white marble. A low octagonal parapet wall surrounded the font on seven sides. On the eighth side the parapet opened, apparently to allow the catechumen down in to the water via one step. There is a partial column at one corner of the parapet, suggesting a canopy over the font. This was common in the Early Church, but few of them remain. Often the canopy was decorated on the underside with stars, suggesting the heaven that is entered via baptism. The symbolism of the octagon in this site seems unknown. It would seem that cathedrals (and, later, parish churches) related to Milan (in contrast to Rome) most frequently had octagonal pools with their paschal symbolism: walking down into the water, passing through the water, and then walking up and out of the water. This sense of passage through the water from death to new life is clearest in a site like the Ambrosian baptistery in Milan, and the Vitalis font in Sbeitla in southwestern Tunisia.

Jewish scrolls. For Christians, the place of the book is normally the *pulpit* or *ambo*, although a *lectern* sometimes serves this purpose. In some Protestant churches, the Bible is left on the altar-table as a kind of reserved sacrament, but rarely, if ever, read from this location. Whatever liturgical center is used, it must be visible and audible to the congregation. In recent years, electronic systems have magnified the voices of reader, preacher, and singer. But face to face encounter remains crucial.

The pulpit needs only the space that it occupies, but it must function as a focus for congregational space. Though baptism may be in private, this and all the remaining services we shall discuss are public and need space to accommodate an assembly of worshipers. This means that *congregational space* must be so shaped that the maximum number of those assembled can hear and see what happens at the pulpit and altar-table. Today we think of the assembly as static in fixed pews, but for most of church history (and still today in many Orthodox churches) the people were mobile, requiring only a level floor.

In recent years liturgists have become more sensitive to the need for *gathering space*, in which the people come together to discern the body of Christ. This may be the most important single action of worship, and failure to take it seriously could have dire consequences as Paul warns (1 Cor. 11:29). Gathering space can be exterior, such as the atrium at Sant' Ambrogio in Milan, or interior, as in a narthex or concourse.

Hexagonal Fonts

The six-sided form for fonts began to appear in both Europe and North Africa in the fifth century. They were especially popular in northern Italy. The usual interpretation was that the number six is a reference to the sixth day of the week, Friday, the day on which Christ was crucified and died. Thus the hexagonal font may refer to baptism as being united with Christ in his death (see Rom. 6:3–5). The symbolism can be especially poignant when the font is a hexagon surrounded by an octagonal baptistery—the catechumen walks into the dark baptistery and down several steps into a six-sided font into death with Christ, and then comes up from the waters into the octagonal baptistery into eighth-day resurrection with Christ.

The original in-ground font at Grado, Italy, was hexagonal. The present medieval font, built on top of the earlier one, is also hexagonal. Such an arrangement was very common in northern Italy.

Square Fonts

In the West, square fonts are rather rare. Ruins of several are in Algeria, but only two have been identified in Tunisia. In Europe several have been found, but none in either France or Italy. It is likely that the symbolism is similar to that of the rectangular fonts, since they are both rectilinear, resembling sarcophagi/coffins.

A well-conserved one (except that the font bottom is missing, making it a dangerous site to visit) is in the baptistery of Hildeguns in Maktar, Tunisia. It seems to date to the sixth century.

Cruciform Fonts

These are among the most interesting fonts, perhaps because their symbolism seems so clearly paschal. The candidate can walk down the steps into the water,

But it marks the transition from the world outside to the community gathered in Christ's name inside. Worshipers come to meet their God and immediately encounter their neighbor in this space.

A third type of space demanded by most forms of public worship is *movement space.* Even baptism once demanded a processional path from doorway (world) to font (church). Much of worship revolves around worshiping with the feet: they gather together, they approach the table for communion, they bring their offerings, they process and recess at weddings and funerals. For the Shakers, who danced before the Lord, the whole interior was movement space.

Finally, many churches have found that music can be an important part of the service of the word. This implies the use of instruments and choirs, which we can speak of collectively as *choir space.* There exists no consensus as to where this is best located in relation to the other spaces. Obviously musicians need to be situated so as

be baptized, and walk up facing the opposite direction. It is likely that the bishop or priest faced the candidate while he/she was in the water (in the earliest days, bishops did the baptizing—or a deacon went into the water with the candidate, while the bishop spoke the words from the top of another side).

In Thuburbo Majus, Tunisia, a cruciform font was constructed with a circle inscribed at the center of the top level.[9]

An interesting cruciform/quadrilobe font is that of El Kantara, Tunisia, now displayed in the Bardo Museum in Tunis. The arms of the cross are rounded, unlike those at Thuburbo Majus.

Quadrilobe Fonts

This four-lobed shape developed as a variation of the cruciform shape. The symbolism thus is likely to be the same: participation via baptism in Christ's death and resurrection. These fonts were common in Tunisia as well as in what is now Israel.

Perhaps the best example of a sixth-century quadrilobe font is that from Kélibia, Tunisia. This font is highly decorated with mosaic figures related to sea life and baptism. In addition to the paschal symbolism of the four lobes, it is appropriate to understand baptism as a proleptic entry into the abundant life of Paradise.[10] On and above the four lobes are fish and dolphins. In Christian iconography of this period and region, the dolphin was a frequent symbol of Christ. One is quickly reminded of what Tertullian had earlier said about baptism: "We, being little fishes, as Jesus Christ is our great fish, begin our life in the water,

to be best heard. But their best location must be determined on the basis of the chief roles they play in worship.

The service of the word, then, demands a liturgical center such as the pulpit and a variety of liturgical spaces: congregational, gathering, movement, and choir. As we shall see, the configurations of these have varied enormously over the centuries and at present. We shall survey briefly how these arrangements of centers and spaces have developed over the centuries and are still evolving.

Earliest Christian worship apparently occurred in private homes, temporarily adapted for that purpose. In such makeshift circumstances, it merely meant the re-arrangement of some household furniture. L. Michael White says of this period: "For the most part private houses were used for casual assembly. Otherwise they remained in domestic use."[17]

But by the third century, at least, more permanent arrangements were becoming possible. "In general, it appears that the first steps toward adaptation occurred in an edifice in which Christians were already accustomed to meeting."[18] Most likely, we have an example of this in the third-century renovations at Dura-Europos where a wall was knocked out in a private dwelling to make a single large room for the assembly [see illustration in chapter 2]. Probably similar adaptations happened to some private dwellings in Rome, reflecting a move from a house church to a church house.

By the late third century, new buildings were being constructed in various parts of the empire when persecution allowed. Eusebius speaks of Christians erecting "churches

and only while we abide in the water are we safe and sound."[11] The interior corners of the four lobes (at the top register) bear images of lighted mosaic candles, perhaps an iconographic reference to baptism as enlightenment or illumination, common metaphors in the early church. Or perhaps the symbolic reference is to the paschal candle (although we do not know for sure whether baptism was held at the Easter vigil in Kélibia).

Polylobe Fonts

This form is basically circular, with a varying number of small projecting lobes or alveoli. In Tunisia the remaining fonts available for study usually have eight lobes, but six and twelve are not unknown in North Africa. Generally they date to the sixth century. They are probably unrelated to quadrilobe fonts, being more likely to carry number symbolism. However, one must be careful in "retrofitting" medieval number symbolism on earlier fonts. Likewise, it is risky to transfer symbolic meaning from one type of polylobe to others; they may have completely different histories. The meaning and purpose of the lobes are unknown, though there has been ample speculation.

The polylobe fonts that remain are in very poor condition, so it is difficult to examine them. Among them, perhaps the best preserved is that near Hergla, Tunisia, where most of the eight lobes (set within a circle) are somewhat visible, though yet unexcavated.

Notes

[1] For two indispensable sources related to shapes, see A. Khatchatrian, *Les baptistères paléochrétiens* (Paris: Imprimerie Nationale, 1962) and *Origine et typologie des baptistères paléochrétiens* (Mulhouse: Centre de Culture Chrétien, 1982).

[2] S. Anita Stauffer, *On Baptismal Fonts: Ancient and Modern* (Bramcote, Notts: Alcuin/GROW Liturgical Studies 29–30), color plates 2 and 3, following page 30.

[3] Introduction to "Iconography of Medieval Architecture," in Richard Krautheimer, *Studies in Early Christian, Medieval, and Renaissance Art* (New York: New York University Press, 1969) 122.

[4] For an excellent full-page rendering of the font and frescoes prior to flooding damage, see the frontispiece in Wolfred Nelson Cote, *The Archaeology of Baptism* (London: Yates and Alexander, 1876).

[5] For a translation of the inscription, see that by Aidan Kavanagh in his *The Shape of Baptism: The Rite of Christian Initiation* (New York: Pueblo, 1978) 49.

[6] S. Anita Stauffer, "Fonts: Baptism, Pascha, and Paradise," *Studia Liturgica* 24 (1994) 58–65.

[7] For insightful text and graphics, see Mario Mirabella Roberti, *Milano Romana* (Milan: Rusconi, 1984); and Mirabella Roberti with Angelo Paredi, the seminal volume, *Il Battistero Ambrosiano di San Giovanni alle Fonti* (Veneranda Fabbrica del Duomo di Milano, n.d.).

[8] For a translation, see Stauffer, *On Baptismal Fonts*, 24.

[9] For a photograph before the excavation was completed, see *On Baptismal Fonts* p. 35.

[10] For detailed attention to the symbolism of this font, see Stauffer, "Fonts," 61–63. It should be noted, however, that some of the mosaic figures are controversial in their interpretation.

[11] *De Baptismo* 1, *Tertullian's Homily on Baptism*. trans. Ernest Evans (London: SPCK, 1964) 4–5.

The interior of San Clemente, Rome. The twelfth-century basilica is built over the site of a fourth-century basilica and still earlier buildings. The current renovated space retains some characteristics of the arrangement of the fourth-century predecessor including the combination of altar and martyr's tomb, the chair of the bishop in the apse, the ambo for the reading of the scriptures, and seating space for cantors of the psalms. BRIDGEMAN ART LIBRARY, LONDON

of spacious foundations in every city,"[19] although these church halls were vulnerable to sporadic destruction as long as persecution persisted. Still they provided experiments in arranging space for services of word and table.

The greatest single change came in the fourth century, when under Constantine and his successors Christianity became respectable and then advantageous. Imperial architects built monumental churches in Rome, Jerusalem, and Bethlehem. It is significant that the form chosen, the basilica, was a secular building used for law courts, not the religious architecture of the temple. The basilica enclosed the community; the temple excluded it. Basically the basilica was a large hall that might have side aisles with clerestory windows above and a semicircular apse at one short end. The Christian bishop and clergy simply took the place of the judge and lawyers in the apse. An altar-table stood at the entrance to the apse; an ambo or pulpit was a bit closer to the people who stood where they best could hear. A short screen might enclose the choir before the altar-table. Men and women were separated and women might be in a rear or side gallery.

Originally, preaching was done by the bishop seated in his cathedra in the apse. Saint John Chrysostom, a great preacher with a weak voice, began preaching from the ambo so as better to be seen and heard, and most preachers since have followed this adaptation by going to the people to preach. The rest of the service was led from ambo, throne, and altar-table. The pulpit had become a distinct liturgical center in its own right and could be quite remote from the altar-table, wherever the people could see and hear best.

Many medieval pulpits stood on the north side of the middle of the nave, where listeners could gather to hear the preacher. This implied a mobile congregation such as still exists in much of the Orthodox world. The biggest single change in worship in the West came late in time, after the Black Death of the fourteenth century, when pews began to encroach on open territory. The congregation, hitherto mobile, sat down on the job and ended with a single orientation, facing the east end. For a thousand years and more they had been on their feet; now their attention was fixed in a single direction. The nave, which had been entirely movement space, now was mostly seating with movement limited to the aisles. Such acts as prostration were no longer feasible.

Mendicant orders, beginning in the thirteenth century, occasionally built hall churches specifically for the needs of preaching to a large congregation. They usually involved wide aisles with narrow piers between them and the nave so that sight lines to the pulpit were not blocked. Essentially these churches allowed a crowd to surround the pulpit. A small chancel stood at the east end.

The typical Western medieval parish church consisted of two spaces: the chancel, whose functions we shall describe shortly, and the nave, where the congregation gathered for mass, to hear preaching, and for a wide variety of social occasions.[20] The clergy were responsible for upkeep of the chancel, the laity for the nave, often resulting in a disparity in size and style.

These were the buildings that both the Protestant and Catholic Reformations inherited by the thousands in western Europe. Both groups found major changes necessary in the configuration of space. For Catholics, especially after the reforms of Saint Charles Borromeo[21] and with the advent of Jesuit Baroque in the Church of Il Gesù in Rome, this meant the advent of a much more theatrical type of space. Visibility of the altar-table was enhanced by destruction of hundreds of rood screens that had separated chancel and nave. Renewed attention was devoted to pulpits and acoustics, for preaching became a major concern. New churches avoided long chancels. For Catholics, such novelties as communion rails, confessionals, the tabernacle on the altar-table, and the destruction of no-longer-favored icons (such as the Trinity as three men with beards) made major changes in the organization of space.

Changes were equally drastic for many Protestant groups that inherited the same type of buildings. Anglicans were the most conservative at first, accepting the two-volume division with a rood screen between. They simply divided the functions, making the chancel the eucharistic room and the nave the space for the service of the word. As the eucharist became more and more an occasional service, new church buildings tended to provide space for it in the nave. All of this was reversed in the Catholic Revival of the nineteenth century when a valiant effort was made to recover the medieval spaces and functions. The efforts of the Cambridge Movement frequently succeeded in restoring or rebuilding chancels, divided from the nave by a rood screen. Whereas the eighteenth century had generally provided a single liturgical center, consisting of clerk's desk, reading desk, and pulpit (the three-decker), the gothicists split these functions between two liturgical centers, a lectern for readings, psalms, and prayers, and a pulpit for the sermon. Such an arrangement remained common, if not universal, in Anglican churches until the closing decades of the twentieth century and was widely copied in many Protestant traditions as the so-called divided chancel. The choir occupied the chancel and was divided on either side. Whatever may be said of such an arrangement in function, it did provide visual symmetry. The late twentieth century found Anglicans experimenting with a variety of other configurations of space for the service of the word and the service of the table.

The Lutheran reformation saw less iconoclasm than the Anglican. In many places, the eucharist remained the normal Sunday service until the end of the eighteenth century. This allowed the old arrangements to be suitable, but frequently the altar-table was made freestanding. As new buildings were built, it became increasingly common for altar-table, pulpit, and font to be grouped together, often surrounded by a communion rail. This *prinzipalstück* arrangement became common and gave the building a single liturgical focus by proclaiming the unity of word and sacrament. Lutheranism tended to be most receptive to baroque architecture. This reached its climax in buildings that resembled opera houses, with multiple balconies. Paul Tillich claimed that the Frauenkirche in Dresden (1726–1945; rededicated 2005) was the ideal Protestant church. Here multiple balconies focused on a stage containing pulpit and altar-table. In recent decades, various experiments have been tried, often retaining the *prinzipalstück* arrangement.

The Reformed tradition (Presbyterians and others) tended to make more radical changes. Although Calvin wanted the eucharist "at least once a week," this did not happen. The result was to make the pulpit the prime liturgical center for the service of the word with most of the service led from it. Frequently the baptismal basin was attached to it. Chancels were often walled off or destroyed. Old buildings were often reoriented to focus on a pulpit, surmounted by impressive sounding boards and surrounded by pews.

New buildings in the Netherlands, France, and Scotland focused largely on the pulpit and tended to be central in plan: squares, octagons, Greek crosses, or T-shaped buildings. The famous temple of Charenton near Paris seated between four and five thousand on the main floor and two rows of balconies around the perimeter. After the destruction of all these churches in 1685, worshipers gathered in secret in woods and barns about a portable pulpit.

America provided a vast laboratory for building meetinghouses for Reformed and Puritan worship. Almost invariably these focused on elegant pulpits ornamented by sounding boards and pulpit windows. Ornate entrances led to pews on the main floor and balconies (eventually horseshoe in shape). Pulpits tended to resemble a wineglass in form.

A major shift began about 1835 with Charles G. Finney's New York building, the Broadway Tabernacle Congregational Church.[22] Here was a large circular building, accommodating thousands with every eye fixed on a large platform with a desk pulpit. A balcony surrounded the space except for a pipe organ behind the platform. In some ways, it was the outdoor camp meeting brought indoors, although large tabernacles continued to be built in rural regions for camp meeting. Broadway Tabernacle soon became the model for thousands of churches, all having balconies to bring the largest number of people close to the platform. Revival preachers could dash about on the platform seeking to save souls. Sloping floors improved the sight lines and the gradual advent of choirs found a home in a concert stage arrangement behind the pulpit. The Akron plan brought all this to a climax by placing the liturgical centers in a corner with floor and balconies sloping toward them.

Methodists were expected to worship in the Anglican parish church but soon began to build

Wethersfield meetinghouse. The meeting house, built in 1764 in Wethersfield, Connecticut, was furnished with box pews to help insulate worshipers during the winter months. A sounding board is suspended above the raised pulpit to aid in the amplification of the voice. First Church of Christ still uses the building for worship. PHOTOGRAPH BY R. PERRON/ART RESOURCE, NY

preaching houses. For a period, John Wesley insisted that octagonal buildings with balconies enabled the most people to see and hear the preacher at least expense.[23] But this model was eventually abandoned in favor of buildings similar to those that the Reformed tradition adopted. In the twentieth century, worship tended to shift from an emotional focus to an aesthetic one. Aping the Anglicans was vigorously promoted by a church bureaucrat named Elbert M. Conover, who stressed Gothic or at least Georgian buildings with a divided chancel.[24] Thus an arrangement functional for medieval parishes was replicated across much of American Protestantism.

The third of a century since Vatican II saw much experimentation by both Protestants and Catholics. Many of these moved to a central type building with a vertical axis. Many churches were remodeled or even reoriented. The emerging favorite among new Catholic churches seemed to be a fan shaped arrangement with ambo and altar-table in the middle of a long side. This brings the largest number of people in close proximity to both liturgical centers. As participation becomes the key word in liturgical vocabularies, proximity to the action seems key in architectural terms.

The latest major shift has been in Protestant circles to the building of megachurches in church growth circles. These tend to avoid any liturgical symbols, including liturgical centers. Theater seating is often provided and balconies are common. A platform usually presents space for professional musicians. The service is led from a portable desk more like a lectern than a pulpit. Movable furniture may be present for dramatic skits or monologues. High technology sound equipment is used.

Another pattern appears in praise and worship services, where the musicians again may be prominent and a screen is dropped to have texts projected on it. Again the pulpit resembles more a teacher's lectern, and the sermon may be called teaching. Participation is largely through congregational song.

The arrangement of space for the service of the word continues to evolve as concepts and practices of this type of worship changes. But all have a common function of bringing together the people and the message of scripture.

The Service of the Table

The needs of the service of the table are quite different from those of the service of the word and most churches represent a compromise between the two. It is as if there were a compromise between an upper room or dining room and a synagogue or auditorium. The service of the table focuses on food and drink held in containers and placed on an altar-table at a convenient height for a standing person. Unlike the Bible, which simply needs to be where it can be read, the bread and wine need a place on which they can be consecrated and from which they can be distributed.

In terms of space, the altar-table needs to be accessible. Accessibility can take a wide variety of forms, each with specific meaning. Tables, benches, communion rails each brought people to the sacrament; pew communions brought the sacrament to the people. The only constant seems to be the need for the clergy to touch the vessels containing the bread and wine, and this implies close proximity. Catholics call *altar-table space* "sanctuary" while Protestants use this term for the entire church interior.

From the fourth to the sixteenth century the service of the word and the service of the table were invariably united. No early altar-tables have survived. Some paintings in the catacombs show a "D"-shaped table at the Last Supper with the apostles reclining around it, but there is no evidence that this was imitated in early Christian practice. Dura-Europos has a dais at one end of the worship space but no evidence of what stood on it.

With the coming of the basilica as the archetype, the altar-table stood on the chord of the apse, the bishop facing the people. As such, the altar-table had a simple function of holding the bread and wine but foreshadowed a number of symbolic meanings: the center of unity, the presence of Christ in the midst of the community, the presence of his sacrifice among his followers, and the offering of their sacrifice of praise and thanksgiving. The moving of relics in the fifth century also brought the burial of saints' bodies beneath the altar-table. The celebrant faced the people across the altar-table in what was known as the "basilican position," his actions visible to all.

In both East and West the altar-table tended to withdraw from such a conspicuous location during the Middle Ages. In the East, it retreated behind a partition, the iconostasis, but remained basically a rather small cube. Doors could open to reveal its presence at appropriate times in the liturgy. In the West, the withdrawal went hand in hand with a greater clerical dominance in worship and infrequent communion of the laity. In most instances, the altar-table eventually lodged against the east wall in a numinous sacred space far removed from the laity. There it became a strictly clerical center, often with candles and a small cross for the priest's own devotions. The table form was lost in favor of a solid rectangle, containing relics. Usually a carved wood or stone reredos or a stained glass window surmounted it so that the altar-table appeared more like a shelf than a freestanding table.

Spatially, the chancel stretched between the laity in the nave and the clergy at the altar-table. Frequently a wood or stone rood screen with a large cross over it separated clergy and flock. The priest had long ago turned his back to the congregation as the altar-table was tied to the east wall and one could celebrate mass thirty feet or more from any people. The one action that could be seen was at the elevation for so-called "ocular communion." On the rare occasions when communion was received by the people it would be at the steps into the chancel.

As masses for the dead proliferated, chantry chapels were built facing east. Each of these contained an additional altar-table, but these were essentially for private masses that were sometimes conducted simultaneously with that at the high altar-table. The result frequently was an array of altar-tables but none closely related to the space the people occupied.

Saint Mary's Cathedral, Killarney, Republic of Ireland. The cathedral nave, completed in 1855, was designed by Augustus W. Pugin. THE ART ARCHIVE/JERROLD PUBLISHING

Much was to change in the Catholic Reformation. The Gesù Church represented a major reconfiguration of space. Since the Jesuits had no need of choir space, altar-table space was moved much closer to the nave. The whole east end became a visual presentation having much in common with changes going on in Italian theater design at the time.[25] It was as if the altar-table had become the centerpiece of a stage set. Rood screens were destroyed as churches were remodeled. The essence was to make the altar-table visually accessible to the nave.

These changes were also promoted by the new fashion for having the tabernacle squarely on the altar-table instead of a reserved sacrament in a pyx, ambry, or sacrament house. New devotions of adoration led to exposition in a monstrance even during mass. At the same time, communion was facilitated by the introduction of communion rails. Thus altar-table space was visually accessible but still carefully demarcated from profanation by the laity. The new baroque concept of church space as essentially one volume changed Catholic churches everywhere and usually thwarted the attempts of gothicists to reintroduce rood screens in the nineteenth century.

As we have already indicated, the Anglican tradition at first held on to the chancel as eucharistic space. But an important change was in the freeing of the altar-table from the wall and making it stand lengthwise in the chancel or "tablewise." There communicants could kneel about it, the priest standing on the north side. Most surviving stone altar-tables were destroyed and replaced by wood tables.[26] As communion Sundays became less and less frequent, chancels were often walled off and used for schools or abandoned. The seventeenth century saw the altar-table usually placed against the east wall of the nave. Above it were placed the texts of the Apostles' Creed, the Decalogue, and the Lord's prayer, thus tying it directly to the main points of the catechism. In front appeared a new device, communion rails, usually returned on the sides to make a rectangular altar-table space. It was quite common for a triple-decker pulpit to stand in the central aisle in front of the altar-table.

Sir Christopher Wren canonized the single volume arrangement. Experiments continued in America, such as pulpit and altar-table at opposite ends of the building or at right angles to each other. Nineteenth-century gothicists attempted to correct all this by restoring the full medieval arrangement with altar-table space at the east end of a long chancel. Battles were waged about the return of stone altars and the placement of candles on them. Rood screens were restored or built anew. It was as if neither Catholics nor Protestants had moved beyond the fourteenth century. The neomedieval arrangement predominated for a century and a half.

Lutherans tended to make the altar-table a central focus of the buildings. The baroque appealed to them, especially with its possibilities of a burst of natural light over the altar-table. In various ways, the altar-table was combined with the pulpit and font to make a triple focus at the east end. Communion rails became and remain common. The altar-table is visible throughout the church and in recent years most have become freestanding, allowing the presider to face the congregation.

Reformed churches made major changes. As the pulpit became the major liturgical center, attention focused away from the altar-table and it became an occasional item. For three centuries, Presbyterians resorted to temporary tables set up or built into the front pew and surrounded by benches. Sometimes these extended down the aisles. The minister broke the bread and passed it and the cup the length of

Saint Stephen's Walbrook, London. The architect Christopher Wren oversaw the construction of the building from 1672 to 1687. Watercolor (1811) by John Coney (1786–1833). GUILHALL LIBRARY, CORPORATION OF LONDON/BRIDGEMAN ART LIBRARY

the table to sitting communicants. This practice still survives in some Dutch Reformed churches but most Presbyterians gave it up for pew communion. This was the preferred practice of English and American Puritans who did not want to seem to be kneeling in adoration of the communion elements. Apparently, a number of Anglican parishes eventually followed suit. Many Puritan meetinghouses simply had a hinged table immediately below the pulpit. These were in time replaced by small tables beneath the pulpit.

Wesleyan chapels were distinguished from those of the Puritans by retaining the communion rails. This has remained the chief feature distinguishing Methodist churches from those of Reformed and Puritan traditions. Quite frequently, the communion rails also enclose the pulpit and lectern (if any). Several of Wesley's chapels followed the contemporary Anglican practice of placing the altar-table directly behind the pulpit. By the nineteenth century, Methodists, Presbyterians, Baptists, and others substituted a small table immediately below the pulpit. The efforts of Elbert M. Conover and others led to a divided chancel with the altar-table once again retreating toward the east wall. Many were and still are attached to the wall. Quite commonly they now contain an open Bible, which is never used. And almost invariably a brass cross and candlesticks appear on the altar-table as if for a priest's own devotions.

Major changes occurred in many churches in the last decades of the twentieth century. Roman Catholics decreed in September 1964 that the altar-table should be freestanding. It took a while to dispose of the tabernacle on it, ideally to a side chapel. At first, many churches simply added a wooden table in front of the old stone altar. Many churches were eventually reoriented to bring the congregation in a semicircle around the altar-table, now on one of the long sides of the building. Newly-built Catholic churches tended to favor the fan-shaped floor plan with the altar-table on a thrust stage toward the middle of congregational space. Communion rails all but disappeared or were recycled for other uses. Table forms became common, frequently of wood. Altar-table space is defined only by a rise in the floor level, necessary to ensure good sight lines. Thus altar-table space is often surrounded on 180 degrees by congregational space. Chapels for devotions often contain the tabernacle. Communion is usually received standing.

Many similar features occur in the more liturgically minded Protestant churches, although few Methodists, Episcopalians, and Lutherans have relinquished communion rails. In many cases, altar-tables have been moved away from the walls and the presider can stand behind them. Many have been unencumbered of Bible, cross, and candlesticks, although far from all. The altar-table is used more and more, not only for more frequent eucharists but as the center for offering prayer in all services. Some churches have adopted communion in a standing posture; many still kneel for communion, making the rails necessary. And the majority of American Protestants seem most comfortable with pew communion. Many congregations

Korean Presbyterian Church. A contemporary building in Queens, New York. PHOTOGRAPH BY JAMES F. WHITE

partake of the bread and wine in unison. This necessitates small glasses for the wine and glass holders on the backs of pews.

Although the altar-tables and the space about them have become more prominent in liturgically-minded congregations, many churches remain content with a small altar-table crouched beneath the pulpit. This is probably a good indication of the relative infrequency and unimportance of the service of the table as compared to the service of the word. Even in churches with a weekly eucharist, such as Disciples of Christ, the altar-table is usually muted in importance compared to the pulpit.

Daily Public Prayer

We have yet to consider a worship pattern unfamiliar to most Christians today outside of intentional religious communities. This is a pattern of daily public prayer that has flourished at various times and places. It is not considered a sacrament and lay people frequently preside. Music may or may not be an important ingredient. Such services consist essentially of prayer and praise. In time, reading of scripture lessons and psalms became important parts and, eventually, hymns, nonscriptural readings, and various responses.

Architecturally, nothing is needed for a group of Christians to pray together. But for convenience, shelter from the weather is needed and some form of grouping the community in close proximity to each other, so the prayers and praise can be heard is certainly desirable. This means a priority is given to community space. The only requisite liturgical center is a lectern for whoever does the readings. Movement is minimal, but some spaces for gathering and taking one's place is needed. Musicians may need to be accommodated, but frequently the whole community is the choir and needs no special space.

There is evidence that even under persecution some early Christian communities were accustomed to gather daily for prayer and for instruction. When persecution ended, a fourth-century writer tells us "throughout the whole world . . . hymns, praises, and truly divine delights are offered to God at the morning going forth of the sun and at evening time."[27] These assemblies were ordinary people on a daily basis. In most of the world, such gatherings eventually came to an end. They were superseded by much smaller communities of monks and nuns for whom to "pray without ceasing" became their chief work, the *opus Dei*. By the sixth century, their prayer life had become thoroughly organized into eight daily and nightly services (the choir office).

A major portion of this revolved around the psalter. Saint Benedict had instructed that "the whole psalter, of a hundred and fifty psalms, be sung every week." As communities evolved, one of the most felicitous ways of doing this was antiphonally back and forth between two groups. (The Puritans, much later, compared this to a game of tennis!) It was only natural that an architectural form evolved with half the community facing the other half across a central aisle in parallel rows of stalls. In the central aisle might stand a lectern for the various readings of scripture, legends, and patristic homilies. The community might be enclosed by a wall to the west to separate its worship from that of visitors. To the east stood an altar-table for mass.

All in all, it was a very functional form and developed in great size in such monasteries as Cluny in France with over a thousand monks. In time, what was normal worship practice for monastic communities was also imposed on parish clergy, so that each clerical community (and clergy in major and minor orders were numerous) were obliged to keep the hours in choir also. This meant that the small chancels that had once been sufficient to house the altar-table were progressively enlarged throughout the Middle Ages to accommodate a community of clerics saying or singing the hours several times a day. The lord of the manor might also have a stall for his family in choir but otherwise laity were excluded and few attended the offices anyhow except for Sunday vespers. Some chancels were half as long as the nave or even more. In the case of college chapels, where the whole community prayed together on a daily basis, the chancel became the whole building except for a small gathering space or ante-chapel.

Thus the parish church had developed on the eve of the Reformation for two quite distinct types of worship, the mass and daily public (or at least clerical) prayer. It was, then, a shock when the Jesuits in the sixteenth-century were dispensed from the obligation of saying the office together so that they might be engaged in labors in the Lord's vineyard. This is vividly expressed in the Gesù Church in Rome, where choir space simply disappeared. And similar baroque churches built the world around by Jesuit missionaries simply erased this once familiar space, so that Catholic parish churches built right up to Vatican II carry little reminder that a long choir space once intervened between nave and altar-table.

More than any other Reformation group, Anglicanism retained a daily office of morning and evening prayer. Still semimonastic in stressing a daily regimen of scripture and psalmody, it was enjoined on the parish priest and for all "such as be disposed . . . to hear God's word, and to pray with him." It could take place in nave, chapel, or chancel as long "as the people may best hear." Frequently this meant the nave with a reading desk or lectern for the clergy. This was often united with the pulpit to form a double- or triple-decker. On Sundays, the office, litany, ante-communion, and sermon were joined. The nave and one liturgical center served them all.

The gothic revival of the nineteenth century brought a sea change. Without altering a single letter of the Prayer Book, the whole ethos of Anglican liturgy changed. This time the battle cry was for the restoration of chancels. Few if any monks were around, but the space could be filled with a choir of lay people dressed in surplices. One pamphlet for the restoration of churches and building anew declared that the chancel should be two-thirds as long as the nave. And so chancels reappeared or sprouted on new buildings in parish churches. Cathedral and collegiate churches had long continued a daily office, where usually community and choir were one and the same. Parish churches now developed choirs that occupied the chancel. The arrangement frustrated many a musician, and still does, for few choirs sing antiphonally. Only in monastic communities did it, and does it still, make sense.

What, then, is the future of space designed for daily public prayer? Such worship has maintained a bare toehold in some Orthodox churches in the Mediterranean world but has been largely lost to the West outside of religious communities. Intentional communities such as the Shakers maintain daily prayer services, but Shakers are near extinction. Roman Catholic parishes are rarely familiar with any pattern other than the mass, for which small weekday chapels may suffice. Some monastic communities have combined space for the office with a university chapel as at Saint John's Abbey in Minnesota. The chief Protestant examples seem to be seminary chapels, where emphasis tends to fall on preaching services. So space designed for daily public prayer seems to be largely marginal in our society. But it is worth remembering that it once built the largest church in the world (Cluny) and many other great abbeys.

Occasional Services

Although they may occur only infrequently, occasional services are a major portion of Christian worship. They are also Christianity's widest outreach to those beyond its borders. Everyone goes to a niece's wedding, an uncle's funeral, and these are prime occasions for portraying the meaning of Christianity to marginal or lapsed members and to the public at large. These services mark climactic events in the lives of those immediately involved. And recurrent rites of reconciliation and healing are deeply important to those participating.

Marriage is common to all societies, Christian or not. For most of church history, weddings took place elsewhere than in church buildings. It was not until three-quarters of the way through the first two Christian millennia that the whole service was finally moved inside church doors. Even the theologians, most of whom were celibate, finally included it as last and least among the list of sacraments.

At the center is the view of marriage as a contract, a view long held and reflected by some theologians today.[28] This is reinforced by the legal language, "to have and to hold," the insistence on witnesses, and the importance of keeping written records. For a thousand years, the home or tavern was the appropriate venue for weddings. With the emergence of legal systems, the presence of someone literate to keep records became imperative, hopefully the parish priest. Eventually, weddings came to be held at the church porch, where legal contracts were ratified (selling land, inheritances, etc.). The same space had a liturgical function in baptism, but here the porch represented not the world outside the church but the world of law. The couple who gave themselves to each other through their vows might then process inside the church for another sacrament, the mass, presided over by the priest.

Chaucer's fourteenth-century wife of Bath had had five husbands "at the church door" and was looking for number six. Exterior and interior spaces were still in use in Saxony when Luther produced his wedding rite of 1529. His Hans and Greta exchanged vows "at the entrance to the church" and then processed to "before the altar," where Genesis 2 was read and Luther preached and blessed them. By Thomas Cranmer's time, two decades later, the whole ceremony at last occurred in "the body of the church [nave] with their friends and neighbors." There it has been ever since.

Obviously space is necessary for those "friends and neighbors" who play an important role as witnesses to the contract and join in celebrating the joyful occasion. In Orthodox churches, vows and rings are exchanged in the narthex before processing inside the church (which symbolizes the kingdom of God). Both partners are crowned as heirs of the kingdom and then process three times around a table set in the nave for this purpose. For most Western churches, a temporary *prie dieu* or kneeler is often placed before the altar-table, although sometimes the communion rail suffices for the final blessing.

In all traditions, movement is an essential part of the service and largely dictated by the space available. A central aisle is usually preferred for procession of two individuals and recession of a married couple. These transitions in space signify a major change in one's being.

Ordinations do not seem to require distinct liturgical centers or spaces. This is partly because they may occur in parish churches, cathedrals, or convention halls. The congregation again plays an important role in testifying that the candidates are "worthy" as "all give consent" (*Apostolic Tradition*) so congregational space is very important. Some traditions require a stool for the bishop to use for the laying-on-of-hands. And many may use the pulpit and altar-table for the newly ordained to read and share in the offering of eucharistic prayer. In some traditions, the candidates kneel or prostrate themselves, requiring an open space, usually in front of the altar-table.

Reconciliation is sometimes known as confession or penance. Major changes have occurred over time in the form it has taken. In the Early Church, it was reserved for notorious sinners and took the form of expulsion from public worship and then reconciliation to the worshiping community. Few sinners were involved and it only occurred once in their life but it did involve moving out of the public worship space and then back into it.

By the seventh century, confession was becoming a reality for all Christians, and it became repeated and private. The Fourth Lateran Council (1215) required annual confession as a minimum for all communicants. In the Middle Ages, the person confessing usually knelt outside of the rood screen or chantry screen with the confessor sitting just inside. This more or less makeshift arrangement seems to have functioned well.

A much more deliberate arrangement eventuated in the late sixteenth century, the introduction of the confessional. This brought to a climax the individualization of the sacrament and made it a judicial tribunal rather than a communal attempt to restore an erring member. Saint Charles Borromeo more than any other promoted confessionals as "a convenient and proper way" to hear confessions. His *Instructions* of 1577 mandated at least two confessionals in each church so that the men and women would not mingle on the way. Space was provided only for the penitent and priest.

In general, Protestant churches did without such spaces, although penitents were sometimes required to face public humiliation and rebuke from a stool before the congregation. Some Anglo-Catholics installed confessionals in churches that had never had any for what was known as "auricular confession." But for the most part, Protestants were content with general confessions as part of Sunday worship for all involved. Serious offenders could be excommunicated: "no person shall be admitted to the Lord's Supper among us who is guilty of any practice for which we would exclude a member of our Church" (Methodist Episcopal Church, South, 1858 on). Communion tokens or tickets had separated the godly from the ungodly for eighteenth-century Presbyterians and Methodists. Thus discipline had spatial overtones at a time when communicants gathered at benches and tables or communion rails. The fencing of tables made some spaces forbidden for the unrepentant.

The years since Vatican II have seen the confessional disappear from most Catholic churches to be replaced by reconciliation rooms, rather nondescript spaces with seating for both penitent and confessor. For whatever reasons, confession, now known as reconciliation, does not seem to play a major role in the piety of most contemporary Catholics.

Healing of the sick has largely been a private matter performed in the sickroom or hospital as part of the visitation of the sick. But there are important exceptions in the case of pilgrimages and public healing services. For much of the early period, the sick person might anoint himself or herself with oil blessed by a bishop. Friends might participate through anointing and prayer, and healing of body and soul were hoped for. In the twelfth century this rite was renamed "extreme unction" and became a final preparation for dying through a final purgation of one's sins. Since Vatican II, it has been recast in a more positive light as anointing of the sick with hope for improvement in health.

Part of the perplexity of ministry to the sick was their removal from the space of the worshiping congregation. Anglicans made provision in 1549 to take communion to them from the parish celebration, but in 1552 a fresh sickroom communion was demanded. The Puritan *Westminister Directory* of 1644 gave careful detail as to how to counsel and pray with the sick in their own space.

There has been a long tradition of Christians journeying to seek healing. Chaucer's Canterbury pilgrims were on their way, "the holy blissful martyr for to seek, / that them had helped when that they were sick." Pilgrimage meant a temporary exile from home for purposes of thanksgiving, forgiveness, or divine help. This usually meant contact with the remains of some holy person or place. Tombs of saints were built so one could not only see but also touch (or even crawl through) the tomb containing the relics. Since large numbers of people came to major shrines, churches were built with ambulatories, so crowds could move past the tomb in an orderly fashion. Offerings could be collected and helped finance many cathedrals and other large churches. Thus the holy was made tangible, whether in such form as the holy house of Nazareth at Walsingham in England or a pit of healing earth at Chimayo in New Mexico. Thousands each day come to be in the presence of a single bone at Saint Anne de Beaupré, near Quebec City, or a body at Saint Joseph's Oratory in Montreal, many of them seeking healing of body and mind.

The eighteenth century saw the restoration of anointing of sick in the Church of the Brethren. Healing became a major function in various nineteenth-century churches, with stress on faith healing. For the Pentecostals, healing is a gift of the Spirit frequently practiced in Sunday services.

Today, many mainline churches have public healing service, often, but not always, in the context of the eucharist. Usually the same liturgical spaces and centers needed for the eucharist function well. Movement space becomes especially important, for such services usually entail coming forward to receive laying-on-of hands and/or anointing. Communion rails function well as the place for these actions, although a standing posture is possible. With an aging population, there is every indication that services of this kind will seem ever more desirable.

Care of the dead is common to all societies as they seek to show respect for the deceased and to bind up the wounds of the bereaved. The spatial demands in Christian worship have varied, especially revolving around the presence or absence of the body of the deceased. When the body is present, a catafalque or bier is usually necessary to hold the coffin. Movement space becomes significant as the body is brought into the community for the last time and then departs on its solitary journey. If a eucharist is celebrated, the usual centers and spaces are necessary. In any case, congregational space is necessary as the community surrounds and supports the bereaved. A pulpit or lectern is necessary as Christian hope is proclaimed in the face of death.

Until recently, burial space surrounded the church in a nearby graveyard or sometimes beneath the floor. Now the dead, too, usually reside in suburban cemeteries and the presence of the church triumphant is often overlooked by the church militant. In medieval times, a lych-gate usually formed the place where the clergy met the coffin and preceded it into the church. Now most of this is done without ceremony. There is a growing popularity of columbaria within or outside the church walls for placing the ashes of those cremated.

Burial spaces have interacted on worship spaces especially in the shape of baptisteries that took the form of mausoleums. Most new burial rites mention the connection of dying and rising with Christ in baptism. Baptism by immersion strongly suggests the threat to life and the deliverance of being raised with Christ.

In some places such as Rome, the *refrigerium* from pagan religions continued to suggest Christian services for the dead, especially on anniversaries of deaths. Annual remembrances at the grave became common and eventually collectively at All Saints' and All Souls' days. The fifth century saw the removal of saints' relics to churches, where they were placed beneath the altar-table. Others sought to be near such holiness and were buried beneath the church. Monuments came to surround worshipers on all sides as memorials to those who had gone on before. Ordinary people were allowed their thirty years in a grave outside and then, like *Hamlet*'s Yorick, dug up to be replaced by someone else. In the seventeenth century, ordinary people began to have their graves marked by tombstones to keep their name alive, if nothing else. In the nineteenth century most people were accorded coffins and embalming became common in the 1860s.

In modern times, preparation of the body has been almost completely taken over by commercial firms although, in earlier times, friends washed the body in farewell just as they had washed a new-born baby in welcome. Commercial funeral "chapels" provide a space for many funerals, especially those without church affiliations. But a strong case can be made that the familiar church space is most appropriate as in itself a statement of Christian hope. Space where the full gamut of Christian worship has been experienced throughout a lifetime has far more a sense of hope for the bereaved. The community filling that space shows that care of the dead continues in remembering them and in ministry to those left behind. The church building functions as a memorial and thanksgiving to those who have passed the faith on to another generation.

Bibliography

Addleshaw, George William Outram, and Frederick Etchells. *The Architectural Setting of Anglican Worship : An Inquiry into the Arrangements for Public Worship in the Church of England from the Reformation to the Present Day*. London: Faber and Faber, 1948.

Cook, George Henry. *The English Mediaeval Parish Church*. London: Phoenix House, 1954.

Davies, J. G. *The Architectural Setting of Baptism*. London: Barrie and Rockliff, 1962.

Hammond, Peter. *Liturgy and Architecture*. London: Barrie and Rockliff, 1960.

Hay, George. *The Architecture of Scottish Post-Reformation Churches, 1560–1843*. Oxford: Clarendon, 1957.

Krautheimer, Richard. *Early Christian and Byzantine Architecture*. Baltimore, Md.: Penguin Books, 1965.

Simson, Otto von. *The Gothic Cathedral: Origins of Gothic Architecture and the Medieval Concept of Order*. New York: Pantheon Books, 1962.

Upton, Dell. *Holy Things and Profane: Anglican Parish Churches in Colonial Virginia*. New Haven, Conn.: Yale University Press, 1977.

White, James F. *Protestant Worship and Church Architecture*. New York: Oxford University Press, 1964.

White, L. Michael. *The Social Origins of Christian Architecture*. 2 vols. Valley Forge, Pa.: Trinity Press International, 1996–1997.

Williams, Peter W. *Houses of God: Region, Religion, and Architecture in the United States*. Urbana: University of Illinois Press, 1997.

Wittkower, Rudolf, and Irma B. Jaffe, eds. *Baroque Art: The Jesuit Contribution.* New York: Fordham University Press, 1972.

Notes

[1] Davies, *The Architectural Setting of Baptism*; and S. Anita Stauffer, "Re-examining Baptismal Fonts" [video] (Collegeville, Minn.: Liturgical Press, 1991).

[2] Francis Bond, *Fonts and Font Covers* (London: Oxford University Press, 1908).

[3] See Ann Eljenholm Nichols, *Seeable Signs: The Iconography of the Seven Sacraments, 1350–1544* (Woodbridge, Suffolk: Boydell, 1994).

[4] Hughes O. Old, *The Shaping of the Reformed Baptismal Rite in the Sixteenth Century* (Grand Rapids, Mich.: Eerdmans, 1992) 265.

[5] Johan van Parys, "A Place for Baptism: New Trends in Baptismal Architecture since the Second Vatican Council" (Ph.D. diss., University of Notre Dame, 1998).

[6] White, *The Social Origins of Christian Architecture*, 1:105.

[7] White, *Social Origins*, 114.

[8] Quoted, White, *Social Origins*, 127.

[9] J. G. Davies, *The Secular Use of Church Buildings* (New York: Seabury, 1968).

[10] Cf. Evelyn Carole Voelker, "Charles Borromeo's *Instructiones Fabricae et Supellectilis Ecclesiasticae, 1577*" (Ph.D. diss., Syracuse University, 1977).

[11] Jeanne Halgren Kilde, *When Church Became Theatre* (New York: Oxford University Press, 2002) 22–55.

[12] Karen B. Westerfield Tucker, "'Plain and Decent': Octagonal Space and Methodist Worship," *Studia Liturgica* 24 (1994) 129–144.

[13] See Elbert M. Conover, *Building the House of God* (New York: Methodist Book Concern, 1928); and *The Church Builder* (New York: Interdenominational Bureau of Architecture, 1948).

[14] Cf. Wittkower and Jaffe, eds., *Baroque Art*, plates 55–60.

[15] Addleshaw and Etchells, *The Architectural Setting of Anglican Worship*; also Nigel Yates, *Buildings, Faith, and Worship* (Oxford: Clarendon, 1991).

[16] Eusebius of Caesarea, Commentary on Psalm 64:10, *PG* 23:650.

[17] Edward Schillebeeckx, *Marriage: Human Reality and Saving Mystery*, trans. N. D. Smith (New York: Sheed and Ward, 1965).

32

Visual Arts

MARCHITA MAUCK

A Bridge to a Higher World

In the early twelfth century, abbot Suger celebrated the rebuilding of the church of the royal Abbey of Saint-Denis, north of Paris, by describing the project in a small book recording work done under his administration. He recounted looking around at the beauty of the building with its stained glass lavish jeweled and sculpted adornments of the altar, and numerous vessels and other objects. He reflected:

> When . . . the loveliness of the many colored gems has called me away from external cares, and worthy meditation has induced me to reflect, transferring that which is material to that which is immaterial. . . . then it seems to me that I see myself dwelling, as it were, in some strange region of the universe which neither exists entirely in the slime of the earth nor entirely in the purity of Heaven, and that by the grace of God, I can be transported from this inferior to that higher world in an anagogical manner.[1]

The abbot expressed a sensuous delight in a grand, if not ostentatious, display of precious jewels, stained glass, and other expensive, beautiful materials. His expectation, though, was that contemplation of these objects should lead the viewer in some mysterious way to heightened spiritual awareness.

Abbot Suger's vivid poetic account of the transformation wrought by contemplation of the beauty of his new church, with its astonishing wreath of stained glass windows embracing the apse, provides an apt context for discussing the role of art in the Christian tradition and its worship. In every age the visual arts have offered a means of enticing the viewer beyond the temporal here and now to a larger experience of an eternal world of grace. Art is the bridge between the tangible mundane and the intangible realm of the spiritual.

Painting

The earliest Christian imagery we have dates from the third century A.D. Small wall paintings survived in the catacombs in Rome and in the "house church" in Dura-Europos, Syria.[2] In both these places, the pictures are surprising to a modern viewer because they do not illustrate biblical stories in a merely narrative way. Scenes from

The Good Shepherd. Wall painting from the Crypt of Lucina in the catacomb of Saint Callistus, Rome. SCALA/ART RESOURCE, NY

the Old Testament do not include all the significant details that elaborate a story. Certainly, subjects such as the crossing of the Red Sea, Daniel in the lions' den, the three youths in the fiery furnace, Jonah thrown into the sea, or Moses striking the rock are scattered over the narrow spaces between the tombs carved out of the walls of corridors or in small chapels in the catacombs. Carefully selected New Testament themes appear, such as the Good Shepherd, the raising of Lazarus, the multiplication of loaves and fishes, or the wedding at Cana. The early-third-century baptistery in the house church in Dura-Europos includes among the surviving fragments an image of the Good Shepherd, Christ healing the paralytic, Christ walking on the water, the woman at the well, and several Old Testament themes. Clearly, however, the early images have an agenda other than the simple illustration of texts. Both at Dura-Europos and in the catacombs, the visual jottings of seemingly disconnected scenes serve to answer the question: Who is our God? And, by visual analogies, they express the triumph over death, of which baptism is the beginning. Blessed be the faithful God who saved the Israelites through the waters of the sea, who saved Jonah from the belly of the whale, who saved Daniel and the three youths, who provided water in the desert! Blessed be the God who, like a shepherd, finds and rescues the lost, who heals the sick and feeds the hungry! Blessed be the God who raised Lazarus from the dead, and who lifts to eternal life all that go down into the tomb of baptism! Blessed be God who will do for us the great deeds he wrought for our ancestors! The theme of salvation in all its dimensions is particularly prominent in the catacombs, where Christians gathered to commemorate their dead—both martyrs and others—before the living God, in whose keeping their departed and they themselves were.

From these humble beginnings, wall paintings evolved into a monumental art form whose content gradually expanded to more comprehensive narrative themes. The legal recognition of Christianity by Emperor Constantine, and then its establishment as the state religion by Emperor Theodosius later in the fourth century, gave access to immense public basilicas that provided opportunities for imagery on a new scale. The large mosaic compositions filling the apse walls of the basilicas served to affirm the identity of God. The image, however, shifted from the simple shepherd of the catacombs or Dura-Europos to the imperial Christ, clothed in gold and floating in the clouds of heaven. With the establishment of Christianity as the state religion came the courtly dignity deemed appropriate for the new status.[3] By the early fifth century, a double row of fresco paintings depicting Old Testament scenes—now lost—filled the length of the nave walls at Old Saint Peter's in Rome.[4]

The surviving fifth-century mosaics along the nave walls of Santa Maria Maggiore in Rome attest to the vitality of an extended narrative scheme.[5] Rather than providing a detailed continuous history, however, these scenes focus on moments in the story of

The Parting of Abraham and Lot.
Wall mosaic from the nave of Santa
Maria Maggiore, Rome, 432–440.
Scala/Art Resource, NY

salvation that highlight the ways in
which God characteristically works
in the world. In a dramatic panel at
Santa Maria Maggiore, Abraham and
Lot cast fierce glances at each other
across a gap in the center: Abraham
and his family, heading toward
Canaan, choose the good, while Lot
and his crowd turn toward Sodom
and evil. The golden background
lifts the scene out of its own time into all times, and the story catapults from an inci-
dent in the book of Genesis to a reminder to all the faithful in all ages that choices
must be made, and that choices carry consequences.

Large wall paintings or mosaics filling the apse, the side walls of the nave, and even
occasionally the ceiling—as at the French church of Saint-Savin-sur-Gartempe—
persisted through the twelfth century.[6] The barrel vault of the nave at the church of

Painted vault. Building of the Tower of Babel and Joseph thrown into prison. Twelfth-
century painting in the church of Saint Savin, Saint-Savin-sur-Gartempe, France.
Giraudon/Art Resource, NY

Saint-Savin (near Poitiers), dating from around 1095–1115, accommodated four registers of Old Testament scenes, part of a much larger cycle of paintings throughout the building, including the infancy of Christ, the Passion of Christ, and the lives of the saints, completed by scenes from the Apocalypse filling the vaults and the walls of the porch. Painted in the contemporary style of flat, segmented color areas with overlapping planes, the figures are animated and energetic. A famous scene illustrates the building of the Tower of Babel, with swaying figures handing stones up to the masons at the top of the rising tower.

The end of medieval monumental wall painting coincides with the emergence of Gothic architecture. Abbot Suger's yearning to be somehow transported to a higher, more spiritual world reflected a contemporary fascination with Neoplatonic thought among university theologians and philosophers. In contrast to their sturdy, massive, anchored-to-the-ground Romanesque predecessors, the new Gothic cathedrals arched toward the heavens like giant skeletons. Great arches, galleries, and clerestory windows pierced the interior nave walls, while the exterior buttresses formed a bridge from which a curtain of stained glass windows hung, forming translucent swags from bay to bay. Although stained glass had long been known as a medium, it now came into its own as the means to express the divine presence as light. Jewel-like colors, primarily red and blue, transform ordinary light into a royal purple, infusing the vast liturgical spaces with mystery and beauty. Thousands of figures inhabit geometric panels narrating the stories of the Old Testament, Christ, the Virgin, the book of Revelation, lives of the saints, and even heroes of classical antiquity. No matter that the viewer could not make out all the details of images several stories overhead. Modern visitors may arrive with their binoculars in hand, but they soon abandon them and simply revel in the kaleidoscopic color washing over surfaces. The walls were now no denser than the thickness of the glass in the windows. The building had dissolved into air and light. The lack of apparent substance created a "spiritual," dematerialized structure of the most glorious sort. In the Western Christian tradition, wall painting disappeared because the walls on which to paint disappeared.

Circumstances were somewhat different in the Eastern Christian or Byzantine world from the fourth-century establishment of Constantinople as the eastern capital of the Roman Empire, through the eleventh and twelfth centuries, and further through the fifteenth century until the fall of Constantinople in 1453. The icon is the singular imagery that most often comes to mind when Byzantine art is mentioned. Images of Christ, the Virgin, and the saints bear testimony to the complex theological disputes concerning the appropriateness of images of holy personages at all, particularly in the challenging demand of addressing the dual natures of the one Christ, his humanity and his divinity. No image at all of the crucified Christ appeared before the fifth century. The image of the dead Christ on the Cross emerged for the first time in the seventh century. Before that, the crucifixion was represented by a live Christ on the Cross, head up with open eyes—the Christ who triumphs over death at the moment of crucifixion. Icons were understood to be portals to the reality they represented. Thus, the images themselves were holy, transporting the faithful into a relationship of worship. Veneration transcended the materiality of paint and wooden panels, communicating prayers and petitions to God. The images had to be familiar, and their power available for all time.

Unlike the Roman West, where we find a preference for longitudinal basilicas that lend themselves to extended image cycles along the nave walls, the Orthodox East preferred domed, central-plan churches. Apses, domes, and the undersides of arches were available for imagery. A spiritualized ideal appeared very early, visible in the earliest surviving icon panels, and additionally in the works associated with the court of the Eastern emperor Justinian in the sixth century. The famous images of Justinian and his empress, Theodora, in the Italian church of San Vitale in Ravenna, flank the apse on opposite sides of the altar, appearing as if the couple was present at the dedication of the church. There is an air of unreality in the representations: the tiny feet do not quite rest firmly on the ground; the background is not a landscape but a golden sky; rich brocades form flat, decorative costume patterns rather than suggest volume; small faces with large eyes stare out at us from elongated figures swaying slightly to one side in a dreamy eternal silence. In these mosaics, Justinian and Theodora are analogous to Christ and the Virgin Mary (Theodora's dress even has the three Magi embroidered along its hem). The timeless spiritual and political authority of church and state marry in these two figures floating in a celestial cosmos.

The iconoclastic crisis interrupted the tradition of painting in the East. For more than one hundred years, from the iconoclast Emperor Leo III's prohibition of images in 726 until the success of the iconodules, who definitively reinstated the use of images in 843, painting and mosaics languished.[7] They blossomed once again during the Middle Byzantine years between the ninth and early twelfth centuries. Mosaics at two Greek monasteries demonstrate new schemas as well as stylistic and iconographic innovations in support of liturgical formation. At both the monastery of Hosios Loukas (c. 1020) and the monastery at Daphni (c. 1100), traditional motifs of events from the life of Christ and of Mary are now arranged according to the feast cycle of the Orthodox liturgy. Events of the Passion and the mature bearded image of Christ as Pantocrator, Ruler of the Universe, take on new prominence. The Pantocrator stares down from the central dome. Directly below, images of the Annunciation and Christ's nativity, baptism, and transfiguration fill the squinches of the dome, asserting Christ's dual humanity and divinity. An image of the Virgin, hovering in a shimmering golden heaven, fills the apse, with saints occupying levels below her, on piers, or under the arches supporting the dome; these figures testify that the earthly liturgy is experienced as participation in the worship of heaven. The scenes at Daphni introduce an extraordinary new expressive quality, a restrained pathos born of the classical spirit that draws the viewer into the suffering Christ underwent for the sake of humankind.

Christ Pantocrator. Monastery church, Daphni, Greece. VANNI/ART RESOURCE, NY

In the West, a new and different spirit began to eclipse the splendors of the Gothic ideal that was born in France and enthusiastically adopted throughout Europe. The Brancacci Chapel in the Florentine church of Santa Maria del Carmine houses a series of scenes depicting the life of Saint Peter. The Early Renaissance artist Masaccio painted these images between about 1423 and 1428.[8] Masaccio's masterful employment of aerial perspective, chiaroscuro (the use of light and dark to create the illusion of solid, three-dimensional figures in a credible space), and portraits of the Apostles that astonishingly betray their individual human foibles and strengths, set painting on a new course that even Michelangelo admired and studied almost a century later. The most famous three panels represent the story of the tribute money, Christ's telling Peter to retrieve a coin from the mouth of a fish along the shore of the Sea of Galilee in order to pay the tax collector. The choice of an otherwise rather obscure biblical story—depicting in a majestic and solemn way Peter's encounter with the tax collector, his confrontation with Christ about the demand to pay the tax, and Peter's retrieval of the coin and payment to the official—probably served a political purpose: Christ's instruction to pay the tax collector supported Florence's desperate efforts to tax everyone, including the clergy and church, for defense efforts in its war against Milan.

An additional scene in the Brancacci Chapel's story of Saint Peter demonstrates the evocative power of painting to open up to the viewer the impact of a narrative event. In the panel representing Peter baptizing the neophytes, he pours water over the head of a nearly nude man kneeling in shallow river water [see color plate 28]. Slightly behind on the shore stands another man waiting his turn for baptism. He hugs his crossed arms close to his chest, visibly shivering in the cold air. A third man dries himself with a towel as others gather around. The vulnerability of being wet and cold in mountain air lends poignancy to the vulnerability of giving assent to baptism.

Michelangelo's admiration for Masaccio's work can be seen in the figures of Adam and Eve in the expulsion from the garden on the ceiling of the Sistine Chapel in the Vatican, painted 1508–1512.[9] The intense human anguish in Masaccio's painting on the same theme in the Brancacci Chapel is matched in Michelangelo's cowering pair, stumbling before the fierce, sword-brandishing angel who thrusts them away. The nine major panels filling the center of the ceiling continue the centuries-long custom of selecting biblical themes to convey a particular idea. Here the idea is no less than the collective story of the creation of the world, the creation of humanity, the fall of humanity through the fall of Adam, further detailed in the degradation of Noah, and finally God's redemption. Nine events from the book of Genesis summarize the theology of salvation, supported by prophets and sibyls, and figures representing forty generations of the ancestors of Christ. They foreshadow the coming of Christ and God's redemptive power. In the most renowned scene of the Sistine program, the *Creation of Adam*, God with one mighty yet sublime gesture of his arm "quickens" Adam, investing him with life, drawing Adam toward himself. This deed of power foretells God's instilling divine life in humanity by fiat at the Incarnation, when the Word was made flesh, the new Adam.

The naturalism and intensity of the figures in Masaccio's Brancacci Chapel, and Michelangelo's later Sistine Chapel program, reflect the concerns of the times in which they were produced. Their work embodied an attitude about the grandeur of nature and the increasingly elevated concept of the artist as a person of genius. Their task was to accomplish the integration of classical style and Christian content in a manner worthy of both the legacy of ancient art and the complexity of contemporary theology.[10]

By the late sixteenth century, the Protestant Reformation stirred the Roman Church to reassess the essentials of the faith. The iconoclastic fervor of many of the Reformers stood midwife to new secular genres in northern Europe, while the Roman Church saw the Holy Spirit hovering "over the bent world with ah! Bright wings," to borrow words from Gerard Manley Hopkins's "God's Grandeur." El Greco's agitated, flamelike brushstrokes imbue the tumultuous moment of Christ's baptism with a shudder reverberating through all creation. The intensity of the painting conveys the profound spirituality characteristic of the Spanish mystics Saint Teresa of Avila and Saint John of the Cross.

An initial Protestant fear of images as an occasion for idolatry subordinated images to the primacy of the word. A range of attitudes emerged, from Calvin's iconoclasm to Luther's more indifferent stance regarding the role of images in churches.[11] Patronage of artists shifted from the church to the bourgeoisie. The new secular subjects—portraiture, still life, landscape, and genre painting—celebrated middle-class prosperity and aspirations. As what one might call an evangelical tool of the Catholic Counter-Reformation, El Greco's supernatural mysticism contrasts sharply with the direct human experience related in Rembrandt's painting *The Return of the Prodigal Son* or quiet, poignant drawings such as his *Christ in the House of Mary and Martha* in the Teyler Museum in Haarlem, or the British Museum's *The Good Samaritan Bringing the Wounded Man into the Inn*. Deeply moved and inspired by Bible study, Rembrandt sought the human dimension of spirituality, the earth-rooted perception of the divine.[12]

The acute compassion for the human condition found in Rembrandt's work emerged once again in the work of his fellowcountryman Vincent Van Gogh (1853–1890), the son of a Protestant minister who himself was a perhaps too intense evangelist ministering to coal-mining Belgian peasants. Van Gogh's bold early drawings of hard-working peasants endow simple folk with strength and God-given dignity. Even when his subject matter moves beyond the darkness of his early drawings of peasants or paintings such as *The Potato Eaters*, the density and agitation of the painted surface continue to affirm his conviction of the presence of the divine in the materiality and substance of the earth.[13]

The last-gasp triumphalism of the Counter-Reformation and the shift in patronage away from the Church in the Protestant north eventually conspired, by the nineteenth century, to diminish the role and place of significant art within churches. Religious art in churches lapsed into a stupor of pious décor, while artists sought the spiritual in what is ordinarily thought of as secular subject matter. In more recent times, the nonobjective paintings of Mark Rothko, or the clown paintings as well as the images of the suffering Christ by the expressionist artist Georges Rouault, exemplify the search for the profound in human experience. Pablo Picasso plumbs the tension between hope and despair in the waiflike figures of his blue period, or in a monumental work like *Guernica*. Dorothea Lange's depression-era photographs and the work of painters of the New York Harlem Renaissance such as Aaron Douglas explore the challenges of biblical precepts of dignity and justice. But their work was not commissioned for churches.

Altarpieces

Somewhere between wall painting and sculpture, between liturgy and devotional piety, altarpieces emerged. In the Early Church, altars were free-standing, movable tables within the assembly. Altars of stone began to appear in the fourth century, customarily located at the crossing of the nave and transept and therefore close to the assembled people. Throughout these centuries, nothing was allowed on the altar that did not have to do with celebrating the eucharist.

Two new developments encouraged the introduction of other objects on the altar or attached to its back. By the sixth and seventh centuries, it became customary to place relics of saints within or under an altar, making martyrial shrines of all altars. The ninth century saw the appearance of reliquaries (elaborate cases for relics) resting on altars, and by the early eleventh century there is evidence of altars looking less like tables and more like sarcophagi, occasionally with a panel of sculpted or painted images along the back edge. These images focused attention on the cult of the saint over whose tomb the altar was built, or whose relics were placed within the altar or on top within a reliquary. The imagery expressed the cult dedication of the altar.

In addition to the interring of relics in altars, the increasing emphasis in the liturgy on the actions of the presider and not of the congregation enabled, if not demanded, an elaboration of the altar. As the clergy took over almost all roles in the liturgy and were separated from the congregation by railings, the altar gradually moved farther and farther away from the people until it was up against the back wall. Enormous architectural structures called retables eventually evolved, attached to the back of the altar or standing directly behind it, housing multiple paintings and sometimes sculptures. Most often the imagery had to do with the saints to whom the church or altar was dedicated. By the fifteenth century, aristocratic donors and guilds and lay organizations became significant players in the development of altarpieces. These patrons commissioned devotional altars for endowed side chapels in churches, proliferating pious images and introducing portraits of the donors as participants in religious scenes.

The simplest of the altarpieces consisted of a central panel of Christ, the Virgin, or a saint, flanked by panels of other saints. This horizontal arrangement of panels gave way to multilevel, gabled structures. Duccio di Buoninsegna's golden *Maestà*, painted for Siena's cathedral (1308–1311), is a glorious example of these free-standing structures.[14] Painted in tempera on wood, surviving panels on the front accompany the image of Mary and the heavenly court, while on the back numerous small panels depict the life of Christ [see color plate 27C]. Altarpieces of the scale of the *Maestà* (7 feet tall by over 13 feet wide) overwhelmed the altar, becoming the major focal point in the church.

In the Netherlands, the preferred medium was oil paint on wooden panels. Unlike tempera paint, which quickly dries into hard, opaque layers, oil paint can be built up in thin glazes through which light penetrates and is then reflected back to the surface; this produces a luminosity and glow that was particularly prized by painters in the north. Completed in 1432, the *Ghent Altarpiece* by Hubert and Jan van Eyck for Saint Bavo Church in that city is the most magnificent example of Flemish altarpieces.[15] In its closed position, an Annunciation to the Virgin fills the upper half, with donor portraits and images of John the Evangelist and John the Baptist, painted to simulate sculpture, inhabiting four painted niches on the lower level. Opened, the altarpiece is some 11 feet tall by over 14 feet wide. Enthroned portraits of Christ, the Virgin, and John form a triptych dominating the upper panels. They are flanked by organ-playing angels in sumptuous array, and nude figures of Adam and Eve. Below, throngs of saints, martyrs, hermits, and ordinary folk surge across five panels to converge in the center at the Lamb upon an altar encircled by worshiping angels. Tall church spires emerge from Flemish cityscapes nestled along the horizon of an illusionistic landscape made credible by masterful use of atmospheric perspective. The apocalyptic vision of the Adoration of the Lamb is at home in fifteenth-century Flanders.

Matthias Grünewald's *Isenheim Altar* (c. 1510–1515) is an even larger and more complex example.[16] Painted for the hospital of the abbey of Saint Anthony in Isenheim, it has multiple wings allowing different arrangements of scenes to be opened at various times of the week or liturgical year. The painted panels cover a carved shrine of Saint Anthony flanked by saints Augustine and Jerome. The altarpiece, including its large reliquary-like shrine and multiple painted panels, serves both as a vehicle for the cult of a saint, Anthony, and as a visual focus changing according to liturgical needs. When it is in its closed position, the viewer confronts a rather horrifying putrefying body of Christ on the cross, his fingers distended in rigor mortis. Such graphic imagery of physical suffering surely comforted the patients who gazed upon it, for the hospital treated those suffering from terrible skin diseases, including leprosy. When the altarpiece is open, luminous panels of the Annunciation, Nativity, and Resurrection dazzle the viewer. The body of the ascending Christ dissolves into radiant light. The second-level opening of the altarpiece reveals the prized limewood sculpture of Saint Anthony enthroned with saints Augustine and Jerome at his sides. This sculpture by Nikolaus Hagenauer provided a focal point for celebrations in honor of Saint Anthony.

The work of the Austrian woodcarver and painter Michael Pacher demonstrates the combination of painting and sculpture in which the dominant art is woodcarving.[17] An elaborate gilded carving of the coronation of the Virgin fills the center panel of his *Saint Wolfgang Altarpiece* (1471–1481). Painted panels of the life of Mary form a triptych with the coronation carving. A towering carved Gothic spire, including the crucifixion of Christ, thrusts upward into the vault of the apse.

With the work of the German woodcarver Tilman Riemenschneider, the carved altarpiece came into its own.[18] The wood is neither painted nor gilded; its natural state reveals the splendor of the carver's art. Riemenschneider's *Altarpiece of the Holy Blood* (1501–1505), with the Last Supper as its central motif, stands almost 30 feet tall in the Church of Sankt Jakob in Rothenburg ob der Tauber, Germany.

By the beginning of the Renaissance in Italy, a new sobriety had been introduced into altarpieces. They now took on the form of a large single, framed panel, frequently representing the *sacra conversazione*, a group of saints gathered around an image of the Virgin and Child. Domenico Veneziano's *Saint Lucy Altarpiece* (c. 1445) is a good example: saints Francis, John the Baptist, Zenobius, and Lucy stand to either side of the Virgin enthroned under an elaborate, vaulted architectural structure.

The role of the single-panel altarpiece set in an architectural framework as a window through which the viewer could see another space and reality gave way to Baroque drama and ultimately to a complete blurring of the distinction between the image and its architectural setting. The altar became a sculptural element in the flurry of painted images, sculpted hosts of angels amid clouds that blur from two-dimensional illusionistic painting into three-dimensional forms, or vice versa, and illusionistic architecture that blends into the actual architecture. The main altar in the German Church of Sankt Johannes, Landsberg am Lech, by Dominikus Zimmermann (1752), admirably represents this genre.[19]

The Last Supper. Scene from the Holy Blood altar (c. 1501) by Tilman Riemenschneider (c. 1460–1531) in the Church of Sankt Jakob, Rothenburg ob der Tauber, Germany. ERICH LESSING/ ART RESOURCE, NY

The mystical intensity, not to mention extravagance, of such enormous eighteenth-century constructions remains unsurpassed. Reformation iconoclasm, combined with a shift in the nineteenth century away from religious piety to a refined sort of aestheticism, rendered the altarpiece a shadow of its former self. Twentieth-century liturgical study and reforms, particularly as articulated in the documents of the Second Vatican Council, obviate the design of elaborate main altars. The reclaiming of early Christianity's emphasis on the altar as a focal point within the assembly, as well as the position of the presider facing the congregation, call for freestanding altars unencumbered by elaborate decorative and devotional apparatus.

Tapestry and Other Textile Arts

Although woven fabrics with designs survive from as early as ancient Egypt, textiles in the Early Church were primarily influenced by Coptic art, Byzantine textiles and embroidery, and intricate Sassanian Persian silks.[20] Very few examples survive from the early centuries of Christian art. The most famous textile of the early Middle Ages, the eleventh-century *Bayeux Tapestry*,[21] is not technically a woven tapestry, but embroidery on linen. Across its length of more than 230 feet, hundreds of figures chronicle the Battle of Hastings in 1066, which resulted in the Norman conquest of England. A work of such magnitude could be commissioned only by wealthy aristocratic or ecclesiastical patrons. Especially during the height of tapestry production during the thirteenth and fourteenth centuries and again in the sixteenth century, this expensive art flourished within the orbit of royal and aristocratic courts. Because tapestry weaving is dependent on artists who produce designs for the weavers, and because the scale of tapestries often equaled that of monumental wall painting, the two arts are closely related. But weavers do not simply render a painting in another medium. The nature of the medium makes its own demands on successful designs. For example, large areas of solid color for sky or water can be much more interesting with the patterned texture of a woven piece than in a painting. A limited palette of colors and linear hatching for edges produce rich contrasts and an animated surface natural to the medium.

The *Angers Apocalypse* tapestry, woven in France between 1375 and 1382, is one of the great treasures of religious tapestry design.[22] Commissioned by Louis I of Angers, the designs were produced by his court painter, Hennequin de Bruges. Nicolas Bataille and Robert Poinçon wove more than one hundred scenes, seventy of which have survived. The original work was 19 feet tall and more than 551 feet long. Louis of Angers's grandson bequeathed the tapestry in 1480 to Angers Cathedral, where it was hung for ceremonial celebrations for some three hundred years. The scenes represent the visions of Saint John on Patmos, as narrated in the book of Revelation. Alternating patterned red and blue backgrounds provide the setting for the elegant Gothic figures swaying in the foreground. The seventy vibrant panels that survived the destruction of the French Revolution—as well as post-Revolution service as floor coverings, winter protection for citrus trees, and padding for horse stalls—can now be seen in the château of Angers.

In 1515 Pope Leo X commissioned Raphael to design ten tapestries of the Acts of the Apostles for the Sistine Chapel.[23] Raphael painted gouache cartoons for the weavers in the Brussels workshop of Pieter van Aelst. By 1519 seven of the tapestries were finished, competing in the same chapel with the ceiling paintings completed by Michelangelo between 1508 and 1512. The commission indicates both the high es-teem in which the Belgian tapestry weavers were held and the significance of tapestries as a serious Christian art form. It was even said with wonder at the time that the designing and weaving of the tapestries cost more than did Michelangelo's ceiling paintings. The naturalism achieved in Raphael's cartoons, the powerful expressions of faces, and the luminous quality of the landscapes achieved in the tapestries influenced artists for generations to come. Modern viewers continue to marvel at the transparency of the water, the beauty of the water birds, and the poignancy of the scene of the miraculous draught of fishes from the Acts of the Apostles series.

By the nineteenth century, tapestry production had fallen into a great decline, useful primarily as a means of copying paintings. Aesthetic delight in the nature of tapestry and the characteristics of its textures gave way to a demand for the illusions created by gradations of thousands of newly standardized colors. The demise of court patronage after the French Revolution, as well as the economic and political turmoil through the Napoleonic era and nineteenth-century revolutions, led to a decrease in commissions and production. Many workshops closed as tastes changed. The introduction of aniline dyes at the end of the nineteenth century was an attempt to engage artists once more in designing tapestries, lured by the attraction of brilliant new colors. The effort was not successful. It took the desolation following World War II in Europe and the concerted efforts of French church authorities to raise up new, inspirational, and significant art to awaken tapestry weaving from its somnolence.

Sculpture

When we peruse the art of the past through twenty-first-century lenses, we bring expectations that might never have been envisioned by the original artists. We often do not recognize the questions to which an image suggests an answer. Ignorance of the history and context from which art emerged limits the possibility of empathy with its content. Three-dimensional works are often more challenging in this respect, intruding as they do into the same space occupied by the viewer.

The upper center panel from the fourth-century sarcophagus of Junius Bassus exemplifies the conflict between modern expectations and original intention. Christ is enthroned between Peter and Paul. Christ, youthful and beardless, holds a scroll in one hand, the image in the ancient world of teacher and philosopher. His feet rest on the head of Aeolus, the wind god, who holds in both hands a veil that billows like a sail above his head. One can hear viewers ask, "But is it Jesus? It doesn't look like Jesus!" Never mind that they don't recognize Aeolus either and have no idea what that pagan figure is doing with this image of Christ. A modern viewer cannot fathom that the fourth-century viewer would never have thought to ask such a question. In its own time, images like this or those of Christ as the Good Shepherd, or any of the catacomb paintings including Christ, represented no intention of suggesting what Christ looked like. They were all about who Christ is! Twenty different images of Christ from the early Christian era probably have twenty quite different faces. A modern viewer might judge this image of Christ inadequate because it doesn't "look like" Jesus, ignoring the larger implications and insight that this composition brings. But seeing the wind god and his veil as a symbol of the heavens over which Christ has dominion might inspire us to imagine a contemporary equivalent which is equally poetic. The Apollo 8 mission photograph of the earth from space, a view seen by no one in the whole history of humankind before 1968, evokes in a contemporary viewer something of the wonder and poetry of the cosmos understood by a fourth-century onlooker seeing Christ enthroned with his feet atop Aeolus.

Could it be that an image can remind us of truths we have known, but long since forgotten? A twelfth-century polychromed wooden statue of the Virgin holding Christ on her lap, now in the collection of the Metropolitan Museum of Art in New York, challenges our understanding. At first glance the figures look austere and sober. Both Mary and the child stare directly out at the viewer. The child is not an infant but a young man, holding the book of the word of God in one hand and raising the other in a gesture of blessing. The context is not intimacy, but theology. Mary here is the Church, the seat of wisdom; her throne recalls the throne of Solomon, of wisdom. Christ in turn is enthroned on her lap. In this image Mary the mother is the Christ-bearer, the Church. Her son is God's wisdom incarnate.

A fourteenth-century gilt and enamel statue of the Virgin and Child given as a gift by Jeanne d'Evreux, wife of Charles IV of France, to the Abbey of Saint-Denis represents a shift in the depiction of Mary. No longer the rigid throne of wisdom, this figure stands elegantly in an exaggerated hip-slung stance, her proportions elongated and slender beyond those of most mortal women, then or now. This regal image originally included a crown, and she carries a jeweled fleur-de-lis scepter. The child is a playful infant, touching his fingers to her lips, grasping an apple in his other hand.

Intimate and appealing, the image invites empathy with the maternal, approachable side of Mary while at the same time invoking a spiritualized, otherworldly perception. All is not sweetness and light, though, as the base of the statue includes enameled scenes of the Passion of Christ, the sorrow that will engulf this mother later in the story. The joy of the birth and infancy of Christ is tempered by the larger narrative.

Simultaneously with the elegance and beauty of the Virgin of Jeanne d'Evreux, another impulse existed. The dark, graphic side of suffering found expression in the devotional images known as *Vesperbilder* ("vespers pictures," to contemplate at evening prayers) or *Andachtsbilder* ("meditation pictures"). Images such as a German Pietà now in the Landesmuseum in Bonn represent a tangible interpretation of the pious devotional literature then in vogue, emphasizing the horrors and agonies of Christ's suffering. The body of Christ slumps across Mary's lap, distorted and emaciated. Sticky clots of blood adhere to his wounds. Mary is physically and emotionally exhausted, stricken with grief. An abstract exaggeration of proportions

Statue of the Virgin and Child. A gift of Jeanne d'Evreux to the Abbey of Saint-Denis, France (c. 1324–1329). MUSÉE DU LOUVRE, PARIS/GIRAUDON/ BRIDGEMAN ART LIBRARY

and gestures serves to amplify the horrors of the scene. Exaggerated elegance and grotesqueness thus appear in the same era, exploring the profundity of human experience.

Formation of the Christian into a lifestyle of discipleship happens by analogy and empathy when a viewer is drawn into the intimacy of an image of the holy mother and child. All mothers share with Mary the bringing of life into the world. All who carry Christ within themselves are Christ-bearers. And all who find an image of the Pietà a portal to redemptive suffering, both Christ's and their own, deepen their faith and enlarge their lives.

Images such as the Virgin and Child or the Pietà have a certain objective and narrative character that provides immediate access. How does one convey a more abstract notion like union with God? Poetry and metaphor can mediate the tension between the ineffable and the tangible, providing a path to new insight. The seventeenth-century Baroque sculptor Gianlorenzo Bernini, a devout Catholic, drew on Saint Teresa of Avila's poetic contemplation of her ecstatic union with God as an inspiration for conveying to viewers the intensity and sensuality of the experience. Union with God was not an intellectual assent. For Teresa and for Bernini the experience was best expressed in sensual, even sexual imagery. Teresa wrote:

> I would see beside me, on my left hand, an angel in bodily form. . . . In his hands I saw a long golden spear and at the end of the iron tip I seemed to see a point of fire. . . .With this he seemed to pierce my heart several times. . . .The pain was so sharp that it made me utter several moans; and so excessive was the sweetness caused me by this intense pain that one can never wish to lose it, nor will one's soul be content with anything less than God.[24]

In Bernini's sculpture, Saint Teresa swoons on a bed of clouds, her eyes closed, mouth open. The angel with the golden barb hovers next to her, soft garments billowing. The sculpture has not been without its critics, who see in it a pandering to sensuality. Bernini took the risk of expressing the miracle of divine love, basing his interpretation directly on Teresa's words. The sculpture's intimacy may seem daunting, but it continues to challenge viewers to broaden an understanding of the mystery of divine love.

Metalwork

Tourists in Florence have been awed for centuries by the baptistery's east doors, so beautiful that Michelangelo called them the "Gates of Paradise." The sculptor Lorenzo Ghiberti worked on these doors for a quarter-century, from 1425 to 1452.[25] They were his second set of doors for the cathedral baptistery, and the third to be installed on the building. Ten panels teem with figures, multiple scenes, and elaborate architectural perspectives. Cast in bronze and gilded, these doors are worthy expressions of the understanding that church portals are doors to the New Jerusalem, to the City of God, to a splendid new reality. The tradition of historiated doors reaches back to the early years of the Church. Eighteen carved wooden panels of the original twenty-eight survive at Santa Sabina in Rome, dated by inscription to 432. These panels incorporated both Old and New Testament scenes. Three panels survive from the carved fifth-century doors depicting the life of David at Sant' Ambrogio in Milan.

A revival of the art of bronze casting in Carolingian times led to the installation of three sets of bronze doors at Charlemagne's Palace Chapel in Aachen.[26] Impressive as these plain framed panels were, the most famous early medieval doors were those

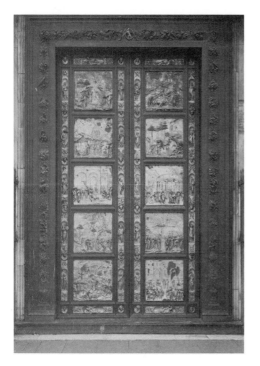

Gates of paradise. East doors of the baptistery in Florence by Lorenzo Ghiberti (1370–1455). SCALA/ART RESOURCE, NY

Baptism of Christ. Detail of the east doors of the baptistery, Florence, by Lorenzo Ghiberti. SCALA/ART RESOURCE, NY

commissioned for Saint Michael's at Hildesheim by that city's bishop, Bernward. These early-eleventh-century doors were cast in one piece, perhaps the largest casting project since antiquity. Old Testament scenes on the left door prefigure New Testament scenes on the right side in an elaborate typological arrangement. Tiny animated figures populate the scenes, betraying their probable source in manuscript illumination. Bishop Bernward had surely seen the doors of Santa Sabina during his time in Rome and was probably familiar also with the doors of Sant' Ambrogio in Milan. Numerous other bronze doors followed in the twelfth century, notably at San Zeno in Verona, the cathedral at Pisa, and at Benevento, where the doors included seventy-two narrative panels of the life of Christ. Although additional projects were undertaken in the fifteenth and sixteenth centuries, none matched the renown or quality of the examples from the eleventh through fifteenth centuries.

The cult of martyrs and saints sustained a precious-materials industry extending from the fourth through the sixteenth centuries for the fabrication of containers for relics. Designed for devotional purposes, for the display of relics for veneration, these reliquaries were found in the private chapels of aristocrats and ecclesiastics as well as in churches. Caught in the frenzy of popular piety in the eleventh and twelfth centuries, churches introduced radiating chapels for the display of relics for thousands of pilgrims traveling from town to town to encounter the holy and miraculous remains of the martyrs and saints.

The earliest reliquaries were decorated boxes, often of silver or ivory with images having to do with salvation. A fourth-century ivory casket from Brescia is an espe-

Brescia Lipsanotheca. Ivory casket, Syrian-Alexandrine, fourth century. (*Top register*) Medallion portaits of Christ and apostles. (*Second register*) Scenes from the life of Jonah. (*Middle register*) Three scenes from the life of Christ: "Noli me tangere" (John 20:17); Christ teaching; Christ enacting the story of the Good Shepherd (John 10:1–16). (*Bottom register*) Scenes from the story of Susannah. Museo Civico dell'Età Cristiana, Brescia, Italy; Scala/Art Resource, NY

cially beautiful example, with scenes from the Old and New Testaments carved on all four sides and the top. Relics of the True Cross were particularly venerated and preserved in rich displays of the goldsmith's art, often in the shape of a cross. The sixth-century Byzantine reliquary cross in the Vatican collection, of gold encrusted with jewels, was a gift of Emperor Justinian to the pope. The *Stavelot Triptych of the True Cross* (twelfth century) is made of gold, jewels, and enamel work.[27] The center panel incorporates two smaller triptychs, and the side wings contain enameled medallions with narrative scenes of the finding of the True Cross.

Typical of the seventh century is the "burse" reliquary, a sort of jeweled purse with a wooden core that is covered with gold, silver, jewels, and sometimes antique gemstones or cameos. From this same period come the earliest "portable altars," small, rectangular embellished stones resting on short legs. Relics were embedded in the portable stone, which was theoretically placed on a table for the celebration of mass in locales where a consecrated altar might not be available. The mid-twelfth-century *Stavelot Altar* is a beautiful example. The sides and top are covered with fifteen richly colored enamel plates in a typological arrangement of Old and New Testament scenes. Twelve enameled images of the martyrdoms of the eleven apostles and Paul encircle the sides. At the four corners are three-dimensional figures of the four evangelists.

"Speaking" reliquaries appeared in the tenth century. These curious reliquaries take the shape of the relic they contain, thus "speaking" or explaining their content. Typical are heads for skull relics, upright arms, fingers, or examples like the golden foot atop a portable altar that purportedly contains the sandal of Saint Andrew, now in the cathedral treasury in Trier.

The reliquaries most popular between the eleventh and thirteenth centuries are also the most opulent in their decoration. These gabled containers are architectural, looking like a basilica. They are adorned with a variety of materials and designs, including gold, silver, champlevé enamel, jewels, and gilded three-dimensional figures. Among the most luxurious is the *Shrine of the Three Kings* in Cologne Cathedral. This shrine, attributed to Nicholas of Verdun at the turn of the thirteenth century, is almost six feet tall by about four feet wide by over six feet long. A masterpiece of the jeweler's art, it is made of gilded bronze and silver with gemstones and enamel work. A gilded relief of the Adoration of the Magi fills the front end, while figures of apostles and prophets are seated in niches along the lower level and clerestory of the structure.

Goldsmiths also produced a magnificent array of liturgical vessels and objects for ritual, including chalices, patens, candlestands, censers, processional crosses, bases for crosses, incense boats, gospel book covers, pyxes, ciboria, and monstrances. In recent years artists have become engaged once again in the design and fabrication of liturgical service items, offering a welcome alternative to the mediocre if not abysmal quality available commercially from church supply companies.

Arts and the Church in the Twentieth and Twenty-first Centuries

The destruction of the two world wars in Europe occasioned a flurry of postwar reconstruction and the design and building of new churches. In some remarkable instances, deliberate collaboration between the Church as patron and the artists opened the way for new creative relationships. Two French Dominicans, P.-R. Régamy and Marie-Alain Couturier, stand at the forefront of the new movement to encourage modern sacred art. An artist himself, Couturier worked in France prior to World War II and became first the codirector with Régamy, and later (in 1939) sole director, of the journal *L'Art Sacré*. Upon his return to France in 1945 after his war years spent in the United States, Couturier took up his mission of the renewal of the dialogue between the Church and art. His guiding principle was that "to keep Christian art alive, every generation must appeal to the masters of living art."[28] It had long been the tradition within the Roman Catholic Church that popes and bishops commissioned the greatest artists of their times. As Couturier points out, "With the nineteenth century all this began to change. One after another the great men were bypassed in favor of secondary talents, then of third-raters, then of quacks, then of hucksters. Thereafter the biggest monuments were also the worst (Lourdes, Fourvière, Lisieux, etc.)."[29] One can only nod in agreement when looking at many very expensive but mediocre efforts of our own time.

Before World War II Couturier had begun conversations with a pastor, abbé Devémy, about planning a new church, Our Lady of All Graces (Notre-Dame-de-Toute-Grâce) in the Alpine town of Assy.[30] A window by Rouault, *Christ Mocked*, was the first acquisition. By the time of its dedication in 1950, the church had become a veritable roll call of the most important French artists. Couturier took the risk of eliciting profoundly spiritual art even from nonbelieving artists, and he was not disappointed. Monumental tapestry was revived in the great *Apocalypse* weaving by Jean Lurçat that fills the apse wall.[31] Lurçat's love affair with the medieval *Angers Apocalypse* led to his assisting the Aubusson tapestry works in modernizing their techniques and processes. In his own work with the factory at the end of his life, he conceived a tapestry series of more than 500 square meters called *Song of the World*, a response to the *Angers Apocalypse*. Nine lyrical tapestries featuring the dangers and joys of the modern world were completed between 1957 and 1964, before his death, and the tenth posthumously.

The façade of the church at Assy is a great mosaic by Fernand Léger. There is a Marian sculpture by Jacques Lipchitz, as well as works by Marc Chagall, Henri Matisse, Georges Braque, Pierre Bonnard, and Jean Bazain. Germaine Richier's emaciated and tortured body of Christ on the Cross for Assy became a *cause célèbre* in subsequent controversies about modernism and the role of modern art in the Church.

Couturier was at the center of three other church projects involving world-famous French artists. At Vence he assisted Matisse as liturgical consultant in designing the chapel for the Dominican sisters, completed in 1951. His participation brought Léger into the 1955 project for the large program of stained glass windows at Audincourt. Léger's designs, based on the instruments of the Passion, encircle the building at the clerestory level. Couturier was also instrumental in the commissioning of Le Corbusier as architect for Notre-Dame-du-Haut at Ronchamp (1950–1955) and the monastery at Sainte-Marie-de-la-Tourette. Le Corbusier initially declined the invitation to design the church at Ronchamp because he was uninterested in working for what he considered a dead institution, but his longtime friend Couturier was able to persuade him to accept the commission. A nonbeliever, Le Corbusier was able to say at the end of the project, "In building this chapel I wanted to create a place of silence, of prayer, of peace, of spiritual joy. A sense of the sacred animated our effort."[32]

The revolution Couturier had begun was short-lived. The debate over modernism choked the goodwill and courage of church leaders and civic underwriters in their efforts to heal the breach between the Church and art, and enthusiasm for commissioning important artists withered in France until the 1980s. Ironically, in a country with minimal involvement with the Church, commissions from the French Ministry of Culture for artworks in churches are now infusing new life into the creation of works of sacred art. A stellar example is the collaboration between the abstract painter Pierre Soulages and master glazier Jean-Dominique Fleury to create 106 stained glass windows for the medieval pilgrimage church of Sainte-Foy de Conques.[33] Given Soulages's understanding of the Church as the celestial city illumined by the glory of God, it was imperative to flood the interior with light. A profound insight for Soulages was that his job was to serve the Church "as it has reached us," and not as it might once have been. There was no need to re-create the illusion of medieval stained glass windows. Instead he invented, with the help of scientists, a new glass medium concentrating opalescent white glass grains to modulate light into warm and cool hues. The new glass is set in abstract linear patterns undulating from window to window, shimmering in a mystical light that changes through the times of day and the seasons of the year.

Couturier's quest for great sacred art from modern artists was matched in other postwar venues. Certainly Coventry Cathedral in England comes to mind.[34] On the morning after the 1940 bombing of the medieval cathedral by the German Luftwaffe, within the smoke and ruins, the decision was made to build a new cathedral as a gesture of faith and hope. The best artists available were to be gathered for the new project. Sir Basil Spence won the competition to design the new building. Graham Sutherland's tapestry of Christ in glory, surrounded with symbols of the Evangelists, 74 by 38 feet in size, clothes the entire east end of the cathedral. Sir Jacob Epstein's statue of Saint Michael the Archangel and the Devil guards the entry portal, whose glass wall, engraved with angels by John Hutton, overlooks the bombed-out ruins of the medieval building. A multistory curved wall embracing the baptistery supports the stained glass window by John Piper depicting the burst of primal creation.

The churches at Assy and Coventry both met with mixed reactions from a public accustomed to a much more conservative and familiar visual environment. A fear-filled objection to the commissioning of modern artists for new church projects is the anxiety that "they will not do what we want." Couturier's response was:

> Thank God! For too often 'what we want,' what people like, is far inferior to what great artists would do even if left to their inspiration alone. And, in any case, experience proves that even when he is left to his own inspiration, what a great artist produces out of himself is infinitely more valid than the inevitable trash done by docile second-raters; these being generally obliging in proportion to their mediocrity.[35]

In Germany too, artists were commissioned to create new works for war-damaged churches. As in France, the best artists were sought, regardless of their faith affiliation or lack of one. Marc Chagall produced nine windows of Old Testament scenes for the Gothic choir of the Church of Sankt Stephan in Mainz, as well as windows for the cathedrals of Metz and Reims in France.[36] Georg Meistermann explored new paths with "colorless" stained glass, working with a palette of whites, grays, and blacks.[37] The monochromatic range, not unlike late medieval "grisaille" or gray glass, brought a new focus to the subtleties and complexities of light. Ludwig Schaffrath eschewed narrative themes, utilizing parallel patterns of white glass and bits of color,[38] while others, including Jochen Poensgen, luxuriated in the extravagant colors of *dalle de verre*, slabs of colored glass set in concrete. Integrating abstract forms and new materials and techniques into ancient buildings jolted the postwar public into seeing the familiar structures in new ways, and discovering a new way of seeing freed from the limitations of narrative and objective images.

On a much smaller scale, in 1977 the American sculptor Louise Nevelson designed and created a small meditation chapel for Saint Peter's Lutheran Church in New York.[39] The church is located in the Citicorp office building on Lexington Avenue, an urban haven for workers in the area. Everything in the chapel is white—the walls, the sculptural reliefs on the walls, and the Cross of the Good Shepherd. The floor, pews, and altar are bleached. The window is frosted white. Nevelson also designed altar cloths and clerical vestments. Three suspended columns imply the Trinity. The stark simplicity conveys strength, presence, peace. It is a healing place.

The purifying light of Nevelson's chapel contrasts with the darkness of the Rothko Chapel in Houston, completed in 1971. Inspired by their friend Couturier's determination to hire the best artists to create significant works of Christian art, Dominique and John de Menil commissioned Mark Rothko to create a series of paintings for a chapel.[40] Three triptychs and five panels occupy the octagonal chapel. The architectural-scale paintings are monochromatic dark colors of blacks, reds, browns, and purples. In them there is somehow a blurring of death and spirituality. After some time getting accustomed to the darkness in the chapel, many visitors feel a great sense of peace and presence. At the inauguration, Dominique de Menil reflected that "Rothko was prophetic in leaving us a nocturnal environment. Night is peaceful. Night is pregnant with life."

Two recent high-profile church building projects reflect worldwide searches for the best architects, designers, and artists to combine modern architecture and art in a

Rothko Chapel. Chapel at Houston, Texas, designed by Mark Rothko (1903–1970). © COPYRIGHT ARS, NY/ ART RESOURCE, NY

place of great spiritual power. The smaller is the Jubilee Church in Rome.[41] Richard Meier, an American Jewish architect, won an invited competition to design a church for a working-class neighborhood in suburban Rome. Dedicated in 2003, the church was commissioned to celebrate Pope John Paul II's twenty-fifth anniversary as pontiff. The church is defined by three tall concrete shapes like sails that arc up to a height of 88 feet. The spaces between them and the ceilings are all glass, so that light cascades throughout the whole inner space. The exterior and interior are white. For Meier, the shafts of sunlight that penetrate the skylights dance in the interior as a metaphor for the presence of God. The space is luminous and wondrous. Meier's hope and intention is that the building will be a model for new churches for the twenty-first century. The architect admits criticism for the traditional, non-innovative arrangement of the liturgical space. It is curious that so daring a sculptural form for the building did not merit more thoughtfulness in the design of the worship space—a missed opportunity.

The second recent effort to gather the best artists and designers for a major church commission is the new Roman Catholic Cathedral of the Angels in Los Angeles.[42] The design competition was won by the Spanish architect Raphael Moneo. Construction began in 1999 and was completed

Palm Sunday. Arrangement by the Japanese artist Gako Ota (died 1972). PHOTOGRAPH COURTESY OF GEOFFREY WAINWRIGHT

The Visual Arts in Africa, East Asia, and the Pacific

Geoffrey Wainwright

The twentieth century witnessed a flourishing of the visual arts among Christians in Africa, East Asia, and the Pacific, more or less directly related to the liturgical life of the churches. Artists and craftspeople typically worked in local materials and genres and represented biblical characters and scenes in the fashions of the local culture.

In Africa, wood has been the chief medium. Carved Stations of the Cross may be found in Nigeria, with palm trees emphasizing the transposed setting. In a Benedictine monastery in Zimbabwe, the stem of the altar-table displays four moments from the Last Supper. The Cameroonian Jesuit Engelbert Mveng (1930-1995)—also a pioneer in the use of African music in the liturgy—created a backdrop for the apse of a college chapel in Douala [see color plate 27A], which he interpreted thus:

> The Christ in majesty which stands above the altar recapitulates the offering of the whole world and humanity in the sacrifice of the Cross. At the foot of Christ crucified stand the martyrs of Uganda; they are the image of all those people in southern Africa who have united the sacrifice of their lives to that of Christ crucified. The Cross rises against a cosmic background of cruciform patters (the four points of the compass), of sun and moon motifs (circles and crescents), and of triangular and diamond shapes, symbols of fertility and life. The whole is in the three fundamental colors: red the color of life, black the color of suffering, white the color of death. Thus Africa, mankind, the whole cosmos, are evoked and comprised in the vast gesture of Christ on the Cross: "Father, into thy hands I commend my breath of life." But the splendor and majesty of this Cross sings the paschal triumph of the Resurrection: "I am the resurrection and the life; he who believes in me, though he die, yet shall he live, and whoever lives and believes in me shall never die. (Quoted in Weber, p. 63.)

The pointed ovals of the heads recall the shape of the nutshells that are carved and inscribed for use as tiles in the local game of *abbia*.

In East Asia, the favored media are textiles and paper. The Indonesian batik painter Bagong Kussudiardja (1928–2004) has created Crucifixion scenes that display Christ as a figure from the Javanese *wayang* puppet theater [see color plate 27B]. In a particularly striking example, Bagong "used the special possibilities of batik painting by letting daringly

Altar-table. Artistic carving in the traditional medium of wood is brought into the service of the central mystery of the Christian faith. Detail from the altar-table at the Benedictine monastery of Christ the Word, Macheke, Zimbabwe, designed by the Art Workshop, Driefontein Mission, Mvuma, Zimbabwe. [For a picture of the entire altar see chapter 26.] PHOTOGRAPH BY ALBAN CROSSLEY, O.S.B.

contrasting colors flow into one another. By this means the apocalyptic dimension of what happened at the Crucifixion, the darkening of the sun and the shaking of the earth, is interpreted in a way never found in European art. Christ looks towards the new dawn at his right-hand side and—symbolizing the new exodus—he jumps from the Cross" (Weber, p. 49).

In 1978 an Asia-wide conference of artists was held in Bali, and from this gathering the Asian Christian Art Association resulted, in which Masao Takenaka (born 1925) of Japan has played a leading part. Christian artists have participated in a widespread revival of folk art in Japan. Its spirit pervades the productions of Sadao Watanabe (1913–1996), a convert to Christianity in his youth, who used the technique of stencil print on handmade *washi* paper, and some of whose works are in the Vatican's collection of modern religious art. In China, He Qi, who specializes in papercuts, writes thus:

> In recent years, our Nanjing Seminary art classes . . . have been exploring and experimenting in the task of indigenization of Chinese Christian art. A number of ink and wash paintings, papercuts, woodcuts and other works in various folk styles have been produced. We hope that our work will add something to the richness of the ecumenical Church, and for this we are willing to work and search tirelessly. (Quoted in Takenaka and O'Grady, p. 12.)

Throughout East Asia, scriptural scenes are used to illustrate Bible translations, for catechetical purposes, and as adornment for calendars. A favorite theme is the Last Supper, but while vestures, gestures and postures there assume a local style, the cultural shift is not often to be found in liturgical practice. An Indian example by Angelo Da Fonseca is reproduced by Takenaka (p. 94); a porcelain work reproduced in *The Gospel in Chinese Art* (p. 49) comes from the Tao Fong Shan Work Shop, established in 1947 to provide former Buddhists with an opportunity to earn a living and express their Christian faith in Chinese art [see color plate 26].

Gako Ota (died 1972) was a Japanese practitioner of *ikebana*, or flower arrangement, and her floral displays were mounted on the altar of her local church every Sunday, often following the festal calendar. Examples created for Palm Sunday and Pentecost are illustrated by Takenaka and O'Grady (p. 129) and by Takenaka (p.123).

References

Dyrness, W. A. *Christian Art in Asia*. Amsterdam: Rodopi, 1979.

The Gospel in Chinese Art. n.p.: Christian Mission to Buddhists, 1991.

Hoefer, Herbert E. *Christian Art in India*. Madras: Gurukul Lutheran Theological College and Research Institute, 1982.

Lehmann, Arno. *Christian Art in Africa and Asia*. Translated by Erich Hopka, et al. Saint Louis: Concordia, 1969.

Ott, Martin. *African Theology in Images*. Blantyre: Christian Literature Association in Malawi, 2000.

Takenaka, Masao. *Christian Art in Asia*. Tokyo: Kyo Bun Kwan, 1975.

Takenaka, Masao, and Ron O'Grady. *The Bible through Asian Eyes*. Auckland: Pace and Asian Christian Art Association (Kyoto, Japan), 1991.

Weber, Hans-Ruedi. *On a Friday Noon: Meditations under the Cross*. Grand Rapids, Mich.: Eerdmans, 1979.

in 2002. Great cast bronze doors by the Mexican-born artist Robert Graham, in the tradition of the great medieval cathedrals, welcome one into the building. Above the doors is Graham's sculpture of Our Lady of the Angels.[43] The interior is lit by the soft light of alabaster windows. The most remarkable of the artworks in the cathedral is the elaborate program of woven tapestries designed by John Nova. Twenty-five large tapestries line both walls of the nave, depicting the communion of saints. Five tapestries forty-seven feet tall and seven feet wide represent the baptism of Christ behind the baptistery, while an additional seven tapestries hang behind the altar. This group represents the streets of Los Angeles converging at the center to create an image of the New Jerusalem. Ancient motifs, the legacy of both the visual tradition and an aural memory of prayers uttered through the centuries, inform the new context in which they now find life.

Bibliography

Belting, Hans. *Likeness and Presence: A History of the Image before the Era of Art.* Translated by Edmund Jephcott. Chicago: University of Chicago Press, 1994.

Favier, Jean. *The World of Chartres.* London: Thames & Hudson; New York: Harry N. Abrams, 1990.

McClinton, Katharine M. *Christian Church Art through the Centuries.* New York: Macmillan, 1962.

Norman, Edward. *The House of God: Church Architecture, Style, and History.* London: Thames & Hudson, 1990.

Ouspensky, Léonide, and Vladimir Lossky. *The Meaning of Icons.* 2nd ed. Crestwood, N.Y.: St. Vladimir's Seminary Press, 1982.

Simpson, James B., and George H. Eatman. *A Treasury of Anglican Art.* New York: Rizzoli, 2002.

Wieck, Roger S. *Painted Prayers: The Book of Hours in Medieval and Renaissance Art.* New York: George Brazillier, in association with the Pierpont Morgan Library, 1997.

Notes

[1] From *Sugerii abbatis sancti Dionysii liber de rebus in administratione sua gestis*, in *Abbot Suger on the Abbey Church of Saint-Denis and its Art Treasures*, ed. and trans. Erwin Panofsky, 2nd ed. by Gerda Panofsky-Soergel (Princeton, N.J.: Princeton University Press, 1979) 63–65. See also Paula Lieber Gerson, ed., *Abbot Suger and Saint-Denis: A Symposium* (New York: Metropolitan Museum of Art, 1986); Caroline Bruzelius, *The Thirteenth Century Church at Saint-Denis* (New Haven, Conn.: Yale University Press, 1985); Sumner McKnight Crosby, *The Royal Abbey of Saint-Denis: From Its Beginnings to the Death of Suger, 475–1151* (New Haven, Conn.: Yale University Press, 1987); and Conrad Rudolph, *Artistic Change at Saint-Denis: Abbot Suger's Program and the Early Twelfth Century Controversy over* Art (Princeton, N.J.: Princeton University Press, 1990).

[2] For the Roman catacombs, see James Stevenson, *The Catacombs: Life and Death in Early Christianity* (Nashville, Tenn.: Thomas Nelson, 1978); Pierre du Bourguet, *Early Christian Painting* (New York: Viking, 1966); Vicenzo Fiocchi Nicolai, Fabrizio Bisconti, and Danilo Mazzoleni, *The Christian Catacombs of Rome: History, Decoration, Inscriptions*, trans. Cristina Carlo Stella and Lori-Ann Touchette (Regensburg: Schnell & Steiner, 1999). For Dura-Europos, see Ann Louise Perkins, *The Art of Dura-Europos* (Oxford: Clarendon, 1973); and *The Excavations at Dura-Europos, conducted by Yale University and the French Academy of Inscriptions and Letters*, ed. M. I. Rostovtzeff, et al. (New Haven, Conn.: Yale University Press, 1929–1959).

[3] For discussion of the shift to images of imperial majesty, see John Beckwith, *Early Christian and*

Byzantine Art, 2nd ed. (New York: Penguin, 1979); and Thomas Mathews, *The Clash of Gods: A Reinterpretation of Early Christian Art* (Princeton, N.J.: Princeton University Press, 1993).

[4]Richard Krautheimer, *Early Christian and Byzantine Architecture*, 4th ed., rev. Richard Krautheimer and Slobodan Ćurčić (New Haven, Conn.: Yale University Press, 1986) 58.

[5]See Heinrich Karpp, *Die frühchristlichen und mittelalterlichen Mosaiken in Santa Maria Maggiore zu Rom* (Baden-Baden: Grimm, 1966).

[6]Georges Guillard, *The Frescoes of Saint-Savin* (New York: Studio, 1944); and R. Oursel, *La Bible de Saint-Savin* (La Pierre-qui-vire: Zodiaque, 1971).

[7]Daniel J. Sahas, *Icon and Logos: Sources in Eighth-Century Iconoclasm* (Toronto: University of Toronto Press, 1986); Léonide Ouspensky and Vladimir Lossky, *The Meaning of Icons*; Henry Maguire, *The Icons of Their Bodies: Saints and Their Images in Byzantium* (Princeton, N.J.: Princeton University Press, 1996); Kurt Weitzmann, *The Monastery of Saint Catherine at Mount Sinai: The Icons* (Princeton, N.J.: Princeton University Press, 1975); Jaroslav Pelikan, *Imago Dei: The Byzantine Apologia for Icons* (Princeton, N.J.: Princeton University Press, 1990); Robin Cormack, *Writing in Gold: Byzantine Society and Its Icons* (London: George Phillip, 1985); and George Galavaris, *The Icon in the Life of the Church: Doctrine, Liturgy, Devotion* (Leiden: E. J. Brill, 1981).

[8]Andrew Ladis, *The Brancacci Chapel, Florence* (New York: George Braziller, 1993).

[9]Marcia B. Hall, *Michelangelo: The Frescoes of the Sistine Chapel* (New York: Harry N. Abrams, 2002); and Carol F. Lewine, *The Sistine Chapel Walls and the Roman Liturgy* (University Park: Pennsylvania State University Press, 1993).

[10]Hans Belting, *Likeness and Presence: A History of the Image before the Era of Art*, offers a magisterial study of the "iconic portrait" in the entire period between Late Antiquity and the Renaissance/Reformation, when the "object of devotion" passed into a "work of art." The book is illustrated and has an appendix containing contemporary interpretative texts. The author deliberately excludes from treatment the "narrative image," which all along served more pedagogical purposes.

[11]See Carlos M. N. Eire, *War against the Idols: The Reformation of Worship from Erasmus to Calvin* (Cambridge: Cambridge University Press, 1986). On the English scene, see Eamon Duffy, *The Stripping of the Altars: Traditional Religion in England c.1400–c.1580* (New Haven, Conn.: Yale University Press, 1992). Lutheran church pictures exalted the Savior on the Cross and showed the appropriation of his saving benefits through baptism, sermon, and supper; see Joseph Leo Koerner, *The Reformation of the Image* (Chicago: University of Chicago Press, 2004); and Ingrid Schulze, *Lucas Cranach der Jüngere und die protestantische Bildkunst in Sachsen und Thüringen* (Bucha bei Jena: Quartus, 2004). The longer-term effects of the Reformation are treated in Werner Hofmann, ed., *Luther und die Folgen für die Kunst* (Munich: Prestel, 1983). Current theological reflections on the visual in worship, with contributions from Orthodox, Catholic, and various Protestant writers, are in an ecumenical symposium published to mark the 1200th anniversary of the Second Council of Nicaea (787): Gennadios Limouris, ed., *Icons: Windows on Eternity*, Faith and Order Paper no. 147 (Geneva: World Council of Churches, 1990).

[12]See W. A. Visser 't Hooft, *Rembrandt and the Gospel*, trans. K. Gregor Smith (London: SCM, 1957).

[13]Judy Sund, *Van Gogh: Art and Ideas* (London: Phaidon, 2002); W. W. Meissner, *Vincent's Religion: The Search for Meaning* (New York: P. Lang, 1997); and Susan Alyson Stein, ed., *Van Gogh: A Retrospective* (New York: Macmillan, 1986).

[14]Luciano Bellosi, *Duccio: The Maestà* (London: Thames & Hudson, 1999).

[15]Lotte Brand Phillip, *The Ghent Altarpiece and the Art of Jan van Eyck* (Princeton, N.J.: Princeton University Press, 1971); Elisabeth Dhanens, *Van Eyck: The Ghent Altarpiece* (New York: Viking, 1973); and Otto Pächt, *Van Eyck and the Founders of Early Netherlandish Painting* (London: H. Miller, 1994).

[16]Andrée Hayum, *The Isenheim Altarpiece: God's Medicine and the Painter's Vision* (Princeton, N.J.: Princeton University Press, 1989); and Horst Ziermann, *Matthias Grünewald* (Munich: Prestel, 2001).

[17]For good photographs of German carved wooden altarpieces see Michael Baxandall, *The Limewood Sculptors of Renaissance Germany* (New Haven, Conn.: Yale University Press, 1980).

[18]Julien Chapuis, Michael Baxandall, et al., *Tilman Riemenschneider: Master Sculptor of the Late Middle Age* (New Haven, Conn.: Yale University Press, 1999).

[19]Karsten Harries, *The Bavarian Rococo Church: Between Faith and Aestheticism* (New Haven, Conn.: Yale University Press, 1983).

[20]A useful (though now outdated) overview of textiles for liturgical use is Marion Ireland, *Textile Art in the Church: Vestments, Paraments, and Hangings in Contemporary Worship, Art, and Architecture* (Nashville, Tenn.: Abingdon, 1971).

[21]See David M. Wilson, The *Bayeux Tapestry: The Complete Tapestry in Colour* (London: Thames & Hudson, 1985); and Wolfgang Grape, *The Bayeux Tapestry: Monument to a Norman Triumph* (Munich: Prestel, 1994), for excellent color photographs of the entire tapestry.

[22]Frederik van der Meer, *Apocalypse: Visions from the Book of Revelation in Western Art* (New York: Alpine Fine Arts Collection, 1978); includes the *Angers Apocalypse*.

[23]John K. G. Shearman, *Raphael's Cartoons in the Collection of Her Majesty the Queen, and the Tapestries for the Sistine Chapel* (London: Phaidon, 1972).

[24]Chap. 29, *La Vida de la Madre Teresa de Jesús*, in *The Life of the Holy Mother Teresa of Jesus, Saint Teresa of Avila*, trans. E. Allison Peers (London: Sheed & Ward, 1979) 192–193.

[25]Richard Krautheimer, *Ghiberti's Bronze Doors* (Princeton, N.J.: Princeton University Press, 1971).

[26]An excellent book including large color photographs of medieval bronze doors is Ursula Mende, *Die Bronzetüren des Mittelalters, 800–1200* (Munich: Hirmer, 1983).

[27]William Voelkle, *The Stavelot Triptych: Mosan Art and the Legend of the True Cross* (New York: Pierpont Morgan Library, 1980). Numerous photographs of northern European metalwork with excellent commentary can be found in the exhibition catalog *Rhein und Maas: Kunst und Kultur 800–1400* (Cologne: Schnütgen Museum, 1972).

[28]M.-A. Couturier, *Sacred Art* (Austin: University of Texas Press, 1989) 52.

[29]Couturier, 34.

[30]See Web site http://www.astoft.co.uk/plateau-d'assy.htm; and William Rubin, *Modern Sacred Art and the Church of Assy* (New York: Columbia University Press, 1961).

[31]See Madeleine Jarry, *La Tapisserie: Art du 20ᵉ siècle* (Fribourg: Office du Livre, 1974).

[32]Le Corbusier, *The Chapel at Ronchamp* (New York: Frederick A. Praeger, 1957) 25.

[33]http://www.conques.com/visite17.htm; see also Christian Heck, *Conques: Les vitraux de Soulages* (Paris: Seuil, 1994); and Marie Renoue, *Sémiotique et perception esthétique: Pierre Soulages et Sainte-Foy de Conques* (Limoges: Presses Universitaires de Limoges, 2001).

[34]Basil Spence, *Phoenix at Coventry: The Building of a Cathedral* (London: G. Bles, 1962).

[35]Couturier, 36.

[36]Robert Marteau, *The Stained Glass Windows of Chagall, 1957–1970* (New York: Tudor, 1973).

[37]Georg Meistermann, *Georg Meistermann: Die Kirchenfenster* (Freiburg im Breisgau: Herder, 1986).

[38]Ludwig Schaffrath, *Stained Glass and Mosaic* (Krefeld: Scherpe Verlag, 1977).

[39]http://www.saintpeters.org/art/index.html.

[40]Sheldon Nodelman, *The Rothko Chapel Paintings: Origins, Structure, Meaning* (Austin: University of Texas Press, 1997).

[41]For photographs, plans, and interviews with the architect, see http://www.archnewsnow.com/features/Feature123.htm; http://archrecord.construction.com/projects/portfolio/archives/0402JubileeChurch-1.asp#;

http://mocra.slu.edu/current_exhibition/JubileeChurch.html;

http://www.archpedia.com/Projects-Richard-Meier_01.html; and

http://www.archpedia.com/Projects-Richard-Meier_01.html

[42]Comprehensive photographs and information about the project and artists for the Cathedral of the Angels can be found on the Cathedral's website: http://www.olacathedral.org/. See also Michael Downey, *The Cathedral: At the Heart of Los Angeles* (Collegeville, Minn.: Liturgical Press, 2002).

[43]Jack Miles, Peggy Fogelman, and Noriko Fujinami, *Robert Graham: The Great Bronze Doors for the Cathedral of Our Lady of the Angels* (Los Angeles: Wave, 2002).

33

Vestments and Objects

JOANNE M. PIERCE

To paraphrase the liturgical historian Aidan Kavanagh, liturgical vestments and objects are not trivial, but sacred, because their meaning derives from the essential "sacredness" of the events in which they participate.[1] It is appropriate, then, for a volume on the history of Christian worship to conclude with a short diachronic overview of the use and meaning of liturgical vestments and objects.

Vestments

The specialized ritual garments worn by the presider and assistants during a liturgical celebration are known as "vestments." Liturgical historians have traced the origins and development of vestments used, with ongoing modifications, in many Christian churches up to the present day.

Eucharistic Vestments in Antiquity

Scholarly consensus today holds that Christian liturgical vestments derive from ordinary clothing worn in Greco-Roman culture during the first century A.D., rather than from the ritual garments used in some Jewish rites of that period.[2] During the second and third centuries, the different "orders" of ordained ministry became fixed. The three key offices were those of bishop, presbyter or priest, and deacon. Another order, that of subdeacon, became increasingly important as well. Each of these orders eventually was assigned specific liturgical vestments. The earliest elements of Christian liturgical clothing seem to have been the alb, the chasuble, and the stole.

The alb, from the Latin word *alba* ("white"), originated from the under-tunic worn in antiquity. The "white garment" given at baptism seems also to have derived from this standard undergarment.[3] As liturgical vestiture became more and more stylized, the alb developed into a floor-length, thin robe or "dress" with narrow sleeves, made of linen. As time went on, the sleeves or hem could be trimmed with embroidered banding ("apparels" or "orphry banding"). It also became customary to wear a special cord or belt tied at the waist of this often full-cut vestment—the cincture (*cingulum* or *zona*). The alb was and still is worn under the chasuble.

The chasuble, a rather full, sleeveless garment similar to a poncho, was derived from certain styles of the ordinary outer cloak worn by both women and men in cold or inclement weather—the *paenula*, as either the fuller *planeta* or the narrower *casula*.[4]

Over time, the chasuble became a stylized and often expansively decorated vestment, worn only by priests and bishops during the celebration of the eucharist.

The stole (*stola* or *orarium*), a scarf-like strip of cloth worn around the neck or on one shoulder, has cloudier origins. Some believe it to have been originally a token of civil rank; others derive it from rectangles of cloth given as imperial gifts to those attending the games; and some earlier writers trace it to Jewish prayer shawls. In Christian use, it became a mark of ordained rank or office: bishops and priests wore it around the neck, with both ends hanging down straight in front, or in later usage, crossed across the chest. Western deacons would later wear it looped on the left shoulder, draped across the torso front and back, and fixed under the right arm.

Somewhat later, another liturgical garment was assigned to the deacon: the dalmatic, which was originally a sleeved overtunic called the *tunica dalmatica* (possibly reflecting its origins in Dalmatia on the northern Adriatic coast). The body of the tunic was decorated by embroidered stripes or bands. Another, plainer, version of this tunic, the tunicle, became the eucharistic vestment of the subdeacon.

Eucharistic Vestments in the Medieval West

After the legalization of Christianity, liturgical vestments became more elaborate and decorated. This tendency continued through the early Middle Ages.[5] As liturgical colors proper to liturgical seasons or feasts became customary (see below), outer liturgical garments like stoles and chasubles were designed to reflect these colors (e.g., purple or "sackcloth" for Lent). Embroidered banding also was often added to these vestments, as well as to the alb. In addition, the act of vesting itself became a ritualized "transition moment," often with an elaborate series of vesting prayers to be recited in the sacristy as the ministers took off their everyday clothing and put on the liturgical vestments of the day. An added complication in the vesting process was the custom of the duplication of vestments. One way this took place was in the addition of special "over" or "under" vestments that were sometimes layered onto the older elements. Another was the stipulation that as the cleric progressed through the major orders, he was to don the vestments of his previous rank as well as those of his present rank. For example, a bishop vesting for mass would be expected to wear the vestments of the subdeacon and deacon

A vested celebrant. The Mass of Saint Giles in the abbey of Saint-Denis, France. The alb and cincture are visible under the chasuble. The scene is that of the early medieval saint receiving angelic delivery of a slip of paper naming the sin that the emperor Charlemagne was reluctant to confess and promising absolution for it. Master of Saint Giles, c. 1500. NATIONAL GALLERY, LONDON/ ERICH LESSING/ART RESOURCE, NY

under his priestly vestments, to which would be added vestments reflecting his episcopal rank.

A bishop of the eleventh century could expect to spend a significant amount of time in preparation for the celebration of mass. Each action of preparation, including the donning of each separate vestment, would be accompanied by a specific prayer, psalm verses, or other short versicle.[6] After the bishop entered the church and prayed for a short time at the altar, he would enter the sacristy. The vesting rite would begin with a ritual handwashing, and then the removal of his ordinary outerwear. He would then don a series of liturgical vestments in layers. The first was the amice (*amictum* or *ephot*), a rectangular piece of cloth worn around the neck and held in place by thin strings tied around the body. Next came the alb, and then the cincture. Sometimes bishops would also wear an embroidered belt or strip of cloth over the cincture called the *precinctorium*. Next, the bishop put on the stole, and then the three overtunics: the tunicle, the undecorated sleeved tunic worn by subdeacons at mass; the dalmatic, the more elaborately decorated sleeved tunic worn by deacons; and the priestly chasuble. The final vestment worn by all priests was the maniple, a stylized and elaborately decorated band of cloth worn on the wrist (as a waiter might wear a napkin or small towel). Next, the bishop would put on a series of "pontifical" vestments, those reserved for episcopal use. Some vesting orders called for the donning of special pontifical stockings (*caligae* or *udones*) and soft shoes or slippers (*sandalia* or *campagi*). Others listed prayers for the bishop to recite as he put on special gloves (*chirothecae*), his episcopal ring (*annulum*), his pallium (a special white circle of cloth, often embroidered with crosses, worn around the neck, granted to certain bishops by the pope), or in some countries, his rationale (a kind of band or small sash worn across the chest). Other vestments might include the mitre (a special kind of stiff cloth cap, often pointed at the top) and the crosier (*baculus* or *pedum*, a staff of pastoral office, often made of precious metals and curved at the end like a shepherd's crook). The vesting rite would conclude with one or two "general vesting" prayers, and a series of verses and responses.

These vesting prayers provide an interesting lens through which to view an important element of medieval piety. These prayers tend to interpret the individual vestments in terms of moral, ethical, or christological allegory.[7] For example, in an eleventh-century *ordo missae*, the presider recited this prayer as he donned the stole:

> Stola iustitiae circumda Domine ceruiem meam. Et ab omni corruptione peccati purifica mentem meam. ("Encircle my neck, Lord, with the stole of justice, and purify my mind from all corruption of sin.")[8]

Vesting prayers were dropped in Protestant churches of the Reformation era, but in Roman Catholicism a required standard set continued to be used until the Second Vatican Council (1963). The prayer for the stole in the Tridentine *Missale Romanum* is different from the eleventh-century example, but it also contains a moral or purificatory message:

> Redde mihi, Domine, stolam immortalitatis, quam perdidi in praevaricatione primi parentis; et, quamvis indignum accedo ad tuum sacrum mysterium, merear tamen gaudium sempiternum. ("Restore unto me, O Lord, the stole of immortality, which I lost through the sin of my first parents and, although unworthy to approach Thy sacred Mystery, may I nevertheless attain to joy eternal.")[9]

The revised *Roman Catholic Missal*, or *Sacramentary* (1970) does not include vesting prayers, which seem widely to have fallen into disuse. The "General Instruction" of the *Roman Missal* lists the vestments to be worn by various liturgical ministers but does not mention the use of vesting prayers as part of the preparation for mass.[10]

The allegorical interpretations ascribed to these vestments through the development of vesting prayers varied from place to place and from century to century during the medieval period.[11] In addition, allegorical interpretations of both vestments and liturgical objects became an important theme in more comprehensive medieval theological and canonical commentaries on the mass and sacraments, from the time of Amalarius of Metz and his *Liber officialis* (823) through the monumental *Rationale divinorum officiorum* (1286–1291) by William Durandus, bishop of Mende.[12] As Joseph Braun notes:

> It is a striking fact that the symbolism of these prayers often pursues its own course without regard to the interpretations of the liturgists. It was not until towards the end of the Middle Ages that a greater agreement arose between the symbolism of the liturgists and what might be called the official symbolism of the Church expressed in the prayers in question; this official symbolism, moreover, differed greatly at different periods and in different places.[13]

Other vestments also came into use during the medieval period for other, noneucharistic liturgical celebrations. The cope (*pluviale*), used by deacons, priests, or bishops for noneucharistic sacramental celebrations such as baptism, is essentially an ornamented, floor-length cape worn over the shoulders and fastened at the neck.[14] The alb and stole would be worn underneath the cope. During processions with the Blessed Sacrament or services for the exposition of the Blessed Sacrament (which became more common from the fourteenth century on), a shawl-like vestment called the *humerale* or humeral veil (from *humerus*, "upper arm") would be worn by the presider. This was usually made from the same kind of material as the chasuble or dalmatic, and was worn draped over the shoulders and covering the arms and hands. For celebrations of the divine office, other vestments were used: the cassock, usually a black, floor-length tunic with long sleeves; and on top of that, the surplice, a waist- or thigh-length version of the alb (the word "surplice" derives from *super-pelliceum*, indicating that it was worn "over" a garment "made from skins"). In England, a warm scarf was also worn in choir; this developed into the modern Anglican tippet.

Basic choir vestiture—the cassock and surplice—would have been worn by clerics in both minor and major orders during the medieval period, and the use spread to anyone assisting at a liturgical celebration. Thus, in some traditions, cassock and surplice (or a shorter version called the cotta) continue to be worn by lay acolytes and choir members today.

The development of one more episcopal vestment should be mentioned here. Bishops presided over many liturgical celebrations involving the use of oil and anointings (confirmations, ordinations, dedication of altars); a short white or colored apron, the gremial, was used to protect their clothing in these situations, and it later came to be draped over the bishop's lap during any mass when he was seated as well.

Vestments after the Reformation

The Protestant reformers, in their attempts to eliminate elements of "human invention" from the liturgy, took different tacks in regard to vestments.[15] The Lutheran tradition regarded vestments as *adiaphora*, to be used at the judgment of the individual or community. In many Lutheran countries, however, the liturgical vestment for pastors came to be modeled after the black gown of the university professor rather than the colorful chasuble of the priest. This gown was often worn with a white ruff at the collar. Germany and Denmark followed this pastor-preacher-teacher model. In Sweden, however, the Lutheran Church remained more "high church" in this regard, retaining the use of the chasuble during the eucharist.[16]

Other reformed churches implemented a stricter reform of liturgical vestiture. In these regions (e.g., Calvinist sections of Switzerland), the black professorial preacher's gown with a white ruff at the collar became a standard for Sunday worship. More radical reform movements (e.g., Anabaptists and later Quakers) discarded the use of any special vestiture for Sunday worship.

The use of vestments in the Anglican tradition became a hotly debated topic for several generations. Little changed during the reign of Henry VIII; the two versions of the *Book of Common Prayer* under Edward VI saw use for only a few years before the death of the young king and the accession of his Catholic half-sister, Mary. Her attempts to reinstate Catholic liturgy and practice failed with her death five years later, and her successor, Elizabeth I, reintroduced the *Second Prayer Book* little changed from Edward's reign. Objections to "popish" elements in Anglican worship led to the general rejection of several vestments, including the chasuble. However, the more extreme Puritans objected even to the wearing of the surplice. Until the nineteenth century, the common Anglican vestiture consisted of the surplice and black scarf or tippet (or academic hood); some clergy wore alb and cope, or even chasuble, while others stayed with the black preaching gown. A return to the more Catholic set of vestments was encouraged in some areas by the "neo-medievalist" and Oxford movements of the nineteenth century.[17]

Western Vestments in the Contemporary Era

The general effects of the two world wars, as well as the more specific influences of the Liturgical Movement of the mid-twentieth century and the Roman Catholic liturgical reforms after the Second Vatican Council, all had repercussions in the use of liturgical vestments for Catholics and Protestants alike. Catholic vestments began to be designed in a more fulsome manner. Chasubles especially expanded greatly in volume and drape in the more expansive "Gothic" style, and the severely cropped, almost stylized Baroque designs (e.g., the "fiddleback" chasuble) fell into disuse in many places. Many Protestant churches began to reappropriate some kinds of "high church" vestments in their worship practices. This had already

"Fiddleback" chasuble. "Totenkasel," or chasuble for a funeral mass, c. 1630. The broken crowns, scepters and papal tiara emphasize, as in the medieval "Totentanz" or "danse macabre," that mortality is the common condition of humankind. KREMS ABBEY, AUSTRIA/ERICH LESSING/ART RESOURCE, NY

begun in the Anglican tradition in the nineteenth century in England (under the influence of the Tractarians, among others) and in the Lutheran Church in Germany (the work of Wilhelm Löhe, for example). In the United States, some Lutheran traditions began to use the alb and chasuble; stoles also became more common and more elaborate in design among some of the more "Reformed" traditions, such as Presbyterians and the United Church of Christ.[18]

Vestments in the East

Liturgical vestments in the Eastern churches share many of the same roots as Western vestments. There are a number of significant differences, however, and several items of vestiture that have no parallel in the Western churches.[19]

In the Byzantine tradition, the *sticharion* is the equivalent to the alb, although it can be more elaborately decorated for a deacon; it is fastened by a cincture (*zone*). The *orarion*, or stole, is worn by deacons; another term, the *epitrachelion*, is used for the priestly stole. It, too, is worn in a fashion similar to the Western use, except that the two arms of the stole are buttoned or fastened near the neck, so the two ends hang close together down the front of the sticharion. Bishops wear this as an "under-stole"; however, the bishop's "outer" stole is referred to as an *omopharion*, and in appearance is similar to the Western pallium.[20] The chasuble worn by priests (and formerly by bishops) is also similar to that in the West (*phenolion*). From the eleventh century until today, however, the bishop has worn another overgarment, the *sakkos*, an elaborately decorated tunic similar to the dalmatic.[21]

Several pieces of Eastern liturgical vestiture appear to have no parallels or common points of origin in the West.[22] Bishops and certain esteemed priests wear an ornately decorated, stiff diamond of material called the *epigonation*, which may have derived from imperial military use (representing a sheath for a dagger).[23] Deacons and higher clergy are also entitled to wear decorated cuffs on the sticharion, called *epimanikia*, possibly derived from decorative imperial bands or *clavi*.[24] Several Eastern liturgical traditions also make use of special liturgical headwear or "crowns." These clerical crowns seem to have come into wide use by bishops after the fall of Constantinople in the fifteenth century; they are made of gold or other metal, and in the Russian tradition they may be worn by certain distinguished priests as well.[25] In the Ethiopian tradition, any minister of the rank of deacon or above may also wear the *zewd*, another type of liturgical crown.[26] It should be noted, however, that liturgical crowns in the Eastern traditions are also used by lay persons in one significant sacramental act, the marriage ritual.

Liturgical Colors

Liturgical colors gradually came into use during late antiquity and the early Middle Ages. In the West, certain colors eventually (perhaps as late as the twelfth century) came to be associated with certain liturgical seasons and feasts or fasts; the use of certain colors could be quite varied, according to location and time period.[27] Very early colors mentioned or depicted include white, purple, and olive green.[28] The nomenclature used for these colors could also vary; thus, a chasuble of the color *blattea* ("the color of clotted blood," probably reddish purple) is mentioned at the turn of the ninth century. Other early medieval colors included brown-purple, brownish gray, black, deep blue, and yellow.[29]

These dark or dun colors (e.g., "sackcloth") were often used for occasions of penitence or certain feasts of the Blessed Virgin Mary, such as Candlemas. Other festal colors—for instance, white and gold—could be used on important feast days. In general, however, on these festive occasions the parish cathedral would use its "best" or most elaborate set of vestments, irrespective of the color. In England and Spain, blue was often used for the season of Advent and feasts of the Blessed Virgin.

Pope Innocent III listed four Roman liturgical colors at the end of the twelfth century: white, red, black, and green.[30] The great French bishop and canonist William Durandus, writing at the end of the thirteenth century, noted the use of the same four liturgical colors. He mentioned that in Rome, others would be added to these four: scarlet to red; violet (or red-violet) to black; "flax" to white; and "saffron" or yellow to green. Violet might also be used in place of black on certain occasions, such as Advent, Lent, and Ember Days.[31]

After the Council of Trent, these colors became more strictly standardized for the Roman Catholic Church: white for festive occasions such as Christmas and its season, or Easter and its season; purple or violet for more penitential seasons including Lent; red for feasts of martyrs, the Holy Spirit, or other occasions such as ordinations; black for funerals, seasons of mourning and occasional feasts of the Virgin, including Candlemas; and green for the Sundays "after Pentecost," or what are today referred to in the Roman Catholic tradition as "Ordinary Time." Since Vatican II, the standard liturgical colors are much the same: white, red, green, and violet or purple.[32] Black has been made an optional color for funerals. The color rose, a light mauve, was and still may be used on two Sundays of the year: Gaudete Sunday in Advent, and Laetare Sunday in Lent. This color signifies a lightening of the penitential mood of these seasons and points ahead to the joyful feasts of Christmas and Easter. Eastern churches also use colored vestments, though not "bound so strictly to adhere to a colour sequence."[33]

Liturgical Objects and Vessels

Through the centuries the array of ceremonial objects used during the liturgy has increased in number and developed in design. These material adjuncts to worship fall into several categories.

Candles and Other Lights

The use of lights, or candles, in the Christian liturgy seems to stem from Roman civil and imperial use. Certain officials, for example, were entitled to be accompanied in the streets by torchbearers. Although in the earliest years there seems to have been a certain resistance to using candles and other lights during Christian liturgy, because this smacked of pagan and imperial cult, references to their use can be seen from at least the fourth century on. The number and size of liturgical candles grew as time progressed, not only during the celebration of mass but also for other liturgical celebrations and devotional purposes.[34]

During the Protestant Reformation, some churches retained the use of candles at the eucharist, while other, more "reformed" traditions did not. For many, the use of candles as votive lights used to reverence statues of the saints and burned in front of a tabernacle or other place of eucharist reservation made them seem generally part and parcel of the "idolatry" the reform of the church was to stamp out. In England, one can see this struggle from the sixteenth through the nineteenth centuries: those of

Puritan leanings in the earlier centuries called for the use of candles to be abandoned, and those of a more "high church" opinion (e.g., the later Tractarians) sought to reintroduce them.[35]

By the eve of the Second Vatican Council, the number and use of candles in the Roman Catholic Church was strictly specified. At least two lighted candles were to be used at low mass, while a third, special candle could be lit during the canon. At least six, and on certain solemn occasions seven, candles were to be lit for high mass. For Benediction and/or exposition of the Blessed Sacrament, at least twelve (and up to twenty) candles were to be used. The composition of these candles was also regulated: these "minimal" numbers of candles (as well as the Paschal candle, mentioned below) were to be at least 65 percent beeswax; other additional candles, 25 percent.[36]

Lights were and are also used in the Eastern churches. In the Byzantine Church, at least two candles are used during the eucharist, although more are permitted. Lights are also carried during the Little Entrance and Great Entrance processions, and during the reading of the gospel. The Coptic Church at one time placed two lights near but not on the altar; today it is permitted to have them on the altar. The Ethiopian Church mandates three candles, two on the altar at the corners of the western side, and one at the center of the eastern side. However, Ethiopian Catholics today have permission to celebrate mass without any candles in use. The Syrian traditions also use two lights.[37]

Some Eastern traditions also call for the bishop to bless the congregation using sets of blessing candles in special candelabra. Either a set of two crossed candles (*dikirotrikira*), signifying the two natures of Christ, or of three crossed candles (*trikirion*), signifying the three persons in one God, may be used.[38]

Other candles were used for special occasions during Holy Week and Easter.[39] In the medieval West, a special late night service called Tenebrae was held during the night of Holy Thursday into Good Friday. About fifteen candles (in some places during medieval period, this could range from 23 to 72 candles) would be ritually extinguished, one by one, during the service. These candles were held in a tall, elaborate candelabrum sometimes called a hearse.[40]

The paschal candle became a major focus of the Easter vigil in Christian liturgy during the fourth century. Its use seems to have originated in the ritual lighting of a lamp during the Christian evening service of *lucernarium*. A prominent candle came to be lighted from the new fire kindled at the beginning of the vigil, and it would be ritually blessed with incense and praised in the singing of the Easter proclamation, the Exsultet. As time went on, the Easter candle came to be ritually carried into the church at the beginning of the vigil; the blessing came to include the insertion of five grains of incense in a cross-like formation, symbolizing the five wounds of Christ. The size and weight of the candle increased markedly over the course of the Middle Ages, as did the height of the stand on which it was placed.[41] The paschal candle is still used in Holy Week ceremonies by Roman Catholics, and its liturgical prominence has been heightened by the reform of these rites. Some other Western Christian traditions, in the course of their own liturgical revisions, have reemphasized or reintroduced the paschal candle in their own Holy Week ceremonies.

Liturgical Vessels for the Eucharist

For the celebration of the eucharist, the two primary liturgical vessels are the chalice (*calyx*, cup) and the plate or paten.[42] The earliest chalices were probably made of glass or ceramic, although we know that other materials (e.g., horn) were used because they were prohibited later. Early chalices also tended to be large, so that many people could drink from them (the "common cup"). Both individual and common cups were used in the domestic sphere in late antiquity. In the early medieval period, large ornamental chalices, given as gifts by dignitaries, might be displayed in close proximity to the altar; so massive were they, however, that it is doubtful whether they were actually used.[43] However, other large but less massive two-handled chalices were clearly designed for actual communal use. Gradually during the Middle Ages the size of the chalice was considerably reduced, reflecting the slow but general withdrawal from the laity of communion under the species of wine. The chalice became a

The Ardagh Chalice, early 8th century.
NATIONAL MUSEUM OF IRELAND, DUBLIN/
SNARK/ART RESOURCE, NY

vessel for the use of the clergy alone. However, as the laity came to rely more and more on actually seeing the consecrated elements, chalices became more elaborately decorated, sometimes even with attached bells.[44]

The paten, or plate, containing the bread for the eucharistic celebration, also underwent development in the West. From the earliest use of baskets or "gold glass" dishes, the paten developed as a specially designed bread plate for use at eucharist. These were often more the size of platters than individual dishes and were made from gold or other precious metal. As the chalice changed during the medieval period, so did the paten. As the breads used for the mass became smaller and flatter (the "host," a term deriving from the Latin *hostia*, "victim or sacrifice"), the paten itself became smaller. As the reception of communion under the species of bread by the laity became less and less frequent, the paten needed only to be the size of the single host to be consecrated by the priest. It also became customary to fit the base of the paten so that it could be placed on top of the chalice.[45]

The Reformation and the shifts in ecclesiology and eucharistic theology that accompanied it precipitated important changes in the design of the paten and chalice in some places. Some Protestant traditions, intent on deemphasizing the adoration of the eucharistic elements and restoring instead the wider reception of both bread and cup to the entire community, stressed the use of plainer plates and chalices, using simple metals, glass, or even wood. These reformers understood their task as a call to simplify ceremonial "of human invention," and they desired to restore what they understood to be the essential meaning of cup and plate. Comments James F. White: "Hubmaier's baptizing with a milk pail was matched by Zwingli celebrating the eucharist using the common wooden platters and cups that each housewife must have scrubbed (we hope) daily. The vessels must have spoken much louder than words."[46]

Others, including the Anglicans and Lutherans, retained the use of more precious metals and added larger pitchers or flagons to refill the smaller communion chalices as needed. Additionally, in some places (e.g., the United States), communion in some churches was distributed to a seated congregation by circulating small individual glasses on communion trays.[47]

Other vessels or instruments were also in use during eucharistic celebrations. By the fourth century, flagons (*amula, urceola*) were used to hold water and wine for use during the offertory. These came to be more commonly known as cruets. They could be large or (as time went on) small, and made of precious metals or glass.[48] In the Byzantine tradition, a special pitcher (*zeon*, *thermarion*, or *kiolion*) is used to hold warm water, which is added to the chalice immediately before the distribution of communion.[49]

The Byzantine tradition also employs a cutting instrument called the lance (*kopyo*, in Slavonic) during the pre-eucharist ritual of the preparation of the bread. The lance is used to cut the portion of the leavened loaf to be used for the eucharist (the *amnos*, or "lamb") from the rest of the loaf, and to make other symbolic ritual incisions in that bread. Until the point of the recitation of the creed, a raised, crossed set of metal bands is placed over the bread on the paten (*diskos*) to keep the cloth veil covering the offering away from the surface of the bread. Because of its shape it is called the asterisk (or *asteriskos*); it is also sometimes decorated with a star at the crossbar.[50]

In the Western tradition, it was permitted in certain circumstances to use other vessels to aid in the distribution of communion. To this day in the Roman Catholic Church, for example, communion may be distributed to the communicant by means of a liturgical spoon (usually by intinction, that is, by dipping a fragment of consecrated bread in the consecrated wine) or a liturgical straw or tube (for sipping the wine alone). The use of these implements is rare, although permitted.[51] However, in some Eastern churches, communion is always distributed with the spoon. At communion time, the priest holds a large chalice containing several small pieces of consecrated bread in the wine. As communicants approach, they cross their arms over their chests and open their mouths. The priest inserts the bowl of the long-handled spoon into the mouth, then turns it over without touching the roof of the mouth or the tongue.

In the East, one frequently finds the use of ceremonial liturgical fans during the course of the eucharistic liturgy. The *ripidion* (in Latin, *flabellum*) used in several traditions has come to resemble a metal wand, with a flat metal figure of an angel or seraph forming the blade of the fan. In some traditions, one of the eucharistic cloths or veils would be waved over the elements during the anaphora (see below).

During the fourth century, beginning in the East, incense came to be used regularly at the celebration of the eucharist.[52] The dish used to hold the burning incense (incense grains poured over glowing charcoal) was called the thurible (from *thus*, "incense") or censer. Eventually these receptacles became larger, and chains with an attached cover were added so that the incense could be dispersed more easily. A smaller covered container, the "boat" or *navicella*, contained reserve grains of incense to be added as needed. For more elaborate celebrations, one acolyte, the thurifer, would be responsible for the incense alone. In some Eastern traditions the chains are shorter, with small bells attached so that they sound whenever the censer (*thymaterion* in Greek) is swung.[53]

Another liturgical object used during the medieval mass in the West was the "pax-board." From antiq-

Priests with censers, 6th century.
MONASTERY OF SAINT CATHERINE, MOUNT SINAI, EGYPT/BRIDGEMAN ART LIBRARY

Pax board. Christ with the Four Evangelists, fourteenth to fifteenth century. PALAZZO PUBBLICO, SIENA, ITALY/ART RESOURCE, NY

uity, members of the Christian community assembled for the eucharist would exchange a kiss of peace during the service, either before the gifts were brought up at the offertory or immediately before communion was distributed. With time, it became the custom for the officiating clerics only to exchange a greeting of peace in descending order of rank. They did so not always by kissing or embracing each other but by ritually circulating and kissing a flat wooden board decorated with religious imagery. This came to be called the "pax-board."[54]

Other Liturgical Vessels

Another set of vessels developed to hold the consecrated elements outside the eucharistic celebration. From earliest times, sources attest to the

Monstrance, cope, and humeral veil. In the great monastic church at El Escorial, King Charles II of Spain (1665–1700) kneels before the Blessed Sacrament. The Escorial was built outside Madrid by King Philip II (1527–1598). Painting by Claudio Coello (1642–1693). SCALA/ART RESOURCE, NY

consecrated bread being carried to those unable to attend the eucharist itself. From this practice, the small portable *arca*, *pyx*, or *theca* ("box") developed. Later, a special cupboard (sometimes a niche or recess called an aumbry) or box was used to reserve the consecrated bread for the use of the sick. This, in turn, led in many places to placing the small container or box in a sacrament tower or eucharistic dove—a metal vessel, often shaped like a dove, suspended from the ceiling of the sanctuary.[55] Finally, in the Roman Catholic tradition, this box was incorporated into the liturgical furnishing of the main sanctuary space as the tabernacle. A particular kind of container also developed in which the consecrated hosts could be reserved with some security, and from which they could be distributed to communicants as needed. This "wide-mouthed dish" came to resemble a flattened chalice, resting on a base with a stem; unlike the chalice, however, it also came with a domed lid that fit tightly over the mouth of the dish. This vessel came to be known as a ciborium, possibly derived from its resemblance to the architectural ciborium over the altar (see below).[56]

One of the most intense areas of controversy during the Reformation was the nature of the eucharist, and more specifically the presence of Christ in relation to the eucharistic elements of bread and wine. The Roman Catholic Church at the Council of Trent continued to stress the real, objective, and permanent change in the bread and wine, expressed "most appropriately" (*aptissime*) in the thirteenth-century doctrine of transubstantiation. Thus, after the Reformation, the Roman Catholic practice of blessing the congregation with the Blessed Sacrament, or exposing the Blessed Sacrament for a period of adoration and prayer, became more widespread. To facilitate this, a special stand or monstrance was used to display the host.[57] The host would be placed into a small round box with glass sides, called a *luna* or *lunette*; often this shallow cylinder was framed with gold or silver metal in the shape of a sunburst, with rays emanating from the center. All of this would be set into a fixed stand consisting of a metal stem and wide base. At the liturgy of what came to be known as Benediction, the priest would put on the humeral veil, and with this special "shawl" draped over his arms and hands, would take the monstrance from the altar, turn, and bless the congregation with the exposed sacrament.

In some Eastern traditions too the eucharistic bread came to be reserved in a cupboard or vessel within the church. One such vessel, the *artophorion*, can be seen as a "mixture of ciborium and tabernacle"[58] and is given a special place within the sanctuary.

In the early Middle Ages, sprinkling with holy water became an important part of a number of liturgical celebrations, the mass included. Appropriate liturgical vessels were used here as well: a small bucket-shaped container for the water itself, and a small staff or baton, which was dipped into the container and then swung to flick drops of holy water onto the clergy and congregation. This came to be known as an aspergil or aspergillum, and the rite itself as the Asperges, from the psalm chant commonly used to accompany it (*Asperges me, Domine*, "Wash me, Lord"; Ps. 51:4).[59]

Other vessels are used for the celebration of noneucharistic liturgies. For example, in both the East and the West (in some traditions), certain special containers are used to hold chrism or other consecrated oils. In some Western churches this is called a chrismatory; in the Byzantine tradition it is called an alabastron (*alavastr*, in Slavonic), and can be made of glass or metal.[60]

Veils, Linens, Frontals, and Rugs

The earliest altar cloths, often embroidered, were called *pallae* or palls. From these early altar cloths evolved a number of different kinds of altar covering. The white linen cloth was called the *palla corporalis* and was used only during the celebration of the eucharist. Other, silken cloths, often donated by the wealthy, developed into colored decorative fabrics. Free-standing altars came to be decorated front and back with elaborate "throw-over" frontals made of fabric or sometimes of metal. Fabric colors did not necessarily match the colors of the feast or season; again, the best or highest-quality frontal would be used for feasts, and those of lesser quality for more "ordinary" days. Later, altars set against walls would be decorated with a similar, one-sided cloth called an antependium. For the celebration of mass, other white cloths would be placed on the altar on top of this one: a longer, narrow white undercloth, and a smaller, square corporal on top, specifically for the chalice and paten.[61] Other small cloths were also provided for use at certain points during the mass: the small linen finger towel, usually used to wipe the presider's fingers dry after the ritual handwashing (the *lavabo*) at the offertory; and the larger purificator, normally used to wipe the lip of the chalice after the presider (and today, other communicants) received the consecrated wine. It could also be used after communion to wipe the chalice clean (to "purify" it) after it had been rinsed.

As time went on, it became the custom to veil the chalice at the start of mass. These "palls" or chalice veils were often heavily embroidered, and the background color came to match the liturgical color of the day. The corporal would also be brought in with the chalice, folded into a stiff, square fabric envelope called a burse. This, too, came to match the chalice veil in color and decoration. These fell into disuse after the liturgical renewal of Vatican II.

Another kind of veil or pall is used during funeral liturgy: the funeral pall. Today this is a large white cloth, often embroidered with a cross or other design, that is ritually spread over the casket after it has been brought in the rear door of the church for the funeral. Family members may take part in this ritual act, which is meant to bring to mind the white garment of baptism donned by the deceased earlier in life.

The Eastern churches also make use of special altar linens or cloths: in Byzantine and Greek use there are several types of veil (*sindon*). The altar is clothed with a large underlying cloth (*katasarkion*), on top of which rests another (*ependysis*). The paten and chalice are veiled by the *aer* (Greek), and a purificator or sponge may also be used (*mousa*, Greek). In the Byzantine rite, a special cloth or veil, the *epitaphion*, is used during Holy Week and Easter. As the name suggests, this cloth is decorated with a picture of the burial of Christ; it is carried in procession twice during Holy Week and remains in the church as a special object of veneration during the Easter season.

Other kinds of larger "architectural" cloths or veils have also been used in Christian liturgy. From the fourth century, references are made to a canopy supported over the altar. These canopies were made of wood or metal, a four-posted frame with a dome over the altar and immediate surrounding area. In the East, the custom of veiling the altar during the eucharist seems to have begun in the fourth century; as time progressed, the chancel barrier and icon stand developed into the sanctuary "wall" known as the iconostasis in some Eastern rites, making these earlier veils obsolete.[62] In the West, from the seventh century, rings or rods for fabric altar veils might be attached to these frames in some places. However, altar veils in the West seem to have fallen into disuse, certainly by the thirteenth century, perhaps because of the shift from "oral" to "ocular" communion and the increasing need for the people to be able to see the newly added elevation of the host at the consecration.[63] It has been suggested that the custom of veiling the sanctuary area during Lent (in England, Germany, parts of Spain and Italy) is a vestige of the more general use of altar veils.[64] For example, in the eleventh century it became the custom in some churches to erect a special veil in front of the altar itself, called a "hunger cloth," from the fifth Sunday of Lent (formerly known as the first Sunday of Passiontide) on.[65] The purpose was to block the altar from the view of the congregation, sometimes explained as a "fast of the eyes."[66] Hunger cloths were later reduced in size; in fact, they are still designed and displayed as objects for meditation today.[67]

The custom of veiling statues of Mary and the saints and crucifixes during Lent also seems to date from the high Middle Ages.[68] This custom continued in Roman Catholic churches until the Second Vatican Council, when it was made an optional observance. It is interesting to note that, while veneration of the wood of the Cross on Good Friday seems to have begun in the fourth century, the use of crucifixes depicting the suffering Christ on the Cross for this Good Friday ceremony (held on other occasions as well) seems to have begun in Germany in the eleventh century.[69]

Finally, an important Eastern liturgical floor covering, one without any corresponding parallel in the West, should be noted. In Byzantine and Slavonic churches, a special rug called the *aetos* (*orletz*), or "eagle," is provided for the bishop when he presides at the liturgy. It is a semicircular rug depicting an eagle flying over a battlemented city, and it appears to have been "a wholesale adoption of the mark of the Byzantine imperial court."[70] It is also used by the candidate during the liturgy for the consecration of a bishop; he stands on different sections of the rug during certain parts of the rite.

Changing Use and Changeless Meaning

It is clear that as the Christian liturgy itself changed and developed over the course of the past twenty centuries, the vestments and vessels used during these celebrations did also. Not only have their various shapes and sizes changed, and their ornamentation become more or less elaborate, but also their significance to the rites has been understood and interpreted differently by different generations. One thing should remain clear, however: in a Christian faith founded on the key theological concept of the incarnation, no physical expression of that incarnate and redeemed reality can be dismissed as insignificant.

Bibliography

Chrysostomos, Archimandrite. *Orthodox Liturgical Dress*. Brookline, Mass.: Holy Cross Orthodox Press, 1981.

Foley, Edward. *From Age to Age: How Christians Have Celebrated the Eucharist*. Chicago: Liturgy Training Publications, 1991.

Holeton, David R. "Vestments." In *The New Westminster Dictionary of Liturgy & Worship*, edited by Paul F. Bradshaw, 464–471. Louisville: Westminster/John Knox, 2002.

Mayo, Janet. *A History of Ecclesiastical Dress*. London: Batsford, 1984.

Norris, Herbert. *Church Vestments: Their Origin and Development*. New York: Dutton, 1950; repr. Mineola, N.Y.: Dover, 2002.

Pierce, Joanne. "Early Medieval Vesting Prayers in the *Ordo Missae* of Sigebert of Minden (1022–1036)." In *Rule of Prayer, Rule of Faith: Essays in Honor of Aidan Kavanagh, O.S.B.*, edited by Nathan Mitchell and John Baldovin, 80–105. Collegeville, Minn.: Liturgical Press, 1996.

Pocknee, Cyril. *The Christian Altar in History and Today*. London: Mowbray, 1963.

Reynolds, Roger. "Vestments, Liturgical." In *Dictionary of the Middle Ages*, vol. 12. New York: Charles Scribner's Sons, 1982.

Notes

[1]Aidan Kavanagh, "Liturgical Vestiture in the Roman Catholic Tradition," in *Raiment for the Lord's Service: A Thousand Years of Western Vestments*, ed. Christa C. Mayer-Thurman (Chicago: Art Institute of Chicago, 1975) 13.

[2]There are several standard works on liturgical vestments. The most comprehensive is Joseph Braun, *Die liturgische Gewandung im Occident und Orient* (Freiburg im Breisgau: Herder, 1907); a much condensed article, "Vestments," appears in *The Catholic Encyclopedia*, vol. 15 (1912) and is accessible at www.newadvent.org. Other summaries include "Vestments," by Gilbert Cope, in *The New Westminster Dictionary of Liturgy and Worship* (Philadelphia: Westminster, 1986), hereafter *NWDLW*; "Vestments, Liturgical," by John D. Laurence, in *The New Dictionary of Sacramental Worship* (Collegeville, Minn.: Liturgical Press, 1990), hereafter *NDSW*; Mayo, *A History of Ecclesiastical Dress*; Cyril Pocknee, *Liturgical Vestiture: Its Origins and Development* (London: Mowbray, 1961); Ludwig Eisenhofer, *Handbuch der katholischen Liturgik*, vol. 1 (Freiburg im Breisgau: Herder, 1932) 342–472. For Roman Catholic vestments on the eve of the Second Vatican Council, see Adrian Fortescue and J. B. O'Connell, *The Ceremonies of the Roman Rite Described* (Westminster, Md.: Newman, 1962) 31–35.

[3]Ronald John Zawilla, "The Alb," in *Clothed in Glory: Vesting the Church*, ed. David Philippart (Chicago: LTP, 1997) 8–11.

[4]Ronald John Zawilla, "Vesting the Ordained," in *Clothed in Glory*, 22–23.

[5]For a complete discussion of the development of medieval vestments in the West, see Roger Reynolds, "Vestments, Liturgical."

[6]See Pierce, "Early Medieval Vesting Prayers." See also Josef A. Jungmann, *The Mass of the Roman Rite*, vol. 1 (New York: Benziger, 1951) 286; and Braun, 149–247.

[7]Jungmann, 1:280–281. Following Braun, he notes three general categories of allusions, from the earliest to the more recent: moral/ethical; the priest as Christ; and the mass as Christ's Passion.

[8]Pierce, 91. A second, slightly longer oration accompanied the act of putting on the stole, alluding to the "easy yoke" of Jesus Christ (Matt. 11:29–30); see p. 92.

[9]Latin text from the *Missale Romanum* (New York: Benziger, 1961) lxvii; approved English translation from *My Sunday Missal* (n.p.: Confraternity of the Precious Blood, 1944) 12.

[10]"General Instruction to the Roman Missal," no. 81.

[11]Braun, "Vestments."

[12]CCCM 140 (1995), 140A (1998), 140B (2000).

[13]Braun, "Vestments."

[14]Ronald John Zawilla, "The Cope," in *Clothed in Glory*, 37–40.

[15]Cope, "Vestments."

[16]For more detail and further bibliography, see Joachim Heubach, "Geistliche Kleidung," in *Evangelisches Kirchenlexikon*, vol. 2 (1988) cols. 34–39.

[17]See *NWDLW*, "Colours, Liturgical," by Gilbert Cope.

[18]Heubach, cols. 37–38; and Cope, "Colours, Liturgical," 180.

[19]See individual entries in Elisabeth Trenkle, *Liturgische Geräte und Gewänder der Ostkirche* (Munich: Slavisches Institut, 1962), and in Peter D. Day, ed., *A Liturgical Dictionary of Eastern Christianity* (Collegeville, Minn.: Liturgical Press, 1993), hereafter *LDEC*. The latter is especially helpful in providing "A Quick Reference Guide" index of names of vestments and objects that vary from rite to rite (315–327), as well as a comparative table of Eastern and Western vestments (Table 6, 333). See also Braun, *Die liturgische Gewandung*. For a more complete discussion in English, see Chrysostomos, *Orthodox Liturgical Dress*.

[20]Chrysostomos, 45–46.

[21]Chrysostomos, 32, 49–50.

[22]Chrysostomos's point here is that these elements were influenced by clothing and other insignia used in the imperial court, and are thus distinctly different from Western vestments.

[23]Chrysostomos, 57.

[24]Chrysostomos, 60.

[25]Chrysostomos, 62–63.

[26]*LDEC*, "Zewd."

[27]Cope, "Colours, Liturgical"; see also Reynolds, "Colors, Liturgical," 484–485; and G. Thomas Ryan, "The Use of Liturgical Colors," in *Clothed in Glory*, 41–43. For a more complete discussion, see William Hope and E. G. Cuthbert F. Atchley, *An Introduction to English Liturgical Colours* (London: SPCK; New York, Macmillan, 1920).

[28]Hope and Atchley, 24–25.

[29]Hope and Atchley, 25–26.

[30]*De sacro altaris in mysterio* 24; cited in Pocknee, *The Christian Altar*, 48.

[31]Cited in Pocknee, 48. For the original citation, see A. Davril and Timothy M. Thibodeau, eds., *Guillelmi Duranti, Rationale Divinorum Officiorum I–IV* (Turnholt: Brepols, 1995), 3.18.1, 8; CCCM 140.

[32]Laurance, "Vestments, Liturgical," 1311–1312. He notes a distinction made in the United States between the bluish violet (Advent) and the reddish purple (Lent).

[33]Cope, "Colours," 179.

[34]See D. R. Dendy, *The Use of Lights in Christian Worship*, Alcuin Club Collections 41 (London: SPCK, 1959) for a more detailed discussion.

[35]Dendy, 151–175.

[36]Fortescue and O'Connell, 28–29.

[37]*LDEC*, "Lights on Altar, The."

[38]Trenkle, "Dikirotrikira"; and Chrysostomos, 64.

[39]See Dendy, 128–150, for an overview.

[40]See Joanne M. Pierce, "Holy Week and Easter in the Middle Ages," in *Passover and Easter: Origin and History to Modern Times*, Two Liturgical Traditions 5, ed. Paul Bradshaw and Lawrence Hoffman (Notre Dame: University of Notre Dame Press, 1999) 167. For a complete description, see A. J. MacGregor, *Fire and Light in the Western Triduum*, Alcuin Club Collections 71 (Collegeville, Minn.: Liturgical Press, 1992) 7–132.

[41]Pierce, "Holy Week," 173–174, and MacGregor, 299–319.

[42]For an introduction to liturgical books, music, and vessels throughout Christian history, see Edward Foley, *From Age to Age*. For a short summary, see also *NDSW*, "Vessels, Sacred," by T. Jerome Overbeck. For a complete discussion of the Christian altar, furnishings, and vessels, see Braun, *Das christliche Altargerät* (Munich: Hueber, 1932).

[43]Overbeck, 1301.

[44]Foley, 37–39, 60–63, 85–86, 110–111.

[45]Foley, 37–38, 58–60, 83–85, 108.

[46]James F. White, *A Brief History of Christian Worship* (Nashville, Tenn.: Abingdon, 1993) 123.

[47]Foley, 136–137, citing James F. White, *Protestant Worship and Church Architecture* (New York: Oxford University Press, 1964).

[48]Foley, 62–63.

[49]*LDEC*, "Zeon."

[50]*LDEC*, "Asterisk."

[51]See *NDSW*, "Chalice, Modes of Distribution of," by John M. Huels, 175–176.

[52]Michael Pfeifer, *Der Weihrauch: Geschichte, Bedeutung, Verwendung* (Regensburg: F. Pustet, 1997) 45–53. Other background reading on incense includes E. G. Cuthbert F. Atchley, *A History of the Use of Incense in Divine Worship* (London: Longmans, Green, 1909); and Roger E. Reynolds, "Incense," DMA, 6:431–433.

[53]See *LDEC* under individual entries; also Trenkle, "Weihrauchfass."

[54]See Jungmann, 1:330–332.

[55]See S. J. P. van Dijk and J. Hazelden Walker, *The Myth of the Aumbry: Notes on Medieval Reservation Practice and Eucharistic Devotion* (London: Burns and Oates, 1957).

[56]Pocknee, 56. See also Nathan Mitchell, *Cult and Controversy* (Collegeville, Minn.: Liturgical Press, 1982); and Miri Rubin, *Corpus Christi: The Eucharist in Late Medieval Culture* (Cambridge: Cambridge University Press, 1991) for more complete treatments.

[57]See Foley, 134–135.

[58]*LDEC*, "Artophorion."

[59]See Overbeck, 1303–1304.

[60]*LDEC*, "Alabastron."

[61]*NWDLW*, "Veil," by C. E. Pocknee and G. D. W. Randall, 518; see also G. Thomas Ryan, "The Altar Cloths and Other Linens," in *Clothed in Glory*, 60–67.

[62]Pocknee, 45–47.

[63]Pocknee, 60; and Foley, 111.

[64]See Pocknee, 56–62, for a more complete discussion.

[65]Pocknee, 62–63.

[66]Adolf Adam, *The Liturgical Year* (New York: Pueblo; Collegeville, Minn.: Liturgical Press, 1981) 106.

67 Adam, 106.

68 Adam, after the eleventh century; Pocknee, from the tenth century. "At that time Christ was depicted on the Cross as alive and triumphant rather than in anguish of death, while statues of the Saints were intended to reflect their heavenly glory. To veil these things during the penitential season of Lent seemed fitting and appropriate" (Pocknee, 63).

69 See Pierce, "Holy Week," 167–169, especially n. 40; and Pierce, "New Research Directions in Medieval Liturgy: The Liturgical Books of Sigebert of Minden (1022–1036)," in *Fountain of Life,* ed. Gerard Austin (Washington, D.C.: Pastoral Press, 1991) 51–67.

70 *LDEC,* "Orletz"; and Chrysostomos, 63.

34

Retrospect and Prospect

GEOFFREY WAINWRIGHT AND
KAREN B. WESTERFIELD TUCKER

In October 1930, the English novelist Evelyn Waugh undertook a journalistic assign-
ment to Ethiopia, a nation whose biblical connections reach back to the queen of
Sheba's visit to King Solomon (1 Kings 10:1–13) and whose introduction to Christianity may have taken place through a court official converted under Philip the Evangelist (Acts 8:27–39). Waugh was to cover the coronation of Ras Tafari as emperor of
Ethiopia under the name Haile Selassie I. His description of the splendid rite combines literary flair with poking gentle fun at liturgical scholarship, even while displaying a disregard for the distinction between the Coptic and Ethiopic traditions:

> The ceremony was immensely long, even according to the original schedule, and the
> clergy succeeded in prolonging it by at least an hour and a half beyond the allotted time.
> The six succeeding days of celebration were to be predominantly military, but the coro-
> nation day itself was to be in the hands of the Church, and they were going to make the
> most of it. Psalms, canticles, and prayers succeeded each other, long passages of Scrip-
> ture were read, all in the extinct ecclesiastical tongue, Ghiz. Candles were lit one by one;
> the coronation oaths were proposed and sworn; the diplomats shifted uncomfortably in
> their gilt chairs, noisy squabbles broke out round the entrance between the imperial
> guard and the retainers of the local chiefs. Professor W., who was an expert of high
> transatlantic reputation on Coptic ritual, occasionally remarked: "They are beginning
> the Mass now," "That was the offertory," "No, I was wrong; it was the consecration,"
> "No, I was wrong; I think it is the secret Gospel," "No, I think it must be the Epistle,"
> "How very curious; I don't believe it was the Mass at all," "*Now* they *are* beginning the
> Mass . . . " and so on.
>   Presently the bishops began to fumble among the bandboxes, and investiture began. At
> long intervals the emperor was presented with robe, orb, spurs, spear, and finally with the
> crown. A salute of guns was fired, and the crowds outside, scattered all over the surround-
> ing waste spaces, began to cheer; the imperial horses reared up, plunged on top of each
> other, kicked the gilding off the front of the coach, and broke their traces. The coachman
> sprang from the box and whipped them from a safe distance. Inside the pavilion there was
> a general sense of relief; it had all been very fine and impressive, now for a cigarette, a
> drink, and a change into less formal costume. Not a bit of it. The next thing was to crown
> the empress and the heir apparent; another salvo of guns followed, during which an Abys-
> sinian groom had two ribs broken in an attempt to unharness a pair of the imperial horses.
> Again we felt for our hats and gloves. But the Coptic choir still sang; the bishops then
> proceeded to take back the regalia with proper prayers, lections, and canticles.
>   "I have noticed some very curious variations in the Canon of the Mass," remarked the
> professor, "particularly with regard to the kiss of peace."

Then the Mass began. . . .

It was now about eleven o'clock, the time at which the emperor was due to leave the pavilion. Punctually to plan, three Abyssinian aeroplanes rose to greet him. They circled round and round over the tent, eagerly demonstrating their newly acquired art by swooping and curvetting within a few feet of the canvas roof. The noise was appalling; the local chiefs stirred in their sleep and rolled on to their faces; only by the opening and closing of their lips and the turning of their music could we discern that the Coptic deacons were still singing.

"A most unfortunate interruption. I missed many of the verses," said the professor.

Eventually, at about half-past twelve, the Mass came to an end.[1]

In October 1962, the Second Vatican Council opened at Saint Peter's basilica in Rome with a ceremony that would doubtless have pleased Evelyn Waugh, a Catholic attached to the old ways, but that was not to the liking of Yves Congar, the French Dominican theologian:

I try to grasp the *genius loci*. St Peter's was made FOR THAT. The colors are enchanting, gold and red predominating. The nave is entirely filled with 2,500 banked seats; in front of the altar of the confession, on the confession itself, the throne of the pope, *Petrus ipse*. To the right, the statue of St. Peter is robed as Boniface VIII; nearby, in the shape of a barrel, the ambo for the speakers. . . . All of it shimmers, sparkles, sings under the spotlights. Very solemn, but a little cold. Decor somewhat in a baroque theatrical style. . . .

At 8.35 one hears over the microphone the distant sound of a half-military march. Then the *Credo* is sung. I came here TO PRAY, to pray WITH, to pray IN. And I did indeed pray a lot. Yet, to kill time, a choir intoned anything and everything. The best known chants: *Credo, Magnificat, Adoro Te, Salve Regina, Veni Sancte Spiritus, Inviolata, Benedictus*. . . . To begin with, one sings along a little, but one gets tired of it. . . .

Dear God, you have brought me here by ways I did not choose. I offer myself to you to be, if you will it, an instrument of your Gospel in this event in the life of your Church, which I love, but I wish it all were less "Renaissance"! Less Constantinian. . . .

Applause from St. Peter's Square. The Pope [John XXIII] must be approaching, entering. . . .

Alternating chant of the *Veni Creator* by the Sistine choir, which is nothing but an opera company. DELENDA [should be abolished]. The Pope, in a firm voice, sings the versicles and the prayers.

The Mass begins, with only the Sistine choir singing: a few items of Gregorian chant (?) and polyphony. The Liturgical Movement has not yet found its way into the Roman Curia. This vast congregation says nothing, sings nothing.

It's said that the Jewish people is a people of the ear, the Greeks a people of the eye. Here we have stuff only for the eye and for the musical ear: no liturgy of the Word. No spiritual word. I know that soon a throne will be installed, to preside over the Council, a Bible. But WILL IT SPEAK? Will it be heard? Will there be a moment for the Word of God?[2]

Things had not changed much by the opening of the second session of the council in September 1963:

About 10 o'clock, distant, then getting closer, the sound of the Sistine choir singing. The Pope [Paul VI] is about to make his entrance. But before him, the Curia: Swiss guards with their halberds, cardinal priests and cardinal deacons topped with very tall miters, prelates in purple and red, chamberlains in sixteenth-century dress, the bearers of the papal tiara and miter, finally the Pope, sandwiched between a deacon and a sub-deacon carrying the ceremonial fans. The Pope enters on foot. As he advances down the nave, the benches applaud his passing. . . .

I can give no ecclesiological interpretation to the shape of the ceremony: between two hedges of bishops as silent spectators, the pontifical court passes, dressed as in the sixteenth century, preceding a pope who thus appears as both a temporal sovereign and a very superior hierarch.

The Sistine choir coos away: the Fathers take up a verse or two of the *Ave Maris Stella*. Will the church keep THIS face? THIS appearance? Will she long continue to give THAT sign? It seems clear to me, at this moment, that the Gospel IS in the Church, but as a prisoner.

Paul VI intones the *Veni Creator*. The Church rediscovers her voice, a voice like many waters, in order to implore God. When the Pope alternates verses with the bishops, it is Peter praying with the Twelve. He is no longer the temporal prince of the sixteenth century.

The bishops have asked to sing the ordinary of the Mass. The Sistine choir coos a Kyrie and will later coo an Agnus Dei, not without displaying admirable voices; but the bishops sing the Gloria, the Credo, the Sanctus. We sing wholeheartedly with them, as far as strength allows. Thus, in the singing as in the entire ceremony, the truth of the *Ecclesia* and the manners of the Renaissance alternate.

Cardinal Tisserant celebrates: badly and unpersuasively.[3]

On 4 December 1963, the Second Vatican Council promulgated as its first text the Constitution on the Sacred Liturgy, *Sacrosanctum Concilium*. The door was thereby opened to implementing many of the desiderata of the Liturgical Movement, epitomized by the phrase "a full, conscious, devout, and active participation of the faithful" (cf. *Sacrosanctum Concilium*, 14, 48, 50). Confluent developments in many Protestant churches in the second half of the twentieth century are chronicled in Chapters 10–22 of this book.

In April 2005, one of us attended the funeral mass for Pope John Paul II, and one of us the inauguration mass of his successor. The papal funeral brought millions of

pilgrims to Rome by rapid means of transportation. People stood for many hours in line to pray before the body of the deceased pontiff lying in state in Saint Peter's. Images of this respect were relayed across the globe by Internet and television.

The mass was celebrated in the open air, on the steps in front of the basilica. The crowds filled the square and stretched back along the Via della Conciliazione as far as the river. Large screens rendered the service electronically visible, and the overflow was accommodated in the larger Roman churches. The event was televised worldwide. The ordinary of the mass and the litany of the saints were prayed and sung in Latin, including Eucharistic Prayer I or the old Roman canon, with the vast throngs joining in the chants. The scripture lessons and the biddings for intercession were read

A papal mass. Pope Benedict XVI censing the altar at the mass in Saint Peter's Square inaugurating his pontificate, April 2005. PHOTOGRAPH BY KAREN WESTERFIELD TUCKER

and spoken in several European, African, and Asian languages, preponderantly by younger men and women. After communion, chants from the Byzantine office of the dead were sung by choirs of the Eastern Catholic rites.

Both the funeral mass and the inauguration mass were presided over by the same man, first as dean of the College of Cardinals, and then after his election as Pope Benedict XVI. As Joseph Ratzinger (born 1927), he had written on the subject of Christian worship with theological insight, pastoral grace, and aesthetic sensitivity – though not without incurring the criticism of some professional liturgical scholars.[4] He celebrated and preached with dignity and vigor in both masses. At the funeral of John Paul II, his eulogy-cum-homily was frequently interrupted by applause and studded with popular cries of "*Santo subito, Santo subito,*" calling for the immediate proclamation of the departed pontiff's sainthood. At Benedict XVI's own inauguration, he preached from the twenty-first chapter of Saint John's Gospel on the twofold vocation of Peter as shepherd and fisherman: to tend and feed Christ's flock, including those who were not yet in the one fold (John 21:15–19; cf. 10:1–18), and to bring home a large catch that yet would not rend the net (21:1–14). Again his homily was punctuated with applause, as if in demonstration of one of the preacher's themes: "*La Chiesa è viva,*" "The Church is alive."

The coronation of an Ethiopian emperor, the opening of a Roman council, the services of transition from one pope to another: these vignettes—each including a eucharistic celebration—illustrate the persistence of accumulated traditions from ancient into recent and contemporary times, with shifts in style and ambience that testify to cultural change and technical development. The history of Christian worship is marked by high points that may occur only once in a lifetime, but (as the present book has shown) its detailed texture is woven Sunday by Sunday, even day by day, in cathedrals and parish churches, in monasteries and mission stations, in dissenting meeting houses and denominational chapels. Liturgy marks and is marked by the natural rhythms of times and seasons; it commemorates by calendar the great events in the story of redemption; it unites the generations in the communion of the saints and anticipates the completion of God's reign.

The ancient churches of both East and West have the longest and perhaps the most colorful record (Chapters 2–7), but the churches of the Reformation—Lutheran, Reformed, Anglican, Mennonite, or Baptist—also have their characteristic stories, confessionally, geographically, and culturally shaped (Chapters 8–20). In the English-speaking world in particular, the linguistic qualities of the prayer books of the sixteenth century have sustained and tolerated a considerable variety of liturgical performance, both official and unofficial, in Anglican churches. The mainstay of Methodist worship has been hymnody, which was for a century and a half chiefly reliant on the Wesleyan *Collection* of 1780; and then the more broadly based *Methodist Hymn Book* of 1933 shaped the entire life of the British Methodist Church for most of the twentieth century. At yet another point on the ecclesiastical spectrum stands the "undenominational conventicle" built around preacher, sermon, and song (with the hymns known by the name of their tunes), whimsically yet not unsympathetically described by the poet John Betjeman, himself of high-church inclination:

> Undenominational
>> But still the church of God
> He stood in his conventicle
>> And ruled it with a rod.

Undenominational
    The walls around him rose,
The lamps within their brackets shook
    To hear the hymns he chose.

"Glory" "Gospel" "Russell Place"
    "Wrestling Jacob" "Rock"
"Saffron Walden" "Safe at Home"
    "Dorking" "Plymouth Dock"

I slipped about the chalky lane
    That runs around the park,
I saw the lone conventicle
    A beacon in the dark.

Revival ran along the hedge
    And made my spirit whole
When steam was on the window panes
    And glory in my soul.[5]

In the nature of the case, this book has been an exercise in retrospect. What are the prospects for Christian worship? Predictions would be foolhardy, but a few trends and challenges may be mentioned.[6]

The Orthodox churches, whose liturgies have shown the fewest structural changes in a thousand years and more, are confronted with the world of late modernity. As long as the Soviet empire lasted, the liturgy proved an unparalleled gathering point for the Christian faith amid the atheistic ideology of Marxism, but now secularism takes the form of Western materialism. In the Western diaspora, the Orthodox face questions concerning ethnic identity as well as cultural assimilation to a wider society about whose dangers the Russian-American priest and liturgical theologian Alexander Schmemann (1921–1983) never ceased to warn his fellow believers and worshipers, tracing its secularism to very deep historical and theological roots.[7]

The Catholic Church, particularly of the "Latin" rite, faces in the realm of worship, as in other areas of its life, the need to discern and define the potential and limits of a pluralism that maintains the historic faith, allowing diversity of expression yet not succumbing to the ideological "dictatorship of relativism" against which Benedict XVI warned on the eve of his election. Already in the later years of Pope John Paul II, the Roman authorities felt impelled to insist on closer adherence to the normative Latin in vernacular translations (*Liturgiam Authenticam*, 2001), on a correct doctrine of Christ's presence and the sacrificial character of the mass (*Ecclesia de Eucharistia*, 2003), and on the proper conduct of the eucharistic celebration (*Redemptionis Sacramentum*, 2004).[8] The question of translation has proved particularly controversial in the English-speaking world, especially perhaps in North America, on account of concerns about "gendered language" and "inclusivity."[9] On the manner and matter of the mass, the Instruction of 2004 lays down, for example:

> The celebration of Holy Mass is not to be inserted in any way into the setting of a common meal, nor joined with this kind of banquet. Mass is not to be celebrated without grave necessity on a dinner table, nor in a dining room or banquet hall, nor in a room where food is present, nor in a place where the participants during the celebration itself are seated at tables. (77).

> The bread used in the celebration of the Most Holy Eucharistic Sacrifice must be un-leavened, purely of wheat, and recently made so that there is no danger of decomposi-

tion. . . . It is a grave abuse to introduce other substances, such as fruit or sugar or honey, into the bread for confecting the Eucharist. (48)

Both the Catholic Church and the churches of the Reformation are suffering steep demographic decline in their historic heartlands of Europe, but over the past two centuries, by migrations and missions, their patterns of worship have spread to other parts of the world. What part will worship play in attempts to "re-evangelize" Europe in the face of secularism, neo-paganism, and the presence of Islam? To invoke Evelyn Waugh for one last time: in his short story of 1933, "Out of Depth," a Mr. Rip Van Winkle is propelled into the twenty-fifth cen-

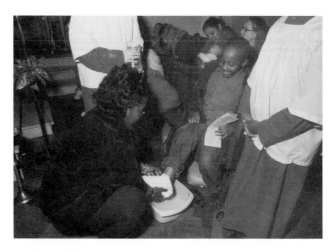

Foot washing. The Maundy Thursday ritual at Saint Joseph's Catholic Church, Roehampton, Surrey, England. Many Western churches have rediscovered this ancient and evangelical gesture of humility and service (John 13:1–19). PHOTOGRAPH BY HELENE ROGERS/ART DIRECTORS AND TRIP

tury, where London has become a village of huts on stilts in the Thames and the land is ruled by African colonizers who treat him as an anthropological specimen. He is taken by cargo boat to the coast, and there encounters "something that was new and yet ageless. The word 'Mission' painted on a board; a black man dressed as a Dominican friar":

> Something was being done . . . something that twenty-five centuries had not altered. . . . In a log-built church at the coast town he was squatting among a native congregation; some of them in cast-off uniforms; the women had shapeless, convent-sewn frocks; all round him, dishevelled white men were staring ahead with vague, uncomprehending eyes, to the end of the room where two candles burned. The priest turned towards them his bland, black face. "Ite, missa est."
> The mass had ended.[10]

Conversely, and in a more proximate future, how will the rapid growth of both Catholicism and Protestantism in parts of Africa and Asia affect the liturgies inherited by the early generations of converts and already to some modest degree "adapted" to local conditions and cultures (as recounted in Chapters 25 and 26)?

More radically, the "southward" shift in the distribution and gravitational center of Christianity is producing ecclesiological and liturgical forms that differ considerably from classical Protestantism or modern Catholicism. In his construction of "the next Christendom," Philip Jenkins wrote in 2002:

> By most accounts, membership in Pentecostal and independent churches already runs into the hundreds of millions, and congregations are located in precisely the regions of fastest population growth. Within a few decades, such denominations will represent a far larger segment of global Christianity, and just conceivably a majority. These newer churches preach deep personal faith and communal orthodoxy, mysticism and puritanism, all founded on clear scriptural authority. They preach messages that, to a Westerner, appear simplistically charismatic, visionary, and apocalyptic. In this thought-world,

A Korean congregation at mass, St. Anne's Catholic Church. Photograph by Hélène Rogers/Art Directors and TRIP

prophecy is an everyday reality, while faith-healing, exorcism, and dream-visions are all basic components of religious sensibility.[11]

Jenkins notes that "in Tanzania, charismatic services are marked by 'rapturous singing and rhythmic hand-clapping, with prayers for healing and miraculous signs'"; and he cites Harvey Cox's *Fire from Heaven* for the view that African Initiated Churches should be placed firmly within the Pentecostal landscape on account of their "free wheeling, Spirit-filled" style of worship, which "exhibits all the features of pentecostal spirituality we have found from Boston to Seoul to Rio de Janeiro."[12]

In the United States, worship practices are diverse and variegated—across the range of ecclesiastical traditions and even within a single denomination—causing some to wonder if a new ecumenism of elective affinities may emerge based on worship style. Many congregations, especially those in "mainline" Protestant denominations that are in decline, are striving to take seriously the new mission field in their backyard by drawing from an array of approaches to worship, some of which depart from the denominationally approved standard that is typically an order indebted to the Liturgical Movement. Among the current forms are a more music-driven "praise and worship" style and "emerging" worship that borrows forms past and present.[13] Yet the willingness to adopt idioms and technological forms from popular culture may come at a price; and some have returned to more "traditional" forms in order to reclaim the sense of mystery lost in an instant-messaging age.

A worldwide electronic culture, with the sights even more important than the sounds, began to develop in the later twentieth century. The Australian Jesuit Richard Leonard writes thus:

> Ignatian spirituality holds that God can be found everywhere but in evil. As liturgists, then, we need to enter the modern media market place where, these days, we have unashamedly to compete with other groups for minds, hearts and values. If we take seriously the idea that liturgy intersects with real life and celebrates it, if as liturgists we are aware that public prayer requires a composition of place, then we need to take very seriously the media the assembly watches *before* they walk into the church so as to enhance what they do in the church and what they take away from it.[14]

Particularly among some Evangelical Protestants, and in moves toward "contemporary worship," electronics have already entered the liturgy through musical forms and as a visual vehicle in preach-

The present and future Church. Three teens profess faith at Neland Avenue Christian Reformed Church, Grand Rapids, Michigan. Photograph by Edwin de Jong, Visual EdJ Productions

ing. At other points along the ecclesiastical and cultural range, the iconic has been re-covered, whether as an instructional aid (like the "bible of the poor" of old) or even as a medium of prayer.

What will, by definition, prolong the history of Christian worship is the continu-ing gathering of people, in faith and in the name of Jesus, to encounter in praise and prayer, in scripture and sermon, in sacrament and song, the God understood to be self-revealed as Father, Son, and Holy Spirit, and thus communally to exercise the vocation and fulfill the destiny for which they as humans were created and redeemed.

Notes

[1]Evelyn Waugh, *Remote People* (London: Duckworth, 1931) 56–58.

[2]Yves Congar, *Mon journal du concile*, vol. 1 (Paris: Cerf, 2002) 106–107 (Wainwright translation).

[3]Congar, 401–402.

[4]Joseph Ratzinger, *Das Fest des Glaubens: Versuche zur Theologie des Gottesdienstes* (Einsiedeln: Johannes, 1981); English ed., *The Feast of Faith: Approaches to a Theology of the Liturgy*, trans. Graham Harrison (San Francisco: Ignatius, 1986); Ratzinger, *Neues Lied für den Herrn* (Freiburg im Breisgau: Herder, 1995); English ed., *A New Song for the Lord: Faith in Christ and Liturgy Today*, trans. Martha M. Matesich (New York: Crossroad, 1996); Ratzinger, *Der Geist der Liturgie: Eine Einführung* (Freiburg im Breisgau: Herder, 2000); English ed., *The Spirit of the Liturgy*, trans. John Saward (San Francisco: Ignatius, 2000). Criticisms in Angelus A. Häussling, "*Der Geist der Liturgie*: Zu Joseph Ratzingers gleichnamiger Publikation," *Archiv für Liturgiewissenschaft* 43–44 (2001–2002) 362–395 (including references to other criticisms and Cardinal Ratzinger's responses). A nuanced appreciation is found in John Baldovin, "Cardinal Ratzinger as Liturgical Critic," in *Studia Liturgica Diversa: Essays in Honor of Paul F. Bradshaw*, ed. Maxwell E. Johnson and L. Edward Phillips (Portland, Ore.: Pastoral Press, 2004) 211–27.

[5]John Betjeman, "Undenominational," originally published in *Continual Dew* (1937), from *John Betjeman's Collected Poems*, 2nd ed. (London: John Murray, 1962) 35–36.

[6]A dozen essays by Roman Catholic writers (mainly Jesuits) on some of these issues can be found in Keith Pecklers, ed., *Liturgy in a Postmodern World* (London and New York: Continuum, 2003).

[7]See, characteristically, Alexander Schmemann, *Church, World, Mission: Reflections on Orthodoxy in the West* (Crestwood, N.Y.: St. Vladimir's Seminary Press, 1979).

[8]Congregation for Divine Worship and the Disci-pline of the Sacraments, "*Liturgiam Authenticam*": *Fifth Instruction on Vernacular Translation of the Ro-man Liturgy*, Latin-English edition (Washington, D.C.: United States Conference of Catholic Bish-ops, 2001). Pope John Paul II, "*Ecclesia de Eucharistia*": *Encyclical Letter on the Eucharist in Its Relation to the Church* (Vatican City: Libreria Editrice Vaticana, 2003); cf. Geoffrey Wainwright, "*Ecclesia de Eucharistia Vivit*: An Ecumenical Reading" in *Ecu-menical Trends* no. 33/9 (October 2004) 1–9. Con-gregation for Divine Worship and the Discipline of the Sacraments, "*Redemptionis Sacramentum*": *In-struction on Certain Matters To Be Observed or To Be Avoided Regarding the Most Holy Eucharist* (Vatican City: Libreria Editrice Vaticana, 2004).

[9]See *The Voice of the Church: A Forum on Liturgical Translation* (Washington, D.C.: United States Cath-olic Conference, 2001).

[10]*The Complete Stories of Evelyn Waugh* (Boston: Little, Brown, 1999) 130–39.

[11]Philip Jenkins, *The Next Christendom: The Coming of Global Christianity* (New York: Oxford University Press, 2002) 7–8.

[12]Jenkins, 68; quoting Frieder Ludwig, *Church and State in Tanzania* (Leiden: Brill, 1999) 182, and Harvey Cox, *Fire from Heaven: The Rise of Pente-costal Spirituality and the Reshaping of Religion in the Twenty-first Century* (Reading, Mass.: Addison-Wesley, 1995) 249, 246.

[13]For an ecumenical discussion, see Cornelius Plantinga and Sue A. Rozeboom, *Discerning the Spir-its: A Guide to Thinking about Christian Worship To-day* (Grand Rapids, Mich.: Eerdmans, 2003).

[14]Richard Leonard, "'Lights! Camera! Worship!' The Cinema and its Challenges to Roman Catholic Worship in Postmodernity" in Pecklers, *Liturgy in a Postmodern World*, 27–31.

Biblical Index

Index

Page numbers in italics indicate illustrations.